# Encyclopedia of
# CRIMINOLOGY
## Volume 3

# Encyclopedia of
# CRIMINOLOGY

## Volume 3
## Q-Z
### INDEX

Richard A. Wright
J. Mitchell Miller

Editors

WITHDRAWN

**ROUTLEDGE**
New York • London

Published in 2005 by

Routledge
An Imprint of the Taylor & Francis Group
270 Madison Avenue
New York, NY 10016

Published in Great Britain by
Routledge
An Imprint of the Taylor & Francis Group
2 Park Square
Milton Park, Abingdon
Oxon, OX14 4RN, U.K.

10   9   8   7   6   5   4   3   2   1

**Library of Congress Cataloging-in-Publication Data**

Encyclopedia of criminology/Richard A. Wright, editor, J. Mitchell Miller,
  editor.
    p.   cm.
    Includes bibliographical references and index.
    ISBN 1-57958-387-3 (set: alk. paper) — ISBN 1-57958-465-9 (vol. 1: alk.
paper) — ISBN 1-57958-466-7 (vol. 2: alk. paper) — ISBN 1-57958-467-5
(vol. 3: alk. paper) 1. Criminology—Encyclopedias. I. Wright, Richard A.
(Richard Alan), 1953- II. Miller, J. Mitchell.

HV6017.E5295 2005
364'.03—dc22                                              2004004861

# ADVISORY BOARD MEMBERS

# DEDICATION

*To Richard A. Wright, an outstanding scholar, colleague, and friend*

# CONTENTS

# ALPHABETICAL LIST OF ENTRIES

# Q

## Qualitative Research

Qualitative research, often referred to as fieldwork or ethnography, is employed by social scientists to discover answers to questions through the application of systematic procedures. In general, the procedures utilized by qualitative researchers result in nominal rather than numerical data, thus making for a fundamental distinction between qualitative and quantitative forms of research. Prior to observing the particular qualitative research methods, it is necessary to consider the philosophical underpinnings of the qualitative approach in contrast to the scientific logic supporting quantitative methods.

### The Qualitative Versus Quantitative Debate

Certainly, one of the longest and most pronounced controversial issues throughout the social sciences is the qualitative versus the quantitative debate (Fitzgerald & Cox, 1987). Differences emerge from different epistemological stances—positivist vs. interpretative. Positivism is a philosophy of science that utilizes empirical methods borrowed from the natural or "hard" sciences to investigate phenomena. The positivistic model employs the strategy of variable analysis wherein attempts are made to capture social realities through a reductionist logic based on specifying and measuring causes and effects. Measurement allows rigorous, verifiable, and reliable conclusions based on the statistical testing of hypotheses denoting relationships or correlations between observed variables. It is generally held that there are finite sets of discernable

relationships and it is the social scientists' goal to uncover these objective realities (Binder & Geis, 1983).

The principle of objectivity entails conscious attempts to ensure that steps in the research process leading to conclusions, and therefore the conclusions themselves, are based on a careful and systematic observation rather than personal prejudices. While scientists as humans cannot be altogether free of personal biases, positivists feel that through awareness and attention to detail, biases can be checked and controlled so as not to affect outcomes.

Qualitative research is based on a much different model that stresses a subjective orientation to the creation of knowledge (Patton, 1990). Stressing an interpretative epistemology, qualitative research involves data collection and analysis that emphasizes the interrelationships between understanding, culture, symbolism, temporally and spatially bounded meaning, and—especially for criminologists—behavior. The emphasis placed on the measurement of concepts by positivists is replaced with the objective of understanding social realities in many situationally specific contexts that may or may not be generalizable. One pronounced difference, and trade-off, between qualitative and quantitative forms of research is breadth vs. depth (Berg, 2001).

Qualitative methods allow a detailed and in-depth examination of selected phenomena because of the absence of the limiting variable analysis process that requires study of only what is measured in predetermined categories. With fieldwork, information is discovered and accumulated in an evolving and cross-referencing manner, allowing greater insight that can lead to the identification and exploration of new knowledge. It is typically less generalizable than with quantitative methods that, through sampling and the analysis of aggregate data, offer greater applicability of findings (Berg, 2001).

To better understand these philosophical trade-offs, it is helpful to consider the practical realities of specific quantitative and qualitative research methods. The primary data collection instrument for positivistic social scientists, that is, quantitative researchers, is the survey, be it administered via mail, via telephone, or face-to-face. It is important to note that the foremost advantages to such an approach include (1) the acquisition of knowledge through responses by a large number of respondents quickly and efficiently, and (2) the value of sampling, especially when the subject population is known. The disadvantages of the quantitative approach include (1) that the research process is limited to variable-specific realities known to and measured by the researcher in an *a priori* fashion, (2) the issues of measurement and sampling error, and (3) the sterility of the positivistic paradigm (Berg, 2001). In respect to the last issue, many qualitative researchers take issue with a form of social science that can be practiced altogether outside of a societal context without any or with minimal human interaction. Such views are particularly pronounced in criminological and deviance research wherein much of the research occurs in clandestine and esoteric settings. One cannot, for example, conduct random sampling among a population of prostitutes or burglars because the total population of these groups is unknown.

## Qualitative Research Techniques

Qualitative research techniques have been defined broadly to include types of inquiries ranging from historical document analysis to image impression. The overwhelming majority of qualitative research, however, can be dichotomized into either an observational or interview category. Qualitative interviews are sometimes confused with quantitative oriented surveys in that they both pose questions to subjects. Several marked distinctions exist, however, that serve as examples for the differences between positivistic and interpretative forms of research. Surveys pose only questions that have been predetermined to be of value and typically have a limited set of possible responses. This close-ended approach does not resonate well with subjectivists who question whether answers unknown to the researcher, and thus absent from survey response choices, are addressed by the research question at hand (Binder & Geis, 1983).

Qualitative researchers instead pose open-ended, less assuming questions that are intended to identify and explore the respondents' worlds. Whereas surveys may take but a few minutes and follow a set agenda, interviews, often termed "in-depth interviews," may involve many hours with a single subject or small group of subjects. The rigidity of questioning in an in-depth interview varies according to the specificity of the research topic, the extant knowledge base, practical matters such as time frame and financial considerations, and the degree of rapport established with subject(s). Thus, in-depth interviews may assume a set sequence of questioning to ensure topic coverage or be totally unstructured (Patton, 1990).

Observational types of qualitative research assume three main forms: direct, participant, or covert. Direct observation is the most straightforward of these forms involving the simple observation and recording of events or behavior. The researcher may position himself or herself in a public place, such as a city park or library, in order to observe a range of phenomena (e.g., illicit drug activity, stranger interaction) transpiring in such locales. In other instances, the researcher may directly observe activities occurring within the context of a social program for evaluation purposes (e.g., school-based early intervention mentoring).

Whereas direct observation involves the researcher as onlooker, participant observation is characterized by some degree of immersion by the researcher into the field setting. The participant observer is fully engaged in experiencing the setting under study while simultaneously attempting to understand the setting through—in addition to firsthand observation—personal experience and verbal exchange with fellow participants. The participant observer attempts to share, as fully and intimately as possible, in the daily life activities of chosen settings. In short, the researcher seeks to develop an insider's view of research topics.

When studying crime and criminal justice, direct or participant observation is often not possible (Miller, 1995). The very nature of most crime is such that it is not subject to public scrutiny, nor can qualitative researchers typically observe the natural behavior of criminals or criminal justice system actors because of the potential problem known as the Hawthorne effect. The Hawthorne effect refers to a situation in the data gathering stage of the research process where the normalcy of routine or natural activities is affected by the researcher's presence. One cannot reasonably expect, for example, to observe gang behavior as a participant (short of joining the gang) or police misconduct by direct observation via citizen ride-along programs. Because so much of the subject material of interest to criminologists is secret in nature, qualitative researchers occasionally engage in covert participant observation.

Covert participant observation is a term that has been used interchangeably with other labels, including "secret observation" (Roth, 1962), "investigative social research" (Douglas, 1976), "sociological snooping" (Von Hoffman, 1970), and most frequently "disguised observation" (Erikson, 1967; Denzin, 1968). Disguised observation has been defined broadly as "research in which the researcher hides his or her presence or purpose for interacting with a group" (Hagan, 1993). The distinguishing feature is that the researcher's intent to conduct research is not made known to subjects within the field setting.

Disguised observation is too inclusive a term to use in reference to those who simply hide in disguise or secret to observe, such as Stein's (1974) observation of prostitutes servicing customers via a hidden two-way mirror. Covert participant observation likewise involves disguise; however, the researcher is always immersed in the field setting. Additional elements that are entailed include intentional misrepresentation, interpersonal deception, and maintenance of a false identity, often for prolonged periods of time. Covert participant observation is therefore a more accurate term than disguised observation because it better indicates the active nature of the fieldwork essential to the technique (Jorgensen, 1989).

Covert participant observation is essentially "opportunistic research" (Ronai and Ellis, 1989) conducted by "complete-member researchers" (Adler and Adler, 1987) who study phenomena in settings where they participate as full members. Admission to otherwise inaccessible settings is gained by undertaking a natural position and then secretly conducting observational research. Some examples of the method include a study of the relationship between personal appearance and suspicion of shoplifting involving students dressed either conventionally or as hippies, Stewart and Cannon's (1977) masquerade as thieves, Tewksbury's (1990) description of adult bookstore patrons, Miller and Selva's (1994) assumption of the police informant role to infiltrate drug enforcement operations, and, most notably, Humphreys' (1970) infamous study of homosexual behavior in public places.

There are other versions of disguised or covert participant observation, where certain confederates are made aware of the researcher's true identity, purpose, and objectives (Formby and Smykla, 1981; Asch, 1951). There are clear advantages to working with confederates. These include easier entry into the research site, quicker familiarity with the nomenclature and standards of conduct of those being studied, enhanced opportunities for the observation of pivotal interactions, and the minimization of potential danger to the researcher. Reliance on confederates may be counterproductive though, because observations and analysis of the social setting may be tainted by their values, perceptions, and positions relative to one another within the field setting.

Even if only a few individuals within a research site are aware of the researcher's true identity, it is possible, indeed likely, that interaction still will be affected adversely, especially if knowledge of the researcher's identity spreads to others. The use of confederates in such a case may cause data distortion (i.e., validity and reliability problems). The covert participant observer role *sans* confederates avoids these problems.

The goals of covert participant observation are no different than the standard objectives of overt participant observation: exploration, description, and occasionally, evaluation (Berg, 1989). An epistemological justification is rooted in interpretive and naturalistic inquiries (Patton, 1990). Most aspects of the methodological process, such as defining a problem, observing and gathering information, analyzing notes and records, and communicating results, are nearly identical to conventional participant observation as well. The covert approach is thus a type of participant observation rather than a distinctive method.

## References and Further Reading

Adler, P.A. and Adler, P. (1987). The past and future of ethnography. *Contemp. Ethnogr.* 16, 4–24.

Asch, S. (1951). Effects of group pressure upon the modification and distortion of judgement. In: *Groups, Leadership and Men*, H. Guetzkow, ed., Carnegie Press, Pittsburgh.

Berg, B. (1989). *Qualitative Research Methods for the Social Sciences*. Allyn and Bacon, Boston.

Berg, B. (2001). *Qualitative Research Methods for the Social Sciences*, 4th ed., Allyn and Bacon, Boston.

Binder, A. and Geis, G. (1983). *Methods of Research in Criminology and Criminal Justice*. McGraw-Hill, New York.

Denzin, N. (1968). On the ethics of disguised observation. *Soc. Probl.* 115, 502–504.

Douglas, J. (1976). *Investigative and Social Research: Individual and Team Field Research*. Sage, Beverly Hills, CA.

Erikson, K. (1967). Disguised observation in sociology. *Soc. Probl.* 14, 366–372.

Fitzgerald, J.D. and Cox, S.M. (1987). *Research Methods in Criminal Justice*. Nelson Hall, Chicago, IL.

Formby, W. and Smykla, J. (1981). Citizen awareness in crime prevention: Do they really get involved? *J. Police Sci. Admin.* 9, 398–403.

Hagan, F. (1993). *Research Methods in Criminal Justice*. MacMillan, New York. p. 234.

Humphreys, L. (1970). *Tearoom Trade: Impersonal Sex in Public Places*, Aldine, New York.

Jorgensen, D. (1989). *Participant Observation: A Methodology for Human Studies*. Sage, Newbury Park, CA.

Miller, J.M. (1995). Covert participant observation: reconsidering the least used method. *J. Contemp. Crim. Justice* 112, 97–105.

Miller, J. and Selva, L. (1994). Drug enforcement's double-edged sword: an assessment of asset forfeiture programs. *Justice* 11, 313–335.

Patton, M. (1990). *Qualitative Evaluation and Research Methods*. Sage, Newbury Park, CA.

Ronai, C. and Ellis, C. (1989). Turn-ons for money: interactional strategies of the table dancer. *J. Contemp. Ethnogr.* 18, 271–298.

Roth, J. (1962). Comments on secret observation. *Soc. Probl.* 9, 283–284.

Stein, M. (1974). *Lovers, Friends, Slaves...: The Nine Male Sexual Types.* Berkeley Publishing, Berkeley.

Stewart, J. and Cannon, D. (1977). Effects of perpetrator status and bystander commitment on response to a simulated crime. *J. Police Sci. Admin.* 5, 318–323.

Tewksbury, R. (1990). Patrons of porn: research notes on the clientele of adult bookstores. *Deviant Behav.* 11, 259–271.

Von Hoffman, N. (1970). Sociological snoopers. *Washington Post* (Jan. 30).

J. MITCHELL MILLER

# Quetelet, Adolphe

Adolphe Quetelet (1796–1874) was a Belgian astronomer, mathematician, and statistician. Along with his French contemporary Andre Michel Guerry, Quetelet was a pioneer in the use of quantitative techniques in the study of social phenomena. Quetelet's positivistic influence spans the range of the social sciences, including the disciplines of sociology, geography, and criminology. In criminology, his influence is particularly pronounced in positivistic criminology, modern crime analysis, and crime mapping.

As a quintessential positivist, Quetelet believed that social phenomena can be analyzed just like phenomena in the physical world. For Quetelet, the key to understanding patterns in social phenomena was the proper application of the laws of probability. Influenced by his interdisciplinary background and the mathematicians Laplace and Fournier, Quetelet believed that the application of probabilistic models was pivotal in the study of the social world.

In the 1820s, Quetelet was commissioned by the government of the Low Countries to improve the compilation and interpretation of census data. His investigations of crime, mortality, and other social characteristics yielded empirical ammunition for his seminal 1835 publication *A Treatise on Man, and the Development of His Faculties*, which detailed his theories of the influence of probability on social affairs.

In 1846, Quetelet published a book on probability and social science that demonstrated a diverse collection of human measurements based on the heights of French conscripts and the chest circumferences of Scottish soldiers. From these measurements, Quetelet observed that the data could be interpreted as approximately normally distributed. These findings, he argued, made it possible to identify the underlying regularities of both normal and abnormal behavior. Quetelet surmised that knowledge about the "average man" could be determined from graphically displaying the "facts of life" as bell shaped curves. Among his many contributions in this area was his introduction of the use of the normal curve (the probability distribution for a normal variable) in applications beyond that of an error law. It is the opinion of some commentators that Quetelet's application of the normal curve in disciplines outside its original home (astronomy) had a powerful influence on Francis Galton (the creator of eugenics), and may have influenced James Clark Maxwell in his formulating the kinetic theory of gases.

This book, as well as his earlier work, lost in the arena of influence to Darwin's *Origin of Species*. Unwittingly, Quetelet perhaps contributed to his own demise regarding his future influence on criminology. Piers Beirne has noted that Quetelet's influence on positivist criminology eclipses that of others. The stories of the early positivist criminologists such as Cesare Lombroso, influenced as much by Quetelet's idea of the "average man" and his overall program of empiricism as Darwin's evolutionary theory, have become standard features of contemporary texts in criminology. Lombroso is sometimes, mistakenly, referred to as the "father of criminology" in some of these texts. Meanwhile, Quetelet and his contemporaries are frequently relegated to the dustbin of history as far as contemporary textbooks are concerned. Their influence is ignored altogether or given only brief attention in such texts.

Quetelet's snub by many criminologists is curious, given the profound influence Quetelet had had on the development of the ecological perspective in criminology in the 20th century, especially in the U.S. The first major sphere of influence on ecological criminology (also known as "environmental criminology") concerns the pathbreaking research emanating from the University of Chicago, known as the "Chicago School."

To the extent that Quetelet studied variations in sociological phenomena (such as crime), across time and place, his work anticipated the work of the more famous Chicago School researchers such as E.W. Burgess, Clifford Shaw, Henry McKay, and their colleagues and students. It is not too far-fetched to say that the empirical work of the Chicago School sociologists examining the correlations of crime, and particularly that of Shaw and McKay and "delinquency areas," and perhaps their entire theoretical program, is but a replication of the work of Quetelet and his 19th century contemporaries. The works of several environmental criminologists in the late 20th century, such as the Brantinghams and Dennis Roncek, while groundbreaking in their own right, were influenced, if not at least indirectly, by the work of Quetelet, Guerry, and other early empirical social scientists. Moreover, the work of Quetelet and his contemporaries anticipates an important development of both the Chicago School and of contemporary environmental criminology: the importance of *opportunities* for crime.

Another area of influence is almost entirely missed by textbook writers and others in the field. Quetelet was among the pioneers (along with Guerry) of modern crime analysis and mapping. He made frequent use of pictorial illustrations of the distribution of crime, education, and other sociological features. Albeit crude compared to the output from today's computerized crime mapping programs (easily developed by anyone with a desktop computer), Quetelet's maps demonstrated the utility of graphical displays of the distribution of crime. The notion of summarizing human activities with summary statistics and graphical displays is clearly a prologue to modern crime analysis and report writing. Crime trends and statistics, calls for service, population density and degree of urbanization, variations in composition of the population (particularly youth concentration), stability of population with respect to residents' mobility, commuting patterns and transient factors, modes of transportation and highway systems, economic conditions (including median income, poverty level, and job availability), educational, recreational, and religious characteristics, family conditions with respect to divorce and family cohesiveness, citizens' attitudes toward crime, beat information, and other features of crime analysis can be viewed simply as developments of the work of Quetelet, Guerry, and their contemporaries.

In addition to his contributions to criminology, Quetelet organized the first international statistics conference in 1853. He was instrumental in the forming of the Statistical Society of London, the International Statistics Congresses, and the Statistical Section of the British Association for the Advancement of Science. Quetelet was the first foreign member of the American Statistical Association. Historian of science George Sarton called him the "patriarch of statistics." In addition, he developed the internationally used measure of obesity, the *Quetelet Index*, sometimes also called the *Body Mass Index* (BMI).

KEVIN M. BRYANT

## Biography

Born In Flanders, Belgium, 22 Feb 1796; received his first doctorate in 1819 from the University of Ghent; taught mathematics in Brussels after 1819 and founded and directed the Royal Observatory there; elected to the Royal Academy of Sciences in 1820; studied astronomy and probability for three months in Paris in 1824; first director of the Royal Observatory at Brussels (1828); established observatory in Brussels in 1833; published *A Treatise on Man, and the Development of His Faculties* in 1835; organized the first international statistics conference in 1853; died in Brussels, Belgium 17 Feb 1874.

## Selected Writings

*Research on the Propensity for Crime at Different Ages*. Translated and introduced by Sawyer F. Sylvester. Cincinnati: Anderson, 1831, 1984.
*Sur l'homme et sur developpement de ses facultés, ou Essai de physique sociale*. Paris: Bachelier, 1835.
*A Treatise on Man*. Translated by R. Knox and T. Smibert. Edinburgh: Chambers, 1842.
Letters addressed to H.R.H. the Grand Duke of Saxe Coburg and Gotha, on the Theory of Probabilities. Translated by Olinthus Gregory.
Downes. London: Charles & Edwin Layton, 1846.

## References and Further Reading

Quetelet, A. (1977). 1796–1874: contributions en hommage à son role de sociologue, Brussels.
Beirne, P. (1987). Adolphe Quetelet and the origins of positivist criminology. *Am. J. Soc.* 92, 1140–1169.
Hankins, F.H. (1908). *Quetelet as a Statistician*. New York.
Lazarsfeld, P. (1961). Notes on the history of quantification in sociology—trends, sources and problems. *Isis,* 52, 277–333.
McDonald, L. (1993). *The Early Origins of the Social Sciences.* McGill-Queen's University Press.
McDonald, L. (1998). *Women Theorists on Society and Politics.* Wilfred Laurier University Press, Waterloo.
Stigler, S. (1986). *The History of Statistics.* Harvard University Press, Cambridge, MA.
Terence, M. (1957). Some ecological studies of the 19th century, In: *The Criminal Area.* Routledge & Kegan Paul and Humanities Press, New York, 42–53.
Tomasi, L. (2001). *New Horizons in Sociological Theory and Research.* Ashgate, Aldershot, England; Burlington, VT.

# Quinney, Richard

At a meeting of the East Coast Conference of Socialist Sociologists in 1979 a gathering of leftist-oriented sociologists and criminologists anticipated hearing Richard Quinney—the best-known, most frequently cited, most prolific, and most controversial radical criminologist of the late twentieth century period—present a neo-Marxist analysis of law and crime. Instead, Quinney began to speak of the need to bring God and the spiritual into our thoughts and analysis. Quinney has always refused to conform to the expectations of others and to conventional career patterns. He has been a unique and singular figure in contemporary American criminology.

Richard Quinney grew up on a farm in southern Wisconsin. He originally thought of becoming a forest ranger or a hospital administrator and got into criminology almost accidentally, after a mentor died unexpectedly. His Ph.D. dissertation at the University of Wisconsin under the supervision of Marshall B. Clinard was on prescription violations committed by retail pharmacists—one of the few studies of that time focusing on white-collar crime. He subsequently wrote an influential article on conceptualizing white-collar crime.

After relatively brief service at St. Lawrence University and the University of Kentucky, Quinney accepted an appointment at New York University. Some of his earliest published work fell generally within the parameters of mainstream criminology, but even at this stage of his career Quinney evinced an interest in broader and more philosophical questions (e.g., on the political nature of crime). In 1967 he collaborated with his old professor Clinard in producing *Criminal Behavior Systems: A Typology*. This typology originally identified eight types of criminal behavior, with corporate crime added as a ninth type in the second edition. It classifies criminal behavior by several different characteristics: legal aspects; the criminal career of the offender; group support for the criminal behavior; correspondence of criminal behavior with legitimate behavior; and societal reactions and legal processing. Although it has been criticized as insufficiently attentive to variable patterns within each type of criminal behavior and neglectful of such dimensions as offender motivations, it has been an exceptionally influential and widely adopted typology.

The late 1960s was a period of much turmoil and conflict in American society, and Quinney was certainly affected by these developments. In 1970 he published *The Social Reality of Crime*, a landmark work that offered a politically informed approach to understanding crime, defining it as a social construct. He formulated a series of propositions designed to demonstrate how law is created and applied by authorized agents in a politically organized society, reflecting and advancing the interests of the powerful and privileged. This book came to be regarded as a seminal articulation of a conflict theory approach to understanding crime and criminal law.

*The Social Reality of Crime* had little to say about the specifically capitalist character of American society. In several books published in the 1970s—*Critique of Legal Order* (1974); *Criminology* (1975; 1979); and *Class, State and Crime* (1977; 1980)—Quinney specifically applied a neo-Marxist interpretation of capitalist society to an understanding of crime and criminal justice. In the first of these books, for example, Quinney argued that law in a capitalist society functions to legitimate the system, and to facilitate oppression and exploitation. He asked whether we really need law, and whether we might be better off without it. In 1982 Quinney co-edited a widely read anthology, *Marxism and Law*.

By the end of the 1970s Richard Quinney had become somewhat disenchanted with the conventional concerns of academic scholars. In the early 1970s he had relinquished his tenured professorship at New York University to embark on a peripatetic career as a researcher or visiting professor at various universities, including the University of North Carolina—Chapel Hill, CUNY—Brooklyn, Brown University, and Boston College. From 1979 on, his published books and articles often explored the links between Marxism and theological concerns (à la Paul Tillich), metaphysical questions in the social sciences, and reflexive or autobiographical accounts of his own life, with some of his striking black-and-white photographs published in conjunction with this work.

In 1984, when Richard Quinney received arguably criminology's highest honor (the Edwin H. Sutherland Award of the American Society of Criminology), it seemed possible that he had abandoned the discipline. The year before he had returned to his native midwest, accepting a professorship at Northern Illinois University in DeKalb. While maintaining his broad new interests, however, Quinney began to re-engage with criminology. With Harold E. Pepinsky he published an influential collection of readings, *Criminology as Peacemaking* (1991). Peacemaking criminology calls for a repudiation of the "war on crime" approach, to be replaced by a response to crime as a form of suffering, and a reconciliatory approach to the offender and the problem of crime. The inseparable character of our personal and public lives is one recurrent theme of Quinney's work during this period. We must be at peace with ourselves if we want to contribute effectively to a more peaceful world.

During the 1990s, Quinney found in the work of Erich Fromm one source of inspiration for an understanding of crime, and human existence, that transcended conventional disciplinary boundaries. He continues to publish autobiographical, reflexive works (e.g., *Journey to a Far Place*, 1991; *For the Time Being*, 1998). His book *Bearing Witness to Crime and Social Justice* (2000) provides readers with a retrospective reprise of some of his most significant criminology articles published over a period of several decades.

Richard Quinney has been a thoroughly unique figure within criminological thought from a period extending from the early 1960s into the new century. He has drawn upon especially broad and diverse sources of inspiration, and has moved through many stages in his intellectual and personal orientation. Quinney himself has described some of the influences on his thought as social constructionism, phenomenology, Marxism, critical philosophy, liberation theology, Buddhism, and existentialism. He has engaged in a lifelong search for a home in the world, driven by an enduring sense of wonder at the nature of reality. He has long subscribed to the conviction that individuals cannot make meaningful separations between the personal, spiritual, and professional aspects of their lives. He is among the most cited of criminologists; he has inspired much criminological work in response to what he has written. Several generations of radical and critical criminologists, in particular, have drawn inspiration from his work. In addition to its substance, his later work in particular can be read for the sheer aesthetic pleasure of his poetic prose and his evocative photographs. Richard Quinney reminds criminologists that they have choices in their lives, and he compels his readers to reflect on the meaning of their own lives and work in this world.

DAVID O. FRIEDRICHS

## Biography

Born in Elkhorn, Wisconsin, 16 May 1934; son of a farmer. Educated at Carroll College, B.S., 1956; Northwestern University, M.S., 1957; University of Wisconsin, Ph.D. in Sociology, 1962. Instructor, St. Lawrence University, 1960–1962; assistant professor, University of Kentucky, 1962–1965; assistant to full professor, New York University, 1965–1972; on leave research/writing, University of North Carolina, 1972–1974; visiting professor, CUNY—Brooklyn, 1974–1975; visiting/adjunct professor, Brown University, 1975–1978; distinguished visiting professor/adjunct professor, Boston College, 1978–1983; professor, Northern Illinois University, 1983–1997; professor emeritus, Northern Illinois University, 1998– . Edwin H. Sutherland Award, American Society of Criminology, 1984; President's Award, Western Society of Criminology, 1992; Fellow, American Society of Criminology, 1995; Major Achievement Award, Division on Critical Criminology, American Society of Criminology, 1998.

## Selected Writings

*Criminal Behavior Systems: A Typology*, with Marshall B. Clinard, 1967; 3rd edition 1994 (with John Wildeman).
*The Problem of Crime*, 1970; 3rd edition, 1991 (with John Wildeman).
*The Social Reality of Crime*, 1970; reprinted, 2001.
*Critique of Legal Order: Crime Control in Capitalist Society*, 1974.
*Criminology*, 1975; 2nd edition, 1979.
*Class, State, and Crime*, 1977; 2nd edition, 1980.
*Providence: The Reconstruction of Social and Moral Order*, 1980.
*Marxism and Law* (edited with Piers Beirne), 1982.
*Social Existence: Metaphysics, Marxism, and the Social Sciences*, 1982.
*Criminology as Peacemaking* (edited with Harold E. Pepinsky), 1991.
*Journey to a Far Place: Autobiographical Reflections*, 1991.
*For the Time Being: Ethnography of Everyday Life*, 1998.
*Erich Fromm and Critical Criminology: Beyond the Punitive Society* (edited with Kevin Anderson), 2000.
*Bearing Witness to Crime and Social Justice*, 2000.
*Home is Where One Starts From: Tales of the Borderland*, 2001.

## References and Further Reading

Dion, D. (1989). Richard Quinney: an interview. *Crit. Criminol.*, 1.
Friedrichs, D. O. (1980). Radical criminology in the United States: an interpretive understanding. In: *Radical Criminology: The Coming Crises*, J. Inciardi, ed., Sage, Beverly Hills, CA.
Goldwyn, E. (1971). Dialogue with Richard Quinney. *Issues Criminol.*, 6.
Martin, R., Mutchnick, R. J., and Austin, W.T. (1990). Earl Richard Quinney. In: *Criminological Thought: Pioneer Past and Present*, MacMillan, New York.
Pepinsky, H.E. (1985). An overview on Richard Quinney on law and crime. *Legal Stud. Forum*, 9.
Tifft, L. and Sullivan, D. (1999). A stranger in search of home: a conversation with United States criminologist Richard Quinney. *Contemp. Justice Rev.*, 2, 3.
Trevino, A.J. (1989). Richard Quinney: a Wisconsin sociologist. *Wisconsin Sociol.*, Fall.
Trevino, A.J. (2001). Introduction to the transaction edition. In: *The Social Reality of Crime*, Transaction Press, New Brunswick, NJ.

*See also* **Marxist Theories of Criminal Behavior; Peacemaking Criminology; Radical Theories of Criminal Behavior.**

# R

# Race and Ethnicity and Criminal Behavior

Few topics have the potential for raising hackles on both sides of the ideological divide than the topic of race or ethnicity and criminal behavior. The volatility of the topic is so great that many countries have ceased to collect crime data broken down by race or ethnicity. There are still debates about whether race is a biological entity or a social construct. Those who favor the latter argument stress that there are no "pure" races, and that racial boundaries are ambiguous and shifting. Those who favor the former acknowledge that there are no pure races, but point out that forensic scientists routinely identify race by skeletal remains and body fluid samples. They also insist that although it may be more fruitful in some circumstance to think in terms of clines (a graded series of physiological and morphological changes along lines of geographical transition) rather than races, data can be analyzed in terms of discrete categories. Crime data, of course, comes to us in these discrete racial categories, not as continua. The discrete categories roughly correspond with the three major continents of the Old World—Africa, Asia, and Europe.

Many criminologists avoid making comparisons along racial lines because of the disagreeable tendency to label those who do as racist if the comparison is unfavorable to minorities. Others ignore the subject out of a genuine concern that already disadvantaged groups will be further stigmatized. Whatever the reason for the neglect, it has resulted in to "an unproductive mix of controversy and silence" (Sampson and Wilson, 2000, 149). There are those, on the other hand, who argue that the crime-race connection should be studied honestly because the racial or ethnic groups who commit most of the crimes also suffer as most of the victims, and these groups are the ones who may benefit most from a candid examination of race or ethnicity and crime issue. "All roads in American criminology eventually lead to issues of race," wrote LaFree and Russell (1993, 273). If we desire to be informed, we cannot avoid making comparisons, however unpleasant it may be for some to contrast the behaviors of "us" and "them."

## African Americans

When Americans speak of race and crime in the same sentence they are almost invariably thinking of Black crime. No one really doubts that crime is rampant in America's inner cities, where most African Americans reside. According to the 2000 Census, African Americans constitute 12.8% of the U.S. population. Arrest rates for African Americans would fluctuate randomly around that percentage if race were irrelevant to predicting the probability of criminal behavior. However, according to 2000 Uniform Crime Report (UCR), the percentages of Blacks arrested for each Part I Index crime in 1999 were: murder (53.4%), rape (37.5%), robbery (55.3%), aggravated assault (36.3%), burglary (29.5%), larceny or theft (31.8%), motor vehicle theft (39.2%), and arson (24.2%). African Americans are thus overrepresented by large margins in each of the eight most serious crimes. By way of contrast, European Americans (Whites) are underrepresented relative to their proportion of the population. Whites constituted

82.2% of the American population in 1999 (U.S. Bureau of the Census, 2000), with arrest rates for murder (45.9%), rape (61.5%), robbery (43.9%), aggravated assault (63%), burglary (68.6%), larceny or theft (66.1%), motor vehicle theft (54.9%), and arson (74.4%).

African Americans are also arrested at a rate 2.3 times greater than Whites for white-collar crimes listed in the UCR, such as forgery, fraud, and embezzlement, and 1.4:1 times greater for hate crimes. The only crimes for which African Americans are not overrepresented are antitrust offenses (99.1% White), securities fraud (99.6% White), drunk driving (87.4% White), and liquor law violations (85.5% White) (Ellis and Walsh, 2000). The pattern of Black overrepresentation in crime, particularly violent crime, has been consistently observed as long as crime statistics have been collected in the U.S. (Flowers, 1988).

Ellis and Walsh (2000) reviewed 174 studies from five different countries comparing Black and White differences based on official statistics. Only one, for property offenses in Canada, found Black offending to be lower than White offending. The remaining 173 studies found Blacks to be significantly more criminally involved than Whites, particularly for violent offenses. Their examination of 83 self-report studies, however, revealed an almost equal number of significant and insignificant results, and even some for which the Black rate was lower than the White rate. This suggests to some that studies based on official statistics could be the result of systemic biases against Blacks rather than real differences in criminal behavior between the races.

There are at least three reasons for doubting such a conclusion. First, self-report studies rely heavily on asking about trivial offenses (smoking, stealing something worth $2, fighting, and so forth) and are typically conducted in high schools and colleges, which are not places where one expects to find many criminally involved individuals. There may indeed be no significant differences between the races as far as trivial offenses are concerned. Second, the vast majority of crime is intraracial, and unless we believe that the high rate of victimization in the Black community is the result of Whites going into Black neighborhoods to victimize Blacks, we have to acknowledge the reality of racial differences in criminal behavior. For instance, African American females have had a higher rate of homicide than White males since at least 1930 (Barak, 1998). Their victims, who are typically killed in acts of self-defense (about 70%), are overwhelmingly boyfriends and spouses, which makes it very hard to attribute the arrest of these women to racism and police bias (Mann, 1990). Third, studies comparing official arrest data from the Uniform Crime Reports with *National Crime Survey* data find that these victimization studies yield the same racial differentials as do official statistics (Wilbanks, 1987). For example, about 60% of robbery victims describe their assailants as Black, and about 60% of the suspects arrested for robbery are Black (Wilson and Herrnstein, 1985). The consensus among criminologists specializing in the area is that the Black to White arrest ratio is primarily (perhaps entirely) because of actual racial differences in crime participation (Blumstein and Cohen, 1987).

## Asian Americans

Asian Americans (particularly East Asians such as the Japanese and Chinese) have long been considered America's "model minority." In the heyday of ecological theory that favored "kinds of places" over "kinds of people" explanations for criminal behavior, research in city after city showed that Asian Americans living in high crime areas had lower crime rates than any other racial or ethnic group living in the same areas (Shaw and McKay, 1972). Wilson and Herrnstein (1985) point out that although a Chinese neighborhood in San Francisco in the 1960s had the highest rate of poverty and unemployment, the greatest percentage of substandard housing, as well as other disabilities, only five Chinese Americans were committed to prison in 1965 in the whole state of California.

Asian Americans are doing substantially better financially today; they tend to report significantly greater family income than any other group except Jewish Americans, despite a history in this country of considerable discrimination (Jencks, 1992). Asian Americans remain almost as underrepresented in the crime statistics as African Americans are overrepresented. Asians (including Pacific Islanders) constituted 4.1% of the American population in 1999 (U.S. Bureau of the Census, 2000), but were arrested for only 1.2% of all violent crimes and 1.7% of all property crimes in 1999 (FBI, 2000). Asians were only overrepresented for gambling offenses (an arrest rate of 5.3% rather than the expected rate of 4.1% based on this group's proportion of the population).

Although East Asian to White comparisons are less often made than Black to White comparisons, Ellis and Walsh's (2000) review of 24 studies based on official statistics conducted in England and the U.S. found that East Asians committed fewer crimes than Whites in all cases. In 14 self-report studies, Whites reported more offenses in 11 studies, with the remaining three being insignificant. These studies reported on East Asians only, and did not include Pacific Islanders in the same category, as the UCR does. The inclusion of Pacific Islanders in the same category as Asians leads to an overestimation of the involvement of East Asians in criminal activity since Pacific Islanders typically have crime rates higher than their proportion of the population would lead us to believe (Ellis and Walsh, 2000). The underrepresentation of Asian Americans in official crime statistics is likely to be an accurate indicator of their actual involvement in crime. It is doubtful whether those who ascribe higher arrest rates to antiminority bias where other groups are concerned would likewise ascribe low Asian rates to pro-Asian bias.

## Hispanic Americans

Hispanic Americans are rapidly becoming the most populous minority group in the U.S. The FBI ceased to report arrest data broken down by Hispanic or non-Hispanic categories after the 1986 edition of the UCR. Hispanics are now recorded in the UCR as "Black" (about 6%), "White" (about 91%), or "other" (3%). The present data thus refer to 1986, when Hispanics constituted 6.9% of the American population. The percentages of Hispanics arrested for all Part I Index crimes for that year were: murder (15.7%), rape (11.5%), robbery (13.9%), aggravated assault (15.3%), burglary (14.7%), larceny or theft (12.0%), motor vehicle theft (16.3%), and arson (7.8%). Thus, in the last year for which national statistics are available for comparing Hispanics and non-Hispanics, Hispanics were arrested about twice as often as their percentage in the population would lead us to predict on the assumption that ethnicity is irrelevant to predicting criminal behavior.

Ellis and Walsh's (2000) review of 31 studies based on official statistics comparing Hispanics with Anglos found Hispanic offending to be higher in 30 studies, with one study finding no significant difference. Self-report studies included 12 in which Hispanic rates were higher than Anglo rates, 11 that found no significant difference, and five that found Anglo rates to be higher.

Parenthetically, placing Hispanic Whites in the same category as Anglos leads to some curious hate crime statistics. Hispanics are listed separately as victims, but as Whites as perpetrators. If a Hispanic assaults an Anglo, both the victim and perpetrator are listed as White, and if a Hispanic assaults a Black, the hate crime will go into the record as a White-on-Black crime. This curiosity inflates the number of hate crimes attributable to "Whites."

## American Indian or Alaskan Native

Ironically, Native Americans are one of the North American continent's smallest major minorities today, constituting only 0.9% of the American population in 1999 (U.S. Bureau of the Census, 2000). Native Americans or Alaskan Natives were arrested for 1.0% of all Part I Index violent crimes and 1.2% of all property crimes. This group is thus slightly overrepresented in

arrest rates. This group is particularly overrepresented in alcohol-related offenses and vagrancy (Part II offenses).

Studies comparing North American Indians and Whites have been conducted in both Canada and the U.S. Ellis and Walsh's (2000) examination of these studies found that Native American involvement in crime was higher than that for Whites in 43 of 45 studies, with one being insignificant and the other showing Whites' involvement greater for property crimes. In terms of self-report studies, 27 of 29 studies showed Native Americans more involved in drug and alcohol abuse offenses.

## Other Ethnic and Religious Minorities

There are other ethnic minority groups for which criminal behavior data are available, albeit not recorded in official statistics according to their minority status. Immigrants in general have typically had higher rates of offending than host nationals in many countries around the world. A review of 54 studies conducted in 12 different countries comparing immigrant with native criminality found that 48 studies reported rates to be higher among immigrants, three to be insignificant, and one in which the natives (Germans) were more criminally involved (Ellis and Walsh, 2000). Many immigrants are young, single males living in crowded urban centers, a fact that may account for the greater criminality of immigrant groups by itself. The country of origin also seems to be important in assessing immigrant crime. British studies show that immigrants from Asia (mostly Indians and Pakistanis) have lower crime rates than the native population, but those from African and Caribbean countries have higher rates than British natives. Canadian, French, and Israeli studies show similar results.

Jews constitute an important ethnic or religious minority group in many countries around the world. Despite centuries of horrible oppression, as a group, Jews have generally been found to be more law-abiding than the majority population among whom they reside. Ellis and Walsh (2000) reviewed 29 studies from 10 different countries that examined crime or delinquency and religious denomination and found that Jews committed fewer offenses than non-Jews in 27 of them.

## Explaining Race or Ethnic Differences in Criminal Behavior

Examining the issue of differential racial or ethnic group involvement in criminal behavior would be a much less controversial enterprise if one did not have to attempt to explain the reasons for group variation. It is the explanation rather than the description of group differences that criminologists either avoid or address in circumscribed ways. Nevertheless, criminological theories do offer a smorgasbord of reasons for why race-differentiated crime rates exist. Some theories focus on cultural and structural factors, others on subcultural and situational factors, and still others on individual factors. No theory can claim a definitive explanation; all have at least something to offer, and all of them combined do not exhaust all possible explanations. Needless to say, no explanation should be uncritically embraced or summarily rejected because they do or do not cohere with one's ideological leanings. Because African Americans have historically had higher crime rates than any other racial or ethnic group, and because far more studies have been conducted with Blacks than with any other minority group, we focus our attention on them.

## Racism

The explanation for high crime rates among Blacks favored by radical and conflict theories is racism. Most theorists in this tradition no longer doubt the reality of the high Black crime rates, and readily acknowledge (so-called "left realism") that the crux of the problem is Black-on-Black crime. There is no denying that Blacks have historically experienced more prejudice and discrimination than other races and ethnic groups, and we should expect these experiences to have an effect on their behavior, but are the disabilities suffered by previous generations adequate to account for current levels of crime? Why should African Americans be more affected by their victimization than other racial or ethnic minorities, such as Native Americans and Chinese Americans, who have far lower crime rates and who have also been severely victimized in America (Flowers, 1988)?

The Chinese have made great strides in the U.S. since being afforded full access to educational and occupational opportunities, but Black crime rates rose even as Black income and educational attainment rose from 1957 to 1988 (LaFree, Drass, and O'Day, 1992). The increase of African American crime rates during the 30-year period of Black political, legal, economic, and educational gain renders it difficult to maintain the notion that racism is the cause of Black crime.

However, perhaps subjective factors that are difficult to measure intrude, even though objective measures may reveal little or no difference in the current conditions and treatment between Blacks and Whites. According to LaFree, Drass, and O'Day (1992), increased education among African Americans may have led to stronger *perceptions* of blocked opportunities and racial discrimination than actually exists, giving rise to a sense of injustice. It has also been

theorized that members of "subcultures of poverty" have a greater tendency to attribute blameworthiness to outside factors for their frequent anger. Regardless of whether or not these perceptions are groundless, a person's perception of reality *is* that person's reality. These perceptions, and the sense of injustice they generate, may lead to "Black rage" or "angry aggression," and to increases in illegal activity (Bernard, 1990).

## Poverty

The most popular explanations for differences in crime rates between Blacks and Whites are socioeconomic. Although most poor people are relatively law abiding, most so- called street crimes are committed by people living in lower-class urban America. Thus, poverty is frequently invoked as a major cause of crime, and therefore as a major explanation of differences in crime rates as well.

The most popular theory invoking socioeconomic explanations for crime is, arguably, anomie theory. Anomie theory basically states that in the U.S. there is a disjunction between the value of material success, for which everyone is supposed to strive, and the equal availability to all races and classes of legitimate means of attaining it (Merton, 1957). According to the theory, lower-class people are pushed towards criminal behavior by the frustration they feel at being denied access to legitimate means of attaining middle-class status and all the material things that go with it. Some anomie theorists emphasize systemic denial of opportunities (Merton, 1957), whereas others emphasize personal disabilities that may prevent some lower-class individuals from taking advantage of the opportunities that they do have (Agnew, 1997). In either case, the result is the same—frustration, alienation, envy, rage, and so forth—all of which are easily translated into criminal activity. In short, anomie theory avers that crime is a way that disadvantaged people obtain what their culture has taught them to want.

How do the major racial or ethnic groups fare in terms of poverty? U.S. Census (2000) data listed median 1999 household income for each of these groups. In ascending order, they are: Black ($27,910), American Indian or Alaskan Native ($30,784), Hispanic ($30,735), Anglo ($44,366), and Asian or Pacific Islander ($51,205). This is almost a perfect inverse correlation with the crime rates of these groups, and will be viewed as evidence that poverty causes crime by some (and perhaps by others that crime leads to poverty). But are there other factors that may be causally linked to both poverty and crime?

According to the United States Census Bureau (1999), 8% of Whites and 26% of Blacks live in poverty. However, there is no significant difference in poverty rates between Blacks and Whites when household composition is considered. The census data appear to indicate that family structure is a major factor in explaining the high rate of Black poverty. Among African Americans Blacks, 53% of households contained only one parent, compared with 18% among non-Hispanic Whites. However, Blacks in two-parent families are less likely to be living in poverty than are Whites in one-parent families, with only 20.8% of Black two-parent households having an income of less than $25,000 compared to 46% of White single-parent households. Whites living in single-parent households are thus more than twice as likely to be living in poverty as Blacks living in two-parent households. Given these data, and given that individuals make their own decisions about whether to divorce, separate, or have children out of wedlock, it is difficult to make the case that Black poverty is caused by discrimination.

## Family Breakdown

The dearth of two-parent families in the African American community points to large-scale breakdown in the family, a variable that control theorists consider a major factor in the explanation of antisocial behavior. In addition to being highly related to poverty, single-parent households are also independently related to criminal behavior.

The four controls, or bonds, focused on by control theory—attachment, commitment, involvement, and belief—are highly dependent upon stable, loving, and responsible family environments. Criminal and antisocial behavior thrives when these controls are absent. Control theorists share the classical assumption that children have to learn to be good, and in the absence of such learning will default to a hedonistic, selfish, and predatory lifestyle.

According to control theory, the family is the nursery of human nature in that it cultivates and nurtures the raw biological organism into a socialized human being. When social control theorists speak of "the family," they are referring to the nuclear family of modern Western societies. They recognize that there are a variety of childrearing strategies around the world, and that family forms respond to ecological, economic, and cultural contingencies. In evolutionary terms, the "best" family form is that which optimally nurtures and protects its progeny to reproductive age, and the optimal rearing environment is one in which children are surrounded by as many genetically related individuals as possible. Such an arrangement no longer fits the economic and social requirements of modern societies, and we are left with the nuclear family as that which works best to produce socially responsible human beings.

A large number of studies attest to the disabilities suffered by the typical child born out of wedlock (reviewed in Walsh, 1995), and a number also show that children born to teenage single mothers are at substantially greater risk for antisocial behavior than children born into two-parent families (Gruber, Levine, and Staiger, 2000). It follows that groups with unusually high rates of illegitimacy will have higher crime (and poverty) rates than groups with more stable families. A study by Messner and Sampson (1991) found the percentage of female-headed households to be the best predictor of serious crime rates in 151 U.S. cities with a population over 100,000. Children in such households often lack supervision, and are at high risk for involvement with predatory youth gangs.

In short, control theorists would attribute the high rate of Black crime to weaker attachments to social institutions, such as the family, school, and the legitimate economy. This, in turn, may be attributed to high rates of illegitimacy, which is itself related to poverty, lax supervision, and a greatly increased risk of abuse and neglect. David Lykken (1995), for instance, has speculated that most of the discrepancy between Black and White crime rates would disappear if Black and White illegitimacy rates were similar, and Gottfredson and Hirschi (1997) have opined that reducing illegitimacy would do more to lessen crime than all other criminal justice policy proposals combined.

## Subculture of Violence

Marvin Wolfgang and Franco Ferracuti (1967) advanced the thesis that a culture of violence is one that tolerates, and even values, the use of violence to settle disputes. The theory can be rescued from its alleged circularity (rates of violence in a subculture is used to define it as violent, and then the subculture is used to explain rates of violence) if factors other than crime rates are used to define and explain the emergence of a violent subculture.

Historical data indicate that Black-on-Black violence has always been remarkably high in the U.S. James Clarke (1996) explains that this is so because the criminal justice system cared nothing about Black crime after emancipation unless it impinged on White interests. Since Blacks did not expect to find justice in the law, they took to settling disputes themselves, often violently. Clarke traces the high rates of crime, domestic violence, illegitimacy, and child abuse and neglect in the Black community today to an evolved system of cultural values born out of slavery and other grave injustices, and which now "accounts for the social and sexual chaos that reigns in America's inner cities" (1996, 50).

Clarke's explanation of the origins of the Black subculture of violence in the U.S., however, does not explain the existence of similar violent Black subcultures (albeit less violent than in the U.S.) in countries without histories of slavery or Jim Crow laws, or in which large Black populations are of relatively recent origin, such as Canada or Great Britain. This may lead some to speculate that values underlying the use of violence to settle disputes may have originated in Africa (most African nations have extraordinarily high rates of violent crime). If such values were imported from Africa, they would have been preserved and exaggerated by the grave injustices Blacks have experienced in the U.S.

## Social Disorganization

The subculture of violence and social disorganization theories are similar in that they trace differential crime rates to subcultures. The former explains high levels of Black crime to the patterned way of life (norms, values) in the Black subculture, whereas the latter concentrates more on the (mostly physical) conditions obtaining in a specific area that may eventually spawn a violent subculture.

Social disorganization theory avers that areas of cities containing a mix of transient peoples with limited resources who bring with them a variety of conflicting cultural conditions will experience a breakdown of social control, and thus social disorganization. Social disorganization facilitates crime both by failing to inhibit it and by providing a set of values supportive of it. The most important finding of the Chicago School of social disorganization was that Chicago's poor transitional neighborhoods always had the highest crime rates regardless of their racial or ethnic composition (Shaw and McKay, 1972). Shaw and McKay acknowledge that crime rates differed in these neighborhoods when different racial or ethnic groups inhabited them (even though the neighborhoods *per se* always remained the most crime ridden), but chose to downplay it in favor of asserting the power of "place" in explaining crime rates rather than the differential criminality of groups.

The issue of "peoples vs. places" has been examined by a large number of studies, most of which have found that the percentage of African Americans in a state, city, or neighborhood is the best predictor of the crime rate in those areas (reviewed in Walsh, 2002). These results persist controlling for variables such as population density, poverty, income inequality, education, and unemployment. However, social disorganization theorists concern themselves with differences between neighborhoods in the same cities, not between crime rates in states and cities as a whole. Just because

African Americans and Whites live in the same cities does not mean that they share the same neighborhoods, and neighborhoods define the pulse of an individual's life far more strongly than do the more distant residential concepts of "state" or "city."

Poor Blacks face vastly different environments in which to live, work, and raise their children than do poor Whites. White poverty is more dispersed than Black poverty, which is highly concentrated in single neighborhoods (Sampson and Wilson, 2000). For instance, among the 90 neighborhoods in Pittsburgh, the most advantaged neighborhoods have zero percent African American residents, whereas the most disadvantaged had 99% (Wikstrom and Loeber, 2000). According to African American sociologist Elijah Anderson (1999), the concentration of disadvantages in many Black neighborhoods has spawned a hostile and violent oppositional subculture that spurns everything mainstream America values. Anderson thus combines the insights of the subculture of violence and social disorganization theories to explain the high rate of Black crime.

## Theories Emphasizing Individual Differences

Theories emphasizing individual differences have not been well received by mainstream criminologists as there is no way to discuss them without giving offense. Robert Agnew's (1992) general strain theory posits that it is not strain *per se* that provides the impetus to criminal behavior, but rather how one copes with it. Two of the primary traits he mentions in terms of coping poorly or well with strain are temperament and intelligence. Although Agnew does not address race or ethnicity specifically, average IQ and temperamental differences between the races have been invoked as possible explanations for racial differences in criminal activity by a number of theorists.

Robert Gordon (1976) used categorized Differential Aptitude Test (DAT) scores, which are highly correlated with IQ scores, to predict official delinquency rates. He reasoned that if structural variables such as racism and poverty were important in explaining Black or White differences in delinquency, then DAT scores would be irrelevant, and delinquency rates for each race within each DAT category would fluctuate randomly. Gordon found that the percentage of Black and White youths with a police record in each of four DAT categories to be essentially similar, and concluded that the intellectual abilities tapped by the DAT predict delinquency equally well for both races. Gordon explained the 4:1 ratio in Black or White delinquency rates by pointing out that Blacks fell into the lower DAT categories about four times more often than Whites.

Wilson and Herrnstein (1985) emphasize IQ and temperament in their "net advantage" theory, which they assert integrates strain and deterrence theories. They state that Blacks, on average, are more impulsive and have lower IQs than Whites or Asians, and that they are thus less likely to take into account the deferred reinforcements of a prosocial lifestyle, or the deferred punishments of an antisocial lifestyle. In agreement with Gottfredson and Hirschi's (1990) self-control theory, Wilson and Herrnstein trace impulsiveness (or low self-control) to inadequate parenting, and this, in turn, to the high rate of young, single mothers in the Black community. If this argument has any merit, it may also explain the low crime rates of Asian Americans. A large number of studies (reviewed in Rushton, 1995) show that, on average, Asian Americans have greater self-control, higher IQ scores, and greater family stability than African or European Americans.

The most controversial theory of racial differences in crime rates is J. Philippe Rushton's (1995) r or K theory. Rushton's theory is the only one that attempts to explain Black, White, and Asian crime rates simultaneously within the same theoretical structure. The theory is borrowed from population biology and refers to the range of reproductive strategies that exist between and within species. Simply put, a K-strategy emphasizes parental effort, and an r-strategy emphasizes mating effort. These strategies covary with many heritable traits helpful in the maintenance of the used strategy, such as altruism for the K-strategy and aggression for the r-strategy.

According to Rushton, racial populations aggregate at different points along the r or K continuum such that Asians are more K-selected than Whites, who are more K-selected than Blacks. Because reproductive strategies carry with them factors related positively (e.g., aggression) or negatively (e.g., altruism) to criminal behavior, r or K theory has intrigued some criminologists. Lee Ellis has shown that traits used to identify r-selection are more typical of criminals than of noncriminals, and that traits used to identify K-selection were more typical of noncriminals than of criminals. That is, persons with serious criminal histories appear to have the following six r-selected traits to a greater extent than persons in general: (1) shorter gestation periods; (2) earlier onset of sexual activity; (3) greater sexual activity (or at least a preference for such) outside bonded relationships; (4) less stable bonding; (5) lower parental investment (high rates of abuse, neglect, and abandonment of offspring); (6) shorter life expectancy.

Rushton includes other traits such as achievement, sexuality, and social organization, in which socialization is heavily involved, and others, such as morphology, speed of physical maturation, and gamete production, in which social variables are involved minimally, if at all. He finds a consistent pattern in 26 different traits in which Blacks are more "r-selected" than Whites, who are, in turn, more "r-selected" than Asians. This led Rushton to examine INTERPOL data for murder, rape, and serious assault in countries in which the majority of inhabitants could be identified as originating or living in Africa, Europe, or Asia. Summing rates for these crimes across years, he found aggregate rates per 100,000 of 142, 74, and 43, respectively. There were exceptions within categories, however, with the Philippines (Asia) reporting one of the highest violent crime rates in the world, and Togo (Africa) reporting the lowest crime rate in the world.

The consistent Black > White > Asian ordering on r-selected traits does not imply the genetic fixation of the traits involved. Rushton, who characterizes his own theory as a mixed evolutionary or environmental one, readily acknowledges that others who have used the r or K approach have used an environmental model. This model posits that individuals living in unpredictable and harsh environments will "select" an r-strategy emphasizing mating effort, and individuals living in predictable and comfortable environments will "select" a K-strategy emphasizing parenting effort (Draper and Harpending, 1982). These strategies are not consciously selected, but rather flow from expectations learned early in life about the dependability of interpersonal relationships. The major factor emphasized by these theorists is father absence versus father presence, which is consistent with both versions of control theory and the subculture of violence and social disorganization theories.

ANTHONY WALSH

## References and Further Reading

Agnew, R. 1992. Foundations for a general strain theory of crime and delinquency, *Criminology*, 30, 47–87.

Agnew, R. 1997. Stability and change in crime over the life-course: A strain theory explanation, in Thornberry, T., Ed., *Developmental Theories of Crime and Delinquency*, pp. 101–132, New Brunswick, NJ, Transaction.

Anderson, E. 1999. *Code of the Street: Decency, Violence, and the Moral Life of the Inner City*, New York, W.W. Norton.

Barak, G. 1998. *Integrating Criminologies*, Boston, Allyn and Bacon.

Bernard, T. 1990. Angry aggression among the "truly disadvantaged," *Criminology*, 28, 73–96.

Blumstein, A. and Cohen, J. 1987. Characterizing criminal careers, *Science*, 237, 985–991.

Clarke, J. 1996. Black-on-Black violence, *Society,* 33, 46–50.

Draper, P. and Harpending, H. 1982. Father absence and reproductive strategies: An evolutionary perspective, *Journal of Anthropological Research,* 38, 255–273.

Ellis, L. and Walsh, A. 2000. *Criminology: A Global Perspective,* Boston, MA, Allyn and Bacon.

Federal Bureau of Investigation, 2000. Uniform Crime Reports—1999, Washington, DC, Government Printing Office.

Flowers, R. 1988. *Minorities and Criminality,* New York, Greenwood.

Gordon, R., Prevalence: The rare datum in delinquency measurement and its implications for the theory of delinquency, in Klein, M.W., Ed., *The Juvenile Justice System,* pp. 201–284, Beverly Hills, CA, Sage.

Gottfredson, M. and Hirschi, H. 1997. National crime control policies, in Fisch, M., Ed., *Criminology 97/98,* pp. 27–33, Guilford, CT, Dushkin Publishing.

Gruber, J., Levine, P.B. and Staiger, D. 2000. Abortion legalization and child living circumstances: Who is the 'marginal child?', *Quarterly Journal of Economics,* CXIV, 263–291.

Jencks, C. 1992. *Rethinking Social Policy: Race, Poverty and the Underclass.* Cambridge, MA, Harvard University Press.

Lafree, G. and Russell, K. 1993. The argument for studying race and crime, *Journal of Criminal Justice Education,* 4, 273–289.

LaFree, G., Drass, K. and O'Day, P. 1992. Race and crime in postwar America: Determinants of African–American and white rates, *Criminology,* 30, 157–185.

Lykken, D. 1995. *The Antisocial Personalities,* Hillsdale, NJ, Lawrence Erlbaum.

Mann, C.R. 1990. Black female homicides in the U.S., *Journal of Interpersonal Violence,* 5, 176–201.

Merton, R. 1967. *Social Theory and Social Structure,* Glencoe, IL, Free Press.

Messner, S. and Sampson, R. 1991. The sex ratio, family disruption, and rates of violent crime: The paradox of demographic structure, *Social Forces,* 69, 693–723.

Rushton, J.P., *Race, Evolution, and Behavior: A Life History Perspective,* New Brunswick, NJ, Transaction,

Sampson, R. and Wilson, W.J. 2000. Toward a theory of race, crime, and urban inequality, in Cooper, S., Ed., *Criminology,* 149–160.

Shaw, C. and McKay, H. 1972. *Juvenile Delinquency and Urban Areas,* Chicago, IL, University of Chicago Press.

U.S. Census Bureau, 1999. *The Black Population in the United States.,* U.S. Census Bureau, Washington, DC.

U.S. Census Bureau, 2000. *The Black Population in the United States.,* U.S. Census Bureau, Washington, DC.

Walsh, A. 1995. *Biosociology: An Emerging Paradigm,* New York, Praeger.

Walsh, A. 2002. *Biosocial Criminology: An Introduction and Integration,* Cincinnati, OH, Anderson Publishing.

Wikstrom, P. and Loeber, R. 2000. Do disadvantaged neighborhoods cause well-adjusted children to become adolescent delinquents? A study of male juvenile serious offending, individual risk and protective factors and neighborhood context, *Criminology,* 38, 1109–1142.

Wilbanks, W. 1987. The myth of a racist criminal justice system, *Criminal Justice Research Bulletin,* Vol. 3, Huntsville, TX, Sam Houston State University.

Wilson, W.J. 1987. *The Truly Disadvantaged,* Chicago, University of Chicago Press.

Wilson, J.Q. and Herrnstein, R. 1985. *Crime and Human Nature,* New York, Simon and Schuster.

Wolfgang, M. and Ferracutti, F. 1967. *The Subculture of Violence: Towards an Integrated Theory in Criminology,* London, Tavistock.

*See also* **Discrimination in Justice: Gender, Race, and Social Class; Police: Race and Racial Profiling**

# Radical Theories of Criminology

Radical criminology is a theoretical perspective for the analysis of crime, justice, and the broader social context in which these ideas exist. Radical criminology is materialist in that it is a product of Marxist philosophy. According to Lynch and Groves (1989, viii), "As theory, radical criminology attempts to explore and verify connections between social phenomena and economic reality." In practice, radical criminology tends to be activist in nature with regard to issues of social and economic justice. As Schwartz and Friedrichs (1994, 221) state, "[Radical theories are] characterized by an argument that it is impossible to separate values from the research agenda, and by a need to advance a progressive agenda favoring dispriviledged peoples."

Since its first widespread elucidation in the late 1960s, radical criminologic theories have been variously referred to as "critical criminology," "new criminology," "Marxist criminology," "Socialist criminology," "dialectical criminology" and "left realism," among others. Although each of these terms speaks to a particular focus within the area, the name radical criminology is perhaps the most general and encompassing. Accordingly, it, along with "critical criminology," is often used as generic references for theories within this perspective. Radical or critical criminological theories are, in the words of Vold, Bernard, and Snipes (1998, 260), "difficult to summarize," "extremely complex," and as a consequence, "lead ... to profound disagreements among theorists within the same area."

Reflecting a renewed academic interest in Marxist philosophy, radical criminology starts with an examination of the power relations within society and the processes by which acts are defined as criminal. Radical criminology is in many ways a refutation of more traditional functionalist theories of crime. Radical criminologists assert that functionalist explanations place too much emphasis on the structural origins of crime and deviance while neglecting the role that rational choice plays in determining behavior. This functionalist tendency to "over-determine" behavior has been characterized by Dennis Wrong (1961) as, "the over-socialized conception of Man."

Taylor, Walton, and Young (1975) argue that a consequence of Functionalist or "Orthodox" criminology has been an over-identification of social science with agencies of formal social control (i.e. the police, the judiciary and government generally). According to this perspective, Orthodox criminology simply assents to the legal definition of "crime" without an exploration of whose interests are served by these official definitions or from whence these definitions are derived. Further, Richard Quinney (1974, 16), a proponent of so-called "Instrumental Marxism," asserts, "criminal law is an instrument of the state and ruling class to maintain and perpetuate the existing social and economic order."

The views of Richard Quinney stand in opposition to what has been deemed the consensus theory of law. The consensus perspective is an outgrowth of "social contract" theories of the 18th and 19th centuries (Lynch and Groves, 1989, 19). In brief, these theories state that formalized law is a product of a broad social consensus, derived by mutual agreement to abandon what would be an otherwise dominating clash of self-interests. A Marxist perspective challenges this assumption about both law and human nature, characterizing it as an historical abstract and based "on some imaginary primordial condition" (Marx, 1975, 323). Consistent with this position, radicals seek to explain laws in terms of specific historical circumstances and within the context of particular power relationships (i.e. those of economic, political, and gender bases).

Another important aspect of radical criminology is the process by which acts come to be defined as crime. Nettler (1984, 16) states, "crime is a word not a deed." In this Nettler asserts that acts in and of themselves are not crimes. Rather, it is only through the socially derived definition of a particular act as a crime that the act "becomes" a crime. In this respect, radical theories of crime are also a product of labeling theory.

In *The Social Reality of Crime*, Quinney (1970, 15) shows how this characterization of crime fits within the radical perspective, "[C]rime is a definition of human conduct that is created by authorized agents in a politically organized society." For Quinney (1970, 18), this process of definition is shaped by opposing power interests in society, "[T]he probability that criminal definitions will be applied varies according to the extent to which the behaviors of the powerless conflict with the interests of the powerful..." In this, Quinney makes the point that the definition of "crime" is not a fixed construct. It is variable and may be used by one group to force its will onto another.

The question of who defines "what constitutes crime" is central to radical criminology. Many have argued for a definition expanded beyond merely that which is defined as illegal (Schwendinger and Schwendinger, 1970; Freidricks, 1980; Reiman, 1984; Groves and Newman, 1987). Radical criminologists have suggested that acts such as racism, sexism, unsafe working conditions, price fixing, pollution, and deprivation of basic survival necessities are all arguably criminal. To the contrary, Austin Turk (1975) and Paul Tappan (1947) have argued that the radical push for broader definitions often leads to overly broad, subjective, and vague concepts of crime.

Collateral to the radical argument for broader definitions of crime, some radicals also contend that the crimes of the politically and economically powerful often go unnoticed or at least unpunished. Michalowski (1985, 314) calls these "crimes of capital." Michalowski asserts that corporate and political crimes are ultimately more expensive for society than so-called street crime.

As to the root causes of crime, many radical theorists look to the works of Engels (1981) and Bonger (1916). Following a Marxist perspective, some radicals theorize that a capitalist economic system is itself the major stimulus for crime. Engles and Bonger argue that crime is a direct response to the strain of life under a capitalist economy. Engels' basic argument is that workers are embedded in a competitive social and economic structure. Crime for Engels arises out of this competition for scarce resources. Modern scholars such as Gordon (1973) echo this position.

Bonger's argument is similar to that of Engels. In *Criminality and Economic Conditions*, Bonger (1916) argues that this competition for resources manifests itself as egoism. For Bonger, egoism is the source of crime. Many scholars have taken these ideas and incorporated them into examinations of other variables. Colvin and Pauly (1983) studied economic stratification and educational opportunities. Wallace and Humphries (1981) analyzed the forces of urbanization with regard to capitalism. Daly and Chesney-Lind (1988), as well as Box and Hale (1983), have extended radical methodology to feminist criminology.

Although radical theory is firmly rooted in Marx, it is by no means limited to Marx. The language of strain theory is, in many respects, similar to elements of radical thought. Merton (1979) framed his theory in terms of the pressures exerted by social structures that promote nonconformist behavior. This pressure (strain) is composed of two elements: the socially acquired goals for achievement and the unequal opportunities for achievement of those goals. Analyzed in terms of class structures, this perspective integrates well into radical thinking. In particular, both strain theorists and radicals agree that crime is not the exclusive purview of "isolated or abnormal individuals," but that it exists as a regular and institutional feature of a highly stratified society (Lynch and Groves, 1989, 75). Where strain theory falls short for radicals is in its failure to address the structural source of differential opportunities (Colvin and Pauly, 1983, 517). Lynch and Groves (1989, 77) discuss the similarities of the two positions:

> [B]oth strain and radical theories view materialistic cultural aspirations as contributing to criminal behavior. Consistent with the general Marxist approach to culture, radicals deepen the strain theory position by explaining those aspirations as logical expressions of the needs and functional necessities of a capitalist political economy. Second, both explanations recognize the centrality of social classes as it bears on the unequal distribution of opportunities and incentives for criminality.

Where the perspectives diverge is in radical theory's situation of opportunity structures within a Marxist vision of class conflict. Whereas a focus on political economies (i.e., capitalism) is the most prevalent manifestation of these, radical theories explore many different sources of social power inequity (i.e., race, gender, sexuality).

Radical criminology is also informed by aspects of control theory. Central to the argument made by control theorists is Travis Hirschi's (1969, 16) observation that, "delinquent acts occur when the individual's bond to society is weak or broken." For radical theorists, the important extension of this is to inquire as to how bonds are established and maintained. Kornhauser (1978), a control theorist, characterized the process in terms of gratification and punishment. In brief, society must make conformity to norms sufficiently attractive (gratifying) and deviance sufficiently unattractive (deprivation) as to ensure conformity. Kornhauser (1978, 39), however, stated that, "the means by which wants are gratified are unequally distributed." The net result of this, according to Kornhauser, is that social controls are not equally distributed throughout society and that they vary according to an individual's structural position. This sort of characterization squares with many radical theorists' ideas about power and the process of criminalization.

Taylor, Walton, and Young (1974, 453) take up this argument with their assertion that individuals at different locations within the social structure will have different levels of commitment to the social order. Where control theorists and radicals differ is that control theories tend to describe only community characteristics (i.e. Kornhauser's "exogenous" variables) without a focus on the source of the structural inequalities.

Although radical theories of crime clearly arise out of several traditional sources, chief among them Marxism, radical criminology has reached into almost indescribably varied sectors. As it is not possible within this format to describe each of these in detail, the following is a sample of three vigorously attended research areas: postmodern criminology; feminist criminology; and justice system or police studies.

Of all the varieties of criminological theory, postmodern theory is perhaps the most difficult to adequately represent in a concise, yet detailed format. As Schwartz and Friedrichs (1994, 221–246) observe, "[T]here seems to be an almost infinite number of postmodern perspectives." In short, postmodern criminology encompasses a great many, often inaccessibly obscure, perspectives. Vold, Bernard, and Snipes (1998, 270) observe that postmodernist criminology treats scientifically derived knowledge on an equal footing with other types of knowledge. Hence, the positivist foundations of modern social science are assuaged in favor of deconstruction and legitimization of "disparaged" points of view. In some regard, postmodern criminology arose as an examination of language and society's power to both shape and be shaped by it. As evidenced by the preceding discussion of defining acts as "criminal," postmodern theorists explore methods by which the powerful in society may oppress the powerless through language systems. As Arrigo (1993, 27–75) asserts, language is not neutral. It is used to convey meaning and support dominant interpretations of social discourse (i.e. legalistic definitions of criminality). Drawing on Marx, postmodern theorists assert that this support of dominant interpretations in turn supports a litany of oppression scenarios. As an attempt to understand this dynamic, Henry and Milovanovic (1996) use "discourse analysis" to study the linguistic construction of sense and meaning.

As an alternative to the oppressive language of domination, many postmodern theorists have called for the creation of alternative or "replacement discourses" such as the "appreciative relativism" or the "communal celebration" of Albert Borgman (1999). Harold Pepinsky (1991, 301), also working from a postmodern perspective, cautions against a response to crime through oppressive social policy. However, Pepinsky goes on to state, "Someone who is closer to God, natural wisdom, or scientific truth has to keep wayward subordinates in line or social order goes to hell."

As with postmodern theories, there are numerous perspectives in the area of feminist criminology. Not surprisingly, both postmodernist and Marxist (along with many other) orientations are represented in the current body of feminist criminology. Feminist criminology arose out of similar discontent with traditional criminological theories. For feminist scholars, however, the general focus has been to provide an alternative to the treatment of gender issues in traditional criminology. In particular, early feminist criminology was a repudiation of theorists such as Lombroso, Ferrero, and Pollock, who each dealt with gender issues in stereotyped and simplistic terms (Vold, Bernard, and Snipes, 1998, 275). Alternative motives are represented in the works of Carol Smart (1976) and Eileen Leonard (1982), both of whom view traditional criminology as largely having failed to address gender issues at all. Likewise, James Messerschmidt (1993) explores the disparity of treatment between men and women in the criminal justice system.

Two works that were important in the formative days of feminist scholarship were Freda Adler's *Sisters in Crime: The Rise of the New Female Criminal* (1975) and Rita James Simon's *Women and Crime* (1975). Both argued that changing women's roles would result in an increase in crimes committed by women. Where Adler predicts a rise in violent crime, Simon predicts a rise in property and white-collar crimes. Additional research lends more support to Simon's work, but neither has seen strong subsequent validation. According to Simpson (1989, 611), there is scant evidence that a "new female criminal" exists at all. Although Adler's and Simon's studies were significant in that they opened the field of feminist studies more broadly, later feminist scholars have been extremely critical of their work (Simpson, 1989; Morris, 1987; Daly and Chesney–Lind, 1988). Morris (1987, 16) even argues that these studies should not be considered feminist.

As radical feminism developed, writers such as Kate Millet (1970) began to explore the implications of "patriarchy" for social systems. For Millet, the term denotes a system where men and women are socialized into particular gender identities that support the oppression and domination of women. This line of reasoning was subsequently built upon by Marxist feminists such as Polly Radosh (1990). Radosh combines the concept of patriarchal domination with the fact that men own most of the means of production. As such, Marxist feminism ties together what may be characterized as the dually oppressive structures of both patriarchy and capitalism.

As a variant of this perspective, socialist feminism focuses on the "sexual division of labor" (Firestone, 1970). According to socialist feminism, the physical demands of childbearing (before modern birth control) placed women in a position of greater dependency upon men. This dependency became institutionalized such that men worked outside the home and women assumed the tasks of childrearing and householding. For socialist feminists, the keys to social parity with men lay not only in women seeking an economic equality through ownership of production, but also taking control of their own bodies and reproductive functions.

Messerschmidt (1993) observes that feminist arguments against patriarchy and gendered sex roles have in many instances transformed from a discussion of socialized roles to an indictment of the "essential" character of men. In this, Messerschmidt refutes the contention that men are biologically determined to be more aggressive, as some feminists have argued.

Building on postmodern ideas, feminists such as Kathleen Daly and Meda Chesney-Lind (1998) and Carol Smart (1989) have expanded criminology to consideration of differences in the kind of criminology done by male versus female criminologists. According to Daly and Chesney-Lind (1989, 518) women criminologists tend to employ methods such as case studies that provide "texture" and "social context" and further, that these methods tend to be less valued or "trivialized" by traditional criminology, which is couched in "grand theory" and "high-tech statistical" analysis. This, however, points to an irony in postmodern feminist thought: postmodern thought refutes the validity of grand theory, while asserting that women are systematically oppressed.

Radical theory as applied to studies of the criminal justice system and to the role of police frequently depicts laws and those who enforce them as tools of the ruling class for order maintenance (Quinney, 1970; Hall, 1978). In his studies of street crime and the media, Stuart Hall et al. (1978) asserts that British police during the 1970s targeted petty crime as a distraction from the broader economic and social problems facing that nation. Hall further argues that this served to reassert the certainty of official responses to crime, promoted social solidarity by creating "hate figures" (the criminals), and legitimized the repression of "inner city youth." In so doing, the police were serving the interests of the ruling class in terms of aggressive order maintenance.

Influenced by Vold's group conflict theory, Richard Quinney (1970) argues that the legal system provides a mechanism for the ruling class to maintain order in the rest of society. Quinney organized his theory around six propositions articulated in the study, *The Social Reality of Crime.* Quinney's arguments employ techniques borrowed from the sociology of knowledge. In particular, he asserts that reality is subjective and socially constructed. Quinney argues that this construction of knowledge (i.e., conceptions of crime) can be manipulated by the powerful in society to serve their own interests.

In a similar vein, William Chambliss (1975) performed a six-year participant observation study of policing in Seattle, Washington. From this study, Chambliss reports that street crimes were encouraged by local authorities as part of a broad web of corruption and bribery. Chambliss found that those persons who controlled organized criminal activities such as gambling, prostitution, and usury were able to coopt the police into a sinister symbiotic relationship, the net effect of which was a police department almost solely focused on crimes of petty offenses outside the interests of organized crime.

Although radical theories of criminology have arguably driven the canon of modern theory, they are not without shortcomings. In general terms, radical criminology, as an extension of Marxist theory, attempts to analyze crime and criminality in a wide social context. This analytical perspective invariably includes discussion of modes of production, power relationships, and positions of relative influence within society. Whereas this is a necessary component to the perspective, radical criminology often deals with these topics in such abstraction and detail that the focus on crime gets shortchanged. Radical criminology also suffers from a tendency to overly romanticize criminal behavior, both in terms of viewing criminals as victims in an unequal power struggle and in terms of portraying criminals as a threat to the ruling class. Lastly, radical criminology has been termed by Jock Young as a form of "left-wing functionalism." Just as functionalists characterize laws as functioning in the interests of society generally, radical criminologists depict laws as functioning to protect the interests of a ruling class.

MATTHEW PATE

## References and Further Reading

Adler, F. 1975. *Sisters in Crime: The Rise of the New Female Criminal,* New York, McGraw-Hill.

Arrigo, B. 1993. *Madness, Language and the Law,* Albany, NY, Harrow and Heston.

Bonger, W. 1916. *Criminality and Economic Conditions,* Boston, Little, Brown and Co.

Borgman, A. 1999. *Holding on to Reality: The Nature of Information at the Turn of the Millennium,* Chicago, IL, The University of Chicago Press.

Box, S. and Hale, C. 1983. Liberation and female criminality in England and Wales revisited, *British Journal of Criminology,* 22, 35–49.

Chambliss, W.J., Toward a political economy of crime, *Theory and Society,* 2, 2, 149–170.

Colvin, M. and Pauly, J. 1983. A critique of criminology: Toward an integrated structural-Marxist theory of delinquency production, *American Journal of Sociology,* 90(3), 513–551.

Daly, K. and Chesney-Lind, M. 1988. Feminism and criminology, *Justice Quarterly,* 5, 4.

Engels, F. 1978. *Anti-Durhing,* Moscow, Progress Publishers.

Firestone, S. 1970. *The Dialectics of Sex: The Case for Feminist Revolution,* New York, William Morrow.

Freidrichs, D.O. 1980. Radical criminology in the United States, An interpretive understanding, in Inciardi, J., Ed., *Radical Criminology: The Coming Crisis,* Beverly Hills, CA, Sage.

Gordon, D.M. 1971. Class and the economics of crime, *Review of Radical Political Economics,* 3, 51–75 (Summer).

Gordon, D.M. 1973. Capitalism, class and crime in America, *Crime and Delinquency,* 19, 163–186 (April).

Groves, W.B. and Newman, G. 1987. *Punishment and Privilege,* New York, Harrow and Heston.

Hall, S., Critcher, C., Jefferson, T., Clarke, J., Robert, R. 1978. *Policing the Crisis: Mugging, the State, and Law and Order,* London, Macmillan.

Henry, S. and Milovanovic, D. 1996. *Constitutive Criminology: Beyond Postmodernism,* London, Sage.

Hirschi, T. 1969. *Causes of Delinquency,* Berkeley, CA, University of California Press.

Kornhauser, R. 1978. *Social Sources of Delinquency,* Chicago, IL, University of Chicago Press.

Leonard, E.B. 1982. *Women, Crime and Society: A Critique of Criminology Theory,* New York, Longman.

Lynch, M.J. and Groves, W.B. 1989. *A Primer in Radical Criminology,* New York, Harrow and Heston.

Marx, K. 1975. *The Paris Manuscripts in Karl Marx's Early Writings,* New York, Vintage.

Merton, R.K. 1979. Social structure and anomie, in Jacoby, J., Ed., *Classics of Criminology,* Oak Parks, IL, Moore Publishing.

Messerschmidt, J.W. 1993. *Masculinities and Crime,* Lanham, MA, Rowman and Littlefield.

Michalowski, R.J. 1985. *Order, Law and Crime: An Introduction to Criminology,* New York, Random House.

Millet, K. 1970. *Sexual Politics,* New York, Doubleday.

Morris, A. 1987. *Women, Crime and Criminal Justice,* New York, Blackwell.

Nettler, G. 1984. *Explaining Crime,* New York, McGraw Hill.

Pepinsky, H. 1991. Peacemaking in criminology and criminal justice, in Pepinsky, H. and Quinney, R., Eds., *Criminology as Peacemaking,* Bloomington, IN, Indiana University Press.

Quinney, R. 1974. *Critique of Legal Order,* Boston, MA, Little, Brown and Co.

Quinney, R. 1970. *The Social Reality of Crime,* Boston, MA, Little, Brown and Co.

Reiman, J.1984. *The Rich Get Richer and the Poor Get Prison,* New York, Wiley.

Radosh, P. 1991. Woman and crime in the United States: A Marxian explanation, *Sociological Spectrum,* 10, 105–31.

Schwartz, M.D. and Friedrichs, D.O. 1994. Postmodern thought and criminological discontent: New metaphors for understanding violence, *Criminology,* 32, 221–46 (May).

Schwendinger, H. and Schwendinger, J. 1970. Defenders of order or guardians of human rights? *Issues in Criminology,* 5, 113–146.

Simon, R.J. 1975. *Women and Crime,* Lexington, MA, Lexington Books.

Simpson, S.S. 1989. Feminist theory, crime and justice, *Criminology,* 27, 4, 605–631.

Smart, C. 1976. *Women, Crime and Criminology: A Feminist Critique,* Boston, MA, Routledge and Keegan Paul.

Tappan, P. 1947. Who is the criminal? *American Sociological Review,* 12, 97–12.

Taylor, I., Walton, P. and Young, J. 1973. *The New Criminology,* New York, Harper and Row.

Turk, A. 1975. Prospects and pitfalls for radical criminology: A critical response to Platt, *Crime and Social Justice,* 4, 41–42.

Wallace, D. and Humphries, D. 1981. Urban crime and capitalist accumulation: 1950–1971, in Greenberg, D., Ed., *Crime and Capitalism,* Palo Alto, CA, Mayfield.

Vold, G.B., Bernard, T.J. and Snipes, J.B. 1998. *Theoretical Criminology,* New York, Oxford University Press.

*See also* **Bonger, William; Critical Criminology: An Overview; Left Realism; Marxist Theories of Criminal Behavior**

# Radzinowicz, Sir Leon

Sir Leon Radzinowicz was a noted and revered criminological scholar, tackling issues of British penology (in the UK) and crime on an international level.

## Education

Sir Leon's life began on August 15, 1906, and ended 93 years later on December 29, 1999. He was born in Poland but did not stay there for long. He started his education in the Faculty of Law at the Sorbonne in the 1920s. He earned a master's degree from the University of Geneva in 1927 and then began working on his doctorate in Rome. In 1930, Sir Leon prepared a report on British penology that resulted in his designation as Chevalier de l'Ordre Leopold. In 1932 he returned to Poland to receive his doctorate from the University of Krakow and began teaching as an assistant professor at the Free University of Warsaw. It was not until the late 1930s that Sir Leon traveled in and out of Britain, eventually settling in Cambridge in 1940.

## Family

Sir Leon married two times. In the first marriage to Mary Anne Nevens (1958–1979), she bore two children, a son and a daughter. His second marriage to Isolde Klarmann did not produce children; he remained married to her until his death.

## Contributions to the Field of Criminology

In 1945 Sir Leon worked for the UN in regard to social defense and international collaboration on criminal justice. His work with the UN was the catalyst for the remainder of his career by establishing an international voice on crime and the criminal justice system. In 1948 he embarked on authoring numerous notable publications, including five volumes of his *A History of English Criminal Law,* which he did not complete until 1986.

From 1949–1953 Sir Leon Radzinowicz was a member of the Royal Commission on Capital Punishment. The commission's purpose was to examine the utility of capital punishment by determining if sentencing laws should be changed, and if they should be changed, suggestions for the reduction of liability were made. The commission concluded, somewhat liberally, that: (1) mitigating circumstances should reduce capital sentences to life imprisonment, (2) verbal provocation is equal to other forms of provocation, and (3) clarification and different verbiage in terms of criminal responsibility for the mentally insane should be written into law (www.bopcris.ac.uk). These recommendations were grounded in *a priori* research, yet they were modern for the time and state of the British criminal justice system.

In 1959 Sir Leon founded the Institute of Criminology at the University of Cambridge. He tenured the position of Wolfson Professor of Criminology until 1973 (department chair), during which he published numerous works advancing knowledge of crime and punishment (three that are commonly cited and his 1999 memoir are discussed below).

Also during his tenure, he taught in law schools across the U.S., such as Yale, Columbia, Virginia, Rutgers, University of Pennsylvania, and others. In 1966 Sir Leon published *Ideology and Crime*, which chronicled the development of modern thought towards reducing and managing crime and criminals. In this publication, he speaks of previous theoretical works and how they aided in the furtherance of modern methodologies to more accurately study and explain crime.

In 1970 Queen Elizabeth II honored Sir Leon by knighting him for services rendered to the Royal Court, and for the previous work he had done in the field of criminology.

In 1972 Sir Leon and Marvin Wolfgang compiled and published *Crime and Justice*, which is a three volume series of selected topics in criminal justice. The first volume suggests explanations for causes of crime (environmental and individual), and the response the criminal justice system should have to criminal behavior. The second and third volumes examine the usefulness and hindrance of the police and court structures.

In 1973 Sir Leon retired from the Wolfson Chair and did not publish another book until 1977 (*The Growth of Crime*). *The Growth of Crime* was Sir Leon and Joan King's international perspective on the crime problem. In this book, they traversed through research and theory while suggesting which policies work and which do not. Their eloquent deduction of the purposes of any criminal justice system is worth attention.

Other published works by Sir Leon address issues in the prison setting, court proceedings, sentencing, law making, policing, etc. The above works are mentioned because they are the most popular of his publications.

The last publication from Sir Leon came in 1999, titled *Adventures in Criminology*. In this work, Sir Leon discussed the growth of criminology and often paralleled such growth to his own career. He uses a modest tone detailing his experiences in the field, personal and professional. This work comprehensively describes the components and functions of the criminal justice system and crime, along with Sir Leon's criticisms and praises.

## Bequest

Sir Leon left a bequest to further supplement and enhance the work of the Institute of Criminology.

Under the bequest, opportunities for students to receive an award have been made possible. The Nigel Walker Prize is an annual award for an outstanding piece of criminological work. The main purpose of this award is to honor the work of Ph.D. students. The bequest also specified a visiting fellowship and a lecture series to be held every other year by a leading public figure. The goal of the series is to continue the relationship between criminology and criminal policy (www.cam.ac.uk).

## Conclusion

In life and death Sir Leon contributed to the field of criminology. He was a highly published scholar and solely contributed to the international perspective of crime and public policy. In some ways, he was ahead of his time in his view of political and governmental aspects that create criminal policy. Sir Leon's work helped to improve the field in examination and measurement of crime.

MEGAN HOWELL

## Biography

Born in Lodz, Poland, August 15 1906. Began education in the Faculty of Law at the Sorbonne; acquired M.A. from University of Geneva, 1927; earned Ph.D. from University of Krakow, 1932; Assistant Professor at Free University of Warsaw, 1932; traveled in Britain reporting on English penal policy, 1933–1939; settled in Cambridge in 1940. Worked for U.N. section on Social Defense and International Collaboration on Criminal Justice, 1945; published five volumes of the history of English penology, 1948–1986; member of Royal Commission on Capital Punishment, 1949–1953. Founder and Wolfson Professor of Criminology at the University of Cambridge, 1959–1973; Knighted by Queen Elizabeth, 1970; wrote and published a memoir, 1999. Died in Haverford, PA, 29 December 1999.

## Selected Writings

*Ideology and Crime*. London: Heinemann, 1966.
*Crime and Justice* (with M. Wolfgang, eds.). New York: Basic Books, 1972.
*The Growth of Crime* (with J. King). NY: Basic Books, 1977.
*Adventures in Criminology*. London and NY: Routledge, 1999.

## References and Further Reading

Maxwell, et al. (1953). *Royal Commission on Capital Punishment 1949–1954; Report,* August, 2003. Available at: http://www.bopcris.ac.uk/bop1940/ref908.html.
University of Cambridge. (2003). Founding Father Leaves Bequest, August, 2003. Available at: http://www.admin.cam.ac.uk/news/dp/2003051601.

# Rape, Acquaintance and Date

Rape is legally defined as the act of nonconsensual penetration of an adolescent or adult obtained by physical force, threatened use of physical force, or when the victim is incapable of giving consent by virtue of mental illness, mental disability, or intoxication from alcohol or drugs. Absent from this definition is any mention of the victim-offender relationship. However, the victim-offender relationship in the commission of a rape has been and continues to be the focus of debate.

Beginning in the mid-1970s, the feminist movement in the U.S. achieved major reforms in state-level rape statutes. By 1980, every state had considered rape reform legislation. Forty-one states passed significant rape law reforms. In 1986, Congress passed a bill making the federal rape law conform to most state statutes. Nonetheless, there still are persons, including some criminal justice personnel, who believe that "real" rape is a crime committed by a person who is a stranger to the victim (see Searles and Berger, 1987; Bohmer and Parrot, 1993). Feminist researchers have steadfastly responded to these critics by arguing that regardless of the nature of the relationship between the victim and the offender, all rapes are "real" rapes and should be treated equally in the rape laws and by institutional structures that adjudicate rape (see Crowell and Burgess, 1996).

Research suggests that the victim-offender relationship influences whether or not a woman considers her experience as a rape. To illustrate, Koss et al. (1988) reported that 55% of the women raped by a stranger acknowledged their experience as a rape compared to only 23% of women who were raped by someone that they knew.

For clarification purposes, two commonly used words—acquaintance and date—describe the victim-offender relationship in which some rapes take place. The terms acquaintance rape and date rape are not legal categories but used in a sociological sense (Bohemer and Parrot, 1993). Rape in which the victim and offender know each other prior to the nonconsensual sexual act is commonly referred to as an acquaintance rape. The acquaintance relationship can be one of many different types of acquaintanceships, including platonic, dating, marital, professional, academic, or familial. Date rape is a subset of acquaintance rape in which nonconsensual sex occurs between two parties who are in a self-defined "dating" relationship (Parrot and Bechhofer, 1991).

The estimates of the extent of acquaintance rape and date rape provided by many researchers suggest that these types are more common than many have thought or have been willing to accept. Reports of rape between individuals who know each other date back to biblical times. The more contemporary pioneering works of Kanin (1957), Amir (1971), and Russell (1982) are among the first published research efforts to examine acquaintance rape.

Since these first generation studies, a countless number of case studies have focused on rape experiences among college women. Many of these studies have consistently reported that college women are at high risk of acquaintance rape and date rape (see Marx, Van Wie, and Gross, 1996). For example, Abbey, Ross, McDuffie, and McAuslan (1996) collected sexual victimization data from 1160 undergraduate women attending a large urban commuter university. They reported that in 91% of the attempted or completed rapes committed against these women, the offender was not a stranger to the victim.

There are numerous localized case studies of the extent and nature of rape among college women, although only two national-level studies have been done to date. In the early 1980s, Koss, Gidycz, and Wisnewski (1987) conducted the first national-level study of acquaintance rape and date rape among college women. Koss et al. reported that of the 468 rape victims in their sample of 3187 college women, 89% (416) of the victims reported that the rape was committed by an acquaintance (i.e., friend, coworker, neighbor, casual date, steady boyfriend or lover, or family member).

In the mid-1990s, Fisher, Cullen, and Turner (2000) completed a nationally representative study of the sexual victimization of 4446 college women enrolled in two-year or four-year colleges or universities. They reported that in 153 completed and attempted rape incidents involving a single offender, 86.9% (133) involved someone that the victim knew or had seen before (e.g., a current boyfriend or lover, an ex-boyfriend or lover, or a classmate). In 21.8% of these incidents (29), the victim and offender were on a date when the rape occurred.

Data from the Canadian National Survey show that experiencing rape in dating relationships is not restricted to college women and men in the U.S. Of the 1835 college women interviewed, 10.5% stated that they had been raped and 10.2% stated that they had experienced an attempted rape in the past year by a dating partner (DeKeseredy and Schwartz, 1998). Further, 2.8% of the males indicated that they had raped a dating partner in the last year; another 2.8% reported that they had attempted to rape a dating partner. Using a larger reporting period, Muehlenhard and Linton (1987) found that 7.1% of all the male college students in their sample admitted raping a woman while on a date during high school or college.

Koss (1985) proposed three theoretical models to explain how women experience a rape: (1) the social control model, (2) the victim precipitation model, and (3) the situational blame model. Briefly, the social control model posits that women are socialized through sex roles to accept rape-supportive beliefs and attitudes. This model suggests that women who accept these beliefs and attitudes are more vulnerable to experiencing a rape. The victim precipitation model proposes that a woman's vulnerability to rape can be increased by unknowingly engaging in specific behaviors or having certain personality characteristics. These may include passivity, over submissiveness, or insensitivity to social nuances. The situational blame model states that rape is more likely in certain environmental or structural locations (bars or slum neighborhoods). The placement of women in these situations increases the likelihood of a rape.

Numerous researchers have used these three models to test hypotheses concerning factors that may increase a woman's vulnerability to being raped by an acquaintance or dating partner. Overall, the research results suggest that the best prediction comes from a combination of factors rather than just one. First, researchers have shown that childhood experiences may increase the vulnerability to date rape. Sanders and Moore (1999) reported that college women who experienced a date rape were significantly more likely than women who have not been raped to report an abusive sexual experience that occurred during their childhood or early adolescence along with more overall childhood stress (for a different conclusion, see Himelein, 1995). Second, prior victimization in dating may account, in part, for future date rape vulnerability. Himelein's (1995) results from a longitudinal study of college women showed that precollege sexual victimization in dating was the strongest predictor of college dating victimization. Third, researchers have examined the role, if any, that alcohol plays in date rape experiences. Consistent with previous research results that report that heavy use of alcohol is associated with greater risk of sexual victimization, Himelein (1995) reported that alcohol use in dating was associated with date rape at the

two time periods she collected data. Some researchers have suggested that a male may view his intoxicated date as a signal of her willingness to engage in sex with him (see Muehlenhard and Linton, 1987). Fourth, several studies have examined the relationship between victim behaviors and the occurrence of date rape. Using vignettes where "suggestive" behaviors were manipulated, Muehlenhard, Friedman, and Thomas (1985) reported that respondents viewed rape as more justified when a man pays for the dating expenses. Consistent with these findings, Muehlenhard (1988), using a similar vignette design, reported that college men and women viewed rape as justifiable when the woman asks the man out, when she went to his apartment, and when she let him pay for the dating expenses. And last, it is difficult at this time to draw conclusions about whether victim's attitudes play or do not play a significant role in vulnerability to acquaintance rape or date rape. The attitudinal studies are limited with respect to acquaintance rape and date rape for two reasons. First, some studies did examine the specific context of an acquaintance or a date rape (see Koss 1985; Koss and Dinero, 1989). Second, other studies examined the broader concept of sexual aggression that included unwanted sexual activity (e.g., kissed with tongue contact or touched buttocks under clothing) without separate analyses for rape (see Muehlenhard and Linton, 1987).

Researchers have also examined resistance strategies used by those who have experienced a rape. Koss et al. (1988) reported that college women who experienced an acquaintance rape used similar resistance strategies as women who experienced a stranger rape (e.g., turning cold, reasoning or pleading, crying or sobbing, and physically struggling). In contrast, evidence from other studies reported that women are less likely to physically resist more intimate offenders than strangers and acquaintances (see Ullman, 1997).

The examination of the characteristics of date rapists is limited in number and scope. Aside from Kanin's study (1984, 1985) of 71 self-disclosed date rapists, there are very few extensive investigations of the characteristics or attitudes of date rapists. Kanin reported that 75% of his samples were from middle class backgrounds and 82% were college students. Relative to the control group, the date rapists were more sexually experienced, dated frequently, and participated in more sexual activity. Kanin further reported that date rapists were more dissatisfied with the frequency of their sexual experiences, and as a result, were frustrated by their relative sexual deprivation.

Another line of research uses role playing and vignettes to examine male sexual arousal and acquaintance and date rape. The results from these studies suggest that male sexual arousal may play a role in date rape and that arousal levels are determined, in part, by such situational factors as perceived female consent, arousal of the female, and repeated exposure to violent sexual stimuli (see Marx et al., 1996).

Contextual and situational characteristics also can play a role in acquaintance and date rapes. First, a number of studies have shown that any level of familiarity is possible—a platonic friend, blind date, or intimate partner involved in a long-term relationship—for a rape to occur (see Koss et al., 1988). To illustrate, Skelton (1982) found that 36% of rapes occurred on the first date or by an acquaintance, 26% by an occasional date, and 31% by a regular suitor. Kanin's (1984) investigation of self-admitted date rapists revealed that the rape occurred after having two to five dates prior to the rape. Of the 416 rape victims identified by Koss et al. (1987), 60% of the offenders were casual or steady dates. The remaining victims reported that the offender was a nonromantic acquaintance (29%) or a spouse or other family member (11%). Second, most date rapes occur in isolated locations. Miller and Marshall's (1987) study of college men and women at a large university revealed that date rapes most frequently happened in apartments or private homes (55%), followed by a residence hall (15%), and parked cars (15%). Five percent of the women in their study reported experiencing a date rape in a fraternity. Third, the time of day when an acquaintance rape occurs differs from when a stranger rape occurs. Date rapes, in particular, are more likely to occur on weekends, between the hours of 10:00 PM and 1:00 AM. The duration of the rape experience also differs by type of rape. Date rapes last longer than stranger rapes—sometimes four hours or more (Allison and Wrightsman, 1993). Fourth, stranger rapists are more likely than an acquaintance rapist to carry a weapon, in particular, a gun (Ullman, 1997).

There is consistent evidence from different sources of data that suggests that experiencing a rape by an acquaintance or a date, just as experiencing a stranger rape, is a traumatic, destructive, life-altering experience that takes a negative toll on the victim (see Gidycz and Koss, 1991). Numerous studies have found no difference between those who have been raped by an acquaintance and those who have been raped by a stranger in terms of post-rape symptoms (e.g., depression, fear, and anxiety). To illustrate, Koss, Dinero, Seibel, and Cox (1988), using Koss et al.'s (1987) national-level survey data of college women, reported that victims of stranger rape and victims of acquaintance rape were not significantly different with respect to psychological symptoms. Both reported significantly elevated levels of anxiety and depression and decreased levels of sexual and relationship satisfaction. Kilpatrick, Saunders, Veronen, Best, and Von (1987) also reported no significant difference in psychological disorders between victims of stranger and victims of acquaintance rapes. More recently, Frazier and Seales (1997), using both hospital-based rape crisis center data and survey data from a sample of college women at a large Midwestern university, reported that victims of acquaintance rape are as traumatized as victims of stranger rape. Their results revealed that victims of acquaintance rape did not differ from women who had experienced a rape by a stranger in terms of depression, hostility, anxiety, or posttraumatic stress disorder. They also reported that "acquaintance rape victims tend to blame themselves more for the assault and to report more disrupted beliefs than victims of stranger rape" (Frazier and Seales, 1997, 62). Further, comparisons made between college women who experienced a date rape and college women who had never been raped are consistent with this previous research: those who had experienced a date rape reported higher levels of dissociation, depression, and various other trauma symptoms than, those who had not experienced a date rape (Shapiro and Schwarz, 1997). Only a limited number of studies have found stranger rape victims more distressed than acquaintance rape victims in terms of depression, fear, and posttraumatic stress disorder (see Frazier and Seales, 1997).

Despite the high frequency of acquaintance and date rape and the documented negative effects on women who have such experiences, reporting of these incidents to law enforcement is quite low, and hence, few acquaintance rapists ever confront the criminal justice system for their behaviors. Fisher et al. (1999), for example, reported few women reported their experience to law enforcement. Only 3.8% (5) of the rapes in which the victim knew or had seen the offender before were reported to the police. Identical to Findelson and Oswalt's results, Fisher et al. reported that none of the date rapes were reported to law enforcement.

Women who were raped by someone they knew are less likely to seek professional services compared to women who were raped by a stranger, although neither of the two types of victims does so very often. Koss et al. (1988) reported that 19.2% of the stranger rape victims sought crisis services compared to 1.7% of the acquaintance rape victims.

Women, however, do report talking about their acquaintance rape or date rape with another person. To illustrate, Dunn, Vail–Smith, and Knight (1999) examined the extent to which a woman discloses to another college student her experience with an acquaintance rape or a date rape. Dunn et al. reported that about 33% of their 828 undergraduate respondents reported knowing one or more women who had experienced an acquaintance rape or a date rape. More than half (52.5%) of the women respondents reported that they had been the recipients of a woman's date or acquaintance rape disclosure whereas 37.8% of the men said they had been the recipients. These results also showed that disclosure to another student typically involved detailed information about the incident and not just casual mention of the rape experience.

A variety of interested groups, including women's advocacy and victim's rights groups, medical and legal professionals, the criminal justice community, college student advocacy groups (e.g., Security On Campus), the media (e.g., *The Chronicle of Higher Education*), the U.S. Congress, parents and students, as well as the general public have all shown concern as to the extent of acquaintance and date rape and taken some action. Despite the increased awareness, there is a lack of a consensus about how to address these problems.

In recent years, many different types of strategies and educational programs have been implemented—many on college and university campuses—to prevent acquaintance and date rape. These strategies and programs include installing blue light emergency telephones or trimming shrubbery (this ignores the consistent findings that a large proportion of rapes are committed by acquaintances), educational programs that teach women assertiveness or self-defense skills, and mixed-sex programs that address cross-sex communication and dating expectations or target changing rape supportive attitudes or misinformation about rape mythology. At least two campus-based case study evaluations of programs designed to change attitudes toward date rape have been published. These concluded that (1) women readily changed their rape supportive attitudes in the desirable direction, whereas males maintained their beliefs even after exposure to a program designed to challenge their attitudes, and (2) a theoretical production based on social learning theory and risk-factor reduction resulted in a significant improvement in attitudes related to date rape among both female and male students (Lenihan, Rawlins, Eberly, Buckley, and Masters, 1992; Lanier, Elliot, Martin, and Kapadia, 1997). Clearly, replication of these programs and evaluations at different types of colleges and universities are needed before any generalizations about the success of programs can be made.

In a similar vein, researchers know very little about the effectiveness of any particular acquaintance or date rape strategy or program in reducing the number of women who have been raped or preventing these types of rape. To date, few rigorous evaluations of the effectiveness of strategies or programs aimed at preventing rape or reducing the number of women who have experienced rape have been completed (see Lonsway, 1996). In part, campus-based program evaluators are struggling with conceptualizing outcome measures and using experimental designs. Until rigorous evaluations of these programs and strategies are done, the promise of acquaintance and date rape prevention (along with stranger rape prevention) cannot be realized fully.

BONNIE S. FISHER

## References and Further Reading

Abbey, A., Ross, L.T., McDuffie, D. and McAuslan, P. 1996. Alcohol and dating risk factors for sexual assault among college women, *Psychology of Women Quarterly,* 20.

Allison, J.A. and Wrightsman, L.S. 1993. *Rape: The Misunderstood Crime,* London, Sage Publications.

Amir, M. 1971. *Patterns in Forcible Rape,* Chicago, IL, University of Chicago Press.

Bohmer, C. and Parrot, A. 1993. *Sexual Assault on Campus: The Problem and the Solution,* New York, Lexington Books.

Crowell, N.A. and Burgess, A.W. 1996. *Understanding Violence Against Women,* Washington, DC, National Academy Press.

DeKeseredy, W.S. and Schwartz, M.D 1998. Woman abuse: Results from the Canadian National Survey, in Renzetti, C.M. and Edleson, J.L., Eds., *Sage Series on Violence Against Women,* Vol. 5, Thousand Oaks, CA, Sage Publications.

Dunn, P., Vail-Smith, K. and Knight, S.M. 1999. What date or acquaintance rape victims tell others: A study of college student recipients of disclosure, *Journal of American College Health,* 47.

Fisher, B.S., Cullen, F.T. and Turner, M. 2000. Sexual Victimization Among College Women: Results from Two National-Level Studies. Research Report at the National Institute of Justice, Washington, DC, National Institute of Justice.

Findelson, L. and Oswalt, R. 1995. College date rape: Incidence and reporting, *Psychological Reports,* 77.

Frazier, P.A. and Seales, L.M. 1997. Acquaintance rape is real rape, in Schwarz, M.D., Ed., *Research of Sexual Violence Against Women: Methodological and Personal Perspectives,* Thousand Oaks, CA, Sage Publications.

Gidycz, C.A. and Koss, M.P. 1991. The effects of acquaintance rape on the female victim, Parrot, A. and Bechhofer, L., Eds., *Acquaintance Rape the Hidden Crime.* New York, Wiley.

Himelein, M.J. 1995. Risk factors for sexual victimization in dating, *Psychology of Women Quarterly,* 19.

Kanin, E. 1957. Male aggression in dating-courtship relations, *American Journal of Sociology,* 10.

Kanin, E. 1984. Date rape: Unofficial criminals and victims, *Victimology,* 9.

Kanin, E. 1985. Date rapists: Differential sexual socialization and relative deprivation, *Archives of Sexual Behavior,* 14.

Kilpatrick, D.G., Saunders, B.E., Veronen, L.J., Best, C.L. and Von, J.M. 1988. Criminal victimization: Lifetime prevalence, reporting to police, and psychological impact, *Crime and Delinquency,* 33.

Koss, M.P. 1985. The hidden rape victim: Personality attitudes and situational characteristics, *Psychology of Women Quarterly,* 9.

Koss, M.P., Gidycz, C.A. and Wisniewski, N.J. 1987. The scope of rape: Incidence and prevalence of sexual aggression and victimization in a national sample of higher education students, *Journal of Consulting and Clinical Psychology,* 55.

Koss, M.P., Dinero, T.E., Seibel, C.A. and Cox, S.L. 1988. Stranger and acquaintance rape: Are there differences in the victim experience? *Psychology of Women Quarterly,* 12.

Koss, M.P. and Dinero, T.E. 1989. Discriminant analysis of risk factors for sexual victimization among a national sample of college women, *Journal of Consulting and Clinical Psychology,* 57.

Lanier, C.A., Elliot, M.N., Martin, D.W. and Kapadia, A. 1998. Evaluation of an intervention to change attitudes toward date rape, *Journal of American College Health,* 46.

Lenihan, G.O., Rawlins, M.E., Eberly, C.G., Buckley, B. and Masters, B. 1992. Gender differences in rape supportive attitudes before and after a date rape education intervention, *Journal of College Student Development,* 33.

Lonsway, K.A. 1996. Preventing acquaintance rape through education, *Psychology of Women Quarterly,* 20.

Marx, B.P., Van Wie, V. and Gross, A.M. 1996. Date rape risk factors: A preview and methodological critique of the literature, *Aggression and Violent Behavior,* 1.

Miller, B. and Marshall, J.C. 1987. Coercive sex on the university campus, *Journal of College Student Personnel,* 28.

Muchlenhard, C.L. and Linton, M.A. 1987. Date rape and sexual aggression in dating situations: Incidence and risk factors, *Journal of Counseling Psychology,* 34.

Muchlenhard, C.L., Friedman, D.E. and Thomas, C.M. 1985. Is date rape justifiable? The effects of dating activity, who initiated, who paid, and man's attitudes toward women, *Psychology of Women Quarterly,* 9.

Muehlenhard, C.L. 1988. Misinterpreted dating behaviors and the risk of date rape, *Journal of Social and Clinical Psychology,* 6.

Parrot, A. and Bechhofer, L., Eds. 1991. *Acquaintance Rape the Hidden Crime,* New York, Wiley.

Russell, D.E.H. 1982. The prevalence and incidence of forcible rape of females, *Victimology,* 7.

Russell, D.E.H. 1984. *Sexual Exploitation: Rape, Child Sexual Abuse, and Workplace Harassment,* Beverly Hills, CA, Sage Publications.

Sanders, B. and Moore, D.L. 1999. Childhood maltreatment and date rape, *Journal of Interpersonal Violence,* 14.

Searles, P. and Berger, R.J. 1987. The current status of rape reform legislation: An examination of state statutes, *Women's Rights Law Reporter,* 10.

Shapiro, B.L. and Schwarz, J.C. 1997. Date rape: Its relationship to trauma symptoms and sexual self-expression, *Journal of Interpersonal Violence,* 12.

Skelton, C.A., *Situational and Personological Correlates of Sexual Victimization in College Women,* Ph.D. dissertation, Auburn University, 1982, (Unpublished).

Ullman, S.E. 1997. Review and critique of empirical studies of rape avoidance, *Criminal Justice and Behavior,* 24.

*See also* **Rape, Forcible: Extent and Correlates; Rape, Forcible: Law; Rape, Forcible: Theories; Rape, Marital; Rape, Statutory**

# Rape, Forcible: Extent and Correlates

In the U.S., rape is a criminal act defined by legal statutes as a felony. As a result of the rape law reforms that began in the last quarter of the 20th century, a variety of terms are used to legally label "rape" (e.g., "sexual assault," "sexual battery," "sexual abuse"). Although all definitions of rape include the notion of nonconsensual sexual behavior, the legal definition of rape varies across the state statutes, the District of Columbia, and the federal government's U.S. code. All states criminalize certain types of forcible sexual penetrations (e.g., vaginal intercourse, anal intercourse, cunnilingus, and fellatio), although some states do not criminalize sexual penetration unless certain extreme circumstances are present. Those circumstances vary but typically include that: the victim was physically forced or threatened with bodily harm or force; the victim was unconscious or unable to give consent because of mental illness, mental retardation, or the administration of an intoxicating or anesthetic substance; or the victim was of a very young age (Horney and Spohn, 1992). The sex classification of the offender and victim also varies across states. To illustrate, the majority of states use sex neutral terminology for both offender and victim because rape can occur to a heterosexual, homosexual, or lesbian. Other states, such as Alabama and Maine, use the term "male offender" and "female victim" (Searles and Berger, 1987, table 4).

There are two national-level sources of the annual incidence of rape in the U.S.: (1) the Federal Bureau of Investigation's Uniform Crime Report (UCR), and (2) the Bureau of Justice Statistics' National Crime Victimization Survey (NCVS). Relying on rapes reported to the police, the UCR reports that 95,136 forcible rapes, or 33 forcible rapes per 100,000 persons, were committed in the U.S. in 2002. The UCR defines forcible rape as: "the carnal knowledge of a female forcibly and against her will." This definition includes assaults and attempts to commit forcible rape but does not include statutory rape and other sex offenses (see http://www.fbi.gov/ucr/ucr.htm). Providing estimates for reported and unreported rapes to the police, the NCVS indicates that in 2002, there were 90,390 completed rape and 77,470 attempted rapes, equaling 167,860 total rapes or 0.7 rapes per 1000 persons (see http://www.ojp.usdoj.gov/bjs/pub/pdf/cvus02.pdf). The NCVS defines rape as: forced sexual intercourse including both psychological coercion as well as physical force. Forced sexual intercourse means penetration by the offender(s) and includes attempted rapes, male as well as female victims, and both heterosexual and homosexual rape. Attempted rape includes verbal threats of rape (see http://www.ojp.usdoj.gov/bjs/glance/rape.htm). Notably, both the UCR and NCVS have reported a gradual, yet steady, decline in the annual incidence of rape since 1992.

Other national-level sources of lifetime prevalence and annual incidence of rape estimates are based on self-report surveys that employ behaviorally specific questions to measure rape. The two most widely cited studies that employ a sample of women from the general public include Kilpatrick and his colleagues' (1992) *Rape in America*, and Tjaden and Thoennes' (1998) National Violence Against Women (NVAW) survey. For example, the NVAW survey found that 1 of 6 women (17,722,672) and 1 of 33 men (2,782,440) have experienced an attempted or completed rape in their lifetime. Tjaden and Thoennes define rape as an "event that occurred without the victim's consent, that involved the use or threat of force to penetrate the victim's vagina or anus by penis, tongue, fingers, or objects, or the victim's mouth by penis" (Tjaden and Thoennes, 1998, 8).

Two national-level studies of college women provide estimates of rape for college women. First, using the Sexual Experience Survey, Koss, Gidycz, and Wiseniewski (1987) provide rape estimates since the age of 14 and incidence of rape during the previous year. Koss et al. (1987, 166) used the state of Ohio

definition of rape: "vaginal intercourse between male and female, and anal intercourse, fellatio, and cunnilingus between persons regardless of sex. Penetration, however slight, is sufficient to complete vaginal or anal intercourse...No person shall engage in sexual contact with another person...." They reported that 15.4% of the college sample self-reported being raped and 12.1% reported experiencing an attempted rape since the age of 14 (Koss, Gidycz, and Wiseniewski, 1987).

Second, Fisher, Cullen, and Turner (2000), using a two-stage measurement strategy with behaviorally specific screen questions, provide rape estimates for an academic year. Fisher et al. (2000) reported that 28 per 1000 female students had experienced either a completed or attempted rape since school had started in the fall of the current academic term. Fisher et al. (2000) differentiates between completed and attempted rape. Completed rape is defined as ". . . unwanted completed penetration by force or the threat of force. Penetration includes: penile-vaginal, mouth on your genitals, mouth on someone else's genitals, penile-anal, digital-vaginal, digital-anal, object-vaginal, and object-anal." The definition for attempted rape is the same as completed rape except it includes only attempted penetration (Fisher et al., 2000, 65).

Men have also been the focus of rape studies. Several studies reported that 25–57% of college men acknowledged committing rape, with 7–15% of these acts meeting the legal standards for rape (see Abbey, McAuslan, Zawacki, Clinton, and Buck, 2001).

Criminal justice statistics concerning rape reveal several noteworthy points. First, rape is most likely to go unreported to law enforcement. Results from several studies, including the NCVS, have consistently reported that approximately two-thirds of all rapes are not reported to law enforcement (see Fisher, Cullen and Turner, 2000). Second, law enforcement has success in clearing rape cases. Of those rapes that do get reported to law enforcement, close to half (49%) get cleared nationwide (http://www.fbi.gov/ucr/Cius_99/99crime/99c2_04.pdf). Third, type of locale does not seem related to clearance rates. For instance, there is little urban to suburban/rural difference in clearance rates for forcible rape (49% and 50%, respectively) (http://www.fbi.gov/ucr/Cius_99/99crime/99c2_04.pdf). However, there appears to be regional variation in clearance rates. The clearance rates for rape are slightly higher in the South (53%) and Northeast (52%) compared to those in the Midwest (45%) and West (45%) (http://www.fbi.gov/ucr/Cius_99/99crime/99c2_04.pdf). Fourth, court data add further insight into the processing of rape cases. The UCR indicate that approximately one in 20 violent felony filings are for rape (http://www.fbi.gov/ucr/Cius_99/99crime/99c2_04.pdf). Once rape cases reach the courts, 8 in 10 convicted rapists enter a plea of not guilty. Of these pleas of not guilty, two-thirds receive a prison sentence, with an average sentence length of 14 years; 19% serve their term in the local jail with an average sentence of 8 months; and 13% receive probation supervision, with an average sentence length of 6 years (Bureau of Justice Statistics, 1997).

Theories of why a person rapes can be divided into two broad categories: (1) those theories that focus on individual factors that are internal to the person, and (2) those theories that focus on societal factors that are external to the person. The internal theoretical perspective addresses such questions as, "Are rapists psychologically 'normal'?" The external theoretical perspective examines such questions as, "Does our culture foster and support attitudes that support the act of rape?"

The internal theoretical perspective has three main theories of rapist behavior. First, the traditional psychiatric view holds that rapists have some sort of psychopathology (Allison and Wrightsman, 1993). This explanation suggests that rapists are mentally ill—they are "crazy," "sexually starved," or "psychotic." According to this perspective, the rapist has a psychological impairment or abnormality that "causes" him or her to rape.

The biological and socio-biological (evolutionary) theories are the second explanation of rapist behavior that focuses on factors internal to the rapist. Advocates of this perspective argue that the urge to rape is present in every man and that, in fact, all men are potential rapists. Darwinists argue that only the fittest genes survive and rape serves to produce offspring to continue the rapist's genealogy, thus satisfying genetic survival. So rape is an adaptive behavior that increases the rapist's genetic fitness.

The third explanation of rape that deals with factors internal to the rapist is offered by social psychologists. Proponents of this theory do not see rapists as abnormal individuals. While continuing to study internal factors of the rapist, they argue that internal factors are influenced by external factors. Rapists may merely be over-conforming to a social and cultural environment that condones and perpetuates rape myths, male dominance, and female passivity (Allison and Wrightsman, 1993).

The second major category of rapist theories, the external theoretical perspective, focuses on social factors that influence a person to commit rape. Two main external explanations are found in the rape research. First, social learning theory argues that aggressive behavior is learned through intimate social interaction with others, such as with parents and peer groups. According to this theory, the rapist learns attitudes and values in his or her intimate group that increases the chance that he or she will commit rape. Second, feminist theory argues that rape is merely one manifestation of many "social traditions in which males have dominated nearly all important political and economic activities" (Ellis, 1989). According to feminists, our society promotes gender and social inequity that influences the rapist. The act of rape, according to this theory, is the manifestation of male entitlement perpetuated by social inequity. Feminists further argue that rapists believe, and society reinforces, that women are to be dominated, possessed, and demeaned.

Many researchers have empirically tested internal and external theories of rape. In several studies, rapists are studied along with other sex offenders as a group. This group is then compared to non-sex offenders (see the meta-analyses of Hanson and Bussière, 1998). By design, these studies overlook similarities and differences that rapists may have from other sex offenders because these offenders are combined into one group. This entry will review only those studies that have separated rapists from other types of sexual offenders and then compared the rapist group to other sex offender groups or to a non-sex offender group.

Research reveals that several correlates are related to those who rape. They will be discussed according to their underlying theory. First, the psychological perspective has one major correlate. Proponents of the psychological perspective assert that psychopathology and other such psychological abnormalities cause a person to commit rape. The literature, however, does not find consistent evidence of psychopathology among rapists (Malamuth, 1986; Prentky and Knight, 1991). Since the role of psychopathology in rape remains unclear, psychological theory is currently limited.

The correlates most often studied in the literature emerge from the sociological perspective, the second category of correlates. First, the most consistent social correlate in the literature is the intuitive finding that rapists have hostile attitudes toward women (Allison and Wrightsman, 1993). Hostility toward women is comprised of feelings of inadequacy, self-aggrandizing and protective behavior, anger, and the need to control women (Malamuth et al., 1991). Furthermore, rapists who have feelings of hostility toward women also tend to support rape myths. The most common rape myth portrays women as secretly desirous of rape and, therefore, as responsible for inciting the rape event (Allison and Wrightsman, 1993). A second common rape myth among rapists is that when a woman refuses sex, she really does not mean it (Allison and Wrightsman, 1993). Therefore, rapists do not seriously consider a woman's verbal communication in response to their sexual aggression. To these rapists, regardless of what a woman says, she agrees to sex.

A second social correlate of rapists is the role of domination in the act of rape. Research suggests that rapists wish to dominate their victims and use the act of sex with an unwilling participant as a means to achieve domination (Malamuth, 1986). Not surprisingly, rapists also tend to have an aggressive and manipulative style in everyday life (Prentky and Knight, 1991; Allison and Wrightsman, 1993).

The third social factor of rapists, traditional attitudes toward women, is controversial among researchers. To illustrate, Rapaport and Burkhart (1984) did not find traditional attitudes toward women to be significantly prevalent among self-reported rapists. Their study, however, supports the prevalence among rapists of hostile attitudes toward women and the acceptance of violence as a means to resolve situations (Rapaport and Burkhart, 1984). However, Allison and Wrightsman (1993) indicate that belief in traditional sex roles is one of the most consistent findings in the literature.

The fourth social correlate among rapists is that they tend to interpret their relationships with women as adversarial. This may be the result of general negative attitudes toward women (Allison and Wrightsman, 1993), and a high acceptance of aggression against others in general, and against women in particular (Rapaport and Burkhart, 1984; Malamuth, 1986).

The fifth social correlate among rapists is that they have been found to have low social perception and social skills—including immaturity, irresponsibility, and impulsivity (Prentky and Knight, 1991; Allison and Wrightsman, 1993). Such factors are assumed to lead to problems in relationships. Not only do rapists have problematic relationships with women, they also tend to have more problematic relationships with their fathers than reported by non-sexually aggressive men (Lisak, 1994).

The sixth social correlate may exist because of low social skills demonstrated by rapists. Researchers argue that ambiguity in consenting cues for sex may cause rape (Johnson and Jackson, 1998). Ambiguity in cue interpretation is argued by other researchers to reside solely with the offender. For instance, Kowalski (1993) found that men's interpretation of cues is mediated by the offender's attitude toward women (1993).

The seventh social correlate, the role of violence among rapists, has a debatable etiology. Generally, rapists have a high sexual response to violence. Several researchers have found that rapists have a higher stimulus response to rape descriptions than nonrapists (Prentky and Knight, 1991; Lalumière and Quinsey, 1994). Similarly, rapists have a higher sexual response (phallometric measurement) to rape cues than to consenting cues (Lalumière and Quinsey, 1994). More generally, Malamuth (1986) finds that the rapists' sexual experience offers the opportunity and ability for other correlates to manifest in the rape.

Whether driven by biology or the social environment, the eighth correlate, alcohol use, is prevalent among rapists. Shotland (1992) suggests that alcohol usage directly and indirectly causes rape. First, alcohol usage directly makes the rapist more aggressive and causes the violence necessary to commit the rape. Second, alcohol usage indirectly lessens the inhibitions in the rapist that may prevent rape.

When taken together the results from these studies suggest two major conclusions concerning the correlates of rapists. First, there appears to be no one internal or external correlate that fully explains why someone commits rape (Malamuth et al., 1991; Lalumière and Quinsey, 1994). There are multiple influences, which range from the individual level to the societal level, that determine whether a person commits rape. Second, the multiple correlates that apply to a rapist are, most likely, interactive rather than additive (Malamuth, 1986). The nature of this interaction is still unclear (Malamuth et al., 1991).

Rape is a gender-neutral crime. However, research has consistently reported that most victims are females and most offenders are males. Two recent studies are illustrative of the gender differences in rape estimates. First, in 1999, the NVCS reported that for females, the estimated rate of rape was 1.5 per 1000 persons age 12 and over, and for males the estimated rate of rape was almost 8 times lower—0.2 per 1000 persons age 12 and over (see http://www.ojp.usdoj.gov/bjs/pub/pdf/cvus99.pdf). Supportive of this large discrepancy between rape estimates for females and males, the NVAW survey found that 0.3% of women (302,091) and 1% of men (92,748) said they had experienced an attempted or completed rape in the previous 12 months. Second, the NVAW survey also reported that 99.4% of the female victims and 81.9% of the male victims were raped by a male aggressor (Tjaden and Thoennes, 2001).

Researchers have also examined why particular women are the targets of rape. The rape victimization research has identified several individual factors that are associated with the likelihood of experiencing rape. First, some demographic characteristics appear to increase the risk of being raped. Rape victims tend to be young. The NCVS has consistently reported that women between 16 and 19 years old have the highest rate of rape, followed by women between 20 and 24 years old, and girls 12–15 years old. Other than age, few demographic variables significantly distinguish between women who have been raped and those who have not (e.g., race, ethnicity) (see Harney and Mue-hlenhard, 1991; Tjaden and Thoennes, 2001). Second, there is mixed support for whether women's belief systems and personality factors influence their risk of being raped (see Koss, 1985; Muehlenhard and Linton, 1987). Third, research indicates that women who are sexually assaulted as children or adolescents are more likely to be raped as adults (Crowell and Burgess, 1996). Fourth, the victim–offender research reveals that most rape victims know their rapist. Of all rapes committed by men, 80–90% are acquainted with the victim (Crowell and Burgess, 1996). This includes inti-mates (e.g., current or former boyfriends, husbands, and cohabiting partners), nonromantic acquaintances (e.g., a friend), and authority figures (e.g., a professor or boss). Approximately 77% of all male victims were raped by a nonstranger (Tjaden and Thoennes, 2001). Overall, female rape victims were more likely to be raped by current or former intimates (e.g., spouse, partner, date), whereas male victims were more likely to be raped by acquaintances (e.g. friend, neighbor, coworker) (Tjaden and Thoennes, 2001).

Situational factors have been shown to increase the risk of rape. First, it appears that more rape attempts occur indoors, typically in a private setting, rather than outdoors. To illustrate, research has shown that date rape most frequently occurs in locations such as the offender's home, a car, or an isolated location (see Harney and Muehlenhard, 1991). Second, research focusing on stranger rapes finds that rapes are more likely to occur in the summer months and at night (Belknap, 2000). Third, a number of studies have reported that alcohol use on the part of the victim and the offender is common, especially in date rapes (see Crowell and Burgess, 1996).

There is much debate, mostly focused on meth-odological issues, within the rapist and rape victim-ization research as to the results of these studies. For example, in the correlates of rapist research, debate centers on (1) whether rapists are a homogeneous subgroup of sexual offender (Knight, Rosenberg, and Schneider, 1985; Mosher and Anderson, 1986; and Prentky and Knight, 1991), (2) the pervasive use of convenience sampling, and (3) the nature of the causal relationship between variables (Malamuth, 1986; and Malamuth et al., 1991). In the rape vic-timization research, debates between feminist and conservative scholars center on the extent of rape—that is, who gets counted as a rape victim. These discussions focus on several methodological issues that include: (1) how rape is operationalized, and (2) if and when women acknowledge their experience as a rape and report such behavior to the police (see Fisher and Cullen, 2000).

In summary, the research that has offered theoret-ical explanations and empirical results as to who com-mits rape and why, and who experiences rape and why, has advanced our identification and understand-ing of the multiple factors influencing the occurrence of these two phenomena. Future researchers should continue to address the previous methodological issues in both the rape offender and victim studies in an attempt to expand our current state of knowledge (see Fisher and Cullen, 2000). We need to better understand the correlates of rape offending and vic-timization so that this knowledge can be applied to treatment and other intervention programs for rapists, and to prevention and postrape medical, mental health, and legal services for those who have experi-enced rape.

GEORGIA SPIROPOULOS AND BONNIE S. FISHER

## References and Further Reading

Abbey, A., McAuslan, P., Zawacki, T., Clinton, A.M. and Buck, P.O. 2001. Attitudinal, experiential, and situational predictors of sexual assault perpetration, *Journal of Interpersonal Violence* 16(8).

Allison, J.A. and Wrightsman, L.S. 1993. *Rape: The Misunder-stood Crime*, Newbury Park, CA, Sage Publications.

Belknap, J. 2001. *The Invisible Woman*, Toronto, Canada, Wad-sworth Publishing.

Bureau of Justice Statistics 1987. *Sex Offenses and Offenders: An Analysis of Data on Rape and Sexual Assault*, Bureau of Justice Statistics, U.S. Department of Justice.

Crowell, N.A. and Burgess, A.W. 1996. Causes and conse-quences of violence against women, *Understanding Violence Against Women*, Washington, DC, National Academy Press.

Ellis, L. 1989. *Theories of Rape: Inquiries into the Causes of Sexual Aggression*, New York, Hemisphere Publishing.

Fisher, B.S. and Cullen, F.T., Measuring the sexual victimiza-tion of women: Evolution, current controversies, and future research, in *Measurement and Analysis of Crime and Jus-tice*, Duffee, D., Ed., Washington, DC, U.S. Department of Justice.

Fisher, B.S., Cullen, F.T. and Turner, M.G. 2001. The extent and nature of the sexual victimization of college women: A national-level analysis, Bureau of Justice Statistics, U.S. Department of Justice.

Hanson, R.K. and Bussière, M.T. 1998. Predicting relapse: A meta-analysis of sexual offender recidivism studies, *Journal of Consulting and Clinical Psychology*, 66(2).

Harney, P.A. and Muehlenhard, C.L. 1991. *Sexual Coercion: A Sourcebook on Its Nature, Causes, and Prevention*, Lexington, MA, Lexington Books or D.C. Heath and Company.

Johnson, J.D. and Jackson, L.A., Jr. 1988. Assessing the factors that might underlie the differential perception of acquain-tance and stranger rape, *Sex Roles*, 19(1 and 2).

Kilpatrick, D.G., Edmunds, C.N. and Seymour, A.K. 1992. *Rape in America: A Report to the Nation*, Arlington, VA, National Victim Center.

Knight, R.A., Rosenberg, R. and Schneider, B.A. 1985. Clas-sification of sexual offenders; perspectives, methods, and validation, in Burgess, A.W., Ed., *Rape and Sexual Assault: A Research Handbook*, New York, Garland Publishing.

Koss, M.P. 1985. The hidden rape victim: Personality, attitudinal, and situational characteristics, *Psychology of Women Quarterly,* 9(2).

Koss, M.P., Gidycz, C.A. and Wisniewski, N. 1987. The scope of rape: Incidence and prevalence of sexual aggression and victimization in a national sample of higher education students, *Journal of Consulting and Clinical Psychology,* 55(2).

Kowalski, R.M. 1993. Inferring sexual interest from behavioral cues: Effects of gender and sexually relevant attitudes, *Sex Roles,* 29(1 and 2).

Lalumière, M.L. and Quinsey, V.L. 1994. The discriminability of rapists from non-sex offenders using phallometric measures: A meta-analysis, *Criminal Justice and Behavior,* 21(1).

Lisak, D. 1994. Subjective assessment of relationships with parents by sexually aggressive and nonaggressive men, *Journal of Interpersonal Violence* 9(3).

Malamuth, N.M. 1986. Predictors of naturalistic sexual aggression, *Journal of Personality and Social Psychology,* 50(5).

Malamuth, N.M., Sockloskie, R.J., Koss, M.P. and Tanaka, J.S. 1991. Characteristics of aggressors against women: Testing a model using a national sample of college students, *Journal of Consulting and Clinical Psychology,* 59(5).

Mosher, D.L. and Anderson, R.D. 1986. Macho personality, sexual aggression, and reactions to guided imagery of realistic rape, *Journal of Research In Personality,* 20.

Muehlenhard, C.L. and Linton, M.A. 1987. Date rape and sexual aggression in dating situations: Incidence and risk factors, *Journal of Counseling Psychology,* 34(2).

Prentky, R.A. and Knight, R.A. 1991. Identifying critical dimensions for discriminating among rapists, *Journal of Consulting and Clinical Psychology,* 59(5).

Rapaport, K. and Burkhart, B.R. 1984. Personality and attitudinal characteristics of sexually coercive college males, *Journal of Abnormal Psychology,* 93(2).

Searles, P. and Berger, R.J. 1987. The current state of rape reform legislation: An examination of state statutes, *Women's Rights Law Reporter,* 10(1).

Shotland, R.L. 1992. Theory of the causes of courtship rape: Part 2, *Journal of Social Issues,* 48(1).

Sourcebook of Criminal Justice Statistics 1998. Estimated Number and Rate (per 100,000 inhabitants) of Offenders Known to Police by Offenses, United States, 1960–1997, U.S. Department of Justice.

Spohn, C. and Horney, J. 1992. *Rape Law Reform: A Grassroots Revolution and Its Impact,* New York, Plenum Press.

Tjaden, P. and Thoennes, N. 2001. Extent, *Nature, and Consequences of Rape: Findings from the National Violence Against Women Survey,* National Institute of Justice and the Centers for Disease Control and Prevention: Research in Brief.

*See also* **Rape, Forcible: The Law; Rape, Forcible: Theories; Rape, Statutory; Sexual Harassment**

# Rape, Forcible: The Law

During the colonial period in the U.S., for the most part, rape was defined as, "the carnal knowledge of a woman not one's wife by force or against her will" (Donat and D'Emilio, 1992). That definition excluded many sexual acts and meant that men and wives could not be raped. Since that period rape laws have undergone a significant evolution and broadening. Most are now gender neutral and include many sexual acts. It is not possible, however, to understand the evolution of rape laws without first understanding the historical position of women in the U.S.

Women were treated quite differently during the colonial period than they are today. The laws then, as they do now, reflected the beliefs and customs of the time. During this period, men and the law held that women were objects and the property of individual men. A woman's value within society was based totally on her ability to marry and her sexual purity (Donat and D'Emilio, 1992). Women who engaged in sex outside of marriage, even if against their will, were considered "fallen" and often blamed for their victimization. This meant that the rape of an unmarried woman made her impure and an unwelcome economic burden on her father. Subsequently, if an unwed woman was raped, the offender paid the women's father a sum to compensate for his loss.

Sexual purity was also a measure a woman's trustworthiness (Spohn and Horney, 1992). It was believed unchaste woman would deliberately lie about being raped to explain away premarital intercourse or to retaliate against an ex-lover or some other man. These images concerned the courts so much that some provided cautionary instructions to the jury about the difficulty of determining the truth about the victim's testimony (Spohn and Horney, 1992). To ensure the rape victim was not lying, the law also required the victim to immediately call out in order to notify others that she was being attacked. Additionally, the victimization also had to be corroborated by other witnesses and the victim had to show that she had physically resisted her attacker (Donat and D'Emilio, 1992; Spohn and Horney, 1992). Moreover, under common law, evidence of the victim's sexual history was admissible in court to prove that she was pure and had not consented to intercourse or to impeach her credibility.

As with daughters, and their fathers, married women were considered the property of their husbands under common law. This meant that a husband could also be financially compensated for the violation of his sexual property. It also meant that a husband could not be charged with the rape of his wife (Russell, 1990). Indeed, a husband's sexual advances could not be turned down by his wife. It was his right under common law to have access to his wife's body anytime he wanted (Donant and D'Emilo, 1992). A number of researchers have traced this law back to Chief Justice Sir Matthew Hale, Chief Justice in England in the 17th century, who wrote, "But the husband cannot be guilty of rape committed by himself upon his lawful wife, for by their mutual matrimonial consent and contract the wife hath given up herself in this kind unto the husband which she cannot retract" (Pagelow, 1984; Russell, 1990). Additionally in the late 1760s, the British legal thinker William Blackstone wrote "by marriage the husband and wife are one person in the law; that is, the very being or legal existence of the women is suspended in marriage" (Pagelow, 1984).

The evolution of rape laws concerning African Americans is also important. During the slavery period in the United State laws against rape openly treated Black and White offenders differently (LaFree, 1989). Statutes in many states provided the death penalty for rape when the convicted man was Black and the victim was White; however, the rape of a Black woman was legal in many jurisdictions. In areas where it was not legal, fines and punishments were less severe for convicted White rapists than for convicted Black rapists. A penal code of antebellum Georgia, for example, required capital punishment for slaves and free persons of color who were convicted of committing a rape or attempting it against a free White female. In contrast, a White man convicted of raping a Black female slave or a free Black women was to be fined, imprisoned, or both at the court's discretion (LaFree, 1989).

After the Civil War, state legislators made their rape statutes race-neutral but the legal system treated rape in much the same way as it had before the war. Defense attorneys' often used statistics to show the court was discriminating against their clients because they were Black. For example, in the 1949 trial of the "Martinsville Seven" in Virginia, the defense attorneys showed that between 1887 and 1949, the state had executed 45

Black men for rape; however, no White men had been executed for the same crime (Kennedy, 1997). In Florida, several defense attorneys challenged the death sentences by showing that in 24 years, 23 Blacks had been executed for rape but only one White (Kennedy, 1997). A modern researcher who examined the characteristics of executions in the U.S. found that since 1930, 89% of 453 men executed for rape in the U.S. were Black (LaFree 1989). Additionally, the 11 states making up the old southern confederacy accounted for 86% of these executions for and for 91% of all Black men executed for rape.

These findings do not account for illegal executions. Between 1882 and 1946 at least 4715 persons were lynched, about three-quarters of whom where Black, many of whom were accused of having raped a White woman (LaFree, 1989). Even if legally found guilty and executed, many courts were coerced by violent mobs, who threatened to execute the defendant themselves unless the court convicted the accused (Kennedy, 1997). The issue of racial discrimination in the death penalty for rape ended in 1977 when the U.S. Supreme Court in *Coker v. Georgia* ruled the death sentence was unconstitutional for the crime of rape. It should be noted, however, that the Court did not address the issue of racial discrimination in this case; instead the justices ruled on issues of the 8th Amendment and that the death penalty was cruel and excessive punishment for rape.

Most of the evolutionary changes in rape laws did not occur until the late 1970s, when the women's movement set out to change the way society viewed women and to challenge the common law definition of rape. Intense lobbying efforts and public campaigns from these powerful groups resulted in reforms that were both symbolic and instrumental (Spohn and Horney, 1992). Reformers hoped that legal changes would serve a symbolic purpose by educating the public about the seriousness of all forms of sexual assault and decrease the stigma and stereotypes associated with rape victims. Instrumentally, reformists set out to change the nature and scope of the law. Reformists charged that traditional rape law was not designed to protect women from rape, but to preserve common-law male rights to possess and subjugate women. They argued that the traditional criminal law definition of forcible rape was inadequate and needed to be revised. Reformers also charged that laws concerning the rules of evidence were legally irrelevant evaluations of the victim's character, behavior, and relationship with the accused and called upon legislators to change consent standards, corroboration requirements, and the admissibility of evidence concerning the victim's past sexual conduct. Reformers expected that the elimination of common law barriers would improve the likelihood of prosecution and conviction because legal hurdles would no longer hamper officials in cases with no corroborating evidence or with no evidence of resistance by the victim. They also predicted that reforms would produce an increase in the number of victims reporting rape to the police because women would not have to fear being harassed at trial about their sexual histories (Spohn and Horney, 1992).

Although reformers' negotiations with the federal and individual state governments produced a wide range of rape law definitions, rules of evidence, and acts that were criminalized, a number of changes can be summarized. Many states expanded rape laws to include: (1) gender-neutral themes that incorporated males as victims; (2) acts other than sexual intercourse, such as fellatio, cunnilingus, anal sex, or the unwanted touching of the sexual organs and the use of inanimate objects; (3) elements of covert force such as acts placing victims in duress or fear of harm; and finally (4) incidents where consent is not possible because of the use of a controlled substance, unconsciousness, or other forms of mental powerlessness (Searles and Berger, 1987). Additionally, laws limited or abolished (1) spousal exemption laws, (2) the cross examination of the victim about her sexual history, (3) cautionary instructions given to juries, (4) special corroboration requirements, and (5) proof of resistance requirements. Reform statutes also created rape shield laws that limited admissibility of evidence regarding the victim's prior sexual history (Spohn and Horney, 1992). Many states and federal governments also dropped the term rape in favor of sexual assault, sexual battery, or sexual abuse and substituted a series of graded offenses such as aggravated sexual abuse, abusive contact, and so on. These contemporary changes resulted in a drastic advancement from the limited definition of common law rape to more complex but less discriminating individual state and federal laws.

The evolution of rape law can be epitomized by the modern federal law definition of sexual abuse. According to Federal Code 18 U.S.C. § 2242, sexual abuse occurs when a person knowingly causes another person to engage in a sexual act, by threatening or placing that other person in fear, or engages in a sexual act with another person when that other person is incapable of apprising the nature of the conduct, or physically incapable of declining in, or communicating unwillingness to engage in, that sexual act. Aggravated sexual abuse, according to 18 U.S.C. § 2241, occurs when a person knowingly causes another person to engage in a sexual act by using force against that person, or by threatening or placing that person in fear that any person will be subjected to death, serious bodily injury, or kidnapping.

Aggravated sexual assault under this statute also occurs when a person renders another person unconscious and thereby engages in a sexual act, or administers to another person without their knowledge or permission, a drug, intoxicant, or other similar substance and thereby impairs the ability of that other person to appraise or control conduct, and engages in a sexual act with that other person or attempts to do so. Sexual assault under 18 U.S.C. § 224 includes contact between the penis, mouth, or any object and the genitalia or anus and the unwanted touching of the genitalia, anus, groin, breast, inner thigh, or buttocks, either directly or through the clothing. This definition of rape is gender neutral, graded, and includes a wide range of acts and use of force. It is far more evolved than the common law definition used not too long ago.

In addition to intense activism by women's groups, the 1970s also saw a new era of scholarly research on many different aspects of rape. Findings from these studies are difficult to interpret, however, because they come from different samples, different definitions of rape, different types of measurement, different units of analysis, and from different time periods (DeKeserdey and Schwartz, 2001; Desai and Saltzman, 2001). Varying definitions of rape make it particularly difficult to compare prevalence and incidence studies. For example, researchers using broad definitions that may include acts that are not considered illegal in some areas may uncover more incidents than researchers utilizing narrower definitions that only include illegal acts. Additionally, counting the number of victims results in different rates than counting the number of incidents. The same person may have raped victims more than once. Findings may be corrupted by the victim's ability to recall rape incidents, particularly if the victim has been raped frequently or if the victimization took place long ago. The intrusive nature of rape investigation can be quite overwhelming to victims who may feel reluctant to divulge their experiences. Victims may fear physical retaliation as well, especially involving research utilizing phone interviews when spouses who rape may be nearby. All research has its strengths and limitations but that does not discount its significance. The important thing to remember when reviewing research findings in rape studies is that various researchers often measure different things using different techniques.

Findings from prevalence and incidence studies show that rape rates are found with varying frequency. The *National Women's Study* (NWS), a longitudinal survey of a national probability of household sample of about 4000 adult women between 1989 and 1991, found that approximately 13% of adult women had been victims of completed rape during their lifetime. This equates to an estimated 683,000 adult American women who were raped during a twelve-month period (Kirkpatrick et al., 1992). Researchers utilizing the *National Violence Against Women Survey* (NVAW) interviewed a national representative sample of about 8000 adult men and women between 1995 and 1996. The data revealed that 18% of the women and 3% of the men experienced completed rape at some point in their lives, with just a little over half occurring before the age of 18. Additionally, 0.3% of women surveyed and 0.1% of men surveyed said they experienced a completed or attempted rape in the previous 12 months. According to estimates, this means that approximately 302,000 women and 93,000 men are raped each year in the U.S. (Tjaden and Thoennes, 1998). Contemporary studies utilizing government-collected data usually find smaller rates. For example, according to the latest Federal Bureau of Investigation *Crime in America* report from the Uniform Crime Reports (UCR), only 90,500 forcible rapes were reported to the police in 2001. A report utilizing the National Institute of Justice's National Crime Victimization Survey shows that approximately 0.4 persons per 1000 households in 2001 were victims of rape (Rennison, 2002). One report also revealed that rates of rape victimization are dropping. Between 1993 and 2001 the rates dropped nearly 43%, from one rape per 1000 persons, to only 0.4 rapes per 1000 persons, according to the NCVS (Rennison, 2002).

Many studies find rape is one of the most under-reported crimes in the U.S. According to the NCVS report, only 38% of the victims in the survey made police reports of their victimization (Rennison, 2002). More notably, rape was the lowest violent crime reported to the police and one of the lowest reported overall. For every two victims that reported a rape to the police, there were about five victims who did not. The NWS found only 16% of the incidents of completed rape were reported to the police (Kirkpatrick et al., 1992).

Victims are more likely to be women and women are more likely to be raped by someone they know than by a complete stranger. According to the NCVS, about 90% of the victims reporting rape were women. The majority of these women reported being raped by a nonstranger, most of whom were friends or acquaintances (Rennison, 2002). The NWS found about 76% of the adult women who reported being raped were victimized by a non-stranger and nearly 30% of all rapes were conducted by victims' husbands (Kirkpatrick, et al., 1992).

Studies of the criminal justice response to rape events reveal that the ability of rape law reforms to produce instrumental change is limited. Despite the fact that it has now been nearly three decades since reformers began their campaign to change public attitudes and the law of rape, many criminal justice officials today continue to rely on irrelevant factors that reformers have fought so adamantly against. Modern studies have shown that outcomes of sexual assault continue to be affected by the victim's background, reputation, risk taking behaviors, the relationship between the victim and the offender, or interaction effects between some of these factors (Frohman, 1991; LaFree, 1989; Spohn, 2002). Similarly, although the death penalty for rape has been declared unconstitutional, empirical evidence reveals that statutory penalty for rape continues to be applied in a discriminatory manner. A number of studies show that the rapist's race or the racial combination of the offender and victim continues to influence the manner in which the police, prosecutors, and judges handle the case. Accused Black men, in general, and principally Black men who are accused of raping White women, have a better chance of arrest, prosecution, and conviction, and will probably spend more time in jail than Whites who are convicted of rape (Lafree, 1989; Spohn, 1994).

There is some evidence, however, that some reforms might be working in some cases. Spohn and Horney (1992) found justice officials in all six jurisdictions they studied indicated that evidence relating to a complainant's sexual history not too significant. Additionally, in the hypothetical cases in their study, surveyed officials judged such evidence would have little chance of being admitted to trial. Data taken from the NCVS from 1992 through 1994 showed that victim and suspect demographic factors, as well as marital status, victim or offender relationship, weapon use, and presence of a injury did not affect police arrest decisions (Bachman, 1998).

This review of rape laws in the U.S. suggests that although the law has undergone a significant evolution and is now broader and less discriminating, actions by officials who enforce the law may not have changed much. Practices continue to reflect beliefs that existed years ago. However, because there is some evidence of changing attitudes, some hope exists that criminal justice behavior will soon echo the law and reform efforts.

STEVE WILSON

## References and Further Reading

Bachman, R. 1998. The factors related to rape reporting behavior and arrest: New evidence from the national crime victimization survey, *Criminal Justice and Behavior*, 25.

DeKeseredy, W.S. and Schwartz, M.D. 2001 Definitional issues, in Renzxetti, C.M., Edleson, J.L. and Bergen, R.K., Eds., *Sourcebook on Violence Against Women,* Thousand Oaks, CA, Sage Publications.

Desai, S. and Saltzman, L.E. 2001. Measurement issues for violence against women in Renzxetti, C.M., Edleson, J.L. and Bergen, R.K., Eds., *Sourcebook on Violence Against Women,* Thousand Oaks, CA, Sage Publications.

Donat, P.L.N. and D'Emilio, J. 1992. A feminist redefinition of rape and sexual assault: Historical foundations and change, *Journal of Social Issues,* 48.

Federal Bureau of Investigation. 2001. *Crime in America, 2001,* Washington DC, Government Printing Office.

Frohmann, L. 1991. Discrediting victims' allegation of sexual assault: Prosecution accounts of case rejections, *Social Problems,* 38.

LaFree, G.D. 1989. *Rape and Criminal Justice: The Social Construction of Sexual Assault,* Belmont, CA, Wadsworth Publishing.

Kennedy, R. 1998. *Race, Crime, and the Law,* New York, Vintage Books.

Kilpatrick, D.G., Edmunds, C.N. and Seymour, A. 1992. *Rape in American: A Report to the Nation,* Arlington, VA, National Victim Center, and Charleston, SC, Crime Victims Research and Treatment Center.

Pagelow, M.D. 1984. *Family Violence,* New York, Praeger Publishers.

Rennison, C., *Criminal Victimization 2001: Changes 2001 with Trends 1993–2001,* Bureau of Justice Statistics, Washington, DC, Government Printing Office.

Russell, D.E.H. 1990. *Rape in Marriage,* Bloomington, IN, Indiana University Press.

Searles, P. and Berger, R.J. 1987. The current status of rape reform legislation: An examination of state statutes, *Women's Rights Law Reporter,* 10.

Spohn, C. 2002. *How do Judges Decide: The Search For Fairness and Justice in Punishment,* Thousand Oaks, CA, Sage Publications.

Spohn, C. and Horney, J. 1992. *Rape Law Reform: Grassroots Revolution and its Impact,* New York, Plenum Press.

Tjaden, P. and Thoennes, N. 1998. *Prevalence, Incidence, and Consequences of Violence Against Women: Findings from the National Violence Against Women Survey,* U.S. Department of Justice, Washington, DC, Printing Office.

*See also* **Rape, Acquaintance and Date; Rape: Forcible: Extent and Correlates; Rape, Forcible: Theories**

# Rape, Forcible: Theories

Because of the horrifying nature of rape, it is imperative that we understand it so that we can do everything we can to prevent it. Unfortunately, theories of rape have been more ideologically infused than theories of crime in general. The three primary theories of rape are the *feminist, social learning,* and *evolutionary* theories. Each theory explains some of the reasons for rape, and none should be uncritically embraced or summarily dismissed. There is no single feminist, social learning, or evolutionary theory; what is presented here represents mainstream versions of these theories. A fourth theory—the synthesized biosocial theory—that integrates insights from each of the other three theories will also be explored.

## The Feminist Theory of Rape

Feminist theories of rape were partly developed in reaction to the *victim-precipitated* perspective (Amir, 1971) that views rape as the culmination of a series of events in which the behavior of the victim was interpreted by the offender as inviting sexual activity. The victim was seen as inadvertently *contributing* to, not *causing,* her rape by her passive behavior or by her initial assent to kissing and necking. Feminists were outraged by this de-emphasis of the assailant's culpability, and by what they saw as dressing prevailing cultural stereotypes of rape and rape victims (e.g., "She asked for it") in scientific clothing.

The victim-precipitated view of rape took it for granted that rape was motivated by the rapist's sexual desire, whereas the bedrock assumption of the feminist theory is that rape is not motivated by sexual desire but rather by power. Feminists also see rape as a crime of violence and degradation designed to intimidate women and keep them "in their place" (Brownmiller, 1975).

To understand the feminist position we have to understand that view of gender relations in modern society. Feminists assert that there are large power differentials between men and women that affect all social interactions between the genders. Men enjoy the advantage and use all means possible, such as subtle coercion, overt force, and ideologies supporting male superiority and dominance, to maintain it. Many feminists aver that males in our society are socialized to rape via the many gender-role messages society sends them asserting their authority and dominance over women (Gilmartin, 1994). Rape is the major weapon males have used to establish and maintain both the general social patriarchy and the dominance of individual men over individual women. Feminists further maintain that the threat of rape forces a woman to seek the protection of a man from the predations of other men, thus forcing her into permanent subjugation. This position is exemplified by Susan Brownmiller (1975, 5), who alleged that rape "is nothing more or less than a conscious process of intimidation by which *all* men keep *all* women in a state of fear." Brownmiller was aware that most men do not rape and that most women are not raped, but to her the act of rape—as a violent *political* act, not a sexual act—is central to understanding the social, economic, and political relationships between the sexes.

Brownmiller's book (*Against Our Will*) politicized rape, and it has had a tremendous impact on social science views of rape. This view leads many feminist theorists to see it as the master symbol of women's oppression. They also view it not as an act committed by a few psychologically unhealthy men, but as an act that practically all men may commit, and one that is indicative of a general hatred of women that characterizes the behavior of "normal" adult men. Feminists point to a number of studies that indicate between 35% and 69% of surveyed males admit that they would commit rape, given assurances of never being exposed and punished, to support this notion (reviewed in Skinner et al., 1995). It has also been pointed out that the American Psychiatric Association's (APA) *Diagnostic and Statistical Manual* has never listed rape as a sexual deviation, which is interpreted as meaning that the APA does not consider rape to be clinically abnormal behavior, but rather as part of the behavioral repertoire of clinically normal males (Walsh, 2001).

Some more radical feminists such as Catharine MacKinnon (1989) do view rape as a sexual act, but only after redefining sex as a "social construct of sexism for male dominance." In other words, sexuality has been created by male power as another way of controlling females. Having redefined sexuality to suit her purpose, McKinnon can state that an assault with a penis is no different than an assault with a fist since both, in addition to being violent, are sexual. Sex, violence, and power thus become synonymous in this view that goes so far as to extend Brownmiller's definition of rape to all acts of heterosexual sex. Males engaging in consensual sex are therefore also motivated by power and control, according to this social constructionist view.

The main contribution of feminist theory is political and legal. It has managed to make us more aware of the horrible nature of rape, it has challenged stereotypes associated with rape and rape victims, and it has demonstrated the link between sociocultural factors and the propensity to rape.

## Social Learning Theory of Rape

Social learning theory shares the general social science assumption that culture is entirely separate from biology, and that culture causes behavior through the process of learning. Social learning theory is thus similar to the feminist theory in that both theories view rape as caused by differences in the way women and men are sexually socialized; that is, they learn different things regarding sexually appropriate behavior. Men are socialized to aggressively pursue sexual opportunities while women are socialized to be passive and to delay sex until a male has committed to them. Under the assumption of biologically free sexual proclivities, if women were socialized like men they would be equally as likely to use sexually coercive tactics, and if men were socialized like women they would be equally unlikely to use such tactics. The major difference between the two theories is that social learning theory places less emphasis on sexual politics and is generally agnostic about what the "ultimate" purpose of rape is (i.e., to "keep women in their place"). Social learning theorists are also unlikely to view rapists as "normal" men, and more as men who have been the recipients of deviant sexual socialization (Groth, 1979).

Social learning theorists agree with feminists that the images of women as the sexual playthings of men circulated in advertising, pornography, rap music, and in other media, play a critical role in increasing the probability of rape. Studies have shown that sex offenders are about three times more likely to own pornography than male control subjects, and that frequent consumers of pornography are less satisfied with "normal" sex and with their partners (Russell, 1998). The cumulative effect of pairing women with eroticized violence and impersonal sex is that men become immune to the suffering inherent in the content of these images and to objectify women as "things" that are useful only insofar as they can be used so satisfy sexual needs.

Part of the process of learning behavior involves learning reasons for it. Rapists can be expected, then, to subscribe to stereotyped images of women that provide them with justifications for their behavior. Indeed, many convicted rapists hold traditional masculine values that glorify sexual prowess and divide women into "whores" and "madonnas." Whores are considered legitimate targets for rape because they are "teasers" and thus deserve, and even want to be, raped. Many rapists have difficulty understanding how their victims could accuse them of rape, feeling that once a woman's initial protests are overcome in the forceful "masculine" way of the movie tough guy, she should just melt into their arms.

Another major difference between the feminist and social learning theories is that the feminist theory is primarily a structural theory that emphasizes that patriarchal dominance puts *all* men at risk for committing rape. The social learning theory, on the other hand, attempts to explain rape at the individual level; that is, it explores the characteristics of *specific individuals* who have actually committed rape.

## Evolutionary Theory of Rape

The evolutionary theory of rape holds the view that coercive sexuality is a male adaptation designed by natural selection (Thornhill and Thornhill, 1992). For evolutionary theorists, the key to understanding rape is the wide disparity in parental investment between the sexes. Having no *necessary* parental investment other than insemination, males have evolved a propensity to seek copulation with multiple partners. The more successful a male is in this endeavor the greater is his reproductive success, and the greater the representation of his genes in subsequent generations. A female's parental investment, however, is enormous. Her best reproductive strategy is to secure investment from a male to assist her in this task. Females cannot increase their reproductive success by promiscuous mating; indeed, such a strategy would be more likely to minimize reproductive success because few men would be expected to assist a female in rearing offspring whose paternity is in doubt. Because our ancient female ancestors faced this problem, women today are more inclined to resist casual copulation than are men.

Evolutionary theory posits two conflicting reproductive strategies arising from these different levels of parental investment: the careful and discriminating strategy of the female, and the reckless and indiscriminate strategy of the male. Rape is sometimes the result of this discrepancy, and is viewed by evolutionary psychologists as a maladaptive consequence of a general male mating strategy of men that may have been adaptive in ancestral environments (Thornhill and Palmer, 2000).

Evolutionary theorists argue about whether rape is an adaptation per se, or a "side-effect" of other adaptations that themselves aid male reproductive success, such as aggressiveness and strength of sex drive (Thornhill and Palmer, 2000). If rape is an adaptation rather than a side effect, it means that rape behavior was *specifically* designed by natural selection because of its effectiveness in promoting male reproductive success. As is the case with any other trait, the more coercive sexuality aided reproductive success in evolutionary environments the more strongly it was selected for. Many evolutionary theorists (in uneasy agreement with feminist theory) believe that any genes underlying rape behavior are virtually invariant in the male gene pool, thus the male use of coercive tactics will not vary with genetic differences but with environmental differences.

The environmental factors stressed by evolutionary theorists are differences in male status and resources. Because older high status males can monopolize females by virtue of their control over resources valued by females, forced copulation in many animal species is a strategy employed primarily by young, resource-poor males. Human females have also been found cross-culturally to prefer to mate with males of high status, or who at least have the potential of achieving it. Because of this preference, many younger and low-status males may be denied the opportunity to mate legitimately with the most attractive females. Evolutionary theory therefore predicts that most of the stranger rapists will be young males of low socioeconomic status, a prediction confirmed with data from around the world (Ellis and Walsh, 1997).

## Evaluation of the Theories

The major problematic area in both the feminist and social learning theories is the insistence that rape is a pseudosexual act. Though it is obvious that rape is a violent act, it is just as obvious to critics of these theories that it is also a sexual act. Most clinicians engaged in the treatment of rapists insist that rape is primarily sexually motivated (Barbaree and Marshll, 1991), and very few laypersons (about 9% of males and 18% of females) believe that power and anger are the primary motives for rape (Hall, 1987). Some recent feminist writings recognize the sexual, as well as the violent, nature of rape, and insist that the "not-sex" argument was necessary initially to emphasize that women received no sexual pleasure from being raped (Herman, 1990). Some theorists even consider the "not sex" belief to be dangerous because it prevents us from learning more about the causes of rape, and that the cost of such ignorance is an increased number of rape victims (Palmer, 1994).

Because few social scientists are familiar with evolutionary biology, and because its claims give many people the impression that it dehumanizes both women and men, evolutionary theory draws the most severe criticism. Critics aver that by claiming that rape is a natural or normal phenomenon (i.e., a product of natural selection), evolutionary theorists dignify and justify it, or imply that it is inevitable and even morally acceptable. Such criticisms are examples of what philosophers call the *naturalistic fallacy* (the confusion of "is" with "ought"). Nature simply *is,* what *ought* to be is a moral judgment. To say that forced copulation is normal primate behavior from a scientific viewpoint is no more a moral statement than it is to say that disease and death, unwelcome as they may be, are natural and normal processes. Evolution is morally blind in that it selects traits to the extent that they aid in reproductive success regardless of how morally reprehensible they may be. Evolutionary theorists are among the first to denounce rape as a crime in need of severe punishment precisely *because* they view it as a potential behavior of all men (Thornhill and Palmer, 2000).

This emphasis on reproduction success has led to the criticism that evolutionary theory cannot explain instances of sexual assault in which reproduction cannot occur, such as the rape of males, children, and postmenopausal women, and rapes that do not include vaginal intercourse. This is another misunderstanding of evolutionary logic. Organisms are not adapted to directly seek ultimate goals (reproductive success), rather they are selected to seek proximate goals (in this case, sexual pleasure) that themselves blindly served ultimate goals in ancestral environments. Even voluntary copulation is rarely engaged in to increase "reproductive success"; instead, we often take pains to subvert this "goal" via the use of contraception. Nonreproductive sex can be likened to the diffusion of the human nurturing of animals that has no fitness-promoting advantage at all for the nurturer. Both nonreproductive sex and animal nurturing provide us with pleasurable effects that are themselves wholly extraneous to the effects responsible for their evolutionary selection.

## Synthesized Theory of Rape

If rape behavior is an adaptation or a side effect of more general adaptations, how useful can such knowledge be? To say that men rape because such behavior is part of our primate heritage may well be true, but it also begs an awful lot of questions. Most men never exercise this "rape potential," so we would like to know what the differences are between those who do and who do not. In short, we need a theory that goes beyond examining phenomena common to all men, whether it is a common biology or a common patriarchal society. Such a theory is Lee Ellis's (1991) synthesized *biosocial theory.* Ellis incorporates the most empirically supportable claims of other theories, and adds neurohormonal (brain functioning and chromosome) variables.

The basis of the biosocial theory is that the sex drive and the drive to possess and control motivate all sexual behavior, including rape. All sexually producing organisms possess an unlearned sex drive, although the manner in which it is expressed is mostly learned. The contention that rape is sexually motivated rests on many kinds of evidence. For instance, nonstranger rapists (the vast majority of rapists are known to their victim) are overwhelmingly likely to use force only when other tactics, such as use of alcohol, pleading, or false claims of love have failed. This makes it difficult to claim that rape is nonsexual. It is also pointed out that forced copulation exists in a number of animal species, making it difficult to maintain claims that similar behavior among human males is motivated by hatred of females, that it occurs because of gender specific socialization, or that males are attempting to protect their privileged political and economic positions when they rape.

Animals also possess a strong drive to possess and control, which is especially strong where sex partners are concerned. Among humans there is plentiful evidence that men and women are extremely possessive of one another. Jealousy and male sexual proprietariness is responsible for an overwhelming percentage of spousal and lover homicides in the U.S., and probably elsewhere also.

Ellis also maintains that the average sex drive of men is stronger than the average sex drive of women. He offers as evidence the fact that males commit the vast majority of sexual crimes, consume the vast majority of pornography, constitute practically all the customers of prostitutes of both sexes, masturbate more frequently, and have a much greater interest in casual sex with multiple partners. These and other indices of gender differences in strength of sex drive are found across cultures and among all other primate species. The strength of the sex drive renders it easy for males to learn forceful copulatory tactics. Opposing the male tendency to readily learn forceful tactics is the evolved female tendency to resist them. As pointed out earlier, the disparity in parental investment between the sexes has produced these opposing tendencies, and the tension generated by them sometimes results in rape.

Biosocial theory contends that although the motivation for rape is not learned, the specific behavior surrounding it is. Rape behavior is learned via operant conditioning, with individuals possessing the strongest sex drive learning it more readily than individuals with weak sex drives. The basic principle of operant conditioning is that behavior tends to be repeated when it is reinforced. Thus, men who have successfully used "pushy" (but not necessarily forceful) tactics to gain sexual favors in the past have learned that those tactics pay off. The initial "pay off" may be little more than a necking or petting session, but if a male finds that each time he escalates his pushiness he succeeds in gaining greater sexual access, his behavior will be gradually shaped by reinforcement in ways that could lead to rape. Biosocial theory does not deny that other kinds of learning (e.g., attitudinal or modeling) can affect the probability of rape; however, the kind of learning it emphasizes is the most powerful method of learning known to psychology.

The final point made by Ellis is that people differ in the strength of their sex drives and in their sensitivity to threats of punishment. All mammalian brains are destined to remain female unless masculinized by androgen hormones *in utero*. This "sexing" of the brain results not only in a stronger male sex drive, but also in variations in the strength of the sex drive among both males and females. The exposure of the brain to higher levels of androgens during fetal development means that males are more likely than females to forcefully seek sexual copulation. Exposure to fetal androgens also results in lessened sensitivity to environmental stimuli later in life. Compared to females, males in many species are less sensitive to noxious stimuli, leading them to somewhat discount the consequences of their behavior, both for themselves and for their victims. Unfortunately, individuals with the strongest sex drives are usually the same individuals who are the most insensitive to environmental stimuli because the same neurohormonal factors are responsible for both. These are the individuals who are most likely to rape and to be engaged in criminal activity in general.

ANTHONY WALSH

## References and Further Reading

Amir, M. 1971. *Patterns in Forcible Rape,* Chicago, IL, University of Chicago Press.

Barbaree, H.E. and Marshall, W.L. 1991. The role of male sexual arousal in rape: Six models, *Journal of Consulting and Clinical Psychology,* 59, 621–630.

Brownmiller, S. 1975. *Against Our Will: Men, Women, and Rape,* New York, Simon and Shuster.

Burgess, J. 1998. *Rape: A Philosophical Investigation,* Aldershot, U.K., Dartmouth Publishers.

Ellis, L. 1989. *Theories of Rape: Inquiries into the Causes of Rape,* New York, Hemisphere.

Ellis, L. 1991. A synthesized (Biosocial) theory of rape, *Journal of Consulting and Clinical Psychology,* 59, 631–642.

Ellis, L. and Walsh, A. 1997. Gene-based evolutionary theories in criminology, *Criminology,* 35, 229–276.

Gilmartin, P. 1994. *Rape, Incest, and Child Sexual Abuse: Consequences and Recovery,* New York, Garland Press.

Groth, N., *Men Who Rape,* New York, Plenum.

Hall, E. 1987. Adolescents' perceptions of sexual assault, *Journal of Sex Education and Therapy,* 13, 37–42.

Marshall, W.L., Laws, D.R. and Barbaree, H.E. 1990. *Handbook of Sexual Assault: Issues,* Theories, and Treatment of the Offender, New York, Plenum.

MacKinnon, C. 1989. *Toward a Feminist Theory of State,* Cambridge, MA, Harvard University Press.

Palmer, C., Twelve reasons why rape is not sexually motivated: A skeptical examination, in Francoeur, R., Ed., *Taking Sides: Clashing Views on Controversial Issues in Human Sexuality,* Guilford, CT, Dushkin Press.

Russell, D. 1998. *Dangerous Relationships: Pornography, Misogyny, and Rape,* Thousand Oakes, CA, Sage.

Skinner, L., Carroll, K. and Berry, K. 1995. A typology for sexually aggressive males in dating relationships, *Journal of Offender Rehabilitation,* 22, 29–45.

Thornhill, R. and Palmer, C. 2000. *A Natural History of Rape: Biological Bases of Sexual Coercion,* Cambridge, MA, MIT Press.

Thornhill, R. and Thornhill, N. 1992. The evolutionary psychology of men's sexual coercion, *Behavioral and Brain Sciences,* 15, 363–375.

Walsh, A. 2001. *Correctional Assessment, Casework, and Counseling,* 3rd ed., Lanham, MD, American Correctional Association.

*See also* **Evolutionary Theories of Criminal Behavior; Feminist Theories of Criminal Behavior; Rape, Forcible: Extent and Correlates; Social Learning Theory**

# Rape, Marital

Occasionally something is so integrated into our culture that it does not seem worth the effort to justify why we allow or forbid it. Although it is barely studied, prosecuted or punished today, before the 1970s this was certainly the case with marital rape throughout the English-speaking world. Essentially if the rape victim was married to the rapist, there was no crime, no matter what the circumstances. Yet for the most part there was no case law, legal comment, or law review study to support that point of view. Where such a justification did exist, it almost always consisted of a reference to the 17th century jurist Sir Matthew Hale. He argued that women consent to sexual intercourse by their marriage vows, and they cannot withdraw that consent just because they do not like a particular time, locale, or circumstance. Since the crime of rape requires a finding of lack of consent, Hale's formulation removes wives from the possibility of victimization by their husbands. Although the legal position of women today is rather dramatically different than it was in the 1650s, this did not seem to have affected many rape laws in the intervening period.

Generally there are two reasons why such laws remained in place for so long. First is that marital rape is a form of domestic violence. Through this era much of society was ambivalent about domestic violence and whether the state has a right to step in and interfere with a man's marital rights to domesticate and physically regulate his wife. When the crime is formulated as coercing an unwilling wife to submit to her agreed upon marital duty, rather than as an uncalled for violent physical assault, the sympathy for the victim is even lower. That many men consider a women's sexuality a commodity that could be owned by her husband further contributed to this opinion.

Second is that the American legal system generally (and those of most other English-speaking countries) was very much stacked against convicting men of rape except in what was considered the most extreme of circumstances, such as interracial rape or violent rape between persons known to be strangers. To this day, there is very little prosecution in America, Canada, or England of violent rape of acquaintances, let alone of wives or girlfriends or for that matter, of dating partners.

Thus, to the extent that the system conceives of marriage as an arrangement held together by the strength of the husband in providing discipline and leadership, and the obedience and subservience of the wife, an exemption on rape laws for husbands makes sense to some people. To the extent that one sees marriage as based on partnership and equality, the spousal exemption makes no sense.

Since the 1970s, every American state has changed its laws on marital rape, generally in response to the same pressures that led to major changes in domestic violence law and stranger rape law. Some states have totally removed the exemption, while others have removed the exemption for first-degree rape but retained it for other violent felony crimes. For example, in Ohio it is legal to administer chemicals to a spouse for the purpose of being able to blunt resistance to rape or to commit a marital rape using various instruments (e.g., a bottle or a gun barrel rather than the penis).

Virtually all scholars of the subject agree that marital rape is significantly more common than stranger rape, with Jasinski and Williams citing several reasons to believe that it accounts for as much as one-third of all rapes in America (only general acquaintance rape is probably more common). Virtually all shelter houses for battered women report that many or most clients report that forced sexual intercourse was a part of the violence in their lives. Of course, this is not representative of all women. One often-quoted statistic comes from Diane E.H. Russell, who conducted a random survey of 644 San Francisco married or formerly married women of all ages, races, and classes, and found that 14% of them had experienced rape or attempted rape by their husbands or ex-husbands. This did not, she reports, include women who always submitted to their husband's demands in orders to avoid rape. Similarly, Finkelhor and Yllo found in a similar sample of Boston mothers a rate of 10% victimization. Many of these women were victims in particularly extreme and brutal circumstances with a high percentage of them reporting multiple victimizations, with 20 or more rapes during their marriage.

Qualitative and clinical research, however, has shown us many things about marital rape. It is known, for example, that few women report marital rape, or even define marital rape as forcible rape. After all, the dominant image of the rapist is a stranger, so husbands are not seen as rapists. This does not mean that the women are not terrorized, beaten, or mentally and physically scarred. Raquel Kennedy Bergen, for example, found that the emotional damage from marital rape could be as great or even greater than with stranger rape. The violation of trust involved can be worse or at least the same as a stranger victimization. Frazier and Seales discovered that although women raped by acquaintances were less likely to self-define as rape victims, they were just as likely as women raped by strangers to suffer from severe psychological trauma. After all, a woman raped outdoors can retreat to the supposed safety of the home, but there is little psychological retreat for a woman raped in her own home by her own husband.

There also is much confusion of marital rape with marital problems. The issue is not whether the man has been deprived of sex, as rape is not a sex crime in the usual sense of the world. Rather, rape largely is a crime of humiliation, domination, and subjugation designed to leave emotional scars, and the fact that the offender is married to the victim does not change the motivation, the act, or the outcome.

MARTIN D. SCHWARTZ

## References and Further Reading

Bergen, R.K. 1998. *Wife Rape: Understanding the Response of Survivors and Service Providers*, Thousand Oaks, CA, Sage.

Finkelhor, D. and Yllo, K. 1985. *License to Rape: Sexual Abuse of Wives*, New York, Holt, Rinehart and Winston.

Frazier, P.A. and Seales, L.M. 1997. Acquaintance rape is real rape, in Schwartz, M.D., Ed., *Researching Sexual Violence Against Women: Methodological and Personal Perspectives*, Thousand Oaks, CA, Sage.

Mahoney, P. and Williams, L.M. 1998. Sexual assault in marriage: Prevalence, consequences, and treatment of wife rape, in Jasinski, J.L. and Williams, L.M., Eds., *Partner Violence: A Comprehensive Review of 20 Years of Research*, Thousand Oaks, CA, Sage.

Peacock, P.L. 1995. Marital rape, in Wiehe, V.R. and Richards, A.L., Eds., *Intimate Betrayal*, Thousand Oaks, CA, Sage.

Russell, D.E.H. 1990. *Rape in Marriage*, revised ed., Indianapolis, IN, Indiana University Press.

Ryan, R.M. 1995. The sex right: A legal history of the marital rape exemption, *Law and Social Inquiry*, 20.

Schwartz, M.D. 1982. The spousal rape exemption for criminal rape prosecution, *Vermont Law Review*, 7.

*See also* **Domestic Assault: Extent and Correlates; Domestic Assault: Law; Domestic Assault: Prevention and Treatment; Rape, Acquaintance and Date; Rape, Forcible: Extent and Correlates; Rape, Forcible: Law**

---

# Rape, Statutory

---

Recent attention has been given by prosecutors and service providers to the ever-increasing problems surrounding the crime of statutory rape. Not only a violation of the law, statutory rape is also associated with a range of corresponding problems for the victim, the offender, and justice professionals. In part because of these issues, many states have begun to reexamine their current approach to handling this particular sex crime against juveniles. Concurrently, the widespread media attention that recently publicized cases has garnered has also contributed to the interest in the development and application of effective statutory rape laws.

## Statutory Rape Laws

The law often regulates the behavior of individuals in their interactions with others. In doing so, one category of offenses deemed punishable under the criminal law is crimes against persons. A specific type of these crimes deals with criminal acts of a sexual nature. Perhaps the most recognized type of sexual offense is the crime of rape. In general, the common law crime of rape occurs when a man has unlawful carnal knowledge of a woman without her consent or against her will by either using force or instilling fear. A more contemporary delineation of rape related to statutory rape is found in the *Model Penal Code*. According to this code, a child under the age of ten cannot legally consent to sexual intercourse; thus any time a person has sex with such a child they are guilty of committing rape. The *Model Penal Code* does not, however, specifically address consensual sexual intercourse engaged in with persons who are over the age of ten.

It should be noted that actual state sexual victimization laws vary in terms of their wording and the potential sentence an offender may receive for their violation. Furthermore, not all sexual offenses are rapes; rather, there are varying degrees of acts, which although not characterized by the same elements of rape, are nonetheless criminal. Statutory rape, as legislatively prescribed, is a unique sexual offense in which the victim is by definition underage.

As such, the term "statutory rape" is actually a misnomer, as key elements of rape are actually not present in crimes of statutory rape. Specifically, statutory rape laws prohibit sexual intercourse, even intercourse that is consensual, with individuals who are under a prescribed age. Illustrative of this point, most state statutes do not include the term statutory rape, but instead have provisions in their rape, sexual assault, or unlawful sexual intercourse laws that dictate the age under which an individual cannot legally give consent to engage in sexual intercourse.

### Implementation of Statutory Rape Laws

Although all 50 states and the federal law currently have such provisions, the law has not always identified a minimum age of consent. Under early common law in England, it was legal to have sexual intercourse with a female child as long as she gave consent. This practice was later criminalized in English statutes that located the age of consent for a female at twelve years.

Under these laws, by having sex with a female child under the age of twelve, a man was committing the crime of rape. The law was later modified in 1576 to effectively decrease the age of consent to ten. Through the adoption of English common law, laws were created in the U.S. that mirrored this practice of identifying the age at which a female became capable of consenting to sexual intercourse.

This age was first determined to be ten years old, but was raised during the 19th century through various state legislative actions. As states were free to determine the age of consent, a lack of consensus resulted in the adoption of differential age standards across states. As such, currently the minimum age of consent ranges from 14 to 18 years of age, with over half of the states utilizing 16 as the age of consent. That is, in states such as Massachusetts, it is a crime to have sexual intercourse with a person under the age of 16. Other states have age-graded laws that prescribe different crimes and penalties depending on the victim's age. According to Kentucky's statutory law, it is first-degree sexual abuse if a person has sexual contact with a child who is less than twelve years of age and second-degree sexual abuse if the child is younger than 14-years-old.

In addition to the minimum age requirement, 23 states also consider the difference in age between the offender and the victim in their statutory rape laws. In doing so, the level and type of offense is determined in part based upon these age considerations. For example, in Minnesota it is first-degree criminal sexual conduct to have intercourse with a person who is less than 13 years old if the actor is more than three years older than the person. In instances that involve a person aged 13 to 15 years old and an actor who is more than two years older, it is third-degree criminal sexual conduct. Most typically, the age differential is three or four years; however, some states require as little as two years difference or as much as six years difference for statutory rape laws to be applied. Consideration of age differentials can also be a factor in sentencing, with stiff penalties being reserved for sexual encounters with younger minors. In Delaware, individuals convicted of having sex with a person who is under the age of 16 when they themselves are ten or more years older than the minor, face a prison sentence of two to 20 years.

### Justification of Statutory Rape Laws

Despite the lack of consensus across states about what constitutes statutory rape, the primary justification for having such laws is less debated. Statutory rape laws were originally implemented to prevent the sexual exploitation of young girls by older, adult men. It is generally believed that young girls lack the necessary sophistication to be able to discern the potentially sexually exploitative motives of older men and thus they may consensually engage in sexual acts without understanding their nature and quality. Because minor females may be susceptible to this sexual coercion by males and because they cannot fully appreciate the decision to engage in sex, statutory rape laws prohibit such activity. In short, statutory rape laws make females under a prescribed age legally unable to give their consent, thus making their sexual encounters criminal. This concern regarding coercion seems to be a valid one. Adolescents who begin having sex at an early age are more likely to have a sexual experience that is coerced than those who begin having sex at an older age. Likewise, other studies have shown that young girls who engage in sex are likely to have sex partners who are older than they are. One study showed that almost 20% of 13-year-old girls who lose their virginity do so to males who are five or more years older (Moore and Driscoll, 1995).

A second major justification for the adoption and enforcement of statutory rape laws is to prevent young girls from getting pregnant and having babies out of wedlock. This justification has recently been used to resuscitate the enforcement of statutory rape laws throughout the country. In fact, as part of welfare reform legislation instituted in 1996, states were advised to "aggressively enforce" statutory rape laws. It was believed that older males are responsible for impregnating young girls and that these girls often turn to welfare and other public assistance programs for support. If statutory rape laws could prevent such pregnancies then it could also be possible to reduce welfare rolls and the amount of money the government would expend on young mothers and their children.

Programs designed for the enforcement of statutory rape laws have recently been implemented in California and other states. The California program, called California's Statutory Rape Vertical Prosecution Program, gives funding to counties specifically for the prosecution of statutory rape. This program alone accounted for the conviction of more than 1400 offenders in its first three years. Despite the seemingly successful implementation of the program, it is less clear whether the program has actually resulted in a decrease in the number of teenage pregnancies or if enforcement has deterred adult men from engaging in sex with underage girls.

Along with questioning the effectiveness of such programs, concerns have also been raised concerning the effects enforcement may have on sexually active young girls. In particular, if states target young pregnant girls and their partners as potential sources of statutory rape prosecution, then pregnant adolescents may be reluctant to seek prenatal care for fear of being reported to the authorities. Similar concerns have been raised in regards to teen girls seeking treatment for sexually transmitted diseases and having an investigation started into the context of their sexual activity.

## Current Issues in the Application of Statutory Rape Laws

In addition to these concerns raised by medical professionals, recent attention has also been given to the enforcement of statutory rape laws. One recent development in statutory rape law has been holding parents of adolescents responsible for their sexual activities. This application is in accordance with the movement towards abstinence-only education and programming that has blossomed during the early 2000s. In part to convince parents to disallow their children to engage in sexual intercourse, a woman in Illinois was charged under the Illinois Wrongs to Children Act after it was learned that her 13-year-old daughter was having sex with her 17-year-old boyfriend. Under more common statutory rape provisions, the young man in this scenario would typically be charged; however, because the mother knew about the sexual relationship, provided her daughter with birth control pills, and allowed her daughter's boyfriend to spend the night in her home, the mother was held criminally liable. The statute was later deemed unconstitutional by the Illinois Supreme Court since the statute was vague and it is unclear how parents can take steps to prevent criminal sexual activities involving their children. Despite being deemed invalid in Illinois, it is possible that other states may seek to adopt similar laws that place a locus of responsibility on parents.

Perhaps more widely publicized than these parental liability laws are other changes in statutory rape laws that have made them gender-neutral. Historically, statutory rape laws were exclusively designed to protect underage female children from the exploitative behavior of older males. As such, the laws did little to prevent young males from engaging in sex with older females. This discrepancy reflects a general belief that males are not capable of being sexually coerced and that young boys who have sex with older females are not victims.

Modern statutes have been crafted in gender-neutral terms so that both underage males and females can be protected. One case involving a minor male that drew widespread attention was the case of Mary K. Letourneau. Letourneau was 35 years old and a sixth grade teacher when she entered into a sexual relationship with one of her 13-year-old students. She was charged with two counts of second-degree rape of a child and spent 180 days in jail. After her release, she was found with her victim after being ordered by the court to refrain from having contact with him. Her violation resulted in her being sentenced to 89 months in prison. It should also be noted that the young, male victim fathered two children with Letourneau.

Despite what seems to be a movement towards gender equality in rape statutory laws, it has been argued that female offenders receive more lenient sentences than their male counterparts. The Letourneau case has been targeted as an example of such disparity, as the sentence Letourneau originally received was not severe given the large age differential between her and her victim and the fact that she abused her power and authority as a schoolteacher. Others have pointed out that male victims of statutory rape remain financially responsible for any children they father with their victimizer despite the fact that they are not legally able to give their consent to have sexual intercourse. This disjuncture reflects the system's general refusal to treat male victims of statutory rape as "true" victims.

In addition to gender-related issues, states have also recently changed their statutory laws to include civil remedies and to increase criminal penalties. Some states allow fines to be imposed upon individuals who are convicted of statutory rape and in the state of California, civil penalties can be imposed. In other states, offenders may face registration as a sex offender if they are convicted of statutory rape, without exceptions or consideration of the circumstances of the individual case. Finally, other states have adopted provisions that increase the sentence for statutory rape offenders if the victimization results in a pregnancy. This sentence enhancement is in accordance with the aforementioned focus of statutory rape laws for the purpose of pregnancy prevention.

Such changes reflect the general concern Americans have for children and the diligence that protection of children requires. As such, it is likely that this increased attention to statutory rape laws across the states will remain as society views sexual abuse of children to be particularly repugnant and the polity continues to be concerned with reducing the occurrence of teen pregnancies.

LEAH E. DAIGLE

## References and Further Reading

Allen, T.M., (2002). Gender-neutral statutory rape laws: Legal fictions disguised as remedies to male child exploitation, *University of Detroit Mercy Law Review*, 80, 111–126.

Davis, N.S. and Twombly, J. (2000). *State Legislators' Handbook for Statutory Rape Issues,* Washington, DC, American Bar Association, Center on Children and the Law, U.S. Department of Justice, Office of Justice Programs, Office for Victims of Crime.

Jones, R. (2002). Inequality from gender-neutral laws: Why must male victims of statutory rape pay child support for children resulting from their victimization? *Georgia Law Review,* 36, 411–463.

Levine, J. (2002). *Harmful to Minors: The Perils of Protecting Children from Sex,* Minneapolis, MN, University of Minnesota Press.

Lynch, M.W. (1998). Enforcing 'statutory rape'? *Public Interest,* 132, 3–17.

Moore, K.A. and Driscoll, A. (1995). Partners, *Predators, Peers, Protectors: Males and Teen Pregnancy: New Data Analyses of the 1995 National Survey of Family Growth,* Washington, DC, The National Campaign to Prevent Teen Pregnancy.

Phipps, C.A. (2003). Misdirected reform: On regulating consensual sexual activity between teenagers, *Cornell Journal of Law and Public Policy,* 12, 373–445.

Russell, D.E.H. and Bolen, R.M. (2000). *The Epidemic of Rape and Child Sexual Abuse in the United States,* Thousand Oaks, CA, Sage Publications, Inc.

Sutherland, K. (2003). From jailbird to jailbait: Age of consent laws and the construction of teenage sexualities, *William and Mary Journal of Women and the Law,* 9, 313–349.

*See also* **Rape, Acquaintance and Date; Rape, Forcible; Rape, Marital**

# Rational Choice Theory

Until the later years of the 20th century there was a general consensus among criminologists and criminal justice professionals that intervention directed at actual or potential criminals, by policing, deterrent sentencing, or effective training, was the only way of restraining the growth of crime. But the failure of programs and policies based upon this view of the crime problem and the underlying assumption that offenders were deviants in need of correction became evident as levels of crime in Western countries continued to rise. It was clear that attempts to restrain the growth of crime through the treatment or retraining of convicted offenders were largely ineffective, and that the threat of judicial punishment seldom deters others from joining their ranks. On the other hand, practical measures designed to make the commission of crime more difficult or less profitable were yielding promising results. Some of these involved "target hardening"—for example, fitting steering locks and immobilizers to automobiles; others improved surveillance of shopping centers and streets by means of closed circuit television, or encouraged informal surveillance by members of the public, such as neighborhood watch schemes and better street lighting; other strategies were used to eliminate common targets of criminals (e.g., ceasing to pay employees in cash and using checks instead). Many such schemes that came to be called "situational crime prevention," are described in a fascinating book edited by Ronald V. Clarke (1992). It is true that situational crime prevention was not always successful, and occasionally produced unexpected and paradoxical results (Barr and Pease, 1990; Newman, Clarke, and Shoham, 1997), but for the most part they did show substantial, robust, and measurable effects.

These practical strategies for the control of crime were not, in the first place, inspired by a formal theory, or a particular view of the motivation of the criminal, and indeed Cornish and Clarke emphasize the futility of trying to construct a general theory of criminality:

> Unlike other approaches…which attempt to impose a conceptual unity upon divergent criminal behaviors (by subsuming them under more general concepts such as delinquency, deviance, rule breaking, short-run hedonism, criminality, etc.), our rational choice formulation sees these differences as crucial to the tasks of explanation and control. Unlike existing theories that tend to concentrate on factors disposing individuals to criminal behavior (the initial involvement model), the rational choice approach, in addition, emphasizes subsequent decisions in the offender's career (1986, 6).

Clarke and his colleagues are reluctant to describe their thinking as the development of a theory, since that term has come to denote a general explanation of criminality; they usually refer to the "rational choice perspective." They emphasize the practical utility of their approach: "The synthesis we had suggested—a rational choice perspective on criminal behavior—was intended to locate criminological findings within a framework particularly suitable for thinking about policy-relevant research" (Cornish and Clarke, 1986). According to Clarke and Felson (1993) "the ultimate purpose of criminological theory [is] not 'understanding' in the abstract, but rather understanding to help control a variety of mostly selfish acts injuring society and often, in time, the perpetrators themselves" (Clarke and Felson, 1993).

The first sketch for the rational choice perspective was established by a conference of social scientists from several disciplines—psychology, sociology, criminology, economics, and law—in Cambridge, England, in 1985. It was generally agreed that progress in crime policy had been retarded by the common assumption that criminal activity was essentially deviant and pathological in nature, and therefore not governed by the principles that dominated other forms of human action. As Clarke and Cornish (1985) have argued:

> Most theories about criminal behavior have tended to ignore the offender's decision-making—the conscious thought processes that give purpose to and justify conduct, and the underlying cognitive mechanisms by which information about the world is selected, attended to, and processed. The source of this neglect is the apparent conflict between decision-making concepts and the prevailing determinism of most criminological theories... [T]hese theories have traditionally been concerned to explain the criminal dispositions of particular individuals or groups... [T]he criminal appears as a relatively passive figure; thus he or she is seen either as prey to internal or external forces outside personal control, or as the battlefield upon which these forces resolve their struggle for the control of behavioral outcomes.

This emphasis on rationality was familiar and attractive to the economists, who were accustomed to working with the exacting principles of expected utility theory (see Lattimore and Witte, 1986) but less so to criminologists, accustomed to the opportunistic and often clumsy activities of burglars and robbers. Acknowledging this problem, Cornish and Clarke (1986) write that the starting point of the rational choice perspective on criminal behavior is:

> the assumption that offenders seek to benefit themselves by their criminal behavior; that this involves the making of decisions and of choices, however rudimentary on occasion these choices might be; and that these processes exhibit a measure of rationality, albeit constrained by limits of time and ability and the availability of relevant information...even in the case of offenses that seemed to be pathologically motivated or impulsively executed.

This raises two basic questions to be asked of the rational choice model: Do the notions of rationality and conscious choice furnish a recognizable characterization of what happens at the time of the commission of a crime? Second, does this theoretical stance enable us to make better predictions about the occurrence of crime or to devise better ways of curbing crime?

The experience of situational crime prevention provides support for the contention that in many situations thieves, fraudsters, and others who steal property ("instrumental offenders") are at least trying to maximize gain and minimize risk of capture, and to that extent they may be described as behaving rationally. It is problematic whether the same can be said of "expressive" offenders—those who commit violent assaults, woundings, and homicides without expectation of profit. The legitimacy of the rational choice perspective as it is applied to criminal activities partly depends upon the definition of rational behavior.

In its most robust form, a rational choice model is based on the assumption that the individual actor is, at the point of committing a crime, in possession of full and accurate information concerning the risks and potential gains that attend a given course of action, and that he or she is capable of processing this information competently *and simultaneously*. This may be an unrealistic assumption, since many burglars, for example, rely upon 'rules of thumb' or habits born of previous successful or disastrous experiences in targeting particular properties at particular times and in given circumstances, for example, choosing isolated houses at night when no domestic lights are visible and when there are no signs of a guard dog or an active burglar alarm. Such stipulations are clearly prior to the contemporary decision and limit the scope of the calculations that have to be made; they reflect routine practices or what Cooke (1980) calls "standing decisions." This is not inconsistent with the notion of rationality; most of us rely upon such habitual and usually unchallenged assumptions about what is safe and what is too dangerous to contemplate, even in minor matters concerning motoring or responding to telephone calls or unsolicited letters. The curious aspect of these basic assumptions is that they have a superstitious quality, because they remain untested; they simply close off certain opportunities. This means that the notion of *simultaneous* processing of all available information is substantially eroded. Partly because of this, there have been several interesting debates concerning the appropriate model of imperfect, limited, or 'bounded' rationality that ought to be adopted. There are difficulties about representing the potential offender as a rational, dispassionate, calculating decision-maker. Many offenders seem to be very vague about such matters as the probability of being apprehended, the likelihood of being convicted, and the "going rate" of penalties for a crime. (It has been pointed out that although the potential criminal may be mistaken in his assessments of the probable consequences of an action, he may still be acting rationally in deriving logical inferences from his erroneous estimates.)

Perhaps the most instructive approach to the problem of bounded rationality begins with Elster's (1986) definition of [fully] rational conduct:

> Rational choice theory appeals to three distinct elements in the choice situation. The first element is the feasible set, that is, the set of all courses of action that (are rationally believed to) satisfy various logical, physical and economic constraints. The second is (a set of rational beliefs about) the causal structure of the situation, which determines what courses of action will lead to what outcomes. The third is a subjective ranking of the feasible alternatives, derived from a ranking of the outcomes to which they (are expected to) lead. To act rationally, then, simply means to choose the highest-ranking element in the feasible set.

There are several aspects of this description that are of particular significance. It refers to the choices and decisions of individuals in specific situations, rather than categories of situations; it implies simultaneous processing of information, rather than serial processing; and it attributes to the individual the capacity to handle what may be complex information in the form of probabilities. As many authors have pointed out, these circumstances are very unlikely to obtain in relation to criminal activities. To the extent that people employ subjective rather than objective probabilities in arriving at decisions, allowance must presumably be made for individual differences (for instance, in appreciation of risks) that may be substantial. Studies that have sought to test the adequacy of the expected utility model against aggregate data are, for that reason, misconceived. On the whole, this debate leads to the conclusion that offenders do try to act rationally in deciding whether to go ahead with the temptation to commit another crime, but lack accurate information about the risks and possible gains from doing so. In this respect they share a handicap with criminologists, who also know little about the prospects of detection and conviction for identifiable breaches of the criminal law.

Criminals operate in conditions of uncertainty, and their predicament is well represented in a masterly analysis by John Watkins (1970). Watkins identifies three circumstances in which formal models of rational behavior do or do not not apply:

> [Under conditions of certainty] the decision-maker proceeds as if he knew (a) all the alternative decisions open to him in the given choice-situation, and (b) the outcome for him that would infallibly follow from each of these possible decisions. [In conditions of risk] the decision-maker is again assumed to know all the alternative decisions that are open to him in the given choice-situation. And while he does not know what outcome a decision would have, he does know, in the case of each possible decision, each of the possible outcomes it might have; and he is able to assign a non-arbitrary numerical probability to every possible outcome of every possible decision. Under conditions of uncertainty, the decision-maker is again assumed to know all the alternative decisions open to him in the given choice-situation and, for each possible decision, all the alternative outcomes it might have; but though he may judge one outcome to be more, or less, or equally likely than another, he is *not* able to assign to each outcome a non-arbitrary numerical probability.

As Watkins comments, "According to normative decision theory, a decision-scheme should consist of a complete specification of the possible outcomes, a complete preference-map or a complete allocation of pay-off values to the outcomes, and (where appropriate) a comprehensive apparatus for dealing risks and uncertainties. Judged by this, an actual decision-scheme is usually very imperfect indeed." In the present context, the implication of his analysis is not that one should abandon the notion that rational decision making has a role in the genesis of or restraint from criminal behavior, but that the individual is operating in, and adapting to, conditions of great uncertainty. Watkins remarks that "An ideal decision-scheme is pictured as being present to the agent's mind in its entirety, a complete whole in which the several components simultaneously play their due role. An actual decision-scheme is usually built up bit-by-bit, so that the arrival of an isolated bit of situational information may have a quite disproportionate influence.... Not only is an actual decision-scheme more or less vague and fragmentary compared with the ideal, but the agent will usually reduce and simplify it further as he proceeds towards a decision" (Watkins, 1970). (This might well be a reference to the opportunistic character of much minor crime, in which the sudden recognition of a chance to carry out a profitable burglary or robbery overrides the habitual caution that normally protects the individual from the risk of apprehension and arrest.) This is a state of affairs that is known as "akratic behavior" or—more simply—"weakness of will." An example is yielding to temptation after having taken a firm decision to give up smoking or to avoid alcohol. Such behavior illustrates two principles: (1) the sequential nature of decision-making—the observation that considerations that are distant in temporal terms from the situation in which a certain kind of behavior is a viable option may have less weight than those that obtain at the relevant time; and (2) that appetites or temptations may override long-term strategic decisions, typically in circumstances in which the long-term decisions are rational, and the immediate temptations are visceral or emotional (Elster, 1986).

An orthodox interpretation of expected utility theory would imply that standing decisions to refrain from crime would be arrived at by an evaluation of the probable gains and risks of engaging in crime in general, in a way that parallels the potential offender's calculations in relation to a particular opportunity for crime. Yet Tyler's study of *Why People Obey the Law* (1990) does not support such an interpretation. He makes a general distinction between "instrumental" and "normative" mechanisms of conformity, the first of these corresponding fairly closely to the model presented by the rational choice perspective:

> [P]eople are viewed as shaping their behavior to respond to changes in the tangible, immediate incentives and penalties associated with following the law — to judgments about the personal gains and losses resulting from different kinds of behavior … a normative perspective … is concerned with the influence of what people regard as just and moral as opposed to what is in their self-interest … They will feel personally committed to obeying the law, irrespective of whether they risk punishment for breaking the law.

Tyler found, in his Chicago sample, that normative mechanisms were more important in securing conformity with the law than instrumental mechanisms—in other words, that personal morality, or recognition of the legitimate authority of the law, rather than fear of punishment was the usual reason for refraining from crime. Several other studies have led to similar conclusions (Tittle, 1977; Grasmick and Green, 1980; Piliavin, Thornton, Gartner and Matsueda, 1986).

The normative sources of conformity described by Tyler reflect several of the characteristics of what is commonly called "conscience." They do not depend upon the threat of punishment or calculations of the gains that might be secured by a criminal act; they represent a general orientation, in the sense that they effectively remove certain classes or types of behavior from the individual's repertoire. This implies that the normative sources of conformity occur prior to any decisions concerning the commission of any particular criminal opportunity or crime, essentially preempting such decisions. This feature is consistent with the notion of sequential decision-making rather than simultaneous decision-making; normative sources involve convictions (not simply opinions) about what is right and what is wrong. But even this emphasis on the normative sources of conformity shares with rational choice theory an exclusive emphasis on cognitive processes and a corresponding neglect of the affective aspects of behavior. An adequate description of what is experienced as conscience must surely embrace *feelings* of obligation, aversion, self-regard, and the anticipation of guilt.

This essentially informal or intuitive nature of what are sometimes called "gut feelings" of right and wrong—the mechanisms that can, and often do, override rational considerations of the prospect of personal gain and risk, is strongly supported by a substantial body of experimental research into the process by which moral training secures the blocking of highly motivated behavior. The existence of such a mechanism is, of course, the basic requirement of a "dispositional" or personality theory of criminality, which has the task of explaining how it is that individuals are induced to develop an antipathy to illegal, immoral, or dishonest behavior that causes them to ignore, or even not to perceive, opportunities for gain or gratification. In the strict terms of the expected utility model, an individual is clearly irrational who insists that, whatever the possibilities of personal gain and the remoteness of risk, he or she will refrain from criminal opportunities is clearly irrational.

GORDON B. TRASLER

## References and Further Reading

Barr, R. and Pease, K. 1990. Crime placement, displacement and deflection, in Tonry, M. and Morris, N., Eds., *Crime and Justice: A Review of Research,* Vol. 12, Chicago, IL, University of Chicago Press.

Clarke, R.V. 1986. Situational crime prevention: Theory and practice, *British Journal of Criminology,* 20.

Clarke, R.V., Ed. 1992. *Situational Crime Prevention: Successful Case Studies,* Albany, NY, Harrow and Heston.

Clarke, R.V. 1995. Opportunity-reducing crime prevention strategies and the role of motivation, in Wikstrom, P.-O., Clarke, R.V. and McCord, J., Eds. *Integrating Crime Prevention Strategies: Propensity and Opportunity,* Stockholm, Sweden, National Council for Crime Prevention.

Clarke, R.V. and Felson, M., Eds. 1993. *Advances in Criminal Theory, Vol. 5, Routine Activity and Rational Choice,* New Brunswick, NJ, Transaction Publishers.

Cooke, P.J. 1980. Research in criminal deterrence: Laying the groundwork for the second decade, in Morris, N. and Tonry, M., Eds., *Crime and Justice: A Review of Research,* Vol. 2, Chicago, IL, University of Chicago Press.

Cornish, D.B. and Clarke, R.V. Eds. 1986. *The Reasoning Criminal: Rational Choice Perspectives on Offending,* New York, Springer-Verlag.

Elster, J. 1986. *Rational Choice*, Oxford, U.K., Blackwell.

Newman, G., Clarke, R.V. and Shoham, S.G., Eds. 1997. *Rational Choice and Situational Crime Prevention*, Brookfield, VT, Ashgate.

Tyler, T. 1990. *Why People Obey the Law*, New Haven, CT, Yale University Press.

Watkins, J. 1970. Imperfect rationality, in Borger, R. and Cioffi, F., Eds. *Explanation in the Behavioural Sciences*, Cambridge, England, Cambridge University Press.

*See also* **Psychological Theories of Criminal Behavior**

---

# Receiving Stolen Goods

There are many paths that stolen goods may take from thieves to eventual consumers. On the simplest and shortest route the thief is the ultimate consumer, using what he steals. Other paths are also relatively uncomplicated and involve the thief or his agent selling to friends, neighbors, and acquaintances under the cover of friendly or neighborly privacy. Still others lead through sheltered markets such as bars, luncheonettes, beauty parlors, bowling alleys, dormitories, and country clubs, all part of the complex fabric of the underground economy (Henry, 1976). Some paths are so narrow, rarified, and obscure that only the most exotic merchandise ever travels them. Others are long-established routes, habitually cluttered with quantities, both large and small, of the most mundane stolen products. With a few exceptions, adequate descriptions of these and other pathways along which stolen property travels are lacking in the literature of criminology and no reliable information is available on the relative contribution of different patterns of sale, purchase, and distribution to the overall flow of stolen property from thieves to eventual consumers.

Despite the paucity of information on the overall composition of the total traffic in stolen property, some specific roles, distinctive actors, and obligatory performances have been well-specified. Among the oldest and probably the easiest to identify is that of the dealer in stolen property—the fence. The fence has been a central figure in the traffic in stolen property at least since the early 17th century when Mary Frith, alias Moll Cutpurse, organized a massive clearinghouse for stolen property in Elizabethan London. An outrageous woman who dressed in mens' clothes and claimed to be the first woman to smoke tobacco, her substantial fencing operation paled in comparison to the enormous organization of Jonathan Wild, the fence who dominated the London underworld between 1715 and 1725. Although Daniel Defoe's claim that Wild employed some 7000 thieves may be

an exaggeration, Gerald Howson (1970) maintains that Wild's operation may well have been the largest criminal enterprise in English history. Wild, memorialized in Henry Fielding's *Life of Mr. Jonathan Wild the Great* (1743), enjoys a literary legacy second only to Charles Dickens' Fagin, a character from *Oliver Twist* that Dickens based on the 19th century London "Prince of Fences," Ikey Solomons (Tobias, 1974). In the 20th century the recognition of high profile fences continued with Mother, alias "Marm," Mandelbaum (Asbury, 1928) and "Cammi" Grizzard (Humphreys, 1929) as well as the contemporary fences "Vincent Swaggi" (Klockars, 1974), "Sam Goodwin" (Steffensmeier, 1986), and others (Walsh, 1977) whose true identities social scientists had to conceal under pseudonyms.

Although the criminal careers of dealers in stolen property are as varied and diverse as the careers of other entrepreneurs, all must solve three general problems in their fencing careers.

## Buying

The first is the problem of *buying*. Persons engaged in certain occupations—auctioneers, pawnbrokers, and dealers in second-hand and general merchandise—regularly find themselves approached by sellers of stolen property because of the similarity between common stolen merchandise and the kinds of legitimate merchandise they routinely handle and the informal manner in which they purchase it. Similarly, persons engaged in other occupations—gamblers, bartenders, criminal lawyers, social workers, and private investigators—find themselves approached by sellers of stolen property because thieves are common among the type of clientele they routinely serve. Although workers in these occupations may buy stolen property occasionally and opportunistically, the fence, the dealer in stolen property, must maintain a steady stream of sellers to sustain his or her business. Doing so requires some form of *advertisement* that he or she is a willing and able buyer. The experience of numerous police "sting" operations in which police pose as fences in order to entice thieves into selling stolen property to them suggests that such advertisement is not difficult; it need only consist of "spreading the word" of the fence's willingness to buy stolen property. Indeed, for the real fence the challenge is not how to generate sellers but how to restrict the flow of willing sellers to those vending desirable merchandise.

## Selling

The second and more difficult general problem every fence must solve is the problem of selling. From the thief's perspective, the fence provides three services, each of which is a reflection of the fence's ability to sell. The first is the fence's ability to buy large quantities of merchandise. A man who steals a trailer loaded with cigarettes may be able to peddle a few dozen cartons to friends, but if he wishes to sell the entire load in a single transaction, the fence can accommodate him. An industrious thief may peddle an entire trailer load of cigarettes because smokers are easy to locate. But the thief who steals a rare manuscript, a case of dentist drills, or a carload of popsicle sticks may have no idea where to sell them. Finally, whether the thief has large quantities of common merchandise or small quantities of exotic property, the fence permits the thief to quickly convert those products into money without the inconvenience of searching for or developing unknown markets.

These three services bear witness to the crucial role of fences in property theft because of their ready access to markets that are effectively closed to many if not most thieves. How, then, does the fence gain access to these markets when the thief cannot? Probably the most common answer to this question is that by virtue of a second, legitimate occupation the fence is in these markets already. Thus, the art fence is likely to be an art dealer, the jewelry fence a jeweler, and the automobile fence a dealer in automobile parts. However, this generalization is limited by the size of the market for specific types of stolen property and the extent to which that market is regulated. Some markets are simply so small that a fence specializing in certain products (popsicle sticks for example) is simply preposterous. If such stolen products are to be sold (and they may simply be abandoned by a thief who is unable to find a fence for them), it is likely that they will be sold back to the manufacturer through a private investigator or attorney acting as a fence. Similarly, the registration of automobiles is so tightly regulated that stolen automobiles must normally be removed to less regulated markets (e.g., smuggled out of the country) or converted into untraceable parts before they can be sold.

## Success

The third general, and normally the most difficult, problem for fences is to become successful. Achieving success as a fence means buying and selling stolen property regularly, profitably, and without getting caught. Making a profit in the stolen property market must be understood in light of the fact that stolen property must generally be sold well below legitimate market prices. Because thieves can steal property at far less cost than legitimate manufacturers can make it, fences customarily purchase goods at one-quarter of their legitimate value. However, the fence may then be obliged to sell it at only a third of its legitimate market value. This is so because less-than-legitimate market prices are the chief inducement for consumers to buy stolen property and assume the risks and disadvantages of doing so.

A fence may operate profitably with just such a profit structure. However, a profit margin of that order may be less than what is available in the legitimate market and barely worth the risks of dealing in stolen property. The economics of the trade in stolen property suggest a superior solution: Buy property from thieves at stolen-property market prices and sell it at or just slightly below legitimate-property market prices. One of the ways of doing so is to maintain a legitimate business that carries the same products as the fence purchases illegally. The legally and illegally purchased merchandise may then be merged and sold together at legitimate market prices.

Being successful as a fence is not simply a matter of making a profit; it also means not getting caught. The occasional consumer of stolen property or even the occasional dealer may rely on the cover of friendship, anonymity, or luck to shield him or her from apprehension, but the fence who buys and sells regularly and who develops a reputation for doing so must engage in active defenses against apprehension and conviction in order to survive. In this effort, the fence's legitimate business front that was so economically advantageous also serves in the fence's effort to thwart apprehension and conviction. In order to convict someone for receiving stolen property it must be proven: (1) that the goods in question are in fact stolen, (2) that the person accused actually received them, and (3) that the person who received them had reasonable cause to believe they were stolen. Consider how the fence may use a legitimate business front to shield against attempts to prove these necessary evidentiary elements.

## Defenses against Proof that Goods Are Stolen

In order to prove that particular goods belong to someone else, the owner must be able to uniquely identify them, distinguishing them from other goods that may be similar in appearance. The fence's legitimate business front often permits the merging of stolen and legitimate stock to make them indistinguishable. Mass-produced products, foodstuffs, metals, loose precious and semiprecious stones, chemicals, clothing, and many types of livestock are virtually indistinguishable as stolen once they are merged with quantities of similar products. Products that bear uniquely identifying marks or labels can be altered or modified so as to make them unidentifiable as the property of another. Gold and other precious metals can be melted down, jewels may be removed from their distinct settings, labels can be cut from suits, automobiles and animals can be reduced to their valuable parts. Although they may not have the exact duplicate of a specific stolen product in stock at the time of purchase, fences may, if necessary, produce receipts from earlier purchases of identical property to establish the appearance of legitimate ownership of the stolen property.

## Defenses against Proof of Possession

If fences merge legitimate and stolen stock, remove labels and other identifying characteristics, and keep a supply of receipts for the purchase of legitimate goods that cover the purchase of stolen goods, they defend against proof of possession with the same stroke that they defend against proof that they are stolen. In addition to these strategies, fences may add the speed with which they can execute transactions to their defenses. If, for example, a fence can purchase stolen goods from a thief and distribute them to other dealers or their ultimate consumers within a few hours, he or she greatly reduces the chance that the goods will be found in his or her possession. Such an expeditious strategy rests on the assumption that there will be a lag between the time of the theft and when it is discovered, reported, and investigated.

Proof of possession may also be frustrated by a strategy known as the "drop." This involves instructing the thief to deposit the stolen merchandise at a neutral location where the fence, the fence's agent, or the consumer can take possession of it after it has been determined that the goods are not being kept under surveillance. In a functionally equivalent strategy, the thief is told to keep possession of the merchandise until the fence sells it on the basis of a sample. Such a strategy forces the thief to assume most of the risks of possession.

## Defenses against Proof of Reasonable Cause to Believe Goods Are Stolen

In advancing this proof it is typically argued that something about the character of the goods, their price, or the person selling them should alert a reasonable person to the probability they are stolen. For the fence whose dealing in stolen property is done behind a legitimate business front, defending against any such proof involves creating a false but plausible account of the illicit transaction that cannot be distinguished from a legitimate one. It should be kept in mind that the ability of the fence to craft a plausible account is a reflection of the fence's knowledge of real business practices and creative ingenuity. If, for example, an unemployed man drives up in a dilapidated vehicle loaded with new merchandise he offers for sale at a tenth of its legitimate market value, the law may well reason that a prospective buyer should have reasonable cause to believe the goods were stolen. How might the fence use his or her ingenuity and knowledge of business practices to fashion a plausible fictional account?

The fence argues that the man presented himself as the friend or relative of a merchant who was going out of business and was attempting to liquidate stock by selling it to other dealers. Such an account may be vulnerable on the suspiciously low sale price, but not if the fence can support his fraudulent story by showing a receipt and cancelled check for purchase of the merchandise from the man at a fair market price. Doing so involves generating a false receipt backed up by a check in an appropriate amount made out to the man, endorsed, falsely if necessary, by him. The check is then deposited in the fence's business account. If questioned about the transaction, the fence explains that he paid the seller the amount shown on the check and then cashed the check at the seller's request. The story is totally untrue, but it gives the fence a receipt and a cancelled check to support his fictitious account that he paid a fair market price for the goods.

## The Fence and the Law

Because the fence has long been recognized as a central figure in property theft (Colquhoun, 1796), distinguishable from the mere consumer or occasional buyer of stolen goods, it has prompted separate legal and police attention. Jerome Hall (1952) pioneered legal writing on the subject in the U.S., offering a typology that distinguished the "professional receiver" from the "occasional receiver" and "lay receiver." Hall's approach to distinguishing the professional receiver, a dealer in the business of buying and selling stolen property, from more ordinary receivers may be found reflected in contemporary federal sentencing guidelines. Such guidelines provide a four-level sentence enhancement for offenders found to be "in the business of receiving and selling stolen property" (*U.S. Sentencing Guidelines Manual*, 1991).

Individual states have sought to strengthen the capacity of law enforcement to attack the fence by modifying the essential elements of the crime of criminal receiving. For example, following a recommendation in the *Model Penal Code* (§ 223.6), Colorado did away with the requirement that the goods be stolen, requiring only that the goods be "of another" (Colo. Rev Stat. § 18-4-410 [1978]). This makes it possible for undercover police officers to offer legitimate merchandise to probable fences under circumstances that lead them to believe the merchandise is stolen. Efforts of this kind are complemented by increasingly stringent requirements that individual products bear identifying marks through which their ownership can be established. Similarly, other states have vastly expanded the concept of "possession" to include receiving, concealing, buying, controlling, disposing, and redistributing, in an attempt to close the loopholes that the simple concept of "possession" may provide. Finally, while some states still adhere to the requirement that the fence know that property he or she receives is stolen, most require only the less stringent standard that the fence have reasonable cause to believe it was stolen. Still other states require dealers to make inquiries about the origins of all merchandise purchased or raise presumptions that it is stolen when the transaction is "out of the regular course of business" (Fla. Stat. Ann. § 812.022 (1981 Supp.)).

## Corruption and Informing

Two final strategies complete the fence's general defenses against apprehension and conviction. The first is to corrupt those who are charged with prosecution. Unlike the sporadic or occasional dealer who may keep his dealings private for years, the full-time fence will inevitably become a public figure and thus an attractive target for enforcement efforts. In some jurisdictions it is possible to thwart such efforts by paying officers with gifts or money to allow a fence to operate unencumbered by police attentions.

The more common general defense against arrest and prosecution is for the fence to play the role of informant in exchange for a police "license" to deal in stolen property. There are numerous advantages in such a relationship for both police and fences. For the police, the informant fence is a source of criminal intelligence, someone to go to when they are under special pressure to recover particular stolen property or arrest a particularly troublesome thief. For the fence, a police relationship offers a way of eliminating troublesome or dangerous thieves, sabotaging competition, and disposing of goods "too hot to handle." Advantageous though the relationship may be for both sides, it involves genuine risks for both sides as well. For the police the relationship risks their being corrupted and manipulated, possibly serving to promote theft rather than control it. For the fence it risks the violent reaction of thieves whose criminal confidence is betrayed.

CARL B. KLOCKARS

## References and Further Reading

Asbury, H. 1928. *The Gangs of New York: An Informal History of the Underworld,* New York, Knopf.

Blakely, R.G. and Goldsmith, M. 1976. Criminal redistribution of stolen property: The need for law reform, *Michigan Law Review,* 74.

Hall, J. 1952. *Theft, Law, and Society,* 2nd. ed., Bobbs-Merrill.

Henry, S. 1978. *The Hidden Economy: The Context and Control of Borderline Crime,* Oxford, U.K., Martin Robertson.

Henry, S. 1976. The other side of the fence, *Sociological Review,* 24, 793–806.

Humphreys, C. 1929. *The Great Pearl Robbery of 1913,* London, William Heinemann.

Howson, G. 1970. *Thief Taker General, The Rise and Fall of Jonathan Wild.*

Klockars, C. 1983. The modern sting, in Carl B. Klockars, Ed., *Thinking About Police,* New York, McGraw-Hill.

1974. *The Professional Fence,* New York, The Free Press.

Lanter, D. 1999. In the business of fencing: Making sense of federal sentencing enhancements for dealers in stolen goods, *Texas Law Review,* 6.

Mars, G. 1978. Crime at work: The social construction of amateur property theft, *Sociology,* 12.

McIntosh, M. 1976. Thieves and fences: Markets and power in professional crime, *British Journal of Criminology,* 16.

Richard R. 1984. The effect of antifencing operations on encouraging crime, *Criminal Justice Review,* 9.

Roselius, T., Hoel, R., Benton, D., Howard, M. and Sciglimpaglia, D. 1975. *The Design of Anti-Fencing Strategies,* Fort Collins, CO, Colorado State University Press.

Steffensmeier, D.J. 1986. *The Fence: In the Shadow of Two Worlds,* Totowa, NJ, Rowman and Littlefield.

Tobias, J.J. 1974. *The Prince of Fences. The Life and Crimes of Ikey Solomons,* London, Valentine Mitchell.

Walsh, M.E. 1977. *The Fence: A New Look at the World of Property Theft,* Westport, CT, Greenwood.

Weiner, K.A., Strephens, C.K. and Besachuk, D.J. 1983. Making inroads into property crime: An analysis of the Detroit anti-fencing program, *Journal of Police Science and Administration,* 11.

*U.S. Sentencing Guidelines Manual* 2B1.2b(4)(A) (1991).

*See also* **Criminal Careers or Chronic Offenders; Theft, Professional**

# Recidivism

The study of recidivism has long been of interest to criminologists. At its most basic level, recidivism is defined as "the reversion of an individual to criminal behavior after he or she has been convicted of a prior offense, sentenced and (presumably) corrected" (Maltz, 1984, 1). The practical importance for recidivism analysis lies in prediction, presumably because the ability to predict outcomes accurately is of immense practical use (Farrington and Tarling, 1985; Schmidt and Witte, 1988). The use of prediction in identifying offenders who will reoffend has received a great deal of attention in the study of criminology and criminal justice. A wide variety of scholars has attempted to design different ways, including relying on statistical methods, to increase the accuracy of prediction, in order to predict those offenders who are most likely to reoffend (Burgess, 1928; Glueck and Glueck, 1959; Greenwood, 1982; Farrington and Tarling, 1985; Gottfredson and Tonry, 1987).

The ability to predict future behavior is central to the prevention and control of crime. As Gottfredson (1987, 6) notes, "if one seeks to control criminal behavior, one needs first to be able to predict it." Prediction is also pivotal to the various decision-making processes made throughout the criminal justice system with specific attention given to decisions to arrest, file charges, release on bail, sentence, as well as release on parole. Prediction can also serve as a useful tool in identifying ways to spend limited resources more wisely. As suggested by the selective incapacitation literature, if chronic offenders are prospectively and correctly identified, directing reformation efforts at them could result in both a reduction in unnecessary prison crowding as well as a reduction in crime rates. The ability to predict offenders' future criminal patterns offers a great deal of promise for the criminal justice system, but it is not without a serious complication: the inability to accurately measure and predict future offending (Gottfredson and Hirschi, 1990).

Predicting those offenders who pose a high risk of recidivism has been of interest to criminologists for years. The most common use for the term recidivism is as an outcome measure for evaluating the effectiveness of correctional programs. Numerous evaluations report recidivism rates to judge program effectiveness; however, problems arise when trying to compare the results across studies. Perhaps the biggest problem facing recidivism research is the lack of agreement as to how to define and measure recidivism (Hoffman and Stone-Meierhoefer, 1980). Studies vary in the way they define or operationalize recidivism, as well as the length of time used as a follow-up period.

Most studies rely on official data in order to assess recidivism. Because official data contains only those crimes known to the police (or other criminal justice agencies), this source of data collection cannot account for the dark figure of crime (those crimes that go unreported). This is a critical point to keep in mind especially given that when studying recidivism, researchers are trying to predict the future behavior of offenders.

Since researchers are unlikely to be able to obtain information on all criminal activities committed during a certain time period (e.g., accurate self-reports of offending), they often must rely on the information regarding all transactions offenders have with the criminal justice system (i.e., official data). Even with the use of official data, there are still a number of different ways in which recidivism may be defined. Recidivism refers to any number of outcomes or events that can be defined as negative. These can include but are not limited to new arrests, new convictions, returns to prison, or revocations because of any number of technical violations (e.g., failing to report to a supervising agent or positive drug tests). Therefore, it goes without saying that in order to compare recidivism rates across studies, it is essential that any report must be accompanied by an explicit operational definition of the criterion used as the negative outcome.

Many scholars have indicated that despite the numerous (officially) available outcomes, the best and most practical definitions of recidivism are those which are based on rearrest (Maltz, 1984; Visher et al., 1991; Smith and Akers, 1993). This argument is based on two specific factors. First, rearrest is closer to the actual commission of a crime than any other measure of recidivism (e.g., reconviction or reincarceration) and therefore better reflects the subject's actual delinquent activity (Sellin, 1931; Moffitt et al., 1994). In this regard, time until next arrest can serve as a proxy for the frequency of future offending. Second, rearrest is not subject to the same amount of manipulation from the criminal justice system as are other official outcome variables. Though arrest records are highly dependent upon the reporting and enforcement practices and policies of police departments, they are not subject to the discretions of other components of the criminal justice system. The circumstances that led to reconviction and reincarceration may not be related to characteristics of the current offense but rather to circumstances inherent to other parts of the criminal justice system (Schmidt and Witte, 1988; Maltz, 1984). For example, the decisions of prosecutors may produce notable discrepancies between the charges levied at time of arrest and those for which the offender is actually convicted (Maltz, 1984; Moffitt et al., 1994).

In addition to identifying the criterion measure to be used to define a negative outcome, there have also been a number of ways in which researchers have enumerated the future offending patterns of offenders. For example, early studies frequently used a binary measure of recidivism. This type of measure indicates either the success or failure of a person by determining whether or not the defined negative event (e.g., a new arrest or conviction) was present during some defined time period after the offender completed their sanction. In addition to this conventional measure of recidivism, Murray and Cox's (1979) study of juvenile delinquents in Chicago redefined the outcome measure of recidivism by reporting the number of arrests per month that were charged against a group of delinquents before and after being exposed to a treatment program. By using this reformulated measure of recidivism, they found a difference in results depending upon enumeration. When they used the binary outcome measure those who were rearrested at any point during the study, 82% of the sample were defined as recidivists; but when using the new rate measure, they were able to determine that the frequency at which the offenders were rearrested declined by two-thirds. This bears significance in pointing out the importance of examining the way in which the outcome variable is measured.

Recidivism has also been defined as an outcome variable that contains information on the timing of recidivism events as well as the severity of offense or the escalation effect of criminal behavior (Wolfgang et al., 1972; Schmidt and Witte, 1988). Because of the difficulties in statistical modeling, much focus in recidivism research has been on the timing associated with negative events as opposed to the severity of the event(s).

The use of the event timing as the dependent variable is preferable to the use of the binary outcome measure (Maltz, 1984; Farrington and Tarling, 1985; Schmidt and Witte, 1988). Schmidt and Witte (1988) point toward two main advantages of examining recidivism as the timing of events. First, this particular outcome measure contains valuable information that is statistically inefficient to simply ignore. Second, estimating the distribution of length of time until recidivism allows one to predict the rate of recidivism for any desired time period after release and not just for the time period used to estimate the particular model. Thus, researchers can examine how soon individuals "fail" after some program participation or release rather than just examining whether someone fails or not. This timing information may provide unique insight into the level of criminal propensity evidenced by offenders (Schmidt and Witte, 1988).

One additional definitional issue raised in recidivism research is the length of time the sample is followed. Although there is no standard way to define or measure recidivism, there is also no standard length of time for the follow-up period. Hoffman and Stone-Meierhoefer (1980, 54) note that a serious problem arises when researchers define the follow-up period as a given number of years or the period of supervision, whichever is less. There is wide variation in the length of the follow-up period examined by researchers, although it is commonly believed in correctional research that unfavorable outcomes (however defined) will occur within the first year after release (Hoffman and Stone–Meierhoefer, 1980; for differing views, see Gottfredson and Ballard, 1965 and Kitchener et al., 1972).

Research on recidivism during the past two decades can be grouped into two general categories (Hepburn and Albonetti, 1994). The first group of studies focuses on evaluating the deterrent effect of some form of intervention and the second group of studies examines the relationship between offender characteristics and recidivism. Both groups of studies have employed a variety of operational definitions of recidivism, time periods of observation, analytic procedures, and sample characteristics. As previously mentioned, recidivism is most commonly used as a measure of effectiveness for correctional programs. A wide variety of correctional interventions such as time served in jail, probation supervision, shock incarceration, intensive supervision, home confinement, and drug treatment programs have been implemented and evaluated (with regard to offender recidivism rates) across the country.

The second group of recidivism studies examines the effects of personal characteristics on rates of recidivism. Across a variety of different sample populations, personal factors such as age, race, educational level, income level, marital status, prior criminal record, as well as current offense factors (i.e., type of crime committed) have been significantly related to recidivism (Benedict and Huff–Corzine, 1997). For example, using a sample of youthful offenders, Visher and her colleagues (1991) found that prior criminal history, current offense variables, substance abuse problems, and experiencing school problems significantly influenced recidivism. Taxman and Piquero (1998) also found that age and prior convictions were consistent predictors of recidivism within a sample of drunk drivers.

Similar results have also been observed with research specifically examining the recidivism rates of probationers in terms of program effectiveness. In general, studies have demonstrated that younger persons, minority group members, the lower class, the unmarried, and those with prior criminal records are more likely to recidivate (Roundtree et al., 1984; Petersilia, 1985; Rhodes, 1986; Benedict and Huff–Corzine, 1997). Despite a common target population (i.e., probationers), there were few other similarities among these studies. For example, Petersilia (1985) and Benedict and Huff–Corzine (1997) specifically focused on felony probationers; Roundtree and his colleagues (1984) examined probationers as well as parolees. The criterion measure for recidivism also varied among these probation-focused studies. Roundtree and his colleagues (1984) used the broadest definition of recidivism by including any event classified as "unsatisfactory termination or revocation of probation." Two of the studies used length of time until a rearrest as the measure of recidivism (Rhodes, 1986; Benedict and Huff–Corzine, 1997) and Petersilia (1985) counted both rearrest and official charges filed as measures of recidivism.

Gendreau and his colleagues (1996) used a meta-analytic approach in order to reach a statistical conclusion in determining which variables were the best predictors of adult offender recidivism. Their results confirm those presented above. They found that the strongest and most potent predictors of recidivism were age, criminal history, criminal companions, family-related factors (e.g., divorce and child abuse), male gender, social class, and substance abuse (Gendreau et al., 1996). In sum, although measurement protocols vary, similar substantive conclusions can be gleaned from extant research.

A handful of scholars have specifically examined the impact of social bonds or "stakes in conformity" on recidivism. From the very beginning, control theorists have believed that an individual's ties to conventional society serve to reduce the probability of criminal offending. Several studies have examined the connection between social bonds or "stakes in conformity" and future offending patterns and have generally found in favor of the relationship. For example, Horney and her colleagues (1995) explored whether local life circumstances strengthen or weaken the influence of social bonds on offending for relatively short periods of time. Utilizing a life history calendar as well as a crime calendar, they asked a sample of serious male offenders to recall on a month-by-month basis their involvement with criminal offenses and local life circumstances. Findings revealed that these men were more likely to engage in criminal activity when they were using illegal drugs and less likely to engage in crime when they were living with a wife or girlfriend. Also employing life history calendars, MacKenzie and her colleagues (1999) examined the effects of monthly activities and probation on the self-reported criminal activities for 106 probationers from northern Virginia. These findings also revealed that the presence of a significant other decreased participation in certain criminal activities.

Using data from male arrestees detained in the Manhattan central booking facility, DeJong (1997) examined whether arrestees with greater ties to conventional society were more easily deterred than arrestees with fewer ties to conventional society. To examine this issue, DeJong (1997) created two groups of offenders, those with high stakes in conformity, and other with low stakes. The former was measured by the presence of at least two measures (married, employment, and graduation from high school), whereas the latter consisted of arrestees with none or only one of these stakes. The analysis revealed that individuals with fewer ties to conventional society were more likely to reoffend following incarceration; however, for individuals with few ties, longer periods of incarceration were more effective deterrents than shorter periods of incarceration. This latter result may signify that longer periods of incarceration are needed to stimulate offenders' reevaluation of the certainty and severity of punishment.

Though it may seem that recidivism research has been plagued with many difficulties, it is not the case that all of the efforts of researchers thus far have been for naught. In fact, this trial and error system of research that has been employed when examining the recidivism rates of offenders has led to some insightful findings. For example, researchers seem to have reached a consensus regarding the high prevalence of recidivism as well as the lack of a deterrent effect for intervention programs. There also seems to be agreement in terms of the best methodological approach to take in studying offender recidivism. Many scholars contend that the best measure of recidivism is rearrest and few would argue against the use survival or time to failure models when examining patterns of recidivism (Maltz, 1984; Schmidt and Witte, 1988). Finally, recidivism research examining personal characteristics consistently has shown that certain factors, primarily those which give the offender a "stake in conformity," are associated with reductions in reoffending.

Despite the deficiencies in the data, whether it be in terms of data collection or in definitions of which negative outcomes to use, few scholars disagree that recidivism rates are generally very high. Hoffman and Stone-Meierhoefer (1980) note that repeater rates fall somewhere between 50% and 80% whereas Baumer (1997) notes that, depending upon certain criteria (such as composition of the sample, the specific definition of recidivism, and the length of follow-up period), approximately one-third to two-thirds of all persons released from prison will return to criminal behavior. In reviewing felony probation follow-up studies, Geerken and Hayes (1993) found that felony rearrest rates ranged anywhere from 12–65%. Therefore, most studies find considerable likelihood of future offending (recidivism).

Despite numerous efforts by correctional officials to introduce new ways of correcting (or rehabilitating) offenders, to date, few deterrence and prevention efforts have significantly affected either the likelihood of failure or time to failure (Albonetti and Hepburn, 1997). In particular, a variety of evaluation studies conducted on different correctional intervention strategies, such as intensive supervision, shock incarceration, and treatment programs, have evidenced similar recidivism rates to those observed for control groups. Therefore, in general, offenders who have been exposed to the latest developments and interventions in corrections fare no better nor any worse than those who have gone through traditional correctional programs. This is not to say that offenders cannot be rehabilitated; rather, this pattern of findings is better attributed to the difficulties in program implementation. A statement made by Maltz (1984, 1) early in the study of recidivism still holds true today: "we truly do not know enough about recidivism to make either absolute or comparative statements about its extent." This is not to imply that nothing has been learned from previous research; rather, much more research is needed before any definitive conclusions can be made.

NICOLE LEEPER PIQUERO

## References and Further Reading

Albonetti, C.A. and Hepburn, J.R. (1997). Probation revocation: A proportional hazards model of the conditioning effects of social disadvantage, *Social Problems,* 44(1), 124–138.

Baumer, E. (1997). Levels and predictors of recidivism: The Malta experience, *Criminology,* 35(4), 601–628.

Reed, B.W. and Huff-Corzine, L. (1997). Return to the scene of the punishment: Recidivism of adult male property offenders on felony probation, 1986–1989, *Journal of Research in Crime and Delinquency,* 34(2), 237–252.

Benekos, P.J. and Merlo, A.V., (1997). Three strikes and you're out: The political sentencing game, in Marquart, J.W. and Sorensen, J.R., *Correctional Contexts: Contemporary and Classical Readings,* Los Angles: Roxbury Publishing Company, pp. 418–427.

Burgess, E.W. (1928). Factors determining success or failure on parole, in Bruce, A.A., Harno, A.J. and Burgess, E.W., Eds., *The Working of the Intermediate Sentence Law and the Parole System in Illinois,* Springfield, IL, Illinois State Board of Parole.

DeJong, C. (1997). Survival analysis and specific deterrence: Integrating theoretical and empirical models of recidivism, *Criminology,* 35(4), 561–575.

Farrington, D. and Tarling, R. (1985). *Prediction in Criminology,* Albany, State University of New York Press.

Geerken, M.R. and Hayes, H.D. (1993). Probation and parole: Public risk and the future of incarceration alternatives, *Criminology,* 31(4), 549–564.

Gendreau, P., cy Little, T. and Goggin, C. (1996). A meta-analysis of the predictors of adult offender recidivism: What works! *Criminology,* 34(4), 575–607.

Glueck, S. and Glueck, E., (1959). *Predicting Delinquency and Crime.* Cambridge, MA, Harvard University Press.

Gottfredson, D.M. (1987). Prediction and classification in criminal justice decision making, pp. 1–20 in *Prediction and Classification: Criminal Justice Decision Making,* (Volume 9) edited by D. M. Gottfredson and M. Tonry Chicago: University of Chicago Press.

Gottfredson, D.M. and Ballard, K.B. (1965). *The Validity of Two Parole Prediction Scales: An Eight Year Follow-up Study,* Vacaville, CA, Institute for the Study of Crime and Delinquency.

Gottfredson, D.M. and Tonry, M. (1987). *Prediction and Classification: Criminal Justice Decision Making,* Vol. 9, Chicago, University of Chicago Press.

Gottfredson, M.R. and Hirschi, T. (1990). *A General Theory of Crime.* Stanford, CA, Stanford University Press.

Hepburn, J.R. and Albonetti, C.A., (1994). Recidivism among drug offenders: A survival analysis of the effects of offender characteristics, type of offense, and two types of intervention, *Journal of Quantitative Criminology,* 10(2), 159–179.

Hoffman, P.B. and Stone-Meierhoeffer, B., (1980). Reporting recidivism rates: The criterion and follow-up issues, *Journal of Criminal Justice,* 8, 53–60.

Horney, J., Osgood, D.W. and Marshall, I.H., (1995). Criminal careers in the short-term: Intra-individual variability in crime and its relation to local life circumstances, *American Sociological Review,* 60, 655–673.

Kitchener, H., Schmidt, A.K. and Glaser, D. (1977). How Persistent is Post-Prison Success, *Federal Probation,* 41, 9–15.

MacKenzie, D.L., Browning, K., Skroban, S.B. and Smith, D.A. (1999). The Impact of Probation on the Criminal Activities of Offenders. *Journal of Research in Crime and Delinquency,* 36(4), 423–453.

Maltz, M.D. (1984). *Recidivism,* New York, Academic Press, Inc.

Moffitt, T.E., Lynam, D.R. and Silva, P.A. (1994). Neuropsychological tests predicting persistent male delinquency, *Criminology,* 32, 277–300.

Murray, C.A. and Cox, L.A., Jr. (1979). *Beyond Probation: Juvenile Corrections and the Chronic Delinquent.* Beverly Hills, CA, Sage.

Petersilia, J. (1985). *Probation and Felony Offenders,* Washington, DC, Department of Justice.

Rhodes, W. (1986). A Survival Model with Dependent Competing Events and Right-Hand Censoring, Probation and Parole as an Illustration, *Journal of Quantitative Criminology,* 2(2), 113–137.

Roundtree, G.A., Edwards, D.W. and Parker, J.B. (1984). A study of the personal characteristics of probationers as related to recidivism, *Journal of Offender Counseling, Services and Rehabilitation,* 8(3), 53–61.

Schmidt, P. and Witte, D.A. (1988). *Predicting Recidivism Using Survival Models,* New York, Springer-Verlag.

Sellin, T. (1931) The basis of a crime index, *Journal of Criminal Law and Criminology,* September, 346.

Smith, L.G. and Akers, R.L. (1993). A comparison of recidivism of florida's community control and prison: A five-year survival analysis, *Journal of Research in Crime and Delinquency,* 30(3), 267–292.

Taxman, F.S. and Piquero, A., (1998). On preventing drunk driving recidivism: An examination of rehabilitation and punishment approaches, *Journal of Criminal Justice,* 26(2): 129–143.

Visher, C.A., Lattimore, P.K. and Linster, R.L., (1991). Predicting the recidivism of serious youthful offenders using survival models, *Criminology,* 39(3), 329–366.

Wolfgang, M.E., Figlio, R.M. and Sellin, T. (1972). *Delinquency in a Birth Cohort,* Chicago, IL, University of Chicago Press.

*See also* **Criminal Careers or Chronic Offenders**

# Reckless Driving *See* **Traffic Offenses**

# Reckless, Walter C.

An aspiring musician, Walter Reckless came to the field of criminology after a tragic automobile accident left him unable to pursue a career as a violinist. Reckless redirected his talents when he was persuaded by Robert Park and Ernest Burgess to enter the graduate program at the University of Chicago. As a graduate student he was intrigued by the work being done in the Chicago slums and throughout his teaching career he strongly urged students to be involved in fieldwork. During his graduate career his fiddle playing allowed him entrance as a participant observer into the roadhouses that operated during Prohibition. His doctoral dissertation explores the many personalities of the roadhouse clientele and is an exemplary model of qualitative research. In 1931 Reckless published his findings in *Vice in Chicago.*

Reckless began his professional career in 1924 when he joined the faculty at Vanderbilt University. While at Vanderbilt he published prolifically and played a major role in the development of a highly reputed undergraduate program in criminology. In 1940 Reckless left Vanderbilt to take a position at Ohio State University where he remained until his retirement in 1969. At Ohio State, Reckless and his associates conducted research that led to his most famous contribution to criminology: the development of containment theory. The successful merging of the prevailing psychological explanations of crime with sociological interpretations makes containment theory unique.

A major focus of criminological theory is the quest to answer the question, "Why are some people deviant and others not?" Containment theory approaches this question differently and seeks to answer why some people are not criminal. Reckless proposed that all individuals are affected by a number of internal and external forces that propel them toward delinquency and opposite forces that inhibit delinquent behavior. Unlike his contemporaries who stressed the learned behavior of criminality, Reckless focused on the identification of factors that act within and upon the individual to determine behavior.

Containment theory sees behavior as a result of the "social pressures" and "social pulls" from the external environment and "inner pushes" of the individual that struggle against one another. Social pressures refer to external environmental conditions and include such factors as poverty, unemployment, minority status, class inequality, and family conflicts. Social pulls refer to the external factors that make deviance attractive. They include bad companions, deviant role models, mass media, etc. Inner pushes refer to a host of factors, including discontent, hostility, aggressiveness, the need for immediate gratification, rebellion, hypersensitivity, and feelings of inferiority or inadequacy. Also included in inner pushes are organic or mental conditions such as brain damage or psychoses.

Intervening between internal and external pressures are " inner controls" and "outer controls" that serve as a buffer to delinquent behavior. Outer controls are structural factors that guide the individual toward conformity. These buffers include institutional reinforcement of norms, supervision and discipline, and a sense of acceptance and identity. If outer controls fail, then inner controls may be sufficient to prevent deviance. Inner controls include self-control, a good self-concept, ego strength, a well-developed super-ego, high resistance to diversions, a heightened sense of responsibility, etc. If inner or outer containments, or a mixture of the two, are strong enough, the individual is most likely to conform to societal expectations. When containments are weak deviance is likely to occur.

Reckless and his colleagues tested containment theory empirically by following the delinquent behavior of juveniles in high delinquency areas in Columbus, Ohio. Beginning in 1955 Reckless undertook a program to evaluate the differential behavior of sixth grade "good boys" and "bad boy" as identified by teachers and school administrators. The study identified two groups of boys; those who were expected to become delinquent and those who were not. Over a period of about 15 years the differences in the self-concept of the boys was assessed. Reckless and his associates concluded that the self-concept helps to explain why some individuals are susceptible to delinquency and others are not.

According to Reckless, the child learns a positive self-concept or a negative self-concept during familial socialization. The "good boy" or "bad boy" research has been used to explain why all youth in high delinquency areas do not become delinquent. In areas where all youth face similar pressures, pushes, and pulls toward delinquency, the "good boy" is insulated from crime by a strong self-concept. Reckless saw containment theory as an explanatory theory of both conformity and delinquency but admitted that the theory falls short in explaining all types of delinquency especially those crimes related to personality disorders or crime that is considered to be a normal role in certain subcultures. The specificity of containment theory led to its classification as a "middle-range" theory.

Reckless was eager to translate his theoretical ideas in the real world. While at Ohio State he was indefatigable in his efforts in the development of juvenile delinquency prevention programs. He was also involved in the juvenile court system and often testified on correctional policies. After his retirement, Reckless remained active both at home and abroad where he lectured, established training programs, and inspected and evaluated juvenile delinquency facilities. Reckless was also actively involved in the professional community. Among his honors are: the Sutherland Award (1963), President of the American Society of Criminology (1964–1966), Chair of the Criminology Section of the American Sociological Association, and the Ohio State Distinguished Service Award (1981).

The relevance of containment theory has been debated on many fronts. Containment theory was initially praised as a viable alternative to strain theories because of its empirical value. The testability of factors such as external pressures and self-concept were appealing to researchers. Today containment theory is considered to be an important precursor to more contemporary control theories particularly Hirschi's social bonding theory but the theory is criticized for its methodological shortcomings. Critics charge that Reckless did not clearly operationalize his concepts especially the self-concept that they argue is more complex than containment theory allows. Reckless is also criticized for limiting his research to boys in high crime rate neighborhoods where a motivation toward delinquency was assumed but not measured. Another major criticism is the inability of containment theory to account for differential mixtures of external and internal controls in predicting crime. These deficiencies have caused many theorists to relegate the work of Reckless to a minor status.

LAUREL HOLLAND

## Biography

Born in Philadelphia, Pennsylvania, 19 January 1899; son of a textile industrialist. Educated at the University of Chicago, Ph.D. in Sociology, 1925. Professor, Vanderbilt, 1924–1940; professor, Ohio State University, 1940–1969. Chair of the Criminology Section of the American Sociological Association; president of the American Society of Criminology, 1964–1966. Died 20 September 1988.

## Selected Writings

"Self concept as an insulator against delinquency," *American Sociological Review* 21 (1956) with Dinitz, S. and Murray, E.
"The self component in potential delinquency and potential non-delinquency," *American Sociological Review* 22 (1957) with Dinitz, S. and Kay, B.
*Vice in Chicago,* 1933
*Criminal Behavior,* 1940
"The 'good boy' in a high delinquency area," *Journal of Criminal Law, Criminology and Police Science* 48 (1957) with Dinitz, S. and Murray, E.
"A new theory of delinquency and crime," *Federal Probation* 25 (1961)
The Crime Problem, 1967

## References and Further Reading

Bloch, H.A. and Geis, G. 1970. *Man, Crime and Society,* 2nd ed., New York, Random House.
Hirschi, T. 1969. *Causes of Delinquency,* Berkeley, CA, University of California Press.
Jensen, G.F. 1970. Containment and delinquency: Analysis of a theory, *Washington Journal of Sociology,* 2.
Orcutt, J.D. 1970. Self-concept and insulation against delinquency: Some critical notes, *Sociological Quarterly,* 2.
Reiss, A.J. 1951. Delinquency as the failure of personal and social controls, *American Sociological Review,* 16.

Schwartz, M. and Tangri, S.S. 1965. A note on self-concept as an insulator against delinquency, *American Sociological Review,* 30.

Shoemaker, D.J. 1984. *Theories of Delinquency: An Examination of Explanations of Delinquent Behavior,* New York, Oxford University Press.

Vold, G.B. and Bernard, T.J. 1986. *Theoretical Criminology,* 3rd ed., New York, Oxford University Press.

Voss, H.L. 1969. Differential association and containment theory: A theoretical convergence, *Social Forces,* 47.

Wiatrowski, M.D., Griswold, D.B. and Roberts, M.K. 1981. Social control theory and delinquency, *American Sociological Review,* 46.

*See also* **Containment Theory**

# Rehabilitation and Treatment

Many people think of rehabilitation and treatment as the core of the American correctional system. In fact, the mere name of this third part of the criminal justice system, "corrections," is taken by many as an indication that these agencies and actors are supposed to be focused on working with offenders so as to "correct" their behavior. At times this view has not only been popular, but also the guiding perspective for our correctional efforts. However, at other times, this has not been the case. Understanding what rehabilitation and treatment in corrections means, why it has (and has not) been popular at varying times, and what types of rehabilitative and treatment efforts are used in correctional systems is important for understanding both what society expects of corrections, and why there may be problems in carrying out these efforts.

Rehabilitation is one of the five basic ideologies that can serve as the basis for determining the specific goals and activities of correctional systems. (Retribution, deterrence, incapacitation, and reintegration are the other possible ideologies that can and sometimes do structure correctional efforts.) When a rehabilitative, treatment-focused ideology is held the primary belief is that criminal offenders need to be provided services and interventions that address deficiencies or weaknesses in their mental, medical, emotional, cognitive, or social functioning. When "experts" are used to "correct" what is wrong with offenders (presumably the reason that the individual engages in criminal activities) this will return the individual to healthy and socially acceptable ways of behaving.

Americans expect several different things to be achieved by our criminal justice system, and corrections specifically. Providing opportunities for offenders to change their behavior, through rehabilitation or treatment programs, is one of these commonly identified goals for the system. Some people expect more; not only should such programs and opportunities be offered, but they should also be a mandatory part of an offender's criminal sentence. According to some views treatment should be required, and we should expect all (or, almost all) offenders should have their behavior changed. Others believe the primary goal of the criminal justice and correctional systems is quite different: the system is about either punishing or segregating offenders from society, with little concern about changing anything about individual offenders.

When rehabilitation and treatment programs are provided they are expected to address the reasons offenders commit crimes. Once the root cause of crime is identified treatment programs are then expected to achieve one of two goals. First, some believe that treatment programs should eliminate (or "correct") the conditions in offenders (such as a lack of job skills, illiteracy, or drug addiction) that are at the root of their criminality. Second, some believe that treatment programs should provide offenders with skills, perspectives, and thinking that encourage or facilitate law-abiding lifestyles. These goals are similar, but differ in their emphasis. The first focuses on a negative state presumed to be present in an offender and eliminating or reducing such conditions so that they no longer push people into crime. The second focuses on a positive state and is based on the idea that correctional programs should provide offenders with the (additional or new) resources that will allow them to avoid being pulled into a criminal lifestyle.

There are many different types of treatment programs offered in prisons and jails. Some of these, like psychological counseling, academic education, and vocational training are found in almost all institutions and are fairly similar across institutions. Other, more unique types of programs are less frequently found and may vary widely in their structure and content. This would include things such as parent education and sex offender treatment. Below are overviews of some of the most common types of treatment programs.

Psychological counseling programs include both one-on-one and group counseling formats. Just as with psychological services in the community, these programs are designed to identify mental illnesses and problems that individuals have in perceiving the world accurately and coping with stressful life situations. The goal of psychological counseling programs is to assist offenders in understanding their problems and finding ways to better control and manage their disturbances. Many times psychological counseling will be combined with the use of psychotropic drugs as an additional way of redirecting an offender's thinking patterns and (mis)perceptions of reality. The idea behind psychological counseling programs is that mental illness or psychological disturbances are the cause of the individual's criminal behavior.

A number of different approaches are commonly used in psychological counseling with correctional clients. Reality therapy is an approach that emphasizes a therapist working to facilitate an inmate understanding the need to take personal responsibility for his or her actions and to behave in ways that are consistent with the realities of the social world. Confrontation therapy is a group approach where a group leader encourages group members to confront individuals when the individual attempts to rationalize his or her behaviors or manipulate others. Confrontational approaches are most often used with offenders who express strong denial of their offenses, and the consequences their behaviors have had for others (i.e. victims). Transactional analysis is an approach that focuses on how a person interacts with others, with special attention to the ways that individuals construct roles for their relationships that minimize the individual's responsibility for his or her actions. Cognitive skills approaches focus on changing the way individuals think and reason out their behaviors. Therapists using a cognitive approach focus on restructuring an offender's thinking and seek to replace old, "criminal" ways of thinking with new skills and patterns that emphasize ways to successfully (i.e., in a law-abiding way) navigate day-to-day life.

Vocational training programs are attempts to teach inmates relevant job skills that will assist them in obtaining a job when they are released from incarceration. These programs are based on the idea that one reason individuals commit crimes is because they do not have the ability to get jobs that provide them with sufficient economic resources. Also, without a marketable job skill individuals would be expected to have low self esteem, large amounts of unstructured free time, and therefore greater opportunities for engaging in criminal behavior.

Vocational training programs come in two basic forms. First, there are actual instructional programs where inmates are students in both classroom instruction and hands-on practice at particular job skills. A wide range of types of job training programs are found in American correctional facilities, including carpentry, auto mechanics, computer programming, data entry, electrical work, plumbing, cosmetology, child care services, construction, furniture manufacturing, textiles, and printing and graphic design.

A second model of vocational training program is the employment of inmates at institutional jobs—such as janitorial work, agriculture, legal aides, and landscaping—as a way of learning a set of skills. This approach to vocational training will often be in the form of correctional industries, in which an actual business is operated inside the correctional institution to make and sell a product. Sometimes these industries are operated by the state (either as a unit of the department of corrections or some other state agency) or by an outside corporation that contracts with the department of corrections. Many critics, however, point out that many of the vocational training programs in correctional facilities are outdated, use old and poor quality materials and equipment, and often do not provide inmates with a truly marketable job skill. Usually inmates who complete structured a job training program will receive a certificate of program completion that they can use to demonstrate to potential employers outside of the institution that they in fact have received training.

Although many do not think of it as such, recreational activities are an important form of institutional programming. Recreational programs are largely focused on providing inmates with activities and keeping them busy. However, many recreational activities—team sports, music, arts and crafts—also teach inmates important skills such as teamwork, patience, and creativity.

Religious programs are probably the oldest form of treatment in American corrections. Prisons, and to a lesser extent jails, provide numerous opportunities for inmates to participate in religious services, engage in religious study, meet with clergy and laypersons in a religious context, and to pursue their own forms of spirituality. There are dozens of religions practiced by prisoners, with Christianity and Islam being the two most common. Correctional facilities often also have some type of programs for Jewish inmates as well as Native American religions, Buddhism, Hindu, Wicca, and many other less common religious sects. Religious programs are very inexpensive to provide and are seen as very valuable because of both their presumed effects on inmates and the fact that many inmates highly value the opportunity to participate.

Substance abuse treatment programs are commonplace in correctional institutions, because estimates suggest that as many as 75–80% of inmates have histories of drug or alcohol use and abuse. Substance abuse programs face significant challenges, regardless of whether conducted in a correctional facility or in free society, but in a prison or jail they can face especially strong barriers. Substance abuse treatment is found in two basic structures. First, there are programs that look very similar to psychological counseling programs, combining individual counseling and group therapy. Second, a more recent development is the idea of the therapeutic community. This is a model where participating inmates are immersed in "healthy living" environments where substance use or abuse education and therapy guide all that the inmate does. Usually a therapeutic community will have separate housing for participating inmates, as well as having participants segregated from the general institutional population for programming, work, eating, and recreation. Research suggests that therapeutic communities are more successful and lead to higher rates of inmates abstaining from use and criminal behavior once they are released (Lipton, 1995). However, therapeutic communities require significantly more resources (personnel, money, space, etc.) than traditional forms of substance abuse treatment, and therefore are less common.

Academic education programs are widely recognized as perhaps the most effective (and often most cost-effective) variety of correctional treatment program. In simple terms, academic education is the most successful form of programming for reducing recidivism and producing law-abiding, productive citizens from criminal offenders. For several decades researchers have shown that all education at all levels—from basic literacy training all the way through college degree programs—are related with significant decreases in recidivism. Some of the most compelling evidence in support of the value of educational programs comes from a 2003 study of educational programs in three states (Steurer and Smith, 2003). Not only did offenders who participated in educational programs show lower rates of criminal recidivism than inmates who did not participate in academic education programs, but so too did the inmates in academic programs have higher rates of employment after release, and substantially

higher incomes. Education provides not only the tools for facilitating law-abiding lifestyles, but it is also associated with former offenders actually changing their behavior.

Despite the popularity of treatment programs, one discouraging fact is that for many years social scientists have shown that many rehabilitation and treatment programs are not very successful. This means that many policy makers and correctional officials have adopted the view that "nothing works" (Martinson, 1975). As a result, support—financial, ideological, political, and social—has remained low for rehabilitation and treatment programs, which in turn has made it yet more difficult for such efforts to succeed. This means that research has continued to show, at best, minimal "success" rates for treatment programs.

Correctional officials, systems, institutions, and programs are often and widely criticized as ineffective and inefficient. The basis of these criticisms is usually grounded in the idea that offenders who participate in rehabilitation and treatment programs often recidivate. It is true that many participating offenders, including those who complete programs, do return to crime, and often return to jail or prison. However do not return to crime after treatment. One major review of the outcomes of prison-based treatment programs reports that well-run, focused, and highly structured programs yield an average of 25–30% reduction in crime for participants (Correctional Service Canada, 2003). However, criticism remains; many people believe that reducing crime by "only" 25–30% is not enough, and view this as largely a failure. Criticisms of correctional rehabilitation programs often have as a foundation the argument that correctional administrations—and political leaders—have focused on management styles and legal requirements that are very restrictive toward which inmates may be allowed to participate in programs, the content of programs, and the contexts in which programs operate. It has only been in the rare prison, jail, or community corrections program that administrators and policy makers have been innovative and worked to prevent problems and truly support rehabilitation and treatment programs. However, it is important to remember that corrections is largely viewed and conceived of as a reactive institution, not a proactive one. This means that creative thinking and the use of true team approaches to rehabilitation and treatment have been rare.

The idea of a true team approach for offender treatment programs was first put forth seriously by the Federal Bureau of Prisons. Today this approach has become a dominant and popular one throughout correctional systems. Not only are treatment professionals (psychologists, psychiatrists, counselors, teachers, social workers, and others) involved in such teams, but so too are correctional officers. As a team, these various actors consider and take into account an inmate's treatment program when making many decisions about inmates. This includes classification, assignment to housing units, assignment of institutional jobs, and other daily life activities that staff members can and often do control. By bringing security staff into the team those correctional staff members who have the greatest amount and frequency of contact with inmates are informed and involved in guiding the offender through the treatment process. If nothing else, having security staff members knowledgeable about inmates' treatment programs can limit the negative impact correctional officers may have on inmates psychologically, socially, emotionally, and behaviorally. Hopefully, however, this integrated team approach will help further the inmate's pursuit of his or her treatment goals.

Most people, including those who work in correctional institutions, tend to have very strong beliefs about whether or not rehabilitative programs should be offered to inmates, required for inmates, or simply not even available. Many corrections professionals do believe in the value of treatment programs, and do believe that at least some offenders can in fact be rehabilitated. National studies of correctional staff members (Cullen, Latessa, Burton, and Lombardo, 1993) have shown that institutional administrators are strong advocates of treatment programs. Other research has shown that all varieties of correctional staff members recognize the importance and contributions of treatment programs. Interestingly, however, as individuals work in corrections for longer periods of time their degree of support for treatment programs decreases. This is most probably because of seeing programming failures—offenders who complete treatment programs and after release recidivate and return to prison. Other research has shown that regular citizens also believe having rehabilitation programs in our prisons is an important and valuable tool.

Although there is significant promise in many types of treatment programs, and many types of benefits for such efforts, treatment programs are not universal. Not all inmates have access or opportunities to participate in rehabilitative programs and not all prisons offer many treatment programs. As prison populations grew rapidly in the 1980s and 1990s many prisons were forced to cut back (or in some cases even eliminate) many of their treatment programs in order to meet the basic needs of housing, feeding, clothing, and watching over inmates. Space and money became extremely scarce resources, and treatment programs came to be seen as "extras" that were targeted by politicians and administrators seeking to save costs wherever possible. Many newer prisons—especially the highest security level institutions (i.e., supermax and maximum security prisons) are designed to emphasize retribution and incapacitation. This means that both physical space and financial resources for treatment programs are minimal if present at all. Even in many correctional institutions that do value and emphasize a rehabilitative ideal, there is only a small proportion of offenders who participate in treatment programs. In most institutions only a small number of both offenders and correctional staff members are involved in rehabilitation and treatment programs. Most treatment programs suffer from low levels of funding, meaning that there are few staff persons and in turn relatively few inmates are able to be involved. Most often inmates who are involved in treatment programs are not participating completely voluntarily. Staff persons who work in treatment programs also have to maintain the position of all institutional corrections employees, emphasizing security and custody issues over all other goals and priorities. Therefore, it is no surprise that treatment programs are often viewed as ineffective (i.e., "failures"). This is especially true for higher level security institutions. When the inmates participating in programs are more serious offenders, often with longer criminal histories, there are more and tighter restrictions placed on all aspects of prison life, and this means that treatment programs are also more tightly controlled. Treatment success and custody levels of institutions are usually inversely related.

Rehabilitation and treatment programs are present in prisons and most larger jails, and both the public and correctional officials express the belief that they should be there. However, a number of structural and political obstacles reduce the likelihood of such programs being successful (i.e., producing ex-offenders who do not return to crime). Treatment programs come in a variety of forms and focus on many different aspects of offenders' psychological, social, emotional, cognitive, and behavioral aspects.

RICHARD TEWKSBURY

## References and Further Reading

Cullen, F.T., Latessa, E.J., Burton, V.S., Jr. and Lombardo, L.X., 1993. The correctional orientation of prison wardens: Is the rehabilitative ideal supported? *Criminology*, 31(1), 69–92.

Lipton, D.S., 1995. *The Effectiveness of Treatment for Drug Abusers Under Criminal Supervision*, Washington, DC, National Institute of Justice.

Martinson, R., 1975. What works? Questions and answers about prison reform, *Public Interest,* 35, 22–54.

Steurer, S. and Smith, L.G., 2003. *Education Reduces Crime: Three State Recidivism Study,* Lanham, MD, Correctional Education Association.

Tewksbury, R., 2003. *Principles of Effective Correctional Programming,* Toronto, Canada, Correctional Service Canada.

*See also* **Drug Control Policy: Prevention and Treatment; Women and Addictions; Work Release**

# Reiss, Albert John, Jr.

Albert J. Reiss, Jr. received his Ph.D. in sociology from the University of Chicago in 1949. In his dissertation (1951), he analyzed court records of juvenile probationers and attempted to identify factors that would predict revocation. He provided one of the earliest statements of control theory by attributing the cause of delinquency to the failure of "personal" and "social" controls. Personal controls are internalized, whereas social controls operate through external formal and informal sanctions dispensed by family, peers, and community. Conduct itself incorporates norms because it implies disciplined behavior.

His work with Rhodes (1961a) established interviewing as the favored technique for collecting information from delinquents. They concluded from self-reports that there was a strong relationship between socioeconomic status and delinquency. Lower-class boys were more likely to drop out of school and more likely to be delinquent. Reiss argued that norms originate through conflict avoidance or resolution. His (1961b) study of boy prostitutes explained how lower-class boys were able to maintain their masculine self-concepts while selling sex to adult males. Subcultural rules strictly regulated permissible sex acts, roles, and attitudes. Peer norms allowed the boys to perform masculine roles devoid of emotion for money without threatening their male identity.

In the mid-1960s, at the request of the President's Crime Commission, Reiss (1971a) and Donald Black conducted the first and still the most comprehensive study of police behavior. Reiss used a new methodology he termed systematic social observation in which standardized protocols are used to record and quantify direct observations of social phenomena in their natural setting (Reiss, 1971b). Ten thousand police-citizen "encounters" were recorded by 36 trained observers who rode in patrol cars on all shifts on all days of the week for seven weeks in Boston, Chicago, and Washington, DC.

What emerged was a sympathetic portrait of police work. Their findings revealed that police discretion is not exercised in a social vacuum. Official decisions are responsive to situational influences such as the preference of the complainant, the relationship between victim and offender, and the demeanor of the suspect. Police mobilization was primarily reactive, responding to citizen complaints and intervening more as arbitrators than as law enforcers. Race was not an important factor in the decision to stop or arrest a suspect. Blacks were arrested more often than whites because they committed more serious offenses, were more antagonistic toward police, and black complainants were more likely to demand an arrest.

Reiss and Bordua (1966) were the first to categorize police organizations and practices as "reactive" and "proactive." Reactive organizations permit greater citizen participation whereas proactive agencies are centrally directed and use more intrusive methods of detection and investigation. Reiss and his students later applied this typology to a wide variety of law enforcement and regulatory agencies. The theme of Reiss and Black's police research was that selective enforcement is inherent within a democratic legal system because it reflects the "moral diversity" of the citizenry rather than official policy.

Reiss conducted pilot studies to identify methodological problems and he helped design the national victimization survey. He noted that commercial establishments were at much higher risk of victimization than households or individuals. He developed concepts and statistical models of co-offending and serial victimization to focus attention to the web of social organization and relationships in which crime is embedded. He coined the term co-offending to refer to the fact that a large percentage of crime is committed by offenders behaving in networks or groups. He first applied the concept (1980) to estimate its effect on incarceration rates and crime. Increased incarceration may not reduce crime if groups generate new members who might not otherwise become criminal. People acting in concert also commit crime at higher rates than individuals (Reiss and Farrington, 1991)

Reiss helped enlarge the domain of criminology to include organizational deviance and those agencies charged with its regulation and control. In their study of the prospects of a national reporting system for white-collar lawbreaking, Reiss and Biderman (1980) reviewed existing sources of data from a range of federal agencies, discussed conceptual and measurement problems, and introduced a compliance or deterrence typology to describe regulatory enforcement. They defined white-collar lawbreaking as violations by someone "using a position of power, influence or trust in the legitimate institutional order for a legal, personal or institutional gain."

Because victimization is diffuse, invisible, or distant, the complaint mechanism may be ineffective in policing organizational violations. Many agencies possess proactive intelligence methods such as self-report, audit, inspection, or subpoena authority, but most adopt the compliance rather than the deterrence enforcement strategy (Reiss, 1984a). Rather than agency capture or corruption, however, Reiss argued that government regulation is largely determined by the structure of an agency's intelligence and mobilization systems. Premonitory control lies at the heart of controlling the behavior of organizations and their agents (Reiss, 1984b). Regulators depend upon negotiated informal relationships with those subject to their authority and fear the unanticipated consequences of formal legal action. Reiss (1993) criticized criminologists for neglecting organizational victimization and failing to distinguish criminal from administrative violations.

Reiss directed interdisciplinary research for the National Academy of Sciences on the prevention and control of violence (Reiss and Roth, 1993). The studies identified biological factors in crime but also found rates of physical and sexual abuse six times higher in lower-class families. Reiss helped design and launch the Project on Human Development in Chicago Neighborhoods. This is an accelerated longitudinal study tracking the influence of individual, family, peer, and neighborhood characteristics on the development of thousands of children. The study is unique in that ecological and demographic characteristics of hundreds of neighborhoods are recorded using Reiss' systematic observation methodology. Preliminary findings show that crime and disorder usually stem from certain neighborhood characteristics, most notably concentrated poverty and lack of social cohesion (Earls and Reiss, 1994).

Albert J. Reiss, Jr., has made major contributions to the study of social organization, community research, the causes of crime and delinquency, police organization and behavior, measurement and methodology, and the social control of organizational deviance. His work examines how the organization of crime and the organization of law enforcement interface and shape the resulting nature and patterns of behavior. Throughout his career, Reiss has been a prominent advocate of collaborative research projects involving different generations of scholars, practitioners, and policymakers.

DONALD SCOTT

## Biography

Born in Cascade, Wisconsin, 9 December 1922. Educated at Marquette University in Milwaukee, Wisconsin, Ph.B., 1944; University of Chicago, M.A., 1948; University of Chicago, Ph.D. in Sociology, 1949. Instructor, University of Chicago, 1947–1949; Assistant Professor, University of Chicago, 1949–1952; Associate Professor, 1952–1954, Professor, 1954–58, and Chairman, 1952–1958, Department of Sociology and Anthropology, Vanderbilt University; Professor of Sociology, 1958–60; Chairman, 1959–60; Department of Sociology and Anthropology, State University of Iowa; Professor of Sociology, 1960–61; Department of Sociology, University of Wisconsin, Director, 1960–61; Professor of Sociology, University of Michigan, 1961–1970, Chairman, 1964–1970; Director, 1961–1970, Center for Research on Social Organization, University of Michigan; Consultant, President's Commission on Law Enforcement, 1966–67; Consultant, the National Advisory Commission on Civil Disorders, 1967–1968; Lecturer, 1968–1970, University of Michigan Law School; William Graham Sumner Professor of Sociology, 1977–1993; Professor of Sociology, 1970–1977, Chairman, 1972–1978, 1985–1989; Chairman, Institute for Social and Policy Studies, Yale University, 1970–1987; Lecturer, Yale Law School, 1972–1993; William Graham Sumner Professor Emeritus of Sociology, Yale University, 1993–. Chair, the National Academy of Sciences Panel on the Understanding and Control of Violent Behavior, 1989–1992; Co-Director, Project on Human Development in Chicago Neighborhoods, 1991–1997. Professional Memberships: American Association for the Advancement of Science; Ohio Valley Sociological Society (President, 1968–1969); Society for the Study of Social Problems (President, 1969); American Society of Criminology (President, 1983–84); American Sociological Association; American Statistical Association; International Society of Criminology (President, 1990–1995).

## Selected Writings

Delinquency as a Failure of Personal and Social Controls, *American Sociological Review* 16 (1951).

The Distribution of Juvenile Delinquency in the Social Class Structure (with Albert J. Rhodes), *American Sociological Review* 26 (1961a).

The Social Integration of Peers and Queers, *Social Problems* 9 (1961b).

Environment and Organization: A Perspective on the Police (with David Bordua), in *The Police* edited by David Bordua (1967).

*The Police and the Public*, 1971a.

Systematic Observation of Natural Social Phenomena, in *Sociological Methodology* edited by Herbert Costner (1971).

Discretionary Justice, in *The Handbook of Criminology* edited by Daniel Glaser (1974).

*Data Sources on White-Collar Lawbreaking* (with Alfred D. Biderman), 1980.

Consequences of Compliance and Deterrence Models of Law Enforcement for the Exercise of Police Discretion, *Journal of Law and Contemporary Problems* 47 (1984a).

Selecting Strategies of Control over Organizational Life, in *Enforcing Regulation* edited by Keith Hawkins and John M. Thomas (1984b).

Why Are Communities Important in Understanding Crime? in *Communities and Crime* edited by Albert J. Reiss Jr. and Michael Tonry (1986).

Co-Offender and Criminal Careers, in *Crime and Justice: A Review of Research* edited by Michael Tonry and Norval Morris (1988).

*Understanding and Preventing Violence* (edited with Jeffrey A. Roth), 1993a.

*Beyond the Law: Crime in Complex Organizations* edited by Albert J. Reiss, Jr. and Michael Tonry (1993b).

*Breaking the Cycle: Predicting and Preventing Crime* (with Felton J. Earls), 1994.

*See also* **Social Control Theories**

---

# Religion and Criminal Behavior

---

The association of religion with crime and crime control originates with the earliest societies when social norms and mores coalesced into institutional arrangements such that they were the source of both organized religious doctrine and codified into law. That is to say, early cultural values, beliefs, norms, and mores are the common or root sources of both the criminal law and religious doctrine. In turn, law and religion, as stable institutional arrangements, tend to be mutually supportive and interdependent. Furthermore, both institutions provide social control functions.

This association between religion and crime was not lost on classical sociological theorists. Max Weber, for example, in his cross-cultural logical experiment in the sociology of religion, asserted that the modern Western culture was the inadvertent product of the rise of Protestantism that encouraged its followers to work hard, reduce consumption, accumulate capital, and avoid sensual indulgences. Likewise, Karl Marx argued that religion was the "opium of the people," directing proletarian attention away from the source of their oppression, thereby serving to reduce class conflict. Finally, Emile Durkheim, by comparing statistical data from France and Germany showed that religion reduced the incidence of suicide by integrating people into moral communities. Whether focusing on sensual indulgences, class conflict, or suicide, these classical examples all posit that religion, as an agent of social control, promotes conformity and inhibits crime or delinquency by encouraging the internalization of moral values and the acceptance of social norms.

The study of these associations between religion and law has a long and complex history involving among others, legal scholars, theologians, philosophers, and social scientists. This essay limits its coverage to contemporary social scientific research examining the relationship(s) between religious commitment and criminal or delinquent behavior.

## Religion and Criminal or Delinquent Behavior

Although a rather narrow area of scholarly interest, the association of religious commitment to involvement in criminal or delinquent activity has generated a fairly substantial amount of research activity within both the U.S. and outside (though very little of this research is cross-cultural in nature). Within this body of literature can be found a variety of scholarly arguments regarding: (1) whether strength of religious commitment is related to criminal or delinquent behavior, (2) if related, why is religion related to criminal or delinquent conduct, and

(3) how is religion related to crime or delinquency? This essay reviews each of these issues.

## Is Strength of Religious Commitment Correlated with Criminal or Delinquent Behavior?

This area of scholarly debate concerns the question of whether or not religious commitment and crime or delinquency are correlated. The classical and dominant view, as we saw above, holds that religion plays an active role in shaping society and controlling human behavior. This view is reflected today in the popular belief, held by at least a third of the U.S. population, that a lack of religious commitment is a major factor in the cause of criminal or delinquent behavior. This view is also evident in the once common practice of requiring, or at least encouraging, regular church attendance as a condition of probation or parole or as a part of a general crime or delinquency prevention program (Fitzpatrick, 1967). Finally, research on the issue yields tremendous empirical support for this view. With but only two or three exceptions, virtually every study published over the last several decades both within the U.S. and in other societies (typically other English-speaking countries such as Canada, the U.K., Australia and New Zealand) has reported significant inverse effects of religiosity on criminal or delinquent behavior. These findings are so consistently reported that some scholars (Cochran and Akers, 1989, 221) have been moved to assert the establishment of a sociological law: as strength of religious commitment increases, involvement in criminal or delinquent behavior decreases.

Although this traditional view is widely held and may seem self-evident, not all scholars agree with it. Some have argued, in fact, that religion actually encourages crime or delinquency while others argue religion and crime or delinquency are unrelated. For the most part, those who argue that religion and crime or delinquency are positively associated are not claiming that religious individuals are more apt to engage in criminal or delinquent acts than those who are irreligious. Instead, they are claiming that societies or communities in which the institution of religion is strong are more inclined to define acts or persons as criminal or delinquent than those societies or communities in which organized religion is weak. Because faith groups often concern themselves with moral issues, they play a very significant role as moral entrepreneurs in making attributions of immorality and criminality. They are most effective at criminalizing sins when the church is a powerful and influential element of community life. It should be pointed out, however, that there are special cases in which religious persons are more prone toward crime; religiously motivated war crimes, acts of terrorism by Islamic fundamentalists, polygamy among some Mormons, the bombing or vandalism of abortion clinics and adult bookstores by some Christian fundamentalists, and the denial of needed medical interventions among Christian Scientists are some examples.

The classical view of the association between religious commitment and criminal or delinquent behavior is also challenged by those who argue that it is either nonexistent or that it is spurious. Robert K. Merton, for instance, agrees that society achieves its unity through commonly held beliefs and values, but adds that there is no evidence to suggest that religiously devoted persons uphold these beliefs and values more so than the nonreligious (for evidence to the contrary, see Evans and Scott, 1984). Many other skeptics claim that the observed correlations between strength of religious commitment and criminal or delinquent behavior are substantively insignificant (i.e., weak to modest, at best, in strength). There is considerable truth to this claim. Indeed, it is important to note that although statistically significant inverse associations between religiosity and criminal or delinquent behavior are consistently observed in the research literature, with few exceptions these associations are, at best, only modest in strength. The weak effect of religious commitment on criminal or delinquent behavior has led some researchers to study the social contexts in which the religious factor expresses its strongest effects.

Perhaps the most challenging critique of the classical view is offered by those who assert that the relationship between religious commitment and criminal or delinquent behavior is spurious. There are two versions of this critique; the first raised by arousal theorists and the second by social control theorists. The basic premise of arousal theory is that persons vary in the degree to which they are neurologically predisposed toward deviancy (Ellis and Thompson, 1989). Those most prone toward crime or delinquency are said to be suboptimally aroused; that is, they bore quickly and easily and, thus, need to seek out new and more intense stimulations than normal daily experiences provide. These stimulus-seeking activities may, if an opportunity should present itself, include criminal or delinquent and criminal behavior. Such suboptimally aroused persons are unlikely to find religion and religious services neurologically satisfying. In sum, these persons are neurologically predisposed toward criminal or delinquent behavior and simultaneously directed away from religion. Hence, arousal theorists argue that "the inverse relationship between religion and crime is largely a spurious correlation of neurological origin" (Ellis and Thompson 1989, 134).

Social control theorists also argue that the relationship between religion and criminal or delinquent behavior is spurious (Elifson, Petersen, and Hadaway, 1983). They argue that religion is one of multiple sources of social control. As such, its direct contribution toward the inhibition of crime or delinquency is almost totally negated by the effects of other moral influences and agents of social control. That is, other powerful but more proximate sources of social control (such as the family, neighbors, friends, and the school) mask or duplicate the influence of religion. Once these other secular sources of social control are added to the religion-crime or delinquency equation, the inverse, bivariate relationship between religious commitment and criminal or delinquent behavior reduces to insignificance. Cochran, Wood, and Arneklev (1994) tested each of these two forms of claims of spuriousness and found merit in both. Similarly, Burkett and Warren (1987) observed that the relationship between religious commitment and adolescent marijuana use was mediated by association with marijuana using peers. However, religious commitment did play a role in the selection of friends; religious kids tend to select religious and nondelinquent friends. Despite these findings, the vast majority of the research examining the effects of strength of religious commitment on involvement in criminal or delinquent activities consistently reveals that criminal or delinquent behavior is associated with weak religious commitment (see Evans, Cullen, Dunaway, and Burton, 1995 and Benda, 1995).

## Why is Religious Commitment Related to Criminal or Delinquent Behavior?

Tittle and Welch (1983, 656–658) show how the influence of religious commitment on criminal or delinquent behavior can be subsumed within several theoretical perspectives. These are: (1) structure-functionalism, (2) social control theory, (3) differential association theory, (4) various psychological approaches, (5) deterrence theory, and (6) conflict approaches.

According to the functionalist approach, conformity and social order are, in part, dependent upon the extent to which individuals have internalized collective social values and moral commitments. Those who have internalized these values are believed to be less inclined to contemplate behaviors that violate them; moreover, they would feel such strong feelings of guilt and moral revulsion that they would be inhibited from acting on

such contemplations. Religion plays a powerful role in both the determination and the internalization of these moral values. In addition, religion further inhibits the violation of these moral values by linking supernatural sanctions to these moral precepts. Finally, participation in religious services and organizations reinforces these internalized moral sentiments and exposes the individuals to a moral community of others who, in turn, serve as a source of social condemnation. Thus, strong religious commitments are associated with conformity to social rules (at least those with a religious or moral foundation) and to an aversion to crime or delinquency.

A second theoretical perspective that attempts to account for why strength of religious commitment is inversely associated with involvement in criminal or delinquent behavior is social control theory. According to this approach, strong bonds to conventional social institutions restrain criminal or delinquent behavior. Attachment to conventional persons or institutions, involvement in conventional activities, commitment to conventional institutions, and holding conventional beliefs serve to bond individuals to society by simultaneously increasing their stakes in conformity and by restraining crime or delinquency through the resulting network of normative obligations. Religion is one institutional arrangement in which these processes take place. Because mainstream religious beliefs are conventional and because participation in religious activities involves attachments to conventional others, a commitment to a conventional social institution, and involvement in conventional activities, it follows that as strength of religious commitment increases, persons' inclinations to participate in criminal or delinquent activities should decrease.

The differential association approach to the study of criminal or delinquent behavior can also account for why religious commitment is inversely associated with criminal or delinquent behavior. Differential association theory argues that exposure to social definitions favorable to criminal or delinquent behavior will result in that behavior. Because mainstream religious faith groups are dedicated to the practice and promotion of moral behavior, participation in these faith groups should increase individuals' exposure to moral messages and definitions unfavorable to the violation of social or moral norms. Thus strength of religious commitment is expected, once again, to be inversely related to involvement in criminal or delinquent behaviors.

Most psychological approaches to the study of criminal or delinquent behavior see crime or delinquency as symptomatic of psychological maladjustment. Religious training in childhood through adulthood is seen as an important element of normal psychological development. Participation in religious groups and activities prevents crime or delinquency: (1) by building a strong superego able to suppress basic, selfish impulses, (2) by developing respect for authority through worship of God, and (3) by reinforcing internalized social or moral values such that the consideration of their violation would produce discomforting sensations of cognitive dissonance.

The deterrence doctrine maintains that people conform when the costs of crime or delinquency are perceived as greater than the potential benefits. Participation in and commitment to religion can serve several deterrent functions. First, the threat of supernatural sanctions (i.e., eternal hellfire and damnation) may make the cost of criminal or delinquent behavior too great for those who believe. Second involvement in a faith group exposes one to increased levels of interpersonal surveillance (more people watching), thus increasing the likelihood of getting caught and of receiving costly, informal social sanctions for criminal or delinquent activities.

Finally, several of the conflict or radical approaches to the study of criminal or delinquent behavior argue that organized religions are often used by rulers to control and placate the ruled (1) by portraying existing social arrangements as divinely ordained, and (2) by promising an afterlife for those who embrace its ideology (religion as the opiate of the people). In this manner religious commitment inhibits criminal or delinquent behavior by generating passive acceptance of the social order.

## How Is Religiosity Associated with Criminal or Delinquent Behavior?

If we accept the claim that strongly religious individuals are less involved in criminal or delinquent activities than are the irreligious, than the final issue for social scientists working in this area is to determine the nature of that relationship; how is religiosity associated with criminal or delinquent behavior? In general, four separate perspectives dominate this area of inquiry: (1) the hellfire hypothesis, which claims that increased religious commitment is associated with decreased involvement in criminal or delinquent behavior of all ilk; (2) the anti-asceticism hypothesis, which restricts the inhibiting influence of religious commitment to those forms of criminal or delinquent behavior that violate religious moral proscriptions, but which are less opposed by other agents of our society, such as premarital sex, gambling, or alcohol use; (3) the norm qualities hypothesis, which restricts the inhibitory effects of religious commitments not only to certain forms of criminal

or delinquent behavior, but also only among those who are affiliated with certain faith groups; and (4) the moral communities hypothesis which argues that the influence of individuals' religious commitment on their involvement in criminal or delinquent behavior is, itself, influenced by the strength of religious commitment within the community in which these individuals reside.

Although the connection of religion to crime or delinquency is an old one, it was relatively dormant as a research question until 1969 when the publication of "Hellfire and Delinquency" by Travis Hirschi and Rodney Stark brought the issue into prominence. Using self-report data on adolescents' religious and delinquent behavior, Hirschi and Stark (1969, 202) tested the hypothesis that "religious sanctioning systems play an important role in ensuring and maintaining conformity to social norms." Religion was said to perform this role: (1) through its system of beliefs that legitimize social values, (2) through its rites and rituals that reinforce one's commitment to these values, and (3) through its system of eternal rewards (heaven) and punishment (hellfire and damnation) that ensures the embodiment of these values in actual behavior. Thus religion both ensures conformity through its beliefs, rites, and rituals and deters crime or delinquency through the threat of hellfire for sinners. These effects are general across all forms of immoral conduct. Stated formally, the hellfire hypothesis asserts that the greater the strength of religious commitment (religiosity), the lower the probability or level of involvement in criminal or delinquent behavior.

Whereas Hirschi and Stark (1969) observed that church attendance and belief in supernatural sanctions were not significantly related to self-reported delinquency, many other studies subsequently have observed that strength of religious commitment is, indeed, inversely associated with involvement in criminal or delinquent activities in support of the hellfire hypothesis (see Cochran and Akers, 1989 for a review of these studies). Nevertheless, others have questioned the validity of this perspective, suggesting that it is too broad and is in need of modification and respecification.

Using a distinction between ascetic and secular ethical standards, Burkett and White (1974) argued that only when secular values are ambiguous in their definition of an activity as wrong can strength of religious commitment have an important inhibitory impact on criminal or delinquent behavior. They suggest that behaviors that simultaneously violate ascetic values but are not consistently disapproved in secular settings, such as premarital sex, gambling, and drug and alcohol use, are more likely than personal or property crimes to be affected by religiosity. Stated formally, this anti-asceticism hypothesis avows that the inhibitory influence of religious commitment is strongest for anti-ascetic behaviors.

Using the same data employed by Hirschi and Stark (1969), Burkett and White found strength of religious commitment to be more predictive of adolescent alcohol and marijuana use than of a delinquency index based on property crimes and violent offenses. They concluded that "blanket generalizations regarding the relationship between religious participation and delinquency are not warranted," and that "religious participation is ... more closely related to some kinds of delinquent behavior than others" (Burkett and White, 1974, 459). Many subsequent studies have also found measures of religious commitment to be more strongly and inversely associated with indicators of such antiascetic behaviors than with forms of criminal or delinquent behavior that are also strongly proscribed by secular influences (for a review of these studies, see Cochran and Akers, 1989).

Some argue that the anti-asceticism hypothesis is also too broad; that it too is limited in the contexts in which it is supported. Jensen and Erickson (1979), for instance, found that the effects of strength of religious commitment on measures of antiascetic behavior vary by religious affiliation. That is, some religious faith groups have more pronounced moral messages (norm qualities) proscribing these antiascetic behaviors than do other faiths. For instance, fundamentalist Protestant faith groups more strongly proscribe alcohol use than do most other mainstream American faith groups. As such, devout members of these faiths are less likely to drink alcoholic beverages than equally devout members of other faiths. Thus, the inhibitory influence of religious commitment on involvement in antiascetic behaviors is strongest among members of those faith groups that proscribe such conduct very strongly. Although the research evidence on this issue is far from conclusive (again, see Cochran and Akers, 1989, for a review), it is likely that religious affiliations may constitute important normative climates that affect the relationship between religious commitment and antiascetic behavior.

According to Stark, Kent, and Doyle (1982), it is in "moral communities," where religious influences permeate culture and social interactions and where a majority profess religious faith, that religious commitment should most effectively control criminal or delinquent behavior. In communities where religion is not as pervasive, the inhibitory effect of religious commitment is substantially reduced, even among the strongly devout. This argument suggests that the relationship between religious commitment and criminal or delinquent behavior is, itself, influenced by social structural and cultural forces that beg for cross-cultural research.

Yet, to date, no cross-cultural studies have examined this issue. However, limited tests of this argument have been conducted within the U.S. For instance, Stark and his colleagues (1982) observed exactly this; they found the strongest negative relationship between religiosity and criminal or delinquent behavior within those secondary schools in which religious students were the majority. The strength of this negative relationship diminished as the proportion of religious students decreased. Title and Welch (1983), however, found just the opposite to be the case. That is, they observed the influence of religious commitment to be strongest in the most secularly disorganized (nonmoral) communities. So the evidence is again, unclear. Nevertheless, both Stark et al. (1982) and Tittle and Welch (1983) argue that the influence of religious commitment on criminal or delinquent behavior varies with the degree of aggregate religiosity. This moral communities hypothesis can be stated formally as: the greater the level of aggregate religiosity, the stronger the inverse effect of religiosity on criminal or delinquent behavior.

Though there may be a variety of social conditions and contexts under which the influence of religion on criminal or delinquent behavior varies, and though there are a variety of theoretical perspectives that have been proffered to account for why religion has this influence, it is clear that religious commitment inhibits criminal or delinquent conduct.

JOHN K. COCHRAN

## References and Further Reading

Benda, B., 1995. The effect of religion on adolescent delinquency revisited, *Journal of Research in Crime and Delinquency, 32,* 446–466.

Burkett, S.R. and Warren, B.O., 1987. Religiosity, peer associations and adolescent marijuana use: A panel study of underlying causal structures, *Criminology, 25,* 109–125.

Burkett, S.R. and White, M., 1974. Hellfire and delinquency: Another look, *Journal for the Scientific Study of Religion, 13,* 455–462.

Cochran, J.K. and Akers, R.L., 1989. Beyond hellfire: An exploration of the variable effects of religiosity on adolescent marijuana and alcohol use, *Journal of Research in Crime and Delinquency, 26,* 198–225.

Cochran, J.K., Wood, P.B. and Arneklev, B.J., 1994. Is the religiosity-delinquency relationship spurious? A test of arousal and social control theories, *Journal of Research in Crime and Delinquency, 31,* 92–123.

Elifson, K.W., Petersen, D.M. and Hadaway, C.K., 1983. Religiosity and delinquency: A contextual analysis, *Criminology, 21,* 505–527.

Ellis, L. and Thompson, R., 1989. Relating religion, crime, arousal and boredom, *Sociology and Social Research, 73,* 132–139.

Evans, D., Cullen, F., Dunaway, R.G. and Burton, V.S., Jr., 1995. Religion and crime reexamined: The impact of religion, secular controls, and social ecology on adult criminality, *Criminology, 33,* 195–224.

Evans, S.A. and Scott, J.E., 1984. The seriousness of crime cross-culturally, *Criminology*, 22, 39–59.

Fitzpatrick, J.P., 1967. The role of religion in programs for the prevention and correction of crime and delinquency, pp. 315–330 in *President's Commission on Law Enforcement and Administration of Justice, Task Force Report: Juvenile Delinquency*, Washington, DC, Government Printing Office.

Hirschi, T. and Stark, R. 1969. Hellfire and Delinquency, *Social Problems*, 17: 202–213.

Jensen, G.F. and Erickson, M.L., 1979. The religious factor and delinquency: Another look at the hellfire hypothesis, in Wuthnow, R., Ed., *The Religious Dimension: New Directions for Quantitative Research*, New York: Academic Press, pp. 157–177.

Stark, R., Kent, L. and Doyle, D.P., 1982. Religion and delinquency: The ecology of a 'Lost' relationship, *Journal of Research in Crime and Delinquency*, 19, 4–24.

Tittle, C.R. and Welch, M.R., 1983. Religiosity and deviance: Toward a contingency theory of constraining effects, *Social Forces*, 61, 653–682.

*See also* **Juvenile Delinquency, Theories of; Marxist Theories of Criminal Behavior; Sociological Theories of Criminal Behavior**

# Repeat Offenders *See* Recidivism

# Restorative Justice

Restorative justice can be viewed as an alternative to retributive or traditional responses to crime. Although restorative justice processes and practices are many and varied (Daly, 1999; Daly and Hayes, 2001), all aim to bring about social harmony, to afford admitted offenders an opportunity to make amends for their wrongdoing, to allow the families of offenders an opportunity to speak about how the offense has affected them, to allow the victims of crime an opportunity to voice their anger and distress, and to move all affected parties of an offense closer to reparation and resolution. The theory of restorative justice derives from the informal justice movements and victim-offender programs of the 1970s and 1980s. Contemporary restorative justice initiatives commonly center on youth offenders.

Interest and academic scrutiny about restorative justice escalated during the 1990s. Restorative justice initiatives have appeared in many jurisdictions around the world, including New Zealand, Australia, North America, and Europe. Although jurisdictions in the Northern Hemisphere have made substantial progress in developing various restorative justice initiatives (e.g., sentencing circles, victim-offender mediation programs, victim-offender reconciliation programs, police accountability conferences; see Hudson and Galaway, 1996; Umbreit, 1996; McCold and Wachtel, 1998), Australia and New Zealand are leaders in diversionary conferencing. Conferencing and restorative justice seem almost synonymous in various writings on the subject, and in Australia and New Zealand, conferences are aimed at diverting young offenders from youth court or are used concurrently with court.

Conferencing was first introduced into legislation in New Zealand under the Children, Young Persons and Their Families Act 1989, making New Zealand the first jurisdiction in the world to provide a legislative basis for diversionary conferences (Maxwell and Morris, 1993, 1994, and 1996). Conferencing was first tried in Australia in Wagga Wagga, New South Wales, under a police-run scheme in 1991. The first legislatively based conferencing scheme in Australia appeared in South Australia in 1994. Since then all but two Australian jurisdictions (Victoria and the Australian Capital Territory) have developed a legislative basis for diversionary conferencing. However, there is a substantial degree of variation across jurisdictions within Australia regarding the way conferencing is administered and run (Daly and Hayes, 2001).

A diversionary conference is a place where a young offender, his or her family members, the victim(s), representatives of the juvenile justice system (e.g., arresting police officers), and community representatives (e.g., mediators, facilitators) come together to discuss the offending behavior of the young person. The context in which this discussion takes place is one of compassion and understanding, as opposed to the adversarial, judgmental, and stigmatizing environment associated with the youth court. Young people who have admitted to an offense are given the opportunity to talk about the circumstances associated with their offending behavior (e.g., what they think brought about the offense, why they think they became involved in the offense). The young person's family members are able to discuss how the offense committed by their child has affected them, the victim is able to voice his or her anger, distress, and concerns regarding future victimization, and policing officials are able to provide details regarding the offense and other potential legal consequences.

Conferences usually move from the arresting officers' factual description of the offense to offenders' and their families' perspective on the illicit events. Victims are then given an opportunity to convey (often emotionally) how the offense has affected them and seek answers to any questions they may have about motive and retaliation. The conference coordinator or facilitator, offenders and their families, and victims then discuss appropriate reparations. Reparations (agreements or outcomes) vary within and across programs but typically include an apology to the victim and the performance of work for the community or victim. Some agreements may include a monetary payment to the victim for damages incurred as a result of the offense.

Depending upon the jurisdiction in which conferences are operating, victims may be involved in discussions about the conference outcomes. In New Zealand, for example, victims do not play a significant role in deliberations regarding reparation (Hassall, 1996). However, in the Australian jurisdiction of Queensland, victims have the right to veto police referrals to conference and play a major role in deciding appropriate reparations.

Although restorative justice is poised to become an important grounding theory for criminal justice policy in the future, there remain many questions about this "new justice." Critics are wary because there is a dearth of systematic empirical research that clearly shows restorative justice practices meet the stated aims of repairing harms, restoring relationships, and reducing reoffending. At issue too are the rights of young offenders. Following are some of the questions raised by academic and legal observers.

Are restorative justice conferences fair and procedurally just? Based on research conducted overseas and around Australia, the findings are the most consistent on this issue. Participants of diversionary conferences report that they were treated with respect, were dealt with fairly, had an opportunity to voice their concerns, and were involved in framing a solution to the conflict (Umbreit, 1996; Sherman et al., 1998; Hayes et al., 1998; Strang et al., 1999; Trimboli, 2000).

Are conferences restorative? Conferences are grounded on restorative justice principles. They are a place where victim, offender, and community representatives come together to discuss the offense and what should be done about it. Results scattered across studies conducted in Australia and overseas seem to indicate that there are restorative features present in diversionary conferences (Umbreit, 1996; Daly and Hayes, 2001).

Do conferences result in fewer reoffenses? Are conferences cost-effective? These questions are difficult to answer at present. There are efforts under way to examine the longer-term effects of conferencing on recidivism. For example, research in New Zealand has shown that conferences have the potential to reduce reoffending (Maxwell and Morris, 1999). Other research currently under way in Australia will examine the crime reduction potential of restorative justice initiatives in the Australian Capital Territory and South Australia, as well as gauge the cost-effectiveness of police-run conferences in the Australian Capital Territory (Daly et al., 1998; Strang et al., 1999). Other research in America has compared the effects of court- to police-run conferences in Bethlehem, Pennsylvania (McCold and Stahr, 1996). Although reduced reoffending is not always the primary objective of restorative justice initiatives, Braithwaite (1998) suggests that "restorative justice will never become a mainstream alternative to retributive justice unless long-term R and D programs show that it does have the capacity to reduce crime." To date, research has not definitively shown that restorative justice programs do have the capacity to reduce reoffending.

These are a few of the most pressing questions raised by observers. Others include: Are conference outcomes a "soft option" to the youth court? Is there potential for "net-widening"? (Net-widening refers to increased levels of state intervention that result from the introduction of new justice programs. For example, young offenders who normally would have been released in the care of their parents may be referred to conference simply because the alternative exists.) Are conferences coercive of young people and minority cultures? Are the rights of young offenders protected? Do conferences meet the needs of children?

The future of restorative justice is an optimistic one. As an alternative to court, restorative practices yield many benefits for those embroiled in conflict (i.e., offenders, victims, and their supporters). Nevertheless, what remains unclear is whether restorative justice practices work. Depending on how one views the success of these initiatives, results of recent research show that restorative justice practices have the potential to repair harms but, for some offenders, may be no more effective in reducing reoffending than court.

HENNESSEY HAYES

## References and Further Reading

Daly, K. 2000. Revisiting the relationship between retributive and restorative justice, in Strang, H. and Braithwaite, J., Eds., *Restorative Justice: From Philosophy to Practice,* Burlington, VT, Ashgate.

Daly, K. and Hayes, H. 2001. Restorative justice and conferencing in Australia, *Trends and Issues,* 186.

Daly, K. et al. 1998. *South Australian Juvenile Justice (SAJJ) Research on Conferencing,* Technical Report No. 1, Project Overview and Research Instruments, Brisbane, Australia, School of Criminology and Criminal Justice, Griffith University.

Hassall, I.B. 1996. Origin and development of family group conferences, in Hudson, J. et al., *Family Group Conferences: Perspectives on Policy and Practice,* Eds., Monsey, New York, Criminal Justice Press.

Hayes, H., Prenzer, T. and Wortley, R. 1998. *Making Amends: Final Evaluation of the Queensland Community Conferencing Pilot,* Brisbane, Australia, Centre for Crime Policy and Public Safety, School of Criminology and Criminal Justice, Griffith University.

Galaway, B. and Hudson, J., Eds. 1996. *Restorative Justice: International Perspectives,* Monsey, New York, Criminal Justice Press.

Maxwell, G.M. and Morris, A. 1993. *Family, Victims, and Culture: Youth Justice in New Zealand,* Wellington, New Zealand, Institute of Criminology, Victoria University of Wellington.

Maxwell, G.M. and Morris, A. 1994. The New Zealand model of family group conferences, in Alder, C. and Wundersitz, J., Eds. 1994. *Family Conferencing and Juvenile Justice: The Way Forward or Misplaced Optimism?* Canberra, Australian Institute of Criminology.

Maxwell, G.M. and Morris, A. 1996. Research on family group conferences with young offenders, in Maxwell, G.M., Morris, A. et al., Eds., *Family Group Conferences: Perspectives on Policy and Practice,* Monsey, New York, Criminal Justice Press and Willow Tree Press.

Maxwell, G.M. and Morris, A. 1999. *Understanding Reoffending: Full Report,* Wellington, New Zealand, Institute of Criminology, Victoria University of Wellington.

Real Justice Website, *Restorative Policing Experiment: The Bethlehem Pennsylvania Police Family Conferencing Project.* Available at: www.realjustice.org.

Sherman, L. et al. 1998. *Experiments in Restorative Justice: A Progress Report on the Canberra Reintegrative Shaming Experiments (RISE),* Canberra, Australian, National University.

Strang, H., et al. 1999. *Experiments in Restorative Justice: A Progress Report on the Canberra Reintegrative Shaming Experiments (RISE),* Canberra, Australian National University.

Trimboli, L. 2000. *An Evaluation of the NSW Youth Justice Conferencing Scheme,* Sydney, Australia, New South Wales Bureau of Crime Statistics and Research.

Umbreit, M. 1996. Restorative justice through mediation: The impact of programs in four Canadian provinces, in Galaway, B. and Hudson, J., Eds., *Restorative Justice: International Perspectives,* Monsey, New York, Criminal Justice Press.

*See also* **Community Corrections; Community Service and Restitution Programs; Retribution**

# Retribution

Retribution as a sentencing philosophy can best be understood in contrast to the principal alternative: utilitarianism. Exponents of utilitarian sentencing aim to reduce the incidence of crime. Several specific mechanisms exist to accomplish this: offenders can be deterred by the infliction or threat of punishment (specific or general deterrence), they can be prevented physically from reoffending (incapacitation), or they can be rehabilitated. Utilitarian sentences look to the future, using punishments to prevent future crimes from occurring. If an offender is very likely to reoffend, a utilitarian judge would impose a severe sentence.

Retribution on the other hand looks towards the past. Retributive sentencing focuses not on the probability that the offender will reoffend, but on punishing the offender for the crime of which he has just been convicted. In short, retributivists impose punishments according to the seriousness of the offense of conviction; utilitarianism sentences offenders according to the likelihood of future offending.

Since the 1970s, retributive justice has been the primary sentencing philosophy in many western nations, including the U.S., England, Finland, and Sweden. Even countries such as Canada that employ a mixed sentencing model subscribe to the principle of proportionality that lies at the heart of the retributive perspective. Retributive justice requires that the severity of punishment be proportionate to the seriousness of the offense and the blameworthiness of the offender.

Contemporary retributive theory owes much of its popularity to the influential book *Doing Justice* by Andrew von Hirsch and published in 1976. For von Hirsch (1993), the sentence imposed conveys a sense of the wrongfulness of the crime and is a reflection of how much an offender is to blame for his or her harmful conduct and therefore is deserving of legal censure. Thus retribution is not simply punishing for punishment's sake: it is about treating offenders as responsible moral agents, capable of making decisions about right and wrong.

The principles of equity and proportionality lie at the heart of retributive sentencing. This contrasts with utilitarian philosophies such as rehabilitation and deterrence that focus more on crime reduction by changing the offender or generating sufficient fear to dissuade other potential offenders. Retributive justice is concerned with a just outcome whereas utilitarian philosophies are concerned with outcomes that reduce crime, even if they are unjust. Retributive justice encourages compliance with criminal laws by means of a sanctioning system that reflects the community values of fairness and the community norms of appropriate moral conduct. A criminal justice system that the public believes is built on a foundation of public values and norms has more legitimacy and the public is more likely to respect, assist, and follow the law. Several empirical studies in the U.S. and Canada have demonstrated that the retributive concept of "just deserts" is central to public sentencing preferences (e.g., Darley, Carlsmith, and Robinson, 2000; Roberts and Gebotys, 1989).

Just deserts (or retributive) sentencing has several defining characteristics. First, retributive justice reduces uncertainty about the amount of punishment. At the time of sentencing, offenders know exactly the maximum amount of punishment that they will receive. Retributive justice provides structure to the sentencing decision and reduces judicial discretion about the amount of punishment that can be imposed on the offender. By constraining judges' discretion to sentence offenders, retributive justice reduces the potential for misuse of authority and discrimination based on an offender's race, gender, social class, or other extralegal characteristics. The seriousness of the offense and the culpability of the offender are the factors that determine the severity of the punishment. The background and demographic characteristics of offenders receive little consideration in determining the nature and severity of the punishment imposed.

The concept of retributive justice has been around for centuries and has clear links to the Judeo–Christian tradition. For example, the Old Testament calls for "an eye for an eye and a tooth for a tooth, and a life for a life." Despite misunderstandings about this well-known biblical quote, retributive justice neither requires nor is consistent with the imposition of severe, harsh, or humiliating punishments. Retributive justice simply requires that offenders who commit more serious harm be punished more severely than offenders who commit less serious harm. Crimes are ranked according to their seriousness and are related to a ranking of severity of potential penalties (this is known as "cardinal proportionality"). Retributive justice treats crimes that have similar seriousness with a similar amount of punishment.

Retributive justice requires that judges or legislative guidelines adhere to the principle of proportionality that requires imposing a punishment that is proportionate to the seriousness of the harm done, and to restrain from providing more severe punishment than is warranted in light of the seriousness of the crime and the culpability of the offender. A scale of the severity of punishment must be appropriately anchored and must be constrained by maximum penalties that define the outer limits of punishment (this is known as "cardinal proportionality"). According to a retributive rationale in sentencing, judges should not impose very harsh sentences in order to achieve some goal such as lowering the crime rate. An increase of bank robberies, for example, should not lead a judge to impose a very harsh sentence in the hope that this will "send a message" to other potential robbers. To do so would be to violate the principle of proportionality.

Disproportionate punishments exist across the U.S. and in other jurisdictions as well. The best examples of disproportionate punishments are the "three strikes and you're out" laws that exist in some American states, and that can result in the imposition of life imprisonment or very long prison terms on offenders convicted of property offenses. These laws are inconsistent with retributive justice sentencing principles because the punishment prescribed is disproportionate to the seriousness of the criminal conduct of which the offender has been convicted. Public opposition to these three strikes laws that count property crimes as a "strike" is further evidence of public support for retributive sentencing.

Another characteristic of retributive justice is that it focuses on various amounts of punishment, and can incorporate community-based sanctions including intermediate punishments such as house arrest, community service, intensive supervision probation, electronic monitoring, fines, and weekend imprisonment. It is the severity or "penal bite" of the punishment that must be proportionate to the seriousness of the offense, not the type of the punishment. Most sentencing guidelines and legislative statutes are guided by retributive justice principles that focus on whether imprisonment should be used and, if imprisonment is an appropriate punishment, the length of imprisonment. This reflects the fact that it is easier to relate a ranking of the seriousness of crimes to a penalty scale that has the same unit of measurement (such as number of months in prison). However, retributive justice does permit the use of intermediate community-based sanctions.

In order to incorporate such sanctions into a structured sentencing system, community judgment about the severity of these community-based sanctions needs to be gauged. Harlow, Darley, and Robinson (1995) have demonstrated the feasibility of measuring community judgments about the severity of intermediate sanctions. Some scholars have proposed that intermediate sanctions should only be used for crimes of moderate seriousness so that the severity of punishment for less serious crimes does not become disproportionate to the seriousness of the offense. Moreover, when retributive justice is the primary goal of sentencing, a structured sentencing guideline could indicate the "penal bite" or the severity of the punishment required and allow the judge to tailor the sentence by choosing different punishments to achieve a sentence that carries the appropriate degree of "bite." For example, a judge may combine a fine, some community service, and a period of intensive supervision probation instead of imposing a two-year prison term, if the public perceived these two sentences as having approximately the same impact on the offender.

The retributive justice model of sentencing also assumes that the public can agree on the relative seriousness of different offenses and the relative severity of different punishments. In support of this assumption, studies on public perceptions of crime seriousness find a general consensus about which crimes are more serious relative to other crimes. Moreover, this general consensus exists across cultures. People in Great Britain, U.S., Canada, Denmark, Finland, Kuwait, Norway, and Holland generally agree about the relative seriousness of different crimes. Men and women, people from different social classes and ethnicities, and even victims and nonvictims agree about the relative seriousness of different crimes, with more disagreement about how to rank the moderately serious crimes such as burglary.

Although there is adequate agreement about relative seriousness of different crime categories, there is marked disagreement about which acts are more serious within a broad crime category such as victimless crimes, white-collar crimes, or property crimes. Thus, a rough scale of crime seriousness can be constructed with general consensus, but a scale with more refined demarcations within crime categories may be more difficult to achieve based on consensus in public perceptions of crime seriousness.

If the seriousness of the crime is essential to a retributive model of sentencing, it is important to understand the various components of the concept of "seriousness." What elements of an offense determine its seriousness? This question can be answered either by reference to empirical research on public perceptions, or by resorting to a prescriptive scheme to reflect crime seriousness. Von Hirsch and Jareborg have proposed just such a prescriptive scheme for judging the seriousness of crimes involving individual victims. According to this scheme, the seriousness of crimes should be determined by the extent to which the victim's capabilities for achieving a certain standard of living are restricted. Standard of living refers both to material resources—such as shelter and money—and nonmaterial quality of life issues such as good health, privacy, autonomy, and avoidance of demeaning treatment.

The problem with using public ratings of the seriousness of crimes to establish a rank-ordering of offenses is that public ratings of crime seriousness can be distorted by excessive media coverage of certain types of offending. One advantage of the prescriptive approach is that it is less influenced by media attention to certain crimes and can be adapted to a particular culture or society. Thus, a high degree of consensus with respect to crime seriousness would not be required to obtain a valid ranking of crimes according to their seriousness. A prescriptive scheme, moreover, could be validated through varying relevant dimensions of harm and obtaining empirical analysis of public judgments about the seriousness of different crimes. Thus, a prescriptive scheme can be a guiding theory to obtain data on public judgments, and does not necessarily eliminate the need for empirical data on public judgments about crime seriousness.

Studies on public perceptions of crime seriousness have identified additional dimensions underlying public judgments of crime seriousness. An obvious dimension is the amount of physical and economic harm inflicted, or the potential for physical or economic harm (as in the case of attempted crimes), with almost all violent crimes seen as being more serious as than most property crimes. Another dimension that affects judgments of the seriousness of crime is the level of premeditation, with premeditated harm being seen as more serious than impulsive responses that are in turn viewed as being less serious than negligence or recklessness. Another dimension of crime seriousness is the degree to which the offender was aware, or should have been aware, of the potential harmful effects of his or her behavior.

Both an offender's awareness of potential harmful effects and intentions are related to his or her blameworthiness (culpability). Other doctrines of legal excuses could also reduce the seriousness of the offense. For example, offenders who have diminished mental capabilities to understand fully the wrongfulness or potential harmfulness of their conduct should receive more lenient sentences. Juvenile delinquents are considered to be less blameworthy than adults convicted of the same kinds of crimes.

The offender's motive for the crime also may affect the degree of blameworthiness. An offender who steals food to feed his family is less blameworthy than an offender who steals for profit. A person who commits voluntary manslaughter to relieve the pain and suffering of a terminally-ill parent deserves less punishment than someone who commits voluntary manslaughter during a heated argument with his terminally-ill father about whether to hire full-time nursing care or go to a cheaper nursing home. An offender who has suffered severe personal consequences as a result of a crime also may deserve a less severe sentence. For example, a man who forgot to buckle his son's seatbelt and lost his son in an accidental car crash may well deserve less punishment for vehicular homicide because he has suffered substantially for his reckless conduct.

All of these examples illustrate that mercy can and should be incorporated into a retributive justice scheme of sentencing. Consideration of mercy arises in situations where offenders commit harmful and even perhaps immoral acts but the motives or circumstances surrounding the commission of the crimes make the usual punishment undeserved and unjust. As Von Hirsch notes, mercy is a normative concept concerned with the deservingness of punishment and can be incorporated into retributive justice. Retributive justice theorists, however, have given little consideration to the concept of mercy.

Another more controversial element of culpability is an offender's prior record. Some retributive supporters believe that only the seriousness of the current offense should affect the severity of punishment imposed. Other retributive supporters such as von Hirsch believe that the seriousness of the current offense should be the most important, but not the exclusive criterion. Von Hirsch asserts that offenders with no prior record (or almost no record) should receive a discounted sentence to recognize human fallibility and the potential to be responsive to censure. However, this discount should progressively diminish and eventually disappear as the prior record becomes more extensive. After three or so offenses, the offender has had a second chance, and can no longer plausibly argue that the crime was an aberration that was "out of character." Studies of public judgments also find that the public perceives a crime as more serious if a recidivist commits it than if a first-time offender commits it.

Most retributive supporters agree that the sentence should not be more severe than the seriousness of the offense even when an offender has a long criminal record. The use of prior record in sentencing is one critical difference between utilitarian philosophies and retributive justice: the sentencing strategies of incapacitation and deterrence place more importance on prior criminal record than does retributive justice, reasoning that if the offender has committed many offenses in the past, he or she is likely to commit offenses in the future, and therefore requires a harsh sentence.

Retributive sentencing theories have attracted criticism, mostly from advocates of utilitarian perspectives. The most recent challenge to retributive "just deserts" sentencing comes from proponents of restorative justice, who focus on restoring the links between the offender and the community to which he or she belongs. Clearly, these links are difficult to restore when offenders are sitting in prison serving retributive-based sentences.

LORETTA J. STALANS AND JULIAN V. ROBERTS

## References and Further Reading

Ashworth, A. 1995. *Sentencing and Criminal Justice,* London, U.K., Butterworths.

Darley, J.M., Carlsmith, K.M. and Robinson, P.R. 2000. Incapacitation and just deserts as motives for punishment, *Law and Human Behavior,* 24(6), 659–684.

Duff, A. 1986. *Trials and Punishments,* Cambridge, MA, Cambridge University Press.

Duff, A., Marshall, S., Dobash, R.E. and Dobash, R.P., Eds. 1994. *Penal Theory and Practice: Tradition and Innovation in Criminal Justice,* New York, St. Martin's Press.

Harlow, R.E., Darley, J.M. and Robinson, P.R. 1995. The severity of intermediate penal sanctions: A psychophysical scaling approach for obtaining community perceptions, *Journal of Quantitative Criminology,* 11(1), 71–95.

Roberts, J.V. and Gebotys, R. 1989. The purposes of sentencing: Public support for competing aims, *Behavioral Sciences and the Law,* 7, 387–402.

Tonry, M. 1996. *Sentencing Matters,* Oxford, U.K., Oxford University Press.

von Hirsch, A. 1976. *Doing Justice: The Choice of Punishments,* New York, Hill and Wang.

von Hirsch, A. 1993. *Censure and Sanctions,* Oxford, U.K., Clarendon Press.

von Hirsch, A. and Ashworth, A., Eds. 1992. *Principled Sentencing,* Boston, MA, Northeastern University Press.

*See also* **Community Service and Restitution Programs; Punishment Justifications; Sentences and Sentencing: Types**

# Riots: Extent and Correlates

Riots are a form of collective behavior in which people act together in a mob or large group and engage in a variety of acts that often constitute crimes (Blumer, 1975). Looting, assault, vandalism, and arson are behaviors common to riots. But there is another dimension to riots that make them more fascinating than the crimes that occur. Riots are often a form of symbolic protest (Fogelson, 1968). They give voice to the powerless to challenge the rule and domination of the powerful in society. However, we should be careful not to think of riots in a romantic way, because they can also be used as a form of recreation and excitement, as when a football team wins the Super Bowl. At those times, the violence associated with the riot has no symbolic or political value.

In order to appreciate fully the nature of riots, we need to understand that the motive to riot varies by many factors. Goode (1992) presents a typology of riots based on the motives and goals of the rioters. His categories are the purposive riot, the symbolic riot, the revelous riot, and the issueless riot. Depending on the type of riot, the lawbreaking and violence will be different in type, scope, and geographic dispersion. For example, in the revelous riot after a win (or sometimes loss) of a big game, the riot is usually confined to a distinct area, such as a street near campus. The violence is part of the fun such as turning over police cars and starting fires in the middle of the street while the crowd stands around and cheers. This revelous riot can be contrasted with the symbolic riot, such as the urban riots of the 1960s when African-American citizens protested the institutional racism that existed at the time. In these urban riots, the violence was not confined to small areas, and it included arson, looting and, in some cities, gunfire. Consequently, the term "riot" can have many manifestations. The real nature of this form of collective behavior can be difficult to understand.

Although they may have many similarities, protest riots need to be differentiated from revolts and revolutions. Revolts and revolutions are aimed at taking down the government and replacing it with some alternative form of power. The American Revolution revolted against a government that had lost the allegiance of many people because of a tax system that was consider unfair and the refusal to include the colonists in decision-making systems. The aim of the revolution was to replace the government. By contrast, the urban riots of the 1960s were simply trying to get the government's attention focused on the unjust economic and social conditions faced by minorities. These riots were not trying to change the values of society but simply the norms (Fogelson, 1968). The American dream of economic prosperity and social freedom was systematically being denied to large groups of people because of who they were rather than what they had done.

How common are riots? Although the history of the U.S. is littered with examples of riots, it is fair to say that they do not occur very often. However, when riots do occur they sometimes come in groups, as if there is some kind of contagion or copycat effect. Barkan and Snowden (2001) provide an excellent brief history of riots in the U.S. They contend that, in order to understand history, we must appreciate the role riots have played in forming this country. In the colonial period, citizens rioted against the British. After the victory over England, they continued to riot against the states over issues such as debt. In the 19th century, mob violence pitted Whites against Blacks, Catholics, and Chinese immigrants. Additionally, there were labor riots in Northern cities, the most famous of which was the Haymarket Riot of 1886 in Chicago.

The 20th century is replete with riots also. Race riots erupted in many cities such as East St. Louis, Illinois (1917), and Washington D.C. and Chicago (1919) (Barkan and Snowden, 2001). The 1960s saw large urban riots that need to be understood as different from the earlier race riots. In the urban riots, African-Americans were not the target of marauding bands of Whites as they were in the race riots. In the urban riots, African-Americans took to the streets as a form of symbolic protest to call attention to the unjust social and economic conditions that were being highlighted by the civil rights movement. It is important to note here that the civil rights movement raised the expectations of minorities to a point where the dominant power structure would not or could not respond fast enough. Consequently, many individuals believed that rioting was necessary to convince the nation that the injustices of racism would not be tolerated.

More recently, there have been riots associated with perceived injustices of the criminal justice system, such as the acquittal of the Los Angeles police officers accused of beating motorist Rodney King (Fuller,

1993). This case is especially interesting because the riots didn't occur until a year after the alleged beating (which incidentally was filmed and shown repeatedly on television). The riots occurred only after the criminal justice system failed to convict the officers. Many individuals saw the failure to punish the officers as a clear example of a double standard in American life where the color of one's skin determines the quality of justice. Another fascinating feature of the Rodney King verdict riots was that they were not confined to Los Angeles. Because television presented live pictures of the rioting in California, the riots quickly spread to several major cities across the nation. In this sense, the local news of the riots in Los Angeles became national news and influenced behaviors of individuals who have never had to deal with the Los Angeles Police Department.

The most recent example of riots were the protests aimed at the World Trade Organization (WTO) when it held its 2000 meeting in Seattle. This riot was interesting because the participants were not protesting against a particular government, but instead against an organization that represented the interests of several governments. The protesters objected to the economic and environmental policies of the WTO and took to the streets of Seattle to call attention to their cause. The local government, the people, and the Seattle police were only involved because the WTO meetings were in their city. These riots could have happened in any city in which the WTO met, but Seattle had to cope with the violence and pay the expense of the damage and police protection.

Many scholars have attempted to explain why riots happen. One particularly interesting explanation is provided by sociologist Neil Smelser (1962) with his "value-added" theory of collective behavior. Smelser believes a chain of events happen in collective behavior situations. As events progress along that chain, it's more likely that a riot will happen. At the beginning of the chain is structural conduciveness. There are some situations that make riots more likely to occur. For instance, people are unlikely to gather on a street during a 20-degree Fahrenheit day in a Chicago winter. However, a 90-degree Fahrenheit day in the summer makes it much more likely that a critical mass of people will gather.

Next, Smelser sees structural strain as a necessary condition for the formation of a riot. The strain felt by the crowd can be the pain felt from years of racism or the uncertainty of what to do when the home team wins a national championship. The long history of complaints against the Los Angeles Police Department provided the backdrop for the riots after the Rodney King verdict (Cannon, 1997).

The third step along Smelser's chain is called generalized beliefs. Here, the crowd must believe they are not responsible for the strain but that the authorities are. The videotape of the beating of Rodney King convinced many individuals that the complaints about the excessive use of force by the police were justified. In some ways, it is surprising that the riots did not occur when the tapes were first shown, but rather a year later when the police officers were acquitted.

Smelser's precipitating factors is the next step in the process. In the Rodney King case, this can clearly be seen as the acquittal of the police officers accused in the incident. This acted as a trigger that set off the tempers of many who thought a great injustice was done. Because of television, mobilization for action, the next step in the chain, actually occurred in many cities. People took to the streets and as crowds grew, looting and violence broke out.

Finally, Smelser's last step in the chain, operation of social control, occurred in each city in different ways. In Los Angeles, the police were slow to respond, and the result was large-scale violence that was filmed from network helicopters and shared with the world. Other cities handled the disturbances in more effective ways and actually prevented the collective behavior situations from turning into riots.

If we accept the idea that riots can be purposive and a form of symbolic protest, then we need to ask if they are effective in achieving their goals. The evidence here is mixed (Smith, 1968). For the urban riots of the 1960s, there was a tradeoff in calling attention to the plight of African-American poverty in the inner city and the backlash of white-dominated police forces that clamped down on the violence. The promise of the civil rights movement patterned after Dr. Martin Luther King's method of nonviolent social protest was compromised by the riots. Many individuals, both White and Black, came to see the challenge to the status quo as dangerously rending the delicate social fabric of the country. In the short run, there were public and private programs aimed at infusing the inner cities with economic stimulus, but now, 40 years later, it is clear that many of the conditions that led to the riots are still present.

There are some intangible results of riots that are not only hard to measure but controversial. The question can be legitimately asked, did the riots give African-American people a sense of pride? It is possible to argue that the riots gave inner-city people a sense that they could challenge the entrenched power structure and start to control their own communities. There is some evidence that this has happened. The democratic representation of minority politicians has notably improved. In many large cities, African-Americans control the city council and the mayor's office.

Although controversial, there are a number of programs, such as affirmative action, that are designed to address the structural conditions that are believed to have led to urban riots. There is some danger in attributing these improvements to riots. It may be that the urban riots actually delayed these advances in the status and power of African-Americans. What cannot be denied, however, is the fact that riotous behavior is part of the historic fabric of the nation. When enough people feel that the government or the power structure does not give them a fair opportunity to participate in addressing their concerns, then the only option they have is to challenge the status quo through rioting. Perhaps the best way to prevent riots is to give people a sense of input through our democratic processes (National Commission on the Causes and Prevention of Violence, 1970). Additionally, there should be toleration for groups who want to engage in nonviolent social protest. Freedom of speech and assembly are constitutionally protected in the U.S., and only by preserving these rights in ways that people can feel that their voices are heard can riots be made unnecessary.

JOHN R. FULLER

### References and Further Reading

Barkan, S.E. and Snowden, L.L. 2001. *Collective Violence,* Boston, MA, Allyn and Bacon.

Blumer, H. 1975. Outline of collective behavior, in Evans, R.R., Ed., *Readings in Collective Behavior,* Chicago, IL, Rand McNally.

Cannon, L. 1997. *Official Negligence: How Rodney King and the Riots Changed Los Angeles and the LAPD,* New York, Times Books.

Fogelson, R.M. 1968. Violence as protest, in Connery, R.H., Ed., *Urban Riots: Violence and Social Change,* New York, Vintage Books.

Fuller, J.R. 1993. The Rodney King verdict riots: A value-added theory perspective, *Journal of Police and Criminal Psychology,* 9(2).

Goode, E. 1992. *Collective Behavior,* Fort Worth, Harcourt Brace Jovanovich.

National Commission on the Causes and Prevention of Violence 1970. *To Establish Justice, To Insure Domestic Tranquility,* New York, Bantam Books.

Smelser, N.J. 1962. *Theory of Collective Behavior,* New York, Free Press.

Smith, B.L.R. 1968. The politics of protest: How effective is it? in Connery, R.H., Ed., *Urban Riots: Violence and Social Change,* New York, Vintage Books.

*See also* **Prison Riots; Riots: The Law**

# Riots: The Law

The crime of riot is one of several related offenses against public order involving group violence or the threat of violence. Riot is often the starting point of rebellion and insurrection, and thus the law of riot provides a means for governmental control over actual or perceived threats to established political authority. Frequently, riots are a form of political or ideological expression by groups lacking access to or meaningful participation in the political process. Riot control involves not just the suppression of violent disorder in the streets, but the government's assertion of its ideological supremacy through actual or threatened violence. In many instances of ethnic riots, however, law enforcement personnel, out of lethargy, sympathy, or connivance, make little or no attempt to enforce public order (Horowitz, 2001).

Under modern definitions of riot, such as that of the *Model Penal Code* (1962), riot is committed when three or more persons participate in a course of disorderly conduct in order to commit or facilitate a felony or misdemeanor. In some states, however, participation by more than three and as many as twelve persons may be required. The *Model Penal Code* grades riot as a third-degree felony, punishable by a maximum of five years imprisonment, and a fine of $2,500. As such, it is the most serious of the violence against public order offenses, although some states grade riot as a misdemeanor.

The crime of disorderly conduct, referenced in the definition of riot, is a separate, less serious crime, defined to include a wide range of behavior intended to cause public inconvenience, annoyance, or alarm: engaging in fights, violent, or tumultuous behavior, making threats, using obscene language or gestures, or creating a hazardous or physically offensive condition. Unlike riot, disorderly conduct can be committed by an individual acting alone; riot requires the participation of at least three individuals.

Closely related to riot is the crime of failing to disperse, typically graded as a misdemeanor, in which three or more persons engaging in disorderly conduct posing a reasonable risk of substantial harm or inconvenience, annoyance, or alarm, fail to disperse upon the order by a law enforcement officer. Additionally, the crime of obstructing streets or other public passages, graded as summary offense (maximum sentence of 90 days and fine of $300), involves the intentional or reckless blocking of streets or other places of public passage.

Riot laws traditionally are state laws, enforced in state courts. In 1968, however, in response to the dubious theory that the numerous public disorders of that decade were generated by "outside agitators," the U.S. Congress enacted a federal riot law that prohibits interstate travel for the purpose of inciting or encouraging a riot. Certain organizers of civil rights and anti-Vietnam War demonstrations at the 1968 Democratic National Convention were unsuccessfully prosecuted under this statute (the "Chicago Eight"), and it has rarely been used since then.

In its early English common law origins, riot was the last of a series of crimes involving escalating levels of public disorder. According to William Blackstone, unlawful assembly involved the assembly of three or more persons with the purpose of doing an unlawful act, but if such persons made an advance toward their objective, the offense became "rout." Riot was committed when the group committed an unlawful act of violence. In 1549, the original Riot Act was enacted as a felony, requiring the participation of 12 or more persons for the purpose of committing any traitorous, rebellious, or felonious act. Such persons were guilty of treason upon failure to disperse within two hours. Later, the Riot Act of 1714 established the statutory felony punishing 12 or more persons who remained together for one hour after being read a proclamation to disperse. The reading of this proclamation, and not the Riot Act itself, gave rise to the expression "reading the Riot Act." This definition of riot survives in the Public Order Act 1986 (U.K.).

Throughout U.S. history, federal and state officials have frequently employed both National Guard and regular army troops for riot duty (Higham, 1971). The law imposes few if any restrictions on the use of force by law enforcement or military personnel to control riots. Police may use deadly force when an individual suspected of having committed a felony, such as riot, attempts to flee and avoid arrest when the police believe that the fleeing individual poses a threat of serious physical injury to the police or others by continuing riotous conduct at another location. Only when feasible must the police warn the individual of their intention to use deadly force to stop the escape. The laws of many states also immunize law enforcement personnel, including state militias, from criminal or civil liability for their actions, resulting in injury or death, when suppressing a riot or dispersing or apprehending rioters, as long as those actions are necessary and proper to suppress the riot. Nevertheless, the use of deadly force is often difficult to justify, as was the case in May 1970, when five students were killed by Ohio National Guardsmen at Kent State University and two students were killed at Jackson State College by Mississippi State Troopers during antiwar demonstrations. No criminal prosecutions were brought against those responsible for the students' deaths. In response to politically significant riots, governmental commissions have been appointed, both to investigate and report on the underlying social causes of the disturbance, as well as to assess or justify the government's response, including its use of force (Platt, 1971).

Enforcement of public disorder laws is limited by recognition of the political right to public assembly, such as that included in the U.S. Constitution's First Amendment (1791) that bars laws against peaceful, nonviolent public assemblies. The U.S. Supreme Court has upheld the constitutionality of public disorder statutes, however, ruling that it is not an abridgement of free speech or assembly to punish those who promote, encourage, or aid a public gathering the purpose of which is to engage in violence. The *Model Penal Code* definition of riot was intended to differentiate between peaceful, constitutionally protected conduct and violent, unprotected conduct. Differentiating between peaceable assembly and riot, however, is difficult when a large group assembles to challenge official authority on a controversial political or social issue and some individuals and police engage in escalating acts of violence.

The actual enforcement of public disorder laws, however, can abridge the rights of speech and assembly through selective prosecution and issuance of orders to disperse based on the political views expressed. Moreover, under legal principles of accomplice liability and conspiracy, participants in a group protest may face criminal charges for the riotous acts of other members of the group.

DAVID W. WEBBER

## References and Further Reading

Donald L.H. 2001. *The Deadly Ethnic Riot,* Berkeley, CA, University of California Press.

*Report of the National Advisory Commission on Civil Disorders* 1968. (Kerner Commission Report) Washington, DC, U.S. Government Printing Office.

Walker, D. 1968. *Rights in Conflict: Chicago's Seven Brutal Days,* New York, Grosset and Dunlap.

Platt, A.M., Ed. 1971. *The Politics of Riot Commissions, 1917–1970* (New York: MacMillan).

Higham, R. 1969. Ed., *Bayonets in the Streets: The Use of Troops in Civil Disturbances,* Lawrence, KS, University of Kansas Press.

Waskow, A.I. 1975. *From Race Riot to Sit-In, 1919 and the 1960s,* Glouster, MA, Peter Smith.

*See also* **Prison Riots; Riots: Extent and Correlates**

# Risk Assessment *See* **Prediction of Criminal Behavior**

---

# Robbery as an Occupation

---

Robbery is arguably the quintessential street crime, tracing its roots to antiquity. As a crime that incorporates the elements of violation of assumed rights of property and the given right to personhood, robbery is essentially an act of domination by threat or the actual commission of violence for the purpose of financial or other property gain. As such, it is an instrumental act of force to obtain a desired object—money or goods. Primitive in its characteristics, robbery is a simple crime that requires little skill (only daring) on the part of the offender or offenders (robbery is frequently committed in pairs or groups), a willingness to place the victim in fear, and a readiness to use physical force and violence to achieve the goal of depriving victims of money or goods. Hence, robbery is always potentially a violent form of crime, although actual violence in the sense of physical harm need not occur. It may be only necessary to place the victim in such fear that the probability of violence is believed to be strong.

The crime of robbery is universally recognized. There has been a long fascination and concern about robbery and robbers that has resulted in a body of research. Some scholars of an early form of organized robbery, such as the brigands and bandits of rural Europe, see these bands of outlaws as a phenomenon of social protest (Hobsbawm, 1969). Modern robbery, for the most part, does not have this political character; although it may be argued that since most robbers are at the lower reaches of the socioeconomic ladder and emerge from a street culture (Jacobs and Wright, 1999), their criminal acts have an inherent political element in their expression.

From the perspective of history, the extent of robbery in England in the mid to the late 18th century is instructive. This was the era of highwaymen or robbers of the rich who traveled on the roads leading to and from London during a period of great class division.

These acts of highway robbery were perceived as a real threat to the then existing system of unequal distribution of economic and social resources. Thus, robbery was a subject of great concern to those who had the most to lose (i.e., the established hierarchy of power). Considerable debate ensued as to what actions could be taken to eliminate this threat. The expression of this concern was made famous by the writings of Henry Fielding in the late 18th century, in particular his well-known tract, *An Enquiry into the Causes of the Late Increase of Robbers* (Zirker, 1988). Though Fielding is perhaps best known as the author of the novel *Tom Jones,* he was also a magistrate, and it was in that capacity that Fielding organized the forerunner of what was to become the beginnings of modern policing in the next century. Known as the Bow Street Runners of London, founded largely on the perception of the increase of crime generally and robbery in particular, this force was the first to institute foot and horse patrols and the investigation of crimes. This development also points to the fact that whereas in earlier eras robbery may have been primarily a rural phenomenon, in the 18th century it became and has remained a crime largely associated with urban development and the problems that such development spawns, particularly for those populations that become dislocated in the socioeconomic divisions of society. In other words, the act of robbery, by and large, is engaged in by those who find themselves in the lower economic stratum in the context of a system of relative economic depravation.

The rise of robbery in the U.S. is usually associated in popular culture with the western movement and the emphasis on individualism. The historical records, however, suggest those patterns of robbery and outlawry on the expanding western frontier in the post–Civil War period was not the individualistic expression of a violent brand of cowboys often portrayed in films and stories. Rather these violent encounters were the result of economic group conflict in great part between cattle and sheep ranchers' interests. It was the social context of the time, much as the culture of the street is today, that provided the rationale for the acceptability of robbery and outlaw styles of violence as a means to satisfy what was perceived by the offending parties as their just due (Einstadter, 1978).

Much of the criminological research on robbery has been descriptive in nature, outlining various features and characteristics of the crime and its offenders. In a recent study of active robbers, however, Jacobs and Wright (1999), attempt to ascertain the motivation involved to engage in robbery. The authors argue that although certain background variables may predispose persons to offend, it is the street culture that becomes the enabling environment that links motivation to background risk factors. In this context, robbery tends to arise when potential offenders perceive that they have the need for immediate cash. But why must robbery become the occupational activity of choice to satisfy the perceived financial need? Given the fact that the population most involved in robbery is poorly prepared for profitable employment and has few marketable skills, the type of legitimate employment that may be available does not provide the amount of instant cash that a street lifestyle demands, according to Jacobs and Wright. Hence, for this population legitimate employment is not a viable option. Moreover, working in a real job with its inherent rules and time requirements impedes the potential robber's style of living and compromises the independence a street life entails. In these circumstances, robbery becomes a crime that offers unique possibilities as an alternative to legitimate employment. With its minimal need for skill and the likelihood of instant cash on demand, robbery becomes the illicit analogue to the ubiquitous automated teller machines (ATM). This does not imply that certain types of robbery do not require planning and organizational skills (e.g., sophisticated bank or jewel robberies), but for the common and most prevalent robberies such skills are not a requisite. Therefore, robbery is a job opportunity, albeit an illegitimate one.

There is another feature of robbery that makes it a preferred crime occupation for some. This is a feature that has taken on a mythic quality in the folklore depiction of the heroic robber and is a point of reference for the street robber. Robbery is an offense where the perpetrator directly confronts his or her target, in contrast to other offenses such as ordinary thefts or burglary where the victim is not necessarily present. Indeed, if the victim of a burglary is at home or on the premises and is confronted, the offense is considered

to be a robbery in legal terms; it is deemed a more serious offense of the law because of its confrontational nature. Yet, it is precisely this distinction of victim confrontation that is often used by those involved in robbery in an exculpatory fashion to indicate that their crime was "honest" because there is no fraud or guise in its commission. (Einstadter, 1969). It is also this confrontational feature of robbery that has generated the myth of the independent, carefree, and individualistic robber glorified in western and gangster films and novels. Referring to a study by Shover and Honaker (1992), Jacobs and Wright (1999) conclude that conspicuous display of independence "is a bedrock value on which street-corner culture rests."

A number of studies from the past have made it clear that robbery is not a unitary form of criminal behavior. De Baun (1950) concentrated on the gang nature of robbery. An early study by McClintock and Gibson (1961) developed a typology of robberies in London, England, by investigating the various types of robbery that occurred between 1950 and 1960. The focus was on incidents from which the authors made inferences concerning the pattern of robberies. Five types of robberies were identified: (1) robbery of persons who in the course of their employment had responsibility for large amounts of money, (2) robbery that was in the form of a sudden attack in a public area (e.g., mugging), (3) robbery committed in a private setting (e.g., a residence), (4) robbery of a person with whom the offender had a short relationship, and (5) robbery of a victim with whom the offender has had an association over time (e.g., friend or colleague). Normandeau (1968) supported this typology in a study in Philadelphia, for the years 1960 and 1966. (For a comparison between the U.S. and England and Wales, see Langan and Farrington, 1998.)

Conklin (1972) developed a typology of robbers on the basis of interviews with imprisoned robbers in Massachusetts prisons. He distinguished four types of robbers on the basis of style and motivation. The *professional* plans his robberies for financial gain to support a hedonistic lifestyle. The *opportunist* uses robbery for extra pocket money and selects victims who may not have much money on their person. The *addict* robber, though preferring other types of theft, is an occasional robber who gains money to support a drug habit. Lastly, the *alcoholic* robber, usually in an intoxicated state, robs a victim sometimes subsequent to an assault. Einstadter (1969) studied armed robbers who engaged in robbery on a career basis and found the organization of robbery groups to differ significantly from earlier studies of professional thieves. Other studies by De Baun (1950), Roebuck (1967), and Letkeman (1973) tended to see the diverse and occupational nature of robbery. Cook (1983) goes too far as to suggest that most street "robbers" are in fact crime "generalists," who opportunistically commit other crimes (especially drug sales and burglary).

A recent review of research by Gabor et al. (1987) suggests that robbery has changed from a career or a profession becoming a more unplanned, careless, and even random event (see Camp, 1967; Feeney and Weir, 1975; Petersilia, Greenwood and Lavin, 1977; Katz, 1991). Given this finding, one could surmise that robbery may be impulsive, a form of *temporary work* to procure cash for what they perceive as an immediate need.

A significant portion of robbery is related to the illegal drug market. Robberies are often committed to raise finances for the maintenance of a drug habit, but those who are the suppliers and sellers of drugs are not immune from being robbed. Research suggests that these types of robberies are common and present special problems to the offender involving retaliation by the victim (Jacobs, Topalli, and Wright, 2000). Nevertheless, drug dealers are attractive targets despite the risk, as Wright and Decker (1997) learned from the active robbers they studied. Robbing drug dealers offers the double advantage of gaining instant cash and free drugs to feed drug habits. Moreover, the authors note that robberies against victims who are themselves criminal are rarely reported and thus do not show up in official crime statistical reports. However, they are important because they contribute to the violent reputations certain high crime neighborhoods receive (Wright and Decker, 2000) and affect the strategies employed to prevent robberies.

Most street robberies involve victims unknown to the robber along with merchants (e.g., liquor stores, convenience stores, gas stations) from whom the robber may have bought items in the past. A relatively newly recognized form of robbery, however, has been given the title of *acquaintance robbery*. According to Felson et al., (2000), acquaintance robbery involves people who know each other in some fashion and consists of more than a third of the robberies reported in the U.S. National Crime Victimization Survey (NCVS) during the years 1992–1995. Those most vulnerable to acquaintance robbery were young, single, poor, and African American. These are opportunistic robberies where the robber may have information on whether the victim is carrying cash or other items of interest; sometimes these robberies are also carried out for purposes of revenge. In these kinds of robberies the offender relies on the hesitancy of victims to report the incident to the police.

As to who commits robbery, there is a consensus among all those who have studied the matter that young males dominate as the perpetrators (Cook, 1983). For example 90.1% of the arrests for robbery in 1997 were male, however, females who commit robbery mostly do so in partnership with men. However, research that focuses more clearly on female involvement in robbery specifically and violent crime in general is only of recent origin (Miller, 2000; Maher, 1997; West and Zimmerman, 1987). Women's involvement in violent crime has been portrayed as a defensive response to male aggression, although as Miller points out, not all women's street violence can be considered as resistance to male oppression. Women caught up in the street culture may rob for similar reasons as their male counterparts, but at a lesser rate. Robbery is for them the same instrumental vehicle for quick cash and for the acquisition of items such as jewelry and other objects that may have "flash" value in building social status in the culture of the street.

Fear of possible harm is the hallmark of robbery and is the element that the robber relies upon in the commission of the crime. Those who make robbery their occupation must rely on their ability to instill this fear whether or not a weapon is used.

Research regarding robbery has in recent years become more sophisticated and more reliable in the sense that researchers have relied less on imprisoned populations to gather data but have gone "where the action is" on the streets of inner cities. This type of ethnographic research is difficult, time consuming, and often dangerous. It relies on informants and demands the establishment of utmost trust between the researcher and the subjects of the research. The research often poses ethical dilemmas because the subjects of the research may still be extensively involved in criminal activity. How these dilemmas are resolved may have important consequences for the outcome of the studies and the researchers themselves.

It is clear that robbery will not vanish as form of criminal activity. As Wright and Decker conclude from their research, preventing or reducing the scope of robbery is a daunting task.

The street culture is not removed from the larger pervasive consumer culture in which we are all enmeshed and cajoled by omnipresent media assaults to acquire all types of goods. The culture's emphasis on materialistic acquisition and its equating of material possession and wealth with personal worth is not lost to those on the street. Indeed, the *street* is an extreme perverse reflection of these values, expressed in robbery. The street does offer for some an opportunity for a life on the margin of extreme individuality based on noncommitment, an ability to demonstrate raw power, and a chance to gain the cash to support the lifestyle the street offers.

As an antidote to street culture, Wright and Decker (1997) suggest job creation as an important long-term strategy, although they admit that practicing robbers may not be willing to abandon the street lifestyle they find attractive. Even if legitimate employment were available, robbers do not make the most reliable employees. In addition, the type of minimum wage jobs that would fit the lack of skills most robbers have are insufficient inducement for behavioral change.

These researchers also point out that as a practical matter, perhaps a strategy that centers on situational change such as creating an increasingly cashless society would strike at the robber's most fundamental desire, the ready availability of fast cash. In some ways society seems to be heading in that direction. It still remains, however, that the structural conditions that create the milieu that germinates the street culture out of which the robber and robbery as alternative occupation arise must, in the long term, be addressed creatively.

WERNER J. EINSTADTER

## References and Further Reading

Camp, G. 1967. *Nothing to Lose: A Study of Bank Robbery in America,* Ann Arbor, MI, University Microfilms.

Conklin, J.E. 1972. *Robbery and the Criminal Justice System,* Philadelphia, PA, B. Lippincott Company.

Cook, P.J. 1983. *Robbery in the United States: An Analysis of Recent Trends and Patterns,* U.S. Department of Justice. National Institute of Justice.

De Baun, E. 1950. The Heist: The Theory and Practice of Armed Robbery, *Harpers* 200.

Einstadter, W.J. 1969. The social organization of armed robbery, *Social Problems,* 17.

Einstadter, W.J. 1978. Robbery and outlawry on the U.S. frontier, 1863–1890: A reexamination, in Inciardi, J.A. and Pottieger, A.E., Eds., *Violent Crime, Historical and contemporary issues,* Beverly Hills, CA, Sage.

Feeney, F. and Weir, A. 1975. The Prevention and control of armed robbery, *Criminology,* 13.

Gabor, T., Baril, M., Cusson, M., Elie, D., LeBlanc, M. and Normendeau, A. 1987. *Armed Robbery: Cops, Robbers, and Victims, Springfield,* IL, Charles C. Thomas.

Hobsbawm, E.J. 1959. *Primitive Rebels: Studies in Archaic Forms of Social Movement in the 19th and 20th Centuries,* Manchester, U.K., Manchester University Press.

Hobsbawm, E.J. 1969. *Bandits,* Hardmondsworth, U.K., Penguin.

Jacobs, B.A., Topalli, V. and Wright, R. 2000. Managing retaliation: Drug robbery and informal sanction threats, *Criminology,* 38.

Jacobs, B.A. and Wright, R. 1999. Stick-up, Street Culture, and Offender Motivation, *Criminology,* 37.

Katz, J. 1991. The motivation of the persistent robber, in Tonry, M., Ed., *Crime and Justice: A review of Research,* Chicago, IL, University of Chicago Press.

Langan, P.A. and David, P.F. 1998. *Crime and Justice in the U.S. and England and Wales, 1981–96,* U.S. Department of Justice, Bureau of Justice Statistics.

Letkemann, P. 1973. *Crime as Work,* Englewood Cliffs, Prentice Hall.

Maher, L. 1997. *Sexed Work: Gender, Race and Resistance in a Brooklyn Drug Market,* Oxford, Clarendon Press.

McClintock, F.H. and Gibson, E. 1961. *Robbery in London,* London, Macmillan.

Miller, Jody 1998. Up it up: Gender and the accomplishment of street robbery, *Criminology,* 36.

Normendeau, A. 1968. *Trends and Patterns in Crimes of Robbery in Philadelphia,* Philadelphia, PA, University of Pennsylvania.

Petersilia, J., Greenwood, P.W. and Lavin, M. 1977. *Criminal Careers of Habitual Felons,* Santa Monica, CA, Rand.

Roebuck, J.B. 1967. *Criminal Typology,* Springfield, IL, Charles C. Thomas.

Shover, N. and Honaker, D. 1992. The Socially-bounded decision making of persistent property offenders, *Howard Journal of Criminal Justice,* 31.

U.S. Department of Justice 1998. Bureau of Justice Statistics, Sourcebook of Criminal Justice Statistics.

West, C. and Zimmerman, D.H. 1987. Doing gender, *Gender and Society,* 1.

Wright, R.T. and Decker, S.H. 1997. *Armed Robbery in Action: Stickups and Street Culture,* Boston, MA, Northeastern University Press.

Zirker, M.R., Ed. 1988. An Enquiry into the causes of the late increase of robbers and related writings, *The Wesleyan Edition of the Works of Henry Fielding,* Middletown, CT, Wesleyan University Press.

*See also* **Bank Robbery; Criminal Careers or Chronic Offenders; Robbery: Extent and Correlates; Robbery: Law**

---

# Robbery: Extent and Correlates

---

Robbery is the taking or attempting to take anything of value from the care, custody, or control of someone by force or by threat of force or violence. If a weapon is used, the offense is termed "armed robbery" and is usually considered by the police and courts to be more serious than robbery without a weapon. Robbery is a unique crime because it is at once a violent crime *and* a property crime. It involves not only the loss of property but also the threat or use of violence. Robbery occurs more frequently than either rape or homicide.

Robberies occur in varied settings. Environmental criminologists typically find a strong association between robbery and places conducive to low informal social control. Robberies may occur on the street, in the home, in a park, on public transportation, or in a business such as a bank, store, hotel, gas station, or restaurant. Places where informal social control is low and where cash is readily available, such as 24-hour convenience stores, video stores, and automatic tellers (ATMs), are attractive targets for robbers (see Duffala, 1976). When placed in or near to residential areas, research has shown that these places may serve as "magnets" for crime; levels of other types of crime can rise in neighborhoods were a convenience store is located, for example.

Environmental design has played a significant role in strategies to reduce robbery. Criminologists have worked with city planners and others to make infrastructures safe from interpersonal predatory crimes such as robbery. Computer technologies such as GIS (geographic information systems) have made it easier to identify actual and potential robbery "hot spots," and how they are associated with streets, highways, and neighborhoods. At the micro-level, target hardening measures such as increased lighting, drop boxes, and other security measures have lowered the incidence of robberies in some locations.

Although criminologists are well aware of the predatory nature of robbery, most of their attention has been paid to the robbery of ostensibly "innocent" victims: law-abiding citizens who are victimized during the routine transactions of their daily lives. Conversely, little attention has been paid to victimization of offenders, specifically the robbery of street criminals by other criminals. One reason for this is that offenders who are robbed by fellow offenders are unlikely to report the crime to the police. By some estimates, the robbery of criminals exceeds that of law-abiders. Jacobs' (2000) ethnography of drug robbery provides an illuminating account of this oft-neglected area. This study shows the inherent irrationality of this type of robbery: why increase the chance of being killed merely to reduce the chance of arrest? Of course, drug robbers do not rob other criminals to reduce the chance of arrest; they rob other offenders because they offer attractive, potentially lucrative targets.

The official extent of robbery, like that of any other major crime, is reported to the public using two main sources—crimes known to the police, sometimes referred to as "official" data, and victimization data, generally regarded as "unofficial" data because it is recorded beyond the auspices of law enforcement by private or pubic agencies. Robberies known to the police are reported to the Federal Bureau of Investigation (FBI), and summarized in the Bureau's annual Uniform Crime Reports (UCR). Robbery is included in the UCR as a Part 1 offense. According to the Federal Bureau of Investigation's UCR, there were 422,921 robberies in the U.S. in 2001, or approximately 148.5 robberies per 100,000 residents.

In 1999, there were 388,588 reported robberies in the U.S., according to law enforcement agencies participating in the UCR, as well as selected agencies contributing data to the "enhanced UCR" known as the National Incident-Based Reporting System, or NIBRS. Based on combined UCR/NIBRS data, the robbery rate in the U.S. in 1999 was 150.2 per 100,000 residents.

According to the UCR, in 1999, 171,504 robberies occurred on highways. Commercial establishments (other than convenience stores) accounted for 47,570 robberies. Residences were robbed 43,203 times. Convenience stores (20,917), gas stations (8229), and banks (6717), traditionally thought of as the most likely targets of robbery, are the fourth, fifth, and sixth most common locations for robbery, respectively. Although NIBRS agencies reported similar findings for highways and residences, they reported parking lots as the third most common target of robbery. Convenience stores and gas stations were just behind parking lots in terms of common robbery locations.

Robbery, by definition, involves a larceny component. NIBRS data provides a rich source of information on the nature of stolen property in robberies because it provides information on every offense committed, thus it is not handicapped by the "hierarchy rule" (where only the most serious felony is reported) that plagues the UCR. Moreover, it is commonly understood that robbery is frequently combined with other crimes, including other offenses that involve stolen property. NIBRS reveals that burglary and kidnapping are the most common offenses that involve stolen property that were combined with robbery in 1999. Other offenses involving stolen property that were combined with robbery include motor vehicle theft, larceny, extortion, fraud, or some combination of these.

According to NIBRS, money is the most commonly stolen property associated with robbery. Jewelry, precious metals, and automobiles are also frequently connected to robbery. Other frequently stolen items associated with robbery include clothing and furs, purses and wallets, bicycles, and electronic goods, including televisions, radios, VCRs, and stereo equipment.

Robberies frequently involve the use, or threatened use, of a weapon. According to the UCR (1999), firearms are the most popular choice in robberies involving weapons. NIBRS data specifies the types of firearm used in robberies. The firearm of choice for most robbers is the handgun. Using NIBRS data, of 7788 robberies involving firearms in 1999, 5765 involved handguns.

Strong-armed robberies, where the robber uses brute physical force, is the next most likely type of robbery with a weapon, followed by knives, according to UCR data. Other weapons, according to NIBRS, are blunt objects, motor vehicles, and drug intoxication or asphyxiation.

The Federal Bureau of Investigation also reports the following statistics:

- In1999, one robbery occurred every minute in the U.S.
- The national loss because of robberies was an estimated $463 million in 1999. According to the Federal Bureau of Investigation, however, the impact of this violent crime on its victims cannot be measured in terms of monetary loss alone. (*Crime in the United States 1999*. Washington, DC: Federal Bureau of Investigation, 2000)
- In 1999, 40% of all robberies were committed with firearms. (*Crime in the U.S. 1999*. Washington, DC: Federal Bureau of Investigation, 2000)
- In 1999, 74% of male victims of robbery and 42% of female victims of robbery stated that the robber was a stranger. (*Criminal Victimization in the United States 1999*. Washington, DC: Bureau of Justice Statistics, 2000)
- In 1999, 48% of all robbery offenses were committed on streets and highways, 24% occurred in commercial establishments, and 12% occurred at residences. (*Crime in the United States 1999*. Washington, DC: Federal Bureau of Investigation, 2000)
- Victims sustain some physical injury in 32% of all robberies. (*Criminal Victimization in the United States 1994*. Washington, DC: Bureau of Justice Statistics, 1997)

As for the demographic correlates of robbery, offenders and victims are generally young males. According to NIBRS data, approximately 60% of robbery offenders are Black males. Conversely, over 40% of all robbery victims are White males. Victims and offenders tend to be in their late teens to early 20s.

Because of the interpersonal nature of robbery (as opposed to burglary), robbery victims often feel total and immediate loss of control. Unlike victims of rape or other personal assaults, robbery victims seldom know their assailants. Victims know their robbers in only about 26% of robberies. Of all violent crimes, robbery is the most likely to be committed by more than one offender. When a weapon is involved, the sense of helplessness and the fear of death is amplified and that can lead to both short-term and long-term crisis reactions.

The National Crime Victimization Survey (NCVS) is the nation's primary source of information on criminal victimization. Each year, data are obtained from a nationally representative sample of roughly 45,000 households comprising more than 94,000 persons on the frequency, characteristics, and consequences of criminal victimization in the U.S. The survey fully reports the likelihood of victimization by rape, sexual assault, robbery, assault, theft, household burglary, and motor vehicle theft for the population as a whole as well as for segments of the population such as women, the elderly, members of various racial groups, city dwellers, or other groups. The NCVS provides the largest national forum for victims to describe the impact of crime and characteristics of violent offenders.

KEVIN M. BRYANT

## References and Further Reading

Duffala, D.C., 1976. Convenience stores, armed robbery, and physical environmental features, *American Behavioral Scientist,* 20, 239–240.

Felson, M., 1998. *Crime and Everyday Life,* Thousand Oaks, CA, Pine Forge Press.

Flagg, D., 1985. *Convenience store robberies: An intervention strategy by the City of Gainesville, Florida* (Unpublished Report).

Gabor, T., Baril, M., Cusson, M., Elie, D., LeBlanc, M. and Normandeau, A., 1987. *Armed Robbery,* Springfield, IL, Charles C. Thomas.

Jacobs, B.A., 2000. *Robbing Drug Dealers: Violence Beyond the Law,* Aldine de Gruyter.

U.S. Department of Justice (Several Years). *Criminal Victimization in the United States,* Washington, DC, U.S. Government printing office.

U.S. Department of Justice (Several Years*). Crime in the United States,* Uniform Crime Reports, Washington, DC, U.S. Government Printing Office.

*See also* **Robbery as an Occupation; Robbery: The Law**

# Robbery: The Law

According to the Uniform Crime Report (UCR), issued annually by the Federal Bureau of Investigation (FBI), the criminal offense of robbery is described as "the taking or attempting to take anything of value from the care, custody, or control of a person or persons by force or threat of force; includes commercial establishments and carjackings, armed or unarmed." In reality this often translates to a person thrusting a weapon into someone's face, screaming obscenities, threatening to kill them if they don't surrender their cash or possessions. Robbery is the most violent interpersonal crime suffered by the majority of crime victims. It is a situation earmarked both by its suddenness and potential for injury, normally occurring outside the presumed safety of one's home. Robberies can occur at work, on the street, in parking lots, and schoolyards— anyplace where face-to-face confrontations are possible. The crime of robbery has several typologies other than the accepted "gimme your money" at gunpoint: purse-snatchings, muggings, car-jackings, and strong-arm "thefts"; all involve the taking of another person's property by force.

The crime of robbery is often used interchangeably with the crimes of theft and extortion, but the three crime types are distinct. Theft is the taking of a physical object, usually without the owner's knowledge or permission, with no force involved (shoplifting, pick pocketing, etc.). Extortion is obtaining something of value from one party by another under the threat, or infliction, of harm. However, extortive efforts can concern abstract or immovable rewards that is, reputation, outcome of sporting events, awarding of contracts, and ownership in businesses or buildings. Also, robberies involve the taking of a physical object at the time of the robbery whereas extortion can concern future rewards. Extortion can also involve payments for the prevention of violence, whereas robberies use present violence to facilitate the crime at hand (theoretically reducing resistance).

Robberies range in economic value from the Great Train Robbery of 1963, with $3 million being taken, to the late night employee being robbed of bus fare while waiting for public transportation. The perpetrators can be as prolific as John Dillinger or Billy the Kid; or as nondescript as the neighborhood drug addict. The incident may be front-page headlines news if the victim is of social rank or status; or buried in the rear of the paper if the victim is an ordinary non-newsworthy person. The crime of robbery and its impact on policing and judicial systems has long been a problem. Fielding's (1751) treatise on robbery and other early writings have studied the cause, impact, and possible deterrence of robberies. Many of the criminals on the early FBI's Most Wanted List were bank robbers. According to FBI calculations a robbery occurs once every 1.3 minutes, with 407,842 robberies committed in the year 2000. Additionally 8% of that year's 15,517 homicides involved robberies. The number of annually reported robberies to the FBI has surpassed 400,000 every year since 1974. The number of robberies calculated by national victimization studies is much higher, with 810,000 robberies reported in 1999. For many people, being the victim of an armed robbery is their first involvement in a crime against person. For those and others it is their first experience with a potential life-or-death situation; for some others who have been victims of multiple robberies, the police are not even contacted. Because of both the physical and psychological damages suffered, many armed robbery victims display symptoms of anger, distrust, and generalized depression subsequent to the robbery incident; with some victims altering their daily lifestyle in significant ways for months after the incident. The public concern has been so great that a psychological diagnostic category has been created: harpaxophobia, described as the fear of crime victimization, specifically robbery. Because of the damages caused by the crime of robbery, all 50 states, the federal government, and other legislated political subdivisions have enacted laws concerning the crime of robbery, both in definition and penalty.

Individual jurisdictions have criminal statutes that identify the crime of robbery from different perspectives: presence of a weapon, number of victims, number of perpetrators, level of injury inflicted, location of offense, and original intent. Robbery is considered by many to be a hybrid crime—a crime against property while being a crime against person (as noted by the fact that some states include robbery statutes in the property crimes codes whereas others place robbery statutes in the crimes against person codes). Similarly, robbery charges can be combined with other criminal statutes: assault, battery, extortion, kidnapping, and homicide. However, most states generally utilize two subclassifications of robberies: armed and unarmed, with additional delineated categories.

Armed (often referred to as aggravated) robbery statutes contain references to either the display or use of a deadly weapon. In most jurisdictions the term "weapon" is not specifically identified as the mode of weapon used is only limited to an item's availability and its usage by a potential offender. Weapons used in the past have included: guns, sharp objects (knives, razors, broken bottles, scalpels), blunt objects (clubs, bats, pipes, table legs, golf clubs), hypodermic needles, caustic substances, HIV contaminated fluids, fire, explosive devices, and electrical devices (stun guns, cattle prods). It is the assumption of the statute, as well as the belief of the person being robbed, that the item used could inflict serious if not deadly harm.

Some statutes apply aggravated robbery statutes based not only on weapon usage but also upon the status of the victim, that is, over 65 years of age or disabled, as noted in Texas statutes, whereas in some statutes the location is a deciding factor. In Florida statutes, a home-invasion robbery is classified as a "felony of the first degree," the same as an armed robbery in which a deadly weapon is used.

In many jurisdictions the implication that a deadly weapon is present, that is, a hand under a shirt, alleged explosive device, container labeled contaminated fluids or caustic liquids, is treated the same as if the "weapon" was real—the fear of serious or deadly harm the victim perceived, as created by the offender's action, was real to the victim even though the weapon was not capable of inflicting that harm.

Some armed robbery crime types have been codified into separate criminal statutes, specifically carjacking. Several states, as well as the federal government, have enacted criminal legislation specifically for the crime of carjacking—an armed robbery committed against the owner or driver of a vehicle. Often specific types of commercial operations have been granted special status that is, bank robbery and postal office robberies have specific criminal codes in federal laws, as do pharmacies under the Alabama criminal code.

In the majority of criminal codes the crime of armed (aggravated) robbery is considered the most serious of robbery offenses and carries more stringent penalties, ranging as high as 99 years. Within the codes further delineation would involve robberies with fatal injuries (most likely to be prosecuted as homicides), robberies with serious injuries, robberies with minor injuries, and robberies with no physical injuries (psychological injuries are generally not considered—other than in the sentencing phase). Within the criminal statutes, the degree or seriousness of the charges filed will take into consideration the totality of circumstances concerning the injuries suffered by the victim(s).

Additionally, in states where permissible, that is, California and Louisiana among others, the usage of "multiple billing" laws are often associated with robbery convictions. These specific statutes allow for enhanced incarceration periods for repeat offenders, creating sentences of several hundred years for some robbery offenders with prior robbery convictions. Louisiana specifically allows for "triple billing," in which prosecutors can ask for sentences triple the length of what a first offender could receive. The length of sentences may also be impacted by the number of victims, not necessarily related to statutes increasing penalties for more than one victim; but because of the fact the each victim is a separate count of robbery. If four persons are held at gunpoint and relieved of their property, four counts of robbery have occurred even though the incidents took place at the same place at the same time. The four victims could be a combination of employees and customers, if the robbery took place at a retail location—but each person who was relieved of money, property, or asked to surrender same is generally considered to be a separate robbery count.

As not all robbery attempts are successful most states also employ attempted armed robbery statutes. These statutes cover any actions up to the completion of an armed robbery. The offender may have fled before completion of the act, the victim may have fled or in some manner thwarted the robbery, or the robbery was interrupted as part of a police operation (sting, robbery decoy unit, or fortuitous police patrol). The lack of monetary gain does not generally impact the crime classification; if a victim has no money to surrender a robbery still took place. Therefore any robbery act that was not consummated is eligible to be classified as an attempted robbery, and prosecuted accordingly. The presence of attempted robbery statutes also allow for plea bargaining arrangements to occur.

Simple robbery statutes generally refer to robbery incidents in which no serious or deadly threat was present or intimidated. Robberies of this type are often identified by less "criminal" sounding names, including mugging, strong-arm theft, purse-snatching, and till-tapping. These robbery types imply a property crime rather than a crime against person. However, the intent of the crime is the usage of some force or threat of force to facilitate the commission of the crime. Some state laws, such as those in Montana, presume that the original crime was a theft that accelerated to the level of a robbery. Other states utilize the concept that the underlying was a robbery, with the intent to utilize force as part of the criminal calculus process. The threat of force or force requirement applies to both paradigms, as well as to actions before, during, or after the robbery. Violence committed by an offender affecting their escape is sufficient enough to meet the force requirement equally as if the violence occurred during the commission of the robbery. Additionally, self-defense by an offender is not accepted as a defense when force is used.

The simple robbery crime of mugging often refers to the robbery of individual(s) by another individual, not necessarily armed but who uses the threat of force to complete the robbery attempt. Another phrasing for this robbery typology is "strong-arm," meant to convey that although physical force was used, it was in the form of punches and kicks—no "weapon" was present other than the body of the offender. Various jurisdictions have varying interpretations on what constitutes physical force. In New Orleans, Louisiana, robbery convictions have been secured against persons who, after declined money from panhandling, would offer to shake the person's hand as a sign of no "hard" feelings, and would proceed to forcibly squeeze the person's hand until they surrendered some money. Some jurisdictions utilize the phrases "till-tapping" or "snatching," often referring to criminal incidents in which offenders grab money from a cashier or cash register. If there is any touching (pushing away or grabbing the hand of the victim) or threat of physical violence the threshold for robbery has been breached. If the incident involved grabbing money with no physical interaction or threat of same the robbery threshold was not crossed. Some jurisdictions, Baton Rouge, Louisiana, for example, will charge property offenders who violate spatial boundaries with robbery. Specifically, persons have entered convenience stores and have proceeded to the area behind the counter and informed the cashier that they were committing a theft (of cigarette cartons) not a robbery and that they meant no harm to the cashier. The police and prosecutors have determined that the entry into the secured area produced a type of physical intimidation and therefore qualified as robbery. Simple robbery charges generally carry less severe penalties that armed robbery charges, with some jurisdictions granting intensive probation in some cases.

PATRICK D. WALSH

## References and Further Reading

Calder, J. and Bauer, J. 1992. Convenience store robberies: Security measures and store robbery incidents, *Journal of Criminal Justice,* 20, 553–566.

Conklin, J. 1972. *Robbery and the Criminal Justice System,* New York, Lippincott.

Cook, P., *Robbery in the United States: An Analysis of Recent Trends and Patterns,* Washington, DC, National Institute of Justice.

Gabor, T., Baril, M., Cusson, M., Elie, D., Leblanc, M. and Normandeau, 1987. *Armed Robbery: Cops, Robbers, and Victims*, Springfield, Illinois: Charles Thomas.

Luckenbill, D. 1980. Patterns of force in robbery, *Deviant Behavior,* 1, 361–378.

Matthews, R. 2002. *Armed Robbery,* Portland, Oregon, Willan Publishing.

Petersilia, J. 1994. Violent crime and violent criminals: The response of the justice system, in Costanzo, M. and Oskamp, S., Eds., *Violence and the Law,* Thousand Oaks, CA, Sage.

Wright, R. and Decker, S., *Armed Robbers in Action*: *Stick Ups and Street Culture,* Boston, MA, Northeastern University Press.

*See also* **Robbery as an Occupation; Robbery: Extent and Correlates**

# Roe v. Wade *See* **Abortion**

# Routine Activities Theory

One of the most useful theoretical approaches to understanding criminal victimization and offending patterns available today is routine activities (lifestyle) theory. Originally put forth by Lawrence Cohen and Marcus Felson in 1979, routine activities theory is today one of the most influential and policy-relevant theories for explaining the dynamics of criminal events, patterns in criminal victimization, and predictions of victimization risks or likelihood. Routine activities theory argues that there must be three elements of a situation present for any crime to occur: potential offenders (individuals seeking, able, or willing to commit offenses), suitable targets (individuals or property that are vulnerable or available) and incapable, unwilling, or absent guardians (a lack of protection or supervision or individuals or devices unable to ward off an offender).

Routine activities theory is based on two central propositions: First, routine activities create criminal opportunity structures by increasing the frequency and intensity of contacts between motivated or potential offenders and suitable targets. Second, the subjective value of a target and accompanying means of guardianship (or lack thereof) determine the choice of a particular victim by an offender. Routine activities theory differs from most other criminological theories in that it essentially disregards the motivations or reasons for crime to be committed and it provides primary emphasis on explaining victimization rather than offending behavior.

Based on the three core concepts then, a person may be willing to commit crime given sufficient opportunity, but if that opportunity never comes, the crime will not occur. Opportunities may not come for several reasons. It may be that the potential offender does not find any person sufficiently vulnerable, or property sufficiently valuable to merit interest. Also possible is the circumstance of finding a suitable target, but one that is too well guarded to merit an attempt. As such, both structural aspects of specific environmental contexts (where one lives and works, and the conditions and structures that are present in those locations that may increase the number of potential offenders and the types of guardianship that is available in the general area) and individual choices (where one goes, what one does, with whom one is, and any self-protective measures one takes to increase or decrease their vulnerability or suitability as a target) are important for understanding the occurrence of criminal events (Miethe and Meier, 1990; Mustaine and Tewksbury, 1997a). Routine activities theory is an extension of Opportunity theory, adding spatial and temporal features to the opportunity parameters.

A number of factors have been correlated with increased likelihood of criminal victimization. However, one of the primary weaknesses with this type of criminological research on victimization is that it relies upon inferences drawn from indirect indicators of lifestyle (see Mustaine and Tewksbury, 1997a). Although some research is available using specific measures, generalizable findings that provide direct, policy-relevant implications based on specific measures of risk factors remain scarce. Researchers have identified five major categories of risk factors that are important influences on the occurrence of criminal events. What we know about these five categories of risks are summarized below.

## Lifestyle Factors that Correlate with Victimization

There are five important components of individuals' lifestyles revealed in the research that contribute to opportunities for, and likelihood of, criminal victimization. Although each of these categories of factors has important influences on crime, it is the combination of these factors, as indications of "lifestyle," that may best explain criminal victimization.

### Demographics

Perhaps the most well established risk factors for criminal victimization are demographic factors. For decades, research has consistently shown that victimization rates are highest for men, adolescents, and young adults, African Americans, those who have never been married, and persons who live in central cities.

Routine activities theory scholars often rely on these types of variables as indicators of lifestyle activities. For example, research usually finds that married individuals are less likely to be victimized than single people. The explanation for this is that single persons usually live lifestyles that take them out of the home, especially at night, to places that attract potential offenders, such as bars or nightclubs. However, the validity of these types of conclusions drawn from such research must be questioned. Presuming what people do and where they do these things based on demographic characteristics provides, at best, weak links to policy and practice. Although knowing the personal characteristics of criminal victims is useful, it may not be as useful as understanding their actual lifestyle activities. Therefore, demographic variables should be included in research, but should not be relied on exclusively.

### Alcohol and Drug Use

The role of alcohol and illicit drugs in crime is among the most well known of all criminological research findings. Across all types of settings, alcohol and other drugs are strongly related to violence. Especially when looking at young victims (and offenders), alcohol is overwhelmingly associated with violence and criminality. Routine activities theory suggests that this relationship can be explained in several ways. First, since alcohol is so closely associated with criminal behavior, engaging in activities, or frequenting places where alcohol is present would increase one's exposure to potential offenders. Further, drinking alcohol may reduce one's ability to protect himself and his belongings.

### Economic Status

Although crime affects all segments of society, and no persons or parts of society are immune to crime, it remains that crime is disproportionately found among lower socioeconomic segments of communities. Although employed persons are more likely to be crime victims, this may be because of increased exposure to potential offenders because they must leave the home every weekday. However, unemployed persons who spend time in public are more likely to be victimized than individuals who remain in their homes. Routine activities theory suggests that unemployed persons are more likely to be victimized because they have characteristics (or at least one characteristic) in common with many motivated offenders. Simply stated, both unemployed persons and many motivated offenders lack sufficient activities to occupy their time and also lack a ready pool of financial and material resources.

### Social Activities

As direct indicators of lifestyle, social activities have significant influences on victimization risks. As addressed, alcohol and other drugs have a clear relationship with crime. Although it is also important to look at additional social activities for possible relationships with victimization, research has not done so very often. Some research, however, does suggest that some relatively common social activities (such as going to shopping malls, eating out frequently, participating in school-related clubs and organizations, and going to a gym or playing team sports) are related to criminal victimization. In summary, what is known about social activities and victimization is that "an active lifestyle thus appears to influence victimization risk by increasing exposure to potential offenders in a context where guardianship is low" (Sampson, 1987, 331). The types of social activities in which an individual engages, and where and with whom they do so are clearly related to victimization risks.

### Community Structural Variables

In general, once someone leaves the home his or her risks of being a victim of crime increase. When leaving the home individuals will encounter a variety of things in their community, some of which may attract potential offenders. For example, the research has shown that community aspects such as the appearance of a neighborhood or neighbor incivility have an effect on property crime and some forms of violent crimes. Also, neighborhoods with businesses that attract potential offenders have higher rates of crime and criminal offenders. For example, the presence of bars or taverns in a community has been related to increased rates of crimes, as are high schools, fast food restaurants, public parks, and liquor stores. These are places where potential offenders gather and where guardianship may be low (or absent). Also, alcohol is often present, and the frequent coming and going of people may also increase the chances of crime happening.

Individuals' perceptions of community safety and quality of life are also important factors in crime. For example, property crime victimizations are more common in communities where residents perceive "too much crime" and high levels of noise. Clearly, there is a relationship between a perception of crime in one's community and the likelihood of being a victim of crime.

Characteristics of one's home life may influence victimization risks, especially for women. When women are victimized, it is most often by someone they know or with whom they have a close relationship. Finally, the amount of time a home is left unattended, as well as an appearance of someone being home, can also influence property crime that takes place there.

## Research Difficulties and Routine Activities Theory

Numerous researchers argue that although routine activities theory is important, it is in need of refinements if it is to become more valuable for explaining crime. Two general areas of difficulties have been identified in routine activities theory research. First, the issues of where crimes occur (their "domains") have received very little attention from routine activities theory researchers. Second, the way researchers define and measure activities or routines has been criticized for being less than precise. Although many researchers and theorists recognize these problems, to date only limited progress has been made in addressing these two major forms of difficulties.

### Domain-Based Research

One of the clearest problems with routine activities theory is the need to include consideration of where crimes actually occur. This is also one of the great promises of routine activities theory. Rather than simply trying to explain crime in a general way, this theory allows a more direct focus on identifying criminal behavior patterns within specific settings. For example, behaviors we engage in while at leisure are different than activities we engage in at home. Nonetheless, in each of these locations there are behaviors that are associated with higher levels of victimization. Routine activities theory can look both at differences in the sources and patterns of victimization across different domains (school, work, home, leisure settings) or between characteristics of individuals within a particular domain.

Domain-specific research is a significantly underdeveloped area of routine activities theory. However, starting in the late 1980s researchers have applied routine activities theory to crimes in specific settings. What has been seen is that certain types of crimes have similar types of offenders, victims, and patterns in all types of settings, whereas other types of crimes have different participants and relationships that are domain specific. For instance, both assault and drug offenders are similar across individuals involved and settings, whereas offenses such as sexual assault and work-related theft are domain-specific.

In support of the need for domain-based research, Lynch (1987) has argued that focusing on domains can actually provide greater ease and efficiency in research. By highlighting only one specific domain, it may be possible to provide more complete and precise definitions and measurements of activities within that domain. Here is where some of the greatest weaknesses in routine activities theory are found. Research has consistently failed to account for: (1) variations in persons and activities within specific domains, and (2) the movement of offenders and victims between domains.

By focusing on domains relationships can be more clearly seen between victimization and daily activities. Rather than only looking at status-based differences in victimization, domain-specific research allows for a much higher level of confidence and specificity in theory.

### Gender Specific Research

Another weakness of routine activities theory is the frequent use of research samples that are very broad and do not take into consideration important lifestyle variations. Although some researchers have focused on only men or women, this has not been common. Similarly, research focusing on other relevant subgroups or categories (racial, ethnic and age groups for example) has also been limited. What this means is that researchers and theorists may have missed important opportunities to truly focus on routine activities theory's core concept of suitable targets.

Schwartz and Pitts (1995) note that although much of routine activities theory research has approached the idea of suitable targets through measurements of objects (i.e. homes and VCRs) or places where strangers can find victims (bars, out-of-the-home entertainment), in the case of victimization of women, it is frequently the individual woman who is the target simply because of her sex. It may be also that some women are more suitable targets than others simply because offenders interpret "vulnerability" in different ways. In simple terms, women may be more suitable targets than men for some crimes.

Researchers also suggest that the core routine activities theory element of guardianship may be more complex for women than it is for men. For instance, women who associate with men more frequently are more likely to be sexually assaulted, and women who associate with men who like to get women drunk, so they offer less resistance to sexual advances, are also more likely to be sexually assaulted. However, routine activities theory argues that people who are with others should be less likely to be victimized, since the presence of others can act as a guardianship measure. For women, however, this relationship appears to be more complex. The implication is that those men that women associate with could act as guardians, but also may act as offenders. Thus, routine activities theory, with the help of feminist theory can explain how women are less free than men in their movements in society. So, although lifestyle is important for understanding victimization risks, it is also important to examine victimization risks specific to particular population groups.

## Methodological Problems in Routine Activities Theory Research

There have been two primary methodological problems identified in tests of routine activities theory. First, there have been a number of problems pointed out regarding measurement of the three core theoretical concepts (motivated offenders, potential targets and guardianship). Second, researchers have relied heavily on indirect, rather than direct, measures of theoretical concepts. The reliance on indirect indicators, especially demographic characteristics (i.e. sex, race, age, marital status) as indicators for lifestyle activities, is perhaps the most important limitation of existing routine activities theory research.

Near universally, routine activities theory scholars recognize lifestyle activities as the most important variables to assess. Even so, however, scholars have usually relied on status variables as indirect measures of lifestyle patterns and behaviors.

This is not to say that demographic variables should not be included in routine activities theory research. Rather, looking at these types of variables, such as sex, is important because of the real differences between male and female victimization patterns. However, what is important is to avoid relying on demographic variables without complementing these with direct measures of lifestyles activities.

Specifically, what is needed to adequately assess routine activities theory is research that focuses on domain-, sex-, and crime-specific analyses. But, this is not enough in itself. It is additionally necessary to overcome common limitations of the literature seen in insufficient specificity, reliance on indirect or proxy measurements, inadequate operationalizations of core concepts.

## International Scope of Routine Activities Theory

In addition to the large body of literature on routine activities theory that has come out of American research, there are also important contributions that have come from researchers in numerous other nations. Most notable is the work out of the U.K. that has been used in crime prevention programming and research drawing on the British Crime Survey (Maxfield, 1987; Sampson, 1987; Lasley, 1989; Sampson and Lauritsen, 1990; Mawby, Brunt, and Hambly, 1999). This work has taken routine activities theory research and thinking and applied the concepts to ideas of how to make various domains less crime-prone, primarily as a result of making targets less suitable and increasing guardianship measures.

Other important theoretical advances in routine activities theory that has come from researchers either outside the U.S. or analyzing data from other nations. Most include the work of Kennedy and Force (1990) in Canada; Braga and Clarke (1994) looking at thefts from automobiles in Germany; Beki, Zeelenberg, and van Montfort (1999) looking at crime rate changes; and Wittebrood and Nieuwbeerta (1997) assessing criminal victimization risks over the life course in The Netherlands. Routine activities theory has also been put to productive use outside of North America and Europe. Most notable here is the work of Bjarnason, Sigurdardottir, and Thorlindsson (1999) assessing the applicability of routine activities theory to youth violence in Iceland and Natarajan (1995) who assessed the utility of routine activities theory to explain dowry deaths in India.

## Summary

Routine activities theory is one of the newer theoretical perspectives to emerge as an attempt to explain criminal incidents and victimization risks. Central to this perspective is the idea that crimes can and will occur only when three elements of a situation are present: potential offenders, suitable targets, and incapable, unwilling, or absent guardians. When these three situational elements converge the likelihood of a criminal event taking place is greatly increased.

Since its inception, routine activities theory researchers have tested many elements of the criminal incident to fully identify the lifestyles and lifestyle components that have higher risks for victimization than others. Researchers have identified several factors that increase risk. Factors such as demographics, community structures, economic status, alcohol and drug use, and social activities have been consistently shown to be related to the risk of victimization.

Researchers have also studied the logical complexities associated with activities that influence the impact of lifestyle on a person's chances for criminal victimization. Researchers in recent routine activities theory analyses have addressed factors such as gender, domain of criminal incident, and methodological difficulties.

Routine activities theory is most useful, and makes important contributions to social policy by predicting conditions under which victimization risks are enhanced and identifying patterns of social events associated with criminal incidents. Additionally, by identifying when, where, and under what conditions crime is more likely to occur we can develop greater understandings of how crime occurs in patterned ways in society. In this respect, routine activities theory allows for more informed efforts to prevent and intervene in crime. As such, perhaps the strongest application for routine activities theory is in the area of crime prevention. Using the concepts, principles, and findings of routine activities theory research, we can begin to identify how individuals in various settings can take steps to protect themselves and their belongings from criminal victimization.

Some prevention strategies can include awareness of increased danger, thus an increase in guardianship behavior. For example, knowing that leaving one's home unattended for long periods of time increases the chances for household burglary, one can install a burglar alarm. Additionally, knowing that going to a bar to get drunk with like-minded males increases a person's chances for criminal victimization, one can carry a form of personal protection, or leave other valuables at home. This type of knowledge can greatly enhance a person's safety and well-being.

Another prevention strategy can include more community-wide efforts. Since routine activities theory suggests that certain types of community structures increase the probability of criminal victimization in a neighborhood, then communities with these structures can take steps to reduce potential criminal efforts. For example, research has found that fast food restaurants increase the chances of criminal behavior in a community. Using this knowledge, a community with fast food restaurants present can form a neighborhood watch program to keep a closer look out for mischief makers.

Although there are noted difficulties associated with defining and measuring concepts and the testing of routine activities theory, it is still a very popular and highly informative criminological theory. With further research addressing the noted complexities and issues, routine activities theory promises to be a lasting theory that informs students, practitioners, and scholars for years to come.

RICHARD TEWKSBURY
AND ELIZABETH EHRHARDT MUSTAINE

## References and Further Reading

Beki, C., Zeelenberg, K. and van Montfort, K. 1999. An analysis of the crime rate in the Netherlands, 1950–93, *British Journal of Criminology,* 39.

Bjarnason, T., Sigurdardottir, T.J. and Thorlindsson, T. 1999. Human agency, capable guardians, and structural constraints: A lifestyle approach to the study of violent victimization, *Journal of Youth and Adolescence,* 28.

Braga, A.A. and Clarke, R.V. 1994. Improved radios and more stripped cars in Germany: A routine activities analysis, *Security Journal,* 5.

Cohen, L. and Felson, M. 1979. Social change and crime rate trends: A routine activity approach, *American Sociological Review,* 44.

Kennedy, L. and Forde, D. 1990. Routine activities and crime: An analysis of victimization in Canada, *Criminology,* 28.

Lasley, J.R. 1989. Routines/lifestyles and predatory victimization: A causal analysis, *Justice Quarterly,* 6.

Lynch, J.P. 1987. Routine activity and victimization at work, *Journal of Quantitative Criminology,* 3.

Mawby, R.I., Brunt, P. and Hambly, Z. 1999. Victimisation on holiday: A British survey, *International Review of Victimology,* 6.

Maxfield, M.G. 1987. Household composition, routine activity, and victimization: A comparative analysis, *Journal of Quantitative Criminology,* 3.

Meithe, T. and Meier, R. 1990. Opportunity, choice, and criminal victimization: A test of a theoretical model, *Journal of Research in Crime and Delinquency,* 27.

Mustaine, E.E. and Tewksbury, R. 1997. Obstacles in the assessment of routine activity theory, *Social Pathology,* 3.

Natarajan, M. 1995. Victimization of women: A theoretical perspective on dowry deaths in India, *International Review of Victimology,* 3.

Sampson, R. 1987. Personal victimization by strangers: An extension and test of the opportunity model of predatory victimization, *The Journal of Criminal Law and Criminology,* 78.

Sampson, R.J. and Lauritsen, J.L. 1990. Deviant lifestyles, proximity to crime, and the offender-victim link in personal violence, *Journal of Research in Crime and Delinquency,* 27.

Schwartz, M.D. and Pitts, V.L. 1995. Exploring a feminist routine activities approach to explaining sexual assault, *Justice Quarterly,* 12.

Wittebrood, K. and Nieuwbeerta, P. 1997. *Criminal Victimization During One's Life Course in the Netherlands: The Effects of Routine Activity Patterns and Previous Victimization.*

*See also* **Victimization, Crime: Characteristics of Victims; Victimization, Crime: Theories about Vulnerability**

# Russia, Crime and Justice in Modern

There are numerous factors influencing Russia's legislative, economic, and political efforts to create a modern criminal justice system. Organized crime and political corruption are two principal obstacles Russia must overcome for a new system to succeed. These two interrelated elements jeopardize the economic and political future of Russia, as well as the national security of nations worldwide. Russia's subsequent success or failure with capitalism and democracy will depend heavily on how these issues are handled by not just the Russian Federation but by global policymakers as well. More specifically, Russia's success in its current war on crime will determine whether organized crime dominates an entire economy and political apparatus or whether democracy succeeds.

## Czarist Period

At the beginning of the 19th century, while most Western European states were making tentative moves towards liberal democracy, Russia remained fixed in a feudal system in which most of the population consisted of serfs. The czar's authority was complete and there were no democratic or populist representative institutions. The emancipation of the serfs in 1861 and the judicial reforms of 1864 instituted some reforms, but true constitutional reforms could not be achieved under the monarchial governmental system. Consequently, the failure of the czar to grant criminal justice reforms contributed to an escalation of revolutionary activity.

The impact of centuries of autocracy on Russia's legitimate structures is pertinent to the development of a certain type of consciousness conducive to deviance and criminality. The law operated as an instrument of the strong, providing little or no protection for the vulnerable. In many ways, deviance became a means of survival for the peasant as an attempt to redress the inequities of life. What the peasants manifested as artifice (theft of property) was practiced as large-scale corruption in the legitimate structures of government. The legal and illegal were separated only by blurred and indistinguishable boundaries. The criminal justice system was too corrupt to uphold justice and too dependent on the czar to effect any positive change. Therefore, the Bolsheviks would eventually inherit an entire system of moral and legal corruption. The current state in which Russia finds itself is directly related to the past and specifically to Russia's authoritarian history.

## Soviet Period

Lenin and the Bolsheviks were products of Tsarist Russia and their inheritance included the corruption that prevailed in all the legitimate structures of government. It was in the economic arena that the conflict between Soviet ideology and reality would allow corruption to become a pillar for Soviet Russia. By the time of Stalin's rule, it was clear that the legitimacy of his government would lay in its economic performance. Given the weak structure of government, it was inevitable that it would have to compromise its ideological goals and would have to negotiate with organizations outside the state-run economic system. This led to tolerance for black marketeering and organized crime as means to eliminate consumer shortages. In summary, the Bolsheviks inherited a corrupt criminal justice system and economic and political factors forced men like Stalin to grudgingly form relationships with nongovernmental economic entities.

The repressive conditions of communist rule also influenced the development of the black market economy. The underground economy provided the means to get items necessary for survival. Russia's black market was one of nearly comic credulity where high-ranking political officials, in stately positions of ostensible socialist idealism, personally benefited from this illicit capitalist market. Networks formed from this mutually beneficial arrangement. The *nomenklatura*, the term used to describe the Soviet political bureaucracy and system of political patronage, flourished.

## The Breshnev Years 1964–1982

In the Breshnev government, a new breed of criminal emerged along with a new breed of Communist Party official. Power, prestige, and profits had replaced the commitment to the ideological goals of the Bolshevik Revolution. The formation of direct alliances between organized criminal groups and the political elite took on significant importance. The criminals became suppliers of commodities and service and the political elite offered the sponsorship. It is important to note that, even with this political connection, criminal groups were not able to operate with the degree of autonomy that they later acquired.

Today the black market is primarily under the control of organized crime that has thrived in the free market environment due in large part to the already established relationships with the *nomenklatura*. Many corrupt officials in Russian government still remain in power and the marriage between these officials and organized crime is at the heart of Russia's woes in its capitalist experiment. The *nomenklatura* survived Stalin and it appears likely it will survive capitalism.

## Perestroika and Glasnost

In 1985, when Mikhail Gorbachev became general secretary of the Soviet Union, he knew that tremendous economic problems faced his country. He also understood the need for the acceleration of economic growth that would be required to increase productivity from the Russian labor force. In order to get this desired productivity, he needed to overcome a historic problem. He simply needed to reduce alcoholism, a severe and continuous problem among the labor force. Unfortunately, his anti-alcohol campaign limited the legal availability of alcohol and resulted in organized crime acquiring enormous profits from bootlegging. Parallel to organized crime in the U.S. during Prohibition, these criminal organizations had access to vast sums of money to invest in new business ventures. These criminal organizations then were faced with how to use these huge profits without attracting the attention of uncorrupted law enforcement officials.

Additionally, in 1987, with the passage of the Law of State Enterprises, Gorbachev attempted to change the state's control over state-owned enterprises and started Russia on the path to private ownership. This also presented opportunity for the expansion of organized criminal activities. They were able to partner with foreign investors in the West and launder profits as hard currency through these partnerships. Organized crime was now positioned literally to control the Russian economy in many respects.

## Democratic Reforms and Yelt'sin

The fall of communist Russia brought about a period of great turmoil in the economy. Former President Boris Yeltsin ushered in capitalism and fabricated a great deal of hope for the people of Russia. Ironically, organized criminals prospered even more in this environment, partially because the Russian system was not legally prepared to deal with organized crime in a capitalist environment. A major obstacle was the lack of legislation prohibiting much of the behavior of organized crime. Organized criminals also benefited immensely from the advantages of superior resources, enterprise experience, and ruthless business practices.

In 1994, In the face of a criminal justice system that did not even have definitions of organized crime, President Yeltsin issued a decree entitled "On the Urgent Measures to Defend the Population Against Gangsterism and Other Kinds of Organized Crime." Compared to the existing criminal justice and legal procedures, the decree was aimed at the protection of the life, health, and property interests of citizens. It also introduced strict measures against organized criminal associations and their members. President Yeltsin's decree caused heated debate among the political elite, who felt that it contradicted the Constitution and violated a number of rights and freedoms of the citizens. Vladimir Zhirinovsky and the Liberal Democratic Party considered the decree to be too soft on crime and demanded the use of summary execution to shoot mob leaders. In the end, however, the Russian public considered the limitations of some rights of those suspected of crimes to be due compensation for an increased guarantee of the right to life and safety for the majority of the population.

President Yeltsin's decree was a start, but a far stronger legal system needed to be implemented and enforced. Ironically, Yeltsin himself became the subject of much speculation relating to corruption and organized crime. On the first of the year 2000, Vladimir Putin took power as Russia's acting president. One of his first acts was to sign a decree protecting former President Yeltsin from criminal investigation. It also secured Yeltsin's personal assets and documents against search and seizure.

## President Vladimir Putin

President Putin has advocated a "dictatorship of law." In an open letter in the *Izvestiya Daily*, Putin was quoted in February 2001 as saying, "Russia's two main problems were 'the lack of will' and 'the lack of firmness' that notably allowed criminal gangs to develop throughout the country." In late 2001, the Duma did pass a hastily drafted anti-money laundering law but it has failed to be successfully implemented. Laws with significant teeth still need to be adopted to fight organized crime in the areas of corruption, illicit criminal incomes, and laundering of capital or money. If these laws are effective, organized crime would slowly be forced back to its traditional spheres—drugs, prostitution, gambling—where efficient criminal justice could take over.

Later, duly elected, President Putin became popular with the Russian people because of his stance against the Chechens and his ostensible resolve to control organized crime. In January 2001, he backed away from a pledge to amend criminal code procedures to limit arbitrary arrests by prosecutors. Currently, arrest and searches can be accomplished on the sole authority of the prosecutors without court approval. Regardless, he has failed to turn the tide against the success of organized crime.

## The Russian Twist

As previously mentioned, in Russia there is a criminal tradition that has existed for centuries and is the root of what is known today as organized crime. By far the most common crime throughout Russian history has been crimes against property. This seems to have been true in all societies where the majority of the population was without private property. For example, in the Russian peasantry, it was accepted custom to cut wood illegally in the forest belonging to landowners or the czar. The Robin-Hood-like taking or stealing from the rich was viewed as a folkheroic activity. This long-held and traditional Russian attitude towards theft of private property is a confused combination of superstition, customary law, and the peasant's dream for land ownership. These attitudes and beliefs have contributed to an inconsistent approach to professional criminals on the part of the people of Russia.

There are several mafia groups operating in Russia, varying in size, area of influence, and power. The Russians are, however, the most powerful gangsters in the world. In 1994, former Russian Interior Minister Mikhail Yegorov claimed the number of organized crime groups had grown from 785 during Gorbachev's reign to 5691. These groups have little fear of Russian law enforcement. Generally speaking, the effectiveness of law enforcement in Russia has deteriorated in its fight against organized crime. Police, judicial, and correctional agencies are underpaid, understaffed, and demoralized. Many Russian police forces lack adequate equipment, training, and supplies. Criminal use of bribes and intimidation also contributes to the ineffectiveness of law enforcement.

The direct threat of Russian organized crime to the U.S. is multifaceted. These gangs have connections to criminal organizations in both Europe and the U.S., giving the Russian criminals increased territorial influence. Furthermore, both FBI and CIA officials believe Russian organized crime groups have the frightening potential to influence and contribute to terrorism. The money and influence these criminal organizations possess, coupled with the economic conditions of the Russian economy, may provide many opportunities for organized crime to acquire weapons of mass destruction. With only the motivation of profit, once criminal groups possess such weapons, any terrorist organizations with deep pockets may be able to purchase these weapons.

The Russian Mafia has arguably managed to thrive under the conditions brought about by Russia's economic and political transition. Although these groups existed under communist rule, they have reaped incredible and illicit rewards because of the changes. They have managed to control the conditions and manners of success or failure of Russia's reform. The penetration of organized crime into the economic, political, and even social interests of Russia is a testament to the power and influence these groups have accumulated. The Russian government estimates the Mafia controls 40% of private business and 60% of state-owned companies.

The downfall of communism left behind an economic, moral, and social vacuum that the Mafia readily assumed. Hundreds of ex-KGB men and veterans of the Afghan war, faced with unemployment, offered up their talent. Russian émigré communities in New York, Paris, London, and across Europe proliferated. It is estimated that around $25 billion of dirty Russian money found its way to banks in Switzerland, Cyprus, and Liechtenstein. Another favorite target continues to be Israel. Russian gangsters simply claim Jewish origin and easily acquire an Israeli passport. Russians are also purported to run prostitution rings in Sri Lanka and exploit lucrative business relationships with the Colombian drug cartels. One Russian Mafia group even sought to sell a Soviet-era submarine, crew included, to a Colombian drug runner.

Unfortunately, significant increases in incidents of violence have occurred that provide additional evidence of the presence and success of today's Russian organized crime. In 1992, it was reported that there were 102 contract killings in Russia and in 1994 that figure had increased to 562 killings. Five years later, the Putin administration claimed that 107 contract murders had been solved and that 400 people have been tried for them. Numerous examples highlight the extreme violence that is wielded against any person who would oppose organized crime's goals to advance its business ventures in Russia.

In March 1995, Vladislav Listyev, a popular television host and director of the Ostankin network, was gunned down near his apartment and his death was rumored to have been linked to planned changes in the network's advertising policies. On July 20, 1995, Oleg Kantor, president of Moscow's Yugorshky Bank, was murdered as a result of his bank's connection to the business of an aluminum company. Indeed, in the Tyumen region, four aluminum executives have been murdered or injured between April and August 1995. In August 1995, Ivan Kivelidi, chairman of the Russian Business Roundtable, was poisoned for his efforts to remove criminals from the business world. He is one of nine senior members of the roundtable who have been killed from 1994–1995.

In addition, on April 22, 1998, Vadim Hetman, chairman of Ukraine's Currency Exchange, was shot to death in the elevator of his Kiev apartment building. He was to speak in March 1998 at the European Bank for Reconstruction and Development's annual meeting in Kiev. It was hoped that he could persuade 4000 international financiers and business leaders to invest in the Ukraine. The timing of his murder sparked speculation that it was intended to sabotage any interest from outside investors that the conference might have generated. Organized crime groups hoped to dissuade Western investors, in order to keep prices low and competition out. Crime groups also keep a firm hand on their own members. Two men were killed when a car blew up in the mining town of Vokuta on January 22, 2002, allegedly in an attempt to keep the members of the gang in line.

It is clear that organized crime has targeted business leaders and media officials who would expose them and their activities. It appears that there is evidence that these tactics work, because few of the killings have been solved. In addition, organized crime groups continue to make inroads into financial services, businesses, and all the activities of a free enterprise system. It is estimated that as many as 10 of Russia's 25 largest banks may have criminal connections.

There is a set structure for organized crime groups, but for the larger groups there is a common hierarchy. Each of the Mafiosi has a leader who has excellent contacts in national and local governments. Additionally, he has contacts in business, banking, and industry. Next, there are deputies of various sections such as banking, security, intelligence, strategy, and economics. The next level has team leaders that act as accountants, bankers, extortionists, automobile traders, and the like. At the lowest level of the hierarchy are the soldiers, who are the smugglers, pimps, bodyguards, assassins etc. Within this hierarchy, the characteristics of vertical operation and restricted membership based on family or ethnic affiliations are found. Additionally, tight secrecy, compartmentalization, and the uninhibited use of intimidation or violence are very typical.

Of the six Russian Mafiosi working in Moscow, three are Chechen. They include the Tsentralynaya, Ostankinskaya, and Avtomobilnaya Mafias. Two of the six gangs are the Slav groups, the Solntsevskaya and Podollskaya Mafias. The final group, the 21st Century Association, is an umbrella organization for a number of newly created cooperatives.

As a group, the three Chechen Mafias have about 1500 members. The three gangs maintain a single account (obshak) to be used for paying lawyers, bribing officials, and supporting their fellow countrymen currently serving prison sentences. The Chechen Mafias also share a security and intelligence department. This department deals with corrupt officials and provides information on possible operations against the gags. It is believed that these contacts are at the highest levels in both Moscow City and national level politics. Their main operations are banking, car smuggling, illegal oil deals, drug smuggling, and prostitution.

The first Slav Mafia, the Solntsevskaya Gang, is the single largest gang in Russia with an estimated membership of 3500–4000 members. This gang is active in the Moscow district of Solntsevo, but also operates in the center and south of the city. Their main operations are production and distribution of synthetic drugs, smuggling of arms and automobiles, extortion, prostitution, and kidnapping. They also own and operate hotels, restaurants, retail businesses, banking, and investments. This gang also has international connections. Their interest includes automobiles, drugs, arms, and antiques smuggling as well as interests in illegal trading in oil, metals, and other raw materials.

The Podolskaya Gang is located in the small suburb of Posolsk, where it enjoys exclusive control. It also controls about 25% of the street trade and prostitution in the center of Moscow. It is suspected that its size is about five hundred members. This gang has emerged as a very strong organization and has a reputation for being ruthless, organized, and disciplined. This gang has international operations that include imports and exports of goods to countries all over the world. It is believed that its main activities are centered in the Netherlands. It is also believed that the Podolskaya Gang deals in the sale of illegal oil products, arms and drugs. It also owns and controls the operation of several casinos.

The 21st Century Association was established in Moscow in 1988. The strength of the gang is estimated to be 1000 members. It has operations in 18 Russian regions, the U.S., and six countries in Europe. The 21st Century Association's leadership has strong relationships with corrupt individuals in regional and municipal administrations, but has been unable to make contacts at the highest levels in national government. The gang's main activities are extortion, kidnapping, prostitution, and other traditional Mafia operations. It also controls several hotels, casinos, and restaurants and is also moving into the business world by offering insurance, investments, banking, and pension services. The 21st Century Association is believed to control over 100 companies worldwide and has founded several charities for ex-sportsmen and military personnel. This interest in charities is believed to enable them to take advantage of legal tax loopholes.

Structurally, organized crime has a destabilizing effect on the Russian political system. The ubiquity of organized crime and corruption has also clearly damaged the Russian economy and the spirits of the Russian people. These conditions favor radical nationalist groups, which could possibly rise to power and undermine all efforts at democratic reform. The desire of radical groups to return Russia to its status as a dominant world power is another potential threat to international security interests. The Russian economy is currently also threatened by income loss through illegal business operations because it circumvents taxation and there are no appropriate laws to address the situation. It is estimated that as much as 25%, but probably a lot more of Russia's gross national income is derived illegally from organized crime. Additionally, this economic harm is magnified because the profits made by Russian criminals are often moved out of the country, not reinvested in the Russian economy.

KATHLEEN M. SWEET

## References and Further Reading

Finckenauer, J.O. and Waring, E.J. 2001. *Russian Mafia in America: Immigration, Culture, and Crime,* Northwestern University Press.

Federico, V. 2001. *The Russian Mafia: Private Protection in a New Market Economy,* Oxford University Press.

Brotherton, J. 2000. *A Fistful of Kings,* The Shear's Group Ltd.

Eberwein, W. and Tholen, J. 1997. *Market or Mafia: Russian Managers on the Difficult Road Towards an Open Society,* Ashgate Publishing Company.

Seidman, J., Allingham, P.F. 1995. *Time Bomb: How Terrorists and the Russian Mafia Threaten the World With a Nuclear Nightmare,* National Press Books.

*See also* **Soviet Union, Crime and Justice in**

# S

# Same-Sex Domestic Violence (Formerly Gay Intimate Violence)

Domestic violence is a major social problem in the U.S. It is the number one health risk among American women between 15 and 44 years of age. There are various forms of intimate violence, including physical, psychological, and sexual abuse. Domestic violence is not an exclusively heterosexual problem. It is also prevalent in homosexual relationships. Homosexuality is the sexual attraction toward a member of one's own sex. Gay refers to a male homosexual and lesbian, a female homosexual. Among gay men, it is reported to be the third largest health problem following AIDS and substance abuse (Island and Letellier, 1991). The actual prevalence and incidence of gay and lesbian domestic violence remains unclear. Family violence research has typically ignored homosexual intimate violence because many do not consider these unions to be a legitimate family structure. Rather, they are referred to as "nontraditional" families, which minimizes their value. Research focusing on homosexual violence has concentrated on gay bashing. Interestingly, concentrating on stranger violence contradicts the argument that people are most likely to be injured by someone they love. Sexual orientation does not make one immune from this ideology. Domestic violence is a universal problem affecting all populations. Although studies remain limited, those that exist show similar or higher rates of abuse among homosexual couples in comparison to their heterosexual counterparts. In particular, some studies show domestic violence to be more prevalent among gay males than lesbians or heterosexual couples. This may best be explained by the argument that males tend to be more aggressive than females and there are two males in a gay relationship. In addition, societal norms dictate that women should not be hit and in a gay relationship, there are no women. Males have also been taught to resolve conflict through fighting. For these reasons, there is a higher probability of aggressive behavior among gay couples.

It is difficult to obtain an accurate picture of domestic violence owing to fear of reporting, lack of victim recognition, and definitional problems. Along with the heterosexual population, same-sex domestic violence is highly underreported. In fact, underreporting is an even greater problem within the gay and lesbian populations. This problem may be attributed to fear of backlash from a homophobic society, lack of resources available to gay and lesbian victims, not recognizing abusive behaviors, and varying definitions of abuse. It is essential to understand that all intimate partners are potential victims of abuse.

Same-sex domestic violence has not only been ignored by the heterosexual community, it has also been discounted within the homosexual community. The belief that this may be occurring in their own relationships contradicts the image of domestic violence: a man hitting a woman. Lesbians often have a difficult time accepting the fact that lesbian abuse does exist and it is more prevalent than believed.

Feminists have historically argued that males and females are unequal. Being superior, males have been the aggressor and females, the weaker, have been their victims. The acceptance of lesbian battering conflicts with this ideology. In fact, denying the fact that women are also aggressors in relationships only perpetuates the myth that lesbian abuse does not exist.

Intimate violence does exist in all types of relationships. What is intimate violence? It is just as it is coined, violence against an intimate partner. It does not recognize sexual orientation. Forms of abuse include physical (hitting, scratching, burning, stabbing, etc.), psychological (threats of leaving, name-calling, verbal assaults, isolating, screaming, etc.), and sexual (forced unwanted sexual intercourse, victim subjected to degrading and humiliating sexual acts, forced victim to watch or participate in pornography). No one deserves to be a victim of abuse. Victims, straight or homosexual, face similar problems. Many never report the abuse. They may not tell anyone because of embarrassment or fear. All too often, victims do not leave their abusive partners for various reasons. First, their partner may be their sole economic support. If the victim leaves, his or her financial stability is gone. Second, victims may fear retaliation for attempting to exit the relationship. Perpetrators may stalk, threaten, harass, physically injure, or kill the victim. Third, victims may not leave the abusive relationship because of embarrassment of family, friends, and coworkers finding out about the abuse. Fourth, victims may not leave their abusive partner because they do not recognize they are being victimized. Some victims accept their victimization as a "normal" part of a relationship. Last, victims do not leave because they love their partner. As unusual as this may sound, most victims do love their partners and hope for change. Many victims fall into a trap outlined in the cycle of violence theory. According to Lenore Walker, domestic violence relationships go through a cycle of violence that consists of three phases: the tension-building phase, the acute-battering phase, and the honeymoon phase. In the tension-building phase, minor daily aggravations start to build over the course of a relationship. At some point, those tensions will be released into an explosion of violence outlined in the acute-battering phase. The last stage of the cycle, the honeymoon phase, is the abusers' loving acts and promises of never engaging in future acts of abuse. The never-ending promises are those that keep the victim in the relationship.

Regardless of sexual orientation, abuse has a purpose. It is to dominate and intimidate one's partner. Perpetrators use abusive tactics to maintain control over their partner and relationship. This allows for a sense of ownership over one's partner and relationship. Control may be subtle or blatant. Subtle forms of control include being in charge of the household finances, exclusively selecting activities for the couple, and hanging out with the abuser's friends and family. Blatant control includes not allowing the partner to work or leave the house without permission; not allowing one's partner to have access to bank accounts or household monies; and not allowing one's partner to see his or her own family and friends.

Although both heterosexual and homosexual couples share similar forms of intimate violence, there are unique differences among these populations. A dangerous myth that prevails regarding abusive gay couples is that they are engaged in "mutual combat." Mutual combat, or mutual battering, suggests that each partner is perpetrating violence. Accepting this idea perpetuates the myth that men are not victims of abuse. Rather, it supports the belief that males are violent. In heterosexual couples, mutual battering is not perceived to be a serious problem. Husbands or boyfriends are thought to be abusive and wives or girlfriends the victims of their abuse. It must be recognized that males and females both have the potential to act out aggressively.

Lesbian and gay abusers may use heterosexist control, a unique form of psychological abuse, to dominate their partners. Heterosexism refers to the belief that homosexuality is unnatural and abnormal. Heterosexuality is viewed to be the norm and is accepted as the desirable form of sexual behavior. The acceptance of heterosexism results in a homophobic society. Homophobia is the fear, loathing, and disgust of homosexuals. As Americans suffer from homophobia, lesbians and gays are fearful of disclosing their sexual orientation. They are not only afraid of physical backlash, but also social rejection. How would their family, friends, coworkers, and church react to such abnormal behavior? Abusers may use the fear of disclosure as a psychologically abusive tactic. They may threaten to "out" one's partner, that is, to reveal one's sexual preference to the heterosexual world. The fear of others finding out about one's homosexuality may keep the victim from leaving the abusive relationship.

Although all victims of abuse are reluctant to report it, the fear is even greater among gays and lesbians. Homosexual victims of domestic violence are often afraid to call law enforcement for help because the police may buy into the myth of mutual combat. When two same-sex people are engaged in an assault, the police tend to believe they are equals. This results in ignoring the seriousness of the situation. For gay males, this is an even more serious problem. Police take the attitude that two men are just "men fighting it out" without recognizing a real victim exists. Rather than ensuring the victim's safety, police attempt to "calm" the situation and leave both abuser and victim together. Another fear gays and lesbians encounter if they call the police is the fear of being "outed" to the public. Others finding out about one's sexual orientation is frightening enough to keep homosexuals from calling the police. All too often, gays and lesbians are afraid to call the police for assistance owing to their fear that they will be ridiculed and harassed. Past studies have suggested that police are more homophobic than the general American population. If this is accurate, homosexual abuse will be discounted and ignored by law enforcement agencies.

Another factor impacting the reluctance of gays and lesbians to leave an abusive relationship is the limited amount of resources available to them. The Feminist Movement made great strides for battered women in creating safe havens for them to turn to when placed in danger. Currently, most American cities have shelters for battered women to take refuge. Although many shelters will accept lesbian victims, they do not accept male victims. In the U.S. alone, less than a handful of shelters exist for gay male victims. For this reason, gay victims may have little option but to remain in the abusive relationship. Battered women's shelters may accept lesbian victims, however, they typically do not have the resources available to meet their unique needs. Counselors are not trained to handle same-sex issues. This results in providing necessary shelter for lesbian victims but not wholly treating the problem.

Domestic violence remains a relatively new area of study in that it has only been researched over the past 40 years. More importantly, only within the past 20 years has it truly been socially and academically recognized as a major social problem in American families. Similar recognition for gay and lesbian victims is lagging. Part of the problem lies within the homosexual population itself. Homosexuals' denial that abuse exists in their own relationships only serves to intensify the problem. The belief that domestic violence is a heterosexual problem and that homosexuals would not engage in that type of antisocial behavior is misleading and incorrect. Recognizing gay and lesbian domestic violence would be to support the myth that homosexuality is sick and aberrant behavior. Moreover, it supports the idea that gay and lesbian victims deserve to be abused owing to their deviant sexual practices. Until gays and lesbians acknowledge domestic violence in their populations, the lack of resources available to them will continue. They must realize that abuse occurs in all intimate relationships.

Homosexual couples encounter greater stress than heterosexual relationships. Clearly, homophobia creates a need for secrecy resulting in social isolation. Gays and lesbians may prefer to live in small, secluded neighborhoods where homosexuality is accepted.

When homosexual victims expose their victimization, they may face rejection from their small tight-knit community. Homosexuals who live in primarily heterosexual neighborhoods may not divulge their victimization because of fear of being found out by their heterosexual neighbors.

Alcohol and substance use has been reported to be more prevalent among homosexuals than heterosexuals. This may best be explained by the greater stress experienced in homosexual relationships. Many gay neighborhoods are flooded with liquor stores and bars. After work, this is where gays and lesbians can go to hang out with their peers. Other venues must be created for homosexuals in order to reduce the availability of alcohol within their communities. Although alcohol and drug usage does not cause one to behave aggressively it may serve as a trigger to violence. It should not be tolerated as an excuse for one's behavior.

In conclusion, it is imperative to give similar recognition to gay and lesbian victims of domestic violence as is given to battered women. Domestic violence is painful to all victims regardless of sexual orientation. It impacts all of society not just the actual victim and perpetrator. There are financial consequences to domestic violence. Particularly, medical costs, mental health costs, loss of wages, and loss of productivity. The costs are no different in straight or gay populations. America is one population where all victims have a right to be recognized and supported.

NICKY ALI JACKSON

## References and Further Reading

Farley, N. (1996). A survey of factors contributing to gay and lesbian domestic violence. *Journal of Gay and Lesbian Social Services,* 4, 35–42.

Gelles, R.J. and Straus, M.A. (1988). *Intimate Violence.* New York, NY: Simon and Schuster.

Island, D. and Letellier, P. (1991). *Men Who Beat the Men Who Love Them.* New York, NY: Harrington Park Press.

Jackson, N.A. and Oates, G. (1999). *Violence in Intimate Relationships: Examining Social and Psychological Issues.* Boston, MA: Butterworth-Heinemann.

Kelly, E.E. and Warshafsky, L., (1987). *Partner Abuse in Gay Male and Lesbian Couples.* Paper presented at the Third National Conference for Family Violence Research, Durham, NH.

Letellier, P. (1994). Gay and bisexual male domestic violence victimization: Challenges to feminist theory. *Violence and Victims,* 9, 125–136.

Walker, L.E. (1979). *The Battered Woman.* New York, NY: Harper and Row.

*See also* **Domestic Assault: Extent and Correlates; Domestic Assault: Prevention and Treatment; Homosexuality**

# Sampson, Robert J.

The work of Robert J. Sampson has greatly influenced that subsection of criminological theory that is best summarized as the *etiology of crime*. His association with the University of Chicago, Department of Sociology has provided him an opportunity to carry on the work of such theorists as Clifford R. Shaw, Henry D. McKay, Ernest Burgess, Robert E. Park, and others who first pointed our attention toward the role that community dynamics play in the production of delinquency and crime. Sampson currently serves as the Fairfax M. Cone Distinguished Service Professor in Sociology, and as Scientific Director of the Project on Human Development in Chicago Neighborhoods. In 2001, he was awarded the prestigious Edwin W. Sutherland Award for outstanding contributions to criminological theory and research by the American Society of Criminology.

Earlier works by Sampson (across the 1980s) included both theoretical and methodological developments dealing with such issues as economic inequality and structural density and the role that both play in the production of delinquency or crime and victimization, intergroup conflict, and urban Black violence. In 1987, for example, Sampson asked that criminologists think again about drawing conclusions nested in both the subcultural theory of violence and the culture of poverty thesis, popular explanations for violent crime among urban Black males. Here, he very clearly built on the earlier works of William Julius Wilson (1978, 1981, and 1984), who postulated that the structural determinants of the disruption of the Black family was found in Black male joblessness and subsequent economic deprivation, which, in turn, led to a disproportionate number of young, Black males being represented in criminal justice statistics.

Wilson and others like Sampson sought to interrupt previous notions that held fast to a belief that the Black culture itself accepted violence as a way of life and that a dependence on welfare had produced a cycle of poverty in which the inner city Black family was trapped. Sampson's (1987) findings clearly pointed to his basic argument that Wilson and others were correct: rates of Black violent offending are strongly correlated with variations in the family structure, with Black family disruption having the largest effect on juvenile robbery and homicide, controlling for income, region, age, and race. He concluded that, "The data suggest that social policies be directed toward the structural forces of economic deprivation and labor-market marginality faced by Black

males and the resulting consequences for family disruption and community crime" (Sampson, 1987, 378).

Sampson and Wilson, in 1995, included a chapter in an edited text by Hagan and Peterson on *Crime and Inequality* in which they look again at the nexus between race, crime, and urban inequality. They suggested that for too long, criminologists had been "loath to speak openly on race and crime for fear of being misunderstood or labeled racist" (Sampson and Wilson, 1995, 37). In this particular chapter, they developed further Shaw and McKay's social disorganization theory by introducing such concepts as *social isolation* and *cognitive landscapes*. Social isolation, coined by Wilson in 1987, refers to the "lack of contact or of sustained interaction with individuals and institutions that represent mainstream society" (Sampson and Wilson, 1995, 51). Cognitive landscapes are defined as "ecologically structured norms regarding appropriate standards and expectations of conduct" (Sampson and Wilson, 1995, 50). They conclude that, individualistic and materialistic notions of criminality aside, the changes in the social structure in the inner cities must be taken into account as they relate to the increases in violent crime within those communities.

## Pathways and Turning Points: Toward a Theory of Life Course Criminology

In a reexamination of the Gluecks' data, Sampson, along with Laub (1990), discovered a strong connection between childhood antisocial behavior and adult criminality, joblessness, divorce, welfare dependence, and educational failure, even when controlling for SES and IQ. The coauthoring relationship established with Laub proved fruitful for both, as much of their work has concentrated on sorting out the issues associated with the notion of stability versus change. Sampson and Laub develop their version of *life course criminology* in a series of articles that culminate in the publication of *Crime in the Making: Pathways and Turning Points* published in 1993, a work that received the outstanding book award by both the Academy of Criminal Justice Sciences and the American Society of Criminology. The book presents an early look at findings from a longitudinal study of 1000 men born in Boston during the Great Depression.

Earlier, however, Sampson and Laub published an article on "Crime and Deviance in the Life Course" in which they address head on the paradox that although the evidence overwhelmingly points to a relationship between antisocial behavior in childhood and adult criminality, not all antisocial youths become criminals. In order to account for this apparent contradiction, Sampson and Laub (1992, 75) argue that it is necessary to examine further the notion of change, especially as change relates to "social transitions and adult life events in the life course."

Set within the framework of such concepts as trajectories (pathways) and transitions (turning points), Sampson and Laub (1992) built on the works of such individuals as Block (1971) who studied changes in individual personalities over time, and Jessor et al. (1991) and others (e.g., Rogosa et al., 1982) who used growth curves to measure change in behavior over time. For too long, argue Sampson and Laub (1992), studies in *change*, within sociology and the study of deviance and crime, took a back seat to studies of *stability*. They suggest that:

> Whether derived from heterogeneity among individuals in an early propensity that manifests itself differently across time, state dependence fostered by social reactions to crime and interactional styles, or constancy in ecological context, the fact remains that explanations of stability are inextricably tied to a sociological perspective on the life-course (Sampson and Laub, 1992, 79).

## Calling for a Return to the Roots of Sociological Inquiry

Sampson has, across a work that spans almost 25 years, published in such journals as *Criminology, Journal of Research in Crime and Delinquency, Violence and Victims, Law and Society Review, Journal of Quantitative Criminology, American Journal of Sociology, Journal of Criminal Law and Criminology, Crime and Delinquency, Social Forces*, and many others. He has, along with several coauthors through the years, continued the work of the Chicago School through applying new methods and statistical techniques to the issue of systematic observation of local neighborhoods, much of that work occurring within the City of Chicago itself.

In 1997, along with Morenoff, Sampson looked at the issue of violent crime and the spatial dynamics of neighborhood transition. The authors theorize that high rates of homicide could account for both *population loss* in areas at the core of the inner city and *growth of the population* in areas adjacent to that core, areas that have seen a high out migration of whites. In Chicago School fashion, Morenoff and Sampson (1997) mapped out the city along several dimensions: socioeconomic disadvantage, homicide potential, and residual change in both. They were able to support their hypothesis,

and concluded that "the spatial context of violent crime has played an important role in conditioning the dynamic processes of neighborhood change in many older industrial cities with traditionally high levels of residential segregation over the past several decades" (Morenoff and Sampson, 1997, 58).

Sampson and his many colleagues of a "like mind" have plowed new ground in the study of crime and delinquency as a subfield of sociology in their theoretical assertions and methodological advances. They have done so by focusing attention not only on social structure, but the very processes within local communities that lead to crime and delinquency. They bring the study of both down to a micro level, and without downplaying or discarding macro views that take into account such social phenomena as poverty, unemployment, single-parent homes, etc. Quite the contrary, they include both in theoretical models, as well as statistical models, that explore further the role of the environment in the etiology of crime and delinquency.

This approach is summarized in a short article by Sampson that he so aptly titled, "Whither the Sociological Study of Crime?" He states:

> What is needed is a concerted effort to enhance the science of ecological assessments by developing systematic procedures for directly measuring social mechanisms in community context, and by developing tools to improve the quality of community-level research ... Such a focus is, of course, foundational to the sociological imagination-Chicago-School style (Sampson, 2000, 713).

BARBARA SIMS

## References and Further Reading

Block, J. (1971). *Lives through Time*. Berkely, CA: Bancroft.

Jessor, R., Donovan, J. and Costa, F. (1991) *Beyond Adolescence: Problem Behavior and Young Adult Development*. Cambridge, U.K.: Cambridge University Press.

Morenoff, J.D. and Sampson, R.J. (1997). Violent crime and the spatial dynamics of neighborhood transition: Chicago, 1970–1990. *Social Forces* 76(1):31–64.

Rogosa, D., Brandt, D. and Zimowski, M. (1982). A growth curve approach to the measurement of change. *Psychological Bulletin* 92:726–748.

Sampson, R.J. and Laub, J.H. (1990). Crime and deviance over the life course: The salience of adult social bonds. *American Sociological Review* 55:609–627.

Sampson, R.J. and Laub, J.H. (1992). Crime and deviance in the life course. *Annual Review of Sociology* 18:63–84.

Sampson, R.J. and Wilson, W.J. (1995) Toward a theory of race, crime, and urban inequality. In Hagan, J. and Peterson, R.D. (Eds.), *Crime and Inequality*. Stanford, CA: Stanford University Press.

Sampson, R.J. (2000). Whither the sociological study of crime? *Annual Review of Sociology* 26:711–714.

Wilson, W.J. (1987). The Truly Disadvantaged: The Inner City, the Underclass, *and Public Policy*. Chicago, IL: University of Chicago Press.

# Scandinavia, Crime and Justice in

The Scandinavian countries—here taken to mean Denmark, Finland, Norway, and Sweden, used synonymously with the Nordic countries—can be characterized as being geographically, economically, and socially similar. It is more of an open question as to how homogeneous they are culturally. The macrovalues of the Scandinavian countries are generally seen as being dominated by leftism and egalitarianism, high standards of living, and life satisfaction combined with weak religiosity.

The criminal justice systems in Scandinavia have usually been looked upon as progressive and humanitarian and hence sometimes have been taken as models for other countries.

Some Scandinavian legal scholars have expressed the view that the Scandinavian legal systems because of their continental traditions are different from those of common law countries. However, as far as criminal law is concerned the differences between common law countries such as England and North America on the one hand and the Western European countries on the other seem to be almost nonexistent. The areas of criminalization and penal sanctions are almost identical in all the countries. It is when comparisons are made between criminal procedure, sentencing practices, and their execution that the real differences between the systems emerge (Sveri, 1990).

## Official Crime Statistics

The Scandinavian countries exhibit the same increasing trends for crimes such as theft and assault as the other countries of central Europe. There is a striking similarity between trends over the past 50 years as noted by several authors (EuR, 1997; von Hofer, 1999). One conclusion appears to be that irrespective of the different criminal justice systems, the development in crimes is very much the same.

Looking at all offences registered by the police from 1980 to 1994 Sweden is continuously on the highest level, followed by Denmark, Finland, and Norway. All the curves for the respective countries are increasing and on a fairly parallel path (Yearbook of Nordic Statistics, 1996). However, the curves for Norway and Sweden in 1994 and for Denmark and Finland in 1995 fall somewhat.

This type of official crime statistics based on offenses committed against the criminal code represent though only a small proportion of all crimes committed according to many criminological studies in different countries.

## Clear-Up Rates

One explanation for the deficient official crime statistics is the police clear-up rates. As in other European countries, the clear-up rates have fallen drastically over the years. Over the past 50 years clearance rates have approximately halved in all the Nordic countries. The curves for Norway, Denmark, and Sweden follow fairly close, parallel courses with a drop from around 40–20%, whereas Finland has had a clear-up rate almost double that of the other Nordic countries. It is neither completely obvious how to interpret the difference between Finland and the other Nordic countries nor is it easy to explain the apparent fall in efficiency.

It may be noted though that the number of police per 100,000 of the population is lower in the Nordic countries than in either southern or central Europe; in the mid-1990s the Nordic countries reported a total of 183 police officers per 100,000 of the population while central Europe reported 291 (von Hofer, 1999). The public report more crimes to the police in Sweden than in Finland, although both countries represent a higher than average level of satisfaction with the police than in other countries, with an average level of confidence in the police in Sweden and below average in Finland (Mayhew and van Dijk, 1997).

## International Crime Victims Surveys (ICVS)

Because not all crimes are reported to the police and not all crimes are registered by the police, cross-national comparisons of levels of crime preferably ought to be based on self-report or victimization data. In spite of the methodological problems that are also involved in these types of interview studies, these statistics are most often considered to be more reliable for this type of comparative analysis. As many as 19 countries, have participated in three surveys—1989, 1992, and 1996—carried out through telephone interviews (Mayhew and van Dijk, 1997). Of the Nordic countries, only Finland participated in all three surveys, Sweden in 1992 and 1996, whereas Norway only took part in 1989 and Denmark in none of them. The offense types covered car theft, motorcycle theft, bicycle theft, burglary, and attempted burglary, robbery, theft from the person, sex offenses, and assault or threatening behavior. Summarized victimization over the last year of the respective studies shows Sweden highest with 22.8, followed by Finland 18.7, and Norway lowest with 16.4. The Swedish level is almost the same as the European level of 23.3.

For crimes of violence, victimization data from 1987 can be compared with recorded crimes in the same year. For the recorded crimes, Sweden and Finland rank far higher than Norway and Denmark (6.3 and 5.1 vs. 2.1 and 1.8, respectively per 1000 inhabitants). However, for the victimization data the rank order is quite different with Finland at the top, closely followed by Denmark and Norway, and Sweden at a much lower level: 33, 30, 29, and 23 per 1000 inhabitants.

The differences between these statistics have been explained by the different methods the police use in recording crimes in the respective countries. In Denmark and Norway, prosecutors are obliged to follow the principle of public policy, which means that they only have a duty to prosecute when it is found that prosecution is in the public interest, whereas in Finland and Sweden prosecutors follow the principle of legality, which means that they have a duty to prosecute whenever they are of the opinion that there is enough evidence to obtain a conviction (Sveri, 1990). The principle of public policy—or opportunity as it is also called—in Denmark and Norway thus seems to explain the low levels of recorded crimes in these countries as compared to Finland and Sweden.

## Criminal Justice Systems

Despite the difficulties in measuring in a comparable way cross-national statistics of criminal justice systems, it is obvious that generally speaking there are great variations between the countries for the different sanctions. Especially incarceration rates have been compared between the countries over time, and an interesting conclusion appears to be that there is no simple relationship between crime rates and incarceration rates (Blumstein, 1997; Shinkai and Zvekic, 1999).

In Scandinavia the most common sanction by far is fines. Half a century ago this financial sanction was most common in Sweden but today it is most frequently applied in Finland and least in Norway. With the Nordic invention of the day fine system—where the number of fines is related to the severity of the crime and the amount of each day fine is related to the socioeconomic ability of the offender—the possibility of using financial sanctions has been further expanded. The practice

of converting nonpaid fines into imprisonment was abolished in Sweden in practice as early as the 1930s; the number of prisoners owing to unpaid fines was reduced from approximately 11,000 to 400 within a decade.

Noncustodial sanctions or measures are used most in Sweden, although not more so than what is average in Europe. Probation is used most in Sweden, followed by suspended sentences with supervision in Denmark and Norway, whereas these statistics for Finland are not available in the European Sourcebook on Crime and Criminal Justice Statistics (CoE, 2000).

Community service is used most in Finland, followed by Sweden when including the new sanction of conditional sentence with community service. Sweden has recently also introduced electronic surveillance as a permanent sanction.

The greater use of other noncustodial sanctions in Sweden probably reflects the more pronounced individual preventive philosophy in this country introduced with the Crime Code of 1965 where the concept of punishment was mainly replaced by treatment. In recent years it has, however, been modified by what is termed the penal value of a sanction, which is intended to be the proportionate relationship between crime and punishment.

The great variations in pretrial detention rates across countries generally appear to reflect different practices rather than different types of crime. Thus Denmark and Norway have much higher levels of pretrial detention than Sweden and especially Finland, reflecting varying legal practices.

Over the past 50 years, prison populations have been fairly stable in Denmark, Norway, and Sweden. However, Finland has been a remarkable exception to this. The detention rates per 100,000 have been around 60 in Scandinavia which is only half the mean in the European countries. The formerly extremely high levels of incarceration in Finland have been drastically reduced over the last half century from around 200 to the same level as the other Nordic countries (Christie, 2000).

In 1999, Denmark had a somewhat higher and increasing level of persons deprived of liberty, whereas the other Scandinavian countries have shown decreasing levels over the last 5-year period, with Norway having the lowest figure over time (Nordisk statistic, 1999).

Another characteristic of imprisonment in Scandinavia is the comparatively short length of sentences. With the increasing numbers of drug criminals in prison sentences have become longer though. And with a more repressive criminal justice climate in Sweden in recent years the number of life sentences has also increased, as is also the case in Finland. In Norway, however, life imprisonment has been abolished.

Women constitute only about 5% of the prison populations. This proportion has increased over the last 5-year period somewhat in Norway and decreased in Denmark.

The proportion of foreign citizens is by far the highest in Sweden with 26% and lowest in Finland with an increase of barely 5%. In Norway, the figure is 11% and comparable figures for Denmark are not available (Nordisk statistik, 1999).

Other prison characteristics in Scandinavia are the small and to a large extent open correctional institutions that are highly staffed. The penal institutions usually only have a capacity of under 50 places and never more than 500. Finland has the lowest expenditure on the prison service among the Scandinavian countries (CoE, 2000).

## Effects of Penal Sanctions

Recidivism is remarkably high in the treatment-oriented correctional institutions in Scandinavia. Comparisons between the countries are difficult to make though owing to different methods of calculating relapse into crime.

Owing to the negative results of rehabilitation in correctional institutions, indeterminate sanctions such as youth imprisonment and preventive detention were more or less abolished in the Scandinavian countries as early as the 1970s.

Generally recidivism is greater the younger the person and higher for men than women. There is a great variation, though, in recidivism rates for different crimes; for example, rates are higher for property crimes then for violent crimes. The Swedish Department of Corrections, compiling the most detailed recidivism statistics, publishes figures for the different penal sanctions, which indicate higher figures for imprisonment and for probation combined with deprivation of liberty than for ordinary probation, and with falling rates for community service, contractual treatment and by far the lowest for intensive supervision with electronic surveillance. The latter figure is only 13% which is remarkable because to be considered for this intensive form of supervision a person must first be sentenced to traditional imprisonment and then apply for an electronic surveillance order. However, the official recidivism statistics do not account for differences in clienteles for the various sanctions.

In a comparative and longitudinal investigation of all kinds of correctional institutions in Sweden—training schools, youth prisons, prisons, and preventive detention institutions for both men and women—there was ample evidence of imprisonment prevailing in all the 13 institutions studied. Although the official objective of these institutions was individual prevention, the result was the opposite—that is, negative individual prevention—measuring *inter alia* extensive criminalization in all types of institutions using a panel and multivariate analysis. In a follow-up study over 10 years for all inmates, three quarters relapse in serious crimes, and in a statistical survival analysis there was a significant relationship between criminalization in the institution and later recidivism (Bondeson, 1989).

A quasi-experimental study of conditional sentence and probation in Sweden also shows that the greater the use of treatment intervention, the worse the results. Probation combined with a short period of institutionalization thus results in higher rates of recidivism than ordinary probation, which in its turn, results in higher rates of recidivism than a conditional sentence. The differences in recidivism rates—60, 30, and 12%, respectively—remain significant even when holding constant a great number of background variables with a prediction instrument (Bondeson, 1994).

Prisoner organizations in the Nordic countries have been rather effective in getting the general public and the media to look critically at the use of imprisonment. Mathiesen, who in the 1960s was involved in negotiations with the Department of Corrections in Sweden in his capacity of chairman of the Norwegian KROM, has advocated the abolition of prisons in many books, the latest in 2000. It is more realistic though to implement a reductionist than an abolitionist policy.

In opinion surveys on alternatives to imprisonment, the Nordic populations also demonstrate great willingness to accept other noncustodial sanctions, even ones that have not yet been implemented (Bondeson, 1998).

As a result of the very high costs of construction and administration of prisons in addition to the negative results of treatment, several Nordic legal commissions have in recent decades proposed that imprisonment, should be used to the least possible extent and with the shortest possible sentences.

At an international conference on prisons arranged by HEUNI—in collaboration with the Finnish Department of Prisons and the Council of Europe—Joutsen and Walmsley (1997) concluded by proposing a broad reform package to reduce imprisonment, including crime prevention, improved enforcement, improved treatment, changed legislation, attention to the media, and mobilization of the public, in addition to research and evaluation.

For a reductionist imprisonment policy to be successful, it has to be consistent and long lasting. As rational, economic, and humanitarian values jointly come to the fore, it is considered to be more realistic to try to mobilize support within different groups in society for a more radical reductionism. In this way a rational criminal policy objective advocated by Finnish criminologists could be approached, namely of minimizing the cost and suffering caused both by crime itself and by society's measures to control it while distributing the cost and suffering in a fair manner.

ULLA V. BONDESON

### References and Further Reading

Blumstein, A., The U.S. criminal justice conundrum: Rising prison populations and stable crime rates, *Prison Population in Europe and in North America,* Helsinki, Finland: Department of Prison Administration of the Ministry of Justice of Finland, 1997.

Bondeson, U.V., *Prisoners in Prison Societies,* New Brunswick, NJ and Oxford, U.K.: Transaction Publishers, 1989.

Bondeson, U.V., *Alternatives to Imprisonment—Intentions and Reality,* Boulder, CO, San Francisco, CA, Oxford, U.K.: Westview Press, 1994.

Bondeson, U.V., Global trends in corrections, *Annales Internationales de Criminologie* 36(1, 2), 1998, 91–116.

Christie, N., *Crime Control as Industry,* London, U.K. and New York, NY: Routledge, 2000.

CoE, European Sourcebook of Crime and Criminal Justice Statistics. PC-S-ST (99) 8 DEF, Strasbourg: Council of Europe, 2000.

Hofer, H.von, *Crime and Punishment in Denmark, Finland, Norway and Sweden,* Stockholm, Sweden: Department of Criminology, Reprint series No. 48, 1999.

Joutsen, M. and Walmsley, R., Summary remarks and conclusions presented by the rapporteur general, *Prison Population in Europe and in North America,* Helsinki, Finland: Department of Prison Administration of the Ministry of Justice of Finland, 1997.

Mayhew, P. and van Dijk, J.J.M., *Criminal Victimisation in Eleven Industrialised Countries. Key findings from the 1996 International Crime Victims Survey.* Onderzoek en beleid 162. WODC, 1997

Mathiesen, T., *Prison on Trial,* Criminal Policy Series, Winchester, U.K.: Waterside Press, 2nd ed., 2000.

Nordisk Statistik för kriminalvården i Danmark, Finland, Norge och Sverige 1995–99, Norrköping: Kriminalvården, 1999.

Sveri, K., Criminal Law and Penal Sanctions, *Scandinavian Studies in Criminology,* 1990, 11–28.

Shinkai, H. and Zvekic, U., Punishment, in Newman, G. (Ed.), *Global Report on Crime and Justice,* published for the UN Office for Drug Control and Crime Prevention. Centre for International Crime Prevention. New York, NY and Oxford, U.K.: Oxford University Press, 1999, 89–120.

*See also* **International Crime Statistics: Data Sources and Problems of Interpretation; International Crime Trends**

# School Violence *See* **Schools and Delinquent Behavior**

---

# Schools and Delinquent Behavior

---

Schools and the nature of youths' school experiences are important variables in criminologists' explanations of delinquency. There are three facets to the topic of schools and crime: (1) a considerable amount of delinquent behavior occurs in and around schools; (2) schools have been blamed as a cause of delinquency; and (3) schools are important for delinquency prevention.

### Juvenile Crime in Schools

Although schools are generally safer than many other places in society, there is a growing perception that schools are unsafe places where crime is a common occurrence. A number of factors contribute to this perception. First, incidents of bullying and threats create a climate of fear. Second, violent school-crime incidents receive widespread publicity. Any reports of students making threats, having "hit lists" or weapons are widely publicized, and the national coverage via television, newspapers, and magazines gives the impression that the problem is widespread. There were 47 school-associated violent deaths in the 1998–99 school year, of which 33 involved homicides of school-age children. This number was just 1% of all homicides of youth during that period (DeVoe et al., 2002). Students were more likely to be victims of serious violent crime away from school than at school. Student reports of victimization include 7–9% being threatened or injured with a weapon on school property; 13% reported being in a fight; 8% reported being bullied in the last 6 months at school. Six percent of students feared being attacked at school; 5% avoided one or more places in school for fear of being attacked; and 6% reported carrying a weapon such as a gun, knife, or club on school property (DeVoe et al., 2002). School crime in

U.S. schools has remained stable or declined slightly during the past 10 years. Although students are statistically safer in school than in many other places, incidents of threats and bullying are serious problems that create a climate of fear and lead to defensive posturing, weapon carrying, fighting, absenteeism, and disrupting the learning process.

Many Americans believe that U.S. schools are the most violent in the world, but many other nations are facing similar problems. School shooting incidents have been reported in Germany and Japan. Research on bullying was recognized as a serious problem and addressed by social scientists in Norway, England, and European countries long before criminologists in the U.S. acknowledged it as a problem (Olweus, 1996; Smith et al., 1999). Findings from student and teacher survey data from the Third International Math and Science Study (TIMSS) indicate that a higher percentage of students and teachers in other countries reported being victims of school crime than in the U.S. (Akiba et al., 2002).

## Causes of School Crime

Research studies on school crime and the role of the schools in causing delinquency fall into three main theoretical perspectives: (1) strain theory, (2) labeling theory, and (3) control theory. Strain theorists claim that delinquency is an expression of frustration resulting from academic failure and the inability to meet school demands and expectations. Youths who are disadvantaged or from lower-income families are often not prepared for the demands of school, and act out their frustration through disruptive behavior, truancy, and delinquent acts. Labeling theorists claim that repeated delinquent behavior is caused by societal reaction to minor deviant behavior, and argue that the schools' practice of placing students into "tracks" tends to stigmatize them as low achievers and increases the likelihood that they will become dropouts and delinquents. Control theorists hold that social bonds in youths' lives help them to withstand the tendency toward deviant and delinquent behavior. Youths who do not have a positive attachment to parents and are not committed to and involved in socially acceptable activities such as education are more likely to become involved in delinquency. These theoretical explanations for school crime and delinquency have been supported in numerous research studies, and offer a variety of recommendations for communities, the justice system, and schools to prevent juvenile delinquency (see Lawrence, 1998).

In addition to the theoretical explanations for school crime and delinquency, a number of social, cultural, and legal changes have contributed to the growing problem of disorder and delinquency in schools.

## Changes in the Role of Families and Peers

The family is the primary source for nurturing and socializing a child. Parents are role models for children, providing examples for interacting with others, for ethical and legal behavior, for instilling work habits, and for fulfilling responsibilities. Two trends have made it difficult for parents to fulfill these responsibilities: the increase in divorce and single-parent families, and the increase in both parents being employed outside the home. Schools are now expected to perform many of the functions that were previously the responsibility of parents. Many parents do not take the time or effort to be aware of their child's educational achievements or behavior problems. The absence of communication between teachers and parents allows for distrust and lack of mutual respect to develop. At the same time that school attendance separates children from their parents, peers begin to play a larger role in young people's lives. Schools bring large numbers of peers together for extended time periods. By the time youths reach the junior high years, peers have an equal or greater influence on them than their parents and teachers. Peer relationships are important in encouraging school attendance and achievement, but friends who have no academic or career goals have a negative influence, encouraging disruptive behavior and absenteeism. Youths who are not committed to school tend to associate with like-minded peers, and disruption and delinquency are encouraged by their association.

## Educational Expectations and Compulsory Attendance

Public education of all citizens is viewed as essential in a democratic society, and schools have been expected to serve as the primary institution for social change. The school is a structured environment that places demands and expectations on students. Those who are not prepared for these educational expectations act out in frustration. Many students are disruptive and violate school rules because they do not want to be there. They rebel against the structure and demands of the classroom. They are not there to learn. Their parents have not prepared them for school, and do not provide the encouragement and support for educational success. Many homes are void of positive learning models and parents have not promoted the value of education. Youths who lack the skills for successful school achievement and who are not committed to educational goals resist the structure and demands of school through absenteeism and truancy, which often escalate to disruptive and delinquent behavior.

An obvious question for youths who hate school is: Why don't they just drop out? Some do, but most do not. Three reasons explain why most youths stay in school: compulsory attendance laws, dropout prevention programs, and because most of their friends are there. First, compulsory attendance laws underscore the importance we place on education for employment, life skills, and responsible citizenship. Compulsory school attendance can assure that youths are physically in school, but there is no guarantee that they will be mentally engaged in the learning process. The unintended consequence of compulsory attendance is that many students remain enrolled but against their wishes; these students disrupt the learning process for others. States' adoption of compulsory attendance also brings with it an obligation to provide alternative educational resources for delinquent students who have been expelled for the violation of school rules.

Second, students who are at risk of dropping out are encouraged to stay in school through dropout prevention programs, which aim to retain students in school until they graduate or reach the age at which they can legally drop out. The programs are promoted on the belief that all youths should be in school, regardless of their commitment to education and the problems that they may cause. Dropout prevention is also in part a response to studies that have noted the negative consequences of school dropout that include unemployment, reduced tax revenues, more demand for social services, increased crime, and poor mental and physical health. The programs have been effective in improving retention and increasing the graduate rates. An unintended consequence of retaining resistant students in school, however, is to increase the incidents of school disruption and delinquency.

The third reason students stay in school despite their lack of commitment to education is because school offers many benefits not available to dropouts. Their attendance is irregular and their academic performance is unsatisfactory, but by staying in school they satisfy parental expectations and enjoy more peer associations than they would as dropouts. As students they avoid the negative stigma associated with being a school dropout. That does not mean they are positively involved in school, however. They are physically present, but mentally absent. These are the youths who cause most of the disruption and delinquency in school.

## School Rules versus Students' Rights

Student disruption and school delinquency are partially attributable to a greater emphasis on students' rights than in past years. Students do have rights. In the words of former U.S. Supreme Court Justice Abe Fortas, students do not "shed their rights at the schoolhouse gate."

There were abuses by school authorities in the past, but many believe that the present emphasis on students' civil rights and due process requirements has made it difficult to enforce school regulations. The discipline process now requires that charges be specified in writing, hearings are required, witnesses may testify, and legal appeals are allowed. Just as with society in general, the emphasis on civil rights has encouraged students to emphasize their rights over their responsibilities under the law, and has opened up the threat of litigation by students and their parents. The result has been that school personnel often overlook some disruptive behavior and rule violations, and take disciplinary action only in the most serious cases. The due process requirements have seemingly given more protection to unruly students than to school staff, creating a disorderly school climate for teachers and well-behaved students.

## Weakening of the Authority of Teachers

Compared with the absolute authority they had in the past, many teachers no longer feel in control of the classrooms and hallways of their schools. Most youths regularly test the limits of acceptable behavior, and students with little interest in education test the teachers' tolerance levels with minor violations like tardiness and walking the halls without a pass. Minor infractions quickly escalate to littering, writing on walls, smoking in the restroom, and verbal disruptions, or threats directed at teachers. The growth of disobedience, disruption, and delinquency has been attributed to a "marshmallow effect" (Devine, 1996). When students push a rule, the system, like a marshmallow, gives way. Personal stereos, beepers, hats, bandannas, hoods, and jewelry, for example, are all officially forbidden but unofficially tolerated. When students are challenged by a teacher, they respond only momentarily or not at all and walk away. Hats and other forbidden clothing have become symbols of students' control, as teachers have found it easier to ignore minor rule violations than to face the challenges of students (and often their parents). When students get by with minor rule violations, they are less hesitant to challenge more serious rules like alcohol and drug possession or threats and assaults against fellow students and teachers. A related factor in the growth of school disruption and delinquency is the importation of a street culture into the school hallways. Like drug dealers who fear each other more than they fear the police, students fear one another more than they fear the teachers or even the school security officers. It is this fear, and the need to appear tough, that explains the carrying of weapons (Devine, 1996, 105).

Teachers' authority is also more frequently challenged by parents than in the past. Many parents have grown to tolerate their children's behavior and style of dress as part of the youth culture, and it becomes difficult to enforce restrictions on their children's behavior when "their friends are doing it." To maintain order in schools that house hundreds of students in crowded conditions, educators must set more limits on behavior and dress styles. Some school regulations are viewed by students and their parents as overly restrictive, and teachers' attempts to enforce the regulations are often challenged by students and their parents.

## Policies for Safe Schools

Highly publicized incidents of school violence have prompted government action, making federal funds available to local school administrators and law enforcement authorities to undertake numerous programs for safe and drug-free schools. Several practices and policies have been implemented in schools throughout the U.S. to increase discipline and safety (see DeVoe et al., 2002, 135–136). The first essential step for any school district is to make a careful assessment of school security needs and discipline policies. A physical security assessment of school grounds and buildings should include the number and location of entrances and exits; lighting around the buildings and parking lots; detailed recording of all incidents of assault, theft, and vandalism; and inventory control of all school supplies and equipment. School administrators must determine if law enforcement or security personnel should be hired to patrol the school buildings and grounds and, if so, how they are to be selected. School staff and law enforcement or security officers should communicate regularly and work together closely to identify security needs. Administrators and all school staff should work together to identify safety and discipline concerns and then implement policies and strategies to address those concerns. Resources and training opportunities should be made available for school staff to improve their skills in discipline, classroom management, and conflict mediation. Developing consistent expectations for student behaviors and establishing clear policies for misbehavior will help to improve the school climate. School staff, students, and parents must see that policies are fair, equitable, and consistently applied; and that administrators are serious about maintaining a safe and orderly school environment.

Maintaining safe and drug-free schools requires regular reassessment and evaluation of policies and strategies. Administrators and security and law enforcement personnel should monitor and record all school crime incidents, and share that information. A reluctance to share information has allowed some high-risk, angry youths to carry out school violence that might have been prevented. The highly publicized school shooting incidents have served as a wake-up call, resulting in greater sharing of information among school staff, students, law enforcement, and the community. Although there remains a tendency to blame schools for violent incidents, most recognize that it is a community problem that cannot be solved without the collaborative efforts of students, parents, school staff, security, and law enforcement officials.

Reducing school crime also requires support from citizens and legislators to address a number of issues that directly affect school crime. First, school districts should consider reducing school size, restructuring schools, and providing more resources for school staff. Education experts generally agree that large schools make it extremely difficult to provide quality, individualized education where students are safe from verbal and physical assaults. Large, consolidated schools are more economical and efficient, but they are not more effective. Taxpayers must decide if safe and effective schools are worth the extra cost to pay for them. Second, state and federal legislators must be willing to tackle the controversial issue of gun control legislation. The difference in school crime and violence in the 1990s can be explained by the ready availability of firearms. The number of assaults and fights in schools currently is not that much worse than in the 1960s, but the presence of firearms has contributed to an increase in deaths and serious injuries, and a sharp rise in the fear of victimization at school. Implementing strict regulations and zero tolerance policies against weapons in schools has had some impact, but the threat of expulsion has not been sufficient to keep guns out of schools. As long as young people are able to get firearms on the street and from their own homes, some will find their way into schools. Metal detectors offer some protection, but do not guarantee safe schools and may give a false sense of security. Schools have resorted to other policies such as requiring students to carry clear backpacks, and the elimination of lockers. Policies to improve physical security and procedures aimed at preventing weapons in the schools are important. Physical security alone however, cannot address the climate of fear and hostility that leads to school violence. Most students who have brought guns to school say that their reason for doing so was to protect themselves. The first priority must be to create schools where all students are respected and feel safe. The best approach for preventing school violence is a comprehensive strategy directed at creating a safe school environment where threats and harassment are not tolerated. Preventing school violence requires "mental detectors" more than metal detectors. That is, school staff must be sensitive to students' anger, hostility, fear, and conflict, and encourage students to communicate their concerns and knowledge of any problems among the student body.

## School-Based Delinquency Prevention Programs

Schools are valuable resources for delinquency prevention. They provide access to virtually all students throughout their developmental years, and can help to counter the adverse influences to which young people are exposed in the community. School personnel are well-equipped to help students develop prosocial values, and positive thinking and communication skills. Research supports the importance of education and school involvement in helping youth avoid delinquent behavior. Numerous programs directed at reducing school crime have been implemented in schools. Programs that have shown positive results are those aimed at clarifying acceptable behavioral norms, establishing and consistently enforcing school rules, and school-wide campaigns to reduce bullying and drugs in schools. The most effective school programs are comprehensive instructional programs that focus on social competency skills (self-control, responsible decision making, problem solving, and communication skills) and that are delivered over a period of time to continually reinforce those skills (Gottfredson, 2001).

## Summary and Conclusion

School crime is a reflection of crime in the community, and can only be prevented through the collaborative and cooperative efforts of educators, law enforcement, community leaders, students, and parents. School administrators can significantly reduce crime in schools by implementing security measures, clear and consistent regulations, student behavioral expectations, and training all staff in discipline management skills. Some school-based delinquency prevention programs can be effective in reducing crime in schools and in the community. Federal and state funding is essential to provide the necessary resources to assure that all students can receive a quality education in a safe and drug-free school environment. There are few crime and justice issues that are more important than reducing school crime. No less than the future of public education is at stake.

RICHARD LAWRENCE

## References and Further Reading

Akiba, M., LeTendre, G.K., Baker, D.P. and Goesling, B., Student victimization: National and school system effects on school violence in 37 nations, *American Educational Research Journal* 39, 4, 2002.

Devine, J., *Maximum Security: The Culture of Violence in Inner-City Schools,* Chicago, IL: The University of Chicago Press, 1996.

DeVoe, J.F., Ruddy, S.A., Miller, A.K., Planty, M., Peter, K., Kaufman, P., Snyder, T.D., Duhart, D.T. and Rand, M.R., *Indicators of School Crime and Safety: 2002,* Washington, DC: U.S. Departments of Education and Justice, 2002.

Gottfredson, D.C. *Schools and Delinquency.* Cambridge, U.K.: Cambridge University Press, 2001.

Lawrence, R., *School Crime and Juvenile Justice,* New York, NY: Oxford University Press, 1998.

Olweus, D. *Bullying at School: What We Know and What We Can Do.* Oxford, U.K.: Blackwell, 1996.

Smith, P.K., Morita, Y., Junger–Tas, J., Olweus, D., Slee, P. and Catalano, R.F., *The Nature of School Bullying: A Cross-National Perspective.* New York, NY: Routledge, 1999.

*See also* **Juvenile Delinquency: Extent, Correlates, and Trends; Juvenile Delinquency, Theories of**

# Scientific Evidence *See* **Police: Forensic Evidence**

# Search and Seizure

The protections guaranteed by the Fourth Amendment to the U.S. Constitution were developed ostensibly as a response to the English practice of "writs of assistance." England's celebrated *Seymane's Case* (Coke's Rep. 91a, 77 Eng. Rep. 194, K.B. 1604) established the idea that a homeowner had the right to defend his house against unlawful entry by agents of the Crown, while at the same time, reiterated the authority of agents to enter as a means to serve the king's process. Another contributory cornerstone of English legal precedence was the decision in *Entick v. Carrington* (19 Howell's State Trials 1029, 95 Eng. 807, 1705) that held that the king's agents could not seize all of a person's private papers. Rather, they must restrict their seizure only to those papers alleged to be criminal in nature. Madison and his fellow framers of the Constitution were clearly influenced by their experience with English legal tradition and sought to protect the new nation from the excesses thereof.

Much of the debate as to the proper scope of governmental search and seizure has revolved around the role of warrants and the circumstances under which a warrant may or may not be required. The language of the Fourth Amendment speaks to this concern, "The right of the people to be secure in their persons, houses, papers, and effects, against unreasonable searches and seizures, shall not be violated, and no Warrants shall issue, but upon probable cause, supported by Oath or affirmation, and particularly describing the place to be searched, and the persons or things to be seized."

There have been, however, a series of Supreme Court reversals hinged on whether both clauses of the Amendment must be taken together. One perspective has argued that the only searches and seizures that are "reasonable" are those meeting the requirements of the second clause (e.g., those pursuant to warrants issued under the prescribed limits). Alternatively, it has been argued that the two clauses are independent such that searches under warrant must comply with the second clause, but that there are "reasonable" searches under the first clause that need not necessarily comply with the second clause.

Collateral to the issue of reasonableness is the protection of a person's interests. This too, harkens back to English legal precedence. In *Entick v. Carrington* the issue was framed as one of property rights. As stated by Lord Camden, "The great end for which men entered in society was to secure their property. That right is preserved, sacred, and incommunicable in all instances where it has not been taken away or abridged by some public law for the good of the whole."

Again, the Supreme Court has wavered in its position. In cases such as *Gouled v. U.S.* (255 U.S. 298, 1921) and *Olmstead v. U.S.* (277 U.S. 438, 1928), the Court reaffirmed the property rights basis for the Amendment. These findings were subsequently overturned by *Warden v. Hayden*, "We [the Court] have recognized that the principle object of the Fourth Amendment is the protection of privacy rather than property, and have increasingly discarded fictional and procedural barriers rested on property concepts."

In *Katz v. U.S.* (389 U.S. 347, 1967) the Court further distanced itself from claims that are solely based in notions of property with the assertion that the expectation of privacy can extend into the public sphere, "what [a person] seeks to preserve as private, even in an area accessible to the public may be constitutionally protected." In cases such as *Alderman v. U.S.* (394 U.S. 165, 1969) and *Mincey v. Arizona* (437 U.S. 385, 1978), the right of an individual to exclude the access of others emerged as a factor in determining the legitimacy of privacy expectations. For instance, one's expectation of privacy in one's own home is held to be greater than one's expectation of privacy in an automobile or in the workplace.

What has emerged particularly in the wake of Katz, is a balancing test where the Court must weigh the needs of law enforcement against the expectations of individual privacy. Again, the issue of the warrant requirement has been central. In *MacDonald v. U.S.* the Court recognized, "the exigencies of the situation" may sometimes make exemption from the warrant requirement "imperative." This being said, exceptions to the warrant requirement are no longer weighed solely against the justification for the exception (e.g., existence of exigent circumstances) and the scope of the search is no longer tied to or limited by the particular justification.

As early as 1806, Chief Justice Marshall also construed the Fourth Amendment as a protection against arbitrary arrest. Long established in common law, the arrest of a person in public without a warrant is accepted as a reasonable practice. However, arrest of a person in his or her home (absent exigent circumstances or similar exceptions) generally requires the issuance of a warrant. The Court has since held that seizure of a person need not be a formal arrest in order for the Fourth Amendment protections to apply. In such incidents, law enforcement must be able to justify all seizures, including those that only involve a brief detention.

The justifiability of a given detention was also considered with regard to the admissibility of evidence obtained as a result of the detention. As an extension of the position articulated in *Mapp v. Ohio* (367 U.S. 643, 1961), the Court held in *Davis v. Mississippi* (394 U.S. 721, 1969) that all evidence obtained as the result of an illegal arrest should be suppressed.

The Court has also prescribed the boundaries within which a law enforcement officer may search an individual detained during an investigation. In *Terry v. Ohio* (392 U.S. 1, 20, 1968) the Court approved the practice of an investigative stop and "frisk" of individuals reasonably suspected of potentially criminal behavior. Under Terry, "[the frisk] must therefore be confined in scope to an intrusion reasonably designed to discover guns, knives, clubs, or other hidden instruments for the assault of the police officer." If during the course of the frisk for weapons, an officer discovers through "plain touch" an article he or she believes to be contraband, that article may be seized. However, the search may not be expanded to determine whether the article is in fact contraband. In *Michigan v. Long*

(463 U.S. 1032, 1983) the Court ruled that a Terry sweep for weapons may be extended to the passenger area of a vehicle. In instances where the amount of time a subject was detained has been pivotal, the Court has relied upon a flexible standard of reasonableness. In *U.S. v. Sharpe* (470 U.S. 675, 1985), the Court couched the reasonableness standard as, "... the period of time necessary to either verify or dispel the suspicion."

Regarding searches of persons, incident to arrest there has been relatively little controversy. However, as in *Michigan v. Long*, there has been considerable debate as to the permissibility and extent of searches beyond the physical person of the detained subject. In a number of decisions dating back to *Harris v. U.S.* (331 U.S. 145, 1947), it has been held that police officers may search the area in which the arrest was made and, in some instances, entire residences if reasonably deemed to be within the arrestee's area of "immediate control." This doctrine of the "immediate area" placed a significant restriction on the searches previously allowed under Harris. Further, the Court held in *Chimel v. California* (395 U.S. 752, 1969) that "the facts and circumstances—the total atmosphere of the case" should be used as the standard by which the reasonableness of the search should be determined. In *Vale v. Louisiana* (399 U.S. 30, 35, 1970) the Court found that officers may not search the interior of an individual's residence incident to arrest, if that individual was arrested outside the residence (i.e., in the street in front of the residence).

The Court reiterated the primacy of an individual's expectation of privacy regarding one's residence in *Mincey v. Arizona*. In this case, the Court held invalid a warrantless search of a suspect's whole apartment conducted over a 4-day period after the suspect's arrest. Justice Stewart, writing for the Court stated, "It is one thing to say that one who is legally taken into police custody has a lessened right of privacy in his person. It is quite another to argue that he also has a lessened right of privacy in his entire house."

One important exception to the warrant requirement, particularly as it relates to both residences and vehicles is the "plain view" doctrine. In *Texas v. Brown* (460 U.S. 730, 1983), the Court held that evidence inadvertently discovered by police during the course of an otherwise protected investigation was admissible under certain circumstances. "For the plain view doctrine to apply, not only must the officer be legitimately in a position to view the object, but it must be immediately apparent to the police that they have evidence before them." One notable revision to this ruling occurred in *Horton v. California* (496 U.S. 128, 1990) wherein the Court ruled that the discovery of evidence in plain view need not be "inadvertent."

Closely related to the plain view doctrine is the question of "open fields." In *Hester v. U.S.* (265 U.S. 57, 59, 1924) the Court ruled that "open fields" (i.e., pastures, wooded areas, open water) were not protected under the Fourth Amendment. The Court's assertion in *Katz v. U.S.* that the Amendment "protects people not places" appeared to weaken the open fields principle, but subsequent holdings in *Oliver v. U.S.* (466 U.S. 170, 1984) linked its ruling clearly to the literal wording of the Amendment, "The Framers would have understood the term 'effects' to be limited to personal rather than real property."

Another qualification of the Chimel ruling came in *Maryland v. Buie* (494 U.S. 325, 1990) in which the Court found that officers could extend a search incident to arrest to include other areas of a residence in an effort to detect "unseen third parties in the house." This "protective sweep" according to the Court, "is not a full search of the premises, but may extend only to a cursory inspection of those spaces where a person may be found. The sweep [may] last no longer than is necessary to dispel the reasonable suspicion of danger and in any event no longer than it takes to complete the arrest and depart the premises."

Moving from residences to vehicles, the Court again turned to doctrine established in Chimel. The Court in *New York v. Belton* (453 U.S. 454, 1981) attempted to give police guidance for searches of a vehicle passenger compartment incident to the arrest of the occupants, "[W]e hold that when a policeman has made a lawful custodial arrest of the occupant of an automobile, he may, as a contemporaneous incident of that arrest, search the passenger compartment of that automobile."

The ruling in Belton was in many ways a clarification of *Carroll v. U.S.* (267 U.S. 132, 1925). In *Carroll*, the Court focused on the mobility inherent in vehicles and possible jurisdictional problem that might arise as a consequence of that mobility. The Court, however, initially limited Carroll's reach, holding impermissible the warrantless seizure of a parked vehicle merely because it is movable, and indicating that vehicles may be stopped only while moving or reasonably contemporaneously with movement. Also, the Court ruled that the search must be reasonably contemporaneous with the stop, so that it was not permissible to remove the vehicle to the stationhouse for a warrantless search at the convenience of the police.

As a supplement to the mobility rationale developed in Carroll, the Court in *Arkansas v. Sanders* (442 U.S. 753, 761, 1979) held, "In the absence of exigent circumstances, police are required to obtain a warrant before searching luggage taken from an automobile properly stopped and searched for contraband." Referencing *U.S. v. Chadwick* (433 U.S. 1, 1977), Sanders also clarified related issues of privacy: "There are essentially two reasons for the distinction between automobiles and other private property. First, as the Court repeatedly has recognized, the inherent mobility of automobiles often makes it impracticable to obtain a warrant. . . . In addition, the configuration, use, and regulation of automobiles often may dilute the reasonable expectation of privacy that exists with respect to differently situated property."

The Court has since revised its position on the matter. In *California v. Acevedo* (498 U.S. 807, 1990), the Court held that warrantless searches of a closed container inside a vehicle could be conducted if there were probable cause to believe that the container held contraband.

In a similar vein, the Court held in *Michigan v. Thomas* (458 U.S. 259, 1982), "When police officers have probable cause to believe there is contraband inside an automobile that has been stopped on the road, the officers may conduct a warrantless search of the vehicle, even after it has been impounded and is in police custody." In this particular case, officers expanded an inventory search incident to arrest whereupon they discovered a quantity of marijuana in an unlocked glove box (and subsequently a handgun) inside the defendant's vehicle. The Court held that the discovery of contraband (the marijuana) was sufficient to expand the search (that yielded the handgun) without further "exigent circumstances."

In *Cady v. Dombrowski* (413 U.S. 433, 1973), the Court reaffirmed the validity of a warrantless inventory search of a vehicle in police custody and the admissibility of evidence discovered therein. Justice Rehnquist, writing for the majority, expressed the Court's conditional approach to the holding, "While these general principles are easily stated, the decisions of this Court dealing with the constitutionality of warrantless searches, especially when those searches are of vehicles, suggest that this branch of the law is something less than a seamless web."

Even with the reduced expectation of privacy associated with vehicles, the Court has maintained the need for probable cause to detain or search a vehicle. In *Whren v. U.S.* (517 U.S. 806, 1996) the Court held that the officer's stated probable cause for the stop does not necessarily have to constitute the officer's entire motivation for the stop, "The temporary detention of a motorist upon probable cause to believe that he has violated the traffic laws does not violate the Fourth Amendment's prohibition against unreasonable seizures, even if a reasonable officer would not have stopped the motorist absent some additional law enforcement objective."

Whether police may reasonably extend a warrantless search of a vehicle to the passengers was considered in *U.S. v. DiRe* (332 U.S. 581, 1948). Holding close to its decision in *Carroll v. U.S.* the Court found, "We are not convinced that a person, by mere presence in a suspected car, loses immunities from search of his person to which he would otherwise be entitled."

In *Rakas v. Illinois* (439 U.S. 128, 1978) the debate moved from a warrantless search of a passenger to the warrantless search of the vehicle in which the passengers were seated. In this case, police, "[D]iscovered a box of rifle shells in the glove compartment, which had been locked, and a sawed-off rifle under the front passenger seat." Citing *Jones v. U.S.* (357 U.S. 493, 499, 1958), the petitioners sought to suppress the rifle and shells (in which they claimed no ownership) on the grounds that they had an "expectation of privacy" in the glove box and passenger compartment as they were "legitimately on premises." The Court disagreed "Petitioners, who asserted neither a property nor a possessory interest in the automobile searched nor an interest in the property seized ... were not entitled to challenge a search of those areas."

In addition to those situations outlined above, there are a number of other circumstances where a warrantless search has been sustained by the Court. Foremost among these, are situations where an individual has given authorities consent to conduct the search. In *Amos v. U.S.* (255 U.S. 313, 317, 1921) the Court ruled that an individual may waive his or her Constitutional rights thus allowing the search of individual property even if officers have not complied with the Amendment. The Court in *Bumper v. North Carolina* (391 U.S. 543, 1968) and *Johnson v. U.S.* (333 U.S. 10, 13, 1948), respectively, held that proof of consent as well as the suspect's awareness of their right to deny consent are the burden of the state.

In some instances, the Court has held that a third party may give consent to search. In *U.S. v. Matlock* (415 U.S. 164, 1974), police made a warrantless search of a bedroom cooccupied by the suspect and the person who gave consent. The Court held that the third party by virtue of their joint occupancy, "possessed common authority over or other sufficient relationship to the premises or effects sought to be inspected."

Warrantless searches of students conducted by school officials have also come under consideration by the Court. In *New Jersey v. T.L.O.* (469 U.S. 325, 1985), the Court held that the Fourth Amendment applies to these searches because "school officials act as representatives of the State, not merely as surrogates for the parents." The Court has, however, made some distinction between school officials and law enforcement. Eschewing both the warrant requirement and the probable cause standard, the Court has held that a simple reasonableness standard applies for all student searches made by school officials.

In regulating searches of prison cells, the Court has dropped the reasonableness standard. In *Hudson v. Palmer* (468 U.S. 517, 1984) the Court ruled that, "proscription against unreasonable searches does not apply within the confines of the prison cell." As such, prison administrators are free to conduct so-called "shakedown" searches according to whatever plan or pattern they determine appropriate.

The Court has likewise held that neither a warrant nor probable cause is necessary for search of a probationer's home. In *Griffin v. Wisconsin* (483 U.S. 868, 1987), the Court stated, "A State's operation of a probation system ... presents 'special needs' beyond normal law enforcement that may justify departures from the usual warrant and probable cause requirements."

A similar reasoning produced decisions related to the drug testing of railroad employees. In *Skinner v. Railroad Labor Executives' Association*, 489 U.S. 602 (1989) the Court held that no warrant, probable cause or even individualized suspicion was necessary for mandatory drug testing of employees. In *National Treasury Employees Union v. Von Raab*, 489 U.S. 656 (1987) the Court upheld a requirement for mandatory drug testing of employees seeking a transfer to positions dealing directly with drug interdiction. In both cases, the Court cited the government's "compelling" interest in the particular situations.

Insofar as drug testing of school children is concerned, the Court in *Verona School District 47J v. Acton* upheld random drug testing of students who participate in extracurricular activities. In this ruling the Court refined its definition of "compelling interest." In a statement that is in itself a fitting summary metaphor for the broader issue of search and seizure, the Court stated that the term, "compelling interest," does not denote a "fixed, minimum quantum of governmental concern, [rather it] ... describes an interest which appears important enough to justify the particular search at hand."

MATTHEW PATE

### References and Further Reading

Bloom, R.M. and Brodin, M.S., *Criminal Procedure: Examples and Explanations*. New York, NY: Aspen Publishers, 2001.
Del Carmen, R.V. and Walker, J.T., *Briefs of Leading Cases in Law Enforcement*. Cincinnati, OH: Anderson, 1995.
Klein, I.J., *The Law of Arrest, Search, Seizure, and Liability Issues—Principles, Cases, and Comments*. Miami, FL: Coral Gables, January 1994.
Bloom, R.M., *Searches, Seizures, and Warrants: A Reference Guide to the United States Constitution*. New York, NY: Praeger Publishers, 2003.

*See also* **Fines and Forfeitures**

# Secret Service, U.S.

Originally created as an investigative bureau, the U.S. Secret Service has evolved into a principal law enforcement agency tasked with significant segments of national security. As the Civil War came to an end in April 1865, stringent efforts were made to rebuild and reunify the American states and the federal government. During this time, the nation's economy was extremely unstable, as more than a third of the currency being exchanged was counterfeit. Treasury Secretary Hugh McCullough advised President Abraham Lincoln that the nation's economy was in eminent peril if the counterfeiting problem was not addressed. As a result, President Lincoln established the U.S. Secret Service on April 14, 1865, under the direction of Chief William Wood. The investigative bureau was tremendously effective during its first year of operation, and in 1866, the Secret Service founded its

National Headquarters as an extension of the Department of the Treasury, in Washington, D.C. Today, the U.S. Secret Service comprises 6000 personnel, approximately 1000 of which are special agents whose primary duties include investigation and protection. On March 1, 2003, in accordance with the Homeland Security Act of 2002, the U.S. Secret Service was moved from the umbrella of the Department of the Treasury and became a division of the Department of Homeland Security.

Although established in April 1865, the Secret Service did not officially deploy until July 5, 1865. During its first year, the bureau successfully located and suppressed over 200 counterfeiting operations. Counterfeiting investigations were problematical during this time, as each state printed and minted its own currency. There was no standard currency until 1877 when the

Treasury Department's Bureau of Engraving and Printing assumed the responsibility of producing all U.S. currency. The Secret Service was able to keep counterfeiting in check for some time; however, with the advent of computer and printing technology, "making money" became easier, resulting in a resurgence of counterfeiting operations during the late 1900s. The Department of the Treasury initiated several safeguards to thwart counterfeiting including redesigns of currency, security threads, watermarks, and microprinting. Despite these efforts, counterfeiting remains a significant threat to the U.S. economy.

Besides counterfeiting, the Secret Service has been authorized to investigate a multitude of crimes, particularly related to financial institutions, transactions, obligations, and securities. Among the common crimes investigated by special agents are fraud, money laundering, identity theft, forgery, food stamp violations, and crimes pertaining to credit and debit card theft, and fraud. In essence, the Secret Service is a key component in protecting the stability of the nation's economy at multiple levels. Investigations, though, are not the sole responsibility of the Secret Service. Protection of dignitaries and world ambassadors has become a sizeable facet of a special agent's duties.

Ironically, President Lincoln was assassinated the very day that he established the Secret Service; and, although the Secret Service began limited protection functions in 1894, the agency did not take on full-time protection responsibilities until 1902, following the assassination of President William McKinley. Since 1902, Congress has passed numerous legislative edicts expanding the Secret Service's protection responsibilities. The following individuals have permanently assigned special agent details:

- The president, first lady, and their immediate family;
- The vice president (or second in command of the president) and his or her immediate family;
- Former presidents, for a period not to exceed 10 years after leaving office, their spouses, unless the spouse remarries, and their children, until the age of 16.

The protection of other dignitaries, listed below, is coordinated through temporarily assigned teams comprising field agents:

- Foreign heads of state and governmental leaders and their spouses while visiting the U.S.;
- Official U.S. representatives conducting business abroad; and
- Presidential and vice-presidential candidates and their spouses, during a period of time within 120 days of a presidential election.

Although the Secret Service does not divulge specific protection details, generally, the Secret Service will coordinate activities with local law enforcement and emergency services prior to a protection mission. During this time, proactive measures are taken to locate and map evacuation routes, medical facilities, checkpoint stations, and other vital or potentially hazardous conditions. Upon the completion of a protective mission, the Secret Service conducts "protective research," during which the entire activity is scrutinized to document unusual conditions and to make recommendations for future activities.

The Secret Service Uniformed Division also provides protection services but is primarily focused on the security of government property. The Uniformed Division originated as the White House Police Force in 1922 as a branch of the White House Military Aide. In 1930, however, President Herbert Hoover recommended that all presidential protection activities be functions of the Secret Service, bringing the White House Police under the control of the Secret Service. The White House Police became known as the Executive Protective Service in 1970, upon assuming responsibilities of protection of foreign diplomats. The division was again renamed in 1977 to its current title of the Secret Service Uniformed Division.

The Uniformed Division carries out day-to-day patrol activities on the White House grounds and other presidential office facilities, Department of the Treasury facilities, and the official residence of the vice president. The Division also supplements protection details with special agents patrolling on foot, in vehicles, on bicycles and motorcycles, and providing Emergency Response Teams, Canine, and various other specialized units.

Aside from the primary branches, Special Agents and Uniformed Division, the Secret Service maintains other initiatives such as National Special Security Events coordination, the National Threat Assessment Center, and Forensic Services. Established in 1998 through Presidential Decision Directive 62, the Secret Service assumed the role of coordinator for events deemed National Special Security Events. As with dignitary protection, details concerning the logistics of carrying out security coordination for these events may not be shared, lest they be compromised. Fundamentally, the Secret Service allies with local law enforcement and emergency services, as well as other federal agencies to insure the development of practical security plan.

The National Threat Assessment Center (NTAC) was created as a resource to law enforcement agencies in response to various incidents throughout the world.

Agents working in the NTAC use information gathered from an extensive study of attacks, assassinations, and potentially dangerous approaches of dignitaries to analyze and assess received threats against political leaders, dignitaries, and society as a whole. The NTAC offers training and research resources to the law enforcement community, and assists with establishing local threat assessment plans to address school and workplace violence, security of public officials, and domestic violence encounters.

The Secret Service Forensic Services unit offers a plethora of investigative services to local, state, and federal law enforcement agencies. Handwriting analysis is available for specific crimes as a function of the Questioned Document Section (QDS) of Forensic Services. Documents can be scanned and digitized for comparison to known samples, which may also be submitted by the requesting agency, or which may be on file in the QDS database. To complement the QDS, the Instrument Analysis Services Section (IASS) maintains a database of ink, toner, watermark, and plastics to help determine the writing or printing instrument or paper used, and to establish a timeframe of when a document was generated. The Visual Information Services Section (VISS) offers video and audio enhancement and voice recognition analyses, whereas the Polygraph Examination Program maintains its spot as one of the most advanced programs in the country.

The U.S. Secret Service operates 125 field offices throughout the country and abroad and offers various employment opportunities. Special agent candidates must be U.S. citizens at least 21 years old, but not yet 37, and hold a bachelor's degree, have 3 years of investigations experience, or an equivalent combination of both. Salaries are based on the general schedule (GS) scale, an index of salary ranges based on position and candidate qualifications, but generally ranges from approximately $39,613–$71,678. Special agents must complete a 22-week training regimen prior to assignment to a field office. Candidates for the Uniformed Division must also be U.S. citizens, at least 21 years old, but not yet 37. The Uniform Division requires candidates have a high school diploma, or equivalent, and be in good health. Starting annual salary is approximately $40,345–$72,652, dependent on qualifications. Uniformed Division officers must complete 19 weeks of training prior to being deployed. The Secret Service also has various professional and administrative positions, most of which require a bachelor's or higher degree. Annual salaries for these positions are dependent on the type of position and the candidate's education and qualifications. All positions receive paid holidays, government health and retirement benefits, and accumulate annual and sick leave.

From a dedicated bureau concentrating on counterfeiting in 1865, the U.S. Secret Service has significantly broadened its responsibilities to become a major component in national security and a prestigious employer in the law enforcement community. For more information on the U.S. Secret Service, visit their Internet website at: www.ustreas.gov/usss.

M. PATRICK LONG

## References and Further Reading

Echaore-McDavid, S. (2000). *Career Opportunities in Law Enforcement, Security and Protective Services*. Checkmark Books: New York, NY.

Factmonster.com (downloaded May 27, 2003). U.S. Money History. Taken from *The U.S. Treasury Department Bureau of Engraving and Printing* (www.bep.treas.gov). Available at www.factmonster.com/ipka/A0774856.html.

The White House (downloaded May 27, 2003). *The U.S. Secret Service in History*. Inside the White House website. Available at http://clinton4.nara.gov/WH/kids/inside/html/spring 98-2.html.

U.S. Secret Service (Revised on October, 2001). *The Secret Service Story*. Pamphlet available from the U.S. Secret Service.

U.S. Secret Service. *Secret Service Protection*. Pamphlet available from the U.S. Secret Service.

U.S. Secret Service Internet website. Available at www.ustreas. gov/usss/.

U.S. News and World Report, Inc. (December 9, 2002). Bogus bucks, presidents. U.S. News and World Report, p. 18. (InfoTrac article A94830337.)

USAJOBS.com (downloaded June 10, 2003). Search results for Secret Service jobs. Available at http://jsearch.usajobs. opm.gov/a9.asp.

*See also* **Federal Bureau of Investigation (FBI); Police: Private Security Forces**

# Securities Fraud *See* **Money Laundering; White-Collar Crime**

---

# Sedition and Treason

---

Sedition and treason are the most prominent political crimes against the state and typically included in many of the criminal codes or legislation governing security and intelligence agencies of advanced industrialized countries. All of these actions have existed since the creation of the first state. However, their codification in legal statutes has varied among countries because of the sophistication of legal codes and the availability of alternative mechanisms for quelling dissent. Although misprision of treason (in short, "the concealment or nondisclosure of the known treason of another," Schmalleger, 2002, 455), and criminal syndicalism (in sum, "advocating the use of unlawful acts as a means of accomplishing a change in industrial ownership, or to control political change," Schmalleger, 2002, 455) have been recognized as oppositional political crimes, in the last three decades these charges have been rarely applied in courts against so-called political criminal defendants. Both treason and sedition are easily confused with dissent, subversion, and espionage (Ross, 2002). This entry defines sedition and treason, and places them in a historical context.

## Historical Perspective

One of the oldest political crimes is treason. In short it is "an attempt to overthrow the government of the society of which one is a member" (Schmalleger, 2002, 454). In "early common law it was considered 'high treason' to kill the king or to promote a revolt in the kingdom" (Schmalleger, 2002, 454). Charging individuals with treason, however was a convenient way to eliminate those the king or queen (of England) deemed actual traitors, but more likely the tactic was used to silence real or supposed threats to his or her power. The history of the Tower of London is embedded with stories of such acts. Those who fell prey to the charge of treason were usually taken to nearby Tower Hill for a public execution and usually beheaded by an executioner. Once the deed was done, the executioner would hold up the head for all of the assembled crowd to see, then it would be placed on a pole

and paraded around the streets of London. Then in a final act of barbarity, the head and pole would be placed on Tower Bridge (one of a handful of bridges crossing the River Thames that leads into the city) while crows, ravens, and other birds would strip the head of its flesh. Eventually the skull would fall into the river. It was alleged that almost 1500 individuals lost their lives this way.

Although treason is mentioned in the U.S. Constitution (Article III) and several federal statutes, the legislation concerning sedition, sabotage, and espionage is embedded in a variety of acts and documents. Some of these include the *Espionage Act* (1917), *Sedition Act* (1918), *Smith Act* (1940), *McCarran Act* (1950), *Internal Security Act* (1952), and *Communist Control Act* (1954). For a review of these acts see, for example, Packer (1962). Some of these laws have been struck down as unconstitutional (Turks, 1984). "Similar, and often even more sweeping, laws (such as those against 'criminal syndicalism') have been enacted by state legislatures and by local governments" (Turk, 1982a, 59).

Nevertheless, these crimes represent "the most serious offenses...[mainly] because such conduct jeopardizes the security and well-being of the whole nation and its inhabitants . . . these acts are rarely committed and even more rarely charged" (Canada, 1986, 1).

Regardless of where the codification of these offenses is located, most informed analysts believe that these crimes threaten the security of the state and its society. Because security is an amorphous term and practice (Saltstone, 1991), it makes identification, arrest, and prosecution of individuals committing so-called political crimes variable.

This situation has stimulated a number of reforms of various countries' criminal codes, especially those sections that deal with political crime. For example, in 1986, the Law Reform Commission of Canada noted a series of problems with offenses against the state and suggested that "Part II of the Code and the Official Secrets Act are riddled with defects of both form and content" (Canada, 1986, 25).

## Sedition

Sedition has been defined as the "incitement of resistance to or insurrection against lawful authority" (Websters, 1980, 1037). In other contexts it is "communication or agreement intended to defame the government or to incite treason" (Schmalleger, 2002, 456). In Canada, the Code identifies an individual guilty of sedition if he or she "teaches or advocates … the use, without authority of law, of force as a means to accomplish a governmental change within Canada" (Borovoy, 1985, 156). In the U.S., individuals judged to be engaging in sedition have been charged with violating the Sedition Act of 1798, Ch. 74, 1 Stat. 596. In essence, it criminalizes any scandalous article written about the president or Congress. Later federal law defined seditious conspiracy as "If two or more persons in any State or Territory, or in any place subject to the jurisdiction of the United States, conspire to overthrow, put down, or destroy by force of authority, thereof, or by force to prevent, hinder, or delay the execution of any law of the United States, or by force to seize, take, or possess any property of the United States contrary to the authority thereof …" (18 U.S.C., Section 2384).

More commonly, those determined by authorities to have engaged in sedition are charged with seditious libel. Thus, the problem is embedded in the larger discussion of freedom of speech, especially that which criticizes government (Borovoy, 1985; Foerstel, 1998, Ch. 1). Furthermore, the criteria for defining acts as seditious libel are dynamic and subject to changes in political, economic, and social conditions. In its most expansive form, however, seditious libel may be said to embrace any criticism—true or false—of the form, constitution, policies, laws, officers, symbols, or conduct of government (Stone, 1983, 1425).

Understandably, the biggest difficulty with the crime of sedition is being able to specify "at what point in the continuum between the thought and the deed is it appropriate for the law to intervene" (Borovoy, 1985, 156). In general, "Speech which is likely to result in imminent violence is arguably dangerous enough to warrant legal intervention. On the other hand, speech which is not likely to culminate in this way does not warrant such intervention" (Borovoy, 1985, 156).

In 1918, in an effort to shore up support for the entrance of the U.S. in to World War I, and to prevent criticism of the war, which would damage recruiting efforts, the act was amended, becoming more specific, and was popularly referred to as the Sedition Act.

In the U.S., judges and jurists generally use what is called the "clear and present danger test" to see if communications are seditious. The question is whether or not it is appropriate to label the speech seditious or merely an expression of a political position.

Occasionally, individuals are charged with seditious conspiracy. "Conspiracy is established by inference from the conduct of the parties. It is very rare that the agreement between the parties can be established by direct evidence; the evidence offered is usually purely circumstantial. To prove the agreement, evidence such as hearsay which would normally be inadmissible to establish any other criminal offense, may be admitted to show links in a chain of circumstances form which the common agreement may be inferred" (Grosman, 1972, 142). Seditious conspiracy is found in section 60(3) (4) of the Canadian Criminal Code.

Too often governments have tried to prevent opposition groups from expressing dissent by charging them with sedition. Rather than protecting the common good, sedition charges generally reinforce arbitrary state power. Additionally because of the cumbersome nature of the Sedition Act, the government has found it more convenient to charge and convict individuals under a number of existing acts that virtually put a gag order on the statements of exemployees.

## Treason

Treason refers to overt (i.e., nonsymbolic) acts aimed at overthrowing one's own government or state or murdering or personally injuring the sovereign (king or queen) or their family. In Canada, the Code distinguished between high treason (acts formerly punished as capital offenses) now subject to a mandatory life sentence, and treason (acts formerly punished by anywhere from 14 years imprisonment to death) now subject to life imprisonment, except espionage in peacetime, which still has a 14-year maximum sentence (Canada, 1986, 12).

In the U.S., the Constitution (Article III Section 3) specifically outlines what is meant by treason. According to this document, "Treason against the United States, shall consist only in levying War against them, or in adhering to their Enemies, giving them Aid and Comfort." Federal statutes use similar language such as "Whoever, owing allegiance to the United States, levied war against them or adheres to their enemies, giving them aid and comfort within the United States or elsewhere is guilty of treason and shall suffer death, or shall be imprisoned not less than five years and fined under this title but not less than ten thousand dollars ($10,000); and shall be incapable of holding any office under the United States" (18 U.S.C., Section 2381). Many states either in their legislation or constitutions have specific sections which refer to treason (Schmalleger, 2002, 455).

Thus, it is "a criminal offense to publish false, scandalous, and malicious writings against the government, if done with intent to defame, or to excite the hatred of the people, or to stir up sedition or to excite resistance to law, or to aid the hostile designs of any foreign nation against the United States" (Packer, 1962, 82).

The appropriateness of the charge is always debatable. Historically, treason has been a slippery concept for it is often recognized as criminal, whereas at other times it is not. Furthermore, prosecuting individuals and organizations for treason has been applied by the state in an erratic fashion.

For example, in the history of the U.S. fewer than 100 cases involving treason have been brought to court. Most importantly, because treason is a violation of allegiance, for the charge to have merit, one must either be a citizen or resident alien of the U.S. Thus, if you have lost, renounced, or were never a citizen of the U.S., the charge of treason does not apply (Schmalleger, 2002, 455).

Normally the offense is committed inside the U.S., but jurisdiction has expanded to outside America; several persons were successfully prosecuted for broadcasts deemed treasonous made from Axis countries during World War II" (Packer, 1962, 80). "Most insurrections have been local affairs and have usually been handled under state treason, sedition or subversive conspiracy statutes or under statutes designed to control riots and public disturbances" (Ingraham and Tokoro, 1969, 148).

JEFFREY IAN ROSS

## References and Further Reading

Borovoy, A. (1985). Freedom of expression: Some recurring impediments, in Abella, R. and Rothman, M.L. (Eds.), *Justice Beyond Orwell*. Montreal, Canada: Les Editions Yvon Blais, pp. 125–160.

Foerstel, H.N. (1998). *Banned in the Media*. Westport, CT: Greenwood Press.

Grosman, B.A. (1972). Political crime and emergency measures in Canada, in Adler, F. and Mueller, G.O.W. (Eds.), *Politics, Crime and the American Scene*. San Juan, Puerto Rico: North-South Center Press, pp. 141–146.

Ingraham, B.L. and Tokoro, K. (1969). Political crime in the United States and Japan. *Issues in Criminology*, 4(2): 145–169.

Packer, H.L. (1962). Offenses against the state. *The Annals of the American Academy* 339: 77–89.

Saltstone, S.P. (1991). Some consequences of the failure to define the phrase "National Security." *Conflict Quarterly*, 11 (3): 36–54.

Schmalleger, F. (2002). *Criminal Law Today*. Upper Saddle River, NJ: Prentice Hall.

Stone, G.R. (1983). Sedition, in *Encyclopedia of Crime and Justice*. New York, NY: Free Press, 4, 1425–1431.

Turk, A.T. (1982). *Political Criminality*. Beverly Hills, CA: Sage.

*See also* **Political Crimes against the State; War Crimes**

# Self-Control Theory

The years spanning the late 1970s and 1980s, as far as the criminologists Michael Gottfredson and Travis Hirschi were concerned, saw little evidence of growth in the understanding of crime. First, the two researchers felt that their discipline had lost its leadership role in shaping crime-control policy. Instead, the government agencies that developed (and had a stake in) crime policy dictated the agendas of the field of criminology—mainly because these agencies also controlled most of the money that funded criminal justice research (Gottfredson and Hirschi, 1986). A second broad concern was that criminology was slowly abandoning theory, which is the source of ideas that might inform policy. In response to this situation, the two scholars coauthored a series of widely cited and debated papers that rigorously questioned the direction of criminological research and crime policy. By 1990, Gottfredson and Hirschi had synthesized these papers into a book entitled *A General Theory of Crime*. The theory described in this book argued that one's level of criminal activity is a function of self-control, which is the acquired ability of individuals to appreciate the long-term consequences of their decisions. This concept, Gottfredson and Hirschi claimed, has relevance to virtually every illegal, immoral, and reckless act that people engage in. The success their book has had in shaping the agendas of researchers is evident in the appearance within 10 years of at least 30 empirical tests in important journals. Few theories published before or since have received so much attention or generated so much argument.

The substantive inspiration for self-control theory can be traced to the problem of explaining the age distribution of crime. The basic shape of the age distribution reveals that offense activity peaks during late adolescence and quickly declines throughout the remainder of life. In an article in the *American Journal of Sociology*, Hirschi and Gottfredson (1983) investigated the attempts to explain why young people commit disproportionately high levels of crime and the implications that this fact might have for criminological research and crime policy. The two authors noted that the form of the age distribution apparently remains the same for everyone everywhere, regardless of gender, racial identity, or national background. Nor has the shape of the age distribution of crime changed appreciably between the 1840s to the present day. Hirschi and Gottfredson also found that young folks are disproportionately involved in nearly every major crime type and even for other behavior, like motor vehicle accidents. Interestingly, the *differences* in offense activity between individual high-rate offenders and low-rate offenders were relatively stable throughout the life course. Thus, Hirschi and Gottfredson concluded that offenders do not desist from crime and suddenly become law-abiding—they merely "slow down" as they get older, and this slowing down affects everyone regardless of the individual's relative level of criminal involvement.

Hirschi and Gottfredson drew the following conclusions from their study of the age effect. First, they believed that the criminal justice system could not claim responsibility for the decline in criminal activity in the later periods in an offender's life. This was because the system often became involved only some time *after* an offender's level of criminal involvement had already started to wane. Second, Hirschi and Gottfredson could find no reason to believe that sociological factors could account for the change, because the age distribution transcends all of the traditional sociological variables (culture, time period, gender, racial identity). Nor could Hirschi's (1969) earlier social control theory account for the decrease in crime over the life course, because variations in the strength of social bonds apparently did not account for any reform (see Hirschi and Gottfredson, 2000b). Hirschi and Gottfredson thus felt that it was necessary to develop a theory that could take into account the "fact" of an invariant age distribution and its implications for theory, methods, and policy. The initial reaction to this article on the age distribution indicates that the field of criminology was unanimous that Hirschi and Gottfredson were wrong (e.g., Greenberg, 1985; Steffensmeier et al., 1989). In a series of later papers, however, the two authors continued to defend their understanding of the age distribution and explore its implications. The eventual result was self-control theory.

## Self-Control Theory

Self-control theory shares its most basic assumption with Hirschi's (1969) social control theory. This assumption is the Hobbesian idea that the individual is inherently amoral and self-interested, which means that whether one conforms to the rules or commits crime depends on which alternative leads to greater personal advantage. Thus, the basic question about crime that the theory tries to answer is "Why doesn't everyone do it when tempted?" rather than "What made that person do it?" This assumption makes self-control theory distinct from other important explanations of crime, such as differential association or social learning theories. These latter two theories, for example, do not assume that criminal behavior is natural. Instead, their starting point is that someone must acquire the motivation and skills to commit crime through exposure to procriminal influences in the environment. In self-control theory, on the other hand, the tendency to commit crime is present at birth and the theory must account for the ability to resist this natural tendency.

Self-control theory accounts for the age distribution problem by making a distinction between "crime" and "criminality." Crime that refers to actual events and presupposes such factors as opportunity, victims, and so forth, is a characteristic that is free to change over time. In contrast, criminality (or self-control) refers to time-stable differences between individuals in their tendency to commit crime. In *A General Theory of Crime*, Gottfredson and Hirschi begin with a discussion of the nature of crime.

The important question for the two authors about the nature of crime concerns the elements common to all crimes. First, their investigation led them to believe that most crimes take very little training or skill. Even crimes that cause serious harm do not usually require commensurately high skill. Second, most crimes happen quickly and need little effort. A decision to commit a murder, for example, is often made on the spot and the homicide itself usually takes but an instant. Third, the advantages that crime confers on the individual, though immediate, are short term and minimal. Most larceny, for example, will net scant financial reward.

A fourth element common to all criminal activity is the presence of long-term negative consequences. Borrowing from the English philosopher Jeremy Bentham, Gottfredson and Hirschi argued that crime carries four kinds of consequences or sanctions. Physical or natural sanctions refer to physical danger that follows naturally from the act without intervention by third parties (i.e., nonvictims). Would-be burglars, for instance, risk the possibility that occupants of a residence might violently resist invasion, which could lead to the death or injury of the burglar. Another consequence of crime is moral, where offenders—if caught—face the negative opinion of others (with consequent loss of status, trust, and benefits). Drug use, for instance, risks the condemnation of friends and family. Crimes also entail legal sanctions, which include imprisonment or even death. Finally, crime leads to religious sanctions, which are the dire consequences that emerge in an afterlife.

Because crime happens in spite of the four sanctioning systems that ought to restrain it, Gottfredson and Hirschi reasoned that individuals must differ in their ability to perceive the long-term repercussions of their behavior. The physical consequences of promiscuous sexual activity, such as disease or (for females) pregnancy, may take weeks, months, or even years before they begin to materialize. Gottfredson and Hirschi labeled this ability to appreciate the sanctions associated with crime "low self-control," which attends to the "criminality" distinction mentioned above. Individuals with low self-control typically possess the following traits: the tendency to behave impulsively, take risks, ignore the feelings of others, prefer easy tasks, and to be belligerent. Low self-control also manifests itself in ways that need not be criminal. For instance, low self-control can lead to a greater share of accidents, alcohol consumption, smoking activity, and promiscuous sex. Gottfredson and Hirschi interpret the high degree of correlation between these behaviors as evidence that low self-control is a characteristic with wide-ranging consequences.

Gottfredson and Hirschi self-control is an acquired characteristic. They specifically emphasize child rearing in the family as the primary agent for the development of self-control. In contrast, social learning theories give no particular preeminence to the family, in the causation of crime, whereas classic versions of strain theory and labeling theory hardly acknowledge the family at all. In self-control theory, childhood socialization is the process of educating individuals about the consequences of their actions. Borrowing from the work of Gerald Patterson, Gottfredson, and Hirschi reasoned that three factors must be present before self-control becomes a habit. First, parents must be able and willing to supervise their children. The level of supervision children receive is thus substantially dependent on how intact the family is, as well as the bonds of love between parent and child. Second, parents must also recognize deviant behavior when it occurs. Third, parents must punish the deviant behavior. Once self-control becomes evident in children, approximately around age 8, differences in self-control remain relatively stable—older children who ignore the consequences of their behavior at a higher level than their peers will show similar tendencies as adults.

## Tests and Criticism of Self-Control Theory

This general theory has generated numerous empirical tests, most of which are supportive (see Pratt and Cullen, 2000). Researchers have linked low self-control with higher levels of self-reported delinquency, official criminal convictions, shoplifting, fraud, drinking and driving, drug use, motor vehicle accidents, adverse social consequences, and even victimization. International tests of self-control theory most often employ data from Canadian residents, with the results from these studies being generally supportive (e.g., Keane, Maxim, and Teevan, 1993; LaGrange and Silverman, 1999). The theory does not lack for critics; however, many tests and commentaries identify apparent shortcomings (e.g., Akers, 1991; Sampson and Laub, 1995). The following list, although not exhaustive, represents some of the major objections to the theory that have emerged in the 10 years since its publication.

One of the earliest criticisms of self-control theory is that it is tautological. That is, the theory makes the definitions of crime and self-control identical, where criminal behavior is, logically, evidence of low self-control. If correct, then self-control theory cannot be proven wrong. Hirschi and Gottfredson (1993, 2000a), however, believe that tautology is, in fact, an important strength of their theory—proof that it follows the path of logic. The two authors argue that tautological systems do not necessarily "conform to empirical reality, make accurate predictions, [or] lead to sound social policy" (Hirschi and Gottfredson, 2000a). For instance, research *can* show that smoking, sex, and crime—all of which are theoretically manifestations of low self-control—are unrelated. A problem related to logical tautology rests in how to measure self-control—indicators of self-control must be distinct from the dependent variable. Current research often measures self-control with personality inventories gleaned from the psychological literature (e.g., Grasmick et al., 1993); however, research also employs alternative measures (e.g., Gibbs and Giever, 1995; Keane, Maxim, and Teevan, 1993).

A vigorous debate that predates self-control theory is the assumption that individual differences in their tendency to commit crime are relatively stable throughout the life course. Self-control theory argues that the tendency to commit crime is relatively stable after childhood, whereas other theories (e.g., Sampson and Laub, 1993) stress the role that external factors can play in criminality many years after childhood. Research has not yet definitively resolved this question.

Another criticism is that the general theory oversimplifies the causes of crime. That is, the parsimony of self-control theory glosses the complexity of the myriad causes of human behavior. Some individuals from apparently well-adjusted families get into trouble as teenagers and just as suddenly cease their participation in crime. The research testing these single pathway versus multiple pathway approaches has yet to resolve this issue.

## Policy Implications of Self-Control Theory

The theory indicates that the most far-reaching programs with the greatest long-term benefits would be those that successfully promote the development of self-control in children. In particular, such programs need to target families that are struggling in terms of their ability to supervise and socialize children (see, also, Hirschi, 1995). In order to achieve this, theorists advocate society striving to maximize the number of caregivers available to each child. Moreover, programs should address the sources of weakened or broken families, in particular teenage pregnancy.

Effective crime-control policy need not emphasize the development of self-control, however. Because the age distribution of crime figures prominently in the self-control framework, Hirschi and Gottfredson argued that an effective crime-control policy might target the activities of the teenage population. In particular, effective policies would limit the ability of teenagers to socialize with friends without the immediate supervision of parents or teachers. Research indicates that teenagers who spend more leisure time with peers without adult supervision are more likely to engage in deviant activity (Osgood et al., 1996; Felson, 1998), because friends can serve as facilitators of deviance. Policies designed to restrict the opportunities of teenagers might include curfews and curbs on the easy access of teenagers to guns, cars, alcohol, and unguarded crime targets. As no other age group gets into as much trouble as adolescents, policies that target teenagers might be the most efficient at reducing crime. Moreover, preventing teens from committing crime by eliminating opportunities is much less expensive and disruptive toward society than institutionalization or incarceration.

Given that the criminal act is attractive to the would-be offender because it provides immediate and easy gratification, policies that make the completion of crime more difficult or complex would be particularly successful at preventing crime. Thus, the potential victim may be the most effective actor in crime control. He or she could reduce the likelihood of becoming a victim of burglary, for example, by trimming the foliage around a house (to eliminate cover for the burglar) and locking all doors. Individuals can reduce the risk of robbery or assault by moving in groups. Shopping centers and apartment complexes can prevent victimization on their property by hiring security guards.

Self-control theory, however, is suspicious of current law enforcement policies, particularly proactive policing. Sting operations where undercover officers tempt would-be offenders to commit crime, serve little purpose because such operations only punish individuals simply for being weak when faced with opportunities for easy gratification; it does not follow that these offenders would have considered committing a crime on their own without the temptation offered by the police. Self-control theory sees proactive policing as activity that infringes on civil liberties without providing any additional crime protection.

Self-control theory is also critical of the emphasis of current policy on the courts and corrections systems— at best, these institutions can only play a minor role in crime prevention. Gottfredson and Hirschi (1986) note that the current system is designed around the adult offender, whose offense activity is already slowing down. Current policies like "getting tough," mandatory sentences, and "three strikes" laws further emphasize inefficient crime control. First, the theory indicates that the offenders affected by these policies are less capable of appreciating the long-term consequences of their decisions and will simply ignore the tougher sanctions. Additionally, offenders with lengthy prior records tend to get longer periods of incarceration. Because it often takes time to acquire long records of arrests and convictions—such offenders tend to be older adults—the system tends to incapacitate mostly low-risk individuals. The theory also does not recommend efforts to rehabilitate offenders. First, few rehabilitation programs have shown much promise. Second, offenders eligible for rehabilitation programs already are becoming less likely to participate in crime because they are aging.

CHRISTOPHER J. SCHRECK

## References and Further Reading

Akers, R.L., Self-control as a general theory of crime, *Journal of Quantitative Criminology* 7 (1991).

Felson, M., *Crime and Everyday Life,* Thousand Oaks, CA: Pine Forge Press, 1998.

Gibbs, J.J. and Giever, D., Self-control and its manifestations among university students: An empirical test of Gottfredson and Hirschi's general theory, *Justice Quarterly* 12 (1995).

Gottfredson, M.R. and Hirschi, T., The true value of lambda would appear to be zero: An essay on career criminals, criminal careers, selective incapacitation, cohort studies, and related topics, *Criminology* 24 (1986).

Gottfredson, M.R. and Hirschi, T., *A General Theory of Crime,* Palo Alto, CA: Stanford University Press, 1990.

Grasmick, H.G., Tittle, C.R., Bursik, R.J. and Arneklev, B.J., Testing the core implications of Gottfredson and Hirschi's general theory of crime. *Journal of Research in Crime and Delinquency* 30 (1993).

Greenberg, D.F., Age, crime, and social explanation, *American Journal of Sociology* 91 (1985).

Hirschi, T., *Causes of Delinquency,* Berkeley, CA: University of California Press, 1969.

Hirschi, T., The family, in *Crime,* Wilson, J.Q. and Petersilia, J., San Francisco, CA: ICS Press, 1995.

Hirschi, T. and Gottfredson, M.R., Age and the explanation of crime, *American Journal of Sociology* 89 (1983).

Hirschi, T. and Gottfredson, M.R., Commentary: Testing the general theory of crime, *Journal of Research in Crime and Delinquency* 30 (1993).

Hirschi, T. and Gottfredson, M.R., In defense of self-control, *Theoretical Criminology* 4 (2000a).

Hirschi, T. and Gottfredson, M.R., *Self-control, in Explaining Criminals and Crime: Essays in Contemporary Criminological Theory,* edited by Paternoster, R. and Bachman, R., Los Angeles, CA: Roxbury Publishing Company, 2000b.

Keane, C., Maxim, P.S. and Teevan, J.J., Drinking and driving, self-control, and gender: Testing a general theory of crime, *Journal of Research in Crime and Delinquency* 30 (1993).

LaGrange, T.C. and Silverman, R.A., Low self-control and opportunity: Testing the general theory of crime as an explanation for gender differences in delinquency, *Criminology* 37 (1999).

Osgood, D.W., Wilson, J.K., O'Malley, P.M., Bachman, J.G. and Johnston, L.D., Routine activities and individual deviant behavior, *American Sociological Review* 61 (1996).

Pratt, T.C. and Cullen, F.T., The empirical status of Gottfredson and Hirschi's general theory of crime: A meta-analysis, *Criminology* 38 (2000).

Sampson, R.J. and Laub, J.H., *Crime in the Making,* Cambridge, MA: Harvard University Press, 1993.

Sampson, R.J. and Laub, J.H., Contributions of life course theory, *Studies on Crime and Crime Prevention* 4 (1995).

Steffensmeier, D., Allan, E.A., Harer, M.D. and Streifel, C., Age and the distribution of crime, *American Journal of Sociology* 94 (1989).

*See also* **Age and Criminal Behavior; Social Control Theories of Criminal Behavior**

# Self-Defense as a Defense to Criminal Liability

## Introduction

Self-defense is an affirmative defense raised by the defendant at a criminal trial. If successfully established, it may serve as a complete defense, eliminating criminal liability altogether. An affirmative defense is a response made by the defendant to a charge in a criminal trial. It is raised after the prosecution has established its case, and permits the defendant to avoid liability even when the government has met its burden of proof on the elements of the offense. There are two general defenses of justification and excuse.

The most commonly raised justification defense is self-defense. A justification defense is raised when the defendant admits he is responsible for the act but claims that under the circumstances the act was not criminal, that what he did was lawful. Justified behavior precludes punishment because the conduct lacks blameworthiness. A defendant who claims self-defense argues that he was justified in using force to repel an aggressor. Self-defense is frequently raised as a defense to charges of battery or even murder.

## The Elements of Self-Defense

Self-defense may be successfully claimed if the defendant can demonstrate that he used force to repel an imminent, unprovoked attack that would have caused him serious injury, and he reasonably believed that such an attack was about to occur, or was occurring (Fletcher, 1978). Each of these elements requires some explication, provided below.

### Against Unprovoked Attacks

Force may only be used against unprovoked attacks. The defendant cannot provoke the attack and then claim self-defense, or if he did provoke the attack he must have withdrawn completely from the fight before asserting a right to self-defense. This rule applies even if the defendant starts a nondeadly fight which then escalates. Additionally, the aggressor must be using unlawful force. One cannot claim self-defense against one who is justified in using force, as during an arrest (Hemmens and Levin, 2000).

It is possible for one who is the initial aggressor to withdraw from the conflict, so that if he then uses force to repel an attack, he may claim self-defense. The initial aggressor must completely give up the fight, however, and successfully communicate his withdrawal to the other person involved.

It is often difficult to determine who started a fight when the only witnesses are the two participants. An example is a case that received national media attention in 1974. It involved the killing of a jailer, Clarence

Allgood, in Wilmington, North Carolina by a jail inmate, Joan Little. Little stabbed Allgood 11 times with an ice pick and escaped from the jail. She was subsequently arrested and charged with first-degree murder, with the prosecution alleging she had lured Allgood into her cell with promises of sexual favors, and then killed him and taken his keys to facilitate her escape. Little claimed that Allgood had entered her cell with the ice pick and attempted to rape her, and that she had acted in self-defense when she took the ice pick away from Allgood and stabbed him with it. Because she was African American and Allgood was White, the case received national media attention.

### Imminent Harm

Force may be used only when an attack is either in progress or "imminent"—meaning it will occur immediately. It cannot be used to prevent a future attack, or to retaliate against an old attack. This limitation on self-defense has been heavily criticized in recent years by scholars who argue that the defense should be available to persons such as battered spouses who resort to deadly force after suffering repeated assaults. According to the National Clearinghouse of the Defense of Battered Women, between 500 and 750 women kill abusive spouses or boyfriends each year.

A case that brought self-defense to public prominence in the 1980s involved the shooting by a New York City subway passenger, Bernard Goetz, of four juveniles who approached and demanded he give them $5. A victim of several prior muggings, Goetz was armed with a handgun that he used on the juveniles, shooting all four of them, wounding one severely. Goetz claimed he was in danger of being assaulted at the time he open fired, but the evidence suggested the juveniles were not in fact about to assault him. None of them displayed a weapon, and only one of them moved toward him prior to the shooting. Goetz was prosecuted for several offenses, including attempted murder, on the ground that he had acted too quickly in shooting the juveniles, before it was clear that he was actually in imminent danger.

### Honest Belief in Death or Serious Harm

Force may be used in self-defense only when the defendant honestly and reasonably believes he or she is about to be killed or seriously injured. This test is similar to tort law's "reasonable man" standard. Some states use a subjective test. In these jurisdictions, force is permitted if the actor honestly believed use of force was necessary. This test focuses exclusively on the mind of actor. Threats that cannot be taken seriously do not justify the use of force. In 1994, a homeowner in Baton Rouge, Louisiana shot and killed a Japanese exchange student who, dressed in a costume for a Halloween party, mistakenly approached the wrong house. The homeowner saw the student approaching his house, yelled "freeze," and then opened fire. The homeowner was charged for the death, but a jury found him not guilty.

### Amount of Force that May Be Used

The defendant may only use as much force as he honestly and reasonably believes is necessary to repel the attack. This means the amount of force used must be proportionate (Dressler, 1995). A defendant who uses more force than is necessary to repel an attack cannot successfully claim self-defense. Self-defense applies to both deadly and nondeadly uses of force. One may use deadly force only if faced with it. Less-than-deadly attacks authorize resort to less-than-deadly responses. A person who uses deadly force to repel a nondeadly attack may be prosecuted for either murder, or, in some jurisdictions, use his mistaken belief that he could use deadly force as an imperfect defense, reducing the charge from murder to manslaughter.

### Limitations on the Use of Self-Defense

There are a number of limitations and exceptions to the general rules of self-defense. These include the retreat doctrine, true man doctrine, and the castle exception. These modifications of self-defense law are intended to provide some flexibility to the law. The *retreat doctrine* requires that a person must retreat rather than use deadly force if it is possible to retreat without endangering the retreator. This doctrine places a premium on human life and discourages the use of deadly force unless absolutely necessary, but is endorsed by a minority of states.

Conversely, the majority of states follow the no-retreat rule, or *true man doctrine*, which states that a person need not retreat, even if he or she could do so safely. The justification for this approach is based on the idea that the criminal law should not force a victim to take a cowardly or humiliating position.

The *castle doctrine* states that a person attacked in his or her home does not have to retreat, even if retreat is possible, if the attack threatens death or serious injury. This exception to the retreat doctrine is based on the idea that a person's home is his or her castle, and that one should never be forced by the criminal law to abandon it (Brown, 1991). Several states, such as Colorado and Oklahoma, have passed so-called "make my day laws" applying the castle exception to any home invasion, even if there is no evidence of serious harm to the occupant of the home. Several other jurisdictions have adopted this approach through court decision.

### Application of Self-Defense Doctrine to Other Situations

Self-defense may also apply to defense of others and, in some circumstances, to the defense of property. Historically, defense of others could be raised only by someone who used force to defend a family member. Most states have expanded this restriction to include other special relationships such as lovers and friends, whereas other states have abandoned the special relationship requirement altogether. The "other" must have the right to defend himself for the defender to claim the defense. Thus if A provokes an attack by B, C could not use force against B and claim defense of B.

Most states restrict the use of deadly force for the defense of the person or the home, and allow only nondeadly force for the defense of property. The justification for this is simple enough—although losing property to a thief is unfortunate, theft is not a capital offense and using deadly force to protect property constitutes a disproportionate response. There are a number of cases involving the prosecution of property owners who set up booby traps (such as spring guns or explosive devices) to deter burglars from entering their homes or businesses. Property owners have been convicted of assault or, when the booby trap resulted in the death of the alleged burglar, manslaughter. In 1990, a Denver machine shop owner who had been burglarized eight times in 2 years rigged a shotgun to fire at the door to his business if the door was pried open. A juvenile attempting to break into the business was killed when the shotgun discharged, and the business owner was convicted of manslaughter.

Some states, such as Texas, go further in allowing deadly force to protect land or certain types of property that have a great value, such as natural gas. These situations are the exception rather than the rule, however.

## Conclusion

Self-defense has a long history in the criminal as law. Much of the law of self-defense was developed as common law, and subsequently codified in criminal statutes or codes. As with any legal doctrine, the defense of self-defense is subject to modification over time. As society changes, changes are occasionally made to the criminal law. Examples of this sort of modification include the general elimination of the true man doctrine as society became more civilized and a higher premium was placed on human life; this in turn has been modified by "make my day" laws that seek to protect the sanctity of the home at the cost of human life.

The law of self-defense is intended to provide those who are compelled to use force to defend themselves with protection from criminal liability. When it is clear from the facts that a people are justified in using force to defend themselves, no charges will be filed. Often, however, it is not clear that self-defense was justified. Thus it is not infrequently raised as an affirmative defense at trial. Frequently, the issue is not whether a defendant was justified in using force in self-defense, but whether the defendant used the appropriate amount of force. This is often a close question. As society has become more civilized, courts have become more reluctant to allow claims of self-defense without close inspection of the underlying facts.

CRAIG HEMMENS

### References and Further Reading

Brown, R.M. (1991). *No Duty to Retreat: Violence and Values in American History and Society.* New York, NY: Oxford University Press.

Dressler, J. (1995). *Understanding Criminal Law.* New York, NY: Matthew Bender.

Fletcher, G. (1978). *Rethinking Criminal Law.* Boston, MA: Little, Brown.

Hemmens, C. and Levin, D. (2000). Resistance is futile: The right to resist unlawful arrest in an era of aggressive policing. *Crime and Delinquency* 46:472.

Kadish, S. (1987). Excusing crime. *California Law Review* 75:257.

*See also* **Defense to Criminal Liability: Justifications and Excuses**

# Self-Esteem and Criminal Behavior

Because the pursuit of expressions of approval, esteem, or respect from others is considered to be one of the most powerful motivating forces shaping human behavior, most criminological theories incorporate some consideration of the personal meaning or interpersonal significance of criminal behavior for its participants. When applied to the specific link between criminal behavior and self-esteem, several distinct and contrasting positions can be identified, ranging from the popular view that such behavior is a reflection of low self-esteem to the view that criminal behavior is a source of self-esteem, honor, or respect in certain subcultures.

Although rarely discussed, the major sociological perspectives on criminal behavior share two basic social psychological assumptions in common: (1) Variations in self-esteem reflect variations in the allocation of esteem by significant others in the individual's social environment and (2) such esteem is likely to be accorded for behaviors that reflect commitment to group norms and contributions to the achievement of group goals. The implications of these shared assumptions for the specific manner in which self-esteem and criminal behavior are linked varies considerably from theory to theory, depending on conceptions of the group standards for allocating esteem and the normative expectations of diverse groups in modern societies.

Social control or social bond theories imply that self-esteem is anchored most often in socially endorsed accomplishments and that involvement in law breaking is likely to be associated with low self-esteem. Such theories assume that there is consensus on the impropriety of law breaking and that crime is a culturally disapproved route for attaining esteem (Hirschi, 1969). In such social environments, crime is likely to result in disapproval and loss of esteem and accomplishments through acceptable channels enhances self-esteem. This perspective is quite consistent with the "self-esteem" movement among policy makers in the later decades of the 20th century that was characterized by the view that boosting feelings of personal worth among the young would act as a barrier to a variety of problematic behaviors. This perspective is supported by the general finding that delinquent youth tend to score lower on measures of self-esteem than nondelinquent youth (Jensen, 1972, 82–103).

Social control theory implies an inverse relation between self-esteem and criminal behavior. People low in self-esteem have less to lose through law breaking and, hence, are more likely to do so. However, law breaking is not viewed as a source of self-esteem, or as a solution to problems of low self-esteem. This perspective stands in marked contrast to theories that depict criminal and delinquent behavior as a problem-solving response to status frustration. One of the earliest statements of this type of theory is Albert Cohen's *Delinquent Boys* (1955, 121) in which youth "denied status in respectable society" are depicted as constructing a delinquent contra-culture with "criteria of status which these children *can* meet." From this perspective, one solution to status problems among similarly disadvantaged youths is to develop their own subculture in which esteem is allocated for demonstrations of rebellion and flaunting attacks on conventional society.

Howard Kaplan proposes a similar problem-solving view of delinquency based on a universal "self-esteem" motive. The self-esteem motive is defined as "the personal need to maximize the experience of positive self-attitudes and to minimize the experience of negative self-attitudes" (1980, 8). He views many forms of adolescent deviance as "deviant behavior in defense of self." Youth who have suffered status losses will be highly receptive to situations where they can redeem self-esteem through defensive behaviors. In this type of theory the correlation between self-esteem and criminal behavior depends on the subject's stage in the problem-solving process. Initially, low self-esteem or a threat to self-esteem generates a status problem and criminal or delinquent behavior can be one of the outcomes. However, if it solves the status problem, then self-esteem is restored or enhanced. Tests of this type of theory require data collected over time because low self-esteem is supposed to prompt delinquency, but delinquency is supposed to enhance self-esteem, a theory requires.

Research on this type of problem-solving theory has yielded mixed results. Two studies have found that when youths are followed over time, those who initially have low self-esteem have a subsequently higher probability of delinquency, and that self-esteem appears to increase after such involvement. In contrast, two studies report no significant enhancement of self-esteem following participation in delinquency. Testing his own theory, Kaplan found some support for the problem-solving view of delinquency, but he also reports that it applies only to certain categories of boys who lack other means of coping with or mitigating rejection. In short, there is as much evidence challenging the theory as supporting it. However, none of these studies specifically examines group delinquency, although it is the allocation of status by other similarly situated youth which is supposed to help solve status problems.

A third type of criminological theory implying specific links between criminal behavior and self-esteem are cultural deviance theories. For example, Walter Miller (1958, 5–19) specifically rejects problem-solving theories and argues that in some social settings there are long-enduring, subcultural traditions that encourage delinquency. Youths may gain status through law breaking, but it is because such activity conforms with subcultural expectations, not because they are collectively repudiating conventional society's standards. This type of theory implies that criminal and delinquent behavior may be positively related to self-esteem in specific subcultures. Only one study has focused on that possibility. In a study of black and white youth in different status categories, the relationship between delinquency and self-esteem was found to vary considerably, but no significant positive relationships were found (Jensen, 1972, 82–103). There are some categories of youth where delinquency is unrelated to self-esteem, but there is little evidence that delinquent youth fare better than nondelinquent youth. If law breaking were approved behavior in the sizeable subcultures identified by cultural deviance theorists, there should be some categories of youth where those involved in delinquency are higher in self-esteem.

Another criminological theory relevant to the relationship between criminal behavior and self-esteem is labeling theory (Schur, 1973). Labeling theory focuses on the consequences of apprehension and correctional interventions for the self-images of offenders. One of the concepts central to such approaches is stigmatization, the application of labels with negative or derogatory implications. These labels can be derivatives of legal processing (e.g., "ex-con"), clinical diagnosis (e.g., pedophile), or they can be colloquial labels (e.g., "troublemaker," "bad kid," "pervert").

Along similar lines, John Braithwaite (1989) argues that the U.S. compounds the crime problem through punitive and derogatory labeling processes that isolate and stigmatize offenders.

Whether punitive labeling has negative consequences for the self-esteem of those labeled has yet to be thoroughly investigated.

GARY JENSEN

### References and Further Reading

Braithwaite, J., *Crime, Shame, and Reintegration*. Cambridge, U.K.: Cambridge University Press, 1989.

Cohen, A.K., *Delinquent Boys*. New York, NY: Free Press, 1955.

Hirschi, T., *Causes of Delinquency*. Berkeley, CA: University of California Press, 1969.

Jensen, G.F., Delinquency and adolescent self-conceptions: A study of the personal relevance of infraction. *Social Problems* 20 (1972).

Kaplan, H., *Deviant Behavior in Defense of Self*. New York, NY: Academic Press, 1980.

McCarthy, J.D. and Hoge, D.R., The dynamics of self-esteem and delinquency. *American Journal of Sociology* 90 (1984).

Miller, W., Lower class culture as a generating milieu of gang delinquency. *Journal of Social Issues* 14 (1958).

Schur, E., *Radical Non-Intervention: Rethinking the Delinquency Problem*. Englewood Cliffs, NJ: Prentice-Hall, 1973.

Wells, E.L. and Rankin, J.H., Self-concept as a mediating factor in delinquency. *Social Psychology Quarterly* 46 (1983).

*See also* **Psychological Theories of Criminal Behavior: An Overview**

# Self-Incrimination, The Privilege Against

The privilege against self-incrimination in the U.S. is embodied in the Fifth Amendment of the U.S. Constitution, which states that "no person shall ... be compelled in any criminal case to be a witness against himself."

## The Privilege in Historical Context

The origins of the privilege have been described as complex and obscure, and the discussions of this topic are prolific. Nevertheless, some generalizations can be drawn. The earliest beginnings of the privilege may be found in the hated device of the oath *ex officio* used by the courts of High Commission and Star Chamber in England. The motto of *nemo tenetuer seipsum prodere* (no man is required to accuse himself) became the rallying cry against the oath and the courts that used it. By the time these courts had been abolished, "compulsory examination of the accused had acquired a bad name" (Schulhofer, 1991), and the use of the privilege gradually began to grow in common law courts. The privilege was traditionally viewed as an idea that no one should be compelled to answer a case brought without well-grounded suspicion or under torture. In its American incarnation, it encompassed even broader protections involving not just the initiation of criminal proceedings, but the conduct of criminal trials as well (Alschuler, 1996).

## The Basic Privilege in the U.S.

As embodied in the Fifth Amendment, the privilege against self-incrimination has its limits. It applies only to criminal proceedings, it applies only to compelled—not voluntary—statements, and it applies only to testimonial evidence. Defendants can still be required to provide physical evidence—for example, weapons or drugs (see *Schember v. California,* 384 U.S. 757, 1966). Since 1966, however, the U.S. version of the privilege has closely intertwined with the rules of *Miranda v. Arizona* (384 U.S. 436, 1966), which replaced the case-by-case determinations of voluntariness and reliability. This, now famous, case held that custodial interrogations inherently involved coercion. Absent procedural safeguards—namely the Miranda warnings—designed to counteract that coercion, any confessions or incriminating statements must be seen as compelled, in violation of the Fifth Amendment (Id. at 467, 478–479).

Under *Miranda,* once suspects are taken into custody, they must be told that they have a right to remain silent, that anything they say may be used against them in court, that they have a right to have an attorney present during questioning, and that an attorney will be provided for them in cases of need. Before the police can use any statements from suspects, it must be shown that they understood these rights, and that they were knowingly and voluntarily waived. Once a defendant invokes the right to silence, all questioning on that particular matter must cease unless reinitiated by the suspect or the suspect's attorney (see *Michigan v. Mosley,* 423 U.S. 96, 1975).

Once an arrestee has invoked the right to silence, not only are any further statements inadmissible at trial, but no comment can be made at trial regarding the invocation of that right or the refusal to testify (*Griffin v. California,* 380 U.S. 609, 1965). Even if the defendant does testify at trial, the U.S. Supreme Court has held that it would be "fundamentally unfair and a deprivation of due process to allow the arrested person's silence to be used to impeach an explanation subsequently offered at trial" (see *Doyle v. Ohio,* 426 U.S. 610, 618, 1976). However, a defendant's silence before arrest can be used to impeach a defense claim raised later at trial (see *Jenkins v. Anderson,* 447 U.S. 231, 1980).

## Inferences and the U.K.: A Comparative Perspective

In England, the rules against such negative inferences are not so strict. In 1994, Parliament passed the Criminal Justice and Public Order Act. Under Section 34 of the act:

> In any proceeding against a person for an offense, evidence given that the accused, after being cautioned by the police, failed to mention any fact [later] relied on in his defense, and that fact is one which under the circumstances existing at the time could reasonably been expected to be mentioned, the trier of fact may draw such inferences from the failure as appear proper.

Cases interpreting the Act have imposed a number of requirements that must be met before any adverse inferences can be drawn. These include: (1) the jury must be informed of the prosecution's burden to prove the state's case beyond a reasonable doubt; (2) the jury must be informed that the defendant retains a right to remain silent; (3) the jury must find and believe that the prosecution has established an answerable case *before* drawing any inference; and (4) an inference alone cannot prove guilt (Van Kessel, 1998).

One of the most renowned supporters of such inferences is A.A.S. Zuckerman, a legal scholar who writes heavily in the area of evidence. He argues that as long as procedural fairness exists, including access to a solicitor attorney, there may be advantages to allowing such inferences to be drawn at trial (Zuckerman, 1989). Zuckerman argues for allowing such inferences as a way to balance the need to protect a suspect from improper police pressure while reducing obstacles to police investigations.

Another argument in support of these types of inferences notes that today, many persons make false statements during interrogations, not out of fear, but because they think they can talk their way out of suspicion. If this is the case, then allowing the inferences would diminish the potential benefits of such fabrications while still protecting basic rights. Along those same lines, Albert Alschuler of the University of Chicago Law School argues that:

> [T]he virtues of an 'accusatorial' system in which defendants are privileged to remain passive are far from obvious. The person who knows the most about the guilt or innocence of a criminal defendant is ordinarily the criminal herself. Unless expecting her to respond to inquiry is immoral or inhuman, ... renouncing all claim to her evidence is costly and foolish (Alschuler, 1996, 2636).

Nevertheless, it is unlikely that these inferences will be transported to the U.S. anytime soon. Unlike the U.K., the U.S. privilege is ingrained in a written constitution and thus much harder to alter. Recently, the U.S. Supreme Court reaffirmed the Miranda warnings—with all that implies for the basis and importance of the privilege—as being required by the Fifth Amendment's Due Process Clause (see *U.S. v. Dickerson*, 530 U.S. 428, 2000).

STEPHANIE MIZRAHI

### References and Further Reading

Alschuler, A.W., A peculiar privilege in historical perspective: The right to remain silent, *Michigan Law Review* 94 (1996).

Helmholz, R.H., et al., *The Privilege against Self-Incrimination: Its Origins and Development,* Chicago, IL: University of Chicago Press, 1997.

Langbein, J.H., The historical origins of the privilege against self-incrimination at common law, *Michigan Law Review* 92 (1994).

Leo, R.A. and Thomas, G.C., (Eds.) *The Miranda Debate: Law, Justice, and Policing,* Boston, MA: Northeastern University Press, 1998.

Levy, L.W., *The Origins of the Fifth Amendment: The Right against Self-Incrimination,* London, U.K. and New York, NY: Oxford University Press, 1968.

Samaha, J., *Criminal Procedure,* St. Paul, MN: West, 1990; 4th ed., Belmont, CA: West or Wadsworth, 1999.

Schulhofer, S.J., Some kind words for the privilege against self-incrimination, *Valparaiso University Law Review* 26 (1991).

Schulhofer, S.J., Miranda's practical effect: Substantial benefits and vanishingly small social costs, *Northwestern University Law Review* 90 (1996).

Van Kessel, G., European perspectives on the accused as a source of testimonial evidence, *West Virginia Law Review* 100 (1998).

Whitebread, C.H., *Criminal Procedure: An Analysis of Constitutional Cases and Concepts,* Mineola, NY: Foundation Press, 1980; 4th ed., as *Criminal Procedure: An Analysis of Cases and Concepts,* by Whitebread and Slobogin, C., New York, NY: Foundation Press, 2000.

*See also* **Interrogation and Confessions**

---

# Self-Report Research

---

Self-report research asks respondents to report on their substance use, both licit and illicit, and other illegal behavior, usually within a relatively recent period of time. The typical format of the lead-in to self-report questions is, "In the past (day/week/month/six months/year), have you…" (for *prevalence,* or *whether* an offense was committed; also as a screening question before asking about frequency of offending), or "In the past (day/week/month/six months/year), *how many times* have you…", (for *frequency or incidence*, or how many times an offense was committed). The lead-in is followed by the specific offenses or behaviors: "… attacked someone with the idea of seriously hurting or killing them," "… stolen something worth more than $50," "…used cocaine," and so forth. In some self-report studies, especially some of the earlier studies, respondents were asked whether they had "ever" committed various offenses. Some self-report studies also ask follow-up questions about the details of the most recent or most serious offense (or more than one offense), including questions about how seriously the victim was injured (knocked down or bruised or cut or bleeding or unconscious; whether the victim required medical care); the dollar value of property stolen in a theft or destroyed by vandalism; whether

the crime was committed alone or with a group; and whether, in the case of offenses other than substance use, the respondent had been drinking or using drugs at the time of the offense (Huizinga and Elliott, 1986; Elliott and Huizinga, 1989).

The first self-report studies were conducted in the 1940s, a decade after the first collection of national data on arrests and crimes known to the police by the Federal Bureau of Investigation's Uniform Crime Reports (UCR), and two decades before collection of the first national data on crime victimization in what was to become the National Crime Victimization Survey (NCVS). Researchers developed self-report measures out of concern over crime, delinquency, and substance use not represented in official records, which actually measure *reactions* of individuals (police arrests or victim reports) to the *perceived* illegal behavior of an alleged perpetrator (who may or may not be guilty of the act in question). Austin Porterfield (1943) pioneered the method, comparing self-reports of college students to court charges against (noncollege) adolescents brought before the juvenile court in Fort Worth, Texas. In 1940–1942, he asked the college students about their illegal behavior, including serious assaults, thefts, and less serious offenses, and found that the seriousness of offenses was similar for the court and college respondents. A few years later, James S. Wallerstein and Clement J. Wyle (1947), citing Porterfield's work, conducted a self-report study of adults, primarily in New York, Westchester, and Long Island, and asked about a wide range of offenses. They found that individuals from all walks of life admitted having committed illegal acts, with some differences in the specific types of acts committed related to profession. For example, "Businessmen and lawyers were highest in perjury, falsification, fraud, and tax evasion; teachers and social workers in malicious mischief; writers and artists in indecency, criminal libel, and gambling; military and government employees in simple larceny" (Wallerstein and Wyle, 1947, 110).

## Testing the Self-Report Method: Reliability and Validity

From the 1950s through the 1970s, self-report studies were conducted on local populations, and studies of their reliability and validity were undertaken, sometimes with considerable creativity and ingenuity. Clark and Tifft (1966) used a three-stage procedure in which the respondents were first asked to fill out a questionnaire, then told that they would be examined using a polygraph, then actually examined using a polygraph. The respondents were allowed to change their answers at the beginning of the second and third stages. The experimenters found that everyone made some changes (most often to correct previous underreporting), but that the changes were minor and did not substantially affect the results. Although some items were more reliable than others, the overall accuracy of respondents at stage one (when they did not know they would be examined further) was over 80%. Although the polygraph was not actually used to assess the validity of the respondents' answers, the "threat" of the "lie detector" led to increased reporting of illegal behavior.

Martin Gold (1966) attempted to confirm interviews by using friends of the respondents as informants. Based on the reports of the informants, 17% of the interview respondents were deemed unreliable. Several researchers compared self-reported police or court involvement with officially recorded police or court involvement (see reviews in Hindelang et al., 1981; Elliott et al., 1989). These studies have produced fairly consistent results regarding the overall accuracy of self-report data, but somewhat mixed results regarding their accuracy for specific sociodemographic groups. In different studies, males have been more truthful than females, or females have been more truthful than males, in reporting their known arrests or illegal behavior. Some studies (Hindelang et al., 1981; Huizinga and Elliott, 1986) have found that African American respondents are more likely to underreport their arrests or offenses than white respondents, but data from Gold (1966) suggest that underreporting is related less to sex, race, or class, than to the seriousness of the offense. Whether there is a race-related error in the self-reported measure or in the official records (or both) is unclear, but these findings do suggest caution when comparing delinquency rates for African American and white respondents.

There is considerable evidence that reliability and validity of self-reports is worse for longer recall periods and for offenders with higher frequencies of offending (Huizinga and Elliott, 1986, 314–322; Elliott and Huizinga, 1989, 163–169; Zhang et al., 2000, 286). Put simply, it appears that individuals tend to forget offenses that were committed a long time ago, and individuals who have committed a small number of offenses or who have had few arrests or police contacts are more likely to remember all of those offenses or encounters with the police than individuals who have committed many offenses or who have been arrested or otherwise contacted by the police many times. Reliability and validity estimates tend to be higher when broad categories of offenses rather than specific offenses are used as the criterion (Gold, 1966; Huizinga and Elliott, 1986). In general, based on these and later studies, short-term reliability for self-reports appears to be about 90%, and overall validity appears to be about 80% (Elliott et al., 1989).

Self-reports of illicit drug use have been compared with radioimmunoassay of hair (RIAH) and urinalysis (enzyme multiplied immune test, or EMIT) for incarcerated samples, with mixed results (Harrison, 1995). Generally, comparison of the results of self-report and EMIT testing indicated that they were highly concordant, with correlations in the range that one would expect for two measures of the same phenomenon, but EMIT finds more heroin and cocaine use, about the same amount of amphetamine and PCP use (more if the self-reports refer to the past 72 hours, less if the self-reports refer to the past 30 days), and about the same or less marijuana use (for which false negative rates are highest for EMIT), than self-reports. RIAH finds more illicit substance use than either self-reports or EMIT, but Harrison (1995, 99) suggests that although RIAH indicates more drug use than either EMIT or self-reports, RIAH is presently regarded as experimental, and "cannot be described as useable with acceptable accuracy." Harrison also notes that results from these studies must also be regarded with caution because incarcerated individuals may have a strong motivation to lie, especially about heroin and cocaine use. Inferences about the validity of self-reports of substance use in the general population cannot legitimately be made based solely on results for incarcerated offenders.

## The National Survey of Youth and the National Youth Survey

Self-report studies were used extensively in the 1960s and 1970s to study the distribution of delinquency among local populations by gender, race, socioeconomic status, age, place of residence, and a variety of variables thought to be related to juvenile delinquency, but few studies involved national samples at two or more different times. Fewer still involved national longitudinal samples *and* the inclusion of a broad range of illegal behavior: not only status offenses and drug use, but also crimes such as assault, robbery, burglary, and larceny, which might appear in the FBI Crime Index. Two major exceptions were the similarly named National Survey of Youth (Gold and Reimer, 1975) and the National Youth Survey (Elliott et al., 1989). The National Survey of Youth consisted of two samples (847 in 1967 and 661 in 1972) of males and females 13–16 years old. The range of offenses in the survey included assault, theft, and minor offenses. Gold and Reimer (1975) found that from 1967 to 1972, in contrast to upward trends in official crime rates, there appeared to be little change in rates of delinquent behavior, except for an increase in drug use among males and alcohol use among females.

In 1977, Delbert S. Elliott and his colleagues collected data for the first wave of the National Youth Survey (NYS), a national, longitudinal, household-based probability sample of 1725 respondents who were 11–17 years old in the first year of the interview, 27–33 years old in the most recent year for which data are available (1992), and who continue to be followed into their late 30s and early 40s. The NYS provides data on prevalence, frequency, and developmental trends in self-reported licit and illicit substance use, problem substance use, criminal and delinquent behavior, mental health, relationships in the family, school, peer group, neighborhood, and work contexts, and sociodemographic characteristics. It includes dropouts as well as individuals in school during adolescence, and institutionalized (military, students, and prisoners) as well as noninstitutionalized respondents, in proportion to their representation in the population for the age groups in question. In over 80 publications to date, the NYS has been used to provide epidemiological estimates of illegal behavior and substance use; to examine correlates of crime, delinquency, substance use, domestic violence, mental health problems, and victimization; and to test theories of crime and delinquency including strain, control, social learning, and integrated theories.

The NYS was designed to overcome some of the limitations of earlier studies of self-reported illegal behavior. First, self-reports in the 1950s and 1960s often had very limited ranges of offenses, focusing on less serious forms of illegal behavior for which, as indicated below, there is a greater risk of reporting trivial events. Second, these studies had categorical scores with limited response sets (e.g., often or sometimes or occasionally or never, or never or once or twice or three or more times) which made no distinction between low-frequency offenders and very high-frequency offenders. Third, some studies used extended recall periods, sometimes asking whether the respondent had "ever" committed an offense, thus increasing the likelihood of respondent recall failure and underreporting. Other problems included item overlap, leading to double counting of offenses; ambiguous item wording, resulting in inappropriate classification of offenses; and a failure to distinguish between prevalence and frequency (see above) of offending (Hindelang et al., 1981; Elliott and Huizinga, 1989).

Extensive research has been done on the methodology of the NYS, including studies of respondent attrition rates, interviewer effects, panel conditioning, reliability and validity of responses, and the extent of inappropriate or trivial responses to questions about illegal behavior and criminal victimization (see, e.g., Huizinga and Elliott, 1986; Elliott and Huizinga, 1989), with generally encouraging results. Sample attrition was less than 10% for the first five waves of data, and generally at or below 20% thereafter, with no systematic pattern of loss with respect to sociodemographic characteristics, substance use, or illegal behavior. Test–retest reliabilities for the self-reported offending items over a 4-week interval were about 70–90% in the total sample, except for the minor assault prevalence scale, which had marginal (50–67%) reliabilities in some demographic subgroups.

Validity analyses included analysis of follow-up questions to determine whether the self-report items in the SRD inventory were eliciting appropriate responses; analysis of the proportion of reported behaviors that were too trivial to evoke an official response; and comparison of official arrest records and self-reported arrests and offenses. Ninety-six percent of responses were judged appropriate to the specific question asked; two third of responses were judged to be nontrivial behaviors (with the exception that 75% of the offenses in the minor assault scale were classified as trivial); and officially recorded arrests were matched approximately two thirds of the time with self-reported arrests and nearly 80% of the time with self-reported offenses. As noted above, comparison of official arrest data and self-reported arrests and offenses revealed a lower rate of matching for African American than for whites. There are several possible reasons for the apparent underreporting of arrests, including errors by the respondents in interpreting the police contact or errors in the official records themselves (Huizinga and Elliott, 1986), but these underreporting rates are nonetheless high compared to those in other, similar, studies.

Tests of the integrated theory and the separate component theories have provided evidence that the dominant influence on illegal behavior in adolescence is exposure to delinquent friends (social learning), which is in turn influenced by belief that it is wrong to violate the law (social control) and normlessness in the family and school contexts (strain and control), which are themselves influenced by stress or strain in the school context (strain), involvement in the family and school contexts (social control), and by social disorganization or urban as opposed to rural residence (social ecology). Exposure to delinquent friends appears to be both a cause and a consequence of delinquency, although exposure appears to have a stronger influence on delinquency than delinquency on exposure (Menard and Elliott, 1993). The influences on illicit drug use are similar to the influences on delinquency, but belief plays a stronger, more direct role for illicit drug use than for other forms of illegal behavior. Race and socioeconomic status are at most weakly and indirectly related to illicit drug use and delinquency, primarily via their impacts on school normlessness and school strain, but being male appears to directly increase the extent of involvement in delinquency, but not illicit drug use. Illicit drug use itself does not appear to be involved in the *initiation* of other forms of illegal behavior, as is often suggested, but instead appears to contribute to the *continuation* of that behavior, once it has already been initiated. Most of these and other findings from the first six waves of the study (the first 12 years) of the NYS are presented in Elliott et al. (1989). Elliott et al. (1989) also found that mental health problems in adolescence appear to arise primarily in response to stress in the family and school context, and although they do not appear to have the same set of causes as illicit drug use, illicit drug use and mental health problems do tend to be significantly associated.

Later research on the NYS has also been used to examine patterns of involvement in illicit drug dealing (as opposed to mere drug use), spouse or partner violence perpetration and victimization, and victimization by violent and property crime in general. Just as illicit drug use appears to be associated with continued involvement in other forms of illegal behavior in adolescence, illicit drug use and to an even greater extent involvement in illicit drug markets appears to be predictive of violent crime and victimization, as well as

drug use, in adulthood (Menard and Mihalic, 2001). Morse (1995) found that, as reported by both males and females, females were actually more often perpetrators of partner violence than males, but that they tended to be involved in relatively minor forms of violence, whereas males, although less often perpetrators of partner violence generally, were more likely to be perpetrators and females were more likely to be victims in serious incidents involving injury. Finally, with respect to violent victimization more generally, Menard (2000) found that victimization by violent crime in adolescence tends to occur repeatedly and intermittently, and that it has pervasive effects on adult outcomes, significantly increasing the odds of a wide range of adult problem behaviors, including posttraumatic stress disorder, both perpetration of and victimization by partner violence, perpetration of and revictimization by violent crimes more generally, and problem drug use. Data on the NYS are presently being collected to examine intergenerational transmission of problem behaviors, including the collection of DNA to examine interactions between genetics and environment in the familial transmission of problem behaviors.

## Other National and International Self-Report Surveys

Annual data from national self-report surveys are routinely published by the Bureau of Justice Statistics (annual), including data from the Monitoring the Future (MTF) study, the National Household Survey on Drug Abuse (NHSDA), and the National Parents Resource for Drug Education (PRIDE). MTF has provided data on prevalence and categorical scores of self-reported licit and illicit substance use and selected offenses, victimization, health, sociodemographic characteristics, personality attributes, interpersonal relationships, and a wide range of attitudes on social and political issues, major social institutions, and happiness and life satisfaction, for a national probability sample of high school seniors from over 100 public and private high schools since 1975, and on eighth and tenth grade students since 1991. The sample excludes individuals who have dropped out of school, and sometimes individuals who are absent from class at the time of data collection. Completion rates are approximately 75–80% of sampled students with nonwhites having lower completion rates. A subsample of respondents is included in a longitudinal follow-up with retention rates about 80% for the first follow-up and declining thereafter. Attrition in the longitudinal sample appears to be associated with substance use and with being African American. MTF data have been used primarily to provide epidemiological data on rates and trends of substance use among American high school seniors, but they have also been used in some studies of the correlates of crime and substance use.

NHSDA provides lifetime, annual, and past month prevalence data and data on annual and lifetime trends in prevalence for licit and illicit substance use, plus information on demographic characteristics, problems associated with substance use, perceptions of harm associated with substance use, and, since 1991, information about other illegal behavior, for a national household-based probability sample of respondents 12 years old and older, and for several major metropolitan statistical areas. Data are reported separately for different age groups, males and females, and white, African American, and Hispanic ethnic groups. There is evidence of underreporting on NHSDA relative to other surveys but the underreporting appears to be consistent from year to year, and estimates of trends appear to be reliable and valid. NHSDA has been used primarily to provide epidemiological estimates of rates and trends in substance use.

PRIDE provides information on self-reported prevalence, categorical scores, and period trends of substance use, intensity of use, where drugs were used, related behaviors (carrying weapons, gang involvement, and getting into trouble with the police), and interactions with parents and friends for a national school-based sample of over 100,000 high school and junior high school students in grades 6–12. Dropouts and absentees are excluded from the sample. Annual surveys of students have been conducted since the 1987–88 school year. Participating schools are sent the PRIDE questionnaire with instructions for its administration. Schools that administer the PRIDE questionnaire do so voluntarily or in compliance with a school district or state request. Like NHSDA, PRIDE is used primarily to provide epidemiological estimates of rates and trends of substance use.

In addition to these national surveys, there are numerous local self-report studies, some of which are longitudinal in nature, following the same respondents for multiple years. On a broader scale, the International Self-Report Delinquency (ISRD) project, using a self-report instrument modeled on the NYS, has surveyed youth in Belgium, Finland, Germany, Greece, Italy, the Netherlands, New Zealand, Northern Ireland, Portugal, Spain, Switzerland, the U.K., and the U.S. Findings from the ISRD suggest that among these Western nations there is a great deal of cross-national similarity in rates, patterns, and risk factors for delinquent behavior in the different countries (Zhang et al., 2000). Their results also demonstrate the feasibility of collecting comparative, cross-national data on illegal behavior, even when laws and official responses to illegal behavior may vary systematically across countries.

## Comparisons with Other Data Collection Methods

Self-report studies have been compared with each other and with official UCR crimes known to police or UCR arrests and victimization data, often with the NYS as the representative self-report dataset. Estimates of the amount of criminal or delinquent behavior are highest in the NYS, lowest in official data, and intermediate in victimization data, and the differences are substantial, even with attempts to adjust the data for differences in operational definitions and methodology (Jackson, 1990). Short-term trends have also been examined using the NYS and the earlier National Survey of Youth, both of which indicated stable or declining trends, consistent with victimization data but contrasting with the increasing trends found in UCR for comparable periods (Gold and Reimer, 1975; Jackson, 1990; Menard and Elliott, 1993).

Self-reports contrast not only with other types of data, but also with each other. Data from the Monitoring the Future (MTF) study were somewhat more consistent with increasing trends in UCR data for certain offenses than were trends in the NYS. Menard and Elliott (1993) examined the differences between the NYS and MTF, and concluded that differences in administration, question context, question wording, and sampling between the two surveys limited the ability to compare the two, even when limiting coverage in the NYS to high school seniors to maximize comparability with MTF. The differences between the NYS and the MTF emphasize the point that there is no single self-report method, but rather several approaches to self-reports that differ in important ways and can produce different conclusions about the extent, trends, and correlates and causes of illegal behavior.

SCOTT MENARD

### References and Further Reading

Clark, J.P. and Tifft, L.L., Polygraph and interview validation of self-reported deviant behavior, *American Sociological Review* 31 (1966).

Elliott, D.S. and Huizinga, D., Improving self-reported measures of delinquency, in *Cross-National Research in Self-Reported Crime and Delinquency*, Klein, M.W. (Ed.), Dordrecht, the Netherlands: Kluwer, 1989.

Elliott, D.S., Huizinga, D. and Menard, S., *Multiple Problem Youth: Delinquency, Substance Use, and Mental Health Problems*, New York, NY: Springer-Verlag, 1989.

Gold, M., Undetected delinquent behavior, *Journal of Research in Crime and Delinquency* 3 (1966).

Gold, M. and Reimer, D.J., Changing patterns of delinquent behavior among Americans 13-through 16-years-old: 1967–1972, *Crime and Delinquency Literature* 7 (1975).

Harrison, L., The validity of self-reported data on drug use, *Journal of Drug Issues* 35 (1995).

Hindelang, M.J., Hirschi, T. and Weis, J.G., *Measuring Delinquency*, Beverly Hills, CA: Sage, 1981.

Huizinga, D. and Elliott, D.S., Reassessing the reliability and validity of self-report delinquency measures, *Journal of Quantitative Criminology* 2 (1986).

Jackson, P.G., Sources of data, in *Measurement Issues in Criminology,* Kempf, K.L., (Ed.), New York, NY: Springer-Verlag, 1990.

Menard, S., Short- and long-term consequences of adolescent victimization, *Youth Violence Research Bulletin,* Washington, DC: Office of Juvenile Justice and Delinquency Prevention and Centers for Disease Control and Prevention, 2002.

Menard, S. and Elliott, D.S., Data set comparability and short-term trends in crime and delinquency, *Journal of Criminal Justice* 21 (1993).

Menard, S. and Mihalic, S., The tripartite conceptual framework in adolescence and adulthood: Evidence from a national sample, *Journal of Drug Issues* 31 (2001).

Morse, B.J., Beyond the conflict tactics scale: Assessing gender differences in partner violence, *Violence and Victims* 10 (1995).

Porterfield, A.L., Delinquency and its outcome in court and college, *American Journal of Sociology* 49 (1943).

Wallerstein, J.S. and Wyle, C.J., Our law-abiding lawbreakers, *Probation* 25 (1947).

Zhang, S., Benson, T. and Deng, X., A test–retest reliability assessment of the international self-report delinquency instrument, *Journal of Criminal Justice* 28 (2000).

*See also* **National Crime Victimization Survey (NCVS); Survey Research**

# Self-Representation, The Right to

Although the U.S. Supreme Court has interpreted the Sixth Amendment of the Constitution to mean that a defendant in a criminal case of any magnitude has the right to be represented by counsel, the Court has also held that an individual does not have to be represented by counsel at all, if he or she does not want to be. In other words, an individual has the right to represent himself or herself in a criminal case. This is sometimes referred to as "pro se" representation. That this right existed was first determined authoritatively by the Court in *Faretta v. California* (422 U. S. 806, 1975). In that case, Justice Potter Stewart, writing for a 6–3 majority, held, (at 821), "The language and spirit of the Sixth Amendment contemplate that counsel, like other defensive tools guaranteed by the amendment shall be an aid to a willing defendant—not an organ of the state interposed between an unwilling defendant and his right to defend himself personally. To thrust counsel upon the accused, against his considered wish, thus violates the logic of the amendment."

The Court also held in this case that, before proceeding "pro se," the defendant must "knowingly and intelligently" waive his or her right to an attorney. Moreover, he or she must be apprised of the pitfalls of self-representation before proceeding on his or her own. A defendant who does waive the right to counsel cannot later on appeal raise the issue of ineffective assistance of counsel. The Court has also held that the accused's competency standard for pleading guilty or for waiving right to counsel is not, under the U.S. Constitution, higher than the standard that is used for determining his or her ability to stand trial, though state courts have the right to set higher standards: *Godinez v. Moran*, 509 U.S. 389 (1993). The standard for competency to stand trial is whether the defendant has the present ability to consult with his attorney with a reasonable degree of rational understanding, and whether he has a rational as well as factual understanding of the proceedings against him: *Dusky v. U.S.* (362 U.S. 402, 1960). This is not a very strict standard.

Although the right of self-representation does exist, it is not an absolute right. It can be denied, for instance, if the court deems a request for self-representation to be a delaying tactic: *U.S. v. Kaczynski* 239 F. 3d 1108 (9th Cir., 2001). Appellate courts have also held that, if the defendant is not willing or able to abide by the rules of procedure or courtroom protocol, he or she may have the right to self-representation revoked, see *U.S. v. Romano*, 849 F. 2d 812 (3rd Cir., 1988). Moreover, the Supreme Court decided in a fairly recent case that although the right to self-representation may apply to trial proceedings, it does not apply to appellate processes. Thus, the Court held, in *Martinez v. Court of Appeals* (528 U.S. 152, 2000), that a "lay" appellant who wished to represent himself was held not to have been deprived of his rights under the U.S. constitution when the California courts required him to accept a state-appointed attorney on direct appeal from a state criminal conviction.

A major concern of many, including some Supreme Court Justices, is that the defendant may not realize the difficulties associated with self-representation, and perform poorly in his or her "pro se" role. An example of this might be the case of Mr. Colin Ferguson, who was eventually convicted of shooting and killing a number of passengers on a New York transit line. He insisted on representing himself at his trial. His defense was that, while he was sleeping, a white man—who was part of a government plot to persecute Ferguson—opened the defendant's bag, stole a gun that was located therein, and started shooting the train's passengers. As part of his defense, Ferguson asked the Court to subpoena an exorcist and a parapsychologist to prove the government had implanted a microchip in his head. He also sought to subpoena the President of the U.S. and the Governor of New York to prove the existence of the widespread conspiracy against him (Bardwell and Arrigo, 2002). Ferguson was convicted, and upon appeal the New York Appellate Court found him to have been competent to stand trial and competent to defend himself.

A mechanism used in some instances as a halfway measure between pure self-representation and the more traditional approach of representation by counsel is the "hybrid" approach of "standby counsel." Under this arrangement, although the bulk of the representation is undertaken by the defendant, a licensed attorney is present to intervene at appropriate times. Under the Court's interpretation of the Sixth Amendment, the trial judge may, but is not required to, appoint such an attorney. Such an arrangement is used in many cases where the defendant insists on exercising the right to self-representation. Indeed, in the case of *McKaskle v. Wiggins* (465 U.S. 168, 1984), the U.S. Supreme Court decided that "A defendant's Sixth Amendment rights are not violated when a trial judge appoints standby counsel—even over defendant's objection—to relieve the judge of the need to explain and enforce basic rules of courtroom protocol or to assist the defendant in overcoming routine obstacles that stand in the way of the defendant's achievement of his own clearly indicated goals. Participation by counsel to steer a defendant through the basic procedures of trial is permissible even in the unlikely event that it somewhat undermines the 'pro se' defendant's appearance of control over his own defense." (p. 173).

How such arrangements work out in practice depends upon the particular case. In some instances, there may be conflict between the defendant and counsel. In others, the arrangement may be more amicable. The relationship between the two may even vary during the course of a trial, although under *Mckaskle*, the appearance (and reality) of the situation should be that the defendant is in charge, at least as long as he or she wants that to be the case.

Whatever the situation, any defendant in a criminal trial should understand that, although he or she has the right to conduct his or her own defense, "one who is his own lawyer has a fool for a client."

DAVID M. JONES

## References and Further Reading

Amar, A.R., *The Bill of Rights: Creation and Reconstruction,* New Haven, CT: Yale University Press, 1998.

Bardwell, M.C. and Arrigo, B.A., *Criminal Competency on Trial: The Case of Colin Ferguson,* Durham, NC: Carolina Academic Press, 2000.

Bloom, L. and Hershkoff , H., Federal courts, magistrate judges, and the pro se plaintiff. *Notre Dame Journal of Law, Ethics, and Public Policy* 16 (2002).

Gardner, M.R., The Sixth Amendment Right to counsel and its underlying values: Defining the scope of privacy protection. *Journal of Criminal Law and Criminology* 90 (2000).

Mello, M., The non-trial of the century: Representations of the Unabomber. *Vermont Law Review* 24 (2000).

Poulin, A.B., The role of standby counsel in criminal cases: In the twilight zone of the criminal justice system. *New York University Law Review* 75 (2000).

Sabelli, M. and Leyton, S., Train wrecks and freeway crashes: An argument for fairness and against self representation in the criminal justice system. *Journal of Criminal Law and Criminology* 91 (2000).

Williams, M.H., The pro se criminal defendant, standby counsel, and the judge: A proposal for better-defined roles. *Colorado Law Review* 71 (2000).

*See also* **Counsel, The Right to**

# Sellin, Thorsten

The first time I personally encountered Thorsten Sellin, he was at the Third Congress of the UN on the Prevention of Crime and the Treatment of Offenders that was held in Stockholm in August 1965. Sellin attended this international congress as a research expert and his sound and relevant contributions attracted my attention. A month later, in September 1965, the "International Society of Criminology" held its Fifth International Congress in Montreal that I also attended as a young criminologist. At that time, Sellin was president of the society and in Montreal he made one of the keynote lectures on the historical origin and present-day application of imprisonment. His critical attitude toward imprisonment and his humanistic intention impressed me deeply. Sellin played a decisive role at both international congresses. In 1966, I attended, for the first time, the Annual Meeting of the American Society of Criminology that was then held in Philadelphia. At that time we were a group of about a hundred participants and I was the only one from abroad. Sellin invited me to his home. He received me in his large private library. I came to know a scholar who loved to learn and teach, to read and to collect, and personally write scholarly articles and books. Sellin was a man of exceptional knowledge and very extensive reading. He had an encyclopedic mind and knew European criminology as well, quoting it as frequently in his scholarly work as North American criminology.

Sellin was a great phenomenologist. His publications mostly encompass comprehensive, internationally based analyses of the literature that bring forth the essential aspects in a form that is both concise and brief, and clearly understandable. His works represent a differentiated and detached presentation of the facts. His first book was his analysis entitled *Research Memorandum on Crime in the Depression*, published in the year 1937, which he had written for the Social Science Research Council. He presents a very differentiated view of the relationship between the economic crisis and the genesis of crime. Even a serious depression does not evoke a wave of criminal activity. The economic crisis influences the reporting behavior of the population and the reactions of criminal justice. It is not the extent of crime but rather the structure of crime that undergoes changes.

In his book *Culture Conflict and Crime* (1938) Sellin develops the culture conflict theory. He proceeds from conduct norms that are determined by social groups and which, in case of violation, are informally sanctioned by these same groups. Culture conflicts are conflicts of behavioral norms. Sellin distinguishes between external and internal conflicts. The external conflict is a conflict of group codes. The internal conflict is a clash between antagonistic conduct norms internalized in the personality. Sellin further distinguishes between primary and secondary culture conflicts. Primary culture conflicts are conflicts of norms drawn from different cultural systems or areas. Secondary culture conflicts grow out of the process of social differentiation, of the transformation of a culture.

The culture conflict theory, therefore, holds a particular significance for countries of mass immigration and rapid social change, such as Israel (Shoham, 1968). In a time of globalization and rapid social change, the theory has lost none of its topicality. On the contrary, multicultural societies are evolving all over the present-day world in which culture conflicts are on the increase. Today, this theory is even more topical than ever.

Throughout his professional career Sellin had an intensive interest in improving statistical data on crime and criminal justice. He wrote his first article on the index of crime, published in the *Journal of Criminal Law and Criminology* in 1931. This article also appeared in Germany in Aschaffenburg's and von Hentig's journal. Initially Sellin supported the concept of police statistics. With his index of crime he then strived to develop an alternative. In his book *The Measurement of Delinquency* (1964) he worked out an index of crime together with his disciple Marvin E. Wolfgang that seeks to take the following factors into account: Only those violations of the law are considered for assessing the threat of crime that show a high and stable reporting probability. The index of crime does not center on the penal standardization of the crimes, but is based on objective features of a case such as physical harm and damage to property suffered by the victim. Empirical investigations aimed at measuring the judgments of public opinion on crime and its severity are needed to select the different case characteristics and their respective weight. The Sellin–Wolfgang index has been discussed in numerous countries. In 1972, Sellin and his coworkers Marvin E. Wolfgang and Robert M. Figlio published a longitudinal study of a birth cohort that evaluated the official school and police records of all boys born in 1945 who lived in Philadelphia at least between their tenth and eighteenth birthdays. A group of 627 chronic offenders (out of a total of 9945 cohort subjects) who had committed more than four violations (18% of the total number of offenders) was responsible for over one half of all offenses. This groundbreaking study promoted many longitudinal studies to be conducted worldwide from the 1970s to the 1990s.

Sellin's studies on the history of punishment and corrections clearly document the influence that Georg Rusche and Otto Kirchheimer's book on *Punishment and Social Structure* (1939), the foreword of which was written by Sellin, had on him. In his historical research he investigates the transformation of the different penal systems within the societal structures of the respective periods of time, and the close interrelationships between punishment and the culture that has produced them. In his book *Pioneering in Penology* (1944) that was inspired by the German lawyer Robert von Hippel, as Sellin writes in the preface, he describes the Amsterdam houses of correction in the 16th and 17th centuries. He rates these houses as fruitful experimentations, marking the first time in the history of criminal punishment that labor and religious training were used as treatment-oriented corrective instruments. The work on his book *Slavery and the Penal System* (1976) gave him great enjoyment, as the reading of the Greek and Roman sources helped him to expand his intellectual horizon (Laub, 1983). The work reflects the impressions he gained during his first visit to Rome in the years 1924–25 and was also inspired by Gustav Radbruch's contention, quoted by Sellin in the preface of his book, that "To be punished means to be treated like a slave. Slavish treatment meant not just a social but also a moral degradation." Sellin investigates slavery and the penal system in ancient Greece, in ancient Rome, and in the Germanic nations of the Middle Ages. He describes penal servitude such as galley slavery. He depicts penal slavery in Russia and in the antebellum Southern U.S.

Sellin was an outspoken opponent of capital punishment. He rejected it on the basis of its ineffectiveness. About 10% of his publications, several published in foreign languages, are devoted to this theme. He questions the deterrent power of capital punishment. He untiringly investigates the truth or falsity of the assertions that the death penalty is a unique means of deterring people from committing capital crimes. He makes a crime-statistical comparison between the homicide rates of abolitionist and retentionist states and finds no difference. He questions the validity of contentions maintaining that the police are better protected by the death penalty and that the death penalty leads to a lower number of homicides in state and federal prisons. All of his studies on the death penalty are summarized in his latest book entitled *The Penalty of Death* (1980). It is not a philosophical work, but rather an analysis of the international theoretical and empirical studies on the death penalty.

His last work is a review of my book on criminology. He read the work, written in German and comprising almost a thousand pages, at the age of over 90 with a magnifying glass because of eye problems. In his review of the book (1989) he focused on the essential aspects of the work with remarkable intellectual acuity and a precision that is to be admired.

Thorsten Sellin was a great personality, a great scholar, but at the same time a reliable team worker. His modesty, integrity, and his internationality deserve merit. He spoke several languages. He was a visiting professor at numerous universities worldwide. He was an honorary doctor of many universities in different countries. More than 20% of his publications appeared in languages other than English. All his publications had an international flavor. He had set his heart on the development of a true science of criminology. But he never sacrificed self-criticism. At the International Congress of Criminology in Paris in 1950, he coined the phrase: "Criminologists are kings without a country." He had his doubts about the interdisciplinarity of criminology. He believed more in a cooperation of several disciplines (multidisciplinarity) with sociology and psychology forming the center. In his own understanding he saw himself as a sociological criminologist.

He felt a certain sympathy for the political Left. During his visit to Florence in 1925, he witnessed a riot by fascists aimed against the socialists. He wrote an article about this entitled "Fascism at Work" for the *Nation*. Enrico Ferri, whose biography he had worked on, had greatly impressed him (1960). The left-wing tried to win him over to their side (Shank, 1978). He found it amusing that he was considered to be a "radical criminologist" (Laub, 1983). He rated "Marxist criminology" as an ideology lacking an empirical foundation and having no practical relevance.

He loved the French *savoir-vivre*. His enjoyment of French culture is why he spent the winter months in Paris during the 1980s and the beginning of the 1990s. In the summer, he preferred the closeness to nature offered by his house in Gilmanton, New Hampshire. He had an ambivalent relationship toward German criminology. Critical German criminologists had a major influence on his thinking. This finds its expression not only in his publications. Also many conversations in the 1970s and 1980s and an extensive exchange of letters that he sent me from Paris bear witness to this. He reported on Gustav Aschaffenburg and Hans von Hentig who had to leave Germany for political reasons during the National-Socialist period (1933–1945) and emigrated to the U.S. Sellin helped both of them to gain a foothold in the U.S. He valued the influence that North American criminology had on its West German counterpart. But he was also concerned that German criminologists could fall back into their old attitudes of provincialism and arrogant nationalistic self-isolation.

HANS JOACHIM SCHNEIDER

## Biography

Born in Örnsköldsvik, northern Sweden, on October 26, 1896. High school and early college education in Sweden. Emigration at age 17 with his family to Canada, then U.S. Educated at the Swedish-American Augustana College in Rock Island, Illinois (A.B. 1915), University of Pennsylvania (M.A. 1916, Ph.D. 1922). Teacher of languages (German, Swedish) at Minnesota College and Central High School in Minneapolis, from 1916 to 1920. Instructor at the University of Pennsylvania in the Department of Sociology in 1921, full Professor in 1930, chairman of the Department from 1944 to 1959. Professor emeritus in 1968. Visiting professor at the universities of Paris, Brussels, Cambridge, Lund, Stockholm, Uppsala. Honorary doctorates from the universities of Leiden, the Netherlands, Kopenhagen, Denmark, Brussels, Belgium and the University of Pennsylvania. Cesare Beccaria Gold Medal of the German Society of Criminology (1964). President of the International Society of Criminology from 1956 to 1965. Honorary President of the International Society of Criminology from 1965 to 1994. Editor of the *Annals of the American Academy of the Political and Social Sciences* from 1929 to 1968. Associate Editor of the *Journal of Criminal Law and Criminology* from 1927 to 1941. Member of the Social Science Research Council from 1933 to 1968. Member of the American Philosophical Society since 1949. Died in Gilmanton, New Hampshire, September 17, 1994.

## Selected Writings

*Research Memorandum on Crime in the Depression,* 1937.
*Culture Conflict and Crime,* 1938.
*Pioneering in Penology,* 1944.
*The Measurement of Delinquency* (with Wolfgang, M.E.), 1964.
*Delinquency in a Birth Cohort* (with Wolfgang, M.E. and Figlio, R.E.), 1972.
*Slavery and the Penal System,* 1976.
*The Penalty of Death,* 1980.

Book Review of Hans Joachim Schneider's *Kriminologie, The Journal of Criminal Law and Criminology* 79, 4 (1989).

## References and Further Reading

Ferracuti, F., European migration and crime, in *Crime and Culture. Essays in Honor of Sellin, T.,* Wolfgang, M.E., (Ed.), New York, NY, London, U.K., Sydney, Australia, Toronto, Canada: Wiley, 1968.
Laub, J.H., *Criminology in the Making,* Boston, MA: Northeastern University Press, 1983.
Lejins, P.P., Thorsten Sellin: A life dedicated to criminology, *Criminology* 25, 4 (1987).
Pinatel, J., Thorsten Sellin and the principal trends in modern criminology, *Crime and Culture. Essays in Honor of Thorsten Sellin,* Wolfgang, M.E. (Ed.), New York, NY, London, U.K., Sydney, Australia, Toronto, Canada: Wiley, 1968.
Rusche, G. and Kirchheimer, O., *Punishment and Social Structure,* New York, NY: Columbia University Press, 1939.
Shank, G., Book reviews: Sellin, J.T., Pioneering in Penology and Slavery and the Penal System, *Crime and Social Justice* 10 (1978).
Shoham, S., Culture conflict as a frame of reference for research in criminology and social deviation, in *Crime and Culture. Essays in Honor of Thorsten Sellin,* Wolfgang, M.E. (Ed.), New York, NY, London, U.K., Sydney, Australia, Toronto, Canada: Wiley, 1968.

# Sentences and Sentencing: Disparities

Sentencing disparity refers to the situation in which legally similar offenders commit the same or very similar crimes, but receive substantially different sentences. Disparity could exist in potentially any aspect of criminal punishment: whether one is incarcerated or not, whether one is incarcerated in jail or prison, the length of incarceration, the amount of fines, or the length or restrictiveness of intermediate punishments.

Most observers distinguish between "warranted disparity" and "unwarranted disparity." Sentencing disparities are attributable to differences that are considered defensible from a legal standpoint. For example, sentencing disparities between offenders and offenses that seem similar on the surface may sometimes be attributable to legally defensible factors, such as special characteristics of crimes, or aggravating or mitigating features of the offenders' prior criminal records. Much more commonly, the focus is on unwarranted disparity—sentencing differences between similar offenses and offenders that are not attributable

to legally prescribed factors. It is important to note, however, that there is no objective standard for deciding what constitutes warranted or unwarranted disparity. These are value judgments that are open to interpretation.

Below, this chapter reviews several theoretical perspectives on sentencing disparity found in criminology. Then, the chapter summarizes empirical research findings on sentencing disparity based on race and ethnicity, class, gender, age, and mode of conviction. Finally, the chapter concludes with a discussion of gaps in the literature on sentencing disparity that should be addressed by future research.

## Theoretical Perspectives

As Dixon (1995) notes, a number of theoretical perspectives can be found in the literature on criminal courts, sentencing, and sentencing disparity. Although these theories appear to be competing, they are actually complementary in important respects, and each is "capable of predicting the organization of sentencing in various contexts" (Dixon, 1995, 1191).

Most broadly, two theoretical orientations have traditionally framed criminological discussions of sentencing disparity. First, the normative consensus perspective is rooted in interpretations of the classical sociologist Emile Durkheim's writings on deviance and social control. Legalistic or normative theory holds that law and its enforcement by the criminal justice system reflect societal consensus about deeply held norms such as justice, accountability, and retribution (see Wilbank, 1987). The legalistic or normative perspective argues that once one fully accounts for legally relevant factors such as offense characteristics, prior record, and legal facts, extralegal factors play little role in criminal justice decision making. The conflict approach is rooted in the work of Karl Marx and especially Max Weber (see discussions by Savelsberg, 1992). Though individual conflict theorists disagree on specific points, most agree that criminal justice and criminal punishment: (1) will reflect and reproduce inequalities of class, status, or power in the larger society; and (2) will reflect the various organizational interests of participants in the criminal justice system. Congruent with this latter conflict perspective are several theories that focus specifically on sentencing disparity.

First, several scholars who study sentencing disparity emphasize the role of social contexts of courts and their decision-making processes. These scholars, such as Myers and Talarico (1987), Flemming, Nardulli, and Eisenstein (1992), Savelsberg (1992), Dixon (1995), Ulmer (1997), and Ulmer and Kramer (1998) argue that any understanding of sentencing and sentencing disparity must include a focus on local courts' organizational structures, organizational cultures, case-processing strategies, and relationship networks. For example, the court community perspective focuses on the interactional dynamics of courtroom workgroups, and views courts as communities of action and communication based on participants' shared workplace, interdependent working relations between key sponsoring agencies (prosecutor's office, bench, defense bar), and local legal and organizational culture. This localized "community" shapes sentencing outcomes and processes as least as much as formal policies and legal structure, and may produce various types of sentencing disparity.

Other recent theoretical developments in the literature expand on the court community perspective's themes. For example, Savelsberg (1992) posits that the substantive rationality of local contexts and individual interests, ideologies, and biases may tend to subvert formally rational decision-making criteria like sentencing guidelines,

especially those that are externally imposed on local arenas and individuals. These local substantive interests potentially produce variation in the degree and type of sentencing disparity. Dixon's (1995) "organizational context theory," which builds on and incorporates the court community perspective, emphasizes factors such as the bureaucratization of prosecutors' offices and the judges' bench as variables that exert particular influence on sentencing and sentencing disparity, even under sentencing guidelines.

Second, the focal concerns theory of sentencing (Steffensmeier, Ulmer, and Kramer, 1998; Steffensmeier and DeMuth, 2000) is an explicit extension of the court community perspective. Sentencing is a situation of bounded rationality in which court actors make highly consequential decisions with insufficient information, and this produces considerable uncertainty. To manage this uncertainty, court actors make attributions about case and defendant characteristics in terms of four focal concerns: *blameworthiness, dangerousness, rehabilitative potential, and practical constraints and consequences*. In the abstract, the use and reliance on these focal concerns is universal, but the meaning, relative emphasis and priority, and situational interpretation of them is embedded in local court community culture, organizational contexts, and politics. The important point for sentencing disparity is that court community actors make these attributions and interpretations regarding the focal concerns mostly on the basis of legally relevant factors, but they may also draw on racial, gender, class, or age stereotypes about defendants. For example, some judges may perceive young black males as particularly dangerous or lacking rehabilitative potential compared to other types of defendants, and sentence accordingly.

Third, Engen and Steen (2000) delineate an "organizational efficiency model," and contrast it with "substantive rationality model" within which they claim the court community and focal concerns perspectives (described above) belong. In this view, organizational efficiency may be an overriding sentencing goal. It may supercede formal rules like laws or sentencing guidelines, or substantively rational focal concerns like perceived blameworthiness and dangerousness. Prosecutors and judges achieve efficient case processing by encouraging guilty pleas and avoiding trials (Engen and Steen, 2000, 1363):

> The goal of criminal justice processing, according to this perspective, is to induce guilty pleas as an organizationally efficient means to an end. Thus offenders who plead guilty are rewarded with less severe sentences than they could otherwise have received.

This theory therefore predicts that the most common and perhaps primary form of sentencing disparity will be based on the mode of conviction. Those who plead guilty will be sentenced more leniently than those convicted by trial, even for comparable crimes and for offenders with comparable prior records.

Actually, the focal concerns theory would agree with organizational efficiency theory on the potential for disparity based on mode of conviction. Proponents of focal concerns theory would locate pressures for organizational efficiency within the focal concern of *practical constraints and consequences*, and concern for organizational efficiency may manifest itself in sentencing disparity between those who plead guilty and those who go to trial. Also, the need to move cases, avoid court backlogs, as well as the common practice of rewarding guilty pleas and penalizing trials are significant themes in prior research from the court community and organizational context perspectives. On the other hand, the court community and organizational context perspectives emphasize variation between local courts in the perceived importance of efficiency as a practical constraint and consequence.

One overall conclusion from the empirical literature on sentencing disparity is that there appears to be support for the conflict perspective's two key propositions about criminal punishment, at least in the contemporary North American context. It appears that key dimensions of social inequality (e.g., race or ethnicity, gender, age) found in the larger society are also sometimes grounds for sentencing disparity. Furthermore, the organizational interests of prosecutors and courts appear to play a role in producing various kinds of sentencing disparity. More specifically, the court community or organizational context, focal concerns, and organizational efficiency theories all enjoy some degree of empirical support in the research summarized below.

## Empirical Research

### Racial and Ethnic Disparity

Though findings are mixed, the majority of recent analyses that include controls for legally relevant factors find that black and Hispanic defendants receive more severe sanctions than comparable whites. A number of studies find that blacks—particularly young black males (Steffensmeier et al., 1998) and unemployed young black males (Spohn and Holleran, 2000))—are sentenced more harshly than comparable white offenders. In addition, Spohn and Holleran (2000) find that Hispanic defendants (particularly young unemployed males) are sentenced more harshly than whites, and Steffensmeier and DeMuth (2000) find that young Hispanic male drug offenders are sentenced more harshly than comparable whites or blacks (see also Engen and Steen, 2000, 1392–1393).

There is evidence of significant racial disparities in death penalty sentences (Baldus, Woodworth, and Pulaski, 1994). This research on the death penalty also finds that, controlling for legally relevant factors, the race of the offender and the victim interact to produce disparity in the likelihood of receiving a death sentence. For example, black offenders who kill white victims were the most likely to be sentenced to death, whereas white offenders who killed blacks were the least likely.

However, other studies reveal little evidence of racial sentencing disparity (e.g, Wilbanks, 1987) or mixed results (Dixon, 1995). These mixed findings have resulted in mixed interpretations. Some (Wilbanks, 1987) maintain that findings of racial disparity in sentencing are an illusion, an artifact of poor research designs and a failure to adequately control for legal factors like offense severity and prior record. This argument would therefore imply support for the normative consensus perspective.

One interesting and important new direction of research shows that race interacts with other variables and affects sentencing severity only in particular kinds of cases (Spohn and Holleran, 2000) or for particular types of defendants (Albonetti, 1997; Steffensmeier et al., 1998; Steffensmeier and DeMuth, 2000). In other words, racial and ethnic disparity appears to be contextualized by other factors, such as gender and age (Steffensmeier et al., 1998), specific crime types (Albonetti, 1997; Steffensmeier and DeMuth, 2000), and even employment status (Spohn and Holleran, 2000).

In addition, the presence and size of racial and ethnic sentencing differences appear to vary between states, and between different courts in the same state with different contextual characteristics (see Myers and Talarico, 1987; Ulmer, 1997; Ulmer and Kramer, 1998). One potential explanation of this is that from the court community standpoint, sentencing varies according to local context and culture. Therefore, the presence and level of racial disparity is locally and perhaps regionally variable. Taken together, these findings lend substantial empirical support to the court community or organizational context and focal concerns theories (see Steffensmeier and DeMuth, 2000).

### Gender Disparity

Compared to racial and ethnic disparity, relatively few studies focus specifically on gender disparity. Most studies, however, do include gender as a variable in multivariate models of sentencing outcomes, and can therefore speak to the presence and size of sentencing differences, while controlling for legally prescribed factors like offense and prior record. Though there are exceptions, studies consistently find that female offenders are sentenced more leniently than male defendants in a variety of ways (see reviews by Steffensmeier, Kramer, and Streifel, 1993; Albonetti, 1997). For example, most studies find that women are less likely to be incarcerated, are incarcerated for shorter periods of time, and tend to receive departures below sentencing guidelines (sentences that are more lenient than sentencing guidelines recommend) more often than men.

One of the important new findings regarding gender and sentencing is that gender's influence on sentencing may not just be direct, but may also interact with race, ethnicity, age, and other factors (see the above discussion of race disparity). That is, the level of disparity based on race, ethnicity, age, or other factors may differ between men and women offenders.

## Age Disparity

Relatively little research focuses specifically on the role of age in sentencing, but recent research reveals it to be rather complex. On the one hand, most analyses of sentencing merely control for age as a continuous linear variable, and these analyses typically report small or modest age differences (e.g., Myers and Talarico, 1987). On the other hand, several studies comparing categories of "old" versus "young" offenders find that older offenders are treated more leniently than younger ones.

Recent research found a curvilinear, inverted U-shaped relationship between age and sentencing. The curvilinearity was largely because of the more lenient sentencing of youthful (ages 18–20) as compared to young adult offenders (ages 21–29), the peak ages for receiving the harshest sentences. Very young offenders aged 18–20 receive sentences on par with offenders in their 30s, whereas offenders in their 50s and older receive the most lenient sentences. The age–sentencing relationship becomes strictly linear from about age 30 into old age. Interview data showed that judges see youthful offenders as more impressionable and more likely to be harmed by imprisonment than young "adult" offenders, whereas they see older offenders as less dangerous, and as imposing too many costs and constraints (e.g., health care, special needs, etc.) on the correctional system (see Steffensmeier et al., 1998).

Again, recent research also finds that age interacts with other defendant characteristics such as race and gender in its influence on sentencing disparity (see above discussions of race and gender). This again suggests the importance of comparing sentencing differences between different race, gender, and age groups. Recent research shows that young black and Hispanic males receive especially harsh sentences relative to younger white males and to the other race-gender-age groupings (e.g., to older offenders of both races, and to younger and older females).

## Mode of Conviction Disparity

The substantial majority of sentencing studies in the last 20 years find that those who plead guilty receive more lenient sentences, and those who go to trial are sentenced more harshly (see reviews in Flemming et al., 1992; Dixon, 1995; Ulmer, 1997; Albonetti, 1997). Engen and Steen's (2000) analyses of the impact of sentencing reforms on the sentencing of drug offenders in Washington also illustrate several ways in which mode of conviction results in differences both at the individual and aggregate levels. Their individual-level analyses also found that mode of conviction interacted with defendant Hispanic ethnicity and gender—that is, the effects of gender and Hispanic ethnicity on sentencing outcomes among drug offenders varied according to mode of conviction (Engen and Steen, 2000, 1392–1395). They argue that the organizational efficiency model better explains patterns in Washington's case processing and sentencing of drug offenders following key sentencing reforms.

Dixon (1995) found that the amount of size of sentencing disparity stemming from mode of conviction varied according to the degree of bureaucratization of local prosecutors' offices. Guilty pleas resulted in significantly shorter sentences in highly bureaucratized courts, but not in less bureaucratized ones. This finding provides solid support for organizational context theory. Finally, studies applying the court community and focal concerns perspectives find that the single largest and most consistent form of sentencing disparity is between those who plead guilty versus those convicted by trial (Ulmer, 1997; Steffensmeier et al., 1998; Steffensmeier and DeMuth, 2000). On the other hand, sentencing disparity based on mode of conviction is found to be locally variable. Flemming et al. (1992) found that some prosecutor's offices are "efficient firms" and are willing to trade punitiveness for moving caseloads quickly, whereas others are "proactive or reactive clans" that place "getting tough on crime" (proactive clans), or the preservation of local traditions (reactive clans) above efficient case processing. These kinds of differences in prosecutor's offices can be related to local differences in sentencing disparity, especially disparity based on mode of conviction (Ulmer and Kramer, 1998).

## Gaps in the Sentencing Disparity Literature

Even though a great deal of solid research on sentencing disparity has been produced in the past two decades, our knowledge is far from comprehensive. A great deal remains for future research to discover. Below are five directions for future research that are necessary to advance our knowledge of sentencing and sentencing disparity.

First, Spohn and Holleran's (2000) findings regarding the direct and interactive role of offender unemployment in sentencing disparity suggests more attention should be paid to such social status and resource factors in sentencing. Factors such as social class, education, employment, marital status, or background factors might have important direct and interactive effects in sentencing decisions (especially in jurisdictions without sentencing guidelines, or jurisdictions that rely heavily on presentence reports, which commonly emphasize factors such as education, employment, and background). However, high quality data on these kinds of data are difficult to collect, and are not often readily available in publicly available sentencing datasets. For this reason, studies including these social status and resource factors are uncommon in the literature.

Second, more research should also address the decision-making processes by which criminal justice actors wittingly or unwittingly produce individual and aggregate level disparity. There is also a need to look beyond the sentencing stage to charging and even arrest decisions to examine whether disparity in these earlier stages directly or indirectly affects sentencing. In pursuing this goal, collecting qualitative data on decision-making *processes* and integrating them with quantitative data on decision *outcomes* will be especially crucial.

Third, we need more detailed knowledge of the role of social, organizational, and political contexts in sentencing disparity. A worthy goal for future research would be to develop empirically grounded sets of explanatory propositions about the influence of court and community contextual factors on sentencing and sentencing disparity.

Fourth, research should empirically examine the interrelationship between sentencing disparity and larger patterns of social inequality. For example, how might racial and ethnic sentencing disparities relate to racial and ethnic disadvantages in other institutional arenas, both on an individual level and at aggregate levels? How might gender differences in sentencing mirror, reproduce, or challenge gender arrangements in the larger society? What implications for larger patterns of social inequality flow from the finding that gender, race, ethnicity, and age mutually contextualize each other's influence in sentencing?

### International and Comparative Research

Perhaps the most glaring gap in the literature is that almost all of the research on sentencing disparity is limited to the contemporary North American—particularly the U.S.—context. However, particularly useful overviews of the comparatively small amount of international literature on sentencing disparity that do exist can be found in Tonry and Frase's (2001) *Sentencing and Sanctions in Western Countries*. For example, some suggestive information on racial and ethnic disparity comes from Canada and Australia. In Canada, some reports find that Native Americans are sentenced more harshly than whites. In Australia, the imprisonment rate among Aboriginals exceeds that of the general population by 12–17 times, but it is not known whether this reflects discrimination by the court system or differential criminal involvement among Aboriginals (see Freiberg in Tonry and Frase, 2001). Reports from the Netherlands indicate that sentencing disparity of a variety of kinds has long been a concern, and that country is experimenting with a variety of polices, such as prosecutorial guidelines, to address disparity (see Tak in Tonry and Frase, 2001).

More cross-national and comparative research would greatly broaden knowledge of sentencing and sentencing disparity. Without such research, social science's understanding of the overlap between criminal sanctions and social inequality will be limited, especially in the global society of the 21st century.

JEFFERY T. ULMER

### References and Further Reading

Albonetti, C. 1997., Sentencing under the federal sentencing guidelines: Effects of defendant characteristics, guilty pleas, and departures on sentence outcomes for drug offenses, 1991–1992. *Law and Society Review* 31(4):789–822.

Baldus, D., Woodworth, G., and Pulaski, C., 1994. *Equal Justice and the Death Penalty: A Legal and Empirical Analysis.* Boston, MA: Northeastern University Press.

Dixon, J., 1995. The organizational context of criminal. *American Journal of Sociology* 100(5):1157–1198.

Engen, R. and Steen, S. 2000. The power to punish: Discretion and sentencing reform in the war on drugs. *American Journal of Sociology* 105(5):1357–1395.

Flemming, R.B., Nardulli, P.F., and Eisenstein, J., 1992. *The Craft of Justice: Politics and Work in Criminal Court Communities.* Philadelphia, PA: University of Pennsylvania Press.

Myers, M. and Talarico, S., 1987. *The Social Contexts of Criminal Sentencing.* New York, NY: Springer-Verlag.

Savelsberg, J., 1992., Law that does not fit society: Sentencing guidelines as a neoclassical reaction to the dilemmas of substantivized law. *American Journal of Sociology* 97(5):1346–1381.

Spohn, C. and Holleran, D. 2000., The imprisonment penalty paid by young unemployed black and Hispanic male offenders. *Criminology* 38(1):281–306.

Steffensmeier, D., Kramer, J.H., and Streifel, C., 1993. Gender and imprisonment decisions. *Criminology* 31(3):411–446.

Steffensmeier, D.J., Ulmer, J. and Kramer, J., 1998. The interaction of race, gender, and age in criminal sentencing: The punishment costs of being young, black, and male. *Criminology* 36(4):763–797.

Steffensmeier, D.J. and DeMuth, S., 2000. Ethnicity and sentencing outcomes in U.S. federal courts: Who is punished more harshly–white, black, white–Hispanic, or black–Hispanic defendants? *American Sociological Review* 65(5):705–729.

Tonry, M. and Frase, R. (Eds.)., 2001. *Sentencing and Sanctions in Western Countries.* New York, NY: Oxford University Press.

Ulmer, J.T., 1997. *Social Worlds of Sentencing: Court Communities under Sentencing Guidelines.* Albany, NY: State University of New York Press.

Wilbanks, W., 1987. *The Myth of a Racist Criminal Justice System.* Monterey, CA: Brooks Cole.

*See also* **Sentences and Sentencing: Guidelines; Sentences and Sentencing: Types**

# Sentences and Sentencing: Guidelines

From the mid-19th century through much of the 20th century court systems in the U.S. almost exclusively operated under indeterminate sentencing schemes. Indeterminate sentences were established by legislative bodies with minimum and maximum terms, they were imposed by judges, but ultimately the sentence that was served (typically some fraction of the minimum sentence) was determined by the state or federal paroling authority. By the late 1970s liberals and conservatives alike were expressing a great deal of dissatisfaction with indeterminate sentences. Liberals saw these sentences as subject to wide discretion and that this often operated to the detriment of the poor and minorities, whereas conservatives criticized indeterminate sentences as being "soft" on crime or "coddling" criminals. As a result, a number of states created determinate sentences. Judges still possessed considerable discretion on the sentences they handed down, but a specific period of time to be served (sometimes called a "flat-time" or fixed sentence) would be ordered and the offender would be required to serve the sentence imposed, minus any allowances for good time credits received.

Even with the advent of determinate sentences, critics still believed that there was a great deal of unchecked discretion in the judicial system. With indeterminate sentences, discretion largely was shared by the judge and the paroling authority. By contrast, with determinate sentences discretion shifted to judges and prosecuting attorneys. The fact that judges possessed wide latitude in sentencing led some to believe that discretion had the potential of becoming discrimination, and that sentencing disparities were very much a part of the legal system in the U.S. The answer to judicial discretion and the possibility or reality of sentence disparities was the development of guided sentences. Quite often observers talk about sentencing guidelines, and this is the most common term employed, but guided sentences can take on a variety of different forms.

## Development of Sentencing Guidelines

There are a number of stages in the development of guided sentences, and it seems simplest to consider the evolutionary process in terms of three phases. First, the State of Maine abandoned indeterminate sentencing in favor of a determinate sentencing system in 1976. The sentencing scheme adopted by Maine was determinate—that is, the judge imposed a fixed number of years—however, like the indeterminate system it replaced, there was a wide range of prison terms from which the judge could choose. The end result was that sentencing disparities could result from (1) inconsistent sentences imposed by the same judge, or (2) different sentences imposed for similar crimes by different judges.

The second phase of determinate sentencing was ushered in by the State of California in 1977. California's determinate sentencing system best can be described as a "presumptive" dispositional approach. The California legislature established very narrow ranges for its determinate sentences, and the mid-range, or "presumptive" sentence, was the one to be imposed in the typical case. If there were aggravating or mitigating circumstances, the judge could deviate slightly in response to these factors.

The final phase in the evolutionary process of creating sentencing guidelines is exemplified by the States of Washington and Minnesota, both of which created guided determinate sentences in the early to mid-1980s. In both Washington and Minnesota, the state legislatures created sentencing guideline commissions to establish new criminal sentences that then would be approved by the legislature and enacted into law. Other states and the federal government have followed the examples of Washington and Minnesota, and in most instances the sentencing guideline commission becomes a permanent agency that regularly reviews the sentences imposed and sentencing trends and makes recommendations to the legislative branch.

A final consideration in the development of sentencing guidelines is important to mention at this point. In most states, as was true with the federal courts, once sentencing guidelines have been adopted they must be taken into consideration by the judges, and departures from the mandated sentences must be justified in writing. However, in a few states (Maryland being one of them), the guidelines that have been established are voluntary or advisory. Obviously, in jurisdictions operating under legislatively mandated guidelines, the level of adherence to the prescribed sentences is relatively high. By contrast, in states that have taken the voluntary or advisory route, departures are fairly common and the written justifications provided for departures may be somewhat rare.

Although the process of creating and implementing sentencing guidelines has been relatively slow—occasionally because of organized opposition from the bench and bar—nevertheless, by the end of 1999, 18 states had sentencing guideline systems that were operational, four other states had guideline proposals that were pending, and three additional states and the District of Columbia were engaged in the process of studying sentencing guidelines. In all of the states that had adopted guided sentences the process has varied somewhat; however, in the final analysis state and federal guidelines look very similar.

## Purposes of Sentencing Guidelines

As previously mentioned, one of the major impetuses for the establishment of sentencing guidelines has been concern over sentencing disparities. Furthermore, there has been acknowledgment by many observers familiar with the judicial process in the U.S. that sentencing is one of the most difficult tasks undertaken by judges, and that some judges might be receptive to additional help or guidance in this area. Beyond these two particular factors, a number of states have articulated very specific justifications for the creation of sentencing guidelines. For example, the State of Washington, which first considered sentencing guidelines in 1981 and which enacted them in 1983, lists seven

reasons, or what the state identifies as goals, for using sentencing guidelines. The Washington Sentencing Guidelines Commission says that sentencing guidelines are designed to:

> Ensure that the punishment for a criminal offense is proportionate to the seriousness of the offense and the offender's criminal history;
>
> Promote respect for the law by providing punishment which is just;
>
> Ensure that the punishment imposed on any offender is commensurate with the punishment imposed on others committing similar offenses;
> Protect the public;
> Offer the offender an opportunity to improve him or herself;
> Make frugal use of the state's and local government's resources; and
> Reduce the risk of re-offending by offenders in the community.

The list of goals provided by the Minnesota Sentencing Guidelines Commission is similar. They say that their guidelines are:

> To assure public safety—The violent offenders who pose a danger to the community are more likely to be incarcerated and for longer periods of time.
> To promote uniformity in sentencing—Offenders who are convicted of similar crimes and who have similar criminal records are to be similarly sentenced.
> To promote proportionality in sentencing—The guidelines support a 'just desserts' philosophy by recommending to the sentencing judge a proportionally more severe sentence based first, on the severity of the conviction offense and second, on the offender's criminal history.
> To provide truth and certainty in sentencing—The period of time to be served in prison is pronounced by the judge at sentencing and that time is fixed. Those sentenced to prison will serve two-thirds of their executed sentences in prison.
> To coordinate sentencing practices with correctional resources—To assure available resources, the guidelines recommend who should be imprisoned and for how long. The need for prison resources is therefore more predictable and the Legislature can fund accordingly.

Other states have similar lists, but in the end the core values promoted by most sentencing guideline systems are uniformity, proportionality, equity, and (to a lesser extent) correctional resource planning and management.

## Elements of Sentencing Guidelines

Under the traditional system of indeterminate sentencing, judges were free to craft what many of them considered to be "individualized" sentences. That is, judges could be take into consideration factors that were legally relevant, as well as factors personal to the offender or victim that might be incorporated into deciding the final sentence. With the establishment of sentencing guidelines, the notion of individualized sentences gave way to the overriding principle of sentencing consistency. Therefore, in most instances, state and federal governments that use sentencing guidelines have adhered to a two-dimensional sentencing grid. Along one axis of the grid is the offender's criminal history, ranked by category of number and type of previous offenses. Along the other axis of the grid is the offense with which the offender currently is charged, or the "instant offense." These two elements—criminal history and instant offense—become legally relevant variables, and all other factors (income, community standing, education, employment history, family situation, chemical dependency, etc.) are extra-legal and, by definition, not relevant to the sentencing decision.

Virtually all states adhere to the two-dimensional grids that have been published since the first sentencing guidelines were implemented. However, five other features of sentencing guidelines and sentencing grids should be noted. First, in some states sentencing guidelines apply only to felonies, whereas in other states they apply to felonies and misdemeanors. Second, some states use multiple grids for certain categories of crimes. For instance, there might be one grid for crimes against persons, one for property crimes, and another one for drug offenses. Third, some of the grids also incorporate an "in or out" element, or what might be called a presumptive incarceration threshold. This element advises the judge on whether the presumptive sentence should be probation, incarceration, or some type of intermediate sanction that falls between probation and prison. Fourth, states with both mandatory and voluntary or advisory guidelines allow judges to depart from the sentencing guidelines. The State of Washington permits judges to impose "exceptional sentences" if there is a "substantial and compelling reason." Other states provide for departures in situations where the presumptive sentence would result in a "manifest injustice." Whatever the state, departures from guidelines normally require a written justification by the judge (although, as previously noted, in about 75% of the cases in Maryland where there have been departures the reason has not been provided). Departures from the standard or presumptive sentences then provide grounds for appeal by either the prosecutor or the defense attorney. Finally, a few states have moved in the direction of developing sentencing guidelines for juvenile offenders. This is the clearest manifestation of the movement away from individualized sentencing toward sanctions that are offense based.

## Early Release under Sentencing Guidelines

Under indeterminate sentencing systems, early release came through the process of discretionary parole decision making. The assumption was that once inmates had been rehabilitated they were eligible for release prior to completion of their prison sentences. With the advent of determinate sentencing (and guided sentences), discretionary parole was abandoned in favor of the accumulation of good time credits. Some states added meritorious good time or "gain time" credits into the process as well. Earning good time and gain time credits could result in substantial reductions in the original sentences imposed by the judge. In fact, it is fairly common for some states to offer good time discounts of as much as 50% off of the executed sentence, or one day of good time credit received for each day served. When the good time credit amount equals the remainder of the sentence the inmate is released, and the remainder of the sentence is served in the community under some type of supervision.

When the federal government developed its sentencing guidelines, concern was expressed over, the potential for generous good time credits such as those available in some states. Therefore, Congress provided for a 15% discount rate, or 54 days of good time credit per year. Some states have followed the lead of the federal government under the banner of "truth-in-sentencing," and pursuit of this policy requires inmates serve 85% of their sentences behind bars. This approach has obvious implications for prison populations and, as a result, some states now use "truth-in-sentencing" policies for only the most serious personal offenders, particularly those who previously have been convicted of crimes of violence.

## Results of Guided Sentences

States that have adopted determinate sentences, with or without guidelines, have experienced many of the same outcomes. Some of the outcomes were anticipated and some were not. For example, states with mandatory guidelines have found that guided sentences have become an accepted part of the criminal justice apparatus. Additionally, guided sentences have proven to be more uniform and consistent, as originally envisioned. The result has been a substantial decrease in sentence disparities, although research indicates that not all of the disparities have been removed. A somewhat unexpected result of nearly two decades of experience with sentencing guidelines has been the broad-based political support for them in the states where they have been implemented. Democrats and Republicans, liberals and conservatives all have rallied to the cause of sentencing guidelines.

By contrast, some results were not necessarily anticipated, although perhaps they should have been. Beginning with the early phases of the movement toward determinate sentencing, there often was not a legislative mandate relative to the impact on prison populations. Thus, if determinate sentencing eliminated parole and substituted good time credits in its place (as was done in Maine and many other states), such a change was not tied to any specific impact that this might have on state prison populations. The consequence in most states (and the federal system) has been that the change to determinate sentences has increased the average sentence served by inmates. This means that even if there was not an increase in the number of people sent to prison, the inmate population would expand anyway simply because the average sentence length has increased.

The early experience with prison population growth and determinate sentences convinced states such as Washington and Minnesota to factor prison populations into the establishment of their sentencing guidelines. Not all states have chosen to do this, but for those that have it has meant a slower net growth (compared to other states) resulting from sentencing changes. Nevertheless, even states such as Washington that have a clear legislative mandate to "make frugal use of the state's and local government's resources," have seen a doubling of their state prison inmate population since 1984 (1 year after the sentencing guidelines were enacted into law). In Minnesota, the sentencing guidelines commission is charged with coordinating "sentencing practices with correctional resources." Although this may not result in zero growth in prison populations, it does make "The need for prison resources . . . more predictable and the Legislature can fund accordingly." Virtually all states have experienced expanding prison inmate populations in the past two decades, but states with sentencing guidelines explicitly based on prison capacities have employed this mechanism to slow some of the population growth.

## Future of Sentencing Guidelines

The future of sentencing guidelines is clear on some points, and unclear on others. For example, although the sentencing guidelines movement has not been embraced equally by all states or all regions of the country, no state that has implemented guidelines has decided at a later time to abandon them. Thus, it is fair to say that sentencing guidelines no longer can be considered an experiment in the criminal procedure of courts in the U.S. However, the states that have established sentencing guidelines have not done so with a consistent vision of what their sentencing philosophy should be. In some states, a retributive or "get-tough" on crime approach has driven sentencing policies. This was true in the states of Minnesota, Oregon, and Washington. In North Carolina, multiple sentencing objectives were employed, with incarceration or incapacitation reserved for the most serious offenders.

In terms of the future, the emerging philosophy of restorative justice presents a unique problem for states with guided sentences. On the one hand, the foundation for restorative justice is an individualized response to the offender and the victim's circumstances. On the other hand, sentencing guidelines have rejected individualization in favor of equity and consistency. Are these two notions incompatible? Perhaps they are. However, as we enter what might be considered a fourth phase in the evolution of guided, determinate sentences, it is possible that we will see some new types of sentences emerge that will take into consideration both uniformity and the ability to craft a reasonable, but personal, response to the particular case.

G. LARRY MAYS

## References and Further Reading

Block, M.K. and Rhodes, W.M., (1987). *The Impact of the Federal Sentencing Guidelines*. Washington, DC: National Institute of Justice.

Champion, D.J., (Ed.) (1989). *The U.S. Sentencing Guidelines: Implications for Criminal Justice*. New York, NY: Praeger Publishing Co.

Knapp, K.A. (1984). *The Impact of the Minnesota Guidelines*. St. Paul, MN: Minnesota Sentencing Commission.

Lubitz, R.I. and Ross, T.W. (2001). *Sentencing Guidelines: Reflections on the Future*. Washington, DC: National Institute of Justice.

Mears, D.P. (2002). Sentencing guidelines and the transformation of juvenile justice in the 21st century. *Journal of Contemporary Criminal Justice* 18(1):6–19.

Petersilia, J. M. (1987). *Expanding Options for Criminal Sentencing*. Santa Monica, CA: Rand.

Petersilia, J.M. and Turner, S. (1985). *Guideline-Based Justice: The Implications for Racial Minorities*. Santa Monica, CA: Rand.

von Hirsch, A, Knapp, K.A. and Tonry, M. (1987). *The Sentencing Commission and Its Guidelines*. Boston, MA: Northeastern University Press.

*See also* **Sentences and Sentencing: Disparities; Sentences and Sentencing: Types; Sentencing Guidelines: U.S.**

# Sentences and Sentencing: Types

A sentence is the penalty imposed on a person who has been convicted on a criminal charge, imposed as a result of that conviction. Sentencing is the process by which the sentencing authority, which is nearly always the judge in the U.S., selects and imposes the sentence. (The court-martial panel usually selects and imposes the sentence in a court-martial case. Texas is very unusual in that it has traditionally allowed a role for the jury in nondeath penalty criminal sentencing.)

A criminal sentence can include one or more sanctions including, among others, a fine, probation, intermediate sanctions (between probation and imprisonment in severity) (Byrne, Lurigio, and Petersilia, 1992), incarceration (confinement in an institution), or death. This discussion concerns nearly exclusively sentences to incarceration.

To understand types of sentences, sentencing, and sentencing law, one must understand two concepts: sentencing discretion and determinacy of sentence.

Sentencing discretion involves how free the sentencing authority is to select the type and severity of the sentence imposed for a particular conviction. As an example, prior to the enactment of Fair Sentencing in North Carolina in 1981, judges could, for a robbery conviction, impose a sentence from probation to an unsuspended lengthy term of years. Those judges had very great and wide sentencing discretion. North Carolina's Structured Sentencing (Clarke, 1997), enacted in 1994, requires that the sentencing judge impose a sentence within a fairly narrow range of months for a particular conviction. Therefore, North Carolina judges now have relatively little sentencing discretion.

Determinacy of sentence involves the degree of certainty one can have at the time of sentencing that the convicted person will serve a very high percentage of a term of confinement. If a person receives a sentence of 10 years of incarceration, and one can be sure at the time of sentencing that the person will serve at least 9 years, there is high sentence determinacy. If the person may serve as little as 1.5 years or as much as 9.5 years, there is low sentence determinacy. Applicable laws concerning parole (see von Hirsch and Hanrahan, 1979) and time off for good behavior (good time) are by far the most important influences on determinacy of sentence. If state law allows discretionary parole and early release as a result of awarding of good time, incarceration sentences under that state's law will be low in determinacy.

*Types of Sentences.* We are now prepared to list and describe many types of sentences to confinement.

*Flat-Term Sentence.* This is a sentence to a particular number of months or years of confinement. Depending on relevant parole and good time law, such a sentence can be either high or low in determinacy.

*Minimum–Maximum Sentence.* This is a sentence that provides a minimum period of confinement that the person must serve and a maximum period beyond which the person cannot serve. If there is a substantial difference between the minimum and maximum, the sentence is indeterminate. If there is little difference between the minimum and maximum, as is the case under Truth-in-Sentencing Law (see Tonry, 1999b), the sentence is actually determinate.

*Indeterminate Sentence.* A sentence is indeterminate when there is little or no certainty that the defendant will serve a high percentage of an imposed term of confinement. An entirely indeterminate sentence is one that authorizes correctional (ordinarily parole) officials to release the person the day incarceration starts or to keep the person incarcerated indefinitely (for life). In the juvenile justice context, an entirely indeterminate sentence ordinarily allows incarcerating the person until he reaches the age of 21.

*Mandatory Minimum Sentence.* This is an incarceration sentence that is imposed under a statute that provides that persons convicted on a particular charge must serve at least a particular number of months or years (Vincent and Hofer, 1994). Convictions on crimes committed with a fire arm and "drunk driving" convictions often result in mandatory minimum sentences. Such a requirement increases the determinacy of a sentence.

*Life without Possibility of Parole.* A person receiving such a sentence cannot receive discretionary parole under any statute existing at the time of sentencing. It is not unlawful, however, for such a person to receive a pardon or some type of commutation (lessening of severity) of sentence.

*Suspended Sentence.* Although various types of criminal punishment can be suspended, suspended sentences usually involve the sentencing judge suspending the operation of an incarceration sentence, on conditions and for a particular period. A person receiving a suspended incarceration sentence can receive supervision, which constitutes probation, or no supervision. As the law relating to incarceration sentences evolved in the early 1800s, judges were often held to have the inherent authority to suspend the execution of an incarceration sentence because the judge's powers came down from those of the all-powerful King of England.

*Split Sentence.* This is a sentence that includes a term of confinement followed by a period of probation. Judges generally cannot impose a split sentence without a statute specifically allowing such a sentence. One can reasonably expect that split sentences will become popular in states that abolish parole because some crimes require some incarceration, whereas the interests of the state, the victim, and the defendant can be served by some period of supervision in the community. For example, a defendant guilty of a serious fraud offense requiring some incarceration may have the ability to pay a large amount of restitution under supervision after the confinement.

*Shock Incarceration.* This is similar to a split sentence, but the term of confinement is generally shorter. It is hoped that the short period of incarceration will shock the person into complying with the criminal law. After the short incarceration, the person ordinarily serves a period of probation.

*Habitual Offender Sentences.* These are sentences to lengthy or indefinite terms of confinement that are imposed after the person has had a specific number of qualifying convictions. Some habitual offender statutes concern sexual offenses.

*Concurrent and Consecutive Sentences.* This phrase does not refer to a type of sentence. It concerns whether a person will serve all incarceration sentences starting at the same time (concurrently) or serve each incarceration sentence separately and sequentially (consecutively). In the U.S., the sentencing judge generally has the power to determine whether service of incarceration sentences will be concurrent or consecutive.

*Boot Camp.* States can require confinement in a "boot camp" program by various means. A legislature can authorize judges to impose a sentence requiring incarceration with specification that the incarceration is to be in a boot camp program. Confinement in the boot camp program can be the incarceration under a shock-incarceration or split-sentence sentence. North Carolina takes the novel approach of requiring service in a boot camp program as a condition of probation

(N.C.G.S. sec. 15A-1343(b1)(2a), -1343.1). If the person fails to successfully complete the boot camp program, his probation can be revoked and a term of imprisonment activated or imposed.

*Presumptive Sentences.* One type of sentencing law that guides the judge's sentencing discretion is presumptive sentencing law, such as North Carolina Fair Sentencing (Clarke, 1984), which was in effect 1981–1994. The use of a sentencing grid including prior criminal record results in identification of a "presumptive sentence." To deviate from the presumptive sentence either higher or lower, the sentencing judge must provide written justification on the record.

*Types of Sentencing.* Because the criminal court judge who presided at any trial nearly always has the power to select and impose sentence in the U.S., only sentencing by that official will be discussed.

*Sentencing Pursuant to a Plea Bargain.* Research has consistently indicated that more than 80% of criminal convictions result from a guilty plea and that a very high percentage of guilty pleas are pursuant to a plea bargain between the defense and the prosecution (see Borland and Sones, 1986). When there has been a plea bargain, the sentencing is nearly always perfunctory because the prosecution and defense have for all practical purposes agreed on the sentence. When judges have wide sentencing discretion, plea bargaining takes the form of sentence bargaining, with the prosecutor and defense counsel obtaining agreement of the judge to impose a sentence consistent with the bargain. When judges have very little sentencing discretion, plea bargaining can be expected to take the form of charge bargaining, with the prosecutor dismissing charges sufficiently for the agreed-upon term of confinement to be imposed.

*Sentencing not Pursuant to a Plea Bargain.* Sentencing is not pursuant to a plea bargain when the defendant pleads guilty or no contest (*nolo contendere*) without an agreement with the prosecution and when there has been a trial and a guilty verdict. In both circumstances, sentencing ordinarily occurs after the verdict is accepted by the judge and the conviction announced. There is usually a sentencing hearing at which the defendant has substantial due process rights including the rights to confront adverse witnesses, present evidence, and be heard by the sentencing judge. If a presentence investigation has been prepared by a probation officer, it is received by the judge, who may or may not give it serious consideration.

If the judge has wide sentencing discretion, this sentencing hearing can be more important than the trial. If the judge has little sentencing discretion, there may be little doubt among the judge, defense counsel, and prosecutor—the courtroom work group—concerning what the correct sentence is (see Neubauer, 2002).

To understand variation in sentencing procedures, one needs to learn about different types of sentencing law.

*Types of Sentencing Law.* Because imprisonment was first commonly used as a criminal punishment in the U.S. in the late 1700s and early 1800s, development of the governing law here has been important and influential. During nearly 225 years, the states and the federal government have enacted countless types of sentencing law, so generalizing is difficult. Following the history of developments is instructive. It is beyond the scope of this article to describe the variety of earliest laws in the states authorizing imprisonment as a criminal penalty.

Soon after the use of imprisonment as a criminal penalty began, and prisons were built in all or most of the states, crowding of prisons, with deterioration of conditions, began. This was one of the factors that contributed to the invention and use of probation, parole, and time off for good behavior during the 1800s. Another factor was the emerging belief that science can provide the means for correctional experts to rehabilitate criminals. According to this view, judges should have discretion to individualize sentences to meet the needs of defendants. Parole was expected to promote rehabilitation of inmates, reduction of undesirable inmate behavior, and limitation of prison population. Time off for good behavior was expected to achieve the same three goals. This set the stage for a distinctive type of sentencing law.

*Indeterminate Sentencing Law.* During the 1800s, many states enacted laws allowing judges to impose indeterminate sentences that allowed the operation of parole and good time or other correctional official decision making to determine how long the sentenced person would stay in confinement.

Indeterminate sentencing law was quite common as the U.S. entered the turbulent 1960s (Bureau of Justice Statistics, 1984). During the 1960s and 1970s, as the Civil Rights Movement continued to make important headway, research indicated that discrimination on the basis of race in sentencing was not uncommon in the U.S. (Gibson, 1978; Forst, 1982; Carroll and Cornell, 1985). In *Gregg v. Georgia* (428 U.S. 153, 1976), the U.S. Supreme Court approved guided-discretion sentencing in death penalty cases to reduce arbitrariness and the possibility of discrimination in the imposition of the death penalty. About that time, many adherents of the Justice and Just-Deserts models argued that it was important to increase certainty regarding what sentences would be imposed in particular types of

cases and regarding determinacy of sentence (Griset, 1991). The result was the development of three types of guided-discretion incarceration sentencing law.

*Presumptive Sentencing Law.* As previously mentioned, presumptive sentencing law involved use of a sentencing grid including prior criminal record in identification of a presumptive sentence. To deviate from the presumptive sentence either higher or lower, the sentencing judge had to provide written justification on the record. The degree to which sentencing discretion was guided was determined heavily by the amount of deviation from the presumptive sentence the law allowed. North Carolina Fair Sentencing (1981–1994) was a type of presumptive sentencing.

*Sentencing Guidelines Law.* The U.S. Congress has elected to direct use of sentencing guidelines developed by a commission and approved by the Congress in sentencing in federal courts. These guidelines require consideration of criminal history and circumstances of the offense in determination of a sentence that presumably will be imposed (Frase, 1995). In conjunction with sentencing guidelines, the U.S. Congress abolished federal parole and time off for good behavior in federal prisons. Several states also have criminal sentencing under sentencing guidelines.

*Truth-in-Sentencing Law.* The U.S. Congress was so pleased with experiences with federal sentencing guidelines and abolition of federal parole and federal good time, that in 1994, it created incentives for states to enact guided-discretion sentencing that would require that defendants serve at least 85% of any term of confinement (Violent Crime Control and Law Enforcement Act of 1994, Title I, Subtitle A). It was virtually impossible for a state to qualify for funding without abolishing parole and good time. North Carolina Structured Sentencing Law that was passed in 1994 in conjunction with abolition of parole and good time, has been ruled to be a qualifying example of Truth-in-Sentencing law. The governing statute includes a grid including a criminal history score, which indicates a presumptive sentence. If the judge believes there is justification to impose a sentence above or below the presumptive sentence in length, he must make supportive findings of aggravating or mitigating circumstances. A list of permissible aggravating and mitigating circumstances is provided in the statute. In some cases the judge has discretion to decide whether the sentence will be "A" (active term of incarceration), "I" (intermediate, including intensive-supervision probation, residence in a halfway house or residential treatment center, or home confinement with electronic surveillance), or "C" (community, which usually involves a fine, probation, or both).

During the recent decades of heavy conservative influence of sentencing law, the Congress and several states have adopted a particular type of habitual offender sentencing law.

*Three-Strikes-and-You're-Out Law.* Such a law, which can be applied in conjunction with several different types of underlying sentencing law, provides that, when a person has had a cumulative total of at least three separate qualifying convictions on a total of three separate occasions, the person is required to receive a sentence of life without possibility of parole (see Clark, Austin, and Henry, 1997). California has adopted this type of law and has been the site of important developments in the evolution of its application, practice, and interpretation. Some experts believe that this law will result in very lengthy and costly incarceration of many persons who present little criminal threat.

*Overview of Sentencing and Correctional Law.* To correctly assess criminal sentencing in a state, one needs to know how much discretion the judge has in sentencing and how determinate the sentences are. Generally, there are nine categories based on variations in these two factors.

Category 1 involves high judge sentencing discretion and low sentence determinacy, which equates to high criminal justice discretion. One can assume that many of the U.S. states during the 1950s had law that would fit in this category.

Category 3 involves low sentencing discretion and low sentence determinacy. Although one might argue that judges under North Carolina Fair Sentencing (1981–1994) had a medium level of sentencing discretion, it will be assumed here that they exercised low sentencing discretion. The extensive availability of parole and good time made sentence determinacy quite low. Therefore, category 3 was exemplified.

One can assume that, soon after imprisonment as a criminal penalty came into use in the U.S., some states granted judges a high degree of sentencing discretion. Before emergence of parole and good time, sentence determinacy was high. This situation would have exemplified category 7.

Category 9 involves low judge sentencing discretion and high sentence determinacy. You can argue that North Carolina law currently fits in this category because North Carolina structured sentencing provides little judicial discretion in sentencing and requires that inmates serve nearly 85% of confinement sentences.

Legislative decision making that determines the extent of criminal justice discretion relating to criminal sentences is important and difficult. When judges lose sentencing discretion, they lose some of their ability to individualize sentences to meet the needs of victims, the public, and the offender. Two criminal cases, each of which involved rape by a person with three prior criminal convictions, can be substantially different. Also, research by Memory et al. (1999) has shown that the abolition of parole and good time can reduce the ability of correctional officers and officials to control undesirable behavior of inmates.

*Myths Relating to Criminal Sentencing.* Many of one's seemingly logical assumptions about sentencing are unsound. For example, one might assume that a legislature could confidently require that all persons who have stolen money or property with a value of at least $250 will receive and serve a sentence of 3 years. Actually, victims and police officers could and would refuse to report offenses because of excessive severity. Prosecutors could dismiss or reduce charges or divert from prosecution because of excessive severity. Juries could engage in jury nullification by refusing to convict because of excessive severity of the required sentence.

One would assume that, as crime goes up, imprisonment necessarily goes up. In fact, during the 1960s, as a tremendous increase in crime was occurring, the rate of imprisonment in the U.S. declined slightly (see Schmalleger, 1999). From 1970 through 2000, the rate of imprisonment in the U.S. increased by about 400% (see Schmalleger, 1999). One might assume that this occurred as a result of a substantial increase in crime. Actually, although there was no pattern of substantial increase in crime during the 1970s and 1980s, crime *declined* significantly during the 1990s, as the rate of imprisonment continued to grow (see Schmalleger, 1999). The U.S. now has a higher rate of imprisonment than any other country.

It seems reasonable that a person cannot under any circumstances be kept incarcerated after the entire period of confinement has been served. In fact, some states allow correctional officials to petition a court in a civil action for continued incarceration of a person who, it is believed, would present an especially great risk of violent crime to the community if released. A court can, in such a case, enter a civil order requiring continued confinement.

*The Future of Sentencing in the U.S.* History tells us that changes in sentencing law will continue to occur. Although federal and state coffers overflowed with money in the 1990s, the federal government now has giant annual deficits, and many states are experiencing budget crises. Correctional officials in South Carolina are being required to incarcerate the same number of inmates with a significantly reduced budget.

Legislatures and correctional officials must develop "smart" and less expensive ways to limit the threat of dangerous persons. Although three-strikes-and-you're-out laws result in lengthy and costly confinement of persons who either are no longer or never were very dangerous, there are no obvious reasons why states and the federal government cannot do better jobs of identifying especially dangerous and high-frequency offenders at a relatively young age and incarcerating them for a high percentage of the years during which they will be most dangerous.

Because the prison incarceration rate of black persons in the U.S. is about seven times as high as the prison incarceration rate of white persons (see Senna and Siegel, 1999), the public, legislatures, researchers, the courts, and other criminal justice officials should continue to investigate to determine whether discrimination on the basis of race in sentencing is occurring. If such discrimination is found, remedial action should be taken. It is relevant that for many years the rates of serious violent crime (murder, rape, and robbery) of black persons in the U.S. have been six to eight times as high as the corresponding rates for white persons (see Senna and Siegel, 1999).

JOHN MEMORY

## References and Further Reading

Blumstein, A., Cohen, J., Martin, S. and Tonry, M. (Eds.), (1983). *Research on Sentencing: The Search for Reform* (Vol. 1). Washington, DC: National Academy Press.

Borland, B. and Sones, R. (1986). *Prosecution of Felony Arrests, 1981*. Washington, DC: Bureau of Justice Statistics.

Brown, J., Langan, P. and Levin, D. (1999). *Felony Sentences in State Courts, 1996*. Washington, DC: Bureau of Justice Statistics.

Bureau of Justice Assistance. (1996). *National Assessment of Structured Sentencing*. Washington, DC: Bureau of Justice Assistance.

Bureau of Justice Statistics. (1984). *Sentencing Practices in Thirteen States*. Washington, DC: U.S. Department of Justice.

Bureau of Justice Statistics. (1997). *Correctional Populations in the United States, 1995*. Washington, DC: U.S. Department of Justice.

Byrne, J., Lurigio, A. and Petersilia, J. (1992). *Smart Sentencing: The Emergence of Intermediate Sanctions*. Newbury Park, CA: Sage.

Carroll, L. and Cornell, C. (1985). Racial composition, sentencing reforms, and rates of incarceration, 1970–1980. *Justice Quarterly, 2*, 473–490.

Chaiken, M. and Chaiken, J. (1990). Redefining the Career Criminal: Priority Prosecution of High-Rate Dangerous Offenders. Washington, DC: U.S. Department of Justice.

Clark, J., Austin, J. and Henry, D.A. (1997). *Three Strikes and You're Out: A Review of State Legislation*. Washington, DC: National Institute of Justice.

Clarke, S. (1997). *Law of sentencing, probation, and parole in North Carolina*. Chapel Hill, NC: Institute of Government, The University of North Carolina at Chapel Hill.

Clarke, S. (1984). North Carolina's determinate sentencing legislation. *Judicature, 68*, 140–152.

Clear, T. (1994). *Harm in American Penology: Offenders, Victims, and Their Communities*. Albany, NY: State University of New York Press.

Ditton, P. and Wilson, D. (1999). *Truth in Sentencing in State Prisons*. Washington, DC: Bureau of Justice Statistics.

Forst, M. (1982). *Sentencing Reform: Experiments in Reducing Disparity*. Beverly Hills, CA: Sage.

Forst, M. (1982). Sentencing disparity: An overview of research and issues. In M. Forst (Ed.), *Sentencing Reform: Experiments in Reducing Disparity*. Beverly Hills, CA: Sage.

Frase, R. (1995). State sentencing guidelines: Still going strong. *Judicature, 78*, 173–179.

Gibson, J. (1978). Race as a determinant of criminal sentences: A methodological critique and a case study. *Law and Society Review, 12*, 455–478.

Goodstein, L. and Hepburn, J. (1983). *Determinate Sentencing and Imprisonment*. Cincinnati, OH: Anderson.

Griset, P. (1991). *Determinate Sentencing: The Promise and the Reality of Retributive Justice*. Albany, NY: State University of New York Press.

Kramer, J. and Steffensmeier, D. (1993). Race and imprisonment decisions. *The Sociological Quarterly, 13*, 81–106.

Mauer, M. (1999). *The Race to Incarcerate*. New York, NY: The New Press.

McDonald, D. and Carlson, K. (1993). *Sentencing in the federal courts: Does race matter? The transition to sentencing guidelines, 1986–1990*. Washington, DC: Bureau of Justice Statistics.

Memory, J., Guo, G., Parker, K. and Sutton, T. (1999). Comparing disciplinary infraction rates of North Carolina Fair Sentencing and Structured Sentencing inmates: A natural experiment. *The Prison Journal, 79*, 45–71.

Morris, N. and Tonry, M. (1990). *Between Prison and Probation: Intermediate Punishments in a Rational Sentencing System*. Oxford, U.K.: Oxford University Press.

Schmalleger, F. (1999). *Criminal Justice Today: An Introductory Text for the Twenty-First Century*. Upper Saddle River, NJ: Prentice Hall.

Senna, J. and Siegel, L. (1999). *Introduction to Criminal Justice*. Belmont, CA: West or Wadsworth.

Steffensmeier, D., Ulmer, J. and Kramer, J. (1998). The interaction of race, gender, and age in criminal sentencing: The punishment cost of being young, black, and male. *Criminology, 36*, 763–798.

Tonry, M. (1996). *Sentencing Matters*. New York, NY: Oxford University Press.

Tonry, M. (1999a). The fragmentation of sentencing and corrections in America. *Sentencing and Corrections Issues for the Twenty-First Century, 1*, 1–8.

Tonry, M. (1999b). *Reconsidering Indeterminate and Structured Sentencing*. Office of Justice Programs, Washington, DC: U.S. Department of Justice.

Ulmer, J. (1997). *Social Worlds of Sentencing: Court Communities under Sentencing Guidelines*. Albany, NY: State University of New York Press.

Vincent, B. and Hofer, P. (1994). *The Consequences of Mandatory Minimum Prison Terms: A Summary of Recent Findings*. Washington, DC: Federal Judicial Center.

von Hirsch, A. and Hanrahan, K. (1979). *The Question of Parole*. Cambridge, MA: Ballinger.

*See also* **Sentencing Guidelines: U.S.; Sentences and Sentencing: Guidelines**

# Sentencing Guidelines, U.S.

Former President Ronald Reagan signed the Comprehensive Crime Control Bill into law on October 12, 1984. This bill included the Sentencing Reform Act of 1984, which mandated the establishment of the U.S. Sentencing Commission, whose purpose would be to promulgate new sentencing guidelines to be followed by U.S. district court judges in sentencing federal offenders. The primary reasons for establishing new sentencing guidelines were to foster consistency in punishment, promote deterrence, provide for specific periods of incapacitation for each federal offense, and promote offender rehabilitation.

The U.S. Sentencing Commission was established in 1985 and consisted of seven voting members. Members would be appointed for 6-year terms. These members included one district court judge, two circuit court judges, a former member of the U.S. Parole Commission, and three persons from academics. Designated as Commissioners, these original Commission members would serve staggered terms of 2, 4, and 6 years in order to promote continuity by preventing a complete Commission turnover every 6 years. The goals of the U.S. Sentencing Commission were to promote honesty, uniformity, and proportionality in the sentencing of federal offenders.

In a historical context, the idea of federal sentencing reform was spawned during the presidential administration of Lyndon B. Johnson in 1966. At the recommendation of President Johnson, Congress created the National Commission on Reform of Federal Criminal Laws. This Commission was chaired by former California governor Edmund G. Brown, Sr., and it issued its final report to Congress in 1968. Known informally as the Brown Commission, this Commission recommended a model criminal code. Such a code was introduced to Congress in 1973 but was not passed. Subsequent to the Brown Commission, various sentencing reform proposals were made by interested congressmen as well as several judges. One judge, Marvin E. Frankels, proposed the creation of a federal sentencing commission that would develop rules for sentencing which would be presumptively applied and could be appealed to higher courts. This proposal received support from several influential congressmen, such as Edward Kennedy and Strom Thurmond. No further action was taken in the furtherance of establishing a Commission throughout the 1970s and early 1980s until the passage of the Comprehensive Crime Control Bill in 1984.

During this interim, several states, including Pennsylvania and Minnesota established their own sentencing commissions and devised sentencing guidelines for state offenders. California adopted a more structured sentencing scheme during the late 1970s. The subsequent successfulness of these state schemes did not go unnoticed by the federal government and Congress. The nature of the influence of state sentencing reforms upon the U.S. Congress is unclear, although it is likely that favorable sentencing results from these state jurisdictions under their new sentencing guidelines formats was moderately persuasive in leading to the ultimate signing of the Comprehensive Crime Control Bill in 1984.

The chief motivating factor behind all sentencing reform leading to the creation of sentencing guidelines is sentencing disparity. Sentencing disparity is the unequal application of punishment to different offenders in the same jurisdiction, where the unequal punishment is primarily attributable to extralegal factors such as race, ethnicity, socioeconomic status, and gender. It is most apparent when two convicted offenders with identical criminal histories are sentenced by the same judge to widely disparate terms or given substantially unequal punishments, and where no legal explanations for these sentencing differences exist or are articulated. An extreme example would involve two 35-year-old Atlanta, Georgia male first offenders convicted of armed robbery and murder. In each case, these offenders might hold up a bank and kill a police officer while escaping. Subsequently, each of these offenders are captured and brought to trial in the same Georgia criminal court but at different times, perhaps a few weeks apart. The same judge presides in both cases. Both men are convicted. One man receives the death penalty, whereas the other man receives 25 years to life. The man receiving the death penalty is black, whereas the man receiving 25 years to life is white. Factually similar circumstances cannot distinguish the two cases. Only the race of the offenders is the primary distinguishing feature. This is an example of sentencing disparity.

On a larger scale and in numerous state and federal jurisdictions, the prevalence of sentencing disparities attributable to extralegal factors has been apparent. Civil liberties organizations, such as the American Civil Liberties Union and Amnesty International, Inc., have investigated and reported such disparities in various public forums and outlets. Research by criminal justice scholars and criminologists has been conducted extensively, addressing sentencing disparities. Widespread sentencing disparities exist throughout the U.S. Furthermore, such disparities have been linked directly with the nature of sentencing schemes used by different state and federal jurisdictions. In order to understand how some of these sentencing schemes promote and perpetuate sentencing disparities, it is important to examine their variations.

Four major sentencing schemes are used in the U.S. today. These are indeterminate sentencing, determinate sentencing, mandatory sentencing, and presumptive or guidelines-based sentencing. The various sentencing schemes are described as follows.

Indeterminate sentencing is used by a majority of state courts. Indeterminate sentencing occurs when upper and lower limits on the time to be served are imposed, either on probation, or in jail, or prison. If offenders are incarcerated under indeterminate sentencing, a parole board determines their early release. Usually, offenders must serve at least the minimum sentence as prescribed by the judge before parole can be granted. This is known as the minimum–maximum sentence. An example of indeterminate sentencing might be where a judge sentences an offender to "not less than one year nor more than 10 years" for robbery. The offender must serve at least 1 year of this sentence before a parole board can grant early release. Another version of indeterminate sentencing is fixed indeterminate sentencing. Under fixed indeterminate sentencing, judges sentence offenders to a single prison term that is treated as the maximum sentence for all practical purposes. The implied minimum might be zero for all sentences, 1 year for all sentences, or a fixed proportion of the maximum.

Determinate sentencing prescribes that judges fix the term of an offender's incarceration that must be served in full, less any good time credits that might be applicable. Good time credits are days earned and deducted from one's maximum sentence as the result of good institutional behavior. For example, in 1995, most U.S. state correctional systems awarded either 15 days, 20 days, or 30 days a month off of an inmate's maximum sentence for every 30 days served in prison. Thus, if an inmate was sentenced to a maximum of 10 years, under a 30-day-per-month good time scenario, it is possible that the inmate would serve only half of the original maximum sentence of 10 years. Essentially, an inmate would have an equivalent amount of time deducted from his sentence for every month or year served. A 5-year incarcerative period would earn 5 years' worth of good time credit. Under this determinate sentencing scheme, good time credit accumulations would determine one's specific release date.

This is a key reason such a scheme is called determinate sentencing, because inmates know approximately when they must be released from custody.

The basic difference between indeterminate and determinate sentencing is that judges must impose a fixed sentence under determinate sentencing and early release is governed by the accumulation of good time credit; under indeterminate sentencing, parole boards make early-release decisions following a minimum–maximum sentence imposed by the sentencing judge. Theoretically, at least, determinate sentencing reduces or minimizes the abuse of judicial and parole board discretion in determining early release for inmates. It is arguable, however, whether judicial discretion has been affected seriously by determinate sentencing.

Mandatory sentencing is a sentencing system where the judge is required to impose an incarcerative sentence, often of a specified length, for certain crimes or for particular categories of offenders. There is no option of probation, suspended sentence, or immediate parole eligibility. In Michigan, for example, the use of a firearm during the commission of a felony adds an additional 2 years to one's sentence. This 2-year sentence must be served in its entirety. There is no time off for good behavior. Virginia has Virginia Exile, a 5-year penalty for the use of a firearm during the commission of a felony. This 5-year sentence must be served in its entirety in addition to any penalty imposed for the crime in which the firearm was used.

Most states have mandatory penalties for particular offenses, especially for drug trafficking. The most well-known mandatory penalty is life imprisonment for being convicted as a habitual offender. Habitual offenders are punished under habitual offender laws, which usually carry life-without-parole sentences. Recidivists, especially those who commit violent crimes, are targeted by habitual offender legislation, such as that enacted in Florida. Offenders convicted of a third felony may receive life imprisonment as a mandatory sentence. However, mandatory sentences are seldom imposed in most jurisdictions. Instead, they are frequently used as leverage by prosecutors to elicit guilty pleas from defendants to lesser-included charges. Thus, many persons who could be charged as habitual offenders aren't charged as such, and this means that mandatory sentencing is often regarded as a cosmetic get-tough measure.

The fourth type of sentencing scheme used in the U.S. is presumptive or guidelines-based sentencing. Under such a scheme, predetermined punishments accompanying each offense are established and imposed. The range of punishments under presumptive sentencing may or may not involve incarceration. These punishments are usually expressed in numbers of months to be served, either on probation or incarceration. A formula is used to arrive at the specified range of numbers of months imposed by the sentencing judge. The formula is based on an offender's prior record or criminal history, mitigating or aggravating circumstances or both, the length of previous incarcerations, and other factors. The word "presumptive" refers to the mid-range of months in any sentencing range for any particular offense. Thus, if a particular punishment has associated with it 25–35 months, the presumptive punishment would be 30 months, because it is midway between 25 and 35 months. Upward or downward departures from the presumptive sentence of 30 months would depend upon the presence of aggravating or mitigating factors. Thus, judges could lower the punishment to 25 months if there were one or more mitigating factors, such as assistance rendered to law enforcement officers in the apprehension of others, mental retardation, or youthfulness. The punishment could be increased toward 35 months if one or more aggravating factors were present, such as whether the offender played the leadership role in carrying out the crime, or whether extreme cruelty was imposed on the victim. Mitigating and aggravating factors are usually considered together, and they may be offsetting. Thus, if there were three mitigating factors and three aggravating ones, these would offset one another and the judge would impose the presumptive sentence of 30 months. However, if there were two mitigating circumstances and three aggravating ones, the judge might raise the punishment to 33 months. Raising or lowering the numbers of months from the presumptive sentence is discretionary with the judge and depends on the weight given these factors.

Presumptive sentencing guidelines supposedly curb judicial discretion by obligating judges to stay within certain boundaries (expressed in month ranges) when sentencing offenders. The intent of presumptive guidelines is to create greater consistency among judges in the sentences they impose on different offenders convicted of the same offenses under similar circumstances. However, judges may depart from these statutory ranges by as much as a year or more. But if judges impose either harsher or more lenient sentences, they must provide a written explanation to justify these upward or downward departures.

When the U.S. Sentencing Commission was formed in 1985 and convened to revise the existing federal sentencing provisions for all crimes, it was a massive and time-consuming undertaking. Virtually every punishment for every federal crime identified in Title 18 of the U.S. Code was reexamined and assigned an offense seriousness score. To assist the Commission in undertaking this task, a sample of 10,500 cases sentenced in federal court between October 1, 1984 and September 30, 1985 was examined. An automated dataset was provided by the Administrative Office of the U.S. Courts, which included offense descriptions, information about each offender's background and criminal history, the method of disposition, such as a guilty plea or conviction following a trial, and the sentence imposed.

Further, the Commission obtained information from the Federal Bureau of Prisons about all offenders in the sample who had been sentenced to prison. This information included estimates of the amount of time served; time scheduled to be served in prison if a parole date had been set; and the time served in prison if a parole date had not been set. The Commission wanted to know how much time is served on the average by convicted federal offenders. Also, how does this average time served vary with the characteristics of the offense, the offender's background and criminal history, and method of disposition? The Commission wanted to know the amount of variation among federal judges and their average sentencing practices on an offense-by-offense basis. It was believed that this information would be beneficial in establishing new parameters for different offense punishments. At the same time, the Commission solicited comments and suggestions from a wide variety of experts in sentencing practices, including some professionals in the academic community. Lawyers, prosecutors, judges, public defenders, probation and parole officers, and others were called upon for opinions and suggestions.

Congress gave the Commission wide latitude in determining the relevance of both offense and offender characteristics insofar as punishment variations were concerned. Offense characteristics included grade of the offense (misdemeanor or felony); aggravating and mitigating circumstances; nature and degree of harm caused by the offense; the community view of the gravity of the offense; the public concern generated by the offense; the potential deterrent effect of a particular sentence for the offense; and the current incidence of the offense in the community and in the nation as a whole. Offender characteristics included age; education; vocational skills; mental and emotional condition as a mitigating factor or as otherwise relevant; physical condition, including drug dependence; employment record; family ties and responsibilities; community ties; role in the offense; criminal history; and dependence upon criminal activity for a livelihood. With the exception of (1) role in the offense; (2) criminal history; and (3) dependence upon criminal activity for a livelihood, the Commission decided that none of the other characteristics were relevant to the purposes of sentencing. Thus, the Commission sought to objectify their projected presumptive sentencing scheme.

It is beyond the scope of this entry to detail the Commission deliberations or explore the rationale provided for all offense scores. However, it should be noted that the Commission gave great weight to offense seriousness according to whether offenders used dangerous weapons to commit their crimes; whether one or more victims were harmed or killed; and the value of merchandise taken in larceny, robbery, or any other type of property offense.

After considerable work, the U.S. Sentencing Commission produced a comprehensive document listing all federal offenses, including specific probationary, incarcerative, or fine punishments or both. A sentencing table was generated. The table consisted of six criminal history categories, ranging from I (the least serious criminal history) to VI (the most serious criminal history). Scoring an offender's criminal history is calculated on the basis of the length of prior sentences of imprisonment (not the amount of time actually served) in any jurisdiction, local, state or federal. For instance, 3 points are added for each prior sentence exceeding 1 year and 1 month; 2 points are added for each shorter sentence of imprisonment that is of at least 60 days; and 1 point is added for each sentence of imprisonment that did not receive 2 or 3 points. A sentence is counted only if that sentence was imposed no more than 15 years prior to the beginning of the offense of conviction. Points are also added if (1) the offense was committed while the offender was under any type of criminal justice sentence (e.g., community supervision, probation, parole, work release); (2) if the offense was committed within 2 years after release from imprisonment on a sentence worth 2 or 3 points; or (3) if the offender was convicted of a crime of violence whose sentence did not receive any points as described above. Summing these points would serve to classify offenders according to one of the six criminal history categories.

These criminal history categories were graduated horizontally across the top of the sentencing table. Down the left-hand side of the table were 43 offense levels, numbered from 1 to 43. Where one's criminal history category intersected in the body of the table with the offense level were ranges of months. For offense level I and criminal history category I, for example, the month range was 0-1. For offense level 43, "life" was indicated as the maximum punishment. At that time, the death penalty was suspended for all federal offenses, with life imprisonment as the most serious punishment. For an offense level score of 35 and a criminal history category of IV, for example, the range of months was 262–327. Thus, month ranges were provided for all intersecting points in the table. Table 1 shows the sentencing guidelines.

Thus, progressively serious punishments or longer periods of incarceration were provided for more serious types of offenses and for offenders with more serious criminal histories. Those categories in Table 1 where zeros occur (e.g., 0–1, 0–2, 0–3, etc.) mean that probation may be imposed as a sentencing option at

**Table 1.** Similarities and differences between the qualifications in the States of California, Oregon, South Carolina, Ohio, and Georgia

| | Peace Officer Certification | Citizenship | Age | Education | Sworn Service | Supervisory Experience | Time Frame | In-Service Mandate |
|---|---|---|---|---|---|---|---|---|
| California | Active or inactive | NR | NR | MS | 1 yr | NR | Within 5 yrs | NR |
| | | NR | NR | BS | 2 yr | NR | Within 5 yrs | NR |
| | | NR | NR | AS | 3 yr | NR | Within 5 yrs | NR |
| | | NR | NR | HD or GED | 4 yr | NR | Within 5 yrs | NR |
| Oregon* | No—must obtain within 1 yr | NR | 21 | AS | 4 yr | NR | NR | NR |
| South Carolina | Yes | 1 yr in county | 21 | HD or GED | 5 yr | NR | NR | Yes |
| | | 1 yr in county | 21 | AS | 3 yr | NR | NR | Yes |
| | | 1 yr in county | 21 | BS | 1 yr | NR | NR | Yes |
| | | 1 yr in county | 21 | Summary court judge | 10 yr | NR | NR | Yes |
| Ohio** | Yes | 1 yr | 21 | HD or GED | NR | 2 yr | Within 4 yrs | Yes |
| | Yes | 1 yr | 21 | AS | NR | NR | | Yes |
| Georgia | No—must obtain within 6 Mo | 2 yrs in county | 25 | HD or GED | NR | NR | NR | Yes |

\* Requires professional certification as supervisor, manager, or administrator based on county size.

\** Requires sworn service within the prior four years before running or three years of continuous service just prior to running.

the discretion of the judge. Provisions for probation are limited to less than 10% of all offenses, however. These provisions subsequently curtailed drastically the use of probation by district court judges, decreasing the percentage of probationary sentences from 36.5% in the preguideline period to 21.2% a decade later in the post-guideline period.

The U.S. sentencing guidelines became effective November 1, 1987 and apply to all federal offenses committed on or following that date. Shortly following the implementation of these guidelines, sentenced federal offenders in various district courts sought to challenge their constitutionality in various ways. The primary challenges targeted two important points: (1) improper legislative delegation; and (2) violation of the separation-of-powers doctrine. Challenges of these guidelines emanated from the district courts as well as from convicted federal offenders. Approximately 150 federal judges refused to use these guidelines in their courtrooms when sentencing federal offenders, and their reasons for rejecting the guidelines were diverse. However, the landmark case of *Mistretta v. U.S.* (488 U.S. 361) in 1989, served to uphold the constitutionality of the guidelines and compel federal district court judges to follow them.

John Mistretta was convicted of selling cocaine. The U.S. sentencing guidelines were officially in effect after November 1, 1987. Mistretta's criminal acts and conviction occurred after this date, and thus he was subject to guidelines-based sentencing rather than indeterminate sentencing, which the federal district courts had previously followed. Under the former sentencing scheme, Mistretta might have been granted probation. However, the new guidelines greatly restricted the use of probation as a sentence in federal courts and thus, Mistretta's sentence involved serving an amount of time in prison. Mistretta appealed his conviction, arguing that the new guidelines violated the separation-of-powers doctrine, as several federal judges were members of the U.S. Sentencing Commission and helped to formulate laws and punishments, an exclusive function of Congress. The U.S. Supreme Court in a vote of 8–1 upheld Mistretta's conviction and declared the new guidelines to be constitutional and not in violation of the separation-of-powers doctrine. The lone dissenting Justice was Antonin Scalia, the newest U.S. Supreme Court Justice, who wrote a lengthy and compelling argument for why the separation-of-powers doctrine had been violated. But the majority prevailed and this action served to abbreviate the number and nature of subsequent appeals concerning the U.S. sentencing guidelines and their constitutionality.

The separation-of-powers criticism of the U.S. Sentencing Commission adheres to the fact that several federal judges comprised the Commission. This fact placed judges in the position of rewriting the federal criminal laws, which is a Congressional function, not a judicial one. Nevertheless, the U.S. Supreme Court regarded this criticism as trivial, declaring that judges are as capable of determining appropriate punishments for offenses as any other participant in the criminal justice system. In fact, the U.S. Supreme Court took offense that somehow the judicial members of the Commission were incapable of making such punishment revisions. This was not the point, according to Justice Scalia, who noted that the very presence of federal judiciary on a Commission dedicated to rewriting federal criminal laws is a clear violation of the separation-of-powers doctrine, where the responsibility for law change is with the U.S. Congress, not the judiciary who are supposed to apply the law, not make it.

Since the guidelines were implemented, more than a little controversy concerning their use and configuration has been generated. The primary goal of eliminating sentencing disparity by implementing sentencing guidelines has not been achieved. Indeed, the guidelines seem to have increased punishments for street crimes and drug offenses disproportionate to other types of federal crimes, such as white-collar offenses. On an abstract level, it would appear that the guidelines have increased punishments for crimes committed largely by persons in the lower socioeconomic classes compared with the upper socioeconomic classes. This is a Marxian argument that has merit in view of the priority given to prosecuting drug offenders and street criminals in the federal courts. In the preguideline years, federal drug prosecutions have more than doubled as well as the federal prison population. Further, sentence lengths for those convicted of drug offenses have more than doubled compared with other federal crime categories. Especially vulnerable to enhanced punishments under these guidelines were repeat offenders and violent criminals.

Because the guidelines were implemented at a time when the federal government was moving toward greater truth-in-sentencing, wherein sentenced federal offenders would have to serve at least 85% of their sentences before being considered for parole or supervised release, this fact alone is sufficient to account for the burgeoning federal prison population. In the postguideline years, federal offenders may now accrue good time credit at the rate of 54 days per year to be applied against their maximum sentences for early-release eligibility. The 54-day-a-year good time credit amount is roughly equivalent to 15% of the year, which relates to the truth-in-sentencing provision of 85% of one's sentence that must be served.

The guidelines have also made it more difficult for federal prosecutors to plea bargain with defendants and offer plea discounts, because federal probation officers are under a duty to report all factual information concerning the federal crime committed. In preguideline years, U.S. probation officers could work with federal prosecutors and conveniently omit certain factual information from their presentence investigation reports such as whether a firearm was used in the commission of the crime. Thus, prosecutors could effectively suppress such information from a PSI report with cooperation from probation officers. Today in the postguideline years, such information must be included as a general policy, and prosecutors cannot ignore this information when formulating plea agreements. Despite this new policy for full factual reporting in PSIs, prosecutors may still engage in guidelines bargaining, wherein they may negotiate with defense counsel over guidelines factors, such as the leadership role played by the defendant in the crime's commission; the defendant's acceptance of responsibility for the crime; and whether the defendant willfully impeded the criminal investigation. Thus, there is still some wiggle room for prosecutors to negotiate over several factual circumstances that may not be clearly articulated in final versions of PSI reports.

The Commission also formulated various adjustments that could be made depending upon the circumstances under which the federal crime was committed. The proximity of the crime's perpetration in relation to a school would increase one's offense level score as would the use of a firearm during the crime's commission. The quantity of drugs seized also leads to substantial variations in point adjustments, either upward or downward, from the base offense level. The Commission advanced various statutory factors that could be used by probation officers and judges for determining one's offense level. However, the Commission encouraged federal judges to be creative in formulating several nonstatutory factors of their own in determining a convicted offender's offense level score.

The clear-cut nature of guidelines application is illusory in fact. Subsequent to the passage and implementation of these guidelines, federal judges have been advised indirectly by the U.S. Supreme Court that these guidelines are in fact guidelines, and not rigid parameters that can never be circumvented. Thus, it is possible for judges to impose sentences that depart, either upward or downward, from the presumptive months designated. Furthermore, these departures may extend beyond month ranges appreciably, provided that federal judges justify these departures with a carefully written rationale.

A good example of how federal judges may depart from these guidelines is the case of *Koon v. U.S.* (518 U.S. 81, 1996). Police officers Stacey Koon and Laurence Powell were convicted in federal court of violating the constitutional rights of a motorist, Rodney King, under color of law during King's arrest, and they were sentenced to 30 months' imprisonment. A U.S. district court trial judge used U.S. sentencing guidelines and justified a downward departure of eight offense levels from "27" to "19" to arrive at a 30–37-month sentence. The government appealed, contending that the downward departure of eight offense levels from "27" to "19" was an abuse of judicial discretion and that the factors cited for the downward departure were not statutory. An original offense seriousness level of "27" would have meant imposing a sentence of 70–87 months. The 9th Circuit Court of Appeals rejected all of the trial court's reasons for the downward departure and Koon and Powell petitioned the U.S. Supreme Court. The U.S. Supreme Court upheld the Circuit Court of Appeals in part and reversed it in part. Specifically, the U.S. Supreme Court said that the primary question to be answered on appeal is whether the trial judge abused his discretion by the downward departure in sentencing. The reasons given by the trial judge for the downward departure from an offense level of "27" to "19" were that: (1) the victim's misconduct provoked police use of force; (2) Koon and Powell had been subjected to successive state and federal criminal prosecutions; (3) Koon and Powell posed a low risk of recidivism; (4) Koon and Powell would probably lose their jobs and be precluded from employment in law enforcement; and (5) Koon and Powell would be unusually susceptible to abuse in prison. The U.S. Supreme Court concluded that a 5-level downward departure based on the victim's misconduct that provoked officer use of force was justified, because victim misconduct is an encouraged basis (by the U.S. Sentencing Commission) for a guideline departure. The U.S. Supreme Court said that the remaining 3-level departure was an abuse of judicial discretion. Federal district judges may not consider a convicted offender's career loss as a downward departure factor. Further, trial judges may not consider an offender's low likelihood of recidivism, because this factor is already incorporated into the criminal history category in the sentencing guideline table. Considering this factor to justify a downward departure, therefore, would be tantamount to counting the factor *twice*. The U.S. Supreme Court upheld the trial judge's reliance upon the offenders' susceptibility to prison abuse and the burdens of successive state and federal prosecutions, however. The U.S. Supreme Court remanded the case back to the district court where a new sentence could be determined. Thus, a new offense level must be chosen on the basis of the victim's own misconduct that provoked the officers and where offender susceptibility to prison abuse and the burden of successive state and federal prosecutions could be considered. The significance of this case is that specific factors are identified by the U.S. Supreme Court to guide federal judges in imposing sentences on police officers convicted of misconduct and violating citizen rights under color of law. Victim response that provokes police use of force, an officer's susceptibility to abuse in prison, and the burden of successive state and federal prosecutions are acceptable factors to be considered to justify downward departures in offense seriousness, whereas one's low recidivism potential and loss of employment opportunity in law enforcement are not legitimate factors to justify downward departure in offense seriousness. Following the U.S. Supreme Court decision, the U.S. district court judge took no further action against former officers Koon and Powell, and they were released on the basis of time they had already served.

In the postguideline period, federal district court judges have increasingly departed from the sentencing ranges provided under the guidelines. In 1991, for instance, about 6% of all sentences imposed on federal offenders by district court judges involved downward departures, whereas only about 1.7% of these sentences were upward departures. In 1997, 12.1% of all imposed sentences involved downward departures, whereas the percentage of upward departures declined insignificantly. Thus, there seems to be a trend among federal judges over the years toward downward departures from guideline recommendations. Thus, more judges are finding ways to craft sentences that they believe are more appropriate and not provided for in the guidelines.

Apart from exerting little influence on judicial discretion in sentencing federal offenders, the guidelines have effectively eliminated federal parole. Federal parole is now termed supervised release, and former parolees are now designated as supervised releasees. Since the U.S. sentencing guidelines are not retroactive, all federal prisoners sentenced in the preguideline period continue to be subject to the discretionary authority of the U.S. Parole Commission. However, those sentenced under the guidelines may be released short of serving their full terms by accumulating good time credit at the rate of 54 days per year. These postguidelines offenders are not subject to discretionary release by U.S. Parole Commission action. But U.S. district court judges may order offenders sentenced to prison as well as to a period of supervised release following their incarceration. Such discretionary authority is exercised whenever offenders are sentenced to

terms longer than 1 year, or required by statute, or following imprisonment in any other case. The length of supervised release may range from 1–5 years, depending upon the offense. Therefore, community corrections may be used as a means of effectively reintegrating federal offenders back into society following their incarceration terms.

One negative consequence of the guidelines is that under their usage, there is no objective body to assess whether an offender should be released short of serving his or her full sentence. An otherwise dangerous offender may be released after accumulating sufficient good time credit without any consideration given this early release by a body such as the U.S. Parole Commission. This is the same criticism leveled against determinate sentencing. The argument has some validity, especially in view of certain offenders who have been freed under determinate sentencing schemes by various states. An example of a heinous offender who was released under determinate sentencing was Larry Singleton, an ex-merchant seaman who raped and attempted to murder a 16-year-old girl, Mary Vincent, in California during the 1970s. Singleton picked up Vincent who was hitchhiking, raped her in his van, and then chopped off her arms at the elbows and dumped her in a ditch. Vincent miraculously survived this ordeal and lived to identify her attacker. Singleton was apprehended and convicted. He was sentenced to 15 years in a California prison for aggravated rape. After serving seven and half years, California had to release Singleton, because the state had adopted determinate sentencing shortly before Singleton committed the rape and attempted murder. California awarded offenders 30 days of good time credit for every 30 days served in prison. Thus, no paroling authority released Singleton. The State of California had to release him under their new sentencing plan. Had a parole board considered Singleton for early release, he probably would have been denied parole. Nevertheless, Singleton eventually left California and moved to Florida, where he killed a man during the 1980s. He was convicted of first-degree murder and sentenced to death. But he died in prison of natural causes. The Singleton case illustrates indirectly how the guidelines can permit certain dangerous offenders to be released short of serving their incarceration terms, because a parole board judgment is not permitted. This is one of several criticisms leveled against the guidelines.

The guidelines continue to undergo periodic revision as the Commission seeks to comply with their congressional mandate. One continuing criticism is that considerable dehumanization has occurred, as mathematical calculations of one's offense level have taken priority over individualized judgments of one's crime(s) and the circumstances surrounding the crime(s). One troubling fact is that there are unequal incremental values assigned to crimes involving monetary losses or the amount of drugs possessed in arriving at one's final offense level score. For instance, in money-laundering transactions, 1 point is added to one's base offense level score for monetary amounts of $100,000–$200,000. However, 2 points are added if the monetary amount ranges from $200,000 to $350,000. We must add 3 points if the amount of money laundered is from $350,000 to $600,000, and so on. If the 2-point addition between $200,000 and $350,000 is divided into the difference between these two amounts, we would have the average value per point to be added to one's basic offense level. Thus, $350,000 − $200,000 = $150,000. $150,000/2 = $75,000. We would conclude, therefore, that each point must be worth $75,000. Or is it? The difference between $350,000 and $600,000 is $250,000, and if we divide this difference by 3, the number of points to be added to one's base offense level score, the new point value per point is approximately $83,333. Therefore, these figures and points have no logical or consistent relation with one another, and as such, they appear to be arbitrarily assigned. Arbitrariness is not mandated by Congress as a goal for the U.S. Sentencing Commission. If rationality and proportionality are to be achieved, a more logical numbering system should be devised and used.

Finally, several of the goals originally sought by the U.S. Sentencing Commission and Congress (e.g., deterring crime, incapacitating the offender, providing just punishment, and rehabilitating the offender) have not been realized. Rehabilitation occurs either in prison or in the community. In the Federal Bureau of Prisons, chronic overcrowding means that not all prisoners have equal access to rehabilitation-oriented programs and work opportunities. Although the Federal Bureau of Prisons operates a prison industries program, only about 20% of all federal offenders have a chance to work in this program and learn potentially useful skills that will assist in their eventual community reintegration and rehabilitation. At the same time, supervised releasees have limited opportunities for federal assistance while on supervised release. Presently, supervised release requirements include payment of restitution; refraining from owning or possessing firearms; refraining from using drugs or alcohol; paying debt obligations; maintaining employment, if possible; paying any fines imposed; giving probation officers access to financial information; undergoing home detention; and submitted to occupational restrictions. None of these conditions of supervised release are connected with rehabilitation in any aggressive sense.

It is also doubtful that federal offenders have been deterred from committing crime. The Federal Bureau of Prisons; inmate population has more than doubled since 1987, when the guidelines were implemented. Offender incapacitation has definitely occurred. This is perhaps the only objective realistically achieved as a result of the guidelines. Recidivism rates of persons released from federal custody following probationary terms or incarceration are approximately 65%, usually over a period of 3 or more years, resembling closely the recidivism rates of prisoners, probationers, and parolees in all state jurisdictions. Therefore, there is nothing of a statistical nature serving to differentiate the U.S. sentencing guidelines from any other sentencing protocol presently used in the U.S.

Nevertheless, the Commission is charged with ongoing responsibilities of evaluating the effects of the sentencing guidelines on the criminal justice system, recommending to Congress appropriate modifications of substantive criminal law and sentencing procedures, and establishing a research and development program on sentencing issues. Among the accomplished innovations of the Commission have been (1) more structured judicial discretion; (2) appellate review of sentences; (3) reasons for the sentences received stated on the record; (4) determinate or "real time" sentencing; and (5) defendants' payment of supervision and imprisonment costs.

DEAN JOHN CHAMPION

## References and Further Reading

Dean, J.C. (Ed.) (1989). *The U.S. Sentencing Guidelines: Implications for Criminal Justice.* Westport, CT: Praeger Publishing Company.

Dean J.C. (2005). *Corrections in the United States: A Contemporary Perspective,* 4th ed. Upper Saddle River, NJ: Prentice Hall. (forthcoming)

U.S. Sentencing Commission (2001). *The U.S. Sentencing Guidelines.* Washington, DC: U.S. Government Printing Office.

*See also* **Sentences and Sentencing: Disparities; Sentences and Sentencing: Guidelines**

# Serial Killers *See* **Homicide: Mass Murder and Serial Killings**

# Sexual Harassment

Although no statute prohibits it, sexual harassment is a crime. Government guidelines at all levels—federal, state, and local—codify the behaviors that constitute sexual harassment. When complaints are filed, government agencies draw upon these guidelines to decide who should be held liable (i.e., responsible) when sexual harassment has occurred. When government agencies are unable to resolve complaints, most victims take their claims to court. Precedents established by 30 years of lawsuits determine the range of possible penalties for those deemed liable for it.

In the U.S., the Office of Equal Employment Opportunity (EEOC) was the first government agency to prohibit the practice of sexual harassment. In 1981, the federal agency defined sexual harassment as any form of unwanted sexual attention that unfairly impacts a person's employment. Along with such crimes as disparate pay and unfair dismissal or demotion, sexual harassment was added to the EEOC's list of sex discriminations that employers should avoid. Annually, the EEOC issues guidelines to assist employers in identifying sexual harassment, preventing it, and most importantly, resolving complaints regarding it. Failure to follow the guidelines risks disqualification for federal funding and civil litigation.

Since the EEOC issued its first set of guidelines, other federal agencies have followed suit, and today, most have antisexual harassment policies appropriate for their respective domains. The Office of Civil Rights (OCR), for example, defines sexual harassment as unwanted sexual attention that unfairly impacts a person's education. Schools, colleges, or universities that fail to comply with the OCR's guidelines risk the withdrawal of federal funding and civil liability.

Responding to trends at the federal level, most state and local agencies responsible for matters of discrimination have issued statements prohibiting sexual harassment. How vigorously their policies are enforced depends upon the agency's budget and the politics of the community it serves. As a result, in states where discrimination has a high priority, sexual harassment policies are actively enforced. In others, sexual harassment policies are largely ignored—it is a crime that exists only on the books. In states where discrimination is an issue but the agencies responsible for handling it are underfunded, extensive backlogs exist of complaints in need of investigation. Even though enforcement varies considerably between states and between agencies, it is exceptionally rare to find a place where sexual harassment remains legal. Even the White House now has a specific policy prohibiting it.

Because sexual harassment is a form of discrimination prohibited by government policy, legally speaking, it is a civil offense. Therefore, in most cases sexual harassment lawsuits are filed in civil court. In a sexual harassment trial the defending party is not the individual perpetrator, but the institution deemed responsible for policy compliance. As is typical for civil claims, the vast majority of sexual harassment cases are settled before they ever go to trial. The threshold for establishing legal liability for sexual harassment is high, as a consequence less than a third of those that take their claims to court win.

In civil court, the purpose of a trial is not to determine guilt, but rather to assess liability. Liable parties are not punished with prison time or community service, instead, they are ordered to compensate plaintiffs for the harms done. When neglect by an institution is found to be especially egregious, a court can punish it by requiring additional payments (called punitive damages) beyond those needed to restore losses. Thus, when sexual harassment claims are found to have legal merit, the liable party is usually an employer or educational institution. Usually, compensations are ordered for lost wages or promotions, legal fees, and expenses incurred for medical and psychological treatment. In a few rare cases, corporations have had to pay millions of dollars in punitive damages.

A growing number of sexual harassment complaints include reports of statutory violations (e.g., stalking, sexual assault, and sexual abuse). In these types of cases, in addition to civil charges filed against the employer, individual harassers may be arrested and charged as criminals.

Before government agencies prohibited it, sexual harassment was so endemic that most considered it a natural outcome of contact between the sexes. In fact, those opposing the integration of women into male dominated workplaces and campuses commonly used women's complaints about sexual harassment as an excuse to deny women jobs and degrees. But in the wake of the Women's Movements, feminist values such as gender equality and the right to choose have gained legitimacy, whereas belief that sexual harassment was "natural" has waned. Nevertheless, many continue to believe that sexual harassment is an unavoidable consequence of gender integration. As a result, the problem of sexual harassment has been used as an excuse to exclude women from military schools, the armed forces, and particularly from combat assignments.

In the 1970s, it was primarily women who demanded the prohibition of sexual harassment. Today it continues to be a crime that disproportionately affects women. In fact, between one third and one half of all women are expected to experience at least one form of legally actionable harassment during their lifetimes. Because reprisals in the form of job loss, demotion, and stigmatization are common, only a handful of those who experience it ever report their problems to authorities. Instead, most women handle their sexual harassment problems by avoiding their sexual harassers, requesting transfers, changing shifts, quitting their jobs, dropping classes, changing their majors, or leaving school altogether.

Even though far more women than men are sexually harassed, men are not immune, and the number who feel victimized appears to be growing. Because nearly all perpetrators are men, male domination remains the primary risk factor. In other words, those who work or learn in male-dominated places or who pursue careers in male-identified occupations experience far more harassment than those who do not. Furthermore, sexual harassment is most prevalent in military and paramilitary organizations—places indelibly marked by a history of male dominance.

In the late 1990s, a heterosexual man employed as an off-shore oil rigger filed a sexual harassment complaint against his employer, Sundowner Offshore Services. According to Oncale, while working offshore, his heterosexual male coworkers taunted him with sexualized threats of violence and attempted to sexually assault him. The case was appealed all the way to the Supreme Court where without dissent, the judges agreed that same-sex sexual harassment was an actionable offense. (*Oncale v. Sundowner Officer Services Incorporated*, 118, S.Ct. 998, 1998).

As a result, gay men and lesbian women are using newly revised sexual harassment policies to demand compensations for unwanted sexual attentions motivated by homophobia.

Today all countries in the U.K., European Union, and Australia have policies prohibiting sexual harassment. In most cases, the policies are very similar to those used in the U.S. They conceptualize sexual harassment as a form of discrimination and hold employers liable for the consequences. The primary difference between the U.S. and these countries is how the cases are litigated. Most notably, the possible dollar amount for punitive damages is much higher in the U.S. than elsewhere. Although in the U.S. sexual harassment lawsuits have earned millions of dollars, in Australia the award average is $1,500.00.

Today, the public no longer accepts the belief that sexual harassment is normal, and few would disagree that the practice should be prohibited. Yet, how serious the problem is and what should be done about it continue to be hotly debated. In fact, like support for the right to choose an abortion, concern about the sexual harassment problem has become a reliable litmus test for determining one's place on the liberal or conservative continuum, with liberal administrations granting the sexual harassment problem higher priority than conservative ones. As a result, what exactly warrants legal action and how high the penalty should be varies from one political administration to another. To the frustration of the institutions held responsible for policing it and to the confusion of the general public, sexual harassment law remains a moving target.

PHOEBE MORGAN

### References and Further Reading

Gruber, J. and Morgan, P., *In the Company of Men: Male Dominance and Sexual Harassment*. Boston, MA: Northeastern University Press, 2004.

MacKinnon, C. *The Sexual Harassment of Working Women*. New Haven, CT: Yale University Press, 1979.

Mink, G. *Hostile Environment: The Political Betrayal of Sexually Harassed Women*, Ithaca, NY and London, U.K.: Cornell University Press 2000.

Morgan, P. Sexual harassment: Violence against women at work, in Renzetti, C., Edleson, J. and Bergen, R. (Eds.) *The Source Book for Violence against Women*. Thousand Oaks, Sage, 2001.

U.S. Merit Systems Protection Board. *Sexual Harassment In the Workplace: Trends, Progress, Continuing Challenges: A Report to the President and Congress of the United States*. Washington, DC: Government Printing Office, 1994.

*See also* **Workplace Violence**

# Sexual Violence *See* **Rape**

# Sheriff's Departments *See* **Sheriffs**

---

# Sheriffs

---

The office of sheriff is perhaps one of the most enduring offices in history. It has transcended monarchies and democracies, tyrants, kings, and presidents. Adaptability to changing social and government characteristics has long been the sheriff's strong suit, perhaps because their very survival depended upon it. From king's agent to tax collector and code enforcer to jailer and law enforcer, the sheriff has worn many hats. Those hats continue to change today.

## History

The office of sheriff is the oldest law enforcement office in the world, tracing its roots to the Anglo-Saxons in England. The Anglo-Saxons lived in rural communities known as tuns (source of the modern English word town). Each tun was divided into groups of ten families, which were called tithings. Groups of ten tuns (or 100 families) were formed to create a unit of government, primarily for the defense of the land. The elected leader of that group was called gerefa, which was later shortened to reeve. Over the next couple of centuries, the groups of tuns eventually evolved into shires, which were the equivalent of a county.

The next great leap for sheriffs occurred in 871 A.D. with England's King Alfred the Great. During this era, the principal law enforcement officer was appointed by each county's noblemen. The term used to describe the chief law enforcement official of the county was shire-reeve (http://www.sheriffs.org/defaults/defaults_s_links.htm, 2003). After the fall of England to the Normans, government became more centralized, resulting in the appointment of the shire-reeve by the king. The office, however, still maintained its significant status. Under Norman rule, the shire-reeve was assigned to maintain order and collect taxes in the shire.

The next significant event in the history of the sheriff involved the signing of the Magna Carta by King John in 1215. The Magna Carta contains references to the role of the sheriff nine times. This established the importance of local representation and election to the office of sheriff. One point of irony is that if the sheriff did not collect all of the taxes in his county, he had to pay the difference out of his own pocket. The sheriff was also required to administer punishment, such as flogging, whipping, and other various and sundry physical punishments to criminals. When the method of punishment in England changed to confining prisoners, the sheriff assumed the responsibility for the county jail. There were many problems that needed to be addressed with the jail system, thus, this responsibility proved a daunting one.

Perhaps one of the most famous sheriffs from a corrections point of view is the High Sheriff of Bedford, John Howard. John Howard became the High Sheriff of Bedford in 1773 and devoted his service in this capacity to God. One of Howard's responsibilities as High Sheriff was to inspect the county prison. He was appalled by what he found at Bedford Gaol, which had replaced the earlier gaol in 1659 (Bedfordshire, 2002). Initially, Howard believed that the suffering of the prisoners there was largely being caused by the system where the gaoler received money from the prisoner for his board and lodging. Howard suggested to Bedford justices that the gaoler should be paid a salary (Bedfordshire, 2002).

The Bedford justices refused to follow his recommendation unless the rest of the country adopted the policy. To move the rest of England in that direction, Howard toured prisons in England and noted their conditions, taking his results to the House of Commons in 1774. As a result of the testimony that John Howard provided to a committee of the House of Commons, Parliament passed the 1774 Gaol Act. The terms of this legislation abolished gaolers' fees and suggested ways for improving the sanitary state of prisons and the better preservation of prisoners' health. Although Howard had copies of these acts printed and sent to every prison in England, the justices and the gaolers tended to ignore these new measures (Bedfordshire, 2002).

Howard continued to be an advocate for prison reform and began touring foreign prisons in 1775. He visited prisons in France, Belgium, Holland, Italy, Germany, Spain, Portugal, Denmark, Sweden, Russia, Switzerland, Malta, Asia Minor, and Turkey. He found one prison that he deemed superior, the Maison de Force in Ghent, whose operations served as a model for England's prison system. Upon returning to England, he began a second tour of the nation's prisons to ascertain the results of the Gaol Act of 1774 only to be appalled at the lack of implementation. As a result, he published his investigations in 1777 in a book entitled, *The State of Prisons in England and Wales, with an Account of some Foreign Prisons.* The contents of Howard's book were so shocking that in some countries, such as France, authorities refused to allow it to be published. It includes a general study of the distress in prisons, proposed improvements, a detailed analysis of prison conditions and statistical tables.

Aware of the discrepancy between law and practice, the English Parliament passed two more prison acts in 1778 and 1781. Howard continued touring the prisons of England and Europe, not only collecting information about conditions, but also revisiting many institutions to monitor the progress of reforms (Godber, 1977, 10–11). This, perhaps, makes him the first known "prison inspector." The following excerpts from Howard's *State of Prisons* (1777) illustrate the type of information that he recorded:

> Food—Many criminals are half starved: some come out almost famished, scarce able to move, and for weeks incapable of any labour.
>
> Bedding: In many gaols, and in most bridewells, there is no allowance of bedding or straw for prisoners to sleep on. Some lie upon rags, others upon the bare floor.
>
> Use of Irons: Loading prisoners with heavy irons which make their walking, and even lying down to sleep, difficult and painful, is another custom which I cannot but condemn. Even the women do not escape this severity.
>
> The Insane: In some few gaols are confined idiots and lunatics. Where these are not kept separate, they distract and terrify other prisoners.

Additional excerpts from Howard's *State of Prisons* (1777) illustrate what is perhaps the first recorded inspection report for prisons and jails:

> Knaresboro Prison: Earth floor: no fire; very offensive; a common sewer from the town running through it uncovered. I was informed that an officer, confined here some years since, took in with him a dog to defend him from vermin; but the dog was soon destroyed and the prisoner's face much disfigured.

> Plymouth Gaol: Three rooms for felons, etc., and two rooms over them for debtors. One of the former, the clink, 15 feet by 8 feet 3 inches and about 6 feet high, with a wicket in the door 7 inches by 5 to admit light and air. To this, as I was informed, three men, who were confined near two months under sentence for transportation, came by turns for breath.

Although the office of sheriff remained essentially the same for centuries in England prior to the American experience, the position became more influential throughout America's history. The first American sheriff can be traced to the Virginia Colony in 1634. William Stone was appointed the first sworn sheriff in America by becoming the sheriff in the County of Accomac (Buffardi, 1998). The office of sheriff in early America was a position of prominence. For example, George Washington's father was an early sheriff in colonial Virginia. Describing the sheriff in "The Value of Constitutions," Thomas Jefferson wrote: "the Office of Sheriff is the most important of all the executive offices of the county." In addition, the office of sheriff is also mentioned in the Constitutions of nearly every state.

One of the most popular terms associated with the sheriff is the "posse."

The sheriff had the power to summon assistance from the citizenry when needed. When the sheriff raised the "hue and cry," as it was called in England, a group of able-bodied individuals would come to assist him in maintaining the peace. This group was known in America as the "posse comitatus." One of the first times that the posse comitatus was used occurred during the War of 1812 when the British passed through Upper Marborough, Maryland on their way to Washington, D.C. After burning Washington, D.C., the British returned through Upper Marborough and began looting the town. A gentleman by the name of Dr. William Beanes raised the "hue and cry" and gathered a group of citizens together and arrested the British soldiers as criminals. The British were transferred to the custody of the sheriff and jailed. After this event, the British arrested Dr. Beanes and some of his group who were held on a warship in Baltimore Harbor. Among those sent to negotiate Dr. Beanes's release was Francis Scott Key, who, while on a ship overlooking Fort McHenry, noticed that the American Flag was still flying, indicating that the fort had not fallen. He was so inspired by this sight that he penned "The Star Spangled Banner" (Buffardi, 1998). Thus, had Dr. Beanes not used the posse comitatus, our National Anthem may have never been written.

## Western Sheriff

The only exposure many individuals have to the term sheriff involves watching television or movie westerns wherein the character "shoots it out" with bad guys. This stereotype, although popular, is far from the truth. Sheriffs effected law enforcement through reputation and community partnerships, relying on citizens to report and, in some cases, assist in apprehending the criminals. Some of the more interesting sheriffs have originated in the Wild West, most notably Wyatt Earp, Wild Bill Hickok, Bat Masterson, and Pat Garrett. Wyatt Earp was most famous for his Tombstone, Arizona exploits involving the Clantons and the OK Corral. Wild Bill Hickok had the distinction of being the sheriff who killed the most men, perhaps as few as 30 and as many as 85 (Buffardi, 1998). Bat Masterson teamed with Wyatt Earp in Dodge City and later befriended Theodore Roosevelt, the 26th president of the U.S. Pat Garrett shot and killed perhaps the most prolific and legend-inspiring criminal figure in the West, William H. Bonney, better known as Billy the Kid. Although not serving in the office of sheriff, Theodore Roosevelt did assist a posse in catching the thieves who stole his small boat from his ranch in the West and received a sum of $50 from the Billings County Sheriff (Buffardi, 1998). Another U.S. president began his political career as sheriff of Erie County, New York, namely Grover Cleveland, who used the office to further his political career as governor of New York and then the presidency.

## Modern Sheriff

The modern sheriff must be immersed in the political field as well as in the field of public safety. As an elected official, sheriffs must constantly confront the issue of keeping voters happy while maintaining law and order, sometimes contradictory realities. Sheriffs have been elected who have political popularity, but lack the necessary skills to competently perform the duties of the office. In other instances, sheriffs with good administrative skills have not been elected owing to political unpopularity. Thus, the most qualified individual for the position of sheriff may not be the one who wins elections.

Only recently have states begun to institute qualifications for the office of sheriff that must be satisfied prior to running for election. Five states have passed legislation providing for professional standards and criteria for an individual seeking the office of sheriff: Georgia, South Carolina, Ohio, California, and Oregon. California, Oregon, South Carolina, and Ohio have educational requirements beyond that of a high school diploma or equivalent. Each of those states makes allowances for college degrees or equivalents by reducing the number of years of supervision or law enforce-

ment experience required to qualify for candidacy for sheriff.

Every state requires U.S. citizenship, but only California does not specify a minimum county residency requirement (with the notable exception of Rhode Island, which does not use the office of sheriff, instead relying on town police chiefs and state police to cover its comparatively small area). Only Oregon and Georgia allow candidates to qualify for the office of sheriff without a valid peace officer certification at the time of employment. Surprisingly, the only state that requires that a candidate have any supervisory experience is Ohio. Oregon and Georgia require that a newly elected sheriff obtain state law enforcement certification within 1 year and 6 months, respectively. Ohio, South Carolina, and Georgia require that each newly elected sheriff attend some sort of training regarding the basic requirements of managing the office. Each of these states also requires the sheriff to obtain a minimum number of hours of in-service training each year he or she holds office, taking the steps necessary to begin professionalizing the office.

Meeting the qualifications for sheriff and the challenges of politics at the county level are just the beginning of the sheriff's job in the U.S. In addition to political adversity, the sheriff faces other challenges. According to Falcone and Wells (1995), the sheriff has up to eight functional dimensions:

1. Criminal law enforcement and other general police services;
2. Correctional services, involving the transportation of prisoners and the management of the county jail;
3. The processing of judicial writs and court orders, both criminal and civil;
4. Security of the court;
5. Miscellaneous services, such as the transportation and commitment of the mentally ill;
6. Seizure of property claimed by the county;
7. Collection of county fees and taxes; and
8. Sale of licenses and permits; plus other services that do not fall neatly under the statutory responsibilities of other law enforcement or social service agencies.

To accomplish these responsibilities, sheriffs' offices across the U.S. have developed four distinctive organizational models (Brown, 1978):

1. Full service model—Carries out law enforcement and judicial and correctional duties.
2. Law enforcement model—Carries out only law enforcement duties, with other duties assumed by separate civil process and correctional agencies.

3. Civil–judicial model—Carries out only court-related duties.
4. Correctional–judicial model—Carries out all functions except law enforcement.

Although maintaining the peace, more popularly known as law enforcement, is the most recognized job of the sheriff, the position differs significantly from police chiefs in how legal authority is realized. In 35 of the 50 states, the office of sheriff is a constitutional office legally authorized in the states' charters (National Sheriffs' Association, 1979). Further exemplifying the sheriffs' independence is the fact that they are separated from other political offices by being elected in all but two states, Rhode Island and Hawaii (Falcone and Wells, 1995). Today, there are some 3088 sheriffs' offices in the U.S.

Sheriffs' offices throughout the nation were surveyed by the U.S. Department of Justice's Bureau of Justice Statistics in 2000. This survey represents the most comprehensive data on sheriffs' offices to date. According to the survey, sheriffs' offices employed 293,823 full-time employees, of which approximately 165,000 were sworn (certified) law enforcement officers (Bureau of Justice Statistics, 2003).

In regard to duties, Table 1 illustrates the four basic functions reported to the Bureau of Justice Statistics in the survey.

In 2000, the sheriffs' salary ranged, based on population, from a minimum of $33,800 in small jurisdictions to a maximum of $105,400 in large jurisdictions (1,000,000 or more) (Bureau of Justice Assistance, 2003). Only 6% require at least a 2-year degree to be considered, but the data suggest there is increasing professionalization in terms of formal higher educational attainment (Bureau of Justice Assistance, 2003).

There have been many colorful sheriffs over the years, but some modern firsts and interesting individuals are what make the office of sheriff so mesmerizing. The first African American female sheriff in the U.S. was elected in Fulton County, Georgia in 1992. Jacquelyn H. Barrett of Fulton County is the only female sheriff in Georgia and holds the distinction as the first African American female sheriff in U.S. history (http://www.georgiasheriffs.org/offsheriff.html). According to CNN,

Maricopa County, Arizona, Sheriff Joe Arpaio runs the only all-female chain gang in history. In addition to this, he has over 2000 inmates housed in tents in the Arizona sun, where temperatures often rise above 120 degrees (Reuters, 2003). From 1992, when Arpaio first took office, until 1999, there were over 800 lawsuits filed on behalf of inmates, by far the most of any U.S. sheriff (Ortega, 1999). The first female sheriff in the U.S. was Emma Susan Daugherty Banister. She took office in 1918 after her husband, who was the sitting sheriff, died and served the remainder of his term before declining to have her name put on the ballot for reelection.

## Conclusion

The office of sheriff has been one of transition for over 1000 years. Its survival has depended upon adaptability to the changing tides of government, social, political, and sometimes, even religious influences. From England to the U.S., the office of sheriff has served a variety of different roles. Ultimately, it is the individual who makes the sheriff. Fortunately, the individuals attracted to this honored position have been, for the most part, solid in moral character and professional in demeanor. With the legacy that the office of sheriff brings into the 21st century, it is unlikely that we will see the disappearance of this office.

SCOTT BLOUGH

## References and Further Reading

Bedfordshire and Luton Archives and Records Service Newsletter, 2002. Available at http://www.bedfordshire.gov.uk/Bedscc/Sdcountyrec.nsf/Web/ThePage/The+Newsletter+-Gaol+Article.
Bohm, R. and Haley, K., 2002. *Introduction to Criminal Justice*, 3rd ed., New York, NY: Glencoe McGraw-Hill.
Brown, L.P, 1977. *The Role of the Sheriff*, in Cohen, A.W. (Ed.), *The Future of Policing*, Beverly Hills, CA: Sage, pp. 227–228.
Buffardi, H., 1998. *The History of the Office of Sheriff*.
Bureau of Justice Statistics, 2003. *Sheriffs' Offices 2000*, U.S. Department of Justice, Washington, DC.
Celebrating 1,000 years of the office of sheriff, 1992. *Sheriff*, 44(3), 10–13.
Falcone, D. and Wells, L., 1993. *The County Sheriffs' Office: A Distinctive Policing Modality*, Paper presented to the American Society of Criminology meeting, Phoenix, AZ.
Godber, J., 1977. *John Howard the Philanthropist*, Bedfordshire, U.K.: Bedfordshire County Council Arts and Recreation Department.
Howard, J., 1777. *The State of Prisons in England and Wales, with an Account of some Foreign Prisons*.
National Sheriffs' Association, 1979. *County Law Enforcement: An Assessment of Capabilities and Needs*, National Sheriffs' Association, Washington, DC.
Ortega, T., Detention mounts. *Phoenix New Times*, April 1999.
Reuters, Sheriff runs female chain gang. CNN.Com, 2003. Available at http://www.cnn.com/2003/US/Southwest/10/29/chain.gang.reut/.

**Table 1.** The four basic functions reported to the Bureau of Justice Statistics

| Operation | Percentage |
| --- | --- |
| Executing arrest warrants | 100% |
| Serving civil process | 99% |
| Providing court security | 97% |
| Operating jail | 81% |

# Sherman, Lawrence W.

Lawrence W. Sherman is the director of the Jerry Lee Center of Criminology and chair of the Graduate Group of Criminology at the University of Pennsylvania. In 2000, under his leadership, the University of Pennsylvania became the first Ivy League University to establish a Ph.D. in criminology as a separate field. Sherman is also the director of the Fels Center of Government and the Albert M. Greenfield Professor of Human Relations in the Department of Sociology at the University of Pennsylvania. He holds the position of adjunct professor of law at the Australian National University, and is the president of the Crime Control Research Corporation. In 2001, Sherman was elected president of the American Society of Criminology. He is also serving as president of the International Society of Criminology and the American Academy of Political and Social Science, and is the founding president of the Academy of Experimental Criminology. Sherman is a fellow of both the American Society of Criminology and the Academy of Experimental Criminology. In 1998, while serving as chair of the Department of Criminology and Criminal Justice at the University of Maryland, Sherman was named a Distinguished University Professor.

Sherman is a prolific writer and researcher who, by 2001, had published 6 books, 30 book chapters, 43 peer-reviewed journal articles, and 20 monographs on a wide variety of topics. In 1993, he received the American Sociological Association's Distinguished Scholarship Award in Crime, Law and Deviance for his book, *Policing Domestic Violence: Experiments and Dilemmas*. The following year, the Academy of Criminal Justice Sciences honored him with the Bruce Smith Sr. Award for leadership and research in the field of criminal justice. In 1999, he received the Edwin H. Sutherland Award from the American Society of Criminology, in recognition for his outstanding contributions to the field. He has received over $20 million in funded research support from a wide variety of public and private agencies, including the National Institute of Justice, the National Science Foundation, the National Institute of Mental Health, the National Endowment for the Humanities, the McKnight Foundation, the Australian Criminological Research Council, and many others. Sherman is a member of the National Academy of Sciences Panel of Policing Research, serves on the Board of Directors of the American Academy of Political and Social Sciences, and is a member of the Advisory Board of the FBI Academy Behavioral Sciences Unit.

Sherman is best known as an experimental criminologist. His use of randomized controlled experiments to study deterrence and crime prevention has led him to examine such wide-ranging issues as domestic violence, police crackdowns and saturation patrol, gun crime, crack houses, and reintegrative shaming. His ground-breaking research on domestic violence began in the 1980s with the highly influential Minneapolis Domestic Violence Experiment. His early experimental research into the influence of arrest on recidivism in spouse abuse led to changes in police department policies and procedures nationwide, encouraged state legislatures to modify state statutes to allow for misdemeanor arrest, and eventually resulted in five federally-funded replications, one of which he conducted. The process and outcomes of these experiments have been detailed by Sherman in his 1992 book, *Policing Domestic Violence: Experiments and Dilemmas*. In the late 1980s, Sherman's experimental research into the effect of directed police patrol in high-crime locations led to his development of the concept of "hot spots." In the early 1990s, Sherman's Kansas City Gun Experiment studied the effect of concentrated police patrol on gun crime and violence. Directed police patrol in gun crime "hot spots" led to an increase in seizures of illegally carried guns and a decrease in gun crimes.

In addition to his experimental research, Sherman has published articles and book chapters on a wide variety of topics, including police corruption, police education, police discretion, police crackdowns, restorative justice, investigations, police use of deadly force, and fear reduction. In 1997, Sherman led a team of University of Maryland criminologists in producing *Preventing Crime: What Works, What Doesn't, What's Promising*, a Congressionally-mandated evaluation of over 500 state and local crime-prevention programs.

Research on the prestige of scholars in criminology and criminal justice has listed Sherman as one of the most highly cited, and thus arguably one of the most influential scholars in the field today. A study of faculty in doctoral programs in criminology, conducted while Sherman was chair of the Department of Criminology and Criminal Justice at the University of Maryland, found that under his leadership this program was ranked first both on citations of faculty and publications by faculty in major criminology and criminal justice journals.

Sherman teaches criminology at both the undergraduate and doctoral levels. He has served on or chaired numerous Ph.D. dissertation committees. He has testified before the U.S. Senate and the U.S. House of Representatives almost a dozen times on issues including police use of deadly force; police, drugs, and homicide; domestic violence; crime prevention; and youth violence. He has also testified before the U.S. Civil Rights Commission, the Mollen Commission on Police Corruption, the Maryland General Assembly, the Ohio State Legislature, and even the Legislative Council of Parliament of New South Wales (Sydney, Australia). He is in great demand as a guest lecturer and has received invitations not only from notable American institutions such as Yale, Harvard, Northwestern, and Duke Universities, but from international educational institutions including Cambridge University (England), Kobe University (Japan), Hebrew University (Israel), Australian National University, and the Australian Institute of Criminology.

## Biography

Born in Schenectady, NY, October 25, 1949. Educated at Denison University, B.A. in Political Science, 1970; University of Chicago, M.A. in Social Science, 1970; Cambridge University (England), Diploma in Criminology, 1973; Yale University, M.A., 1974, Ph.D in Sociology, 1976. Research Employment: Urban Fellow, New York City Office of the Mayor, 1970–1971; Program Research Analyst, New York City Police Department, 1971–72; Director of Research, Police Foundation, 1979–1984; Vice President for Research, 1984–85; President, Crime Control Research Corporation, 1981–Present. Academic Employment: Assistant Professor, University at Albany, 1976–1979; Associate Professor, 1979–1982; Seth Boyden Distinguished Visiting Professor, Rutgers University, 1987; Adjunct Professor of Law, Australian National University, 1994–1999; Associate Professor, University of Maryland, 1982–1984; Professor, 1984–1999; Chair, 1995–1999; Albert M. Greenfield Professor of Human Relations and Professor of Sociology, University of Pennsylvania, 1999–Present; Director, Fels Center of Government, 1999–Present; Director, Jerry Lee Center of Criminology, 2000–Present; Chair, Graduate Group in Criminology, 2000–Present. Fellow of the American Society of Criminology and the Academy of Experimental Criminology. President of the American Society of Criminology, 2001; President of the International Society of Criminology, 2000–2005; President of the American Academy of Political and Social Science, 2001–2004; Founding President of the of Experimental Criminology, 1999–2001.

## Selected Writings

Sherman, L.W., Gottfredson, D., MacKenzie, D., Reuter, P., Eck, J. and Bushway, S. (1997). *Preventing Crime: What Works, What Doesn't, What's Promising.* Report to the U.S. Congress. Washington, DC: U.S. Dept. of Justice.

Sherman, L.W. and Rogan, D.P. (1995). Effects of gun seizures on gun violence: Hot spot patrols in Kansas City. *Justice Quarterly,* 12(4).

Sherman, L.W. and Weisburd, D. (1995). General deterrent effects of police patrol in crime hot spots: A randomized, controlled trial. *Justice Quarterly,* 12(4).

Sherman, L.W. (1992). Policing Domestic Violence: Experiments and Dilemmas. New York, NY: Free Press.

Sherman, L.W. and Smith, D.A. (1992). Crime, punishment and stake in conformity: Legal and informal control of domestic violence. *American Sociological Review,* 57(5), 680–690.

Sherman, L.W., Schmidt, J.D., Rogan, D.P., Gartin, P.R., Cohn, E.G., Collins, D.J. and Bacich, A.R. (1991). From initial deterrence to long-term escalation: Short-custody arrest for poverty ghetto domestic violence. *Criminology,* 29(4): 1101–1130.

Sherman, L.W., Gartin, P.R. and Buerger, M.E. (1989). Hot spots of predatory crime: Routine activities and the criminology of place. *Criminology* 27:27–55.

Sherman, L.W., Steele, L., Laufersweiler, D., Hoffer, N. and Julian, S.A. (1989). Stray bullets and "mushrooms": Random shootings of bystanders in four cities, 1977–88. *Journal of Quantitative Criminology,* 5(4):297–316.

Sherman, L.W. and Berk, R.A. (1984). The specific deterrent effects of arrest for domestic assault. *American Sociological Review,* 49(2):261–272.

Sherman, L.W. (1978) *Scandal and Reform: Controlling Police Corruption.* Berkeley, CA: University of California Press.

# Shock Incarceration *See* **Boot Camps and Shock Incarceration**

# Shoplifting

What is shoplifting and is it a crime? The word shoplifting is a term used to describe theft from a merchant or a business; though little is available on the origin of the word, shoplifting was at first just shopping, which means to visit, or purchase merchandise from a small business; then called shops, now called stores. Therefore to steal from a shop is now known as shoplifting. Shoplifting (i.e., stealing from a store) is technically larceny, which makes it one of the FBI's Big 8; and is what makes shoplifting a crime.

Whether the shoplifting (i.e., theft) is a felony or misdemeanor (and at what level) is, obviously determined by each individual state. The classification is based on the value of the amount stolen and what is stolen. For example, in the State of Alabama, merchandise stolen that exceeds $250.00 in value constitutes a felony charge of theft of property (Code of Alabama, 13A-8-1 thru 8-5). In Tennessee the threshold for a felony theft of property charge is merchandise with a value of more than $500.00 (Code of Tennessee, 39-14-103 and 105). Additionally in Alabama, the actor's prior offenses affects the classification of charges, in that anyone with a prior first- or second-degree theft of property conviction and the value of merchandise stolen is more than $100.00 would now be charged with a felony. Also in Alabama, if the merchandise stolen is a firearm, credit card, debit card, controlled substance, or livestock, if any of these items are stolen it is a felony regardless of the value (Code of Alabama, 13a-8-4).

In charging a person with shoplifting certain elements of crime must be met. When *Asportation* (the taking and carrying away of merchandise with intent to steal) occurs once an item has been concealed and a suspect makes movement, the crime of shoplifting has occurred. In 1984, an Alabama case indicated that if an individual moves merchandise from one area of the store to another with the intent to steal it, then a sufficient taking has occurred to constitute the crime regardless of how far the movement was (*Towns v. State*, 449 So. 2d 1273 Ala. Crim. App., 1984).

*Probable cause* is another key element in the prosecution of shoplifting which, simply stated, is a person's knowledge of facts that a crime has been committed. This knowledge can be either firsthand, from a reliable witness or electronic (Bishop, 1985). Along with the key elements of probable cause and asportation some states have (or should have) another important tool for prosecuting shoplifters and that is a *merchant protection law*. Illustrative of this is Alabama's Merchant Protection Statute.

Alabama's law allows a merchant to stop and detain a suspect as long as he or she has probable cause to believe that a crime or theft has occurred. A merchant may detain for a reasonable amount of time for the purpose of attempting to recover merchandise. Along with the detention a merchant may also perform a reasonable search for the recovery of merchandise. A reasonable search is considered to be a pat-down or frisk of a suspect, along with a request to empty pockets and or purse. Such statutes are important because they protect merchants from being sued for false imprisonment and false arrest; as long probable cause exists.

It must be kept in mind that shoplifting occurs from stores (and malls) and that many stores today are "national," that is, they exist in many states. Therefore, the personnel of each store must be familiar with their state's laws and the policies of their organization. Although Alabama's shoplifting laws, for example, are written strongly in favor of the merchant, not all states have taken such an approach. As such, problems often arise because of a lack of knowledge of these laws and because of lack of training in this area. Although the merchant protection statutes protects from false imprisonment and false arrest, it does not protect a merchant from being sued for slander and libel. If a merchant accuses a suspect of stealing in public and then consequently the suspect is not arrested or not found guilty, the suspect can sue for slander. Libel cases come into play when merchants often circulate pictures of suspected shoplifters.

Because of the threat of such lawsuits and because of the interstate nature of many retail establishments, many retailers have developed policies and procedures, to try and minimize the threat of such cases. Most large retail establishment have put into use what has commonly become known as the six-step stop. The six-step stop is:

1. You must see the shoplifter approach the merchandise.
2. You must see the shoplifter select the merchandise.
3. You must see the shoplifter conceal, convert, or carry away the merchandise.
4. You must maintain continuous observation of the shoplifter.
5. You must observe the shoplifter fail to pay for the merchandise.
6. You must apprehend the shoplifter outside the store.

Some retail stores use these steps specifically whereas others use these steps as a guideline to create their own steps.

For instance the following procedures belong to a major retail store in Alabama. "Loss prevention personnel must adhere to the guidelines listed below prior to initiating contact with a subject for shoplifting. If you are not certain whether all of the listed requirements have been met, *Do Not Approach the Subject*.

1. *Selection*: Did I see the subject select my store's merchandise from the selling floor?
2. *Concealment*: Did I see the subject conceal the merchandise?
3. *Unbroken Surveillance*: Did I maintain unbroken surveillance of the subject to ensure the merchandise was not discarded? *(Broken surveillance is acceptable ONLY when Loss Prevention associate is working and ONLY if concealment is on videotape and the container or device in which merchandise is concealed appears the same when you approach the suspect as it did on the monitor in the camera room.)*
4. *Within Boundaries*: Did I approach the subject at an appropriate time and within approved physical boundaries?
   a. *Permissible Zone of Contact*: At no time shall a loss prevention associate travel beyond physical boundaries as defined herein to apprehend, question, or otherwise engage an individual for the purpose of investigation or apprehension.
      i. *Within the Store–Within 25 Feet*: Apprehensions within the store must occur within 25 feet of the exit.
      ii. *Exterior Store Entrances–Before Curb or Within Ten Feet in Absence of Curb*: A loss prevention associate may not apprehend a suspect beyond the area defined as public sidewalk or beyond the curb. If the suspect has left the sidewalk or curb, the associate must discontinue apprehension. In the event that the store feeds directly into a parking lot and is not bordered by a sidewalk, the associate must apprehend the suspect within TEN FEET of the exterior door.
      iii. *Mall Entrances*: A loss prevention associate may not apprehend a suspect beyond 25 feet outside the store's mall entrance.
      iv. Subject should not be approached or apprehended after entering another retail establishment or reaching and or entering a vehicle.
   b. *Appropriate Timing*: Contact with the subject may be initiated *ONLY* if the loss prevention associate has adhered to all elements of the Ethical Standards and the decision to apprehend was made *before* the subject exited the store."

The five- and six-step process and the modified versions for specific stores make frivolous lawsuits almost nonexistent. However if a store's loss prevention or security force follows these rules absolutely, then there will be many shoplifters walking away without ever being approached. Marquis points out in a recent article that these five-step programs have been put into place for several decades now and were adopted by the insurance industry solely to avoid liability making insurance carriers the driving force behind the use of these policies. How often do you see an insurance carrier working loss prevention? They do not. He also notes that given that these steps have been in use for more than two decades it is quite apparent that they were developed before modern technology. With the use of equipment such as electronic alarm systems and CCTV systems that give very reliable probable cause for making a stop, and with probable cause the *key* element in prosecution, it may be time for insurance carriers and security or loss prevention management to revaluate the five- and six-step process and bring it up-to-date.

In the mean time many loss prevention officers are currently faced with the ongoing fact that shoplifting is on the rise, with 5000 shoplifters being arrested every day (http://www.shoplifting.com). According to a recent article in *Loss Prevention*, "There is an estimated 200 million shoplifting incidents occurring each year, retailers are experiencing approximately 550,000 shoplifting incidents each day, resulting in losses totaling almost $30 million per day." With this kind of numbers, loss prevention officers are forced to find ways around their stiff policies in order to make arrest and to prevent the word on the street marking them as an easy target. The key is to have the word on the street mark you as a place that *will prosecute, and will not play.* In order to do this, some loss prevention officers are teaming up with their mall security staff to "take it" to the shoplifters. Because most mall security officers are not in the business to stop shoplifters, they do not have a five-step process. They are in the business to assist loss prevention officers.

The following are just a few ways that security and loss prevention have teamed up to make a stop and curb around policies. For instance a retail store may have a shoplifter on video stealing an item; this gives the loss prevention officer probable cause to make a stop, but unfortunately the officer will have to leave the camera room in order to make the stop and will more than likely lose sight of the suspect. Also in most cases there are many exits through which a suspect could leave placing the loss prevention officer in a difficult position. So in a team effort loss prevention will radio mall security and advise of the situation and mall security then will post an officer at each exit with a description of the suspect and a security officer will also enter the store and meet up with the loss prevention officer. If the suspect has made it to an exit before the loss prevention officer has been able to catch up with the suspect, the security officer at the door will make the stop, being very careful in his or her reason for the stop making sure not to accuse the suspect of anything, usually just asking the suspect to return to the store. When questioned by the suspect as to why, the security officer has been instructed to reply with such responses as "I'm not sure why, they may have forgotten to give you change for all I know." Usually at this time the suspect, faced by a uniformed officer, decides to return to the store at which point the loss prevention officer(s) takes over, placing the suspect in detention and writing it up to indicate that the suspect

was observed on videotape concealing merchandise and then was stopped at the exit. On the few occasions when a suspect becomes belligerent with the security officer when asked to return to a store, the security officer has then been instructed to inform the suspect that this kind of behavior is totally unacceptable and is against mall rules and informs the suspect that if he or she does not quietly return to the store, then security will take him or her into custody and escort the suspect to the mall security office to deal with the violation of mall rules and will have them banned from the mall property. Upon arrival in the mall security office a safety pat down and search will be conducted and the police will be called to issue a trespass warning to the suspect. At the time of the safety pat down and search if the stolen merchandise is found on the suspect, security will notify the store's loss prevention, and if loss prevention has the suspect on video, and security just "happened" to stop him with the merchandise, loss prevention will prosecute. Loss prevention has gotten around its policy by not making the stop after losing contact with the shoplifter, but by law has sufficient probable cause to make an arrest. In this way, loss prevention uses the law to its advantage when its policy might have allowed the shoplifter to escape. When retail loss prevention and mall security work together in this way, shoplifters (many of whom "rip off" more than one store in the mall) are caught, shoplifting is prevented and, perhaps, just perhaps, prices will remain stable or even be lowered; thus making life better for everyone.

JEFFREY P. RUSH AND DEBORAH PACE

## References and Further Reading

Bishop, B. 1988. The Law of Shoplifting: A Guide for Lawyers and Merchants. Agora Publishing.
Code of Alabama, Title 13a.
Code of Tennessee, Chapter 14.

*See also* **Larceny or Theft: Extent and Correlates**

# Short, James F., Jr.

James F. Short, Jr. is an officer, a scholar, and a gentleman. This brief essay will introduce his background, and then turn to his contributions. Jim grew up in small town America and graduated to become one of our most

influential sociologists and criminologists. After a stint in the Marine Corps, he began his career as a graduate student at the University of Chicago. At Chicago, he studied and worked with William F. Ogburn and developed his interest in gang research. After earning his Ph.D. from the University of Chicago in 1951, he took a job at State College of Washington, which was soon to become Washington State University (WSU). Although he took leaves of absence to work at places such as Chicago, Oxford, Stanford Law School, and the Center for the Advanced Study in the Behavioral Sciences, he has spent his entire career at WSU in Pullman, Washington.

Jim has made numerous contributions to sociology and criminology during his career. Early in his career, he measured juvenile delinquency by the means of self-reports and compared those reports to official data on offending. His work has been associated with the advancements made in research with self-report data. Unfortunately, many who cite his work simplistically assume that all self-report data are valid and reliable. His contribution was the emphasis on "triangulating" information, validity, and reliability.

Another contribution Jim made in his early work involved qualitative research methods. He recognized the need to have someone be accepted into the research environment before any data collection began. His work with the detached worker in gang research is a good example. In this environment, he recognized the need to have a person with intimate knowledge of the group available to explain the actions and reactions of those being observed. Jim was always careful to collect the highest quality information possible.

In 1964, Jim (and Fred Strodtbeck) wrote an article in *Social Problems*, titled: "Aleatory Risks Versus Short-Run Hedonism in explanation of Gang Action." Although mentioned in earlier works, the concept of "aleatory risks" was now introduced into the language of social science. Aleatory risks explain that the social world is not deterministic, or preset, but that some degree of "randomness" exists and forms a concrete factor in our lives. This randomness can be systematized as some events have a greater propensity to occur than others. His point was that we must distinguish between behavior and what we know about the causes of that behavior. Although used to explain gang behavior in his research, this concept had a wide base of application in the social sciences.

In the 1980s, Jim became interested in the broader area of risk analysis. His interests in the other social sciences, including political science, economics, and psychology, as well as his understanding of the "hard" sciences and medicine, led him to look at the world of risk analysis. He honed his skills in organizational theory and research and developed a scholarly and applied interest on the interrelations of risk and society. In fact, he used this area of interest to craft his presidential address to the American Sociological Association in 1984.

In late 1997, Jim was elected to the presidency of the American Society of Criminology. He is the only person to serve as president of both the American Sociological Association and the American Society of Criminology. He has been tireless in his involvement in professional organizations, and influential in their scholarly development.

Jim's contributions to sociology, criminology, and society involve strategies of data collection to test and build theories. From his early days working on gang research in Chicago to his later efforts to understand risk, he has always shown an interest in developing ways to understand and explain social phenomena.

As a teacher, he had the ability to whet a student's appetite by introducing a topic in an interesting and inquisitive manner. He forced the student to explore, investigate and think independently. He would guide his students and show them where to find the relevant information. He would also show students how to understand and incorporate information into the "big picture." One of the lessons passed to his graduate students was to collect one's own data for a dissertation. He always made his students grapple with the methodological problems and prospects of collecting field data. He would challenge his students but show them how to learn.

James F. Short, Jr. has earned a place in the history of American criminology. His contributions speak for themselves and his willingness to share his ideas and his time will never be forgotten.

GEOFFREY P. ALPERT

## Biography

Born in a farm in Sangamon County, Illinois (in the same home in which his mother was born and on land homesteaded by his great grandfather) on June 22, 1924. Graduated from Dennison University in 1947; M.A. 1949; Ph.D in sociology from the University of Chicago, 1951. Accepted a faculty position at Washington State University after graduation and has remained at WSU throughout his career. Visiting appointments at the University of Chicago (1959–1962), Stanford University (1975), University of Cambridge (1976), Oxford University (1986), University of Notre Dame (1987), and Kokugakuin University (1998). Fellow, Center for the Advanced Study in the Behavioral Sciences (1969–70). Awards include the Edwin Sutherland Award from the American Society of Criminology, the Bruce Smith Award from the Academy of Criminal Justice Sciences, and the Wolfgang Award for Distinguished Achievement in Criminology. President of the American Society of Criminology (1997), and the American Sociological Association (1984). Editor, American Sociological Review (1972–1974).

## Selected Writings

Short, J.F. Jr. and Strodtbeck, F.L. 1965. *Group Process and Gang Delinquency*. Chicago, IL: University of Chicago Press.
Short, James F., Jr. and Nye, F.N. 1958. "Extent of unrecorded juvenile delinquency: Tentative conclusions." *Journal of Criminal Law, Criminology and Police Science* 49 (December):296–302.
Cohen, A.K. and Short, J.F., Jr. 1958. Research in delinquent subcultures. *Journal of Social Issues* 14(3):20–37.
Short, James F. Jr. 1990.*Delinquency and Society*. Englewood Cliffs, NJ: Prentice Hall.
Short, J.F., Jr. 1999. Introduction: Revitalizing criminology and studies of deviance, *Theoretical Criminology*, 3(3):355–358.
Short, J.F., Jr. 1999. Review essay: Criminology through the lens of theory, ideology, and research, *Sociological Inquiry*, 69(4):659–664.
Short, J.F., Jr. 2002. Criminology, the Chicago School, and sociological theory, *Crime, Law and Social Change*, 37 (March):107–115.

## References and Further Reading

Short, J.F., Jr. 1988. Aleatory elements in a criminologist's career, *The Criminologist*. 13, 3:1, 3, 6–7.
Jensen, E.L. 1994. Interview and focus on History: An interview with James F. Short, Jr. *Journal of Gang Research*, 2(2):61–68.
Meier, R.F. 1988. "Discovering delinquency (a biographical sketch of James F. Short, Jr.), *Sociological Inquiry*, 58(Summer):231–239.

# Simon, Rita

In the 1960s, when Rita Simon began her career, she entered an academic world that was primarily male-dominated. Simon quickly became a luminary as her research agenda, partly based on personal experiences, set new standards for women in academia and substantially expanded the study of women and the criminal justice system. When she and her husband Julian Simon (who became a well-known professor of business administration) entered the job market, nepotism rules at universities were common. Simon was hired as a "visiting associate professor," unable to secure a tenured faculty appointment because her husband also was a member of the faculty at the University of Illinois in Champaign–Urbana. Her persistence and high caliber of scholarship, however, resulted in a tenured position, and in 1968 she was promoted to full professor.

Simon, who was disturbed by the bias against women at many American universities, sought out and received a grant from the Department of Education. The work resulted in the publication "Of Nepotism, Marriage and the Pursuit of an Academic Career" in 1966 and "The Woman Ph.D." in 1967. The research compared the productivity of women Ph.D.s against that of the male Ph.D.s and productivity among married and unmarried women Ph.D.s. The research showed that women who had received doctorate degrees between 1960 and 1966 believed that their careers had been damaged by antinepotism rules. According to the women in the study, they were able to enter into academic positions, though their employment included restrictions on mobility, lower professorial ranks, more frequent denial of tenure, and inferior salaries compared to their male counterparts. The women affected by antinepotism rules, however, published more than respondents in the other groups (i.e., men, single women, and women with husbands not in academia).

Simon's interest in the jury system developed in the 1950s when she began working as a research associate with the University of Chicago Jury Project. The project sampled over 1000 jurors from trial courts in Chicago, St. Louis, and Minneapolis. The jurors listened to recorded trials, deliberated under the jurisdiction of the courts, and reported their verdicts to a trial court judge. The project revealed the competency, seriousness, and dedication of jurors in the decision-making process, despite growing attacks on the effectiveness and efficacy of the jury system. The results of the studies showed that jurors understood their role, paid careful attention to testimony, considered the evidence during deliberations, and arrived at verdicts that were consistent with the facts of the case and the law. Simon also has studied jurors' reactions to the insanity defense and to pretrial media coverage, along with their understanding of the rules of law and expert psychiatric testimony.

Simon was serving on the Advisory Board of the Center for the Study of Crime and Delinquency of the National Institutes of Mental Health when she was asked to write a monograph on women and crime.

Simon quickly discovered a paucity of research on female criminality. Early literature included, for example, Cesare Lombroso's view that women were unlikely to engage in crime because of low intelligence and that the women who do commit crimes were more masculine; Eleanor and Sheldon Glueck's 1930s study of delinquency that concluded that the major problem for girls was their lack of control of their sexual impulses; and Rose Giallombardo, who in 1966, found that women who commit criminal offenses were misguided creatures who needed protection.

Simon undertook her work to organize and interpret the data in order to gain a better understanding of women and crime. She examined the proportion of women who had engaged in various types of crimes and examined how they had been treated by police, the courts, and prison officials. Simon found that women historically have been treated more leniently than men by the criminal justice system. The other objective of her research was to make predictions about the future course of female criminality as an increasing number of women entered the public sphere. Simon predicted that women's participation in financial and white-collar offenses would increase as more women became employed in higher status occupations. In 1991, after working with Freda Adler and Jean Landis, Simon discovered that the overall pattern of women's participation in criminal activities had not changed dramatically since 1975. Increases in female criminality that occurred in the 1980s were limited to property and white-collar crimes, as Simon had earlier predicted.

There has been considerable debate regarding Simon's conclusions and scholars disagree over the extent and form of female criminality. Darrell Steffensmeier, for example, discovered a substantial increase in the rate of violent offending by women between 1960 and 1975. Helen Boritch's research found data that women have been treated more harshly than men by the criminal justice system. The literature on gender and crime, however disparate, has undergone a tremendous amount of growth since Simon began her work in the mid-1970s.

Simon is the leading authority on transracial and intercountry adoption. In 1971, Simon began her research on the impact of transracial adoptions. The 20-year longitudinal study included in-depth interviews with parents, birth children, and transracially adopted children who lived in the Midwest. The result provided no empirical support for the arguments used to oppose transracial adoption. The adopted children were successful in their lives and had no problems identifying themselves as Black Americans.

Several organizations opposed to transracial adoption took issue with Simon's position, including the National Association of Black Social Workers (NABSW) and some councils of Native Americans. The NABSW labeled interracial adoptions as racial genocide and condemned the practice of American black children being adopted by white families, even when the alternative was long-term institutionalization or foster care. Opponents also argued that black children who grow up in white families suffer identity problems and fail to develop necessary coping skills to survive in a racist society. Simon's research, however, found that the majority of transracial adoptees believed that racial differences were less important than a loving, secure relationship in a family. Simon's years of difficult work paid off when, in 1996, President Clinton signed a law that prohibited states that received federal assistance from denying any person the opportunity to become an adoptive or foster parent solely on the basis of the race, color, or national origin of the persons or the child involved.

Over the course of her career, Simon has researched and written about women as immigrants, rabbis and ministers, lawyers, professors, and political terrorists. She has authored or edited 13 books and over 200 articles with colleagues, students, her children, and her husband. She published a study of black–white friendships in collaboration with her son Daniel, who was 14 years old at the time. In 1993, she founded the Women's Freedom Network, an organization devoted to the empowerment of women and the promotion of equality. Simon's illustrious career has affected not only sociology, law, criminology, and public policy, but has also made a profound impact on individual families.

MARY DODGE

## Biography

Born in Brooklyn, New York, November 26, 1931. Educated at University of Wisconsin, B.A., 1952; University of Chicago, PhD, 1957. Research associate, University of Chicago, 1958–1961; visiting professor and research associate, Columbia University, 1961–1963; associate professor, University of Illinois, 1963–1967; visiting lecturer, Hebrew University, Jerusalem, 1967–68; professor, University of Illinois, 1968–1983; director of law and society program, University Illinois, 1975–1980; dean, School of Justice, The American University, 1983–1987; professor, The American University, 1988-present. Guggenheim Fellowship, 1966; Ford Foundation Fellowship, 1971; editor, *American Sociological Review,* 1978–1980; editor, *Justice Quarterly.*

## Principal Writings

*The Contemporary Woman and Crime,* 1975.
*The Criminology of Deviant Women* (edited with Adler, F.), 1979.
*The Jury: Its Role in American Society,* 1980.
*The Crimes Women Commit, The Punishments They Receive,* (with Landis, J.), 1991.

*Rabbis, Lawyers, Immigrants, Thieves: Exploring Women's Roles,* 1993.
*Editors as Gatekeepers: Getting Published in the Social Sciences* (edited with Fyfe, J.J.), 1994.
*In The Golden Land: A Century of Russian and Soviet Jewish Immigration in America,* 1997.
*The Jury and the Defense of Insanity,* 1967; Revised edition, 1999.
*In Their Own Voices: Transracial Adoptees Tell Their Stories* (with Roorda, R.M.), 2000.

## Further Reading

Adler, F., *Sisters in Crime.* New York, NY: McGraw-Hill, 1975.
Boritch, H., Gender and criminal court outcomes: An historical analysis. *Criminology* 30 (1992).
Geis, G. and Dodge, M., (Eds.), *Lessons in Criminology,* Cincinnati, OH: Anderson Publishing, 2001.
Grow, L. and Shapiro, D., *Black Children, White Parents: A Study of Transracial Adoption,* New York, NY: Research Center, Child Welfare League of America, 1974.
McRoy, R. and Zurcher, L., *Transracial and Inracial Adoptees: The Adolescent Years,* Springfield, IL: Thomas, 1983.
Steffensmeier, D.J., Crime and the contemporary woman. *Social Forces,* 57 (1978).
Terry, R.M., Trends in female crime: A comparison of Adler, Simon, and Steffensmeier. *California Sociologist* 2 (1979).

*See also* **Gender and Criminal Behavior; Juries and Juror Selection**

# Sixth Amendment *See* Due Process

# Smuggling *See* Organized Crime

# Social Class and Criminal Behavior

The division of a society into social classes is a fundamental force in shaping the definition of crime, the characteristics of violators and victims, and the favored modes of punishment in contemporary nation-states.

## The Meaning of Social Class

Social classes are frequently identified by terms such as "upper class," "middle class," "lower class," "investor class," or "working class." Although it is often treated strictly as a matter of economic position, social class is about much more than money. The division of society into social classes represents an unequal distribution of three types of resources: economic, political, and cultural resources. Economic resources consist of the income and wealth controlled by members of different social groups. Political resources represent the ability to shape governmental actions, either as a member of the government itself, or through positions outside of government, such as lobbyists. Cultural resources are those that can be used to shape popular consciousness and opinion through mass media, education, religious institutions, or other platforms of public communication.

A society's class structure is determined less by the specific amount of resources held by each class than by the *relationships* among these classes. The investor class in a capitalist society, for instance, receives most of its income in the form of dividends, profits, and capital gains generated by the efforts of those who survive by working for a paycheck. The relationships between social classes are rarely without tension. Advantaged groups continually seek to protect or expand their wealth and power in the face of demands by less privileged groups that these resources be redistributed more evenly. Political battles over matters such as the minimum wage, tax structure, Social Security, Medicare, school funding, or assistance to the least well-off are all examples of contemporary class conflicts. In such struggles, advantaged classes typically object most strenuously to government-mandated transfers of resources to those who have less, whereas those who have less typically support transfers that will help them.

There have been many attempts to create precise determinations of where one social class ends and another begins (see Bartley and Bruce-Briggs, 1979;- Szymanski, 1983; Wright 1985, 1997). Social classes, however, lack precise boundaries because the people who constitute them represent different constellations of economic, political, and cultural resources. The unequal distribution of resources in a society places individuals somewhere along a social continuum that ranges from the most to the least advantaged members of the society. The uppermost reaches of social class formation in the U.S., for instance, are inhabited by individuals who own large shares of the nation's wealth, exert substantial influence over how laws and governmental policy will be made, play important roles in determining the content of mass media, education, and religious teachings, and who live lives that many people envy and would like to emulate. Nearer to the bottom are individuals who earn very little, have no wealth, enjoy little direct influence over government, media, education, or religion, and whose style of speech, dress, and conduct are often judged to be maladjusted, eccentric, or even "dangerous" by those from more advantaged sectors of the society. The middle ranges of this continuum encompass people who blend various levels of access to economic, social, and cultural resources. Although more comfortable than the poor, these middle classes exert less *direct* influence over major political economic decisions in comparison to those from the upper strata of society.

With the end of Soviet-style socialism in the 1990s, capitalism became the dominant form of political economic organization in most of the world's nations. This means that in most countries economic, political, and cultural benefits are increasingly distributed according to market-based competition. Because competition always produces winners and losers, whenever market competition is the central organizing principle of a society, a wide gap between haves and have-nots is an unavoidable structural outcome. This division is a cumulative process. The more wealth and power that any social group can bring to the competition for resources, the more resources it can win. The more it has won in the past, the more likely it is to win in the future. In this way, social class divisions become relatively permanent. Specific individuals may move upward or downward within the class structure, but the division of society into these classes remains.

## Social Class and the Definition of Crime

The division of society into social classes with very different levels of wealth and power means that some groups have more ability to influence government decisions than others. In the U.S., for instance, wealthy groups whose money comes from investments, business ownership, or high status occupations have more opportunities to influence the law-making process than ordinary wage workers, the poor, the unemployed, the young, or the undereducated. Consequently, the laws and policies that shape the meaning of crime are more likely to reflect the values, life experiences, and interests of the upper and middle echelons of society.

The law-making process certainly reflects more than the exclusive interests of the upper classes. There are many areas of agreement between social classes over the definition of crime. Both the rich and the poor, for instance, agree that murder, rape, theft, and burglary should be treated as crimes. It is where there is disagreement, or where the middle- and upper-class harms represent new dangers not yet incorporated into the law, that social class exerts its greatest influence over the definition of crime. The majority of Americans, for instance, view white-collar crimes that lead to death or injury as being serious as being street crimes that lead to death or injury (see Rossi, 1974; National White Collar Crime Center, 1999). Lawmakers, however, are drawn primarily from the stratum of society that has the exclusive ability to commit white-collar crimes. As a result, fewer harmful acts committed in the white-collar world are defined as violations of law, and most of the ones that are treated as legal wrongs are handled through administrative and regulatory legal structures, rather than through more stigmatizing criminal courts (see Sutherland, 1949).

In addition to frequently winning specific political contests with less-advantaged classes, the resource rich also play a key role in shaping broadly-held visions of right and wrong. Historically, dominant definitions of "dangerousness" have focused on people whose behaviors challenged established economic, political, or cultural hierarchies, rather than on the harms committed by those who controlled those hierarchies (see Renee, 1978). Today, even though expanding technologies for producing and marketing goods and services often create new and more complex ways of causing harm, corporate and political sectors promoting these new technologies are frequently able to use their influence in government, media, and education to downplay these dangers, thus minimizing societal awareness of the hazards posed by new, profit-enhancing technologies. One of the starkest examples of how differential power can obscure victimization is the "dumping" of known unsafe products and hazardous wastes on citizens of developing countries. Citizens of less-developed nations often live with the hazardous consequences of industrial waste produced in more developed countries. Meanwhile many citizens of developed countries are often blissfully unaware that their relatively comfortable lifestyles are contributing to illness and even death in less advantaged parts of the world (see Dowie, 1979; Seager, 1993; Michalowski, 1998; LaPierre and Moro, 2002).

At the beginning of the 21st century many countries must decide what levels of environmental damage, what kinds of genetic alteration to food supplies, and how much electronic intrusion into daily life they will accept as the normal and even beneficial consequence of economic development, and what levels should be considered unacceptable and punished by law. Through their control over news media, advertisements, education, and government, those representing the world view of economic and political elites are able to downplay the dangers of these new technologies, and to label those who raise alarms as "extremists," "tree huggers," or simply uninformed. Those outside elite circles of power and influence who represent other sides of these debates have far fewer options for shaping public consciousness regarding the dangers of new products and practices. The long-term cultural effects of this process is that many people will continue to view the vices and street crimes associated with lower-class communities as *real* crime, and the harms resulting from profit-making activities by middle- and upper-class citizens as more "technical" offenses whose perpetrators should not be treated as real threats to human well-being.

The criminal justice system's focus on the kinds of crimes that are more typical among lower classes, obscuring the often greater harm done by those from advantaged social classes. The U.S. Department of Justice, for instance, estimated that the total cost of serious crime in the U.S. in 1992 amounted to 17.6 billion dollars (Klaus, 1994). Although this represents a substantial loss, it is only a fraction of the costs of white-collar crime. According to the U.S. General Accounting Office, fraud and abuse account for 10% of the total money spent on health care in the U.S., with most of this fraud being committed not by health care users, but by insurance companies, health care professionals, and health care organizations. In 1995, the cost from this one area of fraud alone was estimated to be *100 billion dollars*, nearly seven times greater than the cost of all street crime (see Davis, 1992; Thompson, 1992). According to the Association of Certified Fraud Examiners, the annual cost of all frauds within business in U.S. is approximately 400 billion dollars, *twenty-two times higher* than the total cost of serious street crime (see Geis, 1998).

The consequences of wrongdoing by those within the upper strata of society are not limited to economic losses. Every year, for instance, between 9,000 and 10,000 Americans are killed while working, and an additional 50,000 to 70,000 die from preventable diseases contracted owing to toxins in the workplace (see Landragin, 1988). Combining the lowest estimates for deaths because of workplace injuries and illness yields an approximate annual toll of 59,000 deaths from workplace hazards. Although not all of these deaths and illnesses are the result of violations of law, according to one U.S. Government Accounting Office survey, 69% of all workplaces are guilty of at least one willful violation of workplace safety laws serious enough to pose a risk of death or serious physical harm to workers. Based on this estimated rate of violation, approximately 40,000 U.S. workers die each year from law breaking in the workplace, as compared to around 16,000 who are murdered each year (see FBI, 1999). In other words, American workers are more than two-and-a-half times more likely to be killed on the job than by a stranger, friend, or family member. Workplace deaths, like street crime, also victimize lower classes more than upper ones. Blue-collar workers are far more likely to be killed or contract a fatal illness from their jobs than white-collar workers or investors who are exposed to far fewer workplace hazards (see Friedrichs, 1996).

Workplace deaths and injuries are just one example of how social class influences the definition of crime. The financial costs and physical harms resulting from illegal environmental pollution, the marketing of unsafe products, and the array of financial scams that take not only people's money, but destroy their economic security and emotional well-being, exceed the physical and financial costs of street crime by a wide margin every year (see Chasin, 1998; Reiman, 1998; Lynch and Michalowski, 2000). Nevertheless, because the culturally established understanding of danger and the actual definition of crime reflect the worldview of those with the greatest amount of economic and political power, the kinds of crime most associated with lower classes continue to dominate the popular understanding of crime and the agenda of the justice system.

## Class and Criminality

There is disagreement among criminologists regarding whether individuals from lower classes are more likely to commit crime than those from the middle and upper classes. If we ask who is more likely to cause harm, it would appear that the upper- and middle-class sectors pose the greatest danger to life and well-being. If the question is limited to who commits the kinds of crimes to which the justice system devotes most of its attention and resources, the picture becomes less clear.

In the U.S., the Federal Bureau of Investigation provides an annual report on crime that includes information regarding the sex, age, race, and ethnicity of those arrested for street crime. These reports, however, provide very little information about social class characteristics such as income, occupation, or the residence of those arrested. Consequently, the best information we have regarding the social class characteristics of street criminals is based on surveys of prison inmates. According to these surveys there is little question that the vast majority of those serving time for routine criminal offenses come from the poorest segments of the society. In 1992, for instance, although 78% of the general U.S. population had high school diplomas, only 33% of the prisoners surveyed were high school graduates. Similarly, at a time when only 7% of the total labor force was unemployed, 45% of those in prison had been without jobs at the time of their arrest. Finally, although the average yearly wage for full-time employed workers was $27,000, and even the poorest 10% of full-time workers earned an average of $13,000 a year, 53% of those in prison had incomes of $10,000 or less before being arrested (see Bureau of Labor Statistics, 1993). Although these statistics may be somewhat skewed by the fact that better-off offenders charged with street crimes are more likely to avoid imprisonment, there is little reason to believe that there are equivalent numbers of people from the middle and upper class committing the kinds of "street" crimes that land the poorest Americans in prison. A few days spent in any police station or jail quickly reveal how very few middle- or upper-class citizens are being brought to justice for common street crimes (see Irwin, 1985; Irwin and Austin, 1997). Clearly, the criminal justice net hauls in the poorest of the poor. What this tells us about the link between social class and criminal behavior, however, remains controversial.

Attempts by criminologists to explain the relationship between social class and criminality have produced three categories of explanation: individual defect theories, social interaction theories, and structural outcome theories. During the last quarter of the 20th century, individual defect theories focusing on factors such as inadequate social "bonding," or the "moral poverty" of the poor, grew in popularity among both criminologists and policy makers (see Hirschi, 1969; Bennett, DiJullio, and Walters, 1996). These explanations typically locate the cause of crime in the personality or family background of the individual law breaker or potential law breaker. This emphasis on individual or family defects as the cause of crime resonates with Conservative political thought that emphasizes individual rather than societal responsibility. As the Conservative movement gained strength throughout the 1980s and 1990s, crime theories focusing on individual and family defect became increasingly influential in shaping crime-control policies. Individual defect theories are criticized by some criminologists for giving little attention to the ways other forces shape the context within which individuals learn their values and select their behaviors, and for their lack of insight into why upper- and middle-class corporate offenders who typically have strong social "bonds" and good "moral" values in their personal lives will still knowingly harm others in the pursuit of profit.

Social interactionist approaches argue that there is little real difference in the criminality of the affluent and the poor. From this perspective, the poor are disproportionately represented in official crime statistics because the justice system focuses on controlling poor communities. This has two consequences. One is that poor law-breakers are more likely to be arrested than affluent ones. The other is that the experience of arrest, prosecution, and punishment increases the likelihood of future criminality among the poor because many of them are "labeled" as criminals at an early age (see Matza, 1968). The interactionist position, for example, suggests that although the proportion of drug users among middle-class college students is no less than among poor youth, college students have a far lower risk of being prosecuted and labeled as drug offenders because they are not the targets of the "war on drugs"—which, in practice, is a war on poor people (see Currie, 1993; Chambliss, 1995, 2000). Interactionist theories tend to focus on the behavioral similarity among affluent and poorer classes for crimes such as drug abuse and domestic violence. The interactionist approach has been less persuasive in explaining differences in the rates of arrest and prosecution among different social classes for crimes such as robbery, burglary, or theft that do appear to be committed proportionally more often by the poor than by the affluent.

Structural outcome theories propose that poor communities will manifest higher rates of criminal behavior, just as they manifest increased levels of other problems such as hypertension, alcoholism, and diabetes, not because of the individual failings of their members, but because of the physical, cultural, and emotional stresses associated with inequality and poverty. These theories typically explain higher rates of property crime in poorer neighborhoods in terms of the structurally induced gap between people's material wants and the resources they have to fulfill them, and the structural barriers that make it difficult for poorer neighborhoods to create coherent communities. These ideas first became influential within criminology during the Great Depression of 1929–1941, at a time when many people experienced first hand how structural problems could distort individual lives (see Merton, 1938; Sutherland, 1974). Structural outcome approaches explain nonutilitarian crimes such as interpersonal violence or drug use by focusing on how the daily frustrations of living poor can increase tendencies toward interpersonal aggression, or toward self-medication with illegal drugs to ease the sadness and difficulties of daily life (see Bernard, 1990; Jones and Newman, 1998).

Individual defect and structural outcome theories both accept the idea that the lower classes are more likely to engage in street crime than the middle and upper classes, and in this way they differ significantly from interactionist theories that suggest much of the apparent class differences in crime are a measure of justice system behavior rather than the actual criminal activity of wrongdoers. Despite their one area of agreement, individual defect and structural outcome theories mark a central divide in how criminologists have thought about the relationship between social class and crime. Structural explanations revolve around the idea of *social probability*, whereas defect theories focus on *individual specificity*. Structural theories propose that the increases in the level of stress imposed on any population will increase the proportion of that group that will respond in deviant or self-destructive ways. These theories can neither predict *who* is likely to become criminal, nor do they lend themselves to creating social policies aimed at changing the behavioral paths that specific individuals will choose. Rather, structural outcome theories focus on identifying the conditions that will lead to increases or decreases in the proportion of a group likely to commit crime. Individual defect theories, in contrast, are concerned with explaining why, within any given set of social conditions, *specific* individuals become deviant or criminal and others do not. A criticism of structural theories frequently leveled by those proposing individual defect models of criminality is that structural theories fail to explain why the majority of individuals subjected to the pressures of lower-class life do not become criminal (see Gotfredson and Hirschi, 1990). Probability theorists, in turn, counter with the argument that the research evidence is fairly clear that increases in economic distress and social stress leads to higher rates of crime, and that the most effective crime reduction policies are those that reduce such stressors, not those that attempt to change individuals (see Chiricos, 1987; Carlson and Michalowski, 1997).

This is not a debate that can be resolved on purely intellectual or academic grounds. Social class is about money, power, and politics. Thus, the attractiveness of structural or individualistic theories regarding the link between social class and crime is shaped by broader world views as well as intellectual commitments. Liberals and left-of-center thinkers typically favor probability theories because these suggest we can reduce crime through redistribution policies that will narrow the gap between the most and least advantaged, thus reducing stresses that increase the proportion of the least advantaged who will be tempted to crime. More conservative thinkers tend to be attracted to theories that suggest that crime is not a natural response to social stress, but rather that it results from individual failures to resist the temptations of crime. Criminologists operating from this perspective will be more supportive of crime-control policies such as "character education," promotion of "family values," or more punishment of offenders.

## Social Class and Victimization

Although there is debate about the relationship between social class and street crime, the data regarding social class and criminal victimization are less controversial. Since 1973, the Bureau of Justice Statistics has conducted the National Crime Victimization Survey (NCVS) that uses a representative sample of households to estimate the rate of criminal victimization in the U.S. each year. The data provided by the NCVS indicate that although the link between social class and victimization varies according to crime, in general, the less well-off bear a greater burden as crime victims, particularly with respect to crimes of violence. In 2001, for instance, households earning less than $7500 were six times more likely to contain someone who had been the victim of rape or sexual assault that year, nearly four times more likely to contain some who was the victim of a robbery, and three times more to include a victim of assault than households with incomes above $75,000. In most cases victimization rates for middle-class households fell between the richest and the poorest categories. The difference between the rich and poor households as victims of property crime is less dramatic, although for the more serious crime of burglary, poor households face greater risks than rich ones. According to the NCVS, for every 10 burglaries of rich homes there are 26 burglaries of poor ones. Only the least serious crime reported—theft without personal contact or forced entry—victimized rich households more than poor ones. Rich households had a 27% greater chance than poor households of being victims of a theft that did not involve either illegal entry or personal contact (see Bureau of Labor Statistics, 2002). This pattern is not unique to the U.S. Recent research studies in comparably developed countries such as Canada, Britain and Norway, for example, similarly demonstrate that the risk of criminal victimization and the fear of crime tends to increase as income levels decline (see Besserer et al., 1999; Pantazis, 2000; Daly, Wilson, and Vasdev, 2001; Pederson, 2001).

Although the popular image of street crime is often that of the poor preying on the rich, the reality of crime is that most crimes occur within a relatively short distance of where the offender lives. Thus, to the extent that lower classes commit more street crimes, it means that the poor are also more likely to be the victims of these crimes.

## Conclusion

Most efforts to explain the relationship between social class and criminality focus on a single level of analysis such as economic distress, justice system bias, or individual defects. The division of society into social classes, however, affects all levels of social life. At the broadest level, the organization of society according to market competition produces an unequal distribution of economic, political, and cultural resources. This, in turn, has both behavioral and justice system consequences. At the behavioral level, the economic distress experienced by poorer groups will likely increase the proportion of those groups that will resort to crime to achieve material gain or to adapt to the psychological and emotional stresses of inequality and poverty. At the same time, among more affluent classes, pressures for personal achievement and corporate profits increases the proportion of these groups who will be guilty of white-collar and corporate forms of wrongdoing. Resource-rich social classes, however, enjoy greater ability to shape law and culture such that many of the harms and pleasures of resource-poor populations are defined as criminal, whereas those of more advantaged groups remain largely free of criminal prosecution and punishment. As a result, the justice system focuses on poorer criminals who use crude methods of theft or force rather than on more sophisticated middle- and upper-class offenders, thus setting up a feed-back loop whereby the public comes to believe that the street crimes and vice crimes of the poor are the primary threat to social order.

RAYMOND J. MICHALOWSKI

## References and Further Reading

Barak, G., Flavin, J.M. and Leighton, P.S., *Class, Race, Gender, and Crime*. Los Angeles, CA: Roxbury, 2001.

Bartley, R.L. and Bruce-Briggs, B., (Eds.), *The New class?* New Brunswick, NJ: Transaction Books, 1979.

Bennett, W., DiJullio, J. and Walters, J., *Body Count: Moral Poverty—and How to Win America's War against Crime and Drugs,* New York, NY: Simon and Schuster, 1996.

Bernard, T.J., Angry Aggression. *Criminology,* 28, 1990.

Besserer, S. et al., *A Profile of Criminal Victimization: Results of the 1999 General Social Survey*. Canadian Centre for Justice Statistics. Toronto, Canada: 2001.

Bureau of Justice Statistics. U.S. Department of Justice. *Survey of Inmates of State Prisons*. NCJ 136949. Washington, DC: U.S. Government Printing Office, 1993.

Bureau of Justice Statistics, U.S. Department of Justice. *National Crime Victimization Survey*. Washington, DC: U.S. Government Printing Office, 2002. Also available at http://www.ojp.usdoj.gov/bjs/pub/pdf/cvus01.pdf.

Carlson, S. and Michalowski, R., Crime, unemployment, and social structures of accumulation: An inquiry into historical contingency. *Justice Quarterly,* 14(2):209–241, 1997.

Chambliss, W., *Power, Politics, and Crime*. Boulder, CO: Westview Press, 2000.

Chambliss, W., Another lost war: The costs and consequences of drug prohibition. *Social Justice,* 22(2):101–124, 1995.

Chasin, L. *Inequality and Violence in the United States*. New York, NY: Humanity Books, 1998.

Chiricos, T. Rates of crime and unemployment: An analysis of aggregate research evidence. *Social Problems,* 34(2):187–212, 1987.

Crowther, C. *Policing Urban Poverty* (foreword by Alan Walker). New York, NY: St. Martin's Press, 2000.

Currie, E. *Reckoning: Drugs, the Cities, and the American Future*. New York, NY: Hill and Wang, 1993.

Daly, M., Wilson, M. and Vasdev, S., Income inequality and homicide rates in Canada and the United States. *Canadian Journal of Criminology and Criminal Justice,* 43(2), 2001.

Davis, L., Medscam. *Mother Jones*. Available at http://bsd.mojones.com/mother_jones/MA95/davis.html. Thompson, 1992.

Dowie, M., Dumping: The Corporate Crime of the Century. *Mother Jones,* 1979.

Doyle, J., Ehsan, A. and Horn, R.N., The effects of labor markets and income inequality on crime: Evidence from panel data. *Southern Economic Journal,* 65(4):717–738, 1999.

Dyer, J., *The Perpetual Prisoner Machine: How America Profits from Crime*. Boulder, CO: Westview Press, 2000.

Federal Bureau of Investigation, *Uniform Crime Reports—1999*. Washington, DC: U.S. Government Printing Office.

Friedrichs, D., *Trusted Criminals: White Collar Crime in Contemporary Society,* Belmont, CA: Wadsworth, 1996.

Geis, G., *Association of Certified Fraud Examiners: Report to the nation*. Austin, TX: Association of Certified Fraud Examiners, 1998.

Gottfredson, M. and Hirschi, T., *A General Theory of Crime,* Stanford, CA: Stanford University Press, 1990.

Harring, S. and Ray, L.G., Policing a class society: New York City in the 1990s. *Social Justice,* 26(2):63–81, 1999.

Hirschi, T., *The Causes of Delinquency,* Berkeley, CA: University of California Press, 1969.

Irwin, J., *The Jail: Managing the Underclass in American Society,* Berkeley, CA: University of California Press, 1985.

Irwin, J. and Austin, J., *It's about Time: America's Imprisonment Binge,* Belmont, CA: Wadsworth, 1997.

Jones, L. and Newman, L., (with Isay, D.) *Our America: Life and Death on the South Side of Chicago,* New York, NY: Pocket Books, 1998.

Landrigan, P. *Testimony before the Senate Committee on Labor and Human Resources,* April 18, 1988.

LaPierre, D. and Moro, J., *Five Past Midnight in Bhopal*. New York, NY: Warner Books, 2002.

Lynch, M. and Michalowski, R., *The New Primer in Radical Criminology: Critical Perspectives on Crime Power and Identity*. Washington, DC: Criminal Justice Press, 2000.

Matza, D., *On Becoming Deviant,* Englewood Cliffs, NJ: Prentice Hall, 1968.

Merton, R., Social structure and anomie. *American Sociological Review,* 3:672–682, 1938.

Michalowski, R., International environmental issues, In *Environmental Crime: Enforcement, Policy and Social Responsibility,* Clifford, M. (Ed.). Gaithersberg, MD: Aspen, 315–340, 1998.

Michalowski, R. and Carlson, S., Toward and new and much-needed political economy of crime and justice in a globalized world. *Contemporary Journal of Criminal Justice,* 16(3):272–292, 2000.

National White Collar Crime Center, *White Collar Crime: Victimization and Attitudes*. Morgantown, WV: National White Collar Crime Center, 1999.

Pantazis, C., Fear of crime, vulnerability and poverty. *The British Journal of Criminology,* 40:414–436, 2000.

Parenti, C., *Lockdown America.* London, U.K.: Verson, 1999.

Pedersen, W. Adolescent victims of violence in a welfare state sociodemography, ethnicity and risk behaviours. *The British Journal of Criminology,* 41:1–21, 2001.

Reiman, J., *The Rich Get Richer and the Poor Get Prison.* Boston, MA: Allyn and Bacon, 1998.

Renee, Y., *The Search for Criminal Man,* Boston, MA: Sage, 1978.

Rossi, P., The seriousness of crime: Normative structures and individual differences. *American Sociological Review,* 39(1), 224–237, 1974.

Seager, J., *Earth Follies,* New York, NY: Routledge, 1993.

Sutherland, E., *Criminology.* Philadelphia, PA: Lipincott, 1974.

Szymanski, A., *Class Structure.* New York, NY: Praeger, 1983.

Sutherland, E., *White Collar Crime: The Uncut Version,* New Haven, CT: Yale University Press, 1983.

Taylor, I., *Crime and Political Economy.* Brookfield, VT: Ashgate, 1998.

Thompson, L.H., *Health insurance: Vulnerable payers lose billions to fraud and abuse. Report to Chairman, Subcommittee on Human Resources and Intergovernmental Operations, U.S. House of Representatives.* Washington, DC: United States General Accounting Office.

Wright, B.R., Entner, C.-A. and Moffitt, T.E., Reconsidering the relationship between SES and delinquency: Causation but not correlation. *Criminology,* 37(1): 175–194, 1999.

Wright, E.O., *Classes,* London, U.K.: Verso, 1985.

Wright, E.O., *Class Counts: Comparative Studies in Class Analysis,* New York, NY: Cambridge University Press, 1997.

*See also* **Sociological Theories of Criminal Behavior**

# Social Control Theories of Criminal Behavior

Social control theories of crime and delinquency attribute law breaking to the weakness, breakdown, or absence of those social bonds or socialization processes that are presumed to encourage law-abiding conduct. Such theories accord primacy to relationships, commitments, values, norms, and beliefs that are purported to explain why people do not break laws as compared to theories according primacy to motivating forces thought to explain why people do break laws. When taken to the extreme, social control theory can be an "amotivational" theory, dismissing or ignoring the necessity of addressing motivational issues. The most prominent social control theorist in the 20th century, Travis Hirschi, viewed the motivations as so natural to human beings that no special forces were necessary to explain law breaking. Law breaking is often the most immediate source of gratification or conflict resolution, and no special motivation is required to explain such behavior. Human beings are active, flexible organisms who will engage in a wide range of activities, unless the range is limited by processes of socialization and social learning. On the other hand, many control-oriented theorists do introduce motivating forces, pressures, and pulls into their explanations. However, such motivations are viewed as sufficiently common, diverse, transitory, and situational that more explanatory power is to be gained from focusing on the barriers or constraints that inhibit law-breaking outcomes than attempting to discern specific motivating forces. Rather than being generated by one or a few dominant forces, the motives for delinquency are depicted as quite diverse, ranging from instrumental needs (stealing when one is poor and hungry) to emotional rage, frustration, and sheer thrill and excitement. However, because most people are "motivated" to break laws at one time or another, a focus on motives does not explain who will commit criminal and delinquent acts (Briar and Pilavin, 1965).

This type of theory has roots in the perspectives on human society proposed by the English social philosopher, Thomas Hobbes (1588–1679). In his best-known work, *Leviathan, or, Matter, Form, and Power of a Commonwealth Ecclesiastical and Civil* (1651), Hobbes argued that human nature would generate a perennial war of all against all, were choices not constrained by implicit social contracts, agreements, and arrangements among people. From such a perspective, there is nothing mysterious about theft and violence when it has no social or political costs. This argument does not imply that people are "naturally" evil or "bad." Rather, such moral designations are created in the construction of social order, assigning costs and consequences to certain choices and defining some as evil, immoral, or illegal.

Although "social control theory" is most often associated with the version proposed by Hirschi in his classic work, *Causes of Delinquency* (1969), numerous theorists have introduced ideas reflecting a control theory logic. In one of the early control theories, Albert J. Reiss (1951: 196) proposed that delinquency was "behavior consequent to the failure of personal and social controls." Personal control was defined as "the ability of the individual to refrain from meeting needs in ways which conflict with the norms and rules of the community," whereas social control was "the ability of social groups or institutions to make norms or rules effective."

Reiss's version did not specify the sources of such "abilities" nor the specific control mechanisms leading to conformity, but he did identify the failure of such primary groups as the family to provide reinforcement for nondelinquent roles and values as crucial to the explanation of delinquency. His perspective was true to control theory logic in that no specific motivational sources leading to delinquency when social and personal controls failed were identified.

Between 1956 and 1958, the importance of barriers to delinquent behavior was highlighted in works by Walter Reckless and his colleagues (1956), Jackson Toby (1957), and F. Ivan Nye (1958). Reckless began developing a "containment" theory in 1956 by focusing on a youth's self-conception as an "insulator" against delinquency. By 1967, Reckless had developed that perspective into the most elaborate of the early control-based perspectives. A wide range of characteristics of individuals could operate as internal control mechanisms, but Reckless allotted special significance to "self-concepts" or "self-images." Even in the most criminogenic environments, youth who held images of themselves as "good students" or "good kids" could be insulated from pressures and pulls conducive to delinquency. Of course, formation of such self-images was a reflection of strong social relationships with parents, teachers, and other sources of conventional socialization. Delinquent behavior could also be "contained" through processes external to the individual and parents, school, and neighborhood were particularly important. Reckless also introduced inner and outer pressures and pulls that encompassed a variety of potential motivating forces. However, he listed a broad range of possibilities and, in contrast to other theories at that time, no specific motivational force was advocated. Indeed, most of the empirical work by Reckless and his students concentrated on inner containment. His research suggested that internal controls had an impact independent of external constraints, pressures, and pulls.

Another criminologist, Jackson Toby (1957), argued that "the uncommitted adolescent is a candidate for gang socialization." Toby acknowledged "gang socialization" as part of the causal, motivational, dynamic leading to delinquency, but introduced the concept of "stakes in conformity" to explain "candidacy" for such learning experiences. Youth who had few stakes or investments in conformity were more likely to be drawn into gang activity than youth who had a lot to lose. A variety of conventional social relationships and commitments could be jeopardized by involvement in delinquency and youth without such stakes were free to be recruited into gangs (1957). The notion of "stakes in conformity" fit very well with concepts invoked in later versions of social control theory.

In *Family Relationships and Delinquent Behavior* (1958), F. Ivan Nye not only elaborated a social control theory of delinquency, but specified ways to "operationalize" (measure) control mechanisms and related them to self-reports of delinquent behavior. Like Reiss, he focused on the family as a source of control. Moreover, Nye specified different types of control, differentiating between internal, direct, and indirect controls. Youth may be directly controlled through constraints imposed by parents, limiting the opportunity for delinquency, as well as through parental rewards and punishments. However, they may be constrained when free from direct control by their anticipation of parental disapproval (indirect control), or through the development of a conscience, an internal constraint on behavior. The focus on the family as a source of control was in marked contrast to the emphasis on economic circumstances as a source of criminogenic motivation at the time. Although he acknowledged motivational forces by stating that "*some* delinquent behavior results from a *combination* of positive learning and weak and ineffective social control" (1958, 4), he adopts a control-theory position when he proposes that "most delinquent behavior is the result of insufficient social control…" Hirschi was critical of Nye's use of concepts such as internal control, but (together with Gottfredson) proposed "self-control" as a key explanatory variable over 30 years later. Nye's work was the first major presentation of research from a social control perspective and most of his findings are quite consistent with subsequent research using survey data.

Although it was not presented as a social control theory, David Matza's book, *Delinquency and Drift* (1964), incorporated several of the features of that type of theory. Delinquent youth were "neither compelled nor committed to" their delinquent actions deeds, but were "partially unreceptive to other more conventional traditions" (1964: 28). In short, delinquent youth could be depicted as "drifters," relatively free to take part in delinquency. This argument was a challenge to other theories in the 1960s that emphasized status frustration and the adoption of oppositional values by delinquent youth. According to Matza, the delinquent "flirts" with criminal and conventional behavior while drifting among different social worlds. Matza did not identify any specific constraints or controls that keep youth from drifting, but drifters were depicted as youth who have few stakes in conformity and are free to drift into delinquency. Similar to Hirschi's presentation of social control theory, Matza challenged theories emphasizing distinct subcultural or contracultural value systems in the explanation of delinquency.

Scott Briar and Irving Piliavin presented one of the clearest statements of a control theory logic in an article on "Delinquency, situational inducements and commitments to conformity" in 1965. Like Matza, they specifically challenged other theoretical perspectives of the 1960s by emphasizing transitory, situational inducements as the motivating forces for delinquency in contrast to subcultural or contracultural value systems and socially structured status problems. Motivation did not differentiate delinquent and nondelinquent youth as much as variable commitments to conformity. They argued that the "central process of social control" were "commitments to conformity." They included fear of material deprivations if apprehended, self-images, valued relationships, and current and future statuses, and activities. In his version of social control theory, Hirschi limited the concept of commitment to the rational and emotional investments that people make in the pursuit of shared cultural goals.

Although Hirschi was not the first to propose a social control theory, the research monograph based on his doctoral research, *Causes of Delinquency* (1969) established his reputation as the preeminent social control theorist of the 20th century. Indeed, any reference to social control theory was presumed to be a reference to Hirschi's version of the theory. There are several reasons for this preeminence and the fact that *Causes of Delinquency* became the most cited book in criminology. For one, he proposed his theory as a specific contrast to versions of two perspectives that were much better known at that time, so-called "strain" and "cultural conflict" perspectives. Other control theorists had challenged such theories, but Hirschi proposed what he considered to be "crucial" differences among the theories where confirmation of one position was believed to constitute disconfirmation of an alternative. Second, he presented a parsimonious theory with four specific types of constraints rather than a list of examples and attempted to clearly define each as a type of "social bond." Third, he operationalized the concepts and tested his theory and addressed crucial contrasts with other theories using self-report survey data. Analyses of survey data would become the major method for testing theories in the decades to come.

Three crucial contrasts involved conceptions of culture, the role of ambition, and the role of peers. On the first issue, Hirschi argued that there is a general consensus in American society that criminal and delinquent activities involving personal harm and loss or damage to property are improper or immoral. He did not mean that everyone feels strongly about the impropriety of lawbreaking, but that some people accept the morality behind laws as more binding than others, and are less likely to break laws. Some cultural conflict theories (e.g., Walter Miller) had proposed that sizable racial, ethnic, or status groups in America have subcultural systems of values and norms that require criminal or delinquent behavior, and some strain theorists (e.g., Albert Cohen) had argued that delinquent youth embrace an oppositional or contracultural values that accord status based on law breaking. Hirschi's social control perspective challenged both theories by introducing variation in acceptance of one basic moral system as the crucial factor in understanding the relation between moral beliefs and delinquency.

Hirschi also advocated a view on the impact of ambition that was contrary to one of the most popular theories of crime at that time. Robert Merton (1957) had proposed that high rates of crime reflect embracement of widely shared cultural values emphasizing the merits of the pursuit of wealth and success. When coupled with limits on the prospects of realizing such goals in a stratified society, the disadvantaged resort to "innovative" ways of realizing those goals. In contrast, Hirschi proposed that conventional ambitions constituted barriers to delinquency even among youth with few prospects of realizing those dreams.

Finally, Hirschi challenged differential association theory (Edwin Sutherland and Donald Cressey) with regard to the impact of delinquent peers on delinquency. One of the most consistent findings in research on delinquency was that increases in association with delinquent peers were associated with increases in delinquency. One of his most iconoclastic stands was that delinquent peers would be found to have no direct effect on delinquency when social bonds inhibiting delinquency were taken into account. He argued that similarly unattached youth drifted together into delinquent groups. It was weak social bonds that resulted in both delinquency and association with delinquents.

The dominance of Hirschi's social control theory also reflected its simplicity. The version he proposed was quite parsimonious in comparison to lists of inner and outer containments, and the range of phenomena that could be considered commitments to or stakes in conformity. Hirschi argued that there were four basic "social bonds" that could constitute significant barriers to youths' involvement in delinquency, attachment, commitment, involvement, and belief. Attachment encompassed the emotional bonds of youth to other people and attachments to parents and teachers were viewed as particularly crucial. Attachment encompassed the interpersonal, emotional barriers to delinquency.

Commitment was measured in terms of the aspirations and goals of youth, encompassing rational as well as emotional investments. Involvement referred to behavioral investments in conventional lines of action that could preclude involvement in delinquent behavior. Belief referred to the personal embrace of moral or normative conceptions that inhibit delinquent choices. He proposed that each type of social bond should have its own separable effect in the explanation of delinquency and proceeded to test the theory.

Another reason for the preeminence of Hirschi's social control theory was the empirical approach he took to test the theory. Not only did Hirschi attempt to identify crucial contrasts, but he brought survey data collected from a large sample of junior and senior high school students in California to bear on these crucial differences. Such an approach was daring in that precise specification of measures and presentation of data eliminated the ambiguities that allow theorists to ignore troublesome findings. Hirschi's approach allowed replication and detailed attention to the links between concepts and indicators. Moreover, it put his theory to test in competition with others. His analysis showed that measures of attachment, commitment, and belief had significant and independent effects of delinquency, but that mere involvement in conventional activities did not inhibit delinquency. Attachment, commitment, and moral beliefs are the key social bonds. Moreover, contrary to the implications of some "strain" theories of delinquency, commitments to conventional goals inhibited delinquency even among categories of youth with few prospects for realizing those aspirations. Contrary to some subcultural and contracultural theories, he found few relationships between measures of social class and values or attitudes toward the law.

Hirschi was forced to admit that delinquent peers appeared to have a direct effect on delinquency that could not be explained by social control variables. This finding would become the basis for continuing debate between Hirschi and another prominent criminologist, Ronald Akers, who was developing a "social learning theory" in the late 1960s. Social learning theory combined variables that encouraged delinquency (e.g., delinquent peers) with variables that discouraged delinquency (e.g., parental response). In addition, social learning theory posits that the behavior of people that a youth is attached to affects the consequences of such relationships—a prediction that has been substantiated in several studies (see Akers, 2001).

Most references to social control theory are likely to be references to Hirschi's social bond theory. However, the concept of social control is not defined clearly in Hirschi's work or earlier works developing a control framework. It is understood that social control can refer to mechanisms intended to inhibit deviance and encourage conformity, and that social bonds facilitate process. In contrast, Jack Gibbs (1981) has devoted a considerable amount of scholarly attention to defining social control in a manner that distinguishes it from other concepts. Moreover, he has applied it to develop a control theory of homicide.

According to Gibbs, any attempt to get someone else to do something or refrain from doing something can be considered an attempt at "control." To qualify as "social" control, such attempts must involve three parties. Social control is an attempt by one or more individuals to manipulate the behavior of another individual or individuals by or through a third party (by means other than a chain of command). Gibbs' "third party" can be an actual person or a reference to "society," "expectations," or "norms." For example, if one party attempts to influence another by invoking reference to a third party assumed to have authority (such as "I'll tell Mom!"), it is a type of "referential" social control. If one party attempts to control another by punishing a third (e.g., general deterrence), it is a form of vicarious social control. Numerous categories and subcategories of social control are delineated by Gibbs, but the major point is that the third party distinguishes *social* control from mere external behavioral control, simple interpersonal responses, or issuing orders for someone to do something. This definition clearly distinguishes social control from "prophylactic" conceptions of social control, equating it with "reactions to deviance" and from deviant behavior itself. A variety of phenomenon typically thought of as some type of social control are not clearly "reactions to deviance" (such as propaganda, advertising, education, strikes, protests, and governmental regulations). Moreover, deviant behavior, itself, can be a type of social control (in terms of his final definition of it). If deviant behavior can be a form of social control and social control can involve more than reactions to deviance, then the two concepts cannot be equated; nor can one be subsumed by the other.

Gibbs draws on these distinctions to propose a control theory of homicide. Gibbs argues that "Homicide can be described either as control or as resulting from control failure," (1989: 35) and proposes that the homicide rate is a function "not just of the sheer volume of disputes but also of the frequency of recourse to a third party for peaceful dispute settlement" (37). A dispute typically arises when attempts at some form of direct or proximate control by of one person over another fails and homicide itself represents another attempt at direct control. This argument is similar to Donald Black's discussion of crime as "self-help" that he defines as "the expression of a grievance by unilateral aggression such as personal violence or property destruction" (1983: 34). People resort to self-help (e.g., attempts at direct control through violence) when forms of social control are unavailable or fail. Like other social control theories, the emphasis in Gibbs' theory of homicide is one recourse to third-party social control mechanisms.

Gibbs is critical of Hirschi's social control theory because it does not define social control, but merely presumes that social relationships, personal investments, and beliefs that discourage delinquency are social controls. Hirschi's theory is often referred to as a "social bond theory" for that very reason. Social bonds may make youths subject to more effective control attempts (direct and social), but Gibbs' argues that "the conditions themselves are not control" (1981: 147). At this point in the history of criminological theory, there has been very little attention paid to clear conceptual distinctions among a variety of concepts introduced in the explanation of crime and delinquency, including social control, social bonds, socialization, and social learning. Gibbs' has been working on the concept of social control, but careful delineation among related concepts is rare.

Two of the early control theorists included some form of "internal" control or "inner" containment in their theories, and many of Hirschi's social bonds can be conceptualized as part of the personality, character, identity, mind, or self-conception of individual youth. Youths who want to "do well" in conventional contexts, "care" about their parents and teachers and "believe" that acts hurting others are wrong, are unlikely to become seriously delinquent. Although these characteristics are embodied in desires, feelings, and ideas "mentally" embraced by youths, they are "social" in the sense that they constitute constraints on choices established in interaction with other people. In *Causes of Delinquency* (1969), Hirschi distinguished attachment to others from "internal control" by "locating the 'conscience' in the bond to others rather than making it part of the personality" (19). He challenged related notions such as "internalization" and Freud's "superego" on the grounds that externalizing the social bonds made "change or variation in behavior explainable" (1969: 19). Moreover, although there were correlations among the social bonds, Hirschi proposed that each had separable effects that "justifies their separation" (1969: 30). He challenged psychological perspectives that lumped distinct variables together, or viewed them as mere symptoms of some underlying, hidden, or latent construct such as psychopathology. Indeed, an additional reason for the appeal of Hirschi's theory among sociologists was that it incorporated social, normative, and rational bonds as conceptually distinct, measurable characteristics of youth and allowed for variation or changes in behavior over time.

In 1990, Michael Gottfredson and Hirschi published *A General Theory of Crime* that emphasized variations in "self-control" established at a relatively early age and variations in opportunity to commit crimes as the keys to understanding most empirical regularities in criminality. They argued that the crimes people could commit varied by age but that the individual "tendency" to do so is a product of self-control established in interaction with parents and others during childhood. People low in self-control are "free to enjoy the quick and easy and ordinary pleasures of crime without undue concern for the pains that follow from them" (Hirschi and Gottfredson, 2001: 90). People who learn to "consider the long term consequences of their acts" have "self-control." Variations in self-control are established through interaction and socialization processes involving parents who care about their children, monitor their activities, recognize transgressions when they occur, and take steps to correct their children. In the process, "the child learns to avoid acts with log term negative consequences" (2001: 90).

This "self-control" theory retains the logic of a social control theory in that no special motivation is necessary to explain deviance, crime, or delinquency. "Low self-control" is identified as the "natural" state and actions that hurt others need no special motivational explanation. Moreover, the theory retains the emphasis on barriers to deviance and locates the origins of self-control as a barrier in early socialization and relationships with parents and other conventional role models.

This perspective is not a mere extension or reformulation of Hirschi's social control theory. As presented in *A General Theory of Crime*, and subsequent explications of that theory, self-control theory is a major departure from Hirschi's social bond theory as presented in *Causes of Delinquency*. Most of the features of social bond theory that made it appealing to sociologists have been abandoned in Gottfredson and Hirschi. In fact, self-control theory is subject to all of the criticisms Hirschi leveled against psychological theories in *Causes of Delinquency*. In his earlier work, Hirschi challenged theories that focused on internal, unchanging motivations or constraints. In his new work with Gottfredson, the central focus is just on such states. Hirschi challenged perspectives that lumped conceptually distinct social bonds together as well as theories that transformed disparate barriers or constraints into simple latent constructs. Yet, in *A General Theory* internal barriers are lumped together under the rubric of self-control. In short, the arguments concerning the primacy of self-control presented in *A General Theory* are directly contrary to the arguments presented when advocating social bond theory. In *Causes*, Hirschi demonstrated the distinct relevance of different types of bonds, whether conceived of as social or personal aspects of the self. But, in *A General Theory*, variation in criminality is explained by one inclusive, psychological construct, self-control. Absence of self-control explains continuity in crime among individuals over the life course with the form of crime varying by the age-related structure of criminal opportunity.

There have been two types of research relevant to self-control theory. In one line of research, self-control is inferred to be the stable underlying factor that explains the continuity of deviant behavior or conformity over the life course. The correlations between childhood transgressions and more serious offenses later in life are taken as evidence of an underlying lack of self-control. In contrast, conformity at various ages is attributed to the early establishment of self-control. The second line of research attempts to more directly test the theory by operationalizing "low self-control" and relating it to law breaking with other criminogenic variables controlled. According to Gottfredson and Hirschi "people who lack self-control will tend to be impulsive, insensitive, physical, risk-seeking, short-sighted, and nonverbal" (1990: 90–91). The opposite set of characteristics applies to people high in self-control. The attempt to specify the indicators of "low" self-control differentiates Gottfredson and Hirschi's self-control theory from social bond theory in that it introduces quasi-motivational sources of variation (i.e., impulsivity and risk taking), relevant to the question, "Why do people break laws?"

Research attempting to measure self-control directly (e.g., Grasmick et al., 1993) has used survey data assessing attitudes of respondents that are thought to tap variations in these traits. The most recent review of such research concludes that measures of self-control are significantly related to law-breaking, but that it can be challenged as a general theory of crime. Variables central to differential association and social learning theory affect law-breaking, regardless of variations in self-control (Pratt and Cullen, 2000). At present, self-control theory has not been shown to have superior explanatory power over Hirschi's earlier social bond theory.

There is a mounting body of research drawing on social bond theory to argue that discontinuities between juvenile and adult crime are a product of variations in new social bonds. In an award-winning research monograph, *Crime in the Making: Pathways and Turning Points through Life* (1993), Robert Sampson and John Laub, challenge Gottfredson and Hirschi's theory and report that, consistent with social bond theory, such variables as marital attachment and stable employment explain discontinuities in deviance. Discontinuities can be explained by social bond theory, social learning theory, and a variety of new theories categorized under the rubric of "life course" perspectives.

Numerous "new" perspectives on crime emerged in the late 20th century and two of them included the concept of control. John Hagan (Hagan, Gillis, and Simpson, 1985) introduced a variant of control theory named "power-control" theory and Charles Tittle (1995) introduced "control-balance" theory. Power-control theory integrated ideas from feminist theories with some ideas from social control theory to explain variations in "common delinquency" by gender and parental occupation. Girls were predicted to differ the most from boys in patriarchal households where father's occupational power exceeded mother's occupational power. Increases in mother's power relative to father's power would reduce that gap. That prediction was supported in research by Hagan and colleagues, but has not been found in other research (See Jensen and Rojek, 1998). In contrast to earlier versions of social control theory, power-control theory included very limited social bonds and incorporated a motivational variable in the form of "tastes for risks." Thus, power-control theory can be considered an integrated theory as opposed to a social control theory.

Tittle views his control-balance theory as an integrated theory because it incorporates ideas from a variety of perspectives, including social control theory. He also draws on Gibbs' conception of social control. The central premise is that "the amount of control to which people are subject relative to the amount of control they can exercise affects the probability that they will commit specific types of deviance" (1995: 142). Consistent with social control theory, it is presumed that all people are predisposed toward deviance by common desires for "autonomy" and to fulfill "basic needs." When people experience "control deficits" their probability of engaging in predatory, defiant, or submissive deviance increases relative to people with balanced control ratios. When people have "control surpluses," the probability of exploitative and decadent deviance increases. The theory is very elaborate and, at present, crucial differences and appropriate measures of key concepts have not been clearly specified.

Several issues involving social control theory are likely to be the subject of continuing debate and theoretical elaboration in the 21st century. First, the shift to "self-control" theory will continue to be a source of controversy, because it appears that Hirschi's social bond version of the theory may have superior explanatory power compared to newer "general theory." The self-control version of the theory will be contrasted with predictions by theorists operating from "life course" perspectives, including social bond theory, to explain both continuities and discontinuities in criminality. Self-control is likely to be found to have minimal explanatory power when variables central to social bond and social learning theories are taken into account. Second, social control theory might be effectively incorporated into social learning theory in the coming decades. Whenever there has been a test of crucial differences between the two theories, social learning theory has been supported. Of course, several steps will have to be taken for social learning theory to incorporate social control theory. Social control theory was intimately linked with social disorganization perspectives and Hirschi addressed "macro-level" issues (e.g., "Are their class-based subcultures? "Do shared cultural goals help cause crime?") that have not been central to elaborations of learning theory. Social learning theory can encompass both sources of conformity and sources of deviance to provide a more complete model for explaining criminal and delinquent conduct, but will have to address broader etiological issues to broaden its appeal in some disciplines. Third, taking Gibbs' definition of social control as a starting point, concepts used loosely in the presentation of social control theory (and other theories) such as socialization, social bonds, and social control will have to be more clearly defined and differentiated. There has been minimal effort to define each of these concepts in a manner that would facilitate empirical differentiation and more precise incorporation into theories of law breaking. Finally, the crucial differences (if any), between new perspectives such as control-balance theory and social control theory have yet to be fully explicated, and no crucial tests have been identified or attempted. Regardless of the outcome of new debates and new research, social control theory has to be recognized as one of the dominant theoretical perspectives in criminology in the 20th century.

GARY JENSEN

### References and Further Reading

Akers, R.L. *Criminological Theories*. 3rd ed. Los Angeles, CA: Roxbury Publishing Company, 2000.

Briar, S. and Piliavin, I. Delinquency, situational inducements, and commitments to conformity. *Social Problems* 13 (1965).

Gibbs, J.P. *Control: Sociology's Central Notion*. Urbana, IL: University of Illinois Press, 1989.

Gottfredson, M. and Hirschi, T. *A General Theory of Crime*. CA: Stanford University Press, 1990.

Hirschi, T. *Causes of Delinquency*. Berkeley, CA: University of California Press, 1969.

Jensen, G.F. and Rojek, D.G. *Delinquency and Youth Crime*. 3rd ed. Prospect Heights, IL: Waveland Press, 1998.

Krohn, M. and Massey, J. Social control and delinquent behavior: An examination of the elements of the social bond. *Sociological Quarterly* 21 (1980).

Liska, A.E. and Reed M.D. Ties to conventional institutions and delinquency. *American Sociological Review* 50 (1985).

Matsueda, R. Testing control theory and differential association. *American Sociological Review* 47 (1982).

Matza, D. *Delinquency and Drift*. New York, NY: John Wiley, 1964.

Nye, F.I. *Family Relationships and Delinquent Behavior*. New York, NY: John Wiley, 1958.

Gottfredson, M. and Hirschi, T. *A General Theory of Crime*. CA: Stanford University Press, 1990.

Sampson, R J. and Laub, J.H. *Crime in the Making: Pathways and Turning Points through Life*. Cambridge, MA: Harvard University Press, 1993.

*See also* **Containment Theory; Hirschi, Travis**

# Social Disorganization Theory

Social disorganization theory is a type of criminological theory attributing variation in crime and delinquency over time and among territories to the absence or breakdown of communal institutions (e.g., family, school, church, and local government) and communal relationships that traditionally encouraged cooperative relationships among people. The concept is defined in terms of the absence or breakdown of certain types of relationships among people, and is intimately tied to conceptions of those properties of relationships that are indicative of social or communal "organization." Relationships among people in a given territory are presumed to be especially "organized" when there high levels of involvement across age levels in activities coordinated by representatives of communal institutions (e.g., family heads, pastors, school organizations, and local officials). Such organized interaction is presumed to be closely and reciprocally associated with the development of a sense of community or communal bonds among people in close geographic proximity to one another. The concept was developed to refer to the absence of organization among people in relatively small ecological units (neighborhoods, census tracts, communities), but has been used to explain variations in crime among larger units (e.g., counties, states, and nations) as well as variations over time.

The concept of social disorganization was applied to the explanation of crime, delinquency, and other social problems by sociologists at the University of Chicago in the early 1900s. As a booming industrial city, increasingly populated by recent immigrants of diverse racial and ethnic backgrounds, the city of Chicago provided a social laboratory for the development of American criminology. Rapid growth and change were viewed as "disorganizing" or "disintegrative" forces contributing to a breakdown in the teaching and learning of those prior "social rules" that had inhibited crime and delinquency in European peasant society (Thomas and Znanieki, 1918).

Although better known in contemporary criminology for his "differential association" theory of criminal behavior, Edwin Sutherland (1924, 1934, 1939) elaborated on the concept in the development of his theory of systematic criminal behavior, and Clifford Shaw and Henry McKay (1929) applied it to the explanation of specific patterns of delinquency documented for Chicago and its suburbs.

In the early editions of his classic textbook, *Principles of Criminology* (1924, 1934, 1939), Edwin Sutherland invoked the concept of social disorganization to explain increases in crime that accompanied the transformation of preliterate and peasant societies where "influences surrounding a person were steady, uniform, harmonious and consistent" to modern Western civilization which he believed was characterized by inconsistency, conflict and "un-organization" (1934: 64). He believed that the mobility, economic competition, and an individualistic ideology that accompanied capitalist and industrial development had "disintegrated" both the large family and homogenous neighborhoods as agents of social control, expanded the realm of relationships that were not governed by family and neighborhood, and undermined governmental controls. This disorganization of institutions that had traditionally reinforced the law facilitated the development and persistence of "systematic" crime and delinquency. He also believed that such disorganization fosters the cultural traditions and cultural conflicts that support such activity. The seventh proposition in the 1939 version of his textbook was that "social disorganization is the basic cause of systematic criminal behavior." Systematic criminal behavior referred to repetitive, patterned, or organized offending as opposed to random events. He depicted the "law-abiding culture" as "dominant and more extensive" than alternative criminogenic cultural views and capable of "overcoming systematic crime *if* organized for that purpose" (1939: 8). However, because society was "organized around individual and small group interests," society "permits" crime

to persist. Sutherland concluded that "if the society is organized with reference to the values expressed in the law, the crime is eliminated; if it is not organized, crime persists and develops" (1939:8). In later works, he switched from the concept of social disorganization to differential social organization to convey the complexity of overlapping and conflicting levels of organization in a society. This notion has been elaborated in recent reformulations of social disorganization theory (See Bursik and Grasmick, 1993).

One of the most important works in the development of criminology (the scientific study of crime) in the U.S. was Clifford Shaw's work with Henry McKay and other collaborators on *Delinquency Areas* (1929) which described and sought to explain the distribution of a variety of social problems in the city of Chicago. Their study yielded a great deal of information about crime and delinquency, including the following:

> 1) Rates of truancy, delinquency and adult crime tend to vary inversely in proportion to the distance from the center of the city…2) Those communities which show the highest rates of delinquency also show, as a rule, the highest rates of truancy and adult crime…3) High rates occur in areas that are characterized by physical deterioration and declining populations…4) Relatively high rates have persisted in certain areas notwithstanding the fact that the composition of population has changed markedly…(1929: 198–204).

The observation that certain areas tended to keep high rates despite successive changes in the ethnic groups residing in them suggested that those problems were (a) generated by the social conditions experienced by these groups rather than by any genetic or biological predisposition and (b) by "traditions of crime and delinquency" that develop and are perpetuated through interaction among new and established members of social areas. Shaw and McKay argued that "when business and industry invade a community, the community thus invaded ceases to function effectively as a means of social control. Traditional norms and standards of the conventional community weaken and disappear. Resistance on the part of the community to delinquent and criminal behavior is low, and such behavior is tolerated and may even become accepted and approved." (1929). This was the same argument adopted by Sutherland. He argued that crime could become "systematic" (i.e., organized and enduring) when society was "un-organized" for its prevention.

Robert E. L. Farris (1948) extended the concept of social disorganization to explain "social pathologies" and social problems in general, including crime, suicide, mental illness, mob violence, and suicide. Defining organization as "definite and enduring patterns of complementary relations" (1955), he defined social disorganization as "the weakening or destruction of the relationships which hold together a social organization" (1955: 81). Such a concept was to be employed "objectively" as a measurable state of a social system, independent of personal approval or disapproval. When applied to crime, Farris' central proposition was that "A crime rate is … a reflection of the degree of disorganization of the control mechanisms in a society." In turn, crime also contributed to disorganization, a proposition that would be revived four decades later (See Bursik, 1988). Disorganization of such conventional mechanisms was especially likely in large, rapidly growing industrial cities where such disorganization "permits highly organized criminality" as well as less organized forms of group and individual crime and delinquency.

Social disorganization theory and the evidence cited as support for this type of theory generated considerable criticism. One line of criticism came from theorists advocating alternative perspectives that addressed the sources of motivation for crime. In *Delinquent Boys*, Albert Cohen challenged social disorganization theory on the grounds that "It is wholly negative. It accounts for the presence of delinquency by the absence of effective constraints" (1955: 33). Cohen argued that an adequate theory had to explain the presence of impulses or dispositions toward delinquency that were expressed when constraints were absent. Social disorganization theorists assumed that a high crime rates was a natural outcome when communal constraints were weak.

Robert Merton (1957) was critical of all perspectives that assumed high rates of deviance were a natural outcome when social control mechanisms broke down. He believed an adequate sociological theory had to address "how some social structures exert a definite pressure upon certain persons in the society to engage in nonconforming rather than conforming conduct" (1957: 132). In defense of theories that focus on the absence of constraints, Travis Hirschi (1973: 165) notes that this criticism is based on a nonscientific "procedural rule" in the sociology of deviance to the effect that an adequate theory has to address both why people break laws as well as why they do not. The criteria for scientifically adjudicating among competing theories are the degree to which they parsimoniously explain known facts and yield predictions that are confirmed. If an assumption survives theoretical competition, then there is nothing inherently wrong in making that assumption. In short, the merits of the criticism of social disorganization theory for slighting the issue of motivation, or societal pressures toward deviance, depends on the outcome of research proposing such pressures.

Another criticism raised by Cohen (1955) is that the neighborhoods or areas depicted as "socially disorganized" "are by no means lacking in social organization." Cohen argues that from the perspective of the people who live in an area there is "a vast and ramifying network of informal associations among like minded people" as opposed to "a horde of anonymous families and individuals." Acknowledging the "absence of community pressures and concerted action for the repression of delinquency," Cohen proposes that "defects in organization" should not be confused with "the absence of organization." Sutherland had been wary of this type of criticism and introduced the notion of "differential social organization" by his 1947 edition of *Principles of Criminology*. This theme is expressed in recent editions by noting that "social conditions in which the influences on the person are relatively inharmonious and inconsistent themselves constitute a kind of organization" (Sutherland, Cressey and Luckenbill 1992: 105). In *The Social Order of the Slum* (1968), Gerald Subtles introduced the concept of "ordered segmentation" to refer to the type of social organization that existed in the slum. That concept was intended to convey the notion that there was organization at some levels, but not at others, an idea elaborated in later years by Robert Bursik and Harold Grasmick (1993). Because the concept of "social disorganization" had negative connotations and could reflect observer bias in the depiction of social life, the concept was largely abandoned in sociology by the 1960s. It should be noted, however, that no one disputed the facts that there were differences in degrees and types of social organization among areas of cities and that these differences affected crime rates.

Another criticism of social disorganization theory was methodological. The value of the concept for explaining crime and delinquency was problematic because crime and delinquency were often cited as indexes of social disorganization. In *Toward an Understanding of Juvenile Delinquency*, Bernard Lander (1954) depicted delinquency as indicative of disorganization and attempted to explain it in terms of other dimensions of social disorganization. In their analysis of sources of variation in city crime rates, Schuessler and Slatin (1964) directly acknowledge that they "found it necessary to use the dependent variable" (i.e., crime) as "an index of the very condition in which the explanation is concerted to lie" (i.e., social disorganization). As Bursik notes in his review of social disorganization theory (1988), conceptual ambiguity in the definition of social disorganization was compounded by the lack of direct measures of variation in organization and disorganization. Social disorganization was inferred from a complex of related social problems in ecological areas and was used to explain specific problems as well.

Of ourse, the same issue can be raised with regard to other concepts referring to underlying criminogenic conditions such as strain, anomie, or cultural conflict. All such concepts were introduced as the underlying source of variations in crime with no direct measurement across ecological territories.

As there is generally some order to social life even when it is organized around illegal activities, the concept of social disorganization can be misleading, especially when taken to an extreme. Furthermore, the concept itself is vague and difficult to use in a noncircular fashion. Yet, the concept of social disorganization does tie together a variety of explanations of crime and delinquency that focus on the social conditions that affect conventional social institutions, as well as the bonds between people and those institutions. Moreover, some theorists have reintroduced the same central arguments using somewhat different terms to refer to the same causal processes at the ecological level. Crutchfield, Geerken, and Gove (1982) and Stark et al. (1983) hypothesize that the "social integration" of communities is inhibited by population turnover and report supporting evidence in the explanation of variation in crime rates among cities. The greater the mobility of the population in a city, the higher the crime rates. Similarly, Stark et al. (1983: 4–23) argue that population turnover is a satisfactory inferential measure of variation in social integration and provide supporting evidence based on states. The greater the proportion of a state's population that consists of newcomers or transients, the higher the crime rate. These arguments are identical to those proposed by social disorganization theorists and the evidence in support of it is as indirect as the evidence cited by social disorganization theorists. But, by referring to the positive end of a continuum (social integration rather than disintegration), such research has not generated the same degree of criticism as social disorganization theory. Shaw and McKay, Sutherland and Farris were referring to the same criminogenic circumstances as contemporary social integration theorists. However, it should be noted that the social integration theorists argue that the theory is more relevant to property crimes than to interpersonal violence. They attribute this difference to the "impulsive" nature of homicide and assault, but others (Jensen and Rojek, 1998) have argued that it may reflect the fact that homicide and assault involve people who know one another. Hence, population turnover might have different consequences for different crimes.

Ralph Taylor (2001) introduces yet another concept to encompass the positive end of a social organization–disorganization continuum—collective efficacy. He argues that social disorganization is high for a locale when residents do not get along with one another, do not belong to local organizations geared to the betterment of the community, hold different values about acceptable behavior on the street, and are unlikely to intervene when they encounter wrongdoing. In contrast, the opposite end of the continuum is "collective efficacy." When residents do get along, work through local organizations to better the community, and take steps to informally control trouble in their neighborhood, they are high in collective efficacy. Basically, collective efficacy refers to the same characteristics of residents of particular "locales" as the concept of social integration.

Research on social disorganization theory has focused on crime rates as reported in annual Uniform Crime Reports compiled by the Federal Bureau of Investigation, and the measures used to infer social disorganization were some form of census information on cities or areas of cities. Reliance on such data has been viewed as a major limitation for testing all theories that introduce some abstract, underlying social condition as a source of crime. The best solution to the problem is to collect data that allow more direct measurement of the underlying trait. One of the earliest studies to use other sources of data to test social disorganization theory was Robert Kapsis' (1978) study of self-reported as well as officially recorded delinquency in three neighborhoods that were at different stages of racial change or succession. Consistent with social disorganization theory, Kapsis found delinquency to be lowest in the most stable neighborhood and highest in the neighborhood undergoing racial change. A more recent study using self-reports (Simcha-Fagin and Schwartz, 1986) found residential stability and level of organizational participation in neighborhoods affected adolescent delinquent behavior as predicted by social disorganization theory as well.

In a study of "Community Structure and Crime," Robert Sampson and W. Byron Groves (1989) use data from the British Crime Survey for over 200 communities to measure self-reported criminal offending, criminal victimization, and social disorganization. They define the key mediating mechanisms in that type of theory as sparse local friendship networks, unsupervised teenage peer groups and low organizational participation. These mediating conditions are affected by low economic status, ethnic heterogeneity, residential mobility, family disruption, and urbanization. The key measures of community social disorganization were significant correlates of crime and delinquency and mediated "in large part" the impact of other measures of community structure. In 1991, E. Britt Paterson reached similar conclusions using interviews aggregated by neighborhood to measure victimization, residential instability, and neighborhood integration. Paterson concluded that the strongest evidence to emerge from his analysis was that the "non-economic" characteristics of neighborhoods (i.e., those most directly relevant to social disorganization theory) were the strongest correlates of crime. Hence, when research has addressed the criticisms based on prior research, the findings have been quite compatible with social disorganization theory.

Some of these new assessments of social disorganization theory have drawn on the notion of "social networks" as a more precise way of conceptualizing and measuring the organization or disorganization of communities. In 1983, Stark and his colleagues proposed that "Social integration ... can be effectively defined in terms of social networks" and in 1986, Marvin Krohn (1986) and William Freundenberg (1986) both proposed more specific attention to properties of social networks in the study of communities. Krohn proposed that high "network density," defined in terms of direct relationships among members of communities, facilitates informal social control, inhibiting crime and delinquency. Sampson and Groves linked this network terminology to conceptions of social organization and disorganization as "different ends of the same continuum with respect to systemic networks of community control" (1989). Concepts such as network density, social integration, and collective efficacy avoid the negative connotations that critics leveled at social disorganization theory, but the basic criminogenic process is the same.

In addition to the introduction of network terminology to more objectively specify measurable characteristics of neighborhoods or communities, more elaborate conceptions of social organization and disorganization have been proposed. Bursik and Grasmick (1993) differentiate among personal, parochial, and public "levels of social control." Personal social control is high when there are pervasive interpersonal ties among residents of an area or community. Such ties were central to Shaw and Mckay's formulation of social disorganization theory and are encompassed by the concept of network density. The parochial level of social control refers to relationships between the people in an area and social institutions such as the church, schools, and businesses. Interpersonal network ties might be strong even when relationships with social institutions are weak or strained. Finally, Bursik and Grasmick propose that there is a public level of control distinct from personal and parochial social control. When people lack influence with the government or the justice system, they are low in public control. This conception of the different ways in which people in an area can be organized or "disorganized" elaborates on Sutherland's notion of differential social organization and Suttle's conception of "ordered segmentation" (see above). The introduction of levels of social control or

levels of organization helps explain the emergence and persistence of gang problems in ecological settings characterized by residential stability and neighborhood ties.

Another line of research proposed by Bursik (1988: 542–543) is a consideration of the "reciprocal relationship" between crime and social disorganization. Farris proposed such a reciprocal connection in 1948, but research on the topic was not conducted until 40–50 years later. Wesley Skogan (1986) argues that high crime rates in a neighborhood causes fear among the residents, resulting in social disorganization as reflected in physical and psychological withdrawal, weakening of informal control mechanisms, a decline in organizational life, and deteriorating business conditions among other consequences. Most research has considered social disorganization to be the variable that explains crime and delinquency, but there are sound theoretical reasons to consider feedback loops between crime and social disorganization. A recent study by Marowitz et al. (2001) based on three waves of data from the British Crime Survey found support for this type of feedback loop in that decreases in neighborhood cohesion were found to increase crime, but increases in fear also undermined cohesion. Social disorder increases crime and crime increases disorder through its effect on fear of crime.

Because social disorganization theory focuses on the absence or breakdown of social control mechanisms, there are obvious links between disorganization theories and the brand of theory named "social control" theory. Social control theory as presented by Travis Hirschi in *Causes of Delinquency* (1969) was one of the dominant theoretical perspectives in the last three decades of the 20th century. Hirschi argued that variations in delinquent behavior among youth could be explained by variation in attachment to others, commitments to conventional goals, acceptance of conventional moral standards or beliefs, and involvement in conventional activities. These four were considered to be dimensions of the social bond and the greater the social bonds between a youth and society, the lower the odds of involvement in delinquency.

When social bonds to conventional role models, values, and institutions are aggregated for youth in a particular setting, they measure much the same phenomena as captured by concepts such as network ties or social integration. Indeed, in a comparison of theoretical traditions, Gary Jensen and Dean Rojek (1980) categorized social disorganization theory and social control theory together as a common macro–micro theory and outlined their shared contrasts with other perspectives. Social disorganization theory addresses ecological variations in crime addresses variable behavior among individuals. As expressed by Bursik

(1988), social disorganization theory is the "group-level analogue of control theory." Both social disorganization theory and social control theory focus on variations in barriers to crime and delinquency and the absence or breakdown of social institutions as correlates of crime and delinquency at either the ecological or individual level. This shared emphasis is reflected in the common criticism that they are "absence of something" theories. They both presume that crime is most probable when those institutions and control mechanisms that ordinarily function to reinforce conformity are weak or disrupted. Both focus on failures or inconsistencies in the socialization of the young as part of the underlying causal process when explaining delinquency, but disorganization theory highlights the ecological variables assumed to generate those inconsistencies and failures.

As noted above, one of the criticisms leveled at social disorganization theory is that it is an "absence of something" perspective, ignoring societal pressures (Merton) or motivational forces (Cohen), generating crime and delinquency. This criticism has been leveled at both social disorganization theory and social control theory. Both Merton and Cohen propose alternative theories that focus on driving forces rather than barriers. The societal pressure driving crime from Merton's perspective is a cultural value system, widely embraced by Americans, emphasizing the pursuit of economic success. When coupled with limited means for the full realization of such goals, the social system exerts pressures to adopt innovative ways of realizing those goals. Cohen challenges this "illicit means" theory and argues that it is frustration in the pursuit of the good opinions of conventional adults, especially teachers, that generates anger and frustration. A collective solution to status problems is rejection of the conventional system and its values, and formation of oppositional subcultures (contracultures). In such subcultures status is accorded for law breaking. As both Merton and Cohen focus on discrepancies between goals and prospects of realizing goals as the societal pressure (Merton) or source of individual motivation (Cohen) accounting for crime, their theories have been labeled "strain" theories.

Hirschi argues that there are striking contrasts between strain theories and social control theories, and similar contrasts can be noted for social disorganization and such theories. One contrast is the societal pressure toward crime proposed by Merton. In his illicit means theory, it is widely shared commitments to cultural goals, coupled with limits on full realization of such goals, that generates crime. In social disorganization and social control theories, the failure of conventional institutions to instill conventional values and norms is a cause of crime and delinquency.

This difference is a crucial difference in that strain theory introduces the successful learning of widely shared, culturally approved goals as part of the causal nexus generating crime whereas social disorganization or social control theories argue that it is the failure of institutions to instill shared values and establish social bonds that contributes to crime. There has been considerable research on this issue and, at present, no one has actually shown widely-shared aspirations to facilitate crime. Indeed, most research suggests that high aspirations and ambitions toward culturally approved goals inhibit crime (See Jensen and Rojek, 1998; Agnew, 2001).

Social disorganization theories can be contrasted with some cultural deviance theories as well, especially versions of cultural deviance theory that were advocated by theorists who specifically rejected social disorganization and strain theories. The most dramatic rejection of theories attributing crime to status problems or to the failure of conventional institutions was Walter Miller's "Lower Class Culture as a Generating Milieu of Gang Delinquency" (1958). Miller argued that high rates of crime among lower-class youth did not reflect failure to achieve middle-class goals, nor the absence or disorganization of communal life. Rather, crime reflected socialization into a "lower class culture" with values, norms, and beliefs encouraging behaviors that "automatically" violate "certain legal norms," or where illegal acts are the "'demanded' response to certain situations." Stated quite simply, "the dominant component of motivation of 'delinquent' behavior engaged in by members of lower class corner groups involves a positive effort to achieve status, conditions, or qualities valued within the actor's most significant milieu" (1958: 19).

This type of theory focuses on cultural or normative conflict as the macro condition generating crime. Because there are variable subcultural standards, behavior acceptable or tolerated in one context may be unacceptable in another. Because laws are likely to endorse the perspectives of the more advantaged citizens and to be enforced most rigidly when dealing with the disadvantaged, lower-class, and other disadvantaged categories of youth will experience the greatest conflicts with official authorities. However, within their own subcultural environment, they are quite normal products of successful, but subcultural, socialization. They are merely seeking status in terms of the standards characterizing their milieu. In fact, Miller proposes that lower-class gang youth "possess to an unusually high degree both the capacity and motivation to conform to perceived cultural norms." The delinquent is a conformist within a larger subcultural setting.

Hirschi's social control theory contrasts dramatically with Miller's cultural deviance theory in that

Hirschi argues that there are no sizeable subcultural milieus linked to social class where delinquency is either demanded or an automatic outcome of conformity to subcultural traditions. Not only do his survey data fail to reveal different values concerning the impropriety of law breaking among social classes, but youthful interaction with the people who should be perpetuating the traditions of their community (i.e., parents) is inversely related to delinquent behavior. Hirschi proposes that there is a common cultural disapproval of law breaking, but that youths learn the common culture to varying degrees. Those least socialized into that culture are the most likely to break laws.

Despite similarities between social control and social disorganization theories, it is not clear where social disorganization theorists stand on such cultural issues. Most contemporary social disorganization theorists focus on variables that inhibit the development of social networks, communal bonds, or effective social institutions. Early social disorganization theorists also addressed various forms of "cultural" disorganization, normative conflict, or cultural conflict, but are vague about the exact form that such cultural disorganization takes. In his 1939 edition of Principles of Criminology, Sutherland argued that "cultural conflict is a specific aspect of social disorganization and in that sense the two concepts are names for smaller and larger aspects of the same thing." He proposed "law-abiding culture was dominant," but he argued that Differential association is possible because society is composed of different groups with varied cultures (7). "These cultures varied in desirable ways, but they also varied "with reference to values which laws are designed to protect" (6). Mobility was the "universal and most significant element in the process of social disorganization" (1939: 77), but mobility also contributed to the emergence of "cultural conflict." At some points in his discussion the conflict of cultures is illustrated by questionable business practices and the subcultural values and norms that such practices reflect. At other points the focus is on conflicts reflected in the behavior of second-generation immigrants. At other points, it is conflicts generated by the imposition of external colonial control. In short, there were many ways in which culture could be disorganized, but Sutherland did not develop a clear definition that would allow a clear differentiation between social and cultural disorganization.

That ambiguity has not been resolved and is reflected in more recent treatments of the concept of social disorganization. According to Taylor, one of the characteristics of residents in socially disorganized locales is that they "hold different values about what is and is not acceptable behavior on the street" (2001). This characteristic is included together with other characteristics that clearly reflect social relationships and network ties among people. Although shared values should facilitate social integration, "values" and other cultural phenomena (norms and beliefs) are conceptually distinct from social relationships and should be treated as a distinct form of disorganization.

Discussions of the different ways in which the concept of culture has been introduced into the explanation of crime (see Yinger, 1960; Empey, 1967) suggest several distinct ways in which the system of values, norms, and beliefs can be "disorganized." A cultural system can be disorganized in the sense that there are conflicts among values, norms, and beliefs within a widely shared, dominant culture. Matza and Gresham Sykes (1961) propose that in addition to cultural prescriptions stressing the importance of obeying laws, there are widely shared "subterranean" cultural perspectives that encourage crime. While condemning crime in general, law-abiding citizens accord respect and admiration to the person who "pulls off the big con," takes risks and successfully engages in exciting, dangerous activities. Sykes and Matza (1957) also note that despite conventional admonitions prescribing conformity to the law, other cultural norms and beliefs convey the message that breaking the law is not so bad when the victim "had it coming," when those supporting the law are not morally pure themselves; when the offender believes he or she "had no choice"; when "no one was hurt"; or when the offense was motivated by social purposes more important than the law. Such beliefs, or "techniques of neutralization," are learned in quite conventional contexts and are reflected in legal codes as "extenuating circumstances." Thus, the culture shared by people in a society or locale can be "disorganized" in the sense that conflicting moral messages are built into the cultural system itself.

The depiction of a society as a collection of socially differentiated groups with distinct subcultural perspectives that lead some of these groups into conflict with the law is another form of cultural disorganization, typically called cultural conflict. There may be perfectly consistent messages conveyed within a given subculture, but they may conflict with the views of other subcultures. Thorsten Sellin (1938) outlined three ways in which such conflict could occur involving distinct cultural groups. Cultural conflict could occur when (1) groups with different standards overlap or interact in border regions, (2) laws of one group are extended to encompass others, and (3) distinct groups migrate into new territories. Whereas Sellin's conflicts involve culturally distinct groups, Walter Miller and others extend the conflict to distinctive, socially differentiated subcultures within a society as well. Taylor's view that residents of a locale are disorganized if they hold different values about acceptable behavior on the street reflects this subcultural view of conflict as well.

Among the theoretical challenges for criminology in the 21st century will be a more precise delineation among the many different forms of social disorganization that have been introduced in the revival of that theory and a more precise differentiation between social and cultural disorganization. Do concepts such as social integration and collective efficacy encompass distinct dimensions of social disorganization or do they refer to the exact same phenomena? How can cultural disorganization be measured and differentiated from social disorganization? Do they covary so strongly that independent effects on crime cannot be discerned? In addition to attention to conceptual and empirical issues, the unique explanatory power of this type of theory in competition with cultural deviance and structural strain theories will have to be addressed. Such a feat will require careful attention to the differences among abstract concepts such as anomie, strain, and disorganization and far more attention to the link between abstract concepts and empirical indicators than has characterized research thus far.

GARY JENSEN

### References and Further Reading

Akers, R.L. *Criminological Theories: Introduction, Evaluation, and Application.* 3rd ed. Los Angeles, CA: Roxbury Press, 2000.
Bursik, R.J., Jr. Social disorganization and theories of crime and delinquency. *Criminology* 26 (1988).
Bursik, R.J., Jr. and Grasmick, H.G. *Neighborhoods and Crime: The Dimensions of Effective Social Control.* New York, NY: Lexington Books, 1993.
Empey, L.T. Delinquency theory and recent research. *Journal of Research in Crime and Delinquency* 4 (1967).
Faris, R.E.L. *Social Disorganization.* 2nd ed. New York, NY: The Ronald Press Company, 1955.
Hirschi, T. *Causes of Delinquency.* Berkeley, CA: University of California Press, 1969.
Jensen, G.F. and Rojek, D.G. *Delinquency and Youth Crime,* 3rd ed. Prospect Heights, IL: Waveland Press, 1998.
Matza, D. *Delinquency and Drift.* New York, NY: John Wiley, 1964.
Matza, D. and Sykes, G.M. Juvenile delinquency and subterranean values. *American Sociological Review* 26 (1961).
Merton, R.K. *Social Theory and Social Structure.* New York, NY: Free Press, 1957.
Miller, W. Lower class culture as a generating milieu of gang delinquency. *Journal of Social Issues* 14 (1958).
Patterson, E.B. Poverty, income inequality, and community crime rates. *Criminology* 29 (1991).
Sampson, R.J. and Grove, W.B. Community structure and crime: Testing social disorganization theory. *American Journal of Sociology* 94 (1989).
Sellin, T. *Culture, Conflict and Crime.* New York, NY: Research Council, 1938.
Shaw, C., Zorbaugh, F., McKay, H.D. and Contrell, L.S. *Delinquency Areas.* Chicago, IL: University of Chicago Press, 1929.
Stark, R., Bridges, W.S., Crutchfield, R.D., Doyle, D.P. and Finke, R. Crime and delinquency in the roaring twenties. *Journal of Research in Crime and Delinquency* 20 (1983).
Sutherland, E.H. *Principles of Criminology.* Philadelphia, PA: J.B. Lippincott, 1939.
Taylor, R.B. The ecology of crime, fear, and delinquency: Social disorganization versus social efficacy. In Paternoster, R. and Bachman, R., (Eds.), *Explaining Criminals and Crime.* Los Angeles, CA: Roxbury Press, 2001, pp. 124–140.
Voss, H.L. and Petersen, D.M. *Ecology, Crime and Delinquency.* New York, NY: Appleton-Century-Crofts, 1971.

*See also* **Environmental Theory; Routine Activities Perspective; Sampson, Robert; Sutherland, Edwin**

# Social Learning Theory

Social learning theories of crime argue that individuals learn attitudes and motivations from individuals and groups whom they respect, that make them more likely to engage in delinquent and criminal behavior. Theorists ascribing to this argument generally define social learning as the habits, attitudes, behaviors, and knowledge that develop as a result of the reinforcements and punishments an individual encounters in his or her environment.

Social learning theory contains nine key concepts central to the explanation of criminal behavior. These concepts include: positive reinforcement, negative reinforcement, positive punishment, negative punishment, discriminative stimuli, schedules, differential association, and imitation (modeling). According to social learning theorists, reinforcement is any event that follows a behavior and alters and increases the frequency of a behavior. Positive reinforcers, or rewards, directly increase the occurrence of the behavior they follow (e.g., giving a treat to a child for cleaning his room). Negative reinforcers increase the frequency of a behavior by removing something negative from an environment (e.g., a child who behaves well has his number of chores reduced). Positive punishment involves introducing an aversive stimulus to decrease frequency of a behavior (e.g., spanking to stop a child's behavior). Negative punishment removes rewards that would have been provided had the good behavior continued (e.g., children do not get cookies because they did not clean their room). Discriminative stimuli are those internal and environmental stimuli that provide cues or signs for behavior. These cues help an individual determine when a behavior is likely to be reinforced. A schedule (in the context of social learning theory) refers to the probability and frequency with which a particular consequence will occur combined with the length of time between the behavior and its consequence. Consequences immediately following behaviors that have a high probability of occurring will have the strongest effect on an individual. In other words, the behaviors that are regularly reinforced immediately after they occur are those most likely to be repeated; those regularly punished immediately after they occur will be least likely to be repeated. Differential association is the process through which an individual is exposed to normative definitions either favorable or unfavorable to law-abiding behavior. According to social learning theorists, then, an individual learns to define a behavior as legal or illegal from those with whom he associates. Imitation (or modeling) occurs when an individual engages in a behavior after the observation of similar behavior by others. If the individual observes that another individual (the model) is rewarded for a behavior, then that individual is more likely to engage in that behavior.

Social learning theorists argue that individuals use these key concepts to structure their behavior. These theorists suggest that humans commit crime as a result of learning and socialization experiences with significant others. They further suggest that behavior can be modified through manipulation of rewards and punishments to reinforce law-abiding behavior and punish illegal activity.

Social learning theory can be traced historically to Tarde's laws of imitation that he proposed during the 19th century. Tarde suggested that individuals learned ideas through association with other ideas, and behaviors followed from those ideas. His first law stated that people imitate one another in proportion to the amount of close contact they have with one another. Thus, those individuals who come in close contact with others regularly will eventually begin to imitate their behaviors. His second law was that the inferior usually imitates the superior; thus, an individual who is lower in status will imitate an individual whose social status is higher. Finally, his third law stated that newer fashions displaced older ones; an example would be the growing popularity of cell phones that have led to the tremendous decrease in pay phones. His theory was the first attempt to describe criminal behavior in terms of learning instead of psychological or biological defects.

Another important theorist in the school of social learning was Edwin Sutherland. Most scholars suggest that social learning theory emerged as an attempt to expand and clarify differential association theory, which was originally proposed by Sutherland. Sutherland suggests that individuals learn criminal behavior through association, interaction, and communication with intimate others. Through this association, Sutherland suggests that individuals learn not only the techniques for committing criminal behavior, but also the definitions (attitudes, values, drives, and rationalizations) that support involvement in criminal behavior. Sutherland suggests that criminal behavior occurs when an individual has "an excess of definitions" favoring criminal behavior. Those associations that occur first (priority), most frequently (frequency), last longer (duration), and involve others whom the individual feels are important (intensity) will have the greatest effect in an individual's definition of behavior as good or bad. Thus, the theory of differential association does not emphasize the identity of one's associates as much as it emphasizes the importance of the definition of those associations. Thus, "differential association" suggests that individuals will either engage or refuse to engage in crime based on the definitions learned from their associates.

Most scholars suggest that there are really two major theories under the name of social learning theory. The first version was developed by C. Ray Jeffrey. Jeffrey published the first article that attempted to link criminal behavior with operant learning theory in the 1960s. Jeffrey suggested that individuals do not share common past experiences; as such, their conditioning histories are different. Because of this fact, some individuals have historically been punished for engaging in criminal behavior whereas others have been reinforced. Jeffrey suggested that most important forms or reinforcement are material (e.g., money, cars); as such, individuals engaging in crime did not need reinforcement from peers as the objects obtained through criminal behavior often served as reinforcers themselves. Thus, Jeffrey deemphasized the social nature of reinforcement originally suggested by Sutherland's differential association theory.

Although Jeffrey's ideas are important because they began the extension and reformulation of differential association, the social learning theory that has received the most widespread acceptance among criminologists was developed by Robert Burgess and Ronald Akers. Burgess and Akers fully reformulated the nine principles of Sutherland's differential association theory into a final version that have been labeled as the seven propositions of social learning theory. Whereas Burgess was involved with the original version, more recently, Akers has extended social learning theory into its present form in numerous articles and books. Akers argues that the social environment is the most important source of reinforcement for individuals and definitions of behavior as favorable or unfavorable are the most important concepts in his theory. Akers argues that once definitions or behavior are learned, they become a form of discriminative stimuli that provide cues about consequences to be expected from other behaviors.

Akers' version of social learning theory has seven key propositions that he delivers in his book, *Deviant Behavior: A Social Learning Approach*. A brief summary of the propositions is presented below:

1. *Deviant behavior is learned through operant conditioning.* Thus, individuals who receive reinforcement for deviant behavior are likely to engage in that deviant behavior again.
2. *Deviant behavior is learned in both nonsocial and social situations that are reinforcing or discriminating.* Thus, an individual may receive reinforcement from behaviors or attitudes of individuals whose opinion they value (social reinforcement) or from other physical rewards (nonsocial reinforcers).
3. *Learning of deviant behavior occurs in the groups that are the individual's major source of reinforcements.* Individuals that engage in deviance receive reinforcement for that behavior from those groups of individuals whose opinions they value the most, generally, deviant groups.
4. *Learning of deviant attitudes and techniques to engage in deviance and avoidance procedures based on those techniques, is a function of the reinforcers that individual receives from those aforementioned groups.*
5. *The types of behavior learned and their frequency of occurrence are based on the types of reinforcers the individual receives, and the deviant or nondeviant direction of the norms, rules, and definitions that accompany the reinforcement.* In other words, individuals who frequently receive reinforcers when they engage in deviance will engage in further deviance.
6. *The probability that a person will engage in deviant behavior is increased when the reinforcement they receive includes normative statements, definitions, and verbalizations that value deviant behavior over conformist behavior.* Thus, individuals who adapt the deviant norms, beliefs, and attitudes of their group are more likely to engage in deviant behavior in the future.
7. Those individuals who engage in deviance and receive greater amounts of reinforcement, more frequent reinforcements, and a high probability of reinforcement from groups whose opinion they value are more likely to continue in that deviant behavior.

Thus, Akers argues that people learn deviant behavior and the definitions, beliefs, and attitudes that go along with it through reinforcement. That learning can be both direct, through a conditioned response to reinforcement for deviant behavior, and indirect, through imitation or modeling.

Based on the postulates of Akers and the review of Jeffrey's social learning theory, Williams and McShane (1999) suggest that there are eight major points of social learning theory. First, they suggest that human behavior revolves around the quest for pleasure and the avoidance of pain. Second, they suggest that both reinforcement and punishment are important in learning behaviors; punishment decreases the frequency of a behavior whereas reinforcement increases the frequency. Third, they posit that social learning theory suggests that criminal behavior results from a learning process that is based on an individual's past and present experiences; individuals who receive both social and material reinforcements from deviance will learn deviant behavior. Fourth, social reinforcements are important both in learning deviant behavior and structuring the values that define behavior as acceptable or unacceptable. Additionally, these social definitions serve as cues that allow an individual to know whether a particular behavior will or will not be reinforced, and assist in the learning of crime as signals that either a reward or punishment is imminent. Next, criminal behavior is behavior that has been differentially reinforced through either social or material definitions. Finally, even when individuals do not receive social reinforcements for engagement in criminal behavior, the material reinforcement provided by the crime itself may be enough to cause that individual to engage in criminal behavior in the future.

Social learning theory emerged during the 1960s at a time when behavioral themes in psychology were at their peak of popularity. Psychologists believed that behaviors that had previously been untreatable could be treated successfully with behavior modification techniques. Additionally, schools were also using behavior modification in the classroom setting, and the corrections and juvenile justice system used a variety of behavior modification programs with success. It was within this backdrop that Jeffrey, a behavioral psychologist, and Burgess and Akers, sociologists who studied behavioral psychology, began their versions of social learning theory.

As mentioned earlier, social learning theory emerged as a combination of psychological learning and a reformulation and extension of differential association theory. Whereas Jeffrey suggests that reinforcement is at least in part biological, Akers suggests that reinforcement is social. Nevertheless, both Jeffrey and Akers suggest that social learning theory can be integrated well with other explanations of criminal behavior, whether biological, psychological, or sociological. In fact, Akers has written extensively about theory integration and the role of social learning in that integration, suggesting that social learning is the process through which criminal behavior is learned, whereas other key social variables comprise the structure that encourages or deters criminality in an individual.

Social learning theory has a number of important policy implications. Behavior modification programs, used widely in correctional settings throughout the world, find their foundation in social learning theory. These programs, which reward inmates or delinquents for conformist behavior and punish them for nonconformist behavior, are designed to move an individual from deviant to conformist behavior. As an individual is reinforced for conformist behavior, he or she is more likely to choose conformist behaviors at subsequent steps, until the deviant behavior that landed an individual in the correctional setting is replaced almost completely by conformist behavior. The results of these programs tend to be positive when the individual is engaged in the program, but tend to disappear when that individual leaves the environment where the program is delivered.

Another policy implication of social learning theory involves the impact of environmental design on crime. Social learning theorists suggest that the less likely an individual is to receive reinforcement for engaging in crime, the greater the chances that individual will engage in conformist behavior. Thus, making it difficult for an individual to commit a crime; and gaining the material rewards from that crime reduces the likelihood that an individual will engage in criminal behavior. This logic has brought about a number of structural changes in public settings designed to reduce crime (e.g., placing large bills in locked safes in convenience stores, placing convenience store cashiers in mesh cages) as business and government corporations have embraced this idea.

A final policy idea with its roots in social learning theory is school-based instruction programs such as law-related education and gang resistance education training that emphasize the importance of current conformist behavior and its relationship with future opportunities.

Social learning theory continues to be a popular explanation of criminal behavior, particularly among juveniles and Akers and several of his coauthors have used this theory successfully to explain a wide variety of criminal and delinquent behavior. Akers and others have regularly found that social learning variables explain at least as much deviant behavior as variables from other theories. Additionally, social learning theory is often used to integrate criminological theory, regularly combined with social control theory, labeling, and strain theory to explain delinquent behavior. In fact, Akers' most recent work attempts to develop a general theory of crime using social learning theory as the foundation and predicting criminal behavior based on the structural influences that mediate that behavior. Thus, it appears that social learning theory will be an important theoretical predictor of criminal behavior, whether in its present form or in some other, for several years to come.

DAVID C. MAY

### References and Further Reading

Akers, R.L., *Social Learning and Social Structure: A General Theory of Crime and Deviance,* Boston, MA: Northeastern University Press, 1998.
Akers, R.L., *Deviant Behavior: A Social Learning Approach,* 3rd ed., Belmont, CA: Wadsworth, 1985.
Akers, R.L., Krohn, M.D., Lanza-Kaduce, L. and Radosevich, M.J., Social learning and deviant behavior: A specific test of a general theory, *American Sociological Review,* 44, 1979.
Akers, R.L. and Lee, G., A longitudinal test of social learning theory: Adolescent smoking, *Journal of Drug Issues,* 26, 1996.
Bandura, A., *Social Learning Theory,* Englewood Cliffs, NJ: Prentice Hall, 1977.
Burgess, R.L. and Akers, R.L., A differential association-reinforcement theory of criminal behavior, *Social Problems,* 14, 1966.
Jeffrey, C.R., Criminal behavior and learning theory, *Journal of Criminal Law, Criminology, and Police Science,* 56, 1965.
Jeffrey, C.R., *Crime Prevention Through Environmental Design,* 2nd ed., Beverly Hills, CA: Sage, 1977.
Sutherland, E., *Principles of Criminology,* 4th ed., Philadelphia, PA: Lippincott, 1947.
Williams, F.P. and McShane, M.D., *Criminological Theory,* 3rd ed., Upper Saddle River, NJ: Prentice Hall, 1999.

*See also* **Akers, Ronald; Differential Association; Subcultural Theories**

# Social Support Theory

Social support theory is generally used by psychologists to explain the role of social support in health maintenance and disease prevention. For example, many studies show that individuals with friends and relatives who offer them psychological and material resources are healthier than those with few or no supportive significant others. Two models explain these trends: (1) the main- or direct-effect model and (2) the buffering model (Cohen and Wills, 1985). The main-effect model asserts that an increase in social support generates an increase in well-being regardless of whether people are under stress. In other words, well-being is related to the general benefits associated with a person's integration into large social networks. This argument has roots in early sociological work on deviant behavior, such as suicide. Emile Durkheim (1897) maintained that low levels of social integration may result in egoistic suicide.

The buffering model, on the other hand, contends that social support leads to well-being only for persons under stress. Social support, then, "buffers" or protects people from the negative effects of stressful life events, such as divorce and the death of a loved one. For example, many undergraduate students often experience a considerable amount of stress because they have difficulties paying their tuition and rent. Still, they can more easily deal with these problems if their parents lend or give them money. Thus, their parents protect or buffer them from the negative health consequences resulting from a specific type of stress.

Social support theory mainly deals with health issues and not with crime, although starting in the mid-1980s several Canadian theorists and researchers have demonstrated that this school of thought is directly relevant to the sociological and social psychological study of the physical, psychological, and sexual victimization of women in intimate heterosexual relationships. Consider Ellis and Wight's (1987) work on estrangement assault. Using quantitative data gathered in Toronto, Ontario, they found that the type of social support physically abused women received from lawyers influences the probability of being victimized after divorce or separation. For example, wives who were abused before separation and who consulted conciliatory lawyers were more likely to experience post-separation abuse than those who were counseled by adversarial lawyers. Lawyering, as a mode of social support, affects the victimization of battered women.

Beginning in the mid-1980s, several U.S. researchers also crafted studies to discern whether social support lessens the stressful effects of various forms of woman abuse, as well as other types of criminal victimization, such as burglary, larceny, and vandalism (e.g., Popeil and Susskind, 1985; Krause, 1986; Kaniasty and Norris, 1992). Applications of social support theory to criminal offending, however, are in short supply and much of the limited amount of work on this topic emphasizes only the preventative features of social support. For example, Cullen, Wright, and Chamlin (1999, 193) assert that "the logic of social support theory leads to the prediction that efforts to expand social support will result in less crime and other problem behaviors." However, some studies reveal that certain social support resources aimed at alleviating stress associated with marriage, cohabitation, and dating actually contribute to violent crime.

For this reason, DeKeseredy (1988a) constructed a male peer support theory of woman abuse. Briefly, he contends that many men experience various types of stress in intimate heterosexual relationships, ranging from sexual problems to threats to their patriarchal authority. Some men try to deal with these problems themselves, whereas others turn to their male friends for advice, guidance, and various other kinds of social support. Nevertheless, the social support they receive from their peers can, under certain conditions, encourage and legitimate the physical, sexual, and psychological abuse of women. For example, in DeKeseredy's (1988b) early empirical work, he found that for men with high levels of stress in their dating relationships, social ties with men who abuse their dating partners is strongly related to woman abuse in post-secondary school courtship. Canadian national representative sample survey data gathered and analyzed by DeKeseredy and Kelly (1993; 1995) also show that male peer support is an important predictor of woman abuse in college dating. These findings support Vaux's (1985, 102) argument that "social support may facilitate the resolution of problems or the management of distress, but there are no guarantees that such a resolution is free of cost."

Despite having empirical support, DeKeseredy's model focused mainly on individual factors. It tried to explain woman abuse while using only variables related to stress and social support. Quite a number of other related factors can influence whether a man abuses a woman, and this is why Schwartz and DeKeseredy (1997) added four more variables to the early model: the ideology of familial and courtship patriarchy, alcohol consumption, membership in formal social groups (e.g., fraternities), and the absence of deterrence. Although each of the individual elements has been tested, there has not yet been an empirical evaluation of the entire expanded model. Because of its complexity, it is highly unlikely that the entire model could be tested and therefore it has more value as a heuristic approach.

Can social support theory be applied to other types of crime? Future research will attempt to answer this question. Certainly, this perspective has informed calls for numerous crime control and prevention policies aimed at improving people's material conditions. Examples of such policy proposals are quality job creation programs and housing assistance. Many politicians, journalists, and members of the general public are sharply opposed to these initiatives, preferring punitive means of social control (e.g., incarceration). Much research shows that these conservative approaches do little, if anything, to lower crime rates. Thus, as Cullen et al. (1999, 204) remind us, effective and sensible responses to crime "must move beyond harsh sanctions and include public and private efforts to help others and build more supportive social arrangements."

WALTER S. DEKESEREDY

### References and Further Reading

Cohen, S. and Wills, T.A., Stress, social support, and the buffering hypothesis, *Psychological Bulletin* 98 (1985).

Cullen, F.T., Social support as an organizing concept for criminology: Presidential address to the academy of criminal justice sciences, *Justice Quarterly* 11, 4 (1994).

Cullen, F.T., Wright, J.P. and Chamlin, M.B., Social support and social reform: A progressive crime control agenda, *Crime and Delinquency* 45, 2 (1999).

DeKeseredy, W.S., Woman abuse in dating relationships: The relevance of social support theory, *Journal of Family Violence* 3, 1 (1988a).

DeKeseredy, W.S., *Woman Abuse in Dating Relationships: The Role of Male Peer Support,* Toronto. Canada: Canadian Scholars' Press, 1988b.

DeKeseredy, W.S. and Kelly, K., Woman abuse in university and college dating relationships: The contribution of the ideology of familial patriarchy, *Journal of Human Justice* 4, 2 (1993).

DeKeseredy, W.S. and Kelly, K., Sexual abuse in Canadian niversity and college dating relationships: The contribution of male peer support, *Journal of Family Violence* 10, 1 (1995).

Durkheim, E., *Le Suicide,* Paris: Alcan, 1897; as *Suicide,* Spaulding, J.A. and Simpson, G., (translated by), Glencoe, IL: The Free Press, 1951.

Ellis, D. and Wight, L., Postseparation woman abuse: The contribution of lawyers as "barracudas," "advocates," and "counsellors" *International Journal of Law and Psychology* 10, 401–410 (1987).

Kaniasty, K. and Norris, F.H., Social support and victims of crime: Matching event, support, and outcome, *American Journal of Community Psychology* 20, 2 (1992).

Krause, N., Social support, stress, and well-being among older adults, *Journal of Gerontology* 41 (1986).

Popiel, D.A. and Susskind, E.C., The impact of rape: Social support as a moderator of stress, *American Journal of Community Psychology* 13, 6 (1985).

Schwartz, M.D. and DeKeseredy, W.S., *Sexual Assault on the College Campus: The Role of Male Peer Support,* Thousand Oaks, CA: Sage, 1997.

Vaux, A., Variations in social support associated with gender, ethnicity, and age, *Journal of Social Issues* 41, 1 (1985).

*See also* **Family Relationships and Criminal Behavior**

---

# Sociological Theories of Criminal Behavior

---

Sociological theories argue that the social environment causes crime. Such theories describe those features of the social environment that cause crime and explain why these features cause crime. Some sociological theories seek to explain why some individuals are more likely to engage in crime than others (micro-level theories), whereas some seek to explain why certain groups have higher crime rates than other groups (macro-level theories). This entry provides a brief overview of the leading micro- and macro-level theories of crime, concluding with a brief discussion of efforts to integrate these theories with one another and with biological and psychological theories.

### Micro-Level Theories

Micro-level theories tend to focus on the immediate social environment of individuals, including their family, peer group, school, and work environments. The leading theories in this area are strain, social control, self-control, differential association, social learning, labeling, and rational choice theories (see the separate entries for these theories).

Micro-level strain theories argue that crime is more likely when individuals are treated in a negative or disliked manner by others. There are two general types of strain or negative treatment. The first occurs when others prevent you from achieving your goals. Strain theorists have focused on the failure of people to achieve goals like monetary success, status, and—for adolescents—autonomy from adults. It is commonly argued, for example, that many individuals—particularly lower-class and minority individuals—are prevented from achieving monetary success through legal channels. The second type of strain occurs when others take things you value or present you with negative or noxious stimuli. Strain theorists have focused on stressors such as child abuse and neglect; criminal victimization; negative relations with parents, teachers, and others; negative school experiences like failing grades; and a wide range of stressful life events, such as divorce and the death of family members and friends. These types of strain are said to make people feel bad; these bad feelings create pressure for corrective action. Some individuals may cope with their strain by turning to crime as a way to reduce or escape from their strain (e.g., running away from abusive parents, assaulting the peers who harass them), seeking revenge against those who have wronged them, or making themselves feel better through illicit drug use. Whether strained individuals turn to crime depends upon the influence of a number of factors. Crime is most likely among strained individuals who lack the resources and support to cope in a legal manner, who are low in social and self-control (see below), and who are disposed to crime.

Control theories focus on the restraints or controls that prevent people from engaging in crime, and argue that crime is most likely when these restraints are weak. According to control theorists, crime is often the most expedient way to get what we want. It is much easier, for example, to steal something than to work for it. Most people refrain from crime because of the restraints or controls placed on them. Social control theorists focus on several types of control. People high in direct control are in situations where others, like parents and teachers, set clear rules prohibiting crime, closely monitor their behavior, and consistently sanction rule violations. People with a high stake in conformity have a lot to lose by engaging in crime; crime may jeopardize their ties to others, like family members and friends, and threaten the heavy investments they have made in their education, career, and community. People high in internal control have been socialized to believe that crime is wrong or immoral.

Self-control theory focuses on the individual's personality traits, arguing that some individuals possess traits that make it difficult for them to restrain themselves from acting on their immediate impulses and desires. Such traits include impulsivity, irritability, risk-taking, short-sightedness, and insensitivity to others. Individuals low in social and self-control have fewer restraints on their behavior and so are more likely to turn to crime to satisfy their needs and desires.

Differential association and social learning theory argue that individuals learn to engage in crime from others, especially intimate others like family members and friends. Social learning theory represents an extension of differential association theory in that it more precisely specifies the mechanisms by which people learn to engage in crime. Others may teach us to engage in crime by modeling crime for us, teaching us beliefs conducive to crime, and reinforcing our criminal behavior. Data, for example, suggest that some parents inadvertently reinforce aggressive behavior by giving in to the demands of their aggressive children (e.g., responding to a temper tantrum by giving the child the candy he wants). And much data suggest that associating with delinquent peers is one of the best predictors of crime. This is partly because such peers reinforce crime (often with expressions of approval) model crime, and foster beliefs conducive to crime. These beliefs seldom involve the unconditional approval of crime; rather, crime is defined as justifiable or excusable under certain conditions. For example, they define violence as a justifiable response to a wide range of provocations—including provocations that many would consider trivial (see Neutralization or Drift).

Labeling theory makes a very provocative argument, claiming that the efforts of the police and others to control crime often have the effect of increasing crime. According to labeling theory, the act of arresting and punishing people often increases their strain (e.g., makes it difficult to secure a legitimate job), isolates them from conventional others, and leads them to associate with criminal others. All of these effects increase the likelihood of further crime. The evidence on labeling theory is mixed, and there have been some recent efforts to revise the theory. Braithwaite's (1989) theory of reintegrative shaming, for example, argues that labeling increases crime when no effort is made to reintegrate offenders back into conventional society, but labeling reduces crimes when an effort is made to forgive and reintegrate offenders after punishment.

The above theories focus on those factors that create a general predisposition for crime. But criminologists recognize that predisposed people only engage in crime when there are opportunities to do so. Rational choice and routine activities theories have devoted the greatest attention to those situational factors that increase the likelihood of crime. Routine activities theory argues that crime is most likely when motivated offenders encounter attractive targets in the absence of capable guardians. The likelihood that a crime will take place is influenced by our everyday or routine activities, like going to work and socializing with friends. For example, individuals who go out a lot at night are more likely to encounter motivated offenders. Also, their homes are more often left unprotected. Rational choice theory also devotes much attention to those situational factors conducive to crime, arguing that are a range of factors influence the perceived costs and benefits of crime in a particular situation.

## Macro-Level Theories

Several additional theories seek to explain why some groups have higher rates of crime than other groups. The most prominent of these theories are social disorganization theory, subcultural crime theory, strain or anomie theory, and versions of critical, radical, and feminist theories. These theories focus less on the immediate environment of individuals and more on the characteristics of groups, like communities and societies. At the same time, such theories frequently draw on the micro-level theories listed above to explain why group characteristics affect crime rates.

Social disorganization theory focuses on why some communities have higher crime rates than others. This theory draws heavily on social control theory, and argues that community characteristics like economic deprivation, high rates of residential mobility, high rates of family disruption (divorce, single-parent families), and high levels of multiunit housing like apartments increase crime rates by reducing social control in the community. Such characteristics, in particular, reduce the ability and willingness of community residents to exercise direct control, to provide youth with a stake in conformity, and to socialize youth so that they condemn delinquency.

Subcultural crime theory argues that some groups have higher crime rates than others because they hold values or norms conducive to crime. The higher rate of homicide in the South, for example, has been explained by arguing that Southerners are more likely to approve of violence in certain situations. Anomie theories (micro-level variations of strain arguments) typically claim that the cultural and structural characteristics of some groups foster strain and sometimes reduced social control. Merton's (1938) anomie theory, for example, argues that the cultural system in the U.S. encourages everyone to strive for the goals of monetary success, but places little emphasis on the legitimate rules for achieving such success—thus reducing internal

control. Further, the stratification system prevents many lower-class and minority group members from achieving such success through legal channels—thus increasing strain.

Critical and radical theories explain group and societal differences in crime in terms of power differentials, particularly those linked to class position. Some groups in society—like the capitalist class—have more power than other groups. These groups frequently use their power to protect and enhance their privileged position. Among other things, they use their power to influence what acts do and do not get defined as crimes and how the criminal law is enforced. The capitalist class, for example, tries to ensure that the harmful acts it commits are not defined as crimes (e.g., environmental pollution, unsafe working conditions) and that the criminal law is applied most vigorously against the working class and poor. Workers and poor people frequently engage in acts defined as crimes because they have little stake in conformity, they have difficulty obtaining money and other goods through legal channels, and the capitalist system has reduced their concern for the well-being of others.

Feminist theories point to the neglect of gender in most crime theories, even though gender is one of the most important variables distinguishing criminals from noncriminals. Although many versions of feminist theory exist, the relatively lower involvement of females in crime is often explained in terms of gender differences in social learning and control. For example, females are socialized to be passive and males to be aggressive; the lives of females are closely regulated whereas males are given much freedom. The female crime that does occur is often explained in terms of the oppression females experience; for example, the abuse of females often leads them to run away from home and to engage in crimes like theft and prostitution in order to survive on the street.

## Conclusion

As is apparent, there are a good many sociological theories. New theories continue to be developed, and criminologists continue to apply existing theories to new areas. Much attention has focused on the explanation of offending patterns over the life course. There have also been several efforts to combine two or more of the above theories. And most recently, there has been much discussion about how sociological theories might be combined with biological and psychological theories. The social environment affects both biological factors (e.g., head injury, exposure to toxic substances) and psychological traits; likewise, biological and psychological factors affect the social environment (e.g., individuals with traits like impulsivity and irritability tend to elicit negative reactions from others and select themselves into negative social environments, like bad marriages and bad jobs). Further, biological, psychological, and sociological factors likely interact with one another in their effect on crime, so that crime is most likely when individuals with certain biological and psychological traits encounter negative social environments. Although integrated theories of this type are in their infancy, it has become increasingly clear that any comprehensive explanation of crime must draw from a variety of disciplines.

ROBERT AGNEW

### References and Further Reading

Akers, R.L, *Criminological Theories,* Los Angeles, CA: Roxbury, 2000.

Braithwaite, J., *Crime, Shame, and Reintegration,* Cambridge, U.K.: Cambridge University Press, 1989.

Cullen, F.T. and Agnew, R. (Eds.), *Criminological Theory: Past to Present,* Los Angeles, CA: Roxbury, 1999.

Merton, R.K., Social structure and anomie, *American Sociological Review* 3 (1938).

Paternoster, R. and Bachman, R., (Eds.), *Explaining Criminals and Crime,* Los Angeles, CA: Roxbury, 2001.

Simpson, S.S., (Ed.), *Of Crime and Criminality,* Thousand Oaks, CA: Pine Forge, 2000.

Vold, G.B., Bernard, T.J. and Snipes, J.B., *Theoretical Criminology,* New York, NY: Oxford University Press, 1998.

*See also* **Feminist Theories of Criminal Behavior; Life-Course and Developmental Theories of Criminal Behavior; Radical Theories of Criminal Behavior; Rational Choice Perspective; Routine Activities Theory; Self-Control Theory; Social Control Theories of Criminal Behavior; Social Disorganization Theory; Strain Theories: From Durkheim to Merton; Strain Theories: Recent Developments; Subcultural Theories of Criminal Behavior**

# Solicitation to Commit Crime

## Introduction or Definition

Although criminal law primarily punishes offenses that have been carried out, there are some activities which, even though not consummated, are deemed dangerous enough for the law to impose criminal responsibility. These offenses known as "inchoate," "uncompleted," or "anticipatory" offenses comprise attempt, conspiracy, and solicitation.

The crime of solicitation has long been recognized in common law (*Rex v. Higgins,* 102 Eng. Rep 269, 1801), as well as in the statutes of the different jurisdictions in the U.S.

As defined in section 5.02 of the Model Penal Code:

A person is guilty of solicitation to commit a crime if with the purpose of promoting or facilitating its commission he commands, encourages or requests another person to engage in specific conduct that would constitute such crime or an attempt to commit such crime or would establish his complicity in its commission or attempted commission.

The federal government of the U.S. also has statutes that address inchoate offenses. Senate Bill (Criminal Code Reform Bill), 1437 of 1979 (which has since been revised (see endnotes)), replaced "a patchwork of various attempt, conspiracy, and solicitation statutes with comprehensive formulations applicable to all federal offenses" (George Washington Law Review, 1979, 550). According to s. 373 (a) of the 1986 Amendment to the Bill, a solicitor is one who "with intent that another person engage in conduct constituting a felony ... and under circumstances strongly corroborative of that intent, solicits, commands, induces, or otherwise endeavors to persuade such other person..."

## Elements of Solicitation

A person who enlists, orders, entices, directs, persuades, importunes, another person to commit a crime is guilty of solicitation. It is irrelevant that the crime has not yet been carried out, or is not carried out, the solicitor who manifests a criminal intent by instigating a crime is still culpable. In *State v. Furr* (292 N.C. 711, 235 S.E. 2d 193 1977), for instance, the defendant was found guilty of three counts of soliciting the murder of his wife and two others. Even though those solicited never carried out the murders, the court in finding the defendant guilty stated:

Solicitation of another to commit a felony is a crime in North Carolina, even though the solicitation is of no effect and the crime solicited is never committed. The gravamen of the offense of soliciting lies in counseling, enticing or inducing another to commit a crime.

As held in *U.S. v. Korab*, C.A.9 (Ariz.) 1989, 893 F.2d 212 1989, "federal solicitation statute requires a finding, not that a federal offense resulted from the solicitation, but that the defendant intended that acts constituting a federal offense result."

It is also irrelevant that a missive enlisting another's help never reaches its intended recipient (s. 5.02 (2) of the Model Penal Code). The crime of solicitation is complete when the requisite *mens rea* is manifested through a tacit communication of an inducement for another to commit a crime. As the court strenuously concluded in *State v. Schleifer* (99 Conn. 432 121 A. 805, 1923), it is not so much the danger of the communicated message reaching the addressee, rather, it is the resolve of a dangerous person striving to recruit someone to carry out a nefarious act that makes it necessary to punish a solicitor even though the solicited did not receive the message.

Some states however, require the establishment of a communication between the solicitor and the person solicited in order for the crime of solicitation to be complete. A request that fails to reach an intended recipient in some jurisdictions is considered an attempted solicitation. In *State v. Lee*, 804 P.2d 1208 (Or.Ct.App. 1991), the appellant's conviction for solicitation to commit robbery was reversed and the case remanded for resentencing because the appellant successfully argued that a letter which contained his solicited message was never delivered to the intended recipient, hence he could only be guilty of attempted solicitation. The Oregon appellate court stated that "a completed communication is required to prove the crime of solicitation." Short of that, the court agreed that defendant could only be sentenced for attempted solicitation.

In federal cases, even circumstantial evidence may be used to convict a solicitor as long as there is sufficient information from which inferences about the defendant's guilt can be inferred. Thus, in *U.S. v. McNeill*, C.A.3 (Pa.) 1989, 887 F.2d 448, the court was able to secure a conviction for the defendant based on circumstantial evidence of letters allegedly typewritten by defendant (an inmate), to a person out in the community requesting the addressee to inflict bodily harm on defendant's brother-in-law, and to kill the defendant's probation officer. The fact that the defendant's brother-in-law was described in detail, and the typewriter had been consistently in the defendant's possession, and had similar letter characteristics as the one deemed to have produced the letter, provided grounds weighty enough to convict the defendant for criminal solicitation.

In some jurisdictions, the requested crime has to be a felony or a serious misdemeanor for the request to amount to a crime of solicitation. Federal courts require the crime to be a felony. Further, a solicitor can direct his or her criminal communication to an individual or to a group of people. A factual impossibility that precludes a crime from happening (as for instance, when the solicited person is a law enforcement officer), does not negate blameworthiness. As stated in *State v. Keen*, 25 N.C. App. 567, 214 S.E. 2d 242 (1975), "The crime of solicitation…is complete… even though there could never have been an acquiescence in the scheme by the one solicited." According to section 373(c) of the 1986 Federal Criminal Code Reform Bill, it is not a defense to a charge of solicitation simply because the solicited person "lacked the state of mind required for its commission, because he was incompetent or irresponsible, or because he is immune from prosecution or is not subject to prosecution."

Even though solicitation hinges on words, courts are reluctant to consider passive statements void of any inducements tantamount to solicitation. Sometimes however, it is a crime of solicitation even though the words uttered do not provide any incentives for the solicited person to commit a crime. It only suffices that the solicitor intends the request to be complied to. Hence, if a burglar who is avoiding detection and arrest by law enforcement officers requests his friend to assist him in his escape by giving him a ride to another state where he intends to take refuge, the burglar is guilty of requesting a friend to aid and abet his escape. Those words that encourage the crime of aiding and abetting form the *actus reus* of solicitation (see Samaha, 2002, 204–205).

## Reasons for Punishing Crimes of Solicitation

A reason for punishing those who solicit crimes as stated in the comments to s. 5.02 (365–366) of the Model Penal Code is that: "Purposeful solicitation presents dangers calling for preventive intervention and is sufficiently indicative of a disposition towards criminal activity to call for liability."

Accordingly, the following three rationales are given: first, it is necessary that law enforcement steps in to prevent the occurrence of a crime before it occurs. Second, because of the increased danger in group participation, it is necessary that persons intent on recruiting others in a criminal venture be sanctioned. Third, for the sake of justice it is necessary that the solicitor whose scheme fails mainly because of an extraneous factor not escape responsibility. According to the comments to Article 5, 24–26 (Tent. Draft No. 10. 1960), of the Model Penal Code:

> when the actor's failure to commit the substantive offense is due to a fortuity, as . . . when the expected response to solicitation is withheld, his exculpation

on that ground would involve inequality of treatment that would shock the common sense of justice. Such a situation is unthinkable in any mature system designed to serve the proper goals of penal law.

## Defense

According to s. 5.02 (3) of the Model Penal Code, a solicitor can use the defense of voluntary renunciation to exculpate himself or herself of charges of solicitation if the solicitor does everything possible to retract the inducement, and to prevent the commission of the crime. The solicitor must prevent "the commission of the crime, under circumstances manifesting a complete and voluntary renunciation of his criminal purpose." It follows that in order to be considered voluntary renunciation, the solicitant must establish communication with the person solicited, make an affirmative withdrawal of any enticements, and finally take measures to forestall the commission of the crime.

Some states have slightly different requirements for the defense. Arizona, for instance, requires that the solicitor makes known to the solicitee his renunciation, and give law enforcement officers prompt warning, or make "reasonable efforts" to prevent the crime from happening (Ariz. Rev. Stat., Section 13–1005 (B) (1996).

The federal government also recognizes the defense of voluntary renunciation as long as the renunciation is "voluntary and complete," and not "motivated in whole or in part by a decision to postpone the commission of a crime until another time or to substitute another victim or another but similar objective" (s. 373(b)).

## Issues

There is a debate as to whether the crime of solicitation is dangerous enough to warrant strict attention by the criminal justice system. Proponents for strict attention contend that because it generates group participation, and because solicitors may use insidious means to recruit others (even those who ordinarily may lack the requisite intrepid to engage in criminal activities), it is necessary for solicitors to be held accountable for their actions (Dix and Sharlot, 1999; Samaha, 2002).

On the other hand, opponents against strict enforcement argue that because the solicited person can always decide against carrying out the crime, it is not necessary that too much attention be paid to solicitors. Moreover, by asking others to carry out crimes for them, solicitors in effect are reluctant to carry out crimes themselves (Dix and Sharlot, 1999; Samaha, 2002).

It is also argued that by punishing solicitors who have merely uttered words eliciting another to carry out an act, government might be trampling on the free speech of the solicitor in violation of the First Amendment to the U.S. Constitution (Dix and Sharlot, 1999, 348).

According to Dix and Sharlot (1999, 348), safeguards are in place to ascertain that solicitation statutes do not encompass constitutionally protected speech. In that regard as they contend, many state statutes criminalize only severe felonies. Further, some states require that there be some corroboration by another person or through some other circumstances that confirms the solicitation (California Penal Code s. 653f, Colorado Revised Statutes s. 18-2-302(1)).

VICTORIA TIME

## References and Further Reading

Arizona Revised Statute (1996). Section 13–1005 (B).
Dix, G. and Sharlot, M. (1999). *Criminal Law,* 4th ed., Belmont, CA: Wadsworth.
*George Washington Law Review,* Criminal Attempt, Conspiracy, and Solicitation under the Criminal Code Reform Bill of 1978 (From Reform of the Federal Criminal Code-Symposium, 1979—See NCJ—64754), Vol. 47, Issue 3, March 1979, pp. 550–572.
Samaha, J. (2002). *Criminal Law,* 7th ed., Australia, Canada: Wadsworth.

*See also* **Attempts and Incomplete Offenses; Conspiracy to Commit Crime**

# South Africa, Crime and Justice in

## Orientation

South Africa is a multicultural society with 11 official languages and an estimated population of 43,647,658 people, of whom 32% are younger than 15 years of age. Persons of color (African, "coloured" and Asian) constitute about 86% of the population and whites about 14% (CIA World Factbook, 2003).

Expectations that crime, and especially violent crime, would decrease after South Africa's first democratic elections in 1994 did not materialize (Schönteich and Louw, 2001, 1–15). With the launch of the National Crime Prevention Strategy in 1996, (then) Executive Deputy President Thabo Mbeki stressed that the policy formed part of the government's endeavors "to eradicate the unacceptable levels of crime..." (Media Statement, May 22, 1996). Although official accounts of crime stabilized in 1995 and 1996, the overall number of recorded crimes in 1999 was greater than in any year after 1994. This trend continued until May 2000 when the Minister of Safety and Security placed a moratorium on crime statistics. There are some indications to suggest that officially recorded crime rates may since be stabilizing.

It would be difficult to appreciate the challenges and intricacies underlying an analysis of factors pertaining to any discussion on crime and justice in South Africa without contextualizing its position in southern or sub-Sahara Africa—especially as a member of the Southern African Development Community (SADC). The founding principles of the SADC, similar to that of the African Union (AU), are the sovereign equality of all member states; solidarity, peace, and security; human rights, democracy, and the rule of law; equity, balance, and mutual benefit, and the peaceful settlement of disputes (http://www.sadc.int/index.php, 2003; Department of Foreign Affairs, Republic of South Africa, 2002, 1, 4).

Despite these noble goals, several challenges dominate the sub-Sahara region and the context in which South Africa is situated. Factors universally regarded as crime precipitants are associated with demographic variables such as economic strain and deprivation, substance abuse, administrative and judicial subversion, and serve as interactive and inhibiting factors in creating a deprivation trap of poverty, social vulnerability, powerlessness, and frequent victimization. It is therefore not strange that the Southern African region has been characterized by political instability, internal conflict, and liberation struggles for decades. In many cases, unrest still prevails in most of the countries comprising the SADC (Naudé and Prinsloo, 2002, 81–83, 85).

South Africa is the dominant economic force in Africa, generating almost one third of the continent's production. For instance, South Africa contributed 80% of the SADC's economic production in 1995 (Naudé and Prinsloo, 2002, 81–83, 85). The relative economic opportunities presented by the South African economy amid a high rate of social and economic distress in the region, is but one factor imposing an overrepresentation of mostly uneducated young people on the South Africa's financial and social resources. Almost 50% of the population in the region is under the age of 24. Most offenders seem to fall within the age group 15–35 years with the highest peak between the ages of 15 and 24 years, who are physically strong, daring, seek immediate satisfaction of their needs, and are more exposed to opportunities for committing crime (Pelser and De Kock, 2000, 86; Naudé and Prinsloo, 2002, 81–83, 85). Schönteich (Prinsloo and Naudé, 2000, 42) established that 2283 out of every 100,000 South African males aged 18–20 years were convicted for crime in 1995–96 while 42 out of every 100,000 were convicted of murder and 109 for robbery. Sega, Pelo, and Rampa (Prinsloo and Naudé, 2000, 42) confirm that young men from poor areas are responsible for a large proportion of violent crimes in South Africa. Young persons involved in crime indicated broken homes and poverty as two major factors that precipitated their involvement in crime. However, a small number of young offenders also admitted that the abovementioned factors were of secondary significance as "push factors" and that notions of "manhood" and "peer (gang) pressure" were the main reasons for their involvement in street and violent crime. Age-old institutions and traditional rituals that once governed young boys' entry into adult life have been replaced by rites of passage that are often brutal and deadly. The abovementioned is furthermore precipitated by a high rate of urbanization in Southern Africa, which is almost seven times higher than the average of industrialized countries, coupled with large-scale, socioeconomic, and political transition. Young persons from as far as Nigeria, Morocco, Europe, and China recently flocked to South African cities where it is estimated that at least 6 million undocumented immigrants live mainly in South African cities (Pelser and De Kock, 2000, 86). The people who migrate to urban areas are predominantly persons between the ages of 18–30 years. In the cities they encounter massive unemployment without any basic and social support networks. New arrivals to cities are soon to be drawn into the youth subcultures characteristic of cities that may motivate a person to become involved in criminal and gang activities (Crime Information Analysis Centre (CIAC), 1999; Pelser and De Kock, 2000, 86).

The above mentioned urbanization trends impact negatively on the South African labor market. According to Statistics South Africa (http://business.iafrica.com/news/919537.htm) the unemployment rate approached 30% (29.5%) in September 2001 showing a significant rise compared to 26.4% in February 2001, and 25.8% in September 2000. In February 2000, the reported unemployment rate was 22.5%.

As a result of the many liberation struggles and civil wars in the region, a large number of legal and illegal weapons are readily available. For example, it was estimated that there were 6 million AK-47s in circulation in Mozambique, many of which found there way to South Africa (Prinsloo and Naudé, 2000, 44).

AIDS further poses a serious problem. The average life expectancy of South Africans has decreased by 10 years from the age of 65–55 in the past 4 years and may even decline to 41 by the end of the decade (McGreal, 2001). UNAIDS estimates that approximately 12.9% of the adult population is AIDS positive and it is expected that South Africa will see a decline in its Human Development Index (HDI) over the next few years (Barnett and Whiteside, 1999). According to UNAIDS, South Africa's economy will be 17% smaller as a result of AIDS in 2010, by which date the disease will have cost South Africa about U.S. $22 billion. The Medical Research Council (MRC) predicted in 2001 that the number of AIDS deaths can be expected to grow within the next 10 years to more than double the number of deaths owing to all other causes, resulting in 5–7 million cumulative AIDS deaths by 2010 (McGreal, 2001). The Government rejected however the MRC's report as unreliable propaganda that greatly exaggerated the rates of HIV transmission and that AIDS is only responsible for a fraction of deaths among South Africans (McGreal, 2001).

Alcohol and drug abuse by both the offender and the victim is generally a high crime risk factor that is expected to intensify and perpetuate antisocial behavior. A South African study found that 77% arrested burglars, 53% robbers, 52% murderers, and 47% rapists tested positive for the use of at least one drug (Louw, 1999). The results of an empirical study conducted in South Africa in 1996 by Rocha-Silva and Stahmer (1997) revealed that alcohol was taken in large quantities by offenders during their prearrest history, cannabis and Mandrax were frequently used, whereas the use of LSD, cocaine, and heroin seemed to be greater among the offender population than the comparable general population.

## The South African Crime Profile

The recent history of South African crime statistics is fraught with controversy. The Minister of Safety and Security placed a moratorium on all police crime statistics in May 2000 to overhaul the crime information system that was regarded as unreliable for planning and crime prevention purposes. The latest available crime statistics provided by the Crime Information Analysis Centre (CIAC) following the lifting of the moratorium (see http://www.saps.org.za/8_crimeinfo/200112/report.htm, 2003) are reflected in Table 1.

**Table 1.** The Crime Profile of the Republic of South Africa: Representative Percentages of Cases Reported, January–September 2001

| Crime Category | % |
|---|---|
| Murder | 0.8 |
| Attempted murder | 1.1 |
| Robbery with aggravating circumstances | 4.8 |
| Rape | 2.0 |
| Assault GBS (serious) | 10.2 |
| Common assault | 9.9 |
| Housebreaking—residential | 12.1 |
| Housebreaking—business | 3.6 |
| Other robbery | 3.6 |
| Stock theft | 1.7 |
| Shoplifting | 2.7 |
| Theft—motor vehicle | 4.0 |
| Theft—out of or from vehicles | 8.2 |
| Other thefts | 23.1 |
| Commercial crime | 2.5 |
| Arson | 0.4 |
| Malicious damage to property | 5.6 |
| Illegal possession of firearms | 0.6 |
| Drug related crime | 2.0 |
| Driving under the influence of alcohol or drugs | 1.0 |
| Total | 100.0 |

Broadly speaking, the South African crime profile comprises approximately 12.3% very serious crimes against the person (murder, rape, and robbery), 20.1% violent crimes against the person (assault), and 67.5% property related crimes, commercial crime, and crime generated by police action. Comparative (Interpol) crime results, and bearing the usual criticism against such an approach in mind, suggest that South Africa measures unacceptably high with regard to violence (murder, rape, robbery, and assault), whereas South Africa rates quite average as far as property and commercial crime are concerned.

Table 1 indicates that (other or unspecified) theft in general (23%), assault (20%), and housebreaking (16%) account for nearly 60% of all serious crime in the RSA. An analysis of assault cases suggests that most cases take place in the domestic environment and seem to be closely associated with drug (alcohol) abuse. A close association furthermore seems to exist between assault and malicious damage to property. Furthermore, repeated victimization seems to be precipitated by alcohol abuse within long-term abusive relationships. Housebreaking (16%) is believed to be motivated by "need and greed" arising from exceptionally high levels of unemployment, the existence of an illegitimate market and organized groups (http://www.saps.org.za/8_crimeinfo/200112/report.htm, 2003).

Both aggravating as well as "common" robbery contribute 8.4% of the total incidence of reported serious crime. Analysts of the Crime Intelligence Analysis Centre (http://www.saps.org.za/8_crimeinfo/200112/report.htm, 2003) stress that a distinction should be drawn between the more organized and sophisticated robberies such as bank robberies, robberies of cash in transit, hijackings of motor vehicles on the one hand and robberies committed by loosely knit small groups of armed youth who rob people at random of cellular phones, firearms, jewelry, money, etc., on the streets and at their residences. As already indicated, the very serious violent crimes against the person (murder, rape, and robbery) represent 12.3% of all reported serious crime, which ranks South Africa very high as far as these crimes are concerned compared to 90 other Interpol member countries (CIAC) (see http://www.saps.org.za/8_crimeinfo/200112/report.htm, 2003).

Table 2 indicates that murder in South Africa seems to be decreasing since 1994. Although more volatile, the attempted murder trend also seems to be stabilizing. After an initial decline, aggravated robbery increased to extreme levels since 1998. "Common" robbery also

**Table 2.** A Comparison of the 1994–2001 January–September Increase or Decrease in the Crime Ratios (Rounded Off) Per 100,000 of the Population (Based on 1996 Census Results) Related to Specific Crime Categories

| Crime Categories | 1994 | 1995 | 1996 | 1997 | 1998 | 1999 | 2000 | 2001 |
|---|---|---|---|---|---|---|---|---|
| Violent Crimes | | | | | | | | |
| Murder | 51 | 49 | 46 | 43 | 42 | 40 | 35 | 33 |
| Attempted murder | 52 | 49 | 52 | 50 | 51 | 48 | 46 | 47 |
| Robbery with aggravating circumstances | 163 | 153 | 125 | 122 | 151 | 164 | 180 | 194 |
| Social Fabric Crimes | | | | | | | | |
| Rape | 76 | 84 | 90 | 92 | 83 | 84 | 85 | 84 |
| Assault (serious) | 382 | 394 | 403 | 405 | 391 | 411 | 437 | 418 |
| Assault common | 355 | 374 | 370 | 357 | 339 | 360 | 410 | 403 |
| Property Related Crimes | | | | | | | | |
| Housebreaking—residential | 435 | 454 | 457 | 445 | 462 | 491 | 502 | 494 |
| Housebreaking—business | 174 | 164 | 163 | 159 | 165 | 161 | 154 | 149 |
| Other robbery | 61 | 69 | 94 | 92 | 104 | 118 | 139 | 146 |
| Stock theft | 84 | 85 | 77 | 78 | 71 | 73 | 70 | 68 |
| Shoplifting | 130 | 117 | 114 | 116 | 109 | 113 | 114 | 110 |
| Theft—motor vehicle | 200 | 194 | 178 | 181 | 190 | 180 | 169 | 165 |
| Theft—out/from vehicles | 352 | 362 | 339 | 316 | 331 | 335 | 334 | 335 |
| Other thefts | 735 | 730 | 709 | 694 | 742 | 815 | 916 | 944 |
| Commercial Crime | 123 | 118 | 117 | 117 | 110 | 113 | 118 | 103 |
| Violence Aimed at Property | | | | | | | | |
| Arson | 22 | 19 | 19 | 18 | 18 | 17 | 15 | 15 |
| Malicious damage to property | 231 | 235 | 236 | 226 | 219 | 223 | 228 | 229 |
| Crimes Heavily Dependent on Police Action for Detection | 21 | 22 | 24 | 23 | 26 | 26 | 25 | 25 |
| Illegal possession of firearms | 94 | 80 | 75 | 80 | 72 | 72 | 80 | 81 |
| Drug related crime | 51 | 43 | 42 | 44 | 44 | 42 | 42 | 42 |
| Driving under influence | | | | | | | | |
| Crimes accounted for under aggravated robbery | NA | NA | 24.3 | 23.9 | 25.6 | 26.9 | 25.4 | 24.8 |
| Car hijacking | NA | NA | 6.9 | 7.6 | 10.0 | 9.8 | 8.2 | 6.3 |
| Hijacking of trucks | NA | NA | 0.8 | 0.4 | 0.4 | 0.3 | 0.4 | 0.2 |
| Robbery of cash in transit | NA | NA | 1.2 | 0.9 | 0.8 | 0.8 | 0.7 | 0.7 |
| Bank robbery | | | | | | | | |

**Table 3.** Crimes Reported to the Police: International Crime Victimization Survey in Johannesburg, South Africa, 2000

| Crime | % | Rank Order |
|---|---|---|
| Theft of car | 91.0 | 1 |
| Car hijacking | 74.1 | 2 |
| Theft from car | 52.9 | 6 |
| Car vandalism | 56.7 | 4 |
| Theft of motorcycle | 54.5 | 5 |
| Theft of bicycle | 24.1 | 14 |
| Burglary with entry | 61.9 | 3 |
| Attempted burglary | 39.5 | 7 |
| Robbery | 38.5 | 9 |
| Personal theft | 29.4 | 12 |
| Sexual incidents (women only) | 39.0 | 8 |
| Assault | 33.0 | 11 |
| Consumer fraud | 8.7 | 15 |
| Corruption | 25.6 | 13 |
| Stock theft | 36.4 | 10 |

increased significantly since 1994. In the opinion of the Crime Information Analysis Centre (http://www.saps.org.za/8_crimeinfo/200112/report.htm, 2003), rape, aggravated as well as common assault, housebreaking, various thefts, commercial crime, and malicious damage to property seem to have stabilized.

However, the Third International Crime Victim Survey in Johannesburg, South Africa (Naudé, Prinsloo, and Snyman, 2001) indicates that on average only 44.1% of all crime victimizations were reported to the police. The respective reporting rates of crime varied significantly.

Table 3 indicates that theft of a car (91%), car hijacking (74%), and burglary 62%) have the highest reporting rates. Although less than half of all attempted burglary, robbery, personal theft, sexual crimes against women, theft of bicycle, and assault experienced have been reported, the underreporting rate of consumer fraud seems to be exceptional.

Despite all the criticism that can be leveled against victimization surveys, such as telescoping, sample loss, etc., Zvekic and Del Frate (1995) are of the opinion that the ICVS still undercounts crime, although the count is more reliable than police crime statistics.

## The Department of Justice and Constitutional Development

The Department of Justice and Constitutional Development is charged with the responsibility to uphold and protect the Constitution and the rule of law (http://www.doj.gov.za, 2003). The Department comprises six branches, that is, Corporate Services, Legislation Research, Legal Services, Human Resources, Regional Coordination and State Legal Services.

The Constitution of the Republic of South Africa (1996) is the supreme law and binds all legislative, executive, and judicial organs of the State. The judicial authority of the country is vested in independent courts that are subject only to the Constitution and the law. The Department of Justice and Constitutional Development administers the courts in conjunction with the judges and magistrates. The National Prosecuting Authority of South Africa (NPA) was established on August 1, 1998 and comprises the National Director of Public Prosecutions (NDPP) and Directors of Prosecution (DPP). The Office of the NDPP is the head office of the prosecuting authority and consists of three Deputy National Directors, Investigating Directors, and Special Directors. The Directorate Special Operations (DSO) introduced an alternative paradigm into the adversarial legal environment where prosecutor-led investigations probe organized crime. The Human Rights Investigative Unit focuses on cases emanating from the Truth and Reconciliation Commission and investigates and prosecutes gross human rights violators. The Asset Forfeiture Unit (AFU) was set up to operationalize the powers provided by the Prevention of Organized Crime Act (1999) to seize the assets of organized criminals. The Sexual Offences and Community Affairs Unit probes violent and sexual offences committed against women and children, as well as family violence in general. The South African Law Commission (SALC) is constantly revising the law required by a dynamic society to ensure that the principles underlying the legal system are just and in line with governing social views and values (http://www.doj.gov.za, 2003).

The Constitutional Court is the highest court for the interpretation and enforcement of the Constitution. The court deals exclusively with constitutional matters. The Supreme Court of Appeal is the highest court in respect of all other matters and has jurisdiction to hear an appeal against any decision of a high court. High Courts represent an important source of law in terms of their interpretations of existing common law and legislation by means of the legal *stare decisis* doctrine. There are ten high court divisions and three local divisions whose services are supplemented by a number of circuit local division courts and special superior courts. Regional magistrate courts with limited penal jurisdiction hear cases within their jurisdictions. South Africa's nine provinces are divided into 370 magisterial districts, housing 746 court offices. In terms of the Magistrates Act (1993), all magistrates in South Africa fall outside the ambit of the Public Service to strengthen the independence of the judiciary. Although regional courts have a higher jurisdiction than district magistrate's courts, an appeal from the magistrates court is heard by the relevant High Court and if necessary by the Supreme Court of Appeal. If a constitutional issue is raised, there is a further appeal to the Constitutional Court (http://www.doj.gov.za, 2003).

Research by Schönteich (Naudé, Prinsloo, and Snyman, 2001, 22) indicates that spending on the criminal justice system has increased by 450%, from R4.25 billion in 1990–91 to R23.48 billion in the 1999–2000 budget year, whereas the consumer price index only increased by 159%. Although the overall conviction rate remained stable at 75%, the criminal justice system reportedly functioned poorly in terms of cases reported to the police. In 1998, only 46% of murder cases were sent to the prosecutor for a decision to prosecute, compared to 44.9% rape cases, 38.2% of serious assault cases, 13.2% of residential housebreaking cases, 7.7% of car theft cases, and 7.5% car hijacking cases. Subsequent conviction rates for murder were 15.7%, serious assault 12.6%, rape 8.9%, residential housebreaking 8.9%, aggravated robbery 2.6%, car theft 2.3%, and car hijacking 1.9%.

## Policing

The activities of the South African Police Service (SAPS) are divided into administration, crime prevention, operational response, detective and crime intelligence, as well as protection services (Annual Report of the National Commissioner of the South African Police Service, April 1, 2001 to March, 31, 2002). Toward the end of 2001, there were approximately 102,354 police officers and 20,337 civilians in the employment of the South African Police Service (SAPS). In 1999, South Africa had a civilian to police officer ratio of 408:1 (Naudé, Prinsloo, and Snyman, 2001).

Official policing in South Africa has challenges of its own. The rate at which members of the police are murdered is regarded as exceptionally high in terms of international standards. Some 1325 police officers were murdered between January 1994 and June 1999 (Naudé et al., 2001). During the 2000–01 and 2001–02 periods of review, respectively, 69 (39%) and 57 (42%) police officers died on duty compared to 107 and 78 who died while off duty. Corruption remains a problem as indicated by Table 4 (Annual Report of the National Commissioner of the South African Police Service, April 1, 2001 to March 31, 2002).

**Table 4.** Reported Incidences of Corruption (1996–2001)

| Year | Enquiries | Arrests | Convictions |
|------|-----------|---------|-------------|
| 1996 | 2300 | 249 | 30 |
| 1997 | 3108 | 429 | 78 |
| 1998 | 3779 | 475 | 128 |
| 1999 | 4618 | 844 | 147 |
| 2000 | 6974 | 1048 | 193 |
| 2001 | 4275 | 592 | 138 |

The South African Police Services has recently been supplemented by metropolitan police officers in the major metropolitan areas. The city of Johannesburg was the second city to deploy 1000 municipal officers to combat less serious crime. The Durban Metropolitan Police Service was launched in January 2000, with 950 uniformed members and 400 civilian staff (Naudé et al., 2001, 19).

As a result of perceived police inadequacy the private security industry is one of the fastest growing industries in South Africa. The number of active security officers registered with the Security Officers' Interim Board increased with 53% between January 1998 and December 2000 to about 184,328. The number of unregistered in-house security officers has been estimated to be as high as 200,000. Research shows that a significant section of the private security industry is run by exmilitary and expolice officers resulting in the government recently publishing a draft bill with the aim of regulating these operations as well as guards, polygraphists, and private investigators (Naudé et al., 2001, 19).

## Correctional Services

According to the latest annual report of the Department of Correctional Services (2001–02), the Department of Correctional Services pursues its institutional objectives in the form of administration, incarceration, care of offenders, development of offenders, community corrections, reintegration, and resettlement services, as well as asset procurement, maintenance, and operating partnerships. These services were rendered by a total of 32,666 personnel in March 2002, whereas the actual post establishment was 35,281. Close to 20% (18.5%) of the human resources was devoted to administration services and 62.5% to incarceration objectives. Seven (7.5%) percent members handled the development of offenders, 4.3% were in charge of the care of offenders and 5.7% facilitated community corrections (Annual Report, Department of Correctional Services, 2001–02).

The total prison population comprised 178,998 on March 31, 2003, which constituted a general overcrowding in available facilities of 64%. The adult male population comprised 82.03% of the total prison population, adult females 2.14%, young males (under 21 years) 15.55%, and young females 0.28%. Close to one third (31%) of the population comprised unsentenced detainees. Twenty-five percent (24.5%) of the unsentenced population was young males, younger than 21 years (Annual Report, Department of Correctional Services, 2001–02).

On March 31, 2002 the Department managed 241 prisons countrywide (Annual Report, Department of Correctional Services, 2001–02):

- 8 prisons for female prisoners only
- 13 youth correctional facilities
- 132 prisons for male prisoners only
- 72 prisons accommodating both male and female prisoners
- 14 prisons that are temporarily closed down for renovations
- 2 APOPS prisons (managed by private consortiums) for sentenced males only

The majority (47.1%) of sentenced offenders were incapacitated as a consequence of "aggressive" crimes. Approximately one third (31%) of offenders were sentenced for economic crimes, while 12.2% committed sexual crimes. Fifteen percent (15.5%) of inmates served a sentence of incarceration of less than 24 months. Twenty seven (27.5%) percent of inmates served sentences of imprisonment of between 2 and 5 years, with another 27.3% of inmates serving a 5- to 10-year sentence. Twenty-five percent served prison sentences of longer than 10 years (Annual Report, Department of Correctional Services, 2001–02).

A total of 4111 young offenders younger than 18 years of age were either detained in or committed to prison on March 31, 2002 (Annual Report, Department of Correctional Services, 2001–02). A more specific analysis of the young detainees is reflected in Table 5.

**Table 5.** Offenders Younger than 18 Years in South African Prisons on March 31, 2002

| Age | Unsentenced | Sentenced | Total |
|---|---|---|---|
| 7–13 years | 11 | 7 | 18 |
| 14 years | 166 | 29 | 195 |
| 15 years | 370 | 172 | 542 |
| 16 years | 790 | 514 | 1304 |
| 17 years | 985 | 1067 | 2052 |
| Total | 2322 | 1789 | 4111 |

Another 47,006 offenders served community correction sentences on March 31, 2002. The success rate of correctional supervision services was reported to be 86% compared to 79% for parole supervision (Annual Report, Department of Correctional Services, 2001–02).

The mandate of the anticorruption unit has been amended to allow for the prioritization of the investigation of corruption, dishonesty, and malpractice in the department. For the period April 1, 2001 to March 31, 2002 the unit received 236 reports. Twenty-three officials were dismissed, 76 officials were disciplined and 14 were criminally convicted as an outcome of the unit's activities (Annual Report, Department of Correctional Services, 2001–02).

## Policy and Legislative Initiatives

An overview of projects finalized by the South African Law Commission (SALC) in the recent past (see http://www.law.wits.ac.za/salc/anrep/2000.pdf, 2003) as well as current projects (see http://www.law. wits.ac.za/salc/salc.html, 2003) provides a general idea of the impressive number and diversity of tasks already undertaken to reengineer the judicial and criminal justice environments.

The National Crime Prevention Strategy (NCPS) (1996), however, provided the main coordinated policy framework for initiatives to combat crime. This is illustrated in particular by child justice developments, measures to combat transnational and organized crime, as well as newly introduced sentencing aims and objectives. Although the office of the NCPS, which was based at the Ministry of Safety and Security, has since been terminated, the NCPS remains official crime policy and the principles and approaches of the NCPS are still considered to be a philosophy and directives that must be followed by all government departments in all spheres of activity that may have a bearing on crime prevention (Ladikos et al., 2001).

## The South African National Crime Prevention Strategy (NCPS)

The South African National Crime Prevention Strategy (NCPS) was launched on May 22, 1996 as a long-term interdepartmental strategy involving various state departments and civil society to establish a comprehensive integrated policy framework to address South Africa's crime problems and to develop national crime prevention programs. It advocates a wide responsibility for crime prevention and a shift in emphasis from reactive crime control toward proactive crime prevention and from an offender-based criminal justice orientation to a victim-centered approach (Naudé, 2000).

According to the drafters of the NCPS (1996) it had the following objectives:

- The establishment of a comprehensive policy framework to enable government to address crime in a coordinated and focused manner drawing on the resources of all government agencies, as well as civil society.
- The promotion of a shared understanding and common vision of how to prevent and control crime.
- The development of a set of national programs to activate and focus the efforts of the various government departments in delivering quality service aimed at solving the problems leading to high crime levels.
- The maximization of civil society's participation in mobilizing and sustaining crime prevention initiatives.
- Creation of a dedicated and integrated crime prevention capacity that can conduct ongoing research and evaluation of departmental and public campaigns as well as facilitate effective crime prevention programs at provincial and local level.

Four "pillars" or models were developed to determine the different areas in which crime prevention should be implemented at national, provincial, and municipal levels as well as the initiatives that should be driven by civil society (NCPS, 1996):

- Improving the criminal justice process with a view to deterring crime, better accessibility to disempowered groups (women, children, and victims), focusing on priority crimes and improving service delivery, especially with regard to the rights and needs of victims.
- Reducing the opportunities for crime by means of environmental design.
- Public values and education to foster greater citizen responsibility and involvement in crime prevention.
- The prevention of transnational crime through the better regulation of border posts, coordination of border policing resources and other agencies in Southern Africa.

Seven priority crimes were identified for special attention, namely, crimes involving firearms; organized crime; white-collar crimes; gender violence and crimes against children; intergroup conflict and violence that poses a threat to democracy and orderliness; vehicle theft and hijacking; and corruption in the criminal justice system. In 1998, the cabinet decided to prioritize violent crimes and corruption as the key issues for the NCPS (Naudé, 2000).

## Young Persons at Risk

Until relatively recently, South Africa did not have a separate and unique criminal justice system for dealing with children, but relied on limited and incoherent statutory provisions. With the introduction of constitutionalism in South Africa, the focus shifted toward more progressive approaches as a result of which the South African Law Commission began work on the implementation of a Juvenile Justice System in 1997 (Prinsloo, 1998). The protection of the interests of the child has been entrenched in the final Constitution as a consequence of South Africa's ratification of the UN Convention on the Rights of the Child (1989).

In view of these developments it became the obligation of the "juvenile justice project committee" to recommend legislature and mechanisms that should aim to (Skelton, 1997):

- Promote the well-being of the child and deal with each child in an individualized way.
- Divert cases in defined circumstances away from the criminal justice system as early as possible, either to the welfare system, or to suitable diversion programs run by competent staff.
- Ensure a vigilant approach to the protection of due process rights that should take place in the shortest appropriate period of time without any unnecessary delays.
- Involve the family and the community, promote sensitivity to culture, and the empowerment of victims.
- Promote a culture in which young persons are held accountable for their actions in such a way that they are encouraged to turn away from criminal activities.
- Ensure that children going through the criminal justice system should be tried by a competent authority in an atmosphere of understanding conducive to the child's best interests.
- Ensure that the child be able to participate in decision making.
- Ensure that the outcome of any matter involving a child offender be based on the principle of proportionality and balanced in terms of the best interest of the child, the least possible restriction on the child's liberty and the right of the community to live in safety.
- Ensure that children are only deprived of their liberty as a measure of last resort and restricted to the shortest possible period of time while awaiting trial or incapacitated as part of a sentence.

The principles of reference listed above are inter-related to the principles of restorative justice. The South African Law Commission's specific recommendations in terms of substantive law and procedures to cover all actions concerning the child, are embodied in the draft Child Justice Bill (SALC, 2000), with the objective to:

- Establish a criminal justice process for children accused of committing offences that aims to protect children's rights as provided for in the Constitution and the UN Convention on the Rights of the Child.
- Provide for the minimum age of criminal capacity of such children.
- Describe the powers and duties of police and probation officers in relation to such children.
- Describe the circumstances in which such children may be detained and to provide for their release from detention.
- Make diversion of cases away from formal court procedures a central feature of the process.
- Establish an individual assessment of each child and a preliminary inquiry as compulsory procedures in the new process.
- Create special rules for a child justice court.
- Extend the sentencing options available to such children.
- Entrench the notion of restorative justice.
- Provide for legal representation of children in certain circumstances.
- Establish appeal and review procedure as well as an effective monitoring system for the legislation.

## Organized and transnational crime

The NCPS (1996) specifically identified the prevention of transnational crime aimed to restrict across-border criminal activities as well as regional movements and methods employed by crime syndicates as one of its crime-control models. This was preceded by earlier reports by the Commissioner of Police in his report to Parliament in 1990 that large quantities of heroin, cocaine, and methaqualone had been confiscated, which suggested that international drug cartels and organized syndicates were operating in South Africa (Prinsloo and Naudé, 2001).

South Africa's strategic geographical position on the major drug trafficking routes between the Far and Middle East, the Americas, and Europe contributed to the increase of organized crime owing to the opening up of the borders since its democratization in 1994. The large-scale presence of illegal immigrants, some of whom have strong links with organized crime, coinciding with weak state control during the transition process, have made the country a prime target for an unsaturated criminogenic market structure (Prinsloo and Naudé, 2001).

At legislative level, various statutes and measures have been introduced to curb the spread of organized crime. The Office for Serious Economic Offences (OSEO) was established in 1992 in terms of the Investigation of Serious Economic Offences Act 117 of 1991. Although this act has since been repealed, its provisions were reenacted in the National Prosecuting Authority Act 32 of 1998. The National Prosecuting Authority Amendment Act 61 of 2000 amended the National Prosecuting Authority Act, establishing the Directorate of Special Operations that functions under the control and direction of the National Director of Public Prosecutions. Provision is made for an Investigative Directorate with a limited investigation capacity to prioritize and investigate particularly serious criminal conduct committed in an organized fashion (Prinsloo and Naudé, 2001).

Other relevant legislative and policy initiatives include inter alia, the Drugs and Drug Trafficking Act 140 of 1992, the Proceeds of Crime Act 76 of 1996, the Prevention of Organised Crime Second Amendment Act 38 of 1999, and Prevention of Organised Crime Act 121 of 1998 that have been enacted as a procedure to confiscate the illegal proceeds of crime and the apprehend offenders. The Prevention of Organised Crime Act 121 of 1998 Act also makes it an offence for any person to actively participate in or be a member of a criminal gang and to aid and abet the criminal activity, or to threaten or perform any act of violence with the assistance of a criminal gang, or to threaten with retaliation (racketeering). The National Prosecuting Authority Amendment Act 61 of 2000 furthermore amends the Interception and Monitoring Prohibition Act 127 of 1992. In terms of these amendments the Directorate of Special Operations may approach a judge for authorization to legally tap telephones, for interception of postal articles and installing of bugging devices (Prinsloo and Naudé, 2001).

These developments, as well as the introduction of mandatory minimum sentences introduced by the 1997 Criminal Law Amendment Act to ensure that certain serious offences were punished more severely and to ensure greater uniformity and consistency in the sentencing process (South African Law Commission, http://www.law.wits.ac.za/salc/discussn/discussn.html, 2003), may create the impression that a retributive approach is increasingly being developed. However, the SALC clearly defines the balance and sensitivity underlying its approach in its view that "An ideal system should be seen to promote consistency in sentencing, deal appropriately with concerns that particular offences are not being regarded with an appropriate degree of seriousness, allow for victim participation and restorative initiatives and, at the same time, produce sentencing outcomes that are within the capacity of the State to enforce in the long term" (South African Law Commission, http://www.law.wits.ac.za/salc/discussn/discussn.html, 2003). The significance of this commitment should be considered in terms of the fact that 43% of incarcerated offenders in South Africa serve less than 5-year sentences.

## A restorative justice paradigm

As already indicated, a shift in emphasis toward proactive crime prevention and a victim-centered criminal justice approach envisioned in the NCPS, together with a shared understanding and common vision of how to prevent and control crime through a problem solving approach, as well as the maximization of civil society's participation in mobilizing and sustaining crime prevention initiatives, is clearly identifiable in the Sentencing Framework Bill initiative (South African Law Commission, http://www.law.wits.ac.za/salc/discussn/discussn.html, 2003).

Restorative justice represents a way of dealing with victims and offenders by focusing on the settlement of conflicts arising from crime and resolving the underlying problems that caused the conflict. It is also a way of dealing with crime generally in a rational and problem-solving way. Central to the notion of restorative justice is the recognition of the community rather than the criminal justice agencies. In this context, restorative mediation is regarded as an additional type of restorative justice that includes some form of restitution to the victim or the community. Community corrections are similarly aimed at entrenching the principles of restorative justice. The primary purpose of community corrections is assumed to be the restoration of the rights of victims—a way of dealing with crime generally in a rational and problem-solving way—and to allow the offender subject to the sentence, to lead a socially responsible and crime-free life during the period of their sentence and in future.

In the Sentencing Framework Bill, the South African Law Commission (SALC) approaches restorative justice as a form of criminal justice based on reparation by actively considering the restitution of damages to the victim of a crime, the protection of the community from the offender, as well as the creation of an opportunity for the offender to lead a crime-free life in the future. Furthermore, the Bill provides for victim–offender mediation and family group conferencing as part of the conditions that can be attached to the community penalties of correctional supervision and community service. The Bill furthermore determines that reparation in the form of restitution by the offender to the victim may be imposed for damages (including loss or destruction of property or money), physical, psychological, or other injury and loss of income or support.

Restorative justice blends uniquely with the African culture and already found expression in the Truth and Reconciliation Commission (TRC) that serves as a unique model to the international world. The conditions and circumstances in and around South Africa that influence crime and justice directly or indirectly, are challenging and multiple. However, the idealism with which these aspects are approached is equally intriguing.

JOHAN PRINSLOO

## References and Further Reading

Barnett, T. and Whiteside, A. (1999). *HIV/AIDS in Africa: Implications for development and major policy implications.* Paper delivered at ISS AIDS workshop in Pretoria on November 16, 1999:1–19.

CIA World Factbook. (2003). *South Africa.* Available at http://www.cia.gov/cia/publications/factbook/geos/sf.html.

Crime Information Analysis Centre (CIAC). (1999). *The Incidence of Serious Crime.* Report 10 or 99. SAPS: Pretoria.

Crime Information Analysis Centre (CIAC). (2003). *The Reported Serious Crime Situation in South Africa for the Period January–September 2001.* Available at http://www.saps.org.za/8_crimeinfo/200112/report.htm. Downloaded on May 17, 2003.

Crime Information Analysis Centre (CIAC). (2003). *A Comparison of the 1994–2001 January to September Increase or Decrease in the Crime Ratios per 100,000 of the Population Related to Specific Crime Categories.* Available at http://www.saps.org.za/8_crimeinfo/200112/tabel1.htm. Downloaded on May 17, 2003.

Department of Correctional Services. (2003). *Annual Report, Department of Correctional Services,* (2001/2002). Available at http://www.dcs.gov.za/annual_report/annual_%20report2001/. Downloaded on May 27, 2003.

Department of Foreign Affairs, Republic of South Africa. (2003). *Transition from the OAU to the African Union.* Available at http://www.au2002.gov.za. Downloaded on May 20, 2003.

Department of Justice and Constitutional Development. (2003). *Administration of Justice.* Available at http://www.doj.gov.za. Downloaded on May 30, 2003.

Department of Safety and Security. (2003). *Annual Report of the National Commissioner of the South African Police Service, 1 April 2001 to 31 March 2002.* Available at http://www.saps.org.za/areporto2/index.html. Downloaded on May 27, 2003.

Ladikos, A., Naudé, B., Olivier, K., Prinsloo, J. and Snyman, R. (2001). The third international crime (victim) survey in Johannesburg, South Africa. *Acta Criminologica,* 14(3): 75–86.

Louw, A. (1999). Drugs, alcohol and crime: A survey of arrestees. *Nedcor or ISS Crime Index,* 3.

Louw, A. (2001). City crime trends. *Nedbank ISS Crime Index 1.*

McGreal, C. (2001). Aids will kill 700,000 South Africans a year. *The Guardian*. Available at http://www.guardian.co.uk/aids/story.html. Downloaded on May 20, 2003.

Naudé, C.M.B. (2000). The South African Crime Prevention strategy: A critique. *Acta Criminologica*, 13(2):1–11.

Naudé, C.M.B., Prinsloo, J.H. and Snyman, H.F. (2001). *The Third International Crime Victim Survey in Johannesburg, South Africa (2000)*. Unpublished research report. Pretoria: Institute for Criminological Sciences (Unisa).

Naudé, C.M.B. AND Prinsloo, J.H. (2002). Crime victimization in Southern Africa in *Crime victimization in comparative perspective. Results from the International Crime Victims Survey, 1889–2000*, Nieuwbeerta, P. (Ed.). Den Haag, the Netherlands: Boom Juridische Uitgevers (81–83).

Office of the Executive Deputy President. (1996). *Media statement by acting president Thabo Mbeki at the launch of the National Crime Prevention Strategy (NCPS)*, May 22, 1996, Cape Town.

Pelser, A. and De Kock, C. (2000). Violence in South Africa: A note on some trends in the 1990's. *Acta Criminologica*, 13(1):80–94.

Prinsloo, J.H. (1998). Children and the Criminal Justice system in South Africa, in *Children and Childhood in Our Contemporary Societies*, Behera, D. (Ed.). Delhi: Kamla-Raj.

Prinsloo, J.H. and Naudé, C.M.B. (2000). The African Renaissance—A criminological perspective. *Acta Criminologica*, 13(1):40–48.

Prinsloo, J.H. and Naudé, C.M.B. (2001). Organized crime and corruption in South(ern) Africa. *International Journal of Comparative Criminology*, 1(2):65–90.

Reuters Limited. (2002). *Business news in review. Unemployment nears 30%—StatsSA*. Available at http://business.iafrica.com/news/919537.htm. Downloaded on May 20, 2003.

Schönteich, M. and Louw, A. (2001). *Crime in South Africa: A Country and Cities Profile*. Pretoria, South Africa: Institute of Security Studies.

Rocha-Silva, L. and Stahmer, I. (1997). Dangerous liasons. Alcohol, drugs and crime. *Crime and Conflict*, 9(Winter):1–5.

Southern African Development Community (SADC). (2003). Available at http://www.sadc.int/index.php. Downloaded on May 20, 2003.

Shaw, M. (1997). The violence of alcohol: Crime in the Northern Cape. *Crime and Conflict*, 9(Winter):6–10.

Skelton, A. (1997). *Project 106. Juvenile Justice. Issue Paper 9*. Pretoria, South Africa: South African Law Commission.

South African National Crime Prevention Strategy (NCPS). (1996). Pretoria, South Africa: Ministry of Safety and Security.

South African Law Commission. (2003). *Sentencing (A new sentencing framework). Discussion Paper 82*. Available at http://www.law.wits.ac.za/salc/discussn/discussn.html. Downloaded on May 20, 2003.

South African Law Commission (SALC). (2003). *Discussion Paper 79. Project 106. Juvenile Justice*. Available at http://www.law.wits.ac.za/salc/discussn/discussn.html. Downloaded on May 20, 2003.

Statistics South Africa. (2003). Available at http://www/statssa.gov.za. Downloaded on May 20, 2003.

Steinberg, N. (2001). *Background Paper on African Union*. Available at http://wfm.org/ACTION/africanunion1001.html Downloaded on May 20, 2003.

Verhellen, E. (1994). *Convention on the Rights of the Child: Background, Motivation, Strategies, Main Themes*. Leuven, Belgium: Garant.

Zvekic, U. and Del Frate, A.A. (1995). *Criminal Victimization in the Developing World*. Rome: UNICRI.

*See also* **Africa, Crime and Justice in Subsaharan**

# Soviet Union, Crime and Justice in the

The Union of Soviet Socialist Republics (USSR) was founded upon the Russian Empire, which was overthrown in 1917 when the Bolsheviks overthrew the Czarist order. It spanned an area covering the northern half of Europe and the northern third of Asia. Territory added to the USSR after 1938 increased its area to about 8,600,000 square miles, which made it the largest single state with a continuous territory. It occupied about 15% of the land surface of the globe. According to the 1990 census, the USSR was the third most populous country in the world after China and India. The USSR was a multinational state composed of 15 republics with a rich diversity of peoples, cultures, and languages (approximately 100 nationalities), although three quarters of the population was made up of Slavic-speaking peoples, mostly Russians. Beginning in the 1920s, the country experienced extensive urbanization and industrialization, and rose to the ranks of a major world power.

## Political History

Soviet ideology was based on the theories of revolutionary philosophers Karl Marx and Friedrich Engels, which were adapted to imperial Russia by Vladimir Illyich Lenin, founder of the Russian Communist Party and one of the leaders of the Russian Revolution. Marxist–Leninist ideology viewed history and society as reflections of primarily economic relationships. It called for complete and absolute power to be vested in a small group of leaders who were to direct the changes necessary in economic affairs to eliminate inequality based on property and power in order to achieve an ideal society, communist in nature that promised social justice and equal distribution of goods and services. This small leadership group, representing less than 5% of the population, organized into the Communist Party, operated without competition from other political parties, and had full control over other institutions and organizations, including the government, the armed forces, agriculture, trade unions, industrial production, distribution of goods and services, health care, the press, schools, and mass organizations. For all intents and purposes, the Party served as the decision-making center of the Soviet state for over 70 years, supervising the execution of its policies and programs at all levels. The Soviet political system experienced several phases of development since the 1917 revolution. However, beginning with Vladimir Lenin, all Soviet leaders, while representing varying degrees of communist orthodoxy, appeared to show little tolerance for dissidents or criticism of their political ideology or regimes.

After Lenin's death in 1924, the change in leadership took place with virtually no popular involvement. Although there was competition among some prominent political figures such as Leon Trotsky, it was Joseph Stalin who emerged as the Party General Secretary and undisputed leader of the Soviet Communist Party in 1927. Under Stalin the Soviet system was ruled by an omnipotent despot who achieved control through his use of the major instruments of political power including the Communist Party and the secret police (KGB) who employed unprecedented powers including indiscriminate arrests, brutal investigations and interrogations, and the murder of millions of individuals who in any way were suspected of criticizing the regime. Upon Stalin's death in 1953, Nikita Krushchev assumed power by shrewdly adopting a platform that appealed to the rank and file emphasizing a new concern with the quality of life for the average citizen. Under his reign, modest changes in the criminal justice system took place including the collection of limited crime statistics for the USSR. The expansion of rights for individuals to defend themselves in court and the ability of judges to occasionally fend for defendants in political trials were also among the reforms. Leonid Brezhnev succeeded Khrushchev as

Communist Party General Secretary in 1964. His rule that lasted through 1982 was generally associated with a diminishment of human rights and a hardening of the political discipline and ideological orthodoxy inside the Communist Party. Brezhnev's attacks on dissident groups and members of the literary and scientific intelligentsia were reminiscent of the Stalinist era. Any prior rights of citizens were generally suspended and there were sudden invasions of privacy of suspected dissidents by KGB police, prolonged imprisonment of convicted dissidents in labor camps, penitentiaries, and insane asylums, and general harassment of individuals. Following Brezhnev's death in 1982, Yri Andropov (ruling from 1982 to 1984) and Konstantin Chernenko (ruling from 1984 to 1985) each held power for only brief periods of time taking no credit for any significant changes in the structure and functioning of the Soviet system. Despite the Soviet state's achievement of the status of a global power, inconsistencies between a "world image" and Soviet reality were suspected by onlookers from the international community. The USSR's hyper internal and external security systems and relatively "closed" posture regarding information, especially in the realm of domestic affairs and social problems, led many observers to conclude that the successes and achievements presented to the world were not as they seemed.

When Soviet leader Mikhail Gorbachev assumed power in 1985, a new openness (*glasnost*) was introduced. Gorbachev admitted that numerous problems existed, and that under communism mistakes had been made, giving him the impetus to propose plans for the restructuring (*perestroika*) of society. But Gorbachev's attempts to undo past mistakes by opening up the society and deconstructing the central planning system, however, seemed to make matters worse, not better. In 1987, Gorbachev opened the way for the development of private enterprise. Because of the enormous profits that private enterprises or new "businesses" realized, racketeers and organized criminals (Mafia) were immediately attracted. Taking advantage of uncertain conditions, the Mafia seized control of the private restaurant, retail, and trucking industries.

Gorbachev's 1987 amendments to the constitution pertaining to the relationship between the Soviet state and the republics, the role of the Communist party, and economic policies were prophesied by many to bring down the Soviet state. (A popular joke asked the question: "What comes after Perestroika? The answer: Perestrellka (cross-shooting)!") By December 1991, when Gorbachev was forced to resign, the economy was in shambles and the country was experiencing ethnic strife, civil unrest, and what appeared to be a crime wave. With an annual inflation rate of 1000% and a budget deficit of approximately one quarter of the gross national product, which was declining at a yearly average of 20–25%, something that had not been experienced anywhere in the world developed—"a supply-side depression" (Goldman, 1992).

Gorbachev's resignation signaled the collapse of the Soviet Empire as well as the outbreak of civil wars in many parts of the former Soviet Union. The real meaning of the collapse was that the Communist Party had lost its monopoly on policies; however, much of the state administration continued to function. No new class of elites was apparent in what was often referred to as the Second Russian Revolution. Moscow continued to serve as the center of activity for Russia just as it did for the Communist Party and the Soviet Union. After December 1991, the names of "Soviet" ministries were merely replaced by "Russian" ministries, suggesting that practices and traditions were passed on into the new era.

Russian president Boris Yeltsin tried to reform the economic and nationalistic havoc created by communism and Gorbachev's reforms. Critics of Yeltsin claimed that he failed at his attempts to revive the devastating economic conditions. He was not able to arrest the growing crime problem nor was he able to inspire confidence in his leadership. For example, as soon as Yeltsin assumed power in December 1991, he announced that he would decontrol prices. Before his plan could be enacted, goods disappeared from state stores and were sold on the black market.

In June 1992, The Russian Ministry of the Interior reported that operating throughout Russia were as many as 260 major criminal gangs and that approximately 200 were part of international criminal networks. In September, 1992, Yeltsin asked the U.S. for help in fighting organized crime.

Thus, what once seemed a threatening military superpower appeared to be reduced to a highly inefficient industrial society based on a "barter system" economy, with criminal gangs operating much like those reminiscent of the 1920s and 1930s in the U.S. Since the dismantling of the Soviet Union, Russia, and the former republics have entered a new era of ethnic nationalism. To what extent the former Soviet republics will seek to be reunited politically or economically is still unknown. Strong nationalism makes it impossible to ignore the approximately 30 million Russians living in the other republics of the former Soviet Union. Russia is by no means willing to concede the former Soviet economic or military property.

## History of Crime in the USSR

Crime in the Soviet Union was generally believed to be relatively minor. To the rest of the world, irrespective of the question of validity of any crime reports, the Communist Party and Soviet government had a reputation of dealing with offenders in a deliberate and swift manner and to that extent it was assumed that the country did not have a serious crime problem. Little or no information in the form of comprehensive criminal statistics was leaked to the rest of the world, and only a few Soviet citizens were privy to such information. Detention facilities and prisons were also closed except to criminal justice personnel and, of course, those held captive.

Historically, the official emphasis of the Soviet government was placed more on juvenile delinquency than on adult crime. Early accounts indicated that juvenile misbehavior (hooliganism) was acknowledged as a problem both prior to and after the Soviet takeover of the Russian imperial state. Millions of detached children, both war orphans and refugees from civil unrest and World War I, roamed the cities and countryside. By the mid-1920s, juvenile crime was considered to be a serious problem and an estimated 20% of all criminal convictions involved juveniles. From the beginning, the new Soviet government had to address these problems and thus established Commissions of Juvenile Affairs (CJAs) to combat juvenile crime. The CJAs were coordinating centers for all community organizations concerned with the "upbringing of children" and the prevention of juvenile law breaking. In the newly established state, the upbringing of children became a major preoccupation of the reformist government and key to its future survival. Juvenile delinquency remained a serious problem in the Soviet Union in more modern times as well. Juvenile gangs were believed to be on the rise especially during the Gorbachev years and such "group crime" continued to increase substantially through the early 1990s (Thornton and Voigt, 2001). Most of the group crimes were considered to be relatively minor (often called "situational leisure crimes") and were carried out by two to four adolescents. However, more serious crimes were committed by larger more organized groups of juveniles. In September of 1988, at Gorky Park in Moscow, a violent confrontation between antagonistic youth groups resulted in 25 persons killed and over 400 injured. In 1988, overall, approximately 88,000 juveniles committed crimes as part of a group (Thornton and Voigt, 1992).

By and large, males accounted for most crimes committed in the Soviet Union in modern times. Some reports indicated, however, that female crimes increased at a faster pace. Although homicides were always considered rare especially among juveniles, juveniles accounted for about one third of all rapes, with the average age of offenders being 14–18 years. Other crimes commonly committed by juveniles included burglary, automobile theft, and hooliganism. According to reports, a disproportionate share of these offenses were committed by nonworking, nonstudying juveniles often under the influence of alcohol. Interestingly, crime patterns were not uniform in the Soviet Union and large cities did not necessarily have the highest crime rates. Many outlying rural areas and suburbs experienced relatively higher crime rates. The internal passport system that existed allowed Soviet authorities to exile offenders from cities and to deny the entrance of crime prone youth possibly explaining this anomaly (Shelly, 1987).

It was not until relatively late in Soviet history, however, that authorities admitted that there was a high prevalence of organized crime or mafia engaging in such activities as drug and alcohol crimes, prostitution, contract murder, and black market operation. Such criminals were believed to be well-armed and to have contacts in the police and government, and were generally considered to be ruthless in the pursuit of crime.

## Classification and Extent of Crime

Over the history of the Soviet state, there were five constitutions, the last adopted in 1987. The Soviet constitution contained a detailed description of the Communist Party's role, as well as a detailed description of the federal state. The republic governments were supposed to be concerned with the day-to-day routine administration of the republics, whereas the Union government retained responsibility for such matters as determining military and internal security, foreign trade, money and banking, and social policies.

Soviet law dealing with crimes against the person and property were similar in form to the law of some Western countries, especially those modeled after the Roman–Germanic legal system. However, crimes against the State (counterrevolutionary crimes) differed in at least two respects: (1) merely speaking against the Soviet political and social system, if done with intent to weaken the Soviet power, was a crime; and, (2) cases of espionage were tried by military courts.

Gorbachev's new policies of 1987 affected changes in the reporting of crime. When Soviet crime statistics first appeared in 1961 under Khrushchev, only percentages comparing crime incidence with those of previous years were given. With the base rates not shown, it was difficult to interpret the meaning of the results. After some of Gorbachev's reforms, government statistics (Goskomstat) collected by the Ministry of Internal Affairs (MVD) were much more precise, albeit sensitive to the same errors as any official statistics. There was obviously much unreported crime in the Soviet Union, as in any country. For the field of criminology Gorbachev's reforms meant that crime information was treated more openly. Newspaper articles and television programs began to carry accounts of crimes. The media not only presented cases of victimization and special treatment of crime issues, but bolstered them with statistics (something the public was not privy to in the past). Such openness resulted in greater public awareness of crime both inside and outside of the Soviet Union.

Gorbachev's attempt to develop more openness had international consequences. Crime statistics were, for the first time, made available to the UN and to the international community of scholars or criminologists and thus subject to analysis. International exchange of information presupposed a "perestroika" or restructuring of data gathering and reporting techniques (i.e., in order to be part of international crime information networks, Soviet crime data had to meet more standardized forms). The disclosure of the crime problem led not only to a greater awareness of crime but to a widespread fear of crime. Growing fear of crime was quickly related to the public's perception of economic deterioration and a declining quality of life. The perception of a growing crime problem soon became an indication of social disorder and chaos. Daily newspapers such as *Vechnernaia Moskva* (*Moscow's Evening Report*) began to report crimes in the Soviet Union on a routine basis.

Early crime statistics also became available and were used for purposes of trend analysis and discussions of the growing crime problem. Comparisons revealed inconsistent trends in total registered crimes (i.e., the volume of reported property and violent crimes) through the decade of the 1960s with some spotty increases in reported crimes generally occurring through the 1970s and 1980s. A brief decline in registered crimes between 1985 and 1988 took place, and it was suggested that such decreases were in part because of the reduction in alcohol consumption as a result of antialcohol campaigns and shortages of vodka. However, crimes such as murder, armed robbery, and burglary increased during the same time, possibly because of shortages of every conceivable type of consumer goods and the purported rise in criminal activity of the Soviet Mafia. Rather dramatic increases in total registered crime, a 26% increase, took place from 1989 through 1991, the last year that the Soviet Union existed. This statistic among others may have served to discredit Gorbachev's leadership.

As in the U.S., property crimes such as theft, burglary, and other economic crime was the most prevalent type of crime in the Soviet Union, comprising about 60–70% of total registered crime commission in any given year since crime statistics were made public. A distinction was made between theft of state property and theft of private property. More generally, theft of state property was believed to be committed by adults and was seen as more serious than theft of private property. Theft of state property took several forms, for example, factory workers routinely stole raw products or furnished goods for themselves or friends to be used, sold, or bartered on the black market. Most citizens who stole from the State did so on a small basis and were not caught. Younger offenders generally committed more thefts of private property including burglary and robbery. A large number of these crimes were committed in groups, possibly reflecting the Soviet educational and socialization practices emphasizing collective activity.

As is typical of most nations of the world, violent crimes such as murder, armed robbery, and rape generally comprised a small portion of Soviet crimes. In modern times, violent crimes including a wide variety of assaults and batteries generally averaged no more than 15% of total registered crimes. For example, for a 4-year period between 1985 through 1988, premeditated murder and attempted murder averaged about 1% of total registered crimes, rape, and attempted rape averaged about 1% of total registered crimes, and armed robbery averaged about 3% of total registered crimes (Voigt et al., 1994).

Even though the public perception was that the Soviet Union under Gorbachev was experiencing a crime wave, the volume of crime in the Soviet Union, when compared to the U.S. for similar time periods was significantly lower. For example, in Moscow, a city with over 8 million people, weekly figures for 1988 revealed 2 murders, 5 aggravated assaults, 24 robberies, 47 apartment break-ins, and 11 car thefts. In New York City, a city of comparable size, for the same time frame, the weekly figures averaged 32 murders, 1230 aggravated assaults, 1500 robberies, 2445 burglaries, 2306 auto thefts (Motivans, 1990).

## The Criminal Justice System

Three types of law enforcement systems existed in the Soviet Union: state security forces, regular forces, and ancillary forces. The KGB, Committee for State Security, was responsible for state security. By and large, however, the Militia, developed during the early days of the Soviet state, performed most day-to-day police functions such as law enforcement and order maintenance. It was responsible to the MVD (Ministry of Internal Affairs). In addition, the Militia also answered to the local Soviet district. Under the Militia were specialized branches of law enforcement. The Department for Combating the Misappropriation of Socialist Property investigated theft, bribery, and other crimes connected with state property. The Passport Department allowed the Militia to restrict and monitor the movements of citizens. Another department dealt with automobile and traffic control including concentrated efforts to combat drunk driving.

In a revision of their criminal law, the Supreme Soviet of the USSR adopted several new laws in 1958, among them the Law of Criminal Responsibility and the Fundamentals of Criminal Procedure. The intent behind these reforms was to clarify the laws and eliminate the past arbitrary enforcement of such laws. The Criminal Code went into effect in 1960. Although the code specifically delineated criminal offenses, several political crimes in the codes were vague enough to permit arbitrary investigations that led to questionable convictions.

Individuals under age 16 were generally not subject to criminal responsibility, although some exceptions were made for those who committed serious adult crimes such as murder, rape, and assault. Once a complaint was received or an arrest was made by the Militia, a preliminary investigation began leading to an indictment of the defendant or a decision to drop the case. The Militia could make an arrest based on their observance of a crime, an eyewitness account, or evidence collected from a crime scene. Laws of search and seizure existed theoretically limiting the authority of the Militia unless there was sufficient cause (Terrill, 1984; Savitsky and Kogan, 1987).

With few changes the system continues to this day. Most minor criminal and civil cases of first instance were tried in people's courts, similar to district or city courts. More serious criminal and civil cases were tried in regional courts; such courts also functioned as courts of appeal from the people's courts. The once top-of-the court hierarchy, the Supreme Court of the USSR, which functioned much like the U.S. Supreme Court, became the Supreme Court of Russia; it deals with the propriety of the lower courts and serves appellate functions.

Criminal punishments in the Soviet Union included deprivation of liberty in a correctional institution with a term ranging from a few months to 15 years, exile or restricted residence from 2 to 5 years; corrective labor without deprivation of liberty; deprivation of the right to hold certain positions or engage in certain activities; fines and restitutions; and capital punishment (between 1985 and 1988, 63 offenders were executed (Amnesty International, 1989)). Because of a government report finding that about 60–90% of adult recidivists were convicted for their first crimes as youngsters, the Supreme Soviet adopted in August 1989 a resolution "on decisive measures of struggle against crime" that included emphasis on delinquency prevention and the humanization of education or penal colonies in the Soviet Union that confined approximately 28,000 juveniles (Voigt et al., 1994).

## Causal Theories and Policies

Before Gorbachev's policies of glasnost and perestroika, Soviet crime experts or criminologists appeared somewhat restricted in their explanations of crime causation. Early causal explanations were rooted in communist ideology expounding the view that crime was a bourgeois remnant from the pre-Revolutionary capitalist past. Because socialism was assumed to be superior to capitalism, little attention was given to the roots of crime under socialism. The crime (referred to as parasitism) that supposedly existed was expected to disappear with the final development of communism. Rather than focusing on their own crime problem, Soviet criminologists appeared to give undue attention to crime in other Western industrial nations.

Noting some historical inconsistencies between the Party rhetoric regarding the superiority of Soviet socialism with emphasis on the eventual eradication of crime under communism and the practical (or actual) dynamics and growth of crime and delinquency in the USSR, a few Soviet criminologists developed limited explanations of crime patterns in their own country. From the beginning, Soviet criminology generally did not emphasize the biological and psychological causal models of criminal and delinquent behavior. Soviet criminologists focused more on the social structural roots of crime, arguing that the psychological and biological paradigms deal mainly with individual aberrant behavior and rare events. Soviet theorists claimed that sociological variables were associated with fluctuations in the "rates" of crime, and therefore to reduce crime rates, the greatest attention must be given to the social factors (Voigt and Thornton, 1985).

The forces of industralization, urbanization, and modernization were topics covered among Soviet criminologists. Volodya Kudryavtsev and Ninel Kuznetsova (1983) noted that significant urban transformation had occurred in the Soviet Union since 1917. Over 2700 new towns and settlements had emerged by 1980. They projected that 80% of the population would be urbanized by 1990, a reverse of the 1917 figure. They expected that between 1993 and 1998, approximately, 250 new towns, along with 25–30 large cities, would appear. They also reported that the number of cities with a population exceeding 1 million was rising. According to these criminologists the urban transformation along with the demographic trends were associated with future rising crime rates.

Noting similar changes and properties in crime trends globally, cross-cultural criminologists outside the Soviet Union suggested that perhaps the convergence and similarities of crime patterns among different nations of the world (irrespective of their ideological slant) may have been towing to the historically unparalleled changes that resulted from the universal pattern associated with urbanization, industrialization, and modernization. Although these phenomena helped account for the historic rise in crime overall, there were still questions regarding cultural differences that remained. In other words, although it was understood why the former USSR and the U.S. may have shared some comparable crime patterns, what explained the significant differences between these countries with regard to the actual volume of crime? This question and others have continued to challenge cross-cultural specialists around the world.

Soviet criminologists particularly emphasized institutional determinants of criminal behaviors or trends. Soviet officials believed in social engineering as the way to control crime and other social problems. For instance, officials attempted to manipulate and control their basic institutions (primarily the family, school, workplace, and youth organizations) to inculcate socialist principles and morality. In particular, the family was singled out as a basic institution that contributed to the delinquency of minors. Blame was placed on parents' inability to socialize their children to socialist standards of work, obedience, and loyalty. Parents were often held criminally liable for the delinquencies of their children. Lack of parental supervision, excessive drinking in the home, and workplace, and the like were noted in discussions, both scholarly and popular, dealing with Soviet delinquency or hooliganism.

Blame was also placed on the school and its inability to further inculcate loyalty or respect and belief in communist principles and Soviet law. Various governmental youth organizations as well as the workplace were further held accountable for not adequately controlling juveniles or reinforcing communist morality and proper work habits. In essence, all agencies that impinged upon children were held responsible for failings of society.

A range of other contributory factors can be gleaned from Soviet criminological works. Delinquent peer groups and gangs, of course, were the source of constant worry to the authorities and to law-abiding parents. Unemployment, alcoholism, and drug use on the part of school dropouts and young unskilled workers were also cited among chief contributors to youth crime and other forms of hooliganism. The fall of the Soviet state with the perceived lack of control and ensuing disorder in society has only confirmed these past theories of criminality and delinquency in Russia. Many people continued to lament the loss of social control and blamed governmental laxity even for the more recent perceived crime waves.

Discussion of crime causes, especially during the Gorbachev era, frequently suggested that the government itself contributed to increases in criminality. The high expense and relative scarcity of consumer goods of all types, ranging from toilet paper to meat, led to the expansion of a massive black market where most people were forced to purchase goods and services if they were to survive. Shortages in the state run stores and long lines for the purchase of everything, inadequate housing, and general hardships of everyday life were believed to lead to heightened hostility and tension among citizens. Shortages were typically believed to also affect workplace crime in terms of the theft of scarce goods and resources as well as the manufacture of inferior goods.

The Chernobyl disaster and civil wars in places like Azerbaijan created large numbers of homeless people. Many who sought refuge in large cities such as Moscow have remained there after the coup in 1991. The continuing economic difficulties stemming from the former Soviet Union adversely affected these refugees, many of whom have remained homeless. The homeless in contemporary Russia, like those in the U.S., have been treated with contempt and often as criminals. Homelessness was something Muscovites were not used to seeing under communism. The homeless like the criminal have come to symbolize the faltering economy, and the growing gap between poverty and affluence.

In many respects, the current response and treatment of crime in Russia directly reflect theories and practices of the former Soviet Union. In essence, Russian criminologists today are pointing to the same multitude of daily tensions thought to contribute to crime, especially to explain domestic and street crime, organized crime, and drug use. The Russian government seems to be resorting to past ways to control crime. Plans have included increasing the number of police or militia and court personnel to handle rising crime rates and more severe sentencing of offenders. Organized crime has been under attack with harsher laws and special task forces (including international forces) devoted exclusively to the control of the organized criminal networks. Drug and alcohol educational programs have been put into effect, and delinquency-prevention programs of all types are being developed, although lack of funds seems to hamper progress. President Putin who came into power in 2000 and the present government in Russia realize that crime is affecting the quality of life in their country and that to some extent, rising crime and social anomie, if not addressed, will undermine the current government and its policies.

Presently, the Russian people seem to be struggling to institute and preserve certain democratic freedoms "that have been promised to them" (Miller and Ventura, 2003). In some ways the crime problem poses a threat to the general liberalization of the country and some of the important positive changes in its recent history.

Unfortunately, the public's reaction to crime not only bemoans the victimization of individuals and calls forth more efficient handling of offenders, but has much wider implications. On a societal level, the reaction or overreaction to crime carries the potential of the metaphoric imprisonment and victimization of a whole nation through the creation of fear, mistrust, and alienation.

Certainly no one imagined that Gorbachev's *glasnost* or openness would be associated with not only a greater awareness of crime but fear of crime and disappointment in the public handling of the crime problem. Gorbachev's *perestroika* or restructuring obviously was not originally intended to rebuild or add prisons (nor lead to more bolts on people's doors and bars on their windows). It certainly was not aimed at the reconstruction or alteration of people's routines, forcing them to travel alternate paths or to stay home at night. More importantly, neither glasnost nor *perestroika* were intended to result in the reestablishment of a more repressive public order. In light of the enormous transformations that have occurred over the last decade especially with regard to crime reporting and the popular consumption of crime statistics affecting greater public awareness of crime, it is difficult to ascertain how much of the recent increases in crime are because of changes in patterns of perception or to changes in patterns of actual behavior.

LYDIA VOIGT

## References and Further Reading

Amnesty International, *When the State Kills. The Death Penalty*, New York, NY: Amnesty International, 1993.

Avanesov, G., *The Principle of Criminology*, Moscow: Progress Press, 1981.

Borbat, A.V., Problems of juvenile crime in Moscow. In *Crime, Statistics, and the Law,* Dolgova, A.I., (Ed.) Moscow: Criminological Association, 1997 (In Russian).

*Crime and Delinquency, 1996,* Moscow Ministry of Internal Affairs of Russia, Mininistry of Justice of Russia, Statistical Committee of the CIS, (In Russian)

Goldman, M., Needed A Russian Economic Revolution. *Current History: A World Affairs Journal,* October (1992).

Goldman, M., Russian and the Eurasian Republics: Building New Political orders. *Global Studies: Russia, The Eurasian Republics, and Central and Eastern Europe,* Guilford, CT: Dushkin or McGraw Hill, 1999.

Kudryavtsev, V. and Kuznetsova, N., The scientific and technological revolution and crime. In *Problems of the Contemporary World: Combating Crime in Towns,* Kudryavtsev, V., (Ed.) Moscow: USSR Academy of Sciences, 1983

Miller, J.M. and Ventura, H.E., Evaluation of the Moscow Police Command.

College: A note on the benefits of a professional or cultural exchange program, *International Journal of Comparative Criminology,* 3(1), 2003.

Motivans, J., The effects of the changing policies on crime in the Soviet Union, *Criminal Justice International,* 6(2), 1990.

Savitsky, V. and Kogan, M., The Union of Soviet Socialist Republics. In *Major Criminal Justice Systems: A Comparative Survey,* Cole, G., Frankowski, S. and Gertz, M. (Eds.) Beverly Hills, CA: Sage Publications, 1987.

Shelley, L., Interpersonal violence in the USSR, *Violence, Aggression and Terrorism,* 1987.

Shelley, L., *Crime and Modernization: The Impact of Industrialization and Urbanization on Crime,* Carbondale, IL: Southern Illinois University Press, 1981.

Solomon, P., *Soviet Criminologists and Criminal Policy: Specialists in Policy Making,* New York, NY: Columbia University Press, 1978.

Solomon, P., Courts and their reform in Russian history, *Reforming Justice in Russia, 1964–1996: Power, Culture and the Limits of Legal Order,* Solomon, P. (Ed.) Armonk, NY: M.E. Sharpe, 1997.

Terrill, R., *World Criminal Justice Systems,* Cincinnati, OH: Anderson, 1999.

Thornton, W. and Lydia, V., Russia. In *Teen Violence: A Global View,* Hoffman, A.M. and Summers, R.W., (Eds.) Westport, CO: Greenwood Press, 2001.

Thornton, W. and Lydia, V., *Delinquency and Justice,* New York, NY: McGraw Hill, 1992.

*USSR Crime Statistics and Summaries 1989 and 1990.* Serio, J. (Translated by) Chicago, IL: University of Chicago, Office of International Criminal Justice, 1992.

Voigt, L. and Thornton, W., The rhetoric and politics of Soviet delinquency: An American perspective, in *Comparative Social Research,* Tommason, R.F. (Ed. ) Greenwich, CT: JAI Press, 1985.

Voigt, L., Thornton, W., Barrile, L. and Seaman, J., *Criminology and Justice,* New York, NY: McGraw Hill, 1994.

*See also* **Russia, Crime and Justice in Modern; Ukraine, Crime and Justice in**

---

# Spain, Crime and Criminal Justice in

As in most Western democracies, we need to rely on police statistics and victimization surveys in order to learn about different forms of crime in Spain. Spanish police statistics offer some advantages over the Uniform Crime Reports used in the U.S. The two main police bodies in the country (Policia Nacional and Guardia Civil) use a similar form to collect information about any reported crime. This form includes fields as diverse as type of location, victim–offender relationship, type of weapons, economic losses, and so on. The system is also unique in that statistics are collected about every single offense regulated in the Criminal Code, although that does not apply to violations of administrative law. Because these two main police bodies are centralized and they are mandated to collect statistics based on these forms, the problem of voluntary participation in the collection of police statistics by police jurisdictions in the U.S. is not an issue.

Scant research on the topic suggests, however, that there are important variations across departments in the accuracy and reliability of the data collection. Moreover, the growing process of decentralization programmed by the new Spanish Constitution has also had an impact on the territorial fragmentation of the police and the diffusion of data about crime. Finally, the richness of the data collection instruments contrasts with the "secrecy" of the data. The lack of an agency similar to the National Institute of Justice means that access to the data is difficult. Still today the best way to obtain crime data in Spain is not to search the web page or the publications of the Ministry of Interior but to read the annual special issues of two important Spanish newspapers, *El Pais* and *El Mundo* (for current statistics look for "anuario" in www.elmundo.es/especiales).

Spain started to run victimization surveys in the late 1970s. After a decade-long interruption in this program, the Ministry of Interior decided to continue this effort in the 1990s (datasets can be purchased at www.cis.es). In addition, Spain participated in the first wave of the International Crime Survey. These surveys on "seguridad ciudadana" (citizen safety) have for the most part used the same questions regularly, although the sampling schemes and sizes have changed, making longitudinal comparisons difficult. These surveys include a battery of increasingly better questions on fear of crime, a rather complete battery of questions on attitudes toward and experiences with the police, and a not-so-good battery of questions about personal victimization. The questions about victimization are very poor. Instead of presenting behavioral descriptions of the crimes, the survey lists a set of short legal categories (e.g., aggravated assault, minor assault, sexual assault, and robbery) and asks the respondents to say if they have experienced them. Lack of coordination between Guardia Civil and Policia Nacional has translated recently in the duplication of efforts represented by the existence of two different surveys.

To get some local flavor about the problem of crime it is necessary to go beyond these statistics and pay some attention to media and political discourses about crime. Historically two crime categories have played a particularly important role in democratic Spain: drugs and terrorism. As in any other country Spain is also engaged in its particular war on drugs. Because of its geography, Spain has been an entry door for drugs into Europe from South America and Northern Africa. Compared with other countries, the policies are a bit more tolerant, and thus possession is not a criminal offense. Still, a substantial proportion of the prison population is serving time for drug-related offenses.

Basque separatist insurrection, organized by a terrorist group called ETA, is perceived by the majority of Spaniards as the most serious crime problem in Spain. ETA is responsible for the death of 793 people, including 327 civilians. Born during the dictatorial regime of General Franco, it has continued its activities until today. After a several-month long truce in 1999, the group has reinitiated its terrorist activities in a more sanguine way, increasingly targeting politicians and journalists with opposing views. The different political parties have, as a consequence, radicalized their positions. Not surprisingly, the respondents of the Spanish victimization surveys when asked to rank the most pressing social issues in the country place terrorism and drugs in second and third place, followed by crime, with unemployment usually being the first category.

More recently, two new sets of issues are starting to occupy a central position in the discourses about crime in Spain: organized crime and violence against women. The historical experiences with drugs, the redefinition of prostitution (now legal in most cases) as a problem of the traffic of women organized by illegal networks, the emergence of immigration and the participation of organized groups in the process of illegal entry in the country, as well as the presence of known figures from the Italian and Russian mafia in tourist areas of Spain are elements that are contributing to make organized crime a rather visible or publicized problem.

On the other hand, although there were numerous initiatives to advocate for the cause of battered women since the early 1980s, it was not until 1997 that the Spanish society as a whole became aware of the severity of the problem. Following a dramatic case of wife abuse in Granada, the conservative government of Aznar approved a National Plan to Address Wife Abuse that different surveys considered to be the most popular measure of his first governmental mandate.

## Criminal Justice in Spain

Spain is territorially composed of different "autonomous communities" with their own governments and parliaments. These "autonomous communities" have some jurisdiction over public safety and criminal justice matters, but the national parliament still is the only institution with the jurisdiction to approve bills touching upon "fundamental rights" (e.g., civil liberties and rights included in the first part of the Spanish Constitution). The national parliament, thus, preserves the regulatory capacity to approve the Criminal Code, Criminal Procedure Laws, and Correctional Laws.

Several autonomous communities (i.e., Cataluña or the Basque Country) have, however, their own police force, which means that the Policia Nacional and the Guardia Civil are moving out of those territories (or continue in them with limited jurisdictions). In addition, their regulatory capacity is broad enough to have an impact on a growing decentralization of the criminal justice system. The autonomous communities are also increasing their responsibility in the administration of the correctional and juvenile systems and deliver a number of services to victims of crime.

Spain's procedural system is historically based on the inquisitorial system, although more and more elements of an adversarial system are being gradually introduced. The Spanish system had experienced important changes in the last few years and more are to come as a consequence of the process of European homogenization. Since the 1990s, we have seen a new Criminal Code, the introduction of the jury system, the reform of the juvenile justice system, as well as other important innovations. A new law regulating criminal procedure is being developed. A common criticism of these reforms is that the projects in which they are based are normally the product of political negotiations that are not based on sound empirical studies and economic projections about their cost. As a consequence, when they are implemented, economical and institutional infrastructure to carry out the new policies is not in place.

In Spain, there are two main police forces, Policia Nacional and Guardia Civil, although as indicated above the picture is becoming more fragmented. Policia Nacional has jurisdiction in urban areas and thus coexists with the local police forces of each city. The local police forces are part of the municipal administrations whereas the Policia Nacional is part of the national administration. The Policia Nacional, for the most part, has jurisdiction over the "serious stuff," "real" police work and "real" crime, whereas the Policia Local has jurisdiction in traffic control, administrative police, and other "minor matters" that, however, are very relevant to communities (such as incivilities and neighborhood disputes). The Guardia Civil has jurisdiction over rural Spain and also has to coexist with local police forces. Two of the areas receiving the most publicity in the work of the Guardia Civil are the prevention of environmental offenses and border control. From the perspective of the average citizen, jurisdictional boundaries between all these different agencies are somewhat fuzzy leading to situations in which one does not really know who to call. In problematic areas such as the Basque Country these boundary issues lead to more serious organizational conflicts. National surveys measuring institutional trust usually have the Policia Nacional (6.20) and the Guardia Civil (6.09) as the two institutions that the Spanish citizens give a better grade in a scale from 0 to 10, followed in the third place by the press (5.59). About 65% of Spaniards believe that police service is good or very good and in 55% of cases they believe it is getting better (CIS, 2364).

In the last few years the Policia Nacional has experienced important changes. The new direction aims to implement a new way of operating as conceptualized in their plan *Policia 2000*. This plan prioritizes what it is called "proximity police," which is this agency's jargon for community policing. Official documents from the Ministry of Interior claim this initiative has been successful but very little research has been conducted and the model *per se*, as well as the internal perception of what it means across different departments and organizational layers, is not totally clear.

## Criminology in Spain

Spanish criminology has a long but fragmented history. From the late 19th century a number of jurists and social scientists participated in the development of positivist criminology in Europe. Names such as Rafael Salillas, Jimenez de Asua, Concepcion Arenal, or Bernaldo de Quiros contributed to the development of a better understanding of criminal behavior and the criminal justice system.

The Civil War (1936–1939) and Francisco Franco's dictatorial regime (1939–1975) interrupted these developments. It was not until the end of Franco's regime that criminology started flourishing again. A number of today's professors of criminal law were somehow involved in the student protest movement against the regime and became familiar with the criminology of the time, the 1970s critical criminology. Critical criminology constituted a theoretical platform that was useful in that context. Even before the end of the regime, Institutes of Criminology were being created in the Schools of Law and today have expanded to almost every university. The institutes emphasize teaching more than research, work with part-time staff, and their curriculum is heavily influenced by legalistic and forensic approaches.

Whereas jurists played an important role in the still ongoing process of institutionalization of criminology, psychologists were the main protagonists in the scientific development of the discipline. The first major bill approved by the Spanish new democratic regime was the correctional law. This progressive and innovative law, informed by the prison experiences during the times of political repression of some of the parliament members, emphasized the notion of rehabilitation and the role of treatment of offenders. Lack of proper infrastructure would later undermine the possibilities of treatment but this law opened a new terrain of expansion to the then relatively young and growing Spanish psychology. The first psychologists to work on issues of crime focused their attention on offender treatment, but later on expanded their interests into other areas (e.g., victimology, juvenile delinquency, witness testimony, etc.). Spanish sociologists seem generally uninterested in issues of crime and criminal justice.

Spain is said to be a paradoxical place and the situation of criminology is not an exception. It is a country where criminology is not an officially recognized academic discipline despite being the European country with the highest rate of criminology students. Furthermore, Spain remains a country where you cannot hold a full-time research or academic job as a criminologist despite being one of the European countries with a larger representation in the American Society of Criminology. There are signs for hope. In October of 2000, the Spanish Society for Criminological Research (www.criminologia.net) was officially created. Moreover, the Council of Universities is discussing the possibility of approving a degree in criminology. Still, some observers are pessimistic. Many are worried that established disciplines such as psychology or criminal law are not ready to give up their monopoly on crime-related debates and that these conflicts, worsened by the many more general problems of Spanish universities (i.e., entrenched nepotism, lack of research resources, rigid curriculums, excess of scholars in a context of scarce academic jobs, etc.), will handicap the process of institutionalization.

JUAN JOSE MEDINA ARIZA

## References and Further Reading

Dominguez, C., Sendra, G. and Catena, M., 1997. *Derecho Procesal Penal.* Madrid, Spain: Colex.

Garcia-Pablos de Molina, A., 1999. *Tratado de Criminologia.* Valencia, Spain: Tirant lo Blanch.

Garrido, V., Stangeland, P. and Redondo, S., 1999. *Principios de Criminologia.* Valencia, Spain: Tirant lo Blanch.

Jar, G., 1995. *Modelo policial Espanol y Policias Autonomicas.* Madrid, Spain: Dykinson.

Lopez Garido, D., 1987. *El aparato policial en Espana.* Barcelona, Spain: Ariel.

Munoz Conde, F., 2000. *Derecho Penal: Parte Especial.* Valencia, Spain: Tirant lo Blanch.

Munoz Conde, F. and Aran, M.G., 2000. *Derecho Penal: Parte General.* Valencia, Spain: Tirant lo Blanch.

Rechea, C., Barberet, R., Montanez, J. and Arroyo, L., 1995. *La delincuencia juvenil en Espana. Autoinforme de los Jovenes.* Albacete, Spain: Universidad de Castilla-La Mancha.

Stangeland, P., 1995a. La delincuencia en Espana. Un analisis critico de las estadisticas judiciales y policiales. *Revista de Derecho Penal y Criminologia.* Madrid, Spain: UNED.

Stangeland, P., 1995b. *The crime puzzle. Crime patterns and crime displacement in Southern Spain.* Malaga, Spain: Miguel Gomez Publicaciones.

Torrente, D., *La sociedad policial.* Madrid, Spain: CIS.

# Stalking

Stalking as a concept has proven to be remarkably resistant to definitions that can be used in a legal context without diminishing the range of its meanings within popular culture. Stalking has been variously defined as:

- A constellation of behaviors involving repeated and persistent attempts to impose on another person unwanted communication and contact (Mullen et al., 1999, 1244).
- The willful, malicious, and repeated following and harassing of another person that threatens his or her safety (Meloy and Gothard, 1995, 258).
- A course of conduct directed at a specific person that involves repeated physical or visual proximity, nonconsensual communication or verbal, written or implied threats (Tjaden, Thoennes, and Allison, 2000, 11).

In general, stalking possesses sinister and threatening connotations. Victims are being hunted and harassed, powerless, and unable to stop these relentless and threatening pursuits.

The discrete concept of stalking is a surprisingly recent phenomenon, first appearing at the end of the 20th century. Although practices that might be said to constitute stalking have been documented since the early 19th century, these were never officially designated as criminal, or even seen as constituting a particular category of social behavior (Mullen, Pathé, and Purcell, 2000). Throughout the 20th century, those behaviors that are now defined as stalking were dealt with, as far as possible, through a statutory scheme of summary injunctions that differed in detail across each nation and jurisdiction (Goode, 1995). During the 1990s, however, stalking specifically has been legislated against in many American states and in a variety of countries including the Canada, the U.K., and Australia. Although the specific laws within each nation are too various to note, it is fair to say that most jurisdictions tend to define stalking as the repeated or prolonged harassing of another person. Legal definitions of stalking predominantly vary with regard to the issue of "intent"—whether offenders intended to cause serious apprehension and fear or whether they should have known (as reasonable persons) that the end result of their actions would be detrimental.

Increasingly, then, stalking is being taken seriously as a potentially dangerous and terrifying crime, with research on the topic being conducted in the U.K. (Budd, Mattinson, and Myhill, 2000), the U.S. (National Institute of Justice, 1998), Australia (Mullen, Pathé, and Purcell, 2000), and Canada (Manitoba Law Reform Commission, 1997). This research has yielded a number of reasonably consistent findings. Approximately 10% of people have experienced stalking behaviors at some time in their lives. Victims are most likely to be female and younger than their stalkers, who are usually males and between the ages of 35 and 45. The majority of stalkers pursue ex-partners (wives, husbands, lovers) or acquaintances. It appears that stalkers are more likely to be violent if they have had an intimate relationship with the victim. Finally, most stalking episodes last (on average) 1–2 years, with the most common behaviors involving being watched, followed, and telephoned.

Many of these findings need to be qualified, however, because of definitional complexities. For example, although it has been demonstrated that most offenders are male and most victims are female, when the concept of stalking is broadened to include all respondents who repetitively have experienced unwelcome following, telephone calls, and gifts (without experiencing fear or apprehension), gender differences are less substantial. For example, research focusing on college students shows no significant gender differences in reported victimization for this broader range of behavior.

The heterogeneous nature of stalking thus makes identifying the characteristics of offenders difficult. Stalking itself can require very different forms of knowledge, ranging from simple tasks (making a telephone call) to more complex acts (setting up an anonymous remailer on the Internet). Stalking behaviors can range from persistently threatening an expartner to sending thousands of junk emails to a work colleague. Relationships with victims can vary from Hollywood celebrities, whom offenders have never met, to expartners. It is for these reasons that stalking has come to be seen as an extremely complex crime, resistant to easy definition or explanation.

Despite these problems, a number of academic texts have attempted to categorize stalking in terms of both offenders and offences. Typologies can be based upon: the characteristics of the victim (e.g., gender or occupation); the relationship between the stalker and the victim (e.g., workplace acquaintance, Internet acquaintance, or expartner); the motivations of the stalker (e.g., love or revenge); and the psychological characteristics of the stalker (e.g., erotomanic or simple obsessional personality).

These typologies are useful, given that the categorizing offenders, is a first step toward implementing effective policies against stalking. If stalkers typically suffer from mental illness, then imprisonment is unlikely to prevent further stalking behaviors. A finding that most stalking episodes involve dysfunctional intimate relationships would have crucial implications for domestic violence policies. An accurate and comprehensive classification of stalkers would thus facilitate the development of a system by which we could document the course and duration of harassment, the risks of escalation to assaultive behaviors, and, above all, the most successful strategies for ending stalking (Mullen et al., 2000).

Stalking behaviors increasingly are being recognized as dangerous and socially injurious practices that should be prohibited by law. The best way to respond to stalking depends upon how well we understand it, yet current research indicates that stalking is an extremely complicated crime that is difficult to define. As a result, policy responses will be equally difficult to develop. Extensive cooperation among community, criminal justice, academic, and legislative groups is needed to understand and prevent this crime.

EMMA OGILVIE

## References and Further Reading

Budd, T., Mattinson, J. and Myhill, A. (2000) *The Extent and Nature of Stalking: Findings from the 1998 British Crime Survey,* Home Office Research Study 210: London.

Emerson, R., Ferris, K. and Gardner, C.B. (1998) On being stalked, *Social Problems* 45(3): 289–314.

Goode, M. (1995) Stalking: Crime of the nineties? *Criminal Law Journal* 19: 21–31

Manitoba Law Reform Commission (1997) *Stalking: Report No. 98* Law Reform Commission: Manitoba.

Meloy, J. and Gothard, S. (1995) A demographic and clinical comparison of obsessional followers and offenders with mental disorders, *American Journal of Psychiatry* 152: 258–263.

Meloy, J. (1998) (Ed.) *The Psychology of Stalking: Clinical and Forensic Perspectives.* Academic Press: San Diego.

Mullen, P., Pathé, M. Purcell, R. and Stuart, G. (1999) Study of stalkers, *American Journal of Psychiatry* 156(8): 1244–1249.

Mullen, P., Pathe, M. and Purcell, R. (2000) *Stalkers and Their Victims.* Cambridge, U.K.: Cambridge University Press.

National Institute of Justice: Research Report (1998) *Domestic Violence and Stalking: The Third Annual Report to Congress under the Violence against Women Act* U.S. Department of Justice. Office of Justice Programs.

Ogilvie, E. (2000) *Stalking: Legislative, Policing and Prosecution Patterns in Australia,* Research and Public Policy Series: Australian Institute of Criminology.

Pathé, M. and Mullen, P. (1997) The impact of stalkers on their victims, *British Journal of Psychiatry* 174: 170–172.

Tjaden, P., Thoennes, N. and Allison, C. (2000) Comparing stalking victimisation from legal and victim perspectives, *Violence and Victims* 15(1): 7–22.

*See also* **Sexual Harassment**

# State Troopers or Highway Patrol *See* **Law Enforcement; Police: Patrol; Traffic Offenses**

---

# Status Offenses

---

Status offenses represent a complex and controversial part of juvenile court jurisdiction in the U.S. They have been part of the justice system since the creation of the juvenile court, but many jurisdictions struggle in making decisions over how to classify these offenses, how to respond to them, or whether to respond to them at all. A brief history of the juvenile court, definition of status offenses, discussion of various types of status offenses, and the changing methods for dealing with status offenses will illustrate some of the dilemmas these infractions present for the juvenile justice system.

## The Juvenile Court

When the first juvenile court was created in Cook County, Illinois in 1899, the court's subject matter jurisdiction was defined as cases dealing with delinquency, dependency, and neglect. In most instances, these are the types of cases handled by juvenile courts (also called children's courts or family courts) today. Dependency and neglect will be treated only briefly here. A definition is included to help illustrate what status offenses are not, or may not be. Dependency is any situation of want or need in which children may be found, but which results from no fault of the legal guardians. For instance, if poverty prevents parents from adequately meeting their own needs for food, clothing, or shelter—let alone those of their children— a situation of dependency exists. These situations were included in most juvenile codes in order to give the juvenile court the legal authority to intervene and to provide some help and support to the family. In contrast to dependency, neglect (or abuse, in the most extreme forms) cases involve children in situations of want or need that result from some act or failure to act by the legal guardians. Abuse or neglect cases result when the parents have the means to provide for their children, but they choose not to do so. This could involve withholding food, shelter, clothing, education, medical care, or affection from the children.

From the end of the 19th century through the first two thirds of the 20th century, delinquency involved those violations of the law that would be crimes (felonies or misdemeanors) for adults, plus a group of offenses that were violations for children but not adults (that is, status offenses). Thus, age alone is the defining status that makes some acts illegal for children, but not for adults. The definitions of most forms of delinquency have changed very little in the 100 years of the juvenile court's existence. Youngsters who are to be adjudicated as children have committed delinquent offenses any time they have engaged in crimes such as burglary, larceny, auto theft, armed robbery, or even rape or murder. If they are tried as adults, then these no longer constitute delinquent offenses, but rather become adult crimes. In most jurisdictions juvenile codes do not distinguish between felonies and misdemeanors for children: all offenses constitute delinquency. A definitional problem arises when we consider status offenses, or those violations that are not legally prohibited for adults. Under traditional juvenile court procedures, little distinction was made between criminal delinquency and status offenses. Both groups were incorporated under the definition of delinquent behavior or delinquent children. This meant that youngsters who committed status offenses—by definition, much less serious than other forms of delinquency—could be adjudicated delinquent by the juvenile courts and incarcerated along with juveniles who had committed some of the most serious delinquent offenses.

## Types of Status Offenses

Given the status offense definition that has been provided, a discussion of some of the most common status offenses will further illustrate the nature of these infractions. Again, it is essential to remember that status offenses would not constitute crimes if they were committed by adults (in most states adult status begins at age 18 for most activities—alcohol consumption being an obvious exception). Although there can be a wide variety of activities that are legally prohibited for children, the most common are: truancy, running away, being beyond the control of legal guardians, curfew violations, tobacco and alcohol violations, underage gambling, and sexual activity. Some might also suggest drugs as another category, but sale, possession, transportation, manufacturing, and use of drugs constitute crimes for juveniles and adults. Therefore, this is not a true status offense category.

Colorado was the first state to enact a mandatory school attendance law in 1899. Other states soon followed suit. These laws included a stipulation that youngsters who habitually failed to attend school were truant, and they could be taken into custody for truancy. Over the years it has become apparent that some youngsters are truant because they have chosen not to go to school. At times this is the result of learning difficulties or failures experienced because of language or other deficiencies. In some instances, children have been truant because their parents have kept them home to provide childcare or to work in the family business or on the family farm. Most of these are not situations that would be comparable to the commission of a crime. Nevertheless, some states routinely adjudicated youngsters delinquent who habitually were truant, and confined some of these children in state training schools and other juvenile correctional facilities.

Running away from home constitutes another common status offense. Many states still include running away as a violation for individuals who have not reached the age of majority. Runaways are a particularly problematic group for the juvenile justice system. At the most basic level the law takes a very paternalistic view toward youngsters. It assumes that runaways are potential targets for exploitation, especially for prostitution or sexual abuse. Most of the runaways traditionally have been female, although substantial numbers are males. Some have been subjected to physical or sexual abuse in the home, and a small group of these children are more properly defined as "throwaways" than runaways. These children even may be encouraged by the parents to leave home. The custom in most jurisdictions was to take runaways who had been apprehended into custody and to try to return them home. In some cases no further legal action was needed and none was taken. Persistent runaways eventually came to the juvenile court's attention, and judges could order these youngsters to be incarcerated in a juvenile correctional facility for running away.

Persistent runaways, along with other habitually disobedient children, could be petitioned to the juvenile court alleging that they were beyond their parents' or guardians' control (sometimes called "ungovernability," or the catchall term "incorrigibility"). Legal guardians may petition the court for intervention, sometimes as an act of desperation over their inability to control the child. In the past, children who continued to disobey their parents or guardians were subject to legal action and incarceration. Unfortunately, the juvenile courts often were not able to get to the root of the parent–child problems, and they found themselves treating symptoms and not the causes.

In emergency situations, some cities impose curfews on all residents. However, in most instances curfew laws exclusively apply to juveniles. During the 1960s and 1970s a number cities repealed their curfew laws, or simply did not enforce them. By the 1980s, some localities were once again turning to juvenile curfews in order to address youth gang and graffiti problems.

Tobacco and alcohol violations will be treated together since they constitute similar prohibitions for juveniles. Most states prohibit youngsters from buying, selling, possessing, transporting, or consuming alcoholic beverages (this includes low alcohol-by-content beverages such as wine and low-alcohol beer). Federal highway safety regulations require most states to extend this prohibition to 18–20-year-old adults as well. This age group constitutes a unique status offender population, because for all other purposes they are adults. As a result of the health risks posed by tobacco use, states increasingly have prohibited tobacco sales to minors. This includes the sale of all types of smoking and chewing tobacco. With tobacco and alcohol prohibitions, it is a violation of the law (i.e., a crime) for adults to sell or provide in any way to minors, and a violation for minors to buy or possess.

Underage gambling has become an issue in states that have instituted state lotteries and in newly emerging casino gambling jurisdictions. As is the case with alcohol-related offenses, most states have some prohibitions for the 18–20-year-old group. For instance, states may allow these young adults to play the state lottery, but they may not be allowed to gamble in casinos.

Finally, sexual activity presents a unique form of status offenses. States may prohibit youngsters under the "age of consent" from engaging in sexual activity with other youngsters or adults. Sexually active juveniles may be classified as promiscuous and the juvenile court can intervene in such situations. It is important to recognize, however, that in this area of status offense jurisdiction girls may be treated differently than boys by the courts. In fact, some states historically set higher jurisdictional age limits for girls than boys on the assumption that girls needed greater protections against unwanted pregnancies. Such differences in classification and treatment have brought obvious charges of sexism against juvenile courts and, since the 1970s, statutes making these types of distinctions have been struck down by appellate courts.

## Status Offenses in Other Nations

A quick review of the *World Factbook of Criminal Justice Systems* reveals that the U.S. remains relatively unique among the nations of the world in its treatment of status offenses. Most of the nations in Central and South America (including Brazil, Colombia, Costa Rica, Mexico, and Venezuela) treat as juvenile crimes only those offenses that would be crimes for adults. Likewise, Australia, Canada, France, Germany, Italy, Spain, and Sweden either do not specify status offenses in their juvenile codes or they treat these behaviors through social service or child welfare agencies.

## Changes in Methods of Handling Status Offenders

For much of the second half of the 20th century, critics of the juvenile justice system found status offender treatment and incarceration along with serious delinquents an intolerable arrangement. It placed the least serious offenders in a situation where they could be physically and sexually exploited and corrupted by the juvenile justice system's most serious and intractable offenders. These criticisms eventually brought about changes beginning in 1974 with passage of the Juvenile Justice and Delinquency Prevention Act (JJDPA). When the U.S. Congress passed the JJDPA, one of the key provisions was the deinstitutionalization of status offenders. In other words, youngsters convicted of status offenses were not to be incarcerated in secure juvenile correctional facilities. This legislation resulted in almost half of the youngsters then incarcerated being released. However, in the place of secure correctional placements, a variety of secure and nonsecure private facilities were established. Some were hospitals and some were community mental health agencies. The youngsters sent to these private placements no longer were "delinquents." Instead they were identified as having behavior problems or "conduct disorders." Ultimately, the total population of youngsters detained increased substantially, with the greatest growth coming in the private sector institutions.

It is virtually impossible to know how many status offenses are processed by the juvenile courts annually. Although there are relatively uniform definitions of these acts, there are not uniform ways in how they are processed. Nevertheless, passage of the Juvenile Justice and Delinquency Prevention Act of 1974 (and its subsequent amendments) has resulted in some states redefining status offenses. In 1997, nearly 7000 youngsters were detained in some type of facility for status offenses, most for incorrigibility, running away, or truancy. However, in several states status offenders now are classified as children in need of supervision or services (CHINS), and these youngsters are dealt with in nonresidential or nonsecure types of programs. A few states have classified status offenses as a form of dependency. This approach allows the juvenile court to take jurisdiction over the child and family when services are needed, but when they might not be sought voluntarily. Whatever the approach, there continues to be a lingering doubt about the role of the juvenile justice system in addressing status offenses.

Many of the activities classified as status offenses do not seem very serious compared to most delinquent offenses. In fact, some of these activities (particularly periodic truancy and the use of tobacco and alcohol) seem so prevalent that they are considered by most adults as part of growing up. Nevertheless, virtually all state juvenile codes continue to include status offenses among the acts for which the juvenile court can intervene in the lives of children and their parents. Status offenses may no longer be considered delinquency, but these behaviors are believed to be sufficiently problematic to warrant some action. One of the principal assumptions concerning status offenses—although one not established by research—is that if these behaviors are not addressed youngsters will go on to commit more serious delinquent offenses. Some do, but many do not. The problem the juvenile justice system is left with is what, if anything, should be done in regard to status offenses. Should the courts act early and decisively, or should the actions largely be ignored on the assumption that most youngsters will grow out of this type of conduct?

G. Larry Mays

## References and Further Reading

Balcher, J. (Ed.), *When There's No Place like Home,* Baltimore, MD: Brookes, 1994.

Bureau of Justice Statistics, *The World Factbook of Criminal Justice Systems.* Washington, DC: U.S. Department of Justice, 1993, 2002. Available at www.ojp.usdoj.gov/bjs/abstract/wfcj.htm.

Chesney-Lind, M. and Shelden, R.G., *Girls, Delinquency, and Juvenile Justice,* Belmont, CA: Wadsworth, 1992.

Forst, M.L. (Ed.), *The New Juvenile Justice,* Chicago, IL: Nelson-Hall, 1995.

Gallagher, C.A., *Juvenile Offenders in Residential Placement, 1997,* Washington, DC: Office of Juvenile Justice and Delinquency Prevention, 1999.

Garry, E.M., *Truancy: First Step to a Lifetime of Problems,* Washington, DC: Office of Juvenile Justice and Delinquency Prevention, 1996.

Golden, R., *Disposable Children: America's Welfare System,* Belmont, CA: Wadsworth, 1997.

Maguire, K. and Pastore, A.L. (Eds.), *Sourcebook of Criminal Justice Statistics—1998,* Washington, DC: Bureau of Justice Statistics, 1999.

Mays, G.L. and Winfree, L.T., Jr., *Juvenile Justice,* New York, NY: McGraw-Hill, 2000.

Poe-Yamagata, E. and Butts, J.A., *Female Offenders in the Juvenile Justice System,* Washington, DC: Office of Juvenile Justice and Delinquency Prevention, 1996.

Puzzanchera, C., Stahl, A.L., Finnegan, T.A., Snyder, H.N., Poole, R.S. and Tierney, N., *Juvenile Court Statistics, 1997,* Washington, DC: Office of Juvenile Justice and Delinquency Prevention, 2000.

Thomas, C.W., Are status offenders really so different? A comparative and longitudinal assessment, *Crime and Delinquency* 27 (1971).

*See also* **Juvenile Delinquency: Extent, Correlates, and Trends; Juvenile Justice: The Courts; Schools and Delinquent Behavior**

# Statute of Limitations as a Defense to Criminal Liability

Statutes of limitations are legal definitions explaining the amount of time individuals have to file either a criminal case or a civil lawsuit on a matter, or to put it simply, a statute of limitation is a deadline for filing a case in court. The length of time involved in a statute of limitations is highly variable. The precise time line depends upon the jurisdiction—state or federal—and the type of offense in question. When discussing statutes of limitations, therefore, one must remain cognizant of several factors, such as where the event in question took place, what actually happened, and when the statute of limitations takes effect.

Given the complex nature of statute of limitations clauses, it is important to describe briefly how they were first conceived. Similar to many U.S. legal principles, statutes of limitation are based in old English law, and serve as an attempt to relieve the problem of allowing plaintiffs to bring charges against another as long as both parties are alive. This system, obviously, is fraught with the potential of allowing the flagging or possibly even the destruction—through the mere passage of time—of evidence or testimony needed to prepare an adequate defense. It was the Court of Equity—handling only real estate cases—that first instituted the "doctrine of laches," which contended that a plaintiff, since becoming aware of an injury or wrongdoing, waited an unreasonable amount of time before bringing charges, effectively diminishing one's legal defense.

Although the doctrine of laches is the precursor to statute of limitation clauses, it should be noted that they are applied differently, with the doctrine of laches looking to the reasonableness of a delay. Contrary to this, statutes of limitations are concerned only with the amount of time passed and are irreversible once the time limit is reached. Although this makes statute of limitation clauses sound straightforward, they do contain a great amount of confusion. Much of this confusion comes from determining when the statute of limitation begins; that is, when the clock starts recording the amount of time allowed for a plaintiff to bring charges.

These effective decisions cause courts problems in establishing when limitations begin in different cases. In medical malpractice suits, for example, some courts have decided that the time for filing a claim begins when the event or omission takes place, others assert that the time does not start until an injury results from a medical act or omitted act. An alternative is that the time begins when an injury is discovered or *should* have been discovered, and a final view is that the time limit starts when the treatment is finished.

Medical malpractice suits point to the complexity involved in deciding when statute of limitation clauses take effect, and the responsibility placed upon the plaintiff. This responsibility is the expectation that a plaintiff *should* know or discover the wrongdoing. If, for instance, a homeowner contracts to have her roof replaced and upon completion it begins to leak, but goes undiscovered for nearly 20 years, she has missed her opportunity to bring charges against the roofing company. It is reasonable to assume that the homeowner should have known or discovered the faulty work much sooner.

This notion of discovery carries over into many different types of cases including claims of negligent environmental contamination. Environmental contamination, given that much of the damage is below the surface, is not always readily apparent. Regardless of this, it is well-settled that the statute of limitations begins to run when the plaintiff is injured or when the plaintiff should have reasonably discovered the injury and its likely cause.

Discovery rules become increasingly more complicated when dealing with adults sexually abused as children. In a California case, for example, a father was accused of molesting his daughters for nearly 20 years, and the daughters waited almost 25 years from the final episode to file charges. At the time of the offense, the California statute of limitation on child molestation was 3 years after the crime was alleged to have occurred. As mental health evidence pointed to the difficulty in reporting child sexual abuse cases, the California legislature passed a law giving greater latitude in when the statute of limitations would begin in child sexual abuse cases. In this case, unfortunately, the father was able to avoid prosecution because the passage of the new law was after the offense was alleged to have taken place.

There are exceptions to the applicability of statutes of limitations and legal mechanisms put in place to allow for a break in the deadline to file charges. This procedure is referred to as *tolling*, which is a legal mechanism used to stop the time operating on a statute of limitation. Some reasons for limitations to toll are mental disability, underage, and fugitive status. In situations where a victim is a minor or mentally disabled, the statute of limitations is tolled until the victim turns 18, or the disability is removed or a mentally competent guardian is established. When individuals flee from the jurisdiction in which they are accused of wrongdoing, the statute of limitations is tolled until they return for legal proceedings.

Statutes of limitations, obviously, are complicated legal issues depending upon several factors. Indeed, statutes of limitations are relative to the offense type, the jurisdiction the offense was committed, and any tolling considerations effecting the time limit for filing charges.

MATTHEW DEMICHELE

### References and Further Reading

Engle, M. (1988). *Statutes of Limitations.* New York, NY: Alfred A Knopf.

Kerper, H.B. (1972). *Introduction to the Criminal Justice System.* St. Paul, MN: West Publications.

Levy, A.J. (1987). *Solving Statute of Limitations Problems.* Accord Station, Hingham, MA: Kluwer Law Book Publishing.

Skotnicki, T.P. (2002). "Arraignment," in *The Encyclopedia of Crime and Punishment.* Thousand Oaks, CA: Sage Publications.

*See also* **Defenses to Criminal Liability: Justifications and Excuses**

# Strain Theories: From Durkheim to Merton

The core idea of all strain theories is that crime is more likely when people cannot get what they want through legal channels. The inability to get what they want leads to a range of negative emotions like frustration and anger, and these emotions increase the likelihood that they will turn to crime in order to get what they want (e.g., theft to obtain money), strike out at others (e.g., assault, vandalism), or make themselves feel better (e.g., illicit drug use). In extreme cases, they may kill themselves to end their misery. Emile Durkheim (1951) presented the first modern version of strain theory, although Robert K. Merton's (1968) version of strain theory has had a far greater impact on criminology. In fact, Merton's theory and the revisions in it by Cohen (1955) and Cloward and Ohlin (1960) were perhaps the most widely accepted explanations of crime in the 1950s and 1960s. Further, they played a pivotal role in shaping the War on Poverty in the 1960s, which was designed in part to reduce crime by making it easier for people to achieve their goals through legal channels. Merton's strain theory has since come under heavy attack and it is much less influential today, although it continues to stimulate research in the field and it is the inspiration behind recent revisions in strain theory.

## Durkheim

Durkheim presented the most complete version of his strain theory in his book *Suicide: A Study in Sociology,* (1987) (also see Pickering and Walford, 2000; Poggi, 2000). He attempts to explain why some groups have higher suicide rates than others and why suicide rates vary over time. He begins his presentation of strain theory by posing a rather interesting question: why do suicide rates increase during economic crises. The answer might seem obvious: economic crises increase suicide rates because they increase poverty. Durkheim, however, points out that suicide rates also increase during periods of rapid economic expansion that involve increases in prosperity. Further, he notes that many poor areas have very low suicide rates. So we cannot simply argue that poverty or increases in poverty cause suicide. The explanation is more complex. We need to explain why both rapid increases in poverty and in prosperity cause increases in the suicide rate. Durkheim provides a rather creative explanation.

According to Durkheim, all healthy societies set limits on the goals that individuals pursue. These limits are set so that individuals have a reasonable chance of achieving their goals, which makes them "contented with their lot while stimulating them moderately to improve it" (Durkheim, 1951, 250). As Durkheim (1951, 246) states, "no living being can be happy or even exist unless his needs are sufficiently proportioned to his means." During periods of rapid social change or turmoil, however, societies may lose their ability to regulate individual goals. In such cases, individuals may come to pursue goals that are beyond their means. Individuals, according to Durkheim, have trouble setting limits on their desires. Individuals only limit their desires in response to "an authority they respect." That authority is society or "one of its organs." When society is in a state of disruption or turmoil, individuals are freed from societal regulation and may come to pursue goals they cannot achieve. The pursuit of such goals inevitably frustrates them, and this frustration leads many to despair and suicide.

Durkheim describes several situations where societies lose their ability to adequately regulate individual goals. The first involves economic crises, where many individuals experience a sudden loss of position. Such individuals must lower their goals, but "society cannot adjust them instantaneously to this new life and teach them to practice the increased self-repression to which they are unaccustomed" (1951, 252). As a consequence, these individuals continue to pursue the same goals as before, even though they are now ill-equipped to achieve them. The second involves abrupt increases in economic prosperity. A sudden growth in wealth leads many to increase their goals. As Durkheim (1951, 253, 254) states: "with increased prosperity desires increase...Wealth...by the power it bestows, deceives us into thinking that we depend on ourselves only. The less limited one feels, the more intolerable all limitation appears." Even those who do not benefit from the increased prosperity increase their desires, because the good fortune of some increases the desires of others. Many individuals, then, come to desire far more than they able to achieve.

Durkheim also states that the regulation of individual goals has broken down in the economic sphere. In fact, people are encouraged to pursue unlimited goals

in this sphere of life. "For a whole century, economic progress has mainly consisted in freeing industrial relations from all regulation," including regulation by religious institutions, occupational groups, and governmental agencies (1951, 254). Economic institutions have come to dominate industrial societies, and economic progress has stimulated the desire of people throughout society for wealth and power.

> From top to bottom of the ladder, greed is aroused without knowing where to find ultimate foothold. Nothing can calm it, since its goal is far beyond all it can attain. Reality seems valueless by comparison with the dreams of fevered imaginations; reality is therefore abandoned, but so too is possibility abandoned when it becomes reality. A thirst arises for novelties, unfamiliar pleasures, nameless sensations, all of which lose their savor once known...It is everlastingly repeated that it is man's nature to be eternally dissatisfied, constantly to advance, without relief or rest, toward an indefinite goal. The longing for infinity is daily represented as a mark of moral distinction . . . The doctrine of the most ruthless and swift progress has become an article of faith (1951, 256, 257).

In all these cases, society's inability to regulate or limit individual goals leads individuals to pursue goals that are beyond their means. Higher rates of suicide are the result. It is not poverty that causes suicide. In fact, Durkheim argues that poverty sometimes act as a restraint to suicide, because poverty may act as a restraint to one's desires. "The horizon of the lower classes is limited by those above them, and for this same reason their desires are more modest" (1951, 256). Wealth, on the other hand, often stimulates one's desires. "The more one has, the more one wants, since satisfactions received only stimulate instead of filling needs" (1951, 248). Rather than poverty, suicide is caused by the desire for more than one can realistically obtain. If anything, such desires are more likely in the higher than lower classes.

In sum, Durkheim argues that suicide stems from the failure of society to limit or restrain individual goals—with this failure being most common in the economic sphere and during times of rapid economic growth and decline. The failure to restrain individual goals contributes to the development of unattainable goals. In some case, individuals come to pursue everescalating goals or goals that are impossible to achieve. "If one happens almost to have exhausted the range of what is possible, one dreams of the impossible; one thirsts for the non-existent" (Durkheim, 1951, 271).

Although the focus of Durkheim's theory is on suicide, it is not difficult to extend the theory to crime. First, individuals pursuing unattainable goals may turn to crime in a desperate attempt to achieve such goals.

Second, the pursuit of unattainable goals often leaves individuals exhausted and disgusted with life (Durkheim, 1951, 286). Such individuals may seek relief in drug use or other means of escape, with suicide being the ultimate escape. Third, individuals may turn to crime out of the anger that results from the inevitable setbacks that are experienced in the pursuit of unattainable goals. Durkheim, in fact, states that individuals who blame others for their difficulties may commit homicide or assault before turning to suicide (1951, 285).

Although Durkheim's theory is easily extended to crime, it has been largely neglected by criminologists. Perhaps the major reason for this neglect was the development of Merton's strain theory in 1938. Merton reinterpreted Durkheim's theory to fit American society, which was in the midst of a major depression at the time. So rather than focusing on the pursuit of everescalating or impossible-to-achieve goals by the higher classes, Merton focused on the inability of lower-class individuals to achieve more limited economic goals. Merton also extended strain theory to explain a broader range of deviant behavior including many types of crime (see Agnew, 1997). The resultant popularity of Merton's theory may have diverted attention from Durkheim's theory.

The neglect of Durkheim's theory is unfortunate, because certain research suggests that the pursuit of everescalating or unlimited goals may play a role in the explanation of some crime (see Agnew, 1997). Matza and Sykes (1961, 715), for example, observe that many delinquents have "grandiose dreams of quick success" and that "the sudden acquisition of large sums of money" is their goal. The origin of such goals is somewhat unclear, but it is not unreasonable to suppose that they stem at least partly from a lack of societal regulation. Further, Durkheim's theory holds much promise for the explanation of middle- and upper-class crime and delinquency, including white-collar crime. In fact, certain of the more contemporary efforts to explain middle- and upper-class crime draw heavily on Durkheim (see Merton, 1964; Mizruchi, 1964).

## Merton

Like Durkheim, Merton argues that much crime stems from the inability of people to achieve their goals through legal channels. Merton, however, does not argue that the pursuit of such goals stems from a lack of social regulation. In fact, he argues that societies often encourage individuals to pursue lofty goals. (His arguments in this area bear some similarity to Durkheim's views about the economic sphere, where the pursuit of lofty goals is encouraged according to

Durkheim.) Further, Merton focuses on the pursuit of limited goals rather than impossible or everescalating goals. Merton's theory is in two parts.

The first part describes why the U.S. has a higher crime rate than many other societies. Merton states that societies differ in the relative emphasis they place on goals and the rules governing goal achievement. Some societies, like the U.S., place a strong emphasis on goals but little emphasis on the rules governing the pursuit of such goals. In particular, the U.S. places great stress on the goal of economic success, but much less stress on the rules governing the achievement of such success (e.g., honesty, hard work, thrift). We have, in essence, a society where "it's not how you play the game that matters, but whether you win or lose." As a consequence, people in the U.S. are more likely to resort to illegal methods of making money when legal methods are not available or easily employed.

This part of Merton's theory has not been well explored, although it forms a central component of Messner and Rosenfeld's (1997) institutional anomie theory. Messner and Rosenfeld argue that the high rate of violence in the U.S. partly stems from the emphasis placed on the "American Dream": wherein everyone is encouraged to strive for monetary success, but little emphasis is placed on the legitimate norms or rules for achieving such success. Messner and Rosenfeld note that the American Dream has certain positive effects, providing "the motivational dynamic for economic expansion, extraordinary technological innovation, and high rates of social mobility," but their focus is on "the dark side of the American Dream," particularly the crime that it produces (1997, 7). In the words of Merton (1968, 200), "a cardinal American virtue, 'ambition,' promotes a cardinal American vice, 'deviant behavior.'"

The second part of Merton's theory seeks to explain why some groups in the U.S. have higher rates of crime and deviance than other groups; specifically, why lower-class individuals have higher rates of crime than middle- and upper-class individuals. It was thought that crime was overwhelmingly concentrated among the poor at the time the theory was written; we now know that crime is much more common among the higher classes than previously thought, although the precise relationship between crime and class is still a matter of debate. Merton argues that all individuals in the U.S.—regardless of class—are encouraged to strive for monetary success. This encouragement comes from such sources as family, friends, school officials, politicians, and the media. In the words of Merton, "the goal of monetary success is entrenched in American Culture," and "Americans are bombarded on every side by precepts that affirm the right or, often, the duty of retaining the goal even in the face of repeated frustration" (1968, 190–191). As a consequence, substantial number of people—including lower-class individuals—develop a desire for such success. Not everyone, however, is able to achieve such success through legal channels.

Lower-class individuals, in particular, are more likely to find that legal avenues to monetary success are unavailable to them. Their families are less likely to equip them with the attitudes and skills necessary to do well in school. They are more likely to live in communities with limited resources and inferior schools. They more often face discrimination in the larger community, including the educational system and job market. And their families lack the resources to finance an advanced education or help them secure good jobs. So lower-class individuals are encouraged to strive for monetary success on the one hand, but they are prevented from achieving such success through legal channels on the other. Consequently, they are under much strain: they want money, but cannot obtain it legally.

Merton states that there are several ways to adapt to this strain. The first and most common adaptation is conformity. Individuals continue to strive for monetary success through legal channels, even though they are not very successful in their efforts. They may be dissatisfied with their monetary situation, but they live with this dissatisfaction—perhaps thinking that monetary success will eventually be theirs. A second adaptation to strain is ritualism. Individuals reduce their desire for monetary success to the point where it can be achieved. That is, individuals lower their goals. In this area, data suggest that many lower-class individuals have in fact lowered their desire for monetary success—although a substantial number continue to desire such success (see Agnew, 2000).

There are three additional adaptations to strain, each of which may involve crime. The adaptation most closely linked to crime is innovation. Individuals continue to pursue the goal of monetary success, but they try to achieve this goal through illegitimate channels like theft, selling drugs, and prostitution. A fourth adaptation is retreatism; here individuals retreat from society—rejecting the goal of monetary success and abandoning efforts to achieve it. Retreatism may take a number of forms, including alcoholism, drug use, vagrancy, and in the most extreme case, suicide. The final adaptation is rebellion. Here individuals not only reject the goal of monetary success and abandon efforts to achieve it, they substitute new goals and new means to achieve them in their place. Rebellion often manifests itself in political action, but it may also assume nonpolitical forms. Cohen (1955), for example, argues that some lower-class youth have come to define success in terms of one's skill in criminal activities, like fighting and theft.

So individuals may adapt to strain in several ways, some of which involve crime. A central question is why some people adapt to crime whereas most do not. Merton provides some suggestions in this area. For example, he states that lower-class individuals are more likely to adapt to strain with crime because they are less committed to legitimate rules or norms. Merton, however, has been criticized for not providing a fuller, more systematic discussion of the factors that influence whether one adapts to strain with crime or conformity or ritualism. Many of the major revisions in his theory, like those of Cohen (1955) and Cloward and Ohlin (1960), focus on this issue.

In sum, Merton offers a rather interesting explanation for the concentration of crime in the lower classes. As he states, "It is only when a system of cultural values extols, virtually above all else, certain common success goals for the population at large while the social structure vigorously restricts or completely closes access to approved modes of reaching these goals for a considerable part of the same population that deviant behavior ensues on a large scale." (157).

Merton's argument that crime results from the inability to achieve monetary success has been the subject of much attention in criminology. Many embraced the theory at first, although some stated that the theory was in need of further elaboration (some of the more popular elaborations are discussed below). The theory and its elaborations were perhaps the dominant explanations of crime during the 1950s and 1960s, although as Burton and Cullen (1992) point out, this was not because of a mass of empirical research supporting strain theory. Rather, the theory fit in well with "the growing concern in sixties America over equal opportunity" (Burton and Cullen, 1992, 2). The influence of the theory was reflected in the fact that it helped inspire the War on Poverty during the 1960s. The War on Poverty, initiated by President Kennedy and largely implemented by President Johnson, attempted to increase the opportunities of lower-class individuals to achieve monetary success through legal channels. It was felt that this would not only reduce rates of poverty, but also a range of related problems like crime. Many of the programs initiated under the War on Poverty have since been dismantled, but a few remain—like Project Headstart, a preschool enrichment program, and Jobs Corps, a jobs training program. Although the War on Poverty did not achieve its lofty goals, evidence suggests that some of the programs that it spawned—like Project Headstart and Job Corps—may be effective at reducing subsequent crime (Agnew, 2001).

Merton's theory, however, came under heavy criticism and it is no longer as popular today as it once was. The initial criticisms of the theory focused on the argument that lower-class individuals have a strong desire for monetary success. It was claimed that lower-class individuals adapt to their deprived situation by lowering their desire for money (i.e., by adopting the adaptation of ritualism) and so experience little strain. Data suggest that lower-class individuals do desire less money on average than middle-class individuals, but a substantial number of lower-class individuals—a majority in some studies—desire as much money as middle-class individuals. Data also suggest that, relative to what they have, lower-class individuals desire as much or more money than middle-class individuals. Further, data suggest that lower-class individuals are somewhat more likely to report that they do not expect to achieve their monetary goals and that they are dissatisfied with their monetary situation (Agnew, 2000). So there is some support for Merton's argument that lower-class individuals are relatively more likely to find that they cannot achieve monetary success through legal channels. It is important to note, however, that many middle-class individuals also report that they are not achieving their monetary goals and they are dissatisfied with their monetary situation. Although Merton's strain theory predicts that crime will be concentrated in the lower classes, it also recognizes that some middle-class individuals will have difficulty achieving their goals. And the theory can be used to explain middle-class crime (see Merton, 1964; Adler and Laufer, 1995; Passas and Agnew, 1997).

The key proposition of the theory is that the inability to achieve economic goals increases the likelihood of crime. Surprisingly, few studies have directly tested this proposition. A number of studies have focused on the ability to achieve educational and occupational goals (see Agnew, 2000; Burton and Cullen, 1992). These studies typically ask juveniles how much education or what occupations they would ideally like to get, and how much education or what occupations they realistically expect to get. Such studies usually find that delinquency is not related to the disjunction between ideal goals and expectations: that is, delinquency is not higher among those who do not expect to achieve their ideal educational or occupational goals. Such studies played a major role in reducing the popularity of Merton's theory starting in the late 1960s. These studies themselves, however, have been criticized.

Most notably, Merton's theory focuses on the inability to achieve monetary success, not educational or occupational success (also see Agnew, 1997, 2000; Bernard, 1982; Burton and Cullen, 1992; Passas and Agnew, 1997). Some commentators have suggested that those individuals who engage in crime have little concern about their educational or occupational futures, but are quite concerned about their monetary status. So a proper test of the theory should focus on monetary goals. Surprisingly, there has not been much research in this area. The few studies that have been done, however, provide some support for Merton (see Passas and Agnew, 1997; Agnew, 1997, 2000; Cernkovich et al., 2000). Criminals frequently report that they engage in income-generating crime because they want money but cannot easily get it any other way. And some data suggest that individuals who are dissatisfied with their monetary situation are more likely than others to engage in crime. Both lower- and middle-class individuals report dissatisfaction with their monetary situation, although such dissatisfaction is more common in the lower classes. Related to this, some data suggest that lower-class individuals are more likely to engage in serious crime and there is little doubt that street crimes are most common in economically deprived areas.

So there is limited support for the central ideas of Merton's strain theory: the inability to achieve monetary success may increase the likelihood of crime, with the inability to achieve such success being greatest in the lower classes. More research is needed on Merton's theory, however; particularly on those factors that influence the effect of monetary strain on crime.

## Applying Durkheim and Merton's Theories to Crime in the International Community

Most of the research on strain theory has focused on explaining individual differences in crime in the U.S., but several researchers have recently drawn on Durkheim's and especially Merton's strain theories to explain changes in the crime rate in a number of countries and to explain intersocietal differences in crime rates.

A number of countries have experienced large increases in crime in recent decades, particularly those countries that comprised the former Soviet Union, like Russia, and those Eastern European countries that were under Soviet control. These increases have been explained partly in terms of the failure to achieve monetary goals. In particular, it is argued that the collapse of the Soviet Union lead many people in these countries to expect that economic conditions would improve. Instead, economic conditions frequently worsened; resulting in much economic strain and increased crime rates. The increases in crime are also said to be owing to the rapid social change these countries experienced. Political, economic, and other institutions underwent tremendous change in a short period of time. The resulting turmoil created a situation where many of the norms or rules that governed behavior lost their force, but there was not sufficient time to establish new norms. So a state of anomie or normlessness came to exist (see Savelsberg, 1995 for an excellent discussion).

Similar arguments have been made with respect to many developing countries, like Malaysia and Venezuela (see Stephens, 1994; Ariffin, 1995). These countries are undergoing rapid social change as they industrialize. Such change and the factors associated with it, like massive migration to urban areas and increased exposure to Western influences may increase crime for the reasons listed above. Many individuals come to desire economic success, but large segments of the population are unable to achieve such success through legitimate channels. Also, traditional norms lose their force as the society undergoes institutional changes, as migration to urban areas increases, and as exposure to Western influences increases.

Other researchers have drawn on strain theory to explain why some societies have higher crime rates than others. Their research suggests that it is not the absolute poverty that causes high crime rates, but rather income inequality. That is, crime rates are highest not in those societies that are very poor, but in those where there are both poor and wealthy individuals. Researchers have argued that the wealth of some leads others to increase their monetary expectations, thereby creating economic strain. Further, data suggest that crime is especially high in those societies that are high in economic discrimination; that is, societies that deny access to monetary success based on ascribed characteristics like race (see Messner, 1989). The economic inequality in such societies is especially likely to be seen as unjust, which further contributes to the anger and frustration that fuel crime. Finally, there is some suggestion that the breakdown in social norms that often accompanies industrialization may contribute to higher crime rates (Krohn, 1978).

## Revisions to Merton's Theory by Cohen and Cloward and Ohlin

Cohen (1955) was interested in explaining the delinquency of lower- and working-class gang members; such delinquency was a major concern in the 1950s, as it is today. Cohen first discussed the nature of gang delinquency. He claimed that much gang delinquency was nonutilitarian, malicious, and negativistic. Gang members do not steal or engage in other crimes for the purpose of obtaining money or material goods. Rather, their criminal activity is nonutilitarian; for example, they steal "for the hell of it"; frequently taking things they do not need and throwing away what they do steal. Further, their delinquency is malicious: gang members take "keen delight in terrorizing 'good' children, in driving them from playgrounds and gyms for which

the gang itself may have little use, and in general making themselves obnoxious to the virtuous.... There is an element of active spite and malice, contempt and ridicule, challenge and defiance, exquisitely symbolized in an incident...of defecating on the teacher's desk" (1955, 28). Gang members, in sum, have created a negativistic subculture; they have taken the rules of the larger society and "turned them upside down." That is, gang members have come to value those delinquent activities—like theft, vandalism, and fighting—that are condemned by the larger society. How can we explain such delinquent behavior?

According to Cohen, most lower- and working-class boys come to desire middle-class status (Cohen's focus was on male delinquency; see Broidy and Agnew, 1997, for a discussion of strain theory and gender). Such status involves more than monetary success; it involves achieving respect in the eyes of others. Lower- and working-class boys, however, have trouble achieving such status through legal channels. This becomes apparent when they enter the school system, where they often have to compete against middle-class juveniles, live up to the expectations of middle-class teachers, and satisfy the standards of a middle-class institution. Their families and other community members have not equipped them with the skills and values necessary to do well in school, and they are frequently frustrated—even humiliated—in their efforts to do well. As Cohen (1955, 115) states, "the 'good' children are the studious, the obedient, the docile. It is precisely the working-class children who are most likely to be 'problems' because of their relative lack of training in order and discipline, their lack of interest in intellectual achievement and their lack of reinforcement by the home in conformity to requirements of the school." So the working-class boy is "more likely than his middle-class peers to find himself at the bottom of the status hierarchy whenever he moves in a middle-class world...To the degree that he values the good opinion of middle-class persons or has to some degree internalized middle-class standards himself, he faces a problem of adjustment and is in the market for a 'solution'" (Cohen, 1955, 119).

That is to say, lower- and working-class boys frequently find themselves experiencing a particular type of strain: they desire middle-class status but cannot achieve it through legal means. It is not easy to steal or otherwise get middle-class status through illegal means. So how do lower- and working-class boys adapt to their strain? Some come together and set up an alternative status system in which they can successfully compete. And their hostility toward the middle-class that frustrates them, among other things, leads them to set up a status system that values everything the middle-class condemns. So, for example, theft and violence are valued. This adaptation would be described as "rebellion" by Merton; conventional success goals and the means to achieve them are rejected, and new goals and means are substituted in their place.

Cohen's theory has been criticized on several points. Most notably, it has been said that Cohen's depiction of delinquent gangs is not entirely accurate. Much gang delinquency is utilitarian in nature and gang members do not unconditionally approve of acts like fighting and theft. Rather, they tend to condemn delinquent acts, although claim that their own delinquency is justified or excused by their circumstances (see Cloward and Ohlin, 1960). For example, although they believe that fighting and theft are generally bad, they feel that they must fight to protect themselves and their communities and that they must steal because of the barriers they face. At the same time, Cohen's use of strain theory to explain the formation of gangs was a major contribution. And many current attempts to explain the formation of gangs and explain why juveniles join gangs draw heavily on strain theory (see Agnew, 2001). Cohen's work also sheds important light on the factors that influence whether individuals adapt to strain with crime. According to Cohen, people are more likely to adapt to strain with crime when they interact with other strained or delinquent individuals—with such individuals providing support for a criminal response.

Like Cohen, Cloward and Ohlin (1960) use strain theory to explain lower-class gang delinquency. Drawing on Merton, they argue that the primary type of strain affecting lower-class individuals is the inability to achieve monetary success through legal channels. They then argue that some strained males in the lower classes adapt to this strain by forming delinquent gangs. This is most likely when lower-class boys are in communication with one another and they blame their failure to achieve monetary success on the social order. Gang members come to support one another in their crime; developing shared justifications or rationalizations for their behaviors, among other things. In particular, they claim that their crime is "a natural response to a trying situation."

Cloward and Ohlin, however, go on to argue that the nature of gang delinquency depends on the environment of the gang. Some lower-class boys adapt to their strain by forming "criminal" gangs, which specialize in obtaining money and material objects through illegal channels (i.e., they employ Merton's adaptation of innovation). Such gangs are most likely to develop in communities where adult criminals establish close relationships with strained juveniles, teaching them the techniques necessary for many income-generating crimes. Other lower-class boys adapt by forming "conflict" gangs, which specialize in violent crime and accord greatest status to those who are the toughest and most destructive (i.e., they employ the adaptation of rebellion). Such gangs are most likely to form in communities where adult criminals do not provide instruction in and access to illegitimate channels for monetary success. Finally, some lower-class boys form "retreatist" gangs, which focus on the pursuit of pleasure, often through drug and alcohol use. Strained juveniles who are not able to function well in criminal or conflict-oriented gangs are more likely to get involved with retreatist gangs.

Cloward and Ohlin, then, argue that although strain creates a general disposition for crime, the nature of the criminal behavior that results depends on the environment in which strained individuals find themselves. Cloward and Ohlin's theory has also been criticized. Most notably, data suggest that most gang members do not specialize in income-generating crimes or fighting or drug use; rather, most gang members engage in a wide range of criminal behavior. Nevertheless, there is some specialization in gang behavior (see Agnew, 2001) and Cloward and Ohlin make an important contribution when they point out that environmental factors not only influence whether strained individuals engage in crime, but also the types of crime they commit (see Cullen, 1984).

## Summary

Although the strain theories discussed in this entry no longer dominate the field of criminology, they still have some influence contemporary research (Adler and Laufer, 1995; Passas and Agnew, 1997; Cernkovich et al., 2000). And this research suggests that the inability to achieve monetary success or middle-class status may have some impact on crime. More research is needed on these theories, however; particularly research that employs better measures of monetary strain and explores the factors that condition the impact of such strain on crime. More research is also needed on the "macro-side" of these theories, which attempt to explain changes in crime rates over time and intersocietal differences in crime rates. Beyond that, it should be noted that many of the central ideas of these theories have been incorporated into new versions of strain theory, as discussed in the entry on Strain Theory: Recent Developments.

ROBERT AGNEW

## References and Further Reading

Adler, F. and Laufer, W.S., *Advances in Criminological Theory, Volume 6: The Legacy of Anomie Theory,* New Brunswick, NJ: Transaction, 1995.

Ariffin, J., At the crossroads of rapid development: Malaysian society and anomie, *International Journal of Sociology and Social Policy* 15:343–371 (1995).

Agnew, R., Sources of criminality: Strain and subcultural theories, in *Criminology: A Contemporary Handbook,* Sheley, J.F., (Ed.), Belmont, CA: Wadsworth, 2000.

Agnew, R., The nature and determinants of strain: Another look at Durkheim and Merton, in *The Future of Anomie Theory,* Passas, N. and Agnew, R., (Eds.), Boston, MA: Northeastern University Press, 1997.

Agnew, R. *Juvenile Delinquency: Causes and Control.* Los Angeles, CA: Roxbury, 2001.

Bernard, T.J., Control criticisms of strain theories, *Journal of Research in Crime and Delinquency* 21:353–372 (1984).

Broidy, L. and Agnew, R., Gender and crime: A general strain theory perspective, *Journal of Research in Crime and Delinquency* 34:275–306 (1997).

Burton, V.S. and Cullen, F.T., The empirical status of strain theory, *Journal of Criminal Justice* 15:1—30 (1992).

Cernkovich, S.A., Giordano, P.C. and Rudolph, J.L., Race, crime, and the American dream, *Journal of Research in Crime and Delinquency* 37:131–170 (2000).

Cloward, R.A. and Ohlin, L.E., *Delinquency and Opportunity,* New York, NY: Free Press, 1960.

Cohen, A., *Delinquent Boys,* New York, NY: Free Press, 1955.

Cullen, F.T., *Rethinking Crime and Deviance: The Emergence of a Structuring Tradition,* Totowa, NJ: Rowman and Allanheld, 1984.

Durkheim, E., *Suicide: A Study in Sociology,* New York, NY: Free Press, 1987.

Krohn, M.D., A Durkheimian analysis of international crime rates, *Social Forces* 57:654–670 (1878).

Matza, D. and Sykes, G. Juvenile delinquency and subterranean values, *American Sociological Review* 26:713–719 (1961).

Merton, R.K., Social structure and anomie, *American Sociological Review* 3:672–682 (1938).

Merton, R.K., Anomie, anomia, and social interaction: Contexts of deviant behavior, in *Anomie and Deviant Behavior,* Clinard, M.B., (Ed.), New York, NY: Free Press, 1964.

Merton, R.K., *Social Theory and Social Structure,* New York, NY: Free Press, 1968.

Messner, S.F. Economic discrimination and societal crime rates, *American Sociological Review* 54:597–611 (1989).

Pickering, W.S.F. and Walford, G., (Eds.), *Durkheim's Suicide,* New York, NY: Routledge, 2000.

Poggi, G., *Durkheim,* New York, NY: Oxford, 2000.

Savelsberg, J.J. Crime, inequality, and justice in Eastern Europe: Anomie, domination, and revolutionary change, in *Crime and Inequality,* Hagan, J. and Peterson, R., (Eds.), Stanford, CA: Stanford University Press, 1995.

Stephens, G., The global crime wave: And what we can do about it, *Futurist* 28:22–28 (1994).

Messner, S.F. and Rosenfeld, R., *Crime and the American Dream,* Belmont, CA: Wadsworth, 1997.

Mizruchi, E., *Success and Opportunity,* New York, NY: Free Press, 1964.

Passas, N. and Agnew, R., (Eds.), *The Future of Anomie Theory,* Boston, MA: Northeastern University Press, 1997.

*See also* **Durkheim, Emile; Merton, Robert K.; Social Class and Criminal Behavior; Strain Theories: Recent Developments**

# Strain Theories: Recent Developments

The classic strain theories of Durkheim, Merton, Cohen, and Cloward and Ohlin argue that crime is more likely when individuals cannot get what they want through legal channels. Specifically, they argue that crime is more likely when individuals cannot achieve monetary success or middle-class status through legitimate channels. This is said to be especially true of individuals who are low in social control and who associate with other criminals. Recent developments in strain theory expand on these arguments, pointing to other sources of strain or stress besides the inability to achieve monetary success or middle-class status, and pointing to other factors that influence whether people respond to strain with crime. These developments are described below, with a focus on Agnew's (1992) general strain theory.

Strain theory has been used primarily to explain why some individuals are more likely to engage in crime than others, but the theory can also be used to explain why some groups—including societies—have higher crime rates than others. In fact, the classic strain theories were originally developed to explain group differences in crime rates. Unfortunately, few criminologists have pursued the insights of the classic strain theories in this area. Messner and Rosenfeld's (2001a) institutional anomie theory, however, draws on and extends the work of Merton and others in an effort to explain societal differences in crime rates. Institutional anomie theory and the research that it is beginning to inspire are also described.

## Agnew's General Strain Theory

The classic strain theorists tend to focus on one type of strain: the inability to achieve the goal of monetary success. Individuals who cannot achieve this goal through legal channels may try to achieve it through illegal channels like theft, may strike out at others in their anger, or may try to ease their pain through drug and alcohol use. Several more recent theorists argue that we expand classic strain theory by focusing on additional goals besides monetary success. Most of these theorists focus on the explanation of juvenile delinquency, and it is commonly argued that adolescents are concerned with a range of immediate goals—like popularity with peers, romantic success, autonomy from adults, school success, masculine status, and getting along with parents—and that the failure to achieve these goals might also result in delinquency (see Agnew, 2000 for an overview).

Agnew's (1992; 2001) general strain theory (GST) incorporates and extends these arguments; making it the most comprehensive of the recent strain theories. The most recent version of GST argues that there are two major categories of strain: the failure to achieve positively valued goals and the loss of positive stimuli or presentation of negative stimuli. Although the failure to achieve a range of goals may result in crime, Agnew focuses on the inability to achieve four goals: monetary success, particularly the desire for much money in a short period of time; thrills or excitement; high levels of autonomy, and masculine status (being seen as tough, independent, dominant, competitive, and aggressively heterosexual). These are core goals for certain segments of the population. And limited data suggest that the inability to achieve these goals through legitimate channels increases the likelihood of crime. Among other things, criminal behavior is frequently used to get money, obtain thrills or excitement, demonstrate or obtain autonomy, and "accomplish" masculinity (e.g., demonstrate toughness, and dominance).

The loss of positive stimuli refers to things like the loss of a romantic partner and the death of a friend or family member. The presentation of negative or noxious stimuli refers to things like verbal insults and physical assaults. Although a great many specific strains fall under these categories, GST argues that some of these strains are more likely to result in crime than other types. Those strains most likely to result in crime include parental rejection; parental discipline that is overly strict, erratic, excessive, or harsh (use of humiliation or insults, threats, screaming, and physical punishments); child abuse and neglect; negative secondary school experiences, including low grades, negative relations with teachers, and the experience of school as boring and a waste of time; work in the "secondary labor market" (low-paying jobs with few benefits and poor working conditions); homelessness; abuse by peers; criminal victimization; and experiences with prejudice and discrimination. Data suggest that most of these strains increase the likelihood of crime, although the effects of peer abuse and prejudice or discrimination on crime have not been well researched.

According to GST, experiencing the above types of strain makes people feel bad: angry, frustrated, depressed, etc. These negative feelings create pressure for corrective action, and crime is one way to cope with these negative feelings and strain. Limited data suggest that strain does increase negative emotions like anger, and that these emotions explain part of the effect of strain on crime. Crime may be a way of reducing or escaping from strain; for example, individuals may attempt to achieve their monetary goals through illegal channels like theft, prostitution, and drug-selling; they may attempt to end abuse from others by assaulting them; or they may attempt to escape from abusive parents by running away from home. Crime may be a way to obtain revenge against those who have wronged you. And crime may be a way to reduce negative emotions; for example, individuals may use illicit drugs in an effort to make themselves feel better.

Not all strained individuals turn to crime, of course. In fact, most people cope with strain in a noncriminal manner. They may employ cognitive coping strategies, which involve reinterpreting the strain they experience so as to minimize its negative impact. For example, individuals who cannot achieve their monetary goals may try to convince themselves that money is not that important. They may employ behavioral coping strategies of a noncriminal nature. For example, they may avoid the peers who harass them or negotiate with the employer who mistreats them. And they may attempt to reduce their negative emotions through legal means, like listening to music or exercising. A central question, then, is why some people cope with strain in a criminal manner whereas others do not.

GST builds on the classic strain theories by more fully describing those factors that influence the effect of strain on crime. GST argues that people are most likely to respond to strain with crime when (1) their strain is high in magnitude, (2) they have poor coping skills and resources (e.g., low intelligence, poor problem-solving skills, limited social skills, low self-efficacy, limited financial resources), (3) they have few conventional social supports (i.e., they do not have family, friends, or others who provide assistance to them), (4) they are low in social and self-control (i.e., they probably will not be sanctioned by others if they engage in crime, they do not have much to lose—like a good job or a good marriage—by engaging in crime, and they do not believe that crime is wrong), and (5) they are disposed to crime (i.e., they blame their strain on others, they have personality traits like irritability and impulsivity, they hold beliefs that justify or excuse crime, they have been exposed to criminal models, they have been reinforced for criminal coping in the past). Several studies have tried to determine whether factors of the above type influence the effect of strain on crime.

The results of such studies have been mixed, although recent research is beginning to suggest that many of the factors listed above do influence how people react to strain (see Mazerolle and Maahs, 2000).

GST has mainly been used to explain why some people are more likely to engage in crime than others, but the theory can also be used to explain group differences in crime rates. Agnew (1997) argues that adolescents are more likely to engage in crime than children and adults because adolescents are more likely to experience strain than children and adults; in particular, adolescents are more likely to pursue goals they cannot achieve and adolescents are more likely to be mistreated by others, in part because they more often interact with people they do not know well in unsupervised settings. Also, adolescents are less able to cope with strain in a noncriminal manner than children and adults. Parents usually cope on behalf of their children, and adults have more coping skills and resources than adolescents.

Broidy and Agnew (1997) argue that males are more likely to engage in crime than females partly because males are more likely to experience types of strain that are conducive to crime—like criminal victimization and peer abuse. Females are more likely to experience types of strain that limit opportunities for and increase the costs of criminal coping; strains like the burdens associated with childcare and restrictions on behavior (e.g., parental curfews). Further, Broidy and Agnew argue that males more often react to strain with emotions that are conducive to crime. Males frequently respond to strain with moral outrage, whereas the anger of females is more often accompanied by feelings of guilt and concern over hurting others and disrupting relationships. Finally, males are said to be more likely than females to cope with their strain and negative emotions through crime. There are several reasons for this, including the fact that males are more likely to possess traits conducive to crime (e.g., impulsivity and irritability), males have greater opportunities to engage in crime, and males more often associate with others who encourage criminal coping.

Agnew (1999) has also used GST to explain why poor, inner-city communities have higher crime rates. He argues that the individuals in such communities are more likely to experience a wide range of strains. They have more difficulty achieving their economic goals; among other things, decent jobs are scarce in such communities, there are fewer people to model and teach the skills and attitudes necessary for job success, and schools are often of poor quality. Further, individuals in such communities are more often exposed to such strains as poor housing, family disruption, criminal victimization, and discrimination. At the same time, the individuals in such communities are less able to cope with the strains they experience in a legal manner; they more often lack coping resources like money and power, there are fewer organizations in the community to assist them, crime is less likely to be sanctioned in such communities, and they are more likely to be exposed to others who cope with crime. Efforts are under way to apply GST to the explanation of still other group differences in crime rates, like race differences in serious violence.

GST makes two major recommendations for controlling crime (Agnew, 2001). First, we should reduce the likelihood that individuals are exposed to strain. A variety of programs attempt to do this, including programs that try to improve relations between parents and children; help children do better in school, improve the school environment in ways that increase satisfaction with school, reduce the level of peer abuse—such as bullying, and improve the communities in which people live. It is impossible, however, to eliminate all strain. So GST also recommends that we reduce the likelihood that people will react to strain with crime. Several programs attempt to achieve this by doing such things as teaching juveniles social and problem-solving skills (e.g., how to respond to teasing, negotiate with others, better manage one's anger). Other programs attempt to increase juveniles' level of conventional social support, for example; by training parents and teachers to be more supportive, providing juveniles with mentors, and increasing juveniles' access to a range of people who provide services like tutoring, counseling, and conflict resolution. And still other programs attempt to increase juveniles' level of control and reduce their disposition to crime.

## Messner and Rosenfeld's Institutional Anomie Theory

Merton's classic strain theory not only tries to explain why some individuals and groups within the U.S. are more likely to engage in crime, it also tries to explain why the U.S. as a whole has a relatively high rate of crime. In this area, Merton argues that the U.S. places a relatively strong emphasis on the achievement of monetary success, but a relatively weak emphasis on the rules or norms that should be followed when seeking such success (e.g., honesty and hard work). As a consequence, people in the U.S. often resort to illegal methods of making money when legal methods are not readily available; thus explaining the higher crime rate in the U.S. Researchers, however, have largely neglected this part of Merton's theory. Criminologists, in particular, came to focus on the explanation of individual differences in offending in the years after Merton's theory was developed. Criminologists, however, are now starting to devote much more attention to the explanation of group differences in crime rates. In this area, Messner and Rosenfeld (2001a; 2001b) draw heavily on Merton's theory to explain societal differences in crime rates, especially the relatively high rates of certain types of crime—like homicide and robbery–in the U.S.

The first part of Messner and Rosenfeld's institutional anomie argues that the high crime rate in the U.S. is partly because of the emphasis of the cultural system on the "American Dream." They discuss the elements of the American Dream in some detail, but at its core the American Dream emphasizes the unrestrained pursuit of money. That is, most people are encouraged to strive for monetary success, but little emphasis is placed on the rules or norms for achieving such success (thus the term "anomie" or "without norms"). It is easy to see how high rates of crime may result. On the one hand, the American Dream provides the motive for crime—a strong desire for large amounts of money. On the other, the American Dream encourages the pursuit of this goal "by any means necessary."

Messner and Rosenfeld, however, extend Merton's theory by arguing that the American Dream is only part of the explanation for the high crime rate in the U.S. In particular, they argue that the cultural emphasis on money in the U.S. is paralleled by an institutional structure that is dominated by the economy. Noneconomic goals and roles are devalued. For example, little value is placed on the goal of education for its own sake or on the role of homemaker. Noneconomic institutions like the family and school must accommodate themselves to the demands of the economy. For example, parents struggle to find time for their children because of the demands of work. Policies that would allow parents to spend more time with their children—like parental leave and paid maternity—are strongly resisted. And economic norms have come to penetrate noneconomic institutions. For example, schools—like the economy—are organized around the individual competition for external rewards (i.e., grades). As a result, institutions like the family, school, and political system are less able to effectively socialize people and sanction rule violations. For example, it is more difficult for parents to properly socialize and supervise their children when parents must devote the bulk of their time and energy to work. Likewise, it is more difficult for schools to train and supervise youth when schools are underfunded and overcrowded, and students have little concern for education in its own right.

Institutional anomie theory has not been tested in its entirety, but the few limited tests that have been done are generally supportive of the theory (see Savolainen, 2000; Messner and Rosenfeld, 2001a; 2001b). The theory argues that high crime rates stem from the dominance of the economy over other institutions, like the family, school, and political system. If this is true, crime rates should be higher in those countries or areas where economic institutions are relatively strong and lower in those areas where noneconomic institutions are relatively strong. Researchers have measured the strength of noneconomic institutions in terms of such things as the ratio of marriages to divorces, levels of religious participation (church membership), levels of political participation (voter turnout), and the strength of social welfare programs (e.g., family support, social security, and unemployment insurance programs). The data suggest that crime rates are lower in societies and states that are not dominated by the economy; that is, crime rates are lower in societies and states with stronger families, schools, religious institutions, and political systems. Further, data suggest that the effect of economic stressors on crime is lower in societies and states where noneconomic institutions are stronger. In particular, economic stressors like poverty and high rates of income inequality have a lower effect on crime rates in areas where welfare spending is higher and noneconomic institutions like the family and religion are stronger.

## Conclusion

The classic strain theories of Merton, Cohen, and Cloward and Ohlin were perhaps the leading explanations of crime in the 1950s and 1960s. These theories came under heavy attack, however, and strain theory came close to being abandoned in the 1970s and 1980s. Recent developments in strain theory, particularly Agnew's general strain theory and Messner and Rosenfeld's institutional anomie theory, have led to a revival of the theory. Strain theory no longer dominates explanations of crime as it once did, but strain theory is now among the leading explanations of crime. And criminologists continue to develop the theory and apply it to new areas, like the explanation of organizational and transnational crime (for further information on recent developments in strain and anomie theory, see Adler and Laufer, 1995; Savelsberg, 1995; Passas and Agnew, 1997; Passas, 2000).

ROBERT AGNEW

### References and Further Reading

Adler, F. and Laufer, W.S., *Advances in Criminological Theory, Volume 6: The Legacy of Anomie Theory,* New Brunswick, NJ: Transaction, 1995.

Agnew, R., Foundation for a general strain theory of crime and delinquency, *Criminology* 30:47–87 (1992).

Agnew, R., Stability and change in crime over the life-course: A strain theory explanation, in *Advances in Criminological Theory, Volume 7: Developmental Theories of Crime and Delinquency,* Thornberry, T.P., (Ed.), New Brunswick, NJ: Transaction, 1997.

Agnew, R., Sources of criminality: Strain and subcultural theories, in *Criminology: A Contemporary Handbook,* Sheley, J.F., (Ed.), Belmont, CA: Wadsworth, 2000.

Agnew, R., An overview of general strain theory, in *Explaining Crime and Criminals,* Paternoster, R. and Bachman, R., (Eds.), Los Angeles, CA: Roxbury, 2001.

Agnew, R., A general strain theory of community differences in crime rates, *Journal of Research in Crime and Delinquency* 36:123–155 (1999).

Broidy, L. and Agnew, R., Gender and crime: A general strain theory perspective, *Journal of Research in Crime and Delinquency* 34:275–306 (1997).

Mazerolle, P. and Maahs, J., General strain and delinquency: An alternative examination of conditioning influences, *Justice Quarterly* 17:753–778 (2000).

Messner, S.F. and Rosenfeld, R., *Crime and the American Dream,* Belmont, CA: Wadsworth, 2001a.

Messner, S.F. and Rosenfeld, R., An institutional-anomie theory of crime, in *Explaining Criminals and Crime,* Paternoster, R. and Bachman, R., (Eds.), Los Angeles, CA: Roxbury, 2001b.

Passas, N., Global anomie, dysnomie, and economic crime, *Social Justice* 27:16–44 (2000).

Passas, N. and Agnew, R., *The Future of Anomie Theory,* Boston, MA: Northeastern University Press, 1997.

Savelsberg, J.J., Crime, inequality, and justice in Eastern Europe: Anomie, domination, and revolutionary change, in *Crime and Inequality,* Hagan, J. and Peterson, R.D., (Eds.), Stanford, CA: Stanford University Press, 1995.

Savolainen, J., Inequality, welfare state, and homicide: Further support for the institutional anomie theory, *Criminology* 38:1021–1042 (2000).

*See also* **Strain Theories: From Durkheim to Merton**

# Strict Liability

Strict liability is a legal doctrine, which permits conviction of the defendant without proof of his blameworthiness. The doctrine presents a significant exception to the several-century-old principle that all crimes require *mens rea* (guilty mind) concurrent to *actus reus* (wrongful act). Most strict liability offenses were first enacted in England and the U.S. in the late 1800s to address problems such as sanitation, housing condition, and public safety—the unique problems arising in the urban industrialization and modern technology. Some of the earliest cases of strict liability are those regarding sale of liquor and adulterated milk. See for example, *Barnes v. State,* (19 Conn. 398, 1849) and *Commonwealth v. Boynton* (84 Mass. (2 Allen) 160, 1861).

Strict liability often applies to inherently dangerous activities. Speeding, for example, is a violation of law even though drivers may not be aware they are driving in excess of the speed limit. Drivers commit violations of the state traffic law simply by doing what is forbidden. A strict liability statute may simply provide that one is guilty of a crime by doing or not doing so-and-so, or producing such-and-such an outcome. As no proof of intent is required, it is not a defense that the lawbreaker did not mean to break the law. To use speeding as an example again, because speeding is strict liability crime, a defective speedometer is not a defense. (See *People v. Caddy*, 189 Colo. 353, 540 P.2d 1089, 1975). Laws that impose liability without moral impropriety are typically those controlling pure food, liquor, narcotics, and traffic. For a collection of such criminal statutes see Sayre (1933).

Today, strict liability offenses comprise a significant part of criminal law. Many of them are regulatory or public welfare offenses and are committed by corporate entities. In strict products liability, for example, the concept applies in the case of certain manufactured products. Typically anyone who is engaged in the commerce of the product (from the manufacturer to the wholesaler to the retailer, or all of them) can be held responsible if the product is defective and someone is hurt. There is no need to prove negligence but the wounded party must prove that the product is defective. A wide range of environmental laws have also adopted a strict liability standard, making polluters liable for their polluting activities. Although enforcement has relied almost exclusively on civil penalties to punish polluters, federal and state authorities have increased use of criminal sanctions in the last two decades, often with notably increased penalties.

Two crime concepts are helpful in understanding strict liability. *Mala in se* offenses are considered "wrong in themselves." *Mala prohibita* offenses, on the other hand, are deemed "wrong by law." Common law felonies such as murder, rape, robbery, and larceny are *mala in se*. The intent is built-in even if the current statute stipulating such conduct does not explicate intent as an element of the offense. In contrast, many conducts not regarded as criminal in common law are crimes by criminal statutes. Their conviction does not require proof of intent. These offenses are generally classified as *mala prohibita,* also referred to as strict liability offenses.

Many offenses against the public health and environment are *mala prohibita,* including neglect of compliance with required standards or failure to take action required by law. Statutes criminalizing such violations generally require lower level of intent and often impose a standard of strict liability. Adopting strict liability for regulatory offenses is largely owing to enormous difficulty in obtaining convictions if prosecution must secure proof of intent for violations in the course of doing business. For instance, it will be difficult to show that businesses or their owners intentionally broke safety regulations.

The use of strict liability for criminal offense is unpopular among business groups. A major criticism is that the law may impose a criminal conviction on the good businessperson who made a mistake. Some experts argue that strict liability should be applied only to violations that carry no incarceration or stigma; whereas criminal law should be reserved for offences that are clearly *mala in se.* Nevertheless, lawmakers have been disinclined to remove either strict liability or incarceration from regulatory offenses. Congress has decided that public interest requires a higher standard of care. Because businesses often regard fines as cost of doing business, financial sanctions for corporate violations will ultimately be passed onto the consumers. However, imprisonment and stigma are nontransferable costs. Therefore, imposing strict criminal liability on responsible officers has real deterrence effect, especially on unsafe products and environmental pollution.

Some experts observed that in practice, strict liability is by no means tough on businesses (e.g., Croall, 1992). For instance, the penalty is often imposed only after many unsuccessful efforts made to persuade offenders to comply with the law. In addition, provision of statutory defenses mitigates the harshness of strict liability. Legislation and court rulings to this end define the limits of this type of liability. The impossibility defense is an example in point. The Supreme Court established a standard of strict liability for criminal violations of the Food, Drug, and Cosmetic Act (FDCA) by holding that proof of the defendant's intent to commit a violation was not required to obtain a misdemeanor conviction (See *U.S. v. Dotterweich,* 320 U.S. 277, 1943). The Second Circuit held that impossibility defense is available when the corporate officer provides that, although he exercised extraordinary care, he was powerless to prevent the violation. (See *U.S. v. Gel Spice* Co., 773 F.2d 427, 434, 2d Cir. 1986) Upon such a showing, the burden of proof shifts to the government to prove beyond a reasonable doubt that the officer was not powerless to prevent or correct the violation. (See *New England Grocers Supply Co.,* 488 F. Supp. at 236)

Furthermore, strict liability may work to the advantage of defendants who plead guilty. Without having to establish intent, prosecution may not introduce evidence that perhaps would attest deception or culpability. Defendants on the other hand may use strict liability in the sentencing process to present their offense as technical rather than criminal. Therefore, strict criminal liability may aid offenders in denying the criminal nature of their offense and discounting their apparent blameworthiness despite their admission of guilt.

Some legal scholars predict that in the continuing trend of using criminal sanctions for punishing regulatory violations, it is likely that legislatures (or courts of law) will include a *mens rea* requirement in regulatory statutes that subject violators to severe punishment.

OLIVIA YU

### References and Further Reading

Carper, D.L., *Understanding the Law,* St. Paul, MN: West Publishing Company, 1991; 2nd ed., St. Paul, MN: West Publishing Company, 1995.

Croall, H., *White Collar Crime,* Philadelphia, PA: Open University Press, 1992.

LaFave, W.R. and Scott, A.W., Jr., *Criminal Law, Handbook Series,* St. Paul, MN: West Publishing Company, 1972; 2nd ed., St. Paul, MN: West Publishing Company, 1986.

*Morisette v. U.S.,* 342 U.S. 246 (1952) Justice Robert Jackson upheld the power of legislatures to make certain acts criminal even if *mens rea* was absent.

Sayre, F., Public welfare offenses, *Columbia Law Review* 33 (1933).

Scheb, J.M. and Scheb, J.M., II, *American Criminal Law,* St. Paul, MN: West Publishing Company, 1996.

Vandall, F.J., *Strict Liability,* Westport, CT: Quorum Books, 1989.

*See also* **Actus Reus; Rape, Statutory**

# Subcultural Theories of Criminal Behavior

Cultural transmission theories of crime and delinquency rest on the rudimentary postulate that people internalize values and beliefs. Learning is shaped by and perpetuates values that comprise a belief system representing social attitudes, preferences, and sense of group identification. Belief systems come to characterize social environments, but some environments are distinguished by atypical, criminogenic values and normative systems wherein crime is encouraged or at least condoned. *Cultural variation* is thus a fundamental assumption as is the power of conformity. Subscription to the unconventional is rewarded through increased social status and self-esteem denied subgroup members elsewhere in society.

As similarly situated people face social rejection because of socioeconomic status, race, ethnicity, religion, or place of geographic origin, it is common practice and seems only natural that people from the same state or region choose to identify and bond together. This reality becomes more pronounced when the group is outside of their native environment, largely because their culturally-specific practices and patterns of speech and behavior stand out as different. Noticeable differences in dialect, manners, and political or religious attitudes seem to simultaneously push nonnatives outside of the mainstream and pull them into social groups and settings with which they are more familiar and feel more comfortable. College students from the Northeast region of the country enrolled in Southern universities readily identify with one another and form peer groups that replicate practices reflecting their socialization processes and regionally-specific attitudes. The same social pattern holds true for Southern students at Northern schools as people use culture as a means of defining themselves and to engage social interaction.

The study of subcultures from a criminological orientation is necessarily integrated with the study of legal process. Although the production of law has been shown to be aligned with the interests of the populace (Lynch and Groves, 1989), the criminal law is generally regarded (ironically, by the populace) as a product of a normative consensus, a parallel reinforced by both the myths and realities of democratic ideals (Lynch and Groves, 1989). The law thus denotes "conventional" or "dominant" culture. But an important and paradoxical feature of the legal process is the disjuncture between the moral normative value system held by lawmakers and the positional norms of various societal groups.

Positional norms, defined by values correlated with combinations of class status, sex, age, race and ethnicity, religious affiliation, and similar variables, are often underrepresented in the formal definition of authority. That which is considered normal, appropriate, popular and wrong varies considerably across different social groups throughout society. Repudiation of other groups' societal standards and norms, as specified in law and the rules governing societal institutions, fosters greater group cohesion, and amplifies differences between the value systems of the subculture and the larger society. Thus, another defining characteristic of a subculture is *cultural conflict*. Accordingly, it is important to make the conceptual distinction between subculture and population segment. The subcultural values of a gang, for example, may intensify although membership is reduced through criminal justice system actions. In short, normative conflict is inherent in social structure and subcultures are very much a manifestation of this conflict.

The majority of criminology and criminal justice texts begin discussion of subculture theory with the work of Al Cohen (Shoemaker, 1984; Lilly, Cullen, and Ball, 1989; Martin, Mutchnick, and Austin, 1990; Reid, 1990). Cohen focused on internal social conditions of subcultures, culminating in a strain theory dependent on social structural forces, as well as addressing the essence of subculture, ideas (Vold and Bernard, 1986). There has been considerable debate as to whether Cohen is indeed the founder of subculture theory in criminology, evident by Thomas O'Conner's paper "Is Albert Cohen a Strain Theorist?", a 1992 American Society of Criminology Gene Carte Paper Competition winner (The Criminologist, 1992).

Cohen's repute as the founder of a distinct subcultural theory is based on his most famed work, *Delinquent Boys: The Culture of the Gang* (1955). In this revised version of his doctoral dissertation, Cohen develops a general theory of subcultures through a detailed categorization of delinquent gang formation and behavior; prevalence, origins, process, purpose, and problem (Martin et al., 1990). Cohen observed that owing to social structural constraints largely beyond their control, lower-class youths experience a socialization process that devalues success in the classroom, deferred gratification, long-range planning, and the cultivation of etiquette mandatory for survival in the business and social arenas (Cohen, 1955). Cohen also observed that working-class juveniles generally did not participate in wholesome leisure activity, opting instead for activities typified by physical aggression, consequently stunting the development of intellectual and social skills valued in the mainstream culture. The overall learning experience of lower-class males leaves them ill prepared, says Cohen (1955, 129), to compete in a world gauged by a "middle-class measuring rod", a concept capturing the essence of cultural conflict. Deficiencies are most noticeable in the classroom, where working-class youth are frequently overshadowed and belittled by their middle-class counterparts. Turning to membership in a delinquent gang is but a normal adaptation to status frustration resulting from clashing cultures.

Subsequent theories based in subculture and gangs included Walter B. Miller's focal concern theory (1958) and Cloward and Ohlin's subcultural theory of delinquency (1960). Cloward and Ohlin's *Delinquency and Opportunity: A Theory of Delinquent Gangs* (1960) elaborated upon Merton's anomie and Sutherland's differential association theories to account for subculture emergence and the nature of defiant outgroups in a typology of gangs. As an "opportunity theory" (Bartol, 1980; Shoemaker, 1984; Lilly et al., 1989), the basic assumptions of Cloward and Ohlin's theory are: (1) limited and blocked economic aspirations generate frustration and negative self-esteem, and (2) these frustrations prompt youth to form gangs that vary in type. The ratio of conventional and criminal values to which a juvenile is consistently exposed accounts for the variation in gang types. Their basic premise is that lower-class teenagers realize they have minimal opportunity for future success by normative standards and thus resort to membership in one of three types of gangs, the "type" of gang actually representing similar, but distinct, delinquent subcultures.

Their typology of gangs is a hierarchy with the criminal gang at the top. Individuals reacting to frustration from failure may blame society rather than themselves—a rationalization justifying successful illegal activity. Role models for lower-class youth are not the formally educated professionals that middle-class youth seek to emulate, but rather opportunistic hustlers and criminals in their immediate environment. This ecological influence (Shaw and McKay, 1942) suggests that youth learn that crime is an attractive option in environments with virtually no conventional opportunities. Those without the skills and composure to join criminal gangs that primarily steal, organize around violent group behavior. Fighting, arson, and serious vandalism are common for these "conflict gangs" who experience a near absence of social control. Cloward

and Ohlin also observed that potential gang youth who are unsuccessful in criminal endeavors and not prone to violence recoil into a third variety of gang defined by drug use (Cloward and Ohlin, 1960, 183).

Walter B. Miller presented a pure cultural theory of gang delinquency, which he generalized to the lower class. His theory, found in a short article titled "Lower Class Culture as a Generating Milieu of Gang Delinquency" (1958), submitted that the lower class subscribed to a distinct and criminogenic culture. Unlike middle-class values, the lower class operates according to "focal concerns." Specified as trouble, toughness, smartness, excitement, fate, and autonomy, these concerns lead to gang formation and devalue conventional values. Smartness refers to the ability to "con" someone in real life situations and brings respect for successful hustlers and con artists. Fate undermines the work ethic and sabotages self-improvement through belief in predetermined outcomes. Deviance is normal and to be expected in lower-class cultures because the focal concerns make conformity to criminal behavior as natural as acceptance of conventional mores for the middle class. Miller (1958, 167) observes that juveniles accepting a preponderance of these "cultural practices which comprise essential elements of the total life pattern of lower class culture automatically violate legal norms."

Miller's theory is an explanation of delinquency situated in depressed inner cities, wherein the majority of households are headed by females. Evaluation of the theory has centered around two significant criticisms. First, some of the focal concerns contended to be exclusive to the lower class are also observable in the middle class (Shoemaker, 1984). A second and more controversial issue concerns the use of race rather than class in assessing the relationship between delinquency, matriarchal households, and an exaggerated sense of masculinity associated with physical aggression (Moynihan, 1967; Berger and Simon, 1974). Unfortunately, a focus on blacks and the inseparable issue of atypical family structure moves discussion away from the veracity of a lower-class value system to differences in racial groups. It is surprising that critics neglect the possible benefits of a comparative analysis between urban and rural lower classes, which might highlight obvious differences and similarities. Although it is probable that both groups share similar focal concerns because of alienation stemming from economic and social disadvantage, it is also likely that family structure among the rural poor is traditional (Duncan, 1992). Such a comparison may produce significant ramifications for Miller's theory that rests heavily on the absence of positive male role models.

The impact of the theories of Cohen, Cloward, and Ohlin, and Miller were significant in two respects.

First, they developed a general subcultural theory around what was perceived to be a timely issue. Second, the early studies as a whole focused on what was then a novel problem, the emergence of gangs. Gangs in the future were to be defined as delinquent and their subcultures considered inherently deviant. Moreover, subculture became a major concept in sociology, a convenient comparative device for highlighting normative standards.

The subculture theories of the 1950s and 1960s largely dominated criminological thought. Foremost, crime was seen as more or less normal within subcultures and several theorists built upon the initial efforts of Cohen (1955), Miller (1958), Cloward and Ohlin (1960), and Wolfgang and Ferracuti (1967). Systematic descriptions of the generating processes and patterns of delinquency, often in a gang context, became standard criminological practice (Bordua, 1961; Arnold, 1965; Kobrin, Puntil, and Peluso, 1967). Gangs, with their symbolic and collective features, epitomized a social problem of severe proportions: juvenile delinquency. Rebellious youth, associated with the emergence of the rock and roll era and aided by the appearance of automobiles into daily life, presented a new, visible threat to authority. Policing gangs was equated with addressing a larger issue and funding was available for social science attention to the problem. Major studies thus focused on the gang, built upon subcultural explanations of delinquency. In short, the rise of the subculture perspective was aided by the circumstances of social transition, a point that also explains, in part, its decline.

By the 1960s, a number of interrelated social movements (including the civil rights crusade, anti-Vietnam protest, and the counterculture) were under way. In varying degrees they expressed the same themes: distrust and defiance of authority that was perceived to be used by elite factions to create and maintain a social hierarchy, exploitation of crime and delinquency, and opposition to the oppressiveness of the criminal justice system.

As bandwagon shifts to the political left transpired, labeling theory soon replaced subcultural explanations as the leading theory (Bookin-Weiner and Horowitz, 1983). The main thrust of labeling theory is that crime and delinquency are definitions and labels assigned to persons and events by operatives of the criminal justice system. Explaining crime and delinquency, from this perspective then, is explaining the way in which the labeling process works, and how it singles out certain people for labeling and not others. In its more extreme formulations, labeling theory was not concerned with the explanation of the behavior we call crime and delinquency because criminals and delinquents were not assumed to differ very much in their behavior from other people. Rather, the real difference is said to be the degree of vulnerability to the labeling activities of the criminal justice system.

During this period of interest in labeling, theoretically-oriented research on the relationship between crime and culture languished but did not disappear. More moderate versions of labeling theory propelled some research (e.g., research on gang behavior and emphasis on the role of official processing and labeling in the development of that behavior), but the leading cause of crime and delinquency was considered the criminal justice system itself (Werthman, 1967; Armstrong and Wilson, 1973). Specifically, criminal and delinquent behavior was portrayed as a rational and justified response to social inequality and class oppression (Bookin, 1980).

Much of the contemporary literature of the period (1970s), not just on gangs but on social problems generally, was not only indifferent to subculture theory but was actively opposed to it. This literature included works such as Chambliss' *The Saints and the Roughnecks* (1973) that emphasized a conflict perspective that viewed the subculture theories as conservative. Social control was deemed reactionary because crime and delinquency were considered direct, reasonable, and even justifiable adaptations to injustice.

The rise of social control theory (e.g., Hirschi, 1969) did not seriously factor into the subculture perspective either, though seemingly well-suited to do so (Bookin-Weiner and Horowitz, 1983; Vold and Bernard, 1986). The central elements of attachment to others, degrees of commitment to conventionality, daily routine, and belief in a moral order speak to why subcultures exist and have implications for criminal behavior therein. Ensuing research interests moved toward macro-level determinants of crime and further away from culture and group behavior. Consequently, subcultures were largely ignored until the mid-1980s when they were seriously connected with often gang-related drug and violence problems (Curry and Spergel, 1988).

Although historical developments set into motion a chain of events that moved criminological theorizing away from the subculture, the theory was further marred by paradigmatic shifts in social science research methodology. The rise of positivism delivered subculture theory a would-be deathblow. There was suddenly a disjuncture between the subculture approach and the new preferred theoretical–methodological symmetry: variable assignment, measurement, and analysis congruent with causality as established by levels of statistical correlation. Critics of subculture theory (e.g., Kituse and Dietrick, 1959; Ball-Rokeach, 1973; Kornhauser, 1978) focused on the growing belief that acceptable science must subscribe to particular precepts that subculture explanations did not meet. The theory could not, via a variable analysis format, be adequately tested. Beyond the operationalization problems thwarting concept measurement, there was the more fundamental restraint of tautological reasoning. It was argued that there was unclear separation of cause and effect. Did the subculture, as an independent variable, generate crime, the dependant variable, or vice versa? For many, the inability to answer this question satisfactorily rendered the theory obsolete.

J. MITCHELL MILLER

### References and Further Reading

Arnold, W.R. (1965). The concept of the gang. *The Sociological Quarterly* 7:59–75.

Armstrong, G. and Wilson, M. (1973). City politics and deviance amplification. In Taylor, I. and Taylor, L., (eds.). *Politics and Deviance*. New York, NY: Penguin Books.

Ball-Rokeach, S.J. (1973). Values and violence: A test of the subculture of violence thesis. *American Sociological Review* 38:736–749.

Bartol, C.R. (1980). *Criminal Behavior: A Psychosocial Approach*. Englewood Cliffs, NJ: Prentice-Hall.

Berger, A.S. and Simon, W. (1974). Black families and the Moynihan Report: A research evaluation. *Social Problems* 22:145–161.

Bookin, H. (1980). The gangs that didn't go straight. *Presentation to the Society for the Study of Social Problems,* New York.

Bookin-Weiner, H. and Horowitz, (1983). The end of the youth gang: Fad or fact? *Criminology* 21:585–602.

Bordua, D.J. (1961). Delinquent subcultures: Sociological interpretations of gang delinquency. *Annals of the American Academy of Social Science* 338:119–136.

Chambliss, W.J. (1973). The saints and the roughnecks. *Society* 11:1, 24–31.

Cloward, R.A. and Ohlin, L.E. (1960). *Delinquency and Opportunity: A Theory of Delinquent Gangs*. Glencoe, IL: The Free Press.

Cohen, A. (1955). *Delinquent Boys*. Glencoe, IL: The Free Press.

Curry, G.D. and Spergel, I.A. (1988). Gang homicide, delinquency and community. *Criminology* 26:3, 381–406.

Duncan, C. (1992). *Rural Poverty in America*. New York, NY: Auburn House.

Empey, L. (1982). *American Delinquency: Its Meaning and Construction*. Homewood, IL: Dorsey.

Hirschi, T. (1969). *Causes of Delinquency*. Berkeley, CA: University of California Press.

Kitsuse, J. and Dietrick, D.C. (1959). Delinquent boys: A critique. *American Sociological Review* 24:208–215.

Kobrin, S., Puntil, J. and Peluso, E. (1967). Criteria of status among street groups. *Journal of Research in Crime and Delinquency* 4:1, 98–118.

Kornhouser, R.R. (1978). *Social Sources of Delinquency*. Chicago, IL: University of Chicago Press.

Lilly, J.R., Cullen, F.T. and Ball, R.A. (1989). *Criminological Theory: Context and Consequences*. Newbury Park, CA: Sage.

Lynch, M.J. and Groves, W.B. (1986). *A Primer in Radical Criminology*. New York, NY: Harrow and Heston.

Martin, R., Mutchnick, R.J. and Austin, W.T. (1990). *Criminological Thought: Pioneers Past and Present*. New York, NY: Macmillan.

Miller, W.B. (1958). Lower class culture as a generating milieu of gang delinquency. *Journal of Social Issues* 14:5–19.

Moynihan, D.P. (1967). *The Negro Family: The Case for National Action*. Washington, DC: The United States Government Printing Office.

Reid, S.T. (1990). *Crime and Criminology*. Fort Worth, TX: Holt, Rinehart, and Winston, Inc.

Shaw, C.R. and McKay, H.D. (1942). *Juvenile Delinquency and Urban Areas*. Chicago, IL: University of Chicago Press.

Shoemaker, D.J. (1984). *Theories of Delinquency: An Examination of Explanations of Delinquent Behavior*. New York, NY: Oxford University Press.

The Criminologist (1992). *Official Newsletter of the American Society of Criminology* 17:6,13.

Vetter, H.J. and Silverman, I.J. (1978). *The Nature of Crime*. Philadelphia, PA: W.B. Saunders Company.

Vold, G.B. and Bernard, T.J. (1986). *Theoretical Criminology,* 3rd ed. New York, NY: Oxford University Press.

Werthman, C. (1967). The function of social definitions in the development of delinquent careers. *In Becoming Delinquent: Young Offenders and the Correctional Process,* Garabedian, P.G. and Gibbons, D.C. (Eds.). Chicago, IL: Aldine.

Williams, F.P. III. and McShane, M.D. (1988). *Criminological Theory*. Englewood Cliffs, NJ: Prentice Hall.

Wolfgang, M.E. and Ferracuti, F. (1967). *The Subculture of Violence: Towards an Integrated Theory in Criminology*. London, U.K.: Tavistock.

*See also* **Albert Cohen; Gangs: Theories; Lloyd Ohlin; Richard Cloward; Marvin E. Wolfgang; Sociological Theories of Criminal Behavior**

# Sub-Saharan Africa, Crime and Justice in

### General Comments

The label Sub-Saharan reflects the conventional division of the continent into countries largely influenced, for millennia, by Mediterranean and Arabic cultures, trade relations, migrations and conquests, and those subject to colonial domination and rule, with the exception of Ethiopia, by the European powers beginning in the 17th century. The distinction between Sub- and "above"-Saharan countries is not precise for there was much trans-Saharan trade (gold, slaves, salt), an exchange of cultural and religious norms, and strong political relations among west and central African societies and neighboring societies across the Sahara. This mutual influence is still found in the northern tier of countries in Sub-Saharan Africa, stretching from Senegal in the west to Eritrea in the east, which often incorporate traditional, Islamic and Christian religious and cultural beliefs (and their associated legal norms and values) into the organizations and policies of their criminal justice systems. In eastern Africa, Arabic influence and conquest extended as far south as what now is Mozambique. In the most general terms and taking into account the nonisolation of the region, Sub-Saharan refers to societies and regions populated by black people.

The discussion of crime and justice in Sub-Saharan Africa requires a short introduction to the history of the continent, which is normally divided into three periods: the time before colonization, the colonial period, and the postcolonial or independence era.

A major problem in describing crime and justice, which is true for all three periods, is the distinct lack of systematic and precise data on crime and the operations of crime-control agencies in Africa. Traditional societies were preliterate, hence no written records exist describing criminal acts and how societies responded to these. What we know is based on archeological inference, oral traditions, and the writings of visitors, missionaries, and colonizers.

Official crime statistics and data on police practices, courts cases or correctional policies, and the effectiveness or impact of these policies are practically nonexistent for both the colonial and independence eras, for nearly all countries. The major exception, currently, is South Africa. The systematic collection of information on crime and justice simply was not a priority for colonial governments, nor is it for current regimes, many of which are poor, control few resources and lack the inclination, personnel and finances to collect and analyze data systematically.

Another normal potential source for crime and justice information are studies conducted by scholars and research institutions. Again, as with official data, very few such studies exist for Africa and much of the theoretical enterprise that drives data collection and analysis (e.g., is a particular criminological theory supported by the evidence from an African country, or do police practices have a measurable impact on criminal behavior) has simply not been done. Some Western universities (e.g., the Centre for Comparative Criminology at the University of Toronto) attempted to establish research projects in Africa during the 1960s, but these lapsed fairly quickly. In more recent times, UN affiliated regional centers and projects, international assistance programs, human rights groups in Africa and elsewhere, and local universities and research organizations (e.g., IFRA, 1994) have begun to pay serious attention to analyzing the problems of crime and justice. A number of African scholars, trained in the U.S.A, Europe, Japan, and India, on their return home have begun to develop criminology and criminal justice as distinct academic disciplines. But such efforts are in their infancy. For example, the first classes on criminology in Nigerian universities (Nigeria is by far the most populous country in Africa) were not taught until the 1980s.

## The Precolonial Period

Traditional societies experienced the typical crime problems found everywhere. Things were stolen, people got into fights and were injured or killed, social norms were violated, disorders happened, children were molested and spouses abused, and political power was challenged. Traditional societies in Africa ranged from small "village democracies" and "stateless societies"— isolated communities, small in number and economically self-sustaining—to large, hierarchically organized city states, such as the well-known West African empires (Songhay, Ghana), the kingdoms existing in what is now southern Zaire (Vansina, 1965,) or the Islamic city states of the Sahel region (e.g., Smith, 1960)

In village communities, crime control was done informally. Social control was the responsibility of all as guided by the wisdom of elders and sanctioned by tradition and the power of religious worldviews. There were no specialized institutions to control deviance and crime nor were distinctions made between criminal versus civil acts and conflicts. Crime was normally conceived of as the breaking of established order (violations of the status, persons, property, and norms that constituted that order), thought to include the living, the dead, the deities that populated inanimate objects, and the forces of the cosmos. Punishing violators of norms was a moral duty. The general goals were to punish offenders, make good the harm done, and to reintegrate nonpersistent offenders back into the community. Persistent offenders were banished, killed, or placed into slavery.

At the other end of the organizational spectrum, large state systems developed specialized bureaucracies, armies, and crime-control systems, including police functionaries, courts, and punishment schemes. The institution of a prison, or confinement as punishment, did not exist. Crime was defined not merely by norms and folkways, but by edicts and regulations issued by the politically powerful and punished at the discretion and by the interests of the rulers. In state systems influenced by Islamic values, the ruler's authority rested on religious dogma and the institutions of order and social control embodied Islamic values (e.g., prescribed punishments for *Huddud* crimes) and practices (the gendered status of witnesses in trials) (Anderson, 1970).

In sum, there existed a vast variety of crime-control practices and institutions, as these had arisen through indigenous evolution and state creation and through contacts, conflicts, and conquests with other societies. The imposition of colonial rule effectively stopped social evolution to impose its own brand of social control, yet existing practices continued powerfully, legitimately, and informally even under colonial domination.

## Colonial Period

### Background

The imposition of colonial rule, in Africa mainly by Britain, France, Germany, Portugal, and Belgium, required as its foundation a functioning order maintaining system of laws, regulations, enforcement, and punishments. Colonial rule sought to promote economic activities (slaves, cash cropping, labor for mines, and plantations) and developmental efforts (e.g., road-building, domestic servants) of value to the colonizers, and to protect the personal safety and property of colonial officials and enterprises engaged in that work. Each colonial power imposed its own, familiar system of laws and crime control (laws, police, courts, corrections) on the inhabitants of its possessions. In consequences, the criminal justice system imported by colonizers remained an alien, distant, incomprehensible set of institutions and policies that imposed obligations and sanctions on local people without their consent. From the beginnings of colonial rule to the very end, crime control and order maintenance resembled military occupation more than civil law enforcement and sanctions (Clayton and Killingray, 1989).

There were some basic differences among colonial policies. British colonial crime and justice policy left control to functioning local institutions (the system of "indirect rule") as long as these abided by general principles and values of British justice (i.e., nothing "offensive to justice and good conscience" could be done by local authorities). Continental European powers developed a two-fold crime-control system—one for those local individuals who had become assimilated (the French term) or had "evolved" (the Portuguese term) into the colonizers' culture and were treated by the laws and rights reserved for citizens of the home country; and a harsh, punitive, and separate system of control and punishments for the rest of the population.

But under both colonial governing philosophies, much of local order maintenance and control was left to existing informal, community-based mechanisms. The day-to-day presence or penetration of the colonial state into local affairs was always limited and superficial, yet quite powerful and quickly imposed when the colonizers saw their interests and control threatened.

In the parts of Africa where a large settler population arrived (e.g., Kenya, Angola, Zimbabwe, South Africa), harsh ordering and control mechanisms developed to protect the rights and property of the immigrant minority group against expected criminal acts or violent resistance by the local population. In South Africa, this development reaches its apogee with the institutionalization of the *apartheid* regime that treated four groups (Whites, Bantus, Indian, and Colored) differentially in law and crime control by the perceived color of their skin and their ethnic background.

### Crime

Patterns of crime are difficult to describe for this period. One can assume that normal crime continued to exist. New crimes established by the colonizers (e.g., failure to pay taxes or perform mandatory work) and by new opportunities for local people to exploit the weaknesses of colonizers (e.g., theft by domestic servants, illegal alcohol production, commercialized prostitution) added to this picture (van Onselen, 1970; White, 1990). Colonizers created laws and regulations to serve their interests and punished violations harshly, often to create labor required by the colonizers; that is, convicted offenders were sentenced to work. (Shivji, 1986). Transgressions were punished severely, arbitrarily and with little regard to local customs and norms, in order to impress individuals and the general population that resistance and failure to "help" colonial rule were futile. The political nature of crime control (that it serves power) was nakedly expressed in the policies and symbolisms of colonial rule, including social control practices.

Attempts to explain crime and disorder by local populations stressed the backward nature of local people end cultures, their inability to be prudently foresightful, and the lack of fair and rational control mechanisms in traditional societies. In short, such theories were basically racist, uniformed by empathy or accurate information, and designed to justify the control policies imposed on local people (they needed the firm and civilizing hand of colonial rule). More progressive studies stressed the disrupting influences of development on the social fabric and individual lives (e.g., Clifford, 1974; Mushanga, 1976).

### Control Institutions

Colonial rule, as a system of governance, developed fairly late in this period. Most of the early contact and relations between Europeans and local people were concerned with trade. As long as trading could be done (a supply of goods and a local system to facilitate trade existed), Europeans were by and large content to leave local institutions alone. Only toward the second half of the 19th century, as competition for resources and status among European states increased, was Africa formally subdivided into spheres of control and colonies and efforts made to establish a functioning administration.

The police were created to protect that administration and the economy, impose governmental decisions (tax and labor laws, social hygiene regulations), pacify areas of resistance, and deal with normal crime, almost as an afterthought (Jeffries, 1952; Ahire, 1991). Manpower was recruited from local groups, often on the basis of presumed traits of particular ethnic societies ("warlike tribes") and tended to be deployed away from areas of origin. The officer corps was staffed by Europeans (and continued to be so staffed even after formal independence). The work of the police in urban areas consisted mainly of protecting government and foreign buildings and enterprises and patrolling the segregated residential areas were European and a few high level local people lived. Police were normally absent from rural areas, which were basically unpoliced and left to their own devices, except during pacification campaigns.

Law and court systems were systematized during colonial period. It was always difficult for local people to advance personally, unless they adopted the culture and demeanor of their colonial masters. Even so, personal careers were limited, normally to nonthreatening—to colonial rule—areas (medicine, law, journalism). Ambitious and capable Africans, denied access to political and economic avenues, found careers in those areas. In consequence, during the end of colonial rule, lawyering was practiced by many Africans and courts and law services were staffed by local people. Law became the most developed of control institutions, but partook of the legal traditions and systems of the colonial powers (common law for British colonies, civil or code law for the continental powers). Efforts were made to systematize local traditions and norms into a general, written, and codified legal system, in the process depriving traditional folkways of both their salience and legitimacy (Young, 1970; Bryde, 1976; Snyder, 1981).

In practice, courts reflecting colonially imposed law were established to deal with violations of law of interest to the colonizers, yet existing legal institutions were allowed to continue under the general umbrella of colonial law (such as sharia courts in Islamic areas or traditional courts in local societies). A pluralistic system of laws and courts emerged in many colonies, tailored to the status of offenders or victim and by the degree of deference to local traditions.

We know little of what such courts did. Episodic evidence suggests that traditional and Islamic courts were left largely to their own devices; they dealt with civil and criminal cases based on local control and input. The courts imposing imported law dealt with crime affecting the colonizers, serious cases (homicides, robberies) and with violations of regulations established to ensure effectiveness of colonial rule.

Prisons had been unknown in traditional societies. These were created as a new form of punishment and as holding places for persons awaiting trial or execution by the colonial rulers. Again, we know very little of how such prisons functioned, what life was like within them, who was sentenced and for how long. They became places holding those awaiting trial (even for extensive periods), convicted criminals but also political dissidents, especially during the end of colonial rule when agitations by the local elites, often educated outside Africa, to regain independence reached high pitch. Crime-control institutions were used to crack down on protests, dissents, challenges to the right and the power of colonial rule. Many of the leaders of independent countries that emerged after the system of colonial rule proved unsustainable had spent long periods of time in prison for their willingness to stand up to the colonizers.

## Independence Era

### Background

Starting in 1957 (when the Gold Coast became Ghana), reaching dramatic speed and extent during the 1960s when most African states emerged, and ending with the collapse of the apartheid regime in South Africa in 1994, colonial rule was swept aside, and largely in an evolutionary rather then revolutionary manner, the exception being the Portuguese colonies (Angola, Guinea-Bissau, Mozambique). Even South Africa, in the end, experienced a nonviolent transition.

The emerging states inherited and still share a number of characteristics that continue to shape and bedevil the crime-control systems of these countries. For one, practically all are poverty stricken, with few resources, a tough competition for the few things that are available, strong government controls of the economy and fierce partisan electoral struggles for control of the state. When resources are few and competition for control over them is fierce, funding the criminal justice system is not a high priority of governments in power. The police, judges, and corrections personnel tend to be underpaid, overworked, poorly trained, and held to few disciplinary standards.

A second inherited trait of the criminal justice system is its naked political nature. As stated above, the crime-control system was at the beck and call of the colonizers. That practice has continued, except that now the new, local elites control the system and its powers and are not shy about using it to protect themselves and their political allies. Control means that when accusations of corruption or malfeasance are raised, as they are by daring local competitors and by foreign creditors (World Bank, foreign aid donors), such allegations will not be investigated or pursued or they will be whitewashed. Control means that when political competitors appear to become successful, they end up in jail or exiled (if lucky) or dead. In short, the crime-control system has as its major reason for existence service to power rather than the protection of society (e.g., Schatzberg, 1988). People are not uninformed about what matters. Crime-control institution has little credibility with the public. If something needs doing, people tend to take the law into their own hands, and perform crime-control functions and punishment informally and quickly.

A third characteristic of the new states is political instability, often reaching civil war proportions. Every African state has experienced periods of military coup attempts and military rule. When power comes from the barrel of the gun, law and criminal justice are at the discretion of the military and allowed to function as long as military rule remains unchallenged. Sometimes, the military will step in to deal with specific crimes that threaten to undermine its credibility as an effective government (such as special tribunals to deal with armed robbery, currency frauds, or corruption). Such tribunals are little bound by procedural rules, make decisions quickly and in secret, and execute them almost on the spot. But generally, when political order is suspect and fragile, the very underpinnings necessary for stable, routine functions of crime control are absent.

In societies torn by civil conflicts and war (such as Nigeria or Biafra in the 1960s or Somalia in the 1990s), by genocidal rampages in Burundi and Rwanda during numerous periods, or armed insurrections against the ruling government (e.g., Zaire, Sierra Leone, Liberia recently) the rule of law and criminal justice institutions disappear altogether. Control and punishments are exercised arbitrarily by those temporarily successful, and retaliated against when fortunes shift. When the state "disappears" during such periods people fall back on the only recourse they have to protect themselves, which is force (if they have it) or flight across borders or into hiding (if they do not).

A fourth characteristic of current governments is the continuing persistence and vitality of what has come to be called identity politics, that is a process of political competition and decision making that is based on, appeals to and seeks to satisfy the values and demands of dominant and salient groups in society. The most common forms of identity politics are ethnicity and class-based forms of group struggle for power and economic resources. The notion of citizenship beyond one's group has low salience. Government decisions and policies are evaluated by all by whom they favor, who receives a disproportionate share of resources (scholarships, jobs, infrastructure projects, contracts). Crime-control decisions are viewed through the same lens. The actions of the police or courts are always judged more by outcomes (who received what treatment) than whether the rules and rights stated in Constitutions and rhetorically worshiped in public pronouncements were followed. There is simply little trust in the institutions of crime control among the public and very little interaction with the system. People tend to avoid the formal system even when they have been victimized.

### Crime

Crime responds to economic adversity, ethnic and class-based competition, and political instability in numerous ways. Small-scale larcenies, underground economies, theft and exportation of government moneys into foreign accounts, large-scale economically-oriented, and organized crime (smuggling, currency fraud, fake contracts, white-collar crime), struggles over land ownership, bribery, and corruption, and violent forms of economic appropriation (armed robbery, car jacking, burglary rings) dominate the crime picture. Even violent crime seems to be largely economic in motive; yet interpretations of violence often become aspects of ideological struggles to define the limits of legitimate order and control (Marenin, 1986).

As is typical of developing countries in general, antiperson crime constitutes a larger percentage of the overall crime picture than it does in developed regions. Official statistics generally do not include those crimes causing the most harm to societies, the corrupt and criminal acts of the political and economic elites (Marenin and Reisig, 1995).

Violent crime is exacerbated during period of political instability or civil strife. Acts done during such periods (killings, mutilations, rapes), often on a massive scales, are not counted as crimes in official statistics but are considered part of the almost natural violence society and groups experience during periods of social turbulence. If counted as crimes, which such acts are, the rate of violent crimes would be much higher than even the currently available and unreliable statistics indicate. For example, South Africa, which collects and publishes more comprehensive and reliable crime data than any other sub-Saharan state, has experienced a massive wave of violent crimes, often committed by local vigilante groups against drug dealers, squatters, and those with economic resources.

But official crime statistics are of doubtful validity and reliability, hard to compare among countries because definitions and categories under which they are reported differ, and there are few studies (victimization surveys, self-report research) that can compensate for the unreliability of official data. What we do know is that crime has experienced significant increases since independence, sometimes alarmingly steep rises, such as in South Africa. Recent global surveys that include African countries, done by the UN (e.g., Zvekic and del Frate, 1995; del Frate, 1998) suggest that the official data vastly underreport experienced crime, especially crime that is personal (rape, molestation) or so built into economic activity (as corruption, bribery, white-collar fraud) and so widespread that it is perceived as almost normal, the way things are done.

Theories of crime, in the absence of good data that could be statistically analyzed, are largely speculative, but differ in the emphasis on three general themes. Earlier studies, such as Clinard and Abbott's (1973) seminal study of crime in Kampala, Uganda tended to stress crime as a response to the dislocations experienced by societies and individuals as countries are modernizing, becoming drawn into the developing world system economically, politically, and culturally. The anomie and stressful economic conditions experienced by people as their traditional worlds collapse, as vast numbers of people migrate from rural areas where they cannot survive to gigantic and growing urban conglomerations where legitimate job opportunities are scarce (or to foreign countries where economic opportunities seem even slightly better), support systems nonexistent, and survival—the essential daily task—almost normally leads them into crime and violent interactions with other fellow migrants.

Alternatively, yet still focused on economic and unstable conditions at the driving force behind criminal acts, theories of underdevelopment stress the exploitative, class-based nature of economic life in developing countries. Crime, from this perspective, is the rational and normal response to hard times and can be justified or excused as the rebellion of the poor against the rich who have wrongfully appropriated the vast portion of scarce available resources.

A more recent set of studies, mimicking the popularity of routine activity or opportunity theories in developed countries, have used this framework to analyze crime as the individual's response to the changing opportunities, values, and guardianship levels in African countries. Development, by definition, is a change in routine activities. Scholars theorize that individuals, as they try to survive within changing contexts will exploit those opportunities for theft and violence that have low guardianship and relatively high payoffs.

In general though, such theoretical explorations are largely speculative as few comprehensive or accurate data exist to expose such theories to systematic tests (e.g., Mushanga, 1992; Opolot, 1995).

### Police

Policing systems were inherited by independent governments and tended to continue with little change, including keeping the typically white officer corps in place, especially in former French colonies. The negative image acquired by the police during colonial rule has continued, as have the efforts by new governments to control the police for their own partisan political purposes. In consequences, people generally have very little faith in the capacity or integrity of the police. It is generally assumed, and correctly so, that the police will inefficient, corrupt, and arbitrary in the exercise of their powers, especially at the street level (e.g., Cawthra, 1993; Tamuno, et al., 1993). Anyone who has ever traveled in African states has routinely experienced low level police corruption as police extract bribes from motorists, especially those whose livelihood depends on transportation (taxis, bases, long-distance jitneys).

The organization and functions of the police replicate colonial origins. There has been very little transformation in the work of policing since independence (Brogden and Shearing, 1993; Hills, 2000). The standard organizations charts of police forces, typically organized from the national center, repeat the functional divisions of labor normally found in any police organization (patrol, traffic, investigations, etc.). On paper, the organization looks like the police of other regions, yet their work suffers from lack of resources, often ill-prepared and trained personnel, a negative image with the public, attempts at political control, and low professionalism. Very little information exists to measure police performance. Systematic arrest, clearance, or successful case work rates are unknown, nor can the impact of police work on crime, fear of crime, and the maintenance of order be estimated.

Some governments, to compensate for the inefficiency of police and their general absence in rural areas, have sanctioned locally organized crime-control groups (justice brigades in Zambia, or village protection groups in Tanzania, improvement associations in many urban areas). As was true for the colonial period, informal order and control maintenance groups have sprung up in both urban and rural areas to provide some level of protection. Informal control mechanisms often shade into vigilant actions.

International donors (European states, Canada, USA) have recently begun to offer massive assistance programs to create or retrain local forces committed to the observance of the rule of law and human rights, normally under the rubric of community-oriented policing. The impact of such assistance is as yet unclear.

### Law and Courts

Inherited colonial legal systems and court structures continued as well, with two general modifications. Those states that embarked during the 1960s and 1970s on the socialist road to governance and development modified legal systems, in substantive and procedural areas, to fit and follow socialist legal principles; and introduced local level court structures and processes that reflected the principle of mass participation (e.g., Sachs and Welch, 1990). More recently, some countries have become caught up in the resurgence of Islamic civilization and the rejection of Western culture, including laws. For example, some states in Nigeria (which is a federal system) have adopted Sharia law as the governing law for the state, to the dismay of other states in the federation, competing religions and some groups in the national government.

On paper, national court system reflects the standard division of courts of first instance, appellate and supreme courts. The court system, for those cases that actually enter and proceed in the system, probably functions as close to the practices followed in former colonial countries and by standards of evidence, procedures, and human rights normally considered the rule of law (e.g., Seidman, 1974). Cases and precedents are published; law schools graduate practitioners; legal texts lay out the constitutionally and statutorily defined rights and procedures. There also exists a substantial literature on the law (what it means) but very little on how it is carried out.

Yet most cases decided at the local court level are done in summary fashion, quickly, without much regard to procedure or rights. Little systematic evidence is available of the types of cases taken to court or their outcomes, nor do we know much of the decision-making processes in lower level courts (Dubow, 1973; Luckham, 1976; Sevareid, 1976).

### Corrections

Corrections include the institutions that execute sentences imposed by courts or political power (e.g., during military rule) as well as aftercare programs. Generally speaking, prisons in developing countries, including in Africa, are among the most dismal places on earth.

Facilities are severely overcrowded and ill-maintained; prisoners often have to survive by the support of friends and families; few procedural safeguards on safety, hygiene, health services, or the conduct of guards are enforced; and rehabilitative programs are basically non-existent. In the same way, aftercare programs are small, underfunded, and ineffective. Whatever is done to help supervise or reintegrate released prisoners into society is done informally by self-help and welfare groups, often with international assistance. The correctional system is simply not a high priority to governments that are strapped for resources (Milner, 1972; Tanner, 1972). The best source of information on prison conditions currently are human rights groups that monitor what is happening (e.g., Commission, n.d.).

The number of convicted under the control of the criminal justice systems, whether confined or within society, is unknown, but probably increasing slowly.

## Summation

Crime and justice in Africa is a social and governance problem, but it is only beginning to be studied. The overall impression is that the crime problem is increasing quite dramatically in many countries, especially in violent forms, and that the formal control institutions are not sufficiently legitimate, funded, organized, and led to effectively deliver order and law enforcement services. Much needs to be done in practice to improve the system and in analysis to understand better how the formal institutions function and how they might be improved.

OTWIN MARENIN

### References and Further Reading

Ahire, P.T., *Imperial Policing. The Emergence and Role of the Police in Colonial Nigeria 1860–1960,* Milton Keynes: Open University Press, 1991.

Anderson, J.N.D., *Islamic Law in Africa,* London, U.K.: Frank Cass, 1970.

Brodgen, M. and Shearing, C., *Policing for a New South Africa,* London, U.K.: Routledge, 1993.

Bryde, B.-O., *The Politics and Sociology of African Legal Development,* Frankfurt, Germany: Alfred Metzner Verlag, 1976.

Cawthra, G., *Policing South Africa. The SAP and the Transition from Apartheid,* London, U.K.: Zed Books, 1993.

Clayton, A. and Killingray, D., *Khaki and Blue: Military and Police in British Colonial Africa,* Athens, Greece: Ohio University Center for International Studies, 1989.

Clifford, W., *An Introduction to African Criminology,* Nairobi, Kenya: Oxford University Press, 1974.

Clinard, M.B. and Abbott, D.J., *Crime in Developing Countries,* New York, NY: John Wiley and Sons, 1973.

Commission on Human Rights and Administrative Justice, *Report on the Inspection of Ghana's Prisons. Prison Settlement Camps and Police Cells 1996–1997.* Accra: CHRAJ, n.d.

Del Frate, A.A., *Victims of Crime in the Developing World,* Rome: UNICRI, Publication No. 57, 1998

DuBow, F.L., *Justice for People: Law and Politics in the Lower Courts of Tanzania,* PhD dissertation, University of California, Berkeley, 1973.

Hills, A., *Policing Africa. Internal Security and the Limits of Liberalization,* Boulder, CO: Lynne Rienner, 2000.

IFRA (French Institute for Research in Africa) (Ed.), *Urban Management and Urban Violence in Africa,* Volumes I and 2; *Urban Violence in Africa: Pilot Studies,* Ibadan: IFRA, University of Ibadan, 1994.

Jeffries, C., Sir, *The Colonial Police,* London, U.K.: Allen and Unwin, 1952.

Luckham, R., The economic base of private law practice, *Review of Ghana Law,* 8 (1976). Marenin, O. and Reisig, M. (1995), A general theory of crime and patterns of crime in Nigeria: An exploration of methodological assumptions, *Journal of Criminal Justice,* 23 (1995).

Marenin, O., (1987), The 'Anini Saga': Armed robbery and the reproduction of ideology in Nigeria, *Journal of Modern African Studies,* 25 (1987).

Milner, A., *The Nigerian Penal System,* London, U.K.: Sweet and Maxwell, 1972.

Mushanga, T. M., *Crime and Deviance,* Nairobi, Kenya: East African Literature Bureau, 1976.

Mushanga, T. M.,, (Ed.), Criminology in Africa, Rome: United Nations Interregional Crime and Justice Research Institute, UNICRI Series, *Criminology in Developing Countries,* Publication No. 47., 1992.

Opolot, J., *The Crime Problem in Africa: A Wake-Up Call of the 1960s–1990s,* Houston, TX: Univers de Presse, 1995.

Sachs, A. and Welch, G.H., *Liberating the Law. Creating Popular Justice in Mozambique,* London, U.K.: Zed Books, 1990.

Schatzberg, M.G., *The Dialectics of Oppression in Zaire,* Bloomington, MN: Indiana University Press, 1988.

Seidman, R.B., Judicial review and fundamental freedoms in anglophonic independent Africa, *Ohio State Law Journal,* 35 (1974).

Sevareid, P., The work of rural primary courts in Ghana and Kenya, *African Law Studies,* (1976).

Shivji, I.G., *Law, State and the Working Class in Tanzania,* London, U.K.: James Currey, 1986.

Smith, M.G., *Government in Zazzau, 1800–1940,* Oxford, U.K.: Oxford University Press, 1960.

Snyder, F.G., *Capitalism and Legal Change. An African Transformation,* New York, U.K.: Academic Press, 1981.

Tamuno, T., Bashir, I.L., Alemika, E.E.O. and Akano, A.O., (Eds.), *Policing Nigeria. Past, Present and Future,* Lagos, Nigeria, Oxford, U.K.: Malthouse Press, 1993.

Tanner, R.E.S., Penal practice in Africa: Some restrictions on the possibility of reform, *The Journal of Modern African Studies,* 10 (1972).

van Onselen, C., *African Mine Labour in Southern Rhodesia, 1900–1933,* 1970.

Vansina, J., *Kingdoms of the Savanna,* Madison, OH: University of Wisconsin Press, 1965.

White, L., *The Comforts of Home. Prostitution in Colonial Nairobi,* Chicago, IL: University of Chicago Press, 1990.

Young, R., Legal system development, in *The African Experience, Volume I: Essays,* Paden, J. and Soja, E.W., (Eds.), Evanston, IL: Northwestern University Press, 1970.

Zvekic, U. and del Frate, A.A., (Eds.), *Criminal Victimization in the Developing World,* Rome: UNICRI, Publication No. 55, 1995.

*See also* **South Africa, Crime and Justice in**

# Substance Abuse: *See* **Drug Use: Extent and Correlates; Alcohol Use: The Law**

# Suicide: Extent and Correlates

Suicide is one of the ten leading causes of death in the U.S. Unlike most causes of death, however, suicide can be prevented. The suicide rate has varied between 10–13 suicides per 100,000 population for nearly 50 years. This suggests that the causes of suicide may be deeply rooted in the social fabric of society. The effects of suicide go well beyond the annual toll of 30,000 suicide victims. For each victim there are approximately six survivors. There are between 300,000–600,000 suicide attempts each year. At least 5 million living Americans have attempted suicide.

The present entry reviews illustrations of the major sociological correlates of completed suicide. These are grouped into four major theoretical categories: (1) cultural or social learning, (2) strain or economic, (3) social integration or bond, and (4) modernization. These sets of correlates are not mutually exclusive. For example, the economic losses of divorce can increase suicide risk from the standpoint of strain theory, whereas the sociopsychological bonds that are broken through divorce can be interpreted from the standpoint of social integration or bond theory. Modernization is thought to increase suicide risk through decreasing religious bonds, yet it may lead to declines in the long run by decreasing economic strain.

## Cultural or Social Learning Correlates

Cultural explanations stress the socialization process where normative considerations are learnt and internalized. Learning can take place through such mechanisms as the media, gender roles, and racial socialization.

### Media Effects

It has been well-established that societal exposure to media stories about suicide tends to increase suicidal behavior. The population can learn from news stories that suicide is a problem-solving technique when the individual is faced with stressors such as terminal illness, divorce, and work-related strains. Some stories and conditions can maximize (presumably through differential identification) or minimize copycat effects. For example, a recent quantitative review of 293 findings from 42 studies determined that copycat suicide effects are strongest when the suicide story concerns a well-known entertainment or political figure. Such stories are 14.3 times more likely to generate a copycat effect than other stories. Stories about real victims are 4.03 times more likely to generate a copycat effect than ones about fictional suicide victims. The rate of suicide attempts is more closely correlated with media stories than the rate of completed suicide.

### Racial Socialization

Historical discrimination against African Americans in the U.S. has been associated with a cultural response: the externalization of aggression. Frustrations for minorities are more apt to be vented in the form of homicide than suicide. The opposite is true for whites who are apt to internalize aggression owing to the absence of racial discrimination. Blacks have also learnt to hold more negative attitudes toward suicide than whites. Whites have had a suicide rate that is approximately double that of blacks for many decades. The most current data from 1998 are in Table 1. They indicate that the white suicide rate per 100,000 is 12.4 compared to a black rate of 5.4 per 100,000. This yields a ratio of 2.18.

### Gender Socialization

The suicide rate for men is higher than that for women in 41 of 42 nations surveyed. In the U.S. men currently have a suicide rate 4.2 times as high as women (see Table 1). In most nations, after 50 years of convergence,

**Table 1.** Suicide by Gender, Race, and Age, 1988 and 1998, U.S.

| | | Number of Suicides | | Rate per 100,000 people in Group | |
| --- | --- | --- | --- | --- | --- |
| | | 1988 | 1998 | 1988 | 1998 |
| Total Gender | | 30,407 | 30,575 | 12.4 | 11.3 |
| | Males | 24,078 | 24,538 | 20.1 | 18.6 |
| | Females | 6329 | 6037 | 5.0 | 4.4 |
| Race | | | | | |
| | Whites | 27,790 | 27,648 | 13.4 | 12.4 |
| | Blacks | 2022 | 1977 | 6.7 | 5.7 |
| Age | | | | | |
| | 15–24 | 4929 | 4135 | 13.2 | 11.1 |
| | 25–34 | 6710 | 5365 | 15.4 | 13.8 |
| | 35–44 | 5205 | 6837 | 14.8 | 15.4 |
| | 45–54 | 3532 | 5131 | 14.6 | 14.8 |
| | 55–64 | 3406 | 2963 | 15.6 | 13.1 |
| | 65–74 | 3296 | 2597 | 18.4 | 14.1 |
| | 75–84 | 2462 | 2355 | 25.9 | 19.7 |
| | 85+ | 605 | 851 | 20.5 | 21.0 |

*Sources:* U.S. Public Health Service (1990); National Center for Health Statistics (July 2000).

the gap between men and women in suicide has been widening for two decades. Gender socialization may contribute to the gender gap in suicide through such means as (1) women learn to be more religiously involved than men and religiosity lowers suicide risk, (2) women have an alcoholism rate (a key predictor of suicide risk) that is one fifth that of men, (3) women have more extensive social support systems than men, (4) women's cultural acceptance of suicide is lower than that of men, and (5) men have greater access to lethal firearms than women.

### Culture of Suicide

Recent survey evidence on national levels of suicide acceptability in 30 nations has found that the higher the level of approval of suicide in a nation the higher the suicide rate. However, at the micro level, the process of learning of prosuicide attitudes from peers and their potential influence on completed acts of suicide have been understudied.

## Strain or Economic Correlates

### Unemployment

Suicide is often linked to the experience of various strains (stressors and frustrations) experienced over the life course. For example, unemployment can increase suicide risk through such means as lowering the incomes and self-esteem of the unemployed and their families. A review of 17 studies that compared the suicide rates of the unemployed against those of the employed determined that in all 17 the unemployed had a higher suicide rate. For example, in London, England the respective rates were 73 per 100,000 and 14.1 per 100,000; in Austria the figures were 98.3 versus 25.0 per 100,000; in Italy they were 3.2 versus 2.1 per 100,000.

## Socioeconomic Status

The correlates of poverty such as low income, family disruption, and mental troubles can increase suicide risk. Low socioeconomic status tends to be correlated with high suicide rates. For example, in the U.S. laborers have a rate of 94 per 100,000, eight times the national average. In California, farm laborers have a suicide rate five times that of professional workers. In Australia manual workers have a rate 50% higher than all nonmanual workers combined. Although large socioeconomic categories tend to follow this pattern, some specialized occupations with high socioeconomic status (e.g., dentists) nevertheless have high suicide risk.

## Age

As indicated by the data in Table 1, suicide rates for the general population are relatively stable for the pre-retirement cohorts. Retirement can increase suicide risk through loss: loss of job-derived income, job-derived friendships, loss of loved ones through death, loss of health, and so on. Such patterns may be best interpreted from the standpoint of a generalized strain theory.

## Age and Gender

For men, suicide risk tends to increase slightly over the life course and peaks in the retirement years. Retirement constitutes a significant crisis for men as they lose income, status, contact with coworkers, routines, and other meanings of employment. For women, suicide tends to peak at around age 50 and then decreases. It has been argued that the key life crisis or strain for women is the decline of kinkeeping responsibilities marked by the departure of children from the home.

## Social Integration or Bond

### Marital Integration

Strong attachments to others apparently reduce the likelihood of suicide. For example, marriage can lower the egotistical tendencies of the individual through subordination of the individual's needs to those of the group. Marriage both gives and takes emotional support, a factor thought to reduce suicide risk. The pooling of economic resources in marriage may also reduce economic strain and, as a consequence, suicide risk. Divorced persons tend to have a substantially higher rate of depression (a key psychological risk factor in suicide) than the married. In the U.S. depression among the divorced is 40% higher than that of the married.

A review of 789 findings in 132 studies published between 1880 and 1995 determined that 78% found that divorced persons and groups were at high suicide risk. For example, in Austria divorced persons have a suicide rate of 128 per 100,000. This is 4.2 times greater than that for married persons (30.5 per 100,000). In the U.S., this ratio is typically 3 to 4, depending on the age or gender group that is analyzed.

### Religiosity

Religion influences suicide through religious integration, commitment, or networks. Religious integration refers to the sheer number of religious practices and beliefs. It is believed that the greater the number of such traits, the greater the order and meaning in life, and the lower the suicide risk. Religious commitment is the cultivation of just a few, key religious practices and beliefs such as the coping mechanism of prayer and belief in an afterlife as a reward for suffering. Religious networks may reduce suicide not so much through religious beliefs but through the emotional and social support churchgoers receive from one another.

An analysis of suicide rates in 71 nations determined that the greater the religious integration (as measured by the proportion Islam) the lower the suicide rate. Islam is thought to be a religious faith especially high in shared practices and beliefs. Catholicism, formerly thought to be high in religious integration, is no longer associated with a reduction in suicide rates.

Indicators of religious commitment also tend to be predictive of suicide rates. For example, an analysis of 261 Canadian census divisions determined that a 10% increase in the proportion with no religion (low religious commitment) was associated with a 3.2% increase in suicide.

Religions with structures (e.g., nonhierarchical power relations and conservative ideologies) thought to promote social networking tend to be associated with lower suicide rates. For example, for American counties, the greater the percentage evangelical Baptist or the greater the percentage Seventh Day Adventist, the lower the suicide rate.

### Migration

Bonds to such groups as coworkers, extended family, and neighbors can be severed through migration. The presumed loss in integration through migration has tended to be linked to enhanced suicide risk. International migrants tend to have suicide rates higher than those in their native country. Migrants in less cohesive ethnic cultures (e.g., American, English, Welsh, and Scottish) are especially at risk.

### Political Integration

Great international wars and major political events such as presidential elections are often associated with reductions in the social suicide rate. During such times the population may band together and become less self-centered and be marked by a higher level of group consciousness. However, modern research suggests that the influence of political events on suicide is only indirect; wars and elections tend to reduce suicide through lowering unemployment rates.

## Modernization

Classic 19th century treatises on suicide all argued that suicide would continue to increase with the processes of urbanization, industrialization, and secularization. Urbanization substantially decreased social bonds through migration. Early industrialization often increased economic strain through lowered real wages and longer work days. Secularization weakened religious bonds as individuals were increasingly exposed to education and science. With weakened ties to families, religion, and work, suicide potential should increase.

Analyses of data from 20 nations for 1900–1975 determined, however, that there was no continued, automatic relationship between modernization and suicide. In a third of the nations, suicide decreased, in a third it held steady, and in a third it continued to increase. The initial shocks of modernization are perhaps counteracted by extended families resettling together in a city for several generations, by economic prosperity brought about by late industrialization, and by the unanticipated survival of vibrant religious systems.

An analysis of the oldest available data assessed the impact of urbanization on suicide in Finland from 1750 through 1985. Through 1900, a 1% rise in urbanization was associated with a 0.22% rise in suicide. This association declined thereafter so that a 1% rise in urbanization was associated with only a 0.12% rise in suicide. The influence on suicide is thought to weaken with the advent of late modernization.

## Conclusion

Although suicide has many known correlates, the evidence for some is substantially stronger than that for others. Gender, socioeconomic status, unemployment, and marital status are some of the best substantiated correlates with supporting evidence available from around the world. Even for these correlates, however, it is not fully clear exactly what accounts for the association between the risk factor and suicide. For example, mental troubles such as major depression may cause both divorce and suicide, as well as causing both unemployment and suicide. To the extent that chronically depressed people do not make the best marriage partners or employees, and to the extent that depression is a key cause of suicide, depression may account for divorce and unemployment. The direct effect of divorce and unemployment on suicide may have been exaggerated in sociological work on the subject.

Many correlates have been understudied. For example, although the religiosity levels of groups such as cities, counties, and nations tend to be associated with suicide rates, much less is known about the religiosity levels of individuals who do commit suicide. Recent analyses of American mortality data suggest that infrequent church attendance is a key predictor of suicide risk. Future research of this sort should be conducted in other nations.

STEVEN STACK

### References and Further Reading

Lester, D., *Why People Kill Themselves,* 4th ed., Springfield, IL: Charles Thomas, 2000.

Maris, R., Berman, A. and Silverman, M., (Eds.), *Comprehensive Textbook of Suicidology,* New York, NY: Guilford Press, 2000.

National Center for Health Statistics. Deaths: Final data for 1998. *National Vital Statistics Reports,* 48(11):1–102 (July 2000).

Stack, S., Suicide: A decade review of the sociological literature, *Deviant Behavior,* 4:41–66 (1982).

Stack, S. Suicide: A fifteen-year review of the sociological literature, Part I. *Suicide and Life Threatening Behavior,* 30:145–162 (2000).

Stack, S. Suicide: A fifteen-year review of the sociological literature, Part II, *Suicide and Life Threatening Behavior,* 30:163–176 (2000).

U.S. Public Health Service. *Advance Report of Final Mortality Statistics, Monthly Vital Statistics Report,* 39 (7, Suppl.):1–52 (November 1990).

*See also* **Euthanasia and Physician-Assisted Suicide; Suicide: Law; Suicide: Prevention**

# Suicide: Prevention

Three levels of suicide prevention are generally recognized. First, primary or universal preventions are directed toward an entire population. Gun control laws and the detoxification of natural gas in Europe are examples. Second, primary selective prevention specifically targets a group at higher than average risk of becoming suicidal. An educational program to train primary care physicians in the diagnosis of major depression is an illustration. Third, an indicated intervention targets a group with a demonstrated high risk of suicide. A community's decision to establish a suicide hot line or suicide prevention center for use by suicidal individuals would illustrate such a highly focused intervention. The present entry is organized around two broad categories of interventions: micro-oriented interventions that focus on individuals at risk and macro interventions that target larger populations. The present review focuses on intervention strategies that have been the subject of evaluation research.

## Micro-Oriented Suicide Prevention

A meta-analysis of 249 medical research papers on suicide by personality disorder found that of 44 disorders considered, 36 had elevated rates of suicide. Considerable work on suicide prevention has focused on a few of these disorders at especially high risk of suicide. Individual-centered avenues for suicide prevention are reviewed here for three disorders: impulse control, depression, and bipolar disorders.

*Aggression, Serotonin, and SSRI Treatment.* From a biological standpoint, suicide can be viewed as stemming from an aggressive impulse. Such aggressive impulses can be triggered by emotions such as anger and by social psychological processes such as loss of property and loved ones. The probability that an aggressive impulse will provoke suicidal (as opposed to homicidal) behavior is enhanced by such considerations as the presence of major depression, and hopelessness.

Low impulse control and suicidal behavior have and has been associated with low levels of the neurotransmitter serotonin in the cerebrospinal fluid (CSF-5-HIAA). Although serotonin level is, in part, genetically determined, sustained stress from negative life events also reduces serotonin metabolism.

Suicide prevention in this biological model includes pharmacological treatment with serotonin reuptake inhibitors (SSRI) such as paroxetine. SSRIs have been found, for example, to reduce suicidal thoughts. In a follow-up study of 92 depressed patients who had attempted suicide, ones with below the mean level of serotonin were more than twice as likely as their counterparts to have completed suicide (17% vs. 7%). In a similar study the low serotonin group had a suicide rate of 22% on follow up.

*Depression.* A key predictor of suicide risk is depression. Micro-oriented prevention of suicide in depressed populations includes the treatment of depression with appropriate drugs. In a study based in Finland, 45% of suicides were under treatment the week they committed suicide. However, only 3% had received antidepressants in adequate doses. The need for appropriate pharmacological treatment has been documented in a variety of other studies. For example, the risk of suicide among depressed patients who were on antidepressants was 141 per 100,000, much less than the rate among depressed patients not on antidepressants (259 per 100,000). In Sweden, the suicide rate fell by 10% between 1991 and 1994 whereas there was a 50% increase in the use of antidepressants.

*Bipolar Disorder and Lithium.* Persons suffering from extreme mood swings from depression to a manic state (bipolar disorder) have a very high rate of suicide. There is a substantial body of evidence (28 studies) that suggests that pharmacological treatment with lithium lowers suicide risk for this population. The risk of suicide is lowered by five to nine times for persons with bipolar disorders who are undergoing lithium-based treatment as compared to their counterparts with no lithium treatment.

*Other Evidence for Pharmacological Prevention of Suicide.* There is accumulating evidence that the neuroleptic clozapine reduces suicide risk among schizophrenics. A proven avenue to suicide prevention among alcoholics is abstinence from alcohol. The drug naltrexone prolongs abstinence from alcohol with a relapse rate of only 23% compared to a relapse to alcohol-use rate of 54% among controls.

*Psychotherapy.* Reviews of the 10–20 existing psychosocial interventions on outpatients conclude that we currently do not know which interventions are effective or most effective (Ellis, 2001, 142, 147). However, several leads suggest that cognitive therapy directed at changing common irrational beliefs and dysfunctional attitudes among suicidal patients may help in the prevention of suicide. These common beliefs and attitudes include perfectionism, and a belief that emotional problems are caused by external forces as opposed to one's interpretations of events. Other leads for suicide prevention through therapy include restoring a sense of hopefulness, facilitating problem solving, and providing empathy.

*Suicide Prevention Centers.* Suicide prevention centers can reduce suicide by offering services to suicidal persons such as suicide-hot-line counseling. Recently a meta-analysis of 14 studies on the impact of suicide prevention centers on the social suicide rate was completed. The average correlation from the meta-review was $r = -0.16$. Suicide prevention centers tend to reduce the suicide rate, but they can explain only about 3% of the variance in suicide rates. This is probably a conservative estimate as the centers tend to serve suicidal white females and not a cross-section of the general population. Analyses that restrict evaluation to the suicide rate of the group most apt to have contacted the suicide centers often find the strongest results.

## Macro-Suicide Prevention

*Education of Primary Care Physicians.* A key problem facing suicide prevention is that most persons who commit suicide do not seek psychological help. A large number, however, do see a family physician shortly before their suicide. Primary care physicians might be used to combat suicide if they received adequate training on such issues as how to detect major depression in their clients and what drugs are most apt to prevent suicide. A major experiment was done along these lines on the island of Gotland, Sweden. After all general practitioners were appropriately trained, suicide declined by 60%. This was assumed to be a result of a 300% increase in the use of prescribed antidepressants. The suicide rate ultimately returned to its normal level, but this may be attributed to the fact that half of the trained physicians left the island.

*Means Restriction.* The decrease in the availability of the means of suicide has often been thought of as a possible avenue to suicide prevention. Evaluation research on means restriction has been focused on gun control and the detoxification of natural gas. A key concern in this research is whether or not a decrease in suicide from means restriction (e.g., gun control) is simply transferred or displaced to an increase in an alternative means of suicide (e.g., leaping). That is, gun control would lead to no change in the overall suicide rate if gun suicides simply switch to suicide by jumping. The results of the research have been quite mixed. This is, in part, because of substantial methodological differences and inadequacies of the statistical models employed. Often declines in suicide are noted, but these may be because of unmeasured trends (such as those in the economy) and not to means restriction *per se.*

*Gun Control and Availability.* In the aggregate, guns do not appear to have had a substantial impact on suicide. The supply of firearms has more than quadrupled in American society in the last 50 years, whereas the suicide rate has stayed very stable, typically between 10–13 suicides per 100,000. Suicide has declined nearly 10% in the decade of the 1990s, an era with a record level of firearms. However, such simple statistics can be somewhat misleading without controlling out the covariates of guns and suicide. For example, the impact of guns on suicide in the U.S. in recent years may be offset by large improvements in the economy, with unemployment rates being at record lows. In the future, multivariate models are needed to address the complex aggregate relationship between guns and suicide.

The few available multivariate models that weigh the importance of guns against other predictors of suicide risk often find mixed results. A much cited investigation by Kammerman of 438 households with suicides and 438 matched controls determined that households with guns were 4.8 times more likely to report a suicide than ones with no guns. A key shortcoming of this study was that the percentage that actually used the available guns in their suicides was not reported. Guns were, however, only the fifth most important factor of the seven investigated. For example, persons with a psychotropic medication were 35.9 times more likely to suicide than their counterparts; and persons who had been hospitalized for drinking were 16.4 times more likely to commit suicide.

A study of the institution of a handgun control law in Washington, D.C. in 1976 found that gun suicides declined from 2.6 to 2.0 per month or by 23% after the law went into effect. Suicides by other means did not decline significantly. Similar studies of handgun control in Ontario, Canada, found that gun suicides declined after the law was passed in 1978. However, one study based on a 5-year experimental period found a displacement effect: would-be gun suicides became nongun suicides. This resulted in no net drop in suicide.

In contrast, a study extending the experimental period to 10 years found a net drop in the rate. Neither of these studies controlled for possible covariates of law and suicide such as downward trends in divorce nor improvements in the economy. Until such work is done, we cannot determine if any change in suicide rates is because of a law or because of socioeconomic covariates of the law.

*Detoxification of Natural Gas.*  Highly toxic coal gas, used to heat British homes, was the standard method used in suicides in Britain. As natural gas from the North Sea replaced the toxic coal gas, British suicide deceased by 40%. Similar changes brought about similar drops in suicide in Switzerland. However, detoxification of natural gas in the Netherlands, the U.S., and Scotland did not result in as large declines in suicide. In the U.S., for example, about 81% of the decline in domestic gas suicides may have been transferred to suicide by car exhaust. An increase in suicidogenic conditions (e.g., divorce, unemployment) in some nations may have offset any would-be decline in suicide from the detoxification of gas. Research based on more sophisticated statistical models is needed to resolve this issue.

*Changes in Sociological Structures.*  The most macrosociological-oriented suicide preventive programs would change aspects of the social and economic order as a means of reducing the suicide rate. The poor and unemployed have high suicide rates as do the divorced. Social policies designed to change these and other suicidogenic conditions may have a large impact on suicide in the long run. High-cost full-employment policies and substantial improvements in mental health services for the maritally troubled are probably unlikely to be enacted on the basis of the need for suicide prevention *per se*.

*Conclusion.*  The evaluation of many suicide prevention programs tends to be based on misspecified models with little effort to control for the covariates of suicide prevention such as economic trends. Other evaluation research (e.g., that done on suicide prevention centers) needs to measure the suicide rates of the specific groups that are most influenced by the prevention program (e.g., young white females) in order to fairly assess their impact. The independent impact of such programs on suicide rates remains unclear.

Perhaps the strongest evidence for workable suicide prevention programs comes from the medical literature. Increased prescription of adequate dosages of the appropriate drugs tends to reduce suicide risk among persons from some categories of mental disorders (e.g., major depression and bipolar). Control of the serotonin system through drug therapy also provides a promising attack on suicide. However, most persons who are at suicide risk never come in for medical treatment. Hence, a micro approach to suicide prevention will need to be supplemented by macro solutions. These target larger audiences that contain people presently unreached by medical networks.

STEVEN STACK

## References and Further Reading

Ellis, T.E., Psychotherapy with suicidal patients, in *Suicide Prevention: Resources for the Millennium,* Lester, D. (Ed.), New York, NY: Taylor and Francis, 2001.

Harris, E.C. and Barraclough, B.M., Suicide as an outcome of mental disorders, *British Journal of Psychiatry,* 170:205–228 (1997).

Lester, D., The concentration of neurotransmitter metabolites in the cerebrospinal fluid: A meta analysis, *Pharmacopsychiatry,* 28:45–50 (1995).

Lester, D., The effectiveness of suicide prevention centers: A review, *Suicide and Life Threatening Behavior,* 27:304–310 (1997).

Lester, D., *Why People Kill Themselves,* 4th ed., Springfield, IL: Charles Thomas, 2000.

Maris, R., Berman, A., and Silverman, M. (Eds.), *Comprehensive Textbook of Suicidology,* New York, NY: Guilford Press, 2000.

Miller, H., Coombs, D., Leeper, J., and Barton, S., An analysis of the effects of suicide prevention facilities on suicide rates in the U.S., *American Journal of Public Health,* 74:340–343 (1984).

Roy, A., Psychiatric treatment in suicide prevention, in *Suicide Prevention: Resources for the Millennium,* Lester, D. (Ed.), New York, NY: Taylor and Francis, 2001.

Rutz, W., The role of primary physicians in preventing suicide, in *Suicide Prevention: Resources for the Millennium,* Lester, D. (Ed.), New York, NY: Taylor and Francis, 2001.

Stack, S., Suicide: A fifteen-year review of the sociological literature, Part I. *Suicide and Life Threatening Behavior,* 30:145–162 (2000).

Stack, S., Suicide: A fifteen-year review of the sociological literature, Part II, *Suicide and Life Threatening Behavior,* 30:163–176 (2000).

Van Praag, H., Suicide and aggression: Are they biologically two sides of the same coin? in *Suicide Prevention: Resources for the Millennium,* Lester, D. (Ed.), New York, NY: Taylor and Francis, 2001.

*See also* **Suicide: Extent and Correlates**

# Suicide: The Law

Suicide is generally defined as the intentional act of killing oneself. This common definition of the act is not very different from the legal concept. Under English common law, suicide was deemed a form of murder, in specific, the murder of oneself and was considered a common law felony. This was held to be an offence against the King, who as sovereign had an interest in the preservation of the lives of the Crown's subjects. In addition, suicide was an offence against God, as the taking of one's life usurped the authority of God to determine when it was time for a person to die. Historically, the punishment was severe for those who committed suicide; the person would be buried at a crossroads, with a stake driven through their body, and the suicide's lands and chattel properties were subject to forfeiture to the Crown. The exception to this forfeiture was where the successfully suicidal person was insane at the time of the self-killing, because such a person was legally less blameworthy than a person of sound mind.

It was no small irony that forfeiture punished the suicide's surviving relations, who were innocent of suicide by definition. Thus it was that during the American colonial era, the punitive measure of forfeiture was abolished, a concept that was ultimately embraced in Anglo-American law. By the 19th century, suicides in the U.S. no longer conformed to the traditional practice under the English common law, so that a proper burial of the suicide was permitted and forfeiture of properties was not. Indeed, suicide has been decriminalized throughout the U.S. and the U.K.

This does not necessarily mean that suicide has become a legally accepted practice as a matter of Anglo-American law. For example, a person who states an intention to commit suicide may well be subject to civil commitment, either for prevention or for treatment of an underlying psychological condition or illness, which is leading to the suicidal tendencies, ideation, and action. Conversely, assisting in a suicide, even where the assisted person is terminally ill, other than in the state of Oregon.

Assisted suicide is the subject that has generated the most legal controversy in the past decade. Although it is now a well-settled law that committing suicide is not a crime, and attempting a suicide is not treated as a criminal matter, assisting in a suicide is prosecutable as a homicide related offense in most Anglo-American jurisdictions. The related question of whether prohibitions upon, and prosecutions of, physicians who engage in assisting in a suicide violate fundamental rights of due process and equal protection went to the U.S. Supreme Court in 1997. Interestingly, in one of the cases, that from the state of Washington, the Court noted that it had always been a crime to assist in a suicide there (see *Washington v. Glucksberg*, 521 U.S. 702, 117 S.Ct. 2258, 138L.Ed. 2d 772, 1997). In contrast, withholding or withdrawal of life-sustaining treatment did not legally constitute a suicide; so terminating such treatment did not constitute causing, aiding, or assisting in a suicide.

The Supreme Court, in determining that assisting in a suicide should not be deemed a fundamental right, returned to the historical proposition that the state has an interest in protecting and preserving the lives of its citizens. This legally is consistent with the concept that the sanctity of human life must be protected, which emanates from Judeo-Christian constructs. However, the advances in medical technology and the body of law that developed regarding the right to die has been cited as supporting a legal right to die with assistance, or to have assisted suicide, by another phrase. In the 1997 cases from Washington and New York, the Court noted that Oregon has enacted, through ballot initiative, a Death with Dignity Act, which legalized physician-assisted suicide for competent, terminally ill adults under very controlled circumstances.

However, the court declined to state that there is a constitutional or fundamental liberty interest that includes a right to commit suicide, which in turn includes a right to assistance in doing so. In addition, the Court determined that Washington's assisted-suicide ban had a rational relationship to legitimate governmental interests. These interests include the preservation of human life; in protecting vulnerable persons, such as those who are mentally or psychiatrically ill or who have untreated pain and suffering relating to physical illness; in protecting the integrity of the medical profession; in protecting vulnerable groups such as the poor, the elderly, and the disabled from abuse, neglect, mistake, and coercion and to value and accord dignity to all human lives; and to permit states to engage in policies and legal measures that prevent assisted suicide as potentially sliding down a slippery slope from voluntary to nonvoluntary and perhaps even involuntary euthanasia.

In the companion case from New York, the Court determined that a legal ban on assisted suicide by physicians did not violate the equal protection of those who were seeking assisted suicide as compared with those who sought to discontinue treatment, even though that discontinuation could cause death. The Court specifically noted that the criminal statutes did not infringe fundamental rights of patients seeking assisted suicide from physicians, nor did the prohibitions against assisted suicide involve suspect classifications. Additionally, the Court noted that there was a clear distinction between assisting suicides and refusing lifesaving medical treatment, and that this distinction was important, logical, and rational.

In contemplating the way forward as to how the legal treatment of suicide shall develop, it is important to note that although the civil law relating to those who would attempt suicide remains settled, the assisted-suicide debate, which is at the forefront of legal activity relating to the law of suicide, continues earnestly and profoundly. At the time of this writing, the State of Oregon is possibly *en route* to the U.S. Supreme Court as a result of Attorney General John Ashcroft's directive whereby he has declared that assisting in a suicide is not a legitimate medical purpose and that prescribing, dispensing, or administering federally controlled substances to assist in a suicide was in violation of federal law and punishable (see *State of Oregon v. Ashcroft*, 192 F. Supp. 2d 1077, 2002 U.S. Dist. LEXIS 6695, D. Ct. Oregon 2002). One might posit whether this is the close relative of the legal policy of punishing the family of a suicide in centuries past with forfeiture of the suicide's land and properties, with a modern-day equivalent of punishing a surviving physician with forfeiture of a license and liberty.

DEMETRA M. PAPPAS

### References and Further Reading

John-Stevas, St., *Norman, Life, Death and the Law: Law and Christian Morals in England and the United States,* Beard Books (2002).

Williams, G., *The Sanctity of Life and the Criminal Law,* Faber and Faber Ltd. (1958).

The New York State Task Force on Life and the Law, *When Death is Sought: Assisted Suicide in the Medical Context* (1994).

*See also* **Suicide: Extent and Correlates; Suicide: Prevention**

# Superior Orders as a Defense to Criminal Liability

## Definition or Introduction

"Superior orders" as a defense is used by defendants who contend that criminal intent (*mens rea*) did not originate from them because they were acting pursuant to an order from one higher in rank or importance. Hence, because they would not ordinarily have engaged in the acts but for the orders they were complying to, they should not be held criminally responsible.

When defendants act in compliance to a legitimate law, they may not be held accountable for their actions. However, when they misuse or exceed the scope of powers vested in them, their acts may not be justified. The defense of superior orders is sometimes evoked when it is not clear if the act engaged in falls under the exception of public duty; that is, the defense may be used when a soldier "honestly and reasonably" believes the orders to be lawful. According to Osiel (1999, 1), in international law as well as in the military codes of the majority of countries, soldiers are generally excused "for obedience to an illegal order unless its unlawfulness is thoroughly obvious on its face." A "manifestly illegal" order, as Osiel notes, may be ascertained when (1) the act is clearly prohibited, (2) when indulgence in the act will "produce the very gravest human consequences," (3) when the act deviates from the norm and prescribed standards (1999, 83). At critical times (especially during combat) it may be difficult for soldiers to determine if an act is illegal. In the U.S., as discussed in *U.S. v. Calley* (1973) the law relating to obeying orders states that:

> The acts of a subordinate done in compliance with an unlawful order given him by his superior are excused and impose no criminal liability upon him

unless the superior's order is one which a man of ordinary sense and understanding would, under the circumstances, know to be unlawful, or if the order in question is actually known to the accused to be unlawful.

## Origin of the Defense

In ancient Rome, and as evident in Canon Law during the Middle Ages, soldiers were held accountable for acts that were flagrantly illegal; the corollary being that if the acts were less than atrocious the soldiers could be excused if they presumed the superiors' orders to have been lawful.

Osiel (1999, 44), notes that the defense of superior orders in international law has not been clearly established because while it stipulates instances when criminal proceedings can be instituted, it provides limited directives on how violators who act in compliance to superior orders may be handled. The defense of superior orders as Osiel states is incorporated in the military codes of most nations, as such, when international law is evoked, as opposed to a nation's military law in regard to the defense, courts resort to the latter.

In the U.S., according to the *Manual for Courts Martial* (11–109, 1995):

> it is a defense to any offense that the accused was acting pursuant to orders unless the accused knew the orders to be unlawful or a person of ordinary sense and understanding would have known the orders to be lawful.

Although the superior orders defense is mostly associated with military law, facsimile of it may be found in codes of other professions. According to Rule 5.2 of the American Bar Association Model Rules of Professional Conduct, "A subordinate lawyer does not violate the rules of professional conduct if that lawyer acts in accordance with a supervisory lawyer's reasonable resolution of an arguable question of professional duty."

## Who May Use the Defense?

This defense may be used by public authorities, for the most part, those in the military and law enforcement officers. According to Section 2.10 of the Model Penal Code:

> It is an affirmative defense that the actor, in engaging in the conduct charged to constitute an offense, does no more than execute an order of his superior in the armed services that he does not know to be unlawful.

The defense of superior orders has been used by war criminals in several instances, including Nazi war criminals during the Nuremberg trials after the second world war (even though the International Tribunal at Nuremberg claimed not to have allowed use of the defense), and Lieutenant Calley of the U.S., after the Vietnam war. It was used successfully by Erich Priebke, during his trial by an Italian Court for his atrocities in a 1944 massacre in Rome.

The defense of superior orders was not permitted by the Security Council when it was evoked by defendants of the former Yugoslavia, and those of Rwanda. Instead, the Council allowed its use only to mitigate the penalties against the defendants (UN Documents s/25704 (1993), art. 6, para. 57; art. 7, para. 4.

## Discussion

Articles 91 and 92 of the U.S. Uniform Code of Military Justice, stipulate that those in the military must obey lawful orders. It follows that orders to a military personnel are presumed lawful except when they are "patently illegal" or "direct the commission of a crime." The corollary is that, illegal orders are to be disregarded. It would be a justification defense under "execution of public duty" if the conduct is "required or authorized" by law (see Section 3.03 of the Model Penal Code). The Manual for Courts Martial stipulates that an order or regulation is "lawful unless it is contrary to the Constitution, the laws of the United States, or lawful superior orders or for some other reason is beyond the authority of the official issuing it."

Superior orders as a defense has a lengthy history, and when used successfully, the defendant is exonerated of the crime. In *Commonwealth ex. rel. Wadsworth v. Shortall* (206 Pennsylvania, 165, 1903), following orders to "shoot to kill" anyone failing to stop and identify himself or herself when requested to do so, a guardsman with the National Guard shot and killed someone who adamantly refused to comply with the guardsman's urging to stop. Following a charge of manslaughter, the guardsman was successful in using military orders as a defense.

In a more current case, *U.S. v. Calley* (46 C.M.R., 1131 (1973)) the U.S. Court of Military Appeals scrutinized the defense and established parameters within which the defense may not be acceptable in court either as a justification or an excuse to criminal responsibility. In the *Calley* case, the Military Court made it clear that even though conformity to orders is an integral part of discipline in the military, compliance to illegal orders, especially when such orders precipitate loss of life is inexcusable in law. Calley was charged with the murder of unarmed and nonbelligerent Vietnamese at My Lai. He was found guilty and he appealed his conviction. His conviction for murder was upheld because the Military Court rejected Calley's defense that he had acted pursuant to orders from his superior in command.

VICTORIA TIME

**References and Further Reading**

American Bar Association (1995). *Model Rules of Professional Conduct Manual for Courts Martial.*

Osiel M.J. (1999). *Obeying Orders,* Transaction Publishers, New Brunswick, NJ.

Secretary-General's Report on Aspects of Establishing an International Tribunal for the Prosecution of Persons Responsible for Serious Violations of International Humanitarian Law.

*Committed in the Territory of the Former Yugoslavia,* UN SCOR, 48th Session (1993). UN Doc. S/25704.

*Uniform Code of Military Justice.* Available at http://www.nimj.com/Home.asp.

*See also* **Defenses to Criminal Liability; War Crimes**

---

# Survey Research

---

Suppose you are interested in understanding why criminals behave in deviant ways? Or, what are the perceptions police officers have toward their day-to-day duties? To investigate these questions you might use what is known as survey research. Survey research is defined as a process or category of methods used to systematically answer conceptual questions. This process uses "surveys" or "questionnaires" as a tool for data collection. A questionnaire consists of "questions" or "items" designed to elicit responses related to a specified set of research objectives.

Survey research is widely used in the social sciences. This method is also used in every arena of the larger society, such as government, schools, business, and industry. Surveys are also used for an array of purposes. However, most surveys are used to elicit opinions, attitudes, and perceptions of members of a given population on nearly any topic of interest to researchers.

Survey research can be distinguished from survey methods. Survey research is a general term for the numerous theoretical, methodological, and analytical approaches to understanding the world in which we live. Like all research, survey research represents an attempt to systematically address conceptual questions. Conceptual research has the ultimate goal of making inferences about populations from "samples" or subsets of populations. Survey methods tend to be quantitative in nature. That is, surveys often use numerical values to represent some aspect of the social world. Survey items are also coded for the purpose of serving as measures on some dimension of attitudes or perceptions. Quantitative research in general and survey research in particular uses statistical methods of analysis. To this end, computer programs are used to analyze the quantitative data derived from survey analysis.

Survey methods, on the other hand, represent specific tools used to collect data in conducting survey research. There are numerous survey methods including mail surveys, telephone surveys, and face-to-face interviews. Each of these specific survey methods has its strengths as well as weaknesses. The nature of the questions posed determines the appropriate survey method to be selected. Generally, survey methods share similar limitations with other quantitative methods. Survey methods tend to be low in validity. That is, survey methods by their very nature tend to be an examination of the concept rather than the phenomena under investigation. For example, a survey may be designed to elicit responses measuring attitudes concerning the fear of crime. The analysis of the data derived from the survey may in fact be a study of the perception of the fear of crime rather than the phenomena itself. Despite this limitation, survey methods are quite useful in enhancing our understanding of social issues.

What is the scope of survey research? And, how are survey methods used? The use of survey research can be found across public and private sectors of society. Philanthropic organizations use survey research to determine the needs of communities. The business world uses survey research to determine factors within specific economic markets. Schools use survey research to investigate issues related to student academic performance. Police departments may use survey research to examine community attitudes toward foot patrols. There is no segment of the larger society where survey methods cannot be used to examine the nature of attitudes, opinions, and perceptions on a given topic.

A number of academic disciplines use survey methods in pursuing their research interests. Survey methods are powerful tools in addressing a wide range of research questions. Political scientists use surveys in examining voting behavior. For example, what is the tendency of a given voter population to vote for a particular candidate? Similarly, economists use surveys to determine consumer attitudes toward a particular line of products. For instance, the cosmetic industry may be interested in determining the potential appeal of a new line of lipstick. Survey methods have a wide range of applications across intellectual schools of thought. However, survey research may vary by form and the method used.

What are the types of survey methods generally used in the social sciences? As discussed above survey methods can take on myriad forms. Each of these methods also, has its strengths and weaknesses, respectively. To illustrate this point, three survey methods: (1) mail surveys, (2) telephone surveys, and (3) face-to-face interviews will be discussed. Mail surveys, are generally useful with respect to large samples. This advantage is generally shared by all three methods. Surveys can be copied and mailed to very large segments of a population quite efficiently. Surveys are almost never mailed to entire populations. This would be too time-consuming and expensive. They are usually mailed to samples (random) of a given population. Additionally, surveys of an entire population or census are no more accurate than sample surveys. For this reason, surveys of a sample are considered the most practical method. Mail surveys are considered the least expensive among all survey methods. However, mail surveys have a number of disadvantages that should be considered when selecting among the alternative methods. Survey methods in general are limited in the degree of detailed information that can be obtained from respondents. More specifically, mail surveys can obtain superficial information from a large sample of a population. Mail surveys also rely upon current addresses. Human populations tend to be dynamic. People constantly move in and out of geographical areas every day. These factors can have a significant influence upon research findings derived from mail surveys. Additionally, low response rates are also a major concern of mail surveys. The timing of surveys can dramatically affect response rates. Holidays and summer vacation seasons are undesirable times to mail surveys.

Telephone surveys are an alternative survey method. Telephone surveys are usually used by market researchers, academicians, and political pollsters. Compared with mail surveys, this method tends to be more precarious. Telephone surveys have the advantage of ensuring higher response rates than mail surveys. However, respondents often fail to complete mail surveys as well as return them within specified time constraints. Telephone surveys enable researchers to control the rate of completion and expeditious return of surveys. However, compared with mail surveys this method tends to be more expensive. Costs associated with this method include interviewers, facilities, and equipment. Choosing the appropriate time to call respondents can be tricky when employing this method. Should you call after 5 o'clock in the afternoon? Or, should you call early Saturday morning? Deciding when to contact respondents can often pose a problem. This method is also limited to households that possess a telephone. A related problem is the reliance upon accurate listings of current phone numbers. Despite the limitations of this method, with sufficient resources available it tends to be convenient and useful.

Finally, face-to-face interviews are often distributed among special populations. For example, these interviews are conducted in classrooms, prisons, workplaces, malls, and other sectors of society. Compared with the two previous methods, interviews tend to have the highest response rate. The factor of face-to-face interaction between the researcher and respondents is often advantageous. For example, respondents may be more inclined to participate in a study if asked in person. On the other hand, researchers may have an adverse influence upon respondents. This point is illustrated by a visibly disabled researcher who administers a survey concerning attitudes toward the American Disabilities Act to a nondisabled interviewee. Respondents might be inclined to provide socially desirable responses in the presence of the disabled researcher. Social desirability fosters responses that do not reflect a respondent's true opinions.

What are the methods of survey research used in criminology? Criminologists rely upon three sources of data for criminological investigation. They are namely: (1) The Uniform Crime Report (UCR), (2) self-report surveys, (3) and, victimization surveys. These three sources provide information concerning crime rates, criminal behavior, and victimization on specific categories of crime. Survey methods, as the term for two of these sources implies, are used as either primary sources of data or in conjunction with other methods of data collection and analysis. Survey methods are indispensable tools in the study of criminal behavior.

The Uniform Crime Report (UCR) is the most popular source of statistical data on criminal behavior. The UCR is developed by the Federal Bureau of Investigation (FBI) on what is known as "index crimes." Index crimes include murder and non-negligent manslaughter, forcible rape, robbery, aggravated assault, burglary, larceny, arson, and motor vehicle theft. These eight crimes are also referred to as "Part 1" crimes. Law enforcement agencies report the number of index crimes based upon records of crime complaints from victims, officers, and other agencies every month to the FBI. Additionally, law enforcement agencies report the number of complaints they received as well as the number of criminal cases cleared.

The UCR reports its findings based upon the number of crimes reported to the police and the number of arrests made, the crime rates per 100,000 people, and changes in the number and rate of crime over time. The FBI in cooperation with law enforcement agencies across the country work diligently to provide information concerning the extent of criminality. However, there are number of problems associated with the methodology used in the UCR. Among these issues: (1) not all crimes are reported to the FBI, (2) reports are submitted on a voluntary basis, (3) not all police departments submit reports, (4) there are often duplications of incidences of crime reflected in reports, (5) reports are sometimes incomplete, (6) information is sometime omitted, and (7) law enforcement agencies sometime define crimes differently from the FBI. For these reasons crimes reflected in the UCR may be either overreported or underreported.

Because of the problems associated with the UCR criminologists have developed alternative methodologies. Among them are self-report surveys and victimization surveys. Self-reports assure anonymity and confidentiality to respondents. In these surveys respondents are asked to report the nature and extent of their illegal activities. Self-reports examine the attitudes, values, personal characteristics, and behaviors of respondents. These surveys enable criminologists to expand their analysis of crime beyond the scope of the UCR. These surveys include numerous variables concerning factors associated with criminals and criminality. Self-reports also account for the relationship between gender, class, and race and crime. By examining these factors criminologists are able to account for the extent of racial bias is arrests, convictions, and incarceration rates.

Self-reports have indicated that the numbers of crimes committed are greater than those found in official records. For this reason self-reports tend to yield additional insights into what is known as the "dark figures of crime." Self-reports have been called into question concerning their accuracy. Critics of self-report surveys argue that criminals may not honestly report their crimes. They may also tend to exaggerate the frequency and nature of their activities. These surveys also tend to focus upon those offenses that are considered to be less serious. More serious offenders are more likely to provide inaccurate information. Despite the criticisms of self-report surveys they continue to provide researchers with results that tend to be consistent with official statistics.

Victim surveys like self-report surveys provide additional information to official crime statistics. Unlike self-reports, victim surveys provide information on the nature and extent of victimization. In these surveys, victims report their experiences with crime often unaccounted for in official records. These surveys enable researchers to gain insights from respondents who may not officially report their victimization. In these surveys respondents report the frequency, nature, and consequences of their victimization. The most common method for assessing victimization is known as the National Crime Victimization Survey (NCVS). Findings from the NCVS show that the numbers of crimes are much higher than reported to the FBI. A significant number of crimes are never reported to the police. The NCVS accounts for those crimes that go unreported by victims every year. Like all surveys there are a number of limitations associated with the NCVS. Incidences of victimization may be overreported or underreported. Some victims may consider reporting their experiences not worth the trouble of pursuing legal redress. Victims of rape may consider it an embarrassment to report their encounters. However, victim surveys are a useful tool in understanding the scope and nature of members of a population most likely to become victimized.

What are the key elements of surveys? Surveys can be divided into four main parts. These are (1) the instructions, (2) demographic questions, (3) scale items, and (4) open-ended questions. Most surveys contain a set of detailed instructions found at the beginning of the survey. This section often includes more than specific directions for completing surveys. The instructions include three types of statements: a statement of voluntary participation, a statement of anonymity or confidentiality, and specific directions for responding to survey items. Studies using surveys often claim that participation is strictly voluntary. This is usually accompanied by an assurance that there will be no penalty for choosing not to participate in the study. There is also a statement concerning informed consent. This section includes a statement of anonymity or confidentiality or both included in the instructions. Anonymity ensures that the identity of respondents is hidden from the researcher. That is, there is no way to associate individual respondents with specific responses to the survey. Confidentiality promises that, though the researcher may know the identity of respondents, their identities will not be published. To this end, respondents are sometimes instructed not make any identifiable marks on surveys. Last but not least, the instructions include directions for making specific responses to survey items. Respondents may be instructed to check boxes, circle responses, or print their responses in the appropriate spaces. The directions should be thorough and unambiguous. The specificity of the directions will ensure surveys are completed properly.

The second major division of the survey includes demographic questions. Demographic questions include items concerning sex or gender, race, age, education, income, occupation, or other group characteristics. These questions serve a dual purpose. First, they are designed to determine the characteristics of the sample. This enables the researcher to measure the representativeness of the sample with respect to the population under investigation. Secondly, demographic questions serve the purpose of deciphering how discreet categories of respondents tend to respond to each item on the survey.

The next major part of a survey is termed the scaled items. These items serve as indicators on some dimension of attitudes, perceptions, or opinions. Scale items refer directly to the variables of interest to the researcher. For example, a researcher is interested in the explanations among men for the incidences of domestic violence. Explanations for domestic violence by men would serve as a dependent variable. At the same time, specific items related to these explanations would serve as indicators of these explanations. As indicators, these items would point to a specific explanation men tend to give for the incidences of domestic violence. Pretests are often conducted to determine the validity of the scales.

The last major division of the survey contains open-ended questions. Open-ended questions are often found at the end of the survey. Space is provided for respondents to write their responses. These questions tend to address general issues relative to the research topic. In this section researchers typically ask, do you have any other comments related to topic you would like to add? The organization of open-ended questions may vary from survey to survey. Open-ended questions allow respondents to add insights not addressed elsewhere in the survey. These comments are often coded and used to test the validity of the scales. Scales usually consist of a set of items (usually three or more items) on the survey. Surveys may vary in the number of parts and their organization. However, all surveys must include parts essential to satisfying the research goals.

What is the nature of a good survey? It is very easy to construct bad surveys and difficult to construct good ones. Good surveys are composed of items that are short, clear, and direct. The length and the ordering of questions can influence response rates. Additionally, the wording of questions can influence response rates as well. When constructing surveys the study population should be the focus from beginning to the end of the process. Survey items should be easily understood by the respondents in the study. Questions on the survey may be derived from a number of sources. Some questions may be developed from existing theories or scales whereas others may be derived directly from data. It is important to develop good questions to ensure the successful accomplishment of the research goals. Good questions are clear and concise. Respondents should understand what each question is asking with little effort. Good questions should address a single idea at a time. Avoid what is known as "double-barreled" questions. An example of a double-barreled question is: I feel safe in my community when the police are present and armed. The question above addresses more than one issue, and is typical of double-barreled questions. As presently stated, how is the respondent to distinguish from feeling safe with the police present apart from being armed? Thus, this represents the major problem with these types of questions. This problem can be resolved by dividing this complex question into to separate items. For example:

I feel safe in my community when the police are present.

I feel safe in my community when the police are armed.

Good surveys contain appropriate responses to scale items. Surveys must provide respondents with alternative responses that match the intent of the questions posed. An example of inappropriate responses is:

I am confident that the local police will be at my service when I call them.

1. Very Important
2. Important
3. Unsure
4. Not Important
5. Very Unimportant

This problem could be resolved in the following way:

I am confident that the local police will be at my service when I call them.

1. Strongly Agree
2. Agree
3. No Opinion
4. Disagree
5. Strongly Disagree

Designing a survey is a very painstaking process. Good surveys typically go through several revisions before they are ultimately administered. In addition to constructing good questions, it is also essential to determine the best ordering of questions. One rule of thumb is to order questions based on their degree of difficulty. For example, simple questions are asked first. The most difficult questions are asked toward the end of the survey. Many surveys begin with demographic items, followed with items that tend to have strong emotional responses. The strategic ordering of questions can significantly influence the outcome of survey research.

How is survey research applied to problems in everyday life? As stated above survey research has a wide range of uses across segments of society. Generally, survey methods tend to be applied among two groups—academicians and practitioners. Though these groups sometimes work closely together, they often tend to have different objectives for employing survey research. For example, the impact of toxic waste sites near residential areas is a serious problem in the U.S. and abroad. In this case, a law firm may consult with social scientists on conducting a study of the perceived impact of dumping toxic waste in a small town by a large corporation. The role of the social scientist in this instance may be limited to the specific questions of interest to the firm. This is an example of what is known as "applied research," research conducted with some utilitarian objective in mind. Social scientists often engage in this type of research for a variety of reasons such as to help solve social problems like drug and alcohol abuse, domestic violence, and speeding. An alternative scenario might involve social scientists conducting survey research to accumulate knowledge and increase our understanding of this problem. This is an example of what is known as "pure research." Social scientists conduct research for the sake of knowledge alone rather than for some pragmatic purpose. These two distinctly divergent objectives for survey research have very different implications and consequences. However, both applied and pure approaches are necessary in every arena of everyday life.

What are the implications of survey research methods in criminal justice? Criminal justice is a very broad area of both research and practice. This area involves law enforcement, the courts, corrections, forensics, criminology, and a number of local, state, and federal agencies. For this reason, criminal justice is a very extensive and complex subsystem of society. To facilitate its functioning and the coordination of its activities, the generation of scientific findings as well as practical knowledge is indispensable. As stated above, survey research has different implications depending on its objectives. The most significant distinction between these two approaches is between the types of knowledge sought.

Before we discuss the implications of these two approaches, it is important to first make some distinction between pure and applied research in criminal justice. Every area within criminal justice could employ either pure or applied approaches to survey

research. For example, police departments may want to examine the job satisfaction of officers using survey research. The distinguishing factor whether the approach is pure or applied is contingent upon the objective of the study. If the interest is to determine the correlation between the job satisfaction and job performance with the objective of determining promotion schedules the study would be considered applied research. The purpose of the study would be to answer practical concerns with respect to some specific issue. In this example, the study might be conducted by a social scientist working closely with the human resources department. The role of this social scientist would involve addressing questions concerning departmental policy. Their role would include assisting in the development, implementation, and assessment of departmental policies and practices. Again, the focus would be on practical concerns. The implication of the study would be limited to the significance of police satisfaction for policy reasons, rather than the nature of police satisfaction *per se*. In this example of survey research, police satisfaction itself would be of only tangential.

On the other hand, criminologists might be interested in examining job satisfaction for the express purpose of increasing the understanding of job satisfaction. In this case, the study would be categorized as pure research. That is, job satisfaction itself would be central to the study of police attitudes.

The constraints with respect to the scope of applied research tend to be relatively narrow compared with pure research. Given these constraints, applied research is a useful and necessary approach to the acquisition of practical knowledge. One of the legitimate criticisms of pure research has to do with its use. That is, what can anyone do with pure research? This question could be answered with respect to the objective of pure research and that is to know or to understand some aspect of social reality. There is room for both pure and applied research in criminal justice.

Survey research is widely used in criminology as well as every sector of the society. Survey research encompasses numerous methods of data collection. We have discussed only a few of the most commonly used methods—mail surveys, telephone surveys, and face-to-face interviews. In selecting the appropriate method, one must have three points in mind: (1) What type of data do I need to satisfy my research objectives? (2) What is the time frame from the data collection to the analysis and reporting of the findings? and (3) What are the budgetary constraints or what method is most cost effective? Additionally, it is important to determine the research objectives. That is, how will the data be ultimately used? Will the data be used to address practical dilemmas, as found in applied research? Or, will the data serve to increase one's understanding of some social issue? This objective would be better served by the approach of pure research. Survey research is an invaluable tool designed to investigate both scientific as well as practical concerns in everyday life. Criminal justice practitioners and academicians alike can find numerous applications for this effective research tool.

CHAU-PU CHIANG AND DAVID L. MONK

## References and Further Reading

Babbie, E., *Survey Research Methods,* 2nd ed., Belmont, CA, Wadsworth, 1990.

Babbie, E., *The Practice of Social Research,* 8th ed., Belmont, CA, Wadsworth, 1998.

Bogardus, E.S., *Social Distance,* Yellow Springs, OH, Antioch Press, 1959.

Cernkovich, S., Giordano, P. and Pugh, M., Chronic offenders: The missing cases in self-report delinquency research, *Journal of Criminal Law and Criminology,* 76, 705–732 (1985).

Denzin, N.K., *The Research: Act A Theoretical Introduction to Sociological Methods,* 3rd ed., Englewood Cliffs, NJ, Prentice-Hall, 1989.

Dillman, D.A., *Mail and Telephone Surveys: The Total Design Method,* New York, NY, John Wiley, 1978.

Dunford, F. and Elliott, D., Identifying career criminals using self-reported data, *Journal of Research in Crime and Delinquency,* 21, 57–86 (1983).

Groves, R.M. and Kahn, R.L., *Surveys by Telephone,* New York, NY, Academic Press, 1979.

Hagan, F.E., *Research Methods in Criminal Justice and Criminology,* 5th ed., Allyn and Bacon, 2000.

Haskins, L. and Jeffrey, K., *Understanding Quantitative History,* Cambridge, MA, MIT Press, 1990.

Henry, G.T., *Practical Sampling,* Newbury Park, CA, Sage, 1990.

Hood, R. and Sparks, R., *Key Issues in Criminology,* New York, NY, McGraw Hill, 1970.

Hyman, H., Feldman, J. and Stember, C., *Interviewing in Social Research,* Chicago, IL, University of Chicago Press, 1954.

Hyman, H.H., *Interviewing in Social Research,* Chicago, IL, University of Chicago Press, 1975.

Hyman, H.H., *Taking Society's Measure: A Personal History of Survey Research,* New York, NY, Russell Sage, 1991.

Kish, L., *Survey Sampling,* New York, NY, John Wiley, 1965.

Mather, M., Dodder, R. and Sandhu, H., Inmate self-report data: A study of reliability, *Criminal Justic Review,* 17, 258–267 (1992).

McDowall, D. and Loftin, C., Comparing the UCR and NCVS over time, *Criminology,* 30, 125–133 (1992).

Menard, S., Residual gains, reliability, and the UCR-NCVS relationship: A comment on Blumstein, Cohen and Rosenfield (1991), *Criminology,* 30, 105–115 (1992).

Miller, D.C., *Handbook of Research Design and Social Measurement,* 5th ed., Newbury Park, CA, Sage, 1991.

Miller, L.S. and Whitehead, J.T., *Introduction to Criminal Justice Research and Statistics,* Cincinnati, OH Anderson Publishing Co., 1996.

Ritzer, G., *Sociology: A Multi-paradigm Science,* Boston, MA, Allyn and Bacon, 1975.

Schrag, C., *Crime and Justice: American Style,* Washington, DC, U.S. Government Printing Office, 1971, p. 17.

Smith, T.W., *That Which We Call Welfare By Any Other Name Would Smell Sweeter: An Analysis of the Impact of Question Wording on Response Patterns,* 1987.

Sudman, S., *Reducing the Cost of Surveys,* Chicago, IL, Aldine, 1967.

Sudman, S. and Bradburn, N.M., *Asking Questions: A Practical Guide to Questionnaire Design,* San Francisco, CA, Jossey-Bass, 1983.

Vogt, W.P., *Dictionary of Statistics and Methodology: A Nontechnical Guide for the Social Sciences,* Newbury Park, CA, Sage Publications, 1993.

Wells, L.E. and Rankin, J., Juvenile victimization: Convergent validation of alternative measurements, *Journal of Research in Crime and Delinquency,* 32, 287–307 (1995).

*See also* **National Crime Victimization Survey (NCVS); Self-Report Research**

# Sutherland, Edwin H.

In 1921, Edward C. Hayes, chair of the Department of Sociology at the University of Illinois and editor of sociology books for the publisher J. B. Lippincott, invited a professor he had recently hired to write a criminology textbook. At the time, the request may have seemed a bit odd to the prospective author: He had a Ph.D. in sociology from the University of Chicago and had taught courses that dealt with criminology, but his specialization was in political economy, and he was little known, with no publications in crim-

inology. Whatever Hayes' motivations were, the invitation proved fortuitous: Edwin H. Sutherland's *Criminology* (1924), retitled *Principles of Criminology* in 1934, was to become the most influential textbook in the history of criminology.

The first edition of the text was a solid scholarly work but hardly original in its approach. While researching and writing the book, Sutherland quickly mastered the existing literature in criminology, which explained criminal behavior as a product of either "inherited feeble-mindedness" or "multiple-factors." Sutherland largely rejected the claim that criminals were simpleminded but did endorse the latter view, explaining different criminal behaviors through the relative influence of various geographic, economic, political, and sociological factors.

The 1934 edition still endorsed a multiple-factor explanation, although a number of developments in Sutherland's career and thinking were beginning to point him toward proposing a groundbreaking general sociological theory. In 1930, Sutherland accepted a position as a research professor at the University of Chicago. After Sutherland's arrival, Beardsley Ruml, dean of the university's Division of Social Sciences, called a meeting with several faculty members to discuss what researchers knew about the origins of criminal behavior. Sutherland was embarrassed to admit that to date that criminologists had made little progress toward answering this question.

Perhaps in response to Ruml's inquiry, Sutherland's colleague Louis Wirth published an article in 1931 that attributed criminal behavior to "culture conflict." Wirth argued that in complex, heterogeneous societies like that of the U.S., the rules followed by some groups (especially immigrants) clash with the beliefs of the dominant culture. In this circumstance, behavior that is considered obedient in one group may be unorthodox and even criminal in the eyes of society. The important implication is that criminal behavior may actually conform to some subcultural standards.

In 1932, the Bureau of Social Hygiene in New York City published the Michael–Adler Report, a study commissioned to evaluate the desirability of establishing a national institute to train criminological researchers. Authors Jerome Michael and Mortimer Adler were highly critical of existing criminological research; they were especially skeptical of the multiple-factors approach, claiming that criminologists should strive to create abstract, general theories that explain all forms of criminal behavior. Sutherland was stung but still deeply impressed by these views.

Also in 1932, Sutherland had the good fortune to meet Broadway Jones, a fast-talking, boastful, and articulate Chicago-area grifter (confidence man). Jones regaled Sutherland with stories about his many impressive criminal exploits, which the two gradually compiled and published as *The Professional Thief* (1937) (in which Jones used the pseudonym "Chic Conwell"). These conversations convinced Sutherland that professional criminals learn the techniques and attitudes associated with their work from close relationships with other professional criminals.

The 1934 edition of *Principles of Criminology* featured a paragraph claiming that crime occurs when behaviors learned within different cultures and groups come into conflict. Sutherland apparently did not view this as a potential explanation for criminal behavior until Henry McKay, a fellow researcher at the University of Chicago, referred to the passage as "your theory." From that point onward, Sutherland spent much of the remainder of his career formulating, revising, and defending his renowned "differential association theory."

Sutherland came to believe that multiple factors like gender, race, and age cannot in themselves explain criminal behavior. Rather, he theorized that crime is caused by the different interactions and patterns of learning that occur in groups (e.g., juvenile gangs) that happen to be composed primarily of males, minority group members, or young people. By the time the fourth edition appeared (1947), Sutherland clearly stated differential association theory in a set of nine abstract principles listed near the beginning of the textbook. The principles claimed that behavior is learned through a process of communication in intimate personal groups. These groups teach "definitions" (including skills, motivations, attitudes, and rationalizations) either favorable or unfavorable to the violation of the law. Criminal behavior results when one is exposed to an excess of definitions favorable to the violation of the law over unfavorable definitions.

After Sutherland's death in 1950, first Donald R. Cressey and then David F. Luckenbill kept *Principles of Criminology* in print as Sutherland's coauthors (the 11th edition appeared in 1992). Generations of criminologists and their students learned differential association theory as an accepted wisdom through this extremely successful textbook. Numerous empirical studies also supported the key arguments in the theory. Other influential explanations for criminal behavior built upon Sutherland's insights, mostly by blending differential association with related theories. Albert K. Cohen, Richard A. Cloward, and Lloyd E. Ohlin created important theories of delinquent gang behavior by combining differential association with Robert K. Merton's strain theory. C. Ray Jeffery and Ronald L. Akers formulated modern social learning theories of criminal behavior by restating differential association in the language of behavioral psychology. Neutralization theory was inspired by Gresham M. Sykes and David Matza's attempt to clarify the difference between the learning of rationalizations (offered as justifications after criminal behavior occurs) and of "neutralizations," or excuses that offenders communicate and learn before they commit crimes.

Sutherland considered differential association to be a general sociological theory of criminal behavior. He was especially suspicious of theories that related poverty to crime, believing that police statistics were biased when they showed that most crimes occurred in lower-class neighborhoods. To bolster this view, in 1928 he began a study of law violations among the 70 largest corporations in the U.S., eventually coining the term "white-collar crime" to refer to the occupational offenses committed by respectable persons. After 20 years of painstaking research, Sutherland finally completed a book reporting his findings. Fearing lawsuits, his publisher, Dryden Press, insisted that he delete the names of corporations accused but not convicted of crimes. The expurgated version of *White Collar Crime* appeared in 1949; a restored edition was not published until 1983.

Sutherland examined four types of crime committed by large corporations: false advertising, restraint of trade, unfair labor practices, and patent, copyright, and trademark infringement. He uncovered 980 violations of these laws among the 70 businesses that he studied (an average of 14 per company). Ninety percent of the corporations were habitual offenders, with four or more violations. Sutherland relied on differential association theory to explain these crimes, arguing that young executives learn definitions favorable to the violation of the law through the routines of business practice. He considered white-collar crime a greater threat to society than street crime because the former promotes cynicism and distrust of basic social institutions.

The concept of white-collar crime and this pioneering research were immensely important developments. The eminent British criminologist Hermann Mannheim observed that if there were a Nobel Prize in criminology, Sutherland would have received it for these contributions. Sutherland's work quickly inspired such notable criminologists as Cressey, Marshall Clinard, and Frank E. Hartung to conduct studies of embezzlement and the violation of rationing laws through black-market profiteering by corporations during World War II. Some more recent influential examples of research on white-collar crime include studies of the collective embezzlement practiced by top executives during the savings and loan scandal of the 1980s, Medicaid fraud and the performance of unnecessary surgery by physicians, and the dumping of drugs banned in the U.S. into third world countries by the pharmaceutical industry.

Even if Sutherland never proposed differential association theory nor coined the term white-collar crime, he still would be recognized as a major 20th century criminologist. When he abandoned the multiple-factors approach, Sutherland conducted a relentless academic turf war, tirelessly defending the idea that criminology was a specialty within sociology, and not a part of some other discipline. Two important publications, "Mental Deficiency and Crime" (1931) and "The Sexual Psychopath Laws" (1950), vigorously debated psychological explanations for criminal behavior. The former disputed the notion that "feeble-mindedness," as measured through performance on IQ tests, could

be a general explanation for delinquency and crime, given the superior intelligence of some offenders. The latter criticized state laws that defined child molesters and rapists as mentally ill, rejecting the claim that these offenders were sexual psychopaths (or "fiends" with little control over their impulses).

In the 1940s, Sutherland successfully defended a behavioral definition of crime, as supported by social scientists, against a legalistic definition, preferred by some with training in the criminal law. Paul W. Tappan proposed the legalistic approach, arguing that criminologists should study only persons who actually had been convicted of crimes. This view threatened Sutherland's emerging research on white-collar criminals, because many corporations that violate the law are never prosecuted. Sutherland (1945) maintained that conviction is important in the study of public agency (or justice system) responses to crime, but it cannot be used in defining the subject matter of criminology, which must explain all forms of law-violating behavior. This behavioral definition of crime still prevails in modern criminology.

Sutherland's sharpest attacks, though, were directed toward biological explanations of criminal behavior. He saw these as a threat to the first principle of differential association theory ("criminal behavior is learned"). For Sutherland, learning was entirely a social product, disconnected from the functional operation of the body and the mind. In a number of book reviews published from 1934 to 1951, he harshly attacked scholars who attributed criminal behavior to the physical inferiority of offenders (E. A. Hooton), to "mesomorphy" (or a strong, muscular body type; William H. Sheldon), or to a multiple-factors approach that included "constitutional" (or biological) elements (Sheldon Glueck and Eleanor Glueck). These book reviews were a crucial part of Sutherland's campaign to define crime as social behavior.

Sutherland is better remembered for his conceptual and theoretical contributions to criminology than for any advances in research measures. This may be unfair, given his outstanding use of the "life histories" approach (a qualitative technique that offers biographical accounts of individuals or groups) in *The Professional Thief* Clifford R. Shaw is usually credited with introducing life histories research into criminology, but Sutherland mastered the technique in his depiction of the life of Broadway Jones. Apart from skillfully reporting the language, attitudes, and lifestyles of con artists in the early 20th century, *The Professional Thief* is highly entertaining. Hollywood filmmakers borrowed liberally from the book in writing the screenplay for *The Sting* (1973).

In criminology, Sutherland's legacy extends beyond scholarship to teaching and professional service. Several of his graduate students became influential criminologists, including Donald Cressey, Lloyd Ohlin, Mary Owen Cameron, Albert K. Cohen, and Karl Schuessler. Besides serving as chair of the department of sociology at Indiana University in Bloomington for 15 years, Sutherland was elected president of several national sociological societies. By the time of his death in 1950, it had become a colloquialism in sociology to refer to him as the "Dean of American Criminology."

Sutherland's stature has diminished little since his death. Studies evaluating the influence of scholars through citations to their work still rank him as one of the most important figures in contemporary criminology. Revisionist thinkers, however, have begun to question some aspects of his legacy. As modern criminology has evolved into an independent, interdisciplinary field rather than a specialty within sociology, Sutherland's pugnacious rejection of the contributions of biology and psychology to the study of criminal behavior seems misguided. In particular, his insistence that inheritance plays no role in learning is not supported by late 20th century research in biology and psychology. Even worse, speculation has surfaced that Sutherland misrepresented certain details in *The Professional Thief* to suit his theoretical needs. Apparently, Broadway Jones was heavily addicted to narcotics; Sutherland downplayed this part of his biography, fearing that readers would interpret this drug use as an indication of mental illness rather than as a learned behavior. Sutherland insisted on the highest level of academic integrity among scholars toward whom he was critical (the Gluecks, Hooton, and Sheldon); the idea that he may have violated these same standards suggests a troubling hypocrisy.

Despite these observations, Sutherland's impact on criminology was truly revolutionary. In 1921, when Sutherland was asked to write his textbook, criminology was heading in multiple directions, with inherited "feeble-mindedness" as its only general theory. Thirty years later, sociologists firmly dominated criminology, largely because of Sutherland's efforts. Edwin H. Sutherland in criminology, like Albert Einstein in physics, turned accepted wisdom on its head and transformed a discipline.

RICHARD A. WRIGHT

## Biography

Born in Gibbon, Nebraska, August 13, 1883; son of a Baptist minister. Educated at Grand Island College in Nebraska, A.B., 1903; University of Chicago, PhD in Sociology and Political Economy, 1913. Professor, William Jewell College in Missouri, 1913–1919; professor, University of Illinois, 1919–1925; professor, University of Minnesota, 1925–1929; researcher, Bureau of Social Hygiene in New York City, 1929–1930; research professor, University of Chicago, 1930–1935; professor and chair of the department of sociology, Indiana University, 1935–1950. President of American Sociological Society, 1939; president of the Sociological Research Association, 1940; president of the Ohio Valley Sociological Society, 1941. Died in Bloomington, Indiana, October 11, 1950.

## Selected Works

*Criminology,* 1924; 11th ed., as *Principles of Criminology* (with Cressey, D.R. and Luckenbill, D.F.), 1992.
Mental Deficiency and Crime, in *Social Attitudes,* edited by Young, K. (1931) The Professional Thief, 1937.
Is 'White-Collar Crime' Crime? *American Sociological Review* 10 (1945) White Collar Crime, 1949.
The Sexual Psychopath Laws, *Journal of Criminal Law and Criminology* 40 (1950) On Analyzing Crime, 1973.
White Collar Crime: The Uncut Version, 1983.

## References and Further Reading

Cohen, A., Lindesmith, A. and Schuessler, K., (Eds.), *The Sutherland Papers,* Bloomington, IN, Indiana University Press, 1956.
Gaylord, M.S. and Galliher, J.F., *The Criminology of Edwin Sutherland,* New Brunswick, NJ, Transaction, 1988.
Geis, G. and Goff, C., Introduction, in Sutherland, E.H. (Author), *White Collar Crime: The Uncut Version,* New Haven, CT, Yale University Press, 1983.
Goff, C., *Edwin H. Sutherland and White-Collar Crime,* PhD dissertation, University of California, CA, Irvine, 1982.
Laub, J.H. and Sampson, R.J., The Sutherland-Glueck debate: On the sociology of criminological knowledge, *The American Journal of Sociology,* 96(6), (1991).
Schuessler, K., Introduction, in Sutherland, E.H. (Author), *On Analyzing Crime,* Chicago, IL, University of Chicago Press, 1973.
Snodgrass, J., *The American Criminological Tradition: Portraits of the Men and Ideology in a Discipline,* PhD dissertation, University of Pennsylvania, PA, 1972.
Snodgrass, J., The criminologist and his criminal: Edwin H. Sutherland and Broadway Jones, *Issues in Criminology,* 8(1), (1973).

# Switzerland, Crime and Justice in

## Background

Switzerland, situated in the heart of Western Europe, originates from an alliance of rural and urban republics (cantons) that dates back to the 14th century. Conquests during the early 16th century led to Switzerland developing into a multilingual country, with German, French, Italian, and Romansh speaking areas. Formally independent and neutral since 1648, Switzerland became a federal state in 1848, with a constitution heavily inspired by the model used in the USA, which leaves the cantons ("states") largely autonomous, particularly in matters of criminal justice. Since the occupation during the Napeolean wars (1798–1814) and a short civil war (in 1847), Switzerland has not seen any more armed conflict on its territory. Having a population of 7 million (in 2000), with some 46% catholics and 40% protestants, Switzerland has one of the highest proportions of immigrants in Europe (20%). Traditionally most immigrants have come from southern Europe and, more recently, predominantly from Balcanic countries and areas outside of Europe. Despite the lack of natural resources, Switzerland has developed, over the 20th century, to become one of the most affluent countries in Europe. Since the 1950s there has been a shift from emigration (mostly to the USA) to massive immigration. Although Switzerland's largest cities are relatively small (e.g., Zurich has a population of just over 330,000), most of the population live in urbanized (suburban) areas. Less than 5% are employed in agriculture, and less than 10% live in "real" rural areas (i.e., towns with less than 1000 population). (All statistical information is from *Annuaire statistique de la Suisse—2001*, Zurich: Editions "Neue Zürcher Zeitung")

## A Traditional Low Crime Country

Despite its industrialization, high urbanization and affluence, Switzerland has continued over many decades to have one of Europe's lowest crime rates. This has puzzled international observers, including Marshall B. Clinard, who was a former student of Sutherland and the Chicago school. Clinard considered the low crime rate in Switzerland to be an "exception" to the general trend—increasing crime rates following increasing industrialization, urbanization and affluence (Clinard, 1978). This view was

challenged later by Balvig (1988) who criticized Clinard for basing his conclusions on inaccurate data and for offering questionable interpretations of the data. Balvig was in turn criticized for presenting his argument in a pamphlet plagued by many factual errors. The findings of the 1989 international crime victimization survey (comparative crime and justice), however, confirmed Switzerland's low position in comparison to most of the other 14 Western countries that participated in the survey (van Dijk, Mayhew, and Killias, 1990). Similar findings emerged for violent and serious offences, from the first international self-reported juvenile delinquency survey, which was conducted in 12 Western countries including Switzerland (Junger-Tas, Terlouw, and Klein, 1994). However, it seems that over the last decade crime has increased substantially, particularly in urban areas of Switzerland (Eisner, 1997). A longitudinal analysis of all available national crime survey data from 1984 to 2000 found that the crime rate for burglary increased by more than 100%, and by an even greater amount for violent offences (Killias, 2001). This explains why Switzerland has a crime rate—according to the most recent international crime victimization surveys (of 1996 and 2000)—that is just somewhere below the European average.

## Special Features of Crime

There are two main explanations for the recent increase in the crime rate in Switzerland. The first reason is the emergence of a significant drug (heroin) problem. The problem of the "needle-parks" in Zurich and other cities is internationally known. The second reason concerns the development of a significant transborder (organized) crime industry, which resulted from the opening of the borders in Europe and the emergence of significant markets for stolen goods in Eastern Europe. The development of the latter will depend on the shape of Eastern European economies and the eventual decrease in demand for stolen goods from Western Europe (given the foreseeable saturation with consumer goods). In contrast, the heroin problem has been brought back under control by a large-scale substitution treatment program, which included prescribing methadone and heroin to about 3 in 4 drug addicts. This was found to reduce criminal involvement among drug addicts by about 80%, according to all feasible indicators (criminal records, police and survey measures, at the micro and the macro level; Killias, 2001).

The low rate of violence has often been quoted as an illustration of the irrelevance of the availability of guns to citizens. Recent research has shown, however, that gun ownership is far less prevalent in Switzerland than what has been often assumed, with only 13% of the households owing private guns, a rate which increases to 35% if military weapons are included. Beyond that, Switzerland has, within Europe, an average rate of homicide and one of the highest suicide rates. Both are heavily inflated by the wide-spread use of guns in such events (Killias, 2001).

Both Clinard (1978) and Balvig (1988) suspected that Switzerland would have a particularly high rate of white-collar crime; however, the available data offer no support to this popular view. Switzerland, compared to other Western countries, has the lowest rate of untaxed incomes, and one of the lowest rates of corruption, according to data from the international crime surveys. Even the international survey of crime against businesses, conducted in 1994 in eight countries, showed the rate of fraud to be lower in Switzerland than in most other participating countries (Killias, 2001). The reason for this paradox may be that bankers' secrecy laws do not offer much protection against criminal investigations, and that the incentives favoring corruption and economic crime are less pervasive in Switzerland than in many other Western countries.

## Criminal Justice

Switzerland's criminal justice system has been heavily influenced by the French (code Napoleon) and the German model. According to the data from the *European Sourcebook of Crime and Criminal Justice Statistics* (Comparative Crime and Justice), sentences are among the mildest in Europe for virtually all offenses. Police density and incarceration rates are about average within Europe.

MARTIN KILLIAS

### References and Further Reading

Balvig, F., *The Snow-White Image: The Hidden Reality of Crime in Switzerland,* Oslo, Norway, Oxford, U.K., Norwegian University Press, 1988.

Clinard, M.B., *Cities with Little Crime: The Case of Switzerland,* Cambridge and London, U.K., Cambridge University Press, 1978.

Eisner, M., *Das Ende der zivilisierten Stadt,* Frankfurt, Germany, Campus, 1997.

Junger-Tas, J., Terlouw, G.-J., Klein, M., *Delinquent Behavior among Young People in the Western World,* Amsterdam, the Netherlands, Kugler, 1994.

Killias, M., *Précis de criminologie,* Berne, Switzerland, Stämpfli, 2001.

van Dijk, Jan, J.M., Mayhew, P. and Killias, M., *Experiences with Crime Across the World,* Deventer, the Netherlands; and Boston, MA, Kluwer, 1990.

*See also* **France, Crime and Justice in; Germany, Crime and Justice in**

# Sykes, Gresham M.

Gresham Sykes is a sociologist and criminologist. His influence can be seen in the fields of sociological theory, the scholarship and programming surrounding juvenile delinquency, and he has impacted the development of correctional theory and practice. What is fairly unique about Sykes' work is that since the late 1950s it has influenced these interrelated areas and that influence has many contemporary applications.

Starting in the late 1950s, Sykes and coauthor David Matza focused their attention on juvenile delinquency and eventually fashioned an extension to Sutherland's differential association theory with respect to explanations of juvenile deviant behavior. Differential association theory focuses on how humans learn deviant behavior and rationalize that behavior. Sykes and

Matza's (1957) developed their techniques of neutralization typology in part to expand and clarify this theoretical tradition. In 1961, the two authors extended their ideas to incorporate the impact of subculturalization (i.e., subterranean values) and their impact on juvenile deviant behavior. By the mid-1960s Matza had become a solo author and developed these perspectives into what would become known as drift theory.

Many contemporary applications of the techniques of neutralization and subterranean values, and the subsequent manifestation of these ideas as drift theory, can be found in the recent literature. For example, Elder discusses the transition between age specific events that correspond to delinquent acts and the pathways of juvenile life courses, trajectories such as marriage and fatherhood (Hagan, 1991). Other examples of contemporary applications include Hebdige (1991) on subcultures, Campbell (1969) on the manifestations of youth culture as reinforcement of subterranean values, and Minor (1981) who has used these ideas on numerous occasions and within various contexts.

The specific techniques of neutralization, their conceptualization of how juveniles engage deviant behavior and stigma, and the incorporation of the concept of subterranean values are not without critics and detractors (Phohl, 1994). As is typical of learning-based theories, the criticisms focus around how to empirically test their validity and application to real work problems. For example, if the techniques of neutralization allow one to vacillate between normative and deviant behavior, exactly how and why do they develop in the first place? Additionally, critics wonder how do social scientists operationalized and measure these concepts and test if they are present prior to the act of deviance or created *ex post facto* to the juvenile being caught.

In addition to this pioneering work in understanding how juveniles account for their own behavioral and moral agency, Sykes was also the author of an influential treatise on prisons and the social impacts of incarceration. *The Society of Captives* (1958) uses a New Jersey prison to illustrate the idea of a subculture and the impact of its values on the denizens. In this study, Sykes built off of a rich sociological tradition surrounding the development and impact of social groups and incorporated many classic sociological concepts and ideas into his analysis of this institution. His methodology of describing the physical environment, noting the roles and values of the custodians, and finally offering an analysis of the inmates cultural adaptations to this institution allows Sykes to provide a deeper understanding of the social adaptations of inmates to their incarceration. Sykes discusses the techniques of neutralization used in the everyday existence of the inmate and how these neutralizations make tolerable their current status, living conditions, and shape their social reality. The conclusion of this study notes that prisons are unstable institutions and the inmates adapt to the anomic state of their social conditions by use of various techniques, alternative values, and creation of deviant identities. Thus, they can function within the confines of this unstable institution.

Sykes and his work on prisons was part of what has become known as the "golden age" of prison sociology. His work offers an example of the social scientific methodology associated with knowing, and benefits of understanding, prison social order. This knowledge has impacted generations of students, researchers, and prison administrators. Not withstanding this impact, the current flood of imprisonment and public discourse supportive of punishment of criminal wrongdoers stands in stark contrast to his findings.

Together, these two bodies of work offer a portrait of a scholar and dedicated social activist. This work testifies to his place among the elite of 20th century social observers. Whether one is conducting a sociological analysis of deviant behavior or an institutional analysis of prison culture, his work is part of the rich research tradition because it expands the boundaries of the interactionist paradigm and has direct policy implications for those charged with a mandate to effectively and efficiently deal with juvenile delinquents or to run a prison. Research continues to expand the applications of his work. For example, the current trends toward increased punishment and ever increasing incarceration rates may foreshadow a reactive resurgence of the type of social scientific research embodied in his *Society of Captives*.

JAMES DAVID BALLARD

## Biography

Born in Plainfield, New Jersey, May 26, 1922. Son of M'Cready and Beatrice Sykes. Captain in the U.S. Army, Corps of Engineers in the European theater (1942–1946) Served in England, France, Belgium, and Germany. On July 13, 1946 married Carla Adelt. Academic career started at Hofstra College (1946–1947). Attended Mexico City College (1947–1948) and has fluency in reading, writing, and speaking Spanish. Proficient in reading French and German. Finalized undergraduate education at Princeton University (1950) with an A.B. in Sociology and Phi Beta Kappa and Summa cum Laude honors. Woodrow Wilson and University Fellow at Northwestern University (1950–1953) and received Ph.D Sociology in 1953. Studied at the Art Institute of Chicago (1959–1960). Began teaching at Princeton as an instructor (1952–1954) and later as an assistant professor (1954–1958). Promotion to associate professor corresponded with a move to Northwestern University (1958–1960). Full professor in 1960 at Dartmouth and chair (1961–1963). Executive officer of the American Sociological Association (1964–1965). University of Denver (1965–1972). University of Houston, chair (1973). University of Virginia (1974–1988). At retirement in 1988 granted the status of Professor Emeritus from the University of Virginia. Associate editor *American Sociological Review*, *Criminology*, and the *American Sociologist*. Criminology editor for the *Journal of Criminology, Criminal Law and Police Science*. Honorary M.A. degree Dartmouth (1961), the Order of Saint Ives, University of Denver (1968), Edwin H. Sutherland award from the American Society of Criminology (1980) and numerous other honors. Retired since 1988, pursuing interests in art (painting) and currently residing in Virginia.

## Selected Writings

*Crime and Society,* 1956 (2nd edition, 1967).
*The Society of Captives,* 1958 (1965 edition, Atheneum).
Juvenile Delinquency and Subterranean Values, *American Sociological Review,* 26 (1961).
Techniques of Neutralization: A Theory of Delinquency, *American Sociological Review,* 22 (1957).
*Law and the Lawless,* 1969.
*Social Problems in America,* 1971.

*Criminology,* 1978 (revised edition, 1978).

*The Future of Crime,* 1980.

*Theoretical Studies in Social Organizations of the Prison,* 1960 (Social Science Council Monograph).

Criminals and Non-criminals Together: A Modest Proposal, *The Prison Journal,* 48 (1960).

## References and Further Reading

Agnew, R., The techniques of neutralization and violence, *Criminology,* 32 (1994).

Pfhol, S., *Images of Deviance and Social Control,* 1994.

Priest, T.B. and McGrath, J., Techniques of neutralization: Young marijuana smokers, *Criminology,* 8 (1970).

Minor, W.W., Techniques of neutralization: A reconceptualization and empirical examination, *Journal of Research in Crime and Delinquency,* 18 (1981).

Thurman, Q., Deviance and the neutralization of moral commitment: An empirical analysis, *Deviant Behavior,* 5 (1984).

*See also* **Matza, David**

# T

# Tax Evasion and Tax Fraud

## Introduction

Tax fraud, and more specifically tax evasion, cost governments sizable amounts of lost revenue annually. For example, according to the Internal Revenue Service (IRS), in 1998 the amount of unpaid income taxes from individual and corporate sources in the U.S. totaled approximately $280 billion, or well over half of the federal budget deficit for that same year. This article examines our current understanding of tax fraud in the form of tax evasion.

## Defining Tax Fraud

Balter (1993, 2–3) suggests that three factors must be present in order for tax fraud to occur:

> (1) The end to be achieved — the payment of less tax than that known by the taxpayer to be legally due; (2) An accompanying state of mind that is variously described as being 'evil,' 'in bad faith,' 'deliberate and not accidental,' or 'willful'; and (3) An overt act aimed to achieve the nonpayment of taxes known to be due. This course of action typically would be affected by acts or conduct tinged with some element of deceit, misrepresentation, trick, device, concealment, or dishonesty.

Tax evasion, tax avoision and tax avoidance represent varying degrees of tax fraud. Tax evasion is the most serious form of tax fraud and involves intentionally paying less of one's own tax bill than legally is required through the understatement of tax liability. This can occur by either knowingly claiming undeserved tax deductions or by underreporting taxable income.

Tax avoidance is at the other end of the tax fraud continuum and infers behavior that may or may not be legal but ultimately lacks the intent to fraudulently misrepresent tax liability. This can occur inadvertently when an individual or a business makes an honest error in estimating the taxes they owe or a misinterpretation of the law by them or an advisor. Tax avoidance also may take the more deliberate, but legal form of simply reducing tax burden through extraordinary methods such as relocating a business to a jurisdiction with lower tax rates.

Tax avoision represents a form of tax fraud that lies in a gray area somewhere between tax evasion and tax avoidance. It occurs when a taxpayer is highly motivated to make use of practices he or she knows to be questionable to avoid immediately paying taxes that he or she owes. In such cases, tax avoision may represent a strategy for deferring the payment of taxes until some later point in time when the taxes owed are detected or when the taxpayer has the means and motivation to pay his or her share of taxes due.

## The Scope of the Tax Fraud Problem

The 1913 ratification of the Sixteenth Amendment to the U.S. Constitution paved the way for the collection of federal income taxes in the U.S. Soon after, the costs associated with World War I made the implementation of a federal income tax an immediate economic necessity (Brownlee, 1996). Since then, income taxes collected by the federal government have continued as a prominent way of paying for building and maintaining our democracy.

Although the creation of the federal income tax helped to establish a regular mechanism for collecting revenue for operating the government, it also created the opportunity for tax fraud, a problem in the U.S. that was monitored by the IRS's Taxpayer Compliance Measurement Program (TCMP) for many years. The TCMP was established in 1965 to examine random samples of tax returns in order to assess taxpayer noncompliance. Complex models allowed the IRS to estimate the amount of lost revenue and identify the source of losses. It was determined that underreporting income typically accounts for about 80% of lost tax revenue, whereas overstating deductions and the failure to file an income tax return account for the remaining 20% of the income tax gap (Roth, Scholz, and Witte, 1989; Alm, 1999).

In 1973 the TCMP discovered an average of $99 of income underreported per tax return audited. Three years later the average dollars underreported per TCMP audit rose to $142, suggesting that taxpayer noncompliance appears to be a problem that may grow worse over time. Furthermore, although the size of the revenue lost because of a single act of noncompliance might not seem large, the combined impact of the noncompliance among 100 million individual taxpayers can add up to a significant amount of tax revenue lost each year. Such revenue shortfalls ultimately translate into higher tax rates for law abiding taxpayers than would be necessary if every citizen paid his or her taxes in full.

The use of average amounts of income underreported to portray the scope of the tax fraud problem might indicate that most people "cheat" on their taxes by small amounts. However, self-report data from several studies mentioned in the next section suggest that only a minority of Americans actually engages in tax evasion. The relatively low incidence of tax fraud is further illustrated by the fact that in 1979 the TCMP conducted 50,000 individual audits, and of those, only 200 were referred to the IRS's Criminal Investigations Division for more investigation and potential legal sanctions (Roth et al., 1989).

In 1982, the IRS's TCMP found 48% of tax returns had been perfectly reported; 70% of all tax returns were nearly perfect (within $50 dollars of complete accuracy), whereas 90% of all tax returns were within $1000 dollars of total taxable income. Furthermore, the IRS is able to reclaim a large portion of all taxes incorrectly filed that are discovered during an audit (Roth et al., 1989). Unfortunately, because the IRS audits so few individual returns annually, the tax gap

from unaudited, incorrectly filed tax returns remains quite large—in excess of $100 billion each year (Alm, 1999).

The IRS discontinued the use of the TCMP in 1988 and it recently launched the National Research Program (NRP) in September, 2002 to collect data and carry out studies on tax reporting behaviors. The NRP is expected to make use of an updated data collection approach more efficient than that employed by the TCMP (Cano and Brown, 2002). Although the effectiveness of the NRP is still unknown, the IRS expects this new approach will net additional tax revenue such that a compliance rate increase of only 1% in a single year will result in more than a billion dollar impact on the tax gap (Internal Revenue Service, 2002).

## Focus of Research: Individual vs. Corporate Taxpayers

Whereas both corporations and individuals are expected to pay taxes, most tax fraud research has focused on the latter. One reason for this is that individual tax filings account for a considerably larger portion of all income taxes owed and evaded in most countries. According to the IRS, individuals accounted for $94 billion in unpaid taxes in the U.S. in 1992, compared to $33 billion unpaid by corporations (Alm, 1999). Another reason for the focus on individual taxpayers rather than on corporations is that the latter seem to be more effectively deterred by substantially higher IRS audit rates than the average American taxpayer. For example, in 1983, the IRS audited approximately 58 out of every 100 corporations claiming assets of more than $100 million compared to 1.5 out of every 100 individual taxpayers (Grasmick, 1985). Finally, more research has been conducted with individual taxpayers as subjects than corporations probably because of the greater challenges faced by researchers in gaining access and securing permission to study corporate behavior.

## Tax Fraud Research

To date researchers have examined a myriad of variables to better understand individual tax reporting behavior. Research suggests common characteristics among the noncompliant include being self-employed, high nonwage earners, highly educated, young (Vogel, 1974) and wealthy (Hamm and Ricketts, 1999). The findings on gender are somewhat mixed, with most reporting that males are less compliant than females (Vogel, 1974; Mason and Calvin, 1978), though at least one study suggests that females are less compliant (Hamm and Ricketts, 1999).

Research explaining why individual taxpayers might comply or not comply tends to fall into one of two categories. The first category operates from an *ethics* or *morality* basis and focuses on the degree to which guilt affects individual tax reporting practices. The second category looks at this issue from a perspective of *deterrence* and examines how fear of negative consequences or the lack thereof influences tax reporting.

## Ethics and Morality

In a classic study of taxpayer noncompliance, Schwartz and Orleans (1967) administered one of three surveys to 384 taxpayers. One survey emphasized legal punishments for taxpayer noncompliance, whereas a second was designed to appeal to the moral conscience of participants to pay their taxes. Finally, the third emphasized neither the moral nor legal ramifications of noncompliance. Having examined the gross income of all participants in the year prior to and following the survey, Schwartz and Orleans concluded that both appeal to moral conscience and threat of legal sanction had positive effects on taxpayer compliance, with appeal to moral conscience having a much larger impact. Given these findings, other researchers sought to better understand how thought processes and moral conscience might affect individual taxpayer compliance.

For example, some research suggested perceptions of wrongness influence individual tax reporting (Kaplan and Reckers, 1985) whereas others argued that ethics, tax rate and whether an individual owes tax monies or expects a refund will affect taxpayer compliance, thereby suggesting that individuals with low ethics and who owe tax monies are least likely to be tax compliant (Reckers et al., 1994).

Recognizing that not all compliance is intentional, Ghosh and Crain (1995) attempted to examine purposeful noncompliance by offering study participants the opportunity to purchase assistance when figuring tax liabilities in order to ensure that the individuals did not report incorrect information because of an error in calculations or because they lacked knowledge of the tax system and corresponding tax laws. They concluded that high ethics resulted in less purposeful noncompliance, whereas individuals who were more risk inclined were more likely to be purposefully noncompliant.

In perhaps the largest study of morality and tax compliance, Blumenthal, Christian and Slemrod (2001) sent one of three letters to a random sample of 46,775 Minnesota taxpayers. One letter focused on the importance of taxpayer compliance in order to support prosocial community activities, whereas a second letter stressed that taxpayer noncompliance is not common, nor is it socially acceptable. The third letter emphasized neither prosocial community activities nor the rarity of taxpayer noncompliance. The "Support Valuable Services" letter resulted in taxpayers reporting an average of $220 more on federal tax forms and $15 more on state tax forms, whereas the "Join the Compliant Majority" resulted in taxpayers reporting an average $42 less on federal tax forms and $1 less on state tax forms (Christian and Slemrod, 2001, 131–132). Even though the letters altered individual tax reporting, neither change was statistically significant, suggesting "normative appeal" does not influence individual tax compliance (Blumenthal et al., 2001, 135).

Although research suggests that most people will not evade taxes if they think they will feel guilty for doing so (Scott and Grasmick, 1981; Grasmick and Scott, 1982), some research suggests individuals can overcome their moral conscience and justify noncompliance (Yankelovich et al., 1984; Thurman et al., 1984; Thurman, 1991; Forest and Sheffrin, 2002). Low fear of getting caught, believing it is acceptable to cheat on taxes by small amounts (Yankelovich et al., 1984), an unfair tax system (Forest and Sheffrin, 2002), knowing other people who evade taxes (Vogel, 1974; Spicer and Lundstedt, 1976), lack of faith in government spending (Yankelovich et al., 1984; Thurman et al., 1984), and the belief that others pay lower taxes or use loopholes to avoid paying taxes or both (Thurman et al., 1984) have been empirically supported as justifications for reported taxpayer noncompliance.

In regards to how people cheat on their taxes, Thurman (1991) revealed that more people seem comfortable underreporting income than claiming undeserved income tax deductions. He speculated the latter requires a more conscious effort to break the law, and because of this, generates a greater level of guilt that must be neutralized before tax fraud can occur. In contrast, guilt feelings associated with underreporting are less prohibitive because tax fraud, in this case, involves simply "forgetting" to disclose income that the IRS may never discover.

## Deterrence

Measures of deterrence have long been tested as predictors of tax compliance. Fear of detection (Song and Yarbrough, 1978; Mason and Calvin, 1978; Thurman, 1989), threat of legal sanction's (Schwartz and Orleans, 1967), perceived tax inequity, the number of peers who evaded taxes, past history of tax audits (Spicer and Lundstedt, 1976), and perceived visibility of taxable income (Kagan, 1989) have been cited in the past as salient predictors of taxpayer noncompliance.

Advances in research methodology also have allowed for innovative survey techniques ideally suited for understanding taxpaying behavior. For example, using computer-generated vignettes, Thurman (1989) found nearly two thirds (234 of 319) of respondents indicated that regardless of the situation, there was little or no chance they would cheat. Thurman's analysis of factorial survey data from 76 respondents at elevated risk for noncompliance indicated that 42.7% had underreported income and 29.3% overstated deductions in the past 5 years. Among the more compliant portion of the sample, 22.1% had underreported, whereas 11.5% had overstated deductions in any or all of the previous 5 years. For those respondents who said they might evade taxes in the future, the extent of their evasion varied by the tax rates they were required to pay, their chances of being detected if they did not pay, the threat of a prison sentence, and the size of the fine associated with noncompliance.

Recent research also has examined the effect of "embedded intelligent agents" on tax reporting (Masselli et al., 2002, 60). Embedded intelligent agents are computer-generated warnings built into the computer program that appeared on the computer screen when the taxpayer entered an amount that may raise suspicion. Masselli et al. (2002) found study participants with less tax knowledge and access to the warnings reported more taxable income than did students who did not receive warnings, whereas the warnings had no effect on the reporting practices of the more tax savvy students.

## Discussion and Conclusion

Research suggests that tax fraud is a problem of considerable magnitude in terms of the size of the tax gap it produces. However, self-report data also suggest that most citizens in the U.S. do not engage in taxpayer noncompliance to great excess. Studies also indicate that taxpayers are most compliant when they feel a moral obligation to pay what they owe or are scared of the consequences for being caught evading taxes.

We conclude that American taxpayers seemingly employ a somewhat rational decision-making process when deciding the amount of taxes they owe. They consider tax rates, informal and formal sanctions, and excuses for noncompliance in taxpaying decisions, although the importance of these variables differs according to the type of noncompliance in which they might engage.

The challenge for tax fraud research in this millennium will be to examine taxpayer compliance under changing political and technological conditions. A flat tax rate system, for example, might dramatically alter taxpayer noncompliance. Similarly, widespread adoption of electronic filing of tax returns also might affect compliance. The effects of these and other issues should make tax fraud research fertile ground for future study.

BRENDA VOSE AND QUINT C. THURMAN

## References and Further Reading

Alm, J. 1999. Tax compliance and administration, in Hildreth, W.B. and Richardson, J.A., Eds., *Handbook on Taxation,* New York, Marcel Dekker, Inc., pp. 741–768.

Balter, H., 1983. *Tax Fraud and Evasion,* 5th ed., Boston, MA, Warren, MI, Gorham and Lamont.

Blumenthal, M., Christian, C. and Slemrod, J., 2001. Do normative appeals affect tax compliance? Evidence from a controlled experiment in Minnesota, *National Tax Journal,* 54(1), 125–137.

Brownlee, W.E., 1996. *Federal Taxation in America: A Short History,* Washington, DC, Woodrow Wilson Center Press and Cambridge University Press.

Cano, K. and Brown, R., 2002. *Challenges Associated with Collecting Compliance Data,* Paper Presented at the 2002 IRS Research Conference. Available at: http://www.irs. gov/pub/irs-soi/cocompda.pdf. Retrieved on September 3, 2003.

Forest, A. and Sheffrin, S., 2002. Complexity and compliance: An empirical investigation, *National Tax Journal,* 55(1), 75–88.

Ghosh, D. and Crain, T., 1995. Ethical standards, attitudes toward risk, and intentional noncompliance: An experimental investigation, *Journal of Business Ethics,* 14(5), 353–365.

Grasmick, H.G., 1985. *Age and Tax Cheating: Demographic Implications,* Paper presented to the University of Texas Population Research Center on July 26, 1985.

Grasmick, H.G. and Scott, W.J., 1982. Tax evasion and mechanisms of social control: A comparison of grand and petty theft, *Journal of Economic Psychology,* 2, 213–230.

Hamm, J.L. and Ricketts, R.C., 1999. An experimental examination of the separate effects of tax rate and income level on taxpayer compliance, in Porcano, T.A., Ed., *Advances in Taxation,* Vol. 11, Stamford, CT, JAI Press, pp. 89–109.

Internal Revenue Service, 2002. *National Research Program [IRS Release No.: FS-2002–07],* Washington, DC, IRS Media Relations Office. Available at: http://www.irs.gov/pub/irs-so/natresearchprog.pdf. Retrieved on September 3, 2003.

Kagan, R., 1989. On the visibility of income tax law violations, in Roth, J.A. and Scholz, J.T., *Taxpayer Compliance,* Vol. 2, Philadelphia, PA, University of Pennsylvania Press, pp. 76–125.

Kaplan, S. and Reckers, P., 1985. A study of tax evasion, *National Tax Journal,* 38, 97–102.

Mason, R. and Calvin, L.D., 1978. A study of admitted income tax evasion, *National Tax Journal,* 13, 73–89.

Masselli, J., Ricketts, R., Arnold, V. and Sutton, S., 2002. The impact of embedded intelligent agents on tax reporting decisions, *The Journal of American Taxation Association,* 24(2), 60–78.

Reckers, P., Sanders, D. and Roark, S., 1994. The influence of ethical attitudes on taxpayer compliance, *National Tax Journal,* 47(4), 825–836.

Roth, J.A., Scholz, J.T. and Witte, A.D., 1989. *Taxpayer Compliance: An Agenda for Research,* Vol. 1, Philadelphia, PA, University of Pennsylvania Press.

Schwartz, R. and Orleans, S., 1967. On legal sanctions, *University of Chicago Law Review,* 34, 274–300.

Scott, W. and Grasmick, H., 1981. Deterrence and income tax cheating: Testing interaction hypotheses in utilitarian theories, *University of Chicago Law Review,* 34, 395–408.

Song, Y.-d. and Yarbrough, T.E., 1978. Tax ethics and taxpayer attitudes: A survey, *Public Administration Review,* 38, 442–452.

Spicer, M. and Lundstedt, S.B., 1976. Understanding tax evasion, *Public Finance/Finances Publiques,* 31, 295–305.

Thurman, Q.C., 1989. General prevention of tax evasion: A factorial survey approach, *Journal of Quantitative Criminology,* 5(2), 127–146.

Thurman, Q.C., 1991. Taxpayer noncompliance and general prevention: An expansion of the deterrence model, *Public Finance/Finances Publiques,* 46, 289–298.

Thurman, Q.C., Craig, J., St. and Riggs, L.R. 1984. Tax evasion and neutralization: How effective would a moral appeal be in improving tax compliance? *Law and Policy,* 6, 309–327. Vogel, J., 1974. Taxation and public opinion in Sweden: An interpretation of recent survey data, *National Tax Journal,* 27, 499–513.

Yankelovich, S. and White, Inc. 1984. *Taxpayer Attitudes Study Final Report,* Report prepared for the Internal Revenue Service, New York, Yankelovich, Skelly, and White, Inc.

*See also* **Corporate Crime; White-Collar Crime: Definitions**

---

# Terrorism

---

Terrorism has become the most powerful word in any language. Feared in any country, the term is not proprietary to any one nation or people. Over the decades there has been, and continues to be, much debate over the origins of terrorism and what constitutes "terrorist" activities as well as what is terrorism. Some authors and educators alike cite biblical passages as the first true acts of terrorism whereas others refer to actions in the Middle East and the establishment of the state of Israel. Regardless of any one person's interpretation, the modern version of the term "terrorism" can generally be attributed to the Enlightenment Era in the 1800s, also known as the Age of Reason.

The word "terrorism" is recognized as first being coined during the French Revolution (1792–1794), which was led by Maximilien Marie Isidore de Robespierre, when the *régime de la terreur* was initially viewed by Robespierre as a positive political system. This was a political system that used fear and terror to remind citizens of the necessity of virtue. French leaders initially attempted to weed out traitors among the revolutionary ranks and saw terror as the best way to defend liberty. However, as the French Revolution evolved, the word soon took on grim echoes of state violence and guillotines after thousands of people were put to death, a fate eventually dealt upon Robespierre.

Violence and terrorism have been employed to convince people about ideological issues throughout the years. It has continued to expand beyond ideologies and is regularly associated with nationalistic and theological struggles. In recent decades, particularly since the end of the 20th century and the start of the 21st century, it has taken on decidedly negative connotations as a tactic deployed by those who do not have the powers of state at their disposal.

## Introduction

Terrorism has been viewed by some as simply brutal, unthinking violence. This is not the case. Experts who have been researching and writing on the topic of terrorism since the early 1970s agree that there is almost always a strategy behind terrorist actions. Whether terrorism takes the form of bombings, shootings, hijackings, or assassinations, it is not random, spontaneous, nor blind; it is often a deliberate use of violence against individuals to achieve political or religious ends.

## Definition

Even though most people believe they can recognize various forms or methods of terrorism when they see it, international experts have had difficulty developing an ironclad definition that all nations can use. Defining terrorism has been greatly debated and written about for decades largely because of its subjective nature and the way it has been applied or viewed by various governments. Countless books have had entire chapters solely dedicated to the topic of providing a definition of terrorism. Simply put, there are many "working definitions" of terrorism. The U.S. Code 22 U.S.C. § 2656f (d) defines terrorism as "premeditated, politically motivated violence perpetrated against noncombatant targets by subnational groups or clandestine agents, usually intended to influence an audience." In another useful attempt to produce a definition, Paul Pillar, a former deputy chief of the U.S. Central Intelligence Agency's Counterterrorist Center, argues for the Council on Foreign Relations that there are four key elements of terrorism (Pillar, 2003):

> It is premeditated—planned in advance, rather than an impulsive act of rage.
> It is political—not criminal, like the violence that groups such as the mafia use to get money, but designed to change the existing political order.
> It is aimed at civilians—not at military targets or combat-ready troops.
> It is carried out by subnational groups—not by the army of a country.

In 1983 a researcher, Alex Schmid, studied 109 definitions of terrorism and concluded that there were many similarities. In his research Schmid noted 22 total elements that were common among the definitions and ranked them by percentile. He reported that the top five elements were violence and force, 83.5%; political, 65%; fear and terror emphasized, 51%; threat, 47%; and psychological effects and anticipated reactions, 41.5%.

Many government agencies have attempted to define terrorism and many include some of the elements reported by Schmid. However, agencies within one country cannot agree even upon one definition of terrorism for its government. In the U.S. alone, there are many definitions. Three of the more commonly cited definitions originated from the Federal Bureau of Investigation (FBI), the U.S. Department of State, and the U.S. Department of Defense. They are briefly outlined below.

The FBI 2003 definition of terrorism is:

> …the unlawful use of force and violence against persons or property to intimidate or coerce a Government, the civilian population, or any segment thereof, in furtherance of political or social objectives.

The U.S. Department of State in 2003 defined terrorism as:

> …an activity, directed against persons involving violent acts or acts dangerous to human life that would be a criminal violation if committed within the jurisdiction of the U.S.; and is intended to intimidate or coerce a civilian population; to influence the policy of a government by intimidation or coercion; or to affect the conduct of a government by assassination or kidnapping…

In 2003 the Department of Defense defined terrorism as:

> …the calculated use of violence or threat of violence to inculcate fear; intended to coerce or to intimidate governments or societies in the pursuit of goals that are generally political, religious, or ideological.

Regardless of who is defining or researching terrorism or when it is done, the term will not be definitively defined. The reason for this is that, as one researches the topic, one will notice that the meaning has changed with time and events. What may be considered terrorism today may have been viewed as revolutionary acts or disobedience by anarchists when they occurred. Terrorism is not a new phenomenon. It is a term that will never have a single definition that fits all known models of terrorism.

## Historical

With an understanding of several of the working definitions of terrorism in hand, it is important to know some of the historical context from which it has evolved. This will provide the opportunity to gain insight into the growth of the term "terrorism" as well as how terrorism has become a modern day obsession beyond the tragedy of the September 11, 2001 attack in New York City at the World Trade Center Towers.

It has been written that some of the oldest, or first, terrorists were holy warriors who killed civilians. For instance, in 1st century Palestine, Jewish zealots would publicly slit the throats of Romans and their collaborators; in 7th century India, the Thuggee cult ritually strangled passersby as sacrifices to the Hindu deity Kali; and in the 11th-century Middle East, the Shiite sect known as the Assassins ate hashish before murdering civilian foes (Council on Foreign Relations, 2003). Those studying criminal justice may have discounted these as barbaric acts, or from a strictly criminal standpoint, as homicide.

After the French Revolution in the mid-1800s, the term "terrorism" evolved to describe violent revolutionaries who revolted against governments, or antifederal behavior. In the early 1900s in the U.S., the term was used to describe labor organizations and anarchists. However, it was the anarchists who garnered perhaps the most attention from law enforcement and the public alike. Labor organizations during the early 1900s were fighting for the working class and sought to better the work environment, employee rights, and financial equality. Although some disrupted the flow of society, they generally did not create mass hysteria or death. Anarchists, on the other hand, did what they could to disrupt society by whatever means they could employ in order to achieve their end regardless of who got in their way. An example of this would be the assassination of U.S. President William McKinley in 1901 by Leon Czolgosz, a reported anarchist. This is just one example of the long history of political violence in the U.S. that some many view as political terrorism today. Many anarchists in the U.S. would eventually be "rounded-up" after McKinley's death and deported from the U.S.

It is important to note that the U.S. did not hold a monopoly on anarchists in the early 1900s. There were various terrorist activities in other countries, such as Russia, in response to a change in the way intellectuals approached social problems and class-based revolutions or revolts, such as the Russian Revolution. Historians can trace recognizably modern forms of terrorism back to such late 19th century organizations as the People's Will, an antitsarist group in Russia. One particularly successful early case of terrorism was on June 28, 1914, by a member of the Black Hand group, Nedjelko Cabrinovic. The assassination of Austrian Archduke Franz Ferdinand and his wife Sophie by the Serbian nationalist would be an event that helped trigger World War I.

Shortly after World War II, the term changed again to be associated with nationalistic groups revolting against European domination. It was during the turbulent 1940s and 1950s, known as the postcolonial era, that Europeans felt the repercussions of terrorism by nationalists seeking to end colonial rule. The two hardest hit countries were France and England, who both had colonial settlements on various continents. Two of the more commonly cited problem areas of the time were in Algeria and Kenya. The French suffered greatly from terrorist attacks in Africa against colonialism in Algeria by the National Liberation Front (FLN). English colonies in Kenya were targeted by the Mau-Mau. Also during the 1940s, the State of Israel was being formed in the Middle East. When the British replaced the Ottomans as the governing colonial force over the Palestinians and Jews in Palestine, in what became known as the Balfour Declaration of 1917, they promised the Jews a home in Palestine. Over time this grew into a conflict in which the Jews sought to remove the British. In order to do this, the Jews resorted to urban terrorism and established the Irgun Zvai Leumi, commonly referred to as the Irgun, as an underground terrorist organization to conduct actions against the British (Ronczkowski, 2004). The terrorist actions of the Irgun continued until about 1948, when Israel was recognized as a nation by the UN. Becoming a nation did not end the problem in the Middle East for Israel.

Various groups, particularly the Palestinian Liberation Organization (PLO), continue to struggle against non-Arabs in the region.

As the Middle East conflict continued to grow, much of the world saw a rise from the left. From the mid-1960s to the early 1980s, the term terrorism was associated with activities of left-wing groups worldwide, many of whom were opposed to conflicts such as the Vietnam War. Much of the activity experienced in the world during this period was viewed as being perpetrated by left-wing groups also referred to as radicals, revolutionaries, or extremists, such as the Symbonese Liberation Army in the U.S. and the Bader-Meinhoff Gang in Germany. As left-wing groups diminished with the end of the Vietnam War, the rise of religious extremists began to emerge and grow in notoriety. With the rise of the Iranian Revolution in 1979 and the transformation of Iran into an Islamic republic, the world began to experience state sponsored and well organized groups. Shortly after the transformation, and the fall of the Shah of Iran, the Ayatollah Khomeini declared a holy war against Westerners. This is said to be the start of well organized and financed state sponsored terrorist organizations. Iran is also said to have an important role in the establishment of two current terrorist organizations, Hizbollah and Islamic Jihad. Today, terrorism is associated with large groups such as Hizbollah, Hamas, al-Qaeda, and Islamic Jihad, who are capable of operating independently from a state and are considered to be violent religious fanatics or extremists.

One thing is certain, society's interpretation or perception of the meaning and style of terrorism has shifted over time and probably will continue to evolve in years to come. Technology and the media will undoubtedly play a role in this evolution. Some of the more familiar forms of terrorism—often custom-made for TV cameras—first appeared on July 22, 1968, when the Popular Front for the Liberation of Palestine undertook the first terrorist hijacking of a commercial airplane (Council on Foreign Relations, 2003). Regardless of who among the scholars is defining terrorism, they agree fairly consistently upon the fact that the meaning has changed with societies and time. Other driving forces that have changed the meaning of terrorism over time are the mass media, communication capabilities, advancement in sophisticated weapons, and various socioeconomic factors.

## Terrorist Activity

Terrorism acts are generally directed toward a particular audience. They are often deliberately spectacular, designed to rattle and influence a wide audience, beyond the victims of the violence itself. They are often designed to affect their intended audience both physically and emotionally. The objective is to use activities in which the psychological impact or threat of violence effects political change.

Terrorist activity has taken many forms over the decades. Assassinations, bombings, arson, sabotage, hostage taking, property damage, and anarchy are all forms of terrorist activity. Just like the term terrorism, terrorist activity has been loosely defined without a singular definition.

The U.S. Department of State definition of terrorist activity from Section 212 (a) (3) (B) of the Immigration and Nationality Act states:

> ... (ii) TERRORIST ACTIVITY DEFINED—As used in this Act, the term "terrorist activity" means any activity that is unlawful under the laws of the place where it is committed (or which, if committed in the U.S., would be unlawful under the laws of the U.S. or any State) and which involves any of the following: (I) The hijacking or sabotage of any conveyance (including an aircraft, vessel, or vehicle). (II) The seizing or detaining, and threatening to kill, injure, or continue to detain, another individual in order to compel a third person (including a governmental organization) to do or abstain from doing any act as an explicit or implicit condition for the release of the individual seized or detained. (III) A violent attack upon an internationally protected person (as defined in section 1116(b) (4) of title 18, U.S. code) or upon the liberty of such a person. (IV) An assassination. (V) The use on any–
>
> (a) biological agent, chemical agent, or nuclear weapon or device, or
>
> (b) explosive or firearm (other than for mere personal monetary gain), with intent to endanger, directly or indirectly, the safety of one or more individuals or to cause substantial damage to property.
>
> (VI) A threat, attempt, or conspiracy to do any of the foregoing.

Although many events over the centuries can be construed as terrorist activity, terrorism has been consistently manifested in several forms. According to the book, *Terrorism and Organized Hate Crime: Intelligence Gathering, Analysis, and Investigations*, there are six general forms of terrorism. Outlined below are the six common forms of terrorism affecting the world (Ronczkowski, 2004).

Political Terrorism—An act, or series of acts, directed or aimed toward bringing about political or policy change through the use of force, intimidation, or threatened use of force.

Ecological Terrorism—An act, or series of acts, designed to slow, impede, or halt the growth or harvesting of a nation's natural resources.

Agricultural Terrorism—The use of chemicals or toxins (biological means) against some component of the agricultural industry in an attempt to disrupt distribution or consumption of goods by the general public.

Narco Terrorism—Terrorist acts conducted to extend the aims of drug cultivators, manufacturers, and traffickers in an attempt to divert attention from illegal drug and narcotics operations; usually applied to groups that use the drug trade to fund terrorism.

Biological Terrorism—The threat of use or introduction of biological or chemical agents against individuals that are designed to injure, maim, or cause death.

Cyber Terrorism—The use of computing resources to intimidate and infiltrate public, private, and government computer-based infrastructures through the use of viruses or code breaking in an attempt to disrupt service, destroy, or compromise data.

## Terrorist

It has often been said by a wide variety of individuals that one person's terrorist is another man's freedom fighter. A review of an array of publications written throughout the 20th century describes various individuals as terrorists. However, by historical and some modern standards, they are considered as freedom fighters, martyrs, leaders, anarchists, revolutionaries, visionaries, spiritual clerics, and in some cases even presidents. The fact is there is no one definitive way to identify a terrorist.

Although there is not one definitive way to identify a terrorist, there are six generalities that apply to most terrorists. First, terrorists fight for a political objective. Second, they are often motivated by ideology or religion. Third, they are group-focused largely because of the fact that most terrorist activities are well planned and involve many supporters. Fourth, they are consumed with a purpose. They are committed and dedicated to the cause in which they will fight or die. Fifth, terrorists are usually well trained and highly motivated to the mission for which they have chosen or selected. Sixth, they are always on the attack, even if they are assuming a dormant posture prior to an actual event.

## General Beliefs

There are three types of terrorist beliefs or points of view that, in general terms, capture virtually any group or individual that can be construed as a terrorist or terrorist group:

Nationalistic
Ideological
Theological

"Nationalist terrorists seek to form a separate state for their own national group, often by drawing attention to a fight for 'national liberation' that they think the world has ignored." (General Military Training, 2002). Many nationalist groups are not viewed as terrorists but rather are seen by the populous as freedom fighters. An example of a nationalist group would be the Irish Republican Army, which began its struggle not for a Catholic versus Protestant religious conflict, but rather for a fight for independence and establishment of an Irish state. As for ideological terrorists, their actions are simply based on their beliefs. The difference between nationalists and ideologicals are usually found in their goals. Many ideological terrorists have expressed frustration toward social structures and capitalism, and they seek a new order. The third type of belief group is theological or religious terrorists, who believe they speak and work for the divine. They "seek to use violence to further what they see as divinely commanded purposes, often targeting broad categories of foes in an attempt to bring about sweeping changes." (General Military Training, 2002).

James Fraser (former U.S. Army counterterrorist specialist) and Ian Fulton's analysis and writings from 1984 used a pyramid, similar to the National Strategy for Combating Terrorism, to explain the structural needs of a terrorist group or organization. Fraser pointed out that terrorist organizations are divided into four distinctly separate levels that are dependent upon each other: command, active cadre, active supporters, and passive supporters (White, 2002).

Command level members are well educated planners, financial monitors, and target selectors. The second level is the active cadre. This is the hard-core component of the organization that consists of the "field soldiers" and, as some communities have come to experience, "suicide/homicide bombers." It is at this level that the mission is carried out. Active cadre members are aware of the existence of other members and the organization's beliefs but have limited knowledge of missions beyond their role. The third tier in the hierarchal structure is the active supporters. These are the individuals charged with logistics, field support and intelligence gathering for the active cadre. In order to keep one terrorist in the field, it takes several individuals to actively support their mission. The largest group is the passive supporters. Their function is to muster up political or financial support. Many of these individuals do not even know they are supporting an active terrorist organization. It has been suggested by various scholars that it takes 35 to 50 support personnel to keep one terrorist in the field (Ronczkowski, 2004).

Terrorist leaders within these organizations realize the importance of being inconspicuous. Therefore, leaders limit communication, access to information, and mission details on a need-to-know basis, and often use small units, referred to as cells. The use of cells restricts the likelihood that law enforcement, military personnel, informants, or "spies" can gain access to an organization. Cells are generally comprised of four to six members, all with specialties to enhance the mission, and each member has limited knowledge of the overall mission. This ensures that if one is captured or intelligence is leaked, the entire mission is not jeopardized. It also makes infiltration of the group by law enforcement or a source of human intelligence nearly impossible. Cells are not always in the public eye. Many are referred to as "sleeper cells." These are cells sent to a locale to assimilate within a particular society while awaiting direction from superiors or to perform covert activities. Similar to the military, wherein squads are composed of units that make up divisions, a group of terrorist cells consists of what are referred to as columns. It is this organizational structure that has enabled many groups to achieve their desired results throughout the years.

## Significant Terrorist Events

There have been many kidnappings, hijackings, and assassinations over the decades in many countries throughout the world. Outlined below are some of the more significant terrorist incidents that have taken place since 1960, according to the U.S. Department of State, Office of the Historian, Bureau of Public Affairs. It is important for researchers and investigators alike to be cognizant of dates, or anniversaries of prior significant terrorist activities, because some groups find significance in these dates and have attacked on the same date more than once.

- First U.S. aircraft hijacked, May 1, 1961. Puerto Rican born Antuilo Ramierez Ortiz forced at gunpoint a National Airlines plane to fly to Havana, Cuba, where he was given asylum.
- "Bloody Friday," July 21, 1972. An Irish Republican Army (IRA) bomb attack killed 11 people and injured 130 in Belfast, Northern Ireland. Ten days later, three IRA car bomb attacks in the village of Claudy left six dead.
- Munich Olympic massacre, September 5, 1972. Eight Palestinian "Black September" terrorists seized 11 Israeli athletes in the Olympic Village in Munich, West Germany. In a bungled rescue attempt by West German authorities, nine of the hostages and five terrorists were killed.
- Ambassador to Sudan assassinated, March 2, 1973. U.S. Ambassador to Sudan Cleo A. Noel and other diplomats were assassinated at the Saudi Arabian Embassy in Khartoum by members of the Black September organization.

- U.S. domestic terrorism, January 27–29, 1975. Puerto Rican nationalists bombed a Wall Street bar, killing four and injuring 60; two days later, the Weather Underground claimed responsibility for an explosion in a bathroom at the U.S. Department of State in Washington.
- Entebbe hostage crisis, June 27, 1976. Members of the Baader-Meinhof Group and the Popular Front for the Liberation of Palestine (PFLP) seized an Air France airliner and its 258 passengers. They forced the plane to land in Uganda, where on July 3 Israeli commandos successfully rescued the passengers.
- Iran hostage crisis, November 4, 1979. After President Carter agreed to admit the Shah of Iran into the U.S., Iranian radicals seized the U.S. embassy in Tehran and took 66 American diplomats hostage. Thirteen hostages were soon released, but the remaining 53 were held until their release on 20 January 1981.
- Grand Mosque seizure, November 20, 1979. Two hundred Islamic terrorists seized the Grand Mosque in Mecca, Saudi Arabia, taking hundreds of pilgrims hostage. Saudi and French security forces retook the shrine after an intense battle in which some 250 people were killed and 600 wounded.
- U.S. installation bombing, August 31, 1981. The Red Army exploded a bomb at the U.S. Air Force Base at Ramstein, West Germany.
- Bombing of U.S. embassy in Beirut, April 18, 1983. Sixty-three people, including the CIA's Middle East director, were killed, and 120 were injured in a 400-pound suicide truck-bomb attack on the U.S. embassy in Beirut, Lebanon. The Islamic Jihad claimed responsibility.
- Bombing of marine barracks, Beirut, October 23, 1983. Simultaneous suicide truck-bomb attacks were made on American and French compounds in Beirut, Lebanon. A 12,000-pound bomb destroyed the U.S. compound, killing 242 Americans, whereas 58 French troops were killed when a 400-pound device destroyed a French base. Islamic Jihad claimed responsibility.
- Restaurant bombing in Spain, April 12, 1984. Eighteen U.S. servicemen were killed, and 83 people were injured in a bomb attack on a restaurant near a U.S. Air Force Base in Torrejon, Spain.
- Golden Temple seizure, June 5, 1984. Sikh terrorists seized the Golden Temple in Amritsar, India. One hundred people died when Indian security forces retook the Sikh holy shrine.
- TWA hijacking, June 14, 1985. A Trans-World Airlines flight was hijacked en route to Rome from Athens by two Lebanese Hizballah terrorists and forced to fly to Beirut. The eight crew members and 145 passengers were held for 17 days, during which one American hostage, a U.S. Navy sailor, was murdered. After being flown twice to Algiers, the aircraft was returned to Beirut after Israel released 435 Lebanese and Palestinian prisoners.
- Achille Lauro hijacking, October 7, 1985. Four Palestinian Liberation Front terrorists seized the Italian cruise liner in the eastern Mediterranean Sea, taking more than 700 hostages. One U.S. passenger was murdered before the Egyptian government offered the terrorists safe haven in return for the hostages' freedom.
- Egyptian airliner hijacking, November 23, 1985. An EgyptAir airplane bound from Athens to Malta and carrying several U.S. citizens was hijacked by the Abu Nidal Group.
- Pan Am Flight 103 Bombing, December 21, 1988. Pan American Airlines Flight 103 was blown up over Lockerbie, Scotland, by a bomb believed to have been placed on the aircraft in Frankfurt, West Germany, by Libyan terrorists. All 259 people on board were killed.
- U.S. embassy bombed in Peru, January 15, 1990. The Tupac Amaru Revolutionary Movement bombed the U.S. Embassy in Lima, Peru.
- Bombing of the Israeli embassy in Argentina, March 17, 1992. Hizballah claimed responsibility for a blast that leveled the Israeli Embassy in Buenos Aires, Argentina, causing the deaths of 29 and wounding 242.
- World Trade Center bombing, February 26, 1993. The World Trade Center in New York City was badly damaged when a car bomb planted by Islamic terrorists explodes in an underground garage. The bomb left six people dead and 1,000 injured. The men carrying out the attack were followers of Umar Abd al-Rahman, an Egyptian cleric who preached in the New York City area.
- Air France hijacking, December 24, 1994. Members of the Armed Islamic Group seized an Air France Flight to Algeria. The four terrorists were killed during a rescue effort.
- Tokyo subway station attack, March 20, 1995. Twelve persons were killed, and 5,700 were injured in a Sarin nerve gas attack on a crowded subway station in the center of Tokyo, Japan. A similar attack occurred nearly simultaneously in the Yokohama subway system. The Aum Shinrikyu cult was blamed for the attacks.
- Bombing of the federal building in Oklahoma City, April 19, 1995. Right-wing extremists Timothy McVeigh and Terry Nichols destroyed the

federal building in Oklahoma City with a massive truck bomb that killed 166 and injured hundreds more in what was up to then the largest terrorist attack on American soil.

- Tamil Tigers attack, January 31, 1996. Members of the Liberation Tigers of Tamil Eelam (LTTE) rammed an explosives-laden truck into the Central Bank in the heart of downtown Colombo, Sri Lanka, killing 90 civilians and injuring more than 1,400 others, including two U.S. citizens.
- Khobar Towers bombing, June 25, 1996. A fuel truck carrying a bomb exploded outside the U.S. military's Khobar Towers housing facility in Dhahran, killing 19 U.S. military personnel and wounding 515 persons, including 240 U.S. personnel. Several groups claimed responsibility for the attack.
- U.S. embassy bombings in East Africa, August 7, 1998. A bomb exploded at the rear entrance of the U.S. embassy in Nairobi, Kenya, killing 12 U.S. citizens, 32 Foreign Service Nationals (FSNs), and 247 Kenyan citizens. About 5,000 Kenyans, six U.S. citizens, and 13 FSNs were injured. The U.S. embassy building sustained extensive structural damage. Almost simultaneously, a bomb detonated outside the U.S. embassy in Dar es Salaam, Tanzania, killing seven FSNs and three Tanzanian citizens, and injuring one U.S. citizen and 76 Tanzanians. The explosion caused major structural damage to the U.S. embassy facility. The U.S. government held Usama Bin Ladin responsible.
- Attack on U.S.S. *Cole*, October 12, 2000. In Aden, Yemen, a small dingy carrying explosives rammed the destroyer U.S.S. *Cole*, killing 17 sailors and injuring 39 others. Supporters of Usama Bin Laden were suspected.
- Tel-Aviv nightclub bombing, June 1, 2001. Hamas claimed responsibility for the bombing of a popular Israeli nightclub that caused over 140 casualties.
- Hamas restaurant bombing, August 9, 2001. A Hamas-planted bomb detonated in a Jerusalem pizza restaurant, killing 15 people and wounding more than 90.

- Terrorist attacks on U.S. homeland, September 11, 2001. Two hijacked airliners crashed into the twin towers of the World Trade Center. Soon thereafter, the Pentagon was struck by a third hijacked plane. A fourth hijacked plane, suspected to be bound for a high-profile target in Washington D.C., crashed into a field in southern Pennsylvania. In total more than 5,000 U.S. citizens and other nationals were killed as a result of these acts. President Bush and Cabinet officials indicated that Usama Bin Laden was the prime suspect and that they considered the U.S. in a state of war with international terrorism. In the aftermath of the attacks, the U.S. formed the Global Coalition Against Terrorism.

MICHAEL R. RONCZKOWSKI

## References and Further Reading

Bodansky, Y., *Target America and the West: Terrorism Today,* New York, SPI Books, 1993.
*Council on Foreign Relations,* Washington, DC, 2003. Available at: http://www.terrorismanswers.com.
Crenshaw, M. and Pimlott, J., Eds, *Encyclopedia of World Terrorism,* New York, M.E. Sharpe, 1997.
Hoffman, B., *Inside Terrorism,* New York, Columbia University Press, 1999.
Lesser, I.O., Hoffman, B., Arquilla, J., Zanini, M. and Ronfeldt, D., *Countering the New Terrorism,* Washington, DC, RAND, 1999.
Pillar, P.R., *Terrorism and U.S. Foreign Policy,* Washington, DC, The Brookings Institution, 2001.
Reich, W., *Origins of Terrorism: Psychologies, Ideologies, Theologies, States of Mind,* Washington, DC, Woodrow Wilson Center Press, 1998.
Ronczkowski, M.R., *Terrorism and Organized Hate Crimes: Intelligence Gathering, Analysis, and Investigations,* Boca Raton, CRC Press, 2004.
Stohl, M., Ed., Some Characteristics of Political Terrorism in the 1960s, *The Politics of Terrorism,* 3rd ed., 1988, New York, Marcel Dekker, 1979.
White, J.R., *Terrorism: An Introduction,* 4th ed., Florence, Wadsworth, 2003.

*See also* **International Policing: Interpol; Terrorism: The Law**

# Terrorism: The Law

Generally, terrorism can be explained as the random use of staged violence at infrequent intervals to achieve political goals. The term is more strictly defined by the State Department of the U.S. as, "the use or threat of violence to achieve political objectives." A precise definition of terrorism remains difficult and illusive, in part because of its political nature; one person's terrorist can be another person's freedom fighter. In addition to definitional dissension, efforts and approaches to combat terrorism both internationally and domestically also have taken many forms.

Any sovereign nation can decide to legally define terrorism and subsequently pass laws to make it a crime. It has been argued that criminalizing terrorism, however, fails to address the root causes that are both social and political in nature. In the 1980s, terrorism was arguably defined in the U.S. in terms of national policy; policymakers and intelligence analysts pointed to nations that used terrorism to attack U.S. interests worldwide. In the 1990s, terrorism became a domestic reality both in 1993 at the World Trade Center and later in 1995 in Oklahoma City. On September 11, 2001, the attacks on the World Trade Center and the Pentagon using commercial airliners were a major world event that were also the largest and most tragic terrorist attacks on U.S. soil to date. Only relatively recently has the U.S. drafted laws aimed directly at the terrorist.

In the U.S., partly as a response to the bombings of the World Trade Center in 1993 and the Alfred P. Murrah Federal Building in Oklahoma City in 1995, the public demanded more stringent measures to battle the problem. Essentially, the U.S. has attempted to define terrorism legally by passing the Anti-Terrorism and Effective Death Penalty Act of 1996, signed into law by former President William Clinton (Public Law. No. 104–132, 110 Stat. 1214 (1996)). This law specifically defines a terrorist group as any organization that engages in, or has engaged in, terrorist activity as defined by the Secretary of State after consultation with the Secretary of the Treasury. This definition would therefore include not only groups directly involved in violence but also any other groups that allegedly fund terrorist operations. Simply stated, the U.S. chose to combat terrorism through the law.

The 1996 federal law initiated some sweeping changes and includes some controversial aspects. In summary, the act includes provisions to: (1) enable victims to sue sovereign nations that allegedly sponsor terrorism for damages resulting from terrorist acts; (2) establish special courts that oversee the speedy deportation of foreign nationals on U.S. soil suspected of terrorist activities; (3) expand the powers of the U.S. Immigration Service to deport aliens convicted of a crime; and (4) curtail fund-raising efforts in the U.S. by foreign groups suspected of terrorist activities. Provisions to increase wiretap and electronic surveillance powers of law enforcement were rejected by the Congress prior to 9/11.

Critics maintain that the fight against terrorism need not require the curtailment of civil liberties cherished by Americans for over 200 years. They argue that such police and judicial tactics run opposite to the ideals of due process inherent in the U.S. Constitution. The Fifth and the Fourteenth Amendments provide that no person should be deprived of "life, liberty, or property without the due process of law." In the U.S., citizens and aliens alike share this guarantee of due process. The legislated extrajudicial provisions of the 1996 federal law run counter to such a democratic philosophy. On the other hand, policymakers, intent on stiff counter measures, believe that Americans may have to give up some of these rights in order to combat the problem of both international and domestic threats of terrorism effectively.

Efforts to strengthen U.S. law against terrorists began in the 1970s to combat the hijacking of aircraft. On August 5, 1974, Public Law 93–366 was signed by former President Nixon. Title I is known as the Anti-Hijacking Act of 1974; Title II as the Air Transportation Security Act of 1974. The law implemented international agreements adopted under the Hague Convention for the Suppression of Unlawful Seizure of Aircraft. Specifically, the Hague Convention of December 1970 required that every signatory state in which a hijacker is located must either extradite the offender to the state whose aircraft was hijacked or prosecute the hijacker. Signatory states must also provide penalties for the offense of hijacking

In the U.S., the law gives the president statutory authority to suspend "without notice or hearing and for as long as he determines necessary the right of any U.S. or foreign air carrier to engage in air transportation between the U.S. and any nation that permits its territory to be used as a base of operations or sanctuary for terrorist organizations that engage in aircraft piracy." Other provisions give the president the right to suspend foreign air commerce between the U.S. and any foreign nation that maintains air service between itself and an offending foreign nation.

Furthermore, Public Law 93–366 filled in some legal loopholes, expanding the definition of "in flight." Previously, the Federal Aviation Act of 1958 provided that "in flight" meant "from the time power is applied for take-off until the landing run ends." This wording created the situation where an alleged terrorist apprehended prior to a take-off roll was not covered by existing hijacking penal law. Public Law 93–366 currently defines "in flight" to read "from the moment when all external doors are closed following embarkation until the moment when one such door is opened for disembarkation."

Another discrepancy in the law was cleared up concerning weapons onboard aircraft. Initially, the law did not provide for a penalty for carrying a weapon through screening checkpoints. Now, the law provides for "attempting" to carry a weapon onboard an aircraft, either on one's person or in one's property, if the weapon would be accessible to that person in flight. Additionally, the law imposes the death penalty or life imprisonment if the hijacking results in the death of anther person.

Officials have also negotiated international treaties directly related to the increasing global crisis of terrorism. One of the first, the Tokyo Convention, signed in 1963, recognized the inviolability of a hijacked aircraft and passengers, regardless of where the aircraft may be forced to land. The treaty specifically states that, in the event of a hijacking, the country where the aircraft lands must permit the aircraft, passengers and crew and cargo to proceed to its destination as soon as practical. The Montreal Convention of 1971 included provisions pertaining to violence against individuals aboard an aircraft, damage or destruction of an aircraft, and placing devices or substances on an aircraft that could damage or destroy the aircraft. The Montreal Convention also imposed the requirement that states take all "practical measures to prevent the commission of these offenses." The Montreal Protocol of 1988 extended previous treaties to provide for dealing with acts of violence against civil aviation at airports and ticket offices.

Domestically, other western nations have also chosen a variety of methods and approaches to fight terrorism. In the case of Germany, antiterrorist units were given the right to search and seizure without a warrant during a two-year time frame in the mid-1980s. The suspension of their constitutional rights was limited and well controlled. However, the German people had reached a point where the fear of terrorism outweighed the desire to preserve their own civil liberties.

The threat leading up to such a change in their criminal law procedures was the direct result of the continuing terrorist acts of the Baader-Meinhof Gang, including kidnapping, robbery and hijacking of aircraft.

In Northern Ireland, Great Britain has continued to make use of the Terrorism Act. The British decided to expand the administrative powers of the police and courts in the criminal justice system. Security forces were given the power to arrest and intern without warrant or trial. Courts were given the power of secret trials and testimony. Eventually, the Emergency Powers Act of 1973 shifted the burden of proof from the state to the defendant and also shifted the management of terrorists away from the judicial branch to the executive branch. The law has been amended several times over the years but it remains the law of the land. It still permits security forces to treat suspected terrorists differently than regular suspects. However, extrajuridicial courts have been removed and the goal of the Anglo-Irish Peace Accord is to return Ireland to the realm of regular democratic criminal justice procedures.

Spain took another approach. The Basque region of France and Spain has long been a source for major nationalist terrorism in Europe. In addition to expanded criminal justice procedures, the Spanish government seeks to delegitimize terrorism by opening the political system to the Basques. Furthermore, the Spanish police began using programs such as self-policing, wherein both the Spanish and the Basques were able to denounce violence. The terrorists found it harder to operate and potentially repressive police measures arguably have become less necessary.

Control of narco-terrorism has also created a need for target legislation to curb the flow of drugs as well as to stem the tide of this specialized type of terrorism. Pursuant to a congressional request, the U.S. Government Accounting Office (GAO) provided information on drug trafficking and terrorism in the U.S., focusing on the strategies and technologies developed to combat these threats. The GAO noted that: (1) the threat from terrorism within the U.S. has increased and U.S. aviation is a prime target for terrorist groups that are difficult to infiltrate; (2) drug trafficking continues to pose a serious problem for the southwestern border, as most drug shipments are smuggled by cars, trucks, and tractor-trailers; (3) the Federal Aviation Administration (FAA) relies on a strategy of tailored responses to mandate security procedures commensurate with the level of threat at specific times and places; (4) the FAA mandates more stringent security measures for international than for domestic flights, including the use of x-ray screening for checked baggage; (5) the customs service disseminates intelligence on drug trafficking, targets high-threat conveyances and cargoes, and uses detection technologies to detect drug-related activities;

and (6) the FAA has certified an advanced automated explosive detection system for 75 of the busiest domestic airports, but has been unable to deploy it because installation costs could reach as much as $2.2 billion.

September 11, 2001, however, changed everything.

President George W. Bush signed into law the Air Transportation Security Act P.L. 107–71 (ATSA) in November 2001 in an effort to improve the nation's transportation security system. The Act is intended to fundamentally change the way security is performed and overseen as regards the entire transportation industry. The Act contained some specific deadlines for its new administrators. One such deadline was to issue new qualification standards for airport screeners. On December 31, 2001, Secretary Norman Mineta, U.S. Secretary for Transportation, announced the new but very similar to the already mandated requirements for federal airport screeners. They included the need for U.S. citizenship; possession of a high school education or the equivalent; the ability to pass a background and security investigation, including a criminal records check; and the necessity of passing a standardized examination. The standards have already proven problematic.

Resorting back to the private sector for assistance, the TSA and FAA also published training plans for the new aviation security personnel, meeting the Congressional mandate of doing so within 60 days of the Act. The TSA hoped to also meet the deadline of November 19, 2002 to deploy 30,000 trained screeners at over 400 airports and has since claimed to do so. The challenge is a daunting one and they are likely to run up against the same problems currently encountered by the private security firms presently doing the job. The TSA plans to:

- Screen all persons, baggage and cargo
- Provide stress management conflict resolution programs
- Implement policies for professional interaction with passengers

The agency had previously issued Requests for Proposals (RFPs) devoted to screener and law enforcement personnel qualification, recruitment, experience and screener training. They seek to develop an appropriate training regime including a minimum of 40 hours of instruction. As a first step, as of April 30, 2002, 200 federal employees have been deployed at Baltimore Washington Airport marking the initiation of the program.

The airlines are also required, within 60 days, to amend their training programs to incorporate the TCS standards. All airline personnel, particularly aircrews, must receive the training within six months from enactment of the new legislation. The agency also published the procedures for airports to seek portions of the $1.5 billion authorized by Congress to fund security improvements at airports.

## Conclusion

The need to develop aircraft and airport security functions became readily apparent in the early 1970s. Various jurisdictions took various approaches to counter the threat. In the U.S., the Federal Aviation Regulations Part 107 and 108 specifically addressed these issues. Those regulations were differentiated based on the size of the aircraft and the size of the airport. The public was somewhat slow to recognize the requirement to bypass their Fourth Amendment rights and controversy still surrounds the procedures. Additionally, specific incidents of abuse catch the media's attention and bring the issues to the forefront.

The new TSA seeks to provide, in its own words, "excellence in public service." They hope to protect the nation's transportation infrastructure and to ensure freedom of movement of people and commerce. It took 30 years for the nation to recognize and to implement federal control of security at airports. It remains to be seen how effective administration of the system becomes under federal supervision. They face incredible challenges. The responsibility is almost too massive to imagine and critics will be quick to jump on the slightest infraction or outright failure. Additionally, bureaucracies tend to perpetuate themselves, often to the detriment of the agency's original mandate. The public's attention span is also quite short, especially if they perceive that the threat has dissipated. A return to apathy is a major problem. Just as important a problem is when a democracy goes too far in the name of security.

Fundamental constitutional freedoms still need ever vigilance to protect and preserve. It is a very slippery slope to forget the democratic principles upon which this nation was founded—all in the name of perceived external or internal threats. In January 2003, a federal appeals court ruled that the administration has the authority to designate U.S. citizens as "enemy combatants." This enables the government to label citizens and detain them in military custody if they are considered a threat to national security. In the case of Yaser Hamdi, a Louisiana born American citizen who was captured in Afghanistan fighting for the Taliban, a lower court had ordered the government to release more information to the defense. The government has been able to deny him access to his public defender and has not filed charges against him. The court opinion says, "Because it is undisputed that Hamdi was captured in a zone of active combat in a foreign theater of conflict, we hold that the submitted declaration is a sufficient basis upon which to conclude that the commander in chief has constitutionally detained Hamdi pursuant to the war powers entrusted to him by the U.S. Constitution." The ruling comes from one of the most conservative jurisdictions in the nation.

This case parallels but is easily distinguishable from *Padilla vs. Bush.* Jose Padilla, the alleged "dirty bomb" suspect, has also been designated an "enemy combatant." However, he was captured on U.S. soil after arriving at Chicago's O'Hare International Airport as part of an alleged scheme to explode a conventional bomb laced with radioactive material. His attorneys contend that the government should be forced to comply with standard criminal court procedures including the right to counsel. So far he has been denied that access. On the civil side, a Pakistani businessman from Los Angeles has lost a discrimination suit he filed against United Airlines. He had been blocked from boarding a plane following September 11. The jury reasoned that the discrimination was justified.

Another legal controversy, post 9/11, is the FBI's Carnivore program, which allows law enforcement officials to obtain e-mail wiretaps when criminal activity is suspected. But, the program has been criticized by those who fear it will be abused in violation of constitutional rights pertaining to the right to privacy. A similar, formerly classified, program operated by the National Security program, entitled Echelon, permits the NSA to listen as required if an issue of national security is at stake.

As regards future issues of the law and terrorism, at least in the U.S., technological advancements in airport security to control terrorism by more intrusive methods will present their own set of unique legal problems. In general, the U.S. courts have upheld the right of the FAA to institute airline passenger screening procedures, even when those procedures uncover more than just objects threatening to aircraft. According to the President's Commission on Aviation Security and Terrorism, "the more security measures are imposed, the more fundamental freedoms are restricted." Legal questions surrounding the implementation of new passenger screening technologies fall into two types: (1) potential claims for violations of individual rights against unreasonable searches and seizures and (2) potential claims of injury because of the screening process. The public will accept intrusive technological advances in airport security commensurate with perceptions of the current threat from terrorism.

Overall, the method of countering terrorism in the West has focused on the law. These actions are based on a belief in the efficacy of the democratic legal system to distinguish criminal from political acts without unduly compromising due process protections.

KATHLEEN M. SWEET

## References and Further Reading

Combs, C., *Terrorism in the Twenty-First Century,* 2nd ed., Prentice Hall, Upper Saddle, NJ, 1999.

Laquer, W., Post modern terrorism, *Foreign Affairs,* Sept/Oct, 1996.

Panghorn, A., How far has Europe come since Pan Am 103?, *Intersec,* 6, 195, 1996.

Simonsen, C.E. and Spindlove, J.R., *Terrorism Today, The Past, The Players, The Future,* Prentice Hall, Upper Saddle River, NJ, 2000.

Sweet, K., *Terrorism and Airport Security,* Edwin Mellon Press, Lewiston, NY, 2003.

Sweet, K., *Airport and Aviation Security,* Prentice Hall Publisher, Upper Saddle River, NJ, 2003.

U.S. Department of State, *Patterns of Global Terrorism,* U.S. Government Printing Office, Washington, DC, 1996.

White, J.R., *Terrorism an Introduction,* 2nd ed., Wadsworth Publishers, Belmont, CA, 1998.

*See also* **Terrorism**

# Theft *See* **Burglary; Larceny; Robbery; Theft, Professional**

---

# Theft, Professional

---

The expression "professional thieves" has different meanings to different people. These meanings can change depending on the context in which you are examining them. Some people might consider the common thief who has escaped detection for a number of years to be a professional thief. Some would even consider the thief who has numerous arrests for theft as a professional. It may be that the professional status is awarded to one who gains the recognition of law and whose name and modus operandi are known to the law enforcement agencies. It could even be the thief who served many years in prison and who, upon release, returns to a career of theft without having been rehabilitated. Some might consider the petty thief who makes one large score and is considered as having graduated from penny ante crimes to the big time as a professional. Most petty thieves are juveniles and most of these offenders graduate to jail or prison without attaining any kind of professional status. Some graduate out of criminal activity through a maturation process and become law biding adults. Others may graduate to a type of professionalism and survive or supplement their income solely with money or property obtained illegally. There are groups of thieves for whom theft is part of their culture. Children are raised to embrace criminal activity as a viable occupation. Their view of the world is one of targets to be exploited to their advantage. Whether developing a career as a thief through progressive experience in the ability to steal without attracting attention, or being cultured into a way of life where stealing is an honored occupation, the necessary ingredient is the development of certain skills. These skills are necessary for professionals to maximize their profits and avoid detection.

Although the fragmentation of local law enforcement agencies and their reaction to crime have been a boon to thieves, it has become a little better with modern technology. With so many local law enforcement jurisdictions, the ability for thieves to escape detection, and if detected, to escape arrest by crossing jurisdictional lines has long been a loop hole that could be exploited. Whereas this loop hole has been closed to some extent with information sharing and modern technology, like the use of computers, the extensive localization of law enforcement still leaves numerous areas to be exploited.

So, who is a professional thief? Let us take a look at both parts of the concept. There are a variety of definitions of the meaning of "professional." These definitions usually include the acquisition of skills, the maintenance of skills, and success in practicing these skills. There is usually an element of education and standards that must be met before someone can be considered a professional. Membership into professional organizations is part of the recognition as a professional status. "Theft" is generally defined as taking or using another person's property without their permission. If any kind of force or threat of force is added to the theft, it becomes robbery.

Whereas robbery is a theft offense, the professional thief avoids the use of violence in carrying out their operations. One of the biggest reasons that professional thieves avoid the use of force in the commission of their crimes is the attention that law enforcement places on catching suspects of violent crimes. A crime of violence will attract much more law enforcement resources than theft without violence. In most cases departments would not even investigate crimes under $50,000 because of the resources that are required and the cost of prosecution for, in some cases, what results in a minor sentence.

The prosecution could work the case as a racketeering-influenced corrupt organization and combine several crimes to meet the stricter punishment guidelines of the racketeering statutes. This is how the various operations of organized crime have been attacked and with some success have eliminated the top players in these criminal operations. The violence associated with organized crime activity has been a major reason for the stepped-up criminal investigations into their activities.

By combining these two general definitions of "professional" and "theft" we can classify a professional thief as someone who takes or uses another person's property without the owner's permission and in such a manner to avoid attracting the attention of law enforcement and eliminate chances for detection. This is done through the development of skills that reduce the risks involved in the theft operation. The professional thief avoids the attention of law enforcement by reducing the chance that the crime will even be reported to the police. Also, reducing the chance that the crime will be discovered early eliminates early reaction and intervention by law enforcement. The longer it is between the commission of the crime and the investigation, the greater is the chance of escape.

One way that the professional thief reduces the risk of detection is by reducing the chance the crime will be reported to the police. Professional thieves usually get some form of cooperation or participation by the victim in the crime itself. They often become willing or unknowing participants in the crime and it is a period of time before the loss is realized. Sometimes the professional thief will target the victim based on the victim's distrust of law enforcement by convincing them that the thief has their best interest at heart and that the police cannot or will not help them out. Greed is another human failing that the professional thief preys upon in selecting targets. The get-rich schemes and the something-for-nothing opportunities are all schemes to induce the victim to cooperate in their own loss. At the time of prosecution the professional thief can then claim that the victim willingly gave them the money or property and as no theft has occurred and therefore the thief is not guilty.

Some may refer to these as victimless crimes but in real victimless crimes the victim typically gets something in return for their investment. Typically the product or service that is purchased is unable to be obtained legally but can be purchased at an inflated price illegally. The professional thief may offer a product or service but the product or service offered does not exist or is never provided.

Many thefts are the results of opportunity. Opportunity could occur unexpectedly or be created or noticed by planning and innovation. Juvenile and amateur thieves typically search randomly for opportunities to present themselves, like roaming neighborhoods close to where they live to find something to steal or a house to burglarize. Very little planning goes into these random operations and very little planning is done on what to do if stopped by law enforcement or if prosecuted. Professional thieves are much more systematic and calculating. Operations are planned for any contingency. Opportunities are maximized and risks minimized before the theft takes place. These types of theft require the implementation of skills developed over time and perfected to lessen the risks involved in the theft.

Some of the most important skills a professional thief develops are communication skills. The ability to talk others out of their property or distract them while a theft is occurring is important in preventing the discovery of the crime until as long as possible after the event. Another skill is the ability to convince others of their sincerity to show empathy or feelings to be human in the victim's eyes. Also connected to this skill is the development of a very outgoing personality. Professional thieves develop the same skills that would be very beneficial to a top-notch salesperson. Skills in interpersonal communications and knowledge of human beings are critical components for long term success as a professional thief.

Still another skill is for the professional thief to be nondescript. By that I mean the professional thief is better served by not being recognizable at a later time. Use of the telephone to perform the theft is a good way to stay invisible to the victim. Another way is to remain very normal and general. If there are not any features that stand out in the victim's mind, then the suspect will be able to hide in plain sight. Presenting a very conservative appearance and not losing control of emotions are important features to remaining nondescript. When you ask victims to identify suspects the description is usually pretty general and would fit the majority of the population unless the suspect has done some thing to attract attention. Running from the scene of a crime will attract attention; a large scar, a prominent feature, or a tattoo will draw attention to the suspect and cause the victim to remember more about them.

Another skill necessary is the ability to scan for opportunities for theft, being knowledgeable about world events and how different things work. Immediately following the attack on the World Trade Center in September of 2001 professional thieves and amateur thieve both seized upon the opportunities presented to prey on people's hopes and fears. These thieves sounded very convincing in their presentations to not only victims but also to other people who wanted to help. People gave and donated money and property in the millions of dollars to funds that were used to line the pockets of thieves, with little or nothing going to the victims or their families. Natural disasters are another avenue for professional thieves to profit from others' misfortunes. Every disaster that occurs will provide another opportunity for the professional thief to take advantage. Floods, earthquakes, hurricanes, tornados, fires will bring out professional thieves willing to take advantage.

Another skill that professional thieves possess is flexibility. It is critical to have the ability to be very mobile. It is necessary to respond to the scenes or areas where the disasters or opportunities have occurred. To be in place when the need is critical and the opportunity of taking advantage of people is at its apex is important for professional thieves. Timing is critical during a crisis. People are most vulnerable during the time of a crisis and can be taken advantage of in these situations in a far easier way than that in a normal situation. Flexibility also pays off for the professional thief in that by the time things start returning to normal and law enforcement can redirect some of their resources away from the disaster to investigating crime the thief has moved on to other opportunities. The window of opportunity opens with the disaster and can require maximum use of all of a community's resources and sometimes help from other communities to control the loss and injury to citizens. It remains open as long as resources are redirected to handling other problems. It begins to close as the situation returns to normal but it does not return to normal nearly as fast as the original opportunity occurred. This period of time is the professional thief's opportunity to maximize profits and move on to the next target.

Another skill a professional thief needs to maximize their potential is the ability to work alone. The more people associated with any illegal operation, the more opportunity for information to be leaked out to law enforcement. As long as organized crime figures were able to keep their operations within the immediate family the less vulnerable they were to outside infiltration. The old philosophy that says that if more than one person knows about a secret it is not a secret, holds true. The less people have information about an operation the less likely that it will be compromised.

In one particular case a very skilled burglar was undone by the accomplices he used when committing his crimes. After his second trip to jail he decided that he needed to rethink his use of people in helping him. He was very meticulous and would always break into the business by going through the roof. He always used new tools and left them at the crime scene so that they could not be traced back to him. He still needed a driver and found a young woman who was willing to go along with his operation. They were married so that she could not testify against him later at trial if caught. It worked great for a long period, until after disabling the primary alarm system he was caught inside a building when the secondary silent alarm alerted police of the break-in.

Some professional thieves create their own criminal culture and develop accomplices tied to the criminal enterprise through marriage and by birth. This criminal culture helps to indoctrinate members from birth. Interfamily marriage is promoted and a very close-knit organization is developed. This reduces the opportunity for outsiders, particularly law enforcement, to compromise or infiltrate their organization. It is the same acculturization process that occurred in the early organized crime organizations, with members of certain families being the leaders of the organization and limiting law enforcement infiltration of the organization or gaining knowledge of the inner workings of the group by limiting membership to specific individuals related by blood or marriage. As these criminal organizations expanded, so did the need to include more than blood family members into the management of the organization, and this increased their vulnerability to law enforcement investigation and prosecution. Limited memberships and limited contact outside the culture, family, or organization increases secrecy and limits detection and prosecution. The smaller operation is a much better operation for the professional thief.

Innovation is another important skill that serves the professional thief well. As different opportunities present themselves, ways of taking advantage of these opportunities must be maximized. Although people being warned of the different methods used by professional thieves reduces the amount of money and property that can be obtained, it doesn't eliminate the opportunity totally. Some new wrinkle or variation of an old method could maximize profits in situations even when people have been alerted to possible opportunities where thieves will seek to take advantage.

The ability to hide profits and convert property is a valuable skill that professional thieves need to master. By the careful manipulation of profits the professional thief is able to divert attention away from their operation. Someone who is unable to explain profits or purchases attracts attention to their operation. Easily identifiable property must be converted to more liquid assets that can be moved and used without attracting attention. Becoming extravagant can undo many carefully carried out operations.

The types of crimes that professional thieves are attracted to again are crimes that do not require a large support group to accomplish. Most scenarios play out with the involvement of only one or two players and the victim. A popular crime for the professional thief is embezzlement. This crime may take a long period of time to play out, but the rewards often exceed the risks. The thief may have to work their way into a position of trust. Again, using those interpersonal communication skills and an outgoing personality and in some cases providing fake credentials that show qualifications for a particular position are the key to getting into a position. Some amateur embezzlers hatch the plot to cover for other personal losses or because the opportunity presents itself and they are in a position to take advantage of it. They often only take enough to maintain a lifestyle or pay off debt that has surpassed their resources. A professional thief can maximize their income and is constantly planning for the end of the operation. He constantly keeps in mind when the window of opportunity will close and when the best time is to shut down the operation, take the profits and get out. Some larger companies may not even report this type of theft to the police because of the risk of alienating their stockholders on grounds of poor management of internal affairs.

Scams and frauds have a large profit margin for professional thieves. You can go back in history and see the same or similar frauds being perpetrated on people. Probably the most well known swindler of all time was Charles Ponzi, who bilked people out of their savings and earned a fortune before going to jail. He developed the pyramid scam, and since his initial operations there have been a variety of different scams based on the same principles. Early investors make money and later investors actually provide the foundation until it collapses. The pigeon drop, the bank examiner scam, Medicare scams, the different telemarketing scams, the construction scams, real estate property scams, the Nigerian scams—these are all opportunities for professional thieves to appropriate the money and property of others. All of these scams have lots of different variations. The good thieves are flexible—they adapt. You may have heard of these schemes referred to as something else, but they are more or less similar to some of these basic themes.

These professional thieves prey upon the weak, the uneducated, and the naïve; people who trust them are basically either good, or greedy, or elderly or young. That group of prey would include just about everyone in the human race. This is a vast target audience for the real professional thief. What are the risks, to the professional thief? There are very limited risks, especially for the potential profit that can be gained. Not all these crimes are reported to the police, sometimes out of embarrassment, sometimes because the victim is unaware of the crime. If reported, the description of the suspect is limited because of limited or no face-to-face contact with the suspect. The suspect could be long gone from the local jurisdiction where the crime occurred by the time it is reported. If arrested, the chance of prosecution is limited by resources, time and money for the prosecution and the availability of evidence against the defendant. If a plea bargain is arranged, it will usually involve probation or some restitution to some known victims.

Professional theft is organized and requires skills developed through experience. Interpersonal skills, opportunity knowledge, flexibility, secrecy, and planning are necessary.

JOHN BOAL

### References and Further Reading

Abadinsky, H., *Organized Crime,* Wadsworth/Thomson Learning, Belmont, CA, 7th ed.,

Rosoff, S., Pontell, H. and Tillman, R., *Profit Without Honor: White Collar Crime and the Looting of America,* Prentice Hall, Upper Saddle River, NJ, 1998.

Title IX Organized Crime Control Act of 1970, *Federal Racketeer and Corrupt Organizations Act.*

Walker, K. and Schone, M., *Son of a Grifter,* Harper and Collins Publishers Inc., New York.

*See also* **Burglary as an Occupation; Larceny; Robbery as an Occupation**

# Thrasher, Frederic

Thrasher was born in Shelbyville, Indiana. He received his Bachelor of Arts from DePauw University in Indiana. He completed his Master of Arts in Sociology in 1917 and his Ph.D. degree also in Sociology in 1926 from the University of Chicago. In 1917, Frederic Thrasher started teaching as an instructor of sociology at Ohio State University. He became an assistant professor of sociology at the University of Chicago in 1919. Later, he moved to Illinois Wesleyan University in 1923 to take a professor position, where he promoted the establishment of the Department of Sociology, a separation from the Department of Economics and Sociology. Thrasher served as chair of the department at IWU for one year, until he accepted an assistant professor position at New York University in 1927. He was promoted to associate professor in 1930 and full professor in 1937 at NYU.

Today, Dr. Frederic Thrasher is remembered for his two major contributions. First, he is considered one of the pioneers in the establishment of sociology as a discipline in the U.S. From the 1920s through the 1940s, Thrasher conducted many research projects in the fields of applied sociology and educational sociology. Second, Thrasher is noted for his study on gangs in Chicago and subsequently for writing the book, *The Gang: A Study of 1,313 Gangs in Chicago* (1927). The publication was originally his doctoral dissertation completed in 1926. After Thrasher's death in 1962, the University of Chicago Press invited James F. Short to publish an abridged version of the study. The abridged edition, which was published in 1968, dropped two original chapters: Chapter VI, "The Movies and the Dime Novel" and Chapter X, "Wanderlust." In 2000, New Chicago School Press, in cooperation with the National Gang Research Center, published the original manuscript, which contains 23 chapters in four parts, 24 illustrations, 5 maps and diagrams, and 10 tables.

Thrasher originally showed his interest in youth socialization at the University of Chicago in his Master's thesis, entitled "The Boy Scout Movement As a Socializing Agency" (1918). In his thesis he described some basic conceptual ideas that were later developed into his dissertation in 1927. These included the gangs' negative influence and positive impact from adult supervised recreation on youth development and socialization. Between 1923 and 1926 Thrasher collected data on 1313 gangs (about 50,000 members) in Chicago through hanging-out and participant observations, mainly in the southern part of the city. He also obtained considerable information from 25 social agencies through secondary analyses of agency reports and personal interviews with agency officials, including Chicago Police Department, Municipal Court, and Crime Commission of the Association of Commerce, as he claimed in the author's preface.

The significance of his book can be mainly summarized in four ways, although many gang researchers regard the book as a necessary first text to read. Using the Dirty Dozen gang as an example, Thrasher offered in Chapter III his descriptive definition of a gang: spontaneous and unplanned origin, intimate face-to-face relations, and four types of behavioral patterns (circular, linear, combative, and dispersive movements). Further, he described a gang as an interstitial group with unreflective internal structure, esprit de corps, solidarity, morale, group awareness, and attachment to a local territory. In Chapter IV, Thrasher identified four types of gangs in Chicago: diffused, solidified, conventionalized, and criminal. Thrasher suggested that the gang may develop the features of a secret society—secrecy, initiation, ritual, passwords, codes, and so on. Thirdly, Thrasher created a "gang map" to detail the geographical distribution of the Chicago gangs. This research methodology has had a great impact on today's new technology: computerized crime mapping with GIS. Finally, Thrasher presented a very complex diagram, illustrating the stages in the natural history of the gang and its relations to other types of collective behavior. Dr. Frederic Thrasher died in March 1962 at the age of 70 after several years of hospitalization as a result of a traffic accident on February 5, 1959 when his bus collided with a truck.

JOHN Z. WANG

## Biography

Born in Shelbyville, Indiana, 21 February, 1892. Son of Milton B. Thrasher and Eve Dell (Lacy), Thrasher. Educated at DePauw University in Indiana, A.B., 1915; University of Chicago, M.A. in Sociology, 1917 and Ph.D. also in Sociology, 1926. Unmarried. Instructor in Sociology, Ohio State University, 1917–1918; Assistant Professor in Sociology, University of Chicago, 1918–1923; Professor in Sociology, Illinois Wesleyan University, 1923–1927; Chair of the Sociology Department, Illinois Wesleyan University, 1926–1927; Assistant Professor in Educational Sociology, New York University, 1927–1930; Associate Professor, NYU, 1930–1937; Professor, NYU, 1937–1962. Member of President Hoover's White House Conference on Child Health and Delinquency Prevention, 1929–1931; Chairman of the Council of Lower West Side Social Agencies, New York, 1933; Associate Editor of the Journal of Educational Sociology, 1945; Member of Attorney General's Conference on Delinquency prevention, 1946. Died in March, 1962.

## Selected Writings

The Boy Scout Movement as a Socializing Agency, Master's Thesis, University of Chicago, 1918.
The Gang as a Symptom of Community Disorganization, *Journal of Applied Sociology,* (XI) (1926)
The Gang: A Study of 1,313 Gangs in Chicago, Ph.D. Dissertation, University of Chicago, IL, 1926.
How to Study the Boy's Gang in the Open, *Journal of Educational Sociology (I)* 1928.
*The Gang: A Study of 1,313 Gangs in Chicago,* an abridged version by James F. Short, Jr., 1968.
*The Gang: A Study of 1,313 Gangs in Chicago,* an original version, 2000.

## References and Further Reading

Fletcher, C., Value or validity: A Review of Thrasher, *New Society,* 21, (1964).
Jensen, E.L., An interview with James F. Short, Jr., *The Gang Journal: An Interdisciplinary Research Quarterly,* 2(2), (1994–1995).
Knox, G., *An Introduction to Gangs,* 5th ed., New Chicago School Press, Inc., Chicago, IL, 2000.
*Who Was Who In America with World Notables* (p. 941), Vol. IV, 1961–1968.

*See also* **Gangs: Theories**

# Traffic Offenses

Traffic offenses are criminal activities because people are breaking a traffic law, but the public tends not to view most traffic offenses as crimes. Problematically, traffic offenses often contribute to road accidents with serious consequences. The National Highway Traffic Safety Administration (NHTSA, 2002) reports that 42,116 people died in traffic accidents in the U.S. in 2001. Similar problems exist in Great Britain; the Parliamentary Advisory Council for Traffic Safety (PACTS 1999) estimates there are 10 million road traffic offenses and 3600 deaths in Great Britain per year. Around 15,000 road deaths per year are speed related in the European Union (Corbett, 2000). The economic costs of traffic crashes are also very high— estimated at $230.6 billion in 2000 in the U.S. (NHTSA, 2002).

Road traffic laws have been around for more than 150 years and were designed to promote safe driving (PACTS, 1999). Traffic laws set down rules of position on how to drive on the road (lanes, passing), priority of who is to go first (intersections, stop-signs, lights, speed), and responsibility (obtaining and revocation of driver's license, age, drunk-driving).

Most traffic offenses do not lead to a traffic accident, but a strong majority of traffic accidents involve some traffic violation. Ross (1960–1961) reported that at least 88 of 100 vehicle accidents in 1958 involved some sort of violation. Contemporary statistics from the NHTSA show that the vast majority of vehicle fatalities involved some kind of traffic offense. A key point is that people studying vehicle fatalities refer to these as fatal crashes, not fatal accidents (Giacopassi and Forde, 2000).

The notion that traffic offenses are not crime is prevalent. Ross (1960–1961) wrote that public opinion is such that in most cases traffic offenses are not considered as "real" criminality. Michalowski (1977) comments that there is often public outrage about high rates of violent crime, yet, despite vehicle fatality rates much higher than violent crime fatalities, public responses have often gone against traffic safety measures such as seat belts, head restraints, and others. Corbett (2000) discusses how social harm from speeding is largely ignored because the public generally does not see a problem with exceeding the speed limit or driving too fast for driving conditions. Although seven in ten Americans support greater penalties for drunk-driving, there is less support for police use of sobriety checkpoints (NHTSA 2003). This difference is consistent with Jacobs' (1989) classic study of drunk-driving and the difficulties of deterring it.

The Japanese designed a separate prison for traffic offenders but criminalization only occurs for extreme traffic offenses involving death (Johnson, 1991). The Japanese experience goes counter to the NHTSA (2002) and PACTS (1999), which both suggest that bad driving offenses, especially those involving fatalities, are often not dealt with seriously in the courts and may signal to the public that bad driving is not a serious offense.

An early study by Tillman and Hobbs (1949) suggested that personality differences could distinguish between individuals with high and low accident rates. They interviewed 40 Canadian taxi drivers with a history of four or more accidents and compared them to one hundred taxi drivers with no accidents. They suggested that accident-prone drivers were marked by aggressiveness, impulsiveness, lack of thought for others, and lack of respect for authority. They concluded that "…a man drives as he lives. If his personal life is marked by caution, tolerance, foresight, and consideration for others then he will drive in the same manner."

Tillman and Hobbes (1949), Michalowski (1975), and many other researchers suggest that individuals involved in serious vehicular offenses tend to have other criminal histories. There also are several studies showing strong correlations between traffic offenses and criminal statistics (Junger et al., 2001; Keane et al., 1993). Of importance, the term "accident" in serious vehicle offenses obscures the fact that many accidents were risky, social, or violent acts.

Very few studies have attempted to document the extent of traffic offenses. One exception is Clarke's (1996) effort to establish the propensity for exceeding the speed limit. Using data from 1992 for Illinois, Clarke found a normal distribution around a mean of the speed limit of 65 miles per hour. Data for commercial truckers were similar although skewed toward nonconformity (speeding). The implication is that speeding is not particularly unusual because, in a normal distribution, half of the drivers exceed the posted limit.

Traffic offenses, bad driving, and rude behavior on roadways throughout the world are often ignored by police departments and unpunished by the local laws. Nonetheless, traffic violations are one of the most common forms of law enforcement activity. The familiar sight of drivers slowing as they spot a patrol car reflects the efficacy of traffic enforcement as a routine tool for enhancing traffic safety.

Technology such as cameras and radar may also be used to enforce traffic laws. It appears that cameras are an effective tool for reducing the number of vehicles that run red lights and speed. In fact, police departments that use these cameras have diverted staffing from traffic enforcement to anticrime initiatives. One implication in relying on technology, however, is that other traffic offenses may be ignored and bad driving simply increases as there are no longer traffic officers enforcing other traffic laws.

Police in many communities could enhance the quality of life by simply enforcing routine traffic laws. Despite the view by many in policing that traffic enforcement is not real policing because it doesn't deal with real crimes, the public often ranks lack of traffic regulation as a problem. In my own city of Memphis, speeding as a neighborhood issue was ranked as more of a problem than violent crime and gangs combined. Police traffic enforcement can easily control traffic disorderliness. Moreover, traffic enforcement can lead to significant crime prevention. Sherman, Shaw, and Rogan (1995) showed how routine traffic stops in high crime areas brought substantial gun seizures and a reduction in violent gun crimes. The existing literature shows that enforcement of traffic laws would lead to an increase in the quality of life with tangible benefits for traffic safety and a potential reduction in crime rates.

DAVID R. FORDE

### References and Further Reading

Clarke, R.V., The distribution of deviance and exceeding the speed limit, *British Journal of Criminology,* 36(2) (1996).

Corbett, C., The social construction of speeding as not 'Real' crime, *Crime Prevention and Community Safety,* 2(4) (2000).

Giacopassi, D. and Forde, D.R., Broken windows, crumpled fenders, and crime, *Journal of Criminal Justice,* 28(5) (2000).

Jacobs, J.B., *Drunk driving: An American Dilemma,* Chicago, IL, University of Chicago Press, 1989.

Johnson, E.H., Criminalization and traffic offenses: The Japanese experience, *Deviant Behavior,* 12(1) (1991).

Junger, M., West, R. and Timman, R., Crime and risky behavior in traffic: An example of cross-situational consistency, *Journal of Research in Crime and Delinquency,* 38(4) (2001).

Keane, C., Maxim, P.S. and Teavan, J.S., Drinking and driving, self-control, and gender: Testing a general theory of crime, *Journal of Research in Crime and Delinquency,* 30(1) (1993).

Michalowski, R.J., Violence on the road: The crime of vehicular homicide, *Journal of Research in Crime and Delinquency,* 12(1) (1975).

Michalowski, R.J., The social and criminal patterns of urban traffic fatalities, *British Journal of Criminology,* 17(2) (1977).

National Highway Traffic Safety Administration, *Traffic Safety Facts, 2001,* Washington, DC, U.S. Department of Transportation, 2002.

National Highway Traffic Safety Administration, *National Survey of Drinking and Driving Attitudes and Behaviors, 2001,* Washington, DC, U.S. Department of Transportation, 2003.

Parliamentary Advisory Council for Traffic Safety, Road Traffic Law and Enforcement, *A Driving Force for Casualty Reduction,* 1999. Available at: http://www.pacts.org.uk/lawenforce.htm.

Ross, H.L., Traffic law violation: A folk crime, *Social Problems,* 8(5) (1960–1961).

Sherman, L., Shaw, J. and Rogan, D., The Kansas City gun experiment, *Research in Brief,* Washington, DC, National Institute of Justice, 1995.

Tillman, W.A. and Hobbs, G.E., The accident-prone automobile driver, *American Journal of Psychiatry,* 106(5) (1949).

*See also* **Driving Under the Influence (DUI)**

# Transnational Crime *See* **International Crime Statistics**

# Trespass

A general definition of trespass is "an unlawful intrusion that interferes with one's person or property" (*West's Encyclopedia,* 1998, 137). The Federal Bureau of Investigation defines trespass as "to unlawfully enter land, a dwelling, or other real property" (www.fbi.gov). At one time in history, trespassing was considered a fairly major crime, many times punishable by fines or jail time. Currently, in most state jurisdictions, trespassing is considered a misdemeanor, that of a minor crime (*West's Encyclopedia*, 1998; *The Guide to American Law*, 1984).

In early English common law, trespassing on property, particularly that of the king, could be considered a criminal matter. It was only later in the 14th century that land owners could sue the trespasser for civil damages. In the early 13th century in England, under common law, the king considered trespassing a breach of his peace and would summon the trespassers to appear in court. This summons was a writ that the king would use to notify the defendant of the charges against them and to appear before the king to face the charges. Often times the wrongdoer was fined, but many had no money and were sent to jail instead. It was in the later part of the 14th century that the money collected from the fines was given to the land owners as a method of repayment for any damages caused by the trespasser (*West's Encyclopedia*, 1998; *The Guide to American Law*, 1984).

Today, trespassing is generally used as an "intentional and wrongful invasion of another's real property" (*The Guide to American Law*, 1984, 148). In many jurisdictions, the crime of trespass still has many of the common law elements that originally were used in early England. This said, many laws are very confusing as to who can legally enter privately owned land (postal workers) and who may not.

The *Model Penal Code* defines the law of criminal trespass (also known as unwanted intrusion) and divides this up into the trespassing of buildings and the defiant trespasser. According to the *Model Penal Code*, trespassing can "be punished as a misdemeanor, petty misdemeanor or violation" (88). (For further reading see the *Model Penal Code* §221.2.)

Trespassing later was divided into subcategories. A person could be charged with trespassing onto land or trespassing possessions. Trespassing onto land also includes buildings or structures on the land and is a more common crime than possessions. Often times, trespassing on land is done so without any damage, yet the rightful owner of the land may sue the trespasser in civil court. Only if damage of the property or violence was used can the trespassing be considered a criminal matter. Many times people trespass without even realizing that they are doing so. An example of accidental trespass is when a hunter unknowingly hunts on privately owned land where the owners may have not posted signs defining their property. Those who do trespass onto land or into buildings generally do so to commit more serious crimes such as burglary or homicide. Protecting one's land is a right granted to land owners. The owner has the right to dismiss or exclude any wrongful intruder. Trespassing to retain possession is another illegal subcategory of trespassing.

Many times force is used in order to try and regain possession of property or land (*The Guide to American Law*, 1984; *West's Encyclopedia*, 1998). Each state and local jurisdiction varies on its definitions of trespass. Often the person who trespasses may have done so without any criminal intent and the land owner can fine the trespasser. In other jurisdictions it must be proved in court that a warning was given to the trespasser to leave the land before any charge of trespassing can be filed. In regards to criminal trespass, often this is done when the defendant enters a dwelling or building and stays there with the intent to commit a crime such as burglary. In this case, the punishment of trespassing can go beyond fines and result in incarceration (*West's Encyclopedia*, 1998).

In the U.S. Supreme Court case *United Zinc & Chemical Company v. Britt et al.*, 258 U.S. 268 (1922), the justices had to decide if the owners of the poisonous pond were held liable for the deaths of two children even though the owners had no signs or fences prohibiting people from entering the pond at the chemical plant. The justices said "Infants have no greater right to go upon other people's lands than adults; and the mere fact that they are infants imposes no duty upon landowners to expect them, and to prepare for their safety. There can be no general duty on the part of a land owner to keep his land safe for children, or even free from hidden dangers, if he has not, directly or by implication, invited or licensed them to come there" (*United Zinc v. Britt*, 1922). This Supreme Court case shows that trespassing can be dangerous to both the land owner and the trespasser, yet the land owner is entitled to the rights of owning that land.

Because the crime of trespass is generally a misdemeanor, crime statistics, such as the Federal Bureau of Investigation's Uniform Crime Report, do not report or collect statistics on trespassing. Trespassing is also a crime that many times goes unreported to the police by the land owners. Often times trespassing results in a civil matter and the offender may pay a fine to the land owner. This said, trespassing statistics are difficult to record and report because it is just a minor crime. Many times the trespasser goes on to commit a more serious crime and is charged with the greater crime.

CYNTHIA G. ADAMS

## References and Further Reading

American Law Institute (1980). Criminal Trespass, *The Model Penal Code and Commentaries: Part II*. §220.1 to 230.5, Philadelphia, PA.

Trespass, *The Guide to American Law: Everyone's Legal Encyclopedia* (1984). Vol. 10, pp. 147–152, St. Paul, MN, West Publishing Company.

Trespass, *West's Encyclopedia of American Law* (1998). Vol. 10, pp. 137–140, St. Paul, MN, West Group.

# Trial, The Right to

From a modern defendant's perspective, standing trial on criminal charges is no doubt nerve-wracking. Yet in comparison to the methods historically used to ascertain the guilt or innocence of an individual accused of a crime, the modern trial process is actually a vast improvement. In ancient Rome, citizens were sometimes called upon to decide questions of culpability, but the details of this ancient forerunner of the practice of trial by jury remain murky. These origins become clearer when we look at England around the time of the Norman Conquest in the 11th century. Until then, trial by ordeal was conducted to determine guilt or innocence for a crime, or to settle civil disputes between individuals. This meant that a person accused of a wrongdoing could be subjected to a physical ordeal as a test of his or her culpability.

Historical accounts of the ordeals that unfortunate defendants were forced to undergo included having a hot iron placed on the tongue or the hands. If the accused person was burned by the hot metal, this was considered evidence of guilt; but if the metal did not leave a lasting wound, this was taken as evidence of innocence. A related method of ascertaining guilt or innocence was to pour scalding water on part of the defendant's body and then bandage the wounds. After a few days, the wounds were checked for signs of infection, which, if present, were taken as evidence of guilt. Puritan settlers in America subjected suspected "witches" to "the water test"; the person was bound with rope and thrown into the water to see if he or she would float, whereby floating would be taken as a sign of innocence.

Why were defendants subjected to such traumas? Although the notion of "trial by ordeal" seems bizarre today, the practice reflected the assumption that accused people who were innocent would be saved by divine intervention from God. Thus, the practice reflected the religious beliefs of the time and place. In some instances, disputes between men were settled through "trial by battle," where the notion that "might makes right" was quite literally the case. The defendant and his opponent (or someone hired to fight in place of one of the disputants) would fight in a formal duel, with the accused considered innocent if he won the fight.

As Europe emerged from the early medieval period, less lethal forms of trial began to replace trial by ordeal and trial by battle. In England, gradually it became more common to respond to disputes by calling "compurgators," the term for witnesses who presented opinions about the defendant's character and sometimes their guilt or innocence. The church began to frown on trial by ordeal and eventually refused to sanction it, thus removing the stamp of religious approval that had long existed.

The practice of using citizens to pass judgment on the culpability of a person accused of wrongdoing—in essence, trial by jury—thus gradually become more prevalent. In 1215, the Magna Carta, which included the provision for trial by jury, was signed (Levine, 1992). However, these precedents for our current trial by jury system were very different in terms of how participants were selected and how the procedure was conducted.

These examples illustrate the fact that the practice of trial by jury has evolved over hundreds of years to its current form, wherein a group of citizens sworn as jurors observes evidence presented at trial and then collectively decides on the culpability for a crime or civil offense of the accused. When the colonists came to America, they imported the concept of trial by jury as part of their English legal heritage. At this point in history, however, America was still a colony of the British crown, and thus the jury selection and trial procedures were conducted in a manner that favored the crown. When a colonist was accused and tried, the jurors were generally chosen by the king's officials. Not surprisingly, these officials usually chose folks partial to the crown's interests, so impartial justice was an elusive quality in the eyes of independence-minded colonists.

Yet the colonists could see the potential for the jury trial to be a bulwark against oppression by the government, if the jury was chosen such that either the jurors were impartial or juries consisted of even numbers of those partial to the prosecution and those partial to the defense, so that there would be a "balancing of biases" (Abramson, 1994). A notable example of the jury's potential in this regard was the 1735 trial of John Peter Zenger, a publisher who was accused of printing seditious material. At trial, the jurors returned an acquittal despite the fact that it was clear that Zenger had violated the law.

After the American Revolution, the framers of the Constitution considered trial by a jury of peers to be of such importance that Article III, Section Two of the

Constitution provides the right to trial by jury for all crimes except impeachment, and the Seventh Amendment (1791) grants this right in civil cases involving 20 dollars or more. The Sixth Amendment (1791) provides the right to be tried by an impartial jury, meaning a fair and unbiased one.

These Constitutional provisions for trials by jury were originally construed by the U.S. Supreme Court as applicable only in federal trials. In *Palko v. Connecticut* (302 U.S. 319, 1937), the justices reasoned that, unlike some of the other protections in the Bill of Rights, trial by jury was not a "fundamental" right, and thus was not applicable to the states through the Fourteenth Amendment's due process clause. This meant that whereas federal defendants were constitutionally entitled to trial by jury, defendants charged in state court were not. Because the vast majority of criminal charges were brought under state statutes, this meant that relatively few defendants were guaranteed the right to a jury trial. States could, however, voluntarily choose to provide jury trials to criminal defendants, and many states did.

In *Duncan v. Louisiana* (391 U.S. 145, 1968), the Court reversed its position, ruling that trial by jury in criminal cases is a fundamental right applicable to the states. The justices' reasoning in *Duncan* emphasized the importance of jury trials as part of due process and as a significant aspect of participatory democracy. In subsequent cases, the Court clarified the scope of the right to trial by jury, finding it applicable in any case involving a minimum possible sentence of six months' incarceration. However, in *Lewis v. U.S.* (518 U.S. 322, 1996) the Supreme Court ruled that defendants convicted of multiple petty offenses with a combined penalty of more than six months of incarceration are not entitled to a jury trial. In civil cases, states have discretion about whether to provide jury trials, because the provisions of the Seventh Amendment have not been applied to the states.

The right to trial is a key element of the American legal system for several reasons. It is exercised by defendants in only a small percentage of criminal cases (roughly 5%), with most cases handled through plea bargaining. However, the possibility of trial is the background against which critical legal decisions are made, such as the prosecutor's decision on whether to prosecute a case, and if so, what charges to file. The importance of the right to trial is also illustrated during the process of plea bargaining, which involves both parties considering their options in light of their perceptions of what would occur should the case go to trial. The prosecution and defense must both consider how the case would play at trial: What are the weaknesses that might be exposed in the case? How would a jury perceive the case? What are the possible consequences of losing at trial, compared to settling the case? Thus, despite their relative rarity, the prospect of trial plays a central role in the American legal process. Whereas countries such as Canada and England also try criminal cases before juries, this is not the norm in most countries. However, criminal juries have become somewhat more common in many countries in recent years (Vidmar, 1999).

The right to be tried by a jury is a critical part of the due process protections of the accused. Supreme Court rulings affirm the importance of trial by jury as a protection against government oppression of the defendant, or as a buffer between the power of the state embodied in the office of the prosecutor and the rights of the accused. Most defendants who exercise the right to trial choose to be tried before a jury, but in some circumstances a defendant may opt to be tried before the judge alone in a "bench trial."

Trial by jury also provides opportunities for direct citizen participation in the democratic process through serving as a juror.

Many people find it surprising that despite the status of the trial by jury as one of our most important constitutional rights, minors whose cases are adjudicated in juvenile court do not have the right to a jury trial. Because juvenile court proceedings are not considered adversarial (in contrast to adult courts) but instead supposedly consider the best interests of youth, the U.S. Supreme Court has held that jury trials are not required (*In re Gault*, 387 U.S. 1, 1967). This means that although individual states are free to provide jury trials as part of juvenile court proceedings, they are not constitutionally required to do so.

The application of the right to trial to the states in *Duncan* raised questions for the courts regarding the precise nature and scope of this right. You have the right to trial by a jury of your peers. But how are "peers" defined, and how should they be selected? Does the right to trial mean the right to be tried by a jury of 12, or can juries have fewer people? Must the jury be unanimous, or is a majority verdict acceptable?

Historically, juries were composed of 12 people who were required to reach a unanimous verdict. However, as the U.S. Supreme Court has noted, there is no legal requirement supporting these historical traditions. Therefore, it is constitutionally permissible to have juries composed of as few as six people (*Williams v. Florida,* 399 U.S. 78, 1970), although not five (*Ballew v. Georgia,* 435 U.S. 223, 1978). Must the jury's decision be unanimous, according to the U.S. Constitution? That depends upon several factors, including the size of the jury, whether it is a criminal or civil trial, and whether the case is a federal or state matter. In 1972, two U.S. Supreme

Court cases (*Apodaca v. Oregon,* 406 U.S. 404, 1972 and *Johnson v. Louisiana,* 406 U.S. 356, 1972) established the constitutionality of majority verdicts in state criminal trials. However, *Williams* allowed six-person juries in state criminal cases subject to the requirement of a unanimous verdict. States can also use majority decision rules in civil cases. However, federal criminal and civil cases still require a unanimous verdict. Despite the rulings in *Apodaca* and *Johnson,* almost all states continue to require unanimous verdicts in state criminal cases, reserving the use of majority verdicts for civil cases.

Although the idealized image of a trial is that it is a legal process designed to uncover the truth of a disputed matter, a trial can also be conceptualized as a forum where differing interpretations of events are offered by each side, and jurors sift and sort and select the version of events which seems most plausible. The resulting verdict, thus, may be said to reflect a particular subjective construction of "truth" that serves as a formal mechanism for assigning culpability to one party or the other. In this sense the true purpose of a jury trial may be to provide a means for the presentation of competing versions of events, and to provide a practical and symbolic mechanism for pronouncing that justice has been served.

DIANA GRANT

### References and Further Reading

Abramson, J., *We, The Jury,* New York, Basic Books, 1994.
Finkel, N.J., *Commonsense Justice: Jurors' Notions of the Law,* Cambridge, MA, Harvard University Press, 1995.
Kalven, H., Jr. and Zeisel, H., *The American Jury,* Chicago, IL, University of Chicago Press, 1970.
Levine, J.P., *Juries and Politics,* Belmont, CA, Wadsworth, 1992.
Litan, R.E., Ed., *Verdict: Assessing the Civil Jury System,* Washington, DC, The Brookings Institution, 1993.
Vidmar, N., Ed., The common law jury, *Law and Contemporary Problems,* 62(2), 1999.

*See also* **Due Process; Juries and Juror Selection**

# Trials, Criminal

## Introduction

A criminal trial is a fact-finding proceeding that determines the guilt or innocence of an individual, the defendant, who has been charged with a crime but has not pled guilty. The trial has roots in antiquity: Forerunners to the jury system have been noted in ancient Egypt and Rome. During Henry II's reign (1154–1189), criminal trials used ordeals as primitive fact-finding devices, wherein an individual's guilt could be determined by the adverse effects suffered during a painful task, such as carrying a hot iron rod for a short distance. The modern form of criminal trial emerged over centuries through a series of innovations in English law. Henry II developed a system of common law wherein the law was developed by judges based on precedent. A primitive jury system also developed during Henry's reign, and the right to jury trial was later extended to all English citizens by the Magna Carta (1215).

By the mid-19th century, the trial system had assumed its modern form as a formalized, adversarial, and technocratic fact-finding procedure, given sanctioning power by law and governed by common law, statutes, constitutions, and complex evidentiary rules. The fact-finder may be either a judge or a jury.

## The Parties

A criminal trial is an adversarial procedure with two diametrically opposed sides, both seeking to win a favorable outcome in what is generally a zero-sum game. The prosecution, which may be represented by a prosecuting attorney, a police officer, or even a layperson, attempts to establish a defendant's guilt in order to invoke the formal sanctioning power of the criminal law that include fines, restrictions on liberty, or even death. Under the Fifth Amendment, the prosecution has the burden of proof to establish the defendant's guilt beyond a reasonable doubt. A reasonable doubt has been judicially defined as a doubt which would cause a reasonable person to hesitate to act (*Victor v. Nebraska,* 511 U.S. 1 (1994)). The defendant, by contrast, is facing the sanctioning power of the court. He or she may appear *pro se* (without representation) or represented by an attorney. In the American system, a defendant cannot be compelled to testify, need present no evidence, and has no burden of proof. By contrast, in the English system, a defendant has no right against self-incrimination and may be forced to testify.

Ethical behavior in courtrooms has become increasingly important because of poor public perceptions of the court system (see, e.g., Veilleux, 2000). All attorneys are ethically mandated to behave with decorum and candor toward the tribunal (Model Rules of Professional Conduct, Rule 3.3 2003). But the prosecution and defense have additional, differing ethical standards governing their courtroom behavior. Prosecutors are not simply advocates but are ministers of justice, with a special responsibility to ensure that justice is done in any case. By contrast, defense attorneys, while putatively officers of the court, are ethically mandated to be zealous advocates that pursue all available avenues of defense (Code of Professional Responsibility, 1969; Morgan and Rotunda, 1999). As zealous advocates, defense attorneys may occasionally resort to extreme tactics in cross-examination or evidence presentation and may frequently advocate for the expansion and modification of existing laws. In their efforts to secure a fair trial for their clients, defense attorneys perform a potentially corrective function that safeguards fundamental liberties. However, some commentators have argued that the unrestrained influence of zealous advocacy may damage the integrity of the criminal court system (Shutt, 2002; see also Elkins, 1992; Pizzi, 1999). In the English system, by contrast, a defense attorney's court officer status takes precedence over zealous advocacy.

The modern trial is highly technocratized. In serious cases, the prosecution and defense are represented by professional trial advocates. These licensed attorneys generally have graduate degrees from professional schools, have passed a strenuous professional licensing examination, have various degrees of courtroom experience, and regularly engage in mandatory professional education. Trial attorneys generally need a working knowledge of complex statutes, common law, and court rules of evidence.

The complexities of the modern trial place a premium on expert guidance for defendants. In most modern criminal trials, the defendant has a right to legal representation, which is guaranteed by the Sixth Amendment. Prior to 1963, however, the Sixth Amendment was interpreted as merely establishing a right to have an attorney present if the defendant could afford such representation; courts were not required to provide representation for indigent defendants. In *Gideon v. Wainwright*, 372 U.S. 335 (1963), the Supreme Court ruled that a court must appoint counsel to represent indigent defendants charged with felonies. Following *Gideon*, the appointed counsel right was gradually expanded, through *Duncan v. Louisiana*, 391 U.S. 145 (1968), and *Argersinger v. Hamlin*, 407 U.S. 25 (1972), to the present American rule, from *Scott v. Illinois*, 440 U.S. 367 (1979): A defendant has a constitutional right to appointed counsel in cases in which a court makes a pretrial determination that there is a likelihood that the defendant will receive jail time upon conviction. This right to counsel may be waived, although the defendant does not have an absolute waiver right: The court may determine that the defendant is unable to competently represent himself and order representation.

The judge is, in principle, a neutral, unbiased party who referees the prosecution and defense and has ultimate authority to decide how the law is applied. The fairness of the proceeding depends heavily on the judge, whose responsibilities are largely technocratized: The judge has a legally prescribed method for interacting with jurors; his rulings must follow statutes, court rules, and the common law; and his jury charges must follow established legal patterns. The judge is the gatekeeper for evidence presented to the fact-finder. The gate-keeping function is complexly performed, subject to innumerable rules and common law interpretations. Generally, the judge admits relevant evidence, which tends to prove the truth or falsity of the matter at issue, while disallowing evidence that is either irrelevant, unduly inflammatory, or more prejudicial than probative (see, e.g., Federal Rules of Evidence, Rule 803 2003). Like an anachronistic king, the judge has coercive authority over all proceedings, with contempt powers to jail or fine. The judge's power is buttressed by police officers and bailiffs present in the courtroom.

In fairly trying the case, the judge is assisted by a support staff. Higher-court judges typically have a law clerk, who researches case law and handles a judge's calendar. Whenever court is in session, a court reporter records all statements and exhibits made during the course of the trial, thus creating a record that can be reviewed by appellate courts to ensure the integrity and proper working of the court system. (In lesser courts, the court reporter's function is often handled by a mere recording device.) Most jurisdictions also have a clerk of court, who handles the administrative paperwork of trials.

Both the prosecution and the defense strategically tailor their presentations to appeal to the fact-finder in the case, which may be either a judge or a jury. The fact-finder's role is to hear the facts and render a decision based on the admissible evidence presented in the courtroom. The fact-finder delivers a zero-sum verdict of guilty or not guilty.

## Pretrial Processes

After a defendant's arrest and the issuance of charging instruments such as indictments and warrants, the prosecution and defense must typically engage in discovery, a mandatory information-sharing process governed by court rules (see, e.g., Federal Rules of Criminal Procedure, Rule 5 2002). Upon defense motion, the prosecution delivers most of its evidence to the defense, including warrants, incident reports, police records, rap sheets, and copies of items to be placed in evidence. The defense must also be permitted to inspect evidence that the prosecution intends to submit at trial. As ministers of justice, the prosecution has a continuing constitutional duty, under *Brady v. Maryland*, 373 U.S. 83 (1963), to turn over any potentially exculpatory evidence to the defense. Upon filing a discovery motion, most jurisdictions impose a reciprocal duty on defense counsel to provide copies of written statements and tangible evidence to be submitted in the defense's case in chief, upon prosecution motion.

Prior to trial, both sides engage in pretrial preparation that may include interviews, investigations, evidence reviews and preparation, strategy formulation, formulation of direct and cross-examination questions, and the hiring of experts. The amount of pretrial preparation depends largely on the seriousness of the case and the availability of time and resources. Highly compensated private attorneys may devote considerable time and expense to preparing a defense, whereas prosecutors and public defenders with large caseloads may have comparatively little time to devote to particular cases.

Prior to most trials, the prosecution and defense attempt settlement negotiations. The vast majority of cases are settled prior to trial through a plea bargain, a contractual arrangement in which the defendant accepts responsibility for a particular offense in exchange for some consideration, such as a reduced charge or a sentencing recommendation.

The Constitution's Sixth Amendment entitles a defendant to a fair and impartial trial by a jury of the defendant's peers. However, a defendant may waive his or her right to trial by jury and undergo a bench trial, in which a judge is the fact-finder. Such trials frequently occur in magistrate courts and are characterized by brevity, relatively informal evidence presentations, and relaxed admissibility rules. Typically, the prosecution is a police officer who witnessed the case and tells the judge, under oath, what he or she saw. The defense likewise tells its version of events under oath. The judge makes a summary decision, often with no deliberation, and, upon a conviction, sentences the defendant on the spot.

Juvenile trials are conducted in juvenile court, with the judge as the exclusive trier of fact. Although the goal of juvenile court is the best interest of the child, modern American jurisprudence demands many of the same constitutional protections afforded adults, such as the right to counsel, the right against self-incrimination, the right not to present evidence, and the requirement of proof beyond a reasonable doubt.

## The Jury Selection Process

In most trials involving serious cases, defendants exercise their right to have jurors as fact-finders. A complex common-law system has developed interpreting this constitutional right through the stages of jury selection, presentation of evidence, and jury charging. Courts have repeatedly found a fair jury selection process to be essential to a fair trial (see, e.g., *Batson v. Kentucky*, 476 U.S. 79 (1986)). Jury panels, commonly called the *jury venire*, are generally drawn from public-record sources, such as voter registration rolls, property tax records, and driving records. Jury service is mandatory in that failure to serve may lead to criminal sanctions. To serve, jurors must meet basic eligibility requirements: Typically, jurors must be citizens, residents of the jurisdiction, be able to read and write, and lack a serious criminal record.

Through a pretrial screening process called *voir dire*, the judge, prosecution, and defense may question individual jurors to determine whether they can be fair and impartial. In an attempt to ensure a meaningful right to a fair trial, courts generally exclude potential jurors with prior knowledge of the facts of the case; a serious bias regarding aspects of the case; or a strong relationship to the prosecution, the defense, or any potential witnesses. When pretrial publicity is extensive and juror ignorance is impossible, courts typically take prophylactic measures by allowing extensive *voir dire* questioning and even transferring jurisdiction.

After *voir dire*, members of the remaining *jury venire* are randomly chosen and presented before the prosecution and the defense. For serious cases, laws generally require 12-member juries, though lesser courts frequently have 6-member juries. Juror members are selected for presentation until the prescribed number of jurors is met. Each side has a fixed number of peremptory strikes that may be used to bar individual jurors. Originally, such strikes could be used for any reason or no reason at all; however, the absence of restraint led to procedural abuses, such as the blanket elimination of African-American jurors. In *Batson v. Kentucky*, 476 U.S. 79 (1986) and an ensuing line of cases, the U.S. Supreme Court placed restraints on the use of peremptory strikes: Neither the prosecution nor the defense may use peremptory strikes to eliminate members of constitutionally protected classes, such as race or gender. Any peremptory strike must have a facially neutral justification.

## The Fact-finding Process

Trials begin once a full jury has been empaneled, or once a defendant has waived his or her right to a jury trial. Trials use a number of technologies to ensure fairness and the perception of fairness. Except in juvenile trials, the courtroom is generally open to the public, who remain behind the bar, a barrier in front of which the trial participants play their respective roles. Courtroom settings are strategically organized to isolate the relative players: The judge is centrally seated in the courtroom, typically on a raised bench, and prosecution and defense are typically confined to their tables until given permission to approach the bench, jurors, or witnesses. Jurors are deliberately isolated from parties and spectators: In court, they are confined to a box, and, outside of the courtroom, restricted to a jury room. As a protective measure, juror communication with nonjurors is explicitly restricted. A juror may not discuss the facts of the case with any nonjuror, nor may a juror privately contact any parties to the case.

Typically, jury trials begin with opening statements directed to the jury by the judge, prosecution, and defense. The judge technocratically instructs the jury on the law and the courtroom procedures, following an established language. The judge tells the jury the nature of their role as fact-finder, reads the charging instrument, and instructs them as to the legal standards of burden of proof and proof beyond a reasonable doubt. The jury is instructed to refrain from deciding on a verdict until after all the evidence has been heard. Additionally, the jury is told that guilt may only be established based on facts in evidence. The prosecution and defense then follow with opening statements calculated to provide strategic advantage to their respective sides. Such statements typically include basic themes, outlines of anticipated facts, and summaries of relevant law.

Following opening statements, the prosecution begins presentation of its case in chief. The prosecution individually calls witnesses, who are given an oath to tell the truth. The truth-telling function of the oath is reinforced by criminal sanctions: Lying to a tribunal, if proven, subjects the liar not merely to contempt powers but perjury laws.

Argument and evidence presentation is tightly controlled by laws that are invoked by either party through the form of objections. Violation of evidentiary laws may lead to the exclusion of evidence, curative instructions to the jury, or, in extreme cases, the declaration of a mistrial. A mistrial indicates that the proceeding has concluded without reaching a verdict, either because of an error in the proceeding or party misconduct. Typically, if a mistrial is declared, the prosecution could reinitiate the case before a different jury; however, if a mistrial is declared, judges may occasionally find that the prosecution has failed in its one chance to try the defendant and that, to try the defendant again, would result in double jeopardy, a violation of the Fifth Amendment.

After presenting its case in chief, the prosecution rests, at which time the defense typically moves for a directed verdict. Such motions are rarely granted, however, in that most any evidence creating a reasonable inference of guilt is sufficient to create a jury question.

The defense may then present its case. In most jurisdictions, if the defense does not offer any evidence, then the defense has the tactical advantage of giving the final closing argument.

After the conclusion of the prosecution and defense cases, the prosecution and defense deliver summary arguments. Generally lengthier than opening statements, these summations represent the advocates' synthesis of all the evidence, inferences therefrom, and relevant law. In some jurisdictions, the prosecution may give a closing argument and follow with a rebuttal to the defense's closing argument.

After closing statements, the judge instructs the jury on the law, again using carefully created, technocratized language, approved by court rule, statute, and precedent. Jury instructions are extremely technical and precise, providing the jury with statutory and/or common-law definitions of the crime, relevant legal standards, and concrete instructions on when deliberation is to begin and how verdict forms should be filled out. Upon completion of the jury instructions, the jury is placed in the jury room, an isolated area wherein they receive all exhibits and evidence and begin deliberations.

Deliberations are indefinite and may, in principle, last forever. In most jurisdictions, any jury decision must be unanimous, that is, all jurors must agree either on guilty or on not guilty. Should jurors not agree, the judge may declare a mistrial that ends the trial but allows the prosecution the option of reinitiating a case. Alternatively, the judge may address the jurors using a technocratically drafted "dynamite" charge, which is calculated to break the impasse: The judge typically tells the jurors that they should consider carefully the views of others, the case must be resolved at some point, and the case may simply be retried. If a verdict is still not reached, the judge will declare a mistrial.

## Posttrial Processes

Should the defendant be found not guilty, the charge is dismissed with prejudice, and the defendant may never be tried on that charge again, pursuant to the

Fifth Amendment's ban on double jeopardy. Upon a felony conviction, however, the vast majority of jurisdictions have the jury sentence the offender. Whether judge or jury, the sentencer must follow the sentencing range established by the legal authority. In the vast majority of state jurisdictions, the sentencer may sentence the offender to any sentence within range. However, in federal jurisdictions, and in a small number of state jurisdictions, the judge's sentencing discretion is confined by technocratically administered sentencing guidelines.

Consistent with the technocratization of the trial process, procedural errors may be appealed in several ways. The defense may directly appeal any erroneous rulings to which the defense had made a contemporaneous objection. However, any error not objected to is not preserved for appellate review. Should the defendant lose the appeal, there is a secondary appellate avenue available to the defendant, however: The defendant may allege ineffective assistance of counsel, arguing that defense counsel's performance fell below an objective standard of competent representation. By contrast, the prosecution can only appeal any adverse ruling in an extremely limited number of ways, such as the granting of a directed verdict motion. In few circumstances is a "not guilty" verdict appealable.

J. EAGLE SHUTT

### References and Further Reading

*Code of Professional Responsibility,* 1969. American Bar Association.
Elkins, J.R., 1992. The moral labyrinth of zealous advocacy, *Capital Law Review,* 20, 735–796.
*Federal Rules of Criminal Procedure,* 2002. National Institute of Trial Advocacy, Notre Dame, IN, NITA.
*Federal Rules of Evidence 2003–2004,* 2003. New York, West.
*Model Rules of Professional Conduct,* 2004. American Bar Association. Available at: http://www.abanet.org/cpr/mrpc/mrpc_home.html. Retrieved on January 5, 2004.
Morgan, T.D. and Rotunda, R., 1999. *Professional Responsibility,* 7th ed., New York, Foundation Press.
Pizzi, W.T., 1999. *Trials without Truth,* New York, New York University Press.
Shutt, J.E., 2002. From the field: On criminal defense, zealous advocacy, and expanded ethics dialogue, *Journal of Crime and Justice,* 25(2).
Veilleux, R., 2000. Criminal justice poll shows distrust of America's legal system, Available at: http://www.news.uconn.edu/REL00069.htm. Retrieved on January 1, 2004.

*See also* **Criminal Courts; Defense Attorneys; Prosecuting Attorneys; Trial, The Right to**

# Trials, Political

Scholars who have considered the question have not agreed on a single, concise definition of a political trial. In political theorist Otto Kirchheimer's influential view, political trials are trials in which the courts, by some prearranged plan, eliminate a political foe of those in power.

Expanding on this view, one leading scholarly commentator on political trials, Theodore L. Becker, distinguishes such trials—criminal trials, specifically—from other trials as involving defendants who pose a direct threat to established political power. In his view, there are four categories of such trials: trials in which the nature of the crime is political, but the trial process is fair; trials in which the process is unfair and the outcome (conviction) predetermined, albeit with a high risk of reversal on appeal; trials involving selective prosecution or disparate treatment based on political affiliation; and trials combining the second and third categories—the charges are political in nature and the trial process is unfair. As noted by political scientist Michal R. Belknap, however, Becker omits criminal trials in which the law was broken to make political point, as is the case when acts of civil disobedience are prosecuted. Belknap's broad definition of political trial includes any trial that affects the structure, personnel, or policies of government, that is the result of or has its outcome determined by political controversy, or that results from the efforts of ruling elites to use the courts to disadvantage their opponents.

More recently, political scientist Ron Christenson describes four potentially overlapping categories of political trials: trials of public corruption (prosecutions of public office holders for malfeasance in office); trials of dissenters (prosecution of opponents of a government or its policies), trials of nationalists (prosecution designed to assert domination over an ethnic or other subgroup in a society), and trials of regimes (prosecution of government officials in which the legitimacy of their rule is called into question). Christenson also distinguishes between partisan or fraudulent trials, which he defines as exercises in power totally outside the law, and trials in which there is both a legal and a political agenda, and thus take place within the law. Insofar as they fall in this latter category, Christenson concluded that political trials make a positive contribution to an open and democratic society.

The initial question in defining a political trial is determining the purpose underlying the definition. What is the critical inquiry underlying consideration of political trials? The inquiry might be intended to distinguish legitimate from illegitimate proceedings, or fair from unfair results, or justice from injustice, but in that case the criteria for defining any of those categories should be explicit. A trial in a nonadversarial, inquisitorial system, for example, might correctly be labeled "political" not in a pejorative sense, but in the sense that by the trial's own standards, the process is legitimate. Judged from the perspective of a noninquisitorial, adversarial system, however, the process is likely to be categorized illegitimate and unjust. On the other hand, if one of the purposes of adversarial justice systems with independent prosecutorial and judicial branches in open, democratic states is to eliminate political trials, then to label a trial "political" in such a system is indeed pejorative. Consideration of political trials in that context involves assessment of the potentially complex and covert ways in which the purpose of the system is politically subverted.

Any inquiry into political trials touches on two fundamental but potentially irreconcilable purposes of trials. First, trials are viewed as truth determining processes. Much of the design of modern trials is intended, at least in theory, to facilitate this process. Second, trials are ritualized exercises in the maintenance of social order and control.

One critical feature of many, if not all, political criminal trials is that the accused rejects the role the trial process assigns, but instead attempts to redefine the trial's truth-determining goal in a way contrary to that of the prosecution. Thus, for example, an antiwar demonstrator who is prosecuted for breaking the law in an act of civil disobedience asserts that his act was justified because it was in opposition to a greater harm, an illegal war. Now, the court must determine not merely whether he committed the act he is charged with committing; it also faces the question of the legality of the war and whether the act of the accused was justified in its opposition. If the court declines to address these issues and prohibits the accused from raising them in defense, then it faces the objection that the purpose of the trial is merely to maintain social control, not to determine the truth.

The concept of political trials, as distinguished from other, presumably "non-political" trials, poses the risk that what Max Weber called the "myth of legitimacy" will be implicitly reinforced. Viewed this way, because political trials are the rare exception, not the rule, they imply that trials are generally apolitical, neutral, and without bias. However, empirical studies, as described by political scientist Lawrence Baum, for example, demonstrate that ideological or political attitudes do account for judicial behavior. We rarely know, however, whether the outcome in a political trial is determined by a direct command from the authorities in power, the result of the decision-maker's own preexisting attitudes, or the decision-maker's own inference of what is expected by the authorities in power.

Because of the emphasis on the political nature of the trial process, much of the scholarship in this area overlooks the problem of prosecutorial misconduct that results in conviction through a guilty plea, not a trial. In such cases, the accused pleads guilty and accepts a lesser but nevertheless severe jail sentence to avoid the risk of execution or a lengthier jail term that would result from conviction at trial. Prosecutorial misconduct in such cases involves over-charging (bringing charges against the accused that are not adequately supported by the evidence, or based on illegally acquired evidence, but yet pose risk of conviction at trial, particularly for a defendant who has politically unpopular beliefs or affiliations), prejudicial pretrial publicity, and coercive use of the plea bargaining process. The 2002 prosecution of the so-called "American Taliban," 21-year-old John Walker Lindh, for example, was resolved by a plea agreement in which the U.S. government dropped 9 of its 10 highly publicized charges involving allegations that Lindh conspired with Al Queda terrorists to kill Americans. Instead, Lindh plead guilty to a nonviolent felony not directly related to terrorism. Because he originally faced, at minimum, multiple life sentences if convicted at trial, Lindh accepted a 20-year sentence without opportunity for parole, and, because of alleged security considerations, he was forbidden by the government from speaking publicly about his case.

Consideration of the political nature of judicial proceedings need not be limited to the trial court level, because political considerations are just as significant in other courts, such as appeals courts. In courts with authority to resolve constitutional questions, such as the U.S. Supreme Court, much of the decision making can be seen as nothing more than political decision making. In the final outcome of what was perhaps the ultimate political trial—*Bush v. Gore*—the U.S. Supreme Court chose the president of the U.S. in resolving the disputed 2000 presidential election.

Nor need consideration of political trials be limited exclusively to trials before judicial officers. In impeachment trials, the trial process is conducted by a legislative body, not the judiciary, and that process is quintessentially political. The impeachment trial of President Clinton was a trial process that was inherently political, with opposing political interests vying for supremacy.

Although scholarly attention on political trials appears to focus exclusively on criminal trials, the civil trial process has also been used for overtly political and ideological ends. Often premised on claims of libel or slander, for example, some civil actions have been called "SLAPP (strategic lawsuits against public participation) suits." In these cases, business interests—often large, multinational corporations—use lawsuits or the threat of legal action as a means to deter public dissemination of views critical of their business practices. Perhaps the most remarkable example of such a lawsuit is the libel action brought by the McDonald's Corporation in 1990 against London Greenpeace activists who distributed pamphlets critical of McDonald's advertising, environmental, labor relations, animal welfare, food safety, and nutritional practices and standards. After the longest libel trial in British history, the case resulted in a verdict only partially in McDonald's favor. But by that point, the lengthy litigation that exposed many of McDonald's business practices was a public relations disaster for McDonald's regardless of the verdict.

Even if elimination of all political considerations from the judicial process is impossible, modern constitutional protections are intended to prevent the use of the judiciary for political ends. Many features of the U.S. Bill of Rights, for example, were intended to curb the abuses of political trials that occurred previously. Most notable of these features is the strict prohibition against trial solely for one's political or religious beliefs or affiliations. Features of due process and fundamental fairness in the trial process include the right to a public trial by a neutral and impartial judge, trial before a jury of one's peers, fair notice of the charges in advance of trial, access to effective legal counsel and other defense resources, the right to confront one's accusers, the burden of proof beyond a reasonable doubt being placed on the prosecution, not the defendant, and the right to an independent, posttrial review. Proceedings that lack one or more of these features raise questions about their potential for political manipulation. The Bush administration's proposal in 2001 to use military commissions to try foreign nationals designated as suspected terrorists or as aiding terrorism was controversial because it lacked several of these elements.

The role of an independent news media is also significant in regard to the current use of political trials. Without control over information about a trial and the underlying issues, authorities face significant risks in prosecuting such cases. In one of the most notorious

U.S. political trials of the 20th century—the Chicago Eight Trial—the Nixon Justice Department brought eight antiwar activists to trial in 1969, despite their prosecution being declined by the previous, Democratic administration. The prosecutions stemmed from demonstrations at the 1968 Democratic National Convention. The primary charge against the defendants was that they conspired to cross state lines to incite a riot. Although five of the eight defendants were convicted at trial, albeit none on the conspiracy charge, all convictions were reversed on appeal. During the trial, both in and out of court, however, the defendants and their attorneys used the news media attention to publicize their political views in the most explicit and passionate terms concerning the racist nature of U.S. society, the immorality of the Vietnam war, and the lack of the court's legitimacy to try them. Although the trial brought fame to the defendants and their attorneys, subsequent publicity regarding misconduct by the judge, prosecutors, and law enforcement personnel during the trial brought them into disrepute.

The increasing use of transnational or international criminal tribunals to try charges of crimes against humanity, war crimes, or acts of genocide, often against government leaders, raises new questions about the formation, functioning, and staffing of such tribunals, their legitimacy, and the propriety of bringing such cases before them. The use of national tribunals or other adjudicative processes, such as "truth and reconciliation" commissions in the aftermath of widespread political violence presents similar issues. In 1998, a watershed event in this trend was the arrest in London of Augusto Pinochet, the former president of Chile, for extradition to Spain to stand trial for directing the torture and execution of Spanish nationals during his rule in Chile. Because of alleged poor health, however, Pinochet was released and did not face trial.

During the past decade, the UN Security Council has established international criminal courts to prosecute war crimes and acts of genocide arising from recent internal wars and violent ethnic conflicts. These courts include the International Criminal Tribunal for the former Yugoslavia (noteworthy for the trial of the former Yugoslav president, Slobodan Milosevic, for crimes against humanity), the International Criminal Tribunal for Rwanda, and the UN Special Tribunal for Sierra Leone.

Law professor Mark Osiel, among others, has argued that criminal trials stemming from large scale official brutality by authoritarian states, in which there is public complicity, must be conducted with the pedagogical purpose—in mind—of fostering liberal virtues of toleration, moderation, and civil respect. In such cases, the trial process is seen as a form of storytelling with a didactic purpose. But to the extent that such trials become merely show trials, more concerned with the presentation of historical events than with specific evidence of the guilt of the accused, such proceedings may lack legitimacy. Political theorist Judith Shklar concluded that although international tribunals, such as the Nuremberg war crimes trials in 1946, were inherently political, they nevertheless serve an important purpose in contributing to constitutional politics and the development of a fair legal system. The trial of the former Iraqi president Saddam Hussein for war crimes poses similar issues.

The role of the UN international criminal tribunals in prosecuting war crimes and related offenses form the background to the establishment of the International Criminal Court (ICC), an independent international tribunal that has jurisdiction over war crimes, crimes against humanity, and acts of genocide, when such crimes would otherwise go unaddressed because of the failure of criminal justice systems of national states to prosecute them. Although the ICC was established by international agreement, the U.S. opposes its implementation because of concern that it could compromise U.S. sovereignty in conducting its world-wide military and related operations. Given the need to establish the legitimacy of the ICC, the rules governing its functions include a series of safe-guards intended to prevent the ICC from being used for politically

motivated or frivolous prosecutions, including an elaborate process for the approval of criminal prosecutions of complaints brought to the ICC.

DAVID W. WEBBER

### References and Further Reading

Bass, G.J., *Stay the Hand of Vengeance: The Politics of War Crimes Tribunals,* Princeton, NJ, Princeton University Press, 2000.
Baum, L., *The Puzzle of Judicial Behavior,* Ann Arbor, University of Michigan Press, 1997.
Becker, T.L., *Political Trials,* Indianapolis, IN, Bobbs-Merrill, 1971.
Belknap, M.R., Ed., *American Political Trials,* Westport, CT, Greenwood Press, 1994.
Christenson, R., *Political Trials: Gordian Knots in the Law,* New Brunswick, NJ, Transaction Publishers, 1999.
Kirchheimer, O., *Political Justice: The Use of Legal Procedure for Political Ends,* Princeton, NJ, Princeton University Press, 1961.
Osiel, M., *Mass Atrocity, Collective Memory, and the Law,* New Brunswick, NJ, Transaction Publishers, 1997.
Rehnquist. W.H., *Grand Inquests: The Historic Impeachments of Justice Samuel Chase and President Andrew Johnson,* New York, William Morrow, 1992.
Shklar, J.N., *Legalism: Law, Morals, and Political Trials,* Cambridge, MA, Harvard University Press, 1986.

*See also* **Trial, The Right to; War Crimes**

---

# Typologies of Crime and Criminal Behavior

---

There are different ways in which criminological scholars can approach the primary dependent variable that they seek to understand and explain—crime. In this encyclopedia entry, the reader is first provided with a historical overview of how and why scholars have operationalized and theorized about the crime variable. This is followed by the introduction of a particular conceptual orientation toward crime and criminal behavior—what is termed a *typologies approach.* Scholars who adopt this perspective reject the idea that the dependent variable is best operationalized in an all-encompassing fashion and instead lobby for the use of multiple, more focused and conceptually distinct categories of criminal behavior (i.e., violent crime, property crime, and public order crime). By partitioning the subject matter into conceptually meaningful categories, the researcher and theorist alike are able to

discuss and investigate the unique behavioral and cognitive aspects of the actions and actors that are contained in each category.

A set of basic definitional issues (i.e. how professionals choose to approach the phenomenon) pose a formidable stumbling block early on along the road to criminological enlightenment. Buried within the mountain of criminological literature exists a long-standing and feverish debate that involves two very fundamental questions:

1. What is the subject matter that we should be studying?
2. What is the best way to study it?

Let us start with the first question. One would think that there would be little problem defining the concept of crime. After all, people routinely incorporate it in their daily conversations. The media is constantly covering it. Books are constantly being written on crime-related topics. However, upon closer examination, we see that "crime" is a relatively slippery concept. Should "crime" refer to all those act or omissions of acts that are defined by the criminal law? Many sociologists consider this sort of legally-bound definition of crime to be overly constraining. Scholars such as Becker (1963) point out that the "collective conscience" of society can be far more offended by non-criminal acts of deviance (i.e., social norm violations) than they are by some violations of the law. For example, whereas it may not be illegal to cast racial slurs in public, there tends to be a much more resounding public outcry against this form of behavior than there is when a minor law violation such as speeding or littering takes place.

Many scholars acknowledge this point, but opt instead to pursue the path of least resistance—they contend that the subject matter in question should include only violations of the criminal law. This definitional parameter qualifies as the "path of least resistance" because it immediately limits the discussion to a much more identifiable and manageable set of behaviors. However, there is a more substantive justification that guides this logic. Namely, violations of the criminal law (i.e., criminal acts) are subject to formal, state-imposed sanctions whereas violations of customs or norms (i.e., deviant acts) are subject to informal, peer-imposed reprimands. This difference in the nature and process of social control efforts has long been seen as a critical issue that separates crime from deviance.

Note that a definition based solely on existing criminal codes still produces an *exceedingly* long list of offenses. At the most basic level, one must contend with the fact that there is no one definitive criminal code. Each jurisdiction, ranging from the federal to the state to the thousands of local jurisdictions, has in place a slightly different criminal code. As such, an effort to compile an exhaustive list of all of the law violations that are currently "on the books" would result in a truly massive and unmanageable list of statutes.

Let us assume that one could settle on one given criminal code, be it from a select federal, state or local jurisdiction. This code would include those garden variety offenses such as murder, rape, robbery, theft, and so on that quickly come to mind. However, the complete list would be far more extensive as it would include thousands of law violations—everything from jaywalking to first-degree murder. What's more, criminal codes routinely contain a host of obscure, outdated, and rarely enforced statutes that nonetheless must be defined as crimes. Seuling (1975) documents a few of the more ridiculous examples of this point

such as an Oklahoma law that makes killing an animal with "malicious intent" a case of first-degree murder or the Virginia law that makes it a crime to have a bathtub in your house. Few people are willing to grant equal weight to all of the behaviors detailed in a given criminal code. Instead, one is inclined to set aside the "petty" and "outdated" offenses and focus the discussion on the more "serious" categories of crime. Rest assured that most scholars do just that. Some turn to the Federal Bureau of Investigation's (FBI) Uniform Crime Report (UCR) for direction (FBI, 2000). The UCR is an annual effort to document the number of reported and cleared (i.e., where an arrest was made) cases of *murder, sexual assault, aggravated assault, robbery, burglary, larceny, auto theft, and arson* that are encountered by the various law enforcement agencies across the U.S. These eight offense types are called *Part I offenses*. The FBI asks all law enforcement agencies to provide a series of offense and offender-related data that are then used to generate descriptive crime statistics (e.g., demographic profiles and crime rates).

Most scholars applaud the persistent data collection efforts of the FBI but see the Part I offense classification scheme as too restrictive. They contend that reliance on the Part I offenses precludes any discussion of a number of prevalent and pressing forms of criminal behavior (e.g., white collar crime, all forms of public order drug and sex crimes, and organized crime). As a result, scholars such as Roebuck (1967), Gibbons (1992), Farr and Gibbons (1990), Clinard, Quinney and Wildman (1994), Miethe and McCorkle (1998), and Tittle and Patternoster (2000) have sought to provide their own classification schemes. These scholars begin with long lists of criminal offenses (i.e., the criminal code) and seek to group similar offenses into generic, yet meaningful categories. They are not merely trying to generate their own personalized list of crime types for us to consider. They are simultaneously responding to an additional issue. Namely, they are taking a position against criminological scholars who suggest that "crime" is best viewed as a general social construct.

What follows is a brief history lesson, in order to clarify this point. In the 18th, 19th, and early 20th centuries, the systematic study of crime slowly blossomed and began to gain legitimacy. Philosophers such as Lombroso (1912), Beccaria (1963), and Bentham (1988) applied the "scientific method" to the study of crime and sought to offer testable theoretical statements about crime causation. They also provided rudimentary taxonomies of offenders. In the 1920s, 1930s, and 1940s, sociologists at the University of Chicago (Park, Burgess, and McKenzie, 1928; Shaw and McKay, 1942; Thomas and Znaniecki, 1920) stressed the ecological aspects of crime and began to study criminals in their natural environments. Collectively, these early criminological essays brought hope that we might be able to finally understand and prevent criminal behavior. Soon, scholars began to formulate "grand" general theories of crime. There has been Hirschi's (1969) social control theory, Akers' (1973) social learning theory, and Gottfredson and Hirschi's (1990) self control theory, just to mention a few. These theorists share the common assertion that crime was best viewed as a single social construct and that it is possible to identify it with a series of structural and social psychological factors that can account for an individual's involvement in a huge variety of behaviors. In short, they seek to outline the causes of criminality in our society and these causes are said to apply equally to all forms of crime.

The efficiency and effectiveness of this all-encompassing view of crime was called into question during the World War II era. In an impassioned Presidential Address to the membership of the American Sociological Society, Edwin Sutherland (1940) urged scholars to reconsider the stagnant definition of crime. He was critical of scholars who focused exclusively on street crime, blaming criminality on factors such as poverty, social disorganization, or physical or mental anomalies. Sutherland directed our attention toward "white collar crime" as a means of demonstrating (1) the empirical limitations of the predominant theories of the day, and (2) the relative nature of the crime concept. Sutherland maintained that there exists considerable variation in the motivations and behaviors associated with different types of crime. For example, he saw that the average embezzlement offense is far different from the average murder offense. Embezzlement is described as a crime of greed whereas murder is most often described as a crime of passion. The offenders tend to come from different socio-economic circles. Most embezzlement offenses involve planning and stealth whereas most murders are spontaneous acts of brute force. Sutherland's ideas stirred considerable controversy, as for some (like, Farr and Gibbons, 1990; Gibbons, 1968), he had raised doubts about whether scholars could realistically expect to identify one set of theoretical or preventive propositions that can effectively encompass both. Sutherland himself did not seem to be particularly reticent of this interpretation.

In the same presidential address, he asserted that not all crime is different. He cautioned scholars against adopting an overly nearsighted approach that conceives of all types of offenses as separate conceptual categories in need of their own distinctive set of theoretical and preventative propositions. In later writings,

Sutherland came to adopt a shrewd course of action to resolve this conceptual confusion. Whereas, on one hand he was as a champion of "grand" theorizing (i.e., most notably his formulation of differential association theory), he remained sensitive to the complexities of the social world and thus urged researchers and policymakers to construct modest conceptual groupings when engaging crime and criminals in the real world. He stated: "For purposes of understanding criminal behavior, definitive generalizations are needed regarding criminal behavior as a whole, with specifications of the general theory applied to particular criminal behaviors (Sutherland and Cressey, 1974, 69). Sutherland reasoned that patterned social interactions produce a sort of natural order to the way that crimes and criminals are organized and states: "While a general theory of crime such as differential association theory organizes criminological knowledge, and is therefore desirable, in order to make progress in the explanation of crime, it is also desirable to break crime into more homogeneous units (Sutherland and Cressey, 1974, 279). For example, the crimes of murder and assault share much in common as both tend to involve brief exchanges of heated violence that occur between a lone offender and a lone victim. Similarly, pickpockets and shoplifters operate alone and employ measures of stealth to accomplish their crimes. Sutherland warned that researchers and policy makers must be cognizant of these patterned dimensions of crime as they seek to apply broader theoretical propositions. He coined the term "*criminal behavior systems*" to refer to these conceptual groupings of offenses and urged scholars to delineate membership based on the real world behavioral and cognitive elements of crime (Sutherland, 1939). As a reference point, he later provided white collar crime, kidnapping, racketeering, and what he called "professional crime" as examples of criminal behavior systems. According to Sutherland, white collar crime is best viewed as an integrated unit of common offenses and offenders in crimes such as embezzlement, price fixing, corporate collusion, and political corruption have more commonalities than differences and can thus be treated as one large conceptual category or criminal behavior system (Sutherland, 1949).

Sutherland's ideas gave way to a whole new way of thinking about crime and criminals. Whereas some scholars proceeded along with their efforts at grand theorizing, others sought to organize and explain the mechanics of specific categories of crime or criminals. Merton (1949) used to term "*theories of the middle range*" to refer to those systematic scientific observations and propositions that seek to specify the causal factors associated with an individual's involvement in a given criminal behavior system. During the second half of the twentieth century, it became increasingly popular for scholars to engage in focused studies of criminal behavior systems such as white collar crime or murder. These efforts generated middle-range theories and prevention efforts specifically tailored to each one.

It was in the tradition of Sutherland and Merton that scholars such as Roebuck (1967), Gibbons (1992), Farr and Gibbons (1990), Clinard, Quinney and Wildman (1994), Miethe and McCorkle (1998), and Tittle and Patternoster (2000) set out to group similar types of offenses into generic, yet relevant categories. These criminologists share the assertion that a focus on all crime is seen as too broad whereas the categories set forth by the UCR's Part I offenses are seen as too narrow. Instead, they seek a middle ground, one that yields an efficient categorization scheme capable of providing scholars and practitioners alike with a focused understanding of why people commit different varieties of criminal behavior. This tact also provides insight into what can be done to remedy the situation. It is commonly said that these scholars adopt a *"typology"* approach to crime.

Typology scholars rely on logic-based conceptual frameworks to categorize and theorize about crime. There are two mutually dependent facets to a viable typology of crime. First, the scholar must organize the subject matter into a clearly delineated set of conceptual categories. In short, they must answer question number one, as given above, and generate a list of crime types and detail the types of offenses that fit in each conceptual category. These categories, however, must be based on some requisite logic. That is to say, the scholar must identify a set of underlying dimensions that guide his or her selection criteria. This clearly stated set of definitions and descriptions allows the addressed question number two, as given above, and provides the reader with a full understanding of the logic behind the classification scheme. More importantly, these underlying dimensions represent those factors that the scholar sees as the proverbial "ground zero" of criminal behavior systems as they are the core behavioral and motivational aspects of criminal behavior that serve to organize our understanding of this complex subject matter.

A review of the sorts of classification systems that have been produced by the preeminent crime typology scholars is critical in addressing the first of the italicized questions posed above. Gibbons (1968) was among the first to generate a taxonomy of criminal offenses. This list has undergone several revisions but the most recent effort (Farr and Gibbons, 1990) identifies seven theoretically meaningful categories of criminal behavior:

property-predatory crime (i.e., robbery, burglary, auto theft, larceny)
property-fraudulent crime (i.e., embezzlement, fraud, forgery, bribery)
interpersonal violence—general (i.e., homicide and assault)
interpersonal violence—sexual (i.e., rape and other forms of sexual violence)
social order—transactional (i.e., consensual victimless—prostitution, gambling, drugs)
social order—order disruption (i.e., disorderly conduct, escape, resisting arrest)
social order—folk/mundane crime (i.e., jaywalking, speeding, polluting)

Moving on, Clinard, Quinney and Wildman (1994) produced the following nine-part crime-centered classification scheme:

violent personal crime (i.e., homicide, assault, rape)
occasional property crime (i.e., forgery, shoplifting, vandalism, auto theft)
public order crime (i.e., prostitution, homosexuality, drunkenness, drug use)
conventional crime (i.e., robbery, burglary, larceny)
political crime (i.e., bribery, perjury, treason, terrorism)
occupational crime (i.e., employee theft, embezzlement, sexual harassment)
corporate crime (i.e., price-fixing, antitrust, corporate violence, unsafe work conditions)
organized crime (i.e., racketeering, drug smuggling, extortion, money laundering)
professional crime (pickpocketing, counterfeiting, telemarketing fraud)

Note that in both cases, the scholars have generated a manageable list of conceptual categories and then identified a set of offense types that are to be included. Clearly the scope and content of these two lists differ. Clinard, Quinney and Wildman are not so much concerned with the subtleties that exist between different forms of property, violent, and public order offenses. Instead, much of their attention is focused on crimes that are committed in various organizational contexts. For example, they separate crimes by and against government (i.e., acts motivated by ideological or political reasons) into their own category: political crime. Those crimes that are committed to further corporate goals (e.g., unsafe work conditions, price fixing, antitrusts) are afforded their own conceptual space. Trust violations that are committed by employees or professionals in the context of their work roles are said to constitute occupational crimes. Moreover, Clinard, Quinney and Wildman are sensitive to the potential, conspiratorial or habitual aspects of crime, as evidenced by their inclusion of the organized and professional crime categories. The former includes racketeering offenses perpetrated by ethnically-derived collectives such as the Italian or Russian Mafias or Jamaican "posses." The latter refers to individuals such as pickpockets, counterfeiters, and other hustlers who make crime their life's work. In the final analysis, the above taxonomies provide students of criminology with a broad, yet streamlined set of crimes to consider.

Once agreement has been reached in terms of the parameters of the subject matter, attention must then be directed toward determining the best way to study said behavior (question #2 above). In this respect, the specification of a set of underlying behavioral or cognitive factors is critical to the credibility of the typology. Each of the above categorization schemes is based on the premise that the various crime types are made up of their own identifiable set of crime-related behaviors and motivations. These motivations and behaviors take into account critical offender and offense characteristics. This allows scholars to argue that each crime type exists as its own generic, yet distinct criminal behavior system. And whereas, technically, a violation of a larceny statute might well be part of the rap sheet for persons classified under Clinard, Quinney, and Wildman's heading of occasional property crime (e.g., petty shoplifting), conventional crime (e.g., purse snatching), occupational crime (e.g., employee theft), or professional crime (pickpocket), each set of criminal behavior systems are said to possess their own unique combination of factors.

The organization and content of these sets of underlying dimensions are shaped by the behavioral and motivational aspects of criminal behavior that the scholar chooses to emphasize. A review of the typologies literature demonstrates that considerable variation exists on this issue. There are *legal-based typologies* that stress the roles that social control agents within the criminal justice system (i.e., police, courts and corrections) play in defining and reacting to offensive behaviors. Examples of this approach include the distinction between property, violent, and public order offenses or the UCR's description of Part I offenses. One of the more popular legal-based typologies is the rudimentary distinction between felonies and misdemeanors. Felonies include all offenses punishable by at least one year in prison whereas the misdemeanors include all lesser offenses that carry a maximum sentence of less than one year of jail time.

A typology of crime can take on what is referred to as an *offender-based* orientation. Here the underlying dimensions stress the aspects of the social psychology of the offender as the researcher seeks to identify different behavioral and motivational syndromes that are associated with a given criminal behavior system.

For example, Gibbons (1992) argues that it is possible to separate all lawbreakers into an exhaustive list of offender categories. He does this by focusing on the unique social roles that are played out by different offenders. Gibbons contends that offender roles are shaped by behavioral acts, role conceptions (i.e., a cognitive dimension that includes what he calls "self-image patterns" and "role-related attitudes"), and background characteristics (i.e., a social structural dimension that includes social class origin, family background, peer-group associations, and contacts with social control agencies that define their behavior as problematic). This conceptual framework leads Gibbons to separate lawbreakers into 20 distinct types. Included in this list are categories such as "professional thieves," "semiprofessional property criminals," "naive check forgers," "white-collar criminals," "psychopathic assaultists," "opiate addicts," "statutory rapists," "embezzlers," and "violent sex offenders" (Gibbons, 1992, 206).

Victim-based typologies are yet another variation. The underlying dimensions of these typologies emphasize the role that victim routine and behavior play in the initiation and progression of criminal transactions. Scholars in this tradition seek to formulate typologies of victims, not criminal offenses. For example, Mendelsohn (1956) classifies a victim's level of shared responsibility into ascending levels such as complete innocence, minor guilt, as guilty as the offender, more guilty than the offender, and mostly guilty or fully responsible.

The underlying dimensions of *situation-based typologies* concentrate on aspects of physical space. Scholars in this tradition attempt to deconstruct the setting or situational context of crime episodes. For example, Sherman, Gartin and Bueger (1989) used computer programs to geographically map police calls for service. They coined the term "criminology of place" and assert that there exist certain crime "hot spots" (e.g., hospitals, bus depots, bars, malls) that account for a large share of the calls for service. As a result, the criminological discipline has thus come to identify generic crime domains such as work, school, home, and leisure and contend that each one has its own unique set of social norms and ascribed modes of behavior.

The conceptual frameworks set forth by scholars such as Roebuck (1967); Gibbons (1992); Farr and Gibbons (1990); Clinard, Quinney and Wildman (1994); Miethe and McCorkle (1998); and Tittle and Patternoster (2000) are best described as *multitrait typologies*. These scholars stress the joint, interconnected roles that (1) legal aspects, (2) offender behaviors and motivations, (3) victim behaviors and routines, and (4) influences that the audience and physical location play in the overall dynamic of crime. This logic leads Miethe and McCorkle (1998) to identify the following five underlying theoretical dimensions of criminal behavior:

*Criminal Career of the Offender.* The progression and habituation of criminal activity and the associated social roles and self-concept this process produces. Generic categories of novice versus chronic offenders are described.

*Offender Versatility.* Asks whether the offender limits their criminal behaviors to a select type of crime or engages in a host of different violent, property, and public order offense types. Offenders are characterized as either crime "specialists" or "generalists."

*Level of Criminal Planning.* The amount of rational calculation that precedes an individual's criminal involvements. Some crimes are said to be planned or premeditated while others are said to be spontaneous.

*Offender Motivation.* Stresses the underlying reason for perpetrating an offense. Some crimes are described as expressive crimes that are driven by passion and emotion. Other offenses are described as instrumental crimes in that they reflect one's desire to fulfill some direct objective, often monetary in nature.

*Target-Selection Factors.* The exercise of cognitively weighing the costs and benefits associated with a given criminal transaction. Attention is directed toward the importance that convenience and familiarity, perceived level of guardianship, and expected payoff that are present in the criminal decision making process.

Notice that aspects of the legal definition, offender involvement, victim involvement, and situational involvement are sprinkled throughout. The criminal career of the offender and offender versatility components speak to legal-based distinctions. Offender motivation takes into account the mind set of the offender. The target selection element considers how victim methods of defense and routines shape criminal opportunities. The level of planning component is shaped largely by rational assessments of the social environment in which the crime will occur.

These underlying dimensions serve as the basis for the following nine-part typology of crime (Miethe and McCorkle, 1998, 10):

*Violent personal criminal behavior* (including homicide, assault, and rape).
*Occasional property criminal behavior* (including forgery, shoplifting, vandalism, and automobile theft).
*Public-order criminal behavior* (including prostitution, homosexuality, drunkenness, and drug use).
*Conventional criminal behavior* (including larceny, burglary, and robbery).
*Political criminal behavior* (including conspiracy and political demonstrations).
*Occupational criminal behavior* (including such offenses as embezzlement, expense account misuse, bribery of public officials, and selling fraudulent securities).
*Corporate criminal behavior* (including the restraint of trade, false advertising, manufacturing unsafe food and drugs, and environmental pollution).
*Organized criminal behavior* (including drug trafficking, loan sharking, off-track betting, money laundering, and racketeering).
*Professional criminal behavior* (including confidence games, pick pocketing, forgery, and counterfeiting).

Recall Clinard, Quinney and Wildman's (1994) nine-part classification scheme that has been discussed above. This typology of crime is based on the following five underlying dimensions:

*Legal Aspects of the Offense.* Borrowing from the legal-based tradition, this dimension references the criminal law to identify critical behavioral and mental components of the offense.

*Criminal Career of the Offender.* This dimension speaks to the social psychology of the offender and his or her patterned criminal involvements.

*Group Support of Criminal Behavior.* A cultural-level dimension, this facet considers the role that group interaction plays in the patterning of the offender's norms and behaviors.

*Correspondence between Criminal and Legitimate Behaviors.* This dimension adopts a structural level focus and considers the way that the routines and structures of the individual's legitimate and illegitimate lifestyles coincide with one another.

*Societal Reaction and Legal Processing.* This part of the typology stresses the importance of third party reactions, emphasizing that institutions of social control (i.e., the criminal justice system) define and react to criminal behaviors in different ways.

The important point is that the classification scheme and the underlying dimensions work hand in hand for the typologies scholar. In effect, the scholar identifies a set of underlying dimensions that allows him or her to justify and substantiate a given typology of crime. The case is made that this more focused approach to the study of criminal behavior affords us a fuller understanding of the patterns and dynamics of criminal behavior. It allows the discipline to speak to the unique factors associated with a given category of crime. At the same time, we can identify similarities that exist between homicide and aggravated assault, rape, or even burglary. Keep in mind that this means that the differences or similarities on any or all of the theoretical dimensions need not be complete. Instead, it is tacitly implied that partial or conditional similarities or differences can exist across or within conceptual dimensions of the typology. Namely, these typologies of crimes and criminal events are meant to serve as the basis for theories of the middle range that will more effectively allow us the discipline to explain and prevent criminal behavior.

So what is the most useful list of crime types and the best set of underlying theoretical dimensions by which to organize our subject matter? Clearly, each of the above mentioned typologies has merit. However, before we pass judgment, we must realize that many of these scholars never set out to construct an exhaustive and mutually exclusive conceptual framework designed to generate a host of viable theories of the middle range and corresponding prevention efforts. For example, most legal-based typologies are intended as descriptive devices, not theoretically-driven categorization schemes. The founders of the UCR were anything but typologies scholars. Instead, the FBI simply tries to provide crime researchers and law enforcement officials with descriptive categories and statistics that may help to more efficiently document the incidence and prevalence of crime in society. Legal-based typologies are based almost solely on the "black letter of the law" and thus are not powerful enough for the contemporary typologies scholar in search of explanation and a set of comprehensive theoretical constructs. The rigid, impersonal qualities of the criminal code preclude the typology from addressing subtleties in the offender, victim, and situational context that are part and parcel to criminal behavior systems.

Offender-based typologies are another matter. This approach provides a valuable insight into the criminal mind. Few people question the utility of the in-depth social psychological profiles that are associated with this approach. However, their fixation on the offender leads them to lose site of the various roles that victims and the situational context play in criminal outcomes.

Similar merit and criticism can be applied to victim-based or situational-based typologies. The former raises our awareness of the important role that a victim plays in criminal outcomes whereas the latter directs much needed attention to the situational context in which crimes occur. However, neither professes to serve as causal frameworks that can be used to categorize or account for the broad forms of crime that exist in society today.

The multitrait typologies are in a different category. These are viewed as the "cream of the crop." They have been produced by true typologies scholars, individuals that carry on Sutherland's tradition. Recall that their efforts are directed toward (1) formulating theoretical frameworks that seek to explain the causes of criminal behavior, or (2) generating treatment regimens or policy initiatives that seek to alter criminal behavior. As Gibbons (1975) observes, purist typologies scholars have had to deal with considerable criticism and disappointment. Their categorization systems have been criticized for being less than exhaustive and mutually exclusive. Moreover, the underlying dimensions upon which these classification schemes rest have been said to be incomplete, leaving out critical aspects of the criminal enterprise.

It is true, there has yet to be an all encompassing multitrait typology of crime set forth. This, however, is not a fatal flaw. A typology of crime need not set such lofty goals. As the above pages have demonstrated, crime is a slippery concept. Even if we can agree on a list of offenses, we can never overlook the fact that human behavior is inherently unpredictable. Although it is critical that scholars agree on the topic of discussion, nowhere is it written that there must be a predetermined, unwavering list that shall govern all discussions heretofore. Dabney (2002) suggests that typologies scholars need to get back to the basics. Namely, they need to avoid the temptation of trying to hit a home run and concentrate instead on moving around the base path one base at a time. This new approach is one wherein the typology researcher sets their goals on *appreciation*, not *explanation*. The concept of appreciation is based on justifiable sensitizing concepts or ideas that set forth a clear and concise organization of a given topic. Conversely, explanation is based on deductively or inductively derived theoretical propositions that can be tested and replicated in repeated investigations, namely explanatory frameworks that must satisfy the stringent requirement of validity, reliability and generalizability. An explanatory orientation must stand the test of a far different set of criticisms than the scholar who seeks to provide an organizational framework that allows students to get a feel for the varieties of criminal behaviors that exist in society and how each possesses a certain set of unique and yet generic qualities. Dabney (2002) endorses an orientation that produces a broad yet deep appreciation for the social phenomenon that we know as criminal behavior. By definition, it would not seek to provide the definitive list of crime types, or one that satisfies those paramount criteria of being both exhaustive and mutually exclusive. Immediately, the question becomes: why avoid such an exercise? Dabney (2002) argues that this course of action is a "sucker's bet" that exposed the scholar to criticisms that they either have too many or too few categories to work with.

Dabney uses this logic as the basis for a new typology of crimes, dividing the subject matter into the following nine categories: homicide, assault, sexual assault, robbery, burglary, occasional property crime, public order drug crimes, public order sex crimes, and crimes within complex organizations. Clearly, some of these categories are less complex than others. For example, homicide is perceived as a relatively streamlined set of behaviors and motivations. Although it is true that homicides generally follow a generic set of interactional qualities and share observable victim and offender characteristics, there are many subtypes of homicide. For example, there is stranger homicide, intimate homicide, infanticide, parenticide, serial murder, mass murder, and murder-for-hire. Those subtypes at the front of the list are known more for their generic, shared qualities than the more sensational subtypes at the end of the list. Although the sensational forms of murder certainly account for only a small fraction of all known homicides, they are the subjects that most fascinate the armchair criminologist in all of us. And where the goal is to provide breadth and depth to the resulting understandings, it becomes prudent for the typologies scholar to consider these sensational forms of crime.

On the other end of the continuum, the coverage of some of the above nine types of crime can be described as generic and cursory at best. For example, the category "occasional property crime" would beg consideration of topics such as shoplifting, fraud, and auto theft. Certainly, this is not intended as an exhaustive list of property offenses. However, Dabney (2002) argues that the discussion should be framed in such a way that it allows for the consideration of the unique aspects of each variant of property crime as well as the behavioral and motivational similarities that cut across all three. In the final analysis, one observes that these three types of offenses and offenders have a great deal in common with one another.

The same can be said about the public order drug crime or the public order sex crime. The former would include a discussion of the manufacturers, dealers, and users of illicit drugs. The latter encompasses prostitutes, pimps, johns, and other sexual deviants. Overall, this conceptual category allows scholar to highlight the differences and similarities in offenders, victims,

and situational elements that exist across this genre of crime. Finally, the category termed "crimes within complex organizations" represents perhaps the most generic and hence controversial of them all. This heading collapses what many typologies scholars would consider three separate and distinct types or categories of crime: occupational crime, corporate crime, and political crime. This is true. Notwithstanding the long-standing debate about how to best categorize and define the broad rubric that we have grown to know as "white collar crime" or the vast differences in the ways that an embezzler thinks and acts when compared to a corrupt politician, this conceptual category serves as an organizational or instructional category that is held together by a short list of loosely structured sensitizing concepts.

When speaking of criminal behavior systems, Dabney (2002) focuses on a slightly different unit of analysis—the *criminal event*. The criminal event is defined as the social context in which the crime occurs. Every criminal event is comprised of an offender, a victim (or target), and a setting. For example, the garden variety date rape involves a male offender, a female victim and a leisure setting such as the offender's house and all the situational norms and sentiments that exist in that home. Too often, scholars focus exclusively on the offender (criminal) or offense (crime) and lose sight of the important roles that the victim and or setting play in the criminal enterprise. The underlying dimensions of Dabney's (2002) typology are based on the following set of four organizing principles or sensitizing concepts: *behavioral factors, cognitive factors, cultural factors, and societal reactions*. These sensitizing concepts stress the common themes or criteria by which he or she can compare and contrast offender, victim, and setting roles across different types of crime. In other words, these concepts speak to the important multitrait aspects of the criminal event (i.e., the offender, victim, situation, and legal distinctions) and provide organizational or instructional guidance en route to a more complete appreciation for the phenomenon in question. The behavioral aspects of the criminal event must take into account the following factors:

*Legal Definition.* This refers to particular criminal statutes. This includes behavioral (*actus reas*, or the criminal act and mental *mens rea*, or the guilty mind aspects that jurisdictional entities require for an event to be defined as criminal.

*Skills and Techniques.* The "tools of the trade," or the mechanisms that are generally used by the population of offenders to assist them in his or her criminal activities.

*Criminal Transaction.* The form and content of the interactions that occur between the offender, victim, and audience members as they go about constructing a situationally-bound reality for the criminal event.

*Criminal Career.* The habitual offending routines that emerge as individuals enter into, persist through, and exit their criminal lifestyles. Criminals can specialize in a given type of crime or come to be generalists who engage in a wide variety of criminal behaviors.

The following four components are said to comprise the cognitive or social-psychological aspects of the criminal event.

*Criminal Intent.* Stresses the totality of an offender's mental state, in that time period preceding the crime, during the actual commission of the crime, and in the postoffense aftermath.

*Criminal Motivation.* The thought processes that shape an offender's decisions to violate as well as those ongoing thought processes that lead the criminal back to repeated involvement (i.e., the desired end that the offender hopes to achieve).

*Criminal Planning.* The rational decision-making processes that offenders use to map out their gameplan for committing the crime (i.e., what the offender sees as the most effective and efficient set of behavioral processes to achieve said act).

*Normative Neutralizations.* The thoughts and verbalizations that the offender uses to neutralize, excuse, or justify their criminal actions to themselves and others.

Dabney (2002) stresses the following three criteria when referencing the cognitive dimensions of the criminal event.

*Criminal Subculture.* The culturally-based personal and group interactions that help pattern the offender's crime-specific attitudes, beliefs, and behaviors.

*Organizational Alignment.* The structural networking of interactions that shape a given criminal subculture. Best and Luckenbill (1994) argue that criminals carry out their misdeeds within the context of one of the following organizational forms: loners, colleagues, peers, teams, and formal organizations.

*Socialization Contexts.* The process-oriented aspect of criminal subcultures that, namely, the actual content of subcultural messages and interactions that shape criminal learning outcomes.

Finally, the underlying dimensions of Dabney's (2002) typological framework recognize the following aspects of how society reacts to the criminal event.

*Formal Reactions.* The institutional responses (i.e., arrest, adjudication, and sentencing) that entities of the criminal justice system (i.e., law enforcement, courts, and corrections) impose upon offenders.

*Informal Reactions.* The ways in which audience members and valued associates react to the criminal event and how these shape the offender's future behaviors and sentiments.

These sensitizing concepts direct scholars' attention toward common themes or criteria by which he or she can compare and contrast offender, victim, and setting roles across different types of crime. In other words, the sensitizing concepts and the accompanying list of nine crime types represent the most recent effort to produce a multitrait typological framework. The principle difference between this typology and its predecessors is that it shifts the attention to a new unit of analysis (i.e., the criminal event) and is less concerned with the elusive issues of validity, reliability, and generalizability than it is with adding to and rounding out the scholar's stock of knowledge when it comes to the very complex subject matter that we know as crime. Thus the crime typologies are slowly evolving from mutually exclusive and exhaustive categories to more heuristic and pedagogical devices that can be used in the ongoing operationalization and study of the crime phenomenon.

DEAN DABNEY

## References and Further Reading

Akers, R.L., *Deviant Behavior: A Social Learning Approach,* Belmont, CA, Wadsworth/West, 1973.

Beccaria, C., *On Crimes and Punishment,* New York, MacMillan, 1963.

Becker, H.S., *Outsiders: Studies in the Sociology of Deviance,* New York, Free Press, 1963.

Bentham, J., *An Introduction to the Principles of Morals and Legislation,* New York, Hafner Publishing, 1948.

Best, J. and Luckenbill, D.F., *Organizing Deviance,* Englewood Cliffs, NJ, Prentice-Hall, 1994.

Clinard, M.B., Quinney, R. and Wildeman, J. *Criminal Behavior Systems: A Typology,* Cincinnati, OH, Anderson, 1994.

Dabney, D.A., *Criminal Behaviors: A Text/Reader,* Belmont, CA, Wadsworth/West, 2002.

Farr, K.A. and Gibbons, D.C., Observations on the development of crime categories, *International Journal of Offender Therapy and Comparative Criminology,* 34, 223–237 (1990).

Federal Bureau of Investigations, *Crime in America, 1999,* Washington, DC, Federal Bureau of Investigations, 2000.

Gibbons, D.C., *Society, Crime, and Criminal Careers: An Introduction to Criminology,* Englewood Cliffs, NJ, Prentice-Hall, 1992.

Gibbons, D.C., Offender typologies—Two decades later, *British Journal of Criminology,* 15, 140–156 (1975).

Gottfredson, M. and Hirschi, T., *A General Theory of Crime,* Palo Alto, CA, Stanford University Press, 1990.

Hirschi, T., *Causes of Delinquency,* Berkeley, CA, University of California Press, 1969.

Lombroso, C., *Crime: Its Causes and Remedies,* Montclair, NJ, Patterson Smith, 1912.

Mendelson, B., The victimology, in Schafer, S., Ed., *The Victim and His Criminal: A Study of Functional Responsibility,* New York, Random House, 1956.

Merton, R.K., Social structure and anomie, *American Sociological Review,* 3, 672–682, 1938.

Miethe, T.D. and McCorkle, R., *Crime Profiles: The Anatomy of Dangerous Persons, Places and Situations,* Los Angeles, CA, Roxbury, 1998.

Park, R.E.K., Burgess, E.W. and McKenzie, R.D., *The City,* Chicago, IL, University of Chicago Press, 1928.

Roebuck, J.B., *Criminal Typology,* Springfield, IL, Charles C. Thomas Publisher, 1967.

Shaw, C. and McKay, H.D., *Juvenile Delinquency and Urban Areas,* Chicago, IL, University of Chicago Press, 1942.

Sherman, L.W., Gartin, P.R. and Bueger, M.D., Hot spots of predatory crime: Routine activities and the criminology of place, *Criminology,* 27, 27–56 (1989).

Sutherland, E.H., White collar criminality, *American Sociological Review,* 5, 1–12.

Sutherland, E.H., *Principles of Criminology,* 3rd ed., Philadelphia, PA., J. B. Lippincott, 1939.

Sutherland, E.H., *White Collar Crime,* New York, Holt, Rinehart, Winston, 1949.

Sutherland, E.H. and Cressey, D.R., *Principles of Criminology,* 9th ed., Philadelphia, PA, J. B. Lippincott, 1974.

Thomas, W.I and Znaniecki, F., *The Polish Peasant in Europe and America,* Chicago, IL, University of Chicago Press, 1920.

Tittle, C.R. and Patternoster, R., *Social Deviance and Crime: An Organizational and Theoretical Approach,* Los Angeles, CA, Roxbury, 2000.

# U

---

# Ukraine, Crime and Justice in

---

Ukraine, the second (to Russia) largest country in Europe, was declared independent by the Supreme Soviet of Ukraine in August, 1991. The country has a unitary system of government, featuring an executive branch headed by a president serving a five-year term, and a unicameral national parliament (*Verkhovna Rada*), elected partially according to proportional representation and partially by direct constituency mandate. Although the Ukrainian Constitution provides for an independent judiciary, the courts are subject to political interference and corruption, and are very inefficient.

After the 1917 revolution, the Soviet government abolished the judiciary of Tsarist Russia and created new local courts with extensive discretion to deal with cases on the basis of "revolutionary legal consciousness." In 1918, a new judicial system was established consisting of local, district, and regional people's courts, and a Supreme Judicial Council. The Soviet Union was created in 1922, and the Ukraine, along with several formerly independent nations, was incorporated within it. Although there has always been a strong nationalist movement in Ukraine, it wasn't until the late 1980s that citizens demanded more control over their government and economy. In 1990, Ukraine's parliament passed a declaration of sovereignty that stated that the country could enact its own legislation if it did not conflict with the laws of the Soviet Union. On December 25, 1991, the Soviet Union was dissolved and Ukraine and most of the other former Soviet republics formed a loose association called the Commonwealth of Independent States.

Today, Ukraine is making a very difficult transition from a centrally planned to a market-based economy. Whereas the private sector continues to expand and represents a substantial portion of the economy, the country remains in a serious economic crisis and sustained growth in agriculture and industry has not been achieved. Even though unemployment is extremely low by western standards, it is rising and wages average less than U.S. $100 per month. The black market and associated criminal enterprises continue to grow and invade virtually all sectors of the economy. As a result of these worsening economic conditions and a reduction in general crime prevention programs, the crime rate in most categories has increased somewhat since independence.

The militia (police) in Ukraine, a centralized agency of the Ministry of Internal Affairs, has primary responsibility for preventing and combating crime. The Law on Militia clearly outlines the duties and obligations of the militia and is, in many cases, quite specific in its restrictions on police power. For example, the militia has a right to use physical force (including firearms) in most cases except against women who are obviously pregnant, the elderly, persons with obvious disabilities, and minors. An exception can be made where a group of these persons is involved in behavior that threatens the lives and health of others, militia officers, or in cases of armed assault or resistance. According to the Civil Procedure Code of Ukraine, a citizen has a right to file a complaint against any government official, including a militia officer, if he believes that his civil rights have been violated.

Arbitrary arrest and detention continue to be a major problem in Ukraine. Police are required to perform "administrative surveillance" of "people inclined to commit crimes" and the law provides that authorities may detain a suspect up to three days without a warrant, after which an arrest order must be issued by the court. After charges have been filed, the maximum period of detention is 18 months, but the law does not limit the total time of detention before and during the trial. By law a trial must begin within three weeks after indictment but because of the overcrowded courts, this requirement is rarely met.

One particular group that has come under police scrutiny regarding crime control in recent years has been the Roma (Gypsies). In the Transcarpathian region (bordering Hungary, Slovakia, and Romania), which is home to a large Roma population, the authorities have developed a comprehensive crime prevention policy that targets only Roma. All Roma who have been in prison within the last three years are kept on a special list for monitoring, and young Romani men have been subjected to forced registration and finger-printing, often following collective arrests. There are no formal legal mechanisms that have been successfully available to Romani who protest police abuses, and few officers have been held accountable in Ukrainian courts for mistreatment of Roma.

Although it is difficult to measure accurately the true extent of crime and victimization in Ukraine, the UN, through the *World Crime Survey* (conducted in five-year waves), and the *International Crime Victim Survey (ICVS)* (1996–97) provide the best available assessments. In 1997, the total number of crimes recorded in official criminal (police) statistics was 589,208 (1162 per 100,000) down slightly since 1995 but an overall increase since the early 1990s. There were 4231 accounts of intentional homicide (8.35 per 100,000), 256 committed with a firearm. Other crimes against the person included 4873 assaults (9.61 per 100,000), 1510 rapes (9.61 per 100,000), and 24,699 robberies (48.71 per 100,000). Property crime accounts for most of the criminal activity in Ukraine. In 1997, there were 177,800 thefts (350.70 per 100,000) and 4523 automobile thefts (8.92 per 100,000). Incidences of fraud show a marked increase, almost doubling since 1995 (9695 to 18,051). Car vandalism and automobile theft are the crimes with fastest growth rates, primarily because of the increasing number of privately owned cars.

Organized crime is a major problem in Ukraine and, as is the case in many of the other states of the former Soviet Union, a criminal class has emerged with well-established criminal networks, especially in drug trafficking. This is particularly evident in the Donetsk region and Crimea. The central government in Kiev exerts little institutional control and officials in these areas are widely alleged to have ties to organized criminal elements. The criminal underworld fills a void left by an ineffectual government and policing mechanism, in many cases taking the place of legitimate authority, distributing goods and services, providing protection, and influencing governmental decision making.

Drug trafficking controlled by organized crime is not a new phenomena in Ukraine. The former Soviet Union had a drug problem several years before it formally acknowledged the fact and recent attempts to develop free markets in Ukraine without ensuring their integrity and effectiveness, combined with an ineffective criminal justice system, created an ideal climate for trafficking in drugs. With independence came the collapse of many social and economic controls and Ukraine, like many former Soviet states, was left without formal mechanisms to deal with organized crime and it became much easier for these criminal groups to engage in illegal transnational criminal and drug related activity. The Law of Ukraine on Combating Organized Crime provides for the creation of special divisions, such as regional agencies, to address the problem of organized crime but its effectiveness has not been determined.

Although Ukraine is not a world leader in the cultivation, trafficking, and use of narcotics, or the laundering of profits from drug sales, the country's drug industry is very sophisticated. The drug transportation network has expanded, connecting Ukraine with African, Asian, and European drug markets. Although opium poppies (grown in western and northern Ukraine) and hemp cultivation (centered in the eastern and southern regions) have been problems for several years, it was not until the mid-1990s that a true heroin market emerged in the country. In 1999, narcotics officials estimated that there were approximately 60,000 regular heroin users in Ukraine.

Punishment for most offenders, including drug traffickers, is quite severe in Ukraine. Although the criminal code has not undergone any significant changes since independence, many of the most deplorable provisions of the Soviet-era code have been revised or removed. However, the basic foundations remain focused on the protection of the state and judiciary, rather than those of individual citizens. There are still close links between the militia, prosecution, and the judiciary that lead to very few acquittals and extremely harsh penalties, mostly incarceration. For example, in the first six months of 1998, over 126,000 criminal cases were tried in the courts and only 444 resulted in acquittal. In recent years, more than 4000 offenders have been convicted of "illegal currency operations," which provides for a five-year sentence to anyone who has traded in foreign currency over U.S. $100. Amounts larger than U.S. $500 carry a sentence of up to ten years and the confiscation of the offender's property.

Conditions in prison and pretrial detention facilities are very poor, routinely failing to meet minimum international standards and overcrowding, inadequate sanitation and medical care are common problems in penal institutions. According to official information, there are 126 labor farms for convicted adult offenders and 11 such facilities for juveniles housing between 200,000 and 240,000 inmates, twice that of 1992. Approximately 40,000 pretrial detainees are held in 32 facilities operated by the Ministry of the Interior and six facilities of the Security Service. Although the Ukrainian Constitution prohibits torture, Amnesty International periodically reports that police and prison officials regularly beat detainees and sentenced prisoners. Although no official statistics are available, prison murders and suicides are reportedly quite high. Since 1997, it has been illegal for any official to provide information about conditions of incarceration, which is punishable by eight years imprisonment. Inmates generally have no adequate mechanisms to file complaints regarding inhumane treatment while incarcerated.

A general amnesty in August, 1998 on the country's Independence Day resulted in as many as 25,000 prisoners being released from Ukraine's penal institutions. Although there have been similar amnesties in the past, this was the first time that it applied to prisoners who were underage at the time of imprisonment and to inmates with elderly dependents or children under the age of 18. It is estimated that with high unemployment and government benefits at a record low, many of these amnestied prisoners will return to prison.

In March 2000, the president of Ukraine, Leonid Kuchma, signed a law abolishing the death penalty. Although a moratorium on executions was introduced in 1997 and the Constitutional Court in 1999 declared that the death penalty violated the principle of respect for human life and was unconstitutional, it was not officially ratified until 2000. It was reported that 167 prisoners were executed in 1996 in Ukraine, second in number only to China. At the end of 1999, there were 400 Ukrainians under sentence of death whose sentences were likely to be commuted.

CHUCK FIELDS

### References and Further Reading

Chapkey, S.S. and Tochilovsky, V., *World Factbook of Criminal Justice Systems: Ukraine,* Washington, DC, U.S. Department of Justice, Bureau of Justice Statistics.

Dyczok, M., Ukraine: Movement Without Change, Change Without Movement (Postcommunist States and Nations), Reading, U.K., Harwood Academic Publishers, 2000.

Hajda, L.A., Ed., Ukraine in the World: Studies in the International Relations and Security Structure of a Newly Independent State (Harvard Papers in Ukrainian Studies), Cambridge, MA, Harvard University Press, 1999.

Hatalak, O., del Frate, A.A. and Zvekic, U., Ed., *The International Crime Victim Survey in Countries in Transition: National Reports,* Rome, UN Interregional Crime and Justice Research Institute, 1998.

International Helsinki Federation for Human Rights, *Annual Report, 1999: Ukraine,* Vienna, Austria, International Helsinki Federation for Human Rights, 2000.

Shelley, L.I., Political-criminal nexus: Russian-Ukrainian case studies, *Trends in Organized Crime,* 4(3) (1999).

Transnational Crime and Corruption Center, *Organized Crime and Corruption Watch,* 2(2) (2000).

United Nations, *Sixth United Nations Survey of Crime Trends and Operations of Criminal Justice Systems, 1995–1997,* Vienna, Austria, UN Centre for International Crime Prevention, Office for Drug Control and Crime Prevention, 2000.

U.S. Department of State, *1999 Country Reports on Human Rights Practices: Ukraine,* Washington, DC, Bureau of Democracy, Human Rights, and Labor, U.S. Department of State, 2000.

*See also* **Eastern and Central Europe, Crime and Justice in; Soviet Union, Crime and Justice in**

# Uniform Crime Reports (UCR)

When most people refer to U.S. crime statistics, they mean the Uniform Crime Reporting (UCR) Program data compiled and published annually by the Federal Bureau of Investigation (FBI). These are not the only crime statistics, but they are the most well-known; their collection and reporting began in 1930. Other sources of U.S. crime data include those provided by the Bureau of Justice Statistics (BJS) in its annual National Crime Victimization Survey (NCVS); in addition, crime data are now available from the National Incident-Based Reporting System, a modification of the UCR that many agencies have adopted.

Regardless of the source of crime statistics used, there are limits to their accuracy and reliability, because of some very real problems with them that were ignored for decades. In the past few years greater attention has been paid to these problems, resulting in improvements in the data, in our knowledge of their deficiencies, and consequently in our ability to deal with these deficiencies.

This essay describes the history of crime statistics, from the beginnings of the UCR to the present, as well as its uses, its inaccuracies, and improvements, both implemented and planned. It ends with a discussion of the directions in which the reporting of crime is heading, and their expected impact on our knowledge of and ability to deal with problems of crime.

## The Uniform Crime Reporting (UCR) Program

### Development of the "Crime Index"

The initial impetus for the establishment of the UCR was the concern on the part of an association of police administrators (the organization later became the International Association of Chiefs of Police, or IACP) that so-called "crime waves" were being manufactured by newspapers in an effort to build circulation. Having an official source of crime information, it was hoped, would dampen this tendency and allay the fears of the public. Rather than include *all* crimes, after an extensive analysis of different state statutes and police reporting practices, it was decided to count only seven crimes that had a high likelihood of being reported to the police: murder, rape, robbery, aggravated assault, burglary, larceny $50 and over, and auto theft. These are known as *Index crimes*—because they are included in the FBI's Index of Crime—or Part 1 crimes—because they are reported to the FBI on Part 1 of the agencies' submission to the FBI.

Police departments also report a second set of crimes on a second form; they are called "Part 2 crimes" for obvious reasons. On Part 2 of their submission the police report the number of other, non-Index, crimes like simple assault, forgery, fraud, other white collar crimes, larceny under $50, less serious sex offenses, violations of curfew and liquor laws, and so-called "victimless" crimes—those involving drugs, prostitution, and gambling. Some of these crimes may be as serious as the index crimes, but are considered less likely to be reported, and thus not as useful for inclusion in an index of crime.

Soon after its initiation in 1930 as a voluntary effort on the part of many IACP members, administration of the UCR was assumed by the FBI. It remains largely a voluntary effort, although many states now require police departments to provide crime data to state agencies for compilation, publication, and subsequent transmission to the FBI.

There have been some changes in the Crime Index over the years. In 1973, in the wake of reports that some police departments were reducing their Index crime counts by valuing many over-$50 larcenies as under $50, the FBI decided to make *all* larcenies reportable on Part 1 and included in the Crime Index. In addition, in 1979, after what seemed to be an outburst of arsons for profit, Congress mandated the collection and publication of arson data as part of the Crime Index, notwithstanding the fact that, unlike the other Index crimes, reporting on arson has always been spotty. Currently it is omitted from the Crime Index, although the FBI also publishes the *Modified* Crime Index, one in which arson is included.

### Coverage and Missing Data

Coverage has grown considerably over the years of its existence. At its peak (1978), almost 98% of the U.S. population was represented in the crime data in the FBI's annual UCR report *Crime in the U.S*. This high rate of reporting has diminished in recent years, in part because of problems encountered by police agencies in making the transition to the National Incident-Based Reporting System, or NIBRS (described below); in part because of reduced federal funding; and in part because of organizational, administrative, and software problems.

When agencies do not report consistently, the FBI looks at their past statistics and *imputes* their crime data to fill in the gaps. This permits the FBI to make reasonable estimates of crime rates at the state and national level. Although some have tried to use the FBI data to study crime at the county level, the imputation procedures currently used by the FBI are inaccurate below the state level.

Many cities, both large and small, have been shown to either ignore or downgrade many citizen-reported crimes in compiling and transmitting their crime statistics to the FBI. One of the main reasons for this practice is that municipal police chiefs generally serve at the pleasure of the mayor, and have often been fired if increased crime rates become an issue in a mayoral campaign. So the mayor puts pressure on the chief, who puts pressure on the command staff, who put pressure on the street officers to "do something about crime." This too often has resulted in "cooking the books" in one way or another. (Although the FBI does check on the quality of the data it receives, it cannot audit data from over 18,000 agencies. In the past, in egregious cases the FBI did not accept data from some agencies.)

Moreover, not all crimes are reported to the police. There are a number of reasons for this: for example, the victim may be traumatized, or may feel that the police will do nothing, or may be afraid of the police. In such cases the estimate of the extent of crime is skewed; in fact, a police agency that makes it difficult for citizens to report being victimized will have a lower crime rate than one that is more diligent in obtaining reports from victims. It is for these reasons that in 1973 the Bureau of Justice Statistics initiated the National Crime Victimization Survey (NCVS).

### Supplementary Homicide Reports (SHR)

The current UCR data collection program includes a special submission that gives extensive information about each homicide in a jurisdiction. Known as the Supplementary Homicide Report (SHR), it is also submitted monthly by police departments on a voluntary basis. The FBI collects and publishes this crime series, but only electronically. The SHR is much more detailed than the UCR; whereas the monthly Part 1 and 2 submissions to the FBI consist of crime *counts* (e.g., the number of murders that occurred in January 2000), the SHR has *a separate line of data for each person (victim or offender) involved in the incident.* Among the data elements included in the SHR are: age, race, and sex of all victims and offenders, relationship of primary victim to primary offender, weapon used, incident circumstances (e.g., rape, robbery, lovers, triangle, argument over money, and youth gang killing). The comparative wealth of information about each incident (compared to the summary UCR data) has permitted crime analysts and researchers to characterize homicide trends more precisely: to track, for example, the effect of the creation of shelters for battered women on intimate partner homicide; or the effect of parole or weapons policies on youth gang homicides; or the rate of commission of infanticides, to give but a few examples.

As with any voluntary reporting system, there are problems of completeness and accuracy with the SHR as well. Different agencies have different practices when it comes to providing information about, for example, victim-offender relationships or offender characteristics; moreover, the number of homicides accounted for in the UCR and the number in the SHR are not always the same; between 1995–1999 the SHR or UCR ratio ran between 84 and 92%.

### The National Incident-Based Reporting System (NIBRS)

For the most part, the UCR is used as an overall measure of the harm, danger, or risk because of crime. It is limited in this use, because gaps in the data often make it difficult to determine the extent of the problem or how it has changed over time. Moreover, it cannot be readily used as a diagnostic tool of the crime problems faced by a community, any more than a fever thermometer can be used to determine what caused the rise in a person's temperature. Why do some people feel no safer when the crime index goes down—is it because crimes not included in the index are increasing? When homicide goes up, is it intimate partner homicide, infanticide, felony homicide, or gang-related homicide that is the primary factor? If the rape rate is lowered, is it because there are fewer stranger or acquaintance rapes? The answers to these questions have strong policy consequences and can help agencies at all levels of government plan and evaluate the effectiveness of different crime prevention programs. The implementation of the NIBRS by police agencies will permit such analyses.

The NIBRS is considerably more detailed than the SHR, as seen in Table 1, and is much more difficult to implement. Initially police departments were very resistant to this order of magnitude increase in reporting requirements, but now most realize that they will

**Table 1.** Reporting Characteristics of the UCR

| UCR Component | Data reported to the FBI |
| --- | --- |
| UCR Part I | A single record is reported, giving the monthly count of the number of crimes reported to the police, for each crime type in the Crime Index |
| SHR | The number of records reported monthly depends on the number of homicides, offenders and victims. The incident record contains information about the jurisdiction and month of occurrence; weapon used, nature of incident circumstances, among other fields. The victim record contains the age, sex, and race of the victim and (when known) offender and his or her relationship to offender. The offender record contains (when known) the age, sex, and race of the offender and relationship to the victim. |
| NIBRS | The number of records reported monthly depends on the number of incidents, victims, offenders, weapons used, injuries, property loss and damage, arrests made, and vehicles involved. Thus there is one record describing the nature of the incident, its location type, when it occurred, etc.; one record for each victim, describing that victim's characteristics and injuries; one record for each offender, describing that offender's characteristics (when known); one record for each type of property stolen or destroyed; one record for each vehicle involved in the incident; one record for each weapon used |

need to implement the new system. This change has come about because of a number of factors. First, both the FBI and BJS have provided a great deal of assistance to agencies to help them make the change; second, they gather many of the data elements already, in their own automated databases; and third, companies that sell computer-based dispatch and record systems for police departments have developed software that provide the NIBRS reports as well.

The real benefit to the NIBRS is in its use as a diagnostic tool. If we analogize the UCR as equivalent to taking the temperature of the body politic, we can analogize the NIBRS to a more thorough diagnosis. The NIBRS can tell us what kinds of crime are increasing or decreasing, against what kinds of victims, with what kinds of weapons, and in what parts of the country. If one jurisdiction has experienced a drop in assaults compared to its neighbors, comparisons can be made to see if this drop is in specific kinds of assaults (domestic or stranger), whether weapon use has changed (or how it varies by type of victim), if there is a difference in the types of injuries or locations. In other words, the greater detail of the data permits the more accurate analysis of how the crime mix is changing over time, or how it differs from city to city. As police departments continue to change from reactive policing—focusing on catching the bad guys *after* they commit crimes—to proactive, problem-oriented, and *preventive* policing—determining crime patterns and mobilizing resources (of both the police and other agencies) to address emerging problem areas, the benefits of the NIBRS will become more apparent.

The elements of the NIBRS are already found in many police departments' databases, and crime analysts are becoming more adept in tapping them to find crime patterns. In the past the term "crime pattern" referred, for the most part, to the signature of a specific offender, that is, to a *modus operandi* (MO). With the advent of problem-oriented policing, these analysts are tapping the same data to find specific crime hazards— such as a tavern that generates a great many calls for service within a few blocks, or an apartment complex that houses a number of drug sales operations—and furnishing such data to licensing or zoning agencies to bring civil pressure on the owners.

However, these applications at the local level are based on NIBRS-like data that includes something that the NIBRS does not: location information. When it was initially developed in the 1980s, the NIBRS was specifically proscribed from including such data. The question then arises, To what extent will analyses using the NIBRS be hobbled by this exclusion?

To some extent, this exclusion should not matter, as the NIBRS will permit crime analysts and researchers to determine if, for example, states with different laws relating to domestic violence have different patterns of domestic assault, or if different gun laws or sentence structures affect the types of armed robberies that are committed. That is, the NIBRS will provide a picture of offense characteristics with sufficient detail and with a large enough number of cases so that relatively precise questions can be answered.

But the absence of geographical data may reduce the effectiveness of the NIBRS in other policy contexts.

**Table 2.** Comparing the Uniform Crime Reports and The National Crime Victimization Survey

| Source of Crime Statistics | UCR's Index of Crime | NCVS |
|---|---|---|
| Presumed Coverage | All police jurisdictions in the U.S., excluding most federal agencies | Persons age 12 and older living in a random sample of all households in the entire U.S., reflective of the victimization experience of all U.S. households |
| Crimes Included | Murder, rape, robbery, aggravated assault, burglary, larceny, auto theft; with NIBRS, there are 22 offense categories and many subcategories | Rape, robbery, aggravated assault, burglary, larceny, auto theft |
| Geographic Specificity | Good; can be used to look at specific geographic areas, but must be done cautiously. With NIBRS, can be done somewhat more accurately | Poor; too small a sample size to provide geographic detail |
| Specificity in Victim or Offender Characteristics | Poor at present with UCR; with NIBRS very good; does not include socio-demographic or family characteristics of victims | Very good; includes socio-demographic and family characteristics of victims |
| Gaps in Coverage and Other Limitations | Rural jurisdictions that don't report; agencies that don't report all offenses, in an effort to make their cities seem safer; agencies that have problems with their data systems and do not report their crime data to the FBI; victims who choose not to report to the police | Victims who live in other countries; victims under 12 years of age; victims who don't live in households (e.g., in dormitories, homeless shelters, battered women's shelters); victims who choose not to disclose intrafamily assaults to interviewer; victims who can't recall victimizations when interviewed |

For example, if the Census tract of the crime were made available, it would be possible to correlate the commission of specific types of crime with population and housing characteristics that would make the NIBRS data much more useful in making policy.

## The Future

When the NIBRS is adopted fully throughout the U.S., will this mean that we no longer need a national victimization survey like the NCVS? After all, as Table 2 shows, the NIBRS will do almost everything the NCVS does, and with a much greater coverage and detail as to crime characteristics—and the data are collected at the time of the crime, when memories are fresher. However, there is no other way of getting a count of crime that includes crimes that victims do not report to the police. It is also gives the reasons that they are not reported to the police—perhaps because of fear, or because they feel the police can do nothing, or because it is inconvenient. In addition, as long as the UCR program (of which the NIBRS is a component) is voluntary, and as long as police departments continue to "cook the books" by not reporting all crimes, we will continue to need an alternate estimate of the extent of crime in the U.S.

MICHAEL D. MALTZ

### References and Further Reading

BJS and FBI. The nation's two crime measures, Appendix IV in recent issues of *Crime in the United* States. Available at: http://www.ojp.usdoj.gov/bjs/pub/pdf/ntmc.pdf.

FBI (annually), *Crime in the U.S.,* Washington, DC, Available at: http://www.fbi.gov/ucr.htm.

Maltz, M.D. (1977). Crime Statistics: A Historical Perspective, *Crime and Delinquency,* 23(1), 32–40 (1977). Reprinted in Monkkonen, E., Ed., *Crime and Justice in American History,* Meckler, 1990.

Maltz, M.D. (1999). *Bridging Gaps in Police Crime Data,* A discussion paper from the BJS fellows program, Report No. NCJ-1176365, Bureau of Justice Statistics, Office of Justice Programs, U.S. Department of Justice, Washington, DC, Available at: http://www.ojp.usdoj.gov/bjs/pub/pdf/bgpcd.pdf.

Maltz, M.D. and Targonski, J. (2002). A note on the use of county-level UCR data, *Journal of Quantitative Criminology,* 18(3), 297–318.

Maxfield, M.G. and Maltz, M.D. (1999), Editors' introduction: Special issue on the national incident-based reporting system, *Journal of Quantitative Criminology,* 15(2), 115–118.

*See also* **National Crime Victimization Survey (NCVS)**

---

# United Kingdom, Crime and Justice in the

---

The United Kingdom (U.K.), comprising England, Wales, Scotland, Northern Ireland and several dependencies including The Falkland and Channel Islands, Gibraltar and the British Overseas Caribbean Territories of the Commonwealth, is a constitutional monarchy with three distinct legal systems. These legal systems and their corresponding systems of criminal justice operate within England and Wales, Scotland and Northern Ireland. (The U.K.'s Home Office is responsible for maintaining data related to all justice system records and procedures. Each year, the Home Office, through the Office for National Statistics, publishes "The Official Yearbook of the United Kingdom of Great Britain and Northern Ireland" which disseminates information on a wide range of domestic issues, including crime and justice. All statistics documented here are drawn from the 2004 Yearbook unless otherwise noted.)

Although all share a common emphasis on the independence of both prosecuting authorities and the judiciary, no single criminal or penal code exists mandating the principles upon which the justice system operates. Statutes enacted by the Westminster (British) or Scottish Parliaments are the ultimate source of law, but there is also a legal duty to comply with the European Community (EC) law, derived from EC treaties, Community legislation and the decisions of the European Court of Justice. Where the two conflict, courts in the U.K. are obliged to apply the latter.

Law in the U.K. is dichotomized as criminal or civil, which require separate standards of proof. Criminal cases must be proven by prosecuting authorities (the Crown Prosecution Service or CPS) beyond a reasonable doubt, whereas civil cases must meet the lesser standard of the balance of probabilities. In both criminal and civil cases, the courts make their decisions on an adversarial rather than an inquisitorial basis. Judges typically resolve civil disputes whereas the fate of criminal defendants is determined by a jury trial.

Those accused of criminal offenses in the U.K. are afforded several rights similar to those of the accused in the American criminal justice system. Defendants are presumed innocent until proven guilty; they are not required to testify against themselves and are tried by a judge and jury in an open, public trial. Defendants are not, however, guaranteed publicly funded legal services, rather they may apply for a *representation order*. The court must be satisfied that it is in the interests of justice that publicly funded representation should be granted and reserves the right to order the defendant to pay back some or all of the costs of his or her defense at the conclusion of the case.

## Policing the U.K.

### England and Wales

England enjoys a prominent and integral role in the history of modern law enforcement. In 1829, Sir Robert Peel founded the London Metropolitan Police Force ("The Met"), transforming law enforcement and providing a new standard of professionalism for urban policing (Walker, 1977). Presently, there are 43 police forces organized on a local basis in England and Wales, 41 of which are outside metropolitan London. The Metropolitan Police Service and the City of London Force are responsible for law enforcement within the greater London metropolitan area. Local police authorities maintain the 43 forces and set local policing objectives in consultation with the chief constable and the local community. Chief constables, analogous to the American police chief or sheriff, (in London the Commissioner of the City of London Police and the Commissioner of the Metropolitan Police) are appointed by their local police authorities to head each of the forces. These appointments are made with the approval of the government.

Police powers and procedures are governed by legislation and accompanying codes of practice and cover a wide range of issues, including evidence gathering, stopping and detaining suspects, arrest, and interrogation (Hirschel, 1995). Police may stop and search people or vehicles if they *reasonably suspect* the presence of stolen goods, weapons, or other contraband, however, they are responsible for recording the grounds for the search. All those subject to a stop and search are entitled to a copy of the officer's report. Police in England and Wales have recently introduced stricter regulations regarding stop and search making it more difficult for law enforcement to execute arbitrary stops.

The police may arrest a suspect on a warrant issued by a court; however, they can also do so without a warrant for *arrestable offenses*. Arrestable offenses are defined as those for which the sentence is fixed by law (i.e., mandatory sentences) or for which the term of imprisonment is five years or more (i.e., mandatory minimum sentences). Officers are required to caution suspects of their rights before they can pose any questions about an offense. For arrestable offenses, police may detain suspects without bringing charges for up to 24 hours. Individuals suspected of a serious arrestable offense can be held for up to 96 hours, but not more than 36 hours unless a magistrate's court issues a warrant.

Once police gather what they determine "sufficient evidence," they decide whether the detained person should be charged with an offense. If the police institute criminal proceedings against a suspect, the Crown Prosecution Service then takes control of the case. However, for minor offenses, the police may decide to caution an offender rather than prosecute. A caution is not the same as a conviction and will only be given if the person admits the offense.

If the police do decide to bring charges, that person is usually released on bail to attend a magistrate's court hearing. If the defendant is denied bail, he or she must be brought before a magistrate as soon as possible. Although bail is considered a general right, a magistrate does reserve the right to withhold it on several grounds, the most common of which is risk of flight or threat posed to public safety. However, if bail is refused, the accused is afforded the right to apply instead to the Crown Court or to a High Court judge. Conversely, the prosecution may also appeal to the courts against the granting of bail.

### Scotland

Scotland has eight territorial police forces and is also within the jurisdiction of the British Transport Police (the law enforcement agency responsible for policing the U.K.'s railways and ports) as well as the Ministry of Defense police. Elected councilors compose all police authorities and joint police boards throughout Scotland. Police derive their authority from common law and statutory law passed by either the Scottish or British Parliaments (MacQueen, 1993). These powers address matters including the arrest and detention of suspects, criminal investigation and traffic management.

Relative to England and Wales, police in Scotland enjoy greater discretion in the arrest procedure. Under broad common law powers, police are allowed to execute an arrest without a warrant, if suspects are seen or reported as committing a crime, or are considered a danger to themselves or others. Those suspected of imprisonable offenses may be held for police questioning prior to arrest, but for no more than six hours without being charged. Suspects are required to be charged and cautioned if they are arrested. The case is then referred to Scotland's prosecuting authorities, the procurator fiscal.

### Northern Ireland

November 2001 ushered in a new system for policing Northern Ireland, as the Royal Ulster Constabulary became the Police Service of Northern Ireland (PSNI). The Chief Constable is accountable to the new Policing Board, made up of ten political nominees and nine independent members appointed by the Secretary of State. The policies and procedures governing police power in Northern Ireland are identical to those of England and Wales, as the British government exerts more influence within this region compared to Scotland. From initial stop to formal charges, police in Northern Ireland follow the same protocol as do law enforcement in England and Wales. Once police charge a suspect, the case is turned over to the Crown Prosecution Service.

## U.K. Courts

### England and Wales

Criminal acts are characterized as either *summary offenses*, which are the least serious, or *indictable offenses*, which are divided into "indictable-only" (e.g., murder, manslaughter, or robbery) and "either-way," which may be tried either summarily or on indictment (Hirschel, 1995). Once police charge a suspect, they forward the paperwork to the Crown Prosecution Service (CPS), who either elects to move forward with formal charges or discontinue the matter, in which case there is no court action. If the CPS decides on the former, the case is initially heard in a lower court, the magistrate court. Summary offenses remain at this level, whereas triable-either-way offenses can be heard summarily by a magistrate or moved to the higher Crown Court at the request of either the defendant or the magistrate.

Magistrates' courts typically comprise three representatives of the local community who do not have professional legal qualifications and are advised by court clerks regarding law and procedure. Known as "lay magistrates" or "justices of the peace" (JPs), they may impose a fine up to £5,000 or a maximum sentence of six months, or both. If they feel their sentencing powers are not sufficient, they may send the offender to the Crown Court for sentencing.

The Crown Court sits at about 90 venues in England and Wales in six regional areas called *circuits* and is presided over by High Court judges, circuit judges and part-time recorders. Judges are appointed from the ranks of practicing barristers and solicitors and

can be removed only in rare and limited circumstances typically involving misconduct or incapacity. The Lord Chancellor, who recommends the more senior appointments to the Queen, currently oversees arrangements for the appointment of judges. However, the government announced in June 2003 that it would bring forward legislation to abolish the Office of the Lord Chancellor as part of a series of Constitutional changes directed toward modernizing the relationship between the executive, legislature and the judiciary, separating the powers of the legislature and the judiciary.

Crown Court trials are reserved for serious criminal offenses that must be tried on indictment. An indictment is a written accusation against a person, charging him or her with a serious crime triable by jury. After indictment, if a not-guilty plea is entered, the prosecution and defense form opposing sides in an adversarial manner. Both sides call and examine witnesses and present opposing versions of the case. Strict rules of evidence govern how this is done. Evidence is typically taken by witnesses testifying orally under oath, however, written statements by witnesses are allowed with the consent of the other party or in limited circumstances at the court's discretion.

Defendants tried in the Crown Court have their cases heard by juries comprising 12 members of the community drawn from the eligible electorate. In jury trials within England and Wales the judge decides questions of law, summarizes the case for the jury and discharges or sentences the accused. The jury, then, is responsible for deciding questions of fact and offers a verdict of either guilty or not guilty, the latter of which results in acquittal. Juries may reach a verdict by a majority of at least 10–2.

Upon conviction, the court sentences the offender after considering all relevant information, often including a presentence or any other specialist report and a mitigating plea by the defense. A fine is the most common punishment in the U.K. and most offenders are fined for summary offenses. A court may also order compensation requiring the offender to pay for personal injury, loss or damage resulting from an offense or impose a conditional discharge wherein the offender, if he or she offends again, may be sentenced for both the original and the new offense. Additional sentences imposed in the U.K. include community sentences that are a type of intensive supervisory probation, and custodial sentences that result in incarceration (Weiss and South, 1998).

Those convicted by a magistrate's court may appeal to the Crown Court or the High Court on points of law and for a new trial. Appeals from the Crown Court go to the Court of Appeals, Criminal Division. A further appeal can be made to the House of Lords on points of law of public importance, if permission is granted. Appeals to the House of Lords will soon be directed elsewhere as the British Government announced in June 2003 a series of Constitutional changes including the establishment of a Supreme Court to take over the judicial functions of the House of Lords.

## Scotland

Derived from diverse sources (e.g., Roman law, canon law, influence of other legal systems), Scots law is most influenced today by judge-made law, certain legal treatises having institutional authority, legislative statutes and EC law (MacQueen, 1993). Whereas judge-made law and legal treatises are typically referred to as the common law of Scotland, legislation, similar to the rest of the U.K., consists of statutes passed by and subordinate (local) legislation authorized by the British or Scottish Parliaments. Many statutory offenses are, however, shared with England and Wales through U.K.-wide legislation and laws relating to issues such as environmental pollution and public safety (e.g., traffic laws).

The Crown Office and Procurator Fiscal Service provide Scotland's independent public prosecution and deaths investigation service. Procurators fiscal and Crown Office officials prepare prosecutions in the High Court that are conducted by the Lord Advocate and the Solicitor General for Scotland. They in turn delegate the bulk of their work to *advocates depute*, collectively known as the Crown Counsel, of whom there are 18. The local procurator fiscal has discretion whether or not to prosecute based upon reports submitted by police.

There are three criminal courts operating in Scotland: the High Court of the Justiciary, the sheriff court and the district court. Within these courts, two types of criminal procedures exist: the *solemn procedure*, wherein the accused is tried before a judge and jury (of 15 people selected at random from the general public), and the *summary procedure*, which occurs only in sheriff and district courts where a judge alone hears the case. Similar to the English and Welsh legal systems, lower courts, known as district courts, deal with minor offenses and are the administrative responsibility of local authorities.

District court judges, who are typically justices of the peace, can impose a prison sentence of up to 60 days and a maximum fine of £2,500. These courts are responsible for approximately 29% of Scottish criminal proceedings annually. A local authority may also appoint a stipendiary magistrate to sit in a district court. These magistrates must be professional lawyers of at least five years' standing and have the same summary criminal jurisdiction and powers as a sheriff.

Presently, only Glasgow has stipendiary magistrates sitting in the district court.

Sheriff courts, of which 49 exist throughout Scotland, generally handle less serious offenses committed within their area of jurisdiction. Organized into six *sheriff-doms*, a sheriff principal heads each of these and oversees more than 100 permanent sheriffs, most of whom are appointed to particular courts. The sheriff has jurisdiction in both summary and solemn criminal cases. Under the former, the sheriff may impose prison sentences of up to six months or a fine of £5,000, whereas the latter allows for imprisonment up to three years and unlimited financial penalties.

The High Court of the Justiciary is the supreme criminal court in Scotland, sitting in Edinburgh, Glasgow and on circuit in other areas. Responsible for trying the most serious crimes, it has exclusive jurisdiction in cases involving murder, rape and treason. The High Court also serves as the Scottish Court of Criminal Appeal. Whereas the rest of the U.K. makes final appeals to the House of Lords, Scottish defendants may appeal against conviction, sentence, or both to the High Court. The Court may dispose of an appeal in a number of ways, including granting a retrial. Approximately 3% of all convictions in Scotland are appealed to the High Court, of which 1% have verdicts overturned and 11% receive reduced sentences.

## Northern Ireland

Northern Ireland's legal system is similar to that of England and Wales. Jury trials have the same place in the system, except in cases involving acts of terrorism. Additionally, cases go through the same stages in the courts and the legal profession has the same two branches. Two types of courts exist within Northern Ireland, superior and inferior. Superior courts include the Supreme Court of Judicature comprising the Court of Appeal, the High Court and the Crown Court. All matters relating to these courts are under the jurisdiction of the U.K. Parliament and all judges are appointed by the Crown. The inferior courts are the county courts and the magistrates' courts, both of which differ slightly from their English and Welsh counterparts.

The Court of Appeal consists of the Lord Chief Justice (as President) and two Lord Justices of Appeal, whereas the High Court is made up of the Lord Chief Justice and five additional judges. The practice and procedure of these are virtually the same as in the corresponding courts in England and Wales and both courts sit in the Royal Courts of Justice in Belfast. The Crown Court hears all serious criminal cases in Northern Ireland and also shares procedure identical to the English and Welsh Crown Court. Similar to England and Wales, the final destination of appeals is the British House of Lords.

The inferior courts of Northern Ireland include county courts that are primarily civil law courts, and magistrates' courts that hear minor, local criminal cases. In addition to handling civil matters, the county courts may also hear appeals from the magistrates' courts in both criminal and civil cases. The magistrates' courts also serve multiple functions, exercising jurisdiction in certain family law cases and other civil matters.

## U.K. Corrections

More than a quarter of a million people (323,000) were sentenced for indictable offenses in England and Wales during 2001, nearly a third of whom received community sentences. Scotland sentenced 120,000 persons in the same period, although over a third of these were for motoring infractions. Of the 120,000 sentenced, 64% received a monetary penalty, 11% a community sentence, 14% a custodial sentence, and the remaining offenders received another form of sentence.

Community sentences, administered by the National Probation Service, are typically one of two types: a community rehabilitation order requiring the offender to maintain regular contact with a probation officer, or a community punishment order involving unpaid work within the community. Community sentences are particularly common among juvenile offenders as judges generally refrain from handing out custodial sentences to youthful defendants.

Custodial sentences are given to approximately one in four convicts, with life imprisonment as the maximum. Life imprisonment is the mandatory sentence for murder and is also available for certain other serious offenses such as treason. Those given custodial sentences are held in prisons ranging from open to high-security facilities. The Prison Service in England and Wales is an executive agency of the Home Office and is responsible for overseeing the 138 prisons throughout the U.K. Prisoners are classified into risk levels for security purposes and housed in the appropriate correctional facility based on these categories.

The U.K. has experienced recent increases in the prison population, currently numbering more than 72,000. This increase has prompted officials to take measures to alleviate potential overcrowding in the prisons including greater use of community sentences for minor offenders, expanding the capacity of prisons and making effective use of the early release of some prisoners. For example, those inmates serving terms less than four years may be automatically released at specific points in their sentences, whereas those detained for longer require Parole Board approval or the consent of a government minister.

## Crimes and Victimizations

### Recorded Crime

Recorded crime refers to those offenses reported to and documented by law enforcement ranging from the most serious charge of homicide to lesser infractions such as minor theft and criminal damage. Most summary offenses (such as motoring infractions) typically dealt with at the magistrate's level are not included in the recorded crime category. Similarly, both Scotland and Northern Ireland use comparable definitions of recorded crime (exclusion of summary or equivalent offenses). Between 2002–2003 approximately 55% of recorded offenses involved forms of theft or burglary, whereas 16% were violent in nature (e.g., robbery, violence against the person and sex offenses). Fraud, forgery and drug offenses comprised about 9% of recorded crime whereas criminal damage accounted for 19%. Police in England and Wales recorded a total of 5.9 million crimes within 2002–2003, most of which were concentrated in a relatively small number of mainly urban areas.

Crimes are disproportionately committed by young males between the ages of 16 and 24 in the U.K. This demographic has a conviction rate of 584 per 10,000 population compared to a 46 in 10,000 rate for their 35 and older counterparts. The overall rate for males aged 10 and older was 167 per 10,000 compared with a rate of 37 for females. Males are more likely to commit every category of crime, as well as be tried, convicted and sentenced for an offense.

## Crime Measured by Surveys

In addition to official police recording of criminal offenses, crime in the U.K. is also measured by a national telephone survey. Similar to the U.S.' National Crime Victimization Survey (NCVS), the British Crime Survey (BCS) conducts approximately 33,000 telephone interviews within England and Wales (similar crime surveys are conducted in Scotland and Northern Ireland) asking respondents about their experiences with crime in the previous 12 months. The sample does not include children or individuals residing in institutions and excludes questions regarding murder, fraud, sexual offenses and victimless crimes such as illegal drug use. Surveys such as these are typically considered a more accurate measure of crime because they include many offenses that are not reported to the police. Additionally, they provide a more reliable picture of crime trends because they are not affected by variations in police recording practices.

Estimates from the most recent British Crime Survey suggest that 12.3 million crimes were committed against adults living in private households in the 12 months prior to the interview. This is a significant increase compared to the 5.9 million crimes recorded by law enforcement. The risk of victimization is estimated at 27% in England and Wales, and 20% in Scotland and Northern Ireland. In all three cases, crime has fallen since the previous survey.

HOLLY E. VENTURA

### References and Further Reading

Deflem, M. (2002). *Policing World Society,* London, Oxford University Press.

Hirschel, J.D. (1995). *Criminal Justice in England and the U.S.,* London, Oxford University Press.

MacQueen, H.L. (1993). *Studying Scots Law,* Edinburgh, U.K., Butterworths.

Office for National Statistics. (2004). The Official Yearbook of the U.K. of Great Britain and Northern Ireland, 2003. London, Home Office.

Reynolds, J. and Smartt, U. (1996). *Prison Policy and Practice,* Leyhill, Bristol, CT, HM Prison Service.

Smartt, U. (1999). Constitutionalism in the British dependent territories of the Caribbean, *European Journal of Crime, Criminal Law and Criminal Justice,* The Hague, the Netherlands, Kluwer Law International, 300–313.

Walker, N. (1965). *Crime and Punishment in Britain: An Analysis of the Penal System in Theory, Law, and Practice,* Edinburgh, Edinburgh University Press.

Walker, S. (1977). *A Critical History of Police Reform: The Emergence of Professionalism,* Lexington, MA, Lexington Books.

Weiss, R.P. and South, N. (1998). *Comparing Prison Systems: Toward a Comparative and International Penology,* Australia: Gordon and Breach Publishers.

*See also* **Sir Robert Peel; Crime and Justice in Colonial America; International Policing: Cooperation Among Nations in the European Union; Penal Colonies; Police: History in England**

# United States Frontier, Crime and Justice in the

The frontier justice period in 19th century America has been so enmeshed in mythology and folklore that it is difficult to separate truth from fiction. The "facts" of frontier culture are almost impossible to ascertain, because the chronicles of the westward movement are found largely in local newspapers and "Dime Novels" based primarily on word-of-mouth accounts of the exploits of frontiersmen.

The preponderance of evidence, however, indicates two major conclusions:

1. The distinctive character of the Euro-American was honed during this period, as was the unique concept of American justice.
2. The perceptions of "law and order" that emerged from the popular culture of the frontier era continue to be reinforced by media and other myth-makers, making it difficult for lawmakers and criminal justice practitioners to move beyond the "frontier mentality."

Both "frontier" and "justice" attained unique meanings and played significant roles in the conquest and settlement of the west in the U.S.

What was the frontier? The most quoted scholarly definition of the frontier in America was articulated by Frederick Jackson Turner as he declared in 1893 at a gathering of historians at the World's Columbian Exposition in Chicago that the frontier "was closed." He defined the frontier as "the meeting point between savagery and civilization" that had been occurring in America for the 400 years since Columbus arrived in 1492. He argued that the frontier had been advancing across the continent as every American generation returned "to primitive conditions ... along the frontier line." In 1890, the U.S. Census Bureau had pronounced the disappearance of a contiquous frontier line, which Turner interpreted as "the closing of the frontier." According to Turner's "frontier thesis": "The existence of an area of free land, its contenuous recession, and the advance of American settlement westward explain American development." The history of the frontier, Turner argued "begins with the Indian and the hunter; it goes on with the disintegration of savagery by the entrance of the trader ... the pastoral stage in ranch life; the exploitation of the soil by the raising of unrotated crops of corn and wheat in sparsely settled farm communities; the intensive culture of the denser farm settlement; and finally the manufacturing organization with the city and factory system" (New perspectives).

The impact of the frontier, Turner held, was to establish the unique character of the American: coarse and strong, acute and acquisitive, inventive and expedient, masterful grasp of material things, restless, full of nervous energy, and, above all, self-reliant individualist.

This Eurocentric explanation was called "the single most influential piece of writing in the history of American history" by a Turner contemporary and facilitated the framing of western events into the romanticized folklore of the brave pioneer and the noble savage that have dominated the literature. It was more than half a century later before his critics could sustain a "revisionist" movement that argued the "free" land never existed, but was simply property stolen from the Native American tribes, and that there was as much savagery on the advancing side of the frontier as there was on the retreating side. Additionally, the "thesis" simply did not address the history of Americans of color, from the west coast Chinese Americans to the east coast African Americans; in fact, it did not even address the lot of many Euro-Americans, such as the Irish (mostly left behind in the urban slums) or the Spanish (pushed to the south or off the continent as the wave advanced westward).

Further, the revisionists argue that cooperation was more important than individualism to success on the frontier, as settlers moved west in wagon trains, built their settlements together, and depended on each other for safety and survival.

Most Americans saw the frontier as a chance to start over or seek their fortunes, agreeing with *New York Tribune* editor Horace Greeley's admonition in 1841: "Do not lounge in the cities! There is room and health in the country, away from the crowds of idlers and imbeciles. Go west, before you are fitted for no life but that of the factory.... If you have no family or friends to aid you ... turn your face to the Great West and there build up your home and fortune" (Fenimore).

What was frontier justice? Justice on the frontier was truly in the eye of the beholder. It certainly could not be equated to fairness or equity. In the folklore, however, justice in the west has been painted as "good guys" versus "bad guys," with the wages of "sin" (equated with lawbreaking) being "hung by the neck until dead." Violations of the law or more likely "the code of the west," according to mythology, were handled swiftly and surely.

In *America's Frontier Heritage*, Billington (1966) argued the 18th and 19th century American was different from his European contemporaries in that economically

Americans believed in the "universal obligation of all persons to work endlessly in their eternal pursuit of material gain" and thus disliked a leisure class, were unable to enjoy recreation and had a grim determination to win at any endeavor. Politically, Americans believed "upward social mobility was the lot of every man worth his salt."

Because of the need for the skills and comfort provided by women, the wife and mother was elevated "to a pedestal" on the frontier and any disrespect to her was a serious offense.

"Lawlessness was also a consistent fault in the U.S., where people seemed to take malicious pleasure in flaunting authority," Billington (1966, 65) held. This suspicion of authority led to a schizophrenic type of character — demanding freedom from government interference at the same time vigilante mobs sometimes hung guilty and innocent alike during the times of fear and disorder. Acknowledging the "pace of lawlessness accelerated" as the frontier moved westward, Billington nevertheless said the folklore painting cattle and mining towns as "occupied largely by profane, tobacco-spitting, nose-biting, eye-gouging, Sabbath-breaking, drunken, half-horse and half-alligator rip roarers" was distorted because of the tendency of visitors to "single out unusual frontier types for extended description," partly because they "sensed that the market for their books would expand in proportion to the amount of blood and thunder they could capture on the page....

"That this handful of outcasts should be pictured as typical frontiersmen was unfortunate. The true pioneers — those who subdued the West — were the small-propertied farmers, ranchers, and entrepreneurs who formed the bulk of the advancing population" (Billington, 1966, 72–73).

Their belief in individualism led to many criminal offenses (e.g., fighting, fraud, petty theft) being overlooked in most western communities, but their belief in communal organization for safety and protection led to a propensity to pass laws to stem disorder and protect their economic investments. For example, Billington found in many western towns, "[c]itizens were required to sweep the streets before their doors" and laws restricting private behavior included heavy fines for swearing, billiards, and unfair business practices. "Frontiersmen accepted infringements on individual freedom needed to protect the community against gambling, time-wasting entertainment, or sleep-disturbing noise, just as had the Puritans" (Billington, 1966, 147).

Because of their distrust of government power, frontier communities greatly expanded the power of citizen-controlled grand juries and the use of juries to determine guilt in criminal trials. Billington (1966, 178) concluded:

> Along the frontiers, lawyers and judges alike were usually scantily educated in the common law and distrustful of the pettifogging that seemed designed only to bilk the innocent of their rights. They were inclined to judge issues on the basis of common sense rather than legal precedents. As they applied this philosophy to the unique problems faced in the West, they altered imported practices and in certain areas pioneered a distinctly American law.

As to "justice for all," power and politics prevailed in all too many communities, as Native Americans were led to sign multiple treaties negotiated "in good faith," only to see them broken time and again. Most Americans of color, but particularly Chinese and Mexican Americans received few if any rights by law and often less than equal justice in the courts. In addition, as railroaders and land speculators moved west, they often created law enforcement agencies and courts to extend their own interests, usually at the expense of the settlers.

To understand the development of frontier justice, two elements will be helpful: (1) a highlight chronology of the development of the frontier, and (2) a thumbnail sketch of the major outlaws and lawmen of the period.

## Chronology

Arguably the frontier started in 1492, but the "western" frontier of the U.S. has often been seen as the 1840–1890 period. Here events will be chronicled from 1803 to 1893—the year the U.S. first acquired land west of the Mississippi River to the year Turner declared the frontier "closed."

*1803.* Under the Louisiana Purchase, the U.S. acquires 828,000 square miles west of the Mississippi for $15 million.

*1804.* The *Land Act of 1804* allows settlers to buy western land for $1.64 per acre with a minimum purchase of 160 acres.

*1805.* Fort Bellefontaine, near St. Louis, extends U.S. control west of the Mississippi.
Lewis and Clark reach the Pacific Ocean.

*1811.* Western "war hawks" (e.g., Henry Clay of KY and John C. Calhoun of SC) are elected to Congress and advocate western expansion.

*1812.* White settlers are driven out of Michigan by Native Americans.

Louisiana is admitted as the 18th state and first west of the Mississippi.

*1815.* At the end of the Creek War in the Southeast, Andrew Jackson strips the Creeks of their land in Mississippi.

*1816.* At Portage Des Sioux (at the confluence of the Mississippi and Missouri Rivers, treaties of peace and friendship signed with the Native American tribes allow "rapid settlement of these areas."

*1820.* A *Land Act* reduces the minimum purchase of public land to 80 acres at $1.25 per acre, meaning a settler can purchase a farm for $100.

*1821.* The Sante Fe Trail opens between Independence, MO, and Sante Fe (then Mexico) and becomes the principle route for manufactured goods and emigrants bound for the southwest.

*1822.* The Indian Factory System, established to assure Indians a fair price, is abolished because of pressure from white traders interested in this lucrative business.

*1823.* President James Monroe declares that any attempt by Europeans to colonize the Americas or interfere with its internal affairs will be interpreted as an act of aggression by the U.S. (that became known as The Monroe Doctrine).

*1824.* The Bureau of Indian Affairs is established. Texas is incorporated into the Mexican Federal Republic, but the new State of Texas-Coahuila passes a colonization act that allows emigration of American settlers.

*1825.* The Erie Canal opens, cutting travel time by one third and cost of shipping to one tenth its previous level, opening large scale emigration from the east coast to the Mississippi Valley and beyond.

*1830.* President Andrew Jackson signs the *Indian Removal Act*, which calls for general resettlement of Indians to lands west of the Mississippi.

The *Pre-emption Act of 1830* allows settlers to buy land from earnings on their crops after they stake their claims.

Mexico forbids further colonization of Texas by U.S. citizens after refusing an offer by President Jackson to buy the land.

*1831.* The U.S. Supreme Court rules in *Cherokee Nation v. Georgia* that the Cherokee are not a "foreign nation" but are a "dependent nation," and thus can be removed to the west.

*1834.* The English poor law is overhauled, with thousands removed from assistance, vastly increasing emigration to the U.S.

*1836.* Texas declares itself an independent republic; a small band of American emigrants die at the Alamo.

*1840.* U.S. population reaches 17 million (up from 5 million in 1800), including 40,000 Indians from the "Five Civilized Nations" of the East, now relocated in the West.

*1841. New York Tribune* editor Horace Greeley, writes "Go west, young man, go west."

The *Pre-emption Act of 1841* gives "squatters" the right to purchase federal land upon which they have settled at a "minimum price."

Overland migration to California begins as a wagon train reaches Stockton.

*1842.* Migration of white settlers via the Oregon Trail begins.

*1845.* The Republic of Texas is annexed by joint resolution of Congress and Texas is admitted as the 28th state in the Union, leading to war with Mexico.

President James Polk articulates in his first Annual Message the "Polk Doctrine" that become known as "manifest destiny"—that the people of the American continent have exclusive rights to "decide their own destiny."

*1846.* The U.S. and Great Britain sign the *Oregon Treaty* to establish the boundary between the U.S. and the British Northwest Territory; the U.S. acquires the future states of Idaho, Oregon, Washington, and parts of Montana and Wyoming.

The Bear Flag Revolt in California begins as American settlers declare California is U.S. territory.

Brigham Young organizes the westward movement of the Mormons who over the next two years begin settling in what becomes Salt Lake City.

*1848.* The discovery of gold at Sutter's Mill, CA, leads to thousands of new emigrants.

The U.S. defeats Mexico and acquires the Texas territory, including what becomes the states of Texas, California, Nevada, Utah, New Mexico, western Colorado, and most of Arizona.

*1851.* Dakota (Sioux) Native Americans turn over their land in Iowa and most of their territory in Minnesota to the U.S. government; the Treaty of Fort Laramie promises food and gifts to Native Americans

to compensate for white incursions on hunting grounds.

*1853.* The U.S. acquires southern Arizona and the rest of New Mexico from Mexico for $10 million; this purchase completes the permanent continental boundaries of the U.S.

*1857.* James Buchanan becomes the 15th President, announces support for "popular sovereignty in the territories," but sends U.S. troops to the Utah Territory for the "Mormon War" that ends in a bloodless compromise.

*1860.* The Pony Express Mail Service begins its 16-month life, ended in 1861 with the completion of the first transcontinental telegraph line.

*1863.* A new *Homestead Act* entitles anyone who intends to acquire citizenship to acquire 160 acres of public land by settling on it for 5 years and paying a small filing fee.

*1864.* Some 150 Native American men, women, and children are killed by Colorado volunteers in the Sand Creek Massacre.

*1866.* The westward movement begins in earnest with the end of the Civil War.

250,000 head of cattle are driven across the Chisholm Trail in the first great overland cattle drive.

Congress passes a Civil Rights Act over President Andrew Johnson's veto, granting rights to all natural born Americans, including former slaves, but not to Native American people.

"Red Cloud's War" between the U.S. Army and the Lakotas results from Sioux opposition to construction of a road from Wyoming to Montana along the Bozeman Trail.

*1867.* A Congressional Peace Commission initiates a new round of treaties promising to isolate Native Americans from casual contact with whites and to allocate land to individual tribesmen.

*1868.* The Treaty of Ft. Laramie promises no whites will be allowed to "settle, occupy, or pass through the Black Hills' without the consent of the Lakota people.

Gen. George A. Custer kills over 200 Cheyenne in an attack on the sleeping village of Black Kettle.

*1869.* The Union Pacific Railroad joins the Central Pacific at Promontory, UT, completing the first transcontinental railroad line.

*1870.* The U.S. population reaches almost 40 million (from 17 million in 1840).

*1871.* A new tanning process makes buffalo hides valuable and leads to "the big kill"—the slaughter of 3.7 million buffalo.

All Native American people are declared "national wards" and no further treaties are enacted as the Army issues orders forbidding western Indians from leaving the reservation without permission of civilian Indian agents.

*1872.* Yellowstone becomes the nation's first national park, as preservation of land joins exploitation of land as public policy.

*1873.* Immigration to the U.S. reaches a new single-year high of 460,000.

The *Timber Culture Act of 1873* gives settlers an additional 160 acres of land if they plant trees on at least 40 of those acres.

*1875.* Fifteen thousand gold seekers enter the Black Hills and President Ulysses Grant asks the Sioux to relinquish their tribal homes there; more "Indian Wars" are sparked, led by Sitting Bull, Crazy Horse and others, and resulting in the massacre of Gen. Custer's Seventh Calvary at Little Big Horn.

*1876.* Crazy Horse is killed; Sitting Bull takes his people to Canada; and the Nes Perce under Chief George are taken back to the reservation after they are captured by the U.S. Army just short of Canada.

*1878.* The *Timber Cutting Act* allows miners and settlers to cut timber on public land for their own use, free of charge.

*1879.* In one of the largest spontaneous migrations in history, over 6000 African-Americans travel from the southern states to the great plains of Kansas to establish homesteads.

*1881.* Sitting Bull and his band of 187 return from Canada to accept reservation life in the U.S.
Helen Hunt Jackson publishes *A Century of Dishonor* to publicize the desperate plight of Native Americans, perpetuated by U.S. Indian policies.

*1883.* Buffalo Bill Cody organizes the first Wild West Show that eventually brings the romanticized version of the west to easterners and then Europeans.

*1884.* A Native American tries to vote in Nebraska, precipitating a federal court ruling in *Elk v. Wilkins* that the 14th Amendment does not apply to Indians.

*1886.* With the capture of Apache Chief Geronimo, the last major Indian War is ended.

*1887.* The *Dawes Severalty Act* provides for division of Indian Lands among Indian families; designed to force Native Americans to live the lifestyle of Euro-American farmers; instead it breaks up the reservations, with millions of surplus acres going to white settlers.

*1889.* The first Oklahoma land rush sees 20,000 settlers stake their claims in a single day, many of which are on former Indian lands.

*1890.* The last armed conflict between the U.S. Army and the Lakota Indians takes place at Wounded Knee, SD, where 200 Lakotas are killed; earlier Lakota Chief Sitting Bull was killed by soldiers.

The U.S. population reaches 63 million; the Census Bureau announces the demarcation line between civilization and the frontier can no longer be distinguished.

*1891.* Nine hundred thousand acres of Indian land in Oklahoma are opened for general settlement by presidential proclamation.

President Benjamin Harrison sets aside 1.2 million acres of forest lands for federal use in the Yellowstone region and proclaims 14 other forest preserves.

*1892.* The 1.8 million-acre Crow reservation and the 3 million-acre Cheyenne-Arapaho reservation are opened for settlement by whites.

*1893.* The Cherokee Strip between Kansas and Oklahoma is opened for white settlement.

Frederick Jackson Turner declares the frontier is "closed."

## Outlaws and Lawmen

A brief discussion of the major outlaws and lawmen of the frontier era provides insight into the unique character of these frontiersmen and the reasons for the unique style of justice that emerged. The difficulty of such an endeavor can be seen in the story of Joaquin Murieta, one of "five Joaquins" believed to be responsible for a wave of cattle rustling, robberies, and murders in the Mother Lode region of California during the 1850s. On May 11, 1853, California Governor John Bigler signed a legislative act authorizing the organization of a band of California Rangers to hunt down Murieta and the other "Joaquins." Later a $1,000 bonus was paid to a Ranger for allegedly killing Murieta and producing his severed head. The truth is that Murieta probably never existed, but was the product of the "sensational and highly fictional" account of a San Francisco journalist who wrote under the pen name "Yellow Bird." The legend of Joaquin Murieta took on a life of its own and it was only years later that a photograph of Murieta in the Old Timer's Museum in Murphys, CA, was found to be of Frank Marshall Sr., which was donated by the Marshall family "by mistake" (Mace, 1993).

## Some Other "Legendary" Outlaws and Lawmen

*Judge Roy Bean (about 1825–1903).* Born in Kentucky, Roy Bean set out for adventure in the west, but after killing a man in Chihuahua, Mexico, fled to California to stay with his brother, soon to become the first mayor of San Diego. Roy tended bar in his brother's saloon and smuggled guns from Mexico on the side. After marrying a Mexican teenager, he settled in San Antonio, Texas, and supported five children by peddling stolen firewood and watered-down milk. Fleeing his wife and children, Roy became a saloonkeeper in Pecos County, Texas, and was appointed Justice of the Peace. He set up court in a saloon in isolated Langtry, posting a sign proclaiming "Ice Cold Beer" and "Law West of the Pecos." Ignoring the law for the most part, Judge Bean ruled by intuition, once refusing to pass judgment on a man found guilty of killing a Chinese worker, allegedly saying, "Gentlemen, I find the law very explicit on murdering your fellow man, but there's nothing here about killing a Chinaman. Case dismissed." In legend, Judge Bean became known as a merciless "hanging judge," but in reality, as a justice of the peace he had no jurisdiction to try murder or any other felony case. The myth of Judge Bean and his many colorful exploits became part of Texas folklore.

*Charles E. Boles aka Black Bart (1829 – last seen 1888).* Born in England, Bowles (later Boles) emigrated to the U.S. with his family at the age of two. After gold prospecting in California and serving in the Civil War, Boles for some reason began robbing stage coaches in 1875, gaining a reputation as a polite gentleman bandit. Boles is alleged to have taken the moniker "Black Bart" from a Dime Novel serializing a story of a black-bearded, wild-eyed character by that name. Boles built on the legend by leaving poems at the scene of many of his 28 confirmed robberies, such as one that read,

> Here I lay me down to sleep, to wait the coming morrow, Perhaps success perhaps defeat, and everlasting sorrow,

> Let come what will I'll try it on,

> My condition can't be worse, and if there's money in that box,

> Tis munny in my purse.

After being caught and spending four years in San Quentin Prison (shortened from six for good behavior), he told the reporters swarming around him on his release that he was "through with crime." Asked if he'd write more poetry, he laughingly replied: "Now didn't you hear me say I am through with crime."

*Wyatt Earp (1848–1929).* Born in Illinois, Wyatt moved with his family to California, where he became a stagecoach driver. In 1970 he returned to his Monmouth, Illinois, birthplace to become town marshal. But in 1871 Wyatt was jailed in the Cherokee Nation for stealing horses; he paid his bail and then fled before trial. From 1871–1873, he hunted bison and met people like Wild Bill Hickok and gunfighter Bat Masterson, before becoming a deputy sheriff in Wichita, Kansas, and in 1876 he became marshal in Dodge City. For deputies he hired Bat and the three other Masterson brothers. His exploits as marshal were legendary as he required all visitors to check their guns before entering town and depended on guile and trickery rather than gunfights to keep the peace. In 1879, Wyatt, his brothers, and friend cum gunfighter, Doc Holliday, arrived in Tombstone, Arizona. Confrontations with area gunfighters included the famous shootout at the Oklahoma Corral, followed by the bushwhacking deaths of two of Wyatt's brothers two months later. Wyatt and Doc tracked down the alleged killers and killed them. After moving to California and failing to find gold, Earp spent some time raising race horses in San Diego and spent his last years as a popular sports commentator in Los Angeles.

*Crawford "Cherokee Bill" Goldsby (1876–1896).* Hanged at 20 years of age, Cherokee Bill nevertheless became known as possibly the most notorious outlaw in Indian Territory following a two-year reign of terror. Born in Fort Concho, Texas, at the age of two his father left, fleeing murder charges. For the next 16 years, Crawford went to Indian School and later worked at odd jobs, often for room and board. After a confrontation at age 18, Crawford shot a man and fled, later joining two outlaws, Jim and Bill Cook, and becoming involved in a gunfight with a sheriff's posse in which a member of the posse was killed. The gang grew and over the next months robbed and killed throughout the Oklahoma Territory, with Cherokee Bill being credited with most of the murders, by one account 14 men. Panic ensued and the U.S. government sent deputy marshals to capture Bill and his gang, after lawmen in the territory were reluctant to confront Bill, who according to legend, could shoot faster than two ordinary men. Once captured, Bill was tried before legendary Judge Isaac Parker in Fort Smith, Arkansas, and despite a number of "alibis," he was found guilty and sentenced to hang. During the wait in the Fort Smith jail, Bill obtained a gun and shot and killed a guard, then held the jail captive while "gobbling" and scaring the other prisoners.

Talked into giving up, he was tried for the latest murder and sentenced to hang. On the gallows, he was asked if he had any last words. "I came here to die, not make a speech," he said 12 minutes before being pronounced dead.

*John Wesley Hardin (1853–1895).* Texas' most notorious gunfighter (who by his own account killed 40 men), John Wesley Hardin, was the son of a minister and named after the founder of the Methodist Church. After killing a black playmate at age 15, Hardin was sent away by his father, who feared he would not get a fair trial in this Reconstruction Era following the Civil War. Hardin went on to kill other blacks, leading to his status as a folk hero among like-minded Texans, but he also killed even more whites and Mexicans. In his book, *The Last Gunfighter*, psychiatrist Richard Marohn held Hardin was a narcissistic exhibitionist who gained cultural support for his exploits. After his death, Hardin's autobiography, *The Life of John Wesley Hardin, as Written by Himself*, was published; Hardin described his exploits in detail, always blaming the victims. Hardin was once caught by Texas Rangers and served 16 years in Huntsville Prison. After moving to wild and wooly El Paso on his release, he went back to drinking and handing out autographed playing cards he'd shot holes through. On the evening of August 19, 1895, as he was playing cards in a saloon, he was shot in the back of the head by a notorious gunfighter, the then Constable John Selman.

*John Henry "Doc" Holliday (1851–1887).* Born in Georgia and educated at Pennsylvania College of Dental Surgery, Doc practiced dentistry for a short time before being diagnosed with tuberculosis, after which he lost his practice when patients began leaving the coughing doctor. Heading west for profit and adventure, he became a professional gambler with a reputation as being dangerous and homicidal—hot-tempered and quick on the trigger, although his constant drinking was said to have made him less than accurate on occasion. Doc was dealing cards in a saloon in Fort Griffin, Texas, when he met the only woman who remained in his life, a frontier dance hall prostitute known as Big Nose Kate; he also met Wyatt Earp

there, and after helping the Dodge City marshal track down a train robber, they became lifelong friends. After killing a popular local gunman in Las Vegas, New Mexico, Holliday headed for Dodge City only to find Earp and his brothers had moved to Tombstone, Arizona. Holliday followed and the famous gunfight at Oklahoma Corral, likely, was a result of a confrontation Holliday had in a bar earlier with some of the participants. When two Earp brothers were killed later, it was Holliday who joined Wyatt to track down the killers; by the time they finished, a number of persons were dead, some shot in the back as they ran from their pursuers. Holliday was arrested in Denver later, but was seen more as a folklore hero than an outlaw and escaped punishment. During the last five years of his life, Holliday claimed he tried to give up his gunfighter lifestyle, but was the victim of five ambushes and four attempts at hanging. He finally succumbed to tuberculosis at the age of 36.

*Jesse Woodson James (1847–1882).* Known by some as the American Robin Hood and by others as a cold-blooded killer, Jesse James was the son of a Baptist minister. He and brother Frank served in the Confederate Army and were captured and allegedly cruelly treated by Union soldiers. After the war, the brothers are believed to have pulled off the first daylight bank robbery in peace time, killing one man and escaping with $60,000 from a Liberty, Missouri bank near their home town of Kearney. For the next 15 years the James gang, which included the Younger Brothers, roamed the Midwest robbing trains and banks and becoming the most legendary of American bandits. During this period, Jesse, after a 9-year courtship, married his cousin and had two children. Once, while being chased by the Pinkerton Detective Agency, a firebomb was tossed into the James' family home, killing Jesse's half-brother Archie and tearing the hand off his mother. After a bank robbery in Northfield, Minnesota, in 1876, all the members of the James gang except Jesse and Frank were either killed or captured. Jesse retired, took the name Tom Howard, and became a church-going family man until, in the winter of 1882, he was unable to raise the money to buy a farm. Jesse recruited Bob and Charlie Ford to rob the Platte City bank. Later, prompted by the $10,000 reward, Bob Ford shot Jesse in the back of the head. Rather than be rewarded, the Ford brothers were convicted of murder and sentenced to hang, but were pardoned by Governor Tom Crittenden. Charles Ford committed suicide and later Bob Ford was killed in a barroom brawl.

*William Barclay "Bat" Masterson (1855–1921).* An adventurer from birth, Bat was alternately a buffalo hunter, army scout, gunfighter, and lawman. At age 21,

Bat and his brother Jim became deputy marshals with Wyatt Earp in Dodge City, KA. The next year Bat became sheriff of Ford County where his brother Ed was marshal of Dodge. In 1879, Bat was voted out of office and spent time gambling in Tombstone, Arizona, and later took town marshal jobs in Trinidad and then Creed, Colorado. After moving to Denver, where he began drinking heavily, Bat was told by the local sheriff—well aware of Bat's reputation—to give up his gun or leave town. Bat left, but in 1905 was appointed by President Teddy Roosevelt as marshal of the southern district of New York State. When later offered an appointment as marshal of the Oklahoma Territory, Bat declined, saying his reputation would result in too many situations where he would have to kill or be killed. In 1907 Bat retired from law enforcement and took a job as sports editor of a newspaper, a position he kept until his death in 1921.

*Henry McCarthy aka Kid Antrim aka William H. Bonney aka Billy the Kid (1859–1881).* Born in New York City, Henry McCarthy moved with his mother to Silver City, New Mexico, in 1873. A year later his mother died and soon Billy killed a bully who was beating him up at the time. Taking the name Kid Antrim, he fled to Lincoln County and again changing his name, this time to William H. Bonney, he became a Regulator in the Lincoln County War, fought between cattlemen and "corrupt" merchants and politicians. Bill idolized his boss, John Tunstall (possibly a father figure), and was incensed when Tunstall was murdered. Billy became a leader of the Tunstall forces and killed at least four men during the five-day battle that ended the war. Governor Lew Wallace (author of *Ben Hur*) offered Billy a pardon for his testimony, but then reneged. After being sentenced to hang, Billy escaped from jail, allegedly when a guard slipped him a gun, hoping to kill Billy during the escape. Instead Billy killed the guard. Hunting Billy throughout this period was Sheriff Pat Garrett, who shot him dead at the age of 21 in a darkened bedroom of Billy's friend, Pete Maxwell.

Even while he was alive the Dime Novels wrote of his exploits—the boy running a man's war—and after his death the legend grew and became a significant part of American folklore. In January 2004, legal proceedings were under way to exhume the body of Billy's mother, Catherine Antrim, to obtain a sample of her DNA to compare with that of Ollie "Brushy Bill" Roberts of Hico, Texas, who claimed until his death in 1950 that he was the real Billy the Kid. Before her death, Alpolonaria Garrett allegedly said her husband and Billy the Kid killed a drunk and Sheriff Garrett passed the body off as that of Billy. Current Lincoln County Sheriff Tom Sullivan supported the exhumation to "determine the truth," since Garrett's image was on the logo on his deputies' uniforms.

*Isaac "Hanging Judge" Parker (1838–1896).* Born and educated in Ohio (law degree), Parker opened an office in St. Joseph, Missouri, and in 1868 was appointed as a judge, and two years later was elected to Congress. In 1875, he left office and was appointed Federal Judge in the Western District of Arkansas. From his bench in Fort Smith, Arkansas, he presided over the Indian Territory of Oklahoma. With a promise of bringing "law and order" to the territory, Parker told U.S. Marshal James F. Fagan to hire 200 deputies and bring in all the robbers, murderers, and other thieves they could find. For 21 years, he earned the reputation of "Hanging Judge" by sentencing 168 men and four women to death on the gallows just outside the courtroom. About half the condemned were pardoned or won appeals and five were shot dead by hangman George Maledon as they attempted to escape their fate. Whereas Judge Parker sometimes delivered severe lectures to those brought before him, he also petitioned on behalf of several of the men he sentenced, as the law required a death sentence for anyone found guilty of murder by a jury.

These biographical sketches of major figures of the frontier period indicate: (1) outlaws and bandits were often the same persons, supplying evidence in support of The Dualistic Fallacy; (2) legend, folklore, and Dime Novels make it difficult to separate truth from mythology; and (3) "justice" is a product of popular culture, defined by the milieu.

## Conclusions

Frontier justice had an inordinate impact on today's justice system in America. Although the U.S. justice system was based on the common law system in England, law of custom took a whole new meaning as the frontier moved westward. With no police or courts in place, communities often created their own vigilante committees to hire a sheriff and a judge, often one of their own. When they went outside the group for assistance, they often sought someone with a reputation for toughness, such as a soldier or a gunslinger. Sometimes what they got was the stuff of legends.

At the same time, as the frontier proceeded, few professional journalists were on the scene, with town newspapers often being run by settlers seeking a living and writers arriving from the east mostly selling to the sensationalized Dime Novels, the equivalent of today's supermarket tabloids. It was out of this mix that legend, folklore, and mythology grew and truth and accuracy suffered.

Protection of their ethnic group also became a priority, as white Europeans applied what law there was to their own, but often had a harsher brand of justice for "outsiders," such as Native Americans, Chinese immigrants, and Mexican Americans. Some have even suggested the policy toward Native Americans evolved to one close to genocide.

Possibly the most significant outcome was the change in the guiding philosophy of police from the peace officer pledged to prevent crime to the law enforcement officer determined to enforce the law and catch and punish lawbreakers. In the courts, protection of the community became more important than protecting individual rights, leading to the differential treatment of ethnic groups that still exists in many courts today.

GENE STEPHENS

## References and Further Reading

Axelrod, A. and Phillips, C., *What Every American Should Know about American History,* 2nd ed., Avon, MA, Adams Media, 2004.

Barak, G., Ed., *Media, Process, and the Social Construction of Crime,* New York, Garland, 1994.

*Bat Masterson, Marshal, Deputy.* Available at: http://www.linecamp. com/museums/America...names/masterson bat/masterson bat. html. Retrieved on January 8, 2004.

Benke, R., Billy the Kid mystery resurfaces, *The State* (Columbia, SC), Associated Press, January 14, 2004, p. A12.

Billington, R.A., *America's Frontier Heritage,* New York, Holt, Rinehart and Winston, 1966.

*Billy for School Kids.* Available at: http://www.nmia.com; ~btkog/ billyfor.html. Retrieved on January 8, 2004.

Burchell, R.A., Ed., *Westward Expansion,* London, George G. Harrap, 1974.

*Doc Holliday.* Available at: http://thenaturalamerican.com/holliday.html. Retrieved January 9, 2004.

Einstadter, W.J., Crime news in the old west, in Barak, G., Ed., *Media, Process, and the Social Construction of Crime,* New York, Garland, 1994.

*Fort Smith National Historic Site—Myths and Legends Surrounding Judge Parker.* Available at: http://www.nps.gov/fosm/history/judgeparker/mythandlegend.html. Retrieved January 8, 2004.

*Gunfight at the OK Corral—Tombstone, Arizona.* Available at: http://www.ku.edu/heritage/gunfighters/okcorral.html. Retrieved on January 8, 2004.

*History 686: American Social History Outline: Lecture 5: Americans on the Frontier.* Available at: http://history. smsu.edu/GHummasti_internet class/lectures/lecture5.html. Retrieved December 27, 2003.

*History-Part Nine: Cowtown Marshals 'Winged a Few.'* Available at: http://www.candyscorral.com/Library/HoytHistory/history9.shtml. Retrieved on January 8, 2004.

Hollon, W.E., *Frontier Violence: Another Look,* New York, Oxford Press, 1974.

*Isaac 'Hanging Judge' Parker.* Available at: http://www. rollspel.com/engelsk/western/eparker.html. Retrieved on January 8, 2004.

*Jesse James.* Available at: wysiwyg://49/http://www.ci.st-joseph.mo.us//history/jessejames.asp. Retrieved on January 8, 2004.

*Judge Roy Bean.* Available at: http://www. qsl.net/w5www/roybean.html. Retrieved on January 8, 2004.

*Kickin' Down Route 66: A Little History if You Like [19th Century Timeline].* Available at: http://www.synaptic.bc.ca/ejthree/014hist1.html. Retrieved on January 6, 2004.

Mace, O.H., The Legend of Joaquin Morieta in Mace, O.H., Ed., *Between the Rivers,* Jackson, CA, Cenotto Publications, 1993.

Marohn, R., *The Last Gunfighter,* College Station, TX, Creative Publishing/The Early West, 1993.

McRae, B.J., Jr., *Crawford "Cherokee Bill" Goldsby...the Toughest of Them All,* Trotwood, OH, LWF Publications, 1994.

*New Perspectives on the West: Frederick Jackson Turner.* Available at: wysiwyg://4/http://www.pbs.org/weta/thewest/people/s_z/turner.html. Retrieved on January 8, 2004.

Sublett, J., *The Bio of John Wesley Hardin: The Fortysomething Killer.* Available at: http://www.austinchronicle.com/issues/vol15/issue2/arts.books.html. Retrieved on January 10, 2004.

*The History of Lynching: Courtroom Television Network.* Available at: wysiwyg://151/http://www.crimelibrary.comj/classics2/carnival/2.html. Retrieved on January 8, 2004.

*The Story of Charles E. Boles aka Black Bart.* Available at: http://www.sptddog.com/sotp/bbpo8.html. Retrieved on January 7, 2004.

*The Story of Wyatt Earp in Pella, Iowa.* Available at: http://www.pellatuliptime.com/wyatt.html. Retrieved on January 9, 2004.

*Wyatt Earp.* Avilable at: http://www.rollspel.coj/engelsk/western/eearp.html. Retrieved on January 8, 2004.

*Wyatt Earp.* Available at: http://www.sandiegohistory.org/bio/earp/earp.html. Retrieved on January 9, 2004.

*See also* **Colonial America, Crime and Justice in; Retribution; Vigilante Violence**

# V

# Vandalism

The appearance during the 18th century of the term "vandalism," which during the French Revolution denoted the devastation of works of art, could be assessed as accidental. The introduced term was associated with phenomena that took place during the 5th century AD, when the Vandals (together with other barbarian tribes) crossed the Rhine under the pressure of the encroaching Goths, laid waste to Gaul and Spain, and then via those lands and North Africa invaded the disintegrating Western Empire, destroying everything along their path. In 455 AD, the Vandals captured and looted Rome, already previously (410) sacked by Alaric, leader of the Visigoths. History had witnessed many similar cases of mass-scale pillage and destruction of works of art, not only at the hand of victorious states or tribes. During the 4th century BC, Herostratus, a cobbler from Ephesus, set fire to a temple of Artemis in order to gain fame. Condemned to death and oblivion, he stayed in human memory up to our times.

Subsequent years also provided examples of vandalism. The 8th century iconoclastic movement in the Byzantine Empire razed numerous invaluable works of art that depicted human or animal likenesses. The hordes of Genghis Khan that roamed across Asia and Europe during the 13th century, reduced entire cities, celebrated for masterpieces of architecture, to rubble. During the 14th century King Charles V of Spain managed to prevent local zealots from pulling down the Muslim mosque in Cordova. Certain communist states, such as Mongolia, Albania, and China (during the Cultural Revolution), waged a veritable battle against religious cult objects in the 1970s.

Vandalism appears in assorted types of destructive activities. As a rule, we apply the term "destructiveness" to material property regardless of its value, in other words to products of material culture classified, assessed, and recognized as works of art, and to everyday, mass-produced objects possessing only utilitarian value. On the other hand, destruction may pertain solely to spiritual and social culture. Vandalism consisting of a purposeful devastation or waste of the accomplishments of spiritual and social culture is much more difficult to detect, and is penalized to a degree lesser than the destruction of material property. When considering the problem of vandalism—its etiology, function, intensification, and legal and socioeconomic outcomes—we should consider all forms of destructive activities, regardless of the domain of social life against which it is directed.

Contemporary criminological literature discloses a tendency toward an extremely extensive interpretation of the concept of "vandalism." By way of example, A. P. Goldstein (1996) maintains that "while current definitions include deliberately broken windows, graffiti and other acts of damage, disfigurement and destruction, an expanded definition should include behaviors such as environmentally damaging waste disposal, air, water and noise pollution, and other behaviors collectively identified by the environment movement. Each act of vandalism stems from sources in both the environment and person."

The fact that vandalism is a universal phenomenon in the contemporary world inclines us to consider its etiology in general, and the etiology of the contemporary form of vandalism in particular. In everyday life vandalism is basically a destructive act in which persons attack the objects that surround them. An attempted typology of the motivations of vandals would include:

- the accumulated energy that the individual is incapable of expressing because of the necessity of remaining calm in social situations upon which he is dependent; this situation results in a need to react to the ensuing tension;
- the need to give vent to aggression and take revenge for one's failures—a typical shift of reactions from the field in which aggression came into being onto a neutral field, (where the individual will certainly be the winner);
- the destruction of the symbols of someone else's work as a protest against the person or group who produced that work or use those symbols;
- the destruction of the symbols of someone's ownership in a situation when it is impossible to become an owner (jealousy);
- an inferiority and superiority complex toward the creators of certain works;
- insufficient appreciation of and disrespect for a given work;
- hostility toward a certain artistic style, even while accepting the idea;
- hostility toward an idea symbolized in a material object (e.g., the desecration of a flag).

The feature that distinguishes vandalism from other deeds resulting in loss or injury is the fact that even after the discovery of the perpetrator, the motives of his conduct may remain unclear. Acts of vandalism usually appear to be senseless and to have no use for the offender. It is impossible to define the perpetrator by determining who profited from the crime, who resolved an important problem, or who avoided a threat, thanks to the perpetrated wrongdoing.

Stanley Cohen distinguished five primary motivations for vandalism:

1. Game—in this case we are dealing with vandalism committed by children aged 10–12, and containing an element of "showing off." Other particular elements include competition, curiosity, or a desire to demonstrate skillfulness.
2. Revenge—the act of retaliation against a person, group, or organization who has wronged the offender (in his or her view).
3. Displeasure—vicious vandalism that reveals the general frustration of the vandal. With the two remaining categories of motivations, apparent acts of vandalism actually are for other reasons.
4. Vandalism committed for profit—for example, the destruction of a public telephone in order to steal change.
5. Political vandalism—for example, political slogans written as graffiti.

Technology can be used to prevent vandalism, through architectural design and rational spatial planning (e.g., the use of unbreakable window panes or the construction of special seats in buses and trams made of damage-proof material). Also, great significance should be ascribed to education and attempts should be made to introduce social changes in order to limit the number of frustrated young people. Social surveillance over individuals in public places should be expanded. Finally, young persons must be made aware that public property belongs to society as a whole, so that they feel responsible for objects that are potential targets of vandalism.

BRUNON HOLYST

### References and Further Reading

Clinard, M.B. and Wade, A.L., Towards the delineation of vandalism as a sub-type in juvenile delinquency, *Journal of Criminal Law, Criminology and Police Science*, 5(48), (1958).

Cohen, A.K., *Delinquent Boys. The Culture of the Gang*, New York, NY, Free Press, 1955.

Gimbrerer, S.M., van Rappard, C.E., Boot, A.W.A., et al., Judicial Explorations, *Art and criminality*, 1(23), 8–61 (1997).

Goldstein, A.P., *The Psychology of Vandalism*, New York, NY, Plenum Press, 1996.

Ward, C., Ed., *Vandalism*, London, U.K., Architectural Press, 1973.

# Victim Compensation Programs

Victim compensation refers to the use of public funds to reimburse persons who have been victimized by a violent crime or to reimburse persons who survive those killed by such crimes for losses sustained at the hands of criminals. There are two main arguments made by proponents of victim compensation: the "obligation of the state" argument and the "social welfare" argument (Smith and Hillenbrand, 1997). According to the "obligation of the state" perspective, if the state fails in its duty to protect citizens from crime, it has broken its social contract and must compensate those who have been victimized. According to the "social welfare" perspective, the state has a general societal and moral responsibility to help innocent victims of crime.

Providing compensation to innocent victims is not a new concept. The Babylonian Code of Hammurabi (approximately 1775 BC), which is considered to be the oldest written body of criminal law, is often cited as the first legal record of victim compensation (Edwards, 1971). Legal historians have also traced the existence of compensation for victims to ancient Greece and Rome, biblical Israel, Teutonic Germany, Saxony England, Tuscany, Mexico, Switzerland, Cuba, and France. The modern revival of victim compensation took place during the 1950s in Anglo–Saxon legal systems. Much of the credit for the revival of victim compensation can be given to Margery Fry, a Magistrate in England and an advocate for penal change who argued that victims' injuries were the responsibility of the state. Fry's advocacy efforts had a major impact on compensation programs that were subsequently developed in New Zealand in 1963 and in Great Britain in 1964.

The first victim compensation program in the U.S. was developed in California in 1965. By 1982, 36 states had developed programs and by 1993 all 50 states, the District of Columbia, and the Virgin Islands had established victim compensation programs. In 1984, the U.S. Congress passed the Victims of Crime Act (VOCA), which established the "Crime Victims Fund" from fines, penalties, and forfeitures from federal criminal offenders (Sarnoff, 1996). The fund accrues on an annual basis and is used to supplement state victim compensation programs. Nearly 40% of the compensation payments made by states to crime victims are reimbursed annually by the fund. In addition to the federal VOCA monies states receive to subsidize their programs, there are two other primary sources of income for state compensation programs: fines and charges paid by offenders in state and local courts and general state revenues appropriated by state legislatures.

Each state's compensation program is administered in accordance with the state's statute. As a result, there are similarities and differences across programs. All programs, however, provide compensation to victims of serious violent crimes that result in serious physical injury, psychological trauma, or death. Most programs do not compensate victims of property crimes. In addition, compensation awards are granted to "innocent" victims of crimes. Each state's compensation program has a compensation board that reviews each claim that is filed. Members of the compensation board evaluate claims for evidence of whether the victim contributed to the crime or if the victim was involved in criminal activity during the crime. In cases where this occurred, most boards would rule against the claim. Compensation programs have an appeals process whereby victims have an opportunity to address the compensation board if they do not agree with a decision regarding a claim.

Compensation boards also review compensation claims to ensure that victims have exhausted all other financial sources for reimbursement. Before being eligible for compensation, crime victims must first seek reimbursement from private insurance companies or public benefit sources for medical expenses, funeral benefits, or counseling.

There are additional eligibility requirements that victims must meet in order to file a compensation claim. Victims must promptly report the crime to a law enforcement agency in order to receive compensation. Although there is one program that requires victims to report the crime within 24 hours and another that allows victims 3 months to report the crime to law enforcement, the average across programs is 72 hours. In addition, compensation programs require victims to cooperate with law enforcement and prosecutorial officials in order to remain eligible for their claim. Victims also must file a claim with the compensation program in the state where the crime occurred. Programs require victims to submit a timely application to the compensation program after the crime occurred. Six programs have short filing deadlines, such as 6 months, whereas other programs have longer deadlines.

On average programs require victims to file claims within 1 year after the crime occurred (Karmen, 2001).

Reimbursable expenses from most compensation programs include medical expenses, mental health counseling, lost wages for disabled victims, lost wages because of missed work, loss of support for dependents of homicide victims, and funeral expenses. State compensation programs have set maximum compensation award limits that generally range between $10,000 and $25,000 (U.S. Department of Justice, 1998). Six states have set their limits above this range and instead have maximum award limits between $40,000 and $50,000. The average amount of compensation received awarded to a crime victim is $2000. Medical costs make up over half of all victim compensation payments from compensation programs. Lost wages and support make up the next largest category, followed by mental health treatment and funeral expenses. Compensation claims filed for counseling is an area of reimbursement that has been increasing. Currently, 20–40% of compensation awards in a few states are made for counseling services. In addition, 25–30% of the victims compensation recipients nationwide are 17 years and younger.

The majority of states provide emergency compensation awards to crime victims for cases of extreme hardship. Of these states, most provide between $500 and $2000 for an emergency award (U.S. Department of Justice, 1998). However, a few states do not have a maximum limit for an emergency award. Many programs limit emergency award claims to crime victims and dependents suffering a loss of income because of death or disability and are unable to pay for food, shelter, and utilities.

Public awareness about the availability of compensation for victims of crime is crucial so that victims do not miss application deadlines. Typically, victims find out about the existence of state programs from law enforcement, victim service programs, prosecutors' offices, or from public awareness campaigns. In recent years, many states have implemented policies to improve public awareness of victim compensation.

ANGELA GOVER

### References and Further Reading

Edwards, C., *The Hammurabi Code,* Port Washington, New York, NY, Kennikat Press, 1971.

Karmen, A., *Crime Victims,* 4th ed., Belmont, CA, Wadsworth, 2001.

Lamborn, L.L., Victim compensation programs, in Galaway, B. and Hudson, J., Eds., *Perspectives on Crime Victims,* St. Louis, MO, Mosby, 1980.

Meiners, R.E., *Victim Compensation,* Lexington, MA, Lexington Books, 1978.

Sarnoff, S.K., *Paying for Crime,* Westport, CT, Praeger, 1996.

Smith, B.E. and Hillenbrand, S.W., Making victims whole again: Restitution, victim–offender reconciliation programs, and compensation, in Davis, R.C., Lurigio, A.J. and Skogan, W.G., Eds., *Victims of Crime,* Thousand Oaks, CA, Sage, 1997.

U.S. Department of Justice, Office of Justice Programs, Office for Victims of Crime, *New Directions From the Field: Victims Rights and Services for the 21st Century—Crime Victims Compensation,* Washington, DC, U.S. Department of Justice, 1998.

*See also* **Victimization, Crime: Financial Loss and Personal Suffering**

# Victim Precipitation

Criminologists have long recognized that the actions of ordinary citizens are very important in increasing or decreasing one's chances of being a victim. When citizens contribute to their own victimization by being exceptionally careless in their daily activities or by physically attacking another, the resulting crime is said to be victim precipitated. This article will (1) provide a more detailed definition of the term victim precipitation, (2) indicate how often crimes are victim provoked, and (3) discuss the importance of this concept in judgments about the legal guilt of criminal defendants and for reducing the chances of crime victimization.

### Definitions of Victim-Precipitated Crime

Although there are specific differences by type of crime, all definitions of victim precipitation share two characteristics. First, there is a time ordering of events in which the victim is the first to take some action. Second, the particular action by victims is a major factor that contributes to their victimization. The specific action of victims is what distinguishes between different types of victim-precipitated offenses. The concept of victim precipitation was originally developed by Marvin Wolfgang in his study of homicide.

When applied to murder and manslaughter (the killing of one by another), victim precipitation refers to cases in which the victim is "the first in the homicide drama to resort to physical force against the subsequent slayer" (Wolfgang, 1957). An example of this would be a situation where John attacks Mary with a knife and Mary immediately retaliates by killing John. This definition of victim precipitation follows closely the "rules of provocation" in most country's homicide laws. Verbal insults or derogatory comments by the victim are not considered adequate provocation to reduce a murderer's legal responsibility and these verbal acts are also not usually included in the definition of victim precipitation. However, murder victims in most countries are often given some level of blameworthiness for verbal and physical actions that would not fall under the general definition of victim precipitation.

For the crime of aggravated assault (the application of force against another causing serious bodily injury), victim precipitation has been applied to cases in which the victim is the first to use either physical force or insinuating language or gestures against the subsequent attacker or both (Curtis, 1974). The specific types of victim actions under this definition include physical contact (e.g., pushing, slapping, beating, kicking), threats, and verbal abuse (e.g., screaming or shouting profanities). Displaying or using a weapon by the victim has been included as precipitating factors in a study of violent offenses in India (Bajpai and Maheshwari, 1986).

Robbery (the stealing of something from the person with force or threat of force) is considered victim precipitated when the victim is thought to have acted without reasonable self-protection in the handling of money, jewelry, or other valuables (Normandeau, 1968). Accordingly, persons who are robbed after "flashing bills" in public, wearing and flaunting expensive jewelry, or visiting risky and dangerous places alone at night (e.g., bars, deserted streets, transit stations, parking lots) often fall under this category of victim precipitation.

Clearly the most controversial application of victim precipitation involves cases of sexual assault. Here, the concept refers to cases in which the victim "first agrees to sexual relations, or clearly invited them verbally or through gestures, but then retracts before the act" (Curtis, 1974, 600). Menachim Amir (1967, 494) has extended the definition to include cases where the victim used "what could be interpreted as indecency in language or gestures that constituted an invitation to sexual relation." However, based on research on sexual assault in England and Wales, West (1984) argues that the concept of victim precipitation should be confined to incidents in which the female victim encourages sexual foreplay and then declines to complete the act. Regardless of the definition, studies of victim precipitation in sexual assaults have been widely criticized for "blaming the victim."

Various types of property crimes can also be victim precipitated. For example, shoplifting, car theft, and residential burglaries may be victim precipitated by carelessness in the protection of one's valuables. Similar to personal robbery, the application of victim precipitation to property crimes implies that victims create criminal opportunities by not exercising sufficient care in their routine daily activities.

A number of researchers have recognized that previous definitions of victim precipitation are limited in several ways. The major criticisms are that most definitions are too vague (meaning that nearly any type of victim conduct can be viewed as precipitatory) and the concept places too much emphasis on the victim as a causal agent in crime. Terms such as "victim proneness," "victim facilitation," "victim instigation," and "active victims" have also been used to describe crime situations in which victims play a major contributory role in their victimization. However, these alternative concepts suffer from the same definitional problems as victim precipitation.

## The Extent of Victim-Precipitated Crime

Using the definitions provided above, previous research has shown that a sizable proportion of criminal offenses are victim provoked. The extent of victim precipitation, however, varies by type of crime.

Studies of police and court data on criminal homicides reveal that a large proportion of these offenses are victim provoked by the use of physical violence. Rates of victim precipitation range from 22–50% in these studies. If justifiable homicides (especially those resulting from self-defense) are also included, it is clear that over 50% of all homicides are victim provoked. Extending the definition to include verbally abusive actions by victim would push the rate even higher. Victim blameworthiness was identified in nearly 60% of prosecutions for killing in Japan (Fujimoto, 1982). Victim-precipitated homicides are most prevalent in situations of domestic violence and police use of deadly force. Wolfgang (1957) emphasized the importance of victim precipitation by noting that in many homicides it is merely a matter of chance who ends up being labeled the victim and offender.

For other types of crime, the level of victim precipitation appears to be lower. In a study of 17 U.S. cities

(Curtis, 1974), for example, only 14% of the aggravated assaults were classified as victim provoked by either physical force or threatening language. However, over half of the assaults in this study had insufficient information to determine whether there was victim provocation. Anywhere between 4% and 19% of sexual assaults involve an initial agreement by the victim to undertake sexual relations, about 11% of personal robberies are characterized by carelessness on part of the victim, and about 14% of car theft victims had left their keys in the vehicle. When a less stringent definition is used, a higher proportion of these other criminal offenses would be victim precipitated.

## The Importance of Victim Precipitation

The notion of victim-precipitated crime is important in two fundamental respects. First, it has direct bearing on the legal responsibility of offenders. Second, victim precipitation has major implications for the development of crime-control policy.

The actions of victims can reduce offenders' legal responsibility in both criminal and civil cases. In cases of self-defense, the victim's provocation totally exonerates the offender of any legal responsibility. In both cases of forcible rape and robbery, the lack of victim resistance may also reduce offenders' responsibility or the seriousness of the charge because it implies that the victim somehow contributed to the crime. Similarly, the notion of contributory negligence (where the victim's actions are assumed to be part of the cause for the injury) is a major factor in reducing the amount of damages awarded in civil cases.

Studies of actual decision making in criminal cases indicate that the actions of victims strongly influence the disposition of charges. Victim provocation is commonly employed as a defense for criminal liability and as a mitigating circumstance in the sentencing of convicted offenders. The perception of victim provocation may also explain why other factors influence case disposition. For example, the victim–offender relationship is an important factor that leads to differential treatment of criminal defendants throughout the criminal justice system. Defendants who victimize people that they know (e.g., family members, friends, coworkers) tend to be more likely than those involving strangers to have charges dismissed (by police, prosecutors, and judges before trial), to be found not guilty by judges and jurors, and are given less severe sentences upon conviction. This preferential treatment is in large part because of the belief that persons who victimize their close friends or relatives must have been provoked into the action. The importance of victim precipitation in judgments of legal responsibility is found in both Western and non-Western cultures.

Research on victim-precipitated crime is also important because of its implication for developing effective crime-control policies. Over the last two decades, there has been a dramatic increase in citizen-based crime-control efforts designed to reduce people's chances of being crime victims. These programs have included neighborhood watch programs, private security systems, and self-defense training. Interviews of offenders in Canada, England, Germany, the U.S., and other Western countries consistently reveal that victim carelessness is a significant factor in creation of criminal opportunities. Accordingly, research on victim precipitation may provide information to public citizens about the particular actions that encourage their victimization. Citizens with this knowledge may become better informed about hazardous situations and the type of actions that may increase their likelihood of criminal victimization.

Two of the most widely regarded theories about criminal victimization are called "routine activities" and "lifestyle-exposure" theories. According to these theories, some people have a higher chance of being victimized by crime because they are more exposed to risky and vulnerable situations, have high attractiveness as a crime target, and lack adequate protection or guardianship. These theories of criminal victimization further extend the notion of victim precipitation by highlighting the routine activities and lifestyles of ordinary citizens that increase their exposure to dangerous situations.

Finally, the notion of victim-precipitated crime remains highly controversial because of its inevitable implications for blaming the victim. The previous research on victim-precipitated crime clearly reveals that the victim plays an active role in many violent crimes. However, it is a mistake to assume that victim precipitation is the ultimate cause of criminal activity because the typical offender is likely to engage in crime regardless of the particular actions of the victim. Research on victim precipitation seems to be most useful when it is designed to alert ordinary citizens of the ways in which they can reduce their risks of criminal victimization.

TERANCE D. MIETHE

## References and Further Reading

Amir, M., Victim-precipitated forcible rape, *Journal of Criminal Law, Criminology, and Police Science*, 58 (1967).
Bajpai, G.S. and Maheshwari, H.S., Victim-precipitation in some violent offences, *Indian Journal of Criminology*, 125 (1986).
Curtis, L., Victim-precipitation and violent crime, *Social Problems*, 21 (1974).

Foote, W.E., Victim-precipitated homicide, in Hall, H.V., Ed., *Lethal Violence—A Sourcebook on Fatal Domestic, Acquaintance, and Stranger Violence*, Boca Raton, FL, CRC Press, 1999.

Fujimoto, T., The victimological study in Japan, in Schneider, H.J., Ed., *The Victim in International Perspective*, New York, NY, Walter de Gruyter, 1982.

Karmen, A., *Crime Victims: An Introduction to Victimology*, 4th ed., Belmont, CA, Wadsworth, 2001.

Miethe, T.D., The myth or reality of victim involvement in crime: A review and comment on victim-precipitation research, *Sociological Focus*, 18 (1985).

Normandeau, A., *Trends and Patterns in Crimes of Robbery*, PhD dissertation, University of Pennsylvania, PA, 1968.

Polk, K., Reexamination of the concept of victim-precipitated homicide, *Homicide Studies*, 141 (1997).

Wolfgang, M., Victim-precipitated criminal homicide, *Journal of Criminal Law, Criminology, and Police Science*, 48 (1957).

Wolfgang, M., *Patterns of Criminal Homicide*, Philadelphia, PA, University of Pennsylvania Press, 1958.

*See also* **National Crime Victimization Survey (NCVS); Victimization, Crime: Characteristics of Victims; Victimization, Crime: Prevention and Protection; Victimization, Crime: Theories about Vulnerability**

# Victimization, Crime: Characteristics of Victims

In every crime, there are two individuals involved: the perpetrator (the offender) and the individual against whom the crime is committed (the victim). Until recently, the discipline of criminology generally ignored the study of crime victims, concentrating instead on offenders. Common sources of crime-related information used by criminologists in their studies, including the FBI's annually produced Uniform Crime Reports (UCR) and self-report surveys (conducted by researchers typically using samples of juveniles), ignored victims and instead compiled data on offenders, their characteristics and their behavior.

This situation changed, however, in the 1970s with the development of the first national-level victimization survey conducted in the U.S., the *National Crime Survey* (now known as the *National Crime Victimization Survey* or NCVS). Victimization surveys are now regularly conducted in Britain and Wales using the *British Crime Survey* (BCS), in Canada using the *Canadian General Social Survey* (CGSS), and in Australia using the *Australian Crime and Safety Survey*. The UN Interregional Crime Research Institute (UNICRI) recently developed the *International Crime Victimization Survey* (ICVS) that in its most recent sweep was administered in 56 countries around the globe. Smaller, more specialized versions of the NCVS have also been used to analyze subsegments of the population (e.g., workers, junior and senior high school students, and college students). Using these surveys, criminologists are now in a position to better understand crime victims, in particular their characteristics.

What is known about crime victims? What kinds of crime are experienced most commonly by victims? Are certain groups of people more likely to be crime victims than others? This entry answers these questions using victimization data collected from multiple sources, including the NCVS, the BCS, and the CGSS.

## What Patterns Are Associated with Criminal Victimization?

### Characteristics of Crime Victims: Personal Crimes

Data collected by crime victim surveys administered in the U.S., the U.K., Canada, and elsewhere can be used to examine the characteristics of victims of personal crimes (like robbery or assault) and households that experienced a victimization (such as burglary or automobile theft). By examining these data, various conclusions can be reached concerning the major characteristics of crime victims.

Nearly every year since its inception, NCVS data reveal that age, race, ethnicity, income, marital status, and home ownership are strongly related to personal and household victimization in the U.S. Similar conclusions can be reached based on BCS and CGSS data. For example, NCVS, BCS, and CGSS data consistently show that, in general, men experience higher rates of personal victimization than women (the exception is rape and sexual assault). NVCS data from 1999 show that, with the exception

**Table 1.** Rate per 1000 Persons of Violent and Personal Theft Victimization by Sex, Age, Race, Hispanic Origin, Household Income, and Marital Status (1999)

| Victim Characteristic | All Violence | Rape or Sexual Assault | Robbery | Aggravated Assault | Simple Assault | Personal Theft |
|---|---|---|---|---|---|---|
| **Sex** | | | | | | |
| Male | 37.0 | 0.4 | 5.0 | 8.7 | 22.9 | 0.9 |
| Female | 28.8 | 3.0 | 2.3 | 4.8 | 18.8 | 0.9 |
| **Age** | | | | | | |
| 12–15 | 74.4 | 4.0 | 6.7 | 13.1 | 50.6 | 3.1 |
| 16–19 | 77.4 | 6.9 | 8.2 | 16.8 | 45.5 | 1.5 |
| 20–24 | 68.5 | 4.3 | 7.7 | 16.7 | 39.7 | 1.0 |
| 25–34 | 36.3 | 1.7 | 4.1 | 8.3 | 22.2 | 1.2 |
| 35–49 | 25.2 | 0.8 | 2.8 | 4.7 | 16.9 | 0.4 |
| 50–64 | 14.4 | 0.2 | 1.9 | 1.8 | 10.5 | 0.6 |
| 65+ | 3.8 | 0.1 | 0.7 | 1.1 | 1.9 | 0.6 |
| **Race** | | | | | | |
| White | 31.9 | 1.6 | 3.1 | 6.2 | 21.1 | 0.8 |
| Black | 41.6 | 2.6 | 7.7 | 10.6 | 20.8 | 1.3 |
| All Other | 24.5 | 1.7 | 2.5 | 5.7 | 14.6 | 1.5 |
| **Hispanic Origin** | | | | | | |
| Hispanic | 33.8 | 1.9 | 5.6 | 8.9 | 17.4 | 1.5 |
| Non-Hispanic | 32.4 | 1.7 | 3.4 | 6.4 | 20.9 | 0.9 |
| Household income | | | | | | |
| < $7500 | 57.5 | 4.3 | 8.1 | 14.5 | 30.6 | 1.9 |
| $7500–$14,999 | 44.5 | 1.6 | 6.9 | 10.0 | 26.0 | 1.1 |
| $15,000–$24,999 | 35.3 | 3.2 | 4.8 | 7.2 | 20.1 | 0.8 |
| $25,000–$34,999 | 37.9 | 1.2 | 3.1 | 6.9 | 26.7 | 1.2 |
| $35,000–$49,999 | 30.3 | 1.6 | 3.2 | 5.5 | 19.7 | 0.5 |
| $50,000–$74,999 | 33.3 | 1.5 | 2.2 | 7.1 | 22.6 | 0.4 |
| > $75,000 | 22.9 | 0.8 | 1.8 | 4.0 | 16.3 | 1.2 |
| **Marital Status** | | | | | | |
| Never married | 60.6 | 3.9 | 7.2 | 12.6 | 36.9 | 1.6 |
| Married | 14.4 | 0.3 | 1.1 | 2.7 | 10.3 | 0.4 |
| Divorced or Separated | 53.6 | 2.9 | 5.8 | 11.6 | 33.3 | 1.2 |
| Widowed | 6.0 | 0.0 | 1.9 | 1.3 | 2.8 | 1.0 |

*Source:* Adapted from Callie M. Rennison, *Criminal Victimization 1999*, Washington, DC: U.S. Department of Justice, Office of Justice Programs 2000, Table 2 and Table 3.

of rape or sexual assault and personal theft, men's overall personal victimization rates were 1.3 times higher than women's rates. Men's robbery victimization rate was 2.2 times higher, their rate for aggravated assault was about twice the rate for women, and their rate for simple assault was about 1.2 times higher. The rate of rape or sexual assault for women, however, was 7.5 times higher than the rate for men, whereas rates for personal theft were almost identical (see Table 1). BCS data and Canadian victimization data also show that men have higher personal crime victimization rates than women, except for sexual assault and rape. Thus, across three countries, victimization data reveal that men experience generally higher levels of personal victimization, in particular, higher levels of interpersonal violence.

Age is also related to personal victimization. NCVS, BCS, and CGSS data all show that levels of personal victimization decrease as age increases. To illustrate, NCVS data from 1999 showed that overall rates of violence were highest among individuals age 16–19 and lowest for those age 65 or older. Teenagers (ages 12–19), in particular, experienced the highest rates of rape, robbery, aggravated assault, simple assault, and personal theft. In some cases, teenagers in the U.S. had victimization rates 2–3 times higher than adults in their 1930s and 1940s, and 5–6 times higher than adults in their 1960s and 1970s. Similar patterns are found in England and Wales, where BCS data show that individuals between the ages of 16 and 24 had the highest levels of personal victimization in 1999. In Canada, CGSS data from 1999 revealed individuals ages 15–24 had rates of personal victimization that were 1.3–3.2 times higher than rates for the next age group, those ages 25–34, and some 9.5–161 times higher than personal crime rates for those age 65 or higher. Clearly, these data show that the youngest segment of the population suffers the highest levels of personal victimization.

In the U.S., NCVS data reveal that race and ethnicity are related to victimization (the BCS and the CGSS do not report the race or ethnicity of respondents in their main samples). Turning first to race-based differences, during 1999 African Americans in the U.S. experienced far higher rates of personal crime victimization than did whites or other races. Victimization rates for personal crimes experienced by African Americans were 1.3–2.5 times higher than whites' victimization rates, and between 1.4 and 3.1 times higher than rates for other races. Rape or sexual assault rates for blacks were about 1.6 times higher than the rates, for whites, whereas their robbery victimization rates were 2.5 times that of whites, their aggravated assault rates about twice that of whites, and their personal theft rates about 1.6 times higher than whites. Turning to ethnicity, Hispanics generally experienced slightly higher victimization rates than non-Hispanics. These data thus reveal that membership in certain racial groups (African American) and ethnic groups (Hispanic) in the U.S. significantly increased the likelihood of one experiencing a personal victimization like robbery or assault.

Economics is also related to personal victimization. In the U.S., NCVS data show that members of households at the bottom of the economic scale (earning $7500 or less annually) experienced overall rates of personal victimization 2.5 times higher than members of households at the top of the economic ladder (those earning more than $75,000 annually). This pattern of higher income translating to lower victimization rates also held true for each of the personal offenses as well. In Canada, members of households whose annual income was less than $15,000 had overall rates of violence nearly double the rate of members of households whose annual income was $60,000 or more. For personal victimizations involving sexual assault, victimization rates of members of households whose income was less than $15,000 annually were triple the rate of households at the top end of the economic ladder, whereas their rate of simple assault was 1.6 times higher. However, members of Canadian households whose annual income was $60,000 or more had higher robbery and personal theft rates than victims from households whose annual income was less than $15,000 (see Table 2).

Another economic indicator related to personal crime victimization is the employment status of the victim. Although the NCVS does not report employment status of victims of personal crime, the BCS and the CGSS do report this information. In England and Wales, BCS data show that the unemployed had the highest levels of personal victimization during 1999. Overall levels of violent victimization among the unemployed in the U.K. were nearly 2.5 times higher than levels for employed persons. This pattern continued for the specific offenses of domestic assault, acquaintance assault, stranger assault, and robbery or snatch-thefts, where levels of victimization among the unemployed ranged from 2.1 times higher than employed persons to 4.6 times higher. Canadian data show a similar pattern, with the unemployed having rates of personal victimization that ranged from 2.0–82 times higher than the rates for employed persons. Thus, various economic measures indicate that in the U.S., Canada, and in England and Wales, those at the bottom of the economic ladder experienced the highest rates of personal crime victimization, including serious violence.

Finally, NCVS, BCS, and CGSS data all reveal that married persons have lower levels of personal crime victimization. In the U.S., overall rates of violent victimization for married people were 4.2 times lower than the rates for people who were single and 3.7 times lower than the rates for people who were separated or divorced. Married people in the U.S. had robbery victimization rates 6.5 times lower than single people, and rates nearly 4.3 times lower than people who were separated or divorced. BCS and CGSS data reveal dramatically lower personal victimization rates for married people in England and Wales and in Canada as well.

## Characteristics of Crime Victims: Household Crimes

Victimization data from the U.S., Canada, and from England and Wales reveal interesting patterns associated with households experiencing a burglary, a vehicle theft or vehicle-related theft, or household theft. NCVS data reveal that in the U.S., overall victimization rates per 1000 African American households were 1.3 times higher than rates for white households and 1.2 times higher than rates for households of other races. Hispanic households also suffered higher victimization rates than non-Hispanic households in the U.S. Household income showed no clear relationship with household victimization levels. U.S. households with the lowest annual income (less than $7500 annually) had the highest *overall* levels of victimization and had the highest rates of burglary. On the other hand, households earning more than $75,000 annually had *overall*

**Table 2.** Rate per 1000 Households of Property Crime Victimization by Race, Hispanic Origin, Household Income, and Home Ownership (1999)

| Characteristic of Household or Head of Household | All Crimes | Burglary | Motor Vehicle Theft | Theft |
|---|---|---|---|---|
| **Race** | | | | |
| White | 190.0 | 31.5 | 9.0 | 149.5 |
| Black | 249.9 | 52.6 | 16.0 | 181.2 |
| All Others | 206.3 | 31.2 | 11.6 | 163.6 |
| Hispanic Origin | | | | |
| Hispanic | 232.5 | 37.2 | 17.3 | 178.0 |
| Non-Hispanic | 194.6 | 33.7 | 9.3 | 151.2 |
| **Household Income** | | | | |
| < $7500 | 220.8 | 67.0 | 6.2 | 147.6 |
| $7500–$14,999 | 200.1 | 44.2 | 10.1 | 145.9 |
| $15,000–$24,999 | 214.9 | 38.9 | 11.2 | 164.9 |
| $25,000–$34,999 | 199.1 | 37.1 | 10.4 | 151.7 |
| $35,000–$49,999 | 207.6 | 30.9 | 11.7 | 165.0 |
| $50,000–$74,999 | 213.6 | 24.1 | 10.3 | 179.1 |
| > $75,000 | 220.4 | 23.1 | 9.7 | 187.7 |
| **Home Ownership** | | | | |
| Owned | 170.4 | 26.5 | 8.4 | 135.5 |
| Rented | 251.9 | 48.9 | 13.0 | 190.0 |

*Source:* Adapted from Callie M. Rennison, *Criminal Victimization, 1999,* Washington, DC: U.S. Department of Justice, Office of Justice Programs, 2000 Table 6.

levels of victimization almost matching those of the lowest income households, and had the *highest* rates of household theft. Finally, homeowners in the U.S. experienced far lower rates of all forms of household crimes, compared to those who rented.

In England and Wales, BCS data indicate that households whose head was young (ages 16–24) had the highest overall levels of household victimization (that includes burglary and vehicle-related thefts). Households whose head was under the age of 60, was single, and had children present had the highest levels of household victimization compared to other households. Generally, the poorest households in the U.K. had the highest levels of burglary and vehicle theft-related offenses, although households at the high end of the annual income scale suffered the highest levels of all vehicle-related thefts and the highest levels of theft from a vehicle. Renters in the U.K. also had higher rates of household victimization than those who owned their homes, whereas households whose head was employed suffered much lower levels of victimization than households whose head was either unemployed or economically inactive. Finally, detached houses suffered the lowest levels of household victimization, compared to semidetached houses, terraced houses, or flats.

In Canada, households located in urban areas had the highest rates of victimization (breaking and entering,

vehicle-related thefts, theft of household property, and vandalism). Their rates were 1.3–1.6 times higher than rates for households located in rural areas. In contrast to data from the U.S. and from England and Wales, households in Canada earning the highest annual income ($60,000 or more) not only had the highest *overall* levels of household victimization, but also had the *highest* levels of victimization for each of the offenses comprising the household sector. Household size also mattered: households with four or more persons had the highest rates of victimization, whereas households with one person had the lowest. Unlike in England, in Canada single, detached houses generally had higher victimization rates than did apartments, but both detached houses and apartments had lower rates of victimization than semidetached houses, row houses, or duplexes. Finally, as was the case in both the U.K. and in the U.S., renters had much higher rates of household victimization than did owners.

All three victimization surveys asked respondents about their household income and about home ownership. These data reveal that, in general, renters in all three countries suffered higher levels of household victimization than owners. Additionally, with the exception of Canada, households in the U.S. and the U.K. whose annual incomes were at the bottom of the economic ladder suffered higher levels of victimization than did households at the top end of the economic spectrum.

## Conclusion

The systematic study of factors associated with crime victimization such as age, race, sex, ethnicity, and income was made possible by the development and implementation of large-scale victimization surveys administered around the globe. Since then, criminologists have been able to better understand the extent, magnitude, and nature of crime victimization in the U.S. and elsewhere. These data generally show that significant portions of the populations of the U.S., Canada, and the U.K. experience some form of criminal victimization each year. More particularly, men, the young, the poor, racial or ethnic minorities, and those who are renters have the highest rates of victimization. Those individuals "on the margins" of society appear at greatest risk for victimization of all kinds, despite recent (and sometimes dramatic) downward trends in crime levels in the U.S., the U.K., and Canada. Although these trends are encouraging, much remains to be done to help reduce victimization levels among the least powerful members of society.

JOHN J. SLOAN III

## References and Further Reading

Besserer, S. and Trainor, C., *Criminal Victimization in Canada, 1999*, Ottawa, Canada, Canadian Centre for Justice Statistics 2000. Available at: http://www.statcan.ca/english/ IPS/Data/85-002-XIE00010.htm.

Ennis, P., *Criminal Victimization in the United States: Report from a National Survey*, Chicago, IL, National Opinion Research Center, 1967.

Fisher, B.S., Sloan, J.J., Cullen, FT. and Lu, C., Crime in the ivory tower: The level and sources of student victimization, *Criminology*, 26 (1998).

Fisher, B.S., Cullen, F.T. and Turner, M.G., *The Sexual Victimization of College Women*, Washington, DC, Office of Justice Programs, 2001. Available at: http://www.ncjrs.org/pdffiles1/nij/182369.pdf.

Kershaw, C., Budd, T., Kinshott, G., Mattison, J., Mayhew, R. and Myhill, A., *The 2000 British Crime Survey: England and Wales*, London, The Home Office, 2000. Available at: http://www.homeoffice.gov.uk/rds/pdfs/hosb1800.pdf.

Rennison, C.M., *Criminal Victimization 1999 with Changes 1998–1999 and Trends 1993–1999*, Washington, DC, Office of Justice Programs, 2000. Available at: http://www.ojp.usdoj.gov/bjs/pub/pdf/cv99.pdf.

Smith, S.K., Steadman, G.W., Minton, T.D. and Townsend, M., *Criminal Victimization and Perceptions of Community Safety in 12 Cities, 1998*, Washington, DC, Office of Justice Programs, 1999. Available at: http://www.ojp.usdoj.gov/bjs/pub/pdf/cvpcs98.pdf.

*See also* **National Crime Victimization Survey (NCVS); Self-Report Research; Uniform Crime Reports (UCR); Victimization, Crime: Theories about Vulnerability**

# Victimization, Crime: Financial Loss and Personal Suffering

The topic of crime and its associated costs typically elicits strong reactions from the public as well as from individuals involved in the criminal justice field. Crime knows no boundaries in relation to class, race, gender, or age. In the U.S., according to the National Crime Victimization Survey (NCVS) it resulted in approximately 23 million victimizations in 2002 alone. Of the 23 million crimes in the U.S. in 2002 as measured by the NCVS, 5.3 million were violent victimizations such as rape, robbery, and assault, which was the lowest number recorded since the inception of the survey. Record highs in probation and parole caseloads and increasing jail and prison inmate populations have made a substantial impact on the American system of justice. Although it is relatively easy to determine the amount of funding that countries and localities allocate to crime and justice, or to estimate the dollar value of stolen property, it is difficult but perhaps more important to also examine the emotional, cognitive, and moral costs of crime as well. For instance, data for Australia, Belgium, Canada, England and Wales, France, the Netherlands, and the USA show the cost of crime per citizen is approximately $200 for police, courts, and prisons; $100 for private security; and $25 for lost property (ICPC, 2003).

Typically when examining an issue as broad as the "costs of crime" it is broken down into two rough categories, namely, direct costs or financial losses and indirect costs such as personal suffering. Although the categories overlap to some degree, the direct costs of crime are usually measured rather superficially in terms of dollars lost, injuries suffered, and lives taken. In other words, direct costs can be explored by examining the numerical, financial, and physical aspects of crime. Indirect costs pertain to the actual human costs of crime that typically cannot be measured in dollars and cents. Instead they can be understood by examining various emotional, cognitive, and moral issues that are closely intertwined with one another.

## Direct Costs—Financial Loss

Moving to the country may be a solution espoused by many to avoid criminal victimization. Not only is that impractical for most individuals but rural areas where nearly one quarter of the U.S. population resides are not immune to the costs of crime. In fact, elderly rural residents (65 or over) are more likely than their suburban counterparts to have experienced burglary. Of the violent victimizations nationwide, rural areas account for about 16%. Interestingly, rural victims of violence are often accosted by a relative or acquaintance whereas city and suburban victims typically report that a stranger had been the assailant (Duhart, 2000).

Another way to examine the direct costs of crime to the victims is to place a dollar value on property taken or damaged by criminals, and to estimate medical expenses, and time lost from work in relation to injuries sustained through criminal victimization. Although such costs, when reported, seem rather straightforward, actually crimes against property aesthetically destroy productive resources thus extracting a cost from society in yet another way that cannot be measured in financial terms. In relation to financial terms however, the Bureau of Justice Statistics estimated that in 1992 the cost of medical expenses lost pay because of injuries from the crime, and the cost of property taken or damaged by criminal victimization was $17.6 billion (Klaus, 1994). Each year more than 5 million victims are injured in rapes, robberies, and assaults. About one in seven victims of violent crime requires some medical care and one in ten must spend at least one night in the hospital (Harlow, 1989). More than three out of five victims spent $250 or more on their resultant medical bills. In 1992, lost work-time was reported in 8% of all violent crimes that resulted in 6.1 million days lost from work (Klaus, 1994).

Crime financially affects more than the immediate victim. As taxpayers or consumers of government programs and services, each of us is impacted by the financial costs of crime. For instance, money generated by organized crime and other profit-motivated crime in the U.S. alone is estimated at $300 billion each year, not to mention the increased competition in the economy created by organized crime (Lyman and Potter, 2000).

On a broader level, actually state and local governments must shoulder the bulk of financial responsibility for criminal and civil justice. In 1999, for example, they spent 85% of all justice dollars whereas the Federal government spent 15%. Justice spending at all levels has increased. Overall there is about $100 billion spent annually on the criminal justice system in the U.S. (Kappler et al., 2000). In Australia, Canada, the Netherlands, and the USA, justice accounts for more than 5% of the Gross Domestic Product (ICPC, 2003).

The direct financial costs are not the only expenses involved in administering justice. We must not forget the only partially compensated services provided by witnesses and jury members nationwide each year. There are potential costs to the offender as well. If the offender is incarcerated, not only must society shoulder the burden and expense of maintaining the prison, the prisoners, and the staffs, but also the offender suffers the cost of the loss of freedom and dignity. Also, the offender's family may suffer an emotional loss and require welfare assistance, which is yet another cost to society. Additionally, resources that are invested in the justice system are of course not available now for other socially valued uses such as education or social service programs, thus lowering in yet another way the quality of life for many.

From a broad perspective, one could even consider the time that a criminal invests in committing a crime or in serving a sentence a cost to society because that offender could perhaps have engaged in a legitimate and revenue-producing activity instead. In addition to increasing tax rates to fund the justice system, crime has contributed to the increasing government borrowing, which in turn tends to discourage economic activity and investment in the private sector, which reduces the national income and lowers the standard of living for all of us.

The official justice system is not the only way to combat crime. Many individuals and businesses contact for the services of private security personnel and devices to enhance their security. Internationally, the number of private security guards has increased from being half of the number of police officers to being nearly double (ICPC, 2003). Another alternative is for individuals to help themselves, and it has been reported that an increasing number of citizens carry firearms, knives, or other weapons for self-defense. A third alternative is sometimes referred to as a "collective response." A collective response is where individuals bond together to fight crime. Civilian police patrols or "crimewatch" groups and community meetings addressing crime problems are becoming more common. The costs usually associated with these alternative justice efforts are in terms of equipment costs and time investments made by the persons involved. A less tangible but perhaps more important potential cost is that these efforts might escalate into vigilante justice.

In addition to the direct costs associated with typical street and organized crimes, there are other types of crimes that are not easily observed but that result in substantial costs to society. These crimes include business crimes, white-collar crimes, and computer crimes. The costs of white-collar crime usually manifest themselves in the form of physical harm, financial losses, or damage to the moral climate. These costs affect at least three different groups: employees (e.g., unsafe working conditions), consumers (e.g., unsafe products), and society at large (e.g., pollution) (Potter and Miller, 2002). Estimates vary but it has been reported that street crimes cost an estimated $13.3 billion a year whereas the monetary damage for white-collar crimes ranges between $300 billion and $500 billion (Kappeler et al., 2000). This high price tag is borne, often unknowingly, by employees and consumers alike. Perhaps the greatest cost to society at large is primarily moral in nature. Because of the high social standing of most white-collar offenders, such crimes tend to create cynicism and an attitude that such law violations might as well be committed by "ordinary" citizens, thus increasing the number of white-collar crimes and the cycle continues.

## Indirect Costs—Personal Suffering

Indirect costs of crime are typically neither obvious nor easily measurable, let alone quantifiable in financial terms. Nonetheless, we must not forget the pain and suffering and other indirect costs to victims, their families, friends, neighbors, and society as a whole.

Crime can have a major emotional and cognitive or mental impact on the individual who was victimized. Fear, anger, and surprise are common reactions produced by most types of victimization. Dramatic victimization incidents can effect victims' attitudes and behavior for months or even years after the initial incident. In many instances victims will negatively revise their assumptions about their self-worth and the worth of other people in general, at least until the healing process is complete. Although reactions to crime are quite varied, being a crime victim may have profound psychological repercussions resulting in mental health treatment costs, lost time from work, disrupted social functioning with friends and family,

an overall lowered quality of life, and sometimes death from suicide (Janoff-Bulman, 1985; Karmen, 2002).

People such as family members and friends who are emotionally close to victims of crime may also experience emotional problems and costs. Often these "indirect victims" experience difficulties and symptoms such as anger and fear that are quite similar to the actual victims' reactions. The development of these psychological problems of the indirect victim may inadvertently worsen the symptoms of the direct victims, for instance, a husband reacting with guilt and anger instead of compassion toward his wife when she explains she has been raped. In the case of the death of a victim, close family and friends often feel anger and vengefulness in addition to the feelings associated with normal bereavement. Also, necessary extensive contact with the criminal justice system interferes, sometimes severely, with the normal reorganizations and healing processes taking place (Robinson, 2002; Balboni, 2003).

Emotional and cognitive harm comes not only at the hands of the offender but from the way the criminal justice system often neglects victims' needs or, worse yet, tends to blame them for their own victimization. When the response of the criminal justice system has a negative impact on the fresh emotional problems of victims it is often referred to as the "second wound" or being "revictimized" (Lurigo and Resick, 1990). This revictimization also has an effect on the system as is mirrored in the fact that in 2002, less than half (49%) of the violent crimes were reported to law enforcement officials (Rennison and Rand, 2003). Not only must the criminal justice system be concerned from an ethical standpoint about the victim's avoidance of involvement with the system that was set up at least in part to protect them, but realistically because most crimes come to the attention of the police once they are reported by private citizens, a high rate of reporting is crucial to the effective functioning of the criminal justice system. Not only may victim cooperation be critical in providing the information needed for police to make an arrest, but victim testimony may be crucial to allow prosecutors to secure a conviction.

Whether or not one has been directly victimized, a great number of individuals suffer from a form of psychological victimization known as "fear of crime." Interestingly, one's level of fear is seldom in direct relation to their actual risk of becoming a victim but rather it is based on a perceived risk. For instance, generally females and the elderly express a greater fear of crime than do people in demographic groups that actually face a much greater risk (Jerin and Moriarity, 1998; Karmen, 2001).

The fear of crime phenomena can have a very broad impact and cost. Typically, when one's sense of personal security is threatened by crime and their level of fear is high, defensiveness and suspicion are common responses. If these responses are adopted by a number of individuals, the resulting lack of social interaction and faith in society may actually start to destroy the social order of the community and perhaps even our nation (Conklin, 1975).

The costs associated with fear of crime may at times be financial, but often they are more subtle and pervasive. Often because of their fear of crime, those who can afford it may move to a safer but more expensive neighborhood or they may even pay to send their children to private schools. Those who cannot afford such a change in setting may instead have to alter their lifestyle and normal activities. These attempts to reduce victimization result in decreased personal freedom. In an attempt to avoid possible victimization, many individuals may avoid night-time meetings of social groups and organizations, and may even turn down the opportunity to earn overtime pay as they would then have to return home after dark when the danger is more. The increased fear and suspicion of strangers and others who are "different" in some fashion may reinforce existing racial and ethnic prejudices thus lessening the rewards and knowledge offered by cultural diversity and perhaps even triggering further violence and crime. Increased fear among the citizenry may not only create barriers and distrust between individuals but also public belief in the legitimacy of the government may be weakened as individuals become dissatisfied with the criminal justice system's ability to "protect and serve." To take the issue of fear even further, as individuals begin to emotionally isolate into themselves, the sense of community weakens, and informal social controls dwindle. Weakened informal social control often results in higher crime rates and a type of emotional apathy among the residents of the area. This widespread emotional apathy is often one of the first signs of the onset of community decay. Although assessing the monetary, let alone the emotional, costs of community decay is nearly impossible, its damaging effects are widespread and pervasive.

As the fear of crime spreads, community decay increases, as property values begin to drop. Differences in the risk of victimization in certain areas are often reflected in the property values of the area with high perceived risk being correlated with lowered property values, thus negatively impacting the immediate and surrounding areas. To make matters worse, often companies will not be located in low property value and high crime rate areas as they fear damage to their facilities or workers or both. By not being located in these areas fewer jobs are available to the local residents that contribute to a higher unemployment rate, which may in turn be correlated with an increase in crime, and so the cycle continues. With little competition to contend with and high security or damage costs to recoup, local businesses often raise their prices again harming area residents and furthering decay of the community. Occasionally another cost of community decay is that of political corruption that can be created when criminal groups are able to persuade others to allow them to provide illegal goods and services to the high crime areas with minimal interference (Lyman and Potter, 2000).

Perhaps the ultimate cost of crime is that it has lowered the financial and moral standards of living for all of us. It has taken the money or treasured possessions of many and at the same time inflated the price of consumer goods to cover the costs of shoplifting, theft, and embezzlement. Crime has cost many their emotional and physical well-being and destroyed their sense of security. At the same time it intimidates us into spending large amounts of money on self-protection and security devices. Crime has coerced many into losing faith in their government while it raises our tax bills in an attempt to fund criminal justice efforts. Ultimately, crime convinces many to make the moral error of fearing and discriminating against one another when really what is needed is greater cooperation and understanding.

WENDELIN M. HUME AND SHERINA M. HUME

## References and Further Reading

Balboni, J., Balanced and restorative justice, in Sgarzi, J. and McDevitt, J., Eds., *Victimology,* Upper Saddle River, NJ, Prentice Hall, Inc., 2003.

Conklin, J.E., *The Impact of Crime,* New York, NY, Macmillan Publishing Company, 1975.

Duhart, D., Urban, suburban and rural victimization, 1993–1998, *National Crime Victimization Survey,* Washington, DC, U.S. Government Printing Office, 2000.

International Center for the Prevention of Crime, Crime Prevention Digest. Available at www.crime-prevention-intl.org/english/prevention.

Janoff-Bulman, R., Criminal vs. non-criminal victimization: Victim's reactions, *Victimology,* 10 (1985).

Jerin, R. and Moriarty, L., *Victims of Crime,* Chicago, IL, Nelson-Hall Publishers, 1998.

Kappeler, V.E., Blumberg, M. and Potter, G.W., *The Mythology of Crime and Criminal Justice,* 3rd ed., Prospect Heights, IL, Waveland Press, Inc., 2000.

Karmen, A., *Crime Victims*, 4th ed., Belmont, CA, Wadsworth/Thomson Learning, 2001.

Klaus, P., The costs of crime to victims, *Bureau of Justice Statistics Crime Data Brief,* Washington, DC, U.S. Government Printing Office, 1994.

Lurigio, A.J. and Resick, P.A., Healing the psychological wounds of criminal victimization: Predicting postcrime distress and recovery, in Lurigio, A., Skogan, W. and Davis, R., Eds., *Victims of Crime: Problems, Policies, and Programs*, Newbury Park, CA, Sage Publications, Inc., 1990.

Lyman, M. and Potter, G.W., *Organized Crime,* 2nd ed., Upper Saddle River, NJ, Prentice Hall, Inc., 2000.

Potter, G.W. and Miller, K., Thinking about white-collar crime, in Potter, G.W., Ed., *Controversies in White-Collar Crime*, Cincinnati, OH, Anderson Publishing Co., 2002.

Rennison, C. and Rand, M., Criminal victimization 2002, *National Crime Victimization Survey*, U.S. Department of Justice, Washington, DC, U.S. Government Printing Office, 2003.

Robinson, M., *Justice Blind?* Upper Saddle River, NJ, Prentice Hall, Inc., 2002.

*See also* **National Crime Victimization Survey (NCVS); Victimization, Crime: Characteristics of Victims; Victimology; Victims' Rights**

# Victimization, Crime: Prevention and Protection

Crime victimization prevention and protection consist of two frameworks for "action designed to reduce the actual level of crime or the perceived fear of crime" (Lab, 1997, 19). The crime prevention framework is focused on making the environment safe from crime, reducing the potential for crime in high-risk situations, and halting the possibility of future crime. These three areas of action have been conceptualized as primary, secondary, and tertiary prevention (Brantingham and Faust, 1976). The crime protection framework is focused on ensuring victims their rights to assistance and attention to their needs, with particular emphasis on prevention of revictimization. This type of action is best exemplified by ideas contained in the 1948 UN Universal Declaration of Human Rights, but also other governmental and nongovernmental programs involving victim assistance, advocacy, compensation, reparations, reconciliation, restoration, and reintegration. Victim protection includes witness protection programs and legal proceedings advocacy that should be carefully distinguished from self-protective action, such as firearms ownership, self-defense training, and vigilantism that are not part of the crime protection framework, at least not as it has been conceptualized. Self-protective measures such as gun ownership, martial arts training, and possession of chemical agents or other personal defensive devices are a matter of controversy because it is not known if the net effect is to increase or decrease harm (Kleck, 1998).

Since 1973, the Bureau of Justice Statistics has administered the National Crime Victimization Survey (NCVS) based on a system of household interviews that provides the best detailed information on victimization incidents involving nonfatal violence and property crime. Information on homicide generally comes from the Federal Bureau of Investigation's Uniform Crime Reports (UCR), which also measures nonfatal violence and property crime. The NCVS complements the UCR because it is known that about 50% of crime is not reported to police and thus is absent from the UCR (Meadows, 2004). Therefore, although a UCR report might indicate that 20 million crimes have occurred in a given year, the real number according to NCVS figures may be closer to 40 million. In fact, from 1973 until about 1995, between 40 and 50 million violent crimes were reported every year by the NCVS. That number has been steadily declining since 1995, reaching a new low of 23 million in 2002 (BJS, 2003). People do not report crime to police but will in a household interview for many reasons, such as the crime was unsuccessful, not important enough, a private matter, distrust of police, or fear of reprisal. Females are slightly more likely than males to report crime to police, and the elderly are more likely than young people to report crimes (Skogan, 1984).

Overall, about one in four households a year are victimized by crime, according to NCVS data. Females are just as likely to be victimized by intimates as they are by strangers, although males, African Americans, and young adults between the ages of 16 and 19 have consistently had the highest risk of victimization for most offenses (BJS, 2003). People with lower income, who have never married, and reside in an urban area are also victimized at higher rates (BJS, 2003). Less than 29% of violent crime is committed with a weapon, although firearms are used in about seven in ten murders (Meadows, 2004). Much violent crime, particularly homicide, has consistently followed an intraracial pattern where the offender and victim are of the same race.

The impact of victimization is of the utmost importance for the prevention and protection frameworks. More than one third of crime victims have no health insurance, and besides the cost of medical expenses, there is mental health care, property repair, lost wages from missed work, and reduced quality of life as part of the impact. The government pays about $8 million annually in medical reimbursements through victim compensation programs (Meadows, 2004), but no one can calculate the impact in terms of grief, fear, and anger. Victims of crime often carry emotional burdens or exhibit certain symptoms or syndromes that ruin their social, intimate, and work relationships. The aftermath of being a crime victim frequently involves a numbness or geographic relocation in an attempt to reorganize one's life, and it is in this sense that it can be said the victim sometimes contributes to their own revictimization. In other words, the crime protection framework deals with what can be done about the impact or aftermath for victims, whereas the crime prevention framework, especially primary prevention, aims at what can be done about the first instance of victimization and focuses upon keeping potential offenders from becoming actual offenders.

Primary prevention can be done in any context or location, whether a residence, workplace, school, neighborhood, community, or society. Primary prevention involves altering the environment in such a way that the root causes, or at least the facilitators, of crime are eliminated. As such, primary prevention is typically driven by supportable theory about the etiology of crime. An early example of this would be the social disorganization theory of Shaw and McKay (1942) that stated that the residential mobility and racial heterogeneity led people to have little interest in improving their neighborhood and more of an interest in moving out, leaving behind an area where crime could easily occur. More recent examples include Newman's (1972) defensible space theory, Cohen and Felson's (1979) routine activities theory, and Wilson and Kelling's (1982) broken windows theory. The theory of defensible space, like its counterpart in the field of private security called Crime Prevention through Environmental Design (CTPED), tends to have a focus on preventing easy access and exit by potential criminals as well as the elimination of their hiding places and where they can geographically select a target. Routine activities theory posits a high rate of potential victims becoming actual victims whenever three things occur in space and time together: the absence of capable guardians; an abundance of motivated offenders; and suitable targets. Broken windows theory argues that signs of decay, disorder, and incivilities, such as abandoned buildings, broken street lights, and graffiti, all invite potential criminals to an area. On a larger level, primary prevention can be based on macrosocial theories about the causes of crime in society, with examples of such efforts being job, housing, education, healthcare, and religious programs (Lavrakas, 1997).

Secondary prevention involves a focus upon specific problems, places, and times with the twin goals of reducing situation-specific opportunities for crime and increasing the risks for committing crime. Following Clarke (1980), many people call this situational crime prevention. Secondary prevention is most typically based on well-established law enforcement practices, such as problem-oriented policing where the problem drives a team solution; hot spots analysis that targets certain areas for saturation; or directed patrol, surveillance, and target-hardening that increase the risk and effort for committing crime, property identification, security lighting, intrusion alarms, neighborhood watch, citizen patrols, protection personnel, and efforts on the part of victims to change their lifestyles. A major criticism of secondary prevention is that it does not really reduce crime, but displaces it to other areas. Criminological theories that have been developed in this area include routine activities theory, lifestyles theory (Jensen and Brownfield, 1986), and rational choice theory (Cornish and Clarke, 1986). Lifestyles theory posits that individuals who lead deviant lifestyles, such as abuse of drugs or alcohol, spending time on the street, or association with deviant peers, are themselves more likely to be at high risk of victimization. Rational choice theory emphasizes the calculated decision making that offenders engage in, while determining the payoff and risks for certain crimes. Additional reward-risk models can be found in the criminological literature for specific offense categories.

Tertiary prevention is a term taken from the field of medicine to describe procedures to be taken after a disease or threat is manifest. Such procedures typically serve a deterrence or minimization-of-harm purpose, and are almost always characterized by being reactive, or after the fact. Examples would include personal injury or property insurance as well as self-protective measures engaged in by those who have been victimized previously. Carrying a nonconcealed self-protective device or walking in a self-confident manner accomplishes the purpose of deterrence. Carrying a concealed device or whistle to blow for help accomplishes the purpose of minimization, or at least the chance for an unsuccessful criminal outcome. In some cases, a victim's device may be turned against him or her and result in greater harm, but these cases are probably few in number as it is known that less than 5% of homicides involve the killer using the victim's gun (Kleck, 1998). Tertiary prevention is often symbolic, as with get-tough legislation and other legal reforms that make the punishment for crime more certain, severe, and swift.

The crime protection framework involves reactive or after-the-fact measures. One of the ways victims can secure a sense of protection from further victimization is to sue the property owners and managers of establishments in high-crime areas. Known as premises liability, such civil cases generally seek compensation for being victimized and improvements in security. They are based on claims that inadequate security or design flaws are present in the environment. Negligence cases are similar, where third-party defendants, such as landlords and employers, are found in breach of their duty to protect and the breach is a proximate cause of the injury. Civil justice for victims can also involve a finding of liability on the part of an offender who is not found guilty in the criminal justice system. Civil remedies can be an exhaustive, expensive, and risky activity for victims, which like seeking restitution from the offender, depends upon the ability of a liable party to pay.

Victim compensation programs, which originated in 1966 and reached their zenith in 1984 with the Victims of Crime Act (VOCA), use federal funds or incentives to encourage state funding of victim compensation and outreach. Compensation funds come from many sources, such as fines, penalties, forfeited bail, and prisoner income. As an example of the latter, a so-called Son of Sam clause in the VOCA prohibits criminals from profiting by telling their stories while their victims suffer financially. State compensation programs have rather strict eligibility requirements, and the amount of compensation varies.

Victim support service programs are designed to reduce trauma, ensure recovery, and provide orientation and support during criminal justice proceedings. Victim advocacy and sensitivity are integral parts of these programs. Eligibility requirements sometimes allow anyone who has witnessed a crime to qualify, but again, benefits vary from state to state. Since the passing of the 1982 Victim and Witness Protection Act (VWPA), victims have also earned important notification and protection order rights, followed by the 1994 Violent Crime Act that spawned victim impact statements.

Additional rights for the protection of victims have been legislated or come into existence only recently, such as the right for a homicide victim's family to attend the killer's execution, public notification of when a released sexual offender moves into the neighborhood (Megan's Law), mandatory reporting of campus crime statistics, improved efforts to track missing persons and children (Amber Alerts), better coordination of temporary shelter, counseling, and protective custody, and victim or offender reconciliation programs. In addition,

penalties have been increasing for witness tampering, intimidation, and harassment, especially in gang-related cases. A variety of witness protection and victim assistance programs have been developed at different levels, from the federal government all the way down to local nonprofit organizations.

THOMAS O'CONNOR

## References and Further Reading

Brantingham, P. and Faust, F. (1976). A conceptual model of crime prevention, *Crime and Delinquency,* 22, 284–296.

Bureau of Justice Statistics (2003). *Criminal Victimization, 2002,* NCJ 199994, Washington, DC, U.S. Department of Justice.

Clarke, R. (1980). Situational crime prevention: Theory and practice, *British Journal of Criminology,* 20, 136–147.

Cohen, L. and Felson, M. (1979). Social change and crime rate trends: A routine activity approach, *American Sociological Review,* 44, 588–608.

Cornish, D. and Clarke, R. (1986). *The Reasoning Criminal: Rational Choice Perspectives on Offending,* New York, NY, Springer-Verlag.

Jensen, G. and Brownfield, D. (1986). Gender, lifestyles and victimization: Beyond routine activities, *Violence and Victims,* 1, 85–99.

Kennedy, L. and Sacco, V. (1998). *Crime Victims in Context,* Los Angeles, CA, Roxbury.

Kleck, G. (1998). *Point Blank: Guns and Violence in America,* New York, NY, Aldine de Gruyter.

Lab, S.P. (1997). *Crime Prevention: Approaches, Practices and Evaluations,* 3rd ed., Cincinnati, OH, Anderson Publishing Co.

Lavrakas, P. (1997). Politicians, journalists, and the rhetoric of the crime prevention public policy debate, in Lab, S., Ed., *Crime Prevention at a Crossroads,* Cincinnati, OH, Anderson Publishing Co., pp. 161–173.

Meadows, R. (2004). *Understanding Violence and Victimization,* 3rd ed., Upper Saddle River, NJ, Prentice Hall.

Newman, O. (1972). *Defensible Space: Crime Prevention through Urban Design,* New York, NY, Macmillan.

Reninison, C. (2001). *National Crime Victimization Survey,* Bureau of Justice Statistics. Washington, DC, U.S. Department of Justice.

Shaw, C. and McKay, H. (1942). *Juvenile Delinquency and Urban Areas,* Chicago, IL, University of Chicago Press.

Sherman, L. (1996). *Preventing Crime: What Works, What Doesn't, What's Promising,* A Report to U.S. Congress, Washington, DC.

Skogan, W. (1984). Reporting crimes to the police, *Journal of Research in Crime and Delinquency,* 21, 113–137.

Wilson, J.Q. and Kelling, G. (1982) Broken windows: The police and neighborhood safety, *Atlantic Monthly,* 29–38.

*See also* **Victimization, Crime: Characterization of Victims; Victimization, Crime: Theories about Vulnerability; Victims' Rights**

# Victimization, Crime: Theories about Vulnerability

Victimization is a complex concept. Although frequently encountered in the scientific as well as the nonscientific literature, hardly any attempt is made to define "victimization" or to explain it, as if the term were self-explanatory. The word "victimization" has a negative connotation. The sense it conveys is one of an adverse effect, an undesired and undesirable consequence caused or brought about by some external force or by some individual, group, or organization. It implies the incurring of injury, harm, loss, inconvenience, discomfort, pain, and suffering of one sort or another. In simple terms, victimization implies one party preying upon another. Fattah and Sacco (1989) point out that although it might not be too problematic to recognize what is essential to an appropriate conceptualization of victimization, it is quite difficult to set proper conceptual limits to the term, that is, to determine what sorts of predations are to be included in a definition of victimization and what sorts of predations are to be excluded. This difficulty stems from the fact that there is an infinite variety of kinds, forms, and types of victimization to which people may be subjected or from which they may suffer. People may suffer death, injury, harm, or loss as a result of acts or omissions that have little or nothing to do with crime and the criminal law. It is very common to use the word "victim" in a wide variety of areas and contexts totally unrelated to crime. We hear and read about victims of disease, pollution, natural disasters, war, exploitation, oppression, repression, persecution, torture, discrimination, corporate wrongdoing, and so forth. Many forms of wrongdoing and many types of negligence, carelessness, or recklessness causing injury, loss, or harm are not criminal. In fact, the distinction between crime and tort is quite often an arbitrary one, as is the distinction between criminal victimization and victimization by civil wrongs or corporate wrongdoing.

Because victimization can take various shapes and forms, because it is a varied and multifaceted phenomenon, several attempts have been made to identify certain types and to create classifications and typologies. Using the source of victimization as the classification criterion, Fattah (1991) identified six major categories: natural victimization, auto-victimization, industrial or technological victimization, structural victimization, criminal victimization, and noncriminal victimization. Other types discussed by Fattah include corporate victimization, collective victimization, institutional victimization (that occurs in institutions of varying types), multiple victimization, random victimization, instantaneous and continuing victimization, direct and indirect victimization. Sellin and Wolfgang (1964) distinguished between primary victimization, secondary victimization (that they defined as taking place against impersonal, commercial, and collective victims), and tertiary victimization (that is the kind of diffusive victimization that extends to the community at large). At present, the term "secondary victimization" has acquired a different sense from that of Sellin and Wolfgang. Secondary victimization (sometimes also called the second victimization) is now being used to refer to crime victims' mistreatment by, and traumatic experiences with, the criminal justice system (Fattah, 1991).

The word victimization became part of the criminological lexicon in the 1960s. In 1964, the Finnish criminologist Inkeri Anttila published an article in *Excerpta Criminologica* entitled "The criminological significance of unregistered criminality." She suggested that it would be possible by means of surveys to establish how many individuals have been victimized and how many have reported their victimization to the police. Following this original idea, Biderman and Reiss (1967) suggested to the U.S. President's Commission on Law Enforcement and Administration of Justice a pilot survey designed according to Professor Anttila's suggestion. This survey was the beginning of what has become since then a standard measurement tool in criminology. The first large-scale victimization survey was carried out in the USA in 1965 for the same commission (Ennis, 1967). The findings of this pioneering survey were an eye-opener, as they showed that the volume of unreported crime revealed by the survey was far beyond expectations and previous estimates. The survey yielded rates of victimization that were much higher than those reported in the FBI's Uniform Crime Reports.

In their quest for standardized measures, victimization surveys usually use legally defined offenses. But, because victimization is a personal, subjective, and relative experience, the feeling of being victimized does not always coincide with the legal definition of victimization. It is not quite clear, therefore, what exactly victimization surveys are trying to measure. Is their objective to measure those criminal victimizations that meet the legal criteria set by the criminal code, or are they meant to measure the subjective victimizations experienced by the respondents? These, needless to say, are two different realities. In other words, are the surveys designed to measure crime or victimization? The titles "crime survey" and "victimization survey" continue to be used interchangeably (Fattah, 1997, 2000).

Rape is a good case in point because of the enormous gap that may exist between the legal definition and the subjective experience of the female. Also because the sexual act can be experienced in very different ways by different women.

Another major problem is that definitions and experiences of victimization greatly vary from one society to another and from one culture to another (Fattah, 1993). Several types of victimization are culturally constructed. This is particularly the case in the area of sexuality, child labor, child abuse, and neglect, to mention but a few. Even serious acts of violence may not in some cultures be defined or experienced as victimization. This is the case, for example, of many rites of passage and initiation rites in nonindustrial societies (Fattah, 1993). International Crime Surveys, which collect standardized victimization data from a number of countries for comparative purposes, are particularly prone to the problem of the cultural relativity of victimization.

Despite some unresolved conceptual and methodological problems, victimization surveys have greatly enhanced our knowledge of victims and victimization. Probably the major contribution of victimization surveys, over and above the attempt to measure the volume of certain types of crime, is to have revealed that victims of crime do not constitute an unbiased cross-section of the general population and that victimization is not evenly distributed within society. They showed that victimization is clustered within certain groups and certain areas and revealed that there is much greater affinity between offenders and victims than is commonly believed. Criminological studies in Europe, the U.S., Canada, and Australia have always shown that offenders involved in the types of crimes usually covered by victimization surveys are disproportionately male, young, urban residents, of lower socioeconomic status, unemployed (and not in school), unmarried, and, in the U.S., black. Victimization surveys reveal that victims disproportionately share those characteristics and confirm that the demographic profiles of crime victims and of convicted criminals are strikingly similar (Gottfredson, 1984). Although these findings may have come as a surprise to some when first released, they are both logical and understandable. It seems rather obvious that the frequency with which some individuals become involved in violence-prone situations is bound to affect both their chances of using violence and of being recipients of violence, of attacking and being attacked, of injuring and being injured, of killing and being killed. Who will end up being the victim and who will be legally considered the offender depends quite often on chance factors rather than deliberate action, planning, or intent. Thus, victim or offender roles are not necessarily antagonistic or incompatible but are frequently complementary and interchangeable (Fattah, 1994d). This situation is particularly true of brawls, quarrels, disputes, and altercations. In many instances, dangerousness and vulnerability may be regarded as the two sides of the same coin. They often coexist because many of the factors that contribute to dangerousness may create or enhance a state of vulnerability. One such factor is alcohol consumption, which may act simultaneously as a criminogenic and as a victimogenic factor, enhancing the potentiality of violent behavior in one party and of violent victimization in the other (see Fattah and Raic, 1970).

That victim and offender populations are homogeneous populations who share similar characteristics is undoubtedly because of the social and geographical proximity of victims and victimizers. Proximity and accessibility, for instance, are important factors in family violence. Actually, crimes of violence, particularly those not motivated by sex or financial gain, are interpersonal crimes or crimes of relationships. As the motives for the violence do not develop in a vacuum, it is understandable that these crimes are often committed between people who know each other; who interact with one another; and who are bound by family, friendship, or business ties. The typical contexts in which criminal homicide, attempted murder or assault occur are domestic fights, family disputes, quarrels between nonstrangers, or other altercations where insult, abuse, or jealousy is present. The interpersonal and the intraracial character of crimes of violence, particularly criminal homicide, are well-documented in many studies conducted in different cultures (Svalastoga, 1956; Wolfgang, 1958; Driver, 1961).

The notions of social and geographical proximity apply to many property offences as well. Brantingham and Brantingham (1984) point to a well-established distance decay pattern in human spatial behavior. They explain that people interact more with people and things that are close to their home location than with people or things that are far away and that interactions decrease as distance increases (distance decay). They further note that some of this decrease in activity as distance increases is the result of the "costs" of overcoming distance. According to the Brantinghams (1984, 345), "Crimes generally occur close to the home of the criminal. The operational definition of close varies by offence, but the distance decay gradient is evident in all offences.... Generally, violent offences have a high concentration close to home, with many assaults and murders actually occurring in the home. The search pattern is a little broader for property offences, but these are still clustered close to home".

Although sociodemographic characteristics are strong determinants of risks and rates of victimization, research also suggests that delinquency is one of the most important variables influencing the probability of victimization. Empirical evidence shows that criminals are more frequently victimized than noncriminals and indicates that victims of violent crime themselves have considerable criminal involvement (Canadian Centre for Justice Statistics, 1992; Friday, 1995; Fattah, 1997). The evidence also suggests that marginal groups are more involved in crime and more often victimized than nonmarginal groups. Typical examples of those prone to victimization are persons implicated in illicit activities or those who have opted for a deviant lifestyle: gang members, drug pushers, drug addicts, prostitutes, pimps, persons involved in illegal gambling, loan sharks, and so forth.

The rich data collected primarily through victimization surveys have led to the formulation of various interesting theoretical models aimed at providing plausible explanations for the variations in victimization risks, for the clustering of victimization in certain areas and certain groups, as well as for the intriguing phenomenon of repeat victimization. Repeat victimization refers to the fact that victimization in one event enhances the chances and increases the risk of a second victimization and so on (Fattah, 1989; 1991). Ziegenhagen (1977) studied the repeated victimization of some individuals and his findings suggest that recidivist victims can be distinguished from the general population by distinctive individual, social, and attitudinal orientations. All this points to what may be described as "proneness to victimization." This proneness is by no means limited to criminal victimization. Gottfredson's (1984) analysis of the British Crime Survey data showed that the likelihood of being the victim of a personal victimization was twice as high for those who report any one of other misfortunes (motor vehicle accidents, household fires, and other accidents serious enough to cause injury and suffering) as it was for those reporting that they had never experienced one such misfortune.

One of the first and more important models explaining the differential risks of victimization is the *lifestyle model* developed by Hindelang, Gottfredson, and Garofalo (1978). Their model posits that the likelihood an individual will suffer a personal victimization depends heavily on the concept of lifestyle. Using lifestyle to explain variations in risk is neither a novel nor a unique approach. It has been known for a long time that the probability of accidental death or injury is, in many respects, related to people's lifestyle and the kind of activities in which they are engaged. Physicians have repeatedly stressed the close link between life-style and routine activities and the risk of suffering certain diseases such as lung and skin cancer, high blood pressure and cardiovascular ailments, liver cirrhosis, AIDS, etc. As a matter of fact, the lifestyle concept permeates the explanations of a higher or lower susceptibility to a wide variety of diseases. The belief that lifestyle can influence the probability of victimization by increasing or decreasing people's chances of becoming victims of certain crimes may be seen as a simple, and in many ways logical, extension of the concept to the social sphere (Fattah, 1991).

Another explanatory model is the *routine activity approach* developed by Cohen and Felson (1979). The focus in Cohen and Felson's approach is on "direct-contact predatory violations," which are those "involving direct physical contact between at least one offender and at least one person or object which that offender attempts to take or damage." (Cohen and Felson, 1979). They argue that the occurrence of these types of victimization is the outcome of the convergence in space and time of three minimal elements: motivated offenders, suitable targets, and absence of capable guardians. The central factors underlying the routine activity approach are opportunity, proximity or exposure, and facilitating factors.

The *opportunity model* (Cohen, Kluegel, and Land, 1981) is yet another attempt to explain variations in victimization risks. The opportunity model incorporates elements from the previous two and posits that the risk of criminal victimization depends largely on people's lifestyles and routine activities that bring them or their property into direct contact with potential offenders in the absence of capable guardians.

In an attempt to integrate the various models into a comprehensive schema, Fattah (1991) grouped all the seemingly relevant factors under ten different categories. These are

1. *Opportunities:* that are closely linked to the characteristics of potential targets (persons,

households, businesses) and to the activities and behavior of those targets.

2. *Risk factors*: particularly those related to socio-demographic characteristics such as age and gender, area of residence, absence of guardianship, presence of alcohol, and so forth.

3. *Motivated offenders*: this is because offenders, even nonprofessional ones, do not choose their victim or targets at random but select their victims or targets according to specific criteria.

4. *Exposure*: this is because exposure to potential offenders and to high-risk situations and environments enhances the risk of criminal victimization.

5. *Associations*: the homogeneity of the victim and offender populations suggests that differential association is as important to criminal victimization as it is to crime and delinquency. Thus individuals who are in close personal, social, or professional contact with potential delinquents and criminals run a greater chance of being victimized than those who are not.

6. *Dangerous times and dangerous places*: the risks of criminal victimization are not evenly distributed in time or space—there are dangerous times such as evenings, late night hours, and weekends. There are also dangerous places such as places of public entertainment where the risks of becoming victim are higher than at work or at home.

7. *Dangerous behaviors*: this is because certain behaviors such as provocation increase the risk of violent victimization whereas other behaviors such as negligence and carelessness enhance the chances of property victimization. There are other dangerous behaviors that place those engaging in them in dangerous situations where their ability to defend and protect themselves against attacks is greatly reduced. A good example of this is hitchhiking.

8. *High-risk activities:* also increase the potential for victimization. Among such activities is the mutual pursuit of fun, as well as deviant and illegal activities. It is also well-known that certain occupations such as prostitution carry with them a higher than average potential for criminal victimization.

9. *Defensive or avoidance behaviors*: as many risks of criminal victimization could be easily avoided, people's attitudes to those risks can influence their chances of being victimized. It goes without saying that risk takers are bound to be victimized more often than risk avoiders. It also means that fear of crime is an important factor in reducing victimization because those who are fearful, for example the elderly, take more precautions against crime, even curtailing their day and night time activities thus reducing their exposure and vulnerability to victimization.

10. *Structural or cultural proneness*: there is a positive correlation between powerlessness, deprivation, and the frequency of criminal victimization. Cultural stigmatization and marginalization also enhance the risks of criminal victimization by designating certain groups as "fair game" or as culturally legitimate victims.

On the applied side, the impact of victimization on those who are victimized, the short- and long-term effects of the victimizing act on the victim, and the traumatic effects of victimization became not only major areas of study and research in victimology, but also common fields of practice. A new branch of victimology, *Clinical Victimology* (Lopez and Bornstein, 1995; Audet and Katz, 1999), developed to specifically treat victims, to help them cope with the consequences of the victimizing act, and to recover from the traumatic effects of victimization.

Ezzat A. Fattah

## References and Further Reading

Anttila, I., The criminological significance of unregistered criminality, *Excerpta Criminologica*, 4, 411 (1964).

Audet, J. and Katz, J.-F., *Précis de Victimologie Générale*, Dunod, Paris, 1999.

Biderman, A.D., Survey of population samples for estimating crime incidence, *The Annals of the American Academy of Political and Social Science*, 374, 16–33 (1967).

Biderman, A.D. and Reiss, A.J., Jr., On exploring the dark figure of crime, *The Annals of the American Academy of Political and Social Science*, 374, 1–15 (1967).

Bilsky, W., Pfeiffer, C. and Wetzels, P., Eds., *Fear of Crime and Criminal Victimization*, Ferdinand Enke Verlag, Stuttgart, Germany, 1993.

Brantingham, P.J. and Brantingham, P.L., *Patterns in Crime*, New York, NY, Macmillan Publishing Co., 1984.

Canadian Center for Justice Statistics, Homicide in Canada, *Juristat*, 13 (1992).

Cohen, L.E. and Felson, M., Social change and crime rate trends: A routine activities approach, *American Sociological Review*, 44, 588–608 (1979).

Cohen, L.E., Kluegel, J.R. and Land, K.C., Social inequality and predatory criminal victimization: An exposition and test of a formal theory, *American Sociological Review*, 46(October), 505–524 (1981).

Del Frate, A.A., *Victims of Crime in the Developing World*, UNICRI (Publication No. 57), Rome, 1998.

Del Frate, A.A., Zvekic, U. and van Dijk, J.J.M., Eds., *Understanding Crime: Experiences of Crime and Crime Control*, UNICRI (Publication No. 49), Rome, 1993.

Driver, E., Interaction and Criminal homicide in India, *Social Forces*, 40, 153–158 (1961).

Ennis, P.H., *Criminal Victimization in the United States: A Report of a National Survey,* Washington, DC, U.S. Government Printing Office, 1967.

Fattah, E.A., Victims and Victimology: The Facts and the Rhetoric, *International Review of Victimology,* 1(1), 43-66 (1989).

Fattah, E.A., *Understanding Criminal Victimization.* Scarborough, Ontario, Canada, Prentice Hall Canada (1991).

Fattah, E.A., La relativité culturelle de la victimisation—Quelques réflexions sur les problèmes et le potentiel de la victimologie comparée, *Criminologie,* 26(2), 121–136 (1993).

Fattah, E.A., *Criminology: Past, Present and Future—A Critical Overview,* Macmillan Press Limited, London, U.K.; St. Martin's Press, New York, NY, 1997.

Fattah, E.A. and Raic, A., L'alcool en tant que facteur victimogène, *Toxicomanies,* 3(2), 143–173, 1970.

Fattah, E.A. and Sacco, V., *Crime and Victimization of the Elderly,* New York, NY, Springer Verlag, 1989.

Friday, P., *Personal Communication,* March, 1995.

Gottfredson, M.R., *Victims of Crime: The Dimensions of Risk,* Home Office Research and Planning Unit Report (No. 81), London, Her Majesty's Stationery Office, 1984.

Hatalak, O., Del Frate, A.A. and Zvekic, U., Eds., *The International Crime Victim survey in Countries in Transition, National Reports,* UNICRI (Publication No. 62), Rome, 1998.

Hindelang, M.J., Gottfredson, M.R. and Garofalo, J., *Victims of Personal Crime: An Empirical Foundation for a Theory of Personal Victimization,* Cambridge, MA, Ballinger, 1978.

Laub, J.H., Patterns of criminal victimization in the United States, in Davis, R.C., Lurigio, A.J. and Skogan, W.G., Eds., *Victims of Crime,* 2nd ed., Thousand Oaks, CA, Sage Publications, 1997.

Lopez, G. and Bornstein, S., *Victimologie Clinique,* Maloine, Paris, 1995.

Meier, R.F. and Miethe, T.D., Understanding theories of criminal victimization, *Crime and Justice: An Annual Review of Research,* 17, 459–499, 1993.

Reiss, A.J., Jr., Victim proneness in repeat victimization by type of crime, in Fienberg, S.E. and Reiss, A.J., Jr., Eds., *Indicators of Crime and Criminal Justice: Quantitative Studies,* Washington, DC, U.S. Department of Justice, Bureau of Justice Statistics, Government Printing Office, 1980.

Sellin, T. and Wolfgang, M.E., *The Measurement of Delinquency,* New York, NY, John Wiley and Sons, Inc., 1964.

Sparks, R.F., Surveys of victimization: An optimistic assessment, *Crime and Justice: An Annual Review of Research,* 3, 1–60 (1981).

Sparks, R.F., *Research on Victims of Crime,* Washington, DC, Government Printing Office, 1982.

Svalastoga, K., Homicide and social contact in Denmark, *American Journal of Sociology,* 62, 37–41 (1956).

Victims Referral and Assistance Service, *Support for Victims of Crime, Responding to the Challenges of Diversity: Different Cultures; Different Needs,* Proceedings of the Conference, Melbourne, Australia, April 1999.

Wolfgang, M.E., *Patterns in Criminal Homicide,* Philadelphia, PA, University of Pennsylvania Press, 1958.

Zawitz, M.W., Klaus, P.A., Bachman, R., Bastian, L.D., DeBerry, M.M., Rand, M.R. and Taylor, B.M., *Highlights from 20 years of Surveying Crime Victims.* Washington, DC, U.S. Department of Justice, 1993.

Ziegenhagen, E., The recidivist victim of violent crime, *Victimology: An International Journal,* 1(4), 538–50 (1976).

Zvekic, U., *Criminal Victimisation in Countries in Transition,* UNICRI (Publication No. 61), Rome, 1998.

Zvekic, U. and Del Frate, A.A., Eds., *Criminal Victimization in the Developing World,* UNICRI (Publication No. 55), Rome, 1995.

*See also* **Victimization, Crime: Characteristics of Victims; Victimology**

# Victimization, Repeated

Although the term "repeat victimization" is often used as though it described a single phenomenon, it is useful to make a distinction between two types of repeat victimization, multiple victimization and chronic victimization (Menard, 2000). Multiple victimization is victimization that occurs more than once in a single study period (for example, more than once in a single year) and can be measured, for example, as the annual frequency of victimization for a particular individual. Multiple victimization or frequency of victimization is indicative of the intensity of victimization for an individual within a limited time span.

In purely cross-sectional studies of repeat victimization, multiple victimization is the only available measure of repeat victimization.

Chronic victimization is victimization that occurs in more than one study period (for instance, in more than 1 year) in a sample or population with multiple measurement periods. Chronic victimization is indicative of the duration of the victimization experience, or the span of time during which an individual is subjected to criminal victimization. Chronic victimization can only be measured using longitudinal data, either long-term retrospective data that span several years (and which are subject to serious problems of respondent recall error; see Menard, 2000), or data collected in repeated interviews over a span of years. Both multiple and chronic victimization represent repeat victimization, and it is possible to have chronic multiple victimization as a worst case. In addition to the distinction between multiple and chronic victimization, it is also useful for some purposes to distinguish between intermittent victimization (victimization in at least 2 years, with at least 1 intervening year with no victimization) and continuous victimization (victimization at least once in every year of a span of 2 or more years).

## Sources of Data on Repeated Victimization

Data on victimization are available in the U.S. from the National Crime Victimization Survey (NCVS; formerly the National Crime Survey or NCS), and from self-report studies that include victimization as well as illegal behavior, including the National Youth Survey (NYS) and the Monitoring the Future (MTF) study (Wells and Rankin, 1995). The British Crime Survey (BCS), which parallels the NCVS, has also been used, even more extensively than the NCVS, in the study of repeated victimization (Ellingworth et al., 1995; Farrell et al., 1995). Wells and Rankin compared the NCVS, NYS, and MTF with a focus on juvenile victimization. Adolescent victimization is particularly important to the study of repeat victimization because both the NCVS and other sources agree that victimization tends to be higher for younger than for older respondents. Wells and Rankin found that younger individuals were less reliably represented in the NCVS than in the NYS or MTF because of such factors as the sampling frame of the survey, the form of the questionnaire, and the wording of the questions. The NYS and MTF produced estimates of the prevalence (whether a respondent reports being a victim of crime) and frequency or incidence (how many times an individual reports being a victim of crime) that were consistent with one another, but generally higher than the estimates obtained from the NCVS. Lauritsen et al. (1991) reported similar findings.

According to Wells and Rankin, there are several reasons why there may be a discrepancy between the NCVS and the NYS and MTF surveys. First and most obviously, the interview content is different; however, the questions on victimization are quite similar for all three studies. Second, "Because the sampling unit for most national surveys (including the NCVS) is the *household,* people who are not clearly attached to stable household units are either omitted or grossly undersampled. Moreover, such persons (e.g., runaway juveniles,

transients, homeless persons, institutionalized persons, or persons living in temporary or single-room occupancies) are likely to have higher than average levels of victimization, which will be missing or underrepresented in the NCVS estimates" (Wells and Rankin, 1995, 290). Similar criticisms could be applied to the MTF, and to the first waves of the NYS. The MTF samples are school-based, but the NYS includes school dropouts as well as students. NYS respondents in the first wave were living in households with their parents, but subsequent waves follow individuals, not households, and include individuals who were not attached to stable households, who were in the military, or who were under the supervision of the juvenile justice system or, at older ages, the criminal justice system.

Third, the frequency of victimization may be underestimated in the NCVS (and the BCS; see Ellingworth et al., 1995) because they group incidents involving similar patterns of victimization that occur closely in time into a single "series" victimization incident; but this should have no effect on estimates of the prevalence of victimization. Wells and Rankin concluded that discrepancies among the NCVS, MTF, and NYS were too large and consistent to be dismissed as being attributable to normal sampling fluctuations, or slight variations in item wording, or common methods factors (the NYS is more similar procedurally and in the questions it asks to the NCVS than either the NYS or NCVS is to MTF), or overreporting of trivial victimizations (the MTF has no follow-up questions to check for triviality, but the NYS does). Noting the similarity in victimization estimates between the NYS, MTF, and other surveys, in contrast to the NCVS, Wells and Rankin suggested that the large discrepancies in reported adolescent criminal victimization between the NCVS and other surveys may reflect substantial differences in the social dynamics of the interviews.

In addition to the concerns that led Wells and Rankin to characterize the NCVS as providing "uncertain estimates" of adolescent victimization, the data on any individual respondent in the NCVS are available for a maximum of 3 years. The NCVS uses a rotating sample of households, and interviews each household at 6-month intervals over a span of 3 years, at the end of which the household is dropped from the sample and replaced by another household. Historically, then, the NCVS has been a short-term longitudinal sample of households, but not necessarily of individuals. As a result of the combination of a household focus and the short period for which longitudinal data are collected, repeat victimization may be underestimated, especially if victimization occurs intermittently rather than continuously.

## The Extent of Repeated Victimization

Cross-sectional data on victimization from the National Crime Victimization Survey and the British Crime Survey can give the impression that being a victim of crime is a relatively rare event, and that being a victim of crime more than once is rarer still. The title of Nelson's (1980) analysis of NCVS data is illustrative: "Multiple Victimization in American Cities: A Statistical Analysis of Rare Events." A similar impression of the rarity of repeat victimization is conveyed by cross-sectional and short-term data from the BCS (Ellingworth et al., 1995; Farrell et al., 1995). Sparks (1981, 762) remarked that "Without exception, victimization surveys over the past fifteen years have found that the great majority of the surveyed population report that none of the incidents they were asked about had happened to them during the period covered; a minority report that they had experienced *one* incident; and successively smaller proportions generally report having experienced two, three ... n incidents," and concluded that repeat victimization was so rare in general population samples that "Representative samples of the general population are thus unlikely to produce sufficient cases of multiple victimization, except at inordinate cost" (Sparks, 1981, 777).

A somewhat similar picture emerges based on annual data from the NYS (Menard, 2000). Approximately half of the adolescents in the NYS were victims of crime in any given year, and approximately one third of the same individuals as adults were victims of crime in any given year. Also, the seriousness of victimization in the NYS was comparable to the seriousness of victimization in the NCVS, and the distribution of victimization by age (lower for older respondents), sex (higher for males, especially for violent victimization), and ethnicity (small and generally statistically nonsignificant differences in the NYS, but typically in the same direction as NCVS) were similar for both surveys. Differences emerge, however, when repeat victimization is considered in the longer-term perspective afforded by the 17-year span of the NYS.

Most of the respondents in the NYS were multiple victims in at least 1 year, victims in more than 1 year, and intermittent victims. The sociodemographic correlates of repeat victimization (age, sex, and ethnicity) were the same as for victimization more generally—not surprising, as most respondents, let alone victims, were repeat victims. Like criminal offending, criminal victimization is concentrated among a relatively small number of victims. In adolescence, the upper 10% of victims accounted for approximately half to two thirds of all reported property, violent, and total victimizations. The concentration of adult victimization in the NYS was higher, particularly for violent victimization. The 10% of respondents who were the most frequent victims of violent crime in adulthood accounted for over 80% of the total number of violent victimizations reported.

Koppel (1987) estimated the lifetime likelihood of victimization based on NCVS data. Koppel's estimates are based on age-and-gender-specific rates of victimization beginning at age 12, age-specific life expectancies, and an assumption of constant annual rates of victimization. For the total population, Koppel estimated that 83% would be victims of violent crime (89% for males, 73% for females), and that 99% (both male and female) would be victims of property crime. Of those victimized, Koppel estimated that 30% of violent crime victims and 4% of property crime victims would be victims of a single criminal offense, whereas the rest would be multiple victims. Koppel (1987) emphasized that the estimates of lifetime likelihood of victimization he presented, were estimates only, not descriptions of what has been observed over the life course. Still, in the NYS, rates of cumulative victimization were generally consistent with what would have been expected based on Koppel's projections, except that lifetime rates of violent victimization appear to be higher for the NYS than were projected by Koppel for the NCVS (Menard, 2000).

## Explaining Repeated Victimization

Lauritsen and Quinet (1995) used data from the NYS to try to explain rates of victimization, and found that both state dependence (the influence of past victimization on present victimization) and heterogeneity (a latent tendency or propensity for victimization) appeared to affect victimization. In other words, some individuals appear more likely, for as yet unexplained reasons, to be victims of crime, and once an individual has been victimized, they appear to be at higher risk for future victimization. Osborn et al. (1996) also found that initial victimization appears to increase the probability of future victimization, but otherwise found little evidence that repeat victims had characteristics different from individuals who had been victimized only once. This is consistent with the finding noted above that the sociodemographic characteristics of victims generally and repeat victims more specifically are the same in the NYS.

These explanations seem relatively light on theory, although the concern with heterogeneity versus state dependence has been linked to routine activities and rational choice theories (Farrell et al., 1995). Lasley and Rosenbaum (1988) approached victimization from the routine activities perspective, but built in explicit measures derived from that perspective and found that the processes involved in repeat victimization were the same as the processes involved in single victimizations. Housewives and retired individuals, and individuals who spent fewer nights away from home (both indicating guardianship with respect to household victimization) had lower rates of victimization, and individuals with higher levels of alcohol consumption (target vulnerability for personal victimization) had higher rates of victimization. Given the results suggesting that most victims *are* repeat victims, one might expect that predictors of victimization in general should also be predictive of repeat victimization, but more extensive testing of theories of victimization with repeat victimization as the dependent variable remain, as of this writing, for future research. For now, it remains the case, as Farrell et al. (1995, 384) remarked, that "Research into the extent and policy implications of repeat victimization has outpaced understanding of why it occurs."

SCOTT MENARD

### References and Further Reading

Ellingworth, D., Farrell, G. and Pease, K., A victim is a victim is a victim? Chronic victimization in four sweeps of the British crime survey, *British Journal of Criminology,* 35 (1995).

Farrell, G., Phillips, C. and Pease, K., Like taking candy: Why does repeat victimization occur? *British Journal of Criminology,* 35 (1995).
Koppel, H., Lifetime likelihood of victimization, *Bureau of Justice Statistics Technical Report,* Washington, DC, U.S. Department of Justice, 1987.
Lasley, J.R. and Rosenbaum, J.L., Routine activities and multiple personal victimization, *Sociology and Social Research,* 73 (1988).
Lauritsen, J.L. and Quinet, K.F.D., Repeat Victimization among adolescents and young adults, *Criminology,* 11 (1995).
Menard, S., The 'Normality' of repeat victimization from Adolescence through early adulthood, *Justice Quarterly,* 17 (2000).
Nelson, J.F., Multiple victimization in American cities: A statistical analysis of rare events, *American Journal of Sociology,* 85 (1980).
Osborn, D.R., Ellingworth, D., Hope, T. and Trickett, A., Are repeatedly victimized households different? *Journal of Quantitative Criminology,* 12 (1996).
Sparks, R., Multiple victimization: Evidence, theory, and future research, *Journal of Criminal Law and Criminology,* 72 (1981).
Wells, L.E. and Rankin, J.H., Juvenile victimization: Convergent validation of alternative measurements, *Journal of Research in Crime and Delinquency,* 32 (1995).

*See also* **National Crime Victimization Survey (NCVS)**

# Victimless Crime

The term "victimless crime" is used to describe those acts whose criminal status is often contested, because of their nonpredatory nature. These are crimes that defy the notion that laws are based on a widespread consensus regarding "good" and "bad" behaviors. Victimless crime, or "vice," is defined by the concept of *mala prohibita*—literally, "bad because it is prohibited"—whereas violent and property crimes are considered criminal by virtue of their status as *mala in se*—"bad in itself." In other words, victimless crime is unlike other types of crime because it lacks a universal agreement as to whether it is truly "bad" and deserving of criminal sanction. Most often, victimless crimes include those acts whose criminal status has shifted over time, such as homosexuality, drug use, abortion, gambling, euthanasia, prostitution, and pornography.

The debate as to whether victimless crimes that involve consensual acts on the part of all involved should in fact be illegal is one with a rather long history. In the 1800s, John Stuart Mill articulated the libertarian argument, claiming that one should have the "right to go to hell in one's own way." This argument followed from Mill's concern for where individual rights begin and the state's interests end. These libertarian arguments resurfaced in the 20th century, becoming popular legal thought in the 1950s and 1960s through the writings of legal scholar H.L.A. Hart and the release of the Wolfenden Report in England, calling for the repeal of laws criminalizing homosexual conduct, prostitution, and other such victimless crimes. The philosophical arguments for decriminalization hearken back to J.S. Mill's earlier writings on personal liberty. The practical arguments favoring decriminalization note the cost of enforcement, the growth of black markets and organized crime syndicates that meet the demand for illegal goods and services, and a loss of respect for the institutions of law caused by the enforcement of such controversial statutes. Such concerns have led legal scholars to discuss the criminalization of vice using such terms as a "crisis of over-criminalization" (Kadish, 1967), "coercion to virtue" (Skolnick, 1968), and "not the law's business" (Geis, 1979). On the opposite side of the debate, prohibitionists such as Sir Patrick Devlin have argued that all individual choices have societal repercussions, and that legal restrictions on personal behavior are needed for a healthy moral society.

These debates, at the scholarly level at least, have their origins in the U.S. and Great Britain. However, a variety of approaches to victimless crime are apparent in other parts of the world. In most European countries, particularly in the Scandinavian countries, these activities have been treated as either nonissues by the law or as public health concerns, rather than moral crises. For example, drug use, euthanasia, and prostitution are all regulated but legal in the Netherlands. Sexual norms vary widely across different cultures as well. Certain sexual images on Japanese television and in Indian art, for instance, would be considered pornography and therefore illegal in the U.S. Cross-cultural variation in sexual norms is also evident in differing treatments of homosexuality. Whereas many countries, including England and Canada, no longer criminalize homosexual conduct to the extent that the U.S. does, other countries such as Afghanistan and those in the Middle East have far stricter regulations in terms of both homosexual and heterosexual activities. Yet debate over the treatment of such activities is no less contentious in most of these countries.

One of the most contentious and probably the most long-lived of the substantive debates about victimless crime is the legal treatment of drug use, possession, and sales. When considering the status of certain drugs as legal versus illegal, however, it is important to understand that these statuses are not static over time. In fact, the first drug to be criminalized in the U.S. was one of the few that is now legal; nicotine. The first nation-wide legislation aimed at curbing the use of narcotic drugs was the Harrison Act of 1914, which used tax laws to limit the use of opium, heroin, and other drugs that were commonly used—mostly by doctor's prescription—at the time. This was followed by Prohibition, which outlawed the consumption and sale of alcohol from 1920 to 1933. In recent decades, the Reagan-initiated War on Drugs has had a large impact. The Anti-Drug Abuse Act of 1986, which imposed the same mandatory minimum sentence for possession of 1 gram of crack cocaine as for 100 grams of power cocaine, has resulted in a tremendous increase in incarceration for inner city, minority drug offenders. Eventually, the Powder Cocaine Sentencing Act of 2000

lowered the ratio from 100:1 to 10:1. Other laws introduced in the late 1990s and after have followed this pattern of scaling back some of the stringent drug laws of the 1980s, including the measures in California and Hawaii legalizing the medical use of marijuana and California's Proposition 36 that provided treatment rather than incarceration for first-time drug offenders. Still, as of 1999, the U.S. devoted $16 billion a year to the domestic drug war, close to $17 million abroad, and one third of all felony convictions were for drug charges.

In comparison, enforcement of prostitution laws is relatively lax—particularly considering the widespread general consensus among the public in support of such laws. Of all victimless crimes, prostitution has the longest history and has remained the least changed in terms of its legal status. Currently, estimates are that between 500,000 and 1 million prostitutes are working in the U.S., and about 5 million Americans have at one time worked as a prostitute. Approximately, 20% of men have patronized prostitutes at some point in their lives, and these men come from all racial and socio-economic backgrounds. There are about 100,000 prostitution arrests per year, costing the criminal justice system about $2,000 each. In most cases, prostitution offenses are considered misdemeanors, involving fines and minimal jail time. In many jurisdictions, the official policy for dealing with prostitution is one of containment—as long as it is restricted to designated "red light" districts, laws are not strictly enforced. Some prostitutes have organized a social movement calling for the legalization of sex work, although it remains criminal in every state except Nevada.

The public discourse surrounding pornography is far more contentious than that surrounding prostitution. Even its specific definition has been the matter of much contention. Vague obscenity laws that originated 150 years ago are the basis for today's pornography laws. In 1973, the U.S. Supreme Court attempted to define pornography in *Miller v. California* (413 U.S.), but these standards still left much to individual interpretation. Specifically, the court in *Miller* found that the following three conditions must be met in order for something to be considered pornographic: the average person, according to current community standards, would think the material appeals to prurient interests; it depicts sexual conduct in an offensive way; and it lacks serious literary, artistic, political, or scientific value.

The legal status of pornography has continued to be a source of debate. Free speech advocates and libertarians argue that pornography is harmless and that laws against it violate Americans' First Amendment rights. Those opposed to the legalization of pornography come from two distinct camps: religious conservatives, who object on morality grounds, and feminist activists and scholars, who argue that pornography is harmful and degrading to women. In general, the law has tended to support the libertarian argument, opting to keep pornography regulated but legal for the most part. The advent of the Internet and its potential for widespread distribution has pushed legislatures to reconsider the potential harm of pornography and its legal status.

Gambling, like pornography and prostitution, has not been a major focus of law enforcement efforts, despite its presence in nearly all societies and time periods. Perhaps one reason for this lack of attention is access to legal forms of gambling, including lotteries, Native American casinos, riverboat casinos, horseracing, and bingo. In fact, all states in the U.S. except Hawaii and Utah have some form of legal and often state-run gambling. Even when laws prohibit some forms of gambling such as card games, sports wagers, and some casinos, they are not usually enforced. This is evident in the willingness of newspapers to publish gambling odds for certain sporting events. As of the 1990s, gambling in the U.S. produced approximately $329 billion in wagers and $30 billion in revenues. With an increase in legal gambling of nearly fourfold from the 1980s to the 1990s, it seems that gambling is one victimless crime that eventually may be decriminalized.

Euthanasia, or physician-assisted suicide, has not experienced a similar movement toward legalization as has gambling. Euthenasia has existed as a tacit practice in private homes and hospices for years, although it did not receive significant legal attention in the U.S. until the 1990s. In *Cruzan v. Missouri Department of Health* (497 U.S. 261, 1990), the U.S. Supreme Court upheld the legality of a request to withdraw life support from a patient in a vegetative state. This decision drew on the precedent set in a New Jersey Supreme Court decision, *In re Quinlan* (70 N.J. 10, 1976) that resulted in a "Do Not Resuscitate," or DNR, order. These decisions, however, only dealt with the withdrawal or withholding of life support; they did not legalize actual assisted suicide, such as administering a life-ending dose of medication. In 1994, the "Death with Dignity Act" was passed into law by voters in Oregon, allowing doctors to administer an overdose of pain medication at a patient's request, in order to end her or his life. This remains the only euthanasia law of its kind in the U.S.

The rhetoric and debate surrounding the legalization of euthanasia is often compared with the abortion debate because both involve fundamental rights of life and death. Although it is no longer considered a crime in the U.S. and was not enforced as a matter of criminal law prior to the late 19th century, the criminal status

and enforcement of abortion has shifted several times over the course of the last century. In the 1940s, for instance, police raids that resulted in forced deathbed confessions by victims of botched illegal abortions were common. It was not until the late 1950s that doctors and, later, feminists began to call for the legalization of abortion. This was finally accomplished in the landmark 1973 decision in *Roe v. Wade* (410 U.S. 113). Today there are a number of states that prohibit abortions after the second trimester and those for teenagers without their parents' consent, but generally the act remains legal.

Like abortion, the legal status of homosexuality has been hotly contested for many decades in the U.S. Technically, the identity of homosexuality is not a crime. It is the sexual act usually associated with homosexuality—sodomy (most often defined as anal or oral sex)—that defines it as a victimless crime. Until 1961, adult consensual sodomy was illegal everywhere in the U.S. In 2001, it remained criminal in 17 states. Out of those, four (Arkansas, Kansas, Oklahoma, and Missouri) criminalize only same-sex sodomy. There are no federal laws outlawing sodomy or homosexuality, but in the U.S. military a sodomy conviction carries a mandatory prison sentence of 5 years. In 1986, the U.S. Supreme Court protected the states' right to criminalize sodomy, ruling that homosexual acts are not subject to the same constitutional right to privacy as are heterosexual acts (*Bowers v. Hardwick*, 478 U.S. 186). Despite this ruling, sodomy laws are seldom enforced.

These topical examples illustrate the different policy models for dealing with victimless crime. Policies can be positioned along a continuum, ranging from strict prohibition of the criminal activity to outright legalization, such that it is no longer considered a crime. Strict prohibition of vice can often be costly and difficult to enforce, as demonstrated by America's War on Drugs. Often it is easier to opt for a model of regulation, in which the state maintains control over the activity, and does not consider it illegal if the activity is done in the state-mandated way. New drug laws, such as those legalizing the medical use of marijuana, are evidence of a shift toward this policy model. Another intermediary policy alternative is decriminalization, which means that an edict is issued dictating that the particular vice activity in question will not be heavily enforced by police and other law enforcement agents, but will still be considered officially illegal. This is sometimes accomplished through a policy of containment, in which the activity is not prohibited as long as it remains within a certain geographical area, such as a "red light district." This is an oft-used policy in dealing with prostitution. In some cases, the state will opt for a policy of de facto legalization, in which case the vice activity is treated as legal in practice, and is therefore not enforced at all by policing agents, but is still not legal according to the letter of the law. In many states, this has been the policy model for dealing with homosexuality. Finally, as in the case of abortion, an activity that was once considered criminal is officially and completely legalized. Although complete legalization is relatively rare, it demonstrates the provisional and ambiguous nature of victimless crime.

KIMBERLY D. RICHMAN

### References and Further Reading

Geis, G., *Not the Law's Business? An Examination of Homosexuality, Abortion, Prostitution, Narcotics, and Gambling in the United States,* New York, NY, Schocken Books, 1979.

Great Britain, *Wolfenden Report: Report of the Committee on Homosexual Offenses and Prostitution,* London and New York: Lancer Books, 1964.

Gruen, L. and Panichas, J.E., Eds., *Sex, Morality, and the Law,* New York, Routledge, 1997.

Hillyard, D. and Dombrink, J., *Dying Right: The Death with Dignity Movement,* New York, NY, Routledge, 2001.

Kadish, S., The crisis of overcriminalization, *The Annals,* 374 (1967).

Meier, R.F. and Geis, G., *Victimless Crime? Prostitution, Drugs, Homosexuality, Abortion,* Los Angeles, CA, Roxbury Publishing, 1997.

Musto, D.F., *The American Disease: Origins of Narcotics Control,* New Haven, CT, Yale University Press, 1973.

Reagan, L., *When abortion was a crime: Women, medicine, and the law in the United States, 1867–1973,* Berkeley, CA, University of California Press, 1997.

Skolnick, J.H., *Coercion to Virtue,* Chicago, IL, American Bar Foundation, 1968.

Wagner, D., *The New Temperance: The American Obsession with Sin and Vice,* Boulder, CO, Westview Press, 1997.

*See also* **Abortion; Drug Use: Law; Euthanasia and Physician-Assisted Suicide; Gambling, Illegal; Prostitution: Law**

# Victimology

Victimology can be loosely defined as "the study of the victim." The term victimology, a combination of the Latin word "*victima*" (victim) and the Greek word "*logos*" (science) was coined by an American psychiatrist, Frederick Wertham (1949), who used it for the first time in his book "The Show of Violence." Although scientific criminology dates back to the 19th century and the studies of the Italian Positivist School, victimology is a relatively young discipline that began with the publication of Hans von Hentig's seminal work "*The Criminal and his Victim*" in 1948. It is not easy to explain how or why the need for criminology to thoroughly study the victims of crime, a need that today appears rather obvious, even axiomatic, could have escaped the attention of criminologists and other social scientists for almost a century. And although victimology, in recent years, has firmly established itself as a major and indispensable research area within criminology, its nature, place, and standing continue to generate a great deal of comments and debate. The subject matter of victimology is also a matter of controversy. Although some victimologists (Elias, 1986) advocate what may be described as a "global victimology" encompassing not only crime victims but also all other victims, others believe that victimology should concern itself exclusively with those subjected to some form of criminal victimization (Flynn, 1982; Fattah, 1991). They fear that by broadening its field of study to victimization in a generic sense and by adopting such a loose and diffuse subject, victimology would lack the specificity that is essential for rigorous scientific inquiry. They argue that by overextending itself to the unmeasurable phenomenon of global victimization, to the undefinable and unquantifiable phenomenon of human suffering, victimology risks to lose its scientific character.

The raison d'être of victimology is quite simple. It is the dual frame of most crimes, the fact that the majority of conventional criminal acts involve an offender and a victim, and that the motives for criminal behavior do not develop in a vacuum. The motivation to perpetrate a victimizing act comes into being through needs, urges, and drives. It emerges from contacts, communications, interactions, attitudes, and counterattitudes. Not infrequently, the prospective victim is involved consciously or unconsciously in the motivational process as well as in the process of mental reasoning and rationalization the victimizer engages in prior to the commission of the crime (Fattah, 1976; 1991). In most instances victims are not chosen at random and in many cases the motives for the criminal act develop around a specific and nonexchangeable victim. An examination of victim characteristics, of the place the victim occupies and the role the victim plays in these dynamic processes, is therefore essential to understanding why the crime was committed in this given situation and why this particular target was chosen. This explains why offender target selection is an important and a quite promising research area in victimology.

In the early years of victimology literature on crime victims remained relatively small when compared to that on criminology. Starting from the 1980s, however, a spate of important books and articles were published signaling not only the rapidly mounting interest in victims of crime but also the growing realization of the vital importance of the new discipline. At present, it is fair to say that the study of crime victims has become an integral part of criminology. Not only this, but victimology also offers the potential of reshaping the entire field of criminology. It may very well be the long awaited paradigm shift that criminology badly needs, given the failure of its traditional paradigms: search for the causes of crime, deterrence, rehabilitation, treatment, just deserts, etc. (Fattah, 2000).

Theoretical victimology is a scholarly attempt to convert criminology into a dynamic, holistic discipline, to shift the focus of research from the unidimensional study of criminals' traits and attributes to situational and interpersonal dynamics. Its point of departure is that victimizing behavior is dynamic behavior that cannot be adequately explained by the static etiological theories that dominated criminology for more than a century. Crime needs to be explained by a dynamic approach where the offender, the act, and the victim are inseparable elements of a total situation that conditions the dialectic of the victimizing behavior (Fattah, 1976; 1997). Victimology seeks the genesis of victimization not in the characteristics and background of the victimizer, as traditional criminology did, but in a complex model of total interactions. It places a great deal of emphasis on situational factors, on victim–offender relationships and interactions, and the role all of them play in actualizing or triggering criminal behavior. Whereas traditional criminology viewed criminal behavior as simply the product of the offender's traits and personality, victimology sees it as the outcome of a long or brief interaction with the victim. It considers unscientific and futile any attempt to treat the act of victimization as an isolated gesture, to dissociate it from the dynamic forces that have prepared, influenced, conditioned, or determined its commission or from the motivational and situational processes that were vital to its conception. Victimology insists that in most cases crime is not an action but a

reaction (or even an overreaction) to external and environmental stimuli. Some of these stimuli emanate from the victim. The victim is therefore an important, often an integral, element of the criminogenic environment and of the victimogenic situation.

Although these were the premises that guided the earlier studies in victimology, it soon became apparent that the study of the victim is both needed and useful for many other purposes as well. Not only is it necessary to establish the frequency and the patterns of victimization, but it also sheds light on other issues such as proneness to victimization, fear of victimization, responses to victimization, consequences and impact of victimization, and so forth. Such knowledge provides a solid scholarly foundation for "applied victimology," which is mainly concerned with aiding and assisting victims, alleviating the negative consequences of the victimizing act, preventing its reoccurrence, as well as helping victims overcome the traumatic effects of victimization. A thorough knowledge of victims of crime is also essential for the formulation of a rational criminal policy, for the evaluation of crime prevention strategies, and for taking social action aimed at protecting vulnerable targets, increasing safety and security, and improving the quality of life. By studying victims, victimology seeks other types of information that are of great value to law makers and to society. The victim has a strong impact on criminal justice decisions, particularly those of the police and the courts. In the vast majority of cases, it is the victim who decides whether or not to mobilize the criminal justice system by reporting or not reporting the victimization to the authorities. Not only this, but the characteristics, attitudes, and behavior of the victim, and their relationship to the offender do have a significant bearing upon the decision of the police to proceed in a formal or informal way as well as the decision of the prosecutor to lay or not to lay charges. Victim-related factors can have a major impact on the final outcome and on the sanction meted out by the court. Victimology can thus lead to a better understanding of the functioning of the criminal justice system and to improving the decision-making process. A better understanding of the role victims currently play in the criminal justice process is necessary to enhancing victim involvement, and to establishing or improving the modalities of such involvement.

Research in victimology tries to discover why certain individuals or groups of individuals are more frequently victimized than others, why certain targets are repeatedly victimized, and to find sound empirically-based explanations for the differential risks and rates of victimization. By studying victims' characteristics and by analyzing their behavior, victimology attempts to establish whether there exists a certain proneness to criminal victimization, whether there are given predispositions or specific behaviors that enhance the risks and chances of criminal victimization that are responsible for, or conducive to, becoming a victim.

One growing area of interest in victimology is the frequent passage from the state of victim to the state of offender and the interchangeable roles of victim and victimizer. Among the most obvious examples of such a passage are cases of vendetta, vengeance, reprisal, retaliation, getting even, paying back, settling of accounts, self-defense, and so forth. The transformation of the victim into a victimizer has been the subject of many studies, particularly in cases of battered wives who kill their violent husbands, of abusive parents who were themselves abused as children, of rapists and other sexual offenders who had been sexually molested or assaulted during their childhood. The studies suggest that childhood victimization is a precursor to adolescent delinquency and adult offending (Fattah, 1994b). Although the nature of the link between victimization endured in childhood and future delinquency, and the precise mechanisms of the transformation of victim into victimizer have not yet been established, there is mounting empirical evidence suggesting that childhood victims are at a much greater risk of growing up to victimize others (McCord, 1983; Widom, 1990).

Victimology is a very dynamic discipline and recent years have witnessed profound and far-reaching developments. The major ones have been a shift from micro-victimology to macro-victimology, from a victimology of the act to a victimology of action, and the emergence of what may be called "applied victimology" and "clinical victimology." The latter, clinical victimology, is mainly concerned with the diagnosis and treatment of the short- and long-term psychological effects of victimization, particularly the so-called "post traumatic stress disorder" (PTSD) (Lopez and Bornstein, 1995).

The shift from micro-victimology to macro-victimology took place in the 1970s when the pioneering studies of victims of specific crimes (homicide, rape, aggravated assault, robbery, etc.) were overshadowed by large-scale victimization surveys. The surveys' primary objective was to determine the volume and rates of victimization, to identify the victim population, and to establish the sociodemographic characteristics of that population. Although this approach proved to be of great use, yielding massive amounts of data on crime victims, and although several refinements were made and some additional dimensions were introduced in later surveys, it does not seem to have achieved its full potential yet (see entry on victimization).

Another major transformation occurred almost simultaneously to the previous one. Early victimology was mainly theoretical, concerned almost exclusively with causal explanations of crime and the victim's place in those explanations. It focused primarily on characteristics of victims, their relationships and interactions with their victimizers, and the analysis of victim behavior as a situational variable, as a triggering, actualizing, or precipitating factor. Until the 1960s, hardly any concern was expressed for the plight of crime victims and the way they were treated (or mistreated) by the criminal justice system and the global society. In the 1960s, thanks to efforts by a British magistrate, Margery Fry, modest state compensation programs to victims of crime were set up in a few countries such as New Zealand, the U.K., Canada, and the U.S. (Burns, 1980; Miers, 1990). The plight of crime victims started to get serious attention in the 1970s under the impetus of the feminist movement. The movement championed the cause of victims of rape, sexual assault, and domestic violence and succeeded in generating a great deal of empathy and sympathy for a group that, until then, was largely disenfranchised.

In their zeal to defend the victims' cause, to highlight their plight and demand their rights, victims' advocates decided to attack and criticize theoretical victimology and some (Clark and Lewis, 1977) even portrayed it, rather unfairly, as the "art of blaming the victim." Explanatory concepts like "victim precipitation," introduced by Marvin Wolfgang (1958) in his classic study of criminal homicide in Philadelphia, to refer to those homicides in which the victim is a direct, positive precipitator (by having been the first to show and use a deadly weapon or to strike a blow in an altercation) were erroneously interpreted as an attempt to exculpate the offender and to inculpate the victim. A new focus for victimology was taking shape and attracting support: helping and assisting crime victims. A political movement was born, and victimology became increasingly defined and recognized through its applied components. Victimology meetings mirrored this evolution: the transformation of victimology from an academic discipline into a humanistic movement and the shift from scholarly research to political activism. Often, the meetings were turned into platforms for advocacy on behalf of victims.

This political and ideological transformation of victimology was not without serious implications. One was to refocus the notion of criminality on conventional crimes that have a direct, immediate, tangible victim. White-collar crime, corporate actions causing grievous social harm, whether legally defined as crimes or not, were once again relegated to the background. The transformation also had a negative impact on criminal policy. It helped reinforce vengeful and retaliatory responses to crime and provided much needed ammunition to conservative politicians, thus enabling them to implement their punitive agenda (Fattah, 2000).

Be this as it may, the last 20 years have seen the creation and rapid expansion of victims' services in many countries. Victim assistance programs, totally nonexistent a couple of decades ago, have mushroomed all over the globe, from Australia to Europe, from South America to Asia, from the large Islands of Japan to the relatively small Canary Islands.

One of the most important achievements of victim advocates was the formal approval by the General Assembly of the UN on November 11, 1985 of the *UN Declaration of Basic Principles of Justice for Victims of Crime and Abuse of Power*. In adopting it, the General Assembly stated that it was *cognizant that millions of people throughout the world suffer harm as a result of crime and abuse of power and that the rights of these victims have not been adequately recognized.*

Following the adoption of the UN declaration there was a flurry of victim legislation in a number of countries. In almost every American state, legislatures passed various statutes acknowledging basic rights for victims. Among those is the right to be notified about, and to participate in, judicial proceedings; to promptly get back stolen property that was recovered; to be protected from intimidation and harassment; and to receive restitution or compensation (Karmen, 1990).

Similar legislation was passed in Canada, Australia, Britain, and other European countries. In Europe there were other initiatives as well, in particular a convention and two important recommendations by the Council of Europe in 1983, 1985, and 1987 on state compensation, the position of the victim in the criminal justice system, and assistance to victims (Maguire and Shapland, 1997).

At last, crime victims seem to have regained the recognition they deserve. Both theoretical and applied victimology are developing at a very fast pace. The future looks promising and the outlook of the discipline of victimology is very bright.

EZZAT A. FATTAH

## References and Further Reading

Audet, J. and Katz, J.-F., *Précis de Victimologie Générale*, Paris, Dunod, 1999.

Burns, P., *Criminal Injuries Compensation: Social Remedy or Political Palliative for Victims of Crime*, Toronto, Canada, Butterworths, 1980.

Cario, R., *Victimologie, De l'effraction du lien intersubjectif á la restauration sociale*, Paris, L'Harmattan, 2000.

Clark, L. and Lewis, D., *Rape: The Price of Coercive Sexuality*, Toronto, Canada, The Women's Press, 1977.

Cressey, D.R., Research implications of conflicting conceptions of victimology, in Separovic, Z.P., Ed., *Victimology: International Action and Study of Victims*, Zagreb, Croatia, University of Zagreb, pp. 43–54. Reprinted (1992) in Fattah, E.A., Ed., *Towards a Critical Victimology*, London, Macmillan; New York, St. Martin's Press, 1985.

Davis, R.C., Lurigio, A.J. and Skogan, W.J., *Victims of Crime*, 2nd ed. Thousand Oaks, CA, Sage Publications, 1997.

Elias, R., *The Politics of Victimization: Victims, Victimology and Human Rights*, New York, NY, Oxford University Press, 1986.

Fattah, E.A., The use of the victim as an agent of self-legitimization: Toward a dynamic explanation of criminal behavior, *Victimology: An International Journal*, 1(1), 29–53 (1976).

Fattah, E.A., Some theoretical developments in victimology, *Victimology: An International Journal*, 4(2), 198–213 (1978).

Fattah, E.A., Victims and Victimology: The Facts and the Rhetoric. *International Review of Victimology*, 1(1), 43–66 (1989).

Fattah, E.A., *Understanding Criminal Victimization*. Scarborough, Ontario, Canada, Prentice Hall Canada, 1991.

Fattah, E.A., *Towards a Critical Victimology*, London, U.K., Macmillan; New York, NY, St.Martin's Press, 1992.

Fattah, E.A., The United Nations declaration of basic principles of justice for victims of crime and abuse of power: A constructive critique, in Fattah, E.A., Ed., *Towards a Critical Victimology*, London, U.K., Macmillan, 1992.

Fattah, E.A., From crime policy to victim policy—The need for a fundamental policy change, *International Annals of Criminology*, 29(1 and 2), 1993.

Fattah, E.A., *The Interchangeable Roles of Victim and Victimizer*, Helsinki, Finland, The European Institute for Crime Prevention and Control, 1994.

Fattah, E.A., Victimology: Some problematic concepts, unjustified criticism and popular misconceptions, in Kirchoff, G.F., Kosovski, E. and Schneider, H.J., Eds., *International Debates of Victimology*, Mönchengladbach, Germany, WSV Publishing, 1994, pp. 82–103.

Fattah, E.A., *Criminology: Past, Present and Future—A Critical Overview*, Macmillan Press Limited, London; St. Martin's Press, New York, 1997a.

Fattah, E.A., Toward a victim policy aimed at healing not suffering, in Davis, R.C., Lurigio, A.J. and Skogan, W.G., Eds., *Victims of Crime*, 2nd ed., Thousand Oaks, CA, Sage Publications, 1997b, pp. 257–272.

Fattah, E.A., From a handful of dollars to tea and sympathy: The sad history of victim assistance, in Van Dijk, J.J.M., Van Kaam, R.G.H. and Wemmers, J., Eds., *Caring for Crime Victims: Selected Proceedings of the 9th International Symposium on Victimology*, Monsey, NY, Criminal Justice Press, 1999, pp. 187–206.

Fattah, E.A., Victimology: Past, present and future, *Criminologie*, 33(1), 17–46, 2000.

Fattah, E.A. and Peters, T., Eds., *Support for Crime Victims in a Comparative Perspective*, Leuven, Belgium, Leuven University Press, 1998.

Flynn, E.E., Theory development in victimology: An assessment of recent programs and of continuing challenges, in Schneider H.J., Ed., *The Victim in International Perspective*, Berlin, Germany, de Gruyter, 1982, pp. 96–104.

Karmen, A., *Crime Victims, An Introduction to Victimology*, 3rd ed., Belmont, CA, Wadsworth Publishing Co., 1996.

Kennedy, L.W. and Sacco, V.F., *Crime Victims in Context*, Los Angeles, CA, Roxbury Publishing Co., 1998.

Kirchhoff, G.F. and Friday, P.C., Eds., *Victimology at the Transition From the 20th to the 21st Century*, Festschrift for Hans Joachim Schneider, Shaker Verlag in cooperation with

WSVP (World Society of Victimology Publishing), Monchengladbach, Germany, 2000.

Kirchhoff, G.F., Kosovski, E. and Schneider, H.J., Eds., *International Debates of Victimology,* Papers and Essays Given at the VII-th International Symposium on Victimology in Rio de Janeiro 1991, World Society of Victimology Publishing, Monchengladbach, Germany, 1994.

Lopez, G. and Bornstein, S., *Victimologie Clinique,* Paris, Maloine, 1995.

Maguire, M. and Pointing, J., *Victims of Crime—A New Deal?* Milton Keynes, U.K., Open University Press, 1988.

Maguire, M. and Shapland, J., Provisions for victims in an international context, in Davis, R.C., Lurigio, A.J. and Skogan, W.G., Eds., *Victims of Crime,* 2nd ed., London, U.K., Sage Publications, 1997.

McCord, J., A forty year perspective of effects of child abuse and neglect, *Child Abuse and Neglect, 7,* 265–270 (1983).

Mawby, R.I. and Gill, M.L., *Crime Victims: Needs, Services and the Voluntary Sector,* London, U.K., Tavistock, 1987.

McShane, M. and Williams, F.P., III, series Eds., *Criminal Justice: Contemporary Literature in Theory and Practice,* New York, NY and London, U.K., Garland Publishing, Inc. 1997.

Miers, D., *Compensation for Criminal Injuries,* London, Butterworths, 1990.

Neuman, E., El Role de la Victima en Los Delitos Convencionales Y No Convencionales, *Victimologia,* Editorial Universidad, Buenos Aires, Argentina, 1984.

Rock, P., *Helping Crime Victims: The Home Office and the Rise of Victim Support in England and Wales,* Oxford, U.K., Clarendon Press, 1990.

Rock, P., *Victimology,* Dartmouth, MA, Aldershot, 1994.

Schneider, H.J., *Viktimologie: Wissenschaft vom Verbrechensopfer,* J.C.B. Mohr (Paul Siebeck), Tübingen, Germany, 1975.

Shapland, J., et al., *Victims in the Criminal Justice System,* London, Gower, 1985.

Tobolowsky, P.M., *Understanding Victimology,* Selected Readings, Cincinnati, OH, Anderson Publishing Co., 2000.

United Nations, *Declaration of Basic Principles of Justice for Victims of Crime and Abuse of Power,* New York, NY, United Nations, 1985.

Van Dijk, J.J.M., van Kaam, R.G.H. and Wemmers, J., Eds., *Caring for Crime Victims,* Selected Proceedings of the 9th International Symposium on Victimology, Amsterdam, 1997; Monsey, NY, Criminal Justice Press, 1999.

Von Hentig, H., *The Criminal and His Victim,* New Haven, CA, Yale University Press, 1948.

Walklate, S., *Victimology: The Victim and the Criminal Justice Process,* London, Unwin Hyman Ltd., 1989.

Wertham, F., *The Show of Violence,* New York, NY, Doubleday, 1949.

Widom, C.S., *Childhood Victimization: Risk Factors for Delinquency,* in Colten, M.E. and Gore, S., Eds., *Adolescent Stress—Causes and Consequences,* New York, NY, Aldine de Gruyter, 1990.

Wolfgang, M.E., *Patterns in Criminal Homicide,* Philadelphia, PA, University of Pennsylvania Press, 1958.

*See also* **Victimization, Crime: Characteristics of Victims; Victimization, Crime: Theories about Vulnerability**

# Victims' Rights

## Background

Until the 1970s, crime victims were considered the "forgotten persons" of the criminal justice system. Victims had neither services nor rights in the criminal justice process. The justice system did not address the effects of the crime on their lives, nor did it attend to any of their resultant needs, whether financial, psychological, or justice-related concerns. Victims also had no voice in the processing of their offender. In adversarial legal systems like the U.S., England, Canada, or Australia, victims could only make a complaint to officials, who then decided whether to follow through with the crime. The discovery of the victims' plight, and the detailed and disturbing picture of the "secondary victimization" sustained by victims as a result of the system's crime processing, have set the stage for establishing new legislative and programmatic schemes to address victims' needs (Erez, 1989).

In the U.S., the confluence of several developments has led to a long campaign to improve the treatment of crime victims by the criminal justice system. These developments include: the rise of victimology, particularly the interest in victim welfare as the dominant theme in the study of crime victims; the findings of victimization surveys indicating that victims do not report a considerable amount of crime; the increase in "law and order" demands for harsher sentences because of a perceived increase in violent crime; the concurrent move to apply "just deserts" philosophy of punishment, an approach that heavily considers victim harm and offender culpability; and the emergence of several grassroots movements on behalf of various specialized groups of potential and actual victims (Sebba, 1996). Among the groups were women who called attention to the plight of female victims of sexual assault and domestic violence, mothers (of murdered children and mothers against drunk driving), senior citizens, survivors, and children's advocacy groups (Lamborn, 1985; Erez, 1989).

The interest in victims reached its peak in the U.S. with the establishment and report of the President's Task Force on Victims of Crime (1982), which spearheaded numerous recommendations and initiatives for legislative, executive, and other institutional actions on the federal and state levels. In particular, the Task Force report helped to establish the Office for Victims of Crime (OVC). This federally-based initiative is responsible for providing support to state victim assistance programs, developing training programs for criminal justice professionals (judges, prosecutors, and police) to improve their treatment of victims, and establishing additional task forces on specific problems, such as family violence. The President's Task Force on Victims of Crime (1982) also has recommended an amendment to the U.S. Constitution according victims the right to be present and heard at all critical stages of judicial proceedings.

Similar trends have emerged in several European countries, as well as in Australia and Canada. In Europe, the rhetoric of government, criminal justice agents, and voluntary organizations primarily has been focused on improving services for victims rather than bestowing them rights (Maguire and Shapland, 1997). Campaigns on behalf of victims have also emerged on the international level. Following pressures by the World Society of Victimology and the World Federation of Mental Health to address victims' rights and services in official UN statements, the Seventh UN Congress on the Prevention of Crime and the Treatment of the Offender passed in 1985 a Declaration of Basic Principles for Justice for Victims of Crime and Abuse of Power. This declaration, in turn, has further stimulated legislation on behalf of victims on a national level in several countries (Melup, 1991).

## Rights and Services

The reforms and remedies proposed to assist the victims have centered on the coping needs and perceived justice needs of victims. They included providing them with financial assistance, psychological support, and services related to participation in the criminal justice process. The allocation of rights for information access and input into criminal proceedings has also been a significant gain for the victim rights movement. (Erez, 1989). These victim-oriented reforms consisted of transforming and improving traditional criminal justice processes, providing alternatives to existing processes (such as mediation), and designing ameliorative services or procedures to improve the welfare or maintain the dignity of the victims without impinging upon the criminal process (Sebba, 1996).

In terms of the scope of services, the President's Task Force on Victims of Crime (1982) has listed eight basic areas for services that victim-oriented programs should provide. They include crisis intervention, counseling and advocacy, support during criminal investigation, support during prosecution, support after case disposition, crime prevention, public education, and the training of allied professions.

## Services for Victim Coping Needs

Compensation schemes were the first type of aid accorded to victims. Because restitution from offenders was inadequate, the burden of redress was to fall upon the state. Most schemes evolved from a welfare orientation, which developed into a justice approach. Victims were thought to deserve compensation for their victimization, whether they needed the funds or not, because the state had failed to protect them. Compensation was also thought to promote victim involvement in the criminal justice system, propelling victims to report the crime to the police, and in many cases encouraging further cooperation with the prosecution (Young, 1997).

Crisis intervention and other welfare services were the main focus of victim-related reforms. In many countries and most states in the U.S., various victim- or witness-assistance programs were established. Some of their services were directed at witnesses (including victims who are witnesses) and others were designed to solely assist victims *per se*. These services were accorded to victims to prevent hardships consistently documented by studies of victims in the criminal justice process. Among the most prominent of fielded grievances were complaints of delays, insensitive criminal justice practitioners, emotional and financial setbacks as a result of being involved in the criminal justice process, and risk of intimidation by the offender's family. Victim-assistance programs, in an effort to respond to these deficiencies, began furnishing information to victims about case development, offering referrals, emergency aid, psychological counseling, and court advocacy or services related to participation in court hearings. For instance, victims' aid has been directed toward transportation services, childcare during court proceedings, separate space for victims in court, and financial compensation for time spent in appearances before the police and courts. As the victims' rights movement has gained prominence, parallel services have also extended to victims in other criminal justice arenas such as police and judiciary agencies (Erez, 1989).

Although the provision of such services has been highly praised by victim supporters, critics have noted that the criminal justice system's interest in victims was motivated not by humanitarian or social reasons but essentially by the desire to gain the cooperation of victims in their role as witnesses.

## Rights Concerning Perceived Injustice or Input into Proceedings

The most controversial and resisted victim right reform has been provisions to include victim input in criminal justice proceedings. In many countries with adversarial legal systems, victims are afforded the right to submit victim impact statements (VIS). A VIS informs the sentencing judge of any physical, social, or psychological harm, or any loss or damage to property, suffered by the victim as a result of the crime. In some jurisdictions in the U.S., the victim also has a right to a victim statement of opinion (VSO), or input about their perpetrator's proposed sentence. These rights were aimed at reducing victims' frustration and disenchantment with an adversarial legal system in which they had neither status nor voice in the processing of their offenders. Passing legislation that allows a victim's input into proceedings, particularly sentencing outcomes, was expected to reduce victim alienation, increase their satisfaction with justice and sense of fair treatment, and restore their dignity (Erez, 1989; Kelly and Erez, 1997).

Objections to the VIS as inputs into sentencing have centered around three issues. First, it has been argued that these statements potentially undermine adversarial legal system principles and defendants' rights. Second, the VIS may have negative effects on victims and their welfare by creating unrealistic victim expectations about their individual impact on sentence outcome. Third, the VIS may adversely affect criminal justice processes, particularly by increasing sentence harshness, reducing sentence uniformity, and prolonging proceedings or delays for an already overburdened system. VIS reforms have been portrayed as a way to accomplish the goal of harsher punishment and have been criticized for their presumed alliance with conservative demands for "law and order" (Henderson, 1985; Kelly and Erez, 1997).

Studies in various countries have confirmed that, contrary to the fears expressed by opponents of the reform, the VIS has effected positive changes on victims' welfare, criminal justice processes, and court outcomes. Research also demonstrates that the VIS does not increase sentence severity, but rather helps to make the sentence commensurate with the seriousness of the crime. These statements have not led to longer trials, but instead have shortened proceedings by providing judges with ready access to crime impacts in concise summaries. Research has demonstrated that the VIS can simultaneously empower victims and enhance justice processes and outcomes. It can help victims regain a sense of control over their lives, validate the harm they have suffered, and, with appropriate safeguards, increase their satisfaction with justice. Hence, proper use of the VIS in criminal justice proceedings can virtually eliminate the time honored legal tradition of treating victims as invisible, the "forgotten persons" of criminal justice (Erez, 1990; 1999).

## Other Victim-Oriented Reforms

The scope of victim-oriented reforms has expanded in many other areas; traditional criminal processes have been modified and alternatives to existent criminal justice proceedings (such as informal modes of dispute settlement) have been established in different countries with the aim of assisting crime victims. Specialized services have also expanded that assist groups such as children and the elderly, as well as ethnic and minority groups. Statewide hotlines for information and services for victims of various crimes, professional education and training on various topics, and the expansion of program services all suggest a recognition that victim assistance is a significant concern in efforts to combat crime. The most far-reaching victim-oriented reform has been the attempt in the U.S. to pass a victims' rights amendment to the Constitution. Similar legislation is also taking place on the state level concerning a Victims' Bill of Rights.

## Future Trends

Awareness of the importance of victim assistance, and the consequent expansion of victim services and rights, is likely to continue and increase. The globalization of criminal activities, together with diminishing barriers of language, communication, information, technology transfer, economic cooperation, and mobility between countries call for a transnational approach to combating crime (Young, 1997). Attending to the plight of victims is considered an important part of this goal. International forces that transcend national boundaries and justice systems will drive responses to crime that recognize the importance of victims. Increasing victim services and expanding their rights are requisite corollaries to this trend.

EDNA EREZ

### References and Further Reading

Erez, E., The impact of victimology on criminal justice policy, *Criminal Justice Policy Review,* 3(3), 236–256 (1989).

Erez, E., Victim participation in sentencing: And the debate goes on, *International Review of Victimology,* 3, 17–32 (1994).

Erez, E., Who's afraid of the big bad victim? Victim impact statements as victim empowerment and enhancement of justice, *Criminal Law Review,* July, 545–556 (1999).

Henderson, L.N., The wrongs of victims' rights, *Stanford Law Review*, 37, 937–1021 (1985).

Kelly, D.P. and Erez, E., Victim participation in the criminal justice system, in Davis, R.C., Lurigio, A.J. and Skogan, W., Eds., *Victims of Crime,* Thousand Oaks, CA, Sage, 1997, pp. 231–244.

Maguire, M. and Shapland J., Provision for victims in an international context, in Davis, R.C., Lurigio, A.J. and Skogan, W., Eds., *Victims of Crime,* Thousand Oaks, CA, Sage, 1997, pp. 211–228.

Melup, I., UN: Victims of crime—Report of the secretary general, *International Review of Victimology*, 2(1), 29–59 (1991).

President's Task Force on Victims of Crime, *Final Report,* U.S. Government Printing Office, Washington, DC, 1982.

Sebba, L., *Third Parties: Victims and the Criminal Justice System,* Columbus, OH, Ohio State University Press, 1992.

Young, M., Victim rights and services, in Davis, R.C., Lurigio, A.J. and Skogan, W., Eds., *Victims of Crime*, Thousand Oaks, CA, Sage, 1997, pp. 194–210.

*See also* **Punishment Justifications; Victim Compensation Programs; Victimization, Crime: Financial Loss and Personal Suffering**

# Vigilante Violence

## What Is Vigilante Violence?

Vigilante violence is something like pornography—it is hard to define, but we tend to know it when we see it. As a result of this lack of definitional precision, the research literature on vigilante violence tends to be rather underdeveloped. Unlike with other forms of crime and deviance, the prevalence and incidence of vigilante violence have rarely been measured in a reliable or systematic way. Moreover, the failure to tackle this conceptual issue has meant that folk understandings (often based on controversial notions of "mob psychology" or mass hysteria) tend to hold sway in the popular discussion of vigilantism.

Some academic observers simply define vigilante violence as some form of "taking the law into one's own hands" (Little and Sheffield, 1983). Others define vigilante violence as "establishment violence," meaning that the action concerns the defense of established or mainstream values (Rosenbaum and Sederberg, 1976). Contrarily, some argue vigilante violence should be understood as protecting a progressive social order (Culberson, 1990). Neapolitan (1987) describes vigilante violence as "increased use of violence by potential crime victims and more involvement by citizens in patrolling their neighborhoods" (p. 123).

Johnston (1996) offers what is perhaps the most comprehensive definition, which includes the identification of six essential elements that define behavior as vigilantism, planning and premeditation; private citizens acting voluntarily; acting autonomously (in this sense it is a social movement); acting with force or with just the threat of force; acting to defend some set of established norms; and doing all of this by assuring security through the act.

Others have further suggested that vigilante violence is best conceived of as an umbrella term describing a range of behaviors and have began to develop typologies of vigilante activities. Sederberg (1978), for instance, identifies four different types of vigilantism: spontaneous, organized, formal spontaneous, and formal organized. Brown (1975), on the other hand, suggests that there are really just two, basic types of vigilantism: so-called "classic vigilantism" that seeks to informally control crime through the persecution of suspected offenders; and "neo-vigilantism" that seeks to informally control social life. An example of the "classic vigilantism" might be Bernard Goetz, the so-called "Subway Vigilante," who shot and wounded four teenagers who had demanded he give them $5. An example of "neo-vigilantism" might include activities of groups like the Ku Klux Klan that are aimed at intimidating members of various social groups into leaving a neighborhood or area.

## How and Why Does Vigilantism Occur?

Historically, outbursts of vigilante violence have typically been common in areas that could be characterized as relatively "lawless." For instance, so-called "boomtowns" on the American frontier that attracted large numbers of residents because of some valuable natural resource were often the sights of vigilante attacks. The combination of relative lawlessness (these towns lacked formalized systems of security or protection) and the availability of valued resources is believed to have made these areas ideal for the emergence of vigilante violence (Brown, 1975).

Yet, how can one explain acts of vigilante violence in the developed, modern world? Research suggests that areas that are experienced by residents as being on the "margins" of society might be more vulnerable to the occurrence of vigilante violence. For instance, communities plagued by high rates of victimization or low-level street disorder as well as a relative absence of police control (or perceived hostility from the police) are believed to be at higher risk for participation in vigilante violence (Shotland and Goodstein, 1984; Girling, Loader et al., 1998).

Some research suggests that the process of "responsibilization" whereby social control functions are shifted from the state to citizens and communities (evidenced in such things as community policing and neighborhood watch groups) has also contributed to the appearance of recent acts of vigilante violence (Evans, 2003). The idea is that as democracies decentralize and expect a more active role of citizens in policing themselves, gaps in security open, leaving citizens uncertain as to who is really in authority. It has been suggested that this shift has produced a backlash of increased authoritarianism and demands for the harsh treatment of law-breakers (Voruz, 2003).

These sorts of questions are relatively new in social science research. Yet, the theoretical foundations for the study of vigilante violence are central to sociology and social psychology. For instance, the work of Durkheim (1933), Mead (1918), and Freud (2002) is directly related to the question of vigilantism and should serve as the groundwork of any empirical literature in this field.

ANNA KING AND SHADD MARUNA

## Bibliography

Brown, R.M. (1975). *Strain of Violence: American Studies of Violence and Vigilantism*. New York, NY, Oxford University Press.

Durkheim, E. (1933). *The Division of Labour in Society*. NY.

Evans, J. (2003). Vigilance and vigilantes: Thinking psychoanalytically about anti-paedophile action. *Theoretical Criminology* 7(2): 163–189.

Freud, S. (2002). *Civilisation and Its Discontents*. Hammondsworth, Penguin.

Girling, E., Loader, I. et al. (1998). A telling tale: A case of vigilantism and its aftermath in an English town. *British Journal of Sociology* 49(3): 474–490.

Johnston, L. (1996). What is vigilantism? *British Journal of Criminology* 36(2): 220–236.

Little, C.B. and Sheffield, C. (1983). Frontiers and criminal justice: English private prosecution societies and American vigilantism in the 18th and 19th centuries. *American Sociological Review* 48: 796–808.

Mead, G.H. T. P. O. P. J., *American Journal of Sociology,* 23: 577–602. (1918). The psychology of punitive justice. *American Journal of Sociology* 23: 577–602.

Neapolitan, J. (1987). Vigilante behavior and attribution bias. *Criminal Justice and Behavior* 14(2): 123–137.

Rosenbaum, J.H. and Sederberg, P.D., Eds. (1976). *Vigilante Politics*. Philadelphia, PA, University Of Penn Press.

Sederberg, P.C. (1978). The phenomenology of vigilantism in contemporary America: An interpretation. *Terrorism* 1(3, 4): 287–305.

Shotland, R.L. and Goodstein, L.I. (1984). The role of bystanders in crime control. *Journal of Social Issues* 40(1): 9–26.

Voruz, V. (2003). Recent perspectives on penal punitiveness, Ch 6. *Critical Explorations in Crime, Law and Society* 216–249.

*See also* **Durkheim, Emile**

# Violence *See* **Aggression and Criminal Behavior**

# Vollmer, August, and O. W. Wilson

Often cited as the Father of American Policing, August Vollmer was one of the most innovated, farsighted, and influential American police chiefs of the 20th century. In 1905, when Vollmer was elected Berkeley, California's town marshal, the police agency consisted of only three officers and was not operating full time. By the time Vollmer retired as chief of police in 1932, Berkeley was the policing model for which other cities strived. Until his death in 1955, Vollmer would gain a national reputation as a police administrator, educator, author, reformer, innovator, and criminologist.

Vollmer was born in New Orleans to immigrant parents, but moved with his family to the San Francisco Bay Area when he was 12 years old. Lacking an advanced formal education, Vollmer joined the army and was decorated for his heroism during the Spanish American War. Returning home to Berkeley, Vollmer was encouraged to run for the office of town marshal, which he won in 1905. Three years later the town charter was changed and Vollmer became chief of police.

Vollmer is known for such innovations as the early use of bicycle patrol units that evolved into motorized patrol units. Vollmer also applied new technologies to improve communications between the patrol officers in the field and police headquarters. After experiments with call-boxes and call-lights at intersections, to signal officers from police head quarters, Vollmer eventually installed a delicate crystal two-way radio in one of Berkeley's Model-T police cars. This became the first radio-patrol car.

Vollmer, who respected and was comfortable with academics, adopted scientific knowledge and criminological theories into criminal investigations. His innovative creed was that Berkeley Police should use every modern scientific method known, thus keeping his police officers one step ahead of the criminals, not one step behind. This eventually led to the creation of Berkeley's crime laboratory, which at the time, was the only one in the country that had a full-time forensic scientist in charge. Within Berkeley's crime laboratory, many important innovations and developments were made, including the development of the Keeler Polygraph along with classification systems for both fingerprints and handwriting. Though not as large as other crime laboratories, Berkeley's would remain as one of the most respected in the country.

Vollmer saw the freedom that criminals had to move from one city to the next as a major issue facing law enforcement. Thus, he modified the Atcherly criminal classification system into a detailed modus operandi (MO) file system that he urged other police agencies to adopt. This enabled police departments to share information about similar patterns in the ways that criminals committed their affairs. Still stressing the need to share information among departments, Vollmer proposed a national fingerprint system that the FBI eventually created.

It is within the area of police professionalism that Vollmer made his greatest mark. Using his own word, Vollmer was very "fussy" about hiring his police officers. With Vollmer's admiration for higher education and the location of the University of California within his city, he began a campaign to recruit "college cops" into his police force.

Certainly the most famous and successful of the "college cops" was Orlando Winfield (O.W.) Wilson. Wilson's policing career spanned 46 years, beginning as a Berkeley patrol officer in 1921 and retiring as Superintendent of the Chicago Police Department in

1967. Wilson became chief of police in Wichita, Kansas in March 1928 and over the next 11 years he would revolutionize the American police force as only his mentor, August Vollmer, had done previously.

Wilson introduced one-officer patrol cars as well as modernized police record and report keeping. Under Wilson, the Wichita Police Department developed a code of ethics (the "Square Deal Code") in 1928 that was eventually drafted into the "Law Enforcement Code of Ethics" by the International Association of Chiefs of Police (IACP) in 1957.

Vollmer's commitment to higher education within law enforcement would also be carried forward by Wilson when he returned to Berkeley in 1947 to become dean of the new School of Criminology in 1950. It was here that Wilson wrote what was considered at the time the pivotal works on police administration, management, discipline, patrol allotment, preventative patrol, and police records.

Vollmer's vision of police professionalism extended beyond promoting college education for his police officers. In 1908, Vollmer introduced one of his boldest innovations, the police academy. Although called at the time "police school," Vollmer promoted and implemented the idea that police officers needed training before beginning work on the streets. His police school not only included practical subjects such as police methods and procedures, criminal law, first aid, and fingerprinting, but theoretical ones, including criminology, psychiatry, and anthropology. Vollmer eventually became convinced that the most important area that a police officer needed to train was that of human behavior. Vollmer's ideas on police education would soon find their way into the university setting. In 1931, the University of California recognized Vollmer as its first Professor of Police Administration. Later, he helped San Jose State College design the first law enforcement or criminal justice program in the country.

Vollmer also maintained a national reputation as an organizational reformer. During his career, many city governments hired him as an advisor to professionalize their police agencies. In 1919, Vollmer presented his paper, "The Policeman as a Social Worker," where he stressed crime prevention and corporation between the police and other social service agencies. Despite this radical and professionally unpopular idea, Vollmer was elected President of The International Association of Chief of Police in 1921.

Perhaps nowhere did Vollmer state his ideas, professionalism, and ethics better than in the 1931 publications of the *U.S. National Commission on Law Observance and Enforcement*, or what is commonly known as the Wickersham Commission. Vollmer chaired the two volumes that examined law enforcement in the U.S. In Volume 11, *Report on Lawlessness in Law Enforcement*, Vollmer and his staff took the courageous step of not only publicly acknowledging the use of "third degree" interrogation tactics by the police, but then vigorously condemned the practice as well. In Volume 14, *Report on Police*, Vollmer focused on police training and hiring, condemning the corrupting influence that politics had on law enforcement.

Vollmer stayed active in law enforcement after his retirement. Both in teaching and writing Vollmer continued to stress higher levels of training and education, increased communication between agencies, and the separation of the police from political interference. As a measure of Vollmer's importance to law enforcement nationwide, during the 1940s there were 25 police chiefs in the U.S. who had served at one time or another under him. In 1955, almost blind and dying, Vollmer lethally shot himself, although his legacy to American law enforcement still survives.

KENNETH L. MULLEN

## Biography [August Vollmer]

Born in New Orleans, Louisiana, 1876. Town Marshal, Berkeley, California, 1905–1909; Chief of Police, Berkeley, California, 1909–1932; Interim Chief of Police, Los Angeles, California, 1923. Professor of Police Administration, University of Chicago, 1929; Professor of Police Administration, University of California, Berkeley, 1931–1937; President of California Association of Chiefs of Police, 1908; President of International Association of Chiefs of Police, 1921; Committee member, National Commission on Law Observance and Enforcement, 1929–1931. Died in Berkeley, California, 1955.

## Selected Works (August Vollmer)

The school for police as planned at Berkeley, coauthored by Schneider, A., *Journal of Criminal Law and Criminology* VII (1917).
Revision of the Atcherly modus operandi system, *Journal of Criminal Law and Criminology* X (1919).
The prevention and detection of crime as viewed by a police officer, *Annals* CXXV (1926).
The scientific policeman, *American Journal Of Police Science* I (1930).
Police progress in the past twenty-five years, *Journal of Criminal Law and Criminology* XXIV (1933).
*Crime and the State Police*, 1935, coauthored by Parker, A.E.
*The Police and Modern Society*. 1936.
*Crime, crooks, and Cops*, 1937, coauthored by Parker, A.E.
*The Criminal*, 1949.
Report No. 11: Report on lawlessness in law enforcement, *U.S. National Commission on Law Observance and Enforcement* (1931).
Report No. 14: Report on police, *U.S. National Commission on Law Observance and Enforcement* (1931).

## References and Further Reading (August Vollmer)

Carte, G.E., August Vollmer and the origins of police professionalism, *Journal of Police Science and Administration* I (1973).
Douthit, N., August Vollmer, in *Thinking about Police*, Klockars, C.B., and Mastrofski, S.D., Eds., New York, NY: McGraw-Hill, Inc, 1991.
MacNamara, D.E.J., August Vollmer: The vision of police professionalism. In *Pioneers in Policing*, Stead, P.J., Ed., Montclair, NJ: Patterson Smith, 1977.
Parker, A.E., *The Berkeley Police Story*. Springfield, IL.: Charles C. Thomas, 1972.
Roberg, R., Crank, J. and Kuykendall, J., *Police and Society*, 2nd ed., Roxbury, MA: Publishing Company, 1999.
Walker, S. *A Critical History of Police Reform*. Lexington, MA: D.C. Heath, 1977.

## Biography (O. W. Wilson)

Born in Veblen, South Dakota, 1900. Educated at the University of California at Berkeley, B.A. in Economics 1925. Police Patrolman, Berkeley, California, 1921–1925; Chief of Police Fullerton, California, 1925; Chief of Police, Wichita, Kansas, 1928–1939. Consultant, Public Administration Service, 1939; Professor of Police Administration, University of California at Berkeley, 1939–1943; Lt. Colonel, U.S. Army, 1943–1947; Professor of Police Administration, University of California at Berkeley, 1947–1950; Dean, School of Criminology, University of California at Berkeley, 1950–1960; Superintendent, Chicago Police Department, 1960–1967. President, American Society of Criminology, 1942–1949. Died in Poway, California, 18 Oct 1972.

## Principal Writings (O. W. Wilson)

Picking and training police and traffic officers, *American City* 18 (1930).
What can be done about crime, *Journal of the Kansas Bar Association* 213 (1934).
*Police Records: Their Installation and Use*, 1942.
*Police Planning*, 2nd ed., 1958.
*Police Administration*, 5th ed., with Roy McLaren, updated and expanded by James, J.F., Green, J.R. and Walsh, W.F., 1996.

## References and Further Reading (O. W. Wilson)

Bopp, W.J., *O.W.: O.W. Wilson and the Search for a Police Profession*, Port Washington, NY: Kennikat Press, 1977.
Douthit, N., August Vollmer, in *Thinking about Police*, Klockars, C.B. and Mastrofski, S.D., Eds., New York, NY: McGraw-Hill, Inc, 1991.
More, H.W. *Effective Police Administration: A Behavioral Approach*, 2nd ed., St. Paul, MN: West Publishing Co., 1979.
Roberg, R., Crank, J. and Kuykendall, J. *Police and Society*, 2nd ed., Roxbury, MA: Publishing Company, 1999.
Walker, S., *A Critical History of Police Reform*. Lexington, MA: D.C. Heath, 1977.
Walker, S., *Popular Justice: A History of American Criminal Justice*, 2nd ed., New York, NY: Oxford University Press, 1998.

*See also* **Police: History in the U.S.**

# War Crimes

If criminologists ever needed evidence that violence is a relative concept, the existence of war crimes provides it. Even amidst the horrors of war, distinctions are made between violence that is normal and that which is pathological. Whereas most who are not pacifists will at least grudgingly accept the slaughter of armies in battle, and even express admiration for those skilled enough to kill with great efficiency, most consciences are also offended by acts such as the killing of wounded, the mistreatment of prisoners of war, the killing of civilians, rape, and excessive torture.

Understanding war crimes begins with an understanding of the legal underpinnings of the concept. Starting with the principle of legality, that there is no crime without law, this essay explores how international law defines war crimes and related atrocities. Continuing with the principle that there is no crime without punishment, the essay turns to how international law is enforced, with particular attention paid to the newly established International Criminal Court (ICC).

## War Crimes and the Law

The idea that there is both proper and improper conduct during war has ancient roots. Sun Tzu specified behavioral limits in his classic text *The Art of War*. The ancient Greeks viewed some wartime acts as legally prohibited and war crimes are also defined in the Hindu Code of Manu. The modern understanding of war crimes, however, has its origins in 19th century conflicts. In the midst of the brutal U.S. Civil War, President Lincoln instructed military and international law expert Francis Lieber to develop a code of conduct for Union soldiers. Known informally as the Lieber Code, this document was noteworthy, among other things, for the distinctions it made between combatants and noncombatants and its rules for the treatment of prisoners. In the same year, a witness to the Battle of Solferino in the Franco-Austrian War, Swiss businessman Henry Dunant, was appalled by the neglect of the wounded on the battlefield and began a public campaign to lobby governments to provide humanitarian aid to war victims. His efforts led, in 1864, to the first Geneva Convention, which included among its provisions that medical relief workers could treat wounded and sick on the battlefield, protected by the symbol of a red cross on a white background. In the decades between the first Geneva Convention and the outbreak of World War II, several conventions and peace conferences, most notably in Geneva and The Hague, expanded and evolved the principles articulated in these documents, building the framework for International Humanitarian Law. The four Geneva Conventions enacted after World War II, as well as their additional protocols, enacted in 1977, are currently the principal sources of International Humanitarian Law.

International Humanitarian Law is the branch of public international law that defines proper conduct in international armed conflicts. It is often contrasted with International Human Rights Law, which protects people from predations of their own governments. The former is commonly described as the law of warfare whereas the latter is portrayed as applicable in times of international peace. Although the acts the two branches of law prohibit overlap, the proper application of either branch is often problematic. How, for example, should one define the conflicts that emerged in the early 1990s in former Yugoslavia? Are they international or internal wars? Such debates can be submitted, as they were in this case, to a body such as the International Court of Justice, which arbitrates disputes between nations, but there is no decisive answer to the questions.

As in all legal systems, not everything that is illegal is criminal. Most of the prohibitions defined in International Humanitarian and Human Rights Law apply to governments. For an act to be criminal, it must be possible to apply punishment to a responsible individual. International Criminal Law is the branch of public international law that allows for punishment. Overlapping the other two branches, International Criminal Law became crystallized in the aftermath of World War II. In order to provide symbolic justice by placing the Axis leaders on trial, Allied powers needed to articulate humanitarian law principles in terms of criminal law. This was done in the London Agreement, and was partially derived on common law reasoning that the atrocities committed by the accused were violations of the usual and customary laws of warfare and, therefore, subject to criminal prosecution. Individuals could now be punished for actions taken in the name of their nation.

## A Court for War Crimes and Related Atrocities

The first recorded war crimes trial in Western culture appears to be that of Peter van Hagenbach. In 1474, van Hagenbach was tried and sentenced to death by an ad hoc panel of judges from the Holy Roman Empire on principles derived from natural law for allowing his troops to rape and murder civilians and pillage towns.

There appears to be a gap of several centuries before the exercise was repeated, but the temporary and unspecialized structure of the judicial panel became the precedent. The codification of laws that began in the 19th century never included a provision for a permanent tribunal, relying instead, when ad hoc tribunals were not present, on the courts of individual nations to act based on the principle of universal jurisdiction, the right of a nation to try noncitizens for certain crimes even if they occur beyond their national borders. The practical result of this idealistic principle was that instead of all nations vigorously pursuing violators of international law, almost none did. There have been notable exceptions in recent times. Spain's efforts in

the late 1990s to extradite former Chilean dictator Auguste Pinochet from England in order to place him on trial for criminal violations of International Human Rights Law stands out as a fascinating, if ultimately unsuccessful, attempt to exercise such jurisdiction. Several Iraqi citizens have filed war crimes charges against U.S. General Franks in a court in Brussels, citing, among other things, the targeting of civilian areas with cluster bombs in the most recent war in Iraq. And there may be some evidence of a deterrent effect related to universal jurisdiction if one believes reports that Henry Kissinger forgoes foreign travel because of the possibility of facing war crimes trials for his involvement in planning U.S. actions in Laos and Cambodia during the Viet Nam War. The enforcement of International Humanitarian and Human Rights Law, however, has always been better characterized as spotty rather than universal. A legal system without a judicial system is an unbalanced entity, difficult to support.

Terrorism, rather than war crimes, prompted the first real efforts to create an ICC. Internal violence during the economic disruptions of the 1930s led to the League of Nations adopting a proposal for the court in 1937. The treaty, however, failed to achieve the required number of ratifications prior to the outbreak of World War II. When that conflict ended, the lack of an appropriate venue to try Axis officials required the victors to create ad hoc courts in addition to articulating how the customary laws of warfare can be applied as criminal law in order to conduct the war crimes trials in Nuremberg and Tokyo. The difficulties with this procedure prompted the UN to create an International Law Commission (ILC) in 1947 to begin codifying international law and to define appropriate venues for its application. The ILC completed a draft statute for the ICC in 1951, but Cold War tensions made the project untenable.

Its revival was spurred by two trends. First, in the late 1980s, Caribbean and Latin American nations that faced high levels of drug crime and domestic terrorism urged the UN to establish an international court to which they could refer accused criminals who were too powerful to be handled by national justice systems. As the diplomatic work proceeded, the international community found itself faced with the wars in the disintegrating republic of Yugoslavia, with their attendant ethnic cleansings, and the genocide in Rwanda, both events leading to very public outcries for justice.

The world was no more ready to dispense justice in the early 1990s than it was in the late 1940s. Again, ad hoc tribunals needed to be created, one at The Hague to deal with crimes committed in the former Yugoslavia, and another in Arusha, United Republic of Tanzania, to address violations of humanitarian law committed in Rwanda. These tribunals both helped strengthen arguments for a permanent court and provided models for the ICC.

The UN formally asked the ILC to draft a new statute for an ICC in 1993 and the completed draft was presented in 1994. After several more years of diplomatic wrangling, the treaty was officially considered at a conference with the unwieldy title of the UN Diplomatic Conference of Plenipotentiaries on the Establishment of an International Criminal Court, held in Rome from 15 June to 17 July 1998. The final treaty, known popularly as the Rome Statute, was adopted by a vote of 120 for the statute and 7 against, with 21 nations abstaining. Those who voted in opposition to the treaty were the U.S., China, Iraq, Israel, Libya, Qatar, and Yemen. The principal points of the U.S. opposition are discussed below.

The ICC came into legal existence as a functioning body on July 1, 2002, three months after receiving the minimum number of required ratifications by national governments. Although created by the UN, it is constituted as a separate body that is not under UN jurisdiction. Its formal relationship to the UN remains to be established at a later conference of nations, which are parties to the treaty.

Located at The Hague, the court is composed of 18 judges elected by the Assembly of States Parties, a separate organization representing nations who have ratified the treaty. The judicial arm of the court, known as The Chambers, is divided into the appeals, trial, and pretrial divisions. Defendants are granted legal rights common in Western legal systems. There is, for example, a presumption of innocence until proven guilty, the right to legal counsel and provisions for the appointment of counsel if the accused cannot afford his or her own, the right to examine witnesses, the right to discovery of the prosecution's evidence, the right to not be compelled to testify against oneself, and protection from double jeopardy. Because of the international nature of the court, there is also the right to be informed of charges in one's own language, and the right to an interpreter and provisions to appoint interpreters at the court's expense if defendants cannot afford their own. The court may sentence offenders to incarceration for terms of up to 30 years or, in cases of extreme gravity and where warranted by the circumstances of the offender, life imprisonment. Consistent with the practice of Western legal systems except that of the U.S., there is no death penalty. The court may also apply fines and may order the forfeiture of proceeds, property and assets derived from the crime. Although it is not required, forfeited property may be placed in a trust fund earmarked for victim compensation.

The crimes codified as being under the jurisdiction of the court involve only the most serious offenses addressed in customary International Humanitarian and Human Rights Law: genocide, crimes against humanity, and war crimes. Specific definitions of acts included under these crimes are found in Articles 6, 7, and 8, respectively, of the Rome Statute. The treaty also specifies that the crime of aggression will fall under the court's jurisdiction, but at a later time. Participants in the Rome conference could not agree on a definition of aggression, and the compromise was to include the crime in the treaty but exclude it from the court's jurisdiction until a definition had been agreed to at a later review conference of states' parties. The treaty's definitions for war crimes are interesting to scholars of comparative legal systems because of they way they combine common and civil law traditions. For example, besides specifically mentioning "[g]rave breaches of the Geneva Conventions...," Article 8 also includes "[o]ther violations of the laws and customs applicable in international armed conflict, within the established framework of international law..."

It is a bit ironic given current world concerns regarding terrorism and the role that fear of terrorism played in motivating both the League of Nations and UN efforts to create an ICC that terrorism is not, in fact, one of the crimes to which the court is granted explicit jurisdiction. The argument against including terrorism, pressed by the U.S. and members of the League of Arab Nations, was that it would be impossible to reach consensus on a definition, opening the door to politicization of ICC. The compromise reached on terrorism left it in a more tenuous position than the crime of aggression. It was omitted from the treaty, though a consensus resolution was passed that it be considered for inclusion at a future review conference. Even with its omission, it can be argued that sustained campaigns of terrorism could be prosecuted under the definitions given for crimes against humanity.

U.S. opposition to the ICC has placed it at odds with its allies and dismayed many conference participants especially in light of the strong role the U.S. had previously played in the development of International Humanitarian and Human Rights Law. Though the U.S. argued against the inclusion of aggression and terrorism, its main points of disagreement focus on the court's territorial jurisdiction and the possibility that it may interfere with national sovereignty. Most conference participants aligned with the argument pressed strongly by Germany, that the Rome statute should incorporate the customary principle of universal jurisdiction. The U.S. argued for a highly restricted jurisdiction that would require the consent of the nation of the accused, the consent of the nation where the crime occurred, and the consent of the UN Security Council. Under this proposal, any nation committing war crimes would have been able to provide blanket protection for perpetrators from the court, and despite examples such as the Libyan surrender of those who planned the Pan Am bombing over Lockerbie, could reasonably be expected to do so unless the government fell or was overthrown. It would have, in effect, institutionalized the idea of "victor's justice." Also under this proposal, permanent members of the UN Security Council would have been able to exercise their veto to thwart prosecutions.

The compromise enacted in the Rome statute grants the court jurisdiction if either the nation of the accused or the nation in which the crime occurred is a state party to the treaty, or if either of those nations petitions the court for jurisdiction. The UN Security Council does not have the power to refer cases to the court, but it can pass resolutions deferring prosecutions for one year. These deferrals are renewable. The deferral power granted to the UN Security Council eliminates the ability of permanent members to use their veto to halt prosecutions, but it does allow them to veto deferrals. The treaty also forbids the ICC from initiating investigations into cases that are under the jurisdiction, and can be legitimately tried in, national courts.

Not mollified by the compromise, the U.S. continues to oppose the ICC on the grounds that jurisdiction granted in the treaty threatens U.S. national sovereignty. In addition, the U.S. argues that its extensive military involvements expose its citizens to a higher risk of politicized prosecutions. There is obvious truth to the claim that its military activities may result in legal action. The case against General Franks, noted above, is one example. Also, the International Criminal Tribunal for the former Yugoslavia has initiated investigations into the activities of U.S. and other NATO officials with regard to the bombing of civilians in Kosovo. Whether such cases would result in kangaroo court convictions that are miscarriages of justice is an unanswered question.

U.S. opposition to the Rome Statute has involved both international pressure and domestic legislation. The U.S. threatened to withdraw from all UN peacekeeping missions in nations that are party to the treaty unless all UN forces were granted permanent immunity from ICC prosecution. In a compromise, UN forces have been granted immunity for a renewable one-year term. The U.S. Congress has passed legislation that cuts off military aid to any treaty nation, which has not negotiated a separate bilateral treaty with the U.S. forbidding the transfer of U.S. citizens to the court, and which includes an ominous authorization to use "all means necessary and appropriate" to free any U.S. or allied service member taken into the court's custody.

Although the U.S. has been the Rome Statute's most vocal opponent, it is but one of three permanent members of the UN Security Council who are not states parties. China never signed the treaty. The Russian Federation signed, but has not ratified it. It is questionable whether the ICC will ever become an effective judicial body without the support of these powerful nations. With the ICC having yet to try a case, the enforcement of International Criminal Law will probably follow the precedents set in the aftermath of World War II: the creation of ad hoc tribunals by the victors. The trial of Saddam Hussein for crimes against humanity, for example, appears as if it will take this course.

With its primary focus on the legal status of war crimes, little has been said in this essay about the distinct contributions criminologists have made to our understanding of war crimes. This is because criminologists have contributed little. The field of criminology has largely ignored war crimes and other violations of International Criminal Law, abandoning it to legal studies and other branches of the social sciences. A collection of all papers on genocide, for example, published in major criminological journals would make a shockingly slim volume despite the horrific nature of the crime.

At the micro-level, most attempts to apply criminological theory have focused on control theories (e.g., Brannigan and Hardwick, 2003) and their cousins, such as the techniques of neutralization (e.g., Alvarez, 2001), to explain how ordinary people can suspend moral prescriptions and commit extraordinary violence. More has been attempted at the macro-level, where critical theorists, considering state crime in general, have interpreted state sponsored mass killings as one of the tools a ruling elite may use to secure its hegemony (see various essays collected in Friedrichs, 1998). The relative paucity of criminological literature on war crimes makes it an area ripe with possibilities for theoretical development and empirical investigation.

L. EDWARD DAY

## References and Further Reading

Alvarez, A., *Governments, Citizens, and Genocide,* Bloomington, IN, Indiana University Press, 2001.

Bassiouni, M.C., *Introduction to International Criminal Law,* Ardsley, NY, Transnational Publishers, 2003.

Brannigan, A. and Hardwick, K.H., Genocide and general theory, in *Control Theories of Crime and Delinquency,* Vol. 12 in Britt, C.L. and Gottfredson, M., Eds., *Advances in Criminological Theory,* Piscataway, NJ, Transaction Books, 2003.

Friedrichs, D.O., Ed., *State Crime,* Aldershot, U.K. and Brookfield, VT, Ashgate, 1998.

Gutman, R. and Rieff, D., Ed., *Crimes of War: What the Public Should Know,* New York and London, W. W. Norton & Co., 1999.

Kittichaisaree, K., *International Criminal Law,* Oxford and New York, Oxford University Press, 2001.

Markusen, E. and Kopf, D., *The Holocaust and Strategic Bombing: Genocide and Total War in the 20th Century,* Boulder, CO, and Oxford, Westview Press, 1995.

Neier, A., *War Crimes: Brutality, Genocide, Terror, and the Struggle for Justice,* New York, Times Books, 1998.

Schabas, W.A., *Genocide in International Law,* Cambridge and New York, Cambridge University Press, 2000.

*See also* **Political Crimes by the State; Warfare and Criminal Behavior**

# Warfare and Criminal Behavior

## Introduction

The concept of a "war crime" usually conjures up horrific images of genocide, ethnic cleansing, rape and bombardment of cities. These images do indeed fit the legal definitions of war crimes, however, a great deal of other misconduct also evokes international legal prohibition. Simply put, war crimes are those violations of the law of war that incur criminal responsibility. Limitations by nations on conduct during war date back as early as Sun Tzu during the 6th century BCE. The theory of war crimes as defined by law can also be seen in the Hindu codes of around 200 BCE. These notions were to eventually seep into European law.

Before the time of World War I, the law of war as currently known, was codified in the Hague Conventions of 1899 and 1907. Later, the four Geneva Conventions were drafted after the horrors of World War II became evident. Each of the Geneva Conventions contains their own list of "grave breaches." Those definitions were expanded in 1977 by Protocol I. The grave breaches provisions technically apply only during international armed conflicts for acts against protected persons or during battlefield activities. Though perhaps a transparent point, the laws of war only apply during armed conflict. What constitutes armed conflict is much in dispute and some of the century's worst criminal acts are not accounted for in the specific definitions of "war crimes."

## Purpose

The conduct of armed hostilities on land or air is regulated by the law of land or air warfare which is both written and unwritten. It is inspired by the desire to diminish the evils of war by:

> Protecting both combatants and noncombatants from unnecessary suffering:
>
> Safeguarding certain fundamental human rights of persons who fall into the hands of the enemy, particularly prisoners of war, the wounded and sick, and civilians; and
>
> Facilitating the restoration of peace.

## Basic Principals

The law of war places limits on the exercise of a belligerent's power in the interests mentioned above. It requires that belligerents refrain from employing any kind or degree of violence, which is not actually necessary for military purposes, and that they conduct hostilities with regard for the principles of humanity and chivalry. The prohibitory effect of the law of war is not minimized by "military necessity," which has been defined as that principle which justifies those measures not forbidden by international law, which are indispensable for securing the complete submission of the enemy as soon as possible. Military necessity has been generally rejected as a defense for acts forbidden by the customary and conventional laws of war inasmuch as the latter have been developed and framed with consideration for the concept of military necessity.

The law of war is binding not only upon states as such but also upon individuals and, in particular, the members of their armed forces.

## Sources

The law of war is derived from two principal sources. The first source consists of lawmaking treaties like The Hague and Geneva Conventions and the second part is made up of custom. Although some of the law of war has not been incorporated in any treaty or convention to which any nation is a party, this body of unwritten or customary law is firmly established by the custom of nations and well defined by recognized authorities on international law. Lawmaking treaties may be compared with legislative enactments in the national law of any nation and the customary law of war with the unwritten Anglo–American law. The U.S.

is a signatory party to 12 treaties pertaining to the crime and war.

> Hague Convention No. III, 18 October 1907, Relative to the Opening of Hostilities.
>
> Hague Convention No. IV, 18 October 1907, Respecting the Laws and Customs of War on Land.
>
> Hague Convention No. V, 18 October 1907, Respecting the Rights and Duties of Neutral Powers and Persons in Case of War on Land.
>
> Hague Convention No. IX, 18 October 1907, Concerning Bombardment by Naval Forces in Time of War
>
> Hague Convention No. X, 18 October 1907, for the Adaptation to Maritime Warfare of the Principles of the Geneva Convention.
>
> Geneva Convention Relative to the Treatment of Prisoners of War, 27 July 1929.
>
> Geneva Convention for the Amelioration of the Condition of the Wounded and Sick Armies in the Field, 27 July 1929.
>
> Treaty on the Protection of Artistic and Scientific Institutions and Historic Monuments, 15 April 1935.
>
> Geneva Convention for the Amelioration of the Condition of the Wounded and Sick in Armed Forces in the Field, 12 Aug 1949.
>
> Geneva Convention for the Amelioration of the Condition of Wounded, Sick and Shipwrecked Members of the Armed Forces at Sea, 12 Aug 1949.
>
> Geneva Convention Relative to the Treatment of Prisoners of War, 12 August 1949.
>
> Geneva Convention Relative to the Protection of Civilian Persons in Time of War, 12 August 1949.

## War Crimes According to International Law

Any person, whether a member of the armed forces or a civilian, who commits an act that constitutes a crime under international law is responsible therefor and liable to punishment. Such offenses in connection with war comprise crimes against peace, crimes against humanity, and war crimes. Although the law recognizes the criminal responsibility of individuals for those offenses that may comprise any of the foregoing types of crimes, members of the armed forces will normally be concerned with offenses considered war crimes.

"War crimes" is the technical expression for a violation of the law of war by any person or persons, military or civilian. Every violation of the law of war is a war crime. Therefore, conspiracy, direct incitement, and attempts to commit, as well as complicity

in the commission of, crimes against peace, crimes against humanity, and war crimes are punishable. The most famous example of effectuating war crimes is, of course, the Nuremberg trials after World War II.

In some cases, military commanders may be responsible for war crimes committed by subordinate members of the armed forces, or other persons subject to their control. Thus, for instance, when troops commit massacres and atrocities against the civilian population of occupied territory or against prisoners of war, the responsibility may rest not only with the actual perpetrators but also with the commander. Such a responsibility arises directly when the acts in question have been committed in pursuance of an order of the commander concerned. The commander is also responsible if he has actual knowledge, or should have knowledge, through reports received by him or through other means, that troops or other persons subject to his control are about to commit or have committed a war crime. If he fails to take the necessary and reasonable steps to insure compliance with the law of war or to punish violators he will also bear personal responsibility.

## Grave Breaches

The Geneva Convention of 1949 defines "grave breaches" in broad terms. Specific "grave breaches," if committed against persons or property protected by the Conventions, include such acts as willful killing, torture or inhuman treatment, including biological experiments, willfully causing great suffering or serious injury to body or health, and extensive destruction and appropriation of property, not justified by military necessity and carrying out unlawfully and wantonly. Grave breaches are also extended to embody the acts of compelling a prisoner of war to serve in the forces of the hostile power or willfully depriving a prisoner of war of a fair trial.

In addition to the "grave breaches" of the Geneva Convention, the following acts are also representative of violations of the laws of war:

> Making use of poisoned or otherwise forbidden arms or ammunition
>
> Treacherous request for quarter
>
> Maltreatment of dead bodies
>
> Firing on localities that are undefended and without military significance
>
> Abuse of or firing on the flag of truce
>
> Misuse of the Red Cross emblem
>
> Use of civilian clothing by troops to conceal their military character during battle
>
> Improper use of privileged buildings for military purposes
>
> Pillage or purposeless destruction

Poisoning of streams or wells

Compelling prisoners of war to perform prohibited labor

Killing without trial spies or other persons who have committed hostile acts

Compelling civilians to perform prohibited labor

Violation of surrender of terms

## Trials

Any person charged with a war crime has the right to a fair trial on the facts and the law. Persons accused of "grave breaches" are to be tried under conditions no less favorable than any other defendant in a democratic society. War crimes fall within the jurisdiction of general courts martial, military commissions, provost courts, military government courts, and other military tribunals of the U.S. and other international tribunals. As the international law of war is part of the law of the land of the U.S., enemy personnel charged with war crimes are tried directly under international law without recourse to the statutes of the U.S. However, directives declaratory of international law may be promulgated to assist such tribunals in the performance of their function.

## Penal Sanctions

The punishment imposed for a violation of the law of war must be proportionate to the gravity of the offense. The death penalty may be imposed for grave breaches of the law. Corporal punishment is excluded. Punishments should be deterrent, and in imposing a sentence of imprisonment it is not necessary to take into consideration the end of the war that does not of itself limit the imprisonment to be imposed.

## Defense Not Available

The fact that the law of war has been violated pursuant to an order of a superior authority, whether military or civil, does not deprive the act in question of its character of a war crime, nor does it constitute a defense in the trial of an accused individual, unless he did not know and could not have reasonably been expected to know that the act ordered was unlawful. In all cases where the order is held not to constitute a defense to an allegation of war crime, the fact that the individual was acting pursuant to orders may be considered in mitigation of punishment.

In considering the question of whether a superior order constitutes a valid defense, the court shall take into consideration the fact that obedience to lawful military orders is the duty of every member of the armed forces; that the latter cannot be expected, in conditions of war discipline to weigh scrupulously the legal merits of the orders received and that certain rules of warfare may be controversial or that an act otherwise amounting to a war crime may be done in obedience to orders conceived as a measure of reprisal. At the same time it must be borne in mind that members of the armed forces are bound to obey only lawful orders.

## Government Officials and Domestic Law

The fact that a person who committed an act which constitutes a war crime or acted as the head of a state or as a responsible government official does not relieve him from responsibility for his act. Furthermore, the fact that domestic law does not impose a penalty for an act that constitutes a crime under international law does not relieve the person who committed the act from responsibility under international law.

## Historical Use

The war crimes trials of post–World War II represent the most well-known usage of international war crimes law. In August 1945, the Allies established a tribunal at Nuremberg to try military and civilian Axis leaders. The evidence presented included volumes of documents supporting aggressive warfare, the extermination of civilian populations, the widespread use of slave labor, the looting of occupied countries and the maltreatment of prisoners of war. Several men were sentenced to death. A year later, 28 alleged Japanese war criminals were brought to trial. Evidence similar to that presented against the Nazi also resulted in death sentences for some of those involved. Years later the Israelis captured and tried Adolf Eichmann, a Nazi leader using the same laws.

## Conclusion

Critics have challenged some of the charges of the post–World War II trials, arguing that they violated simple concepts of sovereignty. They argued that defendants should generally be found guilty only if they had been involved in developing policy, not just carrying it out.

In 1998, the UN General Assembly authorized a permanent international court for war crimes over the objection of the U.S., China and five other nations. The International Criminal Court is located at The Hague and is authorized to prosecute war crimes, genocide, crimes of aggression and crimes against humanity.

KATHLEEN M. SWEET

**References and Further Reading**

Department of the Army Field Manual, FM 27–10, July 1956, *Treaties Governing Land Warfare.*

Department of the Army, 1956, *International Law,* Volume II.

Department of the Army, December 1962, Pamphlet 27–161, *Protocols to the Geneva Conventions,* August 12, 1949.

Department of the Army, September 1979, Pamphlet 27–14.

Sweet, K.M., *Law of Armed Conflict Training Guide,* Major USAF, 13th Air Force, September 1986.

*See also* **War Crimes**

# Warrants and Subpoenas

## Warrants

A *warrant* is a written legal document obtained from a magistrate or justice of the peace, unless otherwise specified by a legal statute, directing a law officer to execute specific actions appropriate for their position. Numerous types of warrants exist, but the most commonly issued are *warrants of arrest* and *search warrants.*

*Black's Law Dictionary* defines an arrest warrant as "a writ or precept issued by a magistrate, justice, or other competent authority, addressed to a sheriff, constable, or other officer, requiring him to arrest the body of a person therein named, and bring him before the magistrate or court to answer, or be examined, concerning some offense that he is charged with having committed" (Black's Law Dictionary, 1968). Warrants of arrest instruct a law officer to arrest and bring to the court a specified party who is charged with a stated offense. An arrest warrant is issued on the grounds of *probable cause* following a sworn formal charge of an offense by a complaining party who can present facts surrounding the violation and attest that the individual who is charged is guilty. Probable cause is defined as "The fact that it is more likely than not that a crime has been committed by a person whom a law enforcement officer seeks to arrest," (Oran, 1985).

The complaining party can either be a law enforcement officer investigating the crime or the victim of the crime. The accusation for the warrant is based on officer "information and belief" if the officer did not directly observe the crime and depends upon testimony from witnesses, also known as *hearsay,* as opposed to an officer's "personal knowledge" when witnessing a crime. The Supreme Court has established guidelines to prevent arrest based on unreliable hearsay including that the informant must be credible, that the informant must have information based on previously suggestive circumstances, and that the informant has a reliable source of information for making an accusation other than speculation. Anonymous informant information is usually insufficient to establish probable cause because the credibility of the informant is jeopardized when identity is not disclosed. However, officers heavily consider the motives for an informant to maintain anonymity, such as concern for personal safety or vengeful false accusations (Kerper, 1972).

A valid arrest warrant must contain the name or an adequate description if the name of the charged party is unknown (a *John Doe warrant*) and a description of the committed offense (Matheson, 2004). Yet, simply stating that the accused is guilty of a "felony" or "misdemeanor" is an insufficient amount of information for issuance of a legal warrant. Also required is the time of issuance, names or party of the officers in which the warrant is directed, and a signature from the issuing magistrate or another authority. For an arrest to be legitimate a warrant must be obtained, and, unless otherwise specified by statute, the regional legality of a warrant is limited to the jurisdiction of the magistrate or court official issuing it. However, if an officer has probable cause to act immediately, an arrest warrant need not be issued.

Warrants are not valid outside the issuing state; however, many states have adopted the *hot pursuit warrant,* allowing an officer to make an arrest outside the issuing state if the pursuit continues into a second state during the pursuit of a criminal. Officers' possession of the warrant document is not necessary at the time of the arrest provided that the officer can produce the warrant, if requested, following the arrest. Additionally, a warrant does not expire until its execution or withdrawal, though a reasonable time frame from the issuing period until execution period is required (del Carmen, 1995).

In some jurisdictions, a citizen's arrest or testimonial can serve as probable cause. A *citizen's arrest* is an arrest made by a citizen without a warrant when a felony crime has been committed and the citizen has probable cause that the arrested is guilty. Citizen's arrest also applies to misdemeanor arrests for "breach of peace" and an officer's enlistment of citizens to assist with an arrest (del Carmen, 1995).

Search warrants are written authorizations for law enforcement to inspect stated premises, usually to inspect property for the presence of stolen or unlawful goods—for example, weapons, drugs, or gambling devices. Obtaining a search warrant requires presenting probable cause for suspicion that a violation has or will occur. Probable cause must show, as defined by H. B. Kerper (1972), "that the items for which the search is conducted are connected with criminal activity, and that those items can be found in the place that the police desire to search."

The Fourth Amendment to the U.S. Constitution requires that probable cause be supported by an oath, contain a specific description of items or persons to be seized, and contain a detailed description of the premise in question in order to issue a search warrant. Thus if the search warrant describes only large items to be seized, the officer is prohibited from searching small compartments such as drawers or cabinets, unless more evidence is discovered in the process of the search. Officers have the right to seize any illegal items or evidence not listed on the search warrant, only if the items are found unintentionally, under the "plain view" doctrine.

The Fourth Amendment also protects against "unreasonable searches and seizures" as, prior to the American Revolution, British soldiers were given legal "writs of assistance" to rummage and ransack settlers' homes at will. The Fourth Amendment was carefully constructed to guard against such searches, though the judiciousness by which certain searches are permitted has been argued in court and elsewhere. Searches for evidence without a warrant is allowed only in limited circumstances including when an officer lacks time to obtain a search warrant before the search ensues and when the search functions for alternative purposes other than to obtain evidence. The *frisk* is an example allowable warrant-less search functioning to protect law officers from criminals potentially holding weapons. Also, the Supreme Court ruled in *California v. Acevedo* (1991) that searches of bags or other receptacles in car trunks are permissible and not "unreasonable" without a warrant if probable cause is found to exist (McWhirter, 1994; LaFave, 1995).

The terrorist attacks of September 11, 2001 further compromised the rights established in the Fourth Amendment. Following the attacks, Congress established the Patriot Act that allows for such vague authorities as "TITLE I- Sec. 106 Presidential authority" and "TITLE II- Sec. 213 Authority for delaying notice of the execution of a warrant," as well as a whole host of others (Patriot Act, 2004). However, in most cases, any evidence gathered from a premise without a valid search warrant is illegal and not admissible in court under the *exclusionary principle*, as set forth by the Supreme Court decisions in *Weeks v. U.S.* (1914) and *Mapp v. Ohio* (1961) (LaFave, 1995).

Although states' specific statutes vary regarding the service of a warrant, the following guidelines usually pertain to most U.S. jurisdictions. A warrant may be served by any officer in the jurisdiction where the suspect is found, regardless of where the warrant was issued (in states that allow officers to serve warrants outside of their jurisdictions, it is common courtesy to alert local law enforcement of the intent to arrest). With the exception of the "hot pursuit" warrant, a warrant is not valid outside of the state of issuance (del Carmen, 1995). A felony warrant can be served at all hours of the day or night, but misdemeanor warrants must be served during the day. Officers can, however, request that a misdemeanor warrant be served at night. This is commonly called a *nightcapped warrant* (Harr and Hess, 1990).

Authority to arrest also varies from state to state and from one jurisdiction to another, and an arrest is valid only if it has been properly authorized. Whereas some states allow officers to make arrests only when "on duty," other states grant their officers "off duty" authority, compelling them to make arrests 24 hours a day if they find themselves in the presence of criminal activity. Because policy is decided on a state and local level, it varies widely across the country (del Carmen, 1995).

In addition to arrest and search warrants, a multitude of other warrants exist to prohibit or require a party to perform a specified act. A *bench warrant*, issued by a presiding judge, authorizes the arrest of a person for a mandatory appearance in court. Although usually served to an accused party after indictment or a witness to require mandatory attendance in court, bench warrants are also used to produce a wanted or escaped prisoner or have a confined prisoner appear before the judge (Bench Warrant, 2004). A *warrant of commitment* authorizes prison confinement of a person before or after a trial. Purchases of public land require a *land warrant* whereas a *landlord's warrant* authorizes the sale of a tenants' belongings to fulfill the lease contract. *Death warrants* are issued by a governor ordering the death sentence to be imposed on a criminal. *Tax warrants* authorize tax collectors to collect unpaid taxes from citizens and business. *Dividend warrants, treasury warrants, municipal warrants*, and *stock warrants* are other forms of warrants that are issued to financial and commercial establishments (Matheson, 2004).

For minor offenses many state statutes authorize issuing *citations* or *summons* as opposed to arrest warrants because they require less time and resources. Rolando V. del Carmen defines a citation as, "an order issued by a court or law enforcement officer commanding the person to whom the citation is issued to appear in court at a specified date to answer certain charges." Summons he defines as, "a writ directed to the sheriff or other proper officer requiring that officer to notify the person named that he or she is required to appear in court on a day named and to answer the complaint stated in the summons." If the person issued the citation or summons fails to appear in court on the given date, an arrest warrant is issued (del Carmen, 1995).

*Electronic surveillance warrants* must be obtained before police may use any investigative device such as wiretapping or tracking devices. Title III of the Federal Omnibus Crime Control and Safe Streets Act of 1968 defines electronic surveillance as a form of search and seizure governed by the Fourth Amendment. Obtaining electronic surveillance warrants requires probable cause established by the courts, only after all other methods of investigation have been unsuccessful, and they are valid only for a two month time period.

Despite the many specifics of the arrest warrant, *arrest without a warrant* accounts for nearly 95% of all arrests. For felony offenses and some misdemeanor offenses, state and federal laws do not require a law officer to obtain a warrant for an arrest. This substantially high rate of warrant-less arrests highlights the need for officers to be very cautious when making arrests, making sure they have witnessed a crime or that they have probable cause, as they will be expected to give sworn complaint or testimonial of the arrest at a later date (del Carmen, 1995).

The two main types of warrant-less arrests are *arrests for crimes committed in the presence of an officer* and *warrant-less arrests based on probable cause*. As set forth in *State v. Pluth* (1923), an officer cannot merely suspect that a crime will occur. The crime must actually be witnessed by a police officer, and many states require officers to issue warrants for crimes not committed in their presence. In other cases, if the officer has probable cause "sufficient in [himself] to warrant a man of reasonable caution in the belief that an offense" has been committed by him, a warrant-less arrest is legal (Harr and Hess, 1990). Probable cause must be established before the arrest, and any evidence gathered after the arrest does not justify probable cause, but may support the arresting officer's case. Although a warrant is not issued prior to the arrest of an accused, arrest warrants are often issued afterwards to authorize holding the accused in custody until trial. In many states these post arrest warrants are unnecessary and the officer's sworn statement of probable cause is sufficient (Kerper, 1972).

## Subpoenas

A subpoena is a court order requiring a person to be present at a certain time and place or suffer a penalty. Subpoenas, a Latin term meaning *under penalty*, are the traditional tools used by lawyers to ensure that witnesses present themselves at a given place, date and time to make themselves available to testify. A subpoena may also be issued for documents related to pending lawsuits. Representing an intricate part of the trial process, a subpoena provides for the acquisition of necessary testimony and documents pertinent to the disposition of a case.

Subpoenas were originally a chancery practice wherein a mandatory writ was directed to and requiring one or more persons to appear at a time to come, and answer the matters charged against him or them. The writ of subpoena was first a process in the courts of common law to enforce the attendance of a witness to give evidence and then used in the court of chancery for the same purpose as a citation in the courts of civil and canon law to compel the appearance of a defendant and to oblige him to answer upon oath the allegations of the plaintiff. The writ of subpoena is traceable back to John Waltham, Bishop of Salisbury, and Chancellor to Richard II, who was afforded the authority to issue such an order under the statutes of Westminster 2 and 13 Edward I that enabled him to devise new writs.

Today, subpoenas are dichotomized as either *subpoena ad testificandum* or *subpoena duces tecum*. The former is a subpoena that commands a witness to appear and give testimony whereas the latter commands the production of specified evidence in a person's possession. *Duces tecum* subpoenas are the most common way to obtain potentially useful evidence, such as documents and business records, in the possession of a third party. A subpoena duces tecum must specify the documents or types of documents or it will be subject to an objection that the request is "too broad and burdensome." To obtain documents from the opposing party, a "Request for Production of Documents" is more commonly used.

The writ of subpoena carries with it a penalty that may be imposed upon the target of the order if the individual refuses compliance. Noncompliance with a subpoena of either kind may subject that party served with the subpoena to punishment for contempt of court for disobeying a court order. The court's power to punish for contempt (called "citing" one for contempt) includes fines or jail time (called "imposing sanctions") or both. Incarceration is typically just a threat and if imposed, usually brief. Criminal contempt involves contempt with the aim of obstruction of justice, such as threatening a judge or witness or disobeying an order to produce evidence.

Subpoenas exist within the American legal system under the logic of the Sixth Amendment to the U.S. Constitution. The Sixth Amendment provides that "in all criminal prosecutions, the accused shall enjoy the right...to be confronted with the witnesses against him." The right to confrontation exists in all criminal proceedings, including trials, preliminary hearings, and juvenile proceedings in which the juvenile is suspected of having committed a crime. The Sixth Amendment also expressly provides that the accused in a criminal prosecution shall have the right to compulsory process for obtaining witnesses in his or her favor. The right to obtain witnesses includes the power to require the appearance of witnesses and the right to present a defense, which in turn includes the defendant's right to present his or her own witnesses and his or her own version of the facts. Subpoenas are the legal instrument whereby defendants are able to exercise these rights.

Subpoenas and warrants are similar in that both function as a means of discovery, that is, both allow for the acquisition of necessary information. However, subpoenas also differ from warrants significantly in that probable cause does not apply to the former. Whereas a warrant may only be issued upon probable cause determined by a magistrate, the court is free to subpoena any information it deems relevant to the case at hand. Subpoenas allow for tremendous leeway in this respect, in effect circumventing the probable cause requirement that would otherwise apply to evidence needed by the state.

JESSICA MCGOWAN AND HOLLY E. VENTURA

### References and Further Readings

Bench warrant, *Encyclopedia Americana,* Grolier Online, 2004. Available at: http//ea.grolier.com. Retrieved on January 22, 2004.

Del Carmen, R.V. (1995). *Criminal Procedure: Law and Practice,* 3rd ed., Wadsworth Publishing, Belmont, CA.

Harr, J.S. and Hess, K.M. (1997). *Criminal Procedure,* West Publishing Co., St. Paul, MN.

Kerper, H.B. (1972). *Introduction to the Criminal Justice System,* West Publishing Co., St. Paul, MN.

LaFave, W.R. (1995). *Search and Seizure: A Treatise on the Fourth Amendment,* 3rd ed., West Publishing Co., St Paul, MN.

Matheson, A.A. (2004). Warrant, *Encyclopedia Americana,* Grolier Online, 2004. Available at: http://ea.grolier.com. Retrieved on January 21, 2004.

McWhirter, D.A. (1994). *Search, Seizure, and Privacy,* Oryx Press, Phoenix, AZ.

Oran, D. (1985). *Law Dictionary for Non-Lawyers,* 2nd ed., West Publishing Co., St. Paul, MN.

U.S. House of Representatives. (2001). *H.R. 3162, Patriot Act,* Washington, DC, Government Printing Office.

*See also* **Arrest; Due Process; Search and Seizure**

# White-Collar Crime: Definitions

The person most closely associated with the concept of white-collar crime is the U.S. criminologist Edwin H. Sutherland. Throughout his career, Sutherland used several different definitions of white-collar crime. The one for which he is most well known, and that has had the longest staying power, defined white-collar crime "as a crime committed by a person of respectability and high social status in the course of his occupation" (Sutherland, 1983).

This definition is unusual in that it refers to characteristics of the actor. Legal commentators addressing other sorts of crimes typically take great pains to establish clear definitions of the acts that must take place and the state or states of mind that an individual must possess in order for a crime to be committed, but little is said about the characteristics of the actor. Sutherland's definition, however, tells us that only certain types of people can commit white-collar crimes, those with "respectability and high social status." It also specifies that the act must arise out of the course of the actor's occupation. Both the status of the actor and the occupational location of the act determine whether an illegality is a white-collar crime.

Another distinguishing feature of Sutherland's approach was his willingness to include civil and administrative violations as part of white-collar crime. This decision provoked extensive comment and criticism from legal scholars who contend that only acts that are punished under criminal laws can rightly be called crimes. In Sutherland's view, however, including other types of violations was justified because many civil laws deal with practices that are fundamentally similar to criminal offenses. In addition, many illegal business practices can be sanctioned under both criminal and civil law. To exclude offenses that are pursued under civil law arbitrarily limits the range of white-collar offenses. This limitation is especially important in the context of many white-collar crimes, because the organizations and individuals who commit these offenses often use their political power and economic resources to avoid criminal prosecutions. As many white-collar crime commentators have noted that how and under what circumstances business activities are criminalized, are important issues by themselves.

Although Sutherland defined white-collar crime as an act committed by a person, many of the offenses that he analyzed involved corporations or other types of organizational entities. Recognizing that there may be substantial differences between individual and corporate acts, many white-collar crime scholars now accept a broad distinction between occupational crime and organizational or corporate crime. Occupational crime typically is defined as offenses committed by individuals for themselves during the course of their occupations or against their employers. Organizational crime includes illegal behavior that is committed by an actor or group of actors working together to achieve organizational goals. The distinguishing feature of occupational crime is that actors pursue their own interests, whereas in organizational crimes actors are working to forward the interests of the organization rather than their own interests.

A major point of contention regarding Sutherland's definition is whether the social status of offenders should be a defining characteristic of white-collar crime. Sutherland included respectability and high social status in his definition, because he wanted to draw attention to the criminality of business groups. He argued that the criminological theories of his day were class biased and incomplete because they equated crime with lower-class individuals and ignored crime by upper-class individuals. In addition, he was morally outraged by what he regarded as the lenient and preferential treatment afforded to business offenders in the criminal justice system.

Although Sutherland undoubtedly was correct about the narrowness of criminological theory and the unfairness of the criminal justice system of his day, including social status and respectability in the definition of white-collar crime created several problems for research and analysis. The main problem in using social status as a defining element of crime is that it cannot then be used as an explanatory variable because

it is not allowed to vary independently of the crime. Thus, by definitional fiat, white-collar crime researchers are prevented from investigating how the social status of individuals influences the types or the seriousness of the white-collar type offenses they commit. Similar offenses may be committed by corporate executives and by employees at the bottom of the corporate hierarchy, but only the former meet Sutherland's definition of white-collar crime. For example, a corporate executive may take advantage of privileged information about an impending stock event gained in the boardroom to engage in illegal insider trading. A typist transcribing minutes from a meeting may note the same information and use it in the same manner as the executive in order to trade company stock illegally. Some white-collar scholars believe it does not make sense to focus only on the corporate executive and to ignore the typist.

Including social status in the definition of white-collar crime also rules out the possibility of exploring how variation in the status of actors influences societal reactions to their offenses. For example, it is important to investigate whether insider trading by corporate executives and that committed by clerical staff are treated the same or differently by authorities. Are small businesses that engage in consumer fraud treated the same by regulatory officials as are multinational corporations who do so? In order to investigate these issues white-collar crime must be defined in a status neutral manner.

Sutherland's definition is the most well known and influential example of what has been called the "offender-based" approach to defining white-collar crime. Offender-based definitions emphasize as an essential characteristic of white-collar crime the high social status, power, and respectability of the actor. Despite its shortcomings Sutherland's offender-based approach has remained popular. Numerous attempts have been made to define the concept in a manner that is faithful to Sutherland's intentions but that clarify or expand upon his definition. In 1980, Albert J. Reiss and Albert D. Biderman (1980) proposed that "white-collar violations are those violations of law to which penalties are attached that involve the use of a violator's position of significant power, influence, or trust in the legitimate economic or political institutional order for the purpose of illegal gain, or to commit an illegal act for personal or organizational gain." At a 1996 workshop sponsored by the National White-Collar Crime Center's Research and Training Institute, a consortium of white-collar crime scholars proposed an operational definition to which Sutherland probably would not have objected. The group defined white-collar crime as "Illegal or unethical acts that violate fiduciary responsibility or public trust, committed by an individual or organization, usually during the course of legitimate occupational activity, by persons of high or respectable social status for personal or organizational gain." These definitions have several elements in common with Sutherland's approach. They include the social characteristics of the offender, occupational location, and noncriminal acts as defining characteristics of white-collar crime. James Coleman (1998) proposes that white-collar crime be defined as "a violation of the law committed by a person or group of persons in the course of an otherwise respected and legitimate occupation or financial activity." This definition does not refer to the status or respectability of the actor and expands the location of white-collar crime so as to include nonoccupational but presumably legitimate financial activities. A similar definition has been proposed by Jay Albanese (1995), who argues for this formulation: white-collar crime is "planned or organized illegal acts of deception or fraud, usually accomplished during the course of legitimate occupational activity, committed by an individual or corporate entity."

The other major approach to defining white-collar crime is called "offense-based," because the definition is based on the nature of the illegal act. In 1970, Herbert Edelhertz, then an official at the U.S. Department of Justice, proposed a highly influential offense-based definition of white-collar crime. He defined white-collar crime as "an illegal act or series of illegal acts committed by nonphysical means and by concealment or guile to obtain money or property, to avoid the payment or loss of money or property, or to obtain business or personal advantage." This definition defines white-collar crime according to the means by which offenses are carried out—nonphysical means that involve concealment or guile. Any act or series of acts committed by any person that meets these formal requirements is considered white-collar crime.

Another example of the offense-based school of thought on defining white-collar crime was provided in 1990 by Susan Shapiro. Shapiro (1990) argued that the essential characteristic of the acts that are commonly called white-collar crimes is that they involve violations or abuse of trust. She proposed that the concept of white-collar crime be liberated by "disentangling the identification of the perpetrators from their misdeeds." In Shapiro's view, offender based definitions create an imprisoning framework. This framework leads scholars to misunderstand the structural sources of white-collar offenses, the problems they create for social control agencies, and the nature of class bias in the justice system.

Offense-based definitions have proved popular with researchers for several reasons. Because no mention is made of the social status of the actor or the social location of the act, both status and location are free to vary independently of the definition of the offense and can be used as explanatory variables. Researchers who use an offense-based definition have the freedom to explore how variation in the social status of the actor influences characteristics of the white-collar crimes committed and how the status of the actor influences societal reactions to offenses. Researchers can also investigate whether white-collar offenses committed in occupational settings differ from those committed outside occupational settings. Finally, offense-based definitions make it easier for researchers to draw samples of white-collar offenders from official data sources, such as court conviction records. Researchers need only identify a set of statutory offenses that meet certain formal criteria and then sample individuals convicted of those offenses. A number of well-regarded studies published in the 1980s and 1990s used this strategy to identify and investigate white-collar offenders in the U.S. federal judicial system.

Despite its popularity with some researchers, the offense-based approach to white-collar crime raises troubling issues for many other white-collar crime scholars. The very ease with which offense-based definitions can be used to draw samples becomes a trap for investigators, leading them to miss or ignore the most important aspects of the white-collar crime phenomenon. Investigators who use offense-based definitions often end up studying the relatively minor misdeeds of ordinary people of very modest financial means who somehow become caught up in the criminal justice system. Indeed, if construed loosely, Edelhertz's definition would permit the alcoholic who conned a friend out of a bottle of wine to claim the status of white-collar criminal. Even offense-based samples drawn from the Federal judicial system that supposedly has a more white-collar clientele than is found in state courts, tend to be composed primarily of middle class individuals who have committed banal and simplistic offenses. The powerful corporations and corporate executives that originally provoked Sutherland's interest are largely absent. Offense-based approaches tend inevitably to draw researchers toward the study of acts that have been officially defined as illegal. As a result, powerful individuals and corporate actors who are able to avoid official labeling in the first place never appear in the resulting samples. Thus, the major criticism of the offense-based approach is that in practice it misses the crimes of the powerful. The very people that Sutherland originally sought to bring to the attention of criminologists are ignored and in their place small time con men are substituted.

The debate between advocates of offender versus offense based approaches to defining white-collar crime has continued for more than 30 years and shows no signs of diminishing. At present, the field is marked by a certain definitional eclecticism. Researchers and theorists use whichever type of definition best suits the needs of their current project. Those involved in quantitative studies tend to favor offense-based definitions, whereas those who use more qualitative techniques such as case studies tend to favor the offender-based approach. Some researchers have attempted to combine the two approaches by first drawing samples based on offenses and then trying to identify a subset of individuals who can be regarded as "true" white-collar criminals based on their social status or occupational position.

MICHAEL L. BENSON

### References and Further Reading

Albanese, J., *White Collar Crime in America,* Englewood Cliffs, NJ, Prentice Hall (1995).

Braithwaite, J., White-Collar Crime, *Annual Review of Sociology,* 11 (1985).

Clinard, M.B. and Yeager, P.C., *Corporate Crime,* New York, The Free Press, 1980.

Coleman, J.W., *The Criminal Elite: The Sociology of White-Collar Crime,* 4th ed., New York, St. Martin's Press, 1998.

Edelhertz, H., *The Nature, Impact, and Prosecution of White-Collar Crime,* Washington, DC, U.S. Department of Justice, 1970.

Geis, G., From Deuteronomy to Deniability: An Historical Perlustration on White-Collar Crime, *Justice Quarterly,* 5 (1988).

Geis, G., Meier, R.F. and Salinger, L.M., Eds., *White-Collar Crime: Classic and Contemporary Views,* New York, The Free Press, 1995.

National White-Collar Crime Center, *Proceedings of the Academic Workshop: "Definitional Dilemma: Can and Should There Be a Universal Definition of White Collar Crime?"* Training and Research Institute, 1996.

Reiss, A.J. and Biderman, A., *Data Sources on White-Collar Law Breaking.* Washington, DC, U.S. Government Printing Office, 1980.

Shapiro, S.P., Collaring the Crime, Not the Criminal: Reconsidering 'White-Collar Crime,' *American Sociological Review,* 55 (1990).

Sutherland, E.H., *White-Collar Crime: The Uncut Version,* New Haven, CT, Yale University Press, 1983.

Weisburd, D., Wheeler, S., Waring, E. and Bode, N., *Crimes of the Middle Classes: White-Collar Offenders in the Federal Courts,* New Haven, CT, Yale University Press, 1991.

*See also* **White-collar Crime: Theories**

# White-Collar Crime: Enforcement Strategies

Enforcing white-collar crimes poses a challenging task to all levels of law enforcement, and the federal and state regulatory agencies charged with confronting these crimes. Absence of consistent figures detailing the extent of white-collar crime, it is difficult to assess the performance of those tasked with its enforcement. In addition to this, the complex nature of white-collar crime, coupled with decentralized law enforcement and regulatory enforcement approaches results in an overall enforcement approach that lacks the coordination, tenacity, and effectiveness found in the enforcement of traditional crimes. The enforcement of white-collar crimes has also been hampered by the historical views of politicians, the media, and the general public, who generally recognize these crimes as less serious than traditional crimes. Despite these limitations, there is recent evidence of increased societal focus on white-collar crime enforcement that offers promise for more effective white-collar crime enforcement.

Criminal justice systems are primarily designed to address traditional crime, with recent law enforcement attention devoted to confronting terrorist activities. Nalla and Newman (1994) make the argument that separate police organizations exist for the enforcement of white-collar and traditional crimes. They, and others, support the belief that the "blue-collar" police receive much public attention and are responsible for most arrests, whereas "white-collar" police make far fewer arrests and receive far less attention despite their great discretion and seemingly unlimited control. White-collar offenders clearly benefit from the different use of discretion among the two forms of policing (Mann, 1985).

Local law enforcement agencies lack the resources and personnel to properly address white-collar crime, and are generally ill-equipped to do more than merely respond to the cases that are brought to their attention. Local police agencies appear well-positioned to address particular forms of white-collar crime (e.g., consumer frauds, environmental safety violations, etc.), despite many disincentives, including the lack of training, resources, and excitement; the decreased likelihood of resolution; public pressure to address conventional crimes; and media pressure result in limited local police enforcement of white-collar crime (Friedrichs, 1996).

Large local law enforcement agencies may maintain specialized white-collar crime units (sometimes referred to as "economic crime units," "computer crime units," etc.), although most law enforcement agencies are small in size and do not possess the resources for such specialization. The complexity of white-collar crimes, which could involve the need for specialized training in areas such as accounting or computer technology, mandates that local authorities often seek assistance from state and federal authorities. Local policing plays a notably limited role in addressing white-collar crime, as their practices are primarily guided by societal fears of street crime. Absence of increased substantial, societal, and government concern for white-collar crime, it is likely that local law enforcement will continue its limited role in enforcing these offenses.

With greater jurisdiction and resources, state and federal law enforcement agencies are often recognized as better equipped to address white-collar crime than are local law enforcement groups. State law enforcement agencies generally maintain specialized units that in addition to directly enforcing white-collar crimes, typically offer training, information (e.g., databases of information), and other resources for various law enforcement groups. The limited number of personnel working in these specialized units, however, has historically resulted in a sub par response to white-collar crime.

Federal law enforcement agencies provide the most significant reaction to white-collar crime (Friedrichs, 1996) as they maintain greater specialization than state and local agencies, although they too lack the resources to confront and prevent most white-collar crimes. For instance, until the recent concern for terrorism, the Federal Bureau of Investigation (FBI) maintained a steadfast focus on white-collar crime. The agency has shifted its focus in part to address threats of terrorism both home and abroad.

Although the earliest federal regulatory and policing agencies addressed issues pertaining to banking and agriculture, over two dozen federal agencies currently investigate white-collar crimes, with the FBI, the Secret Service, the Customs Service, the Postal Inspection Service, the Inspector Generals, and the Internal Revenue Service Criminal Investigative Division recognized as the principle investigative agencies (Friedrichs, 1996). A lack of resources results in federal agencies primarily reacting to more serious white-collar offenses. The end result is that law enforcement's response to white-collar crime enforcement assumes a selective, reactive approach, despite the need for greater prevention of white-collar crime.

Greater international commerce and expanded global interaction are but two issues dictating greater enforcement of white-collar crime at the international level (e.g., Schlegel, 2000). No particular international form of policing is designed to confront white-collar crime; thus countries must primarily rely on cooperation from other countries in addressing international white-collar offenses. The two groups arguably best situated to enforce white-collar crimes are INTERPOL and the UN, although the former serves primarily an informational role and is not considered an investigative nor an enforcement agency, whereas the latter has much room to grow before it can be considered an effective international law enforcement agency, should it choose to continue growing in this direction. International efforts to enforce white-collar crime are more fragmented than most national efforts, despite the growing need to establish an international enforcement presence. Primary among the reasons for limited international white-collar crime enforcement efforts are differing international laws, jurisdictional issues, lack of coordination, limited cooperation among countries, and the lack of a centralized agency to assume the lead role in enforcing white-collar crime. Law enforcement agencies are assisted by other groups in the enforcement of white-collar crime. Particularly, federal and state regulatory agencies largely contribute to the enforcement of white-collar crime.

The most common response to white-collar crime is through administrative law and regulatory agencies, primarily because regulatory agencies provide greater specialization and maintain special advantages compared to law enforcement agencies (Frank and Lynch, 1992). Among the advantages maintained by regulatory agencies are the authority to enter and inspect corporate facilities without warrants and probable cause, and mandating that entities provide various kinds of information regarding their conduct and products (Frank and Lynch, 1992). Regulatory penalties generally carry with them a more potent penalty than can be imposed under criminal law, although regulatory penalties lack the stigma attached to a criminal conviction and much of the criticism aimed at regulatory enforcement of white-collar crimes stems from an excessive reliance on negotiation, cooperation, and voluntary compliance (Frank and Lynch, 1992). Regulatory agencies face additional difficulties in balancing the interests of the corporate sector (e.g., they must avoid over criminalization) and the general public, and they are often influenced by the political environment in which they operate. Enforcement practices at the Environmental Protection Agency, for example, were, and continue to be heavily influenced by Congress and the Executive Office.

Such limited resources at all levels of government results in a piecemeal approach to white-collar crime enforcement. Enforcement efforts to address white-collar crime will, however, increase as society recognizes the impact of these offenses. Gallo (1998), for instance, believes that particular forms of white-collar crime can be deterred through targeted enforcement and publicized prosecutions. The idea of publicizing enforcement efforts is supported by others who feel that the negative stigma of being labeled "criminal" or "offender" would adversely impact many profit-driven activities. Stressing the importance of societal recognition of white-collar wrongdoing is a principle component of Braithwaite's (1989) suggestion that reintegrative shaming could be an attractive alternative to the more traditional approaches of punishing white-collar offenses.

Aside from law enforcement and regulatory agencies, other groups identify white-collar crimes, which subsequently contribute to enforcement efforts. For instance, private police forces are used to identify white-collar crimes, although Friedrichs (1996) notes that such groups play a limited role in the enforcement of white-collar crime, particularly with regard to harms committed by upper-level executives. Friedrichs (1996) adds that private policing in a business or corporate setting often focuses more on concealing rather than exposing white-collar crime. Accountants and lawyers are also obligated to identify white-collar crimes, whereas the media, whistleblowers, and informants have also been used. Upton Sinclair's 1906 exposure of the harmful practices of the meat packing industry, which ultimately inspired the passage of the Meat Inspection Act of 1906, is recognized as the earliest form of muckraking journalism that has also added to the enforcement of white-collar crime. More recently, *Time* magazine recognized Cynthia Cooper, Coleen Rowley, and Sherron Watkins as "Persons of the Year" for 2002 for their roles in identifying white-collar malfeasance at WorldCom, the FBI, and Enron, respectively. Similarly, victims of white-collar crime have assisted with the enforcement of white-collar crime by drawing attention to the harms they have incurred, although their role has been limited as they are often unaware of the victimization (e.g., Frank and Lynch, 1992).

Bodies of law and the sanctioning of offenders can also be recognized as efforts to enforce white-collar crime. For instance, in an attempt to approach equality in corporate crime sentencing, in 1991 the U.S. Sentencing Commission established sentencing guidelines applicable only to corporations. Similar to the guidelines used by the federal government and many states, these corporate sentencing guidelines attempt to limit judicial discretion and reduce disparity in sentencing. Sentencing judges are restricted to selecting a penalty suitable for the offense with consideration to the guidelines and particular aggravating and mitigating circumstances. One specific consideration during the sentencing phase, as mandated by the U.S. Sentencing Commission, is whether the offending entity had a corporate compliance program. Corporations are rewarded for having in place a self-monitoring program designed to detect and prevent illegal behavior. Self-regulation helps address the issue of limited law enforcement resources by encouraging corporations to monitor and respond to their own behavior.

Self-regulation as a means of enforcing white-collar crimes is becoming increasingly popular, and is used as a primary enforcement tool with regard to environmental crime regulation. The approach, however, does have limitations (e.g., Lynch, Michalowski, and Groves, 2000), most notably the reliance on individuals and corporations to voluntarily disclose information, and the hypocrisy of regulating white-collar activity through expecting self-disclosure but those engaged in traditional crimes are not offered the same liberty. Regardless, some note the benefits of self-regulation (e.g., Gallo, 1998), and the approach does address, in part, the limited available resources to enforce white-collar crimes.

Laws and penalties certainly act as forms of social control and are primarily used as a form of deterrence to those in position to commit white-collar crime. Accordingly, several bodies of law are used to enforce white-collar crimes. Among these laws, which can be used simultaneously, are criminal, civil, and administrative or regulatory law. Administrative laws permit regulatory agencies to guide specific behaviors, and provide greater flexibility and specialization than civil or criminal laws. Among other things, these laws give regulatory agencies power to regulate areas such as worker and consumer safety and the environment. Friedrichs (1996) notes that the differences among civil, criminal, and regulatory justice are not always clear, although regulatory justice generally maintains a lower profile than civil and criminal justice systems, which are more likely to involve an adversarial confrontation.

Civil laws can be used if an individual brings charges against an alleged violative corporation. Civil laws have become an increasingly important tool in addressing white-collar crime primarily because the civil damages awarded are frequently much greater than the maximum fine that could be imposed by the government through criminal prosecution or civil action (Frank and Lynch, 1992). A large civil penalty and subsequent negative publicity could have a deterrent impact on white-collar criminals, although it is argued that a cost-benefit analysis might show that violative behavior is more beneficial than most civil awards or negative publicity. The Ford Motor Company's 1970s calculated decision to continue producing deadly Ford Pintos and financially reimburse victims and families for harms associated with those vehicles is perhaps the most frequently cited example of the limitations of seeking civil awards from large corporations. Many recent white-collar crime enforcement efforts focus on deterrence, which arguably has had a limited impact on addressing corporate crime.

Criminal law is used infrequently, and typically only as a last resort in enforcing white-collar crimes (Frank and Lynch, 1992). Among the difficulties associated with criminally prosecuting white-collar crimes are the rights with which defendants are provided in criminal proceedings, the heavier burden of proof required to secure a conviction in criminal court compared to civil court, the costs of criminal prosecution, and the technical complexity of criminal cases that often require greater resources than civil cases. The smaller penalties often distributed in criminal cases compared to civil cases and conflicting opinions regarding whether criminal penalties are suited for white-collar crimes pose further problems in processing white-collar offenders in criminal court (e.g., Frank and Lynch, 1992).

Sanctions generally applied to those convicted of conventional crimes have been used in attempts to punish and deter white-collar criminals. Probation, in particular, is viewed as appropriately designed for white-collar criminals primarily because these individuals are recognized as capable of remaining productive in society and are not often viewed as dangerous threats to the public. Probation, however, can also be viewed as too lenient as offenders may remain in position to commit additional offenses. Similarly, fines are also used in the enforcement of white-collar crime, primarily because of the impact fines can pose to individuals committing financially motivated crimes. Questions of leniency also surround the use of fines in sanctioning white-collar offenders, and judges may find it difficult to set a fine amount that serves as a punishment or deterrent. Other sentences used to enforce white-collar crimes include restitution, community service, occupational disqualification, organizational reform, corporate dissolution, and perhaps the most severe sanction, incarceration.

Although not often used in sanctioning white-collar crimes, incarceration, it is argued, seems appropriate in certain instances. Whereas it is impossible to incarcerate a corporation, identifying and incarcerating culpable individuals within an offending entity may serve the purposes of providing justice for victims, recognizing

fairness in sentencing all offenders (conventional and white-collar), acting as a deterrent, and punishing rational, calculating individuals who deliberately intended to break the law. Incarceration may seem inappropriate for enforcing white-collar crimes as some argue that the stigma of criminal conviction, the less dangerous threat to society posed by white-collar offenders, and the lack of public and political concern for these crimes dictates that alternative sanctions be applied.

In discussing the work of others who have examined white-collar crime enforcement and sanctioning, Braithwaite (1985) offers a series of alternative solutions to address the difficulties in sanctioning white-collar crimes using traditional punishments. In particular, Braithwaite suggests the use of equity fines through which an offending company is forced to issue and surrender new shares of stock to a victim compensation fund; publicity orders, through which offending companies must advertise in the media the nature and extent of their violation(s); internal discipline orders that require the company to internally confront the violative situation and report their progress to the court; preventive orders that include steps to prevent future violations (e.g., ordering a company to change its standard operating procedures); corporate probation that involves the appointment of an expert to supervise internal reforms designed to address the violative behavior; and community service orders that require the company to perform some relevant service to the community as reparation for its offenses(s). These alternative sanctions undoubtedly address issues related to the difficulties involved in enforcing white-collar crimes and provide attractive avenues to address the differences between enforcing white-collar and traditional crimes.

An additional alternative approach to addressing white-collar crime involves moral appeals to highlight the harms associated with white-collar crime. Such appeals attack the morality of corporate behavior and maintain the potential to have a more lasting impact than more traditional reactive approaches to white-collar crime enforcement (e.g., fines). The potential for moral appeals in attempts to enforce white-collar crime is evidenced in findings from research on informal sanction threats and corporate crime, which noted that the certainty of an offender receiving an informal sanction and the *perceived immorality* of the act were prominent among the variables significantly related to corporate offending decisions (Elis and Simpson, 1995). Appealing to the morality of white-collar crime seems an effective proactive approach to addressing the limited effects of the more traditional reactive efforts toward enforcing white-collar crime, and can be accomplished through the promotion of business ethics courses in university and corporate training curricula, and by stressing business ethics within the business world.

Responding to a series of high-profile acts of corporate crime, the federal government in 2003 issued legislation designed to implement stiff penalties for corporate fraud, tighten accountability in the accounting industry, and among other things, require chief executive officers to verify the accuracy of financial reports. The *Sarbanes-Oxley Act of 2002,* signed by President George W. Bush on July 31, 2003, grants the president power to select a Corporate Fraud Task Force designed to offer recommendations on efforts to enforce financial crime laws. The act also includes severe penalties for altering or destroying vital documents, restrictions on personal loans from companies to top administrators, new regulations to address the conflict of interest among financial analysts and corporations, and extends the time period for victimized investors to file civil charges for fraudulent activity. The impact of this new legislation and other recent attempts to confront white-collar crime remains to be seen. Absence of sound empirical assessments of the nature and given the extent of white-collar crime, it will be difficult to determine the effectiveness of any approach. One could argue that further legislation is needed to assess the extent of white-collar crime and its enforcement that would serve to direct future justice-based efforts.

Edwin Sutherland's (1949) infamous work on crimes of the powerful suggested that white-collar crimes were rationally calculated, deliberate, and more frequent than their prosecutions indicated. Further, he suggested that enforcement of white-collar crimes committed by the 70 largest corporations of the time of his study were seemingly ineffective as roughly 97% of his sample were criminal recidivists. Almost

half a century later we still face many of the crime-related issues identified by Sutherland, and a seemingly similar lackadaisical societal response to these harms. White-collar crime enforcement requires greater societal attention, particularly with regard to increased emphases on proactive, preventive efforts and greater regulatory and law enforcement.

RONALD G. BURNS

## References and Further Reading

Braithwaite, J., *To Punish or Persuade: Enforcement of Coal Mine Safety,* Albany, NY, State University of New York Press, 1985.

Braithwaite, J., *Crime, Shame and Reintegration,* NY, Cambridge University Press, 1989.

Elis, L.A. and Simpson, S.S., Informal Sanction Threats and Corporate Crime: Additive Versus Multiplicative Models, *Journal of Research in Crime and Delinquency,* 32 (1995).

Frank, N.K. and Lynch, M.J., *Corporate Crime, Corporate Violence: A Primer,* New York, Harrow and Heston, 1992.

Friedrichs, D.O., *Trusted Criminals: White Collar Crime in Contemporary Society,* Belmont, CA, Wadsworth, 1996.

Gallo, J.N., Effective law-enforcement techniques for reducing crime, *Journal of Criminal Law and Criminology,* 88 (1998).

Lynch, M.J., Michalowski, R. and Groves, W.B., *The New Primer in Radical Criminology: Critical Perspectives on Crime, Power and Identity,* 3rd ed., Monsey, NY, Criminal Justice Press, 2000.

Mann, K., *Defending White-Collar Crime: A Portrait of Attorneys at Work,* New Haven, CT, Yale University Press, 1985.

Nalla, M.K. and Newman, G.R., Is White Collar Policing, Policing? *Policing and Society,* 3 (1994).

Schlegel, K., Transnational Crime: Implications for Local Law Enforcement, *Journal of Contemporary Criminal Justice,* 16 (2000).

Sutherland, E., *White Collar Crime,* New York, Holt, Rinehart and Winston, 1949.

*See also* **White-Collar Crime: Definitions; White-Collar Crime: The Law; White-Collar Crime: Theories**

---

# White-Collar Crime: The Law

---

White-collar crime has not been a major focus in the law. Most forms of harm by white-collar crimes are not specifically prohibited by the criminal law, but rather by some other form, either civil or administrative law. White-collar crime is a relatively new concept, having first achieved recognition in 1939 by sociologist Edwin H. Sutherland. Despite its short life, white-collar crime has quickly grown to its present

status of being a major focus of the Department of Justice. Sutherland's definition of white-collar crime concentrated on the offender and the individual social status of the person as opposed to the criminal offense involved. White-collar crime has been subject to varying definitions, although a definition that focuses on the offense rather than the offender is prevalent today. The Department of Justice in early 1977 stated that "white-collar offenses shall constitute those classes of nonviolent illegal activities that principally involve traditional notions of deceit, deception, concealment, manipulation, breach of trust, subterfuge, or illegal circumvention." The FBI has a similar working definition of white-collar offenses: "those crimes that are committed by nonphysical means to avoid payment or loss of money or to obtain business or personal advantage where success depends on guile or concealment."

Even when one adopts an offense approach to defining white-collar crime, the scope of the term remains uncertain in that there is no list of included and excluded offenses. The Bureau of Justice Statistics uses five categories of crimes for comparison statistics, including fraud, forgery, embezzlement, counterfeiting and certain regulatory offenses. In contrast to these included offenses, white-collar crime excludes offenses that are violent, property or public order crimes. Thus traditionally, some crimes that would not meet the definition of white-collar crime are homicides, burglaries, rapes, robberies, assaults, drug offenses, and arson.

There are no set categories of offenses that make up white-collar crime, although there are many federal statutes that are relevant. Some of these federal offenses are not limited solely to white-collar crime, but have been used to prosecute street and property crimes as well. These statutes are often used for white-collar criminality because of the broad interpretation given to them by the courts. For example, many white-collar offenses are prosecuted as mail fraud (18 U.S.C. 1341), wire fraud (18 U.S.C. 1343), conspiracy (18 U.S.C. 371), racketeering (18 U.S.C. 1961–1963), bribery (18 U.S.C. 201), false statements (18 U.S.C. 1001), obstruction of justice (18 U.S.C. 1501–1517), and tax crimes (18 U.S.C. 7201–7206).

There are other statutes that are used almost exclusively for white-collar offenses. For example, criminal acts involving bank fraud (18 U.S.C. 1344) and false claims (18 U.S.C. 287) usually fit the white-collar crime category. White-collar crime includes corporate offenses and most offenses involving public corruption. Many white-collar crime prosecutions have employed statutes relating to securities fraud and antitrust violations. More recently criminal acts prohibited by environmental, health and computer laws have also been created at both the federal and state levels.

The first known documents dealing with contracts of land sales and other business transactions have been dated back to the Hammurabi Code of Babylon in 2400 BC. In English law, the Carrier Case (1473) provided the foundation for the modern law of thefts relating to business. Instead of transporting bales of wool from one place to another, the carrier stole the contents. At this time there was no legal difference between possession and ownership, a distinction that was needed given the emerging class of traders and merchants. The Carrier case prompted the passage of a law that defined and prohibited employee theft, embezzlement, and related acts.

Even though laws have been in existence prohibiting forms of white-collar crimes, many were not used until the end of the 19th century, when the U.S. Congress enacted laws regulating and criminalizing a wide range of business activities. The 1890 Sherman Anti-Trust Act was one of the first administrative laws used in the fight against white-collar crime. It was created to fight trusts (legal entities or holding companies that were able to fix prices and control production and create monopolies) and prohibit restraint of trade. With the growth of industrial capitalism, antitrust legislation was passed in other English-speaking countries. Canada passed its Anti-Combines Act in 1889 and Australia passed the Australian Industries Act in 1906. It was not until 1948 when Great Britain enacted the Monopolies and Restrictive Practices Act.

Other regulatory laws that are frequently used in the U.S. are the Occupational Safety and Health laws and environmental protection laws. Very little substantial legal protection for workers existed before 1970. Most organizations blamed the workers for accidents or the "nature of the work." During the 1960s this started to change and in 1970 the Occupational Safety and Health Administration (OSHA) was created. Also in the 1960s, environmental groups were lobbying for action after a series of environmental disasters were featured in the news media. The Environmental Protection Agency (EPA) was established in 1970.

Laws and regulations are a major tool in protecting society. Congress passes laws that govern the U.S. To put those laws into effect, Congress authorizes certain government agencies, including the EPA and OSHA, to create and enforce regulations. When a bill is passed by Congress and signed by the president, the U.S. House of Representatives standardizes the text of the law and publishes it in the U.S. Code. But laws often do not include all the details. The U.S. Code would not tell you, for example, what the speed limit is in front of your house. In order to make the laws work on a day-to-day level, Congress authorizes certain government agencies to create regulations.

Regulations set specific rules about what is and is not legal. An authorized agency, such as the EPA, decides that a regulation may be needed. The agency researches it and, if necessary, proposes a regulation. The proposal is listed in the Federal Register so that members of the public can consider it and send their comments to the agency. The agency considers all the comments, revises the regulation accordingly, and issues a final rule. At each stage in the process, the agency publishes a notice in the Federal Register. These notices include the original proposal, requests for public comment, notices about meetings (open to the public) where the proposal will be discussed, and the text of the final regulation. Once a regulation is completed and has been printed in the Federal Register as a final rule, it is "codified" by being published in the *Code of Federal Regulations* (CFR).

The CFR is the official record of all regulations created by the federal government. It is divided into 50 volumes, called titles, each of which focuses on a particular area. Almost all regulations dealing with criminal behavior, including white-collar and corporate crimes, appear in Title 18. Once the regulation is in effect, the government agency then works to help Americans and businesses comply with the law and to enforce it.

Legislative lawmaking is a complex process that may reflect a variety of influences. New laws need to ensure the general public welfare while protecting the long-term economic interests of business in a free market society. Businesses may be very supportive of new laws but only if they do not affect their profits. Individuals and corporations can influence regulatory policy not only through pressure on legislation and the administration of justice but also on how these regulations are interpreted by those who enforce them. Businesses can persuade regulators to enforce certain laws and not others. Rules need to have meanings applied to them and this is a complicated process. Both the regulators and the regulated help to define these meanings.

Most of the numerous antitrust, consumer protection, environmental protection, and worker safety laws were controversial issues at the time of their enactments. Many powerful interest groups tried to influence the content of these bills and worked to prevent their passage, but grassroots consumer movements helped to promulgate new laws in spite of the various business interest groups. The ratification of a new law, even if it is a strong one, is not the end of a successful reform movement. The enforcement process plays a critical role in determining whether or not the reforms remain symbolic or result in significant social change.

Until the 1970s, civil and administrative laws comprised the major mechanisms for the social control of white-collar crime, with the criminal law and criminal justice system involved as an avenue of last resort. Widely publicized scandals involving the activities of businesses of government (e.g., Watergate) led the FBI to place white-collar crime on top of its list of priorities.

A prosecutor needs a statutory base for indicting white-collar offenders. There has been a growth of statutes added to the federal criminal code that specifically pertain to white-collar criminal conduct. This has been most noticeable in provisions added to combat financial frauds.

White-collar criminal offenses often can be prosecuted by both the federal and state systems. For example,

RICO (the Racketeer Influenced and Corrupt Organization Act) uses state-defined crimes (e.g., bribery or narcotics violations) as a justification for racketeering charges (18 U.S.C., 1961). Predicate acts could have been prosecuted separately as state crimes. Procedural considerations often play a factor in deciding whether the state, federal, or both jurisdictions should prosecute the criminal conduct. In addition to overlapping prosecutions within the federal and state systems, white-collar offenses often find themselves the subject of parallel proceedings in regulatory bodies and civil courts.

White-collar offenses, like other crimes, are subject to the general principles of criminal law. These principles emanate from the U.S. Constitution, federal and state statutes, and court interpretations. They are affected in some instances by the procedures provided by administrative regulations and rulings. General principles relative to *actus reus*, *mens rea* and causation as well as the procedural and evidentiary issues that surface in a white-collar crime case are governed by the same standards that apply to other crime cases. Thus, constitutional rights, such as the right to trial by jury, the right to counsel, the right to a speedy and public trial, the right to be secure from unreasonable searches and seizures, and the right against excessive bail, fully apply to white-collar offenders.

In order to understand the law and white-collar crime it is important to distinguish between occupational and corporate crimes. Occupational crimes are committed on behalf of an individual, usually in the course of one's occupation. Corporate crimes are committed by, or on behalf of, a corporation. Historically, there have not been many criminal laws that apply to corporate crime because crime has been seen as an individual wrong. Social control and the criminal law traditionally have focused on the occupational crimes of individuals (e.g., fraud and embezzlement), not the behavior of organizations. When applying the criminal law to corporate crime the issue of liability and punishment is crucial.

The legal construct of a "juristic person" was invented around the twelfth century to recognize the existence of organizational entities, although the application of criminal liability to organizations took several centuries to evolve. The initial common law view was that a corporation could not be held criminally liable, although the individual members of the corporation could. Lacking a mind, the corporation could not form the *mens rea* (criminal intent) necessary for criminality. Not having a physical body, there was no *actus reus* (criminal act). Additionally, even if convicted of an offense, the corporation could not be imprisoned for the crime.

Not until 1842 did the English courts decide that a strictly commercial corporation could be held criminally liable for failure to perform a legal duty. Corporate criminal liability for affirmative actions was not imposed until the tort theory of vicarious liability was applied to corporations. The development toward corporate criminal liability emerged in response to corporate violations involving acts of omission with respect to regulatory offenses. As these strict liability offenses did not require a *mens rea*, lacked an affirmative act, and had punishment in the form of fines, the acceptance of corporate criminal liability for these crimes was in keeping with the accepted doctrine.

Eventually, corporate criminal liability expanded beyond the strict liability arena and grew to encompass crimes with an intent element, as legislators included within statutes provisions for the specific application of the offense to corporations. Pivotal in this development of corporate criminal liability was the U.S. Supreme Court ruling in *New York Central and Hudson River Railroad v. U.S.* (212 U.S. 481, 1909). The U.S. Supreme Court in 1909 emphasized that if corporations were immunized from criminal prosecution because of a theory that corporations cannot commit crimes, Congress would lose its ability to control corporate misconduct. Corporate criminal liability has played a significant role in the prosecution of environmental crimes and was used to prosecute the Ford Motor Company in 1978 for reckless homicide for the death of three teenage girls who were killed in their Ford Pinto when it exploded. Ford was found not guilty, but this opened the door to future corporate criminal cases. Prosecutors were more successful in a 1985 case in Illinois, where Film Recovery Systems was found guilty of involuntary manslaughter for causing the death of one of its workers.

Although there has been an increasing prosecution rate for white-collar offenses in the past decade, an enormous amount of latitude remains with prosecutors as to whether a criminal action should proceed and what charges should be used in the prosecution. Criminal prosecutions of corporations rely heavily on the introduction of documentary evidence on the activities and motives of corporate officers, directors, and employees such as letters, internal memoranda, and financial records. Corporations are complex, as are their books and records with which prosecutors must often establish a case.

Corporations have talented legal staffs to help them make the task of prosecution more complicated. The complexity of science is itself an impediment to criminal prosecution. Because it is based on probabilities, scientific evidence concerning such matters as pollution, product safety, and occupational safety violations is often uncertain. Proving that a particular action caused a specific result beyond a reasonable doubt is frequently impossible. Corporate criminal prosecutions are lengthy and sometimes ineffective; therefore, administrative and civil laws are relied upon more heavily.

American regulatory agencies produce federal and state administrative law. Regulatory agencies have wide power, to enact, interpret, and enforce the rules. Administrative courts have become an attractive alternative to prosecutors for four main reasons: the burden of proof is lower (preponderance of evidence); no jury is involved; administrative judges understand the cases; and there are large penalties that can be assessed with relative ease.

Currently, the fight against white-collar crime still remains largely in the hands of administrative and civil proceedings even though many regulatory agencies have added criminal provisions. In the wake of savings and loan bankruptcies and scandals, oil spills, stock frauds, and major industrial plant explosions, questions have arisen regarding the efficacy of reliance on administrative and civil sanctions to regulate white-collar and corporate misconduct. New laws that impose tougher penalties on white-collar criminals might well deter some potential offenders. More punitive federal sentencing guidelines have resulted in more white-collar crime convictions—8050 in 1994, up 6% in 24 months. The debate over whether to criminalize certain types of white-collar and corporate behavior is one of the most important social and legal issues facing the U.S.

DEBRA E. ROSS

## References and Further Reading

Blankenship, M., Ed., *Understanding Corporate Criminality,* New York, Garland Publishing, Inc., 1995.

Friedrichs, D.O., *Trusted Criminals: White Collar Crime in Contemporary Society,* Belmont, CA, Wadsworth Publishing Company, 1996.

Lofquist, W.D., Cohen, M.A. and Rabe, G.A., Eds., *Debating Corporate Crime,* Cincinnati, OH, ACJS or Anderson Monograph Series, 1997.

Rosoff, S.M., Pontell H.N. and Tillman, R., *Profit Without Honor: White Collar crime and the Looting of America,* Upper Saddle River, NJ, Prentice Hall, 1998.

Schlegel, K. and Weisburd, D., Eds., *White-Collar Crime Reconsidered,* Boston, MA, Northeastern University Press, 1992.

Shover, N. and Wright, J.P., Eds., *Crime of Privilege: Readings in White-Collar Crime,* New York, Oxford University Press, 2001.

Sutherland, E., *White Collar Crime: The Uncut Version,* New Haven, CT, Yale University Press, 1949/1983.

Tyler, T.R., *Why People Obey the Law,* New Haven, CT, Yale University Press, 1990.

Vaughan, D., *Controlling Unlawful Organizational Behavior: Social Structure and Corporate Misconduct,* Chicago, The University of Chicago Press, 1983.

Wells, C., *Corporations and Criminal Responsibility,* Oxford, Clarendon Press, 1993.

*See also* **Bribery; Forgery; Fraud; Obstruction of Justice; White-Collar Crime: Enforcement Strategies**

# White-Collar Crime: Theories

As is the case with conventional crime, many approaches have been usefully applied in the search for a better understanding of white-collar crime. Variants of differential association, anomie strain, control, rational choice, and integrated theories have been proposed for white-collar crime. These theories have been based on a combination of individual, organizational, cultural and structural variables. The variable or set of variables that is most appropriate for explanatory purposes depends in large measure on the unit of analysis. For some theories of white-collar crime the unit of analysis is individual behavior, whereas for other theories the unit of analysis is corporate or organizational behavior.

At present there is little consensus on how best to explain white-collar crime. Empirical work in this area is difficult to conduct, and researchers rarely have access to the financial resources made available to those who study traditional forms of street crime. Many of the theories to be reviewed here have not been subjected to extensive empirical scrutiny. Thus, their empirical validity remains unknown.

The person most closely associated with the concept of white-collar crime, Edwin H. Sutherland, theorized that the same general processes that cause other sorts of crime also cause white-collar crime. He argued that individual involvement in white-collar crime comes about as a result of differential association. The theory of differential association postulates that "criminal behavior is learned in association with those who define such criminal behavior favorably and in isolation from those who define it unfavorably, and that a person in an appropriate situation engages in white-collar crime if, and only if, the weight of definitions favorable exceeds the weight of the unfavorable definitions."

Sutherland thought that attitudes and cultural orientations that define illegal business behavior in favorable terms are pervasive throughout the business world. Newcomers to the world of business are socialized to accept these attitudes and orientations. They learn how to commit certain types of offenses, and how to rationalize these offenses so that in the offender's mind they are seen as acceptable, ordinary, and necessary business practices. Thus, a white-collar criminal culture permeates the world of business and is passed from one generation of executives and employees to the next.

Sutherland thought that the weight of definitions favorable to the violation of law exceeds the weight of unfavorable definitions because of isolation and social disorganization. Members of the business community are isolated from definitions unfavorable to their law violations because the government, entertainment industry, and news media have traditionally equated crime with the lower socioeconomic classes. Hence, businesspeople rarely are confronted with unfavorable definitions of their behavior, and they are unlikely to experience criminal labeling.

An often overlooked dimension of Sutherland's theory of white-collar crime is his argument that white-collar crime flourishes when communities are socially disorganized. He identified two types of social disorganization: "anomie" refers to a lack of standards regarding behavior in specific areas of social action; "conflict of standards" refers to conflict between social groups with reference to specific practices. Sutherland thought that anomie regarding business practices is widespread for a couple of reasons. First, business behavior is complex, technical, and difficult to observe. Second, because the U.S. was founded on the ideals of competition and free enterprise, the public is ambivalent about government control of business activity. Taken together, these factors have prevented the development of a strong public consensus on the wrongfulness and harmfulness of shady business practices. Lacking clear signals of concern from the public, law enforcers are not vigorous in their pursuit of business misconduct.

Also mitigating against the control of business misconduct is an enduring conflict of standards between the business community and other interests in society. According to Sutherland, the business community is tightly organized against regulatory control of business practices. It always vigorously contests the efforts of government, consumer groups, labor unions, and environmental organizations to expand regulatory controls and to criminalize harmful business practices. The continual conflict between the business community and those who would control it undermines the development of a strong public moral consensus against misconduct.

A strain variation of anomie theory was developed by Robert Merton to explain why some societies have higher crime rates than others. In a thoughtful effort to extend Merton's anomie strain theory to corporate deviance, Nikkos Passas theorizes that societies based on capitalistic economic principles have cultural and structural contradictions that promote widespread corporate deviance. Passas argues that a cultural emphasis on wealth and material success permeates all levels of the class structure and shapes both individual and corporate behavior. Although business corporations can have multiple goals, in capitalist economies the dominant goal is always profit maximization. Corporations compete with one another to maximize profits in a game that is never ending. There is no obvious stopping point at which enough is enough. Weak competitors may fall by the way side, but new ones emerge to take their place. So, even business leaders must always worry about potential competition. Hence, because of the competitive structure of capitalist economies, corporations are continually under pressure to do better. Coupled with the cultural themes of success and endless striving is a cultural uncertainty and confusion about where the line between acceptable and unacceptable business behavior should be drawn. In this anomic environment, there is strong and constant pressure to engage in corporate deviance to achieve profit goals, and corporations often succumb to this pressure. In Passas' view, corporate crime and deviance are the unavoidable by-products of capitalistic economies.

Edward Gross takes a similar view of corporate deviance, but he focuses more on the culture and structure of organizations rather than that of society as a whole. Gross argues that organizations are inherently criminogenic, because they are goal directed entities and their performance is evaluated according to their effectiveness in achieving their goals. Organizations continually confront competition and uncertainty in working toward goals. The emphasis on performance combined with competition and uncertainty creates pressure to break rules and to achieve goals at all costs.

Gross hypothesizes that variation in organizational crime results from several sources. First, the degree of accountability of an organization or an organizational subunit is directly related to the likelihood of rule-breaking. Organizations and their subunits that are held accountable to specific criteria by which success in goal attainment is judged are under greater pressure to perform than organizations whose success in goal attainment is not as strictly judged. Second, pressure to engage in organizational crime is directly related to the objectivity of performance measures. Business corporations can be judged and compared against one another in terms of their profitability. Hence, their relative level of success in meeting this goal can be easily determined by others. Third, within organizations, the more a subunit interacts with the organizational environment the more likely it is to deviate to achieve goals because of the uncertainty generated by the environment. Finally, pressure to engage in organizational crime is inversely related to goal displacement. If an organization that is threatened by lack of success in achieving its manifest goals can shift to other more attainable goals, then the pressure to deviate is lessened. The ability to displace goals is probably less available to private and for profit organizations than it is to nonprofit and governmental organizations. Altogether, accountability, objectivity of performance measures, environmental uncertainty, and flexibility in goal displacement influence the degree of pressure that organizations are under to deviate.

According to Gross, the individuals who are most likely to rise to the top of the organizational hierarchy are "organizational strainers." Strainers are ambitious, shrewd, and morally flexible. They are characterized by a strong desire for occupational achievement, an ability to spot patterns of organizational opportunity, and a willingness to treat organizational goals as their own and to change their moral stance as the situation demands. Organizations, thus, tend to be led by individuals for whom personal success is closely tied to the organization's success in meeting performance goals. Hence, they are especially susceptible to the emphasis on successful performance and to pressures to deviate in pursuit of success.

Another avenue of approach toward explaining white-collar crime takes control theory as its starting point. There are several variants of control theory, but all have in common the idea that deviance is natural and must be controlled by external social forces or internal predispositions. Travis Hirschi's social bond theory is the most well known version of control theory. Social bond theory starts with the premise that delinquent acts are more likely to occur when an individual's bond to society is weak or broken. The social bond is composed of four interrelated elements: attachment to others, commitment to conventional lines of action, involvement in conventional activities, and belief in society's common value system. To the extent that these elements are strong, they restrain individuals from involvement in criminal behavior.

Although control theory is most often applied in the context of juvenile delinquency or ordinary street offending, James R. Lasley argues that it can also be used to explain white-collar crime by corporate executives. To do so requires that the elements of the social bond be reconceptualized within the context of the corporation and its executives. It is the strength of the executive's bond to the corporation, as opposed to society in general, that regulates involvement in executive white-collar crime. Lasley proposes four theorems regarding executive white-collar crime that are straightforward translations of Hirschi's basic propositions regarding juvenile delinquency and the social bond. First, the stronger an executive is attached to other executives, coworkers, and the corporation, the less likely the executive is to commit white-collar crime. Second, the more strongly an executive is committed to corporate lines of action, the lower the frequency of executive white-collar crime. Third, the more strongly an executive is involved in corporate activity, the lower the frequency of white-collar offending. Fourth, the more strongly an executive believes in the rules of the corporation, the lower the frequency of white-collar offending. Lasley tested his theory with data drawn from a survey of 521 executives employed by a multinational automobile company. He found support for all of his theorems.

In the late 1980s and early 1990s Travis Hirschi and Michael Gottfredson developed a new version of control theory that has been called self-control theory. The basic premise of self-control theory is that crime and other forms of deviance result from the combination of low self-control and criminal opportunities. Low self-control is conceived of as a behavioral predisposition to pursue short-term self-interest with little regard for the long-term consequences of one's actions or for the rights and feelings of other people. One's level of self-control is assumed to be established early in life and to remain relatively constant thereafter. Persons with low self-control are more likely to take advantage of criminal opportunities than persons with higher levels of self-control.

Hirschi and Gottfredson argue that self-control theory is a general theory of crime and that it applies to white-collar crime. Indeed, they argue that the pursuit of special theories of white-collar crime is misguided. Based on their theory of self-control, they contend that white-collar crime should be relatively rare compared to street crimes because persons with low self-control are unlikely to succeed in white-collar type occupations. Hence, they have limited opportunities to commit white-collar offenses. Conversely, persons who are likely to succeed in white-collar occupations have high levels of self-control and hence are not likely to take advantage of the criminal opportunities that their occupations provide them. The few white-collar persons who do engage in white-collar crime are assumed to have less self-control than their similarly situated counterparts, though they may have more self-control than ordinary street criminals. The ideas that white-collar crime is rare and that it can be explained by the same control based factors as other crimes have been vigorously contested by many white-collar crime scholars.

Another theoretical perspective that has been applied to white-collar crime is rational choice theory. Rational choice theory assumes that all actors are self-interested and make decisions about whether to engage in criminal or conventional behavior according to a calculus of costs and benefits. In simplified terms, the theory posits that rational actors will choose to engage in crime rather than noncrime when the perceived net benefits of crime (that is, benefits minus costs) are larger than the perceived net benefits of noncrime. Both benefits and costs have subjective and objective dimensions. A subjective cost of crime might be feelings of guilt or fear of apprehension, whereas a subjective benefit of crime would be the thrill and excitement of getting away with something illegal. An objective cost of crime would be formal punishment by the criminal justice system, whereas an objective benefit would be the gains made from the illegal act.

Like other traditional criminological theories, the rational choice perspective has been applied most often to ordinary street offenders. Raymond Paternoster and Sally S. Simpson, however, have explicated a rational choice theory of the decision to commit corporate crime. Their theory is a subjective utility theory of offending. It focuses on benefits and costs as they are subjectively perceived by individuals. Hence, their rational choice theory is aimed at individual decision makers rather than the corporation as a whole. According to their theory, the individual's decision to commit a corporate crime or violate a regulatory rule involves a series of factors. To calculate the potential costs of corporate crime, actors subjectively estimate the certainty and severity of formal legal sanctions, the certainty and severity of informal sanctions, and the certainty and importance of loss of self-respect. Actors also consider the benefits of corporate crime that include the perceived benefits of noncompliance (that is, higher profits, greater market share, or some other organizationally relevant goal) and the perceived cost of rule compliance (that is, avoidance of expenses associated with complying with regulatory standards). Paternoster and Simpson argue that in addition to these standard rational choice variables, the likelihood of offending is also influenced by the strength of the actor's moral beliefs, whether the actor perceives rule enforcers as legitimate and fair, the characteristics of the potential criminal event, and the person's prior history of offending.

Criminologists have begun to explore ways to integrate standard criminological theories, such as differential association, anomie strain, and control theories, in hopes of providing more comprehensive explanations of street crime. John Braithwaite has extended this line of thought to white-collar crime and organizational crime. He argues that to understand the causes of organizational crime, we need to integrate the insights of anomie strain, labeling, subculture, and control theories. From anomie strain theory, he draws the premise that failure to achieve highly valued goals, such as material success, creates pressure or strain to deviate. To relieve strain actors, including corporate actors, may resort to crime as an alternate means of achieving success. Whether actors do resort to crime depends in part on the availability of illegitimate means for achieving the blocked goal. Illegitimate means are made available through deviant subcultures. With respect to corporate crime, business subcultures can transmit knowledge of how organizations and their leaders may successfully violate the law. In addition, deviant subcultures may attempt to force members to conform to the subcultures values and expectations. Thus, strain, the availability of subculturally endorsed illegitimate means, and enforced conformity to deviant subcultural values act as criminogenic forces that foster corporate crime.

Opposition to these criminogenic forces comes from social controls within the organization and from shaming imposed on offenders by the larger society. Drawing from control theory, Braithwaite argues that corporations can reduce the likelihood that their members will violate the law by strengthening internal controls against illegal behavior. This can be accomplished when organizational leaders promote prosocial values, socialize all corporate members to these values, and create strong internal control units to monitor corporate compliance with the law.

Braithwaite introduces the idea of differential shaming to explain how shaming by society may either promote or retard corporate crime. Shaming, which in the case of business corporations is carried out primarily by regulatory agencies, may be either stigmatizing or reintegrative. When actors are stigmatized, they are treated as outcasts and their involvement in deviance is treated as an indication of a true deviant inner character. Reintegrative shaming, on the other hand, is focused on the evil of the deed rather than the evil of the actor. Those who administer the shame attempt to maintain bonds of respect with the offender, and they try to reintegrate the offender back into the social whole after shaming is terminated. Braithwaite argues that stigmatizing shaming tends to create resistance to change in actors and to push them ever more deeply into their deviant subculture. Hence, stigmatizing shaming is counterproductive. It actually promotes rather than deters corporate crime. Reintegrative shaming deters crime because it clearly announces the wrongfulness of the act but then attempts to make the actor feel like a respected member of society, a member who has a vested interest in conforming to society's rules.

Except for control theory, most theories of white-collar crime implicitly or explicitly assume that the pursuit of individual material success or some kind of business advancement is the core motivation behind white-collar crime. White-collar offenders are assumed to be greedy and egocentric. But recent research suggests another motivational route to white-collar crime. White-collar crime may result not only from the drive for material success but also out of a fear of losing what one already has. Some individuals may become involved in white-collar offenses because they fear that if they do not they are at risk of losing their station in life. For people accustomed to high social status and the material comforts of a middle class lifestyle, the prospect of losing it all because of a downturn in the economy or a miscalculation in a business transaction may provoke strong pressure to deviate in defense. For example, someone who runs a small business may be quite willing to abide by the law in return for a comfortable but not extravagant standard of living. However, if the business is threatened by competition or a downturn in the economy, the same individual may feel that the only option is to break the law in order to survive. Thus, fear of failure as well as the drive for success may drive individuals to engage in white-collar crime.

MICHAEL L. BENSON

## References and Further Reading

Braithwaite, J., Criminological Theory and Organizational Crime, *Justice Quarterly,* 6 (1989).
Clinard, M.B. and Yeager, P.C., *Corporate Crime,* New York, The Free Press, 1980.
Coleman, J.W., *The Criminal Elite: Understanding White-Collar Crime,* New York, St. Martin's Press, 1998.
Croall, H., *White Collar Crime: Criminal Justice and Criminology,* Philadelphia, PA, Open University Press, 1992.
Green, G.S., *Occupational Crime,* 2nd ed., Chicago, IL, Nelson-Hall Publishers, 1997.
Hirschi, T. and Gottfredson, M., Causes of white-collar crime, *Criminology,* 25 (1987).
Lasley, J.R., Toward a control theory of white-collar offending, *Journal of Quantitative Criminology,* 4 (1988).
Passas, N., Anomie and corporate deviance, *Contemporary Crises,* 14 (1990).
Paternoster, R. and Simpson, S.S., A rational choice theory of corporate crime, in Clarke, R.V. and Felson, M., Eds., *Routine Activity and Rational Choice,* Vol. 5, New Brunswick, NJ, Transaction Publishers, 1993.
Sutherland, E.H., *White-Collar Crime: The Uncut Version,* New Haven, CT, Yale University Press, 1983.
Weisburd, D., Wheeler, S., Waring, E. and Bode, N., *Crimes of the Middle Classes: White-Collar Offenders in the Federal Courts,* New Haven, CT, Yale University Press, 1991.

*See also* **Sutherland, Edwin H.; White-Collar Crime: Definitions**

# Wilson, James Q.

James Q. Wilson may be one of the more influential individuals in the study of crime and public policy, and this is particularly noteworthy as he has no formal training in sociology, criminology or criminal justice. He entered in through the back door. It is also significant that Wilson, a prolific writer in crime and justice, "has rarely been published in refereed criminology journals" (Delisi, 2003, 661).

Wilson, trained as a political scientist, became interested in the question of crime because of citizen responses to a survey where they indicated that crime and disorder were the most important problems. Running contrary to what he and his colleagues believed would be the response, this response prompted him to begin looking at the problem of crime and criminal justice. He entered the study quite by accident, but as he says, "you can't just touch the crime issue—it sticks with you forever" (personal communication, August 18, 2003). Wilson's work has been influential in a number of areas, including policing, urban politics, crime, morality, and character building, to name a few (Delisi, 2003).

With Wilson's enormous body of work, one would think (certainly this author thought) that "Broken Windows" would have been the work he was most proud of. After all, this article changed, in many ways, how the police go about their business. It was influential in William Bratton's *Turnaround* of crime in New York City and has been often cited and quoted. However it is *Crime and Human Nature* that he is most proud of. Of his work with Richard Herrnstein, Wilson said in 1988, the scholarly collaboration with Herrnstein "became the most rewarding intellectual period in my life" (Wilson, 1988, 14). This book, according to Wilson, "opened up the question (of crime causation) so that the partial answers that various disciplines have typically given to the question, 'what causes crime' are no longer satisfactory" (Wilson, 1988, 15). As Delisi notes, "*Crime and Human Nature* is a call for criminologists to quit denying that individual level constitutional variables are meaningful causes of criminal and noncriminal behavior" (Delisi, 2003, 667).

Having moved (somewhat) away from crime, Wilson is nevertheless still looking at crime. Of late, he has been looking at it (and man's behavior generally) from a moral perspective, looking at why most people do not commit crime. His books *On Character* and *The Moral Sense* attempt to identify and make sense in the decision making of people. This is reflected in, "the ongoing irrationality practiced in the nation's criminal courts" (Delisi, 2003, 668). Wilson believes that common sense should be more often used than such concepts as disadvantage and inequality, and "the general assassination of the concept of personal responsibility" (Delisi, 2003, 668). He also wonders if religion can have an effect on crime, what happens to ex-inmates, and how to understand better how children growing up can have the probability of crime reduced (personal communication, August 18, 2003). Wilson believes the family is the most important social institution (Delisi, 2003) and wonders how to reach men and young boys so as to get them on the right path, and provide young boys (especially) with the "right background" (personal communication). These thoughts are discussed in his book *The Marriage Problem*.

Despite the influence of Wilson and his many writings, as Delisi notes, "Wilson is criticized, rather than praised, by many in the criminological community. Those who criticize him often allude to Wilson's conservatism *as if to suggest that the advocacy of a conservative criminological imagination is itself wrong*" (2003, 669, emphasis in the original). Does Wilson's conservatism reduce his influence or his observations? It is quite the contrary. Again, Delisi, "many of Wilson's more controversial statements are certainly supported by empirical data" (2003, 670). Perhaps it is his conservatism (the greater part of the academy being more liberal), perhaps it is his willingness to engage "unpretty criminological realities directly" (Delisi, 2003, 671), perhaps it is his ability to make complex ideas simple or his ability to translate or look for the application of his work. Whatever it is, James Q. Wilson has been one of the most influential writers on crime and public policy the study of crime, criminals and criminology has seen. His ideas have seen the test of time and manage to retain their logic and applicability. That is a legacy to be proud of and makes him and his work worthy of study.

JEFFREY P. RUSH

## Biography

Born May 27, 1931. Education: University of Redlands, A.B., 1952; University of Chicago A.M., 1957, Ph.D., 1959. Shattuck Professor of Government, Harvard University 1961–1986; Chairman, White House Task Force on Crime, 1966; Chairman, National Advisory Commission on Drug Abuse Prevention, 1972–1973; Member, President's Foreign Intelligence Advisory Board, 1985–1990; Chairman, Council of Academic Advisors of the American Enterprise Institute; Member, American Academy of Arts and Sciences; Fellow, American Philosophical Society; James Madison Award for Distinguished Scholarship from the American Political Science Association; President, American Political Science Association, 1991–1992; James Collins Professor of Management and Public Policy, UCLA, 1986–1997 (retitred).

## Selected Works

Wilson, J.Q. and Herrnstein, R.J. (1985). *Crime and Human Nature: The Definitive Study of the Causes of Crime,* New York, Simon and Schuster.

Wilson, J.Q. and Kelling, G.L. (1982). Broken windows: The police and neighborhood safety, *Atlantic Monthly,* 249, 29–38.

## References and Further Reading

Bratton, W. with Nobler, P. (1998). *Turnaround,* New York, Random House.

Delisi, M. (2003). Conservatism and common sense: The criminological career of James Q. Wilson, *Justice Quarterly,* 20(3), 661 674.

# Witchcraft and Heresy

Stated in relatively objective, behavioral terms, witchcraft refers to individual and group behavior intended to influence natural events through the use of special knowledge of supernatural forces, or hidden spiritual forces governing nature. An individual who regularly engages in such activity and adopts an identity based on that practice is a witch.

Definitions of witchcraft have varied over history as a reflection of the ability of various groups to "demonize" such activity and to differentiate it from dominant religious doctrine. For example, until the 15th century, the Roman Catholic Church's position on witchcraft was that the practices attributed to witches were fantasies because witches could not wield such supernatural powers. Witchcraft was a sin, but it was not heresy. Heresy refers to beliefs or practices condemned and prohibited as ecclesiastical crimes by the church. By the end of the 15th century, the Church had changed its position, redefining witchcraft practices as activities carried out with the assistance of Satan, constituting a grave threat to Christianity. A book on witchcraft by two Dominican Inquisitors (*The Malleus Maleficarum*), published in 1496, reinforced the transformation of witchcraft into the activities of heretical witches who constituted as serious a threat to the Church as other groups that the Church had successfully defeated. Between 50,000–100,000 people, mostly women, were executed as heretic witches during the 16th and 17th centuries, and several times that number were prosecuted for such activities.

The witch trials and executions in Salem, Massachusetts, in 1692 were one of the last major witch hunts targeting witchcraft as heresy.

The categorization of witchcraft as heresy "demonized" a wide range of ordinary folk practices, defining them as indicators of a more serious and hidden threat to Christian society. Secretive practices that had been attributed to earlier heretic groups, such as the cannibalism of Christian children, sexual orgies, group worship of Satan in secret meetings, the invocation of demons, poisoning and spreading disease, became the secretive practices of witches. Coerced confessions of such activities and of secret pacts with Satan legitimized the demonological interpretation.

A considerable volume of historical research suggests that very few of the people charged with witchcraft could be considered to be practicing witches. However, once the official conception that certain behaviors or practices could be an indication of a far more diabolic threat was established, women with "folk" knowledge relevant to disease, health and childbirth were at risk should anything go wrong in providing such aid. Moreover, accusations of witchcraft could emerge out of conflicts among individuals, families and factions within villages or in adjacent communities. Women with histories of conflict, or who violated expectations for proper female conversation and interaction, were vulnerable to witchcraft charges. Accusations could proliferate rapidly, especially when torture was allowed, and witch hunts often ended when accusations began to spread to people who did not fit the common stereotype, or had sufficient power and resources to challenge such accusations.

Several characteristics of early modern societies have been proposed to explain the rise and demise of the hunt for heretic witches. Major witch hunts often coincided with outbreaks of mysterious and devastating disease and research has supported a close correspondence between disease and the intensity of witch hunts, including the timing of the rise and demise of early modern witch hunts. Major shifts in the ratio of men to women may have been a factor. An excess of women following wars and other crises could (1) increase competition and conflicts among women in the pursuit of husbands, (2) increase the visibility of women who were threats to male power as a result of inheritance and (3) increase the number of women in precarious economic positions where they might have to rely on fear of witchcraft to solicit aid. The intensity of witch hunts appears to have been moderated by actual warfare in an area, although the local problems generated by war could result in surges in its aftermath.

Among a variety of explanations for the end of the early modern witch craze, scholars have proposed the increased regulation of local justice by central political authorities, the demise of torture, new standards of evidence, increases in legal representation, moderation of religious conflicts and a decline in epidemic disease. In addition, the emergence of science brought an increased understanding of the natural origins of disease, weather, and other phenomena that had been attributed to demonological forces by religious and political elites.

Belief in witches and the ability of some people to manipulate demonic forces remained widespread (and is still common today), but wars against heretical witchcraft, sustained by Christian ecclesiastical and political authorities for at least two centuries, were largely abandoned by the 18th century. By the late 17th or early 18th century, criminal prosecution of witches had been countered by prosecutions for false accusations, slander and vigilante violence in pursuit of witches. Attacks by villagers on people viewed as responsible for misfortune because of spells and other forms of witchcraft are still occurring in Africa and other nations, but such vigilante activity violates formal laws in such societies.

Interest in witchcraft and neopagan religions has been growing in Europe and in the U.S., and adherents to Wicca, or "The Craft," refer to the early modern witch trials as "The Burning Times." They interpret the burning times as an attempt to suppress the adherents to an ancient belief system. Although some witchcraft scholars have proposed that the witch craze was directed at members of real "witch cults," that view has been criticized by numerous historians. On the other hand, because many "folk" practices do have pagan roots, the demonization of magic, sorcery and witchcraft was an attack on behavior and practices interpreted as pagan and, therefore, Satanic.

Contemporary Wiccans challenge the tendency to lump Satanism as a contemporary religious belief system together with witchcraft. Wiccans do not embrace the Christian belief in Satan and do not worship such a being. The Council of American Witches states that "A Witch seeks to control the forces within him or herself that make life possible in order to live wisely and well, without harm to others, and in harmony with Nature" (Adler, 1986, 103). Many Wiccans honor female and male spiritual forces that they believe can be experienced through ritual and prayer. Despite obvious overlaps in religious imagery between Wicca and more prominent religious belief systems, their beliefs and practices remain in conflict with church doctrines in the Christian tradition, and are occasionally attacked and condemned by representatives of the most fundamentalist denominations.

GARY JENSEN

## References and Further Reading

Barstow, A.L., *Witchcraze: A New History of the European Witch Hunts,* San Francisco, CA, Harper Collins, 1994.

Boyer, P. and Nissenbaum, S., *Salem Possessed: The Social Origins of Witchcraft,* Cambridge, MA, Harvard University Press, 1974.

Briggs, R., *Witches and Neighbors. The Social and Cultural Context of European Witchcraft,* London, Harper Collins Publishers, 1996.

Cohn, N., *Europe's Inner Demons,* New York, New American Library, 1976.

Demos, J.P., *Entertaining Satan: Witchcraft and the Culture of Early New England,* New York, Oxford University Press, 1982.

Karlsen, C.F., *The Devil in the Shape of a Woman,* New York, Vintage Books, 1987.

Klaits, J., *Servants of Satan: The Age of the Witch Hunts,* Bloomington, IN, University of Indiana Press, 1985.

Kramer, H. and Sprenger, J., *Malleus Malficarum,* Translated by Summers, M., New York, Dover Publications, 1971.

Richards, J., *Sex, Dissidence and Damnation: Minority Groups in the Middle Ages,* London and New York, Routledge, 1990.

Russell, J.B., *Witchcraft in the Middle Ages,* London, Thames and Hudson Ltd, 1972.

*See also* **Demonology; Occult Crimes**

# Witnesses, the Right to Confront

The Sixth Amendment to the United States Constitution states, in part,

> In all criminal prosecutions, the accused shall enjoy the right...to be confronted with the witnesses against him; to have compulsory process for obtaining witnesses in his favor, and to have the assistance of counsel for his defense.

A major purpose of this clause is to ensure the reliability of the evidence presented. By mandating the presence of the witness, the theory goes: one can ensure that the person testifying has been duly sworn. Moreover, the witness's presence would allow the "trier of fact" to observe the individual's demeanor. Finally, of great importance, the clause ensures that the witness would be subject to cross-examination.

The Supreme Court held in 1965 that "the Sixth Amendment's right of an accused to confront the witnesses against him is... a fundamental right and is made obligatory on the States by the Fourteenth Amendment." *Pointer v. Texas 380 U.S. 400* (1965), 403. In this case, Pointer and an accomplice were charged with robbery. At the preliminary hearing, the alleged victim testified that Pointer was one of the perpetrators. The witness then moved out of state, and the prosecution successfully sought to introduce the testimony given at the preliminary hearing. Pointer was convicted, and appealed. The Supreme Court reversed his conviction, holding that, absent the right of the defendant to have cross-examination of the witness conducted, his Sixth Amendment rights had been violated.

The right to confront one's accusers, although important, is not absolute. For example, in the 19th century case of *Mattox v. U.S.,* 156 U.S. 237 (1895), witnesses who had testified against Mattox in a previous trial (and who had been appropriately cross-examined) had died. A stenographic transcript of their testimony was admitted into a subsequent trial, and Mattox was convicted. He appealed, arguing that his Sixth Amendment rights had been abrogated. The Supreme Court, while acknowledging that the right of confrontation is important, held "general rules of law... must occasionally give way to consideration of public policy and necessities of the case." (*Mattox v. U.S.*, 1895). This, unfortunately for Mattox, was one of those occasions, and his conviction was upheld.

The state, however, does have an obligation to seek "unavailable witnesses. Failure to do so may lead to the overturning of a conviction: *Barber v. Page,* 390 U.S. 719 (1968). If, however, an individual was cross-examined at the preliminary hearing, and good faith efforts were made to contact that person, those statements can be admitted, provided they bear "indicia of reliability," *Ohio v. Roberts,* 448 U.S. 56 (1980).

There are also situations in which out-of-court statements may be entered. That is true, in many instances, if the statement falls within the parameters of a well-established "hearsay" exception. For instance, the Supreme Court has ruled that the Confrontation Clause does not require that, before a trial court admits testimony under the spontaneous declaration and the medical examination exceptions to the hearsay rule, either the prosecutor or the trial court must find that the "declarant" is unavailable: *White v. Illinois,* 502 U.S. 346 (1992).

Another Confrontation Clause issue involves the meaning of "confrontation" at trial—does it literally mean that the witness must face the defendant in the courtroom? The Supreme Court's current answer is that, although face-to-face confrontation between witness and defendant is an important component of the trial under most circumstances, there may be exceptions to this rule. For instance, the Court has ruled that a state's interest in the physical and psychological well being of a child witness in a child abuse case may be sufficiently important to outweigh the right of the defendant to confront the witness. *Maryland v. Craig,* 497 U.S. 836 (1990). In this case, Maryland had established a procedure in which a hearing would be held to determine whether a child's confronting his or her alleged abuser would be unduly traumatic for the child. If such a finding were made, the child could testify via closed circuit television, a procedure that allowed the defendant, the judge, and the jury to observe the witness and allowed for appropriate cross-examination. The child witness, however, would not have to face the defendant. In such a situation—where there was a case-specific finding that facing the defendant would traumatize the witness—such a procedure is not forbidden.

A third situation in which the Court has dealt with Confrontation Clause issues involves a "joint trial," that is, a trial involving more than one defendant. In such instances, one of the defendants may make a confession prior to trial, and that confession may contain incriminating references to another defendant. If the first defendant does not then testify, is the Confrontation Clause violated? An issue like this arose in *Bruton v. U.S.,* 391 U.S. 123 (1968). In a joint trial the prosecutor used a confession made earlier by one defendant (Evans) that implicated the other (Bruton). Evans did not testify personally, so there was no chance for cross-examination. Although the trial judge instructed the jury that the confession could only be used in determining the guilt of Evans, Bruton was convicted. He appealed, and the Supreme Court held that "because of the substantial risk that the jury, despite instructions to the contrary, looked to the incriminating extrajudicial statements in determining petitioner's guilt, admission of Evans' confession in this joint trial violated petitioner's right of cross-examination secured by the Confrontation Clause of the Sixth Amendment." (*Bruton v. U.S.,* 1968). This does not mean, however, that such confessions may not be admitted under all circumstances, for the Court has also held that the Confrontation Clause is not violated by the admission of a nontestifying codefendant's confession with a proper limiting instruction when the confession is "redacted" to eliminate such things as the defendant's name and other references to her existence. *Richardson v. Marsh*, 481 U.S. 200 (1987). Merely eliminating the defendant's name from the confession, however, does not meet the standards set by the Confrontation Clause: *Gray v. Maryland,* 523 U.S. 185 (1998).

The Confrontation Clause, in short, continues to play an important role in our constitutional jurisprudence, and it will likely continue to do so in the near future.

DAVID M. JONES

### References and Further Reading

Blumenthal, J., Reading the text of the confrontation clause: 'To Be' or not 'To Be' *University of Pennsylvania Journal of Constitutional Law,* 3 (2001).

Dickinson, J.C., The confrontation clause and the hearsay rule: The current state of a failed marriage in need of a quick divorce, *Creighton Law Review,* 33 (2000).

Friedman, R.D., Confrontation clause: The search for basic principles, *Georgetown Law Journal,* 86 (1998).

Garcia, A., *The Sixth Amendment in Modern American Jurisprudence,* Greenwood, CT, Greenwood Press, 1992.

McGough, L.S., *Child Witnesses: Fragile Voices in the American Legal System,* New Haven, CT, Yale University Press, 1994.

White, P.J., Rescuing the confrontation clause, *South Carolina Law Review,* 54 (2003).

*See also* **Evidentiary Standards; Eyewitness Identification**

# Wolfgang, Marvin E.

Marvin E. Wolfgang is generally considered one of the world's leading criminologists. Over his long career he wrote more than 150 articles and had publications in over 30 books.

Wolfgang's intellectual roots were in sociology and philosophy. He began his long relationship with the University of Pennsylvania after serving as an instructor at Lebanon Valley College. He began his teaching career at the University of Pennsylvania in 1952 and remained there until his death in 1998. He was a Professor of Criminology, Legal Studies, and of Law.

While doing graduate work in sociology at the University of Pennsylvania in 1947 he met Thorsten Sellin, who became his mentor. In an interview in 1971, Wolfgang described the powerful intellectual influence Sellin had on him, stating, "If he had been a biologist teaching the bisection of the tse-tse fly, I probably would have gone into that area" (Snodgrass, 1972, 41). That not being the case, Wolfgang found himself drawn to the study of criminology.

Sellin's influence on Wolfgang was evident in his master's thesis, which was a historical study of crime and punishment in Renaissance Florence. Following the advice of Sellin and other professors, he chose a dissertation topic on a more contemporary theme. Wolfgang's dissertation research resulted in the publication of *Patterns in Criminal Homicide* in 1958, an offense about which criminologists at the time knew very little. This volume analyzed all criminal homicides listed by police in Philadelphia, Pennsylvania between 1948 and 1952 (approximately 600 cases). This detailed study of characteristics and circumstances of homicide cases produced the term "victim-precipitated homicide," indicating the importance of looking at the victim's role in the criminal event. This project began Wolfgang's study of criminal violence and is a work that is still widely cited.

A Ford Foundation grant received in 1960 led to the establishment of the Center for Studies in Criminology and Criminal Law at the University of Pennsylvania. Later renamed the Sellin Center in honor of his mentor, Wolfgang served as its director beginning in 1962. During his tenure at the University of Pennsylvania, Wolfgang also served as chair of the Sociology Department from 1968–1972.

Wolfgang published in a number of areas in the 1960s, including corrections, juvenile delinquency, the death penalty (to which he was opposed), and crime and race. His work appeared in a variety of forums, including law and social science journals and authored and edited books. His interest in these topics continued throughout his career. Sellin and Wolfgang collaborated on a number of works, beginning with *The Measurement of Delinquency* in 1964. This work reflected their interest in criminal statistics and emphasized the importance of the precise development of measures of crime and its severity. In 1968, Wolfgang published *The Subculture of Violence* with Franco Ferracuti. This work proposed a theory to explain homicides that were crimes of passion. The authors noted that such crimes were concentrated in specific ecological areas and among certain socioeconomic groups. Specifically, they found that homicide rates were highest among young adult males in lower class urban environments. Wolfgang and Ferracuti drew in part on Edwin H. Sutherland's differential association theory in their work, noting that the development of favorable attitudes toward the use of violence usually involved learned behavior. The immediate causes of these crimes were seen as the norms and values taught and reinforced by the subculture of violence. Violence was seen as an expected, appropriate, and even required, subcultural response to episodes (e.g., arguments and insults) that may seem trivial to persons in the larger culture. One example of the influence of this work is Lynn Curtis' *Violence, Race, and Culture* (1975), which tried to explain violence among African Americans through a subcultural perspective. *The Subculture of Violence* has influenced scholars up into the present day.

The 1970s saw the release of Wolfgang's most influential work, *Delinquency in a Birth Cohort* (Wolfgang, Figlio, and Sellin, 1972). This study followed 9945 boys born in 1945 who resided in Philadelphia from their 10th to their 18th birthdays. This cohort was studied over time, and data were collected on their contacts (if any) with the justice system, as well as school records, socioeconomic information, and demographic variables. This in-depth, longitudinal study of the criminal careers of these males produced the finding that a small percentage of offenders (the "chronics") were responsible for a majority of the crimes committed by the group. This result had a major impact on researchers and policymakers. *Delinquency in a Birth Cohort* was found to be the most cited work in *Crime and Justice: A Review of Research* for the period 1979–1985 (Cohn and Farrington, 1996).

This research led to increased interest in criminal careers and the use of the longitudinal approach in criminology. Other longitudinal studies followed, for example, Lyle Shannon's analysis of birth cohorts in Racine, Wisconsin (Shannon, 1988). Interest in criminal careers was also reflected in the two-volume set produced under the auspices of the National Research Council, *Criminal Careers and "Career Criminals"* (Blumstein et al., Eds., 1986). Wolfgang himself continued in this research tradition, following the 1945 birth cohort into young adulthood with his study *From Boy to Man, from Delinquency to Crime* (Wolfgang, Thornberry, and Figlio, Eds., 1987). Eventually, Wolfgang and his colleagues at the University of Pennsylvania identified a second Philadelphia cohort of males and females born in 1958; these persons were followed over time in the same fashion as the first project. *Delinquency Careers in Two Birth Cohorts* (Tracy, Wolfgang, and Figlio, 1990), which compared the 1945 and 1958 cohorts, was another important contribution to the criminal career literature. Wolfgang collaborated on a 1970 birth cohort study of delinquency by males and females in Puerto Rico (see Nevares, Wolfgang, and Tracy, 1990). Wolfgang also participated in another cross-cultural effort, in the People's Republic of China, in which he was engaged until his death. This study focused on over 5000 persons born in 1973 in the Wuchang district of the city of Wuhan and was projected to continue to the year 2000, extending to the entire city of Wuhan.

The influence of Marvin Wolfgang can be measured in a variety of ways. A review of 20 scholarly journals in criminology and criminal justice published both in the U.S. and abroad found Wolfgang to be the most cited scholar in 1990 (Cohn, Farrington, and Wright, 1998). In 1996, Wright and Soma published the results of their examination of criminology textbooks to determine the most cited scholars for the periods 1963–1968, 1976–1980, and 1989–1993. They concluded that Wolfgang was among the seven "elite scholars" whose work "has had an enduring impact on criminology" (Wright and Soma, 1996, 45). They attribute Wolfgang's prominence to the great breadth of his work and the longevity of his scholarly career.

The esteem in which people held Wolfgang is reflected in the many commissions and directorships he held. These include appointments to the President's Commission on the Causes and Prevention of Violence

(1966), the National Commission on the Causes and Prevention of Violence as codirector of research (1968), and the National Commission on Obscenity and Pornography (1968–1970). He also presented more than 70 invited papers, on topics including the measurement of crime, the death penalty, penology, victimology, youth crime, and longitudinal research.

Wolfgang received numerous prizes and awards, additional indicators of his prestige and influence (Cohn and Farrington, 1994). He received several Guggenheim fellowships, a Fulbright grant, and was elected president of the American Society of Criminology. Guardsmark, Incorporated established an award in his name for distinguished achievement in criminology; Wolfgang himself received the first Wolfgang Award in 1993.

A review of Marvin Wolfgang's career would not be complete without noting his influence as a teacher. He worked with more than 100 doctoral students, many of whom continue his intellectual tradition as deans, department chairs and professors at universities and institutions throughout the world.

PAMELA TONTODONATO

## Biography

Born in Millersburg, Pennsylvania, 14 November 1924. Educated at Dickinson College in Carlisle, Pennsylvania, A.B. in Philosophy and Sociology, 1948 (graduated Phi Beta Kappa) University of Pennsylvania, M.A., 1950; Ph.D. in Sociology, 1955. Instructor, Lebanon Valley College, Annville, Pennsylvania, 1947–1952; Instructor to professor, University of Pennsylvania, 1952–1998. Chair of the Department of Sociology, University of Pennsylvania, 1968–1972; Director of the (Sellin) Center for Studies in Criminology and Criminal Law, University of Pennsylvania,1962–1998; President of the American Academy of Political and Social Science, 1972–1998; President of the American Society of Criminology, 1967. August Vollmer award of the American Society of Criminology for distinguished research in criminology, 1960; shared in honors for the Dennis Carrol Prize, International Society for Criminology, 1960; Member American Philosophical Society, 1975; fellow, American Society of Criminology, 1977. Honorary Doctor of Laws, City University of New York, 1978; honorary Doctor of Laws, Academia Mexicana de Derecho Internacional, 1978. Roscoe Pound Award, National Council on Crime and Delinquency, for distinguished contribution to the field of criminal justice, 1979; Hans von Hentig award, World Society of Victimology, 1988; Edwin H. Sutherland Award of the ASC for outstanding scholarly contributions to the discipline of criminology, 1989; Wolfgang Award for distinguished achievement in criminology, Guardsmark, Incorporated, 1993; Cesare Beccaria Gold Medal for outstanding contribution to criminology from the German, Austrian, and Swiss Society of Criminology, 1997. Died in Philadelphia, Pennsylvania, April 12, 1998.

## Principal Writings

*Patterns in Criminal Homicide,* 1958; Reprinted, 1975.
*The Measurement of Delinquency* (with Thorsten Sellin), 1964; Reprinted, 1978.
*The Subculture of Violence: Towards an Integrated Theory in Criminology* (with Franco Ferracuti), 1967; Reprinted, 1982.
*Delinquency in a Birth Cohort* (with Robert M. Figlio and Thorsten Sellin), 1972; 2nd ed., 1987.
Race, judicial discretion, and the death penalty (with Marc Reidel), *Annals of the American Academy of Political and Social Science,* 407 (1973).
*Criminology Index: Research and Theory in Criminology in the United States, 1945–1972* (with Robert M. Figlio, and Terence P. Thornberry), 1975.
Evaluating Criminology (with Robert M. Figlio and Terence P. Thornberry), 1978.
*The National Survey of Crime Severity* (with Robert M. Figlio, Paul E. Tracy, and Simon I. Singer), 1985.
*From Boy to Man, From Delinquency to Crime* (edited with Terence P. Thornberry and Robert M. Figlio), 1987.
Crime and punishment in renaissance Florence, *Journal of Criminal Law and Criminology,* 81 (1990).
*Delinquency Careers in Two Birth Cohorts* (with Paul E. Tracy and Robert M. Figlio), 1990.
*Delinquency in Puerto Rico: The 1970 Birth Cohort Study* (with Dora Nevares and Paul E. Tracy, and Steven Aurand), 1990.

## References and Further Reading

Block, R. and Block, C.R., Wolfgang's influence on the Chicago homicide data set, *Homicide Studies,* 2(3) (1998).
Blumstein, A., Cohen, J., Roth, J.A. and Visher, C.A., Eds., *Criminal Careers and 'Career Criminals,'* Vol. 1, Washington, DC, National Academy Press, 1986.
Cohn, E.G. and Farrington, D.P., Who are the most influential criminologists in the English-speaking world? *British Journal of Criminology,* 34(2) (1994).
Cohn, E.G. and Farrington, D.P., 'Crime and Justice' and the Criminology and Criminal Justice Literature, in Morris, N. and Tonry, M., Eds., *Crime and Justice: A Review of Research,* Vol. 20, Chicago, IL, University of Chicago Press, 1996.
Cohn, E.G., Farrington, D.P. and Wright, R.A., *Evaluating Criminology and Criminal Justice,* Westport, CT, Greenwood Press, 1998.
Curtis, L.A., *Violence, Race, and Culture,* Lexington, MA, Heath, 1975.
Fox, J.A., Lessons from Wolfgang: The tradition of Penn criminology, *Homicide Studies* 2(3) (1998).
Shannon, L.W., *Criminal Career Continuity: Its Social Context,* New York, Human Sciences Press, Inc., 1988.
Snodgrass, J., Dialogue with Marvin Wolfgang, *Issues in Criminology,* 7(1) (1972)
Wright, R.A. and Soma, C., The Most-cited Scholars in Criminology Textbooks, 1963–1968, 1976–1980, and 1989 to 1993, *Journal of Crime and Justice,* 19(1) (1996)
Zahn, M.A., Marvin Wolfgang: Colleague and friend, *Homicide Studies,* 2(3) (1998).

*See also* **Juvenile Delinquency, Theories of; Sellin, Thorsten**

# Women and Addiction

Women in the criminal justice system are likely to be involved in offenses that are related to substance abuse. The percentage of women incarcerated has grown substantially, nearly double the male increase (van Wormer and Bartollas, 2003). Aside from involvement in the criminal justice system, addicted and substance abusing women are at increased risk for sexual and physical abuse, have more cooccurring mental illnesses, and suffer more severe physical problems as a result of their addiction (Lowinson, Ruiz, Millman, and Langrod, 1992; NIAAA, 1999).

The path to addiction, the progression of addiction, as well as the entry into, retention in and completion of treatment are significant issues for women. The majority of treatment programs in the U.S. today have been developed with the addiction processes of men in mind, and the dimensions of addiction and treatment in men are more clearly understood. Therefore, those interested in increasing the retention and successful completion of treatment by women, need to understand that the dimensions of addiction are not the same for women.

Addicted women differ from men in three important ways: physiological consequences, psychosocial factors, and patterns of drug use (Nelson-Zlupko, Kauffman, and Dore, 1995).

## Physiological Factors

Physiologically, women experience negative physical consequences of their addiction sooner than their male counterparts. Hormones as well as other physiological differences affect the way in which women metabolize drugs and alcohol.

Consumption of alcohol by a woman will result in higher blood alcohol content (BAC) than a man who drinks the same amount. Three factors are associated with this effect. First, women have less of an enzyme called alcohol dehydrogenase in their stomachs. This enzyme begins to break down alcohol immediately after it is consumed. Therefore, more alcohol will enter a woman's blood stream after consumption. Second, men's bodies contain more water than women's bodies. The excess water dilutes the alcohol resulting in lower BAC's for men who drink. Third, fluctuating hormones in a woman's body can have an impact on the subjective experience of intoxication, making it more likely that the woman who abuses alcohol and other chemicals will be more impaired.

Women experience serious physical consequences of substance abuse sooner than their male counterparts. Substance abuse by women leads to higher rates of malnutrition, cirrhosis and liver disease, breast cancer, and cognitive impairment (NIDA, 1995; Wilsnack, Wilsnack, and Miller-Strumhofel, 1994). The net result of this is that substance-abusing women, and in particular alcoholic women, have a higher mortality rate than men.

## Psychosocial Factors

The psychosocial aspects of women's addictions are significantly different from those of men. Women addicted to both alcohol and drugs are also more likely to be diagnosed with comorbid psychiatric problems, most specifically depression and anxiety disorders (Blume, 1992; Boyd, 1993). When comparing women who were addicts to those who were not, Covington (2002) found that 74% of women addicts were sexually abused, 52% were physically abused, and 72% were emotionally abused. As a result, women are more likely to be found with posttraumatic stress disorder (PTSD) (Back, Sonne, Killeen, Dansky, and Brady, 2003). It has also been found that depression and low-self esteem are found in women prior to the diagnosis of substance abuse.

Women with drug and alcohol problems often lack positive social supports and generally have begun their drug and alcohol careers as the result of a significant traumatic event. These events may be childhood abuse or reoccurring abuse in adulthood. Triggering events may also include the death of a loved one, loss of a relationship or a job, or incarceration and the subsequent loss of connection to children.

Patterns of violence are a significant issue for women who are substance abusers. Sexual abuse in women who enter treatment for substance abuse range up to 78% (Root, 1989). Substance-abusing women are often targets of violence by their substance-abusing partners (Covington, 2002). Alcohol has been associated with aggressive behavior by both men and women (Pagliaro and Pagliaro, 2000). When women are perpetrators, the victims of this aggression are more likely to be children. Women addicted to drugs are not typically found to engage in violent acts but commit crimes as a means to meet the growing demands of their drug use.

Women with histories that involve physical or sexual abuse are at higher risk for multiple problems. When an abuse history, either sexual or physical, is present in a substance-abusing individual, positive treatment outcomes are less likely than for nonabused individuals (Root, 1989). Professionals who work with substance abusing women often lack the expertise to identify sexual or psychological trauma as an obstacle to engaging in rehabilitation services. When women who suffer from these traumas are placed in mixed gender groups, they lack a sense of safety and acceptance. The discussion of such trauma is often actively discouraged in treatment, and this can lead to a self-defeating cycle: the trauma and its subsequent effects leads to addiction, yet women entering treatment are actively discouraged from discussing many of the factors contributing to their addiction. As a result, women are often retraumatized when they enter rehabilitation. This cycle contributes to significantly lower retention rates of women in treatment.

Substance abuse by pregnant women remains an ongoing and serious issue. Although pregnant women are more likely to enter treatment than nonpregnant women, substance abuse by pregnant women remains a serious public health threat (SAMSHA, 2002). Fetal alcohol syndrome (FAS) is a severe condition that develops as a result of alcohol consumption during pregnancy. FAS and a less severe form FAE (Fetal Alcohol Effects) accounts for the most significant number of developmental disabilities in children. FAS's most common characteristics are facial abnormalities, growth deficits and mental retardation.

In general, women experience more guilt about their addiction, and have a stronger sense of shame. These feelings of guilt and shame can further complicate feelings of depression and low self-esteem Women who are addicted have less education, fewer marketable skills, fewer work experiences, and fewer financial resources than men. Additionally, they are more likely to carry the responsibility for care of children and other dependents.

## Patterns of Drug Use

The pattern of women's use of drugs and alcohol is markedly different from that of men. These patterns create obstacles to the identification and ultimate treatment of substance abuse problems in this population. Women are more likely to abuse legal drugs such as tranquilizers and other medication often prescribed by doctors (Ross, 1989). Women are more likely to use drugs and alcohol in isolation (Gomberg, 1986). As the progression toward addiction goes unnoticed, the woman's problems with alcohol and other drugs "telescopes; that is, a woman's addiction career generally begins later than a man, yet she will ultimately require treatment at the same time. At the same time, she is likely to accumulate substantially more physical and emotional distress along the way" (Blume, Frances, and Miller, 1998).

Abuse of alcohol is the primary reason that women enter treatment. A recent study found that 40% of women enter treatment with an alcohol related diagnosis, 22% enter for problems with cocaine, 19% for heroin and other opiates, 7% for marijuana as well as stimulants, and 5% of women entered treatment for problems with all other substances (SAMSHA, 2002).

Although individuals of African American descent are overly represented in prisons, their rates of alcohol use, primarily by women, are typically lower than those of white women and women of Hispanic origin. African American women have the highest rates of abstinence from alcohol of any ethnic group (Gomberg, 1999). They are more likely to use illicit drugs, but only by a small margin (10.2% vs. 9.9%). Native American women have the highest rates of both alcohol and illicit drug use, making this group of women among the most vulnerable for all problems associated with addiction.

Age is a determining factor in patterns of drug use. Younger women have a high degree of vulnerability to problems associated with substance abuse. In particular, teenaged girls in the 12–17-year-old age group drink more often than their male counterparts, and their use of illicit drugs equals or surpasses that of boys (NHSDA, 2002). In addition, substance abuse is strongly associated with early sexual activity (Smith, 1996; The National Center on Addiction and Substance Abuse at Columbia University (CASA), 1999).

Young girls are more likely to suffer from eating disorders and to be sexually abused, both of which increase the risk of current or later substance abuse (The National Center on Addiction and Substance Abuse at Columbia University (CASA), 2003). Substance abusing girls are more likely to get involved in school fights, are more depressed, and have a higher likelihood of suicide (The National Center on Addiction and Substance Abuse at Columbia University (CASA), 2003).

Mature women aged 59 or older remain a hidden problem among addicted populations. Substance abuse among members of this group is likely to be unnoticed in medical settings, and when identified, health insurance is less likely to cover required treatment. Although the population is smaller in real numbers, the consequences—that include higher rates of lung cancer, cirrhosis, hip fractures, pancreatic cancer, stroke and heart disease—impact these older women sooner and to a more devastating degree (The National Center on Addiction and Substance Abuse at Columbia University (CASA), 1998).

Pregnancy complicates the assessment and reporting of drug abuse among women. With an increased focus on prosecution of women who abuse substances while pregnant, there has been a shift in the source of referrals for pregnant women to treatment. The number of pregnant women who were self-referred decreased from 33% to 28%, whereas criminal justice referrals increased from 21% to 28%, and health care providers decreased from 14% to 11%. This may reflect the increased likelihood that women who report substance abuse problems to medical personnel are more likely to be charged with a criminal offense. Under those circumstances, women may forego the risk of disclosure to medical personnel and avoid prenatal care entirely.

A serious consideration in drug abuse among women is the problem of HIV/AIDS. The Center for Disease Control has reported that the proportion of women among HIV cases in adults and adolescents has increased steadily from 7% in 1985 to 20% in 1999. The AIDS rate for black and Hispanic women was approximately 16 and 7 times greater, respectively, than that for white women (CDC, 2003). Although typical transmission is through heterosexual contact, it is primarily with men who abuse drugs using intravenous methods. The second leading cause of transmission is intravenous drug use by women. Therefore, in one manner or another substance abuse is the most significant factor in HIV/AIDS infection of women. HIV/AIDS is now the number one leading cause of death for African American women. This makes any dissemination of information (be it practice, research, or policy) that impacts on the course and treatment of women's addiction critical (Center for Disease Control).

Blume (1994) said that there are three stereotypes that women encounter: first, they are women, second they are addicts, and third, they are addicted women. In addition, addicted women bear the stigma of being promiscuous. These negative stereotypes can make conditions for recovery more complex and difficult. In addition, women have the task of tending to children who require day care or foster care services prior to accessing treatment services (Nelson-Zlupko, Kauffman, and Dore, 1995). If they overcome these obstacles, they will still find that there are fewer treatment beds available to them, and if they are pregnant, treatment may be nearly inaccessible (Blume, 1994). These burdens, among others, make the recovery experience for women different from that of men.

## Women and the Criminal Justice System

There are implications for differential treatment of women, particularly when looking at arrest, conviction and punishment for women who drive under the influence of alcohol. Drinking driver programs are a place where early detection and intervention in alcoholism is more likely to occur. In receiving some consequences for their actions, the drinker may break through denial to view the progression of alcoholism before it takes a much more serious toll, both personally and for society.

Substance abuse has been associated with crime for men and women, both as perpetrators and as victims. The criminal justice consequences of women's involvement with illegal drugs are dramatic. Illicit drug use and sales have sparked the 386% rise in the federal and state female prison population, from 12,331 in 1980 to 59,878 in 1994, whereas the number of men rose by 214% from 303,643 to 952,585. By 1996, the number of women in state and federal prisons had increased by 439% to 130,430 individuals. Among state inmates, a third of women had violated drug laws in 1991, compared to one fifth of men. Many more had committed their crimes under the influence of drugs or alcohol, or to get money to buy drugs.

It is estimated that 80% of all inmates, both men and women are addicted to drugs (CASA, 1999). As noted above, the number of women incarcerated because of substance abuse is increasing at a higher rate than men. Women are typically involved in crimes through which they can obtain and maintain their drug supply. Women either engage in illegal activities to obtain money to buy drugs or to obtain drugs directly (Inciardi, Lockwood, and Pottieger, 1993). The types of crimes that are typical for women relating to drugs are theft, fraud, drug possession, forgery, embezzlement, and prostitution (Merlo, 1995).

Incarcerated women present significant challenges to addiction and corrections personnel. Results of a study by Langan and Pelissier (2001) showed that women in prison had more problematic drug abuse histories, came from homes where drug and alcohol addiction was more prevalent, had more serious physical and sexual abuse histories as children, and were more likely to have cooccurring mental illness and physical disabilities.

It is critical that treatment professionals learn to recognize when to address these issues in rehabilitation. Individuals who deal with women in the area of addiction, including counselors, corrections personnel, and police, need specialized training in the area of trauma as it is specifically manifested in women. An understanding of the relationships between sexual and psychological trauma and addiction in women will lead to improvement in outcomes for women in criminal justice settings and in rehabilitation.

Although the number of women requiring treatment in prison has increased, the actual number of women treated for drug and alcohol abuse has declined, according to the U.S. General Accounting Office (1999). This decline is related more to a lack of available treatment services, and the limitations of existing programs. In three jurisdictions studied, there were long waiting lists for women who required residential treatment.

Additionally, the treatment that is generally available has been designed for men whose experiences with addiction may be quite different.

Gender disparities continue to be a problem for women seeking drug and alcohol treatment. Traditional programs are generally based on processes originally designed for men, and are less effective for women (Covington, 2002). Barriers to treatment access include stigma, denial, and lack of gender-specific treatment services (Finkelstein, 1994). Support services that are essential to women's continued success in recovery include but should not be limited to medical care, child care, parenting education, life skills, education and information about domestic violence.

NANCY K. BROWN

### References and Further Reading

Back, S.E., Sonne, S.C., Killeen, T., Dansky, B.S. and Brady, K.T. (2003). Comparative profiles of women with PTSD and comorbid cocaine or alcohol dependence, *American Journal of Drug and Alcohol Abuse,* 29(1), 169–190.

Blume, S.B. (1992). Alcohol and other drug problems in women, in Lowinson, J.H., Ruiz, P., Millman, R.B. and Langrod, J.G.A.E., Eds., *Substance Abuse: A Comprehensive Textbook,* 2nd ed., pp. 794–807, Baltimore, MD, Williams and Wilkins.

Blume, S.B. (1994). Psychoactive substance use disorders in women...papers and abstracts from the Symposium on Women's Mental Health: Issues for the 90s...annual American Psychiatric Association meeting, *Journal of Women's Health,* 3(6), 497.

Blume, S.B., Frances, R. and Miller, S., Eds. (1998). *Clinical Textbook of Addictive Disorders,* 2nd ed. New York, The Guilford Press.

Boyd, C.J. (1993). The antecedents of women's crack cocaine abuse: family substance abuse, sexual abuse, depression and illicit drug use, *Journal of Substance Abuse Treatment,* 150, 1701–1711.

CDC (2003). *HIV/AIDS Among U.S. Women: Minority and Young Women at Continuing Risk,* Available at: http://www.cdc.gov/hiv/pubs/facts/women.htm. Retrieved on October 28, 2003.

Covington, S.S. (2002). Helping women recover: Creating Gender-responsive treatment, in Straussner, S.L.A. and Brown, S., Eds., *The Handbook of Adddiction Treatment for Women,* San Francisco, CA, Jossey-Bass.

Finkelstein, N. (1994). Treatment issues for alcohol- and drug-dependent pregnancy and parenting women, *Health and Social Work,* 19(1), 7–16.

Gomberg, E.S.L. (1986). *Women and Alcohol: Psychosocial Issues* (Research Monograph No. 16). Washington: National Institute on Alcohol Abuse and Alcoholism.

Gomberg, E.S.L. (1999). Women, in McCrady, B.S. and Epstein. E.E., Eds., *Addictions: A Comprehensive Guidebook,* New York, Oxford University Press.

Inciardi, J., Lockwood, D. and Pottieger, A.E. (1993). *Women and Crack-Cocaine,* New York, MacMillan.

Langan, N.P. and Pelissier, B.M.M. (2001). Gender differences among prisoners in drug treatment, *Journal of Substance Abuse,* 13(3), 291–301.

Lowinson, J.H., Ruiz, P., Millman, R.B. and Langrod, J.G.A.E., Eds., (1992). *Substance Abuse: A Comprehensive Textbook,* 2nd ed., Baltimore, MD, Williams and Wilkins.

Merlo, A.V., Ed., (1995). *Female Criminality in the 1990's,* Boston, Allyn and Bacon.

Nelson-Zlupko, L., Kauffman, E. and Dore, M.M. (1995). Gender differences in drug addiction and treatment: Implications for social work intervention with substance-abusing women, *Social Work,* 40, 45–54.

NIAAA. (1999). *Are Women More Vulnerable to Alcohol's Effects?* No. 46. Rockville.

Pagliaro, A.M. and Pagliaro, L.A. (2000). *Substance Use among Women: A Reference and Resource Guide,* Philadelphia, PA, Taylor and Francis.

Root, M.P. (1989). Treatment failures: The rule of victimization in women's addictive behavior, *American Journal of Orthopsychiatry,* 59(4), 542–549.

Ross, H.E. (1989). Alcohol and drug abuse in treated alcoholics: A comparison of men and women, *Alcoholism: Clinical and Experimental Research,* 13, 810–816.

SAMSHA. (July 16, 2003). *Drug and Alcohol Services Information System (DASIS),* Available at: http://www.samhsa. gov/centers/clearinghouse/clearinghouses.html. Retrieved on July 22, 2003.

Smith, C. (1996). The link between childhood maltreatment and teenage pregnancy, *Social Work Research,* 20(3), 131–141.

The National Center on Addiction and Substance Abuse at Columbia University (CASA). (1998). *Under the Rug: Substance Abuse and the Mature Woman,* New York, The National Center on Addiction and Substance Abuse at Columbia University (CASA).

The National Center on Addiction and Substance Abuse at Columbia University (CASA). (1999). *Dangerous Liaisons: Substance Abuse and Sex,* New York, The National Center on Addiction and Substance Abuse at Columbia University.

The National Center on Addiction and Substance Abuse at Columbia University (CASA). (2003). *The Formative Years: Pathways to Substance Abuse Among Girls and Young Women Ages 8–22,* New York: The National Center on Addiction and Substance Abuse at Columbia University.

U.S. General Accounting Office. (1999). *Women in Prison: Issues and Challenges Confronting U.S. Correctional Systems* (No. GAO/GGD-00-22), Washington, DC.

van Wormer, K. and Bartollas, C. (2003). *Women in the Criminal Justice System,* Boston, Allyn and Bacon.

Wilsnack, R.W., Wilsnack, S.C. and Miller-Strumhofel, S. (1994). How women drink: Epidemiology of women's drinking and problem drinking, *Alcohol Health and Research World,* 18, 173–181.

*See also* **Drug Use: Extent and Correlates; Women as Offenders and Victims throughout History**

# Women as Offenders and Victims Throughout History

The female offender–victim dichotomy has functioned in a dualism of the "both or and" complex throughout history—rarely can the two be separated. Although the early trajectory of this phenomenon emphasizes the role of offender, official studies of the female offender did not gestate until the early 1960s. The victimization of women was also not examined until the 1970s in the U.S. However, despite the lack of early sociological evidence tracking these roles and their consequences on society, the persistence of the female offender and victim is obvious throughout history.

The earliest recorded crimes of women are typically that of witchcraft and prostitution. Witchcraft can be traced throughout many histories and cultures of the world. Whereas men were at times accused of participating in maleficia, the females of society were largely the target of this persecution. Typical offenders of this crime were described as women who committed and experienced infidelity, ambition, and lust. Because of the broad nature of these characteristics, the belief and accusation of witchcraft can be traced back to Babylonian times, though official witch hunts did not develop until the 14th century in Europe. The offense of witchcraft itself was characterized in early Europe as a woman "[making] a pact with the devil when she renounced Christianity in exchange for magical power" (Forrest, 1712). Through these offenses new version of criminal procedure evolved; official prosecutors were introduced to the trials and, in 1252, torture was permitted as a confessional method. Female offenses of this kind were often of epidemic proportions and would die down in the same fashion in which they arose. Accusations of witchcraft and witch hunts still exist today in areas of Africa and Southeast Asia. These accusations are typically bred out of unexplained phenomena: disease, famine, and natural disaster. As in ancient times, lust, ambition, and infidelity in women are used today to label females as offenders of this crime.

A study conducted in America from 1962–1995, examining female crime rates in industrialized nations, determined that economically advanced countries produce the highest rate of female offenses. Despite this rise, female offenses constitute a small percentage of all crimes committed. Of all homicide arrests, females comprise only 12%, 5% for robberies, 11%–18% for thefts, and 40% for fraud (Simon, 1717). These numbers, though revealing, do not acknowledge societal and cultural factors, such as age, race, and education. In wealthier nations, those women who have received higher education tend to commit fraud more than homicide. Fertility rates also factor into this schema, as those countries with higher fertility rates produce less female offenders, as well as less crime altogether. Although this study showed an increase in crime in the 30-year time span investigated, the overall increase of female offenses was slight. Ultimately female offenders to do not encompass a majority of all offenders, despite the social presence they have cultivated in the last half century.

Specifically, female American offenders have existed since the Puritan establishments in the New World. Adultery was the most common offense for females of Puritan America and this trend dominated American culture up until the Victorian era at the end of the 19th century. The Victorian era cultivated an objectifying lens through which women were viewed, a lens that can also be applied to the concept of women and crime. Typically women existed either as the Madonna or the whore (Greene, 1722). Women who exhibited any type of independence, either through education, ambition, or sexuality, were considered threats to a male-oriented society. Although previous versions of American culture treated this type of behavior as an offense of witchcraft, the late 19th or early 20th centuries simply diagnosed women as sick or hysterical and ordered S. Weir Mitchell's "rest cure" (Mitchell, 134). If a woman was still unable to align herself with cultural ideals of femininity, she was then labeled as offender.

Despite the Puritan ideals of repressed sexuality that plagued late 19th century America, the rise of industrialism and tenant housing at this time cultivated poverty and, as a result, prostitution in the urban cities of America. Prostitution became a means of survival for many starving young women, as wages for immigrant workers were low. At the time of this capitalist growth, the first female prison opened in Indiana in 1873 (Casey–Acevedo, 1722), demonstrating the correlation between industrial capitalism and female offenses.

This pattern continued with another 49 female prisons built between the years of 1860 and 1927. Since this rise in the late 19th century, female offenses in America have steadily increased, though not dominated the total percentage of crimes committed. Though prostitution still exists as a frequent crime, the most common female offenses, as of 1995, were possession of drugs, minor assaults, theft, and larceny (Greene, 2002, 1723). These crimes are typically committed by minority women who are between the ages of 24 and 29 and were raised in a single-parent home.

Similar to female offenders, women have also been known as victims since Babylonian times. Rape and sexual assault are the two most prevalent crimes committed against women and have been throughout history. However, the victimization of this crime is often difficult to determine, as no universal definition of rape exists. In ancient times, rape was only seen as an offense if the victim was a virgin and that was "viewed as property crime" (Gibbs, 2003, 130). The penalty for committing such an act, under William the Conqueror, was castration and the loss of both eyes (Gibbs, 2003, 130). However, the victim was often urged to marry her attacker, thus preventing any criminal procedure. Although punishment existed for the rape offender of a virgin, a raped married woman was considered an adulteress and she herself would receive a punishment of death. The definition of rape evolved in the late 13th century to include "married women, nuns, widows, and even prostitutes" (Bonilla, 2003, 138).

Modern versions and definitions of rape are often inextricably bound up with racism. With documented accounts of this phenomenon as recently as the 1980's in America, rape was only considered a plausible offense if the victim were a white female and her perpetrator a black male. However, extreme measures have been taken in recent years to recognize this type of female victimization: the term date rape, or acquaintance rape, replaced the previous term of "rape" that seemed to encompass only those women attacked by strangers. Despite these procedures, rape crisis counselors estimate the numbers of unreported female victimization to be much higher than the familiar phrase of "one out of four college women will be the victim of sexual assault" in the U.S.

Other crimes committed against women are that of murder, robbery and theft (Dobbs, 2002, 1725). The notion of female victimization, like female offenders, did not gain serious attention in the U.S. until the 1970s with a special interest in violent crimes. Domestic violence affects an estimated 20–50% of woman and a third of all female homicidal victims are killed by an intimate partner (Dobbs, 2002, 1727). The rate of female victimization are lower than those of male victimization, however women are more often the victims of violent crimes by one they know. From this psychologists suggest that women have a greater fear of crime, as well as a fear of reporting the crime. Outside of the U.S., females experience victimization through genital mutilation and prostitution trafficking, a role in which offender and victim merge. The common factor among female victims is the violence inflicted by the male race—female victimization is rarely committed by another female. For both victims and offenders, females did not receive serious attention until the second half of the 20th century. Female victimization was dismissed in earlier times, a trend which is still obvious in modern judicial systems, whereas suspected female offenders received the harshest punishment of the most extreme measures.

ABBIE E. VENTURA

## References and Further Reading

Bonilla, M., Cultural assault: What feminists are doing to rape ought to be a crime, in Bauknight, L., Ed., *The Carolina Reader*, Columbia, SC, University of South Carolina, Department of English, 2003, pp. 128–132.

Casey-Acevedo, K., Women as offenders, in Levinson, D., Ed., *Encyclopedia of Crime and Punishment*, Thousand Oaks, CA, Sage, 2002. 1722–1725.

Culliver, C.C., *Female Criminality: The State of the Art*, New York: Garland, 1993.

Dobash, R.E., Dobash, R.P. and Noaks, L., *Gender and Crime*, Cardiff, Wales, University of Wales Press, 1995.

Dobbs, R.R., Women as victims, in Levinson, D., Ed., *Encyclopedia of Crime and Punishment*, Thousand Oaks, CA, Sage, 2002, pp. 1725–1728.

Flowers, R.B., *Women and Criminality: The Woman as Victim, Offender, and Practitioner*, New York, Greenwood, 1987.

Forrest, B., Witchcraft, in Levinson, D., Ed., *Encyclopedia of Crime and Punishment*, Thousand Oaks, CA, Sage, 2002, pp. 1710–1715.

Gibbs, N., When is it rape? in Bauknight, L., Ed., *The Carolina Reader*, Columbia, SC, University of South Carolina, Department of English, 2003, pp. 137–143.

Greene, S., Women in Prison, in Levinson, D., Ed., *Encyclopedia of Crime and Punishment*, Thousand Oaks, CA, Sage, 2002, pp. 1729–1732.

Guido, M., California court creates tough standard for defining rape, in Bauknight, L., Ed., *The Carolina Reader*, Columbia, SC, University of South Carolina, Dept. of English, 2003. 143–144.

Heidensohn, F.M. *Women and Crime: The Life of the Female Offender*, New York, New York University Press, 1985.

Mitchell, S.W., Wear and tear, in Bauer, D.M, Ed., *The Yellow Wallpaper: A Bedford Cultural Edition*, Boston, MA, Bedford, 1998, pp. 133–142.

Naffine, N., *Gender, Crime and Feminism*, Cambridge, U.K., Cambridge University Press, 1995.

Paglia, C., Rape and modern sex war, in Bauknight, L., Ed., *The Carolina Reader*, Columbia, SC, University of South Carolina, Department of English, 2003, pp. 135–137.

Simon, R.J. and Landis, J., *The Crimes Women Commit, The Punishments They Receive*, Lexington, MA, Lexington Books, 1991.

Simon, R.J., Women and crime in a global perspective, in Levinson, D., Ed., *Encyclopedia of Crime and Punishment,* Thousand Oaks, CA, Sage, 2002, pp. 1715–1717.

Steffensmeier, D., Gender and crime: Toward a gendered theory of female offending, *Annual Review of Sociology,* 22, 459–487 (1996).

Young, C., Beyond 'No Means No': Redefining date rape, in Bauknight, L., *The Carolina Reader,* Columbia, SC, University of South Carolina, Department of English, 2003, pp. 132–135.

*See also* **Gangs, Girl; Prostitution; Women and Addictions**

# Work Release

During 2001, the U.S. incarcerated almost 2 million males and females in Federal and State prisons and local jails (Harrison and Beck, 2002). Approximately 650,000 offenders will be released from serving time this year alone. This group of offenders faces significant challenges in terms of housing, reestablishing relationships with family and friends, remaining drug-free, and finding employment. Upwards of 60% of offenders who were formerly incarcerated will likely be unemployed 12 months after their release. Unemployment is also closely related to other problems such as substance abuse and family violence (Petersilia, 2000). Many of the offenders released from prisons around the country will be returned for violations to their conditions community supervision and for rearrests.

Proponents of transition programs such as work release argue that these programs are important and even critical to the successful reintegration of offenders back into the community. Work release provides a structured setting, whereby offenders are confined to either correctional institutions or community residential facilities (e.g., halfway houses, prerelease centers, community correctional centers) during the times that they are not working. The structured setting is appealing to policy-makers and the public because it addresses concerns for community safety, a cornerstone of the recent "get-tough" strategies in community corrections. More importantly, work release is viewed as a valuable tool by correctional administrators because of its emphasis on establishing viable employment options for offenders within the community.

## History and Use of Work Release

The first work release program was created under the Huber Act in the state of Wisconsin in 1914. The law authorized counties in Wisconsin to establish programs for misdemeanants who were serving sentences of up to one year. Offenders were permitted to work in the community during specified hours and were paid wages that were similar to civilian workers. Although initial results from the program in Wisconsin appeared to be successful, only three other states (Nebraska, West Virginia, and Hawaii) followed their lead and established programs in their own states. Work release found a new footing in states around the country in 1957 when North Carolina committed to creating a wide array of programs. Many states followed their lead and during the 1960s work release programs became fairly common. The Prisoner Rehabilitation Act of 1965 signaled the beginning of work release opportunities for federal prisoners and by 1975 all states had in place some form of work release programming for its inmates (Silverman, 2001).

Since the 1970s, corrections systems have experienced a decline in the use of these programs. Funding has been a significant reason for this trend. Monies from the Law Enforcement Assistance Administration (LEAA) provided funding for work release programs throughout the 1970s. However, when this funding source discontinued, many programs became obsolete. In addition, as rehabilitation fell out of favor as a goal of corrections, support for programs such as work release waned. During the 1980s, highly publicized incidents involving early release programs such as the case of Willie Horton in Massachusetts resulted in an increasing concern on the part of the public for the safety of their communities (Turner and Petersilia, 1996). Today, work release is still used as a community option throughout the U.S. During 1999, almost 44,000 inmates participated in some form of work release in 35 agencies. States vary in the extent to which they use such programming. States such as New York (7162), Alabama (4103), Illinois (3985), and Florida (3780) used work release most often; whereas the states of Arizona, California, Connecticut, Montana, Nevada, New Hampshire, Wyoming, and the Federal system did not have any offenders participate in work release (The Corrections Yearbook, 2000).

## How Work Release Programs Work

Work release programs are operated at local, state, and federal criminal justice levels. County Sheriff's departments usually operate programs locally through jails for misdemeanants. Programs operating at the state level are usually directed through prisons or community residential facilities such as prerelease centers. These types of programs provide work opportunities to felony inmates who are close to completing their sentences. The Federal Bureau of Prisons operates work release programs for both misdemeanants and felons. Many local, state, and federal agencies contract with private groups to run their work release programs (Silverman, 2001).

Inmates are selected for work release based on various criteria. Participation in such programs is voluntary and selection of inmates is typically related to their classification level, institutional behavior, current offense and criminal history, time remaining on their sentence, and employment opportunities. Work release staff review applicants based on these criteria and their eligibility. A committee comprised of correctional and programmatic staff however, often makes the final decision for admission to the program.

Those inmates who are accepted for participation in the program are expected to undergo an orientation that highlights the rules and regulations that govern the program. In addition, work release participants may be assessed as to their employability in the community. Use of funds earned while on work release typically cover costs that are related to room and board, restitution, family or child support, fines, courts costs and other financial responsibilities. Any remaining funds are credited to the inmate's account to be given to them at the time of their release from supervision (Silverman, 2001).

A primary objective of work release programs is to provide employment opportunities in locations that are close to where the inmates will be paroled or released. In some jurisdictions where no minimum or prerelease facilities exist, correctional administrators may arrange for supervision and housing in local institutional facilities.

## Effectiveness of Work Release Programs

Although the importance of employment among inmates released from prison has been explored in the literature, very few studies have specifically focused on the effectiveness of work release programs. Two such studies examined program costs and recidivism for work release programs in the state of Washington (Turner and Petersilia, 1996). Theses studies were found to be successful in preparing inmates for their release from prison and in transitioning them back into the community. In terms of program costs, the programs did not cost the corrections system any more than if they offenders had instead remained incarcerated.

Those offenders involved in work release also did not pose any additional community safety problems. Very few work release participants (less than 5%) committed new offenses, and when participants violated conditions of their supervision they were expeditiously returned to prison. Researchers found that offenders who were older, white, convicted of person crimes, and had no prior criminal record were more likely to be successful while on work release compared to their counterparts. Recidivism results from the study suggest that there were no significant differences between the control group and work release participants for arrests based on new crimes. There was however, a significant difference between the two groups for violations. Work release participants were much more likely to have infractions compared to the control group (58% vs. 4.7%). Many of these infractions were attributed to either rule violations or drug possession and drug use (Turner and Petersilia, 1996). It remains to be seen whether the use of work release will continue to decrease across the U.S., or whether corrections planners and administrators will recognize the importance of employment for those offenders who are reentering communities after a period of imprisonment.

BARBARA A. KOONS-WITT

## References and Further Reading

Camp, C.G. and Camp, G.M., The corrections yearbook 2000: Adult corrections, Middletown, CT, Criminal Justice Institute, Inc., 2000.
Harrison, P.M. and Beck, A.J., *Prisoners in 2001*, Washington, DC, Bureau of Justice Statitics, July, 2002.
Nelson, M. and Trone, J., Why planning for release matters, New York, Vera Institute of Justice, 2000.
Petersilia, J., Challenges of prisoner reentry and parole in California, *California Policy Research Center Brief*, Vol. 12(3), University of California, 2000.
Silverman, I.J., *Corrections: A Comprehensive View*, Belmont, CA, Wadsworth or Thomson Learning, 2001.
Turner, S. and Petersilia, J., Work release: Recidivism and corrections costs in Washington state, *Research Brief*, Washington, DC, National Institute of Justice, 1996.

*See also* **Community Service and Restitution Programs; Half-Way Houses and Day Reporting**

# Workplace Violence

Workplace violence has become a well-known yet often misunderstood social problem in both the U.S. and around the world. Ever since 1986, when a postal employee in Edmond, Oklahoma, murdered 14 fellow employees and wounded several others, workplace violence has been synonymous with senseless violence directed against coworkers and supervisors by deranged and disgruntled employees (a comprehensive definition of workplace violence, discussed later, also includes forms of verbal abuse and harassment). In a report entitled "Violence on the Job—A Global Problem" released in Geneva and Washington, DC, in July of 1998, the International Labour Organization (ILO) noted that outbursts of violence occurring at workplaces around the globe suggest that this issue transcends the boundaries of a particular country, work setting, or occupational group. According to the ILO, a 1996 European Union survey based on 15,800 interviews in its 15 member states showed that 4% of workers (6 million) were subjected to violence in the preceding year (Chappell and DiMartino, 1998).

In the U.S., data from the National Crime Victimization Surveys (NCVS) for 1992–1996 indicate that an annual average of 2,010,800 citizens experienced violent victimizations while they were working or on duty. Overall, for each year there were about 1.5 million simple assaults, 396,000 aggravated assaults, 51,000 rapes and sexual assaults, and 84,000 robberies. In fact, one in six violent crimes in the entire U.S. occurred in the workplace, including 8% of all rapes, 7% of robberies, and 16% of assaults. The occupations of these survivors of workplace violence varied widely.

Annually, 330,000 retail sales workers became victims of workplace violence. These included 61,000 convenience store clerks and 26,000 bartenders. More than 160,000 medical workers were victimized. An estimated 70,000 nurses, 24,000 technicians, and about 10,000 physicians were victimized each year. Teachers accounted for about 149,000 workplace victimizations and mental health workers accounted for 102,500 violent assaults. Approximately 234,000 police and 71,100 private security officers were assaulted while on duty. Over 76,930 transportation workers were attacked while working. In fact, the taxi driver's job is the most dangerous occupation with 183.8 victimizations per 1000 workers compared to the overall average of 14.8 victimizations per 1000 workers in all occupations (Warchol, 1998). Workplace violence and homicide

have been identified as the fastest growing forms of violence in the U.S., doubling in the past ten years (Carll, 1999).

A study conducted by the Northwestern National Life Insurance Company in 1993 suggests that the number of assaulted employees may be closer to 2.2 million. Furthermore, 6 million workers were threatened and 16 million were harassed. Overall, one in four workers in the U.S. are attacked, threatened, or harassed each year while on the job. Even more tragic are the homicides that occur at the workplace. During the early and mid-1990s, approximately 1000 people were killed at work annually in the U.S., although U.S. Bureau of Labor data for 1999 reveal that 645 American workers fell victim to homicide on the job compared to 714 in 1998. This drop in homicides at work is likely related to the overall drop in violent crime in the U.S. during the late 1990s. Nevertheless, the homicide rate remains higher than existed in the early 1960s, and remains high when compared to many other industrialized nations around the world (Fox and Levin, 2001).

The economic costs of workplace violence are enormous. In the U.S., the National Safe Workplace Institute estimated in the early 1990s that assaults and murders at work cost the economy $4.2 billion (Kinney, 1995). A more recent estimate in 1998 by the Workplace Violence Research Institute identified the cost of workplace violence to be closer to $36 billion once such variables as loss of productivity, work disruptions, employee turnover, litigation, and incident-related costs such as increased security expenditures and higher insurance premiums are considered (Mattman and Kaufer, 1998). Internationally, the total cost of group harassment and individual bullying of German workers has been estimated at 2.5 billion marks per year. In Canada, the British Columbia Worker's Compensation Board has reported that wage loss claims by hospital workers because of acts of violence have increased 88% since 1985 (Chappell and DiMartino, 2000). Although the true value of a lost life can never be expressed in mere economic terms, one study by the U.S. Department of Labor estimated the dollar value of the life of an employee at $7 million (Kinney, 1995). Certainly, any figures such as these must be cautiously interpreted because of variations in fundamental assumptions and the imprecise nature of much financial data. Nevertheless, the enormity of the estimates alone attests to the contemporary significance of the problem.

Notwithstanding increased popular and scholarly attention to workplace violence, there remain disagreements concerning the exact nature and extent of the problem. Some observers believe the actual threat to workers presented by their disgruntled coworkers is vastly exaggerated by the media and numerous self-proclaimed experts who stand to profit through consulting contracts from hasty corporate expenditures designed to protect their workers from a perceived imminent danger (Southerland et al., 1997). Other observers cite statistics indicating that only 59 employees were killed by coworkers or former coworkers in 1993, out of a total national workforce of 120.8 million people. These critics place the odds of murder by a fellow employee at roughly one in 2 million and point out that the National Weather Service puts the odds of getting struck by lighting at one in 600,000 (Larson, 1996). In fact, most murders of employees are committed during robberies of retail establishments. Other workplace homicides center on disputes with customers and clients or involve the murder of police officers while on duty.

A number of scholars also believe the concept of workplace violence has been unduly limited to physical assaults and homicides. There is a belief that much emotional injury results from sexual harassment, bullying, and other forms of psychological aggression that should become part of the international discourse on workplace violence (Keashley 1998; Neuman and Baron, 1998; Denenberg and Braverman, 1999). Accordingly, a more comprehensive definition of workplace violence is "any act against an employee that creates a hostile work environment and negatively affects the employee, either physically or psychologically. These acts include all types of physical or verbal assault, threats, coercion, intimidation, and all forms of harassment" (Shea, 2000).

In an attempt to promote better understanding of workplace violence, a number of perpetrator typologies have been suggested. Such conceptual distinctions would facilitate investigation into the etiology, patterns, and control of the problem. For example, one psychologist has identified five main types of worksite assailants: the angry customer, the medically ill person, the batterer in a domestic dispute, the criminal, and the disgruntled employee of the company (Flannery, 1995). Other experts, after scrutinizing numerous case histories, have identified seven categories of workplace assailants: criminals, personal or domestic disputants, disgruntled employees, mentally ill, disgruntled customers or clients, disgruntled student or trainees, abusive supervisors (Feldman and Johnson, 1996).

An increasingly popular conceptual scheme, however, is that posited by the California Division of Occupational Safety and Health (Cal/OSHA). The key to this typology is the relationship of the perpetrator to the workplace. In Type I violence, the perpetrator has no legitimate connection to the workplace. For example, during the commission of a robbery at a small late-night retail establishment such as a liquor store, gas station, or convenience store, an employee or proprietor is killed or injured. A Type II workplace violence event involves fatal or nonfatal injuries to individuals who provide services to the public. These events involve assaults on public safety personnel, bus or cab drivers, teachers and social workers, sales personnel and medical, psychiatric, and nursing care workers. A Type III workplace violence event consists of an assault by an individual who has some employment-related involvement with the workplace. These events generally involve threats or assaults by a current or former employee, coworker, supervisor, former spouse or lover, or some other person who has a dispute involving an employee of the workplace.

Because the circumstances and targets of workplace violence vary widely, so too do the motivations of various perpetrators. Because of the wide range of workplace violence incident types, no single etiological theory will generalize broadly enough to be universally applicable. Nevertheless, several theoretical approaches have proven useful in understanding the multifarious nature of workplace violence. Workplace violence Type I crimes are generally explained according to conventional social process and social structure theories of criminality such as differential association theory and strain theory. Routine activities theory and the "General Theory of Crime" (self-control theory) are also representative of current criminological thinking applied to workplace violence (Siegel, 2001).

Type II crimes are often explicable through the same theoretical approaches useful in the analysis of Type I crime. There are, however, additional considerations in several instances. For example, medical people may be attacked because of the paranoid delusions of some of their patients. Attacks at schools may result from the combination of youthful developmental insecurities and school cultures that generate or tolerate bullying (Aronson, 2000; Olweus, 1994). Also, as in the case of school shooters, the interaction of personality traits with school, family, and social dynamics may be the best predictor of violent behavior (O'Toole, 2000).

Attempts at explanations of Type III workplace violence often take the form of various profiles describing the disgruntled employee as a narcissistic loner whose ego involvement with his job prevents insight, who feels unappreciated, places blame externally, is infatuated with weapons and violence, and who is characterized as having negative affectivity. Because profiles often produce an unacceptable number of false positives, other observers attribute workplace violence to any of a variety of factors such as perceived injustice, increased worker diversity, downsizing, noxious environmental conditions, hostile attributional bias, and Type A behavior patterns (Neuman and Baron, 1998). Also appropriate to explain many cases of Type III workplace violence between coworkers is Agnew's general strain theory, which discusses how anger may develop as a consequence of failure to achieve positively valued goals, removal of positively valued stimuli, and the actual or anticipated presentation of negatively valued stimuli (Agnew, 1992). Also present in the literature are explanations attributing workplace crime to domestic violence spillover into the workplace and to such psychiatric disorders as Borderline Personality Disorder, Delusional Disorder, Dependent Personality Disorder, Narcisstic Personality Disorder, Histrionic Personality Disorder, and Antisocial Personality Disorder.

Employers can sometimes find themselves liable in tort for those instances of workplace violence that were "substantially certain" to befall their employees and where no preventive action was taken to protect these employees. Causes of action such as negligent hiring, negligent retention, negligent supervision, and negligent entrustment have been successfully brought against employers by injured employees who are not barred by workers compensation laws from bringing suit. To avoid such litigation, to prevent other financial losses, and to fulfill their moral duty to their employees, many employers are adopting "zero tolerance" policies toward aggressive behavior on the part of their employees. Security surveys are being conducted to identify threats to employee safety. Employee Assistance Programs are becoming responsive to victimization prevention needs, and company leaders are forming threat assessment teams to evaluate developing situations that may prove a threat to employee safety.

Both government employers and private sector employers are developing comprehensive violence prevention policies and are sharing information widely. For example, the International Association of Chiefs of Police recently commissioned the development of guidelines for both law enforcement and employers to follow in order to prevent workplace violence, manage acute incidents, and deal with the aftermath. Overall, the best strategies for dealing with the problem of workplace violence will ultimately require this kind of coordinated effort.

DANIEL B. KENNEDY

## References and Further Reading

Agnew, R., Foundation for a general strain theory of crime and delinquency, *Criminology*, 30(1) (1992).

Aronson, E., *Nobody Left to Hate*, New York, W.H. Freeman Company, 2000.

Carll, E.K., *Violence in Our Lives: Impact on Workplace, Home, and Community*, Boston, MA, Allyn and Bacon, 1999.

Chappell, D. and DiMartino, V., *Violence at Work*, Geneva, International Labour Office, 1998. 2nd ed., 2000.

Denenberg, R. and Braverman, M., *The Violence Prone Workplace*, Ithaca, NY, and London, Cornell University Press, 1999.

Feldman, T. and Johnson, P., Workplace violence: A new form of lethal aggression, in Hall, H., Ed., *Lethal Violence 2000*, Kamuela, Hawaii, Pacific Institute for the Study of Conflict and Aggression, 1996.

Flannery, R.B., *Violence in the Workplace*, New York, The Crossroad Publishing Company, 1995.

Fox, J.A. and Levin, J., *The Will to Kill*, Boston, MA, Allyn and Bacon, 2001.

Keashley, L., Emotional abuse in the workplace: Conceptual and empirical issues, *Journal of Emotional Abuse*, 1 (1998).

Kinney, J.A., *Preventing Violence at Work*, Englewood Cliffs, NJ, Prentice Hall, 1995.

Larson, E., Violence in the workplace is not a serious problem, in Barbour, S. and Swisher, K., *Violence: Opposing Viewpoints*, San Diego, Greenhaven Press, 1996.

Mattman, J. and Kaufer, S., Eds., *The Complete Workplace Violence Prevention Manual: Volume I*, Costa Mesa, CA, James Publishing, 1998.

Neuman, J.H. and Baron, R.A., Workplace violence and workplace aggression: Evidence concerning specific forms, potential causes, and preferred targets, *Journal of Management*, 24 (1998).

Olweus, D., Bullying at school, in Hussman, R.L., *Aggressive Behavior*, New York, Plenum Press, 1994.

O'Toole, M.E., *The School Shooter: A Threat Assessment Perspective*, Quantico, VA, National Center for the Analysis of Violent Crime, 2000.

Shea, T.H., Workplace violence: Turning down the heat, *Workplace Violence Prevention Reporter*, 6 (2000).

Siegel, L.J., *Criminology: Theories, Patterns, and Typologies*, 7th ed., Belmont, CA, Wadsworth, 2001.

Southerland, M., Collins, P. and Scarborough, K., *Workplace Violence*, Cincinnati, OH, Anderson Publishing Company, 1997.

Warchol, G., Workplace violence, 1992–1996, *Bureau of Justice Statistics Special Report*, July (1998).

# Young, Jock

In his Foreword to John Lowman and Brian D. MacLean's *Realist Criminology: Crime Control and Policing in the 1990s* (1992), Paul Rock contends that "criminology undergoes a scientific revolution *every* time Jock Young changes his mind" (emphasis in original). For this and many other reasons, it is not surprising that in 1998, he received the American Society of Criminology's Sellin-Glueck Distinguished International Scholar Award.

Currently Head of Middlesex University's Centre for Criminology, Young is one of the pioneers of contemporary critical criminology. There are variations in this school of thought, although most critical criminologists view broader political, economic, social, and cultural forces as key determinants of crime and its control. They also regard major structural and cultural changes within society as essential means of reducing criminality and improving people's overall quality of life. Sharply opposed to individualistic explanations for criminal behavior and to calls for harsher punishments for those who violate social and legal norms, Young helped to develop contemporary critical criminology by becoming a founding member (in 1968) of the British National Deviancy Conference (NDC). The NDC lasted for five years and culminated in some of the most important books in the field, including Young's (1971) *The Drugtakers* and *The New Criminology* (co-authored book with Ian Taylor and Paul Walton, 1973).

*The New Criminology* is still widely read and cited, and has influenced many criminology students around the world to embrace Marxist analyses of crime and to reject conservative theories, research methods, and policies. Following in the footsteps of Taylor, Walton, and Young, these radicals have defined crime as a socially constructed phenomenon and viewed the criminal justice system as an oppressive handmaiden to corporate elites. Most agree with Taylor, Walton and Young, who argued that crime is "a product of inequitable economic relationships in a context of general poverty" (1973).

Deeply committed to major structural change and to challenging conservative research on street crimes committed by the poor, radical criminologists— influenced by *The New Criminology* and other radical works published in the early and mid-1970s—ignored or trivialized the causes and possible control of crime committed by members of the working class against other members of the working class. For these scholars, such crime was a function of a state-sponsored moral panic designed to divert attention away from crimes of the powerful, such as corporate violence and white-collar crime. Moreover, any attempt to promote reform within the current capitalist patriarchal order was simply seen as just another way of oppressing the socially and economically disadvantaged. It was almost as if these new criminologists feared that they would lose their credentials as radicals if they studied street crimes committed by the poor and if they proposed short-term solutions to this problem. Thus, they devoted the bulk of their intellectual energy to studying crimes committed by large corporations, politicians, and other elite members of society. At the same time, they relentlessly attacked imprisonment, the war on drugs, and other right-wing means of curbing crime on the streets.

Jock Young, too, was (and still is) very concerned about crimes committed in corporate and political offices. In the early 1980s, however, he and several other radicals in the U.K., Australia, and the U.S. argued that critical criminology was out of balance. For them, crimes committed by working-class offenders against working-class victims are just as serious as crimes of the elite and require considerable empirical, theoretical, and political attention. Young and his colleagues also argued that critical criminology's general failure to acknowledge predatory street crime in poor urban areas came at a great price to the left. It allowed right-wing politicians in several countries to claim opposition to this social problem as their own issue, giving them the room to generate ideological support for harsh law enforcement policies.

Thanks again to Young, critical criminology underwent another scientific revolution with the creation of left realism that was formally articulated in *What is to be Done about Law and Order?* (coauthored with John Lea, 1984). In addition to taking working-class crime seriously and providing practical, crime control strategies (e.g., community control of the police) that challenge the conservative law and order campaign, left realists provide a sophisticated theoretical perspective on working-class crime. They envision a "square of crime," consisting of four interacting elements: the police and other government agencies of social control, the public, the offender, and the victim. The idea of relative deprivation experienced within subcultures where crime is caused by the frustrations of disadvantaged groups when they compare their circumstances against those of elites is also a major component of the left realist theoretical framework.

Spearheaded by Young, left realism is much more than a theoretical and political enterprise. It is also a school of thought that relies heavily on the use of local victimization surveys to elicit data that challenge conservative interpretations of street crime and domestic violence, along with the effectiveness of right-wing policies for curbing these problems. The Islington Crime Survey is the most famous left realist survey, and Young's book on this study (coauthored with Richard Kinsey and Brian D. MacLean, 1986) was recently ranked number two in a list of the 25 most-cited publications in critical criminology (Wright and Friedrichs, 1998).

Young contributed to yet another revolution in criminological thought with his 1999 book *The Exclusive Society*. Here, he argues that since 1970, a growing number of people throughout the advanced industrial world have been excluded from the labor market and have been denied access to quality education, housing,

and health care. For Young, these structural changes are strongly associated with both rising crime (as a response to oppression and marginalization) and the increased use of imprisonment and other punitive means of excluding people who violate social norms or the law or both.

Regardless of what type of scholarly work he does, Jock Young always insists that critical criminology must be policy relevant. Further, he never fails to oppose the conservative forces that contribute to social exclusion. Despite all his important contributions, Young was denounced as a "liberal threat to civilization" by William Hague, then Leader of the British Conservative Party, in *The Sunday Telegraph*. Young's response was "You can't do much better than that!"

WALTER S. DEKESEREDY

## Biography

Born in Gorebridge, Scotland, March 4, 1942. Educated at London School of Economics, B.Sc. in Sociology, 1965; M.Sc. in Sociology, 1966; London School of Economics, Ph.D. in Sociology, 1972. Lecturer to professor of sociology, Middlesex University, Enfield, England, 1967 to date. Founding member and committee member of National Deviancy Symposium Conference, 1968–1975; Recipient American Society of Criminology's Sellin-Glueck Award for Distinguished International Scholar, 1998.

## Principal Writings

*The Drugtakers: The Social Meaning of Drug Use,* 1971.
*The New Criminology: For a Social Theory of Deviance* (with Ian Taylor and Paul Walton), 1973.
*The Manufacture of News* (edited with Stanley Cohen), 1973; 2nd ed., 1981.
*Critical Criminology* (edited with Ian Taylor and Paul Walton), 1975.
*What is to be Done about Law and Order?* (with John Lea), 1984.
*Losing the Fight against Crime* (with Richard Kinsey and John Lea), 1986.
*The Islington Crime Survey: Crime Victimization and Policing in Inner-City London* (with Trevor Jones and Brian D. Maclean), 1986.
*Confronting Crime* (edited with Roger Matthews), 1986.
*Rethinking Criminology: The Realist Debate* (edited with Roger Matthews), 1992.
*Issues in Realist Criminology* (edited with Roger Matthews), 1992.
*The New Criminology Revisited* (edited with Paul Walton), 1998.
*The Exclusive Society: Social Exclusion, Crime, and Difference in Late Modernity,* 1999.

## References and Further Reading

DeKeseredy, W.S., The left realist approach to law and order, *Justice Quarterly,* 5(4) (1988).
DeKeseredy, W.S. and Schwartz, M.D., British and U.S. left realism: A critical comparison, *International Journal of*

*Offender Therapy and Comparative Criminology,* 35(3), 1991.

Lowman, J. and MacLean, B.D., Eds., *Realist Criminology: Crime Control and Policing in the 1990s,* Toronto, Canada, University of Toronto Press, 1992.

MacLean, B.D. and Milovanovic, D., Eds., *New Directions in Critical Criminology,* Vancouver, Canada, Collective Press, 1991.

MacLean, B.D. and Milovanovic, D., Eds., *Thinking Critically About Crime,* Vancouver, Canada, Collective Press, 1997.

Rock, P., Ed., *A British History of Criminology,* New York, Oxford University Press, 1988.

Rock, P. and Downes, D., *Understanding Deviance: A Guide to the Sociology of Crime and Rule Breaking,* 2nd ed. (revised), New York, Oxford University Press, 1995.

Schwartz, M.D. and DeKeseredy, W.S., Left realist criminology: Strengths, weaknesses and the feminist critique, *Crime, Law and Social Change* 15(1), 1991.

Wright, R.A. and Friedrichs, D., The most-cited scholars and works in critical criminology, *Journal of Criminal Justice Education* 9(2) (1998).

*See also* **Critical Criminology; Marxist Theories of Criminal Behavior; Radical Theories of Criminal Behavior**

# Youth Work and Crime

## Introduction

The labor market is a major life domain among youths enrolled in high school, as approximately 80% of youths participate in some way in the labor market prior to graduating from high school. Moreover, about half of all working high-school seniors average at least 20 hours per week, or what researchers have labeled "intensive work" (Greenberger and Steinberg, 1986; Steinberg and Cauffman, 1995; National Research Council, 1998). Folk wisdom suggests that employment during the school year provides a number of positive benefits for adolescents, by structuring a youth's leisure time, increasing exposure to adult authority figures, fostering independence and maturity, teaching responsibility in the use of money, and promoting the balancing of multiple responsibilities. On the contrary, an extensive literature consistently finds that youths who work during high school tend to engage in higher rates of minor delinquency, serious delinquency, substance use, and school misconduct, and to have higher rates of police contact.

## Empirical Research on the Association Between Adolescent Employment and Problem Behavior

Since the early 1980s, over 30 studies have been conducted on the relationship between youth employment and problem behavior. Greenberger et al. (1981) conducted the first systematic study of the effects of adolescent employment on problem behavior, finding that weekly earnings and time spent in the workplace were consistent predictors of higher levels of excessive alcohol use and marijuana use. Steinberg and Dornbusch (1991) found that longer work hours were associated with higher rates of substance use, minor delinquency, and school misconduct.

Bachman and colleagues (1981 and 2003; also Bachman and Schulenberg, 1993) found that work intensity was predictive of a variety of substance use behaviors. They found similar adverse work intensity effects for theft, interpersonal aggression, and trouble with police. Wright et al. (1997) found that work intensity was associated with increased parent-report problem behavior, controlling for numerous known correlates of delinquency. Mihalic and Elliott (1997) found using the National Youth Survey that entering the labor market at high intensity (over 20 hours) wave was associated with an increase in alcohol and drug use.

The accumulated literature underscores the idea that work intensity, rather than work experience *per se*, is crucial to understanding the relationship between youth employment and problem behavior. That is, high-school youths who work the highest number of hours during the school year also have the highest levels of participation in a wide variety of problem behavior. Robust as the existing findings are, however, there remains considerable uncertainty about whether the adverse work effect on problem behavior is genuinely causal. The issue is the problem of *self-selection*, the idea that adolescents who work at high intensity are systematically different with respect to preexisting characteristics that are correlated with problem behavior. For example, youths who work tend to engage in more delinquency, aggression, substance use, and school misconduct prior to labor market entry, and are more heavily involved with delinquent peers than future nonworking youths. Thus, problem behavior actually *precedes* the transition into the adolescent labor market. One recent study acknowledges the inferential risk posed by ignoring this source of selection bias. Paternoster et al. (2003) estimated a fixed-effects panel model, focusing their attention on the within-individual change in work involvement. They found that changing from nonwork to intensive school-year work had no adverse effect on problem behavior, and in fact the coefficient for intensive work was negative in all three models (and significantly so in one). They concluded from their analysis that the consistently reported positive association between intensive school-year work and adolescent problem behavior is driven by a process of *selection* rather than *causation*.

## Criminological Theory and the Explanation of the Adverse "Intensive Work Effect"

Developmental researchers have identified numerous correlates of intensive youth employment that suggest several theoretical avenues to explain the adverse work intensity effect on delinquency and substance use.

## Causal Mechanisms for the Adverse Work Effect

Several potential causal mechanisms explain the relationship between intensive work during adolescence and elevated involvement in problem behavior. According to these theories, intensive work is simply the first step in a causal sequence, the end result being increased levels of problem behavior.

*Social Control Theory.* Youths who work intensively during high school tend to spend less time with, are less emotionally close to, engage in more disagreements with, and are less closely monitored by, their parents than nonworkers or moderate workers. High-intensity work during high school also tends to be associated with less time spent on homework and studying, cutting class and absenteeism, lower educational expectations and aspirations, and negative school attitudes or school disengagement. The research with respect to grades and test scores is considerably more mixed. Social control theory, for one, predicts that an intensive work commitment during adolescence disrupts emotional attachment to parents ("relational control"), diminishes parental monitoring of adolescent behavior ("instrumental control"), and

erodes commitment to conventional educational pursuits (Hirschi, 1969). The unattached, uncommitted, and uninvolved youth is subject to lower levels of informal social control over his or her behavior. To the extent that intensive work weakens the youth's bond to conventional society, higher levels of delinquency and substance use are a consequence.

*General Strain Theory.* Most adolescents work in minimum-wage jobs concentrated in the secondary labor market, and little of what they do on the job involves opportunities for learning. Work stressors associated with adolescent jobs have been found to increase the likelihood of excessive alcohol use, as well as occupational deviance. In addition to these on-the-job stressors is the concern that extensive employment compromises a youth's central role as student by conflicting with school demands, and leads to poor mental and physical health. According to general strain theory, heavy work involvement creates job dissatisfaction and stress, a form of noxious stimuli that, in the absence of conventional coping mechanisms, is eased through delinquency and drug use (Agnew, 1992). One potent source of strain relevant to adolescent work is the "presentation of negatively valued (or noxious) stimuli" in the workplace. The highly impersonal and demanding workplace of teenage "McJobs" may generate a desire to manage the resulting negative effect inwardly through substance use (smoking, drinking, using marijuana) and poor physical health (lack of sleep, exercise, eating), or through acting out in a delinquent manner.

*Learning Theory.* The adolescent workplace is dominated by youths; consequently an intensive work commitment puts adolescents in contact with a wider circle of young people. Employment may thus increase exposure to delinquent peers in the workplace, which has been linked to occupational deviance as well as a youth's own nonwork delinquency. Learning theories such as differential association and social learning propose that intensive employment puts youths in regular contact with older, less-than-conventional peers in the workplace, who provide a source of antisocial attitude transference, behavioral modeling, and reinforcement (Sutherland, 1947; Akers et al., 1979). Considering that youth job opportunities often originate in low-wage, low-skill, service occupations, older co-workers are expected to be more deviant and unconventional. Consequently, intensive employment potentially alters the balance of definitions favorable and unfavorable to violation of the legal code.

*Routine Activity Theory.* Work intensity does not lead to a reduction in time spent with friends. On the contrary, adolescents who work at high intensity tend to spend more time each week going out on dates, going out for evening fun and recreation, and spending time with friends. Working adolescents also participate in such activities as cruising around, going to parties and movies, shopping, and having informal get-togethers with friends. Thus, employed youths appear to be able to find time for an active social life. Routine activity theory predicts that intensively employed youths spend more time engaging in unstructured leisure activities with peers in the absence of adult authority figures (Osgood et al., 1996). Youths who are intensively employed are more likely to spend their time "being out and about" and "making the scene" (Osgood, 1999), and thereby more often placing themselves in social situations conducive to deviance. The automobile plays a particularly important role in the routine activities of youths. By providing autonomy, having a car presents ample opportunities to cruise around with friends farther away from home and the watchful eyes of parents and other "handlers."

## Spurious Mechanisms for the Work Effect

Other theories propose that the positive relationship between intensive work and problem behavior is a spurious one. These theories view the manifold negative correlates of intensive youth employment as more than a mere coincidence. Rather, they are viewed as multiple outcomes of a common underlying process. Theories that specify spurious mechanisms include precocious development and propensity theories.

*Precocious Development Theory.* Precocious development theory draws attention to the life stage of adolescence *per se*, emphasizing the changes in affiliations, identities, and responsibilities that correspond with a stage-appropriate "drive toward autonomy" (Jessor and Jessor, 1977; Greenberger and Steinberg, 1986; Newcomb and Bentler, 1988; Bachman and Schulenberg, 1993). Early and intensive employment is viewed as one symptom of a broader, latent, stage-specific propensity to expedite the transition to adulthood. The issue is thus one of early timing of work transitions, whereby adolescents have not yet acquired the capabilities necessary to assume adult roles and responsibilities. This idea is consistent with a growing body of literature that links youth employment with dating, sexual intercourse, pregnancy, alcohol use, and smoking, behaviors that are normatively age graded and considered "problem behavior" only when engaged in by teenagers. A dominant theme of precocious development theories is the inability to delay gratification, in that the more rewarding aspects of adulthood are sought at the expense of

the more difficult tasks responsibly gained through experience and maturity.

*Propensity Theory.* Propensity theory proposes that intensive youth employment and such correlates as problem behavior, school disengagement, emotional distance from parents, and exposure to delinquent peers are all diverse manifestations of a single underlying tendency that is established early in life and remains stable over time. Gottfredson and Hirschi (1990) refer to this proclivity as low self-control, or the tendency to pursue short-term gratification without consideration of the long-term consequences of one's actions. Youth employment and its adverse outcomes are simply manifestations of the "versatility" of individuals with low self-control. Studies of youth employment that include a lagged measure of problem behavior—a proxy for "propensity"—consistently find that prior behavior is a strong predictor of present behavior. Propensity theory is somewhat different from precocious development theory in that the underlying "propensity" is generally presumed to be stable rather than transitory. This distinction is especially important given that both theories draw upon a concept of the inability to delay gratification as the basis for the relationship between intensive youth work and problem behavior. According to precocious development theory, the association is motivated by the maturity gap during adolescence. According to propensity theory, the association is a consequence of poor socialization that is set early in life and remains stable thereafter.

## Discussion and Conclusion

A lengthy literature suggests that employment has detrimental consequences for involvement in a wide variety of adolescent problem behaviors, most notably delinquency and substance use. The emphasis in this literature has been almost exclusively on the amount of time that adolescents spend in the workplace, and the accumulated findings suggest that work that is of high intensity is robustly correlated with adolescent problem behavior. The tendency has been to interpret this association as causal. Because of this, scholars have recently called for time limits on youth work to minimize its detrimental impact:

> The Department of Labor should be authorized by Congress to adopt a standard limiting the weekly maximum number of hours of work for 16- and 17-year-olds during the school year. This standard should be based on the extensive research about the adverse effects of high-intensity work while school is in session. (National Research Council, 1998, 227)

Nevertheless, recent evidence urges restraint in inferring causality from this empirical association, as most prior research relies on relatively unsophisticated analytic designs. Although the intensive work effect is robust to control for *observed* heterogeneity, it may not withstand more rigorous control for *unobserved* heterogeneity.

New directions in youth employment research hold some promise for disentangling the positive correlation between employment and problem behavior. Notably, these studies focus on characteristics other than work intensity, emphasizing that youth jobs are not "one size fits all." Apel et al. (2003), for example, consider the impact of work hours in addition to job type (formal vs. informal jobs) and seasonality (school-year vs. summer jobs). Staff and Uggen (2003) consider such diverse measures of "work quality" as work intensity, hourly pay, work-derived peer status, learning opportunities, autonomy, work stressors, and work–school compatibility. Mortimer (2003) examines the consequences of "steady" work on outcomes of interest. Researchers are thus beginning to move beyond a single-minded focus on work intensity, a move that is sure to pay dividends for better understanding the nature of the relationship between youth employment and problem behavior.

ROBERT APEL

## References and Further Reading

Agnew, R., Foundation for a general strain theory of crime and delinquency, *Criminology,* 30 (1992).

Akers, R.L., Krohn, M.D., Lanza-Kaduce, L., and Radosevich, M., Social learning and deviant behavior: A specific test of a general theory, *American Sociological Review,* 44 (1979).

Apel, R., Paternoster, R., Bushway, S., and Brame, R., *Gender and Race Differences in the Impact of Youth Employment on Problem Behavior* (manuscript under review), 2003.

Bachman, J.G., Johnston, L.D., and O'Malley, P.M., Smoking, drinking, and drug use among American high school students: Correlates and trends, 1975–1979, *American Journal of Public Health,* 71 (1981).

Bachman, J.G. and Schulenberg, J., How part-time work intensity relates to drug use, problem behavior, time use, and satisfaction among high school seniors: Are these consequences or merely correlates?, *Developmental Psychology,* 29 (1993).

Bachman, J.G., Safron, D.J., Sy, S.R., and Schulenberg, J.E., Wishing to work: New perspectives on how adolescents' part-time work intensity is linked to educational disengagement, substance use, and other problem behaviours, *International Journal of Behavioral Development,* 27 (2003).

Gottfredson, M.R. and Hirschi, T., *A General Theory of Crime,* Stanford, CA, Stanford University Press, 1990.

Greenberger, E. and Steinberg, L., *When Teenagers Work: Psychological and Social Costs Adolescent Employment,* New York, Basic Books, 1986.

Greenberger, E., Steinberg, L.D. and Vaux, A., Adolescents who work: Health and behavioral consequences of job stress, *Developmental Psychology,* 17 (1981).

Hirschi, T., *Causes of Delinquency,* Berkeley, CA, University of California Press, 1969.

Jessor, R. and Jessor, S.L., *Problem Behavior and Psychosocial Development: A Longitudinal Study of Youth,* New York, Academic Press, 1977.

Mihalic, S.W. and Elliott, D., Short- and long-term consequences of adolescent employment, *Youth and Society,* 28 (1997).

Mortimer, J.T., *Working and Growing Up in America,* Cambridge, MA, Harvard University Press, 2003.

National Research Council, *Protecting Youth at Work: Health, Safety, and Development of Working Children and Adolescents in the United States,* Washington, DC, National Academy Press, 1998.

Newcomb, M.D. and Bentler, P.M., *Consequences of Adolescent Drug Use: Impact on the Lives of Young Adults,* Newbury Park, CA, Sage, 1988.

Osgood, D.W., Having the time of their lives: All work and no play?, in Booth, A., Crouter, A.C., and Shanahan, M.J., Eds., *Transitions to Adulthood in a Changing Economy: No Work, No Family, No Future?* Westport, CT, Praeger, 1999.

Osgood, D.W., Wilson, J.K., O'Malley, P.M., Bachman, J.G., and Johnston, L.D., Routine activities and individual deviant behavior, *American Sociological Review,* 61 (1996).

Paternoster, R., Bushway, S., Brame, R., and Apel, R., The effect of teenage employment on delinquency and problem behaviors, *Social Forces,* 82 (2003).

Staff, J. and Uggen, C., The fruits of good work: Early work experiences and adolescent deviance, *Journal of Research in Crime and Delinquency,* 40 (2003).

Steinberg, L. and Cauffman, E., The impact of employment on adolescent development, *Annals of Child Development,* 11 (1995).

Steinberg, L. and Dornbusch, S.M., Negative correlates of part-time employment during adolescence: Replication and elaboration, *Developmental Psychology,* 27 (1991).

Sutherland, E.H, *Criminology,* Philadelphia, PA, J. B. Lippincott, 1947; 4th edition published as *Principles of Criminology,* Philadelphia: J.B. Lippincott.

Wright, J.P., Cullen, F.T., and Williams, N., Working while in high school and delinquent involvement: Implications for social policy, *Crime and Delinquency,* 43 (1997).

*See also* **Juvenile Delinquency and Youth Crime throughout History**

# CONTRIBUTORS

Howard Abadinsky
St. John's University
*Organized Crime: Activities and Extent; Organized Crime: Definitions and Models; Organized Crime: Italian-American Mafia; Organized Crime: Outlaw Motorcycle Clubs; Organized Crime: Sicilian Mafia; Organized Crime: Theories*

Cynthia G. Adams
Central Missouri State University
*Trespass*

Robert Agnew
Emory University
*Sociological Theories of Criminal Behavior; Strain Theories: From Durkheim to Merton; Strain Theories: Recent Developments*

Ronald L. Akers
University of Florida
*Cressey, Donald*

Leanne Fiftal Alarid
University of Missouri-Kansas City
*Incapacitation (Collective and Selective)*

Geoffrey P. Alpert
University of South Carolina
*Short, James*

Shahid Alvi
University of St. Thomas
*Left Realism*

Robert Apel
University of Maryland
*Youth Work and Crime*

James B. Appel
University of South Carolina
*Lysergic Acid Diethylamide (LSD)*

David Baker
University of Toledo Ohio
*Labeling and Symbolic Interaction Theories of Criminal Behavior; Loan Sharking*

Ralph Baker
Ball State University
*Politics and Crime Policies*

Jeremy D. Ball
University of Nebraska
*Criminal Law: Reform*

James David Ballard
California State University, Northridge
*Sykes, Gresham*

Rosemary Barbaret
Universidad Carlos III, Spain
*International Crime Statistics: Data Sources and Interpretation; International Crime Statistics: Juvenile Delinquency and Youth Crime; International Crime Trends*

Contributors

Thomas Barker
Eastern Kentucky University
*Gambling, Illegal*

Allan R. Barnes
University of Alaska Anchorage
*Jeffery, Clarence Ray*

Ronald Becker
Chaminade University of Honolulu
*Administrative Law; Homicide: The Law*

Gad J. Bensinger
Loyola University Chicago
*Israel, Crime and Justice in*

Michael L. Benson
University of Cincinnati
*White-Collar Crime: Definitions; White-Collar Crime: Theories*

Ashley Blackburn
Sam Houston State University
*Amphetamines*

William P. Bloss
The Citadel
*Accomplices, Aiding, and Abetting; Attempted and Incomplete Offenses*

Scott Blough
Tifflin University
*Sheriffs*

John Boal
University of Akron
*Gangs: The Law; Theft, Professional*

Rachel Boba
Police Foundation
*Crime Mapping*

Robert M. Bohm
University of Central Florida
*Capital Punishment: United States History; Capital Punishment: World History*

Ulla V. Bondeson
University of Copenhagen
*Scandanavia, Crime and Justice in*

Timothy Brezina
Tulane University
*Boot Camps and Shock Incarceration*

Ramona Brockett
Northern Kentucky University
*Criminology and Criminal Justice Careers*

Alison McKenney Brown
Wichita State University
*Assault and Battery: Extent and Correlates; Larceny/Theft: Extent and Correlates; Preliminary Hearings*

Kristine A. Brown
U.S. District Court for the Western District of Virginia
*Due Process; Prisons: Women's Facilities*

Nancy K. Brown
University of South Carolina
*Women and Addictions*

Stephen E. Brown
East Tennessee State University
*Classical Criminology; Criminology: Definition; Peel, Sir Robert*

Clifton D. Bryant
Virginia Tech University
*Military Justice: The Police*

Kevin M. Bryant
Benedictine University
*Robbery: Extent and Correlates; Quetelet, Adolphe*

Michael Bryant
University of Toledo
*Babylonian Legal Tradition; English Legal Traditions; Genocide; Organized Crime: Irish, Jewish, and German Mobsters; Lynching*

Ronald G. Burns
Texas Christian University
*White-Collar Crime: Enforcement Strategie*

James D. Calder
University of Texas at San Antonio
*Hoover, John Edgar; Organized Crime: Black Mafia*

Dawn Caldwell
Isle of Palms Police Department
*Police: Forensic Evidence*

Lisa A. Callahan
Russell Sage College
*Insanity and Diminished Responsibility as Defense to Criminal Liability; Mental Illness and Criminal Behavior*

Dean John Champion
Texas A & M University at Laredo
*Sentencing Guidelines, United States*

Chau-Pu Chiang
California State University, Stanislaus
*Evaluation and Policy Research; Survey Research*

John K. Cochran
University of South Florida
*Religion and Criminal Behavior*

Ellen G. Cohn
Florida International University
*Climate and Criminal Behavior; Farrington, David P.; Citation Research in Criminology and Criminal Justice; Sherman, Lawrence W.*

Anthony J. Connolly
Australian National University
*Clemency and Pardons*

Norman Conti
Duquesne University
*Police: Vice and Special Units*

Heith Copes
University of Alabama Birmingham
*Hackers: History, Motivations, and Activities; Motor Vehicle Theft: Extent and Correlates; Motor Vehicle Theft: The Law*

Gary Cordner
Eastern Kentucky University
*Police: Administration and Organization; Police: Patrol*

Ronald D. Crelinsten
Middle East Technical University
*Hostage Taking and Negotiations*

Michael Cretacci
The Citadel
*Police History: England*

Katherine Culotta
Indiana State University
*Hate Crime*

Eugene H. Czajkoski
Florida State University
*Presentence Investigation Reports (PSIR)*

Contributors

Dean Dabney
Georgia State University
*Typologies of Crime and Criminal Behavior*

Leah E. Daigle
University of North Texas
*Biochemical Theories of Criminal Behavior; Rape, Statutory*

Lanette P. Dalley
Minot State University
*Child Abuse: The Law; Domestic Assault: The Law; Juvenile Delinquency: Definitions and the Law*

Jacqueline Davis
University of Arkansas at Little Rock
*Child Abuse: Prevention and Treatment*

L. Edward Day
Penn State Altoona
*War Crimes*

Mathieu Deflem
University of South Carolina
*International Police Cooperation, History of; International Policing: Role of the United States*

Walter S. DeKeseredy
Ohio University
*Chesney-Lind, Leda; Social Support Theory; Young, Jock*

Alejandro del Carmen
Sam Houston State University
*Central America, Crime and Justice in*

Matthew DeMichele
University of Louisville
*Counterfeiting; Statute of Limitations as a Defense to Criminal Liability*

Linda B. Deutschmann
University-College of the Cariboo
*Canada, Crime and Justice in; Criminal Justice*

*System: Definitions and Components; Halfway Houses and Day Reporting Centers; Inquisitorial Justice*

Mary Dodge
University of Colorado at Denver
*Chambliss, William J.; Simon, Rita*

Kimberly D. Dodson
Indiana University of Pennsylvania
*Prisons and the Rule of Law*

Amy V. D'Unger
Emory University
*Feminist Theories of Criminal Behavior*

Mary Ann Eastep
University of Central Florida
*Pretrial Detention/Preventive Detention*

Werner J. Einstadter
Eastern Michigan University
*Robbery as an Occupation*

O. Oko Elechi
University of Wisconsin-Parkside
*African Indigenous Justice System; Nigeria, Corruption in*

Lee Ellis
Minot State University
*Genetic Theories of Criminal Behavior; Neurophysiological Theories of Criminal Behavior*

Michael C. Elsner
William Paterson University
*Arraignment; Arrest; Drug Use: The Law*

Nicola Epprecht
Ministry of Community, Family and Children's Services and Ministry of Health and Long-Term Care
*Mertin, Robert K.*

Edna Erez
Kent State University
*Victims' Rights*

David P. Farrington
University of Cambridge
*Citation Research in Criminology and Criminal Justice*

Ezzat A. Fattah
Simon Fraser University
*Victimization, Crime: Theories about Vulnerability; Victimology*

Theodore N. Ferdinand
Southern Illinois University
*Historical Research; Juvenile Justice: History and Philosophy*

Jeff Ferrell
Northern Arizona University
*Cultural Crimino-logy*

Chuck Fields
Eastern Kentucky University
*International Imprisonment: Rates and Conditions; Ukraine, Crime and Justice in*

Jim Finckenauer
Rutgers University
*Organized Crime: Russian Mafia*

Bonnie S. Fisher
University of Cincinnati
*Campus Crime; International Crime Statistics: Data Sources and Interpretation; International Crime Statistics: Juvenile Delinquency and Youth Crime; International Crime Trends; Rape, Acquaintance and Date; Rape, Forcible: Extent and Correlates*

Kelly E. Fitz
Chicago, IL
*Electronic Surveillance and Wiretapping*

Ben Fitzpatrick
University of Leeds
*Actus Reus (The Criminal Act)*

David R. Forde
*University of Memphis*
*Traffic Offenses; Official and Unofficial Measures of Criminal Behavior*

Robert A. Foster Jr.
University of South Carolina
*Asset Forfeiture*

David O. Friedrichs
University of Scranton
*Crime, Definitions of; Occupational Crime; Quinney, Richard*

Tina M. Fryling
Mercyhurst College
*Accident as a Defense to Criminal Liability; Assault and Battery: The Law; Bail: Right to; Mistake of Fact as a Defense to Criminal Liability*

John R. Fuller
State University of West Georgia
*Peacemaking Criminology; Riots: Extent and Correlates*

Thomas Gabor
University of Ottawa
*Firearms and Criminal Behavior*

Phyllis P. Gerstenfeld
California State University, Stanislaus
*Habeas Corpus; Juvenile Justice: Due Process; Mens Rea (Criminal Intent)*

Chris L. Gibson
University of South Florida
*Exhibitionism and Voyeurism; Police: Race and Racial Profiling*

## Contributors

Michael J. Gilbert
University of Texas at San Antonio
*Drug Use and Criminal Behavior; Drug Use: Extent and Correlates*

Deirdre Golash
American University
*Punishment Justifications*

Zenta Gomez-Smith
University of Florida
*Elderly in Prison, The*

Jill A. Gordon
Virginia Commonwealth University
*Intensive Supervision Programs (ISP)*

Angela Gover
University of South Carolina
*Victim Compensation Programs*

Peter Grabosky
Australian National University
*Braithwaite, John*

Diana Grant
Sonoma State University
*Discretion and the Criminal Justice System; Juries and Juror Selection; Trial, The Right to*

Patricia Grant
Virginia Commonwealth University
*Perjury*

Robert E. Grubb Jr.
Marshall University
*Police: Rural*

John Hagan
Mercyhurst College
*Homelessness and Criminal Behavior*

James L. Hague
Virginia Commonwealth University
*Public Drunkeness*

Daniel E. Hall
Miami University Hamilton-Ohio
*Aggravating/Mitigating Circumstances; Indictment (Filing an Information); Micronesia, Crime and Justice in*

Mark Halsey
Flinders University of South Australia
*Australia, Crime and Justice in*

Robert D. Hanser
University of Louisiana at Monroe
*Adultery and Fornication; France, Crime and Justice in*

Richard D. Hartley
University of Nebraska at Omaha
*Bail: Reform*

Hennessey Hayes
Griffith University
*Differential Association Theory; Restorative Justice*

Melody M. Heaps
Treatment Alternatives for Safer Communities (TASC)
*Drug Control Policy: Enforcement, Interdiction, and the War on Drugs*

Craig Hemmens
Boise State University
*Defenses to Criminal Liability: Justifications and Excuses; Elements of Crime; Evidentiary Standards: Burden of Proof; Larceny/Theft: The Law; Self-Defense as a Defense to Criminal Liability*

Stuart Henry
Wayne State University
*Critical Criminology; Postmodernism and Constitutive Theories of Criminal Behavior*

Wendy L. Hicks
Michigan State University
*Police: Municipal/Urban*

Laurel Holland
State University of West Georgia
*Cloward, Richard; Reckless, Walter*

Alexander M. Holsinger
University of Missouri-Kansas City
*Classification of Offenders*

Kristy Holtfreter
Michigan State University
*Eyewitness Identification*

Brunon Holyst
University of Lodz, Poland
*Poland, Crime and Justice in; Vandalism*

Ross Homel
Griffith University
*Driving under the Influence (DUI)*

James Houston
Grand Valley State University
*Prisons: Administration and Organization*

Megan Howell
Columbia, SC
*Radzinowicz, Sir Leon*

Wendelin M. Hume
University of North Dakota (with Sherina M. Hume)
*Victimization, Crimes: Financial Loss and Personal Suffering*

Sean Huss
University of Tennessee, Knoxville
*Hackers: History, Motivations, and Activities*

Michelle Inderbitzin
Oregon State University
*Juvenile Justice: Corrections*

David Indermaur
University of Western Australia
*Public Opinion and Criminal Behavior*

Mark Israel
Flinders University
*Australia, Crime and Justice in*

Nicky Ali Jackson
Purdue University
*Same-Sex Domestic Violence*

Marianne James
Australian Institute of Criminology
*Art Crime*

Alison Jamieson
Control Risks Group
*International Policing: Coordination against Organized Crime in Europe*

David Jenks
California State University at Los Angeles
*International Policing: Cooperation among Nations in the European Union*

Wesley Jennings
University of South Carolina
*Drug Enforcement Administration (DEA); Federal Bureau of Investigation (FBI); Genealogical Studies of Crime*

Contributors

Gary Jensen
Vanderbilt University
*Criminology: Historical Development; Self-Esteem and Criminal Behavior; Social Control Theories of Criminal Behavior; Social Disorganization Theory; Witchcraft and Heresy*

Arthur Jipson
University of Dayton
*Occult Crimes*

W. Wesley Johnson
Sam Houston State University
*Amphetamines; Kidnapping*

William Jonas
University of Texas at San Antonio
*Marshals Service, United States*

David M. Jones
University of Wisconsin-Oshkosh
*Self-Representation, The Right to; Witnesses, The Right to Confront*

Matti Joutsen
Ministry of Justice, Finland
*Eastern and Central Europe, Crime and Justice in; International Crime and the United Nations*

Rebecca S. Katz
Morehead State University
*Family Relationships and Criminal Behavior*

David Kauzlarich
Southern Illinois University at Edwardsville
*Crime, Definitions of; Political Crimes of the State*

Michael Kempa
Australian National University
*Police: Contemporary Development; Prisons, Problems and Recent Developments in*

Daniel B. Kennedy
University of Detroit
Mercy *Workplace Violence*

Martin Killias
University of Lausanne
*Comparative Crime and Justice; Switzerland, Crime and Justice in*

Anna King
University of Cambridge
*Vigilante Violence*

Malcolm W. Klein
University of Southern California
*Gangs, Street; Gangs: European Street*

Carl B. Klockars
University of Delaware
*Police: Detectives; Receiving Stolen Goods*

Barbara A. Koons-Witt
University of South Carolina
*Work Release*

Peter Kraska
Eastern Kentucky University
*Criminal Justice Theorizing*

John T. Krimmel
The College of New Jersey
*Arson: Extent and Correlates; Arson: The Law*

Hamid R. Kusha
Texas A&M International University
*Islamic Legal Traditions*

Samantha S. Kwan
University of Maryland
*Natural Law*

Robyn D. Lacks
Virginia Department of Education
*Personality Theories of Criminal Behavior*

Jodi Lane
University of Florida
*Petersilia, Joan*

Lynn Langton
University of Florida
*Forgery*

Dennis Laster
Central Missouri State University
*Elder Abuse; Grand Juries*

Richard Lawrence
St. Cloud State University
*Schools and Delinquent Behavior*

Richard A. Leo
University of California-Irvine
*Interrogation and Confessions*

Kim Michelle Lersch
University of South Florida
*Police: Disciplinary Actions and Internal Affairs*

Michael Levi
Cardiff University
*Money Laundering*

Elena Licu
University of Cincinnati
*International Crime Statistics: Data Sources and Interpretation; International Crime Statistics: Juvenile Delinquency and Youth Crime; International Crime Trends*

John Liederbach
University of North Texas
*Physicians and the Pharmaceutical Industry, Crimes by*

J. Robert Lilly
Northern Kentucky University
*House Arrest and Electronic Monitoring*

Jianhong Liu
Rhode Island College
*China, Crime and Justice in*

Wayne A. Logan
William Mitchell College of Law
*Duress as a Defense to Criminal Liability*

M. Patrick Long
Criminal Justice Academy
*Law Enforcement: Careers; Police: Personalities and Subcultures; Secret Service, United States; Criminal Anthropology*

Arthur J. Lurigio
Loyola University
*Drug Control Policy: Enforcement, Interdiction, and the War on Drugs; Heroin*

Joan Luxenburg
University of Central Oklahoma
*Prostitution: Extent, Correlates, and Forms*

John M. MacDonald
University of South Carolina
*National Institute of Justice (NIJ)*

M. Kimberly MacLin
University of Northern Iowa
*Psychological Theories of Criminal Behavior*

Otto H. MacLin
University of Northern Iowa
*Phrenology*

Sean Maddan
University of Nebraska at Omaha
*Burglary: The Law; Corporal Punishment; Glueck, Sheldon and Eleanor*

Jess Maghan
University of Illinois at Chicago
*Prisons: Correctional Oficers and Staff*

Contributors

Toni Makkai
Australian Institute of Criminology
*Braithwaite, John*

Stephen Mallory
University of Southern Mississippi
*Drug Trafficking as an Occupation*

Michael D. Maltz
University of Illinois at Chicago
*Uniform Crime Reports (UCR)*

Otwin Marenin
Washington State University
*Criminology and Criminal Justice: A Comparison; Sub-Saharan Africa, Crime and Justice in*

Satenik Margaryan
Rutgers University
*Guilty Pleas and Plea Bargaining*

Nancy Marion
University of Akron
*Akers, Ronald L.; Colonial America, Crime and Justice in; Customs Service, United States*

Ineke Haen Marshall
University of Nebraska at Omaha
*Bonger, Willem*

Shadd Maruna
University of Cambridge
*Neutralization/Drift Theory; Vigilante Violence*

Ross L. Matsueda
University of Washington
*Cressey, Donald*

Rick A. Matthews
Ohio University
*Courts in the United States: Supreme Court*

Michael O. Maume
University of North Carolina, Wilmington
*Masculinity Theory*

David C. May
Eastern Kentucky University
*Alcohol, Tobacco, and Firearms, Bureau of (ATF); Body-Type Theories of Criminal Behavior; Community Corrections; Firearms: The Law; Juvenile Delinquency and Youth Crime Throughout History; Juvenile Delinquency: Extent, Correlates, and Trends; Prisons: Inmate Populations and Subcultures; Social Learning Theory; Incivilities Theory*

G. Larry Mays
New Mexico State University
*Conspiracy to Commit a Crime; Courts in the United States: Structure and Functions; Jails: Purposes, Populations, and Problems; Juvenile Justice: The Courts; Sentences and Sentencing: Guidelines; Status Offenses*

Lorraine Green Mazerolle
Griffith University
*Crime Prevention; Law Enforcement: Community Policing*

N. Jane McCandless
State University of West Georgia
*Prostitution as an Occupation*

Bill McCarthy
University of California, Davis
*Homelessness and Criminal Behavior*

Candace McCoy
Rutgers University
*Guilty Pleas and Plea Bargaining*

Jessica McGowan
University of South Carolina
*Drug Control Policy: Legalization and Decriminalization; Immigration and Naturalization Service (INS); Warrants and Subpoenas*

Gill McIvor
University of Stirling
*Community Service and Restitution Programs*

LaVerne McQuiller Williams
Rochester Institute of Technology
*Corpus Delicti*

Juan Jose Medina Ariza
University of Manchester
*Spain, Crime and Justice in*

John Memory
Livingstone College
*Sentences and Sentencing: Types*

Scott Menard
University of Colorado-Boulder
*Cross-Sectional and Longitudinal Research;
Integrated Theories of Criminal Behavior;
Intelligence (IQ) and Criminal Behavior;
Self-Report Research; Victimization, Repeated*

Kenneth Mentor
New Mexico State University
*Mediation and Dispute Resolution Programs*

Fred Meyer
Ball State University
*Politics and Crime Policies*

Raymond J. Michalowski
Northern Arizona University
*Cuba, Crime and Justice in; Social Class
and Criminal Behavior*

Terance D. Miethe
University of Nevada at Las Vegas
*Victim Precipitation*

Alexis J. Miller
Middle Tennessee State University
*Neo-Nazi Groups*

J. Mitchell Miller
University of South Carolina
*Cohen, Albert; Criminology as a Social Science;
Drug Control Policy: Legalization and
Decriminalization; Drug Enforcement
Administration (DEA); Gangs: Theories; Native*

*American Crime and Justice; Penal Colonies;
Qualitative Research; Subcultural Theories of
Criminal Behavior*

Milo Miller
Southeast Missouri State University
*Appeals and Post-Trial Motions*

William J. Miller
*Gambling, Legal*

Patricia Millhoff
University of Akron
*Criminal Courts: Felony*

Dragan Milovanovic
Northeastern Illinois University
*Postmodernism and Constitutive Theories
of Criminal Behavior*

Stephanie Mizrahi
Washington State University
*Counsel, The Right to; Self-Incriminantion, The
Privilege against*

David L. Monk
California State University, Sacramento
*Survey Research*

Reid Montgomery
University of South Carolina
*Prison Riots*

Robert Moore
University of Southern Mississippi
*Criminal Law: Definition, Sources, and Types*

Nathan R. Moran
Midwestern State University
*International Court of Justice (World Court);
Organized Crime: Chinese Tongs and Triads;
Organized Crime: Colombiam Cartels; Organized
Crime: Cuban Gangs; Organized Crime: Enforce-
ment Strategies; Organized Crime: The Law*

Contributors

Stephen J. Morewitz
*Obsession*

Phoebe Morgan
Northern Arizona University
*Sexual Harassment*

Laura J. Moriarity
Virginia Commonwealth University
*Adler, Freda*

Kenneth L. Mullen
Appalachian State University
*Vollmer, August and O. W. Wilson*

Christopher W. Mullins
Southwestern Illinois College
*Medieval Europe, Crime and Justice in*

Roslyn Muraskin
Long Island University–C. W. Post Campus
*Abortion*

Elizabeth Ehrhardt Mustaine
University of Central Florida
*Routine Activities Theory*

David L. Myers
Indiana University of Pennsylvania
*Deterrence, General; Deterrence, Specific*

Greg Newbold
University of Canterbury
*New Zealand, Crime and Justice in*

Grant Niemann
Flinders University
*International Criminal Law; International Criminal Tribunals*

James J. Nolan III
West Virginia University
*Police: Vice and Special Units*

Dana M. Nurge
Northeastern University
*Gangs: Definitions; Prisons, Privatized*

Thomas O'Connor
North Carolina Wesleyan College
*Educational Programs in Criminology and Criminal Justice; Victimization, Crime: Prevention and Protection*

Emma Ogilvie
Australian Institute of Criminology
*Stalking*

Gregory P. Orvis
The University of Texas at Tyler
*Gangs: Enforcement, Intervention, and Prevention Strategies*

Marc Ouimet
Université de Montréal
*Environmental Theory*

Deborah Pace
Mental Health Services, Kainai Indian Reserve
*Shoplifting*

Francis J. Pakes
University of Portsmouth
*Netherlands, Crime and Justice in*

Wilson R. Palacios
University of South Florida
*Club Drugs; Designer Drugs*

Michael J. Palmiotto
Wichita State University
*Police Crime*

Demetra M. Pappas
Bryant College
*Criminalization and Decriminalization; Euthanasia and Physician-Assisted Suicide; Suicide: The Law*

Matthew Pate
University of Arkansas-Little Rock
*Radical Theories of Criminal Behavior; Search and Seizure*

Allan L. Patenaude
University of Arkansas-Little Rock
*Diversion and Diversion Programs; Customary Law*

Marc A. Patenaude
University of Arkansas-Little Rock
*Diversion and Diversion Programs*

Anthony Petrosino
Harvard University
*Experimental Research/ Radomized Experiments*

Heather Pfeifer
University of Baltimore
*Prediction of Criminal Behavior*

Alex R. Piquero
University of Florida
*Criminal Careers/Chronic Offenders; Educational Attainment and Criminal Behavior; Forgery; Life-Course and Developmental Theories of Criminal Behavior*

Nicole Leeper Piquero
University of Florida
*Police: Occupational Problems; Recidivism*

Gary W. Potter
Eastern Kentucky University
*Cocaine; Police History: United States*

Tim Prenzler
Griffith University
*Police: Brutality and Corruption; Private Investigators*

Johan Prinsloo
South Africa University
*South Africa, Crime and Justice in*

Amy Reckdenwald
University of South Florida
*Police: Race and Racial Profiling*

Robert M. Regoli
University of Colorado
*Differential Oppression Theory*

Rosalva Resendiz
Texas Woman's University
*Gangs: Prison*

Stephen C. Richards
Northern Kentucky University
*Convict Criminology*

Kimberly D. Richman
University of San Francisco
*Homosexuality; Victimless Crimes*

Marc Riedel
Southern Illinois University
*Homicide: Mass Murder and Serial Killings; Homicide: Muder-for-Hire*

Julian V. Roberts
University of Ottawa
*Public Opinion and the Criminal Justice System; Retribution*

Amanda L. Robinson
Cardiff University
*Law Enforcement*

Matthew B. Robinson
Appalachian State University
*Burglary: Extent and Correlates; National Crime Victimization Survey (NCVS)*

Michael R. Ronczkowski
RAILE Group and Miami-Dade Police Department
*Terrorism*

Contributors

Debra E. Ross
Grand Valley State University
*Environmental Crimes; White-Collar Crime: The Law*

Jeffrey Ian Ross
University of Baltimore
*Convict Criminology; Political Crimes against the State; Sedition and Treason*

James Rotton
Florida International University
*Climate and Criminal Behavior*

William J. Ruefle
University of South Florida
*Curfews*

Jeffrey P. Rush
University of Tennessee
*Ecclesiastical Law and Justice; Gangs: Enforcement, Intervention, and Prevention Strategies; Shoplifting; Wilson, James Q.*

Steve Russell
Indiana University at Bloomington
*Consent as a Defense to Criminal Liability; Criminal Courts: Personnel; Necessity as a Defense to Criminal Liability; Battered Women Defense to Criminal Liability*

Amie R. Scheigegger
Charleston Southern University
*Consumers, Crimes against*

Hans Joachim Schneider
University of Westfalia
*Germany, Crime and Justice in; Sellin, Thorsten*

Andrea Schoepfer
University of Florida
*Educational Attainment and Criminal Behavior*

Christopher J. Schreck
Illinois State University
*Self-Control Theory; Hirschi, Travis*

Jennifer Schwartz
Pennsylvania State University
*Gender and Criminal Behavior*

Martin D. Schwartz
Ohio University
*Gambling, Legal; Rape, Marital; Prisons, Privatized*

Donald Scott
University of Evansville
*Bank Robbery; Reiss, Albert J.*

Hannah Scott
University of Memphis
*Becker, Howard S.*

Richard W. Sears
Wright State University
*Psychological Autopsy*

Lance Selva
Middle Tennessee State University
*Asset Forfeiture*

Brion Sever
Monmouth University
*Criminal Courts: Administration and Organization; Pornography and Criminal Behavior*

Joseph F. Sheley
California State University, Sacramento
*Conflict and Consensus Theories of Law; Firearms: Controversies over Policies*

William L. Shulman
Middle Tennessee State University
*Exclusionary Rule, The*

J. Eagle Shutt
University of South Carolina
*Criminal Courts: Problems in; Judges; Prosecuting Attorneys; Trials, Criminal*

David R. Simon
University of North Florida
*Bribery and Graft; Prostitution: The Law*

Barbara Sims
The Pennsylvania State University at Harrisburg
*Marxist Theories of Criminal Behavior; Sampson,
Robert*

John J. Sloan III
University of Alabama at Birmingham
*Fear of Crime; Victimization, Crime:
Characteristics of Victims*

Brad Smith
University of South Carolina
*Psychopathy and Criminal Behavior*

Michael R. Smith
University of South Carolina
*Equal Protection*

Jacqueline Smith-Mason
Virginia Commonwealth University
*Blumstein, Alfred*

Georgia Spiropoulos
University of Cincinnati
*Rape, Forcible: Extent and Correlates*

Steven Stack
*Wayne State University*
*Suicide: Extent and Correlates; Suicide: The Law*

Loretta J. Stalans
Loyola University Chicago
*Child Molestation; Incest; Internal Revenue Service
(IRS); Public Opinion and the Criminal Justice Sys-
tem; Retribution*

Debra L. Stanley
Central Connecticut State University
*Domestic Assault: Prevention and Treatment;
Prison History: United States*

Darrell J. Steffensmeier
Pennsylvania State University
*Age and Criminal Behavior; Gender and Criminal
Behavior*

Gene Stephens
University of South Carolina
*Crime Commission Reports; Demonology; Law
Enforcement Assistance Administration; Mass
Media and Crime and Justice; United States Fron-
tier, Crime and Justice in*

Dennis J. Stevens
Salem State College
*Prison History: Continental Europe and England*

Mark Stevens
North Carolina Wesleyan College
*Military Justice: Courts, the Law, and Punishment*

Anna Stewart
Griffith University
*Evolutionary Theories of Criminal Behavior*

Sandra S. Stone
State University of West Georgia
*Child Abuse: Extent and Correlates*

Sean C. Stucker
University of South Carolina
*Immigration and Naturalization Service (INS)*

Yumi Suzuki
SUNY-Albany
*Judeo-Christian Legal Traditions*

Cheryl Swanson
University of West Florida
*Intermediate Sanctions*

Kathleen M. Sweet
Embry-Riddle Aeronautical University
*Russia, Crime and Justice in Modern; Terrorism:
The Law; Warfare and Criminal Behavior*

1799

Noriyoshi Takemura
Toin University of Yokohama
*Japan, Crime and Justice in; Organized Crime:
Japanese Mobsters*

Laura Talbott
University of South Carolina
*Marijuana*

Becky Tatum
University of Houston-Clear Lake
*Discrimination in Justice; Gangs: Race
and Ethnicity*

Jennifer Tatum
University of South Carolina
*Lombroso, Cesare*

Kimberly Tatum
University of West Florida
*Defense Attorneys; Felonies and Misdemeanors*

Faye Taxman
University of Maryland
*Prediction of Criminal Behavior*

Morris A. Taylor
Southern Illinois University
*Criminal Justice System: Models of Operation*

Richard Tewksbury
University of Louisville
*Corrections: Careers; Counterfeiting; Legal
Careers; Rehabilitation and Treatment; Routine
Activities Theory; Statute of Limitations as a
Defense to Criminal Liability*

Amy Thistlethwaite
Northern Kentucky University
*Domestic Assault: Extent and Correlates;
Institutional Corrections; Juvenile Delinquency,
Theories of*

William E. Thornton
Loyola University in New Orleans
*Employee Theft and Inventory Shrinkage;*

*Investigative (Psychological) Profiling; Police:
Private Security Forces*

Gabriel Thrasher
Midwestern State University
*International Court of Justice (World Court)*

Quint C. Thurman
Texas State University-San Marcos
*Tax Evasion and Tax Fraud*

Stephen G. Tibbetts
California State University-San Bernadino
*Obscenity*

Victoria Time
Old Dominion University
*Solicitation to Commit Crime; Superior Orders as
a Defense to Criminal Liability*

Jeffrey A. Tipton
South Carolina Department of Public Safety
*Aggression and Criminal Behavior; Gangs:
Female; Juvenile Delinquency, Girls and*

Misti Tobias
*Sam Houston State University
Kidnapping*

Stephen Tombs
John Moores University
*Corporate Crime*

Pamela Tontodonato
Kent State University
*Cohort Research; Wolfgang, Marvin E.*

Sam Torres
California State University-Long Beach
*Corrections: Federal Bureau of Prisons; Parole;
Probation; Probation and Parole: Careers;
Organized Crime: Mexican Mafia*

Gordon B. Trasler
University of Southampton
*Antisocial Personality Disorder and Criminal
Behavior; Rational Choice Theory*

A. Javier Treviño
Wheaton College
*Beccaria, Cesare; Bentham, Jeremy; Prohibition*

Andromachi Tseloni
University of Macedonia
*Greece, Crime and Justice in*

Ryan Kellus Turner
Texas Municipal Courts Education Center
*Criminal Courts: Lower; Disorderly
Conduct/Disturbing the Peace*

Jeffery T. Ulmer
Penn State University
*Age and Criminal Behavior; Sentences
and Sentencing: Disparities*

N. Prabha Unnithan
Colorado State University
*Alcohol Use and Criminal Behavior; Alcohol Use:
The Law; Hindu Legal Traditions*

Stuart L. Usdan
University of South Carolina
*Alcohol Use: Prevention and Treatment; Drug
Control Policy: Prevention and Treatment;
Marijuana*

Amy C. Van Houten
University of Arkansas, Little Rock
*Police: Use of Deadly Force*

Donna M. Vandiver
Illinois State University
*Pornogrpahy: The Law*

Abbie E. Ventura
University of South Carolina
*Maritime Offenses: Crime at Sea; Women as
Offenders and Victims throughout History*

Holly E. Ventura
University of South Carolina
*Matza, David; Ohlin, Lloyd E.; United Kingdom,
Crime and Justice in; Warrants and Subpoenas*

Arvind Verma
Indiana University at Bloomington
*India, Crime and Justice in*

Livy Visano
York University, Toronto
*Labeling and Symbolic Interaction Theories of
Criminal Behavior*

Lydia Voigt
Loyola University in New Orleans
*Durkheim, Emile; Soviet Union, Crime and Jutsice
in*

Brenda Vose
University of Cincinnati
*Tax Evasion and Tax Fraud*

Jeffery T. Walker
University of Arkansas at Little Rock
*Police: Use of Deadly Force*

Lisa Hutchinson Wallace
Eastern Kentucky University
*Burglary as an Occupation; Extortion and
Blackmail; Obstruction of Justice*

Sam Wallace
University of Tennessee, Knoxville
*Hackers: History, Motivations, and Activities*

Anthony Walsh
Boise State University
*Biological Theories of Criminal Behavior;
Genetic Theories of Criminal Behavior; Race and
Ethnicity and Criminal Behavior; Rape, Forcible:
Theories*

Patrick D. Walsh
Loyola University in New Orleans
*Robbery: The Law*

John Z. Wang
California State University-Long Beach
*Containment Theory; International Policing:
Interpol; Thrasher, Frederic*

Contributors

David W. Webber
Philadelphia, *PA*
*Acquired Immune Deficiency Syndrome (AIDS)
and the Law; Riots: The Law; Trials, Political*

David L. Weisburd
University of Maryland
*Experimental Research/ Radomized Experiments*

Michael Welch
Rutgers University
*Moral Panic*

Laura D. Whitlock
South Carolina Department of Public Safety
*Criminal Justice Funding, The State Role in*

Matthew Williams
Cardiff University
*Computer Offenses*

Heather Williamson
Virginia Commonwealth University
*Personality Theories of Criminal Behavior*

Steve Wilson
University of Nebraska-Omaha
*Rape, Forcible: The Law*

John L. Worrall
California State University-San Bernardino
*Double Jeopardy, Protection against; Entrapment*

*as a Defense to Criminal Liability; Fines, Fees,
and Forfeiture; Intoxication as a Defense to
Criminal Liability*

James D. Wright
University of Central Florida
*Boot Camps and Shock Incarceration*

Richard A. Wright
Arkansas State University
*Physical Attractiveness and Criminal Behavior;
Sutherland, Edwin H.*

Olivia Yu
University of Texas at San Antonio
*Strict Liability*

Margaret A. Zahn
North Carolina State University
*Homicide: Nature, Extent, and Correlates*

Marvin Zalman
Wayne State University
*Publications in Criminal Law*

Christina Zarafonitou
Panteion University
*Greece, Crime and Justice in*

# Index

definition of, 580
elements of, 580–581
of historical documents, 582
Formal reactions, 1675
Formal sanctions
as general deterrent, 388
as specific deterrent, 392–393
Formal social control, 872
Fornication
adultery vs., 16–17
definition of, 16
Forum-shopping, 213
Foucault, Michel, 1128, 1246
"Four Track" rural police program, 1217
Fourteenth Amendment
confession admissibility under, 823
death penalty issues, 470
description of, 466–467
due process, 466–467, 890, 1286
equal protection provisions, 509, 1286
prisoner's rights under, 1286–1287
Fourth Amendment
asset forfeiture and, 76
deadly force rulings involving, 1218–1219
privacy rights, 487
reasonableness clause of, 468
search and seizure issues, 1469–1473
terrorism effects on, 1743
unreasonable search and seizure protections, 1743
warrant clause of, 468, 1743
Fragile X syndrome, 639
Fragment of legislative bodies, 1236–1238
France
criminal justice system in, 583–588
criminal law in, 583
detectives in, 1170
detention centers in, 588
incarceration in, 587–588
investigations in, 584–585
judges in, 586
juveniles in, 587
penal colonies of, 1132–1133
police, 584–585
police forces in, 1130–1131, 1185–1186
prisons in, 588, 1262–1266
prosecution in, 585
Sellin's research in, 1496
sentencing in, 585–587
Supreme Court of Appeals in, 586
terrorism in, 1643–1645
trials in, 585–586
Franco, Francisco, 1581–1582
Frank, Antoinette, 1168–1169
Frankels, Marvin E., 1511
Frankpledge system (England), 1183
Fraser, James, 1643
Fraud
consumer, 228
definition of, 1044
health-care, 1145–1148
by pharmaceutical industry, 1146–1148
police involvement with, in U. S., 1190–1193
as professional theft, 1653
research on, 1628
social class and, 1535

Free speech
pornography law and, 1243
seditious libel vs., 1227–1229, 1477
Free will, 383
"Free-wheeling addict," 448–449
French Connection, 1072
French Criminal Code, 586–587
French Revolution
terrorism during, 1639–1641
vandalism during, 1697–1698
Freud, Sigmund, 342, 560, 985
Friction ridge impressions, 1179–1181
Friere, Paulo, 1246
"Frisk" procedures, 1470–1473
Frith, Mary, 1407
Frontal lobe theory, 1036–1037
Frontier crime
description of, 1688–1696
municipal and urban police development and, 1195–1197
robbery and, 1438–1439
sheriffs' role in, 1522–1523
vigilantism and, 1731–1732
Frotteurism, 1336
Frustration, 1335–1336
Fry, Margery, 1699, 1726
*Frye v. U.S.*, 854, 1180–1181
Full service gang units, 615
Fuller, J., 1126–1127
Fulton, Ian, 1643
Functionalist criminal theory
radical criminology and, 1375–1378
religion and criminal behavior and, 1425–1427
Functions of deviance, 221
Fundamentalist religion
criminal behavior and views of, 1424–1427
terrorism and, 1642–1645
vandalism in name of, 1697–1698
*Furman v. Georgia*, 264, 403
"Future dangerousness rule," 1219

## G

*Gagnon v. Scarpelli*, 1311–1312
*Galas v. McKee*, 1218
Gall, Franz Josef, 1142–1143
Galleys, as prison ships, 1264–1265
Gallows, 202
Gambling
in American colonies, 591–592
bingo, 1070
card playing, 591–592
casino, 594
controversies regarding, 596
crime and, 596
definition of, 591, 1112
history of, 595–596, 1113
horse racing, 592
illegal, 591–595
international, 596
in Las Vegas, 593, 596
legalized, 595–598
lotteries, 592–594
on Native American reservations, 594
in nineteenth century, 592
organized crime and, 593, 1068, 1112–1113
police involvement, history of, 1189–1193

# O